Intimate Relationships,
Marriages, and Families

Intimate Relationships, Marriages, and Families

FIFTH EDITION

Mary Kay DeGenova

F. Philip Rice
University of Maine

Boston   Burr Ridge, IL   Dubuque, IA   Madison, WI   New York   San Francisco   St. Louis
Bangkok   Bogotá   Caracas   Kuala Lumpur   Lisbon   London   Madrid   Mexico City
Milan   Montreal   New Delhi   Santiago   Seoul   Singapore   Sydney   Taipei   Toronto

McGraw-Hill Higher Education

*A Division of The **McGraw-Hill** Companies*

To my children, Louis & Eleanor

To Irma Ann Rice with deepest love

2 3 4 5 6 7 8 9 0 DOW/DOW 0 9 8 7 6 5 4 3 2 1

Library of Congress Cataloging-in-Publication Data
DeGenova, Mary Kay.
   Intimate relationships, marriages, and families / Mary Kay DeGenova, F. Philip Rice.—5th ed.
      p. cm.
   Rev. ed. of: Intimate relationships, marriages, and families / F. Phillip Rice. 4th ed. © 1999.
   Includes bibliographical references and index.
   ISBN 0-7674-2166-3
      1. Family life education—United States. I. Rice, F. Philip. II. Rice, F. Philip. Intimate
   relationships, marriages, and families. III. Title.

HQ10.5.U6R53 2001
306.8—dc21   00-052527

Sponsoring editor, Franklin C. Graham; developmental editor, Barbara Armentrout; production editors, Julianna Scott Feir and Carla Kirschenbaum; manuscript editor, Tom Briggs; design manager, Jean Mailander; text and cover designer, Jean Mailander; cover image, © Celia Johnson SIS and PhotoDisc; illustrator, John and Judy Walter and Judith Ogus; manufacturing manager, Randy Hurst. The text was set in 9.5/12 Palatino by Thompson Type and printed on 45# Somerset Matte by R. R. Donnelley & Sons Company.

Text and illustration credits appear at the back of the book on page 574, which constitutes a continuation of the copyright page.

http://www.mhhe.com

Brief Contents

PART ONE   *Social and Psychological Perspectives: Cognition and Challenge*

   1   Intimate Relationships, Marriages, and Families in the Twentieth Century   1

   2   Family Backgrounds and How They Influence Us   28

   3   Cultural and Ethnic Differences in Families   46

PART TWO   *Intimate Relationships: Choices and Change*

   4   Being Single   68

   5   Dating, Going Together, and Courtship   88

   6   Attraction and Love   116

   7   Gender: Identity, and Roles   134

   8   The Sexual Basis of Relationships   158

   9   Mate Selection, Nonmaital cohabitation, and Transition to Marriage   186

PART THREE   *Marriages and Ramily Relationships: Challenges and Commitment*

  10   Qualities of Successful Marriages   214

  11   Marital Relationships over the Family Life Cycle   232

  12   Work, Ramily Roles, and Material Resources   258

  13   Companionship in and outside the Family   288

  14   Power, Decision Making, and Communication   302

PART FOUR   *Parenthood: Cognition and Challenge*

  15   Family Planning and Parenthood   322

  16   Pregnancy and Childbirth   358

  17   Parent-Child Relationships   380

  18   Parents and Extended Family Relationships   404

PART FIVE   *Family Stress and Reorganization: choices and Commitment*

  19   Conflict, Family Crises, and Crisis Management   424

  20   The Troubled Family and Divorce   460

  21   Coming Together: Remarriage and Stepparenting   488

Glossary 510   •   Bibliography 518   •   Index 575

Contents

Preface xxi

PART ONE — SOCIAL AND PSYCHOLOGICAL PERSPECTIVES: COGNITION AND CHALLENGE

CHAPTER 1

Intimate Relationships, Marriages, and Families in the Twenty-First Century 1

Learning Objectives 1

What Is a Family? 2
Some Definitions 2
Family Forms 3

Changes in Family Philosophy and Emphasis 4
From Institution to Companionship 4
From Patriarchy to Democracy 4

Changes in Marriage and Parenthood 6
Marriage Rates 7
Age at Marriage 7
Birthrates and Family Size 8
Working Mothers 10
One-Parent Families 10
Gay and Lesbian Families 11
■ Family Issues: Lesbian Couples and Children 12
Grandparents as Parents 13

Changes in Divorce and Remarriage 14
Divorce Rates 14
Remarriage Trends 14
Blended Families 15

Changes in Nonmarital Sexual Behavior 16
Sexual Activity 16
■ Perspective: High-Risk Sexual Behavior Among Adolescents 17
The Use of Contraceptives 18
Unmarried Pregnancy 18

Theories to Help Explain Family Behavior 18
Structural-Functional Theory 18
Family Developmental Theory 20
Symbolic Interaction Theory 21
Systems Theory 22
Exchange Theory 22
Conflict Theory 23

Feminist Theory   23
Critique of Family Theories   24

Summary   24

Key Terms   25

Questions for Thought   25

Suggested Readings   26

CHAPTER 2

Family Backgrounds and How They Influence Us   28

Learning Objectives   28

Why Examine Family Background?   30
Understanding the Socializing Influence of the Family   30
Determining Differential Effects   30
Developing Self-Understanding   31
Assuming Personal Responsibility   31
Making Peace with the Past   31
■ Perspective: The Alcoholic Family   32

Parental Attitudes Toward Children   32
■ Perspective: Perfectionist Parents   33
Approval   33
■ Family Issues: Can We Blame Our Parents?   34
Criticism and Rejection   34

Attitudes Toward Intimate Partners   34

Family Closeness: Attitudes Toward Intimacy   36
■ Perspective: Who Needs Intimacy?   37

Attitudes Toward Sex   37
Positive Attitudes and Teachings   37
Negative Attitudes and Teachings   38
Possible Effects on Sexual Behavior   38

Attitudes Toward Marriage and Divorce   38

Gender-Role Socialization in the Family   39

Variations in Family Values and Work Habits   40
Workaholic Families   40
■ Perspective: Values and Marital Satisfaction   41
Family Values   41
Parental Role Models   41

Communicative, Noncommunicative, and Conflictive Families   41
Open, Honest, Tactful Communication   41
■ Perspective: Self-Disclosure   42
Superficial Communication   42
One-Sided Communication   42
False Communication   42
Avoidance of Communication   42
Noncommunication   42
Angry Communication   43

Summary   43

Key Terms   44

Questions for Thought   45

Suggested Readings   45

CHAPTER 3

Cultural and Ethnic Differences in Families   46

Learning Objectives   46

African American Families   48

Class Differences Among African American Families   50

The Increase in One-Parent Families   51

African American Family Ideology   51

▓ Perspective: African American Family
Strengths   52

Socialization of Children   53

Reality and Gender-Role Fulfillment   53

Mexican American Families   54

Familism   54

Divorce Rates and Birthrates   55

Power and Decision Making   55

Child Rearing and Education   56

Native American Families   56

Vital Statistics   57

Economics   57

▓ Perspective: Degrees of Acculturation Among
Native Americans   58

Education   58

Family Life   59

Children   59

Teenage Mothers   59

Cultural Conflict   60

Chinese American Families   60

Immigration   61

Family and Children   61

▓ Perspective: Neither Real Americans
nor Real Asians?   62

Education   63

Prejudices   63

Conclusions   64

Summary   64

Key Terms   65

Questions for Thought   65

Suggested Readings   66

PART TWO   INTIMATE RELATIONSHIPS: CHOICES AND CHANGE

CHAPTER 4

Being Single   68

Learning Objectives   68

Categories of Singles   70

Voluntary Singles   71

Involuntary Singles   72

Marital Delay   72

Why Some People Remain Single   72

Deliberate Choice   73

Fear of Marriage   73

Lack of Opportunity   73

Circumstances   74

**Advantages and Disadvantages of Being
Single   74**

The Health and Well-Being of Singles   75

▓ Perspective: What Makes People Happy?   77

Living Arrangements   78

Shared Living Spaces   78

Living with Parents   79

Living Alone   79

Loneliness and Friendships   79

▓ Family Issues: Flying Back to the Nest   80

The Importance of Companionship   80

Males Versus Females   80

Loneliness Versus Aloneness   80

Sexual Behavior   81

Employment and Income   82

Single Mothers 83

The Never-Married Adult 84

Summary 85

Key Terms 86

Questions for Thought 86

Suggested Readings 87

CHAPTER 5

Dating, Going Together, and Courtship 88

Learning Objectives 88

The Dating System 90
Courtship in Early America 90
The Emergence of Dating 90
The Rating and Dating Complex of the 1930s 91
▦ Perspective: Bundling 92
Dating and Courtship from the 1940s to the 1960s 92
Dating and "Getting Together" Today 93

Reasons for Dating 94

Dating Partners Versus Long-Term Partners 96

Finding and Meeting Dates 96
Singles Bars 96
Personal Ads 96
▦ Perspective: Love Matches Versus Arranged Marriages in China 98
Dating Services and Computer Networks 98
▦ Perspective: Dating Preferences of University Women: The "Nice Guy" Stereotype 99

Changing Gender Roles in Dating 100

Problems in Dating 101
Honesty and Openness 101
▦ Family Issues: Who Controls Dating? 102
Extradyadic Relationships 102
Getting Too Serious 103
Closeness and Distance in Relationships 103

Sexual Aggression and Dating Violence 104
Unwanted Sexual Pressure 105
Verbal Sexual Coercion 105
Date Rape 106
▦ Perspective: "Date Rape" Drugs 107
Physical Violence 107
Correlations with Violence 108
The Progression of Violence 110

Breaking Up a Relationship 110

Summary 112

Key Terms 114

Questions for Thought 114

Suggested Readings 115

CHAPTER 6

Attraction and Love 116

Learning Objectives 116

Attraction 118
Physical Attractiveness 118
Standards of Attractiveness 118

▦ Perspective: Women and Weight: Gendered Messages on Magazine Covers 119
▦ Perspective: What Physical Features Are Most Attracting? 120
Personality and Social Factors 120

Unconscious Influences   121

What Is Love?   121

Romantic Love   121
  Is Romantic Love a Sound Basis for Marriage?   122
  ■ Perspective: Love and Attachment   123

Erotic Love   124
  Are Love and Sex the Same?   124
  Sex as an Expression of Love   124

Dependent Love   125
  Maslow's Theory of Love as Need   125

Friendship Love   127
  Loving and Liking   127

Altruistic Love   127
  Fromm's View of Altruistic Love   127

Components of Love   128
  Research on the Components of Love   129
  ■ Perspective: Achieving and Maintaining Psychological Intimacy   130

Changes Over Time   130
  ■ Perspective: Lee's Love Styles   131

Summary   132

Key Terms   133

Questions for Thought   133

Suggested Readings   133

CHAPTER 7

Gender: Identity and Roles   *134*

Learning Objectives   134

Environmental Influences on Gender   136
  Societal Expectations   136
  Parental Influences   137
  The Influence of Television   138
  School Influences   139

Theories of Gender and Identity   140
  Social Learning Theory   140
  Cognitive Developmental Theory   140
  Gender Schema Theory   141
  Social Structure/Cultural Theories   141
  Evolutionary Theories: Sociobiology and Functionalism   142

Traditional Masculine and Feminine Stereotypes   142
  Masculinity   142
  Femininity   143
  Problems with Gender Stereotypes   144
  ■ Perspective: My Life on the Boundaries of Gender   145

Gender Roles and Body Image   146

Gender Roles in the Family   147
  Ethnic Variations   148
  ■ Family Issues: Gender, Parenthood, and Anger   150
  Housework and Child-Care Roles   150
  ■ Family Issues: Fathers' Participation in Child Care   152
  Roles Over the Family Life Cycle   152

Androgyny   152
  ■ Family Issues: Mothers' Responsibility for Children   153

Summary   154

Key Terms   155

Questions for Thought   156

Suggested Readings   156

CHAPTER 8

The Sexual Basis of Relationships   158

Learning Objectives   158

Sex and a Happy Marriage   160

Phases of Human Sexual Response   160
  ■ Perspective: Nonmarital Sex and
Relationships   161
  Physiological Responses   162
  Summary of Response Patterns   164
  Multiple Orgasms   164
  The Three-Phase Model   166

Sources of Sexual Arousal   166
  Tactile Stimulation   166
  Oral Sex   166
  ■ Perspective: The G-Spot: Myth or Reality?   167
  Visual Stimulation   167
  Auditory Stimulation   168
  Verbal Stimulation   168
  Mental Stimulation   168

Lovemaking Principles   169
  Sexual Initiative   169
  ■ Perspective: Cybersex   170
  Communication   170
  Time Factors   170
  The Physical Setting   171

Frequency of Intercourse   171
Nonmarital Sexual Conflicts   173
Gay and Lesbian Sexual Activity   173

Sexual Dysfunction   174
  Causes of Sexual Dysfunction   176
  Getting Help   176
  ■ Perspective: Viagra   177

Sexually Transmitted Diseases   177
  HIV/AIDS   178
  Herpes Simplex   179
  ■ Family Issues: AIDS and Safer Sex   180
  Hepatitis B   180
  Human Papillomavirus (HPV)/Genital Warts   181
  Chlamydial Infections   181
  Gonorrhea   182
  Syphilis   182
  Parasitic Infections   183

Summary   183

Key Terms   184

Questions for Thought   185

Suggested Readings   185

CHAPTER 9

Mate Selection, Nonmarital Cohabitation, and Transition to Marriage   186

Learning Objectives   186

Theories of Mate Selection   188
  Psychodynamic Theories   188
  Needs Theories   188
  Exchange Theories   189
  Developmental Process Theories   189

**Family Background Factors in Mate
Selection**   190

Socioeconomic Class   191
Education and Intelligence   192
Interracial Marriages   193
Interfaith Marriages   194
  ■ Family Issues: The Marriage
Gradient   195

Personal Characteristics   196
  Individual Traits and Behavior   196

Age Differentials   196

Consensus and Similarity of Attitudes
and Values   197

Gender Roles and Personal Habits   197

**Why Some People Regret Their Choice
of Mate   198**

   ▓ Perspective: Danger Signals in Relationships   200

Nonmarital Cohabitation   200

Patterns of Relationships   200

Reactions to Cohabitation   201

   ▓ Perspective: Facts About Cohabitation   202

The Effect on Marriage   202

The Effect on Children   203

The Transition to Marriage   204

Marital Readiness   204

Marriage and the Law   206

Preparing for Marriage   207

Rites of Passage   209

Engagement   209

The Wedding as a Religious and Civil Rite   210

Summary   211

Key Terms   212

Questions for Thought   213

Suggested Readings   213

PART THREE

MARRIAGES AND FAMILY RELATIONSHIPS:
CHALLENGES AND COMMITMENT

CHAPTER 10

Qualities of Successful Marriages   214

Learning Objectives   214

Criteria for Evaluating Marital Success   216

Durability   216

Approximation of Ideals   216

Fulfillment of Needs   216

Satisfaction   217

Happy Versus Unhappy Marriages   217

   ▓ Family Issues: Patterns of Marital Relationships:
What Type Fits You?   219

**Twelve Characteristics of Successful
Marriages   220**

Communication   222

Admiration and Respect   222

Companionship   223

Spirituality and Values   224

Commitment   224

Affection   226

The Ability to Deal with Crises and Stress   226

Responsibility   226

Unselfishness   227

Empathy and Sensitivity   228

Honesty, Trust, and Fidelity   228

   ▓ Perspective: Trust in Relationships   229

Adaptability, Flexibility, and Tolerance   229

Summary   230

Key Terms   230

Questions for Thought   231

Suggested Readings   231

CHAPTER 11

Marital Relationships over the Family Life Cycle   232

Learning Objectives 232

Marriage and Personal Happiness 234

The Family Life Cycle 235
Data on Family Life Cycles 235
Changes in Marital Satisfaction 236
The Curvilinear Pattern 237
Gay and Lesbian Families 237

Adjustments Early in Marriage 239
Marital Adjustment Tasks 239
Problems During Three Early Stages 239

Adjustments to Parenthood 239
Parenthood as Stress 240
Parenthood and Psychological Well-Being 242

Adjustments During Middle Adulthood 242
Marital Adjustments 243
The Postparental Years 244

Adjustments During Late Adulthood 245
Developmental Tasks 246
■ Perspective: Postretirement
Employment 249
Marital Satisfaction 249
Divorce 250
Parent–Adult Child Relationships 251

Widowhood 252
■ Family Issues: Who Cares for the
Elderly? 253

Summary 255

Key Terms 256

Questions for Thought 257

Suggested Readings 257

CHAPTER 12

Work, Family Roles, and Material Resources   258

Learning Objectives 258

Work and the Family 260
The Provider Role 260
■ Family Issues: Who Supports the Family? 261
Work, Stress, and the Family 261
■ Perspective: Navy Officer Wives 262
The Parents' Child-Care Role 263

Employed Women and the Family 264
Ethics and Value Systems 265
Role Conflict and Strain 265
■ Perspective: Graduate Student Management
of Family and Academic Roles 266
Marital Adjustment 267

Dual-Career Families 268
Benefits of a Dual-Career Marriage 269
Issues for Dual-Career Couples 269
■ Perspective: First-Time Mothers' Styles
of Integrating Parenting and Employment 271
The Quality of Dual-Career Marriages 272

Material Resources 272
Financial Needs 272
The Gender Wage Gap 274
■ Perspective: X Marks the Spot: Generation X
College Students Speak Out on Goals for the
Future 275
Money and Marital Satisfaction 275

Poverty and Family Life   278
   The Poverty Line   278
   The Effects of Poverty   278
   The Feminization of Poverty   279
   The Effects of Poverty on Children   279
   The Widening Gap Between the Rich
   and the Poor   281

Family Issues: Welfare and the Family   282

Summary   284

Key Terms   286

Questions for Thought   286

Suggested Readings   287

CHAPTER 13

Companionship in and outside the Family   288

Learning Objectives   288

Companionship and the Family   290
   Companionship as Motive for Marriage   290
   Styles of Companionship   290
   Togetherness Versus Separateness   291
   Loneliness   291
   Family Issues: No Time for Love   292
   Family Interaction   293

Companionship in Leisure Time
Activities   294
   Sports and Other Recreational Activities   294
   Vacations   294

Television   295
Computers   296

Beyond the Family   297
   Friendships   297
   Gender Differences   298
   Same-Sex and Opposite-Sex Friendships   298

Summary   300

Key Terms   301

Questions for Thought   301

Suggested Readings   301

CHAPTER 14

Power, Decision Making, and Communication   302

Learning Objectives   302

The Meaning of Power   304

Why People Want Power   304
   Self-Actualization   304
   Social Expectations   304
   Family-of-Origin Influences   304
   Psychological Need   305

Sources of Power   305
   Cultural Norms   305

Gender Norms   306
Economic Resources   306
Education and Knowledge   307
Personality Differences   308
Communication Ability   308
Emotional Factors   308
Physical Stature and Strength   308
Life Circumstances   308
Children   308

Marital Power Patterns   309

Power Processes 310
   Power Tactics That Help 310
   Power Tactics That Can Help or Harm 310
   Power Tactics That Harm 311

Consequences of Power Struggles 312
   ■ Perspective: Power Neutralization Strategies 313

Communication 313
   ■ Family Issues: Women's Empowerment 314
   Verbal and Nonverbal Communication 314
   Barriers to Communication 314

Improving Communication Skills 316
   Motivation and Concern 316

Self-Disclosure 316
   ■ Perspective: I-Statements in Family
Communication 317
Clarity 317
Feedback and Reciprocity 317
Arguing Constructively 317

Summary 318

Key Terms 320

Questions for Thought 320

Suggested Readings 320

PART FOUR   PARENTHOOD: COGNITION AND CHALLENGES

CHAPTER 15

Family Planning and Parenting 322

Learning Objectives 322

The Importance of Family Planning 324

Hormonal Control 325
   Oral Contraceptives 325
   ■ Perspective: Why Some People Don't Use
Contraceptives 326
   Other Forms of Hormonal Contraceptives 328
   ■ Family Issues: RU-486 (Mifeprex):
The Abortion Pill 329

Vaginal Spermicides 329

Intrauterine Devices 330

Barrier Methods 331
   Condoms 331
   ■ Perspective: Condom Availability
in U.S. Schools 332
   Diaphragms 333
   Cervical Caps 334

Sterilization 334

Vasectomy 334
   ■ Perspective: Mistakes People Make with
Contraceptives 335
   Tubal Ligation 335

Birth Control Without Devices 336
   Fertility Awareness Methods 336
   Coitus Interruptus 338
   Noncoital Stimulation 338

Choosing a Method of Contraception 338

Abortion 338
   Legal Considerations 338
   Physical and Medical Considerations 342
   Moral Considerations 342
   Social Considerations 342
   Psychological and Personal Considerations 343
   ■ Perspective: Facts About Abortion 344

Infertility 346
   Causes of Infertility 346

Infertility and Subjective Well-being   346

Treatment of Infertility   347

Alternative Means of Conception   347

The Adoption Option   348

To Parent or Not to Parent   350

Delayed Parenthood   350

Reasons for Having Children   351

Choosing a Child-Free Marriage   352

Effects of Children on Parents' Happiness   353

The Decision to Have or Not to Have Children   354

Summary   354

Key Terms   356

Questions for Thought   356

Suggested Readings   357

CHAPTER 16

Pregnancy and Childbirth   358

Learning Objectives   358

Pregnancy   360

Signs and Symptoms of Pregnancy   360

Tests for Pregnancy   360

Calculating the Birth Date   361

Emotional Reactions to Pregnancy   362

Prenatal Care   362

The Importance of Prenatal Care   362

Minor Side Effects of Pregnancy   364

Major Complications of Pregnancy   364

Sexual Relations During Pregnancy   365

■ Perspective: Developmental Tasks of Pregnancy   366

Mental Health   366

■ Perspective: Avoiding Birth Defects   367

Prenatal Development   367

The Germinal Period   367

The Embryonic Period   368

The Fetal Period   369

Prepared Childbirth   369

The Lamaze Method   369

Labor and Delivery   370

The Duration of Labor   370

Stages of Labor   371

The Use of Anesthesia   371

■ Perspective: Options for Delivery   372

Induced or Accelerated Labor   372

Cesarean Section   372

The Postpartum Period   373

Care of the Newborn   373

Parent-Infant Contact and Bonding   373

Rooming In   373

Breast- Versus Bottle-Feeding   373

■ Family Issues: Preterm and Small-for-Gestational-Age Babies   374

Postpartum Adjustments   375

Returning to Work   376

Sexual Relations After Childbirth   376

Summary   377

Key Terms   378

Questions for Thought   378

Suggested Readings   379

CHAPTER 17

Parent-Child Relationships   380

Learning Objectives   380

Philosophies of Child Rearing   382
Parental Differences   382
Parent-Child Differences   382
Cultural Differences   383
Life Circumstances   383
Differences in Children   384

Parental Roles   384
Meeting Children's Needs   384
■ Perspective: Constructive Versus Destructive Parenting   386
Sharing Responsibilities   386

Fostering Cognitive and Intellectual Growth   387
Parental Contributions   387
■ Perspective: Children's Home Environments   388
Language Development and Cultivation   388
Education Defining and Modeling   389

Meeting Emotional Needs   390
Emotional Attachments   390

Effects of Separation and Rejection   390
Child Care   390
Autonomy   392

Socialization and Discipline   392
Meaning and Goals of Discipline   393
Principles of Discipline   394
Corporal Punishment   395

One-Parent Families   395
Unmarried Teenage Mothers   396
Family Structure and Children's Adjustments   396
Special Issues in the Female-Headed Family   397
■ Perspective: Children's Contributions to Household Work   399
Special Issues in the Male-Headed Family   399
Family Work   399

Summary   400

Key Terms   401

Questions for Thought   401

Suggested Readings   402

CHAPTER 18

Parents and Extended Family Relationships   404

Learning Objectives   404
Parent–Adult Child Relationships   406
When Parents Disapprove of Choice of Partner   406
Children's Identification with Parents   408
Interdependence Between Generations   408
Mother-Daughter Relationships   409
Father-Son Support Networks   411
Conflict Between Parents and Adult Children   411
Parent–Adult Child Relationships and Psychological Functioning   411

In-laws   412
Successful In-law Relationships   412
The Roots of Conflict   413
■ Family Issues: Adult Child Contact with Elderly Black Parents   414

Living with Parents or In-laws   414
Effects of Coresidence   414
Sources of Stress   415
Extended Families During Middle Age   415
Sharing Residence with the Elderly   415

Grandparents   416
  What Grandparents Can Do for Grandchildren   417
  Adolescents, Young Adults, and Grandparents   418
  ◾ Family Issues: Grandparents Who Parent Their Grandchildren   419
  What Grandchildren Can Do for Grandparents   420

Summary   420

Key Terms   422

Questions for Thought   422

Suggested Readings   423

PART FIVE   FAMILY STRESS AND REORGANIZATION: CHOICES AND COMMITMENT

CHAPTER 19

Conflict, Family Crises, and Crisis Management   424

Learning Objectives   424

Conflict and Children   426
  The Family Environment   426
  Interparent Conflict   426
  Older Children and Adolescents   427

Sources of Conflict   427
  Personal Sources   427
  Physical Sources   428
  Interpersonal Sources   428
  Situational or Environmental Sources   429

Methods of Dealing with Conflict   429
  Avoidance   429
  Ventilation and Catharsis   430
  Constructive Conflicts   431
  Destructive Conflicts   431
  ◾ Perspective: Spouses' Rules for Marital Conflict   432
  Means of Ending Conflict   433

Family Crises   433
  Stage 1: Onset   433
  Stage 2: Disorganization   433
  Stage 3: Reorganization   434

The Crisis of Infidelity   435
  Reasons for Infidelity   435

Affairs as Crises for Married People   436
  ◾ Perspective: Investing in Your Relationship   437
  ◾ Family Issues: Extramarital Affairs   438

The Crisis of Economic Distress   438
  Types of Economic Distress   438
  Effects on Individuals and on Family Relationships   439
  Coping with Economic Distress   440

The Crisis of Violence and Abuse   441
  A Cycle of Violence   442
  Factors Related to Violence   442
  Spouse Abuse   443
  ◾ Perspective: Men Who Abuse   445
  Child Abuse   445
  Treatment for Spouse and Child Abuse   447
  Sexual Abuse of Children   447
  ◾ Family Issues: Sexual Abuse and the Criminal Justice System   449

The Crisis of Death and Grief   450
  Uncertain Death   450
  Certain Death   450
  Premature Death   452
  Unexpected Death   452
  Calamitous Death   453
  Grief   454

Summary 456

Key Terms 458

Questions for Thought 458

Suggested Readings 459

CHAPTER 20

The Troubled Family and Divorce 460

Learning Objectives 460

Probability of Divorce: Social and
Demographic Factors 462
   Marital Age 462
   Religion and Socioeconomic Status 463
   Geographic Area 463
   Parental Divorce 464
   The Presence of Children 464

Causes of Marital Breakup 465
   Spouses' Perceptions 465
   The Marital Disaffection Process 467

The Divorce Decision 468

Alternatives to Divorce 470
   Marriage Counseling 470
   Marriage Enrichment 470
   Separation 470
   ▨ Family Issues: Why Marriage Counseling
   Sometimes Does Not Succeed 472
   No-Fault Divorce and Mediation 473
   ▨ Perspective: Marital Separation Contract 474

Adult Adjustments After Divorce 475
   Emotional Trauma 475
   Societal Attitudes Toward Divorce 476
   Loneliness and Social Readjustment 476
   Adjustments to Custody Arrangements 477
   Finances 477
   Realignment of Responsibilities and Work Roles 478
   Contacts with the Ex-Spouse 478
   Kinship Interaction 479

Children and Divorce 479
   Child Custody 479
   Child Support 480
   Visitation Rights 481
   Reactions of Children 481

Summary 484

Key Terms 485

Questions for Thought 485

Suggested Readings 486

CHAPTER 21

Coming Together: Remarriage and Stepparenting 488

Learning Objectives 488

Remarriage 490
   Divorce and Success in Remarriage 490
   Courtship and Mate Selection in Remarriage 492
   ▨ Perspective: Successful Remarriages 493

Carrying Expectations from One Marriage
to Another 494
Finances 495
Relationships with the Ex-Spouse 496
▨ Family Issues: Stepfamily Turning Points 498

Stepfamilies 498

Stepparent-Stepchild Relationships 500

Child Well-being in Stepfamilies 501

Facilitating Bonds Between Stepparents
and Stepchildren 503

Cohabiting with a New Partner 504

Coparents and Parenting Coalitions 504

▦ Family Issues: Ten Major Issues for Families
of Remarriage 505

Stepsibling Relationships 506

Summary 507

Key Terms 508

Questions for Thought 509

Suggested Readings 509

Glossary **510**

Bibliography **518**

Index **575**

ABOUT THE AUTHORS

Mary Kay DeGenova received her Ph.D. in 1992 from Purdue University in Child Development and Family Studies. She was an associate professor of Family Studies at Central Michigan University and the University of New Hampshire and has taught various courses on marriage and the family for ten years. Her work on this text is a direct result of her experiences in the classroom and her experiences with diversity, including work as a Peace Corps Volunteer in West Africa and a Fulbright Scholar in Chile. In addition to her recent work on this text DeGenova has written *Families in Cultural Context: Strengths and Challenges in Diversity,* also published by Mayfield Publishing Company. She has written numerous journal articles, presented papers at many conferences, and appeared in anthologies. DeGenova is the recipient of many honors and awards, including the Excellence in Teaching Award, Purdue University Summer Research Fellow, and the Fulbright-Hays Seminar Abroad Scholarship. She is a member of the National Council on Family Relations and Groves Conference on Marriage and the Family. She is currently working from home on numerous writing projects while caring for her two children.

F. Philip Rice received his Ed.D. in Marriage and Family Relationships from Teachers College of Columbia University. He is a Professor Emeritus at the University of Maine-Orono, where he taught courses in the field of Marriage and Family for many years. His years of experience teaching courses on Marriage and the Family, Human Sexuality, Contemporary Marriage, Human Development, and many others come through in this text. In addition to writing *Intimate Relationships, Marriages and Families* he has written more than twenty other texts on Marriage and Family, Stepparenting, Working Mothers, Human Sexuality, Human Development, and numerous others in related fields. His principal areas of research include Human Development, Child Development, Adolescent Development, Adult Development, and Marriage and Family Relations.

Preface

The desire for intimacy is a universal need of human beings. Almost all adult men and women seek to marry or form a permanent stable relationship with another person. Most people will want to bear children and raise a family in a secure, loving, and fulfilling environment.

The real question each human being faces is, How do I create such relationships? As students studying relationships you must ask: How do families sustain relationships given the structure and changes in today's social world? This book was written to help you understand how intimate relationships are formed and maintained, and why they sometimes fail. Throughout the discussion, the focus is on motivation and commitment, on diversity and individual choice, and on our capacity to understand, grow, and change.

FIVE THEMES

Five major themes serve to organize the content and emphasis in this book:

Cognition—developing knowledge and understanding

Change—personal growth

Challenge—being motivated

Choice—making wise decisions

Commitment—the importance of dedication

Each of us has a tremendous capacity to grow and change, but to grow and change in ways that are best for us, we need a cognitive understanding of what is involved, what choices we have, and what the consequences of these choices may be. It is here that the information provided by the social and behavioral sciences can help. For instance, we know more about the biology of sex and reproduction than ever before, and such knowledge can contribute immeasurably to a successful marriage.

As we grow in knowledge, we may also grow in other ways, especially in objectivity and tolerance for others. The more we study intimate relationships, marriages, and family patterns, the more we see that no one way can be considered the "right way" or the ideal for everyone. We also can grow by examining and clarifying our personal attitudes and values directly. We can grow in our ability to love, to express warmth and affection, and to show empathy with others. Also, we can develop social skills and seek friendships that fulfill us and enrich our lives. We can learn to resolve interpersonal conflicts. Throughout this book we focus on these various dimensions of growth.

One of the questions most frequently asked of a therapist or counselor is, Do you believe people ever really change? The conclusion of experts and researchers is that we do change. And although we can't expect to change others and probably shouldn't try, we can change ourselves. We can change if we want to, and sometimes we must change if we are to grow in ways that are healthy for us. Obviously, such change is more likely to be fruitful if it is the result of informed choice based on sound knowledge.

This book gives particular attention to changes that occur over the life cycle. Life is not static, and neither are intimate relationships. People change, situations change, relationships change. The love we may feel today may not be exactly the same as the love we feel ten years from now. However, there is also continuity to life; what happens now greatly influences tomorrow. And there is similarity as well as diversity in the ways humans develop and cope with events. To show students how others have responded to change and how those responses have affected the quality of their intimate relationships is an important aim of this book.

Life involves many choices. Shall I marry or remain single? What should I look for in a partner? What are my priorities in life? Do I want marriage, a career, or both? Do I want children? If I cannot have children of my own, is adoption a desirable choice? How do I raise a child? If I find myself in a troubled marriage or other relationship, do I choose to end it or try to save it? How does one choose a counselor? If divorced, will I choose to marry again? What should my relationship be with my parents, and what is the best way to help them if they cannot help themselves? One purpose of this book is to challenge and motivate readers to commit themselves to finding their own individual answers to such questions as these and to make wise choices in the light of realistic expectations.

ORGANIZATION AND CONTENT

Part One, Social and Psychological Perspectives: Cognition and Challenge, places our study in social and historical context. Chapter 1 examines the changes that took place in marriage and family during the 20th century and how different theoretical perspectives interpret those changes. Chapter 2 describes ways that family background influences our attitudes toward intimate relationships, gender roles, marriage and divorce, parenthood, and communication within the family. Chapter 3 reports current research about cultural and ethnic variations in families.

Part Two, Intimate Relationships: Choices and Change, explores relationships before marriage, ranging from singlehood to dating to partner selection (Chapters 4–9). The chapters in this part explore such questions as these: What are the effects of race and gender on never marrying? What are successful strategies in initiating romantic relationships? Does breaking up follow a predictable script? What attributes are important for dating partners and for marriage partners? Is being in love a valid criteria for marriage? How do gender identity and gender role affect self-concept and behavior in intimate relationships? How do people express their sexual and intimacy needs? How do people find a partner and know if the partner is really the right one? What effect does living together before marriage have on marital success?

Marriage brings with it a new set of demands for growth and change. Part Three, Marriages and Family Relationships: Challenges and Commitment, considers first the qualities essential to happy and successful marriages (Chapter 10) and then discusses changes in marital relationships over the life cycle (Chapter 11). The remaining chapters (12–14) explore work and family roles and the effect of economic status; companionship in and outside the family; and power, decision making, and communication.

In Part Four, Parenthood: Cognition and Challenges, the presentation shifts from an emphasis on couples to a focus on the family. Chapter 15 discusses the decisions involved in parenthood and family planning, and Chapter 16 follows the birth process from conception through pregnancy and the preparations made by the family for a new baby. Chapter 17 examines parent-child relationships, while Chapter 18 considers relationships among members of the extended family, especially aging relatives.

Most families at one time or another experience some conflict or face a period of crisis. Part Five, Family Stress and Reorganization: Choices and Commitment, explores conflict and family crises (Chapter 19), causes and effects of divorce (Chapter 20), and the special challenges of remarriage and stepparenting (Chapter 21).

SPECIAL FEATURES

Several features distinguish *Intimate Relationships, Marriage, and Families* from other textbooks.

First is its emphasis on understanding ourselves by examining our family backgrounds. Throughout this book, especially in Chapter 2, Family Backgrounds and How They Influence Us, the family and social experiences that shape our personal roles, values, and attitudes about intimacy and relationships are examined in detail.

As students become aware of the remarkable range of individual and cultural differences in human relationships, they not only gain tolerance for others but also control over their own lives; yet few textbooks devote much attention to such diversity. This book emphasizes diversity from the outset, especially in Chapter 3, Cultural and Ethnic Differences in Families. While acknowledging differences, however, this text stresses that there are also many universals in intimate and family relationships.

New information is most meaningful to students when it is placed within the context of the personal narrative, the case study, the carefully chosen excerpt from a client interview. This book offers students the benefit of many real experiences drawn from the notes of counselors and therapists, including one of the authors. Although the details have been altered to protect the anonymity of clients, the experiences described are real.

Though concrete and thoroughly practical in its aims, this book gives students a sound research base for the information it offers. Family theories are now discussed in Chapter 1 (rather than in the Appendix), and a new discussion of feminist theory has been added. Where appropriate throughout the text, specific theories are discussed in relation to particular topics. For example, Chapter 7, on gender, considers applications of cognitive developmental theory, gender schema theory, social structure and cultural theories, and evolutionary theories. Information from some 2,000 research references has been incorporated into the text; more than 400 new references have been added to this edition to replace older references.

Two types of special-focus boxes appear throughout this book. *Perspective* boxes present interesting research findings or viewpoints related to the chapters. Among the topics these boxes cover are the dating preferences of university women, messages that magazine covers send about women's weight, cybersex, Viagra, and Gen-X college students' goals for the future. *Family Issues* boxes present important situations or problems facing families today. Lesbian couples with children, grandparents who par-

ent their grandchildren, fathers' participation in child care, and the effects of welfare reform are some of the issues discussed in these boxes.

Pedagogical aids for the student include detailed outlines and learning objectives at the beginning of each chapter; and a summary, key terms, questions for thought, and a list of suggested readings at the end of each chapter.

NEW TO THE FIFTH EDITION

For the fifth edition, all chapters were carefully revised and updated to incorporate current research and statistics and newly emerging topics. The following list gives a sample of some of the new, updated, or expanded topics addressed in this edition:

- Grandparents as parents

- The influence of family-of-origin experiences on intimate relationships, with a focus on social learning theory and attachment theory

- The relationship between parental approval and children's self-concept

- The feminization of poverty

- Variations among African American families

- The socialization of children in African American families

- The strength of intergenerational relationships in Mexican American families

- Power in Mexican American marriages

- The effect of gaming on Native American tribes

- The dilemma of discrimination for third-, fourth-, and fifth-generation Japanese and Chinese Americans

- The current trends of delaying marriage and the greater social acceptance of single adults

- The effects of age, ethnicity, and gender on never marrying

- Social support and life satisfaction among the never-married

- Young adults living with their parents

- "Getting together" as a current trend in dating

- Ideal qualities sought in intimate partners

- Changing gender roles

- Successful strategies used in initiating romantic relationships
- Sexual activity outside a dating relationship
- Closeness and distance in relationships, discussed in terms of attachment theory
- Sexual aggression and violence in dating relationships
- Date and acquaintance rape
- Breaking up and relationship dissolution scripts, discussed in terms of process theory and social exchange theory
- Current body ideals, including extremely thin fashion models and buffed athletes
- Body dissatisfaction among younger women
- Decrease in passion over time in a relationship
- Gendered messages on magazine covers about women and weight
- Transgendered people and transsexuals in terms of gender identity
- Representation of men and women on television during the last three decades
- Gender roles and body image, including the effect of gender differences in media presentations on self-esteem and body satisfaction
- Ethnic variations in gender-role behaviors
- The effect of pornography on men and women
- The correlation between communication about sexual preferences and satisfaction with the relationship
- A comparison of the importance men and women place on various types of intimacy
- Differences in qualities of mates selected for cohabitation and for marriage
- Definition of common-law marriage
- Happy and unhappy marriages, based on research into communication patterns and attributions
- Life stages and parental roles in gay and lesbian families
- Fathers as primary caregivers for young children
- The effect of wives' income on marital discord and the dynamics of power in marriage
- The "gender wage gap"

- Families living below the poverty line and the minimum costs of supporting a family
- Homeless families
- The widening gap between the rich and the poor
- The psychological need for power discussed in terms of attachment theory, social control theory, and feminist theory
- Gender barriers to communication over the lifespan
- How to argue constructively
- Parent-child differences in terms of developmental stake theory and intergenerational stake theory
- Interdependence between generations as parents age
- Divorce statistics and trends through the 1990s
- Causes of marital breakup, including critical periods of a marriage and the failure to show positive affect
- Legal aspects of divorce
- Child custody arrangements and the quality of father-child relationships across time (based on the National Survey of Families and Households)
- Poverty in single-parent families and child-support payments
- Effects of divorce on children versus effects of high levels of parental conflict in intact families
- Success in remarriage
- Stages of separation with an ex-spouse and the effect on a new marriage
- Stepparents' attempts to discipline stepchildren
- Factors that affect stepchildren's adjustment in stepfamilies
- Affinity-seeking strategies of stepparents toward their stepchildren

ANCILLARY MATERIALS

This book is accompanied by a complete package of supplemental materials. New to this edition is an Instructor's CD-ROM that includes PowerPoint slides, an Image Set, and the Instructor's Research Guide. Also new to this edition is a book-specific

Web site (www.mhhe.com/relationships5) with materials for both students and instructors. It includes an online study guide, Internet activities, Web links, key terms, and more.

The Instructor's Manual has been revised by Elizabeth Butchart Carroll of East Carolina University and includes learning objectives for each chapter; lecture outlines; teaching strategies; individual and classroom activities; and a list of key journals. A set of transparency masters that augment material in the textbook is also included.

The Test Bank, also revised by Elizabeth Butchart Carroll consists of over 1,500 items, including, for every chapter, true/false, multiple choice, matching, short-answer, and essay questions. It is available both in printed form and on CD for IBM-compatible and Macintosh computers. The computerized test bank allows the instructor to select, edit, and add questions, randomize them, keep a record of their use, and print tests (with an answer key) for individual classes.

The *Study Guide to Accompany Intimate Relationships, Marriages, and Families,* by Jeanne Kohl-Welles of the University of Washington and Kyle Jenkins helps students to master and retain the concepts in each chapter of the textbook, prepare for examinations, assess their own personal attitudes and beliefs, and (through exercises) apply their knowledge to real-life situations.

Each chapter of the *Study Guide* has three parts. The first part contains learning objectives, a chapter summary, and a practice test. These components are designed to facilitate student mastery of the content. The types of questions in the Test Bank are also in the practice test.

The second part, the Personal Involvement Assessment, gives students the opportunity to examine in depth one of the important issues discussed or referred to in the textbook chapter and to apply the knowledge gained from the chapter to their own lives (for example, exploring personal stereotypes, testing their awareness of the consequences of AIDS, considering how they would react to a spouse's having extramarital affairs).

The final part of each chapter, Knowledge in Action, highlights key research studies on a specific topic from the textbook. Following a review of the topic, the section suggests a project or projects in which students apply what they have learned to "real-life" situations involving others. Examples of such projects are content analyses of sex roles found in the media, interviews with single parents and married couples about child-care arrangements, and surveys of youth attitudes about alcohol or marijuana use.

The 13 segments on this videotape (each 5 to 15 minutes in length) *Mayfield Relationships and Intimacy Videotape* were selected and edited to complement the topics covered in the text. They include such subjects as gender roles, interracial marriages, parenthood, the "sandwich generation," children of divorce, and stepparenting.

Also available is *Mayfield's Quick View Guide to the Internet for Intimate Relationships, Sexuality, Marriage, and Family,* Version 2.0. Available free with the text, this guide includes tutorials on using the World Wide Web, how to find Web sites related to the study of relationships, family and gender, and how to use them. Throughout the guide, students are taken through the steps needed to find information on the Internet, including library resources, listservs, APA writing guides, and more.

ACKNOWLEDGMENTS

The authors thank the reviewers for their guidance and suggestions: For the first edition, Jeanne H. Ballantine, Wright State University; Bruce L. Campbell, California State University at Los Angeles; Eugene W. Jacobs, Presbyterian College; Jeanne Kohl, University of Washington; Sherrill Richarz, Washington State University; Jay D. Schvaneveidt, Utah State University; Barbara H. Settles, University of Delaware; Benjamin Silliman, Louisiana Technical University; and W. Fred Stultz, California Polytechnic State University.

For the second edition, Scott M. Allgood, Auburn University; Esther DeVall, New Mexico State University; Deborah Gentry, Illinois State University; Jeanne E. Kohl, University of Washington; Lowell J. Krokoff, Florida International University; Estella Martinez, University of New Mexico; Bernita Quoss, University of Wyoming; and Kenrick S. Thompson, Northern Michigan University.

For the third edition, Scott M. Allgood, Utah State University; Esther L. DeVall, New Mexico State University; Bernita Quoss, University of Wyoming; and Kenrick S. Thompson, Northern Michigan University.

For the fourth edition, Glee Absher, University of Central Oklahoma-Edmond; Scott M. Allgood, Utah State University; Elizabeth B. Carroll, East Carolina University; and Patricia A. Levy, University of Southern Colorado. Thanks are also due to Jeanne Kohl-Welles, University of Washington, for her work on the study guide and test bank, both past and present editions; and to Kenrick Thompson, now of Arkansas State University, Mountain Home, for his updating of the test bank.

The authors wish to thank the following people who have reviewed and offered guidance and suggestions for the fifth edition: Scott M. Allgood, Utah State University; Elizabeth B. Carroll, East Carolina University; Bryce Dickey, Western Michigan University; Patricia Gibbs, Foothill College; Joyce M. Johnson, Santa Rosa Junior College; and Michael Traugot, Tennessee State University.

Also, the authors thank Eileen Malone Beach, Amy Voege, and Laura J. Vogel for their support and assistance in revising this text.

The authors also thank the staff of Mayfield Publishing who have been so helpful: Franklin C. Graham, sponsoring editor; Barbara Armentrout, developmental editor; and Kate Schurbert, editorial assistant. Finally, thanks are due to Julianna Scott Fein and Carla Kirschenbaum, Senior Production Editors, for their able production management.

*Intimate Relationships,
Marriages, and Families*

CHAPTER 1

LEARNING OBJECTIVES

After reading the chapter, you should be able to:

Define family and describe various family forms.

Explain the changes in family philosophy and emphasis: the change from institution to companionship and from patriarchy to democracy.

Outline the basic trends in marriage rates, age at first marriage, birthrates and family size, employment of working mothers, and one-parent families.

Summarize the basic trends in divorce rates, remarriage, and blended families.

Describe present trends in premarital sexual behavior, use of contraceptives, and unmarried pregnancy.

Identify family issues relating to various family forms.

Explain behavior and patterns in families using the seven different family theories.

Intimate Relationships, Marriages, and Families in the Twenty-First Century

Learning Objectives

What Is a Family?
Some Definitions
Family Forms

Changes in Family Philosophy and Emphasis
From Institution to Companionship
From Patriarchy to Democracy

Changes in Marriage and Parenthood
Marriage Rates
Age at Marriage
Birthrates and Family Size
Working Mothers
One-Parent Families
Gay and Lesbian Families
Family Issues: Lesbian Couples and Children
Grandparents as Parents

Changes in Divorce and Remarriage
Divorce Rates
Remarriage Trends
Blended Families

Changes in Nonmarital Sexual Behavior
Sexual Activity
Perspective: High-Risk Sexual Behavior Among Adolescents
The Use of Contraceptives
Unmarried Pregnancy

Theories to Help Explain Family Behavior
Structural-Functional Theory
Family Developmental Theory
Symbolic Interaction Theory
Systems Theory
Exchange Theory
Conflict Theory
Feminist Theory
Critique of Family Theories

Summary
Key Terms
Questions for Thought
Suggested Readings

amilies as we know them today are different from those of previous generations (Glick, 1984, 1989). They differ in structure and composition, size, and function. The reasons people marry and their marital expectations have changed. Changes have also occurred in how families are governed, in who supports families, and in how people behave sexually. An analysis of marriage rates and ages, birthrates, the percentages of working mothers, divorce and remarriage rates, the numbers of reconstituted families, rates of pregnancy and parenthood among single women, and some alternative family forms reveals some significant trends.

We are going to examine some of these changes and trends and their effects on the society and the individual. In addition, it's important for each of us to consider: How have these changes affected me?

WHAT IS A FAMILY?

What makes a family? Do its members have to be related by blood? By marriage? Do they have to share the same household? We'll examine a few of the countless definitions of *family* that have been formulated in recent decades, and then we'll look at some of the variations in types of families that have been identified by psychologists, sociologists, and anthropologists (Levin, 1993; Levin and Trost, 1992; Trost, 1993).

Some Definitions

The U.S. Bureau of the Census (1999a) defines a family as "two or more persons related by birth, marriage, or adoption and residing together in a household" (p. 6). Thus, for statistical purposes, the number of families in the United States is equal to the number of households. By this definition, the family may consist of two persons who are not necessarily of different genders: two brothers, two female cousins, a mother and daughter, and so on. They may also be of different genders: a husband and wife, a mother and son, a brother and sister, and so on. If the family includes two adults, they may or may not have children. The common characteristics included in this definition are twofold: (1) The individuals must be related by blood or law, and (2) they must live together in one household.

Thus, according to the Census Bureau, if adult children move out of their parents' household and establish families of their own, they are no longer considered a part of their parents' family.

Other definitions have been proposed. Winch (1971) defined the family as "a set of persons related to each other by blood, marriage, or adoption and whose basic societal function is replacement." But this definition seems to limit family functions to child rearing. Burgess and Locke (1953) defined the family as "a group of persons united by ties of marriage, blood, or adoption; constituting a single household; interacting and communicating with each other in their respective social roles (husband and wife, mother and father, son and daughter, brother and sister); and creating and maintaining a common culture." This definition would eliminate those cohabiting, though not legally related or married. It seems to assume as well that individuals in a family must conform to some sort of prescribed social roles.

None of these definitions seems to cover all types of family situations: nonmarried cohabiting couples, gay and lesbian couples, single-parent households, couples without children, group marriages, and communal living situations. A more comprehensive and less stereotyped definition is used in this book: A **family** is any group of persons united by the ties of marriage, blood, or adoption, or any sexually expressive relationship, in which (1) the adults cooperate financially for their mutual support, (2) the people are committed to one another in an intimate, interpersonal relationship, and (3) the members see their individual identities as importantly attached to the group with an identity of its own.

This definition has a number of advantages. It includes a variety of family structures: the traditional married couple with or without children, single-parent families, families consisting of blood relatives (such as two widowed sisters, a grandparent and grandchildren, and a multigenerational extended family). It also includes persons not related by marriage, blood, or adoption who have a sexual relationship: an unmarried cohabiting couple, a gay or lesbian couple, a group marriage, a communal family. Because this definition insists that the persons be committed and in an intimate, interpersonal relationship, it eliminates cohabiting couples who live together for practical reasons, without commitment, and those who have only a casual relationship

The conventional idea of a family is two parents and one or more children, but in reality, there are many varieties of family structure.

even though they may have sex together. The members must see their individual identities as importantly attached to the group, and the group must have an identity of its own. The definition doesn't say that people have to be together continuously, so it can include commuting couples or family members away at college or in the armed services.

Family Forms

We can categorize families according to their structure and the relationships among the people in them.

A **voluntarily childless family** is a couple who decide not to have children. (Some people refer to this as a child-free family.)

A **single-parent family** consists of a parent (who may or may not have been married) and one or more children.

A **nuclear family** consists of a father, a mother, and their children. This type of family as a proportion of all families has been declining as the family form has become more diverse.

A **family of origin** is the family into which you are born and in which you are raised. The family consists of you, your parents, and your siblings.

A **family of procreation** is the family you establish when you have children of your own.

An **extended family** consists of you, possibly a mate, any children you might have, and other relatives who might live with you in your household or nearby. It can also include grandparents who are helping to care for grandchildren.

A **blended, or reconstituted, family** is formed when a widowed or divorced person, with or without children, remarries another person who may or may not have been married before and who may or may not have children (Dowling, 1983). If either the remarried husband or wife has children from the former marriage, a **stepfamily** is formed.

A **binuclear family** is an original family divided into two by divorce. It consists of two nuclear families: (1) the maternal nuclear family headed by the mother and (2) the paternal family headed by the father. The families include whatever children were in the original family and may be headed by a single parent or two parents if former spouses remarry (Ahrons and Rodgers, 1987).

A **polygamous family** is a single family unit based on the marriage of one person to two or more mates. If the man has more than one wife, a **polygynous family** is formed. If a woman has more than one husband, a **polyandrous family** is formed. Polyandry is rare, but polygyny is practiced in African and Asian countries. Both are illegal in the United States.

A **patriarchal family** is one in which the father is head of the household, with authority over other members of the family.

A **matriarchal family** is one in which the mother is head of the household, with authority over other members of the family.

A **gay or lesbian family** consists of a couple of the same sex, living together and sharing sexual expression and commitment. Some gay or lesbian families include children, usually the offspring of one of the partners.

A **cohabiting family** consists of two people of the opposite sex living together, sharing sexual expression, who are committed to their relationship without formal legal marriage.

When talking about the family, then, we need to specify which type we are referring to. With such a wide variety of family forms, we can no longer assume that the word *family* is synonymous with *nuclear family.*

CHANGES IN FAMILY PHILOSOPHY AND EMPHASIS

Not only has family structure changed over the years, but there have also been significant changes in family functions (Cheal, 1993; Gubrium and Holstein, 1993). These changes have been from institution to companionship and from patriarchy to democracy.

From Institution to Companionship

One of the most important changes in family function has been a shift in emphasis (Mancini and Orthner, 1988; Scanzoni, 1987). Traditional views emphasized the role of the family as an institution whose function was to meet the needs of society; this is the **instrumental role** of the family. More modern views of the family tend to emphasize its role in fulfilling personal needs for emotional security and companionship; this is the **expressive role** of the family (Edwards, 1987).

In an industrial society in which the majority of people live in urban areas, neighbors remain strangers, and it becomes harder for people to find friendship, companionship, and emotional support. Affectional needs may not be met; the individual feels isolated and alone even though surrounded by millions of people. In such an impersonal society, it becomes more important to find intimacy, a sense of belonging, and emotional security in the family itself. There is a universal longing to be attached, to relate, to belong, to be needed, to care. Most humans need a profoundly reaffirming experience of genuine intimacy. Erik Erikson (1959) suggested that the achievement of intimacy is one of the major goals of life. In a highly impersonal society, in which emotional isolation is frequent, developing a close family relationship is vital to one's identity and security.

There has been some shift, therefore, in family functions. In the 1800s, people openly admitted to marrying to obtain economic security, to provide goods and services for one another, to attain social status, to reproduce, and to raise children. By the 1970s, people professed to marry for love, companionship, and the satisfaction of emotional needs. Raising healthy and happy children and having economic security are still important reasons for marriage, but love and affection are people's primary expectations in marriage today (Barich and Bielby, 1996).

This shift has placed a greater burden on the family itself. When people establish a family for love, companionship, and emotional security but don't find fulfillment, they become disappointed, frustrated, and full of feelings of failure. The higher their personal expectations, the greater the possibility of failure. Sometimes expectations are charged with so much romantic fantasy that fulfillment becomes impossible. Some couples begin to feel that their personal happiness no longer depends on their being married (Glenn and Weaver, 1988). This is one reason for the high rate of divorce. Rather than staying together for the sake of the family, couples often separate if their personal needs and expectations are not met.

From Patriarchy to Democracy

Throughout most of our history, the American family was patriarchal (Edwards and Kluck, 1980). The father was considered head of the household, with authority over and responsibilities for other members of the family. He was the supreme authority in making decisions and settling disputes. He was entitled to the deference and respect of other family members, who were expected to be submissive and obedient.

As head of the household, he owned the property, which was passed to the next generation through the male line. This is known as **patrilineal**

The family pictured here was once considered the ideal. The father was traditionally the head of the household, with authority over all the family members.

descent. The wife and children were expected to reside with the husband and with or near the husband's family, according to his choice. This is **patrilocal residence.** The terms that refer to female descent and residence are **matrilineal descent** and **matrilocal residence.** This practice was seen in traditional Iroquois society, in which men were expected to move to the female household, and important lines of descent were traced through the female.

Generally, in the 1950s and before, one characteristic of the traditional patriarchal family was a clear-cut distinction between the husband's and wife's roles in the family. The husband was the breadwinner and was usually responsible for clearly defined chores that were considered "man's work," such as making house repairs or mowing the lawn. The wife was responsible for "woman's work," including housecleaning, cooking, sewing and mending, and caring for the children.

Although the traditional patriarchal family is often portrayed in idealized form, cracks often developed in its structure. The father who was a tyrant was a difficult and unpleasant taskmaster, feared and respected but not necessarily loved by his wife and children. "Life with father" often meant toil and obedience, regardless of personal desires and feelings. Sons waited impatiently for the time when they would inherit family wealth and property and when they could marry and achieve a man's status. A daughter might hope that marriage would fulfill her dreams, but she sometimes experienced friction living in close proximity to her husband's

family. Husband-wife relationships lasted because women had few alternatives, but there may have been little emotional closeness and companionship. Sex was considered "a man's pleasure and a woman's duty" and often resulted in an endless succession of pregnancies.

Not all patriarchal families were unhappy or unsuccessful. The structures were stable, sustained by law and social custom, as well as by the lack of economic and social opportunities. However, with the cultural climate of activism of the civil rights movement of the 1950s and the women's rights movement of the 1960s, the ideals of the patriarchal family were challenged. The patriarchal family was replaced by the democratic family, in which women were treated more as equals and demanded a greater voice in family governance (Vannoy, 1991).

This change had several causes. First, with the rise of the feminist movement, women gained some economic power and freedom. The first feminist movement in the United States was launched at Seneca Falls, New York, in 1848, where the first women's rights convention was held. The delegates asserted that "men *and* women are created equal . . . endowed . . . with certain inalienable rights." Starting with almost no political leverage and no money, and with conventional morality against them, the suffragists won enactment of the Married Women's Property Act in the latter half of the nineteenth century and ratification of the Nineteenth Amendment to the Constitution in 1920, which gave women the right to vote. The Married Women's Property Act

After years of protest, in the latter half of the nineteenth century, women won the right to own property and borrow money with the enactment of the Married Women's Property Act.

recognized the right of women to hold property and borrow money. As some economic power gradually shifted to women, they gained more power and authority in family governance as well. Property could now be passed on through **bilateral descent** (through both the father and the mother).

Second, in the 1960s and 1970s, increasing educational opportunities for women and the gradual increase in the percentage of married women working outside the home encouraged the adoption of more egalitarian gender roles in the family. As more wives earned an income, more husbands were asked to bear equal responsibility for homemaking and child care. While a sharing of responsibilities was the developing ideal, it was not always followed in practice, and working wives continued to do most of the housework (Blumstein and Schwartz, 1983). The general trend, however, is toward a more equal voice in decision making and a more equitable and flexible distribution of family responsibilities; see Chapter 7 for a detailed discussion. In democratic, egalitarian, dual-career families, residence is often **neolocal**—a place where both spouses choose to live, rather than living with either spouse's family.

Third, in the 1960s and 1970s, the demand for equality of sexual expression resulted from the recognition of the sexual needs of women. With such recognition, marriages could be based on the mutual exchange of love and affection. Development of efficient contraceptives also freed women from unwanted childbearing and enabled them to have a personal life of their own and a social life with their husband.

Fourth, the child study movement after World War II catalyzed the development of the child-centered family. No longer was it a matter of what children could do to serve the family; rather, it became a matter of what the family could contribute to the total development of the child. The rights and needs of children as important members of the family were emphasized.

The net result of these and other changes has been the development of a democratic family ideal that emphasizes egalitarian rights and responsibilities in a group concerned with the welfare of all. This ideal has not always been achieved, but family philosophies, forms, and functions continue to change as new needs arise.

CHANGES IN MARRIAGE AND PARENTHOOD

As we will see, trends in marriage and parenthood have changed in recent decades. The marriage rate has gone down, the age at which people marry has

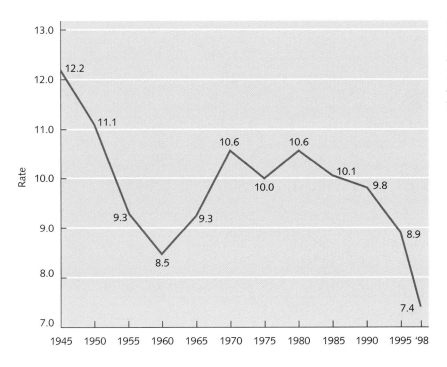

Figure 1.1   Marriage Rate per 1,000 Population (*Note:* From *Statistical Abstract of the United States, 1999* [Table 155, p. 110] by U.S. Bureau of the Census, 1999, Washington, DC: U.S. Government Printing Office.)

gone up, and the number of children per family has declined.

Marriage Rates

The marriage rate is the number of persons who marry during the preceding 12 months per 1,000 population. The rate depends on economic and political conditions, as well as on the percentage of persons of marriageable age in the population. The rate reached a peak of 12.2 per 1,000 population in 1945, the last year of World War II. The rate then declined very rapidly after the war, falling to 8.5 per 1,000 in 1960. The rate varied at a fairly high level for two decades and then began to fall again in 1980, after most of the baby boom babies had married (see Figure 1.1). Today the rate is 7.4 per 1,000 (U.S. Bureau of the Census, 1999).

Age at Marriage

One of the most important trends in the changing family has been the increase in the median age at first marriage (Sporakowski, 1988). The median age at first marriage in 1999 was 27.1 years for men and 24.8 years for women. At the beginning of the twentieth century, the median age at first marriage started a decline that ended in the mid-1950s,

reaching a low of 22.5 years for men and 20.1 years for women. Since then, the estimated median age has been rising, with especially rapid increases since 1980; this trend will be discussed in Chapter 4. Furthermore, the gap in median age of marriage for men and women narrowed to about a 2-year difference in 1995 (U.S. Bureau of the Census, 1999a). Figure 1.2 shows the trend. Not apparent in Figures 1.1 and 1.2 is the fact that marriage and childbearing begin much earlier for women in rural, as opposed to urban, areas (McLaughlin, Lichter, and Johnston, 1993).

A higher age at marriage is associated with an advantaged family background and with school enrollment. Delays in marriage are also associated with underemployment and unemployment. People today marry later and may experience a period of cohabitation prior to marriage (Barich and Bielby, 1996). The reasons for the trend toward marital delay probably include increased opportunities for nonmarital sexual intercourse and increased acceptance of nonmarital cohabitation (Cooney and Hogan, 1991; Miller and Heaton, 1991).

This trend is significant because those who wait until they are in their middle or late twenties to marry have a greater chance of marital success than do those who marry earlier. In fact, one of the strongest and most consistent predictors of the

Figure 1.2 Median Age at First Marriage, by Sex: 1890 to 1999 (*Note:* Data from *Vital Statistics of the United States* by U.S. National Center for Health Statistics [U.S. Department of Health and Human Services], annual, 1890–1999, Washington, DC: U.S. Government Printing Office; *Monthly Vital Statistics Report* by U.S. National Center for Health Statistics, monthly, Washington, DC: U.S. Government Printing Office; and *Statistical Abstract of the United States, 1999* [Table 158, p. 111] by U.S. Bureau of the Census, 1999, Washington, DC: U.S. Government Printing Office.)

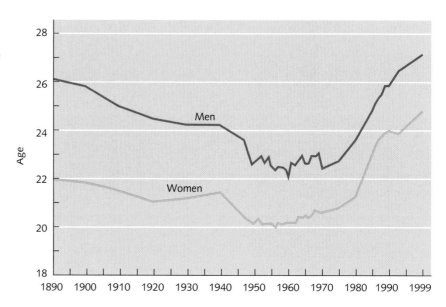

propensity to divorce is the age at which persons marry. Virtually every study of marital dissolution undertaken since the late 1960s has found both spouses' age at marriage to be statistically significant with respect to the probability of divorce (South, 1995). The delay of marriage also has resulted in a marked increase in unmarried young adults in the population. One-half of the men (51%) and over one-third of the women (38.6%) in the country still have not married by 30 years of age (U.S. Bureau of the Census, 1999). This is due to a decline in negative attitudes toward remaining single, a longer life expectancy, smaller families, and more career options for women (Thornton, 1989). See Chapter 4 for a complete discussion.

Birthrates and Family Size

The birthrate in the United States climbed very rapidly after 1945 and stayed high for the next 20 years. This **cohort,** known as the baby boomers, was larger than any that had been born since the years before the 1910s and 1920s. At the present time, birthrates are on the decline. Birthrates for all groups have fallen to their lowest level since 1986 (Hollander, 1997a). Declining birthrates since 1965 have resulted in smaller families. The average number of persons per family was 3.67 in 1960 and 3.18 in 1999. Figure 1.3 shows the change in the average population per family from 1960 to 1999.

As you can see in Figure 1.4, 52% of White families in 1999 had no children of their own under 18 years of age. An additional 20% of White families had only one child of their own at home who was under 18 years of age. Higher percentages of both Black and Hispanic families had greater numbers of children. The birthrate continues to be higher for most minority groups because of cultural differences and different employment opportunities; this trend will be discussed more in Chapter 3.

Seventy-two percent of White families had only one or no children under 18 at home. Among Black families, the figure was 65%. These figures reflect the fact that American women of all races are having fewer children. At the beginning of the twentieth century, the average married woman had five children. By the end of the century, the average number of total births to ever-married women between the ages of 15 and 55 had declined to 1.8.

The decline in family size can be attributed to several factors. Until the twentieth century, women were expected to "be fruitful and multiply." Large families were considered not only a blessing but also an economic asset: More hands were available to work the family farm. Furthermore, reliable birth control methods were largely unavailable. In fact, in 1873, Congress enacted the "Comstock Law," which imposed heavy fines and long prison terms for sending information on contraceptives through the mail. Twenty-four states passed additional statutes that banned advertisements for and the publication and

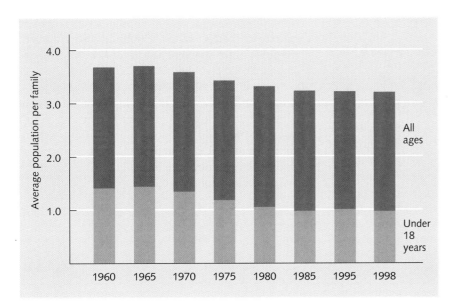

Figure 1.3 Average Population per Family, 1960–1998 (*Note:* Data from *Statistical Abstract of the United States, 1999* [Table 70, p. 60] by U.S. Bureau of the Census, 1999, Washington, DC: U.S. Government Printing Office.)

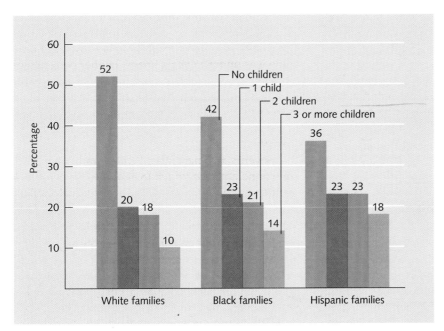

Figure 1.4 Percent Distribution of Families, by Number of Own Children Under 18 Years Old and by Ethnic Group, 1998 (*Note:* Data from *Statistical Abstract of the United States, 1999* [Table 79, p. 65] by U.S. Bureau of the Census, 1999, Washington, DC: U.S. Government Printing Office.)

distribution of information on contraceptives. Another 14 states made it illegal for anyone, including physicians, to provide information about contraception.

As families moved from farms to the city, large numbers of children became a financial burden, so it became economically expedient for women to have fewer children (Margolis, 1984). Also, women began to work in factories and offices and could not take care of large families. At the same time, more efficient means of contraception became available, and couples were more willing to use them. Federal and state laws prohibiting the dispensing of contraceptive information and methods were gradually repealed. When married women began a massive movement into the world of work, the birthrate decreased even more.

Working Mothers

Another important change in family living has been the large influx of married women into the work-force (Floge, 1989). Until the early 1980s, married women with no children under age 18 had higher labor force participation rates than did those with children under age 6. This long-standing pattern began to change during the 1980s and has now reversed. In 1998, married women whose youngest child was between ages 6 and 17 had the highest labor force participation rates (76.8%; see Figure 1.5). Sixty-four percent of married women with the youngest child under age 6 also were employed. This represents a larger percentage than that of married women without children under 18 (U.S. Bureau of the Census, 1999a). This trend will be discussed in more detail in Chapter 12.

Research has revealed some demographic, social, and attitudinal differences between married women who work outside the home and those who do not. Those who do not are more likely to hold traditional attitudes regarding marital roles, mothers' employment outside the home, and sexuality. Married women who are not employed full-time have more children and live in households with less income. Married women who are employed full-time are better educated and have fewer children and more income than married women who are not employed (Glass, 1992). There has also been a marked increase in the proportion of highly educated women who convert their professional training into paid employment (Cooney and Uhlenberg, 1991).

Mothers are entering the workforce for reasons both economic and noneconomic. The major reason is financial need: Many families simply can't make it financially without both parents working. Factors such as inflation, the high cost of living, and the desire for a higher standard of living pressure families to have two incomes. Employment opportunities for women have also increased.

Noneconomic reasons for employment are important as well. Large numbers of women want to work for reasons of personal fulfillment. For many, this is the primary motive.

These trends have only added to women's burdens. Most working wives now try to meet the usual demands for housework and family care in addition to working full-time outside the home. Generally, research indicates that the wife's employment has only a minimal effect on the husband's household responsibilities. Women's satisfaction is greatly enhanced when husbands are willing to assume a fair share of the total responsibilities (Scanzoni, 1987).

Increased employment for mothers has intensified the demand for child care. Eighty-eight percent of mothers working 35 or more hours a week use nonparental child care for their children under 6 years of age (U.S. Bureau of the Census, 1999a). This includes both group care in centers and baby-sitting by relatives or nonrelatives.

One-Parent Families

One of the most far-reaching changes since the 1970s has been the increase in the number of families that consist of a single parent maintaining a household with one or more children. The high rates of separation and divorce, as well as the increased number of births to single women, have contributed to the large increase in this family type.

In 1998, nearly 1 out of every 3 families (27.7%) with children under age 18 was a one-parent family, up from 1 in 10 in 1970. The number of one-parent families tripled between 1970 and 1998 (from 4 million to 12 million; U.S. Bureau of the Census, 1999a). Among one-parent families, 2.1 million were headed by fathers, and 9.8 million were headed by mothers, 42.2% of whom were never married.

Eighty-five percent of one-parent families in 1998 were mother-child families. The older the parent (and the children), the more likely the father is to maintain a one-parent family with his children. Boys are more likely than girls to be living with fathers. However, mother-child families are disproportionately concentrated among African Americans because of high rates of unemployment and underemployment of Black males; this pattern will be discussed further in Chapter 3. Fifty-eight percent of all Black children under 18 are currently living with only their mother, compared with 23% of all White children and 30% of Hispanic children under 18.

Statistics for a particular year fail to show the true extent of one-parent families (Hofferth, 1985). Cross-sectional studies show only the percentages of one-parent families during the year of the survey, not the total number that have ever been one-parent families. According to projections, nearly 60% of all children born in 1986 can expect to spend at least a large part of one year in a one-parent family before reaching the age of 18 (Norton and Glick,

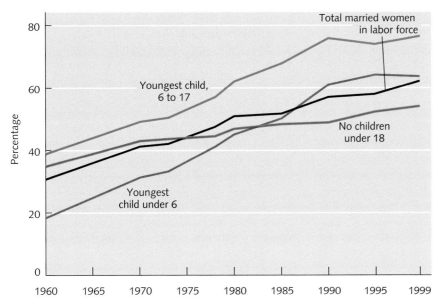

Figure 1.5 Labor Force Participation Rates of Married Women, by Presence of Children and Age of Youngest Child, 1998 (*Note:* Data from *Statistical Abstract of the United States, 1999* [Table 659, p. 417] by U.S. Bureau of the Census, 1999, Washington, DC: U.S. Government Printing Office.)

1986). The effects on mothers and on children are discussed in detail in Chapter 17.

Gay and Lesbian Families

This discussion would not be complete without including gay or lesbian families. Researchers have become increasingly interested in the same-sex relationship form.

As in any family type, there is a wide diversity of gay and lesbian life-styles. Many same-sex couple relationships are of short duration, and a pattern of serial monogamy is common. However, a large number of gays and lesbians have made long-term commitments in stable couple relationships (Masters and Johnson, 1979). Although only a few states have legitimized same-sex marriage, marriagelike liaisons are increasingly accepted by society.

Reverend Philip Zwerling, a California clergyman, wrote:

I had never married two people of the same sex. I finally realized that their sexual orientation did not lessen their commitment to each other, or their love for each other. I cannot now predict the future of their relationship, but I do believe that they freely chose what both believe best for them.

Gay people have the same desire for happiness in our society as heterosexuals. And one of those desires is the chance . . . to create a marital relationship of depth and love. (Zwerling, 1989)

Gays and lesbians are fighting harder than ever before for the right to legally marry. Public support for marriage equality continues to grow, but 30 states and Congress have passed laws that allow them to refuse to honor gay marriages in the event that a state court permits them. By passing some form of antimarriage law, states have sanctioned public policy discriminating against lesbian and gay couples. However, some states have adopted more progressive policies regarding gay and lesbian marriages. For example, the Vermont Supreme Court in December 1999 ordered the state legislature to extend to lesbian and gay couples the same rights, protections, benefits, and obligations available to nongay couples through marriage. While the court held that all the benefits and protections of marriage must be made equally available, the justices explicitly did not rule on whether to allow lesbian and gay couples access to civil marriage.

Many cities and businesses are now recognizing gay and lesbian couples as domestic partners and extending benefits commonly granted only to married couples. Although these laws and policies do not include all of the rights of marriage, they generally grant partners some of the recognition and benefits extended to married couples. The benefits vary depending on city and company but typically include the right to visit a sick or dying partner in the hospital, sick leave to care for a partner, bereavement

It is estimated that between 1 and 5 million lesbians in the United States are biological or adoptive mothers. These figures, however, probably underestimate the actual numbers. Because of fear of discrimination and contests over child custody, lesbian and gay parents are sometimes reluctant to make their sexual orientation known.

Most children in families headed by lesbian mothers were born into the context of a heterosexual relationship between the biological parents. After leaving the heterosexual relationship, some mothers eventually enter a relationship with another woman who may or may not act as a stepparent to the children. If both women are parents, the children may form stepsibling relationships with one another.

Some single lesbians, as well as lesbian couples, conceive children through artificial insemination. Lesbians who want to become mothers through artificial insemination may select a friend, relative, or acquaintance to be the sperm donor, or they may choose to use an anonymous donor.

In one study, researchers interviewed 28 lesbian couples with 51 children (Hare and Richards, 1993). Half of the families had one child; the remainder had between two and eight children. The children's ages ranged from 4 months to 23 years, with a mean of 9.6 years. Thirty-six children (70%) were conceived heterosexually. Eleven (22%) were conceived through artificial insemination using either known or unknown donors. Four (8%) were adopted by one of the women in the couple. In 72% of the families, the mother had full custody of the children; in 18% of the families, there was joint mother-father custody; and in 10% of the families, the father had full custody.

The involvement of biological fathers ranged from low to moderate and tended to vary over time, with some fathers increasing and others decreasing contact with children. The mothers were very supportive of the fathers' involvement, and they felt that the more involvement, the better for the child. Four or five children were conceived

using a known donor; two of the donor fathers were moderately involved, visiting the child once a week. The role of the donor with respect to the child was primarily that of a family friend or male role model. He was acknowledged as "your father" but did not act as an authority figure or parent.

Most women who elected to use an unknown donor still believed that a male role model was important for their children, although not all mothers had been able to identify such a person for their child. One couple asked the husband of a long-time friend to serve as their son's godfather. They reported that this had been a very positive relationship for the child. Of the four adopted children, one had a highly involved surrogate father who lived across the street and saw him daily. The other adopted children had no surrogate father or male role model during the study time period.

The involvement of lesbian partners in the lives of the children varied considerably. In all cases, the birth mother assumed ultimate parental authority for her own child. No children in this group referred to the partner as "mother"; all called the partner by her first name. When both women in the couple were birth mothers, child-care responsibilities were shared to a greater extent than when only one woman was a birth mother. In families in which only one of the women was the birth mother, the partner tended to assume the role of friend and ally of the child. A clear distinction was made between partner and mother in terms of parental authority. Overall, the relationships were very positive; however, some strain was reported between the partner and adolescent children. This was true even when the partner had joined the family when the children were very young.

Families formed by lesbian mothers are described as closely resembling heterosexual stepfamilies. As with heterosexual families, it appears that, when children are born or adopted outside the context of a current relationship, all relationships require adjustment in terms of new roles and responsibilities (Hare and Richards, 1993).

leave to attend a partner's funeral, housing rights such as rent control, and health insurance.

Many gays and lesbians are parents of children who were born during previous heterosexual unions. In the 1990s, many gays and lesbians also used artificial insemination and adoption as avenues to parenthood. There are an estimated 2–6 million gay or lesbian parents, who have 6–14 million children (Patterson, 1992). One of the problems in obtaining more exact numbers is that discrimination still exists, and so many gay and lesbian parents keep their sexual identity relatively hidden. Child custody can be denied if a parent's homosexuality can be proven to adversely affect the child (Patterson and Redding, 1996). Indeed, fear of losing their children is often the biggest barrier to gays' and lesbians' openly declaring their sexual orientation. During custody cases, the courts often are concerned with several issues surrounding the social and psychological development of children being raised by gay or lesbian parents. These include concerns that the parents' homosexuality will adversely affect the child's gender and emotional development, that social stigma or peer rejection will result due to parental homosexuality, and that there is an increased likelihood of the child becoming homosexual (Fitzgerald, 1999). However, the studies that have been conducted on children who grow up in gay and lesbian families show that they develop in a positive manner psychologically, intellectually, behaviorally, and emotionally. They have no greater incidence of homosexuality than do children who grow up in a heterosexual family, and the presence of a heterosexual parent of each gender is not crucial to healthy child development (see Fitzgerald, 1999, for a review of the literature).

Grandparents as Parents

One notable trend in the evolution of the family in recent decades is the dramatic increase in the number of children living in grandparent-maintained households. In 1970, 2.2 million children under age 18 lived in their grandparents' home, with or without parents present; by 1998, that number had grown to almost 4 million (Casper and Bryson, 1998). When these households are categorized by the presence of parents, it becomes evident that the greatest increases have occurred in households in which one parent is also residing in the home. Between 1970 and 1997, households in which the mother was present increased by 118 percent, and households in which the father was present increased by 217 percent (see Figure 1.6). Research has indicated that possible reasons for this trend include an increase in drug use among parents, higher rates of teen pregnancy or divorce, the rapid rise in single-parent households, AIDS, child abuse and neglect, and incarceration of parents (Minkler, 1998).

The arrangement of grandparent as caregiver has benefits and drawbacks, for both grandparents and children. Grandparents may experience a greater sense of purpose for living, a renewed vitality, and a feeling of rejuvenation (Kleiner, Hertzog, and Targ, 1998). They may relish the opportunity to raise a child differently or to nurture family relationships, and they may be rewarded with love and companionship they did not have previously with the grandchild (Burton, Dilworth-Anderson, and Merriwether-de-Vries, 1995).

Children may also benefit from living in grandparent-maintained households. Compared to children in single-parent households, children being raised solely by their grandparents are healthier, have fewer behavioral problems, and are better adapted socially (Solomon and Marx, 1995). And compared to children in foster care, those in grandparent-maintained households may be less traumatized, enjoy the continuation of family identity and culture or ethnicity, and maintain a connection to their siblings (Bell and Garner, 1996).

Much of the research, however, puts more emphasis on the apparent negative effects on grandparents and children in these households. Economic difficulties are prevalent in grandparent-maintained households. Twenty-seven percent of children who live with their grandparents are in poverty, and if the grandmother is raising the children alone, almost two-thirds of the children are living in poverty. Both numbers are significantly greater than the 19 percent of children in poverty who live with their parents (Casper and Bryson, 1998). Figure 1.7 shows the comparison. Grandparents may even be penalized for their willingness to care for their grandchildren, being denied foster-parent benefits because of their blood relation to the children (Kleiner et al., 1998).

Some grandparents also experience increased health problems and loss of stamina. Many report feeling emotionally and physically drained from having to care for their grandchildren (Kleiner et al., 1998). Other drawbacks include loss of time for themselves that they had rediscovered after their own children left home, isolation from their social networks, and resentment based on jealousy and role confusion on the part of other grandchildren and family members (Kleiner et al., 1998).

Aside from being poor, children living with their grandparents are more likely to be living with caregivers who have not graduated from high school: one-third of children in grandparent-headed households versus one-eighth of children in parent-headed households (Casper and Bryson, 1998). Another negative consequence for children in grandparent-maintained households is a lack of health insurance. Fifty-six percent of children residing with both grandparents, with no parent present, are uninsured, compared to 13% of children living with both parents (Bryson and Casper, 1999).

Given the increase in the number of grandparents raising their grandchildren and the impact this arrangement has on both caregiver and child, the

Figure 1.6   Grandchildren in Grandparents' Homes by Presence of Parents, 1970–1997 (*Note:* Data from Bureau of the Census, 1970 and 1980, and "Marital Status and Living Arrangements: March 1994" [Table A-6] and "Marital Status and Living Arrangements: March 1997" [Table 4] by U.S. Bureau of the Census, Current Population Surveys, Washington, DC: U.S. Government Printing Office.)

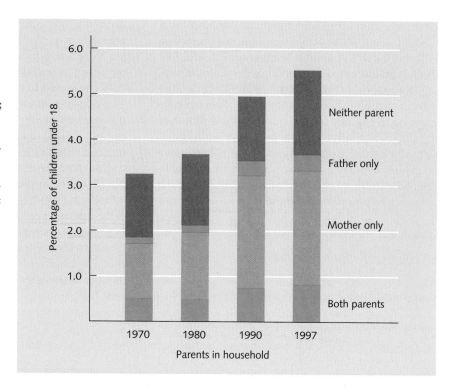

government and the community likely are going to be called upon to provide more support. Policies and programs intended for traditional and foster families could be extended to these families as well, and employers of grandparents remaining in the workforce will expect subsidized child-care and family-friendly policies (Casper and Bryson, 1998).

CHANGES IN DIVORCE AND REMARRIAGE

One of the most dramatic changes in family life in the past generation has been the increase in the rate of divorce and remarriage and the number of step-families (Bray and Hetherington, 1993). In recent years, rates of divorce and remarriage have declined slightly, but they are still at a relatively high level.

Divorce Rates

Divorce rates increased steadily from 1958 until 1979, but since then they have declined slightly (see Figure 1.8). In 1998, 19.4 million adults were currently divorced, representing 9.8% of the popula-

tion. Most scholars believe that the divorce rate has stabilized, with about 50% of new marriages likely to end in divorce. Certainly, there has been a decline in the belief in the ideal of marital permanence, which may have contributed to the increase in marital failure (Glenn, 1991).

Remarriage Trends

The majority of people who divorce eventually remarry. The National Center for Health Statistics estimates that two-thirds of the people who get divorced will eventually marry again (Clarke, 1995). Furthermore, remarriage happens fairly quickly. The median number of years between divorce and remarriage is 3 years for women and 4 years for men (U.S. Bureau of the Census, 1996/1997). Whites remarry more quickly than African Americans, with Latinos the least likely to remarry of the three groups (Coleman and Ganong, 1991; Tiesel and Olson, 1992). These remarriage rates will be discussed in subsequent chapters. However, since the early 1990s, the proportion who remarry appears to be declining. Redivorce rates for remarried persons also show signs of decline, so future rates

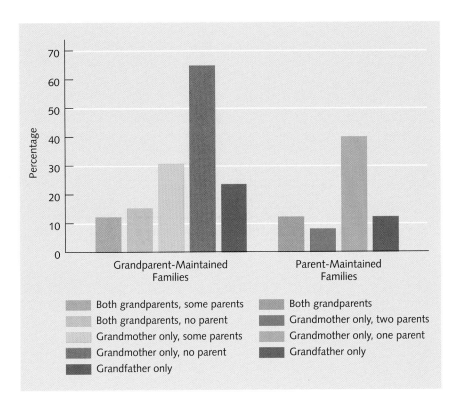

Figure 1.7 Percentage of Children in Different Family Types Who Are in Poverty, 1997 (*Note:* Data from "Coresident Grandparents and Grandchildren" [p. 8] by K. Bryson and L. M. Casper, 1999, Current Population Reports, Series P-20, No. 168, Washington, DC: U.S. Government Printing Office.)

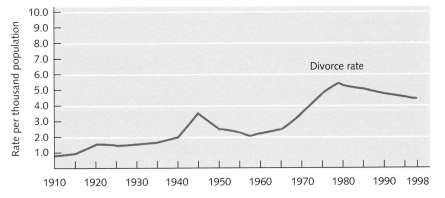

Figure 1.8 Divorce Rates, 1910–1998 (*Note:* Data from *Vital Statistics of the United States* by National Center for Health Statistics [U.S. Department of Health and Human Services], annual, 1910–1998, Washington, DC: U.S. Government Printing Office.)

of redivorce may be quite similar to those of first divorce. This may be due to economic factors, as in the case of divorced men who are paying child support and are reluctant to assume financial responsibility for another family. However, the incidence of divorce in the United States remains among the highest in the world. The net effect of a high rate of divorce and remarriage is an increase in reconstituted, or blended, families.

Blended Families

Overall, about 46% of American marriages are remarriages for the husband, wife, or both (Clarke, 1995). When a parent remarries and brings children from a previous marriage into the new family unit, a blended, or reconstituted, family is formed. If the couple has children together, the blended family may consist of children from her previous marriage,

Figure 1.9   Age of First Intercourse, by Ethnic Group and Sex, 1992 (*Note:* From *Sex in America* [p. 91] by R. T. Michael, J. H. Gagnon, E. O. Laumann, and G. Kolata, 1994, Boston: Little, Brown.)

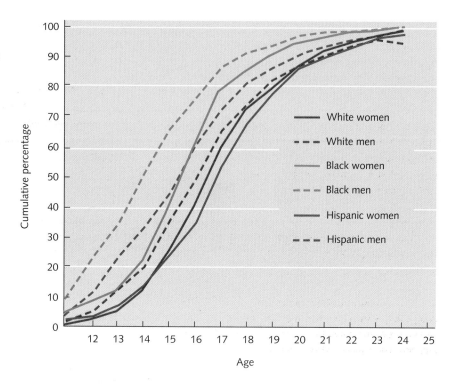

children from his previous marriage, and children born to them since they married each other.

Family relationships in a blended family can become quite complicated, because each parent faces the challenge of forming new relationships with stepchildren, with the children of the new marriage, and perhaps with the spouse's ex-spouse. The children face the challenge of adjusting to stepparents and to stepsiblings, as well as maintaining relationships with natural parents both inside and outside their new family unit. If both their natural parents remarry, the children must adjust to two stepparents and to any stepsiblings in their newly constituted families. Also, both parents and children may have to form new relationships with other relatives on both sides of the families. In short, obviously, many adjustments are required. See Chapter 21 for a detailed discussion of remarriage and stepparenting.

CHANGES IN NONMARITAL SEXUAL BEHAVIOR

Sexual Activity

Researchers have reported significant changes in attitudes toward and behaviors associated with nonmarital sexual activity over the past 40 years. A comprehensive survey conducted in 1992, called the National Health and Social Life Survey, is based on 3,432 interviews with people across the United States. These respondents answered a 90-minute questionnaire about their sexual behavior and other aspects of their sex lives (Michael, Gagnon, Laumann, and Kolata, 1994). One of the trends that the results revealed was, with a few exceptions, a steadily declining age at which people first had sexual intercourse. Men reported first having sex at a younger age than did women, and Blacks reported doing so at a younger age than did Whites.

Another way to look at the age of first intercourse is illustrated in Figure 1.9, which shows the age at which teenagers and young adults first experienced sexual intercourse. The graph shows that half of all Black men have had intercourse by age 15, half of all Hispanic men by age 16½, and half of all White men by age 17. Half of all Black women have had intercourse by age 17, and half of all White and Hispanic women have had intercourse by about age 18. By age 22, about 90% of each group have had intercourse (Heaton and Jacobson, 1994).

When asked why they had intercourse the first time, 51% of the men said curiosity and readiness for sex, and 25% said affection for their partner. Among the women, it was the reverse: About half said affec-

Efforts have been made to identify those students who engage in high-risk sexual behavior in order to decrease the rate of teenage pregnancy and to slow the spread of AIDS and other sexually transmitted diseases. Such behavior includes substance abuse, sex with multiple partners, and condom nonuse.

Students who use marijuana, cocaine, and other illicit drugs are more likely than students who report no substance abuse to have had sexual intercourse and to have had four or more sexual partners; they are also less likely to have used condoms during intercourse. Students who report no substance abuse are least likely to have ever had intercourse or to have had four or more partners (Lowry et al., 1994).

Unmarried American women who have first intercourse when they are younger than age 17 are more likely than other women to have had more than one sexual partner (Seidman, Mosher, and Aral, 1994). Female adolescents who receive little parental supervision are more likely to engage in risky sexual behavior than adolescents who talk more with their parents about birth control. They have more partners and use contraceptives unreliably (Luster and Small, 1994). High-risk sexually active females have a lower mean grade point average than do low-risk sexually active females. Likewise, average alcohol consumption is significantly higher among high-risk young women (Luster and Small). High-risk females are also significantly more likely to have been physically abused than are low-risk teenagers (Donovan, 1995). Males who engage in sexual risk taking are more likely than others to contemplate suicide and to have been sexually abused (Luster and Small).

Maternal disapproval of premarital sex, maternal discussions about birth control, and the quality of the parent-child relationship may have an important influence on male and female adolescent sexual activity and on the consistency of adolescents' contraceptive use (Jaccard, Dittus, and Gordon, 1996).

Both boys and girls are significantly more likely to become sexually active before age 14 if their mother had sex at an early age and if she has worked extensively outside the home (Mott, Fondell, Hu, Kowaleski-Jones, and Menaghan, 1996). Data gathered from 2,168 male and female adolescents in grades 7, 9, and 11 showed that the six strongest predictors of sexual experience were frequent use of alcohol, involvement in a committed relationship, low parental monitoring, permissive parental values, low grade point average, and a history of sexual abuse (Small and Luster, 1994).

Social control factors have an important influence on sexual behavior. For example, religious control systems act as a powerful deterrent to adolescent sexuality in terms of both attitudes and behavior. Data from a national probability sample of single female adolescents, ages 15–19, indicated that geographic mobility was partly related to premarital sex. Migration may lower control, resulting in greater sexual experience (Stack, 1994).

Having both sexually active girlfriends and an adolescent childbearing sister had strong effects on permissive sexual attitudes of adolescent girls (East, Felice, and Morgan, 1993). Maternal conservative attitudes about sex and the presence of dating rules that were enforced delayed development of sexual behavior in male and female White and Latino adolescents (Hovell, Sipan, Blumberg, Atkins, Hofstetter, and Kreigner, 1994).

---

tion for their partner, and about 25% said curiosity and readiness for sex. A very small percentage of both men and women said they had sex because of a desire for physical pleasure. Most of the men said they were not in love with their first sexual partner; most of the women, in contrast, said they were.

Today, American teenagers are having sex earlier than their parents did, but they do not necessarily have more partners. About half of today's young adults begin having intercourse with a partner ages 15–18, and at least four out of five have had intercourse by the time they are 21. Given that the average age of marriage is now the mid-twenties, few Americans are waiting until they marry to have sex. But most sexually active young people show no signs of having large numbers of partners. More than half of the men and women between ages 18 and 24 in 1992 had had just one sex partner in the past year, and 11% had had none.

The National Health and Social Life Survey gives no support to the idea of a promiscuous society or of a dramatic sexual revolution in which large numbers of people have multiple, casual sex partners. Instead, the survey indicates that most people form partnerships and ultimately get married. And no matter how sexually active people are before and between marriages, and no matter whether they live with a sexual partner before marriage or they are virgins on their wedding day, the vast majority, once married, have no other sexual partner; their past is essentially erased. Marriage remains the great leveler (Michael et al., 1994).

The Use of Contraceptives

People in a high-risk category—those who have more than one partner, especially if they do not know them well, and those who have the most frequent sexual relationships—need to use condoms consistently to protect against sexually transmitted diseases, especially AIDS. According to the National Health and Social Life Survey, nearly half the people in the high-risk category never use condoms during vaginal intercourse with their primary partner or a secondary partner (see Figure 1.10). Nevertheless, perhaps because they want to protect their spouse or lover from infection and because they recognize the riskiness of their behavior, people who have several sex partners in a year are more likely to use a condom with their primary partner and with their secondary partners than are people who have only one other partner.

Unmarried Pregnancy

The marked increase in nonmarital sexual activity, accompanied by an inefficient use of contraceptives, the lesbian baby boom, and more single women deciding to have children, has resulted in an increase in unmarried pregnancy. However, the teen birthrate has declined 20% since 1991, from 62.1 per 1,000 females ages 15–19 to 49.6 (Curtin and Martin, 2000). The total number of live births to unmarried women of all groups increased from 827,420 in 1985 to 1,260,000 in 1996 (see Figure 1.11). The nonmarital birthrate peaked in 1994, with 47 births per 1,000 females, and then declined to 44 births per 1,000 females (National Center for Health Statistics, 1999).

THEORIES TO HELP EXPLAIN FAMILY BEHAVIOR

As rational creatures, we seek explanations. When a husband and wife divorce, for instance, family and friends look for answers to a variety of questions: What happened? Why are they getting a divorce? What agreements will be made? What will happen to them and the children after it's all over?

There are dozens of theories related to intimate relationships, marriages, and families. Theories have been formulated to explain why people are attracted

to one another, why people fall in love, why people select the mates they do, how gender roles develop, how families make decisions, what causes sexual dysfunctions, how to raise children, and what causes divorce and remarriage.

Here we are interested in theories related to the family itself. According to scientific methods, theory building is a process of formulating a problem, collecting data to aid in solving the problem, developing a hypothesis, testing it, and then drawing conclusions, which are stated in the form of a theory. A **theory** is a tentative explanation of facts and data that have been observed (Klein and White, 1996).

Psychologists and sociologists have formulated a number of theories about the family (Holman and Burr, 1980). Seven important ones have been selected for discussion here: structural-functional theory, family developmental theory, symbolic interaction theory, systems theory, exchange theory, conflict theory, and feminist theory.

Structural-Functional Theory

Structural-functional theory looks at the family as a social institution and asks, How is the family organized, and what functions does it serve in meeting society's needs? When talking about the family, structural-functionalists usually refer to the nuclear family. From this point of view, the family is considered successful to the extent that it fulfills societal expectations and needs.

Family functions have been described in numerous ways. A generation ago, Murdock (1949) identified four basic functions of the nuclear family: providing a common residence, economic cooperation, reproduction, and sex. Since Murdock's time, the nuclear family has become much less common, and some of the functions he identified are not necessarily confined to the family. In an attempt to provide an even more basic definition of the family, sociologists and family theorists have proposed other functions. However, Murdock's four are a good place to start discussing the family's role in society.

Common Residence   In recent decades, changes in society have created many variations of this function. In commuter marriages, for example, spouses maintain separate residences for much of the time, seeing each other only on weekends or occasionally during the month. Today, family members may share

Condom Use with Primary Partner　　　　**Condom Use with Secondary Partner**

Figure 1.10　Frequency of Condom Use over the Past 12 Months with Primary and Secondary Sex Partners, 1992 (*Note:* From *Sex in America* [p. 197] by R. T. Michael, J. H. Gagnon, E. O. Laumann, and G. Kolata, 1994, Boston: Little, Brown.)

Respondent had two sex partners in past 12 months

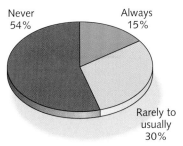

Never 54%　　Always 15%　　Rarely to usually 30%

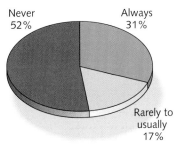

Never 52%　　Always 31%　　Rarely to usually 17%

Respondent had three or more sex partners in past 12 months

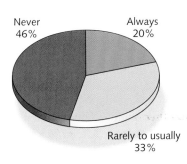

Never 46%　　Always 20%　　Rarely to usually 33%

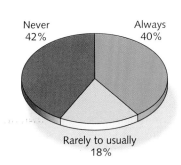

Never 42%　　Always 40%　　Rarely to usually 18%

a common residence only some of the time, but they still form a family.

Economic Cooperation　Economic cooperation is a broad concept that can include a wide range of activities, from cooking, to maintaining a household, to earning an income. It includes the production, allocation, distribution, and management of resources such as money, material goods, food, drink, services, skills, care, time, and space.

Historically, the family was almost a self-sufficient economic unit. The traditional rural family produced much of its own food, housing, and clothing. Family members cooperated in this production and depended on one another for goods and services.

During and after the industrial revolution, many families moved off the family farm and came to depend more on those outside the family for the production of goods and services. As families became consumers rather than producers, earning an income became even more necessary. Partly because of increasing demands for income, wives as well as

husbands were enlisted in the task of providing a living. Thus, spouses become mutually dependent in fulfilling this task.

The economic functions of the family are still important, but the nuclear family has never been able to meet all of them. Some needs have been met by other groups. For example, insurance companies provide health and life insurance, and industries and the Social Security Administration provide pensions for the retired or disabled.

Reproduction　Although the reproductive function of the family has always been important, non-marital reproduction is now common as well. Births to unmarried women now constitute one-fourth of all live births (U.S. Bureau of the Census, 1999a). Advances in reproductive technology—in vitro fertilization, for example—have made it possible for fertilization to take place without any sexual contact between a man and a woman.

Sexual Functions　Murdock's concept of sexuality was synonymous with heterosexual relationships

Figure 1.11   Births to Un-married Women, by Ethnic Origin, as a Percentage of Total Live Births, 1998 (*Note:* Data from "Births: Final Data for 1998" [Tables 13 and 14] by S. J. Ventura, J. A. Martin, S. C. Curtin, T. J. Mathews, and M. M. Park, 2000, *National Vital Statistics Report, 48*(3), Hyattsville, MD: National Center for Health Statistics.)

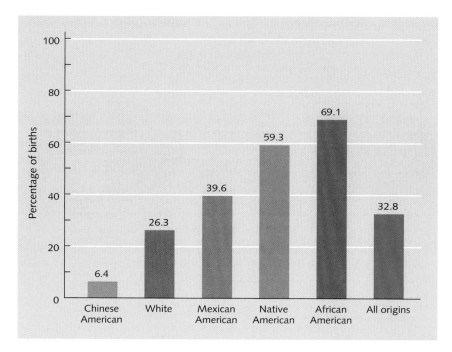

within the family. Obviously, sexual expression, both heterosexual and homosexual, may take place between two people outside a family unit. Some gay and lesbian couples have children from previous heterosexual relationships or have been able to legally adopt children, and some lesbians have given birth.

Nurture and Socialization of Children   Sociologists have described other family functions. Reiss (1980) insists that the only universal function of the family (nuclear, extended, or otherwise) is the nurturance and socialization of children. According to this view, parents do not have to be biologically related to their children (the children may be adopted), but society insists that socialization is the responsibility of the family group (Moss and Abramowitz, 1982). Whether parents are single, separated, divorced, married, or remarried, they are expected to be responsible for meeting their children's physical, emotional, social, intellectual, and moral needs. The family is not the only caregiving or socialization unit. Schools, churches, and social groups such as the Cub Scouts, Brownies, Girl and Boy Scouts, and YMCA participate in the socialization process (Hoge, Petrillo, and Smith, 1982). But society delegates to the family primary responsibility for this process. Failure to meet this function constitutes legal grounds for charges of child ne-

glect or abuse. Additional information on the socialization of children may be found in Chapter 17 on parenting.

Family Developmental Theory

Family developmental theory includes two basic concepts. The first is that of the family life cycle, which divides the family experience into phases, or stages, over the life span and describes changes in family structure and roles during each stage. The traditional family life cycle is an early marriage (with no children), years devoted to childbearing and child rearing, empty-nest years, retirement, and the death of one's spouse and widowhood. Chapter 11 discusses the family life cycle in more detail.

The second concept is that of developmental tasks, which Duvall (1977) defines as growth responsibilities that arise at certain stages in the life of the family. The successful completion of these tasks leads to immediate satisfaction and approval, as well as to success with later tasks. In contrast, failure leads to unhappiness in the family, disapproval of society, and difficulty with later developmental tasks. Examples of developmental tasks are the need to develop parenting skills when a child is born and the need to make adjustments at the time of retirement. For the family to continue to grow, biological requirements, cultural imperatives, and

Families exist in a variety of forms, but the nuclear family is still much in evidence. Its most enduring function may be the care and guidance of children.

personal aspirations need to be satisfied during each stage of the family life cycle.

To be successful, family members need to adapt to the changing needs and demands of other family members and the changing expectations of the larger kin network, the community, and society. Family members also need to attend to tasks that are necessary to ensure family survival. Family tasks can be grouped into five categories: (1) physical maintenance, (2) socialization for roles inside and outside the family, (3) maintenance of family morale and motivation to perform tasks, (4) social control, and (5) the acquisition of family members (through birth or adoption) and their launching when mature (Mattessich and Hill, 1987). Chapter 11 provides a more detailed discussion of developmental tasks over the family life cycle.

Symbolic Interaction Theory

Symbolic interaction theory describes the family as a unity of interacting personalities (Stryker, 1972; Turner, 1970). It focuses attention on the way that family members interact through symbols:

words, gestures, rules, and roles. People are socialized to understand the meaning of various symbols and to use them to communicate messages, feelings, intentions, and actions. Family members interact through symbols, and together they develop roles (such as father, husband, mother, wife, or daughter) and assign roles to others in the family, who "play" the assigned role. Each actor adjusts his or her behavior to what he or she thinks the other person is going to do.

Children derive much of their self-concept, or thoughts and feelings about themselves, from symbolic messages conveyed by their parents. These messages may be expressed in words: "David is a naughty boy," or "Joan is a very smart girl." Or they may be expressed in actions, such as withholding or bestowing rewards. From symbolic messages, children learn to enact expected roles and follow prescribed behavior.

But meanings are conveyed both ways. That is, children influence the way parents act as well. Parents will respond differently to a child who is rebellious and to a child who is a conformist, for example. The same principles of reciprocal interaction by means of symbols apply to the relationship between spouses and other family members.

Symbolic interaction is important because our actions and feelings are determined not just by what happens to us but also by how we interpret those events. For example, people define family violence differently. One woman may regard a slap by her husband as unacceptable violence and seek help from the police or a crisis center; another woman may view a couple of punches as a loss of temper not worth mentioning. Symbolic interaction theory is widely used in family therapy to help individuals understand how they perceive one another and how they can modify their perceptions and behavior to develop a more meaningful and harmonious relationship.

Systems theory emphasizes the interdependence of family members (Broderick and Smith, 1979). Family members do not live in isolation; rather, what one does affects all the others. A person with deepseated fears and anxieties and emotional instability, for example, may upset everyone else in the family. People may be interdependent in terms of not only money, shelter, and food but also love, affection, companionship, socialization, and other nontangible needs.

There may be various subsystems within the total family unit. Three children may constitute one subsystem, and their two parents another. A husband and his mother may constitute a subsystem, a mother and her daughter another, a father and son still another. Knowing how one subsystem relates to others can be an important way of understanding the relationships within a particular family. For example, chronic conflict in the husband-wife subsystem may have a negative effect on children in the family. To help the children, a therapist has to assist the spouses in dealing with their conflict.

The concept of interdependency of family members has been useful in the treatment of dysfunctional families. Chronic alcoholism, for example, is considered a family illness. A woman who is married to an alcoholic but denies the problem and covers up for the husband is an "enabler" because she enables him to continue drinking without suffering more consequences. Family interactions may become habitual and therefore difficult to change, even when they are dysfunctional. By analyzing the patterns of response and behavior, therapists seek to motivate partners to rethink and restructure the way they relate to each other and to other family members (Papp, 1983).

Exchange theory is based on the principle that we enter into relationships in which we can maximize the benefits to us and minimize our costs (Nye, 1978). We form associations that we expect to be rewarding, and we tend to stay away from relationships that bring us pain. At the least, we hope that the rewards from a relationship will be proportional to the costs (Aldous, 1977).

People seek different things in relationships. For example, people marry for many different reasons: love and companionship, sex, procreation, status, prestige, power, and financial security. People are usually satisfied with relationships that at least partially fulfill their expectations and that do not exceed the price they expected to pay.

Some relationships are one-sided; one person does most of the giving, and the other the receiving. Over the long term, the giver is likely to become resentful and angry and to seek a more equal exchange.

Equity theory is a variation of exchange theory holding that exchanges between people have to be fair and balanced so that they mutually give and receive what is needed. People cooperate in finding mutual fulfillment rather than compete for rewards. They learn that they can depend on each other to meet needs, and their commitment involves strong motivations to please each other. Exchange theory is discussed in detail in Chapter 9, on mate selection, and in Chapter 14, on power and decision making.

Conflict Theory

Conflict theory has never achieved the same status in contemporary family life literature as have symbolic interaction theory, systems theory, and exchange theory. Nevertheless, conflict theory is useful in describing and understanding family conflict as members struggle for ascendancy and power (Sprey, 1988).

Conflict theory begins by asserting that conflict in families is the normal state of affairs and that family dynamics can be understood by identifying the sources of conflict and the sources of power. What do family members fight about? Who wins, and how and why? What can be done about the conflict? The issue is not how to avoid conflict, but how to manage it, deal with it, and resolve it. When conflict is disruptive and negative, change is needed, and so resolving the conflict becomes the motivation for establishing a more rewarding and meaningful relationship. Solutions come through establishing better communication, developing empathy and understanding, and being motivated to change. Solutions come as well through bargaining, negotiation, and compromise.

Feminist Theory

Feminist theory is often called a "perspective" rather than a theory because it reflects thinking across the feminist movement and includes a variety of viewpoints that focus on the inequality of power between men and women in society, and especially in family life (MacDermid, Jurich, Myers-Walls, and Pelo, 1992). While there are many varia-

tions within the feminist perspective, at the heart of all of them is the issue of gender roles, particularly traditional gender roles. *Gender* is defined as the learned behaviors and characteristics associated with being male or female, and feminist theories examine how gender differences are related to power differences between men and women. Feminists assert that the female experience is just as important and valuable as the male experience in life but that women are exploited, devalued, and oppressed (Osmond and Thorne, 1993; Walker and Thompson, 1984). Feminist theory argues that family and gender roles have been constructed by society and do not derive from biological conditions, and that these roles were created in order for men to maintain power over women. Feminist theory is similar to conflict theory in that the conflict perspective focuses on the unequal power within groups or larger societies, while feminist theory focuses on the sex-gender system and the way male dominance in the family and society is oppressive to women.

Proponents of feminist theories have a common interest in understanding the subordination of women (Osmond and Thorne, 1993) and working to change conditions in society that promote barriers to opportunities for women (Thompson and Walker, 1995). Unique to the feminist perspective is the use of knowledge to raise the level of awareness of oppression and to end oppression and subordination based on social class, race/ethnicity, age, or sexual orientation. The feminist perspective is concerned with the overall oppression of all groups that are defined on the basis of age, class, race/ethnicity, disability, or sexual orientation (Baber and Allen, 1992).

In general, feminists have challenged the definition of family that is based on traditional roles. They see the family as a dynamic and diverse system whose members are constantly changing, and it should not confine men or women to proscribed roles. While they may have been socialized to perform particular roles (for example, males as provider and decision maker, and females as passive and nurturing), feminists maintain that both men and women can play various roles and be quite functional in all of them. This perspective provides couples with more flexibility, because both men and women can play roles based on their unique skills and interests, as opposed to the roles traditionally assigned based on their gender.

The feminist perspective is about choice and about equally valuing the choices individuals make. For example, if the man wants to stay home and take care of the children while the woman pursues a career, his choice should be valued as equally as a decision to pursue a career. Similarly, if the woman chooses to stay home and be the primary caregiver for the children, her choice, as well as her experience in the home, should be valued as equally as her husband's career. Feminists do not object to the idea of women being "traditional" as long as it is a choice that they make, and not a role imposed on them. Women need to make their own choices about how to live their lives, and they need access to the same opportunities available to men. And those choices need to be supported and valued as equally as the choices men make in their lives.

Critique of Family Theories

No one family theory has a monopoly on the truth. Each time a new theory is introduced, it is described as the "key" to understanding family phenomena (Nye, 1978) or as the wave of the future (Broderick and Smith, 1979; Holman and Burr, 1980). Inevitably, however, each theory falls short of completely explaining family processes. This shortcoming does not detract from the usefulness of theories but rather motivates us to look for additional ways to understand changing families and the interaction of the people in them.

SUMMARY

1. A family is any group of persons united by the ties of marriage, blood, or adoption or any sexually expressive relationship, in which the adults cooperate financially to support and care for the children; the people are committed to one another in an intimate, interpersonal relationship; and the members see their identity as importantly attached to the group with an identity of its own.

2. Different family forms are determined by their structural arrangement, the persons in them, and their relationship to one another.

3. Modern views of the family emphasize its role in fulfilling personal needs for emotional security and companionship.

4. Although historically the American family was patriarchal, there has been a gradual shift to a more democratic power structure.

5. The marriage rate has declined since 1980.

6. The median age at first marriage is increasing for both men and women, resulting in an increase in unmarried young adults in the population.

7. Declining birthrates since 1965 have resulted in smaller families.

8. The percentage of married women in the workforce has been increasing steadily. At the present time, greater percentages of women with either preschool or grade-school children are working outside the home than are women without children.

9. The number of one-parent families, especially mother-child families, has risen considerably in recent years.

10. One increasing family form is gay or lesbian families.

11. Large numbers of gays and lesbians live in stable couple relationships, some with children.

12. Divorce rates increased steadily from 1958 until 1979, at which time they leveled off and even declined. At the present rate, it is predicted that between 50% and 60% of new marriages will end in divorce.

13. Three out of four divorced women and four out of five divorced men will eventually remarry, although those rates appear to be declining. The relatively high rates of divorce and remarriage have resulted in a large number of reconstituted, or blended, families.

14. Over the past 40 years, more adolescents have been engaging in sexual intercourse and at a younger age.

15. Unmarried teenagers are inefficient users of contraceptives. The result has been an increase in unmarried pregnancy. Altogether, over 1,260,000 babies were born to single mothers in the United States in 1996. About 96% of unwed mothers decide to keep their babies.

16. A theory is a tentative explanation of facts and data that have been observed.

17. Psychologists and sociologists have formulated a number of theories about the family. Seven main ones in helping to explain families are structural-functional theory, family developmental theory, symbolic interaction theory, systems theory, exchange theory, conflict theory, and feminist theory.

KEY TERMS

family
voluntarily childless family
single-parent family
nuclear family
family of origin
family of procreation
extended family
blended, or reconstituted, family
stepfamily
binuclear family
polygamous family

polygynous family
polyandrous family
patriarchal family
matriarchal family
gay or lesbian family
cohabiting family
instrumental role
expressive role
patrilineal descent
patrilocal residence
matrilineal descent
matrilocal residence

bilateral descent
neolocal residence
cohort
theory
structural-functional theory
family developmental theory
symbolic interaction theory
systems theory
exchange theory
equity theory
conflict theory
feminist theory

QUESTIONS FOR THOUGHT

1. What is your definition of a family? How is it similar to or different from the definition used in the text?

2. For either your family of origin or your present family (if you are married), how well does it adhere to instrumental and/or expressive roles.

3. What are the various reasons for current trends in marriage rates, age at first marriage, birthrates and family size, percentage of working mothers, and one-parent families?

4. What are your thoughts about current trends in nonmarital sexual behavior? What measures do you believe should be taken, if any, to decrease the incidence of unmarried pregnancy?

5. The text suggests that family philosophy has changed from an emphasis on institution to an emphasis on companionship. If you were to follow this philosophy, what kind of marriage would you strive to have? Explain.

6. Which family theory makes the most sense to you? How would you use that theory to help explain the behaviors and patterns in your family?

SUGGESTED READINGS

Acock, A. P., and Demo, D. H. (1994). *Family Diversity and Well-being.* Thousand Oaks, CA: Sage. Focuses on the impact of family structural variations on family relationships and personal well-being.

Baber, K. M., and Allen, K. R. (1992). *Women and Families: Feminist Reconstructions.* New York: Guilford Press. Discusses women's experiences in families and gender relations.

Brubaker, T. H. (Ed.). (1993). *Family Relations: Challenges for the Future.* Newbury Park, CA: Sage. Traces changes in society and families.

Coontz, S. (1992). *The Way We Never Were: American Families and the Nostalgia Trap.* New York: Basic Books. Dispels myths about the traditional family.

Coontz, S. (1997). *The Way We Really Are: Ending the War over America's Changing Families.* New York: Basic Books. Examines "nontraditional" family life and the way changes in family structure have had both positive and negative effects.

Drucker, J. (1998). *Families of Value: Gay and Lesbian Parents and Their Children Speak Out.* New York: Insight Books/Plenum Press. Presents stories by and about gay fathers and lesbian mothers raising children in various settings and situations.

Ganong, L. H., and Coleman, M. (1999). *Changing Families, Changing Responsibilities: Family Obligations Following Divorce and Remarriage.* Mahwah, NJ: Lawrence Erlbaum. Explores responsibilities of members of stepfamilies.

Gottfried, A. E., and Gottfried, A. W. (Eds.). (1994). *Redefining Families, Implications for Children's Development.* New York: Plenum. Examines nontraditional families.

Jagger, G., and Wright, C. (Eds.). (1999). *Changing Family Values.* London, New York: Routledge. Covers the backlash against single mothers, lesbian and gay families and the law, family and social policy, and the future of the nuclear family.

Kissman, K., and Allen, J. A. (1993). *Single-Parent Families.* Newbury Park, CA: Sage. Discusses characteristics, problems, and interventions.

Laird, J., and Green, R. (Eds.). (1996). *Lesbians and Gays in Couples and Families: A Handbook for Therapists.* San Francisco: Jossey-Bass. Presents a series of readings.

Marciano, T. D., and Sussman, M. B. (Eds.). (1991). *Wider Families: New Traditional Family Forms.* New York: Haworth Press. Explores various relationships that constitute families.

McLanahan, S., and Sandefur, G. (1994). *Growing Up with a Single Parent: What Hurts, What Helps.* Cambridge, MA: Harvard University Press. Argues that the disadvantages for children living with single parents are substantial, occur across several important life domains, and persist long into adulthood.

Michael, R. T., Gagnon, J. H., Laumann, E. O., and Kolata, G. (1994). *Sex in America.* Boston: Little, Brown. Reports on a survey of sexual behavior.

Mulroy, E. A. (1995). *The New Uprooted: Single Mothers in Urban Life.* Westport, CT: Auburn House. Examines how single mothers from a diverse set of social and economic circumstances experience the dual roles of sole family breadwinner and sole resident parent in the changing urban environment.

Slater, S. (1995). *The Lesbian's Family Life Cycle.* New York: The Prepress. Traces five stages of the lesbian family life cycle.

Wood, J. T., and Duck, S. (Eds.). (1995). *Under-studied Relationships: Off the Beaten Track.* Thousand Oaks, CA: Sage. Discusses seven different types of relationships that have been understudied.

CHAPTER 2

LEARNING OBJECTIVES

After reading the chapter, you should be able to:

Explain why it is important to examine our family background.

Describe and explain the relationships between parents' attitudes toward their children and children's attitudes toward themselves.

Describe how attitudes toward intimate partners are formed partly by the relationships experienced in the family of origin.

Show how attitudes toward intimacy and expression of affection are developed in the family.

Describe the role of the family in developing attitudes toward sex.

Explain how attitudes toward marriage and divorce are affected by one's family background.

Describe the role of the family in gender-role socialization.

Describe the role of the family in developing family values toward work and in developing work habits.

Summarize the various patterns of communication in families and the way these carry over into marriage.

Identify some of the characteristics of adult children of alcoholics.

Family Backgrounds
and How They Influence Us

Learning Objectives

Why Examine Family Background?
Understanding the Socializing Influence of the Family
Determining Differential Effects
Developing Self-Understanding
Assuming Personal Responsibility
Making Peace with the Past
■ **Perspective:** The Alcoholic Family

Parental Attitudes Toward Children
■ **Perspective:** Perfectionist Parents
Approval
■ **Family Issues:** Can We Blame Our Parents?
Criticism and Rejection

Attitudes Toward Intimate Partners

Family Closeness: Attitudes Toward Intimacy
■ **Perspective:** Who Needs Intimacy?

Attitudes Toward Sex
Positive Attitudes and Teachings
Negative Attitudes and Teachings
Possible Effects on Sexual Behavior

Attitudes Toward Marriage and Divorce

Gender-Role Socialization in the Family

Variations in Family Values and Work Habits
Workaholic Families
■ **Perspective:** Values and Marital Satisfaction
Family Values
Parental Role Models

Communicative, Noncommunicative, and Conflictive Families
Open, Honest, Tactful Communication
■ **Perspective:** Self-Disclosure
Superficial Communication
One-Sided Communication
False Communication
Avoidance of Communication
Noncommunication
Angry Communication

Summary
Key Terms
Questions for Thought
Suggested Readings

The marital relationship neither exists nor evolves in isolation. It has a family in back of it and usually one in front of it (Klagsbrun, 1985). Every marriage is influenced by the family backgrounds the partners bring to the relationship. Each couple, in turn, influences the family relationships their children will establish after them.

The first purpose of this chapter is to examine a representative variety of family relationships to illustrate their possible effects on the family relationships of the next generation. The second purpose is to stimulate and facilitate the examination of our own family backgrounds to see how they have influenced us.

WHY EXAMINE FAMILY BACKGROUND?

Our values, attitudes, and habits are largely molded by our family, although the influence of parents is subject to a number of variables. By being conscious of the positive and negative aspects of our family background, we can make responsible choices about the kind of partner we want to be and, if we choose to become parents, the kind of parent we want to be. Without understanding what influences behavior, it is very difficult to work toward change.

Understanding the Socializing Influence of the Family

The family is the chief socializing influence on children. In other words, the family is the principal transmitter of knowledge, values, attitudes, roles, and habits from one generation to the next. Through word and example, the family shapes a child's personality and instills modes of thought and ways of acting that become habitual. This process is called **generational transmission** (Peterson and Rollins, 1987).

This learning takes place partly through the formal instruction that parents provide their children and partly through the system of rewards and punishments they use to control children. Learning also takes place through **reciprocal parent-child interaction,** as each influences and modifies the behavior of the other in an intense social process. And learning occurs through **observational modeling,** as children observe, imitate, and model the behavior that they find around them (Bandura, 1976). What par-

Because children observe, imitate, and model the behavior of their parents, parents have the opportunity to exert both positive and negative influence over them.

ents say is important, but what children perceive parents to believe and do influences them most. As adults, our attitudes toward marital and parental roles are strongly related to the marital and parental role attitudes of our parents (Snyder, Velasquez, and Clark, 1997).

Determining Differential Effects

Not all children are influenced to the same degree by their families. The degree of influence that parents exert depends partly on the frequency, duration, intensity, and priority of their social contacts with their children. Parents who are emotionally close to their children and who have long-term loving relationships with them exert more influence than do those who are not so close and who relate to their children less frequently. Moreover, family influence may be either modified or reinforced by influences outside the family: the school, church, other social organizations, peer groups, or the mass media. Here again, the extent of influence depends partly on the duration and intensity of the exposure.

Another important factor in determining the influence of the family is the differences among individual children. Not all children react in the same way to the same family environment because children differ in temperament, cognitive perception, developmental characteristics, and maturational levels. Because A happens does not mean that B will inevitably result. When children are brought up in an unhappy, conflicting family, it is more difficult for them to establish happy marriages themselves (Fine and Hovestadt, 1984), but some still do. A person's marital fate is not cast in concrete.

Developing Self-Understanding

Not all children are influenced by their families to the same degree, and not all react the same way to the same environment. However, background has an effect, whatever it might be. The first task in developing self-understanding is determining what effects our families have had on us and evaluating them and the dynamics of their development.

What we have learned in our family of origin may be either helpful or detrimental to subsequent group living. Thus, a family may instill qualities of truth or deceit, of kindness or cruelty, of cooperation or self-centeredness, or of tolerance or obstinancy (Elliot, 1986). In relation to marriage and family living itself, the family may teach flexible or rigid gender roles. It may exemplify and teach democratic or authoritarian power patterns. It may teach rational communication skills or habits of destructive conflict. It may teach children how to express love and affection or how to withhold it. Parents may model responsibility or irresponsibility; they may teach that sex is healthy and pleasurable or that it is dirty and painful. The family helps children develop positive self-images and self-esteem or negative self-images. The family may teach the value of work and the wise management of money or ways to avoid work and mismanage money. The family may teach what a happy marriage can be like or how miserable marriage can be. By examining family background, we can determine how much influence our family of origin had and whether it was positive or negative.

Assuming Personal Responsibility

Another task in examining family background is to begin to choose the goals and directions we want to take and to assume responsibility for our own selves. We can't continue to blame our parents for our problems if these problems are ever to be solved (Caplan, 1986). Nor can we assume that everything will be all right just because we grew up in a happy home.

When grown children enter into intimate relationships, they bring with them the background of experiences from their own families. They tend to feel that the way they were brought up is either the right way (which they try to duplicate in their own families) or the wrong way (which they try to avoid). By examining our family background, we can develop insight into what our own attitudes, feelings, and habits are, how these might cause us to respond, and whether we need to change any of them. Consider this example:

> One couple in their middle fifties went to a marriage counselor after the wife announced she wanted to divorce her husband. The wife's chief complaint was her husband's authoritarian dominance over the family. The wife explained: "Everything has to be done his way. He never considers my wishes. Several years ago I wanted to remodel the kitchen. It was going to cost five thousand dollars, but I was going to pay for it out of my own salary. He said he didn't want the kitchen remodeled and that was that. Our relationship has always been like that. I never do anything I want to do. So I decided I couldn't stand it any longer. I'm leaving him."
>
> In subsequent counseling sessions, the family backgrounds of the couple were explored. The husband pointed out that his father was a dictator in his family. "I really got so I couldn't stand my father," the husband explained.
>
> "And you're just like him," the wife remarked.
>
> It was difficult for the husband to accept this observation at first, but by talking about his experience with his dad compared to his present role as a father, he was able to determine that he needed to change himself.
>
> He did, and the marriage survived. (Author's counseling notes)

Making Peace with the Past

Examining family background also enables us to "make peace with our past." For example, if we are afraid of marriage because our parents were unhappily married, examining background experiences helps us to face these anxieties honestly and to rid

Much attention has been focused on adult children of alcoholics (ACOAs) and the effects of being brought up in an alcoholic family. In this discussion, we are concerned with the effect of alcoholism in the family on growing children. Approximately 76 million Americans, about 43% of the adult population, have been exposed to alcoholism in the family, with almost one in five adult Americans (18%) having lived with an alcoholic while growing up. There are an estimated 26.8 million children of alcoholics (COAs) in the United States, and 11 million of these are under the age of 18 (Eigen and Rowden, 1995). These children are at high risk for a host of emotional and behavioral difficulties during childhood, adolescence, and adulthood. Fetal alcohol syndrome can cause serious neurological and physical damage to infants born to mothers who drink heavily during pregnancy. There is strong scientific evidence that alcoholism tends to run in families. Children of alcoholics are more at risk for alcoholism and other drug abuse than are children of nonalcoholics. Alcoholics are more likely than nonalcoholics to have an alcoholic father, mother, sibling, or other relative. In addition, COAs are more likely than non-COAs to marry into families in which alcoholism is prevalent. It is estimated that 13–25% of all COAs will become alcoholics themselves (Eigen and Rowden, 1995).

COAs are at high risk for mental health problems, too (Roosa, Tein, Croppenbacher, Michaels, and Dumea, 1993). However, not all children in problem-drinking households experience mental health problems. Therefore, the risk status of children with alcohol-abusing parents may be related to parental dysfunction in general rather than to alcohol use in particular (Roosa et al., 1993). For instance, there appears to be no difference between the mental health risk status of children with a problem-drinking parent and that of children with a psychiatrically disturbed parent. There is no question that COAs experience more stress than non-COAs. But the higher stress is due not simply to alcohol abuse, but to greater family conflict, poorer parental monitoring, and less parental involvement, all of which are related to heavy drinking. Both unreliable parental support and inconsistent parenting produce stress in the child and affect his or her mental health.

Alcoholism disturbs normal patterns of parent-child interaction and marital relationships (Noll, Zucker, Fitzgerald, and Curtis, 1992). In alcoholic families, parental depression, family stress and conflict, and marital discord create problems for the children (Tubman, 1993). Family cohesiveness, positive affect, and pleasant relationships are destroyed, creating stress and antisocial behavior in the children. Three-year-old children of alcoholics are more impulsive and have less control over their actions than other children (Fitzgerald et al., 1993). Family relations and get-togethers during holidays are disrupted because a parent is drunk, so even happy times become occasions for stress and conflict (Jacob, 1992).

In spite of the negative effects just described, some children reared in alcoholic families become happy, well-adjusted adults (Easley and Epstein, 1991). Some children learn how to cope because they are remarkable survivors. In many families in which only one parent is an alcoholic, the other parent is able to provide for the children's needs. In one study of families in which the fathers were alcoholics, Hispanic mothers particularly were able to exert a strong, positive influence on their children's mental health (Roosa et al., 1993).

ourselves of them so that we can dare to marry. Similarly, spouses who become hostile toward their partner because of unhappy experiences with their own parents may have difficulty relating to a partner in a positive, warm way. For example, research has indicated that physical violence witnessed in one's family of origin is predictive of greater psychological distress in adulthood for men and women. Men's reports of symptoms of psychological distress, such as depression or mental illness, in their family of origin indicate that this distress was an important contributor to their own displays of physical and verbal aggression in their marriages (Julian, McKenry, Gavazzi, and Law, 1999). Facing the past squarely, talking about it, and releasing the anger will often help people to change their feelings and behaviors. Similar steps have helped adult children of alcoholics move beyond their damaging histories.

In this chapter, we look at a variety of family patterns and situations and discuss some of their possible effects on individuals. The family situations selected represent only a small fraction of the infinite variety that exists in real life.

PARENTAL ATTITUDES TOWARD CHILDREN

A child's self-concept is strongly influenced by her or his parents. Children who are encouraged and affirmed by their parents are more likely to develop into self-assured adults who feel good about them-

Most parents derive real pleasure from their children's accomplishments. Perfectionist parents carry expectations to an unhealthy extreme. Their standards are beyond reason; they set impossible goals. As a result, their children develop the irrational belief that they must be perfect to be accepted. And since they are not perfect, they are plagued by self-criticism, and their sense of self-worth is minimal. They become defensive and angry when criticized, a behavior that alienates others and causes the very disapproval they fear. Over time, they are filled with emotional turmoil and experience more pain than rewards. As they get older, they avoid intimate relationships because they fear ultimate rejection. The result is a life of loneliness, devoid of intimacy or closeness. Even professional success, which many obtain, seems empty because they can never accept the fact that they are successful enough (Halgin and Leahy, 1989).

selves. Conversely, children who are constantly criticized or even rejected by their parents are likely to be insecure, self-doubting adults. For example, research has shown that mothers who are very dependent and self-critical relate to their daughters in ways that may foster dependency and self-criticism by thwarting their daughters' attempts at autonomy or by being punitive and controlling (Thompson and Zuroff, 1998).

Approval

The most important contribution that parents can make to their children's development is to let the children know that they adore them, love them, approve of them, like them, value them, care about them, and accept them. Parents communicate these attitudes through words of approval, praise, and encouragement; through the interest shown and the care given; and through actions that demonstrate positive feelings and trust. Children base their view of how healthy their family is on whether their parents trust them (Kerr, Stattin, and Trost, 1999). Parents also communicate love through guidance, by caring enough about their children to be concerned.

Children who grow up with approval and positive affirmation and acceptance develop good feelings about themselves, adequate self-concepts, and confidence in their own worth and abilities. Lau and Pun (1999) examined the relationships between parents' evaluation of their children and their children's self-concept in four domains: academic, physical, social, and general. They found significant correlations between parental (especially maternal) evaluations and children's self-concept. Across sex and grade, academic self-concept was most influenced by parents' evaluations. When parents thought their children were bright, the children had a higher self-concept with regard to their intelligence. Feelings of self-worth make the children

Every marriage is influenced by the family backgrounds the partners bring to the relationship. Will these children be influenced by their grandparents? How much of what the parents learned as children will be passed on to the next generation?

This chapter is based on the assumption that family backgrounds do have an influence on our lives. The purpose of the chapter is to help us gain self-understanding through understanding the different ways our families can affect us. But this chapter is also devoted to discussing how personal responsibility comes with self-understanding. Once we know how we became what we are, we have a responsibility to decide how we want to be in the future. Our personalities are not locked in concrete; they can be changed. If someone decides to become a more sociable individual and assumes personal responsibility for trying to achieve this, this is a way of overcoming a negative factor in her or his own life. We can't change what has happened to us, nor can we really change those who influence us. But we can change how we react to what has happened to us, and we can change ourselves if we are highly motivated to do so.

more likely to choose a suitable marital partner. High self-esteem gives them a greater capacity to develop positive relationships because they feel that they are lovable and expect to be loved. They feel they are capable spouses, able to fulfill the expected roles of marriage, and they are confident that they can be good parents to their children.

Criticism and Rejection

Some children are brought up in the opposite type of family situation, in which the parents constantly express their disapproval and criticize them. "You never approve of me and compliment me" and "You always find fault with everything I do" are frequent complaints from the children. Children who are ignored by one or both parents may feel emotionally rejected. Maternal coldness often leads to insecure attachment in the daughter, which leads to self-criticism (Thompson and Zuroff, 1999). If dependency needs are unfulfilled and the child is made to feel undervalued as a person, feelings of inferiority and unworthiness may be carried over into all areas of life. Sometimes a person marries because of a need for an affectionate parent figure rather than a marital partner.

When children grow up with emotional deprivation, they may transfer their needs for attention, love, recognition, and approval to the marriage relationship and expect their spouse to fulfill all the emotional needs that were not met in their own family during childhood. The most frequent example of marriage for neurotic reasons is that of the spouse with exaggerated dependency needs. Such spouses may become clinging, smothering, and insatiable in their demands for attention. Such people may need constant reassurance: "I won't be rejected by you as my parents rejected me" (Messer, 1983).

At the opposite extreme are spouses who won't let their mate love them. They really can't believe that anyone would want to love them, and they won't let anyone get close for fear of being hurt and rejected. Early experiences with parents have an impact on the well-being of both elderly and young people. When parental care is recalled as neither warm nor attentive, unattached elderly people experience lower self-esteem and more loneliness; unattached older men also experience worse subjective health and more anxiety and depression. Apparently, differences in well-being in old age can be at least partially explained by differences in early experiences and interaction with primary caregivers or parents. And individuals' early experiences with parents add to predictability about who will react well when faced with adversity. Those who have learned early in life that their proximity- or support-seeking behavior is rewarded on a reliable basis are less prone to anxiety when an attachment figure is not available (Andersson and Stevens, 1993).

ATTITUDES TOWARD INTIMATE PARTNERS

How we feel toward intimate partners is determined partly by the relationships we have experienced in our family of origin. It has been well documented that current relationship problems often are simply repeated patterns from past relationships. Through case studies, Zimmerman and Cochran (1993) learned that people not only repeat family patterns in other relationships in their lives but also revise these patterns in ways that allow them to heal emotional wounds, switch roles, and strengthen loyalties. How individuals resolve family-of-origin relationship issues determines how they handle similar matters in all of their relationships (Williamson, 1991). Family of origin even affects the attitudes of engaged partners toward premarital counseling and the likelihood that they will attend (Silliman and Schumm, 1995). Thus, it is important to have a good understanding of one's own family patterns in order to avoid repeating dysfunctional patterns (Deacon, 1999).

A large body of research suggests that family-of-origin experiences are related to the quality of the offspring's romantic relationships. Most research suggests that individuals who experience poor relationships with their parents are more likely to have adjustment difficulties in their intimate relationships and that poor marital and parent-child relationships predict lower quality and stability in the offspring's long-term intimate relationships (Rodgers, 1996).

While relationship problems can be transmitted across generations, the mechanisms underlying these patterns are not fully understood (Feldman, 1997). Two theories are often used to try to explain them: (1) social learning theory and (2) attachment theory. **Social learning theory** suggests that parents act as role models for their children and that children learn to imitate their parents' behavior, attitudes, and perceptions. For example, exposure to violence in the family of origin is a consistent predictor of later domestic violence as an adult (Feldman, 1997). Martin (1990) assessed links between marital conflict, parent-child conflict, and conflict between the offspring and their romantic partners. Marital conflict was related to aggressive and avoidant patterns of parent-child conflict, and these patterns were similar to those found in conflicts with romantic partners. Parents who consistently engage in coercion or withdrawal may provide powerful models of negative behaviors and may fail to provide models of positive behavior (for example, expressing affection) that are vital to relationship quality (Stafford and Canary, 1991). Consistent with this idea, young adults' attributions about relationships with parents (both positive and negative) have been linked to their attributions about intimate relationships (Benson, Arditti, Reguero DeAtiles, and Smith, 1992).

Attachment theory suggests that early interactions with parents lead to the formation of attachments that reflect children's perceptions of their self-worth and their expectations about intimate relationships. These ideas about attachment are car-

ried forward into subsequent relationships, where they guide emotional, cognitive, and behavioral responses (Collins and Read, 1994). Several research findings support attachment theory as a means of explaining how family-of-origin experiences are related to romantic relationships. Feeney and Noller (1996) found that adults' attachment style predicts the quality of their dating and marital relationships: Those with insecure attachment show less constructive interaction patterns, which tends to result in lower relationship satisfaction and stability. Kennedy (1999) examined the connection between adult romantic attachment style and measures of psychological well-being, healthy self-concept, attachment to primary caregiver, and family environment in 225 college freshmen. Individuals with a secure attachment style were less likely to experience depression and were more likely to have a positive self-concept, to rate their primary caregivers as higher in encouraging them to be independent, and to rate their families as higher in expressiveness, cohesiveness, participation in family recreational activities, and provision of a stimulating environment than were individuals with insecure or fearful attachment styles. Attachment theory supports the idea that thoughts and behaviors learned from negative family experiences can change over time when individuals' negative expectations about intimate relationships are consistently not confirmed (Feeney and Noller, 1996).

Examples of both of these theories at work can be found in the research of Judith Feeney (1999b). She studied the links between young adults' romantic relationships and their experiences in the family of origin in both newly dating and long-term dating couples. The majority of participants in both groups reported positive and negative links between their family-of-origin experiences and the functioning of their dating relationship. One participant commented:

> I see him as a lot different to me, because of his relationship with his family. They are really close-knit and caring, and that's probably why he's always concerned about whether things are going to affect them. And that's why he's sensitive to me, and always takes account of what I think and feel. I see him as really caring. He cares about what I'm thinking, and whether there are problems between him and me. (Feeney, 1999b, p. 31)

Another participant wrote about communication difficulties with his girlfriend and attributed them to a range of problems in her family of origin, including not only marital conflict and breakdown but also poor parent-child relationships:

> She's been through a lot in her early family life. Yes, she's been through a lot in terms of her family—she's had a very hard life. She's come out—not unscathed—she still has a lot of troubles. She doesn't express her feelings very well. That's because of her life early on. She's been through so much with that and trying to escape from it. Because from what I've seen and what I've heard about, she's got every right to hate the world. So she has a lot of trouble expressing herself. She's frightened of being—she's put a lot of barriers up, throughout her life. (Feeney, 1999b, p. 31)

This comment clearly illustrates the perspective of social learning theory that communication patterns are learned in the home. In contrast, in the following example, the boyfriend described the relationship's problems in attachment-related terms:

> She has a low opinion of herself, and she can't understand herself—and then I look at her mother and what she did to her! And then I see her as a person who really needs someone to help them, and to attach to. But at other times I look at her and I see this evil person who doesn't really want you for what you're worth, it's just using you for what she can get out of you at the moment. She's a very mixed-up person. . . . She doesn't know how to relate to her own emotions, and all that external show she puts on is just a way of hiding what she really thinks of herself. (Feeney, 1999b, p. 32)

FAMILY CLOSENESS: ATTITUDES TOWARD INTIMACY

Some families are huggers, and others limit physical contact to an occasional dutiful peck on the cheek or a handshake. But we all have an inborn need for affection and physical contact.

A common complaint of men and women in intimate relationships is that their partner is not affectionate enough. By affection, they don't always mean sexual intercourse. They mean touching, holding, hugging, cuddling, kissing, and caressing.

The importance of affection in enduring relationships is well established, but this does not always mean sexual intercourse. It can also mean touching, holding, hugging, and caressing.

Ann Landers (1985) asked female readers to reply to the question, "Would you be content to be held close and treated tenderly and forget about the act?" Seventy-two percent of 100,000 respondents answered yes to the question. This survey revealed that these women wanted to feel cared for and to receive tender and loving embraces more than they wanted to have sexual intercourse with an inexpressive male. Other women have offered the same complaint: "I am so hungry for him to touch, hug, or hold me. He will not, or cannot touch—not in the bedroom or anywhere else" (Renshaw, 1984, p. 63). Husbands, too, complain of the need for physical expressions of affection. One husband complained because he and his wife slept on either side of a king-size bed with her poodle in between. He remarked, "I'm so jealous of the attention, loving, stroking, and petting she gives it. . . . I want to touch her, but she will not let me" (Renshaw, 1984, p. 64).

Children's need for physical contact with parents, for "contact comfort," has been well documented (Harlow, 1958). The desire for physical close-

Lauer and Lauer (1991) studied some of the long-term relational consequences of problematic family backgrounds. A sample of 313 volunteers, average age 35.4, from intact-happy, intact-unhappy, death-disrupted, and divorce-disrupted families were compared on the quality of their intimate relationships, the likelihood of their being in intimate relationships in the first place, and the number of children. The researchers found that those from intact-happy families were *less* likely than others to be in an intimate relationship. However, the quality of intimate relationships of individuals from the four groups and the number of children they had did not differ, according to the reports of the respondents.

It was suggested that those from disrupted and intact-unhappy families had an intimacy deficit that made it more imperative for them to be in an intimate relationship than those who came from intact-happy family backgrounds.

While the respondents from the four groups reported that the quality of their intimate relationships was similar, there was some doubt regarding the perception of those who came from unhappy family backgrounds. In response to a question about the effects of family disruption on the quality of their relationships, two-thirds of the respondents reported negative consequences of the kind that would adversely affect their intimate relationships. They said things such as "I have difficulty in trusting others"; "I have difficulty in making a commitment"; "I am too independent and self-reliant"; "I have trouble resolving difficulties in relationships"; "I am afraid of being abandoned." In other words, while they, particularly those in the divorce- and death-disrupted groups, reported that the quality of their relationships was as high as those in intact-happy families, they tended to see deficiencies in their ability to relate in a healthy, stable way (Benson, Arditti, Reguero DeAtiles, and Smith, 1992).

ness seems to be inborn. It is one way that children feel secure and develop positive self-esteem (Barber and Thomas, 1986). By being loved, children see themselves as both lovable and able to love. By being stroked, caressed, cuddled, and loved, children learn to stroke, caress, cuddle, and love others. Often there is perceived favoritism in a family by one of its members. In one study, children who felt disfavored in their family also reported lower family cohesion, higher family disengagement, and more family conflict than did the other members of the family. Children who perceived themselves to be disfavored also reported more frequent shame and more intense fear (Brody, Copeland, Sutton, Richardson, and Guyer, 1998). Receiving parental love and perceiving oneself to be loved are important in learning how to express affection.

Families vary considerably in the way they express love. Leo Buscaglia (1982), a popular lecturer on love, recalls the physical expressiveness of his large Italian family: "Everybody hugs everybody all the time. On holidays, everyone gets together, and it takes 45 minutes just to say hello, and 45 minutes to say goodbye. Babies, parents, dogs—everybody's got to be loved" (p. 116).

Children who grow up in families that do not show affection often have difficulty expressing affection as adults. They may sometimes feel insecure and have difficulty knowing how to give or receive affection. Males especially have difficulty because

they generally receive less affection while growing up than do females. They are often brought up to feel that it is "sissy" or "unmanly" to express tender emotions (Carter and Sokol, 1987).

ATTITUDES TOWARD SEX

Just as their attitudes about physical intimacy influence their children's attitudes, parents' attitudes about sex and expressions of sexuality also leave a legacy. Research has shown that, from generation to generation, the guidance parents give their children about sexuality is very similar to the guidance their parents gave them (Kniveton and Day, 1999). However, negative attitudes can be unlearned, and positive attitudes can be learned.

Positive Attitudes and Teachings

Certain attitudes about sex and sexual expression are developed at home from the time children are young. Some parents are very matter-of-fact about the body and nudity. They don't get upset if their preschool children see them nude or walk in on them while they are in the shower or going to the bathroom. Young children have no embarrassment at exposing their bodies or at seeing their siblings naked. Their interest in how other people look reflects a naive innocence and curiosity. Their interest soon turns to boredom when their curiosity is satisfied. Gradually, as children get older, they tend to want some privacy.

Parents who exhibit matter-of-fact attitudes toward bodily functions are helping their children develop a healthy sense of acceptance toward these things. We know, for example, that parents who prepare their daughters for menstruation in a positive way (Ruble and Brooks-Gunn, 1982) or their sons for nocturnal emissions minimize any negative emotional reactions that otherwise might accompany these natural consequences of puberty. Similarly, parents who try to give positive information about human reproduction, masturbation, and sexual response and expression help their children accept their sexuality as a positive part of their lives.

Negative Attitudes and Teachings

At the opposite extreme are parents who try to repress any interest in or thoughts and feelings about human sexuality. They never allow anyone in the family to see anyone else nude—not even the baby. Toileting always takes place behind closed doors, and dressing and undressing are strictly private, with the sexes separated. Children are brought up to believe that touching their genitals or playing with them is wrong or dirty. For example, when a baby boy innocently holds his penis, his father slaps his hand and shouts, "Don't do that; it's dirty." Or when a baby girl scratches her itchy pubic area, her mother pulls her hand away and warns, "Nice girls don't do that." Normal childhood curiosity about the facts of human reproduction is denied and repressed. The children may not ask any questions about sexual arousal, response, and expression.

Possible Effects on Sexual Behavior

Many parents who initiate sexual discussions with their children, especially with adolescents, do so primarily to try to prevent early sexual activity and pregnancy. They typically communicate with their sons about topics related to sexual exploration, while they discuss physiological and contraceptive issues with their daughters (Downie and Coates, 1999). One national survey of 15- and 16-year-olds revealed that daughters of traditional parents who had communicated with them about sex were less

likely to have had intercourse than were those whose parents had not talked to them (Moore, Peterson, and Furstenberg, 1986). However, family communication about sex had little influence on discouraging early sexual activity of sons.

There is ample clinical evidence that sex education emphasizing repression and abstinence can have a detrimental effect on mature sexual functioning. In trying to prevent their children from being sexually promiscuous or especially in trying to prevent their daughters from becoming pregnant, some parents unwittingly make it harder for their children to achieve mature and loving sexual adjustments. One teenage girl remarked:

> Every time I go out the door my mother says to me, "Now don't get into trouble, don't let anything bad happen to you." After several weeks of this I asked her, "Exactly what do you mean, Mother?" and she replied, "I mean don't let any boy touch you." (Author's counseling notes)

Without realizing it, in trying to keep her daughter "out of trouble," the mother was also making it harder for her to relate to any male in a warm, loving way. Another mother told her daughter over and over again, "All males are lechers and filthy-minded. All they are interested in is one thing." As a result of this mother's teaching, her daughter never dated throughout high school. Only when she went away to college was she able to get out from under her mother's influence and begin to date.

The effects of negative, repressive sex education vary from person to person. Fortunately, many people, given time and perhaps therapeutic assistance, are able to overcome the effects of repressive upbringing. The important issue is whether the individual was brought up with positive or negative attitudes about sex and how this influenced her or him.

ATTITUDES TOWARD MARRIAGE AND DIVORCE

Attitudes toward marriage and divorce are also profoundly affected by one's family background. Some people brought up in very unhappy homes develop very negative attitudes toward marriage itself. They do not want to duplicate the unhappiness that they experienced in their family of origin, so they are hesitant to marry. Some of them never

Knowledge and attitudes about sex are developed from the time children are young. When and in what setting should children learn about sex and sexual expression?

marry, a greater proportion delay marriage, and a still greater proportion get married but have little idea how to make it work. The marriage that they knew as a child serves as a poor model for marital success. A lot of people who have been brought up in unhappy homes resolve that what happened to their parents will never happen to them. Nevertheless, they tend to duplicate the patterns of family relationships in their own marriage that they experienced in their family of origin while growing up.

What about people who come from divorced parents? What effect does divorce have on children's attitudes toward marriage and divorce? In one study, respondents from intact families were generally more likely than those with divorced parents to voice approval of marriage, but having been brought up in a divorced family had little impact on the timing of marriage. This suggests that parental divorce does not influence the perceived desirability of marriage (Trent and South, 1992). Children of divorced parents have goals for and attitudes toward marriage and family that are similar to those of children from intact families: They want long-term, loving, rewarding relationships with their spouses. However, adult children of divorced parents do express more accepting attitudes toward divorce than people who grew up with both biological parents, unless their family was conflictive (Amato and Booth, 1991).

Attitudes toward divorce and marriage have become more liberal as divorce, cohabitation, and never marrying have become more common. Societal disapproval of unmarried mothers also has diminished as their numbers have increased. As nontraditional family forms become more predominant, with successive cohorts, different family forms will gain increased acceptance (Trent and South, 1992).

GENDER-ROLE SOCIALIZATION IN THE FAMILY

Gender role refers to a person's outward expression of maleness or femaleness in a social setting. Traits and behavior thought to be appropriate for a male are considered masculine; those thought to be appropriate for a female are considered feminine. However, gender roles vary according to cultural expectations and are influenced partly by environmental factors, the most important of which is the family. Children learn expected gender roles through identifying with parents and modeling their behavior.

Gender-role learning in the family can be divided into three categories:

1. **Children develop masculine or feminine personality traits.** Children are taught how

men and women are supposed to look and act; they also learn the attitudes and values that their culture considers appropriate for their gender.

2. **Children learn masculine or feminine gender roles and responsibilities in marriage and family living.** These include decision-making roles, the division of household responsibilities, and parental responsibilities.

3. **Children learn vocational roles of men and women in our culture.**

The extent to which identification and modeling take place depends on the amount of time parents spend with their child and the intimacy and intensity of the contact. It also depends on the relative influence that the parents exert. Of course, the gender concepts the child learns depend on the patterns of role models exemplified. Thus, a girl who closely identifies with a masculine mother may only weakly identify with a typically feminine personality. A girl brought up by a mother who is a professional career woman will have a less stereotypic concept of femininity than will a girl whose mother is primarily a homemaker. For example, research has found that mothers and early adolescent daughters in traditional, dual-work, and dual-career family environments held similar attitudes toward marriage, children, and careers (Bohannon and White, 1999). Similarly, a boy brought up by a father who represents very traditional ideas of masculinity and the role of the husband and father in the family will likely develop quite different concepts about the masculine gender role than will a boy brought up by an egalitarian father.

Gender-role expectations are in a state of flux, with many people advocating a more egalitarian distribution of income earning, homemaking, and child rearing. In actual practice, role performance has not kept up with ideology. Large numbers of people still hold to traditional concepts of the roles spouses play in the family. See Chapter 12 for a more detailed discussion.

VARIATIONS IN FAMILY VALUES AND WORK HABITS

Our parents are the primary role models for the kind of life we want to live as adults. If a man's father was a workaholic, he's more than likely to be

This child is learning that doing laundry is a family job, not a "mommy" role. What children are taught about common tasks has a lot to do with their adult attitudes.

one, too—he's never had a good look at any other way to be. If a woman grew up in a well-off family, she's not likely to be happy spending all her time trying to make ends meet.

Workaholic Families

Patterns of work and industry may be developed in one's family of origin. One married man described his family situation as a child:

> When I was growing up, all I ever did was work—from the time I was eight years old. My parents had a corner grocery store. I was expected to come right home from school and help my parents in the store. I never had time to play or have fun like other kids. When I was in high school, I never could join any clubs or participate in activities. I had to work. The store was open seven days a week from eight o'clock in the morning until nine at night. That's where I spent my childhood when I wasn't in school. (Author's counseling notes)

This man had never learned to play. When his spouse wanted him to take time off to enjoy social activities and have fun, he felt very guilty doing so. He could never relax and enjoy himself. His

Having an adequate income can contribute to marital satisfaction, but marital satisfaction is not always the greatest when income is the highest. Many spouses want love more than a lot of money. With regard to income, what is important is whether the partners agree that the level they have achieved is satisfactory. The real problem arises when spouses each have different values in relation to their standard of living and work ethic. If both spouses are workaholics, they may not have much time for leisure activities and a social life. But if they're happy with each other, there is no real problem. If their life goals and life-styles are similar, they can both be content with the level at which they are living. If they both lack ambition, have poor work habits, and simply want to enjoy life without too much effort or without many material possessions, at least they're compatible. A problem may arise when they have been brought up with different value systems.

Orientations toward work and life-style are most influenced by the way we were brought up. Thus, it's helpful to explore our family backgrounds and philosophies in trying to evaluate compatibility.

spouse, in turn, felt isolated and alone because she and her partner never had any companionship. She complained, "He gives everything to his job: all of his time and energy. By the time he works eighty hours a week he's exhausted. He has nothing left to give me" (author's counseling notes).

Family Values

The work habits that people develop are related to family goals and values. Some people are never happy unless they reach a high level of material prosperity. They want to live in a large house, have fine clothes and luxury cars, and take expensive vacations. They are used to a certain standard of living in their family of origin and seek to duplicate this life-style in their own marriage. They are willing to work to achieve what they want. Other people want similar things but haven't developed the work habits and assumed the responsibilities necessary to fulfill their expectations. Still other people have more modest goals, which they're willing to work just hard enough to achieve. They are content with a modest life-style and income.

Parental Role Models

The role models parents provide are crucial in establishing life goals and work patterns in their children. Children whose parents have high expectations and standards of work performance tend to adopt these standards themselves. One man commented, "My father and mother both went to college and held good jobs when we were growing up. They always assumed that we would go to college too, and make something of ourselves. And we all did. They also taught us how to do physical labor around the house." In contrast to this family, some parents present lenient standards of performance, whether on a job or at home. They place less value on working hard, doing a good job, and getting ahead in life.

COMMUNICATIVE, NONCOMMUNICATIVE, AND CONFLICTIVE FAMILIES

Effective communication is one of the most important requirements in intimate relationships. Couples who are close usually have good verbal and nonverbal communication, talk enough and listen carefully, discuss important issues, understand each other, show sensitivity to each other's feelings, say positive things to each other, and keep open the channels of communication. Chapter 14 discusses communication in more detail.

The patterns of communication that exist in a family also influence communication patterns that the children establish in families of their own. These communication patterns may be divided into seven basic categories: (1) open, honest, tactful communication; (2) superficial communication; (3) one-sided communication; (4) false communication; (5) avoidance of communication; (6) noncommunication; and (7) angry communication.

Open, Honest, Tactful Communication

Family members are able to reveal what they think and how they really feel in a tactful, sensitive manner. They voice their concerns and worries and talk about important issues. They each can talk about themselves and their lives and know that others will listen and understand.

41

Successful communication in intimate relationships depends partly on one's willingness to reveal oneself voluntarily, to risk disclosing private information and feelings in order to enhance companionship, affective exchange, understanding, and acceptance. Self-disclosure needs to be mutual and positive, reflecting deep acceptance of and commitment to the relationship (Galvin and Brommel, 1986).

Littlejohn (1983) has summarized the findings of research on self-disclosure as follows:

1. Disclosure increases with increased relational intimacy.
2. Disclosure increases when rewarded.
3. Disclosure increases with the need to reduce uncertainty in a relationship.
4. Disclosure tends to be reciprocal.
5. Women tend to be higher disclosers than men.
6. Women disclose more with individuals they like, whereas men disclose more with people they trust.
7. Disclosure is regulated by norms of appropriateness.
8. Attraction is related to positive disclosure ("I feel comfortable with you") but not to negative disclosure ("I don't think you care about me").
9. Positive disclosure is more likely in nonintimate or moderately intimate relationships.
10. Negative disclosure occurs with greater frequency in highly intimate settings than in less intimate ones.
11. Satisfaction and disclosure have a curvilinear relationship; that is, relational satisfaction is greatest at moderate levels of disclosure.

Superficial Communication

Sometimes family members talk a lot but never about anything important. They avoid disclosing themselves and discussing "gut" issues. Because of denial, fear, or distrust, they haven't learned to share their concerns. They are taught to be independent and strong and to handle their own problems. As a result, they avoid discussing feelings and problems. When someone asks, "How is everything?" the answer is usually "Just fine," even though it may not be true. As a result, no one really knows or understands what the others are thinking and feeling.

One-Sided Communication

In some families, one person does all the talking while the others listen. A woman may do all the talking and not give her spouse a chance to express his opinions. He either sits passively or tries to withdraw so that he won't have to hear it. A man's idea of talking to his spouse or children may be to give them lectures, to talk *to* them rather than *with* them. He wants to tell them something, but he doesn't really want to discuss anything. If others try to talk, they are criticized for interrupting or talking back, and so they learn to be quiet. When the children in such families marry and establish their own families, they often either repeat their passive roles in family interaction or model their behavior after their talkative parent and dominate the conversation in their own families.

False Communication

Communication patterns can be negative. Family members may learn to lie to keep out of trouble. If they are punished or ridiculed when they tell the truth, they learn to make up stories or to tell others what they think they want to hear. Sometimes they say just the opposite of what they really feel to give false impressions.

Avoidance of Communication

In some cases, family members learn not to talk about sensitive issues because such discussions lead to fights. They hate arguments and so avoid touchy, controversial subjects. They repress their own ideas and feelings for the sake of family harmony, and they try to deny problems and hope they will go away. They are taught to inhibit honest feelings and to keep everything in. It becomes very difficult to resolve problems, because they are never discussed.

Noncommunication

Some people are nonverbal. They may not have learned how to express themselves, so they seldom discuss anything. Or they may simply be shy or afraid that others won't like them or accept them,

A family's pattern of communication is reflected in how it handles discussions of feelings and problems.

or will criticize them and think they are stupid. As a result, they keep quiet.

Here again, the important question is, What patterns of communication existed in an individual's family while he or she was growing up, and how have they affected that person?

Angry Communication

Some people are not able to talk about anything without becoming angry. They have a very low tolerance for frustration and experience more emotional arousal than most people when they are frus-

trated. They perceive more life situations as annoying, and they get angry more often, are more likely to express verbal and physical aggression when provoked, have higher general anxiety, and make less effort at constructive coping. Angry people describe their family environments while they were growing up as significantly less cohesive, less emotionally expressive—that is, less tolerant of self-expression—and more conflict-ridden and disorganized than those of less angry people. In families in which the expression of anger is a way of life, the children may carry that pattern into their own marital relationships (Lopez and Thurman, 1993).

SUMMARY

1. The family is the chief socializing influence on children. Examining our own family background helps us understand how our family has affected us. This is necessary if we are to develop self-understanding, assume responsibility for our own behavior, and make peace with our past.

2. Children are affected by alcoholism in their family of origin, but not necessarily to the same degree or in exactly the same way.

3. The most important contribution that parents can make to their children's development is to let children know that they are adored, loved, liked, approved of, valued, cared about, and accepted. This knowledge gives children positive self-esteem and self-acceptance.

4. Children who are criticized or rejected grow up with poor self-images and are starved for affection, which makes mature marriage relationships more difficult for them to establish.

5. Rather than blame parents for our problems, we need to gain self-understanding, assume personal responsibility, and strive to change ourselves.

6. Current relationship problems are often repeated patterns from past relationships. People not only repeat family patterns in other relationships but also revise these patterns in ways that allow them to heal emotional wounds, switch roles, and strengthen loyalties.

7. Family-of-origin experiences are related to the quality of offspring's romantic relationships. Individuals who had poor relationships with their parents are more likely to have adjustment difficulties in their own intimate relationships.

8. Social learning theory suggests that parents act as role models for their children and that children learn to imitate their parents' behavior and adopt their attitudes and perceptions.

9. Attachment theory suggests that early interactions with parents lead to the formation of attachments that reflect children's perceptions of their self-worth and their expectations in intimate relationships.

10. People are born with a need for affection. Some adults need more expressions of affection than others, and spouses sometimes complain that their partner is not affectionate enough. Expressing affection is behavior that is learned in the family.

11. The family is also instrumental in instilling either positive or negative attitudes toward sex, which influence sexual behavior during adolescence and adulthood.

12. Attitudes toward marriage and divorce are developed in relation to our family background. People become more accepting of divorce for themselves if they have grown up in a divorced family.

13. The family also influences gender-role socialization. This socialization includes developing masculine or feminine personality traits, learning masculine or feminine gender roles and responsibilities in marriage, and learning vocational roles of men and women.

14. The roles parents model are crucial in establishing the life goals and work patterns that adults take into their own marriages.

15. Communication patterns are also influenced by one's family of origin. Types of patterns include open, honest, tactful communication; superficial communication; one-sided communication; false communication; avoidance of communication; noncommunication; and angry communication.

KEY TERMS

generational transmission

reciprocal parent-child
   interaction

observational modeling

social learning theory

attachment theory

gender role

QUESTIONS FOR THOUGHT

1. How has your family of origin influenced you in each of the following areas?

   a. Your attitudes toward intimacy and the expression of affection

   b. Your attitude toward sex

   c. Your gender-role socialization

   d. Your basic values and habits in relation to work

2. What pattern of communication best reflects the pattern in your family of origin, and how has this pattern affected each member of your family?

3. If someone in your family of origin was or is a chronic alcoholic, how do you believe he or she has influenced you? Or, if you know someone who is the adult child of an alcoholic, how has that experience influenced him or her?

SUGGESTED READINGS

Barber, N. (1998). *Parenting: Roles, Styles, and Outcomes.* Commack, NY: Nova Science. Discusses parenting in different settings and situations and its effects on children, exploring the theory that antisocial behavior is a response to low parental investment.

Berner, R. T. (1992). *Parents Whose Parents Were Divorced.* New York: Haworth Press. Summarizes research findings.

Freeman, J. (1989). *Women: A Feminist Perspective* (4th ed.). Palo Alto, CA: Mayfield. Represents a classic reader dealing with feminism.

Furstenberg, F. F., Jr., and Cherlin, A. J. (1991). *What Happens to Children When Parents Part?* Cambridge, MA: Harvard University Press. Reviews the effects of marital breakup.

Joselson, R. (1996). *The Space Between Us: Exploring the Dimensions of Human Relationships.* Thousand Oaks, CA: Sage. Focuses on the development of human relationships.

Noller, P. (1993). *Communication in Family Relationships.* Englewood Cliffs, NJ: Prentice-Hall. Covers communication in several types of relationships, including parent-child, sibling, nontraditional family, and troubled family ones.

Quinton, D., and Rutter, M. (1988). *Parenting Breakdown: The Making and Breaking of Inter-Generational Links.* Aldershot, UK: Avebury. Examines the relationship between being a poor parent and having been poorly parented.

Socha, T. J., and Rhunette, C. (Eds.). (1999). *Communication, Race, and Family: Exploring Communication in Black, White, and Biracial Families.* Mahwah, NJ: Lawrence Erlbaum. Offers a collection of works focusing on communication within and about ethnic and biracial families.

Starr, R. H., Jr., and Wolfe, D. A. (Eds.). (1991). *The Effects of Child Abuse and Neglect: Issues and Research.* New York: Guilford Press. Traces the effects of childhood mistreatment.

CHAPTER 3

LEARNING OBJECTIVES

After reading the chapter, you should be able to:

Explain the reasons for the increase in one-parent families among African Americans.

Describe African American families in terms of ideology and class differences.

Summarize the strengths of the African American family.

Describe Mexican American families in terms of familism, divorce rates and birthrates, power and decision making, and child rearing and education.

Summarize the strengths of the Mexican American family.

Describe Native American families in terms of population trends and distribution, education, standard of living, family life, children, and cultural conflict.

Summarize the strengths of the Native American family.

Compare Chinese American families with the general population in terms of family and children, income, and education.

Summarize the strengths of the Chinese American family.

Cultural and Ethnic Differences in Families

Learning Objectives

African American Families

Class Differences Among African American Families

The Increase in One-Parent Families

African American Family Ideology

■ **Perspective:** African American Family Strengths

Socialization of Children

Reality and Gender-Role Fulfillment

Mexican American Families

Familism

Divorce Rates and Birthrates

Power and Decision Making

Child Rearing and Education

Native American Families

Vital Statistics

Economics

■ **Perspective:** Degrees of Acculturation Among
Native Americans

Education

Family Life

Children

Teenage Mothers

Cultural Conflict

Chinese American Families

Immigration

Family and Children

■ **Perspective:** Neither Real Americans
nor Real Asians?

Education

Prejudices

Conclusions

Summary

Key Terms

Questions for Thought

Suggested Readings

ultural and ethnic backgrounds affect family living—and the variety of heritages in the United States is reflected in the variety of family styles. Figure 3.1 shows the composition of the U.S. population by race and Hispanic origin (U.S. Bureau of the Census, 2000a). About 196 million people (72% of the population) are classified as White non-Hispanic; most of their family trees have roots in some European country that date back 200 or 300 years. Non-Hispanic African Americans number 33 million individuals (12% of the population). Latinos—whose family roots stretch from Mexico, to the Spanish-speaking Caribbean, to Central and South America—total about 31.3 million people (11.5% of the population). Most of the Latino population (about 20.6 million, or 65% of the population) hail from Mexico (U.S. Bureau of the Census, 2000b). About 10 million people (3.7% of the population) identify themselves as Asians or Pacific Islanders. Non-Hispanic Native Americans from various tribes number about 2 million (0.74% of the population).

In fact, the United States contains people from virtually all the world's cultures. If people take the time to learn about and benefit from this diversity, the cultural makeup of the nation becomes a significant strength. In a general sense, family **ethnicity** can be thought of as the way people define themselves as part of a group through similarities in ancestry and cultural heritage (race, religion, or national origin). **Culture** can be defined as the sum total of ways of living, including the values, beliefs, aesthetic standards, linguistic expressions, patterns of thinking, behavioral norms, and styles of communication a group of people has developed to ensure its survival in a particular physical and human environment (Hoopes, 1979). Ethnicity and culture are not always the same thing, as culture can encompass many different ethnicities. For example, American culture is a mixture of the arts, beliefs, customs, and other products of human endeavor and thought created by many different ethnic groups.

We have selected four different ethnic groups in order to illustrate how ethnic and cultural differences help shape family life. Each group has some distinctive features, and socioeconomic factors combine with cultural and ethnic characteristics to form particular family patterns. Be aware that you are reading generalizations and that there is

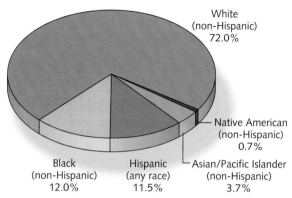

Figure 3.1 U.S. Population by Race and Hispanic Origin, 1999 (*Note:* Data from "Resident Population Estimates of the United States by Sex, Race, and Hispanic Origin: April 1, 1990, to July 1, 1999, with Short-Term Projection to April 1, 2000" [2000, May 24] by U.S. Bureau of the Census, Population Estimates Program, Population Division. Retrieved June 29, 2000, from the World Wide Web: http://www.census. gov/population/estimates/nation/intfile3-1.txt)

tremendous individual and family variation within groups. Ultimately, if you look beyond surface differences, you will find far more similarities than differences with regard to family life and cultures.

AFRICAN AMERICAN FAMILIES

As with all families, the most significant differences among African American families are associated with economic and educational factors (Bryant and Coleman, 1988).

In 1965, Daniel Patrick Moynihan (1965), assistant secretary of labor under President Johnson, issued a report titled *The Negro Family: The Case for National Action.* He reported that the Black community was a "tangle of pathology" and that at the heart of this mess was the deterioration of the Black family. The major problem was the large number of young Blacks growing up in mother-centered families without the helpful influence of two parents. Moynihan argued that this situation was the major reason Blacks were making only limited gains. Moynihan also traced the high percentage of mother-centered families back to the days when slave owners sold slaves as individuals, not as families.

This report raised a storm of protest, primarily because it was erroneous. Gutman (1976) examined

Families differ in many ways. In the United States, cultural and ethnic diversity is reflected in differences in family styles and philosophies of child rearing.

1865–66 census data in Virginia and found that slavery had not destroyed the Black family. Three-fourths of Black households contained either a father or a husband. In fact, the archetypal matrilocal family hardly existed among southern Blacks. Many slave marriages were ripped apart, but people were strong enough that the institution of marriage persisted. Gutman also examined 13,924 Black households in the central Harlem area of New York City in 1925 and found that 85% of the households were headed by both parents. Even at the time of the Moynihan report itself, three-fourths of Black families were headed by a husband and wife (Staples, 1985). Other researchers emphasize that the single-mother African American family is not a result of slavery or of welfare policies, nor is it a traditional African American family form; rather, it is the result of poverty and Black male unemployment. It simply reflects the greater difficulty that Black men have in finding employment (Smith, 1993).

Class Differences Among African American Families

Many variations among Black families stem from differences in socioeconomic status. Wilkinson (1997) described four classes among Black families: (1) families in poverty, (2) the nonpoor working class, (3) the upwardly mobile middle class, and (4) the established upper class. Impoverished families have very different histories, parenting behaviors, and expectations from those for families in other classes. Over one-fourth (25.5%) of African American families were below the poverty level in 1998, compared to 11% of the White population (U.S. Bureau of the Census, 1999c). Families that are poor experience endless complications in trying to meet basic needs, such as finding safe, affordable housing. Proper attention to children's optimal development is difficult when parents are in constant economic distress, and many children of poverty end up on the streets and in the juvenile justice system. Poverty can reduce the quality of parenting due to daily financial and psychological distress (Conger et al., 1992), and research has consistently shown that parents who experience economic stress display less nurturance and more harshness in their responses to their children (McLoyd and Wilson, 1992). However, the custom of the extended family

helping out creates an important support network, and when resources are available, the extended family may help raise the children. Understandably, in families living in poverty because of a lack of education, job market segregation, and struggles with a welfare existence, the parents may be unable to participate in children's schooling or take an active role in community affairs (Wilkinson, 1997).

African American working-class families usually have an annual income of $15,000–$35,000 and differ in composition and functioning from impoverished families. Spouses in these working-class families (31.4% of African American families in 1998; U.S. Bureau of the Census, 1999c) generally do not have the educational achievements of middle-class families, but they desire more education for their children than they have achieved themselves. Solidarity and internal strength are central to the nonpoor working class, and family life is characterized by a constant effort to maintain economic security. This preoccupation with the family's financial condition affects the opportunities for and aspirations of children (Wilkinson, 1997).

Increased educational and economic opportunities have contributed to the growth of a well-educated and economically secure African American middle class (Giles, 1994); in 1998, 30.7% of African American families had an income between $35,000 and $75,000 (U.S. Bureau of the Census, 1999c). Mothers in the middle class are more likely to be married, to have come from intact nuclear families, and to hold values that are more compatible with a nuclear rather than an extended family. Fathers are effective authority figures, and discipline and decision making are joint parental responsibilities. These middle-class families tend to live in suburban areas and participate in various church and community activities. One of the primary expectations of both parents is that their children will attend college and obtain secure professional positions. Essentially, African American middle-class families are characterized by (1) a sufficient family income, (2) conformity to prevailing norms of morality, (3) close supervision of children, (4) dual employment of spouses, (5) at least one spouse with a college education, (6) a belief in upward mobility, (7) a close attachment to and involvement with their children's lives, and (8) the expectation that children will look to their parents as role models (Wilkinson, 1997).

Family life is an important source of life satisfaction for African Americans, especially if the family has a comfortable and steady income.

The number of upper-class African American families is small but growing. In 1998, 12.4% of Black families had incomes over $75,000 (compared with 26.5% of White families; U.S. Bureau of the Census, 1999c). Dual-career marriages are common in the upper class. Although egalitarianism is an expectation in spousal relationships, child rearing is still a key dimension of the mother's role, and kinship bonds are essential. The majority of women have earned professional degrees, and the children often attend private schools, which usually have few Blacks. Intimate relationships in African American upper-middle- and upper-class families are based on gender-role specificity, conservative attitudes toward nonmarital sex, and a strong belief in the value of monogamous relationships. These families are characterized by enduring values, a belief in higher education, exceptional parental role-modeling behaviors, and children's ambitions. Other characteristics of this group include inherited

wealth or ample financial security, home ownership, a history of intergenerational family stability, and a middle- or upper-class background for both spouses (Wilkinson, 1997).

The Increase in One-Parent Families

Moynihan was clearly wrong in his analysis of the Black family. But since his report, there has been a dramatic increase in one-parent families among Blacks, as well as among Whites (Franklin, 1988). In 1970, one-third of Black children under age 18 were living in one-parent families, most with their mother. In 1998, 57% were living in a one-parent family with their mother. This increase is particularly relevant given that 64% of African American single-female-headed households are below the national poverty level. Why the increase?

The primary reason has been the high rate of births to unmarried women. In 1997, births to unmarried Black women accounted for 69% of all live births to Black women (U.S. Bureau of the Census, 1999a). This is attributed largely to high rates of unprotected intercourse among teenagers (Stack and Wasserman, 1995). This trend is problematic in that households headed by never-married mothers experience more persistent poverty and longer spells of welfare receipt than do other types of mother-only households (Franklin, Smith, and McMiller, 1995). Furthermore, unmarried African American women are far less likely to marry or to have an abortion if they become pregnant than are unmarried White women. Another reason for the rise of one-parent Black families is the high divorce rate (Norton and Moorman, 1987). Two out of three Black marriages will eventually dissolve, and African American women are less likely to remarry than are White women. In general, African Americans are significantly less likely than Whites to feel that their marriages are harmonious, and African American women are less likely to be satisfied with their marriages than are White women (Broman, 1993).

African American Family Ideology

The situation of the modern Black family is not caused by any deficiency in ideology in relation to the family. African Americans believe strongly in the institution of the family. In fact, family life is the greatest source of life satisfaction among middle-class

Many of the problems that beset the Black family are due to racial discrimination and the difficult economic conditions under which a disproportionate number of African Americans live. Black families show a number of positive characteristics that have enabled them to function and survive (Crawley, 1988; Gary, Beatty, and Berry, 1986). These characteristics include the following:

- **Strong kinship bonds.** Extended families are common, and family members rely on one another for care, strength, and mutual support (Chatters, Taylor, and Neighbors, 1989; Taylor, 1985, 1986). According to one study, relatives of African American mothers are almost twice as likely as members of Anglo-American families to provide child care when children are sick or out of school (Benin and Keith, 1995). Compared to that of Whites, Black kin networks are more intensive and extensive. Blacks are more likely to live with relatives, to contact kin, and to visit their mothers (Baley, 1995).

- **A favorable attitude toward the elderly.** At all socioeconomic levels, African Americans have a more favorable attitude toward the elderly than do Whites.

- **Flexible roles.** Spousal relationships in most middle-class Black families are egalitarian, with men sharing significantly in the performance of household tasks (Taylor, Chatters, Tucker, and Lewis, 1990). Although the women spend more time than the men as primary caregivers of children, the men appear to be accessible and involved with their children (Ahmeduzzaman and Roopnarine, 1992). Roles of all family members are flexible. An uncle or grandmother can assume the vacated position of an absent parent.

- **Strong achievement orientation.** The median number of years of schooling completed is nearly equal to that for Whites (U.S. Bureau of the Census, 1999a). Moreover, most African Americans are highly motivated to get ahead and have pride in their own accomplishments and those of Black people generally (Belsky, Youngblade, Rovine, and Volling, 1991).

- **Strong religious orientation.** Religion traditionally has been a source of solace for oppressed people, as well as a vehicle for rebellion and social advancement (Coke, 1992). Religiosity has been linked with higher levels of marital interaction and with lower levels of marital conflict. The church contributes to cohesion in the African American community by acting as an agent of moral guidance and the center of community life. The potential benefits of African Americans' religious participation are underscored by research indicating that religious belief and activity form an important coping mechanism for negotiating life's stresses (Brody, Stoneman, Flor, and McCrary, 1994).

Blacks (Thomas, 1990), and married Black people, regardless of gender, tend to be happier than unmarried Black people (Broman, 1988; Zollar and Williams, 1987). There are, however, significant differences according to income level. Family life satisfaction is highly correlated with income level: the higher the income, the greater the marital satisfaction (Ball and Robbins, 1986b; Crohan and Veroff, 1989).

Motherhood and child rearing are also among the most important values for Blacks. The role of mother is regarded as more important than any other role, including that of wife. African Americans also have strong kinship bonds, so the single mother is not necessarily left to raise her child on her own. Rather, she can rely on the assistance of members of her extended family (Hampson, Beavers, and Hulgus, 1990; Jackson and Berg-Cross, 1988; Taylor, Chatters, and Mays, 1988). Blacks report that their personal happiness depends partly on the strength of affectional bonds among extended family members (Ellison, 1990). Both two-parent and single-parent Black families are more likely than White families to reside in extended family households (Fine, McKenry, Donnelly, and Voydanoff, 1992). African American children are also more likely than children of other races to spend significant portions of their childhood in households that are not headed by both parents, and they are more likely to reside with extended family relatives. In addition, the high rates of marital disruption and single parenting among Black families, along with the fluidity of extended family households, suggest that changing living arrangements are a common experience for Black children, because changes in household composition and family structure are common among Black families (Hunter and Ensminger, 1992; Jayakody, Chatters, and Taylor, 1993; Taylor, Chatters, and Jackson, 1993).

Increasing numbers of middle-class African American students are going on to college to receive a higher education. Why are such students sometimes more achievement oriented than their White counterparts?

Socialization of Children

African American parents face the difficult task of raising their children to have positive self-concepts, and racial and personal identities in a society in which racist attitudes, negative media images, and stereotypes are all too common (Thomas and Speight, 1999). Studies have found that a positive racial identity is related to increased psychological health, self-esteem, and achievement, while a negative racial identity is linked to low self-esteem, problems with psychological adjustment, low school achievement, and high rates of school dropout, teenage pregnancy, gang involvement, eating disorders, drug abuse, and involvement in crime. Due to the potential consequences of a negative racial identity, it is important that African Americans develop a positive sense of self that includes feelings of racial pride (Thomas and Speight, 1999).

Socialization depends on the types of messages transmitted to children. Boykin and Toms (1985) identified three types of socialization by African American families. Mainstream socialization is characterized by European American values and beliefs, although the families may demonstrate more African American values through their behavior. The second type, minority socializing, accepts the fact that we live in a society with oppressive and racist beliefs and tries to work within it. Finally, Black cultural socialization includes the teaching of values related to West African traditions of spiritu-

ality, harmony, movement, verve, communalism, expressive individualism, and orality. Nearly all African American parents feel that racial socialization is important in preparing their children to cope with the reality of racism (Thomas and Speight, 1999). Parents in this study reported that they give both their boy and girl children messages of racial pride and self-pride; the importance of achievement, moral values, and family; and the need to overcome negative social messages and racism. However, boys were given more messages on overcoming racism, whereas girls were encouraged to pursue an education and become financially independent.

Reality and Gender-Role Fulfillment

Gender-specific work and family roles have an important impact on members' satisfaction with family life. Among Black women, those who are employed have significantly lower levels of family-life satisfaction than do those who are not employed, regardless of financial status. Employed men who do most of the housework have particularly low levels of family-life satisfaction (Broman, 1991). Apparently, Black men and women are happier when they are fulfilling traditional spousal roles in the family.

When Black men and women are unable to fulfill their family roles, it is often because of situations beyond their control. The most important is the shortage of African American males, especially of those who are economically ready for marriage (Tucker and Taylor, 1989). There are 1.9 million fewer Black men than women over age 14 (U.S. Bureau of the Census, 1999a), and many of the unmarried men are underemployed, can't find jobs, or have dropped out of the labor force (Fossett and Kiecolt, 1993). Another factor in the shortage of eligible Black men is that, although the percentages are small, more African American men than women marry outside their race. The lack of eligible men for all the reasons listed here is one important factor in the increase in Black female-headed households (Joe and Yu, 1984).

The problem is especially acute for college-educated African American women. More Black women than Black men are enrolled in college, and the gap is widening. Not wanting to marry men with less education than they have, almost one-third of college-educated Black women remain unmarried past the age of 30 (Staples, 1981; U.S. Bureau of the Census, 1999a). Compared to White women, African American women place greater importance on having economic supports in place prior to marriage and are more resistant to marrying someone who has few resources (Bulcroft and Bulcroft, 1993). Overall, both Black men and Black women are significantly less likely to marry than are their White counterparts (South, 1993).

African Americans tend to feel that the male's primary role is that of provider. Yet it is the role he finds hardest to fulfill in a racist society. He is the last to be hired and the first to be fired. Even if he is working full-time, in 1998 he earned on average only about 74% of the income of a White man (U.S. Bureau of the Census, 1999c). It may be harder for him to feel good about himself or to be happy in marriage when he believes he is not fulfilling family expectations (Ball and Robbins, 1986a).

MEXICAN AMERICAN FAMILIES

Mexican Americans constitute the second largest minority group in the United States. Most reside in Arizona, California, Colorado, New Mexico, and Texas, with the heaviest concentration in California and Texas. The majority live in urban neighborhoods, or **barrios.**

The strength of the intergenerational relationships in the Mexican American family is well doc-

umented. Studies consistently show stronger levels of obligation, more frequent social interaction, more support exchanged, and a greater likelihood of shared living arrangements with elders in Mexican American families than in Anglo-American families (Holmes and Holmes, 1995). However, family patterns of Mexican Americans are more likely to resemble those of the dominant culture the longer they have resided in the United States (Silverstein and Chen, 1999). Although some research suggests that Mexican Americans are the immigrant group that has had the most success in retaining its culture and language (Holmes and Holmes, 1995), there is also a strong belief that when Mexican Americans achieve economic success they are more likely to adopt the values of the mainstream culture.

Familism

Familism among Mexican Americans means that they emphasize the needs of the family above those of the individual. Either a parent or the older children may stay home from school or work to care for a sick family member or visit a relative who is bedridden. Individuals find their identity and sense of belonging in family groups. There is usually pride in the family and a close emotional bond among members (Hampson et al., 1990). Families are large (Klitsch, 1990a), and extended families are common. Mexican Americans are taught to bring elderly relatives into their homes if they are not able to care for themselves. However, trigenerational households have never been the norm for Mexican Americans, except in times of stress. Rather, Mexican American extended families are groups of independent nuclear households forming social organizational units that might be called "kin-integrated." Family group structures might include first cousins, aunts, and uncles, as well as grandparents, parents, brothers, and sisters. Members of these groups offer aid as needed, provide resources, and help raise children. Interaction between younger Mexican American family members and the older generation is frequent. Mexican Americans are much more likely than European Americans to believe that the younger generation should support and provide living accommodations for the older generation if needed (Burr and Mutchler, 1999). One study examined the attitudes toward family obligations among

The majority of Mexican American families live in urban areas. Most Mexican Americans live in intact families and are less likely to divorce than either Whites or Blacks.

over 800 Mexican American adolescents and found that they possessed stronger values and greater expectations regarding their duty to assist, respect, and support their families than did their peers with European backgrounds (Fuligni et al., 1999). And most adult Mexican American children speak with or see their parents daily (Dietz, 1995).

Traditional families also include **compadres** (godfathers) and **comadres** (godmothers) as part of the extended family network. These people become godparents at a child's baptism and will readily help in time of need. Families that do not have relatives or godparents on whom to rely in times of need may turn to welfare programs (Horowitz, 1983).

Divorce Rates and Birthrates

The majority (72%) of Mexican Americans live in intact families; 20% of the families consist of a female householder with no spouse present; 8% are male householders with no spouse present. Divorce rates are far lower among Mexican Americans than among Blacks and slightly lower than among Whites (U.S. Bureau of the Census, 1996-1997). There is a higher proportion of never-married people and a lower proportion of widowed or divorced people among Mexican Americans than in the general population. Mexican American families are younger and tend to average one more child per family than Anglo-American families do. The rate

of births to unmarried Mexican American mothers is higher than among Whites and Chinese Americans, but lower than among Blacks and Native Americans, who are less likely to marry because of pregnancy. Figure 1.11 shows the comparisons among ethnic groups.

Power and Decision Making

Historically, Mexican American families have been considered patriarchal (male-dominated). In order to prove his **machismo** (masculinity), the male could have extramarital affairs; he could not, however, flaunt them, for that would demonstrate lack of respect for his wife. The sexual purity of women—the faithfulness of wives and the virginity of unmarried women—was symbolized by the Virgin Mary. The honor of a man was besmirched if his wife was unfaithful or his daughter was not a virgin at marriage. Girls were taught to be modest and were not supposed to learn about sexual relations through either conversation or experience. Males learned about sex from other males and from encounters with "bad" girls (Horowitz, 1983). In spite of these traditional views, an increasing number of Mexican American women are sexually active prior to marriage. This is especially evident in the fact that almost a third of Mexican American women are pregnant when they marry (Magana and Carrier, 1991).

The most recent views of Mexican American families emphasize that male dominance is still a persistent feature but that the fathers usually exercise their authority in a dignified and fair manner, showing honor and respect for other family members. The Mexican American family has been characterized as warm and nurturing, with cooperation among family members and with egalitarianism in decision making. Role relations range from patriarchal to completely egalitarian, with the most prevalent the one in which the husband and wife share in decisions. While some studies indicate that Mexican American women follow the traditional role of submission to their spouse's authority, more research rejects the notion that Mexican American women lack power within heterosexual relationships (Gutmann, 1996).

The most important role of Mexican American women still is in the home, primarily as mothers. In the past, working outside the home was frowned upon. Today, it has become a necessity in many households. The marriage bond is based on procreation and expression of love, but much socializing occurs in single-sex groups because of the expanded family network fulfilling companionship needs.

Child Rearing and Education

There are important intergenerational differences in child-rearing practices related to variations in the sociocultural backgrounds of Mexican American families. Parents of first- and second-generation adolescents, especially mothers, are very similar in their socialization practices. Foreign-born mothers stress earlier autonomy, productive use of time, and strict obedience more than do mothers of third-generation adolescents. Immigrant parents generally emphasize socialization practices that revolve around issues of responsibility. This approach is characterized by an expectation of earlier self-reliance and adherence to family rules within an open parent-child relationship. It resembles an authoritative parenting style. In contrast, U.S.-born parents, particularly mothers, emphasize socialization practices that revolve around expressions of concern. This approach is characterized by emotional support and the expectation of proper behavior at home and in school (Buriel, 1993).

Mexican American children are still comparatively poorly educated, as Table 3.1 shows. The low level of education has several causes. There is often a language problem if parents do not speak English at home (Mendelberg, 1984). Teachers may be poorly trained, may not speak Spanish, or may be prejudiced against Mexican American children. Schools in the barrios are more often poorly funded, and educational programs are inferior (Casas and Ponterotto, 1984). Under these circumstances, not surprisingly, scholastic performance often is poor and dropout rates are high.

NATIVE AMERICAN FAMILIES

Currently, the Bureau of Indian Affairs (BIA) defines Native Americans as those with one-fourth or more Indian blood. The latest census figures indicate that in 1999 over 2 million persons identified themselves as Native Americans (U.S. Bureau of the Census, 2000b). Of the total population, about half live in the West and Southwest, especially in Arizona, New Mexico, California, and Oklahoma. Arizona and Oklahoma represent extremes in tribal representation. Arizona has the largest single tribe, the Navajo, living on the largest reservation in the United States. Oklahoma, in contrast, has the largest number of tribes, about 60. Members of these tribes historically were relocated in Oklahoma from all over the country when their tribal lands were taken by Whites. Because the Oklahoma Indians were newcomers, living on land next to their White neighbors (who had also recently immigrated), most lived among the general population, although there are some remote reservations in the

Table 3.1 Percentage of Population Age 25 or Older, by Years of Schooling and Ethnic Origin, 1995

Number of Years of Schooling	White	Black	Mexican American
Elementary: 0–8	7.9	9.8	43.5
Four years or more of high school	87.7	73.7	49.7
Four years or more of college	27.7	13.2	7.1

Note: From *Statistical Abstract of the United States, 1998*, Current Population Report: "Educational Attainment in the United States" (p. 159) by U.S. Bureau of the Census, 1999, Washington, DC: U.S. Government Printing Office.

state. In some states, such as New Mexico and the Dakotas, the majority of the population still live on reservations. In other states, such as North Carolina, California, and New York, the majority either resisted movement to reservations or now live on land over which the government has relinquished control (Rice, 1993).

Since the beginning of World War II, there has been a rapid migration of Native Americans to urban areas. The government encouraged migration and offered assistance through a relocation program that sought to promote rapid integration into the mainstream. But this relocation program created many problems. Native Americans in cities are not integrated but are an alienated, invisible minority group. Many return to the reservation because they dislike the city and its demands.

The federal relocation program and its effects on Native Americans highlight one of the major problems of contemporary Native Americans: the cultural conflict between the way of life on reservations and the way of life in urban America (Rice, 1993).

Vital Statistics

Native Americans have the highest birthrate, the highest death rate, and the shortest life expectancy of any group in the United States (Utter, 1993).

In spite of steady declines over the past 50 years, infant mortality on an Oregon reservation was found to be nearly three times higher than the rate for the United States as a whole (Remez, 1992b).

Native Americans are afflicted with most major diseases to a much greater degree than other Americans. They are more likely than someone in the general population to die from a variety of causes, including tuberculosis (5 times), homicide (1.6 times), suicide (1.3 times), pneumonia and influenza (1.3 times), diabetes (2.6 times), liver disease (3.4 times), and all types of accidents (2.3 times). Interestingly, the rate of cardiovascular disease and cancer among Native Americans is lower than in the general population (Utter, 1993). AIDS experts consider many Native Americans to be at high risk for HIV infections because of unsafe sex habits, alcohol use, IV drug use, and the intermigration between urban centers and Indian country (Erikson, 1991). Middle-ear infection results in widespread hearing loss among Native American children and affects cognitive development (McShane, 1988). Native Americans suffer more from hunger and malnutrition than does any other group in the United States, but they also have high rates of diabetes and obesity due to eating habits (Snow and Harris, 1989).

Rates of fetal alcohol syndrome (FAS) are very high in babies of both adult and adolescent mothers, and FAS is the primary cause of mental retardation (Backover, 1991; McShane, 1988). Suicide is the leading cause of death among Native American youths ages 15–19, with a rate five times the national average (LaFromboise and Bigfoot, 1988). The rate varies tremendously, however, from tribe to tribe.

Economics

Native Americans have a lower standard of living than does any other racial or ethnic group in the United States, with unemployment high and income low. In 1995, about one-third of the households had incomes below the poverty level (U.S. Bureau of the Census, 1998a). Unemployment on some reservations runs as high as 80%–90%. In most communities, life is a matter of bare subsistence; in fact, some of the worst slums in the United States are on reservations. In sum, Native American health, income, and education statistics are among the worst in the country, according to recent Census Bureau reports.

Economic strides have been made. Some tribes are slowly gaining control over their own economic livelihoods. Some Native American lands have large deposits of uranium, coal, or natural gas, and some tribes have made progress in tapping these sources of revenue, but most remain dormant. Moreover, during the twentieth century, periodic mismanagement or corruption within the BIA, as well as within certain state and tribal agencies, resulted in accumulated losses of hundreds of millions of dollars in tribal royalty revenues from oil and gas leases (Washburn, 1988; White, 1990). The Choctaws in Mississippi have auto assembly plants and other businesses that make them the state's 15th largest employer. The Passamaquoddy and Penobscot tribes in Maine received a huge settlement from the government for land claims and have invested it in various money-making enterprises.

Degrees of Acculturation Among Native Americans

The Native American population varies from tribe to tribe, so it is impossible to make general statements that apply to all Native Americans. Nevertheless, researchers have found some common patterns. One study grouped the households on Blackfeet, Sioux, and Navajo reservations and was able to distinguish four types of households:

1. The isolated Native American family lives in a remote area of a reservation and strongly prefers to use the native language.
2. The traditional Native American family has a bilingual home and actively participates in tribal ceremonies.

3. The bicultural Native American family lives on a reservation and engages in traditional ceremonies but prefers speaking English.
4. The acculturated Native American family speaks English as its primary language, and family activity approximates White norms.

Some Native Americans who live and work in cities or nonreservation rural areas return to the reservations to attend ceremonies or visit relatives. Many Native Americans have never lived on reservations and have life-styles similar to those of their neighbors in either nonreservation rural or urban areas (Thomason, 1991).

Some tribes have turned to gambling as a major source of income. This was made possible by the Indian Gaming Regulatory Act (IGRA) of 1988. Gaming is a growing industry on reservations and has brought economic prosperity to some Native American communities. As of March 1999, the National Indian Gaming Commission reported that there were 310 Native American gaming operations in 28 states with estimated revenues of $7.4 billion per year. However, less than one-third of the federally recognized tribes in the United States have casinos. The IGRA mandates that tribal governments, not individuals, control gaming operations, which means that all profits must be funneled to tribal government programs. This revenue has helped to create better schools, medical clinics, and social service programs. In California in 1998, gaming revenues were estimated to have reduced Aid to Families with Dependent Children payments by $50 million, including reductions of $21 million to tribe members and an additional $28.9 million to other former recipients.

Although gaming has led to self-sufficiency for some tribal nations, not everyone agrees that it has been a positive change for Native American family life and culture. Many reservation members worry about gambling's long-range impact on the tribal community. Their concerns range from the fear that many tribal members may become addicted to gambling to the fear that the tribe may pursue economic development strategies that are not compatible with traditional Native American culture (Vinje, 1996).

Education

The record of education for Native Americans is one of broken promises, inadequate resources, incompetent teachers, and—worst—attempts to use education to destroy their culture and way of life in order to make them into White people.

By the turn of the twentieth century, the BIA was operating 147 reservation day schools, 81 reservation boarding schools, and 25 off-reservation boarding schools for Indians in various parts of the country. The goal was complete assimilation. Reading, writing, arithmetic, the manual trades, and home economics were drilled into the students. Life at these boarding schools was regimented. Estranged from family, isolated in an alien culture, and unable to talk to teachers (who did not know the various dialects), many Native American students performed poorly. About three-fourths of the children in boarding schools had emotional or social problems, and about one-third were physically handicapped (McShane, 1988).

At the secondary level, the school curriculum was based on traditional Anglo-American culture. A report on education in Native American schools in Alaska stated that education that gave the Indian, Eskimo, and Aleut knowledge of—and therefore pride in—their historical and cultural heritage was nonexistent (Henninger and Esposito, 1971).

The Indian Education Act of 1972 (known as Title IV) resulted in some improvements. This legislation established funding for special bilingual and bicultural programs, culturally relevant teaching materials, proper training and hiring of counselors, and establishment of the Office of Indian Education within the U.S. Department of Education. More important, the act required participation of Native Americans in the planning of their educational experiences (O'Brien, 1989).

Education for Native Americans has improved remarkably in the past two decades. The BIA is funding many education facilities, which include day schools, on-reservation and off-reservation boarding schools, and BIA-operated dormitories that enable students to attend public schools. The BIA also provides funding to many public school districts around the country. Such financial support is designed to aid the education of more than 225,000 eligible Native American students who attend public school.

One positive development is the rise in the number of Native Americans going to college. Two postsecondary schools are operated by the BIA. The BIA also provides funding for the operation of 22 tribally controlled community colleges. Approximately 15,000 Native American students receive scholarships each year under BIA programs to attend colleges and universities. Between 1980 and 1995, the number of Native Americans enrolled in college rose from 84,000 to 131,000 (U.S. Bureau of the Census, 1998a).

Family Life

There is no such institution as the typical Native American family. Tribal identity is primary, and family structures and values differ from tribe to tribe. Despite the attempt to impose Western family models on Native Americans, various family forms still exist among the different tribal groups. Some families are matrilineal, with descent through the mother's line. For many Native Americans, the extended family is the basic unit for carrying out family functions, despite the absence of extended kin in the same household. Children may be raised by relatives residing in different, noncontiguous households. The existence of multiple households sharing family functions is quite common. Members of the elderly population are likely to reside in independent households but to maintain close functional contact with their children, grandchildren, and great-grandchildren. They fulfill traditional family roles on a daily basis.

Children

Because of the high rates of alcoholism and other problems among parents, large numbers of Native American children are removed from their families and placed in the care of foster parents (McShane, 1988). However, Native Americans view children as important assets to the family. Children are taught that family and tribe are of the utmost importance. Grandmothers are very important, and the aged in general are looked up to for wisdom and counsel. The aged play the important role of storytellers, relating traditions, beliefs, and customs. Children are taught to be independent (there often are no rigid schedules for eating and sleeping) and to be patient and unassuming. They are taught not to show emotions but to maintain a rather severe reserve. The ability to endure pain, hardship, hunger, and frustration without showing discomfort is emphasized, as are bravery and courage.

Teenage Mothers

Birthrates among Native American youths vary substantially by geographic location and tribal affiliation. Overall, the rate of births to teenagers in Native American populations is nearly four times greater than that among comparable populations of non-Hispanic White teenagers. The birthrate among 16- to 19-year-old reservation-residing Navajo youths is approximately 15.8%, a figure substantially higher than that for similar-age youths across the nation (Dalla and Gamble, 1997).

With the birthrate so high among Navajo youths, an important question becomes, How competent are these teenage mothers? In general, mothers who have a high degree of identification with the maternal role and who are intensely committed to that role in relation to their children are the best mothers. These teens report that their lives revolve around their children and that they often make personal sacrifices for their children's well-being. However, some teenage mothers report that they have difficulties coping with motherhood and that they relinquish many maternal responsibilities to their own mothers.

For some Navajo mothers, the relationship with their partner is a critical factor in the determination of parenting competence. Interviews with young mothers revealed that their partners had been

Will these Native American children grow up in urban areas, in which individualism and competition are emphasized? Or will they experience the more traditional values of tribal identity and cooperation some leaders believe is so important to their culture's future?

supportive prior to and immediately following the birth of their children. However, over time, the young mothers implied that the financial strain of parenting and the limited employment opportunities on the Navajo reservation might lead their partners to turn to alcoholism.

Many young Navajo mothers suggest that their own mothers provide essential financial and child-rearing assistance. However, some report that relationships with their own mothers are often tense. Some teens note the absence of emotional and instrumental support from their mothers. Adolescent mothers who choose to leave threatening home environments are those in greatest need (Dalla and Gamble, 1997).

Cultural Conflict

Native Americans are making a determined effort to retain their traditional garb, dances, and crafts and to teach their cultural values to their young people. Religion has always been important, but many practices were banned when the federal government conducted its 60-year (1870–1930) program of enforced enculturation ("The Denial of Indian Civil and Religious Rights," 1975). Puberty rites for girls and boys were banned during the year, except between July 1 and July 4.

Most important, Native American values are at variance with modern Anglo-American culture.

Native American culture is present-oriented and is not concerned with time or the future; White culture is future-oriented, concerned with time and planning ahead. Native Americans see human life as being in harmony with nature; Whites seek conquest over nature. Native American life is group-oriented and emphasizes cooperation; White society emphasizes individualism and competition, which is one reason many Native Americans do not easily succeed and assume positions of leadership in it.

As a result of conflicting cultures, Native Americans today are faced with a dilemma: whether to accommodate themselves to the Anglo-American world and learn to compete in it or to retain traditional customs and values and live apart (Markstrom-Adams, 1990). An ideal solution would be for both Native Americans and all others to appreciate and understand the values of Native American culture and the importance of preserving a rich heritage. The individual who is proud to be a Native American and who is respected by the rest of society can contribute richly to a nation that prides itself on being the world's melting pot (Rice, 1993).

CHINESE AMERICAN FAMILIES

In comparison to the general population of the United States, the Chinese American population includes greater percentages of the college educated and college graduates; its unemployment rate is lower; and it includes a greater percentage with incomes of $25,000 or more per year (U.S. Bureau of the Census, 1999a). These figures result partly from the Chinese American emphasis on education and industriousness and reflect the characteristics of those who have immigrated to the United States.

Immigration

A minority of modern Chinese Americans are descendants of the Chinese who immigrated to the United States during the period of open immigration from 1820 to 1882. After 1882, a series of exclusion acts were passed that restricted Asian immigration. As a result, for a number of years, more Chinese left than entered the United States.

Traditionally, Chinese males entered the United States without their wives and children. Custom required a man to marry before he left China and his spouse to remain in the house of his parents. The man's duty was to send money to his patiently waiting family and to return home eventually. Frequently, years passed before he returned. Many hoped to earn enough to bring their families to the United States, but under the Immigration Act of 1882, no Chinese women were permitted to enter except for a handful from exempt classes and wives of U.S. citizens. This restriction continued until 1943. As a result, many Chinese men who remained in the United States faced a life without intimate family relations. Some joined together in clans and secret societies that provided a sense of family solidarity. Others engaged in gambling, opium smoking, and prostitution and were stereotyped by White Americans as lowly, immoral, and dangerous. In 1930, there were four Chinese males to every Chinese female in the United States. The national origin quota system that discriminated against Asians was abolished in 1965, and today the gender ratio is almost equal. More than 270,000 immigrants born in China were admitted to the United States between 1981 and 1990. The growth in immigration from China has been particularly impressive in recent years, with 65,579 Chinese admitted in 1993 alone. Many of the recent Chinese immigrants who came to the United States on student or exchange visas later became legalized immigrants as a result of a presidential amnesty order (Hwang and Saenz, 1997).

Family and Children

Well-educated Chinese Americans have lower rates of divorce, mental illness, and public assistance—and higher family income—than does the general U.S. population (McLeod, 1986). The percentage of Chinese American women who have never married is higher than that of native-born White women (Ferguson, 1995). In comparison to other minorities, Chinese Americans have more conservative sexual values, a lower fertility rate, fewer births to unmarried women, and more conservative attitudes toward the role of women. Chinese Americans place a great deal of emphasis on the family as the most important societal unit and emphasize the need for interpersonal affection (Feldman, Mont-Reynaud, and Rosenthal, 1992). They have a high sense of duty to family and of filial responsibility, and they blame themselves when a young person fails to live up to expectations. A child who misbehaves brings shame to the family name (Ishii-Kuntz, 1997).

Philosophies and methods of child rearing depend on the degree of acculturation (Ho, 1989). Traditional approaches feature authoritarian methods: a strict interpretation of good and bad behavior, limitation of social interaction, firm discipline involving physical punishment, little verbal communication other than commands or scoldings, an expectation of obedience and conformity, and the absence of overt parental praise.

Americanized Chinese parents use different approaches. The parents are nurturing and expose their children to more varied experiences than do other immigrant families. They use more verbal praise, talk and joke more with their children, and give them more freedom in decision making. Chinese American mothers play a significant role in decision making and discipline in the family. They consider teaching to be an important part of their maternal role, and many give regular formal instruction to children at home.

Chinese American children are taught that everyone has to work for the welfare of the family. They are given a great deal of responsibility and are assigned specific chores. Adolescents are responsible for supervising young children and for working around the house or in the family business. One research study indicated that Chinese American adolescents give a greater priority to parental expectations than to their own personal desires (Yau and

Asian Americans often find themselves caught between not being considered "real" Asians because they have adopted mainstream cultural habits and not being considered "real" Americans because of their looks. Consider the following quotations from the media:

> "You know, I'm tired of the Kristi Yamaguchis and the Michelle Kwans! They're not American . . . when I look at a box of Wheaties, I don't want to see eyes that are slanted and Oriental and almond shaped. I want to see American eyes looking at me."
>
> —Bill Handel, popular morning DJ for KFI-AM, one of the nation's most listened-to talk radio stations.

> "American beats Kwan."
>
> —MSNBC's erroneous headline after figure skater Tara Lipinski beat Michelle Kwan during the 1998 Winter Olympics. Both women are Americans.

Mia Tuan (1999) has explored what she called the "authenticity dilemma" confronting Asian Americans today. She interviewed 95 third-, fourth-, and fifth-generation Chinese and Japanese Americans living in northern and southern California to (1) determine the content, meaning, and salience of ethnicity in their lives, (2) explore the extent to which they felt that ethnicity was an optional rather than imposed facet of their identities, and (3) examine the role played by race in shaping life experiences. The following excerpts are from her interviews:

Q: How do you identify yourself?
A: *That's a really hard question actually. I guess as an Asian-American. I don't consider myself just Japanese, just Chinese. I don't consider myself just American. I don't know. I kinda like terminology like Asian-American and African-American because it's kinda messy. . . . By blood, I'm Chinese and Japanese. By culture, I don't know if I am so much of either. I don't know. . . . Mom would always tell me I used to get confused growing up. "How can I be Japanese and Chinese and American?" "Well, you are half Japanese, half Chinese, and all American." (p. 108)*
A: *I don't think I can be just American just for the fact that I look different from the typical American, white. (Why not just Japanese then?) Because I definitely am Americanized, an American raised in America. And I don't always agree with what Japanese, Japan stands for. (p. 109)*
A: *Usually I say Chinese-American because I realize I'm not Chinese. People from China come over here and*

like, whoa, they're like a foreign species. And I'm not American because just one look and I'm apart. I used to struggle with this question a lot and to make a long story short, Chinese-American is a hybrid of its own. It's kind of like Afro-Americans. Boy, they're not African and they're not American and it's just its own species and that's the way it is. (p. 116)
A: *Like my girlfriend, it's kinda funny because she's of Irish descent, but people would never think that or ask where are you from because they see her as being Caucasian. And if they look at me they would say, "Oh where are you from," because I'm perceived as being Asian first. It's like girl, an Asian girl, and anything that follows after that. For my girlfriend it would be like, she's white, she's of Irish descent but it doesn't really matter. It's like way down the list of whatever. (p. 112)*

These statements go to the heart of the dilemma many Asian Americans face: They have learned that others view them as outsiders in American society. Even though they are lifelong Americans, they are not perceived as such because they do not fit the image of a "real" American. About half the respondents reported having felt out of place or suddenly conscious of their racial background at some time. Reasons for this reaction included stares, comments, and even threats from others who looked upon them as strangers or intruders in a public place. European-Americans see it as a matter of personal choice whether to identify along ethnic lines, but the respondents found that not identifying in ethnic or racial terms was problematic in their interactions with non-Asians. Complicating matters for many Asian Americans was that their foreign-born counterparts saw them as "too American" and not knowledgeable enough about Chinese or Japanese ways (Tuan, 1999).

Tuan (1999) summarizes:

Today, Asian ethnics exercise a great deal of choice regarding the elements of traditional ethnic culture they wish to incorporate or do away with in their personal lives. They befriend whom they please, date and marry whom they please, choose the careers they please, and pursue further knowledge about their cultural heritage if they please. In this sense, ethnicity has indeed become optional in my respondents' personal lives. But in another very real way, being ethnic remains a societal expectation for them despite how far removed they are from their immigrant roots or how much they differ from their foreign-born counterparts. (p. 123)

Chinese American families enjoy a higher standard of living than do most other minority groups and include a greater percentage of college-educated members.

Smetna, 1993). Table 3.2 contrasts a number of traditional Asian values with Western urban industrial values.

Education

Chinese Americans have always stressed the importance of education and hard work as the means of getting ahead. Parents who are shopkeepers or farmers urge their children to go to college to be professionals. The emphasis is on earning money in the technical professions, such as engineering, pharmacy, dentistry, and technology (Leong, 1991). As Rand Corporation's Kevin McCarthy says, "They are the most highly skilled of any immigrant group our country has ever had" (McLeod, 1986, p. 50).

Prejudices

Racial prejudice is still an important limiting factor in the lives of Chinese Americans. Although some employers like to hire Chinese Americans because of the stereotype that they are hardworking and dependable, the employers sometimes pay them below-standard wages. In seeking more desirable employment, many Chinese Americans feel they are not on equal footing with Anglo-Americans. A successful engineer may still be

Table 3.2 Comparison of Traditional Asian Values and Western Urban Industrial Values

Traditional Asian Values	Western Urban Industrial Values
Group/community emphasis	Individual emphasis
Extended family	Nuclear family/ blended family
Interdependence	Independence
Person-to-person orientation	Person-to-object orientation
Past→present→future	Future→present→past
Age	Youth
Conformity/cooperation	Competition
Harmony with nature	Conquest over nature
Fatalism	Master of one's own fate
Logic of the heart	Logic of the mind
Balance	Change
Patience/modesty	Aggression/assertion
Pragmatic outlook	Theoretical outlook
Suppression of emotion	Expression of emotion
Rigidity of role and status	Flexibility of role and status

Note: From "Cultural Factors in Working with Southeast Asian Refugee Adolescents" by E. Lee, June 1988, *Journal of Adolescence*, *11*, pp. 167–179. Used by permission.

labeled a "Chinese engineer," whereas one hardly hears reference to a German or Swedish engineer. Frequent reminders of their ethnic origin make some Chinese Americans feel that they are not fully accepted as Americans. "In the past we had the coolie who slaved," said Jim Tso, president of the Organization of Chinese Americans of Northern Virginia. "Today we have the high-tech coolie" (McLeod, 1986, p. 51).

CONCLUSIONS

As we have seen, family living exhibits a wide range of patterns. Ethnic differences in families are characterized by differences in family structure, household composition, goals and philosophies, power structures, gender roles, spousal relationships, sexual values and behavior, and child-rearing patterns. The United States continues to become more ethnically diverse; therefore, a multicultural perspective on the family is necessary if we are going to understand and appreciate different patterns. The challenges are for members of various groups to develop understanding of other groups and to develop pride in their own group.

Despite the differences, there are many similarities. All families are made up of people with needs, feelings, values, hopes and dreams, problems, and intense desires to love and to relate to others within the family context. The more deeply we explore differences, the more we recognize how very much alike people are, no matter what their country of origin.

This chapter has emphasized that it is a mistake for one group to judge another by its own set of values. The belief that there is a single ideal family form is a narrow, prejudiced, stereotypic view of family relationships. This chapter has also emphasized that there are differences *within* ethnic groups, as well as differences among them. For example, there are educated and uneducated people in every ethnic group, and there are social classes within every ethnic group. Any discussion of ethnic diversity must take into account these differences (DeGenova, 1997). Our goal is not to try to get everyone to think and act alike, but to develop an understanding of each individual family.

SUMMARY

1. African Americans are the largest ethnic minority in the United States.

2. There has been a marked increase in the number and percentage of one-parent Black families. African Americans believe strongly in the institution of the family, but the acute shortage of marriageable Black men leaves large numbers of Black women, especially the educated ones, without husbands.

3. Being able to fulfill gender-specific roles has an important influence on African Americans' satisfaction with family life.

4. The considerable differences among Black families often depend on class.

5. African American families show a number of strengths: strong kinship bonds, a favorable attitude toward the elderly, adaptable roles, strong achievement orientation, and a strong religious orientation.

6. Familism (putting the needs of the family above those of the individual) is common among Mexican Americans. Extended family networks are common and sometimes include *compadres* and *comadres* (godparents).

7. Divorce rates are lower among Mexican Americans than among Blacks. There is a higher proportion of singles and a lower proportion of widowed or divorced persons than in the general population. A high fertility rate results in large families.

8. Historically, the Mexican American family was patriarchal, according to the tradition of *machismo*. The most recent views suggest that, although male dominance still prevails, men usually exercise their authority in a fair manner. The most important role of the woman is in the home.

9. Educational levels of Mexican American children lag behind those of much of the population.

10. Forty-five percent of Native Americans live in the West and Southwest. Some live on reservations, and others among the general population.

11. Large numbers of Native Americans have migrated to urban areas, where they have encountered many problems. They have a higher birthrate, higher death rate, and shorter life expectancy; suffer more hunger and malnutrition; and have a lower standard of living than any other minority group in the United States. But some tribes have made progress in developing the natural resources on their reservations, and others have gained revenues from gaming casinos.

12. Native Americans' education has improved remarkably in the past two decades. One hopeful sign is the number of young Native Americans going on to college.

13. Family forms among Native Americans vary from tribe to tribe. Some families are matrilineal, and extended families are common. Children are often raised by relatives even if they don't live together in the parents' household. Births to unmarried teenage women are common. The aged are important leaders of the people.

14. Native Americans are making a determined effort to retain their culture but have been in conflict with White society's efforts to enculturate them.

15. The Chinese American population has a greater percentage of college graduates, a lower rate of unemployment, and a greater percentage of families with incomes over $25,000 per year than does the general population.

16. Well-educated Chinese Americans have lower rates of divorce, mental illness, and public assistance and have more conservative sexual values, a lower fertility rate, fewer children born to single mothers, and more conservative attitudes toward women than is true in the general population.

17. Chinese Americans have a high sense of duty to family. Methods of child rearing tend to be traditional, although Americanized parents are more nurturing and use more positive approaches to development of their children. Chinese Americans stress the importance of education.

18. Traditional Asian values are sometimes in conflict with urban industrial values in this country.

KEY TERMS

ethnicity	familism	comadres
culture	compadres	machismo
barrios		

QUESTIONS FOR THOUGHT

1. How is the family in which you were brought up (your family of origin) similar to or different from other types of families discussed in this chapter in terms of basic characteristics, philosophies, strengths, and challenges?

2. What are some of the major challenges facing families whose ethnic background is not the same as the mainstream culture's?

3. What is the meaning of the word *machismo*, and how is it manifested in family relationships and in the personal behavior of Mexican American males? How is this similar to and

different from male behavior in other cultural groups?

4. If you could pick the cultural group you were brought up in, which one would it be, and why?

5. Do you think it is important to have cultural diversity in the United States? Why or why not? What have you learned about family life from reading about other cultures?

SUGGESTED READINGS

Coontz, S. (Ed.). (1999). *American Families: A Multicultural Reader.* New York: Routledge. Highlights the socioeconomic and cultural forces that affect family dynamics and organization.

DeGenova, M. K. (1997). *Families in Cultural Context.* Mountain View, CA: Mayfield. Discusses 11 different ethnic families.

Demo, D. H., Allen, K. R., and Fine, M. A. (Eds.). (2000). *Handbook of Family Diversity.* New York: Oxford University Press. Explores ethnic, racial, cultural, and class diversities, as well as gender dynamics in families.

Dosanjh, J. S., and Ghuman, P. A. S. (1996). *Child Rearing in Ethnic Minorities.* Bristol, PA: Taylor & Francis. Summarizes problems and offers guidance.

Hill, R. B., et al. (1993). *Research on the African-American Family: A Holistic Perspective.* Westport, CT: Auburn House. Summarizes research.

Ingoldsby, B. B., and Smith, S. (Eds.). (1995). *Families in Multicultural Perspectives.* New York: Guilford Press. Takes a comparative approach.

Jacobson, C. K. (Ed.). (1995). *American Families: Issues in Race and Ethnicity.* New York: Garland. Carefully illustrates meanings and interpretations regarding the impact ethnicity may have on American families.

Lee, Y., and McCauley, C. (Eds.). (1999). *Personality and Person Perception Across Cultures.* Mahwah, NJ: Lawrence Erlbaum. Explores the links between personality and culture, with the aim of providing information on how we are different from and similar to one another.

McAdoo, H. P. (Ed.). (1999). *Family Ethnicity: Strength in Diversity* (2nd ed.). Newbury Park, CA: Sage. Focuses on African American, Hispanic, Native American, Muslim, and Asian American families.

McFadden, J. (Ed.). (1999). *Transcultural Counseling* (2nd ed.). Alexandria, VA: American Counseling Association. Provides resources for counselors working with clients from various cultural backgrounds.

Mindel, C. (Ed.). (1997). *Ethnic Families in America: Patterns and Variations* (4th ed.). New York: Elsevier North Holland. Offers essays on different ethnic groups.

Pleck, E. H. (2000). *Celebrating the Family: Ethnicity, Consumer Culture, and Family Rituals.* Cambridge, MA: Harvard University Press. Gives a comparative history of American family with insight into the significance of ethnicity as it affects consumer culture.

Sheets, R., and Hollins, E. (Eds.). (1999). *Racial and Ethnic Identity in School Practices: Aspects of Human Development.* Mahwah, NJ: Lawrence Erlbaum. Examines cultural differences in family values among Mexican, Mexican American, and Anglo-American families and the relationship of the parents' family values to the family values and mental health of adolescent children.

Staples, R., and Johnson, L. B. (1993). *Black Families at the Crossroads: Challenges and Prospects.* San Francisco: Jossey-Bass. Traces historical forces shaping the Black family.

Taylor, R. L. (Ed.). (1998). *Minority Families in the United States: A Multicultural Perspective.* Upper Saddle River, NJ: Prentice-Hall. Analyzes various minority families organized around a common set of issues and themes, allowing readers to compare similarities and differences in family structure, contemporary trends, and socioeconomic factors.

LEARNING OBJECTIVES

After reading the chapter, you should be able to:

Identify in general terms the percentages of people in the U.S. population who are married, single, widowed, and divorced and point out cultural and ethnic differences.

Describe the differences between voluntary and involuntary singles.

Sort out myths versus realities about singles.

Explain the reasons for marital delay and the reasons some people remain permanently single.

Understand the advantages and disadvantages of being single and discuss singles' health and well-being.

Describe the various living arrangements of singles, including the increasing phenomenon of adult children living with their parent(s).

Understand the need of singles for companionship, the difference between loneliness and aloneness, and the differences between males and females in relation to companionship issues.

Discuss the sexual behavior of singles.

Compare singles with marrieds in terms of employment and level of income.

Discuss the challenges faced by single mothers.

Discuss the life situations of older, never-married adults.

Examine personal attitudes toward being single.

Being Single

Learning Objectives

Categories of Singles
Voluntary Singles
Involuntary Singles

Marital Delay

Why Some People Remain Single
Deliberate Choice
Fear of Marriage
Lack of Opportunity
Circumstances

Advantages and Disadvantages of Being Single

The Health and Well-Being of Singles
Perspective: What Makes People Happy?

Living Arrangements
Shared Living Spaces
Living with Parents
Living Alone

Loneliness and Friendships
Family Issues: Flying Back to the Nest
The Importance of Companionship
Males Versus Females
Loneliness Versus Aloneness

Sexual Behavior

Employment and Income

Single Mothers

The Never-Married Adult

Summary
Key Terms
Questions for Thought
Suggested Readings

One of the choices adults face is whether to get married. In previous generations, adults had less choice: Society assumed that everyone who could do so would get married, and those who didn't marry faced social disapproval. Today, the number of never-married adults has increased dramatically, reflecting changing social conditions and attitudes.

Figures 4.1 and 4.2 illustrate the marital status of the U.S. population, 18 years of age and older, in 1998. Overall, 59.7% were married, 23.6% were single (never-married), 6.9% were widowed, and 9.8% were divorced. Obviously, the great majority of adults were married, and an additional number had been married at one time. Nevertheless, nearly one in four adults had never been married, but these were primarily in the youngest age groups.

When these figures are examined according to ethnic group, we find some variations. Only 41.8% of Blacks age 18 or older were married. Over one-third had never been married. The percentage of Blacks widowed (7.6%) or divorced (11.7%) was slightly higher than for Whites. The statistics for Hispanics showed that about 29.7% had never been married, compared to 21.7% for Whites. Approximately the same percentage of both groups were married, and slightly fewer Hispanics than Whites were widowed or divorced. Marriage was more popular among White Americans than among other groups.

In this chapter, we examine the facts about being single and the reasons for the increase in those numbers. We examine why some people remain single and what some advantages and disadvantages of being single are. We discuss the lifestyles and living arrangements of singles, as well as factors such as social life and leisure time, loneliness and friendships, sexual behavior, and employment and income. Finally, we examine the situations of single mothers and of older, never-married adults.

CATEGORIES OF SINGLES

Several sociodemographic variables are related to the likelihood of never marrying—namely, age, race, and gender. First, age is negatively related to the likelihood of never marrying: the older one becomes, the greater the likelihood of remaining single. Approximately 74% of the never-married are younger than age 34 (U.S. Bureau of the Census, 1999a). Between 1970 and 1998, the proportion of 25- to 29-year-olds who were never married more than quadrupled, from 11% to 45% (U.S. Bureau of the Census, 1999a). Although this reflects the trend toward delayed marriage, it also could indicate increasing societal acceptance of long-term singlehood (Barrett, 1999). If more people are choosing singlehood as a long-term status, it is reasonable to expect that the social resources and well-being of the never-married now include better social support in and higher satisfaction with their lives (Barrett, 1999).

Second, some research suggests that race is related to social support and well-being among the never-married. Non-White, never-married individuals have more frequent contact with relatives

Figure 4.1 Marital Status of U.S. Population, Age 18 and Older, 1998 (*Note:* Adapted from *Statistical Abstract of the United States, 1999* [pp. 57, 58] by U.S. Bureau of the Census, 1999, Washington, DC: U.S. Government Printing Office.)

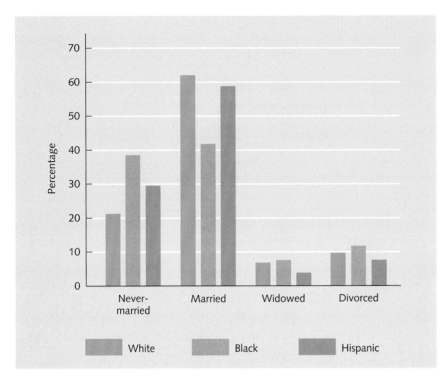

Figure 4.2 Marital Status of U.S. Population, Age 18 and Older, by Ethnic Origin, 1998 (*Note:* Adapted from *Statistical Abstract of the United States, 1999* [p. 57] by U.S. Bureau of the Census, 1999, Washington, DC: U.S. Government Printing Office.)

and are more likely to live with relatives other than their parents than are Whites (Raley, 1995). Research has shown that being never-married is associated with lower satisfaction among White women and men and non-White men, but no difference is observed between unmarried and married non-White women (Mookherjee, 1997). While only 21% of Whites have never married, 39% of African American and 30% of Hispanics have never married (U.S. Bureau of the Census, 1999a). The gap between Whites and African Americans appears to be widening, as the percentage of never-married African Americans is rising at a faster rate than that for Whites (Waite, 1995). It is possible that the higher proportion of never-marrieds among non-Whites makes the single status less stigmatizing (Barrett, 1999).

Third, some research associates being never-married with lower well-being and less social support for men than for women. Among the never-married, women interact more frequently with relatives than do men (Seccombe and Ishii-Kuntz, 1994). Studies on psychological health suggest that, among the never-married, men have more depression and anxiety (Davies, 1995) and a higher risk of suicide (Meehan, Saltzman, and Sattin,

1991). Much research supports the idea that never-married women are better off than their male counterparts.

There are various categories of single persons. Stein (1981) developed a typology of single persons based on whether their status is voluntary or involuntary. Table 4.1 shows the four major categories of singles according to Stein.

Voluntary Singles

The category **voluntary temporary singles** includes young people who have never been married and are not currently looking; they are postponing marriage even though they are not opposed to the idea of marriage. It includes cohabiters who will eventually marry each other or someone else. It includes recently divorced or widowed people who need time to be single, though they may eventually want to marry again. It also includes older never-marrieds who are not actively looking but who would marry if the right person came along.

The category **voluntary stable (permanent) singles** includes never-marrieds of all ages who have no intention of marrying, cohabiters who never

Table 4.1 Typology of Singles		
	Voluntary	**Involuntary**
Temporary	Never-marrieds and previously marrieds who are not opposed to the idea of marriage but are not currently seeking mates	Those who have actively been seeking mates but have not found them
Stable (permanent)	All those (never-marrieds and former-marrieds) who choose to be single	Never-marrieds and former-marrieds who wanted to marry, who have not found a mate, and who have more or less accepted being single

Note: Adapted from *Single Life: Unmarried Adults in Social Context* (pp. 10–12) by P. Stein (Ed.), 1981, New York: St. Martin's Press. Used by permission of Haworth Press.

intend to marry, and formerly married people who never want to marry again. It also includes those who have taken religious vows not to marry.

Involuntary Singles

The category **involuntary temporary singles** includes young adults who have never been married but are actively seeking a mate and divorced or widowed persons who want to remarry soon.

The category **involuntary stable (permanent) singles** includes never-married persons or widowed or divorced people who wanted to marry or remarry but who have not found a mate; they have become reconciled to their single state.

MARITAL DELAY

In fact, most singles are only temporarily unmarried, since by ages 45–54 only 8.9% of males and 7.2% of females have never married (see Figure 4.3). However, the trend is for adults to get married at older ages than they used to.

The reasons for delaying marriage are social, economic, and personal. One particular reason is the changing attitude toward single life. Societal disapproval of single people has diminished, and it is no longer unacceptable for those in their thirties to be unmarried, especially if they have a flourishing career and an active social life. However, often, both family and friends continue to expect that ultimately they will marry. Nevertheless, if they opt to remain single because this is their preferred life-style, family and friends come to accept their decision.

The lengthening of the period of education and economic dependency has greatly influenced the delay of marriage. Women who have career aspirations marry later in life than do those who planned to be homemakers. Lower socioeconomic status individuals, with lower educational and vocational aspirations, are more likely to marry at early ages.

The sexual revolution has also influenced the age at first marriage. The increasing acceptance of nonmarital sexual intercourse has made sexual expression possible at younger ages without necessitating marriage. The increased acceptance of nonmarital cohabitation also provides some benefits of marriage without the commitment—for example, companionship, sex, shared housing, and shared living expenses (Althaus, 1991).

The women's movement has also influenced views of marriage. Women are encouraged to seek their own identity, apart from marital identity, and to find career fulfillment and economic self-sufficiency if that is what they desire. Feminists are in no way opposed to marriage, but women are encouraged to explore opportunities in addition to or as alternatives to family fulfillment. At the least, this attitude has led to marital postponement as women explore other options.

WHY SOME PEOPLE REMAIN SINGLE

Just as marriage may be delayed for any of a number of reasons, there are also a number of reasons for never getting married. As we have seen, some

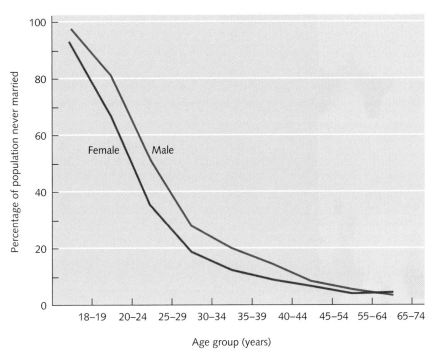

Figure 4.3 Never-Married People as a Percentage of Total Population, Age 18 and Older, by Age and Sex, 1998 (*Note:* Adapted from *Statistical Abstract of the United States, 1999* [p. 58] by U.S. Bureau of the Census, 1999, Washington, DC: U.S. Government Printing Office.)

people remain single because of life circumstances and find singlehood to be the best life-style for themselves.

Deliberate Choice

Some of the small minority who never marry have deliberately chosen to stay single. A survey of 3,000 single men and women from 36 states revealed that one-third of the men and one-fifth of the women were unmarried by choice (Simenauer and Carroll, 1982). For example, members of some religious orders take vows of chastity. Some people perceive marriage as incompatible with their careers. A minority of singles are gay or lesbian and do not share the legal right to marry.

Fear of Marriage

Fear of marriage is a powerful deterrent. Some singles who are afraid of marriage were brought up in unhappy homes in which their parents fought all the time. Others have been disappointed in love and are afraid to try again. Some have been married before and failed; they prefer not to remarry. Lutwak (1985) studied fear of intimacy among col-

lege women and found that, for some, emotional involvement was simply too risky. These women were so terrified of possible dependency that they could not conceive of healthy mutuality and interdependence. They were fearful of possible pain, vulnerability, and—most important—the possible loss of self. Many had a profound sense of insecurity about the consequences of caring. Many thought that marriage was a deception, a farce, and a trap.

Lack of Opportunity

At the other extreme are people who would prefer to marry but have never had the chance. In particular, some women are caught in the "marriage squeeze"; that is, they have difficulty finding eligible male partners. Until 1940, the male population in the United States exceeded the female population. Since then, adult women have outnumbered men; this is especially true for African Americans, as discussed in Chapter 3. The older the age group, the greater the discrepancy in numbers. Both the numbers of eligible men and their employment and education affect women's opportunity to select a mate (South and Lloyd, 1992).

A growing number of adults are delaying marriage or choosing to stay single throughout their lives.

Circumstances

For many people, remaining unmarried permanently is not necessarily a matter of deliberate choice, but rather a result of circumstances such as family situations, geography, social isolation, or financial condition. Consider this case:

> Mary lived with her widowed father, who was very possessive and protective of her. He made her feel she had an obligation to take care of him. Her father was also very critical of every young man she dated or brought home. According to her father, no one was ever good enough for her. She had several chances to marry but was always dissuaded by her father. She vowed that she would marry after her father died, but the years slipped by. Her father lived until his mid-eighties. By this time, Mary was in her sixties and had remained single. (Author's counseling notes)

ADVANTAGES AND DISADVANTAGES OF BEING SINGLE

People find both advantages and disadvantages in being single. Some single people find advantages to include the following:

- **Greater opportunities for self-development and personal growth and fulfillment.** If singles want to take a course, go on to graduate school, or travel, they are freer to do so than are married people, who must consider their spouse's school and career plans and interests.

- **Opportunities to meet different people and to develop and enjoy different friendships.** Singles are free to pursue friendships with either men or women, according to their own preferences.

- **Economic independence and self-sufficiency.** As one single person said, "I don't have to depend on a spouse for money. I earn it myself and I can spend it as I want."

- **More varied sexual experiences.** Singles are free to seek experiences with more than one partner.

- **Freedom to control their own lives.** Singles are free to do what they want without having to consider a spouse's desires; they enjoy more psychological and social autonomy.

- **More opportunities for career change, development, and expansion.** Singles are not locked into family responsibilities and so can be more mobile and flexible in the climb up the career ladder.

Not all of these advantages apply to all singles. For example, not all singles have opportunities to meet different people, nor are all economically well off, nor are all free of family responsibilities. Nevertheless, most singles would list at least some of these items as advantages for them.

Those who are not in favor of remaining single describe a number of disadvantages, some of which include:

- **Loneliness and lack of companionship.** This is a pressing problem for some singles (Ponzetti, 1990).

- **Economic hardship.** This is especially true for single women. Single women earn less than single or married men and, because they do not have access to a spouse's income, have a lower standard of living than do married women. Also, top positions are more often given to married men than to single men or to women.

- **Feeling out of place in some social gatherings.** This may result because many people's social lives tend to be organized around married couples.

- **Sexual frustration.**

- **A lack of children or a family in which to bring up children.**

One study investigated the perceptions of being single among heterosexual single women ages 30–65. Some of these women had never been married; others were divorced. The most salient theme that emerged from the analysis is that single women have unresolved or unrecognized ambivalence about being single. This overarching theme was supported by three self-assertions: (1) Single women are aware of both the advantages and the disadvantages of being single; (2) single women are ambivalent about their single status; (3) although content with being single, many women simultaneously experience feelings of loss and grief (Lewis and Moon, 1997).

About half of the women interviewed said they wished to be married, and half said they did not. Some of the women blamed themselves for being single. These explanations fell primarily into four categories: (1) physical (overweight), (2) personality (shyness, independence or dependence, lack of social skills, lack of competency), (3) psychological (selfishness, low self-esteem, demanding nature, vulnerability, experience of sexual abuse as a child, codependency), and (4) cognitive (too much or too little intelligence, learning disability). An overwhelming majority of the women (including those who blamed themselves for being single) wrote comments that laid blame on men. Some women complained that the men they were meeting were not able to deal with their intelligence, confidence, assertiveness, and accomplishments. One woman remarked, "It scares them. Guys don't want women who are smarter than they unless they are looking for a mother." Another woman said, "I'm intelli-

gent, have a responsible job and money. This makes me inappropriate for ninety-five percent of the men I meet."

The advantages of being single related to having increased freedom: freedom from having to take care of a man; freedom to do what they want, when they want, how they want; and freedom from having to answer to others in terms of time, decisions, and behaviors. The most frequently cited drawbacks to not being married were the absence of being special to a man, the lack of touch, the absence of children, the lack of ready companionship and someone with whom to share interests, and sadness about growing old alone.

Some of the women identified their primary loss in being single as not having children. Others felt that they had lost a lot by investing so much time and energy in previous years on relationships with men. Another major loss was not having assurances about the future. At no point did any of the women know for certain whether marriage would occur in the future. As long as there was hope for marriage, the pain of ambiguity was present. As one woman said, "It'd be easier if I just knew for sure, then I could adjust fine." Another woman said, "If I knew for sure I would never meet a man, I could get on with my life" (Lewis and Moon, 1997).

THE HEALTH AND WELL-BEING OF SINGLES

For years, researchers have been investigating the effects of marriage and singlehood on people's health and sense of well-being (Mastekaasa, 1992). In general, the studies seemed to indicate that married people are healthier and happier than single people, so marriage may have a beneficial effect on well-being (Lee, Seccombe, and Shehan, 1991). However, researchers are now concluding that marriage alone doesn't make the difference; rather, marriage is one of a number of variables that contribute to the quality of life.

In general, single people are less healthy than married people and have higher mortality rates (Trovato and Lauris, 1989). It may be, however, that singles simply *appear* to be less healthy because they go to their physicians more often than do married people; when singles live with other adults, their

Are married people happier and healthier than single people? Recent research says not necessarily; marital status is just one of many variables affecting a person's well-being.

visits to physicians decrease, and they seem to be as healthy as married people (Anson, 1989). Another possible explanation for the better health and greater happiness of married people is that unhealthy and unhappy people are less likely to get married in the first place. In other words, those who have superior health and psychological well-being also have the highest probability of marrying. Or the stress of divorce, separation, or the death of a spouse may take a toll on one's health. In addition, single people who were once married may be older on average than people who are married.

One study analyzed the impact of marriage on mental health. After taking into account premarital levels of mental health, the researchers found that young adults who get married and stay married report better mental health than do those who remain single (Horwitz, White, and Howell-White, 1996).

To determine the relationship between marital status and reported happiness, Glenn and Weaver (1988) evaluated survey data between 1972 and 1988. Consistently, a greater percentage of married men and women reported being very happy than did single men and women (never-married, sepa-

rated, divorced, and widowed). However, the percentage of married people reporting that they were very happy declined between 1972 and 1988, whereas the percentage of single people reporting that they were very happy increased over this period. These results suggest that we may need to reassess the assumption that married people are happier than single people.

Many variables in addition to marital status determine life satisfaction and physical and mental well-being. Employment and socioeconomic status are especially important factors. It has been found that for women a good job and a high family income are positively correlated with good physical and psychological health (Ross, Mirowsky, and Goldstein, 1990). A study of the effects of women's marital status and employment showed that women who are married and have children and a high-prestige job have the highest level of well-being. But it was a high-prestige job rather than a spouse that was the best predictor of well-being. Being single in and of itself was not associated with diminished well-being, but being single and having a low-level job was.

For many people, happiness is the fundamental goal of life. According to Csikszentmihalyi (1999), most people believe that material comforts should be grasped whenever they can be and that these will improve the quality of life. For example, when university students were asked what would improve the quality of their lives, by far the most common answer was "more money" (Cambell, 1981). Yet, even though we are living in a time of unprecedented economic prosperity in the United States, people do not report being any happier than in previous years. Although the adjusted value of after-tax personal income in the United States more than doubled between 1960 and 1990, the percentage of people who described themselves as "very happy" did not change (Myers, 1993). Some research suggests that the wealthiest people in the United States are barely happier than people with average incomes (Diener, Horwitz, and Emmons, 1985). Furthermore, in a recent study of the psychological well-being of American adolescents, Csikszentmihalyi and Schneider (2000) found that wealthy children reported being less happy than children of lower socioeconomic status.

Why might this be the case? Csikszentmihalyi (1999) suggested three reasons material rewards do not necessarily ensure happiness. First, people's expectations are continually increasing. Studies on happiness confirm that goals keep getting pushed upward as soon as a lower level is reached. Thus, people are never satisfied for long with their achievements. Second, people are constantly comparing what they have to what wealthier people around them have. Those with decent incomes can feel poor relative to those who have more, and this can lead to unhappiness. Third, despite an almost universal obsession with wealth, nobody has ever claimed that material rewards alone are sufficient to make us happy. Ironically, if people devote most of their time to making money, they often neglect other aspects of their lives that might ultimately be more important for happiness, such as family life and friends. Eventually, they might even develop a dependence on material rewards and lose the ability to derive happiness from other sources (Benedikt, 1999).

According to Csikszentmihalyi (1999), an alternative to the materialist approach to happiness is a psychological approach in which happiness is a mental state that a person can control. Although it is also possible to use drugs or alcohol to induce artificial well-being, a crucial ingredient to happiness is the knowledge that one is responsible for achieving it. By this definition, chemicals cannot produce real happiness. Csikszentmihalyi suggested that the key to achieving happiness is finding meaning in everyday experiences, and one does not need material wealth to accomplish this. In fact, studies have shown that in comparison to less wealthy adolescents, affluent teenagers have more difficulty finding meaning in activities and tend to be more bored and less involved, enthusiastic, and excited. When the meaning derived from activities comes from active physical, mental, or emotional involvement, one's chances for a happy life improve.

Barrett (1999) investigated social support and life satisfaction among the never-married by analyzing data collected from interviews with 3,178 respondents, age 30 and older. There were 266 never-married, 1,765 married, and 1,147 previously married respondents. She found that, compared with other marital groups, the never-married tended to be younger, better educated, and non-White. Females reported more hassles associated with never being married than did males, and non-Whites reported fewer hassles than did Whites. Women made up smaller proportions of the never-married and currently married than did the previously married. On average, the never-married had incomes between those of the married and the previously married, and they rated their health higher than did the previously married. The never-married reported less informal interaction, more hassles in arranging to go out with friends, and less likelihood of having a confidant than did members of the other groups. They had overall life satisfaction higher than that of the previously married but lower than that of the married. Among respondents ages 30–45, the never-married had more frequent interaction with friends, relatives, and neighbors than did members of the other groups. In those two groups, the pattern of informal interaction reversed, with the married and previously married reporting more interaction. Results indicated that the frequency of interaction increased with age among the ever-married but decreased among the never-married. In addition, results showed that never being married or being previously married was negatively related to life satisfaction. Higher life satisfaction was associated with being older, female, White, married, and healthy.

Many single young adults would prefer to be independent but instead choose to live at home with their parents for financial reasons.

Other research indicates that married women rate their health higher than do divorced, separated, widowed, or never-married women. The better economic circumstances of married women compared to the other groups may be the reason. Clearly, married women have access to higher incomes than do most single women, and higher income is associated with better health. The married woman receives the material benefits that a higher family income provides, as well as a sense of security that her well-being is not entirely dependent on her own earnings (Hahn, 1993).

LIVING ARRANGEMENTS

Most singles meet some of their needs for companionship and economic well-being by sharing a residence with friends or family. Singles who are still in school are most likely to live with their parents or with classmates; singles in their late twenties and early thirties are most likely to live with a roommate or by themselves; and older singles are most likely to live alone or with relatives.

Single elderly people often face worse housing problems than do other singles or elderly people in families. Single elderly people are likely to live in rental housing, where they face the risk of social isolation, and a disproportionate number are

Table 4.2   Percentage of Young Adults Living with Their Parents, by Age, 1998

	18–24 Years of Age	25–34 Years of Age
Total	53	11.5
Men	59	14.5
Women	48	8.5

Note: From Statistical Abstract of the United States, 1999 (p. 57) by U.S. Bureau of the Census, 1999, Washington, DC: U.S. Government Printing Office.

poor. In addition to having low fixed incomes, they are likely to lack any asset "cushion" in the form of home equity, and they may have little or no spousal help available if they become impaired. Under these circumstances, subsidized housing is an important source of affordable housing and companionship for poor, single elderly people (Crystal and Beck, 1992).

Shared Living Spaces

Although large numbers of singles live in singles' complexes or apartment buildings, more live with the general population. The majority occupy individual apartments, usually with roommates. The usual pattern is to share an apartment and living expenses with one or more people who provide emotional support and companionship.

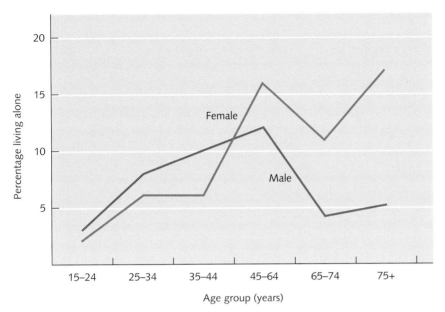

Figure 4.4   Percentage of Persons Living Alone, by Age and Sex, 1998 (*Note:* Data from *Statistical Abstract of the United States, 1999* [p. 69] by U.S. Bureau of the Census, 1999, Washington, DC: U.S. Government Printing Office.)

Living with Parents

The percentage of young adults (ages 18–29) who lived with parents reached a high in 1940, near the end of the Depression. The percentage bottomed out in 1960, near the end of the baby boom, and has risen modestly since then. In 1998, 53% of 18- to 24-year-olds were living with their parents (U.S. Bureau of the Census, 1999a). The increase has occurred because of marriage postponement and high rates of college enrollment, unemployment, divorce and separation, and birth to unmarried mothers. Most adults who live with their parents have a plan for achieving independence, such as saving enough money or getting more education. But while they are living at home, their parents still spend a lot of money on their food, clothes, cars, insurance, and other goods and services (Crispell, 1996). Table 4.2 shows the percentage of young adult men and women of different ages living at home with parents. Note that greater percentages of men than women of all ages live at home with their parents. Women who are married, separated, or divorced and have one or more children are more likely to live at home with their parents or relatives than are women who do not have any children.

Living Alone

Figure 4.4 shows the percentage of the population, by age and sex, living alone in 1998 (U.S. Bureau of the Census, 1999a). This figure includes divorced, separated, and widowed people, as well as the never-married. As illustrated, greater percentages of males than females in the 15–44 age group live alone. With each succeeding age group (45–64, 65–74, and 75 and older), the percentage of females living alone increases rapidly. This is due to the greater numbers of older females in the population. Of all elderly people over 65 years of age, 32% live alone (males, 17%; females, 42%). Health status is the most important factor in determining how long they continue to live alone. When a move is necessary, many elderly people go to live with their children. Declining health increases the likelihood of institutionalization (Spitze, Logan, and Robinson, 1992).

LONELINESS AND FRIENDSHIPS

The greatest need of single people is interpersonal relationships: networks of friendships that provide emotional fulfillment, companionship, and intimacy.

Rob is a 23-year-old who has been living at home since his graduation from college more than 2 years ago. When his mother asked him, "Why don't you move out with your friends?" Rob had a ready answer: "They all live at home, too." Rob and most of his buddies are launching their adult lives back at home where they grew up as children. Across the country, this new breed hangs around refrigerators full of leftovers. Altogether, 59% of men 18–24 years of age and 14.5% of men 25–34 years of age are living at home with their parents (see Table 4.2).

Why are so many young men flying back to the nest? There are a number of reasons. One is that they are delaying getting married; with the median age at marriage 26.7 years, they find it convenient to go back home after graduation until they decide to get married. Living at home is relatively stress-free. Parents often do the laundry, cook the meals, clean the house, and do it all at a very low cost.

Most young men living at home are not unemployed; rather, they want to save money for personal expenses. Rob says, "I could make it on my own, but if I paid hundreds of dollars a month for rent and bills, I would have to cut back considerably on my social life." Many parents welcome their sons back home. They can help out with the small chores, as well as keep them company. Also, many of these parents are divorced and are alone except for their children.

Most young men sadly admit that they sacrifice a considerable degree of independence to live at home. They do not have as much privacy, nor do they feel free to bring their girlfriends back home in many cases.

What about daughters? Fewer daughters return to the nest than do sons, for a number of reasons. Daughters may feel more of a need to prove their ability to live on their own. And daughters are likely to be subject to more parental control than are sons. When daughters are frequently lectured about their personal lives, they are likely to prefer to live on their own. Furthermore, many single daughters are divorced with children. While many grandparents take care of grandchildren, living together 24 hours a day can put a strain on the whole family. In addition, whereas a few parents of live-at-home sons may not object to intimate visits from girlfriends, parents are almost never as liberal with their daughters and their boyfriends (Duff, 1994).

Single people value freedom and varied activities, but they also place a high value on enduring, close friendships.

The Importance of Companionship

When Cargan and Melko (1982) asked both marrieds and singles to describe the greatest advantage of being married, most replied in terms of shared feelings: "companionship and someone to share decisions with," "companionship," "love and companionship," "the opportunity to converse with someone every day," "being able to share your life with someone you love," "togetherness is very important to me," "love is caring and having children and sharing things, and doing things together." A physician (now married) commented:

> Med school for me was the loneliest period of my life. I lived alone, studied alone, and was alone most of the time. I didn't really have any friends or anyone with whom to socialize. I think I married Chris soon after I met her because I was so terribly lonely. At last, I had someone to talk to and do things with. (Author's counseling notes)

One woman remarked, "I'm not lonely every day, only when I have something to share, or want to do something with someone. The rest of the time I'm perfectly content."

Males Versus Females

Loneliness is a problem for a significant minority of never-marrieds. Some evidence suggests that among single young adults male-male friendships are less intimate and spontaneous than are female-female friendships. Single males are more isolated and have fewer intimate relationships than do single females. Although men may belong to more voluntary associations than women do, they spend less time in group activities, and their participation is less stable. Yet both males and females need close, caring friendships that promote a sense of mutuality and provide a major source of social support.

Loneliness Versus Aloneness

However, there is a difference between being alone and being lonely. Loneliness is partly a psychological state; it is independent of the presence of companions (Meer, 1985b). Thus, many never-marrieds do not perceive themselves as especially lonely. Two-thirds of them live at home or with roommates of either the same or the opposite sex (Cargan and Melko, 1982), and most spend considerable time with friends. Conversely, married people who are estranged from their mates may be quite lonely even though they don't live alone.

In addition, being lonely is not the same as doing things alone (which most people enjoy occasionally). Rather, loneliness means having no one to turn to, to call, or to touch when the need is there. We are lonely when we feel there is nobody on whom we can rely, especially when under stress or threatened.

SEXUAL BEHAVIOR

If we are to believe the media, all healthy young Americans are having a great deal of sex; if they are not, they are encouraged to do so as quickly as possible. The truth is far more complex. Americans, we find, are not having much sex at all—at least not much compared to what we are told is a normal and optimal amount. According to the National Health and Social Life Survey (NHSLS), as of 1994, 94–98% of men and women have had sexual intercourse by the time they reach age 25 (Michael, Gagnon, Laumann, and Kolata, 1994). But when we inquire about the frequency of sex in the past 12 months, we get a completely different picture. According to the NHSLS, 23% of noncohabiting men and 32% of noncohabiting women have not had sex in the past 12 months. An additional 25% of men and 23% of women had sex only a few times during the past year. These figures certainly do not present a picture of frequent and promiscuous sex (Michael et al., 1994).

In light of the increase in HIV/AIDS and other sexually transmitted diseases, we are interested not only in the percentages of people having sexual intercourse but also in the number of sex partners they have had. According to the NHSLS, in 1994, 25% of never-married, noncohabiting men and women had no sex partners during the past 12 months, 38% had only one partner, and 28% had two to four. Only a small percentage of the population (9%) had as many as five sex partners during the past year; most of this group were young men

Loneliness is a common problem among single adults. The advantage of the increased freedom of being single is often outweighed by the lack of ready companionship. What are some other advantages and disadvantages of being single?

who had never been married and were not living with anyone. These findings give no support to media images of a promiscuous society. Rather, they suggest that most people do in fact form partnerships and ultimately get married.

These findings, along with those from other studies, indicate, however, that a small percentage of young adults are still engaging in high-risk sexual behavior and thus risking contracting HIV/AIDS. A survey of 671 predominantly young, Black women living in 10 low-income housing developments in five cities revealed that 17% of the women had sex with multiple partners and that 22% had an exclusive partner. That exclusive partner, however, had other sexual partners in the past year or had a history of intravenous drug use. Of those women who had multiple partners, 26% were treated for a sexually transmitted disease. Condom use at previous intercourse and communication about condom use were less frequent

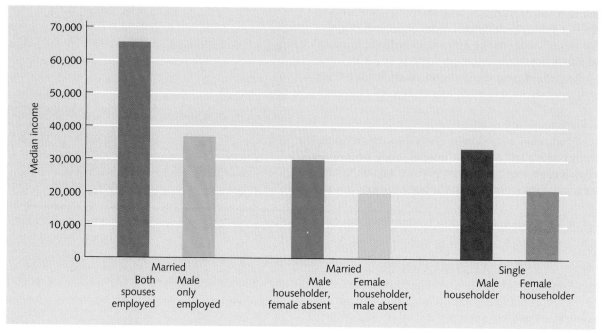

Figure 4.5   Median Income, by Household Type and Marital Status, 1998
(*Note:* Adapted from *Statistical Abstract of the United States, 1999,* by U.S. Bureau of the Census, 1999, Washington, DC: U.S. Government Printing Office.)

among women with an exclusive, risky partner than among those with multiple partners. The more partners there are and the less frequently condoms are used, the riskier sexual behavior becomes (Wagstaff et al., 1995).

A 1991 study of a random sample of heterosexual undergraduates at a midwestern university yielded some disturbing figures, particularly in light of HIV/AIDS. During the 4 years since they first had vaginal intercourse, males reported an average of 8.5 vaginal-sex partners, and females reported an average of 6.1 partners. In addition, 17% of the sexually experienced males and 18% of the sexually experienced females had engaged in heterosexual anal intercourse. Researchers concluded that a substantial number of college students had engaged in sexual behavior that placed them at risk for sexually transmitted diseases, including HIV/AIDS (Reinisch, Hill, Sanders, and Ziemba-Davis, 1995).

Data on substance use and sexual activity from a nationally representative probability-based sample of young adults ages 18–30 in 1990 indicated that those who had used marijuana in the past year and those who had consumed five or more

drinks at a sitting were more likely than others to have had more than one sexual partner. Heavy drinkers were also less likely to use condoms, thus placing themselves at further risk (Graves and Leigh, 1995).

EMPLOYMENT AND INCOME

One stereotype holds that never-marrieds are richer than marrieds: They have no spouses or children to support, they do not require expensive homes, and they can live more cheaply than marrieds. In fact, marrieds are better off financially than never-marrieds. In 1998, the median income of married householders with both spouses employed was $60,669; for married male householders with only the man employed, it was $36,027; and for single male householders it was $32,960. The median income for married female householders with the male absent was $19,872; for single female householders, it was $21,023. Figure 4.5 shows the comparison (U.S. Bureau of the Census, 1999a). According to these figures, greater percentages of married householders are in high-income brackets than are never-married householders.

There are a number of reasons for these differences. Slightly more than half of all married women are employed outside the home, contributing substantially to the total household income. The combined income of two wage earners is likely to be greater than the income of one wage earner.

One reason is a practical one. Married people, especially those with families, have to earn more money because their needs are greater, and they are more motivated to earn higher incomes. Despite many exceptions, this principle generally holds. Many married people are forced to work more than one job to provide sufficient incomes for their family.

In addition, the income discrepancies reflect deep-seated prejudices against women. Overall, the average woman with education and experience comparable to that of a man is paid only about 73% as much for the same work (U.S. Bureau of the Census, 1999a).

SINGLE MOTHERS

Births to unmarried women are no longer unusual. The birthrate among unmarried women rose almost 60% in the 1990s, with about one-third of unmarried women ages 15–44 becoming mothers (U.S. Bureau of the Census, 1999a). Over half have never married. While teenage birthrates have declined 18% since 1991, the overall number of births to unmarried women has risen 3%, to almost 1.3 million, the highest number ever recorded. Most of the increase is linked to the rise in the number of unmarried women of childbearing age (Ventura, Martin, Curtin, Mathews, and Park, 2000). Single White women in this age range have the most rapidly increasing birthrate. The birthrate doubled among never-married college-educated women and almost tripled among never-married women who work in a professional or managerial capacity.

Why do single women become mothers? Aside from the obvious, one answer is that the appeal of marriage may be diminishing for women. The rates of marriage for both men and women have declined. Women's increased options outside of marriage, including the ability to support themselves, are having a large effect on marriage patterns. The most significant of the options available to women

is labor force participation. In ever increasing proportions since the end of World War II, women have entered and remained in the labor force. Today, a greater percentage of women are able to support themselves and do not need a man's income in order to afford children. However, the most common reason for becoming a single mother is the basic desire to be a mother, regardless of economic resources. In the words of a single mother, "[I had a child] for the same reason I think any woman wants a child. I couldn't imagine not having a child. It's a greater passion than anything else" (Siegel, 1995, p. 202). Although they wanted a child, many single mothers were concerned about how their marital status would affect their ability to manage as a mother and how it would affect their child. One mother remarked, "I sorta felt bad but I thought there are so many kids today who grow up without a father. It wouldn't be like it was unique but I was concerned about a male role model and I still am" (Siegel, 1995, p. 202).

Stated very simply, some single women became mothers because they wanted to when it was time to do it. Some single mothers who are satisfied with their marital status tend either to put a low priority on marriage or to feel certain that marriage is not for them. A woman who became a mother by adoption, about 5 years after her divorce, reflected, "It [marriage] is not something that I care whether it happens or not. I think it is wonderful, being in love and finding someone to live with. But I'm not seeking it out. If it happens, it happens" (Siegel, 1995, p. 203). Family sociologists have observed a 30-year trend in American society toward an increasing separation of marriage and childbearing. Older, single women who choose to become mothers are contributing to this trend.

Single mothers who do not marry often express a concern that they will not do well in marriage, either because they are not sure how to make marriage work or because they are not interested in doing what they think is necessary for marriage to work. One woman remarked, "I never wanted to be married. In actuality, I always thought I would be, but I have not wanted to be in the real way and am probably not well suited to it" (Siegel, 1995 p. 204). Some women who bore children have a fear of marriage because they reject their own parents' marriage. Their parents were miserable in

*Many older singles value their inde-
pendence, rarely feel isolated, and are
generally happy with their lives.*

marriage, and these women do not want to repeat the pattern in their own lives (Siegel, 1995).

The research on single versus married people needs to address the all-important factor of the effect of being single or married and having children. Single mothers and married mothers experience parenthood differently. Long-term single parenting, usually performed by employed women, is a chronic stressor. Compared with their married counterparts, most single mothers have little relief from the responsibilities and burdens of parenting. Marriage typically provides social integration, social support, and emotional support; spouses have someone to talk to, someone to listen, someone who cares about them as individuals and who cares about their problems. Research has shown that emotional support reduces depression, anxiety, and other psychological problems. Married mothers also receive instrumental support from their spouses. If they have competing or conflicting demands, they can often rely on their spouses to help out. In contrast, single mothers are often on their own.

Parent-child relationships are also central to mothers' self-esteem and overall well-being. Their children's well-being is one of the strongest and most consistent predictors of their own well-being. Difficulties in relationships with children adversely affect mothers' well-being. For divorced mothers, an important source of distress and de-

pression is the coparenting relationship with their children's nonresidential father (Demo and Acock, 1996).

THE NEVER-MARRIED ADULT

One difference between older adults who have never married and younger ones is that many younger singles consider their status temporary, whereas older singles are often well adjusted to their situation. Older singles usually have an active social life and do a variety of things with a few close friends (Keith and Nauta, 1988), and their patterns of social support differ from those found in married groups. For example, the never-married interact more frequently with friends and less often with relatives than do married people (Stull and Scarisbrick-Hauser, 1989). Substitution theory posits that the never-married use more remote family members or nonfamily individuals for support compared with the married or the previously married (Shanas, 1979). The nonkin relationships that form the social networks of never-marrieds are sometimes referred to as "constructed" ties (Rubinstein, Alexander, Goodman, and Luborsky, 1991). While these relationships resemble friendships, they involve role sets that are similar to those found in families. In support of substitution theory, research has shown that, compared with the other groups, never-marrieds see their relatives less frequently and interact more often with friends and neighbors (Stull and Scarisbrick-Hauser, 1989). However, despite higher levels of interaction with friends, the never-married report less satisfaction from friendships than do the married.

Barrett (1999) suggested that differences in dimensions of social support between the never-married and other marital groups may be greatest in later life. Compared with marrieds, older never-marrieds are at a disadvantage, in part due to their lower probability of having confidants and their lower levels of interaction and perceived support. Analyses of informal interactions indicate that younger never-marrieds (ages 30–45) have more frequent interaction with friends and relatives than do their currently or previously married peers. However, this pattern reverses in two older groups (45–60, 60 and older). It is possible that during middle and later adulthood never-marrieds, in anticipation of health declines in old age, learn to be more self-reliant and independent than do marrieds (Barrett, 1999). A possible explanation for the difference between marrieds and never-marrieds in terms of having confidants in later life could involve the potential differences in the identities of confidants among the groups. For example, never-marrieds are likely to have primary confidants who are significantly older than themselves (such as parents or older siblings), while marrieds tend to have similar-age confidants (such as spouses). A factor in the higher proportion of never-marrieds reporting having no confidants in later life may be the loss of close social ties due to death, a phenomenon that occurs somewhat later among married individuals (Barrett, 1999).

Overall, however, the happiness of single older adults is very dependent on satisfaction with their standard of living and with their level of activity, rather than merely the extent of their social contacts. Adequate financial resources permit mobility and reciprocation in developing and maintaining friendships. Also, people who are satisfied with their level of activity even though they are isolated from family or friends tend to express greater happiness.

SUMMARY

1. Overall, the great majority of people in the United States marry.

2. Adult singles may be divided into four groups: voluntary temporary singles, voluntary stable (permanent) singles, involuntary temporary singles, and involuntary stable (permanent) singles.

3. Most adults who are single delay marriage rather than remain permanently single. By ages 45–54, only 8.9% of men and 7.2% of women have never married.

4. The reasons for marital delay are social, economic, and personal.

5. Reasons people remain single include deliberate choice, fear of marriage, lack of opportunity, circumstances, and lack of a good relationship with their parents.

6. There are both advantages and disadvantages to being single. Advantages include greater opportunities for self-development, personal growth, and fulfillment; opportunities to meet different people and enjoy different friendships; economic independence and self-sufficiency; more varied sexual experiences; freedom to control one's own life; and more opportunities for career change, development, and expansion.

7. Disadvantages include loneliness and lack of companionship, economic hardship, feeling out of place in social gatherings organized for couples, sexual frustration, and the absence of children.

8. Overall, single people are less healthy physically and mentally than married people and have a shorter life expectancy. The divorced, separated, and widowed have the poorest health. There are, however, gender differences. Never-married men have poorer physical and mental health than do married men. Never-married women may fare as well as or better than married women on a number of mental health, physical health, and life satisfaction indexes. However, married women who have children and satisfying high-prestige jobs usually rate very high on measures of happiness and well-being. Many variables in addition to marital status determine life satisfaction.

9. There are wide variations in the life-styles of singles. Singles may share living spaces with friends, live with parents, or live alone.

10. Increasing numbers of singles are returning home to live with parents.

11. One of the greatest needs of single people is to develop fulfilling friendships. Loneliness is often a problem, although it is not necessarily synonymous with being alone. Single men join organizations more often than do single women, but they have more difficulty than women in establishing intimate relationships.

12. Most single adults have had sexual intercourse but confine their sexual experiences to only a few partners during their lifetime. A minority of young adults engage in high-risk sexual behavior.

13. Married people are usually better off financially than are single people.

14. Births to unmarried women have become more common, but births to teenagers have decreased.

15. Many older singles are well adjusted to their situation and interact more frequently with friends and less often with relatives than do married people.

KEY TERMS

voluntary temporary singles

voluntary stable (permanent) singles

involuntary temporary singles

involuntary stable (permanent) singles

QUESTIONS FOR THOUGHT

1. Think of a single person and a married person whom you know. Describe each individual's personality, work life, social life, life goals and values, general outlook, and problems. Then contrast the two as to how they are similar to and how they are different from each other, and how their being single or being married influences each.

2. Describe the advantages and disadvantages of being single, and tell why you prefer being single or being married.

3. What is the ideal age at which to get married for men and for women? Why do you consider this (these) age(s) ideal?

4. What factors ought people to consider in deciding whether to remain single or to get married?

5. Compare singles with marrieds with respect to each of the following:

   a. Loneliness and friendships

   b. Sexual behavior

   c. Employment and income

SUGGESTED READINGS

Allen, K. R. (1989). *Single Women/Family Ties: Life Histories of Older Women.* Newbury Park, CA: Sage. Gives interviews with 30 women (15 never-marrieds and 15 widows).

Clements, M. (1999). *The Improvised Woman: Single Women Reinventing Single Life.* New York: Norton. Represents a compilation of interviews with over 100 single women and essays by the author confronting society's view of single women today.

Michael, R. T., Gagnon, J. H., Laumann, E. O., and Kolata, G. (1994). *Sex in America.* Boston: Little, Brown. Provides a broad overview.

Peiffer, V. (1999). *Positively Single: The Art of Being Single and Happy.* Shaftesbury, UK: Element. Discusses the advantages to being single and presents singlehood from a positive perspective.

Wieland-Burston, J. (1996). *Contemporary Solitude: The Joy and Pain of Being Alone.* York Beach, ME: Nicolas-Hays. Describes how solitude is an important aspect of one's life and how it can also cause a person to stagnate.

CHAPTER 5

LEARNING OBJECTIVES

After reading the chapter, you should be able to:

Trace the history of courtship from colonial America to the present day.

Summarize the reasons for dating.

Explain how dating can be functional or dysfunctional as a means of mate selection, depending on the qualities looked for in a date.

Discuss the problem of finding and meeting dates.

Describe the changes in gender roles in dating.

Understand some of the major problems in dating, such as achieving honesty and openness, maintaining extradyadic relationships, and getting too serious.

Discuss the problem of sexual aggression in dating.

Discuss the problem of violence in dating.

Describe ways to minimize the pain of breaking up a relationship.

Dating, Going Together, and Courtship

Learning Objectives

The Dating System

Courtship in Early America

The Emergence of Dating

The Rating and Dating Complex of the 1930s

Perspective: Bundling

Dating and Courtship from the 1940s to the 1960s

Dating and "Getting Together" Today

Reasons for Dating

Dating Partners Versus Long-Term Partners

Finding and Meeting Dates

Singles Bars

Personal Ads

Perspective: Love Matches Versus Arranged
Marriages in China

Dating Services and Computer Networks

Perspective: Dating Preferences of University
Women: The "Nice Guy" Stereotype

Changing Gender Roles in Dating

Problems in Dating

Honesty and Openness

Family Issues: Who Controls Dating?

Extradyadic Relationships

Getting Too Serious

Closeness and Distance in Relationships

Sexual Aggression and Dating Violence

Unwanted Sexual Pressure

Verbal Sexual Coercion

Date Rape

Perspective: "Date Rape Drugs"

Physical Violence

Correlations with Violence

The Progression of Violence

Breaking Up a Relationship

Summary

Key Terms

Questions for Thought

Suggested Readings

ating is rare in most of the world. It is uncommon in China and India, which together account for over half the world's population, as well as in most areas of Africa and South America and in some Mediterranean countries, such as Greece, Spain, Sicily, and Portugal. It is forbidden by many families in Egypt, Saudi Arabia, Iran, Libya, and other Muslim countries.

Dating is widely practiced in most of western Europe and is most common in the United States, Great Britain, Canada, Australia, and New Zealand. In these countries, it is now recognized as *the* method by which young men and women get to know one another, learn to get along socially, and select mates by mutual choice. In this chapter, we will examine the many issues associated with dating—from systems of and reasons for dating, to the process of obtaining dating partners, to problems with and violence in dating.

THE DATING SYSTEM

Dating is a relatively recent phenomenon in the United States; it did not become firmly established until the years after World War I. Before that time, courtship consisted mainly of the young man paying formal visits to the young woman and her family. Dating evolved when marriage started to become an individual rather than a family decision and when love and mutual attraction started to become the basis for marriage.

Courtship in Early America

In the 1700s and 1800s, casual meetings at unsupervised social affairs were condemned. Parents carefully supervised the activities of their children, especially their daughters. Young women were not left alone to meet young men casually and indiscriminately. If a man desired the company of a woman, he had to meet her family, be formally introduced, and obtain permission to court her, as well as gain her permission to be courted, before they could "step out." Even after a couple had been formally introduced, they often were chaperoned (especially upper-class women) or attended social functions only in the company of friends or relatives. Parents exerted considerable influence, and even veto power, over whom a son or daughter

might see or consider for marriage. Parents were concerned about the social standing and prestige, economic status, education, and family background of potential suitors. And if a young man wanted to marry a woman, he had to ask her father's permission for her hand.

At this time, marriage in Europe was arranged by parents, with little emphasis on romantic attraction. With some arranged marriages, parents sought to merge the property and good name of the families to ensure economic well-being and the perpetuation of family status and prestige. Only a few American marriages were parentally arranged. These were limited to the most aristocratic families, which sought to expand their financial empires through marriage. American courtship was controlled more by the participants, who exercised autonomy and freedom.

The Emergence of Dating

By the late nineteenth and early twentieth centuries, chaperonage and close supervision of courtship had declined. A new pattern of dating emerged whereby young people themselves arranged a time and place to meet so that they could get to know each other better and participate in activities together. The primary purpose was to have fun and enjoy each other's company. Parents might have sought to maintain some control of dating partners, but the system usually allowed a high level of freedom from parental supervision.

In the years following World War I, the dating system was still comparatively stylized and formal. The man was expected to take the initiative in asking the woman for a date. Generally, he was expected to plan the activities, pay all the expenses, and exercise his masculine prerogatives as the leader. Over the years, however, the pattern became less structured and more informal, with greater equality between the sexes in initiating and planning dates. Today, couples frequently simply "get together" to do things or to "go out," without going through a specific ritual. "Going together" has replaced the formal patterns of courtship of previous generations.

The emergence of dating was due to numerous factors. The most important was the industrial revolution. Thousands of families moved from farms to crowded cities, where young people had

In eighteenth-century America, if a man desired the company of a woman, he had to meet her family, be formally introduced, and obtain permission to court her.

increased opportunities for social contact. Lower-class women were employed in the mills and factories, where they met male workers. Some girls from farm families took up residence in boardinghouses away from home and so were separated from parental supervision. The invention of the telephone made regular contact much easier.

At the same time, the late 1800s saw the rise of free public high schools, where large numbers of physically mature youths were brought together for coeducational schooling (private academies had segregated the sexes). These schools offered activities that brought youths together for recreation and companionship and that promoted dating.

Increased affluence and leisure time allowed people to devote more time to their own pursuits and social lives. Having a date became a pleasant way to spend an evening. During and after World War I, middle-class women began to work in offices and stores and attained greater economic and personal freedom. For the first time, they were allowed to wear less restrictive clothing and to engage in strenuous sports. (They participated in the Olympic Games for the first time in 1920.) This new freedom allowed them to engage in many of these activities with men.

The invention and use of the automobile increased mobility and provided transportation to roadhouses, nightclubs, parties, dances, theaters, and restaurants. Dating couples could go from place to place or simply park. The automobile became a bundling bed on wheels.

The 1920s also witnessed an early surge in the women's equality movement. The women's movement encouraged women's rights politically, socially, and sexually and made it possible for young women to participate on a more equal basis with young men in the total life of the community. Liberated women with their bobbed hair and flapper dresses were now free to take a ride in their boyfriend's jalopy and to engage in a little intimacy on the sly without being under the watchful eye of chaperones. As a result, dating emerged as an important part of the life of American youths, replacing the previous system of formalized courtship.

The Rating and Dating Complex of the 1930s

During the 1930s, Willard Waller (1937) observed dating behavior on the campus of Pennsylvania State University and published a paper titled "The Rating and Dating Complex." The report caused quite a stir because it described dating as a superficial, exploitative relationship rather than as a means of finding and selecting a future marriage partner. Men outnumbered women six to one on the campus, which resulted in much competition for dates. The fraternity system was flourishing. Men and women were rated according to their desirability as a date. Class A men belonged to one of the better fraternities, engaged in prestigious activities, had plenty of money and access to an automobile, were

Bundling was a fascinating courtship practice in colonial America that allowed couples to talk and visit while keeping warm on a cold night. If a young man wanted to court a woman, he might have to walk a long distance on a snowy winter evening to see her. The family usually prepared for bed shortly after supper, and if the young man were asked to leave, he had very little time to visit the woman whom he had walked miles to see. Since fuel and candles were scarce, it would be wasteful to burn them exclusively for the couple while they stayed up and visited. The couple was allowed to climb onto a bundling bed and get under the covers with only outer garments removed. There they would talk late into the night. Some beds had a "bundling board" that was placed between the two people. In other instances, the woman got into a sack that was sealed at the neck. Rigid sex codes forbade any sexual contact, so the custom didn't seem to encourage sexual experimentation. Doten (1938) quotes a poem that reflects the attitudes of country folk toward the practice.

Nature's request is, give me rest
Our bodies seek repose;
Night is the time, and 'tis no crime
To bundle in our clothes.

Since in a bed, a man and maid
May bundle and be chaste;
It doth no good to burn up wood
It is a needless waste.

Let coat and shift be turned adrift,
And breeches take their flight,
An honest man and virgin can
Lie quiet all the night. (p. 26)

The practice gradually diminished as transportation improved so that a young man could return home the same evening. As fuel became more plentiful, courting was moved from the bedroom to the parlor. With the advent of the automobile, it moved to the car.

Note: From *The Art of Bundling* by D. Doten, 1938, New York: Farrar.

---

good conversationalists and dancers, were well dressed, and so were considered highly desirable dates. Men who did not rate in Class A were placed in a lower class: B, C, or D. Women with high ratings wore good clothes, were good conversationalists, could dance well, and were considered popular. Coeds tried to give the impression of being sought after even if they did not belong to Class A. Young women often allowed themselves to be paged several times in the dorm when the telephone rang for them. They were never supposed to make themselves available for last-minute dates. They avoided being seen too often with the same young man so as not to discourage others, and they tried to have many partners at dances. Above all, Class A women dated only Class A men, and so forth. The system emphasized emotional excitement. Pretending to be in love was an important part of the game, as each person wanted to feel more involved than he or she was.

Other research has substantiated part of Waller's description of campus life of the 1920s and 1930s, especially the role that fraternities and sororities played in creating social activities. According to Fass (1977), the University of Wisconsin hosted 30 college dances and 80 fraternity and sorority dances each month in 1925. However, other observers looked at campus life in the 1930s and reported that the rating game was already cooling in intensity (Gordon, 1981). Certainly, the Depression altered undergraduate culture. College enrollments dipped, and Greek letter societies declined and were less able to maintain their dominant role on campuses. World War II completed the transformation. Automobiles and partying declined for the duration.

Today, there are still some prestige dimensions to cross-sex socializing, but the rating and dating complex has virtually disappeared. Pluralistic dating has given way to exclusive dating, but not necessarily to relationships oriented toward choosing a mate.

Dating and Courtship from the 1940s to the 1960s

The most important dating pattern to emerge just prior to World War II was that of **steady dating.** This pattern developed as an outgrowth of both romantic contacts at younger ages and the practice

In the 1930s, dating was often a way of gaining prestige rather than a means of finding a future marriage partner. What kinds of changes have occurred in dating and courtship since then?

of group and random dating in junior high school and early high school. Steady dating was an intermediate form between casual dating and engagement, since it involved a transition between the lack of commitment of casual dating and the very high commitment of engagement. This intermediate stage was necessary for individuals who were allowed personal responsibility for the selection of mates.

One of the best descriptions of the dating and courtship system of the 1950s was given by LeMasters (1957) in his book *Modern Courtship and Marriage.* The six stages LeMasters identified are shown in Table 5.1. These stages represented an orderly progression from the first date in the junior high school years until marriage in the late teens or early twenties. An adolescent girl usually had her first crush in junior high school; boys reached this stage 1 or 2 years later. At each stage, the relationship was excessively romantic, with other considerations subordinate to the fact that the two were madly in love. Each successive stage involved a progressively deeper commitment. Each stage also implied an appropriate degree of sexual intimacy: the more commitment, the greater the intimacy that was allowed. This led one young man to remark:

> I often had the uncomfortable feeling that the California coed dispensed passion by some sort of rule book.

It had all been decided beforehand: the first date, so many kisses, the second date, lips apart, tongue enters, fifth date, three buttons, next time, one zipper. . . . (Green, 1964, p. 131)

"Steadies" frequently broke up and realigned themselves with others, but broken engagements were serious matters.

There was sense and logic to the system except when a couple moved too rapidly from the earliest stages to marriage. Speeding up the courtship process was more common among lower socioeconomic status youths than among middle-class youths—resulting in an increasing number of marriages at younger ages—until the trend began to be reversed in the early 1960s.

Dating and "Getting Together" Today

Dating and getting together have undergone many changes since they emerged as a social phenomenon. "Getting together" is a popular term used by many adolescents to describe the practice of going out with a group of friends to get to know potential intimate partners as opposed to going out with one individual on a date. These meetings are usually informal and casual. This change in dating patterns may be due to the reduced pressure to marry. Many

Table 5.1 Stages in Dating and Courtship in the 1950s	
Ages or Grades	**Stage**
7th, 8th grade	Group dating
9th, 10th grade	Random dating between "steadies"
11th, 12th grade	Steady dating
College years (earlier for women, later for men)	Pinning
College years, or post–high school years	Engagement
Ages 19–21 for women, 20–24 for men	Marriage

Note: Adapted from *Modern Courtship and Marriage* by E. E. LeMasters, 1957, New York: Macmillan. Copyright © 1957 by Macmillan. Used with permission.

of today's teens will remain single throughout their twenties and engage in more casual "dating" relationships during the 10 or more years before they settle into marriage.

Another major change in dating is the increased opportunities for informal sexual contacts. For example, high schools and colleges that used to be exclusively for men or women are now coeducational. Many college dormitories have become coed, academic programs that used to attract only one sex or the other now enroll both men and women, and some fraternities are now coeducational. Also, men and women may share apartments and houses. These changes represent a drastic departure from the days when college men and women ate and slept in different parts of the campus. With such segregation, it was more difficult to get together, and often a formal phone call was required to arrange a meeting or a date. Today, group or paired social activities develop as a natural result of daily informal contacts in residences, classrooms, and social centers.

Another major change is the lack of any set pattern of progression of intimacy and commitment from initial meeting to marriage. Earlier generations followed a fairly consistent pattern: casual dating, steady dating, going steady, an understanding (engaged to be engaged), engagement, and marriage. Today, patterns vary. Some partners today do follow the traditional pattern; others decide to date each other exclusively and, after a period of time, decide to live together before getting married.

There may be no formal engagement, but marriage develops out of the cohabitation experience. In other words, not all couples work up to a formal engagement and then marriage. Patterns of dating and courtship vary.

Dating today is also much less formal than in previous generations. It is not necessary for the man to make a formal request in order to arrange a date. This sometimes happens, but a date may be arranged by mutual consent as a result of conversation about the evening activities. In addition, more women are taking the initiative in arranging a get-together. Dress is certainly more casual, and the activities are often less formal or more casually planned. Many times, a social evening cannot really be called a date. Couples simply go out together for an informal evening.

REASONS FOR DATING

One of the most significant changes in dating patterns is in the reasons for dating. Dating fulfills a number of important functions in the lives of today's youth.

First, dating is a form of recreation. One reason couples go out is simply to relax, enjoy themselves, and have fun. It is a form of entertainment and thereby an end in itself.

Second, dating provides companionship, friendship, and personal intimacy. Many young people have an intense desire to develop close, intimate relationships through dating. One study found that those couples who were able to share their most important thoughts and feelings in an egalitarian relationship were those most likely to be compatible and in love (Rubin, Hill, Peplau, and Dunkel-Schetter, 1980).

Third, dating is a means of socialization. Dating helps people learn social skills, gain confidence and poise, and begin to master the arts of conversation, cooperation, and consideration for others.

Fourth, dating contributes to personality development. One way in which individuals can establish their own identity is in relationship to other people. Since individuals mature primarily through successful experiences with others and since an adequate self-concept is partly a result of successful human associations, an important part of personality development is successful dating experiences.

Modern dating couples enjoy a variety of informal activities together.

One of the reasons young people go steady is that such associations give them security and feelings of individual worth.

Fifth, dating provides an opportunity to try out gender roles. Gender roles must be worked out in real-life situations with partners. Many women today find that they cannot accept a traditionally passive role; dating helps them discover this and learn what kinds of roles they find fulfilling in close relationships. Men also try out the roles they want to assume in relationships.

Sixth, dating is a means of fulfilling the need for love and affection. No matter how many casual friends people have, they meet their deepest emotional needs for love and affection in close relationships with other individuals. This need for affection is one of the major motives for dating.

Seventh, dating provides an opportunity for sexual experimentation and satisfaction. Dating has become more sex-oriented, with an increasing per-

centage of young people engaging in sexual intercourse (Michael et al., 1994).

Eighth, dating is a means of mate sorting and selection. In our culture, dating is the method for sorting out compatible pairs. The process involves gradually narrowing the field of eligibles from a pool of many to a specific few and eventually to one individual. Whether dating results in the selection of the most compatible partners will depend on the total experience. Not all dating patterns result in wise mate selection, especially if dating partners are chosen on the basis of superficial traits. Compatibility of mate selection suggests that individuals who are well matched on key characteristics marry each other in part because matching increases the likelihood that they will be able to establish a mutually satisfying partnership. It has been found, for example, that partners who share leisure time interests and have similar role preferences are more compatible and more likely to marry successfully (Houts, Robins, and Huston, 1996).

Finally, dating prepares individuals for marriage. Not only can dating result in the sorting of compatible pairs, but it also can become a means of socialization for marriage itself. Through dating, individuals develop a better understanding of the behavior and attitudes of each other; the partners learn how to get along and how to discuss and solve problems. The longer the dating period before marriage, the more dating fulfills this function of "anticipatory socialization" for marriage (Lloyd and Cate, 1984).

DATING PARTNERS VERSUS LONG-TERM PARTNERS

Physical attraction has always been an important factor in bringing partners together, but it is not the only factor. When college students were asked to paint a mental picture of their ideal partner and relationship, both males and females rated three "partner" factors most highly: (1) personal characteristics relevant to the development of intimacy and loyalty, (2) personality and appearance characteristics relevant to levels of attractiveness, energy, and health, and (3) characteristics relevant to social status and resources. In terms of the ideal relationship, the two most important factors were (1) the importance of intimacy and stability and (2) the degree of passion and excitement (Fletcher, Simpson, Thomas, and Giles, 1999).

However, not everyone chooses a date based on what they desire in a long-term partner or relationship. In one survey, 1,135 college students were asked to name three qualities they considered to be most important in a date and then to name three qualities they considered most important in a spouse. Table 5.2 shows the results. The most important characteristics in a date were primarily *extrinsic* characteristics: being physically attractive, having a congenial personality, having a sense of humor. The most important characteristics in a spouse were primarily *intrinsic* qualities: being loving, affectionate, and honest. This pattern was true for both males and females. These findings suggest that youths tend

to look for somewhat different qualities in a spouse than in a date, a fact that may hinder the selection of a compatible marriage partner (Jorgensen, 1986). If dating is the primary means of mate sorting but different qualities are desired in dates than are expected in spouses, how can suitable mates be discovered through the dating experience?

FINDING AND MEETING DATES

College provides a large pool of potential dating partners, but single men and women who are not in school face a greater challenge in finding dating partners. They may meet through friends or at parties or work, but some single people also try other methods, such as singles bars, personal ads, and dating services.

Strouse (1987) polled two samples of college-age individuals to determine the reasons they frequented singles bars. The first sample comprised 637 students in a University of Michigan class on human sexuality. Over half (51%) of these students indicated that they went to bars "to socialize with friends." Seven percent (11.7% of men and 3.4% of women) said they went to a bar to meet a sexual partner. Thirty-five percent said they went to a bar to meet people of the opposite sex. The second sample comprised 260 patrons of three bars in a town in the north-central United States. The majority (57%) of these people indicated that the main reason for going to bars was to see friends, to meet people, and to socialize. Fourteen percent of the men and 18% of the women went to bars to find a partner for sexual intercourse. Overall, the data suggest that single people go to bars to escape boredom and loneliness, to relax and have fun, to socialize with friends, and to meet a partner.

Newspapers and magazines across the country carry personal advertisements from people seeking a partner. The following are actual ads:

Table 5.2 Rank Order of Desirable Qualities in a Date and in a Spouse for 1,135 College Students

Most Important Qualities of a Date	Most Important Qualities of a Spouse
1. Physical attractiveness	1. Loving and affectionate
2. Congenial personality	2. Honest
3. Sense of humor	3. Congenial personality
4. Intelligent	4. Respectful
5. Manners/being considerate	5. Intelligent
6. Sincere, genuine	6. Mature/responsible
7. Compatible interests	7. Ambitious
8. Conversational ability	8. Loyal and trustworthy
9. Fun to be with	9. Physical attractiveness

Note: From *Marriage and the Family* (p. 260) by S. R. Jorgensen, 1986, New York: Macmillan. Copyright © 1986 by Stephen R. Jorgensen. Used with permission.

LUMINOUS, LITHE, LUSCIOUSLY BEAUTIFUL, tantalizingly bright, relaxed 31 SJW [single Jewish woman] seeks charismatic, handsome, athletic man who, like herself, feels deeply, laughs easily, is tender, warm, strong, sparkling, and playful. Is there a sincere, successful man out there who is in love with his work and looking for an endearing relationship? PO Box 0000, Cambridge, MA 02238.

SOFT SPOKEN, SWM [single White male] 6'0", 30, intelligent, professional, stockbroker seeks single, self-confident, attractive female for dating, perhaps more. PO Box 0000, Boston, MA 02114.

One study of the self-advertisements from a magazine for singles found that the men who placed ads were not looking for the women who placed ads, and vice versa (Bolig, Stein, and McKenry, 1984). Another study of personal advertisements in a national English newspaper found that women were offering physical attributes and seeking financial resources and that men were offering financial resources and seeking physical attributes (Cameron and Collins, 1998). Men were also more prone to stipulate the desire for casual relationships and to spend more money on their ads. In addition, because men tend to prefer younger women, women (particularly those ages 35–50) may decline to declare their age in order to seem younger than they really are (Pawlowski and Dunbar, 1999). Since there are fewer men than women in older cohorts, female advertisers outnumber male advertisers in the 40–50 age group (Pawlowski and Dunbar, 1999). This lack of older eligible males may help explain why older women receive fewer responses to ads than younger ones (Baize and Schroeder, 1995).

Research into singles' ads has raised questions regarding how much of the content of the ads is true. In general, research does not reveal outright lies when comparing information provided on questionnaires returned by advertisers to statements made in the ads themselves, but it does suggest that exaggeration and selective truth telling may be commonplace. For example, single women tend to omit any mention of children in their ads.

Other research has investigated what makes for successful ads. One study of the types of ads that increase the number of responses yielded the following results: For men, factors that increased the number of responses include (1) being older and taller, (2) mentioning educational and professional success or expensive cultural activities, (3) conveying an aura of masculinity, and (4) seeking a generally attractive woman but avoiding sexual references. For women, factors that increased the number of responses include (1) physical attractiveness (for example, being younger and slimmer and mentioning a preference for sports), (2) providing positive or neutral self-descriptions, especially about intelligence, and (3) mentioning or alluding to sex. For both men and women, writing an ad with originality

Love Matches Versus Arranged Marriages in China

Traditionally, in China, mates have been chosen and marriages arranged by parents. Recent data reveal that parental involvement has declined sharply and that young people have more say in the process of spouse selection. Defenders of arranged marriages claim that love matches start out hot and grow cold, while arranged marriages start out cold and grow hot. To what extent is this true?

A study by Xiaohe and Whyte (1990) of 586 ever-married women in the province of Sichuan, China, revealed that it is not exactly true. Marital satisfaction in arranged marriages tends to increase somewhat over 20 years of marriage, but marital satisfaction in love matches is always higher than in arranged marriages. Figure 5.1 shows the trends.

Figure 5.1 Marriage Quality by Mode of Mate Choice in China (*Note:* From "Love Matches and Arranged Marriages: A Chinese Replication" by X. Xiaohe and M. K. Whyte, 1990, *Journal of Marriage and the Family, 52,* p. 710.)

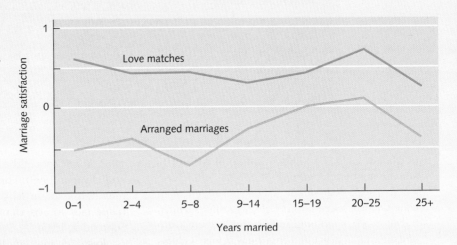

or flair increased the number of respondents, as did having seemingly trivial traits such as a certain hair color. Future research needs to measure an ad's success by its ability to attract good potential matches, not just a large number of responses (Ahuvia and Adelman, 1992).

A variety of dating services have been created to bring people together. One example is Together, which has 95 offices nationwide and which registers people ages 21–71. Applicants are asked to fill out a profile of themselves and their expectations in a partner. The Jewish Dating Service matches Jewish singles, and Chocolate Singles matches African Americans. Preferred Singles brings together those who are overweight.

One innovative method of finding a partner is to have a videotape made of yourself and to put it on file with a company specializing in the service. The company then sends you videotapes of other

people. Videos do a slightly better job of yielding accurate information than do written profiles and pictures (Woll and Young, 1989). Research tends to indicate that those who enroll in video dating services try to match themselves with others with similar traits. For example, the probability of a relationship progressing from viewing each other's videos to repeated dating has been found to be positively related to the similarity in the dating partners' level of physical attractiveness. People tend to look for those who are as physically attractive as they are.

Three variables seem to be most important in determining whether clients will be popular or unpopular: (1) attractiveness, (2) occupational status, and (3) level of education required by a job (Woll and Cozby, 1988). Men are mainly attracted to good-looking women, but women consider both social status and physical attractiveness in their selection of men.

Some organizations sell computer-matched information to members. Individuals are asked to complete a questionnaire, and a computer sorts out the

Dating Preferences of University Women: The "Nice Guy" Stereotype

Do "nice guys" finish last with regard to dating preferences of women? While many researchers have studied what type of men women prefer for relationship partners, one study focused on the appeal of the "nice guy" in the world of dating. Herold and Milhausen (1999) researched university women's perceptions and dating preferences regarding men considered to be nice guys. Specifically, the researchers were interested in whether women perceived so-called nice guys to be more or less sexually successful than men who were considered not nice and whether this mattered to them in choosing a dating partner.

Women were asked how important sex was to them in a dating relationship and what their acceptable upper limits were in terms of a potential partner's level of sexual experience. Seventeen percent of the women reported that sex was "very important," 58% reported that sex was "somewhat important," 17% reported that sex was of "little importance," and 7% reported that sex was "not important." Almost all (95%) of the women were willing to accept a partner who had had intercourse with at least 1 partner. But only 10% of women were willing to accept a partner who had had intercourse with 11 or more women. Almost half (48%) were willing to accept a partner who had had up to 5 previous sexual partners, and 73% were willing to accept a partner who had had up to 3 previous partners.

So do women prefer "nice guys"? The women were given the choice between two hypothetical dates: John, a sexually inexperienced, nice, but somewhat shy man, and Mike, an attractive, fun man who had had sex with 10 women. Fifty-four percent of the women reported that they would prefer John as a date, 28% reported that they would equally prefer John or Mike, and 18% reported that they would prefer Mike. Yet 56% of the women knew of other women who had had the choice of dating nice but sexually inexperienced men but who chose to date men

who were sexually experienced but not so nice. Also, 56% of the women agreed that nice guys were less likely to have as many sexual partners as guys who were not so nice.

Ironically, nice guys who are sensitive, patient, and nurturing appear to be favored as dating partners by many women (Herold and Milhausen, 1999; Regan, 1998), but men who are dominant, confident, and aggressive have reported the most sexual success with women (Reise and Wright, 1996). Perhaps some of the reasons for this irony can be gleaned from the comments of two students:

Nice guys often don't provide the drama and adventure women think they want.

Nice guys are generally not as attractive, and have a great personality to compensate for this shortcoming. Unfortunately, looks, not personality, tend to get a woman into bed.

(Herold and Milhausen, 1999, p. 339)

While university women perceived the nice guys as having such positive traits as a good personality, high standards and morals, and good manners, the nice guys were also perceived to be less physically attractive, and this was considered to be a major weakness. The women believed that the "not-so-nice guys" had more sexual success with women because they were more aggressive, were willing to lie and manipulate a situation, and were more physically and sexually attractive. Also, they were more likely to approach and proposition women because their self-confidence and previous successes with women had made them less fearful of rejection. Women believed that, because of their popularity and sexual successes, the not-so-nice guys were seen by other women as more desirable and appealing (Herold and Milhausen, 1999).

---

information to match those with similar profiles. One organization in Maine, Matchmaker Dating Service of Maine, has more than 6,200 members. It seeks to match people as closely as possible on over 200 characteristics, including geographical area, age, height, build, education, and socioeconomic status. Since these services use computers to match people according to a variety of traits, they could be more successful than a human matchmaker at predicting a couple's compatibility (Ahuvia and Adelman, 1992).

Personal computers may also bring people together. Computer Information Services of Colum-

bus, Ohio, allows individuals to use any of its 36 channels to "talk" with other members. Subscribers send information back and forth on their computers and decide if they want to meet in person.

Computer modems allow for interactive contacts, such as chat rooms and e-mail bulletin board systems. A benefit of computer contacts is that they allow people to get to know each other before screening each other on the basis of physical attraction.

This ability to communicate with others via computer has not been without its disadvantages

Dating services seek to sort out compatible pairs and bring them together.

and even perils. One college-age woman established a romantic relationship via computer with a man whom she visualized as her ideal partner. When she met him, she discovered he was an 80-year-old widower. Others have been even more unlucky. A pedophile lured a young girl to a secluded place and then beat and raped her. Pictures or computer conversations cannot reveal the true character of the individual with whom one is corresponding.

CHANGING GENDER ROLES IN DATING

Male and female roles in the dating process have changed. Traditionally, men initiated, planned, and paid for the date. This arrangement encouraged an unspoken agreement whereby females were expected to reciprocate for benefits received by allowing expressions of affection and sexual intimacies (Sprecher, 1985).

With the advent of the feminist movement, women became more aware of the inequalities between the sexes and more intolerant of the power distribution in sexual relationships. Accordingly, they have sought to equalize control within the dating situation by initiating and paying for dates, thereby altering both male sexual expectations and female sexual obligations. In a study of 400 college women (Korman and Leslie, 1982), approximately 55% reported that they helped pay for the date at least some of the time. Korman (1983) compared the behavior of feminists and nonfeminists in terms of whether they initiated dates and shared the expenses. The subjects were 258 unmarried, undergraduate women attending classes at a large southeastern university. In comparison to nonfeminists, feminists were more likely to initiate dates and to share the expenses when they did so. However, their primary goal was to achieve more egalitarian relationships and not necessarily to reduce sexual obligations. Although both feminists and nonfeminists believed that men who paid for dates were more likely to expect sexual favors, both groups said they were unlikely to engage in unwanted sexual activity.

A more recent study found that among today's college students both men and women may initiate romantic relationships but that men still take the initiative more often (Clark, Shaver, and Abrahams, 1999). The study found that the most successful strategies in initiating romantic relationships were emotional disclosure (for example, talking on the phone or in person and spending time together), being direct (for example, asking directly, using touch, and giving gifts), and manipulating the setting (for example, visiting the partner unexpectedly). Showing off material resources was seen as the phoniest strategy. The most commonly used strategies were talking in person (and over the phone), touching the partner, and asking directly. While men and women perceived themselves as equally successful in initiating relationships, men initiated more romantic relationships than did women. Men were more confident and more likely to use the strategies of manipulating the setting and being direct. A greater percentage of men than women were seeking sexual intimacy in the beginning states of their romantic relationship. Women were more likely to rely on the man to initiate the relationship and were more likely to be concerned about the risk of an unsuccessful initiation attempt. Thus, they were less direct, less motivated, and less likely to initiate a relationship with a potential partner. Women described themselves, and men described them, as being passive and using indirect or subtle strategies in relationship initiation. These findings are consistent with the literature on gender differences in communication. They also coincide with the evolutionary perspective, according to which females are heavily invested in each reproductive act and must be more discriminating than males about the quality of their partners (Clark, Shaver, and Abrahams, 1999). Thus, the researchers concluded that females take a more tentative approach to relationship initiation, making sure to evaluate prospective mates carefully.

PROBLEMS IN DATING

Dating is usually an important part of the social life of young people. Yet some haven't learned the social skills and developed the self-confidence to succeed. A survey of 3,800 undergraduates at the University of Arizona found that a third (37% of men and 25% of women) were "somewhat anxious" or "very anxious" about dating. Half the students in a University of Indiana survey rated dating situations "difficult." Nearly a third of University of Iowa students said they feared meeting new people (Timnick, 1982).

A study of 227 women and 107 men in a random sample of students at East Carolina University sought to identify dating problems (Knox and Wilson, 1983). The most frequent problems reported by the women were unwanted pressure to engage in sexual activity, the decision of where to go and what to do on dates, communication, sexual misunderstandings, and money. Examples of sexual misunderstandings included a man's perception that a woman was leading him on when she really didn't want to have intercourse and disagreement about the desired level of sexual intimacy (Byers and Lewis, 1988).

The problems most frequently mentioned by the men were communication, the decision of where to go and what to do on dates, shyness, money, and honesty/openness. By honesty/openness the men were referring to how much to tell about them-selves, how soon, and how to get their partner to reciprocate.

Honesty and Openness

Men and women both look for honesty and openness in relationships. Because men and women strive to be on their best behavior while dating, a certain amount of pretense or playacting, called **imaging,** is necessary to present themselves in the best possible manner.

Researchers have found that men tend to deceive dating partners about commitment levels and financial resources and that women tend to deceive dating partners about physical attributes (Tooke and Camire, 1991). In one study (Keenan, Gallup, Goulet, and Kulkarni, 1997), researchers surveyed 60 undergraduate students about deception in dating strategies by members of the opposite sex and rated the responses according to financial, commitment, and physical dimensions of deception. For example, on the commitment subscale, one item read, "On a date, a person of the opposite gender would portray themselves as more interested in having a long-term relationship than they actually are." The survey revealed that women expect significantly more deception on financial characteristics from men than men expect from women. Women also expect more deception from men on variables related to commitment than men expect from women. However, men do not anticipate significantly more deception from women about physical characteristics than women expect from men. Overall, women expect significantly more deception from men than men expect from women. Women are especially suspicious of claims made by males who are sexually interested in them. These findings support the idea that women, who bear the greater cost for procreation and thus greater corresponding reproductive risk, are more selective and cautious maters than men are (Keenan et al., 1997).

Despite expecting imaging by dating partners, strikingly high proportions of male and female college students who participated in a study of self-disclosure in dating couples reported that they had disclosed their thoughts and feelings "fully" to their partners in almost all areas. However, women revealed more than men in several specific areas, including their greatest fears. Couples with egalitarian gender-role attitudes disclosed more than

Research into issues of power in sexual relationships has generated a spirited debate over whether men or women have the most power. Here we look at two sides of the argument.

Men Control Dating

The courtship system in the United States is largely patriarchal despite recent efforts to enhance equality in intimate relationships. *Patriarchy* as used here refers to the emotional and financial dependence of women on men. Well before marriage, power is ascribed to the male partner in a relationship (Lloyd, 1991). The theme of male control and female dependence also emphasizes the overriding importance of relationships to women. The stereotypic beliefs about women in relationships include the belief that in order to be fulfilled a woman needs to be married and that upon finding the right man everything will suddenly fall into place. Women's socialization ultimately emphasizes female responsibility for relationship maintenance. The themes of male control and female dependence are reflected in dating practices.

Sexuality is a major source of conflict for dating couples. The patriarchal sexual script grants ownership of sexuality (both his and hers) to the male. According to this script, men have an urgent sex drive, which women are expected to fulfill. Women's resistance to sexual pressure is viewed as token; the male should continue to exert pressure. In the courtship context, the male's control gives him permission to use force to achieve his sexual goals.

Unfortunately, the female courtship themes of dependence and the importance of relationships encourage women to attach nonexploitative meanings to sexual aggression, especially if the relationship is an established one, and to acquiesce in situations of sexual aggression.

Women Control Dating

Women are more likely than men to try to control their partners regardless of the stage of the relationship. This contradicts the hypothesis that men are likely to control interaction. It also contradicts the idea that control in personal relationships is a derivative of control in society, which is based on economic resources and power. But economic resources and power in the public sphere are not the only bases of control. Love is an important basis for control in interpersonal relationships, and it may explain the power that women have in the dating situation. Women's greater control over love is exemplified by the fact that men tend to fall in love more often than women, that women's love for their partners is a better predictor of the health of their relationships than men's love, that more relationships are ended by women than by men, and that ending relationships is a more traumatic experience for men than for women. Gender differences in socialization make women better equipped to manage love in the interpersonal realm (Stets, 1993).

---

those with traditional gender-role attitudes. Self-disclosure was strongly related to respondents' reported love for their partners. The highest level of self-disclosure was found in couples who had been dating for the longest time. The median length of time for high self-disclosure was 8 months of going together (Rubin et al., 1980).

Extradyadic Relationships

One of the considerations in dating is whether to have sexual relationships outside the dating dyad. Certainly, there is ample evidence that both men and women most desire and experience sexual intercourse within a caring relationship (Sherwin and Corbett, 1985). The more involvement, the more men and women both desire and experience intercourse (McCabe, 1987).

The real question, however, is, To what extent do couples in committed dating relationships engage in **extradyadic sexual activity,** and with what effect? Hansen (1987) asked 215 college students who had ever been in a committed dating relationship to respond to the following question: "While in a committed dating relationship, have you ever engaged in the following with someone other than your dating partner?" Erotic kissing, intimate touching, and sexual intercourse were listed; Table 5.3 shows the results. As you can see, 35% of the men and 12% of the women reported having sexual intercourse with someone else while involved in a committed dating relationship. A little more than 40% of men and women were certain or fairly sure their dating partner knew about it. About 40% of both men and women felt their own extradyadic relations had hurt their dating relationships. But

Table 5.3 Percentage of Men and Women Who Have Engaged in Various Types of Extradyadic Behavior		
Type of Behavior	**Men**	**Women**
Erotic kissing	65.2	39.5
Intimate touching	46.7	18.5
Intercourse	35.2	11.9

Note: From "Extradyadic Relations During Courtship" by G. L. Hansen, 1987, *The Journal of Sex Research, 23,* pp. 382–390.

when their partner had had extradyadic relations, more than 70% of both men and women felt it had hurt their dating relationship. Apparently, the students were more accepting of their own extradyadic sexual relations than they were of their partner's.

In another study, Wiederman and Hurd (1999) asked 621 college students about their experiences with extradyadic dating and sexual activity. Despite general disapproval of extradyadic involvement, a majority of the respondents reported having had such an involvement. There were no gender differences in the incidence of extradyadic dating, but men were more likely than women to experience extradyadic fondling, oral sex, and intercourse. In general, extradyadic dating was related to less adherence to the belief that sex, love, and marriage should be associated, to increased sexual sensation seeking, and to a self-perceived ability to deceive one's partner.

Getting Too Serious

Another of the dating problems people face is the situation of one person getting more serious than the other person desires. A University of Maine student wrote:

> I am not ready for and have no immediate intentions of getting married—for the next five to ten years anyway. Through my dates I have made some very close personal male friends. But for the past three years the situations have ended abruptly because each time my partner decided the relationship was more serious than I wanted. How can I keep my enjoyable and good contacts without leading them on? (From a student paper)

Another student complained, "No matter what we're talking about, my partner always gets around

to hinting about marriage, but I'm not ready to settle down. I have two more years of college and then grad school ahead of me."

Sometimes couples make a premature commitment; then one of them has second thoughts and wants to discontinue the relationship. People in new romances tend to expect that their relationship will last longer than it actually does (Buehler, Griffin, and Ross, 1995). Individuals who have made the decision to enter a dating relationship may focus on its present strengths and on their positive feelings and fail to consider the potential challenges to the relationship (MacDonald and Ross, 1999). Women are more likely than men to have second thoughts. One man wrote:

> My current girlfriend is very serious about getting married, but I'm not at all sure about the relationship now. How do I explain this to her (a very sensitive person), especially after I expressed a sincere desire to marry her at one time? (From a student paper)

Sometimes both people begin to realize that something is wrong in the relationship, but each is afraid to tell the other. In most instances, each partner needs to express the doubts, inquire about the other person's feelings, and discuss viewpoints tactfully but openly. Most problems can be dealt with only by honest and sensitive communication.

Closeness and Distance in Relationships

Closeness and distance are both important needs in a dating relationship, and much research has focused on individuals' strategies for balancing closeness and distance (Feeney, 1999a). Romantic relationships involve many such "contradictions," and the need for a balance between autonomy and connection is one of the central ones (Baxter and Simon, 1993). Although any romantic relationship requires each individual to give up some autonomy in order to develop a couple identity, giving up too much of one's own identity can be problematic. This contradiction has been called the "me-we pull," because the individual has a desire both to be true to his or her self and to be flexible enough to make the relationship work (Baxter, 1990). Baxter and Montgomery (1997) suggested that romantic partners deal with these issues over the course of the relationship but never fully resolve them, as the needs for autonomy and distance are constantly changing.

It is important to remember that every individual is unique and has different needs for distance and closeness in a relationship. In general, men and women differ in their interaction patterns in dating relationships. Researchers have found that women want more closeness in their intimate relationships than men do and that these needs are related to differences in patterns of communication. Women push for active discussion of relationship issues, whereas men tend to withdraw from such discussions (Christensen and Heavey, 1990). These differences are related to gender-role socialization whereby women are taught to be caretakers of relationships and men are taught to be independent and self-reliant. Unfortunately, these patterns tend to cause conflicts over intimacy levels in romantic relationships (Baxter and Montgomery, 1997).

People's attachment styles, which are developed early in life, also affect their need for closeness and distance in dating relationships. Studies of adult romantic attachment styles have consistently revealed two major dimensions: (1) comfort with closeness and (2) anxiety over relationships (see Feeney and Noller, 1996, for a review). Individuals who are comfortable with closeness prefer a balanced type of relationship, characterized by high levels of openness and closeness but also by a certain amount of independence. Individuals who are highly anxious about their relationships typically seek extreme closeness to partners and become overdependent on them. Avoidant individuals want the most distance in their relationships and so limit closeness, dependence, and affection (Feeney and Noller, 1991).

In a study of distance regulation in established dating relationships, the overwhelming majority (92%) of participants referred to issues of closeness and distance, such as partners' needs for autonomy and connection, the amount of time spent together versus apart, and involvement in individual versus joint activities (Feeney, 1999a). Couples with two secure partners were less likely to report problems with distance regulation than were couples in which one or both partners were insecure. The following statements highlight the importance of considering the attachment styles of both partners:

I've never let anybody get really close to me. I think it's just like a self-defense mechanism that I have, to not get hurt. I always keep, you know—there's always a thin distance that I don't let people come near me; not a physical touch, but I think, spiritual. To me this is important, my own space. To have someone invade that space that is special to me, I feel violated. I get angry, I get irritated, I get very irritated. (Feeney, 1999a, p. 579)

If they don't want to be with you . . . , you wonder what you've done wrong. Or you wonder why; if they don't love you anymore, or if they don't find you attractive anymore, or if they're bored with you, or if it's the end of the road. That's the hardest thing; if S doesn't want to be with me emotionally or doesn't want to be with me, there's nothing to look forward to [sniffling]. There's nothing at all, nothing I can do. It makes me quite miserable, quite alone and quite neglected; ugly, fat, boring, uninteresting; like a nothing. (Feeney, 1999a, p. 579)

SEXUAL AGGRESSION AND DATING VIOLENCE

Sexual aggression can take many forms. It may be limited to verbal coercion in order to obtain sex, or it may include physical attempts as well. Sometimes those attempts take the form of date rape, which has become an increasingly reported problem. Sometimes conflict on dates escalates into other forms of violence, such as physical abuse.

Evidence from a variety of studies indicates that physical violence occurs in at least 20% of dating relationships. Women age 12 and older were victimized 5 million times annually in 1992 and 1993, and nearly three-quarters of the offenses committed by a lone attacker were by someone the victim knew. In one-quarter of the cases, the offender was a current or former spouse or boyfriend. Because fewer than 50% of all rapes are reported (Dupre, Hampton, Morrison, and Meeks, 1993), the incidence of violence in intimate relationships is probably much higher than the data indicate. For example, a survey of 6,159 college students enrolled in 32 U.S. institutions found the following: (1) 54% of the women had been the victim of some form of sexual abuse, over 25% had been the victim of rape or attempted rape, and 57% of the assaults occurred on dates; (2) 73% of the assailants and 55% of the victims had used alcohol or other drugs prior to the assault; (3) 25% of the men admitted to some degree of sexually aggressive behavior; and (4) 42% of the victims told no one (Koss, Dinero, and Seibel, 1988). Another study revealed that, among students who had ever dated, 36.4% of the females and 37.1% of the males reported physical violence in a dating relationship (Molder and Tolman, 1998).

Societal attitudes toward sexual aggression and dating violence are as troubling as the national numbers. In a survey of high school students, 56% of girls and 76% of boys believed that forced sex was acceptable under some circumstances (White and Humphrey, 1991). In addition, these researchers found the following: (1) 51% of the boys and 41% of the girls said forced sex was acceptable if the boy "spent a lot of money" on the girl; (2) 31% of the boys and 32% of the girls said it was acceptable for a man to rape a woman with past sexual experience; (3) 87% of the boys and 79% of the girls said sexual assault was acceptable if the man and the woman were married; and (4) 65% of the boys and 47% of the girls said it was acceptable for a boy to rape a girl if they had been dating for more than 6 months.

Some men as well as women feel pressured into engaging in sexual activity (Smith, Pine, and Hawley, 1988). In a study of 507 university men and 486 university women, 63% of the men and 46% of the women reported having experienced nonconsensual sexual intercourse (Muehlenhard and Cook, 1988). When asked why they engaged in nonconsensual sexual intercourse, the men listed (in descending order of importance) enticement, altruism (desire to please), inexperience, intoxication, reluctance not to, partner's verbal coercion, gender-role expectations, threat of termination of relationship, peer pressure, physical coercion, and a desire to be popular.

In another study of college students, 35% of men anonymously admitted that under certain circumstances they would commit rape if they believed they could get away with it. One in 12 admitted to committing acts that met the legal definition of rape, and 84% of the men who committed rape

did not label it as rape (Koss, Dinero, and Seibel, 1988). (Legally, **rape** is defined as sexual intercourse, with actual penetration of a woman's vagina with the man's penis, without consent and accomplished through force, threat of violence, or intimidation, such as a threat to harm; lack of consent includes such things as saying no or being too drunk or drug-influenced to be able to either resist or consent [Hill and Hill, 1997].) In another survey of college students, 43% of the men admitted to using coercive behavior to have sex, including ignoring a woman's protests, using physical aggression, and forcing intercourse. Fifteen percent admitted that they had committed acquaintance rape, and 11% acknowledged using physical restraints to force a woman to have sex (Rapaport and Posey, 1991).

Pressure to engage in unwanted sexual activities begins for some during early adolescence. An investigation of a sample of 1,149 adolescent females in grades 7, 9, and 11 found that 20% of the sample reported some type of unwanted sexual contact in the past year. Of this group, over one-third reported that they had been forced to have sexual intercourse; the remaining two-thirds reported unwanted touching. Boyfriends were the most commonly named perpetrators, followed by dates, friends, and acquaintances. Individuals were more vulnerable to unwanted sexual contact if they had a history of sexual abuse, reported excessive alcohol use in the past month, scored high in measures of peer conformity, or had parents who did not closely monitor their behavior or use an authoritative parenting style (Small and Kerns, 1993). Young women who report a history of forced sexual intercourse have their first voluntary sexual experience at a younger age than women who do not report a forced sexual encounter (Mahler, 1996d).

Men are more likely than women to use verbal coercion to obtain sex, but not all men use verbal coercion. A study of 194 undergraduate males at a large state university grouped subjects into three levels of sexual experience (Craig, Kalichman, and Follingstad, 1989). Twelve percent were classified as being sexually inexperienced, 46% had had only consensual sexual relations, and 42% had used

Many instances of date rape go unreported. Help is becoming more available for women who have experienced sexual aggression, although reluctance to report it continues.

verbal coercion to obtain sex. Those in the first two groups approached relationships with women in terms of a broad spectrum of possibilities, including friendship, companionship, and enjoyment. Those in the third group saw relationships with women in terms of sexual possibilities. They placed a great deal of emphasis on the value of sex, devalued—but did not hate—women, and used a wide range of manipulative techniques: They said things they really didn't mean, made promises, and tried to talk women into having sex. The coercive men reported feeling aroused and in need of sex, and they believed they had accomplished a goal when they seduced a woman who was a stranger or acquaintance, particularly on a first or second date. Some admitted trying to get their dates to drink excessively.

Date Rape

Date rape is rape that occurs on a voluntary, pre-arranged date or after a woman meets a man in a social setting and voluntarily accompanies him elsewhere. Date rape and other types of sexual aggression are very common. In a study of 275 undergraduate single women, more than 50% of the participants reported being pressured into being kissed, having their breasts and genitals manipulated, and having oral contact with the male's genitals (Christopher, 1988).

Women are told frequently, "Don't go out with a man whom you don't know. If you do, you're taking a big chance." This is probably sound advice, but one of the purposes of dating is to get to know other people. And no matter how well you know an individual, problems can arise. Date rapes can occur in relationships in which two people have been going out together for a long time. As familiarity grows, the sexually aggressive male may become more insistent and try to coerce his partner into sexual activity that she finds objectionable.

This coercion may reflect a lack of communication and understanding in the relationship. In particular, sexual aggression may occur in a long-term relationship in which there is a lack of disclosure about sexual feelings, attitudes, and desires (Herold and Way, 1988). Some men are brought up to believe that when a woman says no she really means yes and that it's up to the man to do what she really wants him to do. This reflects the same myth that exists in relation to other types of rape: that women want to be forced. It also reflects the social leaning in our culture: that men are supposed to be the sexual aggressors and overcome the reluctance and hesitancy of women. Of course, some men rape their dates out of anger and hostility, and many of these men engage repeatedly in acts of sexual aggression with a series of partners (Heilbrun and Loftus, 1986).

Rohypnol and GHB are known as date rape drugs because, when they are slipped into someone's drink, a sexual assault can take place without the victim being able to control or remember what happened. Rohypnol (also known as "roofies," "roopies," "circles," and "the forget pills") works like a tranquilizer, causing muscle weakness, fatigue, slurred speech, loss of motor coordination and judgment, and amnesia that lasts up to 24 hours. It looks like an aspirin—small, white, round. GHB (also known as "liquid X," "salt water," and "scoop") also causes quick sedation. Its effects include drowsiness, nausea, vomiting, headaches, dizziness, coma, and death. Its most common form is a clear liquid although it can also be a white, grainy powder.

Malamuth (1989a) reported that some men are more attracted to sexual aggression and less attracted to conventional sex. Men who are most attracted to rape are highly aroused by media portrayals of forced sex, are less sensitive to the victims when exposed to sexually violent materials (Byers, 1988; Linz, 1989), and have hostility toward women, the desire to dominate women, and antisocial personality characteristics (Malamuth, 1989b).

Many date rapes are never reported. Women might not realize that such incidents qualify as rape; they sometimes feel ashamed and don't want anyone to know; they might hesitate to report someone they know; and they sometimes feel partially responsible.

According to a study of college men's perceptions of acquaintance rape and date rape scenarios, when a woman engages in some sexual activity but refuses sexual intercourse, perceptions of her accountability for the rape increase dramatically and perceptions of the perpetrator's accountability decrease dramatically (Yescavage, 1999). Women who say no to all sexual activity are not perceived to be as accountable for their victimization. Duration of the relationship also has an impact on perceptions of accountability: If the couple has been together a while and is sexually active, the victim is perceived as more accountable and the perpetrator as less accountable. This pattern of responses suggests that a woman is judged to have given up her right to say no to sex if she allowed sexual activity to reach a certain point, somewhere between light and heavy intimate touching (Yescavage, 1999).

A study that surveyed the prevalence of sexual assault on one college campus found that unwanted sexual experiences of some kind were common among the women respondents (Ward, Chapman, Cohn, White, and Williams, 1991). The experiences typically occurred in residences (university and community), were party related, and involved alcohol use. A range of types of relationships was reported, from "stranger" to "boyfriend." The men commonly ignored the women's protests and used verbal coercion; physical force was less frequent, although it did occur. The resulting psychological damage to the women was high, yet the women did not report the damaging experiences to university or criminal justice officials.

The women were also asked, "In what ways did you show that you did not want the experience?" Verbal protests were common; 91% of the women said no to attempted intercourse, which may explain why some attempts were not completed. Some women also resisted physically, with 28% struggling unsuccessfully against completed intercourse. Altogether, 73% of the instances of unwanted intercourse occurred in spite of the woman's verbal or physical protests.

Eighteen percent of the women reported being psychologically injured as a result of unwanted sexual contact, and 30% as a result of attempted intercourse. Psychological harm from unwanted sexual intercourse appeared to be high, with 51% of the women sustaining harm from the experience. Physical injury was less common but did occur in 10% of the completed intercourse instances.

Unwanted sexual activity continues to be a dilemma for many young people and adults. Many don't know how to cope with unwanted sex but blame themselves if they experience it. Clearly, more education is needed.

Physical Violence

Domestic violence, especially the growing problem of spouse abuse, has received increased attention in the media. But the problems often begin during courtship. Estimates from nationally representative samples suggest that the rates among young adults may be as high as 51% for "general" violence and

23% for "serious" violence (Fagan and Browne, 1994). Rates of partner violence are dramatically higher for young adults than for people in other age groups. Abusers and abused exhibit patterns of violence during courtship that are similar to those seen in marriage (Roscoe and Benaske, 1985). Furthermore, courtship violence appears to be a training ground for marital violence (Flynn, 1987). Male aggressors using violence against a premarital partner are more likely than others to continue being violent in marriage. And women who experience violence in a premarital relationship and stay in the relationship are more likely to remain in an abusive marriage than are those who left a violent relationship before marriage or never experienced one at all (Flynn, 1987).

Acceptance of courtship and marital violence is related to attitudes toward such violence. Some groups of people consider it acceptable for a man to be abusive toward a woman. In two studies, both high school students (Henton, Cate, Koval, Lloyd, and Christopher, 1983) and college students (Cate, Henton, Koval, Christopher, and Lloyd, 1982) who had been involved in an abusive relationship held less negative attitudes toward premarital violence than did students who had never experienced abuse. Those in abusive relationships may enter marriage with a predisposition to be more tolerant of marital abuse than are those in nonabusive premarital pairings.

Studies show that both males and females are abusers and abused, but females suffer more serious forms (being struck with an object or beaten up), while males sustain less serious forms (being hit by thrown objects, pushing, slapping, kicking, biting, punching; Follingstad, Wright, Lloyd, and Sebastian, 1991). Females more often are injured physically (sometimes severely) and more often suffer greater emotional trauma from the experience than do males (Makepeace, 1986). Table 5.4 lists the motives for the use of violence by gender.

Correlations with Violence

A number of factors may contribute to courtship violence. Social learning theory emphasizes that aggression is learned in interactions in intimate personal groups. Those who grow up in families in which parental interactions involve aggressive or

Table 5.4 Motives for Use of Violence, by Gender

Motive	Males (%)	Females (%)
Self-defense	18.1	35.6
To harm	2.4	8.3
To retaliate	16.5	18.9
To intimidate	21.3	6.8
To "get" something	3.9	2.3
Uncontrollable anger	28.3	24.2
Other	10.3	13.7

Columns total more than 100% because many respondents reported multiple motives.

Note: From "Gender Differences in Courtship Violence Victimization" by J. M. Makepeace, 1986, *Family Relations, 35,* pp. 383–388. Copyright © 1986 by the National Council on Family Relations. Reprinted by permission.

violent acts may learn these behavior patterns and later imitate them in their adult relationships (Gwartney-Gibbs, Stockard, and Bohmer, 1987). A large number of studies support a positive relationship between aggression in the family of origin and aggression sustained or inflicted in courtship (Laner and Thompson, 1982). For example, in a study of 156 college males, Ronfeldt, Kimerling, and Arias (1998) found that the men at greatest risk for escalating from psychological to physical acts of control over their partners were those who as children had witnessed their fathers physically abusing their mothers. Although this idea is widely accepted, one investigation into longitudinal data from 113 adolescent boys and their parents yielded mixed results. The researchers found that frequent use of corporal punishment increased the risk of dating violence but that interparental aggression did not. However, parents did have an impact on other antisocial behavior. Low support and involvement by parents was associated with adolescent delinquency and drug use, which was correlated with involvement in dating violence. Other studies, particularly two by DeMaris (1987, 1990), indicate that witnessing parental violence in one's family of origin has an inconsistent effect on later physical aggression during courtship. It may increase courtship violence, decrease it, or have little effect one way or the other. In other words, not all people who grow up in violent families become violent themselves.

Sexual aggression in dating relationships is related not just to learned behavior but also to the environment of the dating relationship itself. Three factors have been found to be related to violence in a relationship: commitment, conflict, and ambivalence. Commitment is a factor in that it allows partners to explore many levels of the relationship and to express themselves fully and honestly without the fear of breaking up. In committed relationships, partners often know how the other person will respond to aggression (Christopher, Madura, and Weaver, 1998). Early and possibly milder acts of aggression may not lead to the dissolution of a committed relationship (Lloyd, 1991), which can reinforce those acts and lead to more violent forms of aggression. This conceptualization may explain why single men and women in more committed dating relationships are more likely than those in casual pairings to use coercive strategies to influence sexual relations (Christopher, Owens, and Strecker, 1993). Intimate relationships are also fertile grounds for conflicts if one partner's ideas and goals for the relationship are not in harmony with the other's. Christopher and colleagues (1993) found that, as conflict in the relationship increased, so did the use of sexually assaultive and coercive strategies for influencing the other person. Premarital sexual aggression also has been linked to relationship ambivalence among single women. Ambivalence can hinder the establishment of relationship goals and cause people's behavior to be more uncertain. One partner may use sexual aggression to try to gain greater control and counteract the other partner's uncertainties (Christopher et al., 1993).

Social factors also relate to courtship violence. Makepeace (1987) surveyed 2,338 students in seven colleges and found that both offenders and victims in courtship violence exhibited certain social profiles. The following factors were of special significance:

- **Socioeconomic status.** Violence was highest in families with both very low and very high incomes from urban areas. Violence was lowest among those with medium incomes from rural areas.
- **Family background.** Rates were highest among those who were reared in one-parent families, who were not very close to their parents, or who had experienced harsh discipline. Those who receive abuse as children are more likely to express and to receive violence in courtship (Marshall and Rose, 1988).
- **Academic achievement.** Students who received the poorest grades (Ds or Fs) or who had been suspended or expelled from school were most likely to exhibit courtship violence.
- **Work record.** Those most likely to exhibit courtship violence were those who had experienced multiple firings from jobs. This was the single factor most related to courtship violence.
- **Alcohol.** Courtship violence was more common among those who drank "somewhat more than most" and for whom alcohol "sometimes" interfered with school or work than among those who admitted drinking "much more than most" or for whom alcohol "often" interfered. This may reflect denial of violence on the part of those who said they drank the most, or denial of drinking by those who said they drank less, or the depressant effects of excessive alcohol consumption.
- **Dating.** Courtship violence was associated with both early dating and poor dating success.
- **Life events stress.** Courtship violence was also related to exposure to life events stress, such as illness, death in the family, a job change, or a move to a new home.

Certain personality traits relate to courtship violence, too. Courtship violence, especially premarital sexual aggression, is more common with men who are hostile toward women, who have a high degree of anger and a low degree of empathy, who have experienced negative relationships in the past, and who are sexually promiscuous (Christopher, Owens, and Strecker, 1993). Physical abusers have been found to be less able to inhibit their aggressive impulses, and they exhibit greater emotional arousal, especially anger, in conflictive situations (Barnes, Greenwood, and Sommer, 1991). Violent people tend to be low in self-esteem and self-mastery (Bird, Stith, and Schladale, 1991). They are very insecure and anxious in relationships because they fear abandonment (Mayseless, 1991).

Courtship violence is also related to the level of emotional commitment in the relationship. In one study of dating partners who had experienced violence, 45% remained in the relationship and 29% reported that the relationship had become more deeply involved (Makepeace, 1981). Between one-fourth and one-third of both the abusers and the abused interpreted the violence as love (Henton et al., 1983). Others viewed violence as a destructive force in the relationship.

When it occurs, violence seems to progress as the relationship becomes more serious (Stets, 1993). In one study of partner violence among young adults in dating versus cohabiting relationships, researchers found that cohabitors were nearly twice as likely as daters to be physically abusive toward their partner (Magdol, Moffitt, Caspi, and Silva, 1998). Relationships defined as serious and meaningful show higher rates of abuse than do those defined as casual, although violence occurs even at the casual dating level. Overall, however, the studies suggest that greater commitment can be an opportunity for greater risk of violence (Billingham, 1987).

The Progression of Violence

Often, violence begins with verbal aggression, which becomes the seed of physical aggression (Stets and Henderson, 1991). Aggression may occur for the first time in a relationship when disagreement over some issue (for example, when to have sex) results in an uncontrollable, emotionally charged response. The response may come as a surprise to both perpetrator and victim. If it is negatively sanctioned by either or both partners, the perpetrator of the aggressive act may make a commitment never to respond that way in the future. If the act is immediately challenged, it may not recur.

Recurring aggression may be the result of persistent, long-term interaction patterns instead of a sensitive issue. An individual's tendency to repeatedly neglect the needs, wishes, and concerns of the other partner, and instead to put his or her wants and desires ahead of the partner's by controlling him or her, may contribute to repeated acts of aggression. In essence, refusal to meet the needs of the other person, together with a desire to maintain control over him or her, so that his or her perspectives and desires are neglected and the wishes

are focused more on the self, creates excessive tension and may be a motivation for violence. When aggression occurs more than once, it may be not so much an expression of how one partner feels as an instrument to get what he or she wants. In such cases the aggression may be deliberate. If the conduct is not challenged, it may quickly enter one's repertoire of behavior as a means to one's own ends. The more time spent with a partner, the greater the likelihood that he or she will be severely hurt. Spending more time with each other may mean a greater likelihood that more sensitive issues will emerge, thus increasing the possibility of severe aggression (Stets, 1992). Therapeutic intervention is often necessary in helping women get out of violent dating relationships (Rosen and Stith, 1993).

BREAKING UP A RELATIONSHIP

Breaking up a relationship can be very painful, especially if the breakup is unilateral, with only one person wanting to end the affair. Contrary to popular belief, however, women more often break off relationships than do men—perhaps because men fall in love more readily than do women (Baumeister, Wotman, and Stillwell, 1993). Men are also more likely to report that they feel depressed, lonely, unhappy, and less free than are women who have broken up. Apparently, the women take a practical approach to the situation. They cannot allow themselves to fall in love too quickly, nor can they afford to stay in a relationship with the wrong person. After carefully evaluating their partner's strengths and weaknesses and comparing them to other potential partners, they make a decision about whether to continue the relationship.

Although not all breakups follow the same course, researchers have developed several theories and models of relationship dissolution. One such model is the process theory of relationship trajectories (Baxter, 1984), which outlines a series of relationship decisions and their possible outcomes. The various courses that the relationship may follow are based on six crucial factors: (1) gradual versus sudden onset of problems, (2) unilateral (one partner's) versus bilateral (both partners') desire to end the relationship, (3) use of direct versus indirect methods to dissolve the relationship, (4) rapid versus protracted disengagement negotiations, (5) the presence versus the absence of attempts to resolve the issues surrounding the breakup, and (6) relationship termination versus relationship survival as the final outcome (Baxter, 1984). The decisions made at each of these intervals will determine the relationship dissolution trajectory.

Another breakup model is based on social exchange theory. The premise of this model is that a relationship will be dissolved when the rewards of staying in the relationship no longer outweigh the costs (Kelley and Thibaut, 1978; Levinger, 1979). The variables used to make this determination are people's personal expectations for and feelings about the current relationship and the value they place on the costs and rewards of alternatives to the relationship (Kelley and Thibaut, 1978). Thus, if someone believes that he or she is receiving more from the relationship than any alternatives might offer, the tendency will be toward reconciliation. But if the current relationship seems to offer less than the alternatives, the tendency will be toward dissolution.

Some theories on relationship dissolution describe a sequential process, suggesting phases of a breakup. One such model involves four phases: the intrapsychic, the dyadic, the social, and the grave-dressing (Duck, 1982). In the intrapsychic phase, each partner privately assesses his or her satisfaction with the relationship and the possible alternatives should the relationship be dissolved. The next phase, the dyadic, begins when the thoughts of dissolution become public; this phase features both attempts at relationship repair and dissolution behaviors. The social phase occurs when the couple reach the decision to break up and begin to accept the societal response. Finally, the grave-dressing phase is characterized by each individual's analysis of what went wrong and eventual recovery (Duck, 1982).

Another sequential process theory is the cascade model for breaking up (Gottman and Levenson, 1992). The elements in this process are the behaviors individuals display when dissolving a close relationship. This process is initiated when one partner begins to complain about and criticize the other partner, resulting in mutual feelings of contempt. As these feelings intensify, first the partner being criticized becomes defensive, and then both partners react defensively; eventually, one part-

ner, usually the male, stonewalls, or avoids interaction. These four phases of this cascade model—complaints/criticism, contempt, defensiveness, and stonewalling—have been referred to as the Four Horsemen of the Apocalypse (Gottman, 1994).

Based on the hypothesis that such relationship dissolution models could indicate a cultural script for breakups, a study was conducted involving 80 undergraduate students who completed questionnaires (Battaglia, Datteri, and Lord, 1998). The resulting information was compiled to create an ordered script that traced the cyclical process of breaking up (Battaglia et al., 1998). The repetition of certain behaviors in this cycle, whose steps are listed in Table 5.5, is characteristic of an approach-avoidance pattern in conflict resolution (Miller, 1944). The script illustrates the tendency for individuals to sway back and forth when attempting to make relationship dissolution decisions. Breaking up is most commonly achieved after the individuals in the relationship repeatedly approach and avoid reconciliation with their partner (Miller, 1944).

Breaking up a relationship—and perhaps making someone you care for unhappy or perhaps angry—can be very uncomfortable. The best way to minimize the pain is through mutual discussion rather than unilateral action, which is the course many are tempted to take. Following are some guidelines to consider when you are thinking of breaking up a relationship:

1. Think very clearly about why you want to end the relationship; weigh the pros and cons very carefully before you make your decision.

2. If you want to maintain the relationship but are troubled by unresolved issues, consider counseling to see if the problems can be resolved before you make the final decision.

3. Discuss your feelings and doubts with your partner as truthfully and tactfully as possible, without putting blame on him or her. The other person deserves to know why you want to end the relationship. Try to arrive at a mutual decision rather than make a unilateral decision that you force the other person to accept.

4. Don't hesitate to bring up the subject of breaking up for fear of hurting the other person. Fear of hurting your partner is no reason to continue an unsatisfactory relationship. It is even possible

Table 5.5   An Ordered Script for Relationship Dissolution
1. Display a lack of interest.
2. Notice other people.
3. Act distant.
4. Try to work things out.
5. Maintain physical distance and use avoidance behaviors.
6. Display a lack of interest.
7. Consider breaking up.
8. Communicate feelings.
9. Try to work things out.
10. Notice other people.
11. Act distant.
12. Date other people.
13. Get back together.
14. Consider breaking up.
15. Move on or recover.
16. Break up.

that your partner will be relieved that you brought up the subject.

5. Break off cleanly; don't try to maintain an on-again, off-again relationship. It merely makes the pain worse. Get back together only if you have obtained counseling and have resolved your problems.

If your partner has unilaterally decided to break off the relationship, you have every right to feel hurt and angry, but you must also get on with your life. The following guidelines may be helpful when your partner announces that he or she wants out of the relationship:

1. Listen carefully and find out why. Accept your partner's feelings even if you don't feel the same way.

2. Don't try to force the continuation of a relationship that your partner doesn't want.

3. Recognize that it takes time to get over some relationships but that time will help the healing process. Get counseling, join a support group, and become involved with other activities, work, and other people as soon as possible. But don't get involved in another serious relationship right away. Wait until you have recovered from the breakup.

4. Don't do anything extreme such as threatening or considering suicide. Your own life is more important and valuable than any relationship. You *will* feel better in time.

SUMMARY

1. Dating as we know it is rare in most of the world. It did not become firmly established in the United States until after World War I. In colonial America, casual meetings were not possible. If a young man wanted to court a woman, he had to meet her family, be formally introduced, and obtain permission to court her.

2. By the late nineteenth and early twentieth centuries, chaperonage and close supervision of courtship had declined. Young people arranged their own get-togethers, and the man was expected to take the leadership role in dating.

3. Dating emerged for a number of reasons: the industrial revolution, the rise of public high schools, increased affluence and leisure time,

the invention of the automobile, and the women's equality movement.

4. Waller described the "rating and dating complex" that existed on university campuses during the 1930s. The most important dating pattern to develop prior to World War II was going steady. In the 1950s, dating and courtship usually followed an orderly progression through six stages—from group dating to marriage.

5. Dating patterns today differ from those of previous generations. Dating has become more casual, there are increased opportunities for informal sexual contacts, and there isn't any set pattern of progression in courtship.

6. Dating fulfills a number of important functions: recreation; companionship, friendship, and personal intimacy; socialization; personality development; the opportunity to try out gender roles; a source of love and affection; the opportunity for sex; mate sorting and selection; and preparation for marriage.

7. Dating does not adequately serve its function of sorting out marital partners if the qualities desired in dating partners are different from those preferred in marital partners.

8. Youths meet prospective dates through a friend, at parties, at work, in classes, and through other means. Bars, personal ads, dating services, and computer networks also bring people together.

9. Gender roles in dating are changing, with females more frequently asking for dates and planning and paying for them. But men still take the initiative more often.

10. From one point of view, the courtship system in the United States is patriarchal, with the male controlling the situation and the female playing a submissive role, including acquiescence to the male's sexual aggression.

11. From another point of view, it is the female who controls the dating situation, since she has greater control over love, with the male dependent on her.

12. Large numbers of youths have dating anxiety. Some common problems experienced by women in dating are unwanted pressure to engage in sexual behavior, decisions about where to go and what to do on dates, communication, sexual misunderstandings, and money. The problems most frequently mentioned by men are communication, decisions about where to go and what to do, shyness, money, and honesty/openness.

13. Other dating problems include extradyadic relationships and one partner getting too serious.

14. Closeness and distance are important issues in dating relationships and are related to the attachment styles people develop early in life. Individuals who are secure prefer a balanced type of relationship, characterized by high levels of openness and closeness, and also a certain degree of autonomy. Individuals who are highly anxious about their relationships typically seek extreme closeness to partners and become overdependent on them. Avoidant individuals want the most distance in their relationships and so limit closeness, dependence, and affection.

15. The primary dating problem females have is unwanted pressure to engage in sexual activities, but some men are also victims of unwanted sexual activity. There are considerable differences among men in their willingness to use verbal coercion to obtain sex.

16. Date rape is involuntary sexual intercourse forced on someone by a dating partner. Many young people and adults don't know how to cope with unwanted sexual aggression. Many date rapes are never reported.

17. Dating violence may be carried over into marriage. A number of factors correlate positively or negatively with dating violence: violence in one's family of origin, race, religion, socioeconomic status, family background, academic achievement, work record, use of alcohol, life events stress, personality traits, and level of emotional commitment in the relationship.

18. Violence in dating tends to progress from verbal aggression to physical aggression unless it is stopped by one of the partners.

19. Breaking up a relationship is always painful. If you're initiating the breakup, the best way to minimize the pain is to discuss your feelings as truthfully and tactfully as possible with the other person. If your partner has initiated the breakup, the best thing to do is to accept his or her feelings and get on with your life.

KEY TERMS

dating

bundling

steady dating

imaging

extradyadic sexual activity

rape

date rape

QUESTIONS FOR THOUGHT

1. Compare dating and courtship patterns today with those of the 1940s and 1960s. Which pattern do you prefer, and why?

2. What do you think of the current dating system as a means of sorting and choosing compatible mates? How could the system be improved?

3. What are the best ways of meeting new people as potential dates? Explain.

4. What are the principal problems you have experienced in dating? Explain. What could be done about those problems?

5. Research has suggested that one of the principal dating problems women experience is unwanted sexual aggression. Look at this from the man's point of view: Why does this happen, and what should he and the woman do about it? Look at this from the woman's point of view: Why does this happen, and what should she and the man do about it?

SUGGESTED READINGS

Andreae, S. (1998). *Anatomy of Desire: The Science and Psychology of Sex, Love, and Marriage.* London: Abacus. Takes a contemporary and scientific look at intimate relationships.

Cate, R. M., and Lloyd, S. A. (1992). *Courtship.* Newbury Park, CA: Sage. Provides a historical sketch of courtship and an overview of courtship today, including sexual and physical expression.

Duck, S. (1991). *Understanding Relationships.* New York: Guilford Press. Reviews sociological, psychological, and communication research to demonstrate how relationships work.

Fisher, H. E. (1994). *Anatomy of Love: A Natural History of Mating, Marriage, and Why We Stray.* New York: Ballantine Books. Discusses the history of romance, new explanations for why men and women fall in love, and the future of sexual behavior.

Kingma, D. R. (2000). *Coming Apart: Why Relationships End and How to Live Through the Ending of Yours.* Berkeley, CA: Conari Press. Offers guidelines for breaking up without guilt and taking the next step in one's personal development.

Kirkwood, C. (1993). *Leaving Abusive Partners.* Newbury Park, CA: Sage. Gives voice to 30 formerly abused women.

Pirog-Good, M. A., and Stets, J. E. (Eds.). (1989). *Violence in Dating Relationships.* New York: Praeger. Examines physical abuse and sexual abuse in dating relationships.

Rutherford, J. (1999). *I Am No Longer Myself Without You: An Anatomy of Love.* London: Flamingo. Discusses love from a psychological perspective.

Whyte, M. D. (1990). *Dating, Mating, and Marriage.* New York: Aldine de Gruyter. Discusses the institutions of dating, mate choice, and marriage over time.

Attraction and Love

Learning Objectives

Attraction

Physical Attractiveness

Standards of Attractiveness

Perspective: Women and Weight: Gendered Messages on Magazine Covers

Perspective: What Physical Features Are Most Attracting?

Personality and Social Factors

Unconscious Influences

What Is Love?

Romantic Love

Is Romantic Love a Sound Basis for Marriage?

Perspective: Love and Attachment

Erotic Love

Are Love and Sex the Same?

Sex as an Expression of Love

Dependent Love

Maslow's Theory of Love as Need

Friendship Love

Loving and Liking

Altruistic Love

Fromm's View of Altruistic Love

Components of Love

Research on the Components of Love

Perspective: Achieving and Maintaining Psychological Intimacy

Perspective: Lee's Love Styles

Changes over Time

Summary

Key Terms

Questions for Thought

Suggested Readings

In this chapter, we are concerned with two major subjects: attraction and love. First, what attracts us to others, and what qualities do men and women find attractive in one another? Second, what is love, how do you know if you're in love, and how important is it in interpersonal relationships? Can love be a reliable guide in mate selection? These are some of the questions that have fascinated social scientists. We now have some of the answers—not all of them, to be sure, but enough to shed considerable light on the subject of interpersonal attraction and love and their role in relationships.

ATTRACTION

The most obvious kind of attraction is physical; our first impression is based on how someone looks. But attraction, especially if the relationship is a lasting one, is also based on the less tangible factors of personality traits and even one's own past experiences and conditioning.

Physical Attractiveness

The most important element in attraction—at least in initial encounters—is physical attractiveness. We are attracted to those who are pleasing to look at, have good builds and well-proportioned bodies, and display other physical characteristics that appeal to our aesthetic sensibilities. Study after study finds physical appearance to be one of the chief ingredients in early attraction. In fact, one study of college students revealed that physical attractiveness was more important than relevant sexual history in making judgments about potential risks and probable future sexual activity with the person. This was especially true for males (Agocha and Cooper, 1999).

There is also something called "couple attractiveness," which is the perception other people have of the couple and the quality of their relationship (Garcia and Khersonsky, 1997). Couples whose members differ in physical attractiveness are perceived differently. A currently dating opposite-sex couple in which both the man and the woman are physically attractive or in which the woman is attractive but the man is unattractive are perceived more favorably than are unattractive male/unattractive female couples and attractive male/unattractive female cou-

ples. They are also perceived as more satisfied with their current relationship than the others and as less likely to break up. In short, couples in which both members are physically attractive and in which the woman is attractive and the man is not are viewed as the most stable and happiest (Garcia and Khersonsky, 1997).

Standards of Attractiveness

Standards of attractiveness are culturally conditioned. In our culture, slender women are considered more attractive than obese ones, tall men more attractive than short ones, and youthful men and women more attractive than the elderly. In contrast, in some Arab cultures, obesity is synonymous with physical beauty.

The standards of beauty by which Miss America contestants are judged have changed over the years.

Women and Weight: Gendered Messages on Magazine Covers

Media messages regarding bodily appearance are very different for men and for women. There has been a strong emphasis on women being slim and beautiful, but that same standard does not apply to men. Malkin, Wornian, and Chrisler (1999) analyzed the covers of several issues of 21 popular women's and men's magazines for gendered messages related to bodily appearance. The cover is the primary sales tool of the magazine and must be provocative, hard-hitting, and full of elements that people are interested in ("Make the Cover," 1998). Magazine covers were categorized according to the targeted readership, and each cover was analyzed in terms of visual images and text. The researchers examined 69 covers of women's magazines and 54 covers of men's magazines.

For the 12 magazines most frequently read by women, 54 of the 69 covers (78%) contained some message about bodily appearance, whereas none of the 53 covers of the men's magazines contained such messages. And whereas the majority of the most popular women's magazines focused on how women could improve themselves by changing their appearance, especially by losing weight, the popular men's magazines focused on news, politics, hobbies, sports, entertainment, activities, and ways to expand knowledge.

When the researchers examined the covers of women's magazines, they found that 94% showed a slender female in excellent shape, whereas only about 3% showed a male on the cover. When they examined the covers of men's magazines, they found that 28% showed a male model or celebrity, whereas almost 50% showed a slim young woman wearing revealing clothing. Apparently, visual images on both men's and women's magazine covers send messages about what women should look like and what men should look for (Malkin et al., 1999).

Perhaps most alarming, noted the researchers, was the position of weight-related messages in relation to other messages on the magazine covers. By their placement of message, magazines seem to suggest that losing weight or changing the shape of one's body will lead to a better life. For example, messages such as "Get the Body You Want" placed next to "How to Get Your Husband to Really Listen" and "Lose 10 Pounds" placed next to "Ways to Make Your Life Easier, Happier, and Better" imply that by changing their appearance people will be happier, sexier, and more lovable.

Furthermore, in our own culture, standards of beauty change over time. For example, the mean bust-waist-hip measurements of Miss America contest winners in the 1920s were 32-25-35, with no winner having a larger bust than hips. In the 1940s, the mean measurements were 35-24-35, with nearly half the winners having a larger bust than hips. In this same era, Hollywood introduced the "sweater girl" Lana Turner and the buxom Jane Russell. Since 1950, the norm has been bust-hip symmetry, with an ideal measurement of 36-24-36.

As the 1950s progressed, the women featured as *Playboy* magazine's "Playmate of the Month" had increasingly larger breasts. This was a period of "mammary madness," with Hollywood and the fashion industry promoting large, cleaved bustlines, tiny waists, and wiggly-hipped walks (Mazur, 1986). Since that time, Playmates have become increasingly taller and leaner, but they still have large breasts in proportion to body size. At the same time, the idealized women shown in fashion magazines and on television often are far below the normal weight recommendations, bordering on the anorexic (Mann, 1994). It is interesting to note that

Miss America contestants work out an average of 14 hours a week, and some as many as 35 hours a week, in order to achieve the current body ideal (Wilfley and Rodin, 1995). Thus, in the 1990s, the body size and shape of the average young adult became increasingly different from the underweight ideal being promoted by the media (Spitzer, Henderson, and Zivian, 1999).

Unfortunately, these standards of attractiveness do not make life easier for the average person. It is no wonder that the current standards of attractiveness for women promoted by the media lead women to rate their bodies negatively (Hamilton and Waller, 1993). Studies have reported body dissatisfaction greater than 60 percent for high school girls (Garner, 1997) and greater than 80 percent for college women (Silberstein, Striegel-Moore, Timko, and Rodin, 1998). A large percentage of younger women feel that they are too heavy and are trying to lose weight even when their weight is within, or even below, the range that is considered healthy (Green et al., 1997). One of the most pervasive criticisms of advertising is that it promotes distorted body images by setting unrealistic standards of

What Physical Features Are Most Attracting?

The Roper Center asked 600 people, "When you are admiring physical appearance, what physical features attract you the most?" Figure 6.1 shows the results for men and women. When admiring a woman, men were most attracted to the face, followed by the legs and the breasts. When admiring a man, women were most attracted to the eyes, followed by the face and the build. As this survey reveals, the face is very important in physical attractiveness, and particularly the eyes for women. However, some men and women reported figure or build as most important, which suggests that there are variations in standards of attractiveness.

Figure 6.1 When You Are Admiring a Person's Physical Appearance, What Physical Feature Attracts You the Most? (*Note:* From Roper Center at University of Connecticut, Public Opinion Online, Copyright 1995. Organization conducting survey: Princeton Survey Research Associates, February 21–24, 1991. Reprinted with permission of the Roper Center.)

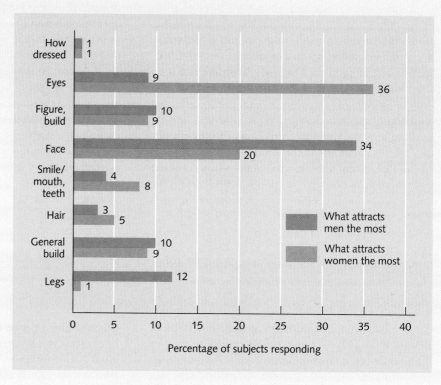

thinness and female beauty (Lavine, Sweeney, and Wagner, 1999), which only increases women's insecurities about and dissatisfaction with their bodies.

Personality and Social Factors

Factors other than physical appearance attract people to each other. In a study of mate selection standards, Regan (1998) found that women required higher levels of agreeableness (attentiveness to a partner's needs, kindness and understanding, honesty and trustworthiness) in a marriage partner than any other attribute, and they rated dominance as the least important trait. In a study of desired characteristics in a spouse, Regan and Berscheid (1997) found that women desired honesty, trustworthiness, and sensitivity above all other characteristics. However, they preferred a different characteristic—namely, physical attractiveness—for short-term and sexual partners (Regan, 1998; Regan and Berscheid, 1997). In contrast, some researchers have reported that women prefer dominant males characterized by high levels of assertiveness and confidence and high financial and social status. For example, Buss and Schmitt (1993) concluded that a man's ability to accrue resources was related to women's desire for either a short- or a long-term relationship. Ambition, industry, income, and status were all considered observable cues to a mate's potential value. Similarly, Botwin, Buss, and Shackelford (1997) reported that power, social ascendance, and resource acquisition were more prevalent in women's preferences for potential mates than in men's preferences. There is a discrepancy in the research findings, however. So-called nice guys, who are sensitive, patient, and nurturing, appear to be favored by many women, but men who are dominant, confident, and aggressive have reported the most sexual success with women (Reise and Wright, 1996).

Other studies have confirmed that personality traits and the way people act are significant factors in whether others find them attractive. In general, people who are warm, kind, gregarious, intelligent, interesting, poised, confident, or humorous or who exhibit generally admired qualities are more attractive than those who are rude, insecure, clumsy, insensitive, unstable, or irresponsible or who manifest other negative traits.

Unconscious Influences

Sometimes people are not aware of why they find another person attractive. Unconscious factors are often at work. If, for example, we experienced love and security with our opposite-sex parent while we were growing up, we may seek to duplicate the relationship and so be attracted to a dating partner or spouse who reminds us of that parent. Or we may be attracted to those who meet our needs and who make us feel good about ourselves. Some people are attracted to those who are helpless, alone, handicapped, or dependent; taking care of someone else makes them feel needed, important, and wanted. Other people are attracted to their "ego ideal," to someone who has all the qualities they wish they had. A smile, a glance, or a mannerism may trigger a positive response because of conditioning that took place years before. We'll look at other factors related to attraction in the discussion of love that follows. Figure 6.2 shows the results of one poll on the possibility of love at first sight.

WHAT IS LOVE?

Each person defines love according to his or her background and experiences. One person may describe love in terms of emotions and strong feelings. Another may describe it as a biological attraction or as a way of acting toward and treating others. Another may frame love in terms of liking and friendship or in terms of care or concern for someone else.

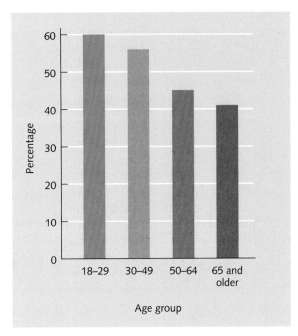

Figure 6.2   Percentage of Adults Who Believe in Love at First Sight, by Age, 1999 (*Note:* From *USA Today*, February 14, 2000.)

Still another may say that there is no such thing as love, that it is just a myth or a delusion.

In fact, there are many different definitions of love. Although, in a sense, love is what each person thinks it is, this subjective view is not always helpful. It leads to misunderstandings between two people who say they love each other but have entirely different concepts of what they mean. When we talk about love, therefore, we need to know what kind of love we mean. The point of view reflected here is that love is not a single concept but has different dimensions. Let's start with a five-dimensional view of love: romantic love, erotic love, dependent love, friendship love, and altruistic love.

ROMANTIC LOVE

Romantic love has been defined as a profoundly tender or passionate affection for another person. Its chief characteristic is strong emotion, marked by intensity of feelings. A glance, a smile, a brushing of the hand of one's beloved may arouse powerful feelings of warmth and affection. Individuals in romantic love report that they become "alive again" and start "to really feel for the first time in years." If the love is mutual and fulfilling, there is a strong sense of joy, exhilaration, and well-being.

Romantic lovers have a strong desire to be together so that they can continue to enjoy the pleasure of love. When apart, these lovers can become obsessed with thoughts of each other. It is also common for romantic love to result in physiological changes and manifestations: palpitations of the heart, a quickening pulse, breathlessness, trembling, a tightness in the chest, or halting speech. Loss of love can be so upsetting that the person can't eat or sleep. The literary portrayal of a debilitated and unhappy person as someone suffering from unrequited or lost love has some basis in fact.

The primary component of romantic love is strong emotion, but current research has indicated that a host of negative emotions, including anxiety and fear, may also be related to increased romantic love. Thus, romantic love appears to be derived from both positive and negative emotions, just as sexual desire may be enhanced by feelings of both intimacy and fear. An extradyadic sexual affair can add excitement to a relationship and may increase the feelings of romantic love (Roberts, 1992).

There is also a strong feeling of sexual attraction and a desire for physical contact in romantic love. In such a state of passion, romantic love is sometimes accompanied by idealization and adoration whereby the lovers focus on those physical traits and qualities of character that embody their ideal of womanhood or manhood. Theodore Reik (1957) theorized that individuals fall in love with people who manifest the characteristics of their ego ideal, and they project these characteristics onto the other person. This is **narcissistic love** in that it really represents love of the self, as reflected in the other person.

But romantic love can also involve altruism and unselfishness, with the lovers filled with feelings of generosity and wanting to shower each other with gifts. The sense of devotion and willingness to serve and to sacrifice is often astounding. Along with this desire to give up much for the sake of love comes a renewed feeling of self-confidence that one is beautiful and capable and can do the impossible.

These feelings have been substantiated by Dorothy Tennov (1979). She found that when the passion is strong the relationship eclipses all else. The lovers are in a wildly emotional state, seesawing between bliss and despair. They are obsessed with their loved one: When their loved one responds, they walk on air; when there is no response, they are crushed. Tennov labeled these feelings **limerence.** She reported that people can be this passionately involved with only one person at a time. For a while at least, the lovers may be completely out of control, and the emotional ups and downs can interfere with their work, study, sleep, and peace of mind.

Is Romantic Love a Sound Basis for Marriage?

An interesting issue regarding romantic love is whether it is a sound basis for marriage. There is no question that romanticism plays a significant role in attraction and the decision to marry. Romanticism brings individuals into serious sexual associations that may eventually lead to marriage. In this sense, romantic love is very functional.

However, if romantic love is taken as the only criterion for marriage, love can become very problematic. People can fall romantically in love with individuals who are completely unsuitable prospective mates and who will make their lives miserable. Having romantic feelings is not an accurate indication of suitability for marriage.

The idealism of romantic love is functional if it approaches reality. Strong, Wilson, Robbins, and Johns (1981) called rational love **conscious love.** They wrote, "When we love someone consciously, we are aware of who that person really is. We do not relate to their image, but to their reality" (p. 201). Romantic love becomes problematic if it blinds us to reality.

In addition, passion, which fuels romantic love, generally fades over time and is a function of a rapid increase in intimacy, which cannot be sustained over the lifetime of a marriage (Baumeister and Bratslavsky, 1999). Sharing new experiences, finding out that the other person cares for one deeply, and learning new things about the other person can all increase passion. In contrast, when people reach a point at which they understand each other completely, know all there is to know about each other, and do not share new experiences together, passion fades. Thus, partners in long-term

Several investigators have made significant breakthroughs in the development of a theory of romantic love. First, attachment theory, originally used to explain an infant's bonding with a parent, has been applied to the formation and maintenance of attachment bonds in adult love relationships. For example, the three styles of infant attachment—secure, anxious/ambivalent, and avoidant—have been applied to romantic relationships. The reaction of children to others is similar to the dynamics of romantic love in that they appear to experience both ecstasy and misery in response to closeness and distance, respectively. Changes in romantic love over time appear to be similar to the process of maintaining a secure attachment in a child when the child begins to take the parent for granted.

Support for attachment theory is found in research on romantic love. For example, people with lasting relationships tend to be secure, those who fall in love often tend to be anxious/ambivalent, and those doubtful of the existence of romantic love tend to be avoidant. In addition, love histories are different for individuals depending on whether they are secure, anxious/ambivalent, or avoidant. Secure individuals view their mothers as dependable; anxious individuals remember them in both positive and negative ways; and avoidant individuals remember them as domineering and cold (Roberts, 1992).

relationships may have to deal with decreased passion even when intimacy and commitment remain high (Baumeister and Bratslavsky, 1999).

Schachter and Singer (1962) developed a two-component theory of human emotional response. They suggested that, for a person to experience true emotion, two factors must coexist: (1) The individual must be physiologically aroused, and (2) the arousal must be interpreted as a particular emotion. Berscheid and Walster (1974) applied Schachter and Singer's theory to romantic love. They suggested that it does not really matter *how* someone produces an agitated state in an individual. Stimuli that cause sexual arousal, gratitude, anxiety, guilt, loneliness, hatred, jealousy, or confusion may increase one's physiological arousal and thus the intensity of emotional experience. As long as the person attributes the agitated state to passion, passionate love exists.

Emotional arousal, even from a frightening source, facilitates attraction. Perhaps this is why lovers who meet under dangerous conditions or who risk discovery experience greater excitement and passion than those who meet under more secure conditions. Perhaps this is why forbidden or secret love can be so intense.

The fear-breeds-passion principle was documented in research in Vancouver, British Columbia. Dutton and Aron (1974) conducted their experiment on two footbridges that cross the Capilano River. One bridge was a narrow, shaky walkway that swayed in the wind 230 feet above the stream. The other was a solid structure only 10 feet above

the water. Near the end of each bridge, an attractive female experimenter approached men who were crossing and asked if they would take part in an experiment on "the effects of exposure to scenic attractions on creative expression." They were asked to write down their associations to a picture she showed them. That the men on the narrow suspension bridge were more sexually aroused than the men on the low, solid bridge was inferred from the amount of sexual imagery in their associations. The men on the suspension bridge also were more likely to call the researcher afterward "to get more information about the study."

Romantic love is influenced not only by negative emotions but by positive ones as well. Sexual arousal produces intense physiological changes in the body, and these changes facilitate attraction. For example, in looking at photographs of different women, men will tend to label as most attractive seminude women who arouse them sexually; if there is no arousal, the women will be seen as less attractive.

There have been efforts to show the relationship between specific changes in the autonomic nervous system and various types of emotions (Ekman, Levenson, and Friesen, 1983). Liebowitz (1983) stated that the excitement and arousal of romantic love are a result of increased levels of **dopamine** and **norepinephrine** in the bloodstream. These neurotransmitters are activated by visual cues (by observing an attractive nude, for example), and they then bathe the pleasure center of the brain in a sea of chemical messages. Liebowitz also argued that romantic love stimulates the secretion of a chemical

123

called **serotonin,** which can produce a feeling of intense pleasure. **Companionate love,** however, defined by Walster and Walster (1978) as "a more low-key emotion with feelings of friendly affection and deep attachment," results in the brain producing narcoticlike substances called **endorphins,** which give a sense of tranquility.

These timeless studies emphasize the importance of emotional excitement as a component of attraction and of romantic love. The more positive excitement a relationship generates, the more likely the participants are to report that they are in love. However, since intense emotional arousal and excitement cannot be sustained, love that is to endure in a marriage must include components other than emotional excitement.

EROTIC LOVE

Erotic love is sensual love. This type of love can be defined as sexual attraction to another person. It is the biological, sensual component of love relationships. What is the relationship between love and sex?

Are Love and Sex the Same?

According to Sigmund Freud, love and sex are really one and the same thing. Freud (1953) defined love as "aim inhibited sex," as a yearning for a "love object"—for another person who could meet one's own sexual needs. Love, to Freud, was narcissistic in that it was measured by the extent to which the love object could satisfy someone's sexual aims.

Freud emphasized two important elements of the sexual aims of adults. One element is physical and sensual. In both men and women, this element consists of the desire for physical pleasure such as the release of sexual tension through orgasm.

The second element of the sexual aims in adults is psychical; it is the affectionate component—the desire for emotional satisfaction. Freud emphasized that a normal sexual life is assured when there is a convergence of the affectionate and sensual components. The desire for true affection and the desire for the release of sexual tension are the needs that motivate individuals to seek love objects. Freud (1953) also claimed that, once an appropriate love object was found, sexual strivings diminished. In

turn, diminished yearnings resulted in a search for only one love object at a time.

While Freud emphasized that love and sex are the same thing, other writers would say that love and sex are two separate entities, that they are not identical, and that a distinction must be made between them. Reik (1957) argued that love and sex are different in origin and nature. Sex, according to Reik, is a biological function whose aim is the release of physical tension. Love stems from psychic needs and provides affection and emotional satisfaction. More recent research indicates only a low correlation between sexual desire and love. This means that many individuals tend to separate the two things—that they can be in love without having sexual desire or they can have sexual desire without being in love (Beck, Bozman, and Qualtrough, 1991).

Still other writers have suggested that romantic love arises when sexual expression is denied. This "sexual blockage" theory emphasizes that romantic love is felt most strongly for those who play "hard to get." Once sexual involvement begins, romantic love declines.

A much more common manifestation of the separation of love and sex today is casual sex. This is sex for its own sake, because it is pleasurable and fun, without the necessity of love and commitment. As one student remarked, "What's wrong with just enjoying one another's bodies? Do people have to be in love to do that?" Commonly cited motives for casual sex are sexual desire, spontaneous urges, interest in sexual exploration and experimentation, and use of alcohol or drugs (Regan and Dreyer, 1999). In general, men and women have similar motives for engaging in short-term sexual relationships, which challenges the idea that sexual desire is an inherent aspect of the male but not the female experience (Regan and Dreyer, 1999). However, more women than men reported having entered a casual sexual encounter to increase their chances of obtaining a long-term commitment from the sex partner. Even though sex is a popular form of adult play, with the rise of STDs, casual sex can be potentially hazardous.

Sex as an Expression of Love

Many couples can't separate sex from all other aspects of their relationship, at least in the long term. One woman summed up her feelings:

Is physical attraction more than skin deep? Freud defined love as "a yearning for a 'love object.'" It's possible that, for some, the appearance of one of these men satisfies Freud's definition of a love object, although another of these friends might satisfy that definition for someone else.

I like sex a lot. But it can only supplement a warm, affectionate, mutually respecting, full personhood relationship. It can't be a relationship. It can't prove love. It can't prove anything. I have found sex with people I don't really like, or who I'm not certain will really like me, or with people I don't feel I know well, to be very shallow and uncomfortable and physically unsatisfying. I don't believe you have to be "in love" and married "till death do us part." But mind and body are one organism and all tied up together, and it isn't even physically fun unless the people involved really like each other. (Hite, 1981, p. 48)

In modern Western society, there has been considerable fusion between love and sex (Weis, Slosnerick, Cate, and Sollie, 1986). Some maintain that love increases the pleasure of sex and that erotic pleasure is reduced when love is at a minimum. Sex can be important as a confirmation of the love relationship; it says to the other person, "I love you." In this view, sex can be both a physical and an emotional expression of deep feeling. But many adults disagree completely with this point of view, arguing that it simply is not true that sexual pleasure is less when the partners do not love each other. Whichever view an individual holds, many people want sex with affection, not without it, and insist that love and sex should go together.

DEPENDENT LOVE

One of the components of a durable love is dependency. **Dependent love** develops when someone's needs are fulfilled by another person. In its simplest form, it works like this: "I have important needs. You fulfill those needs; therefore, I love you." This is the type of love the dependent child feels for the mother who feeds, clothes, and cares for him or her: "You give me my bottle; you keep me warm; you hold me, cuddle me, and talk to me. That's why I love you."

But it is also the kind of love that develops when the intense psychological needs of adults that have been denied in the past are now fulfilled by a lover. For example, a lover who has a strong need for approval may be getting that need met through a partner who is full of compliments and praise.

Maslow's Theory of Love as Need

Abraham Maslow (1970) is one of the chief exponents of love as dependency and need fulfillment. According to him, human needs may be arranged in a hierarchy, ascending from physiological to psychological, as shown in Figure 6.3.

Maslow referred to the first four levels of need as D-needs, or Deficiency-needs, and to the last three levels as B-needs, or Being-needs. He emphasized that the needs at each level must be met before a person can move up to the next level. An individual develops "Deficiency-love" for a person who meets D-needs and "Being-love" for the person who fulfills B-needs.

Maslow emphasized that in marriage **D-love** refers to all forms of self-centered love whereby two people love each other because the needs of each are met by the other. It is a sort of bookkeeping arrangement, with the man meeting certain needs of the woman even as she meets certain needs of his, and vice versa. Since the focus of attention is on the fulfillment of self and personal needs, D-love may be fragmented. For example, a woman may enjoy her spouse as a sexual partner because he meets her

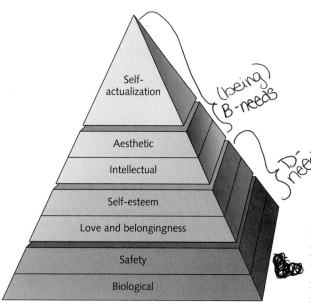

Figure 6.3 Maslow's Hierarchy of Needs *(Note:* From *Motivation and Personality,* 2nd ed., by A. Maslow, 1970, New York: Harper & Row.)

biological and emotional needs but dislike him in some other ways because of his sense of values.

This fragmentation cannot happen in **B-love,** because it is love for the very existence and uniqueness of the other person. The sexual impulse is anchored in the deep love of the qualities of one's mate. With this type of love, neither person feels insecure and threatened, because each feels accepted by the other and is comfortable in the other's presence. The love is not conditioned by the extent to which the other person fills one's needs. It is not possessive, nor is it motivated by any desire to fulfill some personal need or some selfish aim. It is unconditional and offers the kind of relationship in which each person can develop the best that is in him or her.

It is important that need fulfillment be mutual and that partners strive to meet each other's D-needs. This assumes the needs are reasonable and capable of fulfillment. However, difficulty can arise if an individual's D-needs were not met while growing up; he or she may become possessive, domineering, and overly dependent and manipulate the other person only for self-satisfaction. In such a situation, self-actualization and B-love are impossible. There is no room for growth, freedom, and fulfillment, because the partner is only being used. One woman explained:

My husband says that if I really loved him, I would want to be together with him all the time. He didn't want me to go to work (we don't have any children), but I did anyhow. He calls me several times during the day to talk to me. I'd like to go to lunch with the girls once in a while, but he insists on having lunch with me every day. When we're home, he follows me around the house. I can't even go to the bathroom without his following me. If I don't feel like sex, he feels hurt, starts to pout, and starts drinking beer. Sometimes he'll drink the whole weekend because I turned him down (I do so very seldom, however).

In a counseling session, the husband revealed that he had felt very rejected and unloved by his mother when he was growing up, that she was never home for him. Unconsciously, he expected his wife to make up for all the love he had never received as a child. His demands were unreasonable, and the more he expected, the more she came to resent and shun him (author's counseling notes).

If, however, D-needs have been met as one is growing up, the individual does not need to strive for their fulfillment and thus can show an active concern for the life and growth of the loved one. Maslow (1962) recognized that there is some mixture of D-love and B-love in every relationship (see Figure 6.4).

People differ regarding their need for emotional closeness and distance in their family relationships. If they experience excessive emotional distance, their anxiety increases because of fears of rejection and abandonment. They then attempt to reduce the anxiety by seeking increased togetherness. However, if people experience excessive togetherness in their family, they may become anxious over perceived threats to their autonomy and independence. Anxiety about excessive closeness prompts them to increase the emotional distance from other family members.

Functional, or healthy, families have ample tolerance for normal variations in closeness and distance, and low levels of anxiety are sufficient to return the family to a balance between closeness and distance. In dysfunctional families, however, minor variations in closeness or distance frequently provoke intense anxiety. Moreover, intense anxiety and persistent reliance on anxiety to regulate closeness and distance result in chronic anxiety within the family (Benson, Larson, Wilson, and Demo, 1993).

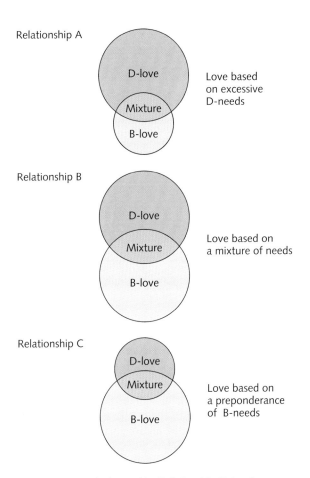

Relationship A
Love based on excessive D-needs

Relationship B
Love based on a mixture of needs

Relationship C
Love based on a preponderance of B-needs

A reciprocal relationship (Relationship B) involves a balanced and mutual give-and-take of D-love and B-love.

Figure 6.4 Degrees of Dominance of D-Love and B-Love in Relationships (*Note:* From *Marriage and Parenthood* [p. 106] by F. P. Rice, 1979, Boston: Allyn & Bacon.)

FRIENDSHIP LOVE

Another important element of love is **friendship love,** similar to what Walster and Walster (1978) call companionate love. This implies a type of love between individuals with common concerns. This type of love may exist between good companions because of similar interests; it may arise out of respect for the personality or character of another. Research has shown that the most comprehensive and profound relationships are between two lovers whose involvement includes friendship. While romance may exist without friendship, love becomes more complete and enduring with it.

There is some evidence to show that loving and liking are separate phenomena and may be measured separately (Davis, 1985). But this research defines love only in romantic terms. Other research emphasizes that as love matures over the years it contains more and more elements of friendship. This means partners grow to like each other. In fact, liking has been called the key to loving. Liking in a relationship brings relaxation in the presence of the beloved; it is a stimulus for two people to want to be with each other. It is friendship in the simplest, most direct terms.

Friendship love is certainly more relaxed and less tense than romantic love. It is less possessive and less emotional, and it affords more security without anxiety. In such a secure environment, partners are free to live, work, and go about their lives supported by their friendship.

ALTRUISTIC LOVE

Altruistic love reflects unselfish concern for the well-being of another. It is the investment of someone's psychic energies and abilities in caring for another individual and in seeking what is best for the other person. By nurturing someone else and doing all one can to make that person happy, the individual finds meaning and satisfaction in his or her own life.

One of the chief exponents of altruistic love was Erich Fromm (1956). Fromm saw love as an activity, not a passive affection; it is a "standing in," not a "falling for." In the most general terms, the active character of love can be described as primarily giving, not receiving. To Fromm, giving did not mean "giving up" something, not being deprived of or sacrificing. Rather, it involved giving of oneself—one's joy, interest, understanding, knowledge, humor, even sadness. Thus, when one gives of one's life, the person one loves is enriched.

In addition to the element of giving, Fromm emphasized <u>four</u> <u>basic</u> <u>components</u> of <u>love</u>: <u>care</u>, <u>responsibility</u>, <u>respect</u>, and <u>knowledge</u>. Fromm used the illustration of a woman who says she loves flowers but forgets to water them; it would be difficult

Research shows that lovers whose involvement includes friendship maintain more enduring relationships.

to believe she really loves her flowers. As Fromm (1956) put it, "Love is the active concern for the life and growth of that which we love" (p. 22). Where concern is lacking, there is no love. Care and concern also imply responsibility, not as a duty imposed from the outside, but as a voluntary act in which one responds to the needs (primarily psychic) of the other person. Love also depends on respect, which involves not fear and awe, but an awareness of the unique individuality of the other person and a concern that he or she grow and unfold as he or she is. Respect is possible only where freedom and independence are granted. It is the opposite of domination. Finally, love also requires knowledge of the other person, in order to see his or her reality and overcome any irrational, distorted image.

The love that Fromm described is an unselfish, caring, giving love. But, ideally, this type of love, like dependent love, should be mutual. If it is not, the relationship will certainly have problems and may not survive.

COMPONENTS OF LOVE

Western culture emphasizes romantic love as the basis for mate selection. Because it is so highly regarded, it cannot be ignored. When based on reality instead of an idealization of the partner, romantic love provides a functional basis for marriage.

Erotic love is an important part of love. Certainly, sexual attraction is an important factor in relationship building, and sexual satisfaction strengthens the bond between two people. Ordinarily, love and sex are interdependent. A loving relationship becomes a firm foundation for a happy sex life, and a fulfilling sexual relationship reinforces the total love of the partners for each other.

Dependent love is an important basis for a strong relationship when it involves mutual dependency. Integration in the relationship takes place to the extent that each person meets the needs of the other. Difficulty arises if the needs of one person are excessive, so that neurotic, possessive dependency becomes the basis for the relationship. Most people need to receive as well as give if they are to remain emotionally healthy. Those who enjoy giving without receiving become either martyrs or masochists.

Friendship love, based on companionship, is an enduring bond between two people who like each other and enjoy each other's company. It can endure over many years. For most people, friendship alone is not enough for marriage, but it is an important ingredient in loving relationships.

Finally, altruistic love adds genuine concern and care to the total relationship. Behavior, rather than feelings, is the active means by which the individual shows care. As in dependent love, giving and receiving must be mutual. Altruistic love allows the person expressing it to gain satisfaction through caring for another. It allows the receiving person to be cared for and loved for his or her own sake.

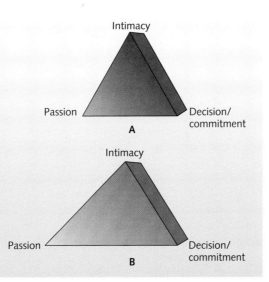

Figure 6.5   The Triangle of Love (*Note:* Adapted from "A Triangular Theory of Love" by R. Sternberg, 1986, *Psychological Review, 93,* pp. 119–135.)

The greater a given component of love, the farther from the center of the triangle. The greater the total love, the greater the area of the triangle. Figure A shows balanced components; Figure B depicts a relationship that has more passion than the other two components.

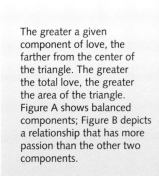

Research on the Components of Love

Research findings support the idea that the most complete love has a number of components. Robert Sternberg (1986) asked subjects to describe their relationships with lovers, parents, siblings, and friends. Analysis of the results revealed three components of close relationships: intimacy, passion, and decision/commitment to maintain the relationships (see Figure 6.5).

Intimacy involves sharing feelings and providing emotional support. It usually involves high levels of self-disclosure through the sharing of personal information not ordinarily revealed because of the risk involved. Intimacy gradually increases as the relationship matures and deepens.

The passion component refers to sexuality, attraction, and romance in a relationship.

The decision/commitment component involves both short- and long-term factors. The short-term factor is the decision, made consciously and unconsciously, to love another person. The long-term factor is the commitment to maintain the love. Sometimes people fall in love but do nothing afterward to maintain it.

Sternberg and Barnes (1988) described eight different combinations of these three components of love:

1. **Absence of intimacy, passion, and commitment**—no love

2. **Intimacy only**—liking (but no passion or commitment)

3. **Passion only**—infatuation (but little intimacy or commitment)

4. **Decision/commitment only**—empty love (with no passion or intimacy)

5. **Intimacy and passion**—romantic love (no commitment)

6. **Intimacy and commitment**—companionate love (without passion)

7. **Passion and commitment**—fatuous love (foolish love, without real intimacy)

8. **Intimacy, passion, and commitment**—consummate love (the most complete love)

Sternberg emphasizes that the most complete love, **consummate love,** results from a combination of all three components (Trotter, 1986). The love relationship is balanced when all three elements are present in relatively equal degrees. People are more likely to be satisfied with their relationship if their love triangles match—that is, if they have fairly equal amounts of the same components of love (Sternberg and Barnes, 1985).

Davis (1985) described love relationships in terms of three categories that differ somewhat from Sternberg's: passion, caring, and friendship. Each of these, in turn, features a cluster of characteristics. The passion cluster includes fascination with each other, a desire for exclusiveness, and sexual desire. The caring cluster includes giving the utmost of oneself, being a champion and advocate of the partner's interests, and making sure that the partner succeeds. The friendship cluster involves enjoy-

Achieving and Maintaining Psychological Intimacy

Even though we sometimes speak of a person as knowing her- or himself intimately, psychological intimacy requires two people. Individuals differ widely in their ability to know quickly what they feel and to label it with words such as *guilt, ambition, sexual desire, envy,* or *anger.* Some people are so self-oriented that they have trouble paying much attention to anything outside themselves. Others occupy the opposite end of the spectrum of self-knowledge: They are so attuned to the external world that they pay relatively little attention to their inner experiences. However, to achieve intimacy, we must do both: We must pay attention to our inner selves and to the world around us.

For intimacy to occur, we have to tell our partner about ourself, and our partner has to respond in a manner that conveys noncritical acceptance of what is being said, an awareness of the importance of the moment to us, and a grasp of what is being said. It also helps a great deal if the listener feels that it is a privilege to hear what the speaker has to say. The ideal condition for intimacy occurs when both the speaker and the listener experience the importance of the moment. If the speaker lacks self-awareness, is unwilling to share, or is unable to express what is felt, or if the listener is critical, disagrees tactlessly, is unable to perceive the importance of the conversation to the speaker, or fails to grasp the speaker's point, any hope of attaining or reestablishing psychological intimacy may be lost.

Intimacy has two basic forms. If the speaker only speaks and the listener only listens, intimacy is one-sided; if they switch roles, the intimacy is two-sided. One-sided psychological intimacies are common between children and their parents or between patients and health care professionals. Two-sided intimacies are the basis of friendships and love relationships.

On the way to the comfort of being understood and to the pleasure and privilege of hearing about another person's inner self, powerful emotions can be generated in the listener and the speaker. Sharing the inner self with a person who receives it well creates a bond between the speaker and the listener, which thereafter causes each to regard the other differently. The two people are together in a new way: They glance at each other differently, touch each other differently, laugh together differently, and continue to readily discuss other aspects of their private selves. Yet much more occurs within the two people than these observable changes in behavior. Within both the speaker and the listener, there is a feeling of attachment, a loss of the usual social indifference, and a vision of the other person as special. Continued intimate sharing by the speaker and listener in a two-sided manner is necessary if psychological intimacy is to be maintained and each partner is to continue to feel enriched by the attachment. This process of attaining and maintaining psychological intimacy soothes the soul. It allows people to be seen, known, accepted, understood, and treated as unique. When these needs are realized, both people feel an inner peace and a sense of security.

Not only does psychological intimacy lay the groundwork for people to become lovers; it enables them to make love again and again and to share their inhibitions during lovemaking so they can eventually discover their sexual potential with each other. Sometimes busy people develop a scheme for bypassing the process of psychological intimacy in order to quickly obtain its results: to have sex. They begin to act as though they believe sex is an efficient substitute for psychological intimacy. This erroneous point of view is understandable. After all, sometimes even a kiss changes a relationship and creates a nonverbal yet profound sense of knowing the other person. Busy people with dwindling time and energy during their day easily come to rely on sexual interaction to re-create closeness. Sex as a substitute for psychological intimacy probably works best in early adulthood, but as men and women reach midlife, they need better psychological conditions to make love in a way that reliably delivers physical and psychological satisfaction (Levine, 1991).

ment, acceptance, trust, respect, mutual assistance, self-disclosure, understanding, and spontaneity.

Moss and Schwebel (1993) described the multidimensional nature of love with a related set of components. They saw intimacy in enduring romantic relationships as depending on the level of commitment and positive affective, cognitive, and physical closeness in a reciprocal (although not necessarily symmetrical) relationship. Their definition specified five components of intimacy: commitment, affective intimacy, cognitive intimacy, physical intimacy, and mutuality. Most people strive to achieve intimacy in their lives.

CHANGES OVER TIME

Some researchers feel that love changes over time, with romantic love becoming more rational and less emotional. Couples' ideas of love may change over

By **J. HAHN** and **T. BLASS**

Eros

This style (which can best be summarized as passionate love) is characterized by having a physical ideal, which is recognized immediately. Individuals with this love style believe in "love at first sight." Erotic lovers want intimacy, including sexual intimacy, right from the beginning of a relationship. They are affectionate and communicate openly. The experience is highly emotional and very intense, but they are not obsessive and do not get jealous. They are secure in love and able to commit themselves to a love relationship. They are also usually aware of the shortcomings of their partner; they are not "blind" in love.

Mania

This is an obsessive, jealous, and very emotional love style. These lovers desire intimacy quickly and are intense in their approach. However, they tend to be insecure about their relationships, often fearing that they will give too much and that it will not be reciprocated or needing reassurance that they are loved. They like to spend much time with their lovers and require a great deal of affection. Manic lovers are often "in love with love" (enjoying the excitement of love). They so desperately want to be in love, that they often begin relationships with people with whom they are not compatible.

Ludus

Ludic lovers or game-playing lovers enjoy playing the game of love. Having no one physically ideal type, they like variety in partners and have no problem dating more than one person at a time. They believe you can love two or more people simultaneously. Ludic lovers are not very emotional; their relationships do not get "serious." They try not to spend too much time with any one person, so as to avoid commitment. These lovers also do not spend time discussing the relationship (e.g., their feelings or where it is going). They would prefer telling partners that they are dating other people, but if they feel their partners would be jealous, ludic lovers do not feel any need to tell them.

Pragma

This style is best described as practical or "shopping-list" love. These lovers seek compatibility (in terms of social and personal qualities). They want the relationship to work well and have each of their basic needs satisfied. Background characteristics (e.g., religion, education, family background) are important to the pragmatic lover, whereas physical appearance is unimportant. They have criteria that one should meet before beginning a relationship. Naturally, then, they are cautious when making a commitment. Pragmatic lovers want to know someone well before becoming intimate. Like storgic lovers, they tend to want a friendship to grow into love. Unlike storgic lovers, however, they do this to be sure the partner meets their criteria for a committed relationship. They feel that seeking an optimal match is the only sensible approach to finding a mate. Pragma is not an emotional type of love.

Storge

[This] "friendship" love values companionship and stability. Love comes in time as an extension of a friendship relationship. Storgic lovers are intimate, sharing activities and common interests. Physical attraction is relatively unimportant; common interests are more important. They like to feel comfortable in the relationship, which is not emotionally charged.

Agape

[This] altruistic (or selfless) love may be more an ideal than a love style that is frequently found. The agapic lover believes in giving love because everyone is deserving of it. They believe this is the only mature way to love. They feel it is their duty to love and do not expect anything in return (they don't feel it is necessary that their partner meet their needs, although they may certainly think it would be nice). They do not feel as if they are making any sacrifices. Of course, they do not have any physical preferences and are generally patient, non-demanding, very forgiving, and supportive. Also, they believe in honesty in relationships. Agapic lovers are not highly emotional.

Note: From "Dating Partner Preferences" by J. Hahn and T. Blass, 1997, *Journal of Social Behavior and Personality, 12*(3), pp. 595–610.

the years, with fewer components of romanticism and more components of friendship, trust, cooperation, dependability, and acceptance.

Montgomery and Sorell (1997) measured differences in love attitudes across family life stages. Their sample included 250 adults in four groups: (1) college-age single young adults, (2) young, childless married adults, (3) married adults with children living at home, and (4) married adults with grown children living on their own. Contrary to expectations, the researchers did not find a smooth developmental progression of love attitudes over the course of the life span involving the peaking of erotic, romantic love early in life and the rising valuation of friendship in midlife. Although a developmental model that includes the rising and falling of different love attitudes throughout the family life course was not evident, a number of differences were found between young singles and older married adults, regardless of family life stage. Possessive, playful love attitudes were held more strongly by young singles than by any of the married adult groups, and unmarried youths were lowest in altruistic love attitudes. Playful as well as obsessive and possessive attitudes are characteristic of courtship. Marriage, in contrast, may encourage self-giving love and altruism. A rational, "shopping-list" attitude was understandably prevalent in younger adulthood because of the emphasis on mate selection.

In this study, child rearing did not appear to be associated with differences in love attitude. The older married adults had practical attitudes reflecting generational pressures to form socially and economically viable partnerships. Consistent with previous research, the erotic and altruistic styles of love were associated with high relationship satisfaction for all the groups. Erotic, altruistic, and friendship types of love seemed to have enhanced importance when children were living in the home. Strategies that maintained eroticism were likely to increase a couple's satisfaction with the relationship, no matter the stage of the life cycle. Exclusive commitment to a partner, partner-supportive attitudes, sexual intimacy, and the passionate valuing of the partner and the relationship were most likely to enhance the partners' satisfaction.

These findings suggest that men and women are quite similar in their love attitudes across adulthood. At all stages of the life course, adults value passion, friendship, and self-giving love attitudes. This research indicates that there are far more similarities than differences between the love attitudes of men and women. Friendship/companionship love attitudes are important for all groups and do not differ by family life stage. The results of this study also indicate that passion and friendship/companionship do not occur consecutively in a romantic relationship after all. Rather, they appear to exist concurrently in both dating and married life stage groups (Montgomery and Sorell, 1997).

SUMMARY

1. The most important element in initial attraction is physical attractiveness. Standards of attractiveness are culturally conditioned and change over the years.

2. Personality and social factors are also important in attraction. Personality traits and behavior are significant factors in whether others find individuals attractive.

3. Sometimes, because of previous conditioning, unconscious factors influence a person's evaluation of the attractiveness of others.

4. Love is not a single concept, but has different dimensions. The five dimensions of love discussed here are romantic (emotional), erotic (sensual), dependent (need), friendship (companionship), and altruistic (unselfish).

5. The five elements of love discussed in this chapter are all important in the most complete love.

6. Researchers have identified various components of love. Sternberg revealed three components—intimacy, passion, and commitment—that he linked together as consummate love. Davis included three categories of love: passion, caring, and friendship. Moss and Schwebel specified five components of intimacy: commitment, affective intimacy, cognitive intimacy, physical intimacy, and mutuality.

7. Psychological intimacy involves two people, with each disclosing, listening, and developing attachment to the other. Intimacy lays the groundwork for making love; sex alone cannot substitute for intimacy.

8. At all stages of life, adults endorse passion, friendship, and self-giving love as highly important. There are far more similarities than differences between the love attitudes of men and women.

KEY TERMS

romantic love	serotonin	D-love
narcissistic love	companionate love	B-love
limerence	endorphins	friendship love
conscious love	erotic love	altruistic love
dopamine	dependent love	consummate love
norepinephrine		

QUESTIONS FOR THOUGHT

1. What factors do you believe are most important in attraction between the sexes? In other words, what qualities or characteristics in another person make that person attractive to you?

2. Have you ever been romantically in love? Describe the relationship. Would it have been a sound basis for marriage? Why or why not? If you have never been romantically in love as described in the text, describe and analyze the reasons. Would you like to be? Why or why not?

3. Describe your views of the relationship between sex and love.

4. Compare friendship love with dependent love. Is one more important than the other in a satisfying marriage? Explain.

5. Describe, evaluate, and write a critique of Fromm's view of altruistic love.

SUGGESTED READINGS

Emener, W. G. (1998). *Adult Loving Relationships.* Commack, NY: Kroshka Books. Discusses self-awareness as it relates to improving loving relationships.

Fromm, E. (1956). *The Art of Loving.* New York: Harper & Row. Is a classic on the subject.

Gaylin, W. (1986). *Rediscovering Love.* New York: Viking Press. Gives a psychoanalyst's view.

Hendrick, S., and Hendrick, C. (1992). *Liking, Loving, and Relating.* Pacific Grove, CA: Brooks/Cole. Discusses liking, attraction, affiliation, friendship, love, sexuality, courtship, mate selection, relationship progress, marriage, conflict, power, and satisfaction, as well as contemporary social issues such as divorce, remarried families, gender roles, and dual-career couples.

Hendrick, S., and Hendrick, C. (1992). *Romantic Love.* Newbury Park, CA: Sage. Examines the nature of love, loving and liking, and differences in love styles.

Lerner, H. G. (1989). *The Dance of Intimacy: A Woman's Guide to Courageous Acts of Change in Key Relationships.* New York: Harper & Row. Traces the development of intimacy from a woman's point of view.

Sternberg, R. J. (1998). *Cupid's Arrow: The Course of Love Through Time.* Cambridge: Cambridge University Press. Discusses the author's "triangular theory" of love through combinations of intimacy, passion, and commitment.

Sternberg, R. J. (1998). *Love Is a Story: A New Theory of Relationships.* New York: Oxford University Press. Identifies 26 types of love stories that individuals carry inside and discusses how they affect relationships.

LEARNING OBJECTIVES

After reading the chapter, you should be able to:

Define sex, gender, gender identity, and gender role.

Explain how concepts of masculinity and femininity vary by society and culture.

Discuss how the following environmental influences mold masculinity and femininity: societal expectations, parents, television, and school.

Discuss how different theoretical views have different ideas about the development of "maleness" and "femaleness."

Describe masculine and feminine stereotypes and norms and the problems they create.

Discuss gender-role influences in interpersonal relationships between men and women.

Discuss gender roles in the family, differing expectations and attitudes of various ethnic groups, and the way they affect housework and child care in families.

Discuss how gender roles tend to change over the family life cycle.

Describe how marital quality can be influenced by gender-role expectations.

Explain the meaning of androgyny and its advantages.

Gender: Identity and Roles

Learning Objectives

Environmental Influences on Gender
Societal Expectations
Parental Influences
The Influence of Television
School Influences

Theories of Gender Role and Identity
Social Learning Theory
Cognitive Developmental Theory
Gender Schema Theory
Social Structure/Cultural Theories
Evolutionary Theories: Sociobiology and Functionalism

Traditional Masculine and Feminine Stereotypes
Masculinity
Femininity
Problems with Gender Stereotypes

Perspective: My Life on the Boundaries of Gender

Gender Roles and Body Image

Gender Roles in the Family
Ethnic Variations
Housework and Child-Care Roles
Family Issues: Gender, Parenthood, and Anger
Family Issues: Fathers' Participation in Child Care
Roles over the Family Life Cycle

Androgyny
Family Issues: Mothers' Responsibility for Children

Summary
Key Terms
Questions for Thought
Suggested Readings

Sex describes who we are biologically—male or female. We also manifest **gender,** or personality traits and behavior that characterize us as men (masculine) or women (feminine). These psychosocial components that characterize us as masculine or feminine are largely acquired behaviors (Lips, 1997). Our outward manifestations and expressions of maleness or femaleness are our **gender roles,** which are influenced by cultural expectations of what is considered socially appropriate for males and for females. There is a trend, however, toward less rigid and more androgynous gender roles. Our personal, internal sense of maleness or femaleness is our **gender identity.** Most children accept cognitively their assigned sex as a boy or a girl and then strive to act according to the expectations of society and the group of which they are a part. Some children and adults, however, have difficulty establishing their gender identity. They may experience gender dysphoria, or the feeling that their biological sex does not match their gender identity. Such **transgendered** people may alter their gender identity occasionally or permanently by cross-dressing or by becoming **transsexuals** with the help of hormones and surgery. In this chapter, we examine the concepts of gender and gender roles and describe some of the influences on their development.

ENVIRONMENTAL INFLUENCES ON GENDER

Sex is determined by biological factors. Gender identities and gender roles are influenced by the environment. Certain qualities of maleness are defined as and become "masculine" because of society's view of what being male means. Society prescribes how a male ought to look and behave, what type of personality he ought to have, and what roles he should perform. Similarly, a female is created not only by genetic conception but also by those psychosocial forces that mold and influence her personality (Lopata, 1993). When we speak of a masculine man, we express a value judgment based on an assessment of the personality and behavioral characteristics of the male according to culturally defined standards of "maleness." Similarly, we label a woman feminine according to culturally determined criteria for "femaleness." In this sense, the development of **masculinity** or **femininity** involves

an education in what it means to be a man or a woman within the context of the culture in which one lives (McCandless, Lueptow, and McClendon, 1989). Gender is as much about a set of beliefs as it is about anatomical differences (Sheinberg and Penn, 1991).

Concepts of masculinity and femininity vary in different societies and cultures. For example, Margaret Mead (1950), in studying three primitive tribes, discovered some interesting differences in conceptions of masculinity and femininity. Arapesh men and women displayed "feminine" personality traits. Both males and females were trained to be cooperative, unaggressive, and responsive to the needs and demands of others. In contrast, Mundugumor men and women developed "masculine" traits. They were ruthless and aggressive, with maternal, nurturant aspects of personality at a minimum. In the third tribe, the Tchambuli, the women were dominant and impersonal, while the men were less responsible and more emotionally dependent.

Conceptions of masculinity and femininity have undergone considerable change in the United States. For example, in colonial times, a "true man," especially a gentleman, could wear hose, a powdered wig, and a lace shirt without being considered unmanly. Today, such attire would be considered quite feminine. Thus, the judgments made about masculinity or the extent of "manliness" are subjective, based on the accepted standards of "maleness" as defined by the culture. These standards vary from culture to culture and from era to era in the same society (Rice, 1989).

Societal Expectations

Because society plays such an important role in the establishment of the criteria for masculinity and femininity and in the development of maleness or femaleness, it is important to understand how gender identification and gender-role learning take place. Almost as soon as a child is born, society expects him or her to begin thinking and acting like a boy or like a girl, according to its own definitions. For example, if the child is a girl, she is often dressed like a girl and is given dolls and other toys considered appropriate for little girls. She may be expected to act like a "little lady" or be encouraged to play girls' games. And as she gets older, she likely will be expected to help her mother around

Concepts of masculinity and femininity have undergone considerable change over the centuries. Is this eighteenth-century regency beau similar to the contemporary image of the "true man"?

the house doing traditionally feminine chores. Thus, what society expects the girl to be and do becomes the basic influence in molding her into a woman. She also observes her older sister, her mother, and other females acting like women, and so she begins to identify with them, to imitate them, and to model her behavior after theirs. In short, as soon as a girl is born, she is programmed to become a woman.

The same process applies to boys: Once he is born, a boy is often expected to manifest masculine traits and to do masculine things. He is programmed to become a man. Because programming begins very early in life, gender stereotyping is very common in early-elementary-age children (Trepanier-Street, Romatowski, and McNair, 1990).

Various social influences play a role in gender identity and gender-role development. Three of the most important influences will be discussed here: parents, television, and school.

Parental Influences

One of the ways that children develop gender identities and appropriate gender roles is through identification with parents and modeling of their behavior. **Parental identification and modeling** is the process by which the child adopts and internalizes parental values, attitudes, behavioral traits, and

Certain qualities of maleness are defined and become "masculine" because of society's view of what being male means.

personality characteristics. Identification begins soon after birth, because of children's early dependency on their parents. This dependency, in turn, normally leads to emotional attachment. Gender identification and gender-role learning take place almost unconsciously and indirectly in this intimate parent-child relationship. Children may learn that their mother is affectionate and nurturing and that their father is playful and strong. Not only does each child receive different care from each parent, but he or she also observes that each parent behaves, speaks, dresses, and acts differently in relation to the other parent, to other children, and to persons outside the family. Thus, the child learns what it is to be a mother, a father, a spouse, a woman, or a man through parental example and through daily contacts and associations.

How traditional the parents' gender roles are can also affect their children's gender-role attitudes. One study showed that early adolescent daughters of mothers who are employed hold less traditional gender-role attitudes than do daughters of women who are not employed (Nelson and Keith, 1990). In addition, the happier the husband is with his wife's employment, the more nontraditional is the daughter. Another study found that the adult offspring of nontraditional parents tend to have nontraditional gender-role attitudes (Booth and Amato, 1994).

The Influence of Television

Television plays a significant role in the socialization process for young and old alike. Children's television shows and the accompanying commercials contain considerable gender bias and sexism. However, children do not watch only children's programs. Prime-time television draws the largest number of viewers from every age group, and prime-time TV often portrays males and females in stereotypical ways. In a study of prime-time television programs from 1967 to 1998, researchers found that women consistently received less recognition than did men (Signorielli and Bacue, 1999). Although programs broadcast in the 1990s had more women than those in the 1960s and 1970s, women were still underrepresented in relation to their numbers in the U.S. population. However, there have been some changes in the ways in which women are depicted. They are still cast to be younger than their male counterparts, but more women char-

acters are employed outside the home. In addition, the percentage of women in more prestigious occupations and in traditional male or gender-neutral jobs has increased significantly.

Television affects the value systems of those who watch it. In most homes, the television is on for more than 7 hours a day, and the average person watches at least 3 hours each day. The messages transmitted into the homes of millions of people every day shape their attitudes, beliefs, and gender roles. Although programming content changes seasonally, television transmits a fairly stable and consistent set of images about men and women (Signorielli, 1998). For example, women are underrepresented in television, with men outnumbering them by at least two to one. Women are typically younger than men, and they age faster. A woman on television is most likely to be in her early thirties, and a man in his mid- to late thirties. Men over the age of 65 are more likely to be cast in younger roles and to be employed and romantically involved, while women over the age of 65 are cast as elderly. Although there are just as many women professionals as there are men professionals, women are more often portrayed as having lower-status professions than men (Signorielli, 1998).

With regard to television's influence on gender roles, the research has found that television viewing, as well as how television portrays gender roles, is related to gender stereotypes among young adult viewers (Signorielli, 1998). In particular, television viewing is related to more sexist responses to questions about the nature of men and women and their treatment and appropriate roles in society (Signorielli, 1998).

One study examined whether exposure to television advertisements that portray women as sex objects causes increased body dissatisfaction among women and men. Results revealed that women exposed to sexist ads judged their current body size to be larger and felt more negative about their actual body size (preferring a thinner body) than did women exposed to nonsexist ads. Men exposed to sexist ads judged their current body size to be thinner and also felt more negative about their actual body size (preferring a larger body) (Lavine, Sweeney, and Wagner, 1999). A word of caution, however: These studies do not prove cause and effect, but they do show a relationship between television viewing and gender stereotypes. Either tele-

Because gender roles have become more flexible, this girl can now study auto mechanics. Today, many school programs encourage students to make choices that are not influenced by gender stereotypes.

vision influences people's gender attitudes, or people who hold traditional gender stereotypes watch more television, or there is some other factor that influences both variables (Doyle, 1985).

School Influences

Gender concepts and roles are taught both informally at home and more formally in school as the child grows up (Brody and Steelman, 1985). Giving children gender-specific toys may have considerable influence on vocational choices. Such toys influence boys to be scientists, astronauts, or football players and girls to be nurses, teachers, or flight attendants. Publishers have made a concerted effort to remove gender stereotypes from reading materials. Without realizing it, however, many teachers still encourage traditional masculine-feminine stereotypical behavior in school.

Studies of teachers' relationships with boys and girls reveal that teachers encourage boys to be more assertive in the classroom (Sadker and Sadker, 1985). For example, when the teacher asks questions, the boys often call out comments without raising their hand, whereas most girls sit patiently with their hand raised. Somewhere along the way, these children have received this message: Boys should be assertive academically; girls should be quiet (Rice, 1989).

Research indicates that teachers also have different beliefs about male and female students' competencies (Li, 1999). For instance, teachers tend to stereotype mathematics as a male domain, which is reflected in their tendency to overrate male students' mathematics capability, to have higher expectations for male students, and to have more positive attitudes toward male students (Li, 1999). This gender bias is also reflected in parents' attitudes toward and beliefs about their children's subject competency in kindergarten and elementary school. Parents perceive boys as more competent than girls in science, and they perceive science as more important for boys and have higher performance standards for them (Andre, Whigham, Hendrickson, and Chambers, 1999). Moreover, jobs related to math or science are seen as more male dominated. All this suggests that gender stereotypes related to subject competency have their roots in the early elementary school years.

However, things are changing. For example, as part of the Equal Opportunity Act of 1972, Congress enacted Title IX to provide more opportunities for girls and women to participate in high school and college athletics—a domain once reserved for males. It affects all schools that receive federal funding of any kind. To comply with Title IX, an athletic department must meet at least one of these requirements: (1) provide athletic opportunities for females and males substantially proportionate to their respective enrollments, (2) consistently expand programs for the underrepresented sex, or (3) show that it fully and effectively meets the interests of the underrepresented sex. Schools that violate Title IX requirements risk losing federal funds. Universities and colleges were given until 1978 to comply with its provisions. Since that time, there have been numerous lawsuits from those trying to block Title IX in their schools, but there is little doubt that Title IX has impacted women athletes. More U.S. women than ever before now compete in the Olympics, and women's teams have won gold medals in gymnastics, basketball, soccer, hockey, and softball. There are now women's professional basketball, soccer, and softball leagues—and in 1999 the women's soccer team won the World Cup. Improvements continue from grade school through college in the area of female sports in large part because of Title IX. This has provided more athletic opportunities for females, as well as role models that go beyond traditional gender expectations and behavior.

THEORIES OF GENDER ROLE AND IDENTITY

While no one theory adequately explains all aspects of gender roles and identities, the various theories do provide helpful ways in which to think about and discuss patterns of behavior. Each theory might hold some of the answer to the mysteries as to why females act one way and males another. Five common theories used to explain gender roles and identities are (1) social learning theory, (2) cognitive developmental theory, (3) gender schema theory, (4) social structure/cultural theories, and (5) evolutionary theories.

Social Learning Theory

Social learning theory emphasizes that boys develop "maleness" and girls "femaleness" through exposure to scores of influences—including parents, television, school, and peers—that teach them what it means to be a man or woman in the culture in which they are brought up. They are encouraged to assume the appropriate gender identity by being rewarded for some behaviors and punished for oth-

ers. Thus, the gender-role concepts and gender stereotypes of a particular culture become self-fulfilling prophecies. Those who live up to societal expectations are accepted as normal; those who do not conform are criticized and pressured to comply.

According to this theory, parental models, particularly those offered by the same-sex parent, are the most influential in shaping gender behavior. Other socializing agents, such as television, teachers, and peers, distinguish and reinforce children's gender roles. By the first year of life, children begin to be aware of the differences in gender roles, and by the third year, it is quite evident how girls and boys have been socialized to behave, play, and dress. A great deal of evidence supports social learning theory, but by itself, it is insufficient to explain the development of gender roles and gender identity (Lips, 1997).

Cognitive Developmental Theory

Cognitive developmental theory suggests that gender, like other things, cannot be learned until a child reaches a certain stage of intellectual development. This theory suggests that between the ages of 3 and 5 children acquire "gender constancy," a fixed concept of gender that cannot be altered by superficial things, such as clothing or appearance. Prior to the development of gender constancy, children may confuse gender classifications and believe that classifications can arbitrarily change. According to cognitive developmental theory, once children categorize themselves as female or male, they will use this self-categorization to figure out how to behave. In response to positive reinforcement, they will attach higher value to gender-appropriate behaviors than to gender-inappropriate behaviors, which receive negative reinforcement (Lips, 1997). As children develop a model for proper gender behavior, they enter a phase of great rigidity. Around the age of 6 or 7, their views of gender roles are oversimplified and inflexible, relying greatly on stereotypes. For example, at this age, children may pretend to give one another "boy shots" or "girl shots" to protect themselves from becoming like members of the other sex. But within a few years, children become secure in their gender identity and so are more comfortable with occasional departures from the stereotypical gender role.

Whereas social learning theory is based on gender typing, such as sex-appropriate activities or occupations, cognitive developmental theory is based on cognitive aspects, such as knowledge of stereotypes and flexibility in applying them. Although some support exists for both theories, neither one can fully explain the development and maintenance of gender roles and gender identity (Lips, 1997).

Gender Schema Theory

A schema is the framework of logic and ideas someone uses to organize information and make sense of things. We all hold a variety of schemas, such as how an older person should act, what behavior is polite, and what it means to dress appropriately. According to **gender schema theory,** a person with a strong gender schema has very definite ideas about how males and females should look and behave. For example, baby girls typically are dressed in pink, and baby boys in blue; there are some blue outfits for baby girls, but virtually no pink outfits for baby boys. In addition, girls are often dressed in lace and bows, while boys are dressed in clothes imprinted with sports- or tool-related images. From the first days of life, individuals' gender schemas (and those of their parents) influence how males and females are thought of and treated.

Here is a hypothetical example of a gender schema at work in the mind of a 4-year-old boy and his friends:

> Philip's sister received a Barbie doll for her birthday. When Philip saw it, he wanted his own Barbie doll. After his parents explained that only girls play with Barbies, Philip was still not satisfied and continued his pleading for his own doll. His parents reluctantly conceded and bought him one. Philip was so happy that he took the doll to school the next day to show his friends. They greeted him with "You must be a girl because only girls play with Barbies" and began to make fun of him. Philip never played with a Barbie doll again.

Of course, people differ in the degree to which they use their gender schemas to process information about themselves and others, with strongly sex-typed individuals tending to have stronger gender schemas (Bem, 1985). Gender schemas are shaped through the socialization of children and the degree to which males and females are treated differently.

Thus, gender schema theory builds on both cognitive developmental and social learning theories in suggesting that children both cognitively construct gender categories and learn to respond to environmental cues about gender roles (Lips, 1997).

Social Structure/Cultural Theories

If we accept that children learn or cognitively develop different ideas about appropriate gender behavior, then an important issue is why society supports the perpetuation of these differences. According to **social structure/cultural theories** of gender, most of the differences between male and female gender roles are established because of the status, power, and division of labor found in most societies. Researchers have shown that gender differences occur more frequently (and in some cases only) when the sexes are in the typical male dominant/female subordinate relationship and that much so-called feminine behavior is actually powerless behavior (Lips, 1991). Cultural theorists argue that, if males and females were seen as equally powerful in society, many of the so-called gender differences would disappear. For example, gender differences in nonverbal communication, such as who touches whom during conversation, parallel those between less powerful and more powerful people. Also, both women and members of lower-status groups are characterized as more controlled and passive, whereas men and members of higher-status groups are characterized as more direct and opinionated (Henley and Freeman, 1995).

These power and status differences are related to the differences in the division of labor between the sexes that still exists. For example, there are still far more male executives and female secretaries than vice versa. However, it is almost impossible to determine if the division of labor by sex is a cause or a consequence of the status differences between women and men, and most likely the process is a kind of vicious cycle (Lips, 1997):

> The way work is divided between women and men in our own society practically guarantees that women will have less control over economic resources than men do. Men's greater control over economic resources, achieved through better jobs with higher salaries and through more continuous participation in the paid labor force, creates the

expectation that women (and children) will depend on men for support. Under this set of expectations, which is communicated to children long before they understand the economic realities on which it is based, it is little wonder that girls and boys, women and men, tend to make choices that emphasize different aspects of these skills, aspirations, and preferences. These choices lead males and females into different types of work, and the cycle repeats itself. Whatever its source, the division of labor by sex and the parallel male-female difference in control over resources contribute to gender differences in behavior. (p. 55)

However, not all theories about gender differences focus on culture, cognition, or learning, and many people believe it is not nurture but rather nature that contributes the most to gender differences. Thus, no discussion of theoretical approaches to gender differences would be complete without a discussion of evolution and biology.

Evolutionary Theories: Sociobiology and Functionalism

Sociobiology and functionalism are two theories rooted in the concept that human genetics have evolved over time so that men and women are best adapted for their biological functions and reproductive success. According to **evolutionary theories** such as these, genetic heritage is more important than the influence of learning and culture for gender roles. Proponents of sociobiology believe that male and female genes have adapted over time to meet each sex's reproductive goals. The inclination for males to attempt to fertilize as many eggs as possible stems from the innate drive to guarantee survival of their own genes, enhanced by the production of millions of sperm with very little energy expenditure. In contrast, the tendency for females to selectively seek a monogamous partner relates to the amount of effort required to produce comparatively few eggs and to support the life of an embryo. Similarly, functionalism suggests that males and females evolved genetically to fulfill reproductive tasks. The presence of a "maternal instinct," according to this theory, is genetically linked to the biological functions of pregnancy, lactation, and childbirth—all of which require tremendous energy. Theorists in the late

1800s actually argued that women expend so much energy on reproductive functions that they have little left over for other pursuits, such as higher education (Lips, 1997).

There is little empirical evidence to support evolutionary theories of gender, but they are still the basis for many societal assumptions. No evidence has linked any of these gender behaviors to a specific gene, and the universality of a trait has not been proven to mean that the trait is necessarily genetic rather than learned. If males are biologically predisposed to be aggressive and females to be submissive, it is certainly also true that society reinforces and accentuates these differences.

TRADITIONAL MASCULINE AND FEMININE STEREOTYPES

Many people develop stereotyped concepts of masculinity and femininity. These **gender stereotypes** are assumed differences, norms, attitudes, and expectations about men and women.

Masculinity

According to traditional masculine stereotypes, men were supposed to be all of the following:

Aggressive	Adventurous
Dominant	Courageous
Strong	Independent
Forceful	Ambitious
Self-confident	Direct
Rugged	Logical
Virile	Unemotional
Instrumental	

These stereotypes of masculinity still are considered socially desirable by some people (but certainly not all) in our society today.

Traditionally, to be a man, the male was supposed to be a provider; he was successful, had status, and was looked up to. To be a man, a male was supposed to be a sturdy rock with an air of toughness, confidence, and self-reliance. Stereotypic masculine heroes are Bruce Willis in *Die Hard*, Clint Eastwood in *Dirty Harry*, and Mel Gibson in *Lethal Weapon*.

Concepts of femininity vary, and they change with time. Strenuous, competitive activity, such as this college women's hockey game, is no longer automatically assumed to be inconsistent with femininity.

Typically, the assertive male was also supposed to be the initiator in relationships between the sexes, and the woman was expected to follow. He was expected to ask *her* out on a date and to decide where to go, what to do, and when to meet. He was expected to court *her* while she demurely but coquettishly responded. He was expected to ask for *her* hand in marriage. The woman who was too bold or forward was regarded as a threat to the traditional relationship. And after marriage, the male continued his dominant role as decision maker and initiator. He was supposed to have the last word over both his wife and his children.

Today, these dimensions of the traditional masculine stereotype can readily be seen in the three avenues by which adolescent boys gain admission to deviant peer groups (Mosher and Tomkins, 1988).

1. They have to fight their way in and demonstrate courage and toughness by being willing to fight.
2. They have to show fearlessness by climbing a water tower or racing a car or demonstrating bravado and courage by some other means.
3. They have to engage in a callous sex act and prove their manhood by "scoring."

Femininity

What are the traditional concepts of femininity as taught by our society? In the past, women were supposed to be all of the following:

Unaggressive	Sentimental
Submissive	Softhearted
Weak	Dependent
Sensitive	Aware of the feelings of others
Gentle and tender	Emotional and excitable
Kind	
Tactful	Somewhat frivolous, fickle, illogical, and talkative
Warm and affectionate	

A "feminine" female was never aggressive, boisterous, loud, or vulgar in speech or behavior. She was expected to cry on occasion and sometimes to get upset over small events. It was all right for her to like laces, frills, and frivolous things. She was expected to be interested primarily in her home.

Along with these stereotyped concepts of femininity, society emphasized gender norms that all women were expected to follow. The primary gender norm was the motherhood mandate. Girls were expected to play with dolls because, in most people's minds, doll play prepared girls to become mothers. When they got older, girls were considered more capable of baby-sitting than boys. When a young woman got married, one of the first questions she would be asked was when she was going to have a baby. If she delayed too long, friends and family began to worry that she was not living up to her expected role. If she had the biological capability of having children, she was expected to use it. Then, when she had a baby, the motherhood mandate said that she should be a good mother by devoting a majority of her time to caring for her baby (Doyle, 1985).

The marriage mandate was second in importance to the motherhood mandate. Women were expected to get married, since it was the rite of passage to the adult world, the way to unlock the shackles of dependency on their parents and best fulfill the motherhood mandate.

As another consequence of stereotypic gender roles, women were taught that their role was to please men, regardless of their own needs and desires. Nowhere was this more evident than in intimate relationships. Some women went through years of marriage attending only to their husband's wants. Many became very dissatisfied and depressed as a result (Whisman and Jacobson, 1989). If women are to achieve true equality in intimate relationships, they can no longer be the passive, pleasing partner who considers their partner's needs without regard for their own. This means learning to communicate their needs to their partner.

Problems with Gender Stereotypes

One problem with gender stereotypes is that, whenever rigid gender standards are applied to all members of one sex, individual personalities can become distorted. Everyone is expected to conform, regardless of individual differences or inclinations. Furthermore, gender identity and gender-role stereotypes place serious limitations on the relationships that people are capable of forming and on career or personal achievements.

Another problem with gender stereotypes is that they lead to different expectations of employment and pay for males and females, even among children. Although the rate of participation in the labor force is not different for boys and girls, their type of work is segregated by gender early on. Girls are more likely to be employed by family and neighbors to perform "benevolent" jobs, such as baby-sitting, whereas boys are more likely to do manual work in more formal work settings, such as bagging groceries, mowing lawns, and bussing dishes (Desmarais and Curtis, 1999). Although boys and girls work the same number of hours per week, girls earn significantly lower hourly wages. This gender inequality in youth employment reflects what is occurring among adult workers. Interestingly, studies show that female college students have lower perceived income entitlement for two main reasons. First, women are socialized to value the social and interpersonal aspects of their work rather than pursue monetary rewards. Second, women learn to downplay their work efforts or contributions when examining whether they are being paid a fair wage and thus tend to compare themselves to other women, who are also underpaid, rather than to men (Desmarais and Curtis, 1999).

Findings from the National Opinion Research Center General Social Surveys show that traditional gender-role ideology in both men and women contributes to lower observed earnings for females, independent of the influences of individual characteristics. More traditional women are more likely to choose female-dominated jobs, which have low average earnings, and men with traditional gender views are more likely to think women belong in low-paid, traditionally female jobs. If a man believes a woman's place is in the home and he is responsible for deciding a woman's promotional opportunities and salary, this may impact her earnings negatively. Traditional gender-role ideology can also impact men's earnings. Employers may view men with sexist views of women as "lacking in openness to diversity" or as open invitations to discrimination lawsuits, which may affect their career success (Firestone, Harris, and Lambert, 1999).

The traditionally unaggressive, submissive, weak female was not able to stand up for herself at home, so she was thought to be unworthy to assume positions of leadership in government or business. (In spite of women's advances, only a few of the Fortune 500 corporations are headed by women.) If our daughters are expected to be breadwinners, if many women remain single, or if some women are required to raise their children alone, then they need the same assertiveness, independence, and rational thinking that we seek to de-

My Life on the Boundaries of Gender

By **BETSY LUCAL,** *Department of Sociology, Indiana University, South Bend*

What does it mean to live on the boundaries of gender? It means being a woman who answers to "Sir" because it is entirely likely that the speaker is talking to me. It means being a woman who thinks twice about using a public restroom in order to avoid comments like "This is the *ladies'* room!" that make it clear someone thinks I'm in the wrong place. It means facing the possibility that someone will challenge my use of a credit card because they're convinced that a card with a woman's name on it could not possibly belong to me. On the other hand, it also means not being afraid to walk alone at night, feeling safer than most women because I'm fairly certain that a potential attacker would not choose someone who appears to be a (relatively big) man. It means being taken seriously in all-male environments, such as auto parts stores, by people who think I'm one of them, and therefore someone who possesses relevant knowledge, rather than a naive woman.

These are among the consequences I deal with every day of my life as a woman who does not conform to the conventions of femininity. However, despite outward appearances, I am female, and I identify as a woman (that is, I am not transgendered—I am not a person whose gender identity is different from my sex). My appearance simply defies the rule that says a person's sex and gender display must match. I am a living illustration of the distinction between sex and gender. I am a female (sex) who is, because of my appearance, regularly mistaken for a man (gender). The fact that this happens shows that gender, contrary to popular belief, is not natural but is instead socially constructed. If gender followed naturally from sex, it would be impossible for a female to display masculinity or for a male to display femininity.

Yet my experiences (and those of other people) show that such a thing *is* possible. They provide a vivid reminder that gender is a set of social characteristics and expectations assigned to men and women, not something biological. Though I possess the physical characteristics of a fe-

male, people often see me as a man. This is not surprising, given my large size (six feet tall), short hair, lack of jewelry and makeup, and nonfeminine clothes (no dresses or skirts, simple pants/shorts and shirts). As a member of our society, I understand that these are masculine gender markers—aspects of my appearance that may be taken as evidence that I am a man (and, therefore, also male).

So, why don't I align my gender display with my sex? At first, I did not do this with any purpose in mind. Growing up, I simply appeared in a way that was comfortable to me. The fact that my appearance confused other people and/or made them uncomfortable was just something I learned to live with. But as I gained a sociological understanding of the world, I realized that my life on the boundaries of gender gave me an opportunity to show people how gender is socially constructed, how sex and gender are distinct from one another. Hoping that my life could help break down the inequality that accompanies gender, I not only continued this practice but also began to use it to help people understand the consequences of gender in our society.

As a person who lives on the boundaries of gender, I get to see both the oppression of women and the privilege of men firsthand. Because I am a woman, I face the prospect of earning less money than a man with comparable credentials. As a woman, I must endure the derogatory media images of women that are ubiquitous in our society. On the other hand, I need not worry about the public harassment many women experience as they move through the world. If men think I am also a man, they will not engage in catcalls, sexual remarks and other verbal harassment. When mistaken for a man, I am treated more respectfully than a woman might be.

Like other social constructions, gender has very real consequences. My experiences show that people are treated differently based on the gender they are perceived to be. My experiences make it clear that gender does matter in our interactions with other people. Life on the boundaries isn't always easy, but it is instructive.

velop in our sons. If women are to succeed, new roles require acceptance of different traits.

Stereotyped concepts of gender roles also result in double standards of behavior. Men as aggressors are encouraged to express their sexual desires, but women are encouraged to inhibit theirs. As a result, men may seek multiple partners, but women who do so are considered "loose." Women are allowed

to be emotional but not erotic. Consequently, women can show emotions and feelings but are supposed to inhibit their sexual desire and expression. Wives complain that their husbands are unfeeling. Husbands complain that their wives aren't interested in sex.

What about the traditional gentler female traits of tenderness, kindness, softheartedness, sensitivity, and awareness of the feelings of others? These traits have always been needed in all types of human relationships (Cook, 1990). Yet men are not supposed to exhibit these traits. They are not supposed to show feelings or to cry; they are supposed to be impervious to sorrow, pain, and tragedy and to be able "to take it like a man." As a result, some men consider it unmanly to tell their wives, "I love you," or to give their children (especially boys) a hug and a kiss. Men are encouraged to be interested in sex because "real men" are virile, but they are often encouraged to be indifferent to love.

The result is insensitive men and sensitive women trying to learn to live together in the same world (Notarius and Johnson, 1982). The very traits that women are supposed to exhibit and that men are expected to suppress expose women to the hurts of intimate living and prevent men from understanding why their partners are upset. It is also difficult for men and women to become real friends and companions.

Trying to follow traditional male gender roles also can be harmful to many men themselves. Adherence to the traditional male role is associated with higher levels of suicide, substance abuse, health problems, stress, and emotional illness (Good and Mintz, 1990). Being openly aggressive, dominant, independent, and unemotional is distinctly disadvantageous. The overaggressive male gets in trouble with friends, family, and society. Yet many of the toys boys are typically expected to play with, such as G.I. Joes and Star Wars figures, still display these aggressive traits.

As far as roles in the family are concerned, highly segregated gender roles result in lack of cooperation, companionship, and intimacy in the family. Cooperative sharing of roles results in greater contentment and companionship among all family members and in greater opportunities for meaningful relationships.

GENDER ROLES AND BODY IMAGE

Gender roles define not only masculine and feminine behavior but also masculine and feminine ideals of appearance. Trying to live up to these prescribed roles can damage self-esteem and even endanger health.

"Body image" most often refers to positive or negative feelings about specific parts of the body and to overall appearance (Feingold and Mazzella, 1998). How people feel about their body depends on many factors, both external and internal. People's body image attitudes are purely subjective and personal, but specific attitudes tend to be common to each gender and based on societal cues.

Today many young girls worry about the shape, size, and muscle tone of their bodies because they are taught that the body is the ultimate expression of the self (Brumberg, 1997). In contrast to women of a century ago, who externally controlled their bodies with corsets and girdles, most of today's young women control their bodies internally, with diet and exercise. Nevertheless, the woman who goes to the gym every day for the sole sake of her looks isn't very different from the woman who wouldn't go out before struggling into a corset (Turkel, 1998).

In contemporary society, both males and females, particularly on television and in the movies, are less modest about their bodies and are showing more skin than ever before. This openness has profound implications for how adolescents handle their bodies, and it is particularly problematic for girls, because their bodies, even more than the bodies of boys, are constantly being displayed and appraised (Brumberg, 1997). It is not surprising, then, that there are now fourth-grade girls who diet dangerously, that one-half of 9-year-old girls have dieted, and that eating disorders, usually acquired in adolescence, can be seen in girls as young as 7 (Turkel, 1998). This preoccupation with weight, perfectionism, and fear of rejection stems from our cultural expectations for females, rather than from individual psychopathology (Turkel, 1998). As Pipher (1994) observed, females measure their bodies against cultural ideals and can't help but feel inferior when measured against today's standard of abnormal thinness, which is unattainable for most females. Thus, in recent decades, females' dissatisfaction with their bodies has increased along with the number of eating disorders.

Adolescents learn a lot about feminine and masculine gender roles through television and popular magazines. Typically, boys watch programs that are activity-driven, with lots of action and movement, and girls watch programs about friendship and relationships. These programs teach boys to be strong and in control; they teach girls to look good and to please their peers. Although most data collected on gender and body image are female-focused, men also are affected by the media's portrayal of them. One study found that the way men were portrayed, in both ads and articles, changed depending on the type of magazine and the intended audience. In magazines with a predominantly male readership, men were most often shown in occupational settings, while in women's magazines, men were shown in nurturing activities (Vigorito and Curry, 1998). Because male portrayals in the media are more about status and success than physicality, males' body images are not so dependent on the images in magazines or popular culture. However, toys depicting males are changing in terms of body characteristics. Although the inappropriate thinness of female dolls has long been noted and criticized, male action figures now also depict inappropriate and most likely impossible ideals of muscularity. One study of the physiques of G.I. Joe and Star Wars figures showed that the action figures today, as well as pop culture icons like Tarzan, are much more muscular than those of 30 years ago (see Figure 7.1) (Pope, Olivardia, Gruber, and Borowiecki, 1999). Though it might be premature to conclude that boys develop body image disorders solely because they are exposed to these muscular ideals at a young age, such toys do have an impact on children.

Advertisements promote the idea that females' personal happiness is linked to physical appearance rather than good character and positive self-esteem. While such ads have boosted profits for manufacturers of skin, hair, and diet products, they sap the creativity of girls and threaten their mental and physical health (Brumberg, 1997). One study found that girls who watched 8 or more hours of television a week reported greater body dissatisfaction than did girls who were less exposed to television (Thompson and Heinberg, 1999). Another study found that women who viewed typical female model images in magazines had higher levels of anger and depression than did women who viewed only images of objects (Pinhas, Toner, Ali, Garfinkel, and Stuckless, 1999). Viewing images of models had an immediate and negative effect on women's moods, creating feelings of depression, guilt, low self-esteem, and failure.

In our culture, females feel more negatively about their body image than do males. Not surprisingly, a study of 21 popular women's and men's magazines found that 78% of the covers of women's magazines contained a message regarding appearance, while none of the men's magazines did. In addition, 25% of the women's magazine covers contained information on weight loss, perpetuating the idea of slimness as the only attractive ideal. And where the men's magazines focused on entertainment, hobbies, and activities, the women's magazines focused on improving one's life by changing one's appearance (Malkin, Wornian, and Chrisler, 1999). Although magazine covers do not fully represent the media and their messages, they do reflect cultural standards and shape attitudes regarding gender behavior. Researchers have also analyzed the content of *Seventeen* magazine over a number of years to identify patterns in the concerns and interests of the modern teenage girl. Although minor changes have occurred in *Seventeen* over the years, its content still conveys the same message that it did when it was first published in 1944: that young women should be concerned only with improving their external appearance and pleasing a man (Schlenker, Caron, and Halteman, 1998). Even in the 1990s, this publication—the most widely distributed teenage magazine—still did not address most of the intellectual issues relevant to young women. Although more women than ever before are pursuing higher education, having careers, and delaying marriage, the content of their publications does not seem to reflect the aspirations and levels of achievement of which they are capable.

GENDER ROLES IN THE FAMILY

Beliefs about masculinity and femininity profoundly affect the roles men and women play in the family (Ferree, 1990). Some adults believe that gender roles are innate, that men and women are "born" to perform certain roles (Mirowsky and Ross, 1987). The male chauvinist, for example, considers women subordinate—lacking equal authority, destined to care for husbands and children, and not suited for many kinds of jobs because of their physical, emotional, and mental shortcomings. According to this view, if they are employed, women cannot expect equal pay for equal work, because men are meant to be the primary breadwinners.

Not surprisingly, men more often than women believe in innate gender roles. People who are older, less educated, and more conservative in their religious beliefs also hold more traditional beliefs about gender roles (Rogler and Procidano, 1986). One important goal of the women's movement has been to motivate women to achieve true egalitarian rights and roles. At the present time, however, there is still an incongruency between ideology and the practice of marital equality (Blaisure and Allen, 1995).

As long as sexist views persist, women will be placed in subordinate, inferior roles. Feminists' emphasis on equality does not mean they desire or expect women and men to be the same or to act identically (Margolin, Talovic, Fernandez, and Onorato, 1983). Rather, the goal has been freedom—the freedom to choose one's own destiny and status. With some conscious effort, partners can construct their own gender roles through the decisions they make concerning work, family, and marriage (Zvonkovic, Greaves, Schmiege, and Hall, 1996).

Ethnic Variations

The attitudes that men and women hold toward gender roles have a significant influence on many aspects of marital and family dynamics. They also help perpetuate gender-differentiated opportunities in education, politics, employment, and other areas. A substantial body of literature has documented the formation of gender-role attitudes in women and girls. Far less attention has been focused on how the attitudes of men and boys are formed and change over time (Blee and Tickamyer, 1995), and researchers have only recently begun to look at differences in gender-role attitudes in different classes and ethnic groups.

The research typically shows that young White women are at higher risk than young White men for depression, suicide attempts, eating disorders, substance abuse, academic underachievement, dropping out, and plummeting self-esteem and self-confidence (Brumberg, 1997). According to Brown and Gilligan (1992), White girls often struggle "against losing something which feels essential: their voice, their mind, their self" (p. 159). They begin "losing voice" and "abandoning self" around age 12, in various aspects of their lives, in exchange for being perceived as a "perfect" girl: passive, quiet, demure, and attractive to boys—qualities that make up the traditional female gender stereotype. They

derive their worth from relationships rather than from their abilities and accomplishments.

Although such gender-role behaviors may be common among middle-class White girls, they are not universal. Today, a growing body of research is focused on female gender identity development among urban adolescents from different social class and ethnic backgrounds. In one sample of 362 girls from five different ethnic groups (Erkut, Fields, Sing, and Marx, 1996), almost half of the girls cited athletic abilities, rather than relationships, as the main thing that made them feel good about themselves. African American adolescent girls often are described not as "losing voice" but as being assertive, powerful, resilient, and resistant (Gibbs, 1996; Ward, 1996; Way, 1995). Among African American families, mothers socialize their daughters to be independent, strong, and self-confident rather than passive (Gayles, 1984). The most important message that African American adolescent girls receive from their mothers is to be self-reliant and resourceful (Collins, 1987).

Body image also seems to differ among different ethnic groups. In a study of 120 university men and women, African Americans reported greater body satisfaction and less overestimation of weight than their White counterparts. African American women also rated themselves as more sexually attractive than did Anglo-American women and had higher self-esteem regarding their weight. Hispanic women rated themselves as less sexually attractive than did African American women but more sexually attractive than did Anglo-American women. Males in all three groups demonstrated little difference (Miller, Gleaves, Hirsch, Green, Snow, and Corbett, 2000).

Recent scholarship about male attitudes toward gender roles has documented a variety of masculine standards that define manhood differently across ethnic, class, sexual, and regional boundaries. Men's attitudes toward female gender roles also vary. The idea that women's roles should be circumscribed by home and family may reflect only a narrow segment of White, middle-class heterosexual men. One study of African American male attitudes toward women's gender roles revealed that African American and White men differ in their attitudes about women's gender roles, that the men's beliefs change over time, and that individual status and life course processes influence these men's attitudes. African American

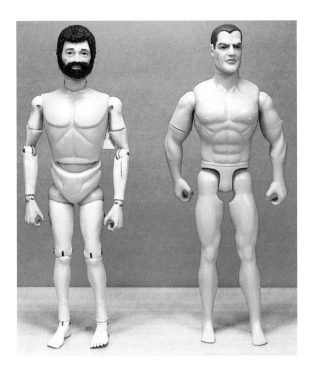

Figure 7.1   The Evolution of the Physiques of Action Figures and Traditional Heros (*Note:* From *Time,* April 24, 2000.)

Gender, Parenthood, and Anger

Using data from a national probability sample of 2,031 adults, a study examined how gender inequality in the family affects anger. The researchers found that women had higher levels of anger than men, that each additional child in the household increased anger, and that children increased anger more for mothers than for fathers. The study revealed two types of stressors in the mothers' lives: (1) economic strain and (2) the strain associated with child care. Women were exposed to both types of strain more than were men. Child-care responsibilities, economic hardships in the household, and difficulty arranging and paying for child care all significantly increased anger and explained the effects of gender and parenthood on anger. Mothers facing the greatest economic inequality and the most inequitable distribution of parental responsibilities had the highest level of anger. Some were more likely than others to express their anger (Ross and Van Willigen, 1996).

men are more liberal in their attitudes toward working wives than White men and are far more likely to have lived in a household with a working wife and/or mother (Blee and Tickamyer, 1995).

Housework and Child-Care Roles

With over half of all married women employed outside the home, fairness demands a willingness on the part of husbands to assume shared responsibility for housework and child care. Some studies indicate that gender-role stereotypes, especially among college students, may be weakening, but most current research continues to find evidence of traditional gender roles (Ridgeway and Smith-Lovin, 1999). For example, although the gap between the amount of time women and men spend in family work is shrinking (Levine and Pittinsky, 1997), women are still doing more family work than men (Demo and Acock, 1993). Overwhelmingly, the evidence suggests that, even when women work as many hours outside the home as their spouses, they retain primary responsibility for home care and child care, although men do participate in domestic work more when their partner is employed (Pleck, 1997). However, men do relatively little domestic labor unless both they and their spouse are somewhat egalitarian in their beliefs about gender roles in marriage (Greenstein, 1996). In dual-earner families, fathers are more involved and engaged in activities with their children, and this involvement increases as the mother's work hours increase, but all other household chores continue to be gender segregated. Indoor work is predominantly completed by women, and outdoor work by men (Gottfried, Gottfried, Killian, and Bathurst, 1999).

A study of 54 Dutch couples who were expecting their first child or had a first child under 12 months of age revealed that there was more conflict about household labor than about paid work. Conflict about household labor was related to women's dissatisfaction with the division of labor. Conflicts about paid work revolved around spouses' dissatisfaction with the man's working hours. The majority of spouses preferred men to spend less time on paid work (Kluwer, Heesink, and Van DeBliert, 1996).

Marital satisfaction depends partly on partners perceiving themselves and their spouses as each doing a fair share of family work (Deater-Deckard and Scarr, 1996; John, Shelton, and Luschen, 1995; Sanchez and Kane, 1996). When women work outside the home and also have to do most of the work around the house and to care for the children, they experience considerable role conflict and strain (Elman and Gilbert, 1984; Katz and Piotrkowski, 1983). Most suffer from overload (Hare-Mustin, 1988). In fact, Kaplan (1990) suggests that successfully combining marriage (or dating if a woman is single), work, and motherhood is impossible.

Individual psychological well-being has been equated with less traditional gender-role orientations (Markides and Vernon, 1984). Furthermore, the quality of child care is related negatively to the amount of housework mothers are expected to perform. In families in which spouses share household chores, mothers have more time to respond to their children's personal and social needs. Sharing is important, therefore, to individual well-being, to the marital relationship, and to quality parent-child relationships (Thompson, 1991). Greater paternal involvement in child care also increases the marital satisfaction of the woman (Harris and Morgan, 1991).

In sum, several studies—including ones of single- and dual-earner families and of upper-middle-class families—reveal that women still spend signifi-

Is cooking the family dinner a gender-typed role? The ability to perform any family task without concern for its gender appropriateness can make it easier for the child, when the time comes, to achieve an egalitarian marriage.

In families in which men help with child care and household responsibilities, working women report considerably less role conflict and stress.

cantly more time doing housework and caring for children than do men (Berardo, Shehan, and Leslie, 1987; Ferree, 1991; Levant, Slattery, and Loiselle, 1987; Levine and Pittinsky, 1997). The man's gender ideology is the best single predictor of sharing housework. This suggests that men share more when they think they should, or perhaps that men who share more adjust their gender-role beliefs accordingly (Pyke and Coltrane, 1996). If the woman has egalitarian views and demands that he share household tasks, his participation is more likely to increase (Hardesty and Bokemeier, 1989). Studies of married women indicate that egalitarian and full-time employed women perceive that their spouses give less support when domestic labor arrangements are more unequal. Women who perceive less support, in turn, experience lower marital and personal happiness than do those who perceive more equal household labor arrangements (Pina and Bengston, 1993).

Many studies have reported that men would like to spend more time doing family work, such as

child care, but a number of factors affect their involvement, including gender-role flexibility and egalitarian views (Pleck, 1997). In some families, a barrier to men's involvement is maternal gatekeeping, which Allen and Hawkins (1999) define as

> the mother's reluctance to relinquish standards, wanting to be ultimately accountable for domestic labor to confirm to others and to herself that family work is truly a woman's domain. . . . [Maternal gatekeeping is] a collection of beliefs and behaviors that ultimately inhibit a collaborative effort between men and women in family work by limiting men's opportunities for learning and growing through caring for home and children. . . . [It is] a schema that builds, maintains, and reinforces the gate to home and family, which, if opened, could encourage more father involvement in housework and child care. (p. 200)

Allen and Hawkins (1999) studied specific gatekeeping beliefs and behaviors and found that 25% of the 1,500 women in their sample were

Fathers' willingness to participate in child care is influenced by a number of variables. Barnett and Baruch's (1987) research with 160 White, middle-class parents revealed the following:

- The more hours the mothers work per week, the more likely the fathers are to participate in child-care tasks. (A few studies disagree with this.)

- Liberal mothers who expect the help of their husbands are more likely to get it than are traditional mothers who do not expect such help.

- Fathers who report dissatisfaction with the quality of fathering they received as children tend to compensate by providing more care for their own children.

- Fathers do a higher proportion of child-care tasks when their child is small.

- Fathers spend more time interacting with their children when the children are younger than when they are older. (The same is true of mothers.) They also spend more time with their sons than with their daughters (Marsiglio, 1991).

- Fathers' proportionate interaction time is greater when there are more children in the family.

- The fewer hours the fathers work per week, the more time they spend caring for their children. This is not true for fathers who are unemployed.

---

gatekeepers. However, it is important to remember that maternal gatekeeping is just one of the many factors in men's involvement in domestic work.

Roles over the Family Life Cycle

The roles that people play depend partly on the family situation. The adolescent who has a baby may be forced into a traditional mother role whether she wants to assume it or not (Krissman, 1990). Having or adopting a baby forces women into traditional domestic roles, at least for a period of time (Hill, 1988). There's some evidence that women's satisfaction with the division of household labor rises and falls and rises again over the life cycle. Although women shoulder a disproportionate share of household labor, the disparity between their contribution and that of their spouses appears to be least in the preparental and postparental years and greatest in the early child-rearing years (Suitor, 1991). Men tend to spend more time performing domestic labor during periods of least occupational involvement—that is, early in their employment career and after retirement (Dorfman and Heckert, 1988; Rexroat and Shehan, 1987). Men's contributions to household labor rise when the woman is employed full-time (Pictman and Blanchard, 1996). The divisions of household labor are, in short, the result of multiple causes. Who does what around the house is shaped by time availability, relative resources, and ideology, and these three factors are intertwined and mutually reinforcing (Coltrane and Ishii-Kuntz, 1992).

In general, if spouses agree on gender-role expectations and performance, couples report higher marital quality than if there is disagreement (Bowen and Orthner, 1983). If a man does not fulfill the roles his spouse expects him to, she will not be completely satisfied with the relationship. Men, too, have certain preconceived expectations about the roles their spouses should fulfill; if the women do not live up to their expectations, their marital satisfaction is less (Bahr, Chappell, and Leigh, 1983). The need for **gender-role congruence** is an important consideration in selecting a compatible mate (Bowen, 1989; Lueptow, Guss, and Hyden, 1989).

ANDROGYNY

What seems to be emerging in today's society is a gradual mixing of gender roles to produce **androgyny,** a gender role that combines both the feminine and the masculine. Androgynous people are not gender-typed with respect to roles, although they are distinctly male or female in sex. They match their behavior to the situation, rather than being limited by what is culturally defined as male or female. For example, an androgynous male feels comfortable cuddling and caring for a young boy; an androgynous female feels comfortable changing the oil in her car. Androgyny expands the range of acceptable behavior, allowing individuals to cope effectively in a variety of situations.

The mixing of roles is advantageous to both sexes. Both sexes are restricted in their behavior and

Child care is still the purview of women. Women, whether they are employed outside the home or not, tend to be responsible for children, both in terms of planning and implementing decisions regarding their care and in terms of the amount of time they spend caring for the children. Although men in dual-career marriages do more with their children than do men whose wives do not work outside the home, the data suggest they do not have the primary responsibility for the children, even when the woman earns a substantial proportion of the family income. The main determinant of responsibility for children seems to be gender: Women are more responsible for children than are men.

Women who work longer hours spend less time with the children, but their husbands do not spend more time. Instead, the gap is filled by nonfamily members (Lesli, Anderson, and Branson, 1991).

relationships by narrow gender-typed roles (Rice, 1989). Both masculine and androgynous people are more independent and less conforming than those identified with femininity, and both feminine and androgynous individuals are more nurturing than those who are traditionally masculine. Some men are beginning to realize that they can gain far more in their lives by caring, loving, and collaborating, and so they have less need to combat, compete with, and overpower one another (Freudenberger, 1987).

Historically, psychologists have taught that mental health depends on a clear-cut separation between male and female roles (Cook, 1985). Now, some studies reveal that androgynous individuals have better social relationships and are better adjusted than people who have more traditional gender identities. For example, a 6-month longitudinal study of college students found that individuals who showed more masculine and androgynous characteristics experienced less depression (Cheng, 1999). Another study revealed that more androgynous individuals possess adaptive capabilities and resources, such as effective coping techniques, emotional integration, communication skills, and a well-defined self-concept with a high level of ego strength (Small, Teagro, and Selz, 1980). Another study, this of 195 new mothers, showed that those classified as either androgynous or masculine scored lower on dimensions reflecting psychological distress than did their feminine or undifferentiated (having low scores on both masculine and feminine traits) counterparts (Bassoff, 1984). A study of adolescent females showed that those with androgynous or masculine gender-role orientation had higher self-esteem than did those classified as feminine or undifferentiated (Mullis and McKinley, 1989). However, many feminists don't agree that androgyny should be a model for women. Rather, women's biological, emotional, and psychological attributes should be valued as

Androgyny expands the range of acceptable behavior. Clothes and hairstyles do not express either maleness or femaleness.

much as men's. Although feminists emphasize equal treatment for women and nonsexist attitudes, many also seek to acknowledge the fundamental difference between men and women and to equally value those differences.

Although researchers may use the categories of masculine, feminine, and androgynous, in reality, our gender self-concept probably changes across

153

the various contexts in which we interact. The gender makeup of the group (that is, same-sex or mixed-sex) may influence the interactional style of the participants. Or the situation itself may influence the traits exhibited by individuals. For example, around her intimate partner, a woman may exhibit traditional feminine qualities, whereas at work she may exhibit more traditional masculine qualities. Smith, Noll, and Bryant (1999) examined the effect of social context on gender self-concept and challenged the assumption that it is static and consistent across contexts. They found that males are more likely to demonstrate feminine traits when

they are with females and to avoid showing feminine characteristics when they are with other males. Being with other males seems to activate males' gender belief system (Deaux and Major, 1987). The females in the study were less likely to change their feminine self-concept across contexts. However, among unfamiliar people, both males and females are less likely to describe themselves according to gender-role stereotypes and are more likely to display androgynous characteristics. Overall, we seem to be developing more flexible and interchangeable gender roles.

SUMMARY

1. Sex refers to one's biological identity, male or female. Gender includes those psychosocial components that characterize one as masculine or feminine. Gender identity is an individual's personal, internal sense of maleness or femaleness that is expressed in personality and behavior. Gender role is the outward manifestation and expression of one's maleness or femaleness in a social setting.

2. Environmental influences are a major determinant of gender identities and gender roles. Society defines the qualities of maleness and femaleness expected of men and women. Three of the major influences on children that mold their individual gender identities and roles are parents, television, and school.

3. Social learning theory asserts that concepts of gender roles and appropriate gender behavior are established through exposure to social influences such as parents, teachers, peers, and media.

4. Cognitive developmental theory suggests that children actively seek out cues and learn gender stereotypes at a particular stage of intellectual development—going through phases of rigidity and flexibility concerning gender behavior.

5. Gender schema theory combines elements of both cognitive developmental and social learning theories, suggesting that children cognitively determine gender categories in response to environmental cues.

6. Social structure and cultural theories directly relate power, status, and division of labor to concepts of gender identity. The view of women as subordinates in the workplace parallels the gender conception of women as less powerful and in need of support.

7. Evolutionary theories assert that gender roles have been established through genetic evolution, based on biological functions of the sexes and reproductive success.

8. People develop stereotyped concepts of masculinity and femininity. Traditionally, males were supposed to be aggressive, dominant, strong, forceful, self-confident, rugged, virile, instrumental, adventurous, courageous, independent, ambitious, direct, logical, and unemotional. To be a man, a male was supposed to be a big wheel, be successful, have status, and be looked up to.

9. Traditionally, females were supposed to be unaggressive, submissive, weak, sensitive, gentle, tender, kind, tactful, warm and affectionate, sentimental, softhearted, dependent, aware of the feelings of others, emotional and excitable, and somewhat frivolous, fickle, illogical, and talkative. Female gender norms included the marriage and motherhood mandates; that is, women were expected to get married and to have children.

10. The problem with stereotypes is that forcing everyone to conform to the same mold severely limits the development of individual

personality and personal achievement. New gender roles encourage women to be more assertive and less passive, and men to be less aggressive and more cooperative. Both sexes need the traditional female traits of tenderness, kindness, softheartedness, sensitivity, and awareness of the feelings of others in all types of human relationships. Cooperative sharing of roles results in greater contentment and companionship among family members.

11. Females are socialized to believe that the body is the ultimate expression of the self. Television, magazines, and advertisements influence the way women feel about themselves and their bodies and create unattainable standards for women to live up to, resulting in an increase in eating disorders and in negative self-image.

12. Beliefs about men and women profoundly affect the roles they play in the family. Those who believe that particular behaviors and attitudes are innate to each sex are more likely to subscribe to traditional conceptions of the subordination of women. Feminists have been working to achieve egalitarian rights and roles for women.

13. Gender-role expectations and attitudes have an effect on marital and family dynamics. African American men are more accepting of working wives than are White men.

14. Research on White adolescent girls has shown that, in addition to having increased rates of depression and suicide, they are more vulnerable to eating disorders, substance abuse, and low self-esteem. White girls also tend to "lose voice" and become more passive in order to fit the traditional gender stereotype. But recent research focusing on minority adolescent girls suggests that they have greater body satisfaction; specifically, African American girls are becoming more assertive and powerful, rather than "losing voice."

15. Egalitarian roles have not been achieved fully, even though marital satisfaction, individual psychological well-being, and child-care quality are improved when spouses share in family tasks. Women still spend significantly more time than men doing housework and caring for children, even when they work full-time outside the home. This unequal division of labor is a source of resentment and anger for many women.

16. Roles tend to change over the family life cycle. Role segregation decreases after the husband retires.

17. Partners who agree on gender-role expectations and performance report higher marital quality than do those who disagree. Gender-role congruence is an important consideration, therefore, in selecting a mate with whom one will be compatible.

18. The present trend is toward androgyny, whereby people are not gender-typed with respect to roles. A mixing of roles is advantageous to both sexes. People may actually change gender roles depending on their social context.

KEY TERMS

gender
gender role
gender identity
transgendered
transsexual
masculinity

femininity
parental identification and
 modeling
social learning theory
cognitive developmental theory
gender schema theory

social structure/cultural theories
evolutionary theories
gender stereotypes
gender-role congruence
androgyny

QUESTIONS FOR THOUGHT

1. What are the traditional conceptions of a masculine person? What effects can such conceptions have on a man's life?

2. What are the traditional conceptions of a feminine person? What effects can such conceptions have on a woman's life?

3. What roles do you believe men and women should play in marriage and the family? Explain your views.

4. Write an essay on the role of television in influencing gender roles. Do you believe television is becoming more or less influential in children's development of gender roles? Explain.

SUGGESTED READINGS

Baber, K. M., and Allen, K. R. (1992). *Women and Families: Feminist Reconstructions.* New York: Guilford Press. Examines gender and how it shapes family life.

Beall, A. E., and Sternberg, R. J. (Eds.). (1994). *The Psychology of Gender.* New York: Guilford Press. Discusses the complexity of gender and the implications of gender for individuals and for society.

Chira, S. (1998). *A Mother's Place: Taking the Debate About Working Mothers Beyond Guilt and Blame.* New York: Harper Perennial. Supports the argument that it is possible for women to be good mothers while working outside the home.

Deeghley, L. (1996). *What Does Your Wife Do? Gender and the Transformation of Family Life.* Boulder, CO: Rescue Press. Investigates how current rates of nonmarital sex, abortion, divorce, and women's employment affect family life.

Fausto-Sterling, A. (2000). *Sexing the Body: Gender Politics and the Construction of Sexuality.* New York: Basic Books. Discusses the argument that choosing to distinguish by gender is a social decision without a scientific basis.

Goodnow, J. J., and Bowes, J. M. (1994). *Men, Women, and Housework.* Melbourne: Oxford University Press. Discusses a study of housework sharing by 50 heterosexual couples in Sydney, Australia.

Lips, H. M. (1993). *Sex and Gender* (2nd ed.). Mountain View, CA: Mayfield. Provides a comprehensive discussion.

Lorber, J. (1994). *Paradoxes of Gender.* New Haven, CT: Yale University Press. Reflects on changing gender roles and some consequences.

Mahoney, R. (1995). *Kidding Ourselves: Breadwinning, Babies and Bargaining Power.* New York: Basic Books. Argues that women will not achieve economic equality until men do half the work involved in raising children.

McMahon, M. (1995). *Engendering Motherhood: Identity and Self-Transformation in Women's Lives.* New York: Guilford Press. Provides a sociological analysis of the meaning of motherhood.

Risman, B. J. (1998). *Gender Vertigo: American Families in Transition.* New Haven, CT; London: Yale University Press. Studies single fathers, married baby boom mothers, and heterosexual egalitarian couples and their children to discover how family relationships succeed without gender as a basis for family organization.

LEARNING OBJECTIVES

After reading the chapter, you should be able to:

Identify the relationship between sex and a happy marriage.

Describe the four phases of human sexual response as outlined by Masters and Johnson, and explain what happens during each stage.

Describe the three phases of sexual response as outlined by Kaplan.

Explain the role of each of the following in sexual arousal: tactile stimulation and oral-genital stimulation, visual stimulation, auditory stimulation, verbal stimulation, and mental stimulation through fantasy and nocturnal dreams.

Explain the importance of each of the following factors in lovemaking: sexual initiative, communication, time, physical setting, inhibition, relaxation, frequency of intercourse, and premarital sexual conflicts.

Describe the major male and female sexual dysfunctions, their characteristics and causes, and four types of help for overcoming sexual problems.

Describe the causes, symptoms, and treatments of the major sexually transmitted diseases, and explain in detail how AIDS is and is not transmitted and how one might protect oneself from AIDS infection and other sexually transmitted diseases.

The Sexual Basis of Relationships

Learning Objectives

Sex and a Happy Marriage

Phases of Human Sexual Response
- **Perspective:** Nonmarital Sex and Relationships
- Physiological Responses
- Summary of Response Patterns
- Multiple Orgasms
- The Three-Phase Model

Sources of Sexual Arousal
- Tactile Stimulation
- Oral Sex
- **Perspective:** The G-Spot: Myth or Reality?
- Visual Stimulation
- Auditory Stimulation
- Verbal Stimulation
- Mental Stimulation

Lovemaking Principles
- Sexual Initiative
- **Perspective:** Cybersex
- Communication
- Time Factors
- The Physical Setting

Frequency of Intercourse
Nonmarital Sexual Conflicts
Gay and Lesbian Sexual Activity

Sexual Dysfunction
- Causes of Sexual Dysfunction
- Getting Help
- **Perspective:** Viagra

Sexually Transmitted Diseases
- HIV/AIDS
- Herpes Simplex
- **Family Issues:** AIDS and Safer Sex
- Hepatitis B
- Human Papillomavirus (HPV)/Genital Warts
- Chlamydial Infections
- Gonorrhea
- Syphilis
- Parasitic Infections

Summary
Key Terms
Questions for Thought
Suggested Readings

Sexual expression is an important component of the couple relationship. As such, it affects the whole relationship and, in turn, is affected by all other aspects of that relationship. It also involves interdependent physical and emotional stimuli and responses. Emotions and feelings affect physical responses, and physical conditions and responses affect feelings. Most sexual adjustments, therefore, require an understanding of both the physical and the emotional aspects of sexual response.

Specifically, in this chapter, we focus on the process of sexual stimulation and response, on the sources of sexual arousal, and on how the body responds during the process. We are concerned with basic principles of lovemaking and ways to make sexual relationships meaningful and satisfying. We are also concerned with some of the most common problems of sexual dysfunction: what they are, what causes them, and how they might be overcome through help and treatment. Finally, we are concerned with understanding and avoiding sexually transmitted diseases.

SEX AND A HAPPY MARRIAGE

What is the relationship between sex and a happy marriage? Can people be happily married without a satisfying sex life? Certainly, the positive expression of sexuality contributes to marital satisfaction in particular and to life satisfaction in general (Maddock, 1989; McCann and Biaggio, 1989). Healthy sexuality is meant to be a blessing, not a problem (Dyk, 1990). However, what is satisfying to one couple may not be acceptable to another. Human beings differ in their sexual appetites, preferences, habits, and aims. Some couples want intercourse every day or several times a day; others would find this frequency unacceptable. If both partners are satisfied with their sex life, it can contribute in a positive way to their overall happiness; but if the partners disagree, or if one or both are frustrated or unhappy with their sex life, it can significantly reduce or even destroy relationship satisfaction.

PHASES OF HUMAN SEXUAL RESPONSE

To gain a better understanding of the total process of sexual response, it is helpful to have a clear understanding of the actual physiological changes that take place during sexual stimulation. According to the research of Masters and Johnson (1966), the phases of sexual response may be divided into four phases: (1) the excitement phase, (2) the plateau

Human beings differ in their sexual appetites, but most people agree that some form of sexual expression is an important component of a happy marriage.

In one study, 302 student volunteers from a large north-western university were asked to respond to a questionnaire about nonmarital sexual relationships. Females represented 61% and males 39% of the sample. Participants were primarily White (90%), with only a small minority representing other ethnic groups. The mean age of the undergraduates was 20.43 years. Forty-one percent of the students were casually dating, 44% were seriously dating, 9% were engaged, and 6% were cohabiting.

Correlational analysis showed strong support for the importance of personal factors in predicting the effects of first intercourse on a nonmarital relationship. As expected, more women than men reported that first intercourse had a more positive effect on their relationship. This supports the argument that women are more likely than men to connect the sexual side of a relationship to the emotional side. The analysis also showed that, the greater the extent to which both men and women considered the quality of their relationship in their decision to have intercourse, the more positive the impact on the developing relationship. The quality of the physical aspect of first intercourse was also predictive of positive impact on the subsequent relationship. For both sexes, as satisfaction with the first intercourse

increased, positive effects on the relationship increased. The greater the feelings of obligation and pressure to engage in first intercourse, the less positive the effect on the subsequent relationship for females. In addition, the higher the reported guilt of having first intercourse, the less positive the effect on the relationship for both men and women. This finding lends further support to the important role of guilt in nonmarital sexuality. If either partner viewed having intercourse as a violation of beliefs and values, this led to a subsequent decrease in sexual satisfaction.

For females, the best predictors of effects on the relationship were if the quality of the relationship was a factor in deciding whether to have intercourse and the sexual satisfaction with the first intercourse experience. For males, the best predictors of effects on the relationship were if the quality of the relationship was a factor in deciding whether to have intercourse, sexual satisfaction with the first intercourse experience, and the degree of sexual permissiveness. The primary predictor for both males and females was the extent to which the quality of the relationship was a factor in the decision to have intercourse with a partner (Cate, Long, Angera, and Draper, 1993).

A, B, and C are three different female sexual response patterns, Female C—one orgasm, Female A—two orgasms, Female B—no orgasm.

The refractory period represents the last, irregular contractions during which sexual tension rapidly subsides.

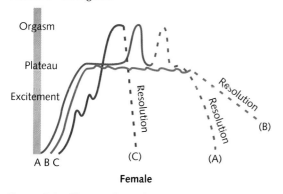

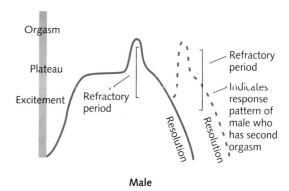

Female   Male

Figure 8.1   Human Sexual Response Cycles (*Note:* From *Human Sexual Response* by W. H. Masters and V. E. Johnson, 1966, Boston: Little, Brown. Used by permission of Masters and Johnson Institute.)

phase, (3) the orgasm phase, and (4) the resolution phase (see Figure 8.1). The **excitement phase** extends from the beginnings of sexual stimulation to the point at which the individual reaches a high degree of sexual excitation. The duration of this phase may be prolonged or shortened depending upon the intensity of the stimulation and individual reactions to it. Cessation of stimulation or some form of

Figure 8.2 Breast Changes During the Female Sexual Response Cycle (*Note:* From *Human Sexuality,* 2nd ed., by W. H. Masters, V. E. Johnson, and R. C. Kolodny, 1983, Boston: Little, Brown. Used by permission of Masters and Johnson Institute.)

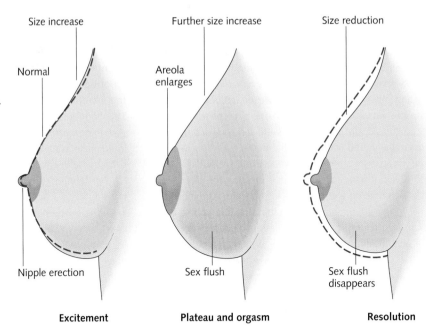

Size increase

Normal

Nipple erection

Excitement

Further size increase

Areola enlarges

Sex flush

Plateau and orgasm

Size reduction

Sex flush disappears

Resolution

interruption (the phone ringing, a displeasing comment, an uncomfortable sexual move) may even abort the process. If sexual stimulation is continued, sexual tensions are intensified, and the individual reaches the **plateau phase** of the sexual cycle, from which he or she may move to orgasm. If sexual stimuli are withdrawn, the individual will not achieve orgasm, and sexual tension will gradually subside.

The **orgasm phase** is limited to those few seconds during which sexual tension is at its maximum and then suddenly released. However, there is usually great variation in the intensity and duration of orgasm from time to time and from person to person. After orgasm, the person enters the last or **resolution phase** of the sexual cycle, during which sexual tension subsides as the individual moves back through the plateau and the excitement phases to the unstimulated state.

Physiological Responses

As sexual excitement increases, both men and women show similar physical responses.

Vasocongestion and Erection The man's penis, the woman's clitoris and nipples (and often the man's nipples), and the woman's labia become en-

gorged with blood—a process known as **vasocongestion**—which causes swelling, enlargement, and **erection** (see Figure 8.2).

One of the most important changes in the female is in the vagina (see Figure 8.3). The outer one-third becomes engorged with blood, reducing the opening, with the outer muscles contracting around the penis. At the same time, the vaginal length increases and the inner portion balloons out, increasing considerably in width. Women who use diaphragms for contraception have to be certain they are fitted quite tightly; otherwise, the ballooning of the inner vagina due to sexual excitement loosens the diaphragm, allowing sperm to pass around the edges or the diaphragm itself to become dislodged.

Another change in the female is in the clitoris. As excitement increases during the plateau phase, the erect clitoris begins to withdraw into the hood, showing a 50% total reduction in length by the end of that phase (see Figure 8.4). It returns to its normal position in 5–10 seconds, and orgasmic contractions stop during the resolution phase.

The important change in the penis is erection and increase in width and length (see Figure 8.5). It is not uncommon for an erection to come and go several times if the excitement phase is prolonged. Erections are also affected by fear, anxiety, changes

Excitement

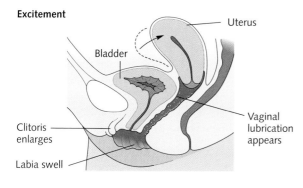

Uterus
Bladder
Clitoris enlarges
Labia swell
Vaginal lubrication appears

Plateau

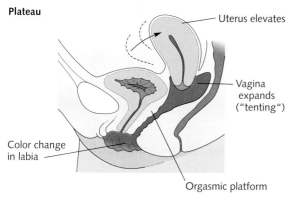

Uterus elevates
Vagina expands ("tenting")
Color change in labia
Orgasmic platform

Orgasm

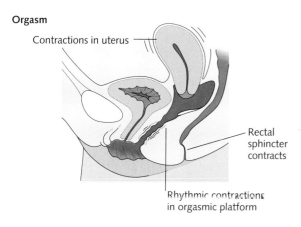

Contractions in uterus
Rectal sphincter contracts
Rhythmic contractions in orgasmic platform

Resolution

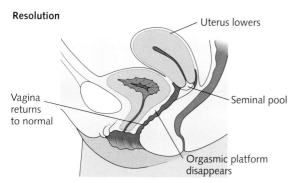

Uterus lowers
Vagina returns to normal
Seminal pool
Orgasmic platform disappears

Figure 8.3   Internal Changes During the Female Sexual Response Cycle

in temperature, loud noises, changes in lighting, and other distractions. The testes also enlarge by at least 50% due to engorgement with blood during sexual excitement.

Myotonia   As excitement increases, there is a tensing—known as **myotonia**—and flexing of the voluntary and involuntary muscles of the arms, legs, abdomen, face, neck, pelvis, buttocks, hands, and feet. Muscular tension may result in facial grimaces, flaring of the nostrils, and strain around the mouth. The cords of the neck become rigid, the back arches, and the long muscles of the thighs become tense. The muscles of the buttocks become voluntarily contracted. There is a semispastic contraction of the hand and foot muscles.

Lubrication   Within 10–30 seconds after sexual stimulation begins, sweating and self-lubrication of the inner walls of the vagina begin. The presence of **lubrication** is one indication of sexual response. The male emits two or three drops of preejaculatory fluid, which is secreted from the Cowper's glands. This, too, can function as a lubricant during coitus, although the secretion does not appear until the plateau phase of response.

Increase in Heart and Pulse Rate, Blood Pressure, Respiration, and Perspiration   The heart, pulse, and respiratory rates may more than double; the blood pressure may increase anywhere from 20% to 80%. About a third of men and women perspire during the resolution phase.

Sex Flush   As excitement increases, the **sex flush,** a noticeable reddening of the skin, usually in the form of a red, splotchy rash, gradually spreads over more and more of the body. About three out of four orgasmic women and one out of four orgasmic men show this reaction.

Orgasm   During **orgasm,** there may be severe involuntary muscular contractions throughout the body, gradually subsiding during the resolution phase. These contractions during orgasm are especially strong in the vagina, uterus, and pelvic region of the female and in the penis, vas deferens, seminal vesicles, and prostate gland of the male. The female may experience 5–12 contractions with gradual lengthening of the intervals between and

Figure 8.4   The Clitoris and Labia During the Female Sexual Response Cycle (*Note:* From *Human Sexuality,* 2nd ed., by W. H. Masters, V. E. Johnson, and R. C. Kolodny, 1985, Boston: Little, Brown. Used by permission of Masters and Johnson Institute.)

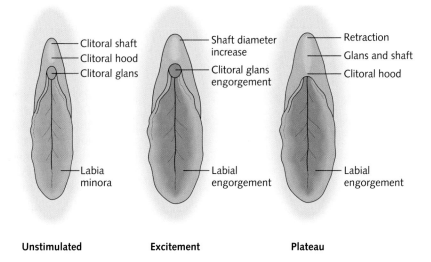

with decreasing intensity. Under sexual excitement, the uterus increases in size by 50% and pushes outward during the contraction of orgasm, expelling any fluids that may be inside. If orgasm occurs while the woman is menstruating, increased flow may result briefly. In the male, contractions of the prostate, vas deferens, seminal vesicles, and penis produce ejaculation.

Summary of Response Patterns

Two observations should be made about these phases of sexual response. First, the responses of the male and female are very similar, even though the actual sexual organs are different. Both males and females show vasocongestion of the sex organs when stimulated, and both have erectile tissue that enlarges and becomes firm. Both show evidence of sex flush (the reddening of the skin) and myotonia (muscular tension). Both show an increase in heart rate, blood pressure, and respiration, and both evidence lubrication. Both experience orgasm, and both perspire during the resolution phase.

Second, the physiological responses to stimulation are similar regardless of the method of stimulation, whether by individual masturbation, mutual foreplay, or intercourse. The only real difference is in the degree of excitation. The important point that Masters and Johnson and others have made is that there is no physical difference between the so-called vaginal orgasm (one achieved by stimulation of the vagina) and the clitoral orgasm (one achieved by

stimulation of the clitoris). Of the two organs, however, the clitoris—not the vagina—is by far the most sexually sensitive. In fact, the nerve endings in the vagina lie deep beneath the surface, so that often no feeling occurs until sexual excitement is already well advanced. Thus, female sexual arousal comes far easier by clitoral than by vaginal stimulation. This knowledge can be used in foreplay to achieve a high level of arousal prior to coitus itself. It must be recognized, however, that intensity of orgasm can vary with any method of stimulation.

Multiple Orgasms

One important male-female difference was "discovered" by Masters and Johnson (1966), even though Kinsey, Pomeroy, Martin, and Gebhard (1953) and others had mentioned it years before: Some females are capable of rapid return to orgasm after an orgasmic experience. Furthermore, these females are capable of maintaining an orgasmic experience for a relatively long period of time. In other words, some females are capable of multiple and more prolonged orgasms, whereas the average male may have difficulty in achieving more than one without some time elapsing in between. Figure 8.1 shows some male and female response patterns (Masters and Johnson, 1966).

In one study, researchers investigated the female multiorgasmic experience in relationship to method of stimulation—namely, masturbation, intimate touching, and sexual intercourse. Of the re-

Excitement

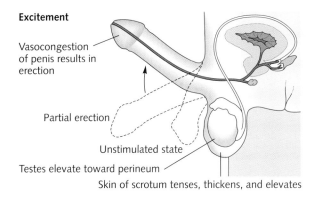

Vasocongestion of penis results in erection

Partial erection

Unstimulated state

Testes elevate toward perineum

Skin of scrotum tenses, thickens, and elevates

Plateau

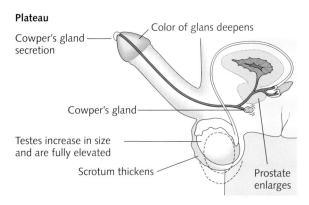

Cowper's gland secretion

Color of glans deepens

Cowper's gland

Testes increase in size and are fully elevated

Scrotum thickens

Prostate enlarges

Orgasm

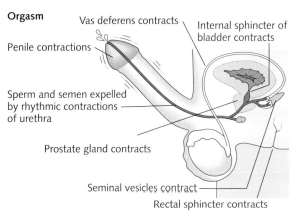

Vas deferens contracts

Internal sphincter of bladder contracts

Penile contractions

Sperm and semen expelled by rhythmic contractions of urethra

Prostate gland contracts

Seminal vesicles contract

Rectal sphincter contracts

Resolution

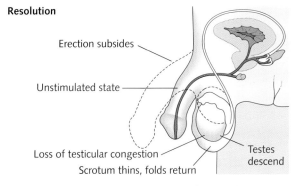

Erection subsides

Unstimulated state

Loss of testicular congestion

Testes descend

Scrotum thins, folds return

Figure 8.5 Changes During the Male Sexual Response Cycle

spondents, 48% had experienced multiple orgasms by some method of stimulation: 26% by means of masturbation, 18% by means of intimate touching, and 25% by means of sexual intercourse. Only 7% had experienced multiple orgasms during all three types of sexual activity. For the multiorgasmic group, 40% reported that each successive orgasm was stronger, 16% that it was weaker, 35% that it varied in strength, and 9% that there was no difference. The number of orgasms reported during a multiorgasmic experience ranged from 2 to 20.

The findings indicated that women who experienced multiple orgasms were more explorative in their sexual activities. Furthermore, their awareness of pleasurable sensations resulting from masturbation occurred at an earlier age than for single-orgasmic women.

A related issue is how satisfied women feel with their sexual activities. Although a majority of women were satisfied with their sex lives, multiorgasmic women were more likely to be physiologically satisfied with sex intercourse than were single-orgasmic women. Partner involvement in sexual intercourse was important, since multiorgasmic women were more likely to receive nipple stimulation, clitoral stimulation, and a variety of vaginal stimulation techniques along with emotional interaction. Thus, through sexual intercourse, multiorgasmic women may satisfy more of their sexual needs (Darling, Davidson, and Jennings, 1991).

There are great individual variations in female responses. Some women desire multiple orgasms while others seem satisfied with one. If women practice contracting their PC (pubococcygeal) and pelvic muscles repeatedly (called Kegel exercises), they can strengthen the vaginal muscles and increase sexual pleasure and orgasm response.

Hartman and Fithian (1984) have been able to teach men to experience multiple, nonejaculatory orgasms by withholding ejaculation until the final orgasm in the series. This is accomplished by tightening the PC and pelvic muscles when orgasm is approaching. (If the man tightens his muscles as he does in holding back urine, this contracts the PC muscles.) By tightening the PC muscles, ejaculation is prevented but orgasm continues just the same. This makes it possible to continue stimulation to produce additional orgasms without ejaculation. The process of resolution does not occur until after the final orgasm with ejaculation.

The Three-Phase Model

Psychiatrist and sex therapist Helen Kaplan (1979) has developed a three-phase model of the sexual response cycle: desire, excitement, and orgasm. Kaplan's **desire phase** is unique since it does not involve the genitals but consists of attitudes, ideas, feelings, and stimuli that motivate a person to want sexual expression. The excitement phase is a stage of sexual arousal characterized primarily by vasocongestion. The orgasm phase is defined primarily by muscular contractions.

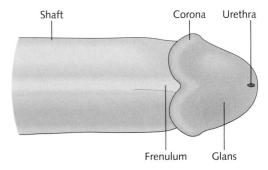

Figure 8.6 Parts of the Penis

SOURCES OF SEXUAL AROUSAL

Not only the genitals themselves, but also the senses and the mind, can be sources of sexual arousal for both men and women. Sources of sexual arousal may include tactile, visual, auditory, verbal, and mental stimulation.

Tactile Stimulation

One of the primary means of sexual arousal is through touch, or tactile stimulation of those parts of the body that are sexually sensitive (Thayer, 1988). These sexually sensitive areas are called **erogenous zones.** The erogenous zones in women include the clitoris (particularly the glans), the mons, the labia minora and the vestibule the labia enclose, the vaginal opening, the outer one-third of the vaginal barrel, the anus, and the perineum (the area between the vagina and the anus). The breasts, especially the nipples, are also sensitive to touch, as are the tongue and lips.

The erogenous zones in men include the penis (Figure 8.6), especially the glans and corona (particularly the underneath area, or the frenulum), the scrotum, the anus, and the tongue and lips. The nipples of some men are also sexually sensitive. Some men and women find other areas to be sexually responsive as well.

Common methods of tactile stimulation include cuddling, hugging, kissing, rubbing, caressing, and stroking. Most couples find these forms of tactile contact to be deeply satisfying, producing feelings of security, warmth, and affection, as well as sexual arousal.

The fingers are the most common instrument of stimulation. **Digital foreplay** involves the use of one or more fingers and sometimes the whole hand in massaging, caressing, rubbing, or vibrating sensitive body parts. Usually, a light touch, especially in the beginning, is more arousing than a forceful or heavy one. The pressure and speed of movement are increased as excitement grows. The mouth is used for oral-genital stimulation and is a preferred method of stimulation for many couples because it is arousing not only to the recipient but also to the person doing it.

Oral Sex

The National Health and Social Life Survey found that about 75% of men, and about 70% of women, had given and received oral sex (Michael et al., 1994).

The stimulation of the clitoris, labia, or vaginal opening with the lips and tongue is called **cunnilingus** (from the Latin for "one who licks the vulva"). The technique involves kissing, licking, nibbling, or sucking the shaft and tip of the clitoris or the labia minora, or thrusting the tongue in and out of the vaginal opening.

Most men enjoy cunnilingus (Petersen, Kretchner, Nellis, Lever, and Hertz, 1983). It turns them on, and they enjoy giving pleasure to their partner. Many women also like cunnilingus. For some, it implies a special kind of acceptance; for others, the erotic sensations are most important. One woman comments, "A tongue offers gentleness and precision and wetness and is the perfect organ for contact. And, besides, it produces sensational orgasms!" (Hite, 1981, p. 361). Some women, however, are embarrassed and self-conscious about it.

Fellatio (from the Latin for "to suck") involves the stimulation of the male genitals, especially the

The G-spot was first recognized by a German gynecologist, Ernst Grafenberg, for whom the spot is named. He identified the spot as a half-dollar-sized area of high sensitivity on the wall of the vagina toward the front of the body. It is located where the urethra runs closest to the top of the vaginal wall, about halfway between the pubic bone and the cervix, 3 inches into the vagina. The G-spot supposedly contains bundles of highly sensitive nerve endings capable of producing intense arousal when stimulated. Some researchers claim that the entire anterior wall of the vagina contains these nerve endings, rather than one specific spot, while other researchers claim that the spot does not exist at all in some women.

It is relatively challenging for women to find and explore their G-spot on their own because most do not have fingers long enough to reach it. With the use of a vibrator or through intercourse, the search can become an enjoyable activity. The spot generally responds only to intense localized pressure, so stimulation is often more effective when done through steady pressure rather than the usual thrusting. Rear-entry and female-on-top positioning for intercourse are two effective ways of producing direct stimulation. Some women are able to climax as a result of such pressure, while others may have significantly heightened arousal. By communicating with her sexual partner about what is pleasurable, a woman will have a more open and liberating sexual experience.

penis, with the mouth, lips, and tongue. It may mean licking various parts of the penis or the scrotum, or sucking the penis, especially the glans. The frenulum is especially sensitive. Fellatio may also involve simultaneous digital caressing of the scrotum, perineum, or anus.

Like most types of sexual expression, oral-genital contact requires the consent and cooperation of both partners. If two people disagree, they need to talk about their feelings and try to reach some sort of consensus. Certainly, trying to force oral sex on one's partner represents coercion and an attempt at domination and will be deeply resented. Some people who have initial misgivings or fears are able to overcome their inhibitions and learn to enjoy this method of arousal. Nevertheless, for many couples, the success of their sexual relationship does not revolve around whether they have oral-genital contact.

Visual Stimulation

Traditionally, men and women have been considered different in the way they respond to visual sexual stimuli. Kinsey and his colleagues (1948, 1953) observed that men are aroused by reading erotic writings, looking at photos of naked women, talking about sex, looking at women with good figures, going to strip clubs, and observing people having sex. Women are thought to be less aroused by these sources than by reading love stories or seeing romantic movies. In this sense, men are considered *erotic* and women *romantic*. One of the first comparative studies found that when women are exposed to erotic photographs they tend to verbally judge them to be less arousing than do men but show almost the same degree of sexual-physiological reactions as men (Sigusch, Schmidt, Reinfeld, and Weideman-Sutor, 1970). In a more recent study, women watching erotic tapes reported sexual arousal, and physical measurements of vaginal responses indicated physiological arousal as well (Heiman, Rowland, Hatch, and Gladue, 1991). Apparently, both men and women are responding to social cues. That is, women are not supposed to be stimulated by pictures, so they report less arousal when, in fact, they are aroused (Kelley, 1985; Przbyla and Byrne, 1984). And men are socialized to accept the fact that they are aroused, which is what they report. In short, there is not as much difference between the sexes in regard to sources of stimulation as was once thought, and the differences that exist may have their foundation in the socialization process.

For example, a study examining the influence of pornography on women found that women who were exposed to pornography earlier in life reported being more influenced by the media in how they viewed their bodies (Keihani, 1999). This finding indicates that, whereas men are socialized to become aroused by visual stimuli, women are socialized to feel that they must live up to these doctored images, and they view their bodies negatively as a result.

Couples need to be aware of the importance of visual stimuli in sexual arousal. Many people thoroughly enjoy seeing their partner dress or undress or wearing sexy clothes. Arousal and lovemaking are enhanced if people can see what they

Do men and women respond the same to visual sexual stimuli, such as the physical features of the "sex object"? What social cues do men and women respond to?

are doing and can watch their partner respond to erotic caresses.

Auditory Stimulation

Sound can also be sexually stimulating (Julien and Over, 1988). An important way that couples use sound in sexual stimulation is through words. Loving, soothing, adoring, flattering words may have a more romantic effect than much preliminary caressing. One wife remarked, "If he'd only tell me he loves me, he could get me in the mood in a hurry. He never talks to me and certainly doesn't whisper 'sweet nothings' in my ear" (author's counseling notes). Vocalization during sexual activity is a great way to inform a partner that what he or she is doing is pleasurable.

Music can also be a relaxing or stimulating addition to a couple's sex life. Playing a favorite CD in the background can set a romantic mood and enhance sexual stimulation. From rock and roll to classical, music can help to create a comfortable environment for sexual expression.

Of course, sound can be a turn-off as well as a turn-on. A sudden loud noise, the voices of children in an adjacent bedroom, or the telephone ringing can dampen sexual ardor.

Verbal Stimulation

The printed word can also be an important source of sexual arousal, which is why millions of dollars worth of erotic literature are sold each year. One woman commented, "I can get more aroused by reading a sexy novel than by any other way." A man admitted, "I like to read dirty books before I masturbate. It really puts me in the mood" (author's counseling notes). Steinman and colleagues (1981) found that both men and women become aroused when listening to tape recordings of erotic stories. Heiman (1980) found that women become aroused when listening to such tapes but sometimes are not consciously aware of their own arousal.

Mental Stimulation

Fantasies   Fantasy plays a big role in sexual stimulation (Ellis and Symons, 1990), and fantasizing before and during intercourse facilitates sexual arousal. During lovemaking, some people find their thoughts wandering to other things or have trouble concentrating on love play. Therapists urge people who are having difficulty responding to conjure up the most sexually arousing images they can think of (Lentz and Zeiss, 1984). Couples are encouraged

Kissing is an important means of sexual expression and arousal, but it also encourages relaxation and feelings of security, warmth, and affection.

to concentrate on these to promote sexual arousal. However, there are large individual differences in the extent to which fantasy can contribute to sexual arousal (Smith and Over, 1990). Some people who have low sexual desire and arousal problems have difficulty fantasizing, and others experience guilt when fantasizing (Gil, 1990).

Nocturnal Dreams   Some fantasies occur as dreams. These can be similar in content to daydream fantasies except that they may end in orgasm because inhibitions are lowered during sleep. Kinsey and his colleagues (1953) found that most men and a majority of women had nocturnal dreams with sexual content and that 83% of males and 37% of females had erotic dreams leading to orgasm. **Nocturnal emissions** and **wet dreams** are most common among adolescent males who do not have other sexual outlets. Dreams that culminate in orgasm are common among adolescent females, and Wells (1983) reported that one-third of his sample of college women had experienced nocturnal orgasm.

However, both men and women of any age may experience nocturnal dreams accompanied by orgasm.

LOVEMAKING PRINCIPLES

Lovemaking is an art that can be developed through knowledge and experience. One key to a satisfying sex life is each partner's responsiveness to the other's needs and feelings. We are concerned here with such things as willingness to initiate sex, the importance of communication, time factors and their relationship to lovemaking, the physical setting for lovemaking, and the frequency of intercourse.

Sexual Initiative

Traditionally, men were the sexual aggressors and women were the recipients, but times have changed. The important thing now is that both the man and the woman feel free to initiate sex and to be sexually assertive and active during sex itself. In one

Methods of sexual expression continue to change with technological advances. With the introduction of the automobile came a new place for sexual exploits, with motion pictures came X-rated films, and with the telephone came phone sex. And so it follows, with cyberspace comes cybersex.

The Internet provides an anonymous environment in which people can participate in sexual activities with little risk of embarrassment or punishment. Lamb (1998) has suggested that cybersex might be harmless when adults use it to enhance one another's fantasies. The danger arises when adults contact children and solicit them to fulfill their fantasies and engage in deviant behavior. According to a survey on online victimization of children, one in five adolescents has been exposed to strangers who wanted cybersex (Finkelhor, Mitchell, and Wolak, 2000). It is estimated that as many as 24 million adolescents ages 10–17 were online regularly in 1999 and so were at risk for unwanted sexual solicitations and sexual materials, as well as threatening and offensive behavior directed at them.

Almost half of the 1,501 youths surveyed believed that the solicitations were from someone under the age of 18. A quarter of those seeking cybersex were perceived as being adults but were actually young adults ages 18–25. Thus, in teaching children about online safety, parents and others need to look beyond the stereotypic older male sexual predator (Finkelhor, Mitchell, and Wolak, 2000).

Other important data in the report included the following:

- One in 33 youths surveyed had received aggressive solicitation—someone asking to meet them, calling them on the phone, or sending regular mail, money, or gifts.
- One in four youths had received unwanted pictures of naked people or people having sex.
- Almost two-thirds of the incidents occurred in a chat room.
- Three-quarters of the advances were brushed off by the adolescent.
- About one-quarter of the youths who experienced a solicitation told a parent, and almost 40% who received sexual material told a parent.
- Only 17% of the youths and approximately 10% of the parents could identify an authority to whom they could report these incidents, such as police or social workers.
- One-third of the parents who had Internet access at home said they had filtering or blocking software on their computers.

As this report suggests, parents and other authority figures must constantly remind youths and teens that people have ulterior motives and hidden agendas, and any meetings with cyberfriends should be under supervision and in a public place.

---

study, assertive women reported higher frequencies of sexual activity and orgasm, rated themselves as having more sexual desire, and reported greater marital and sexual satisfaction (Hurlbert, 1991).

Communication

Once sex is initiated, it is helpful if partners communicate their sexual preferences. James (1983) wrote, "Men are generally pleased with women who let them know what they want and how they want it. With this kind of information the man can perceive her sexual interest as flattering and provocative" (p. 250). The man can also derive pleasure from knowing that he is satisfying the sexual needs of his partner. A few males resent suggestions, preferring to believe they are great lovers and don't need instruction. But this may be a sign of immaturity and insecurity. Communication of sexual

preferences enhances sexual relationships. Interviews with college men and women revealed that sexual self-disclosure increases not only sexual rewards in the relationship but also perhaps overall relationship satisfaction (Byers and Demmons, 1999).

Time Factors

Time plays an important role in sexual arousal. Both men and women show variations in desire over time. Some of the woman's variations in sexual drive relate to her monthly cycle. Overall, some women report an increase in sexual thoughts and feelings just before and during menstruation, while others report increased sexual desire and activity at the time of ovulation (Friedman, Hurt, Arnoff, and Clarkin, 1980; Matteo and Rissman, 1984). Still others report no differences at different stages of the menstrual cycle (Morrell, Dixen, Carter, and Davidson, 1984). Of course, many factors affect desire: general health, the degree of marital harmony, events that happen in and outside the family, and even current events. Whatever is upsetting may influence sexual drive and desire.

Men and women are affected by these factors. People who are sick, who are tired, or who are upset by their relationship with their partner or children or by events at work may have a temporary decrease in sexual drive. As noted previously, female sexual desire may fluctuate at different stages of the menstrual cycle, as well as during pregnancy. Male sexual drive is affected by testosterone levels. Fatigue may lower the level, and, in most men, the testosterone level is highest in the morning and lowest at night; as a result, many men show greater interest in intercourse in the morning than at night. Emotional factors may play a role in influencing sexual desire in both men and women, and both sexes are subject to mood and behavior patterns (Lips, 1997).

When couples have intercourse, they need to give themselves an uninterrupted period of time to make love. Love play should be a leisurely time in which partners have a chance to pleasure and respond to each other. One of the biggest complaints of women is that men are in too much of a hurry (Denny, Field, and Quadagno, 1984). One woman commented, "I like long arousals, but it usually doesn't last as long as I need, because he is rushing to move along toward orgasm" (Hite, 1981, p. 145). Kinsey and his colleagues (1953) found that through coitus alone the average female took 10–20 minutes to achieve an orgasm, whereas the average male achieved an orgasm in 4 minutes. However, with proper stimulation and sufficient love play, females could achieve an orgasm in just under 4 minutes and males in 2–4. The problem is not that women require a longer period to achieve an orgasm. The problem is that they are sometimes not stimulated in the right way so that they are sufficiently aroused before intercourse takes place.

One study outlined those factors that inhibited female orgasm during sexual intercourse. The factors mentioned, in decreasing order of importance, are lack of foreplay, premature ejaculation, fatigue, preoccupation with nonsexual thoughts, conflict between partners, lack of interest in foreplay by the partner, lack of tenderness by the partner, lack of adequate vaginal lubrication, difficulty in sexual

arousal of the partner, desire to perform well, lack of privacy, overindulgence in alcohol, painful intercourse, and overeating (Darling, Davidson, and Cox, 1991).

Ordinarily, an important goal for couples is to ensure that the woman is aroused first and even achieves an orgasm before the man to ensure that his erection is sustained long enough for coitus. If he has his orgasm first, her stimulation can be continued manually or orally. Certainly, it is not necessary to have simultaneous orgasms to have good sex.

Coitus can become so lengthy, however, that it becomes uncomfortable. After a period of time, lubrication ceases, the vaginal tissues become dry, and intercourse becomes painful. Using lubricants and decreasing the time of actual coitus can help. If either partner has trouble achieving orgasm, lengthy foreplay and then brief coitus is one answer.

The Physical Setting

Physical surroundings play a role in enhancing or retarding lovemaking. Some couples can make love freely in their own bedroom but are inhibited in someone else's house. One couple stayed in the husband's mother's house for the first year of marriage, and he was not able to achieve an orgasm the entire year. Obviously, he had been negatively conditioned sexually from the time he was very young (author's counseling notes). Some couples find it exciting to check into a motel, make love in the automobile, or retreat into the woods. Sex need never become boring if couples introduce variety and change from time to time. Certainly, assuring privacy helps couples to be uninhibited. Locked doors add assurance that the children won't walk in unexpectedly.

Frequency of Intercourse

A question often asked is, How frequently do couples have intercourse, and what is the relationship between frequency and sexual satisfaction? It is always dangerous to play the numbers game, because whatever figures are mentioned are going to be disappointing to someone. But, as a starter, let's examine what some couples do.

In general, men experience sexual desire somewhat more frequently than do women, although there is a considerable variation among individuals (Beck et al., 1991). One study of women in the early years of marriage showed that the frequency of intercourse declined from an average of almost 15 times per month during the first years of marriage to about 6 times per month during the sixth year (Greenblat, 1983). However, there was a wide range of frequency: from 4 to 45 times per month for couples married under 1 year. Typically, most couples start out marriage engaging frequently in intercourse, but then the incidence begins to decline, and they settle into their own individual patterns. However, couples report that affection, love, tenderness, companionship, and physical closeness continue to be strong needs.

This does not mean that couples lose interest in sex. One study presented data on marital sex based on the 1988 National Survey of Families and Households. For this representative sample of 7,463 U.S. adults, the incidence and frequency of marital sex declined over the life course. Several factors contributed to this decline, including diminished health, biological aging, and habituation to sex. Age was the most frequent predictor of marital sex frequency, and marital happiness was the next most common predictor. Some factors found to be related to frequency of sex were associated with life changes that either reduced or increased the opportunity for sex; these included pregnancy, the presence of small children, and sterilization. Married couples that had cohabited before marriage and those in which spouses were in their second or later marriage had more frequent sex than couples that had not experienced these events (Call, Strecher, and Schwartz, 1995).

In another study, 62 women and 40 men ages 60–84 were asked to reveal their current sexual interests and activities compared to when they were ages 20–30 (Turner and Adams, 1988). Sixty-eight percent of the respondents were married; the rest were widowed, separated, divorced, or never-married. Overall, there was a reported decline in incidence of sexual activity, frequency of orgasm, interest, urge, pleasure, and satisfaction from young adulthood to old age. However, 47% of the respondents reported stability in preferred sexual activity. That is, those who liked intercourse in young adulthood liked it in old age, and those who preferred intimate touching, fantasizing, or masturbating in young adulthood liked it in old age. In short, sexual interest and activity in old age were highly related to early-life interest and activity.

An investigation of 4,000 respondents revealed that 75% of the men and 61% of the women were sexually active and enjoying sex at age 70 and older (Brecher, 1984). When asked for reasons for no longer having sexual intercourse, many women reported they lacked an interested and capable male partner. A study of Swedish men and women ages 60–79 with partners revealed that 53% of the men and 38% of the women were having intercourse at least once a month (Bergstrom-Walan and Nielsen, 1990); 29% of the men and 16% of the women were having intercourse at least once a week.

A study of sexual interest and behavior of 202 healthy White men and women ages 80–102 revealed that the most common activity was touching and caressing without intercourse (Bretschneider and McCoy, 1988). Masturbation was the second most common activity (only 19% of the women and 29% of the men were presently married), and sexual intercourse the third most. Sixty-two percent of the men and 30% of the women said they had sexual intercourse at least sometimes, with 76% of the men and 39% of the women enjoying it. Only a minority of men in their nineties and women in their eighties reported having no interest in sex.

Another important consideration is how partners feel about the frequency with which they have intercourse. In cases of marked differences in sexual appetite, overlooking the problem is no solution. Doing so creates tension in the marriage or relationship. If partners can't work things out themselves, they may need outside help from a sex therapist.

Sex has long been intertwined with feelings of intimacy in committed relationships. It involves trust and communication by both partners, and as such, their sexual functioning can directly affect their relationship functioning. One study examined how men and women differ in their attitudes toward five categories of intimacy—emotional, social, sexual, intellectual, and recreational—and how that impacts overall relationship and sexual satisfaction. In interviews with 137 males (mean age 33.4) and 102 females (mean age 29.6), the researchers found that the women had higher sexual intimacy scores, thus placing more importance on sexual intimacy. Men placed more importance than women on sexual satisfaction, sexual communication, positive attitudes toward sex, and physical contact. Men and women had similar views on conventionality, sexual behavior, and assessment of their own level of sexual dysfunction. These findings suggest that, while women seek a higher level of intimacy with sexual relations, both men and women place a high value on sexual functioning, directly correlating sex with relationship functioning (McCabe, 1999).

Nonmarital Sexual Conflicts

Sexual interactions outside of marriage have increased markedly in recent years for both men and women. This increased sexual activity in nonmarital relationships provides numerous occasions for conflict between partners. Although gender differences concerning sexual attitudes have been converging, females still have more conservative sexual attitudes than males. This gender difference creates a situation in which both parties may engage in strategies to either decrease or increase sexual involvement.

One study used the Premarital Sexual Conflict Scale to assess nonmarital sexual conflicts among 250 students—51% females and 49% males. The participants were primarily White, with a small proportion representing other ethnic groups (African American, Hispanic, and Native American). The mean age of the undergraduates was 22.2 years. Thirteen percent of the students were casually dating, 68% were seriously dating, 12% were engaged, and 7% were cohabiting. Of the 250 students, 189 (76%) reported having sexual intercourse with their present partner. The average respondent stated that he or she had had sex with five previous partners and currently had sex a mean of seven times per month.

Participants were given a list of 61 sources of sexual conflict and were asked to rate each item in terms of how much conflict they experienced over it. Table 8.1 lists the 12 most common reasons for conflicts, in order of decreasing frequency.

The study showed that satisfaction with the sexual experience is negatively related to nonmarital conflicts with a partner. Individuals who were not sexually satisfied experienced higher levels of conflict than those who were sexually satisfied. The item most frequently mentioned was conflict over appropriate sexual positions to use. Individuals who felt obliged or pressured from peers and/or partners to engage in sexual activity were likely to have higher levels of sexual conflict. Individuals

Table 8.1 Sources of Nonmarital Sexual Conflict

1. Appropriate sexual positions
2. Partner's failure to ask questions about satisfaction with sex
3. Duration of sex
4. Partners' expectations about sexual behavior
5. The kinds of sexual behavior engaged in (intimate touching, oral sex, sexual intercourse, and so forth)
6. Pressure to engage in sex
7. One partner not in the mood for sex
8. Lack of orgasm
9. Lack of mutual orgasm
10. Sex merely a habit
11. Sex only for physical gratification
12. Frequency of sexual involvement

Note: From "A Longitudinal Assessment of a Measure of Premarital Sexual Conflicts" by E. C. J. Long, R. M. Cate, D. A. Fehsenfeld, and K. M. Williams, 1996, *Family Relations, 45,* pp. 302–308.

who reported higher levels of guilt over their sexual involvement and those who were sexually conservative had higher levels of sexual conflict. This finding indicates that people must learn how to make sexual decisions based on their own self-determined values and feelings. If inflated levels of conflict exist, partners may need instruction or information about sexual techniques or about how to communicate effectively with a partner about physical pleasure. Sexual conflict can hinder the development of a satisfying relationship for both males and females. Partners may need assistance in controlling the overall level of conflict by resolving specific issues so that sexual conflict does not erode satisfaction within the relationship (Long, Cate, Fehsenfeld, and Williams, 1996).

Gay and Lesbian Sexual Activity

This chapter is largely focused on the sexual relationships of heterosexual individuals, but homosexual relationships are becoming increasingly visible and accepted in society (Sullivan, 1995). For example, many states have done away with the traditional sodomy laws, which criminalized gay and lesbian relations and oral and anal sex, although some states still have these laws on the books (Sack, 1998). Gay and lesbian sexual relationships are similar to heterosexual relationships. For example, the three-phase model of sexual arousal is the same, as are the physiological changes occurring in the body during sexual arousal. Stimulation is equally effective in homosexual activity, and heterosexual lovemaking principles also apply. Gays, lesbians, and bisexuals experience sexual dysfunction at rates similar to those of heterosexuals. From a purely sexual standpoint, homosexual relationships offer the same potential for intimacy and pleasure that heterosexual relationships do; the only difference is the choice of sexual partners.

SEXUAL DYSFUNCTION

Under most circumstances the body functions quite smoothly, reacting in predictable ways to certain sexual stimuli. Sometimes, however, the sex organs do not respond. For example, the penis remains flaccid when stroked, or the nipples fail to become enlarged and erect when the breasts are stimulated, or partners don't achieve orgasms after copulating for a long period of time. Obviously, something has gone wrong if a particular stimulus does not produce the expected response. Any malfunction of the human sexual response system is termed **sexual dysfunction,** because a person has not reacted as would normally be expected. In this section, we address both male and female dysfunctions.

Premature ejaculation has been defined as a condition wherein a man is unable to exert voluntary control over his ejaculatory reflex, with the result that once he is sexually aroused he reaches orgasm very quickly (Kaplan, 1974; Rowland, Haensel, Blom, and Slob, 1993). A man's ability to control ejaculation helps a couple attain sexual satisfaction. The couple needs to be able to engage in sexual play and in intercourse until both partners are sufficiently aroused for orgasm to take place. If the man climaxes before the woman is aroused sufficiently, the couple may have to rely on other means of stimulation to bring her to orgasm. Premature ejaculation curtails the woman's sensuous enjoyment even if she has an orgasm afterward. The couple's pleasure and lovemaking are heightened if the man can prolong the period of intense excitement prior to orgasm. At best, prematurity restricts the couple's sexuality. If the partners become anxious and worried about their sex life, premature ejaculatory dysfunction can reduce the harmony of the relationship. Fortunately, premature ejaculation is one of the easiest of male sexual dysfunctions to treat (Masters and Johnson, 1970).

If a male is unable to produce an erection so that coital connection can take place or maintain one long enough to complete the sexual act, he has **erectile dysfunction.** Actually, most men experience this condition at some time or another, but it usually is temporary in nature.

Some men are not able to achieve and/or maintain a sufficient erection to accomplish penetration (Simkins-Bullock, Wildman, Bullock, and Sugrue, 1992). If this condition has always existed, it is known as **primary erectile dysfunction.** Some men may develop **secondary erectile dysfunction.** In this case, erection is sufficient for successful intercourse some of the time only; however, episodes of erectile failure have occurred one or many times. If the problem persists, many men withdraw sexually from the partnership. Unfortunately, many women feel they are to blame for their partner's erectile failure (Carroll and Bagley, 1990). Fortunately, the condition is treatable in the great majority of cases (Goldman and Carroll, 1990; Kaplan, 1990; Segraves, Saran, Segraves, and Maguire, 1993; Sonda, Mazo, and Chancellor, 1990).

A minority of males suffer from **ejaculatory inhibition.** They are able to become sexually aroused, to maintain an erection, and to have normal intercourse but are unable to reach a climax. As a result, intercourse becomes frustrating. Even though a man desires an orgasm and is stimulated enough to trigger a climax, he cannot ejaculate.

The severity of ejaculatory inhibition varies considerably. At one extreme is the male who has never experienced an orgasm, although this condition is rare. At the other extreme is the male who occasionally finds himself unable to ejaculate. Mild forms of the disorder may be highly prevalent, as attested to by the increasing number of patients seeking treatment and the huge demand for Viagra.

Hypoactive sexual desire disorder is a deficiency in or absence of sexual fantasies and desire for sexual activity that causes marked distress or interpersonal difficulty. Low sexual desire may involve various forms of sexual expression and may be situational in that it is specific to a given activity or partner (American Psychiatric Association, 1994). Both males and females who have this disorder may also have arousal or orgasm problems.

Thus, desire disorders rarely occur in isolation (Segraves and Segraves, 1991). Although in the minority, these cases are not at all unusual. A person who has hypoactive sexual desire disorder may cause a great deal of misery for a partner who desires regular sexual expression.

Hypoactive sexual desire disorder is far more common in females than in males. Women with this disorder may have little or no interest in sexual activity (O'Carroll, 1991). If they participate, they derive no erotic pleasure from the experience. On a psychological level, they often are averse to sex, consider it a frightening or disgusting ordeal, and so they try to avoid sexual contact. The dysfunction may be situational; that is, a woman may be unresponsive in a particular situation or with a certain partner but not on other occasions or with another partner (Meisler and Carey, 1991). Degrees of sexual interest and responsiveness vary, but complete and permanent lack of sexual interest is rare.

A woman may manifest hypoactive sexual desire disorder in ways other than by refusing to have intercourse most of the time. For example, a woman may allow intercourse with her partner because she desires to please him although she does not derive satisfaction from the experience. For such a woman, sex is like brushing her teeth or combing her hair: It's something that has to be done. Or a woman may be responsive in the beginning of a relationship but become unresponsive later on. Intercourse may cease to offer her pleasure, or other problems may occur in the relationship to make her unresponsive sexually (Henker, 1984).

Some women are able to become sexually aroused but are unable to reach a climax. This condition, referred to as **orgasm dysfunction,** is one of the most common sexual dysfunctions in women. Only a minority have never had an orgasm (primary orgasm dysfunction). Women with secondary orgasm dysfunction can reach a climax under certain circumstances or with a particular partner, but not in other situations or with other partners. Some women are able to achieve an orgasm through masturbation, oral-genital stimulation, or other stimulative techniques, such as the use of a vibrator, but not through coitus. Some may have an occasional "random" orgasm but otherwise be nonorgasmic. Others may have difficulty in reaching a climax under all circumstances. The problem is caused by both biological and psychological factors (Raboch and Raboch, 1992).

Another female difficulty is **dyspareunia,** or painful intercourse (Semmens and Tsai, 1984). The pain may be severe or slight, depending on its origin and the woman's condition. Although dyspareunia is not unusual, it is not "natural." Except for the first few times or soon after childbirth, intercourse should not be a painful experience. Persistent pain is a symptom of an underlying problem that usually requires medical attention.

Vaginismus, which is rather rare, refers to an involuntary contraction and spasm of the vaginal muscles. This spasm becomes apparent not only when intercourse is attempted but also when a physician gives a pelvic examination. As soon as the physician approaches such a patient with a vaginal speculum, the muscles of her vagina go into spasm, making speculum insertion impossible or extremely painful. The woman also may have trouble inserting a tampon. If vaginismus exists in even a mild form, sexual intercourse may be very unpleasant.

How prevalent are sexual dysfunctions in women? The prevalence will depend partially on the group studied. In one study, a standardized sexual function questionnaire was administered to 329 healthy women, ages 18–73, all of whom were enrolled in a women's wellness center. About two-thirds of the sample were married or living with a partner, and most of the women were employed outside of the home. A broad range of sexual behavior frequencies was observed, with 49% reporting at least weekly intercourse and 28% who were not sexually active at the time of the study. Among the most common sexual problems were anxiety or inhibition during sexual activity (38%), lack of sexual pleasure (16%), and difficulty in achieving orgasm (15%). Other common problems were lack of lubrication (14%) and painful intercourse (11%), each of which was significantly more prevalent among postmenopausal women. Despite these difficulties, 69% of the sample rated their overall sexual relationship as satisfactory. Age and relationship status were significant predictors of sexual satisfaction, with older women and singles reporting a higher incidence of sexual problems. Educational level, religious affiliation, and employment status were not predictive of sexual dysfunction (Rosen, Taylor, Leiblum, and Bachmann, 1993).

Causes of Sexual Dysfunction

In general, physical or emotional disorders (or both) cause sexual dysfunction in men and women (LoPiccolo, 1985). From a purely physical point of view, the whole body is involved in sexual expression. Sexual expression also involves people's feelings and emotions. In fact, the emotional component of sex can have a definite effect on physical responses. For example, feelings of love and affection can stimulate sexual response and pleasure, while worry, fear, or disgust may completely inhibit sexual feelings or block the body's normal sexual response systems. Therefore, how people feel about themselves, their bodies, their sex organs, their partners, and sex itself influences their sexual functioning.

Because our physical and emotional makeup influences our sexual expression, an examination of the causes of sexual dysfunction is a complicated matter. For purposes of clarity, these causes may be grouped into six categories:

1. **Ignorance or lack of knowledge and understanding of sexual anatomy, sexual response, or lovemaking techniques.**

2. **Environmental and situational circumstances.**

3. **Inadequate stimulation.** This is usually due to ineffective techniques or insufficient time.

4. **Psychological blocks.** These include negative attitudes toward sex, the human body, the sex organs, masculinity or femininity, or oneself. Fear and anxiety are psychological blocks. Fears of pregnancy and of hurt, rejection, and failure are common causes of difficulties, as are feelings of guilt, embarrassment, or disgust. Guilt may exert a powerful influence on the nature and type of sexual practices in which a person engages (Wyatt and Dunn, 1991). Less frequently, prior sexual trauma and emotional illness can also cause sexual dysfunction (McCarthy, 1990).

5. **Negative feelings toward one's partner or a disturbance in the relationship.** People respond best to those whom they love, admire, and trust, and contrary feelings can influence their ability to respond sexually. Partners who are congruent on the meaning attached to their sexual relationships are more likely to be compatible (Lally and Maddock, 1994). The quality

Just as negative emotions can cause sexual dysfunctions, so can positive feelings enhance sexual response and pleasure.

and emotional tone of a couple's relationship influence sexual function. Anger may be the primary mechanism through which sexual desire and arousal are inhibited (Bozman and Beck, 1991).

6. **Physical abnormalities, illnesses, surgery, or drugs.** Chronic alcoholism is a major cause of sexual dysfunction, for example (Schiavi, 1990).

Getting Help

At some time in their lives, most people experience temporary sexual dysfunction. If the dysfunction persists and is left untreated, it can wreck a relationship. This is even more unfortunate because most difficulties can be cleared up by obtaining help.

There are four types of help: (1) medical treatment for physical problems, (2) psychotherapy for

The recent FDA approval of the drug sildenafil (Viagra) for the treatment of erectile dysfunction has created quite a media stir. The drug has been shown to be effective in producing and maintaining erections in men who were previously unable to do so. The ability to perform sexually is a huge benefit to these men and their partners. In addition, the men's increased confidence allows for a cognitive shift from a focus on performance to a greater immersion in the sex act. These men can then achieve sexual intimacy without worrying about maintaining an erection.

The creation of a pill that can restore sexual capacity is momentous, but Viagra is not without its side effects. Studies have shown an increased rate of heart failure as a result of use of the drug, so men with heart problems must seek alternative treatments. There is also a concern that restoring sexual capacity may result in an increase in sexual behavior associated with negative social consequences and public health risk, such as increased risk of contracting an STD. Viagra has proved to be a legitimate treatment of erectile dysfunction, but, as with anything else, we must be aware of the risks (Perelman, 1998).

emotional problems and hang-ups, (3) marriage counseling to deal with the total marital relationship, and (4) sex therapy, which emphasizes sensate-focus or symptom-focus approaches to an immediate sexual problem. Sex therapy assigns couples sexual tasks that enable the partners to learn how to caress or pleasure each other in a nondemanding way until they are able to respond to each other.

Whatever type of help is needed, and it sometimes involves a combination of one or more of these approaches, most therapists agree that **conjoint therapy,** involving both partners, is desirable because sexual functioning necessarily affects them both. People who are having problems need to decide to get help together.

SEXUALLY TRANSMITTED DISEASES

Sexually transmitted diseases (STDs) are among the most common infections in the United States. An estimated 15 million Americans acquire an STD every year, and 22 million Americans ages 18–59 have contracted STDs. Roughly one-quarter of new cases occur among teenagers, and two-thirds of new cases occur in people under age 25 ("Sexually Transmitted Diseases," 1998). By age 24, at least one in three sexually active people will contract an STD.

Most Americans are unaware of the extent of the STD epidemic. One study found that most men and women of reproductive age (18–44) seriously underestimate the prevalence of STDs and their own risk for contracting an STD. Only 14% of men and 8% of women say they think they are at risk for STDs. Perhaps this is why so many couples do not use condoms consistently; two-thirds of single men and women say they do not "always" use condoms. The story is similar for teenagers ages 15–17: Approximately three-fourths of these girls and boys think the STD rate is 1 in 10 Americans over the lifetime, and only 1 in 5 teens think they are at risk of contracting an STD (Kaiser Family Foundation/Glamour, 1998).

It is difficult to accurately gauge the number of STDs because many infections are asymptotic and social stigma limits discussion of the problem. Many STDs can only be detected through testing, and many Americans do not discuss STDs with health care professionals. Thus, most STDs go undiagnosed. Of the STDs that are diagnosed, health care providers are only required to report cases of gonorrhea, syphilis, and chlamydia to state health departments. There is no national reporting requirement for the other STDs ("Sexually Transmitted Diseases," 1998).

Infection rates for some STDs in the United States are the highest in the developed world; in some cases, they rival those reported in developing countries (Donovan, 1997). STDs can be grouped into three categories according to their cause:

1. Those caused by viruses: HIV/AIDS, herpes simplex, hepatitis B, and genital warts
2. Those caused by bacteria: chlamydia, gonorrhea, syphilis, and various vaginal infections, including pelvic inflammatory disease (PID) and nongonococcal urethritis
3. Those caused by parasites: pubic lice and scabies

Any of the STDs caused by viruses or bacteria can pose serious health problems if left undetected and untreated. Some, including AIDS, herpes, and

177

hepatitis B, do not have a cure. About half the people with an STD seek treatment. In one study, 49% of respondents who had contracted an STD went to a private practitioner for treatment, and 5% sought treatment at an STD clinic. Men were more likely than women to go to STD clinics, and respondents who were young, poor, or Black were more likely to use a family planning clinic for treatment than were those who were older, relatively wealthy, or White (Brackbill, Sternberg, and Fishbein, 1999).

An analysis of a representative national survey of households provided strong evidence that alcohol consumption exceeds illicit drug use as a risk factor for sexually transmitted diseases. Men and women who report a history of an STD are significantly more likely to have a history of problem drinking, independent of high-risk sexual activity and demographic influences. A high rate of change in sexual partners over the past 5 years also increases the risk of STD infections. More than half of teens ages 15–19 have had sex, and these teens are at high risk for STDs. Women under the age of 24 may be at greater risk for acquiring an STD than older women because these diseases easily infect the immature cervix (National Women's Health Resource Center, 1998).

HIV/AIDS

HIV/AIDS is a sexually transmitted disease characterized by virtually irreversible damage to the body's immune system and, eventually, death. An estimated 650,000–900,000 Americans are living with the human immunodeficiency virus (HIV), with 40,000 people becoming infected each year. The total number of reported AIDS cases in the United States at the end of 1999 was 733,374 ("HIV," 1999). New treatments have slowed the progression from HIV to AIDS and from AIDS to death for people infected with HIV. Consequently, rates of both AIDS cases and AIDS deaths have dropped dramatically, and an increasing number of people with HIV are living longer and healthier lives ("Trends," 1998).

A blood test measures the presence of HIV antibodies in the bloodstream. A person who tests positive for HIV antibodies has been exposed to the virus, is infected, and can transmit it to others. People may spread the virus without knowing they are infected. The incubation period may run from sev-

eral years to longer than 10 years. Several new drugs have been developed that, if used in combination, retard the development of the disease, but they are still being tested for their long-term effectiveness. One disadvantage is that these drugs cost thousands of dollars per year; another is their often serious side effects.

It is best to take the HIV antibody test at least 6 months after the last possible exposure to HIV. Almost everyone who is infected develops antibodies within 6 months, although there are rare cases of people who take longer. A negative test result within the first few months after exposure may mean only that the body has not had time to develop antibodies (*Expanded Guide,* 1991). Approximately two-thirds of Americans with HIV and AIDS have been tested confidentially ("HIV," 1999).

HIV is found in semen, blood, urine, vaginal secretions, saliva, tears, and breast milk and is transmitted from male to female, female to male, male to male, and female to female during the exchange of body fluids ("HIV," 1999). HIV is transmitted through direct sexual contact or infected needles or syringes. HIV can also pass from mother to fetus during pregnancy and from mother to nursing infant through breast milk ("HIV," 1999). Although HIV has been found in tears and saliva, no instances of transmission from these body fluids have been reported. It has, however, been transmitted via contaminated blood during a transfusion, and it has also been transmitted from health care worker to patient and from patient to health care worker through blood exchange. Some people fear that HIV might be transmitted in other ways, but there is no scientific evidence to support any of these fears. If HIV were being transmitted through other routes, such as through air, water, or insects, the pattern of reported AIDS cases would be much different from what has been observed ("HIV," 1999). For example AIDS is *not* transmitted through casual, nonsexual social contact such as occurs at home or in offices, restaurants, or schools. Nor is it transmitted through touching, shaking hands, or playing together, unless a person with an open sore or wound comes into contact with the blood of a person who has AIDS. AIDS is also *not* transmitted by sneezing, breathing, or coughing, nor through food or insect bites, nor through door knobs, toilet seats, eating utensils, or water fountains ("HIV," 1999).

Because anyone who is sexually active can get AIDS—and can pass it on before realizing he or she is infected—education in schools and communities about the disease is essential to stopping its spread.

The more sex partners one has, male or female, the greater the risk of becoming infected ("HIV," 1999). In a study of college students seeking HIV testing at a private 4-year urban university, researchers sought to identify common characteristics of those who felt they were at risk for HIV. The 622 subjects completed surveys on initial and follow-up visits on three potential risk factors: multiple partners, condom use, and STDs. The results indicated that multiple partners was the only variable significantly related to getting tested for HIV (Fredericks, 1999).

In the United States, rates of HIV-related death are highest among young and middle-aged adults, particularly those in racial and ethnic minorities. HIV is the fifth-leading cause of death for Americans ages 25–44. Among African American men and women in this age group, it is the leading cause of death. Many of these young adults were infected as teenagers. According to estimates, at least half of new HIV infections in the United States are among people under age 25, and the majority of young

people are infected from heterosexual contact. Even though the number of new AIDS cases diagnosed each year is declining, there has not been a comparable decline in the number of newly diagnosed HIV cases among youths ("HIV," 1999). Obviously, there is a great need for AIDS education in schools and communities to prevent young people from being exposed to HIV. Research has shown that early, clear communication between parents and young people about sex is an important step in helping adolescents develop and maintain safe sexual behaviors ("HIV," 1999).

Herpes Simplex

Herpes simplex is caused by a virus that can produce cold sores or fever blisters on the mouth or face (oral herpes) and similar symptoms in the genital area (genital herpes). Herpes is different from other common viral infections because once it is introduced it lives in the body over a lifetime, often without symptoms or with periodic symptoms. Rates of infection have grown by 30% over the past two decades, and at least 50 million cases have been diagnosed. Genital herpes now affects more than 1 in 5 Americans over age 12, with a million new cases occurring each year. As many as 80–90% of those infected do not recognize the symptoms or have no symptoms at all, but they still transmit the virus ("New Survey," 2000). Although genital herpes is one of the nation's most prevalent STDs, one study showed that many adults in a high-risk category (those having multiple sex partners) saw themselves as having no risk of contracting genital herpes ("New Survey," 2000).

Herpes is most easily spread during or a few days before an active outbreak. The virus can cause some discomfort, but it usually does not affect the immune system or lead to other health problems. It is important to remember that some symptoms are so mild that people don't notice them and that sometimes there are no symptoms at all. If symptoms do occur, they can include itching or tingling followed by a painful eruption of blisters and sores, headaches, flulike symptoms, swollen glands in the lymph nodes, and other breaks or irregularities in the skin, such as a cut, red bumps, or a rash. Signs and symptoms will vary from person to person and from one episode to the next ("Finding Answers," 1999).

Many people are failing to protect themselves against sexually transmitted diseases. In a national survey of 10,630 people ages 18–75, among respondents with multiple partners, only 18% of men and 22% of women always used condoms with their primary partner, and only 28% of men and 32% of women always used them with secondary partners. These proportions did not increase significantly with the number of partners; in general, almost half of men and women with multiple partners never used condoms. The interviews in this survey took place between June 1990 and February 1991 (Dolcini et al., 1993). In a National Survey of Family Growth (NSFG), 10% of sexually active women ages 15–44 in 1990 reported always using condoms to prevent either disease or pregnancy. This represents 6% of married women and 16% of unmarried women (Turner, 1994).

Individuals can do a number of things to protect themselves from the AIDS virus (Reiss and Leik, 1989):

1. Choose your sex partners very carefully (Hearst and Hulley, 1988). Then maintain a mutually faithful, monogamous relationship with a person who is free of the virus.

2. Be aware that asking a potential partner for his or her sexual history is an unreliable means of finding out about possible infection because people do not always tell the truth. Be aware as well that you cannot know if a person is free of the virus unless he or she has tested negative at least 6 months after engaging in risky behavior.

3. Use a high-quality latex condom (the virus passes through lambskin condoms) during oral, vaginal, or anal sex, and use a protective shield over the female genitals to prevent transmission during cunnilingus (Conant, Spicer, and Smith, 1986).

4. Put the condom on carefully, leaving excess at the end of the penis to receive the ejaculate. Use only water-based lubricants. Hold on to the condom when withdrawing to prevent it from slipping off the penis and spilling semen. Although these measures will ensure safer sex, they do not guarantee 100% safe sex (Kost and Forrest, 1992; Maticka-Tyndale, 1991.

5. Do not assume that just because you are heterosexual you can't get AIDS. Straights as well as homosexuals and bisexuals get AIDS from infected persons of either sex (Kane, 1990).

6. Avoid sex with male or female prostitutes (Nahmias, 1989; Redfield et al., 1985).

7. Avoid intravenous drug use and especially sharing syringes and needles (boiling does not guarantee sterility), as well as other items that may pierce the skin or have blood on them.

8. Avoid oral, vaginal, or anal contact with semen.

9. Avoid sex during menses (Edwards, 1992c).

10. Avoid inserting fingers or fist into the anus either as a passive or active partner. Small tears allow direct access to the bloodstream.

11. Do not allow another's urine to enter open sores or cuts, or your mouth, anus, vagina, or eyes.

Herpes is transmitted though anal or vaginal intercourse, oral-anal or oral-genital contact, genital-genital contact, and kissing. If a person gets the virus on his or her fingers and then touches his or her genitals or mouth, or someone else's, those areas may be infected. The best way to prevent the spread of genital herpes is to avoid sex during an active outbreak, to always use condoms between outbreaks, and to use suppressive antiviral therapy to reduce outbreaks ("Finding Answers," 1999). Genital herpes and cancer of the cervix and vulva appear to be associated, so periodic Pap smears and pelvic exams are especially advisable for women who have herpes. If a woman is pregnant and has herpes, it is important that she discuss this with her health care provider. While the spread of herpes to newborns is rare (less than 0.1%), an episode during late pregnancy and delivery can cause serious health problems for the newborn ("Finding Answers," 1999).

Hepatitis B

Hepatitis B is a highly contagious infectious disease of the liver. Despite the availability of a vaccine, hepatitis B remains a leading STD, with 240,000 new cases a year transmitted through sexual contact (Centers for Disease Control and Prevention, 1998). A total of 750,000 people are infected with hepatitis B as a result of sexual transmission ("Hepatitis B," 1998). One out of 20 people in the United States will get hepatitis B at some time during their life.

Many people show no symptoms and only discover they have the virus through blood tests. When symptoms occur, they include fever, nausea, loss of appetite, fatigue, muscular aches, headaches, jaundice, dark urine, abdominal swelling, light-colored feces, and a sweet odor to the breath.

The hepatitis B virus is present in seminal and vaginal fluids, saliva, urine, and blood, so it may be transmitted by contact with contaminated blood, or by vaginal and anal intercourse, oral-genital contact, and kissing. Having intercourse without a condom or performing oral sex without a moisture barrier increases one's risk of becoming infected. Infected needles, ear-piercing and tattooing tools, acupuncture needles, and medical or dental instruments that cut or puncture the skin may also transmit the virus. The virus can pass through defective latex condoms and lambskin condoms as well. A person may develop an immunity to the virus but still be a carrier and infect other people. Hepatitis B is potentially fatal and has no cure, but a vaccine has been developed that gives protection for 5 years. It may prevent infection even after exposure because of the virus's long incubation period ("Hepatitis B," 1998). Treatment consists of bed rest and careful attention to diet; antibiotics are not effective.

Human Papillomavirus (HPV)/Genital Warts

Human papillomavirus (HPV) refers to a group of viruses that infect the skin. There are over 70 HPV types, with about 30 being sexually transmitted and causing **genital warts.** Some 5.5 million new infections occur each year, and at least 20 million Americans currently are infected. An estimated 80% of sexually active people contract HPV at some point in their lives. Anyone who has ever had sexual intercourse can be infected and not know it, as HPV often has no symptoms.

Genital HPV is spread through skin-to-skin contact, not through an exchange of bodily fluids, during vaginal, anal, or oral sex. When symptoms do occur, they can include growths or bumps on the vulva, in or around the vagina or anus, on the cervix, or on the penis, scrotum, or groin. Sometimes, HPV causes such tiny blemishes that they can only be detected with special instruments that magnify the lesions. Warts may appear months or even years after sex with an infected person. Thus,

HPV can be contracted from one sex partner, remain dormant, and then later be unknowingly transmitted to another partner.

Although certain high-risk strains of HPV cause cervical lesions that, over time, can develop into cancer if untreated, most women with an HPV infection will not develop cervical cancer. However, HPV can put men at risk for anal and penile cancers ("HPV Backgrounder," 1999). Electrocautery, cryocautery (use of extreme cold), diathermy (use of heat), laser therapy, and surgery can be used to remove the warts.

Chlamydial Infections

The bacterium *Chlamydia trachomatis* is responsible for a variety of infections that are spread through sexual contact. **Chlamydial** is the most prevalent bacterial sexually transmitted disease and can be cured by antibiotics. The number of new reported chlamydia cases has risen in recent years, but this is due mainly to improved screening. Overall, as more infections have been diagnosed and cured, the number of new cases has fallen from an estimated 4 million to about 3 million a year (American Social Health Association, 2000). The disease may be asymptomatic in 75% of women and 50% of men, so medical tests are important in detecting it (Nordenberg, 1999). Chlamydia must be treated early, or it can do permanent damage to the body. In some cases, it causes infertility for both men and women (American Social Health Association, 2000).

Nongonococcal urethritis (NGU) is the most common chlamydial infection in men. Some men have no symptoms; others experience a burning sensation during urination and discharge a puslike fluid. If anal sexual contact was involved, rectal pain and soreness and rectal discharge may be present. A lab test is used to distinguish NGU from gonorrhea.

Epididymitis is an inflammation of the epididymis; it is most common in sexually active males under age 35. Symptoms include tenderness of the testicles and fever. Epididymitis may cause sterility if left untreated.

Chlamydial infections in women include oral, rectal, and cervical infections. If left untreated, chlamydial infection can cause pelvic inflammatory disease (PID). Cervical smears are used in diagnosis. Tetracycline is used in treatment; pregnant women are given erythromycin. Some babies are exposed to the chlamydia bacterium when passing through the birth canal. Infected newborns are subject to lung, eye, and ear infections ("Some Facts About Chlamydia," 2000). However, pregnant women can take medicine to cure chlamydia and protect the baby.

Pelvic inflammatory disease (PID) is a general term for infections of the uterus, fallopian tubes, and ovaries, most often caused by untreated chlamydial or gonorrheal bacterium. Abdominal pain during intercourse is the most common symptom. Vaginal discharge, nausea, vomiting, high blood pressure, and fever may also occur. Long-term consequences are chronic pain, greater risk of ectopic pregnancy, and infertility from blocked fallopian tubes ("Pelvic Inflammatory Disease," 1996). Early diagnosis and treatment are imperative.

Gonorrhea

Gonorrhea, also called the "drip" or "clap," is a highly contagious, sexually transmitted disease caused by the bacterium *Neisseria gonorrheae.* The number of new cases has declined over the past two decades, from 1 million in 1977 to 324,901 in 1997. However, rates of infection remain disproportionately high among persons under age 24 who have multiple sex partners and engage in unprotected sexual intercourse ("Gonorrhea/Neisseria," 2000). It is spread by oral, genital, or anal contact when the mucous membranes of the throat, genitals, or rectum come into contact with those of an infected person. Newborn infants of infected mothers may get gonorrhea of the eyes when passing through the birth canal. Treatment with silver nitrate or an antibiotic prevents blindness.

Many people who have gonorrhea have no obvious symptoms. Testing of discharge from the penis or vagina is important in detecting gonorrhea. When they do occur, symptoms in men appear from a few days to as long as a month after infection and may include a puslike penile discharge, blood in the urine, a burning sensation during urination, pressure or pain in the genitals, and enlarged lymph glands in the groin. The infection spreads through the urinary and reproductive systems if left untreated. If the disease spreads, it may cause chronic obstructions in the vas deferens and lead to infertility.

When they do occur, symptoms in women include a puslike vaginal discharge, which comes

from cervical infection, and painful and frequent urination from infection of the urethra. The disease may spread to the ovaries, fallopian tubes, and uterus, causing PID. Infection may also occur in the mouth, throat, and rectum. Both men and women may develop gonorrheal arthritis. Treatment usually consists of a dose of antibiotics, although a strain has been discovered that is resistant to antibiotics (Centers for Disease Control, 1998).

Syphilis

Syphilis, caused by the spirochete (spiral-shaped) bacterium *Treponema pallidum,* is far more serious than gonorrhea because it can cause death if not treated. Without a moist, warm environment, the spirochete dies within seconds outside the body. For this reason, it is transmitted exclusively by vaginal or anal intercourse or oral-genital contact. The fetus may contract congenital syphilis from the pregnant woman when the spirochete crosses the placental barrier. The fetus will not develop syphilis if the disease is diagnosed and treated before the fourth month of pregnancy (Dubroff and Papalian, 1982). If a woman is not treated in the early stages of the disease, the baby is likely to die before or shortly after birth. For these reasons, a syphilis test should be done on pregnant women.

Syphilis develops in four stages: primary, secondary, latent, and tertiary. During the primary stages, a chancre, or sore, will develop at the site the spirochete entered. The chancre usually heals in 4–6 weeks, so the disease will seem to have disappeared. However, the spirochetes circulate in the blood, and secondary syphilis develops within 1–6 months. It is characterized by weight and hair loss, constipation, nausea, poor appetite, joint pain, swollen glands, headache, sore throat, fever, and a pinkish or red rash. The disease can be cured at this stage if treatment is initiated.

Without treatment, the symptoms disappear, but the disease enters the latent stage, during which the spirochetes burrow into the brain and spinal cord, blood vessels, bones, and other body tissues. The latent stage may last for years. After a year or two, the disease is no longer infectious except that a fetus may still contract congenital syphilis from a pregnant woman with latent syphilis.

Thirty to 50% of untreated infected people develop tertiary syphilis; the remainder remain in the latent stage the rest of their lives. Tertiary syphilis may damage the brain, spinal cord, nervous system, heart, and major blood vessels, causing paralysis or death.

No blood test for syphilis is 100% accurate in the first 4–6 weeks following infection (during the primary stage), but all are 100% accurate during the secondary stage. Treatment usually consists of injections with penicillin (Centers for Disease Control, 1998). Rates of syphilis in the United States are at the lowest levels in 20 years, with only about 7,000 new cases diagnosed annually. Because the levels are so low, the Centers for Disease Control and Prevention has concluded it should be possible to eliminate syphilis in the United States ("Eliminating Syphilis," n.d.).

Parasitic Infections

These STDs are not really diseases but rather infestations of parasites. **Pubic lice** (*Pediculosis pubis*), or "crabs," are wingless, parasitic insects that suck blood from human hosts, causing itching. They may be identified with a magnifying glass. Permethrin or lindane creams, lotions, or hair shampoos are applied, and the nits removed with a fine-toothed comb (Centers for Disease Control, 1998). Sexual partners should be treated simultaneously, and sheets, pillowcases, pajamas, and underclothing should be washed thoroughly in hot water.

Scabies (*Sarcoptes scabiei*) is a parasitic infection that may be transmitted by contact with infected fabrics or through sexual contact. *Sarcoptes* mites burrow under the skin, lay eggs, and cause itching. Scabies is spread quickly among family members sharing the same living quarters. Treatment includes applying an antiscabies medication to the entire body and washing clothing and fabrics. All family members should be treated at once.

SUMMARY

1. There is a positive correlation between sexual satisfaction and happy marriage.

2. The effect of first intercourse on a nonmarital relationship depends on the quality of the relationship as a factor in sexual decision making.

3. Masters and Johnson have divided the human sexual response cycle into four phases: the excitement phase, the plateau phase, the orgasm phase, and the resolution phase.

4. Physiological responses during the sexual response cycle include vasocongestion and erection; myotonia; lubrication; an increase in heart and pulse rate, blood pressure, respiration, and perspiration; sex flush; and orgasm.

5. The responses of males and females are similar even though the sexual organs are different.

6. One important difference between men and women is that women are able to have multiple orgasms. Some men can also have multiple orgasms; if they tighten the PC muscles during orgasm to prevent ejaculation, continued stimulation will result in excitation to orgasm more than once.

7. Kaplan outlined a three-phase model of human sexual response: desire, excitement, and orgasm.

8. Sources of sexual arousal include tactile stimulation, visual stimulation, auditory stimulation, verbal stimulation, and mental stimulation through fantasy and erotic dreams.

9. Some helpful lovemaking principles include the following: Both partners ought to feel free to initiate sex and need to communicate their desires to each other. Both will show variations in sexual desire over time and need to allow themselves an uninterrupted period of time to make love. The physical setting either enhances or retards lovemaking. Frequency of intercourse varies with each couple and with age. The important consideration is for both people to feel satisfied with the frequency of intercourse.

10. Sexual satisfaction is negatively related to nonmarital conflicts with a partner. Individuals who are not sexually satisfied in their nonmarital relations have higher levels of conflict than those who are sexually satisfied.

11. Male sexual dysfunctions include premature ejaculation, erectile dysfunction, ejaculatory inhibition, and hypoactive sexual desire disorder. Female sexual dysfunctions include hypoactive sexual desire disorder, orgasm dysfunction, vaginismus, and dyspareunia (painful intercourse).

12. The causes of sexual dysfunction can be physical or emotional or both. Causes include ignorance or lack of knowledge and understanding; negative environmental or situational circumstances; inadequate stimulation; psychological blocks; negative feelings toward one's partner or disturbance in the relationship; and physical abnormalities, illness, surgery, or drugs.

13. Four types of help are available: medical help for physical problems, psychotherapy for emotional problems and hang-ups, marriage counseling, and sex therapy that concentrates on the immediate sexual problem. Most therapists agree that conjoint therapy, involving both partners, is desirable.

14. Sexually transmitted diseases can be categorized according to their cause: those caused by viruses (HIV/AIDS, herpes, hepatitis B, and human papillomavirus (HPV)/genital warts), those caused by bacteria (chlamydial infections, gonorrhea, and syphilis), and those caused by parasites (pubic lice and scabies).

15. Any of the sexually transmitted diseases caused by viruses or bacteria can be serious if left undetected and untreated.

16. There are a number of things couples can do to protect themselves against getting HIV, especially using a latex condom.

17. The only truly safe sex is in a relationship with a monogamous partner who is disease-free.

18. Herpes simplex, which is characterized by an eruption of blisters in the infected area, is incurable at the present time.

19. Viral hepatitis B is an incurable infectious disease of the liver.

20. HPV/genital warts are spread through skin-to-skin contact rather than through exchange of bodily fluids. Genital warts may be asymptomatic or not visible externally.

21. The bacterium *Chlamydia trachomatis* is responsible for a variety of infections that are spread by sexual contact, including nongonococcal urethritis (NGU) and epididymitis in men and cervical infections and PID in women.

22. Gonorrhea can infect the urinary and reproductive systems if left untreated and can cause PID in women and infertility in both men and women.

23. Syphilis develops in four stages, starting with a chancre, or sore. If left untreated, the spirochete may attack the brain, heart, or nervous system and cause death.

24. Pubic lice and scabies are parasitic infestations of insects that burrow under the skin, suck blood, and cause itching.

KEY TERMS

excitement phase	desire phase	primary erectile dysfunction
plateau phase	erogenous zones	secondary erectile dysfunction
orgasm phase	digital foreplay	ejaculatory inhibition
resolution phase	cunnilingus	hypoactive sexual desire disorder
vasocongestion	fellatio	
erection	nocturnal emissions	orgasm dysfunction
myotonia	wet dreams	dyspareunia
lubrication	sexual dysfunction	vaginismus
sex flush	premature ejaculation	conjoint therapy
orgasm	erectile dysfunction	sexually transmitted disease (STD)

HIV/AIDS

herpes simplex

hepatitis B

human papillomavirus (HPV)

genital warts

chlamydia

gonorrhea

syphilis

pubic lice

scabies

QUESTIONS FOR THOUGHT

1. Can people be happily married without a satisfying sex life? Explain.

2. What do you consider important principles of lovemaking?

3. If a man has erectile dysfunction, what might be the causes?

4. If a woman is not able to achieve orgasm, what might be the causes?

5. How is AIDS transmitted? How is it not transmitted? How might one protect oneself from AIDS infection?

SUGGESTED READINGS

Boyd-Franklin, N., Steiner, G. L., and Boland, M. G. (Eds.). (1995). *Children, Families, and HIV/AIDS: Psychosocial and Therapeutic Issues.* New York: Guilford Press. Gives a series of readings.

Comfort, A. (1994). *The New Joy of Sex.* London: Mandarin. Represents the latest edition of the classic illustrated guide to sexual technique.

Diamond, J. M. (2000). *Why Is Sex Fun? The Evolution of Human Sexuality.* London: Phoenix. Explores human sexuality from an evolutionary perspective and discusses why we differ from other mammals.

Gullotta, T. P., Adams, G. R., and Montemayor, R. (Eds.). (1993). *Adolescent Sexuality.* Newbury Park, CA: Sage Publications. Includes eight chapters dealing with a variety of topics.

Mahoney, C. (Ed.). (1999). *Human Sexuality: Contending Ideas and Opinions.* St. Paul, MN: Coursewise. Discusses controversial issues surrounding human sexuality.

McKinney, K., and Sprecher, S. (Eds.). (1991). *Sexuality in Close Relationships.* Hillsdale, NJ: Lawrence Erlbaum. Provides a well-written overview of the subject.

Newman, A. J. (1999). *Beyond Viagra: Plain Talk About Treating Male and Female Sexual Dysfunction.* Montgomery, AL: Starrhill Press. Discusses causes of sexual dysfunction, ways it has been treated historically, and answers frequently asked questions about Viagra; written by a doctor.

Rathus, S. A. (2000). *Human Sexuality in a World of Diversity.* Boston: Allyn & Bacon. Takes a multicultural, multiethnic perspective on the sexual experience in today's society.

Reinisch, J. M., with Beasley, R. (1990). *The Kinsey Institute New Report on Sex.* New York: St. Martin's. Gives a broad overview.

Sprecher, S., and McKinney, K. (1993). *Sexuality.* Newbury Park, CA: Sage Publications. Examines sexually based, primary relationships.

Webb, F. S. (1999). *Human Sexuality.* Cincinnati: West Educational Publishing. Represents a comprehensive textbook on sexuality.

LEARNING OBJECTIVES

After reading the chapter, you should be able to:

Understand the psychodynamic theories of mate selection: parent image theory and ideal mate theory.

Describe the traditional exchange theory of mate selection and equity theory.

Explain the components of the developmental process theory of mate selection.

Describe how family background factors are related to mate selection.

Explain the concept of the marriage gradient.

Describe how personal characteristics influence mate selection.

Explain why some people regret their choice of a mate.

Discuss patterns of relationships in and effect on marriage and children of nonmarital cohabitation.

Understand the importance of each of the following factors in marital readiness: age and maturity, timing of and motives of marriage, readiness for sexual exclusiveness, emotional emancipation from parents, and educational and vocational readiness.

Discuss marriage as a civil contract, and summarize the major legal state requirements regulating marriage.

Discuss the need to prepare for marriage and the roles of education, premarital assessment, and counseling.

Describe the functions of engagement as a rite of passage and the wedding as a religious and civil rite.

Mate Selection, Nonmarital Cohabitation, and Transition to Marriage

Learning Objectives

Theories of Mate Selection
Psychodynamic Theories
Needs Theories
Exchange Theories
Developmental Process Theories

Family Background Factors in Mate Selection
Socioeconomic Class
Education and Intelligence
Interracial Marriages
Interfaith Marriages
Family Issues: The Marriage Gradient

Personal Characteristics
Individual Traits and Behavior
Age Differentials
Consensus and Similarity of Attitudes and Values
Gender Roles and Personal Habits

Why Some People Regret Their Choice of Mate
Perspective: Danger Signals in Relationships

Nonmarital Cohabitation
Patterns of Relationships
Reactions to Cohabitation
Perspective: Facts About Cohabitation
The Effect on Marriage
The Effect on Children

The Transition to Marriage
Marital Readiness
Marriage and the Law
Preparing for Marriage

Rites of Passage
Engagement
The Wedding as a Religious and Civil Rite

Summary
Key Terms
Questions for Thought
Suggested Readings

In this chapter, we are concerned with the process by which mate selection, nonmarital cohabitation, and the period of transition to marriage can be used to make marriage more successful and satisfying. Because the responsibility for mate selection in our culture is an individual one, we need to better understand the process so that we can make wise choices.

THEORIES OF MATE SELECTION

Selecting a mate is one of the most important decisions we make during our lifetime. We are concerned here with theories of mate selection and their applicability to real life. What factors influence mate selection? How important is family background? What are the possibilities for intermarriage between people of different socioeconomic classes, educational levels, ethnic groups, and religions? How important is consensus of attitudes and values? How do you know if you are compatible? Is it necessary to have similar role concepts and personal habits?

This section presents the results of years of study by researchers of the mate selection process. If you aren't already married, perhaps the section will help you choose your mate wisely.

Theories of mate selection attempt to explain the process and dynamics by which people select mates. Some theories have proven more valid than others, and no one theory tells the whole story; but together they provide some explanation of what happens (Surra, 1990). The major theories discussed here can be divided into four groups: (1) psychodynamic theories, (2) needs theories, (3) exchange theories, and (4) developmental process theories.

Psychodynamic Theories

Psychodynamic theories of mate selection emphasize the influence of childhood experiences and family background on one's choice of mate.

Parent Image Theory   The **parent image theory** is based upon Freud's psychoanalytic concepts of the Oedipus complex and Electra complex and states that a man will likely marry someone resembling his mother and that a woman will likely marry someone resembling her father. Jedlicka (1984)

tested this theory and found that the resemblance between a man's wife and his mother and between a woman's husband and her father occurred more frequently than expected by chance. In general, the data supported the theory of indirect parental influence on mate choice.

Ideal Mate Theory   The **ideal mate theory** states that people form a fantasy of what an ideal mate should be like, based partly upon early childhood experiences. Schwartz and Schwartz (1980) wrote:

> Somewhere we "remember" how it felt to have another human being take care of us. We take this memory with us as we mature. Ultimately, it becomes our model, our expectation of a loving relationship. (p. 4)

There is little doubt that many people form fantasies of an ideal mate. The problem occurs when people hold unrealistic fantasies and their mate never fulfills them. If they pressure their mate to do so, rather than accept him or her as is, it places a strain on the marriage.

Needs Theories

Needs theories of mate selection are based on the idea that we select a partner who will fill our needs. Various theorists have offered descriptions of how needs influence mate selection. For example, the complementary needs theory, which was originated by Robert Winch (1958), states that people tend to select mates whose needs are opposite but complementary to their own. According to this theory, a nurturant person who likes to care for others would seek out a succorant mate who likes to be cared for. A dominant person would select a submissive person. Winch later (1967) added a third aspect of complementariness: achievement/vicariousness. The person who has a need to achieve tends to select a person whose need is to find vicarious recognition through attainment of a spouse. The individual selects a mate who gives the greatest promise of providing maximum need gratification. This is the person whose needs are complementary to one's own.

Since Winch's formulation, subsequent research has provided either no support or only partial support for this theory (Murstein, 1980). In fact, similarity of need may be more functional than complementarity in mate selection.

Exchange Theories

Exchange theories are a sort of cost-benefit analysis of relationships. These theories are based on the notion that we enter into relationships with those who possess resources (both tangible ones, such as a good income, and intangible ones, such as attractiveness, intelligence, or good humor) that we particularly value. If the emotional costs of the relationship begin to outweigh its benefits, we will probably end the relationship.

Traditional **exchange theory** holds that the basis for a continuing relationship between two partners is that each believes he or she will get at least as much from the relationship as it will cost (Filsinger and Thoma, 1988). Each person tries to maximize her or his chances for a rewarding marriage. Sometimes, the partners end up being equal in their abilities to reward each other. Other times, however, those who are motivated primarily to maximize their own benefits may exploit their partner, which is not conducive to a loving relationship.

An improvement over exchange theory, **equity theory** insists on fairness, on the assumption that people should obtain benefits from a relationship in proportion to what they give. The exchanged benefits might not be the same. People may desire different things, but they are attracted by a deal that is fair to them. Some people are attracted to others not primarily for what they can get, but for what they can give to a relationship. Judging equity, then, is an individual matter.

Developmental Process Theories

Developmental process theories describe mate selection as a process of filtering and weeding out ineligible and incompatible people until one person is selected. These theories describe various factors that are used in the selection process.

The Field of Eligibles The first factor to be considered in the mate selection process is the field of eligibles. For women, shortages of potential mates affect not only the likelihood of marriage but also the quality of the spouse in the event of marriage. A favorable marriage market (measured in terms of the relative number of men to women) increases the likelihood of marrying a high-status man rather than a low-status man (measured in terms of educa-

The ideal mate theory states that people form fantasies of what a mate should be like, but sometimes such fantasy images are not realistic.

tion and occupation) (Lichter, Anderson, and Hayward, 1995). At the same time, it decreases the number of eligible women from whom men can choose.

Propinquity Another factor in mate sorting is **propinquity** (Davis-Brown, Salamon, and Surra, 1987). That is, geographic nearness is a major factor influencing mate selection. However, this does not mean simply residential propinquity; institutional propinquity is equally important. In other words, people meet in places of business, schools, social organizations, and churches.

Attraction People are drawn to those whom they find attractive. This includes physical attraction and attraction because of specific personality traits. Many mate preferences are thought to be sex-linked; in other words, men and women look for different characteristics in potential mates. Women have been shown to look for mates with attributes related to their ability to provide for future offspring, such as intelligence, extraversion, and ambition. Men who possess these characteristics are seen as better providers for offspring. Men, conversely, look for physical signs of health in mates, most often represented in terms of physical attractiveness. While everyone has specific and different needs when choosing a mate, many of these sources of attraction fall within this biological framework (Botwin, Buss, and Shackelford, 1997).

Homogamy and Heterogamy People tend to choose mates who share personal and social characteristics, such as age, race, ethnicity, education, socioeconomic class, and religion (Dressel, 1980; Rogler and Procidano, 1989b; Stevens and Schoen, 1988). This tendency to choose a mate similar to oneself is called **homogamy.** Choosing a mate different from oneself is called **heterogamy.** Homogamous marriages tend to be more stable than heterogamous marriages, although there are exceptions. Various types of heterogamy and homogamy will be explored in detail in later sections of this chapter.

The major reason that marriages are generally homogamous is that we tend to prefer people who are like us and to feel uncomfortable around those who are different. Another important factor, however, is social pressure toward endogamy, or marrying within one's group. People who marry someone who is much older or younger or who belongs to a different ethnic group, religion, or social class may meet with overt or subtle disapproval. Conversely, people are generally prohibited from marrying someone who is too much like them, such as a sibling or a first cousin. This is social pressure for exogamy, or marrying outside one's kin group.

Compatibility The concept of **compatibility** refers to peoples' capability of living together in harmony. Compatibility may be evaluated according to temperament, attitudes and values, needs, role conceptions and enactment, and personal habits. In the process of mate selection, individuals strive to sort out those with whom they are compatible in these various areas.

The Filtering Process Figure 9.1 shows a schematic representation of the **filtering process.** The figure is based on numerous theories and research studies. Rather than relying on any one narrow view, the diagram represents a composite of various theories to show the process in detail.

As the figure shows, we begin the process of filtering with a very wide field of eligibles. This group goes through a series of filters, each of which eliminates ineligibles, so that the numbers are reduced before we pass on to the next filter. Before making a final decision, two people may go through a final trial period, either through cohabitation or formal engagement or both. If they survive this filtering process, the final filter is the decision to marry.

The order is approximate. Obviously, partners are selected according to propinquity first, and physical attraction plays a significant role early in the relationship, followed by attraction based on other personality traits. Gradually, people begin to sort out homogamous mates according to sociocultural factors: age, ethnicity, education, socioeconomic class, and religion. As the relationship develops, they find out if they are compatible according to temperament, attitudes and values, needs, role concepts, and personal habits. Some couples place more emphasis on some factors than on others (Cate and Koval, 1983). Some may explore compatibility without regard for homogamy. Others are more interested in selecting someone with the same socioeconomic background. Generally, both homogamous factors and compatibility factors are important. A testing of the relationship provides further evidence of whether the choice is a wise one.

As you can see, mate selection is a complex process by which people sort out a variety of social, psychological, and personal factors prior to making a final choice. Unfortunately, some people are not this thorough. They move from physical attraction to marriage without going through the intervening filters. Or situational factors, such as pregnancy, pressure them into a marriage that is unwise. The remainder of this chapter discusses factors in mate selection.

FAMILY BACKGROUND FACTORS IN MATE SELECTION

Family background influences everything that people are, want to become, or do. A detailed discussion of family background and its influences may be found in Chapter 2. But we need to look at it

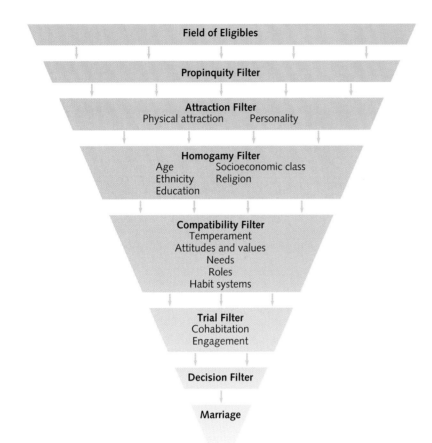

Figure 9.1 The Filtering Process of Mate Selection

from the point of view of mate selection. How people are brought up influences how they view marriage, how they want to bring up their children, and what their gender-role preferences are. It influences their personalities, traits, attitudes, values, and feelings. There is probably no area of living that is unrelated to family background.

For these reasons, it is helpful in mate selection to learn about the family background of a potential marriage partner. There is an old saying, "I'm not marrying his or her family." But that is not completely true. We marry a son or daughter, a person who is the product of his or her family experiences. When we marry someone, we marry everything the family has been able to impart to that individual. Knowing something about the family helps us to know the person who grew up in that family.

When both spouses have been exposed to healthy family-of-origin experiences, they more often achieve greater marital satisfaction than do spouses who have not been exposed to healthy experiences (Wilcoxon and Hovestadt, 1983). If we discover troubling things about a person's background, we can discuss those things to find out how our partner feels or has been affected. These problems may be thought of as caution signals influencing us to slow down while we examine them. Strong feelings about unresolved issues may require professional premarital counseling to see if they can be worked out. If not, they may be reasons to discontinue the relationship.

Socioeconomic Class

The possibilities of marital satisfaction are greater if people marry within their own socioeconomic class. Interclass unions do take place, but partners experience more stress in heterogamous unions. Moreover,

Marriage brings together two families, not just two individuals. Knowing something about a marriage partner's family experiences can be important to successful marital adjustment.

the spouses who marry down are more stressed than the ones who marry up, if status is important to them. That is, if the spouses from a higher class are class-conscious, they are more aware of the lower background of their spouse, and the relationship with their spouse is less affectionate, less emotionally supportive, and subject to less consensus.

Overall, women are less willing than men to marry someone with low earnings or unstable employment. But economic considerations are not irrelevant to men's preferences, either; men are less willing to marry a woman lacking steady employment than one having steady employment. Both men and women with high earnings and education are less willing to marry a formerly married person with children or a person with low socioeconomic status. Among African Americans, both men and women report less willingness than their White counterparts to marry someone of low status

(South, 1991). The increasing reliance of couples and families on two incomes might well be altering the field of eligibles. As the tradition of the man as the family's sole source of income disappears, men increasingly are considering the economic characteristics of potential wives in the mate selection process.

Education and Intelligence

There is a tendency for couples to enter into homogamous marriages with respect to education. Overall, women with 4 years of college tend to marry men who are also 4-year college graduates or who have more education than they do. However, Black women are significantly more likely than White women to marry men who are less educated than they are (Shehan, Berardo, Bera, and Carley, 1991), primarily because the pool of eligible well-educated

Black males is less than the pool of well-educated White males. The tendency toward educational homogamy among males is greatest among those with a high school education. Slightly more than half of males with some elementary education are married to women with more education than they themselves have. Among men with 4 years of college, a majority marry women with less education than they have.

What about the compatibility of spouses who are mixed with respect to education? As a general principle, educationally homogamous marriages tend to be slightly more compatible than educationally heterogamous marriages. In fact, the risk of marital instability is highest among couples who are heterogamous with respect to education (Tzeng, 1992). Among couples with unequal levels of education, the risk of marital disruption is about twice as high if the woman is more educated (Bumpass, Martin, and Sweet, 1991). **Hypergamous unions** (woman marries upward) have lower divorce rates than **hypogamous unions** (woman marries downward).

Obviously, however, educational attainment is not the only important factor. People who lack the advantages of a formal education but who are quite intelligent may be very happily married to those who are well educated. Education and brilliance are not necessarily synonymous. Spouses who are matched according to intelligence levels tend to be more compatible than spouses who differ in intelligence levels.

Interracial Marriages

Marriages tend to be homogamous with respect to race. The 1.35 million interracial couples in the United States in 1998 represented only 2.4% of all married couples (U.S. Bureau of the Census, 1999b). Figure 9.2 shows that 24% of interracial couples were Black-White marriages. Sixty-four percent of Black-White couples had a Black male and a White female and 36% had a White male and a Black female. African American men who marry White women tend to be of high economic and educational status and to marry women younger than themselves (Schoen and Woolridge, 1989). The majority of non–Black-White interracial marriages are between White men and Asian women; intermarriage between Blacks and Asians is uncommon.

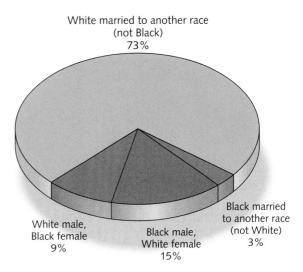

Figure 9.2 Interracial Marriages, 1998 (*Note:* Data from *Statistical Abstract of the United States, 1999* [Tables 11, 13] by U.S. Bureau of the Census, 1999, Washington, DC: U.S. Government Printing Office.)

Twenty-six percent of marriages of Hispanics are to non-Hispanics.

The rate of interracial marriages is increasing rapidly. Between 1960 and 1998, the number of interracial marriages skyrocketed by more than 800% (National Center for Policy Analysis, 1998). This trend results from changes in attitudes, declining social barriers between different groups, and the increase in ethnic diversity and mixed race population in the United States.

Although the rate of interracial marriage is still low for the nation as a whole, the rates in different locales and among different groups vary tremendously. Studies in 1980 of intermarriage between Asians and non-Asians (primarily Whites) in Los Angeles County showed that the rate was 50% for Japanese, 30% for Chinese, and 19% for Koreans (Kitano, Yeung, Chai, and Hatanaka, 1984). The high rate for the Japanese indicates the presence of a third generation growing up with lessening community and family controls.

Comparable studies of Asian-White marriages in Hawaii showed that 25% of adult Whites were married to non-White spouses, a rate far higher than on the mainland (Labov and Jacobs, 1986). This reflects lower levels of prejudice against such unions and a general blending of various racial and ethnic groups (Stephan and Stephan, 1989).

Friends and parents often disapprove of an interracial marriage, creating conflict and hard feelings. In spite of this, the majority of interracial marriages are intact after 10 years.

Generally, divorce rates for interracial couples are higher than for same-race marriages. This is true even in Hawaii, where, as mentioned, prejudices against such unions are less than in some other places (Schwertfeger, 1982). However, many interracial marriages do succeed. Vitousek (1979) found in Hawaii that White males had the lowest divorce rates when they married Chinese women.

In 1967, the U.S. Supreme Court ruled that interracial marriages may not be banned. Although the federal government has recognized the sanctity of interracial marriage for decades, some states have been slow to adjust. Alabama has a law on the books banning marriage between Blacks and Whites dating back to 1901. Although the law has not been enforced for years, many feel it is time to repeal it. Voters in South Carolina are fighting to have a similar law repealed.

Interfaith Marriages

One of the factors that is sometimes considered in choosing a mate is religious preference. There may be strong religious and family pressures to marry within one's own faith, based on the assumption that religiously homogamous marriages are more stable, with less likelihood of dilution of religious principles and greater possibility that the children will grow up with strong religious convictions and well-defined moral standards. The more orthodox and conservative the religious group, the greater the pressures exerted to marry within the faith. For example, Mormon adolescents express great reluctance to date non-Mormons, since their religion emphasizes marrying within the Mormon faith (Markstrom-Adams, 1991).

However, some significant trends may be noted. There has been a substantial decline in pressure toward religious homogamy, especially among younger people (Glenn, 1984). Among Protestants, a great deal of denominational switching takes place for the express purpose of achieving religious homogamy. Among the three main religious groups, the rate of interfaith marriages among Catholics is the highest. It is lowest among Protestants, and Jews are in the middle. The incidence of interfaith marriage is substantially lower if current religion is used as the criterion rather than religious upbringing (Sander, 1993).

Jewish attitudes toward interfaith dating and marriage depend on whether the group is orthodox, conservative, or reformed. The more orthodox the religious group, the greater the sanctions against dating or marriage outside of one's group. The

In the United States, the tendency for young men and women to marry someone like themselves in age, social class, religion, intelligence, ethnicity, education, and attractiveness has been well documented. This means that the pool of eligible partners is filtered based on perceived similarity on a number of social characteristics.

However, the expectation of similarity is not the only expectation in operation in mate choice. Partner asymmetry, sometimes called the **marriage gradient,** has traditionally been encouraged in American culture. Ideally, husbands are supposed to be superior to their wives on certain characteristics (occupational success, education, age). The marriage gradient serves as another filter for the pool of eligibles, but one that results in different effects for women and for men. For men, getting older, achieving more schooling, and becoming occupationally successful increase the number of women who consider them acceptable marriage partners. However, older, well-educated, successful women find that their choices are reduced because fewer men consider them acceptable partners.

In one study, young women expected more success for their future spouses than the young men did for theirs. Both males and females expected men to earn more, reflecting an adherence to the marriage gradient model in which women "marry up" and men "marry down" (Ganong and Coleman, 1992). In particular, young women expected that their spouses would be somewhat superior in intelligence, ability, income, success, and education. Less than 10% of the women expected to exceed their partner on any of the variables measured. These attitudes reflect the fact that women as a group generally have less power than men, so they may strive to gain economic security and status through marriage. One of the consequences of the expectation that men will be more professionally successful is that women may not fully develop their abilities. Another consequence is that men may not fully develop emotionally. In an effort to fulfill their role as primary provider, men may spend more energy and time earning money, leaving less time and energy for developing a close emotional relationship with their wives. Thus, the marriage gradient can lead to frustration for both men and women and to dissatisfaction and conflict in their marriages.

Ultimately, the marriage gradient expectation serves as a filter to eliminate people from consideration as a mate. Men may be threatened by capable, successful, bright women; therefore, they do not perceive them as eligible partners. Women find that personal success reduces their opportunity for marriage. Consequently, career choices of women and men may be influenced by their marriage gradient expectations. Women feel pressured to limit their educational career goals, and men feel compelled to choose high-status, high-paying careers (Ganong and Coleman, 1992).

degree of religious participation is also an important factor. Increased participation provides more opportunities for interaction with one's field of desirable mates and may influence attitudes toward interfaith date and mate selection. The frequency of religious participation may also increase the investment in relationships within the religious community. Jewish men are more likely to marry outside their faith than Jewish women, because the home is the focal point for the practice of Judaism and women set the spiritual tone (Marshall and Markstrom-Adams, 1995).

The Effect on Children   Devout people in particular worry that children of interfaith marriages, in comparison to those of homogamous marriages, are subjected to less intense and less consistent religious socialization and therefore are likely to be weakly religious. However, Petersen (1986) found that offspring of Catholic-Protestant marriages do not consistently score lower on general religiosity measures than do offspring of homogamous marriages. In general, conservative Protestants score higher on religiosity measures than Catholics, who in turn score higher than liberal Protestants. Parental influence varies depending upon how strongly religious they are, not upon whether their marriage is religiously heterogamous (Thomas and Cornwall, 1990). Religious supervision of the children by the mother and the father and their religious commitment are the best predictors of religious beliefs of the children (Hayes and Pittelkow, 1993). Thus, parental influence remains the prime predictor of the current religious beliefs among children.

The Effect on Adults   Adults wonder about the effect of marrying outside their faith. It depends. Petersen (1986) found that Catholics married to liberal Protestants attended Mass and received communion much more often than did Catholics married to conservative Protestants. Liberal Protestants were more tolerant and supportive of their spouse's attempts to practice Catholicism than were conservatives.

The Effect on the Marriage   Another important issue is the effect of interfaith marriage on marital happiness and stability. Most studies have identified a moderate negative effect of religious heterogamy on marital stability (Heaton and Pratt, 1990; Weller and Rofe, 1988). Often, however, these studies have not sorted out the different variables or controlled for age, socioeconomic status, and other factors. For example, rates of interfaith marriage are higher among persons of low socioeconomic status and among the very young. But divorce rates are also higher among these two groups. If divorce rates are higher, which is responsible: the interfaith marriage, the socioeconomic level, or the age? Through statistical analysis, Glenn (1982) determined that "the estimated heterogamy effect for females is positive and nonsignificant, but the one for males is negative and significant" (p. 563). This means that the men in interfaith marriages are more likely to evaluate the marriage negatively than are the men in religiously homogamous marriages. Religious heterogamy produced no negative effects on the women's evaluation of their marriages.

One study of Protestant and Catholic marriages found no differences in marital happiness in religiously heterogamous versus religiously homogamous couples (Ortega, Whitt, and William, 1988). The researchers did find, however, that Protestants married to doctrinally similar Protestants were happier with their marriages than were those married across doctrines. Another study found that, despite the strong position of the Catholic Church on divorce, there is no difference in marital stability between couples in which both partners are Catholic and those in which both are Protestant. However, overall marital disruption rates are 40% higher when one partner is Catholic and the other is not (Bumpass, Martin, and Sweet, 1991).

PERSONAL CHARACTERISTICS

When people choose someone with whom they plan to spend the rest of their life, compatibility is clearly essential. In this section, we will look at various personal characteristics that contribute to compatibility: traits and behavior, age, attitudes and values, and gender-role expectations and personal habits.

Individual Traits and Behavior

Research on individual traits focuses on physical, personality, and mental health factors. Physical illness puts stress on a relationship, making it less satisfying and less stable. Certain personality traits make it difficult for people to have a happy marriage. Neurotic behavior and mental illness weaken marital stability and quality. Depression has been found to be negatively related to marital quality, and impulsivity has been shown to be negatively related to marital stability. High self-esteem and adequate self-concept are positively related to marital satisfaction. Poor interpersonal skill functioning and unconventionality are related to marital dissatisfaction and instability. Sociability (extraversion) has been found to be positively related to marital stability and quality (Larson and Holman, 1994).

Age Differentials

One consideration in selecting a mate is the age difference between the two people. Overall, the median age differential between spouses in a first marriage is about 2.3 years (U.S. Bureau of the Census, 1996/1997). Only 8% of all married couples have an age difference larger than 10 years (Vera, Berardo, and Berardo, 1985). Marriages thus tend to be age homogamous. Age differentials are more common in remarriages and among lower-class groups (Atkinson and Glass, 1985). Older individuals also are more willing than younger ones to consider a wider age span in mate selection. And Black women are more likely than White women to be in age-heterogamous marriages (Shehan, Berardo, Bera, and Carley, 1991). That is, Black women are significantly more likely than White women to marry men who are older than themselves.

What are the effects of age differences on marital quality? When allowances were made for variables of gender, age, ethnicity, and socioeconomic status, Vera, Berardo, and Berardo (1985) found no significant differences in marital quality among couples from various age-dissimilar categories. In another study, the rate of marital disruption was

Declining social barriers between individuals of different ethnic and cultural backgrounds reflect a general decline in prejudice against intergroup marriage.

42% lower for couples in which the woman was older than her spouse by 2 or more years, but the lower divorce rate was due to these couples being older in the first place rather than to their age differential (Bumpass, Martin, and Sweet, 1991). Similarly, if one of the partners is in his or her teens, the probability of divorce is quite high, because of the youthfulness of the person (Booth and Edwards, 1985), and not because of the age disparity of the couple.

There may be considerations in addition to marital quality when contemplating marriage to someone much older or younger. For example, a young woman married to an older man is likely to be widowed at an early age, but both older men and older women tend to live longer if married to a younger spouse (Davidson, 1989; Foster, Klinger-Vartabedian, and Wispe, 1984).

Consensus and Similarity of Attitudes and Values

Marital compatibility is enhanced if spouses develop a high degree of consensus and similar attitudes and values about things that are important to them. Two people can never agree on everything, but ordinarily the greater the consensus, the easier it is to adjust to each other in marriage. People who share attitudes and values usually feel more comfortable with each other. There is less friction and stress in adjusting to each other.

Consensus develops slowly in a relationship. A dating couple may not even get around to talking about important values until after the partners have been together for some time. The more intimate the two people become, the more likely they are to express agreement in a number of important areas. There may be two reasons for this: (1) Being together may create greater understanding and agreement, and (2) those who disagree too much may not progress to the next stage of intimacy. Whichever reason is more valid, value consensus in a couple is related to satisfaction and to progress toward permanence in the relationship.

From this point of view, compatibility may be described partly in terms of the extent of agreement or disagreement about key issues such as employment, residence, money matters, relationships with parents and in-laws, social life and friends, religion and philosophy of life, sex, manners and living habits, children, and gender roles.

Gender Roles and Personal Habits

Compatibility is based, not only on attitudes and values, but also on behavior. A couple will have a more satisfying and successful life together if the partners share common expectations about gender roles and if they can tolerate each other's personal habits.

Compatible Role Concepts One measure of compatibility in marriage is the similarity of male and female role expectations. Every man has certain concepts of the kind of roles he should perform as a husband and certain expectations of what roles

One measure of compatibility in marriage is the similarity of male and female role expectations and the degree to which these are being fulfilled in the relationship. Many partners agree that the male can be a nurturing parent and the woman can have a satisfying professional career.

his spouse should perform. Every woman has certain concepts of what roles she should perform as a wife and certain expectations of what roles her spouse should perform. What the two people expect and what they find, however, may be different. The following examples illustrate instances where role expectations were never realized in marriage:

> **A young husband:** I always wanted a wife who was interested in a home and family. My wife doesn't like housework, hates to cook, and doesn't even want children.

> **A new bride:** In my family, my father always used to help my mother. My husband never lifts a finger to help me. (Author's counseling notes)

Leigh, Holman, and Burr (1984) found that individuals who had been dating their partner for a year were no more likely to have role compatibility than when they first started dating. This indicates that role compatibility is not very important for continuing dating relationships. However, it becomes very important after marriage. Spouses often assume their partner will enact the roles they expect, only to find out afterward that they have very different ideas and expectations. Data collected from 168 couples married for the first time showed that individuals' role preferences and leisure interests were highly related to the quality of their marriage and to their subjective evaluations of their relationship (Houts, Robins, and Huston, 1996). Role expectations should be discussed before marriage.

Habits   Advice columns in newspapers are filled with letters from people complaining about the annoying habits of their mate. Their spouse has terrible table manners, is careless about personal cleanliness, smokes or drinks too much, snores too loudly, goes to bed too late, won't get up in the morning, leaves dirty dishes scattered all over the house, never replaces the cap on the toothpaste, or has other habits the partner finds irritating. The writers have either tried to get their mate to change or tried to learn to accept the habit, often without success. Over the years, some of the habits become serious obstacles to marital harmony. Most personal habits that were annoying before marriage become exasperating in the closer and more continuous shared life of marriage. Most problems can be worked out, however, if people are caring, flexible, and willing to assume responsibility for changing themselves.

WHY SOME PEOPLE REGRET THEIR CHOICE OF MATE

All couples are influenced by the characteristics of their own family of origin. In general, the higher the marital quality in the parents' marriage, the higher the marital quality in their children's marriages. Parental divorce, parental mental illness, and family dysfunction have a negative influence on the children's marital success. Support from parents and in-laws after marriage has a positive influence on marital success.

Several sociocultural factors influence marital quality, including age at marriage, education, income, occupation, social class, and ethnicity. The relationship between young age at marriage and marital instability is among the strongest and most consistently documented in the research literature. Individuals who marry as teenagers are especially likely to separate or divorce. Limited education, income, or occupational status detracts from a person's ability to assume a marital role.

There are a number of reasons people regret their choice of mate. One reason is they don't really get to know the other person (Stafford and Reske, 1990). People who are in too much of a hurry to get married may not give the relationship enough time to develop. Getting to know another person usually takes several years of being together under varying circumstances. Even then, the knowledge is incomplete. Sometimes, the types of activities a couple share are not conducive to developing rapport and communication. The partners may participate in a whirl of social activities, spending all their time with other people or going to movies, concerts, or sporting events. The activities are fun, but the relationship remains superficial because of minimal interpersonal interaction.

Some people choose the wrong mate because they live in a fantasy world. Their concept of marriage has been gleaned from romantic movies and the media, and marriage represents an escape from their own humdrum existence. Their parents may have a troubled marriage, but they are sure it won't happen to them. They completely overlook the faults of their partner and the problems in their relationship. Love will conquer all, and they will live happily ever after. Their views of marriage and their relationship are completely unrealistic.

Other people choose the wrong mate because they look for the wrong qualities in a person. They emphasize physical characteristics and attractiveness without regard for important personal qualities. They don't stop to think about whether their partner is a good person. They are also looking for the wrong things in their relationship—perhaps for excitement instead of stability. They are thrilled with new relationships that are emotionally arousing, forgetting that the high level of emotions will subside and that only more permanent qualities will sustain the relationship.

Some people make the wrong choice because they confuse sex with love. They enjoy each other sexually and have intercourse whenever they are together. Their relationship focuses primarily on sexual passion, and so they assume they are much in love. But, as explained in Chapter 6, theirs is an incomplete love. Other components, such as friendship and care, are needed to sustain the relationship over a period of time. As one man remarked, "After they are married, what are they going to do the other 23 hours of the day?" (author's counseling notes).

Another common reason for marrying the wrong person is a poor self-image and lack of self-esteem. Such people can't believe that anyone desirable would really love them and accept them, so they settle for less than they might. They court rejection and unhappiness because they believe they are unworthy of support, love, and nurturance (Abramson, 1983).

Some people succumb to pressures to marry. One pressure is from their biological clock. One woman remarked, "I'm thirty-two years old and I want to have children. I'm marrying Charlie because I'm afraid I might not find someone else in time. I don't really love him, but I can't wait any longer" (author's counseling notes). Other people have a "now or never" attitude. They are afraid if they don't get married to this person, they may never get another opportunity.

Another pressure is that of pregnancy. The number one reason for marrying while still in school is pregnancy. Yet the prognosis of success for the marriage, particularly if the partners are in their teens, is poor. Most such marriages simply don't work out. Pressure to marry may also come from parents who want their son to marry "that nice girl down the block" (Leslie, Huston, and Johnson, 1986). Or a couple is cohabiting and the parents pressure them to marry. Parental intervention in the process of choosing a mate is more often indirect than direct (Davis-Brown et al., 1987). Instead of actively expressing approval or disapproval, parents try to arrange conditions so that their children will meet and marry suitable partners. Pressure to marry can also come from relatives and friends. When two people have gone together for some time, friends begin to ask, "When are you two going to get married?"

There are also unconscious, neurotic needs that people try to fulfill by marrying. For example, women who have an unconscious need to feel needed marry men they can mother. They may

What are some of the signs that the person selected is potentially a problem person? Here is a list of danger signals. If any of the following exist, exercise caution before you commit yourself to marriage. Encourage your partner to do something about the problems and to get professional help if needed. If your partner is not cooperative in getting help or trying to make changes, remember that you can't change someone yourself. If you try, chances are the problem will get worse. People have to want to change themselves. And marriage doesn't solve anything; it usually makes things worse.

- **Has a substance abuse problem.** This can involve alcohol and/or other drugs (Fu and Goldman, 1996).
- **Shows evidence of severe personality faults.** Examples include mental illness as diagnosed by a professional; extreme criticism of you and others; excessive jealousy and possessiveness; deep-seated insecurity as evident in excessive fears and anxiety; unstable temperament;

very rigid, inflexible, or compulsive thinking and behavior; a cold, insensitive personality; and negativism toward life in general.

- **Has important character flaws.** This person may be dishonest, unfaithful, distrustful, immoral, abusive, arrogant, or condescending.
- **Has serious problems relating to his or her family.** It's important to determine whether these are primarily the family's fault, or the individual's, or both. People who are not able to get along with their family, or whose family of origin is troubled, have more difficulty in creating harmonious family relationships themselves.
- **Can't get along with other people.** This person may lack social skills or be a loner with no friends.
- **Has an unstable job history.** This individual may be unable to hold a job and be irresponsible in job and task performance.

marry men who are immature, who have problems with alcohol or drug abuse, or who can't hold a job. In other situations, people feel uncomfortable with successful, desirable people, so they marry someone they can feel superior to as a means of boosting their own ego. Others boost their ego by choosing a mate they feel will enhance their image in others' eyes—for example, a "trophy wife."

Neurotic people may be drawn together to enable them to play roles in each other's "games" and transactions. Such role combinations include father-daughter, sadist-masochist, pursuer-pursued, beater-battered, and rescuer-victim (Hoyt, 1986). These unconscious feelings and needs may be very powerful motives to marry a particular person.

NONMARITAL COHABITATION

For some couples, cohabitation is only a convenient living arrangement. For others, it is a means of mate selection and preparation for marriage. Cohabitation is usually a short-term arrangement, with most couples either splitting up or marrying within 18 months. Today more than 50% of opposite-sex couples planning on getting married live together first, up from 10% in 1965, and, of those, 40% actually do

get married (Bumpass and Sweet, 1989). As Figure 9.3 shows, the number of live-in, opposite-sex couples increased from less than half a million in 1960 to 4.2 million in 1998 (U.S. Bureau of the Census, 1999a). In 1998, 36% of these couples had children in the household under age 15. A little over half of the women (57%) had never been married, about a third had been divorced, and a few (10%) were married to someone else or widowed.

Patterns of Relationships

One of the most important considerations is what the relationship means to the couple involved. No single pattern and no set meaning can be applied to all cohabitors. Any one relationship may fall along a continuum from friendship to long-term commitment to a substitute for marriage. For purposes of analysis, the relationships may be grouped into five basic types (Tanfer, 1987): (1) utilitarian arrangement, (2) intimate involvement with emotional commitment, (3) trial marriage, (4) prelude to marriage, or (5) alternative to marriage.

In order to avoid misunderstanding, those contemplating cohabitation would be wise to discuss their feelings ahead of time to ascertain the meaning each person associates with the decision to live together. If one partner considers cohabitation para-

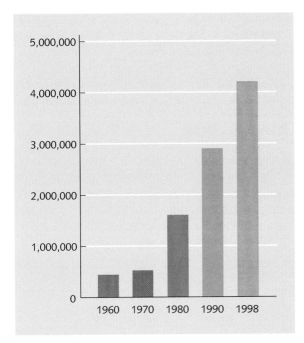

Figure 9.3 Number of Unmarried Couples Cohabiting, 1960–1998 (*Note:* Data from *Statistical Abstract of the United States, 1999* by U.S. Bureau of the Census, 1999, Washington, DC: U.S. Government Printing Office.)

mount to engagement and the other is participating without love and commitment, hard feelings and emotional pain result.

Utilitarian Arrangement   A good number of adults live together for utilitarian reasons. They save money by sharing living quarters and expenses, and they also share the work of housekeeping, laundry, and general maintenance. Some adults don't want to get married because they will lose some financial benefits: alimony, welfare, pension payments, or tax breaks. In such cases, they may or may not have an intimate relationship. They may be lovers or only friends.

Intimate Involvement with Emotional Commitment   This group includes those who love each other, want to have sex together, and want to be together in a monogamous relationship. They usually have a strong commitment to each other but are not planning marriage. They do not consider themselves married and are content to wait and see what happens. There is no statistically significant associ-

ation between cohabitation and the type of relation that eventually evolves—that is, whether the couple marries.

Trial Marriage   Some adults want to live together to test their compatibility, to help them decide if they are meant for each other and if they want to get married. The arrangement is considered "little marriage" to see if a "big marriage" will last.

Prelude to Marriage   A number of adults move in together before they get married. They have already committed themselves to marriage and see no reason to be apart in the meantime.

Alternative to Marriage   Those in this category are cohabiting, not as a prelude to marriage, but as a substitute for it. This includes those who are married to someone else and separated but not divorced and those who have been unhappily married and have become skeptical about the viability of legal marriage. Others have witnessed their friends' unhappy marriages and have concluded that legal marriage is not for them. People have numerous philosophical, legal, and ideological arguments about why they decide not to marry.

Reactions to Cohabitation

Generally, the majority of cohabiting couples report no regret at having cohabited. Among those who later married, Watson (1983) reported that only 9% of the women and 4% of the men expressed regrets. The proportion of dissatisfied cohabitors is higher among those who do not marry, and there is a much higher rate of violence among cohabiting couples than among married couples, especially among the young (Stets, 1991).

Overall, controlling for relationship duration and demographic characteristics, cohabitors in general report poorer relationship quality than their married counterparts. It is hard to know exactly why this is the case, but some researchers speculate that it could be due to less overall commitment in cohabiting relationships and less certainty of a lifetime partnership. In fact, cohabitors who report plans to marry their partner are involved in unions that are not significantly different from marriage (Brown and Booth, 1996).

In 1998, there were more than 4 million unmarried cohabiting couples in the United States (U.S. Bureau of the Census, 1999a). About 60% of cohabitors are between 25 and 44 years old.

About 40% of cohabiting unions in the United States break up without the couple getting married. This tends to occur rather quickly. After about 1½ years, half the cohabiting couples have either married or broken up. Twenty percent of cohabiting couples have lived together for 5 or more years. The duration of cohabiting unions is longer among previously married persons.

Childbearing is becoming increasingly common within nonmarital unions (Hollander, 1995a). One-sixth of never-married cohabiting couples have a child who was born after they began living together. However, entry into motherhood still occurs more often and sooner in marriage than in cohabitation (Manning, 1995).

Cohabitation increases the likelihood that a pregnant unmarried woman will give birth. Cohabitation also increases the odds of marriage before childbirth among pregnant White women, while it decreases these odds among Hispanic women. Among Black women, cohabitation does not appear to have an impact on the likelihood of marriage between conception and birth (Mahler, 1996a).

About a sixth of the women and about a third of the men report that their "freedom to do what they want" would be less if they married. A fairly sizable proportion of cohabiting respondents, especially women, report that their economic security would be better if they were married.

A high proportion of cohabitors are concerned about the stability of their relationship. Clearly, there is a good deal of uncertainty among cohabitors about the potential stability of the union. Compared with married respondents, cohabitors are almost twice as likely to report that they thought their relationship was in trouble over the past year.

Contrary to the popular image of cohabitation as a college student phenomenon, the trend toward cohabitation has been led by the least educated segment of the population, and cohabitation as a substitute for early marriage is most common among people who have not completed high school (Bumpass, Sweet, and Cherlin, 1991).

The net effect of cohabitation depends partially on the level of social attachment in the relationship. The higher the level of social attachment, the lower the level of psychological distress. Social attachment, emotional support, and economic support significantly reduce stress and account for the positive effect of being married and the negative effect of cohabitation if such attachment does not exist (Ross, 1995).

All that can be said with certainty is that cohabitation has been harmful to some and helpful to others. The effect depends upon the individuals involved, on how they feel, and on what happens.

The Effect on Marriage

One of the important issues here is the extent to which cohabitation results in greater satisfaction in subsequent marriage. There is no evidence that cohabitation weeds out incompatible couples and prepares people for successful marriage. One reason is that the kind of person an individual chooses to cohabit with is not necessarily the kind of person he or she would choose to marry (Schoen and Weinick, 1993). For example, in a recent study, those who cohabited with rather than married their partner were found to be less selective with regard to education level and race. There was also less economic egalitarianism among cohabitors, and women were less upwardly selective of partners when they were planning to cohabitate with rather than marry them (Blackwell and Lichter, 2000).

In general, those who cohabit prior to marriage have been shown to be significantly lower on measures of marital quality (Booth and Johnson, 1988) and to have a significantly higher risk of marital dissolution, especially if they have cohabited more than once prior to marriage (Bennett, Blanc, and Bloom, 1988; Booth and Johnson, 1988; Bumpass and Sweet, 1989; Gurak, Falcon, Sandefur, and Torrecilha, 1989; Teachman and Polonko, 1990a; Trussell, Rodriquez, and Vaughan, 1988). According to the 1987–1988 National Survey of Families and Households (Thomson and Colella, 1992), couples who had cohabited before marriage reported lower quality marriages, lower commitment to the institution of marriage, more individualistic views of marriage (women only), and a greater likelihood of divorce than couples who had not cohabited. These consequences were generally more likely for those who had cohabited for longer periods before marriage. One Canadian study found that cohabitation is associated with a greater risk of divorce even after the effects of stepchildren, prior marriage, parental divorce, and age differences are taken into consideration (Hall and Zhao, 1995).

The results seem to be affected partially by how long people have been married at the time of the evaluation. Most research indicates that a period of disillusionment with marriage occurs after the initial glow and excitement have worn off and couples have settled down to daily living. Presumably, the longer couples have lived together before marriage, the earlier in the marriage relationship the period of disillusionment sets in (DeMaris and MacDonald, 1993).

The finding that cohabitation decreases marital quality especially for serial cohabitors may be explained by the reduced commitment to marital permanence (Teachman and Polonko, 1990a). Or the association of cohabitation with greater odds of marital dissolution may be the result of the increased exposure to the problems of living together. DeMaris and Rao (1992) found that cohabiting prior to marriage, regardless of the nature of that cohabitation, is associated with an enhanced risk of later marital dissolution. Contrary to the expectation of many couples, who believe that prior cohabitation is a hedge against marital failure, those who live together before marriage stand a higher chance of ending their marriage. Furthermore, the researchers found that the association of cohabitation with increased odds of dissolution persisted even after accounting for the extra time that cohabitors had been together.

Data taken from the National Survey of Families and Households (NSFH) are based on a national sample of 13,017 individuals who were interviewed. Married and cohabiting individuals described their relationships differently. Cohabitors reported lower levels of happiness with their partnerships, expressed lower degrees of commitment to their relationships, and had poorer quality relationships with their parents (Nock, 1995b).

The Effect on Children

There are practically no data available on the effects of cohabitation on children (King, 1989). The number of children living in cohabiting households is on the rise, however. In 1980, 27% of cohabiting households included children under the age of 15; as of 1994, 35% included children (Rodriguez,

Nonmarital cohabitation increased rapidly in the 1980s and 1990s, reflecting changes in social norms. One factor associated with the increase in cohabitation may be the increase in the average age at first marriage.

1998). The effect on these children depends a great deal on the quality and harmony of the cohabiting relationship—and on the quality of the relationship that nonparent as well as parent cohabitors establish with the children. Children need love, affection, security, stability, and guidance in their lives. If the cohabiting relationship supplies these needs, children will likely benefit; if it does not, they will be affected negatively. This is one reason cohabitors who are parents need to choose partners very carefully. What effect will their live-in partner have on the children involved? Children also need stability in their lives. What will be the effect on them of developing attachment to a nonparent cohabitor only to have that person move out? Certainly, a series of cohabiting experiences would create insecurity in the lives of children (Loomis and Landale, 1994).

Roughly one in seven children in unmarried-parent families also lives with the parent's unmarried partner. The unmarried partner makes an economic contribution to the family that results in a reduction in the proportion of children living in poverty, but the children still fare poorly compared to children in married-couple families (Manning and Lichter, 1996). The 1996 poverty rate for children living in cohabiting households was 43% if their custodial parent's income was used and 31% if their custodial parent's partner's income was available to the family. This is a staggering poverty rate when compared to the 5.6% of children in married families living in poverty (Rodriguez, 1998).

Another important financial difference between children of married parents and cohabiting parents is the entitlement to child support once the relationship has ended. Whereas married couples can file for child support under the federal Divorce Act, cohabiting couples must seek support under the Family Relations Act. This entitles the child to support only until the age of 19, whereas under the Divorce Act child support is payable as long as the child remains a "child of the marriage" (Storey, 2000). This means that child support continues if the child is pursuing a higher education or if the child has a disability that keeps him or her from becoming independent. Both higher education and a disability can be an enormous financial burden for many families.

THE TRANSITION TO MARRIAGE

How do two people know if they are ready for marriage? What legal requirements must they fulfill? What can the couple do to prepare for marriage ahead of time? What kinds of marital education, assessment, and counseling might be considered? How can engagement become a constructive period of preparation? This section attempts to answer these questions.

Marital Readiness

A number of important factors in the transition to marriage determine marital readiness (Holman and Dao Li, 1997). Based upon the research information

we have, the following considerations may be significant:

- Age at the time of marriage
- The level of maturity of the couple
- The timing of marriage
- Motives for getting married
- Readiness for sexual exclusiveness
- Emotional emancipation from parents
- The level of education and vocational aspirations and the degree of their fulfillment

Age and Maturity   Age and level of maturity are important considerations in evaluating marital readiness. Teti, Lamb, and Elster (1987) found that males who married before they turned 19 were more likely to divorce or separate than were those who married later. Booth and Edwards (1985) found that marital instability was higher for men and women who married while in their teens.

There are a number of reasons for the greater instability of teenage marriages (Teti and Lamb, 1989). Teenagers are usually emotionally immature and not able to deal with the problems and stresses of early marriage. They do not have the social skills necessary to deal with a sustained intimate relationship. Their lack of skills leads to dissatisfaction with the way the spouse fulfills certain marital obligations, which leads, in turn, to friction and marital instability. Booth and Edwards (1985) found that the principal sources of marital dissatisfaction among spouses who married young are lack of faithfulness, the presence of jealousy, and the lack of understanding, agreement, and communication. Attempts to dominate or refusal to talk makes communication difficult.

Early marriages often are precipitated by pregnancies and result in couples abandoning educational pursuits in favor of parenthood, or full-time (and lower-status) employment, or both (Haggstrom, Kanouse, and Morrison, 1986). The result is low income and increased stress from trying to deal with the strains of adolescence, marriage, and parenthood. Long-term consequences are especially negative for women, who more frequently are compelled by circumstances to make a career-inhibiting life choice (Lowe and Witt, 1984).

Maneker and Ranking (1985) found that among divorcing couples those married youngest were married somewhat longer when they did divorce

Age and level of maturity at the time of marriage are important factors that determine marital readiness. What other considerations might be significant?

than those married at a later age. The reasons may be complex. Younger couples are more likely to lack financial and emotional resources to pursue the process of divorce, and they may be less aware of the alternatives to stressful marriage. No doubt many are very miserable during the years of marriage. Marriage duration is not synonymous with marital quality.

The Timing of Marriage   Another factor in marital readiness is the extent to which people really choose to get married at the particular time they do. One husband explained:

> Margie and I could not have picked a worse time to get married. I was laid off work a week before we got married. Her mother was sick and later diagnosed as having terminal cancer. Margie and I didn't really give ourselves time enough to know one another well. (Author's counseling notes)

One wife felt she and her husband got off to a bad start because she let him talk her into marriage before she was ready. Such people become disenchanted, not because they are not in love or because they don't want to get married eventually, but because they simply are not ready when they do marry.

Motives for Marriage   The motives for marriage are also important to marital success or failure. Most people in our culture get married for positive reasons, such as love, companionship, and security. Other people get married for essentially negative reasons, such as an attempt to escape from unhappy situations or relationships, to get even with others, to heal a damaged ego on the rebound, or to prove worth and attractiveness. Some people mistake gratitude for love. Very paternal or maternal people are attracted to those who seem to need to be cared for or nurtured. In a society that overromanticizes marriage, some people find it hard to resist the temptation.

Readiness for Sexual Exclusiveness   Ordinarily, monogamous marriage in our society means that spouses desire sexual exclusiveness. Although many adults are quite tolerant of nonmarital sexual intercourse, most are insistent upon the marital fidelity of their mate. Marital readiness for the majority of couples requires an attitude of sexual exclusiveness.

Emotional Emancipation from Parents   Another indication of marital readiness and maturity is emotional emancipation from parents. Individuals who still seek emotional fulfillment primarily from their parents are not yet ready to give their primary loyalty and affection to their spouse, as is necessary for a successful marriage. No spouse, male or female, wants to play "second fiddle" to an in-law. Overall, young adults today stay single longer and live with their parents until later in life than did those in the 1960s ("Young U.S. Adults," 1988). However, the reasons are usually economic, not social.

Educational and Vocational Readiness   There is a significant relationship between educational and vocational aspirations and the time of marriage. The lower the educational and vocational aspirations of youths, the more likely they will marry early. Youths with no post–high school educational plans are likely to feel that, since they have completed their education, marriage is the next step. The higher their educational aspirations, the longer young people wait after graduating from college before they marry. Once married, the higher their educational level, the longer after graduation they wait before beginning their families. Women who are in their twenties and have career aspirations tend to marry later in life than do those who plan to stay home and raise families.

Marriage and the Law

All people who get legally married enter into a civil contract. This means that their marriage is not just a personal affair. It is also of social concern, and each state has set up laws defining people's eligibility to marry and the procedures by which a contract may be established, as well as laws governing the maintenance of the contract once it is made.

Because marital regulation is the responsibility of individual states rather than the federal government, marital laws differ from state to state. However, the following discussion covers most of the major legal requirements regulating getting married.

Age   In most states and territories, males and females may marry without parental consent at age 18. Puerto Rico requires both the male and female to be 21. In Georgia and Hawaii, they need to be only 16; in Nebraska, they need to be only 17; and in Mississippi, men need to be 17 and women 15. The minimum age for marriage with parental consent in most states is 16 for females and males,

although marriages at even younger ages are possible in some states with the parents' and a judge's consent.

Consanguinity   The term **consanguinity** refers to a blood relationship or descent from a common ancestor. Because of the increased possibility of genetic defects in the offspring of people who share some of the same genetic makeup, states forbid marriage to one's consanguineous son, daughter, mother, father, grandmother, grandfather, sister, brother, aunt, uncle, niece, or nephew. About half the states forbid marriages to first cousins. Some states also forbid marriages of second cousins or marriage to a grandniece or grandnephew.

Affinity   The term **affinity** refers to a relationship resulting from marriage. Some states forbid marriage to one's stepparent, stepchild, mother- or father-in-law, son- or daughter-in-law, or aunt- or uncle-in-law. But critics argue that the law has gone overboard in forbidding such marriages, since no biological harm can result from such a marriage.

Mental Deficiency   Because some severely mentally handicapped people are not able to meet the responsibilities of marriage, a number of states forbid their marrying. Other states have no clear definition of mental deficiency and so cannot prevent such marriages. In other instances, sterilization or placement in institutions prevents mentally deficient people from reproducing.

Insanity   Most states prohibit marriages of the legally insane for the reason that an insane person cannot give his or her consent. Additionally, such a marriage could create severe problems for both family and society.

Procedural Requirements   Couples must obtain the legal permission of the state before marrying. This is accomplished through issuance of the marriage license, but the couple must fulfill certain requirements before getting the license. Some states will issue the license the same day the couple applies, but the rest have a waiting period of from 24 hours to 5 days. All but about a dozen states also require marriage within a specified period of time after issuance of the license for the license to be valid.

Some states also require a blood test for sexually transmitted diseases. A few states also require women to be tested for rubella, some states may require sickle cell anemia tests, and some give AIDS tests or information to marriage license applicants.

Common-Law Marriages   A **common-law marriage** is marriage by mutual consent, without a license. About 12 states still permit common-law marriages. The basic requirements to create a common-law marriage are that the partners must (1) have legal capacity (of age, opposite sex, with sufficient mental capacity) to marry, (2) intend to marry and have a current agreement to enter a marital relationship, (3) cohabit as husband and wife, and (4) represent themselves to the world as husband and wife (which means, for example, having the mail delivered to "Mr. and Mrs.," filing joint tax returns, and referring to themselves as husband and wife). With the rising numbers of couples who are opting for cohabitation rather than marriage, it is important to clarify what constitutes a common-law marriage and to point out that cohabiting without meeting the requirements just listed will not result in a common-law marriage. Although common-law marriages are recognized in some states and the District of Columbia, a common-law marriage validly created in one of those jurisdictions may not be recognized in a state that does not normally recognize common-law marriages.

Void or Voidable Marriages   If the legal requirements have not been met, a marriage may be defined as void or voidable. A **void marriage** is never considered valid in the first place, so a court decree is not necessary to set it aside. Marriages may be considered void in cases in which a prior marriage exists (bigamy), the marriage partners are related to each other within certain prohibited degrees, or either party is judged mentally ill or mentally defective. Some states consider marriage to the mentally ill or mentally defective voidable but not void.

Voidable marriages require an act of annulment to set them aside, after legal action has been instituted by one party. Only one spouse needs to take steps to void the marriage, and action must be brought during the lifetime of both spouses. The most common grounds for voiding a marriage are if either party is under the age of consent, either party is physically incapable of having intercourse,

either party consents to the marriage through fraud or duress, or either party lacks the mental capacity to consent to the marriage.

Fraud can be grounds for annulment, as in cases involving concealment of a previous marriage or divorce, financial misrepresentation, concealment of pregnancy, misrepresentation of virginity, concealment of disease, misrepresentation of character, refusal to have children, or breach a promise to have a religious ceremony after a civil ceremony. The injured party must act within a reasonable period of time to have the marriage set aside. If the injured party voluntarily cohabits with the guilty spouse after the fraud becomes known, the suit may be barred.

Preparing for Marriage

The need for marriage preparation has long been recognized by professionals. Studies of high school and college students indicate a need for and interest in marriage preparation programs. There also is evidence that marriage preparation programs are effective; however, such programs are notoriously underattended (Duncan, Box, and Silliman, 1996). It seems ironic that couples will spend months and months planning their wedding but scarcely any time preparing for their marriage. One young man revealed different priorities: "We aren't going to have much of a wedding, but we're going to have a wonderful marriage" (author's counseling notes). To this young man, marriage was more important than the wedding. Why spend thousands of dollars and many hours planning a wedding, only to have the marriage founder shortly after?

The basic theme here is that couples can prepare themselves for marriage in a way that will improve their chances for marital success. There are no guarantees, of course. But why do we often feel that vocational preparation is important and possible, and marital preparation is not? People aren't born knowing how to be good spouses and how to succeed in marriage any more than they are born knowing how to design a bridge. These things must be learned. But how?

We have mentioned elsewhere in this book, especially in Chapter 2, that much of what we know about marriage and family living was learned as we grew up in our family of origin. This is the most important means of learning. But there are other, more formal ways of preparing for marriage. Here we will discuss premarital education, premarital assessment, and premarital counseling.

Premarital Education   Premarital education takes many forms (Mace, 1987). It may include a college-level course in marriage and family living (Sollie and Kaetz, 1992). It may include short courses offered by counselors or by community agencies and organizations such as child and family service agencies, mental health clinics, community counseling centers, women's clubs, service organizations, churches, or schools.

Over the past decade, a vast assortment of premarital and marital enrichment programs have been developed and partially evaluated. These programs are of special interest because of their focus on teaching couples specific communication skills related to individual and couple functioning. In general, research tends to support the claim that these programs have a positive effect on the participants. The most often reported finding is that couples do, in fact, learn the communication skills taught in the programs.

Some clergy and churches require couples to come for instruction before weddings are performed. Such programs are most often designed to interpret the religious meaning of marriage, but they may also include discussion of sexual, emotional, economic, social, and familial aspects of marriage.

Hospitals do an excellent job of offering childbirth education classes to expectant mothers and their partners. Concerned community leaders might well consider doing as thorough a job by offering marriage preparation programs to couples on a regular basis.

Premarital Assessment and Counseling   Marriage preparation includes an evaluation of the extent to which the couple is fit and ready for marriage (Holman, Larson, and Harmer, 1994). The most common form of assessment is health assessment: a physical examination and blood tests for sexually transmitted diseases. In addition to the usual blood test for syphilis, many couples are now tested for AIDS, gonorrhea, and herpes. Certainly, if either partner has a sexually transmitted disease, the other needs to know about it.

Premarital assessment involves more than a health assessment, however. It may profitably include an assessment of a couple's overall relationship. Such an assessment is difficult for the partners to complete themselves because it's hard for them to be objective. A couple can go to a marriage counselor for the express purpose of exploring important areas of the relationship and determining the level of adjustment and any possible unresolved difficulties. Premarital counseling also helps couples, individually or in groups, to address difficulties that have been revealed.

One well-known instrument for predicting marital success is a premarital inventory called PRE-PARE (Fowers and Olson, 1989; Olson, Fournier, and Druckman, 1982). PREPARE is a 125-item inventory designed to identify relationship strengths and weaknesses in 11 relationship areas: realistic expectations, personality issues, communication, conflict resolution, financial management, leisure activities, sexual relationship, children and parenting, family and friends, equalitarian roles, and religious orientation. Additionally, the instrument contains an Idealistic Distortion Scale (Fowers and Olson, 1986). For each scale, an individual score is provided for each spouse. In addition, a Positive Couple Agreement (PCA) score is provided for each category; it measures the couple's consensus on issues in that area (Fowers, Montel, and Olson, 1996; Fowers and Olson, 1986).

Validity tests of PREPARE have shown that the inventory can correctly predict in 80–85% of cases whether partners will be happily married or will end up divorcing, in 79% of cases whether partners will be happily or unhappily married, and in 78% of cases whether partners will be happily married or will cancel marriage plans (Fowers and Olson, 1986; Larsen and Olson, 1989). This high predictive accuracy is exciting news, since it gives counselors a very useful tool for premarital and marital counseling.

Another widely used premarital inventory is FOCCUS (Facilitating Open Couple Communication, Understanding, and Study). FOCCUS has replaced the Pre-Marital Inventory (PMI) as the predominant premarital inventory used in marriage preparation by the Catholic Church. FOCCUS is used by approximately two-thirds of the Roman Catholic dioceses in the United States as well as by over 500 Protestant churches of various denominations (Williams and Jurich, 1995).

Results indicate that FOCCUS and PREPARE are roughly comparable in terms of their predictive

Individual counselors or community agencies and organizations may offer classes and workshops in premarital education.

validity. FOCCUS scores during engagement predict a couple's future marital success 4–5 years later and indicate with 67.6–73.9% accuracy (depending on the scoring method used) whether the couples will have a high-quality or low-quality marriage. FOCCUS scores are able to identify 75% of the couples who later develop distressed marriages. Yet the fact that FOCCUS is not 100% accurate in its predictions is an important reminder that it should not be used as the single, infallible predictor of future marital success.

RITES OF PASSAGE

Rites of passage are ceremonies or rituals by which people pass from one social status to another. In our culture, the rites of passage from a single to a married status include the engagement, the wedding ceremony, and the wedding reception.

Engagement

An engagement to be married is an intermediate stage between courtship and marriage after a couple has announced the intention to marry. Engagement may be informal, at least for a while, during which time the two people have an understanding to marry. Marriage may still be too far off to make a formal announcement, or the couple may want to

further test their relationship. Because many engagements are broken, a couple is probably wise to be very certain before making a formal announcement. Some couples move from informal engagement to marriage without ever formalizing the engagement period.

Engagement also becomes a final testing of compatibility and an opportunity to make additional adjustments. Some problems, such as planning finances or making housing arrangements, are difficult to resolve unless a date has been set for the wedding. One woman commented:

> Sam owns a lot of property. I didn't feel free to bring up anything about ownership until after we were engaged. As it happens, he's going to put my name on all of it too. But I can see how the whole subject could have caused a lot of problems. (Author's counseling notes)

If any problems that have arisen in the couple's relationship have not been worked out before engagement, this period allows an additional opportunity to address them. The more things are worked out prior to marriage, the fewer adjustments and surprises arise afterward.

The engagement period also involves preparation for marriage itself. A most important part of this period, but one often neglected, is premarital education. A couple may choose to take advantage of premarital assessment and counseling. Marriage

While wedding practices vary among different religious groups, all have certain things in common. Four parties are normally represented in the religious wedding rite: the couple, the religious group, the state (witnesses), and the family.

preparation also involves applying for a marriage license and having a physical examination and blood tests for sexually transmitted diseases.

The Wedding as a Religious and Civil Rite

Eighty percent of all people who marry are married by the clergy (Knox, 1985). This means that the majority of marriages are performed under the auspices of a religious group and that the wedding itself is a sacred rite. The Catholic Church considers marriage a sacrament, with special graces bestowed by God through the church to the couple. The marriage bond is considered sacred and indissoluble. Both Judaism and Protestantism consider marriage a covenant of divine significance, sanctified by God and contracted between the spouses and the religious group with God as an unseen partner. While lifelong marriage is considered ideal, divorce and remarriage are allowed under certain circumstances.

Any religious rite is rich in meaning and symbolism. Although the rites vary among different religious groups, they have certain things in common. Four parties are represented in the service: the couple, the religious group (clergy), the state (witnesses), and the parents (usually through the father of the bride). Each party to the marriage rite enters into an agreement, or covenant, with the other parties to fulfill his or her obligations so that the marriage will be blessed "according to the ordinances of God and the laws of the state." The denomination, through the clergy, pledges God's grace, love, and blessing. The man and woman make vows to each other "in the presence of God and these witnesses." The state grants the marriage license once the requirements of the law have been fulfilled.

In the wedding rite, the two people must indicate their complete willingness to be married; they must make certain pledges to each other; they indicate to the clergy their agreement to abide by divine ordinance and civil law. They join hands together as a symbol of their new union. Rings are a sign of eternity (having neither beginning nor end) and so symbolize the eternal nature of love. They are also a sign, seal, and reminder of the vows taken. The license is signed and witnessed as evidence that state law has been fulfilled.

Different religious groups have different rules and customs regarding weddings, but more and more clergy of all faiths are giving couples an opportunity to share in some of the decisions and even to help design their own service if they so desire.

SUMMARY

1. Selecting a mate is one of the most important decisions we make during our lifetime. Various theories have been developed to explain the process: psychodynamic theories, needs theories, exchange theories, and developmental process theories.

2. Family background factors are important influences in a person's life and so need to be investigated when choosing a mate. Marriages tend to be homogamous with respect to socioeconomic class, education, intelligence, and race. Divorce rates are higher in interracial marriages than in racially homogamous marriages.

3. Religious heterogamy produces no negative effects on women's evaluation of their marriage, but men are more likely to evaluate their marriage negatively if they are in a religiously heterogamous relationship. Parents' religious influence upon their children depends on the parents' religiosity and not on whether the marriage is religiously homogamous.

4. The marriage gradient refers to the practice of men marrying women who are younger, are less educated, and have a lower occupational status to maintain a relationship of superiority. The practice is encouraged by women and men, both of whom expect more success for the man. The husband is pressured to succeed professionally and so has less opportunity to develop emotional sensitivity; the woman is not motivated to fully develop her professional capacities.

5. Sociocultural and background factors that influence marital quality include age at marriage, education, income, occupation, social class, and ethnicity.

6. Individual personal characteristics that influence the quality of marriage include physical and mental health, self-esteem and self-concept, interpersonal skills, unconventionality, and sociability. Age differentials are not a significant factor in marital quality, but marriage at a very young age is.

7. Marital compatibility is enhanced if spouses develop a high degree of consensus and similar attitudes and values about things that are important to them. A measure of marital compatibility is similarity of male and female role expectations. It is also helpful if the spouses have compatible personal habits.

8. Danger signals in the choice of a mate include a substance abuse problem, personality and character flaws, family problems, inability to get along with other people, lack of social skills, a lack of friends, and an unstable job history.

9. People regret their choice of mate for a number of reasons: They don't get to know the other person; they live in a fantasy world; they look for the wrong qualities in a person; they confuse sex with love; they have a poor self-image and low self-esteem; they succumb to pressures to marry; or they have unconscious, neurotic needs that they are trying to fulfill by marrying.

10. Rates of nonmarital cohabitation have increased greatly in recent years. In 1998, 36% of cohabitors had children under age 15 in their household. A little more than half of the women (57%) had never been married. About a third had been divorced, and a few were married to someone else or widowed. Childbearing is common in nonmarital unions.

11. Cohabitation may mean different things to different people. A relationship may be a utilitarian arrangement, an intimate involvement with emotional commitment, a trial marriage, a prelude to marriage, or an alternative to marriage.

12. Some cohabitors are hurt, either because the relationship didn't work out or because they expected that it would result in marriage and it did not. Generally, the majority of cohabiting couples report no regret at cohabiting. However, cohabitation seems to be harmful to some people and helpful to others.

13. Those who cohabit prior to marriage have been shown to have lower marital quality and a higher rate of marital dissolution than those who have not cohabited. One reason is a lower commitment to marriage permanence.

14. The effect of marital cohabitation on children depends on the quality and stability of the relationship and the extent to which it meets children's needs.

15. The transition from singlehood to marriage ordinarily takes place over several years. The transition is more successful if couples are ready for marriage.

16. The following considerations may be significant in evaluating partners' marital readiness: age at the time of marriage, level of maturity, the time when marriage takes place, motivation for getting married, readiness for sexual exclusiveness, emotional emancipation from parents, and level of educational and vocational aspirations, as well as the degree of their fulfillment.

17. Getting married involves entering into a civil contract. Each state has its own laws regarding marriage. Laws include age requirements and restrictions on consanguinity and affinity and on marrying mentally deficient and insane people. Procedural requirements include obtaining a marriage license and, usually, blood tests and observing a waiting period.

18. Some states permit common-law marriages.

19. Couples need to prepare for marriage through marriage education, assessment, and premarital counseling. A number of instruments, usually inventories, have been developed to help couples assess their relationship. Two of the most valid are PREPARE and FOCCUS.

20. Rites of passage are ceremonies by which people pass from one social status to another.

21. Engagement is an intermediate stage between courtship and marriage. Engagement is a period of final testing of compatibility.

22. The wedding is a religious and civil rite, rich in meaning and significance. Four parties are usually represented: the couple, the religious group, the state, and the parents. Many couples prefer writing their own wedding service.

KEY TERMS

parent image theory
ideal mate theory
needs theory
exchange theory
equity theory
propinquity
homogamy

heterogamy
compatibility
filtering process
hypergamous union
hypogamous union
marriage gradient

consanguinity
affinity
common-law marriage
void marriage
voidable marriage
rites of passage

QUESTIONS FOR THOUGHT

1. From your viewpoint, which psycho-dynamic theory of mate selection seems to be more valid: parent image theory or ideal mate theory? Explain the reasons for your choice.

2. Do opposites attract? Do opposites make compatible mates? Explain.

3. What are your views on interracial marriages? Explain your views.

4. Why do some people regret their choice of mate?

5. What things would you want to know and consider before you decided to enter into unmarried cohabitation?

SUGGESTED READINGS

Casper, L. M. (1999). *How Does POSSQL Measure Up? Historical Estimates of Cohabitation.* Washington, DC: U.S. Bureau of the Census. Reprints a paper presented at the 1999 annual meeting of the Population Association of America.

Miller, R. R. (Ed.). (1999). *Marriage Systems in Transition: A Multicultural Approach.* Thousand Oaks, CA: Sage. Discusses the transition in marriage from a multicultural perspective.

Miller, R. R., and Browning, S. L. (Ed.). (2000). *With This Ring: Divorce, Intimacy, and Cohabitation from a Multicultural Perspective.* Stamford, CT: JAI Press. Examines intimate relationships from both a sociological and a multicultural perspective.

Resenblatt, P. C., Karis, T. A., and Powell, R. D. (1995). *Multiracial Couples.* Thousand Oaks, CA: Sage. Includes in-depth interviews with 21 high school graduates describing the experiences of interracial couples and opposition from both African American and White family members.

South, S. K., and Tolney, S. E. (Eds.). (1992). *The Changing American Family: Sociological and Demographic Perspectives.* Boulder, CO: Westview Press. Has a social and statistical emphasis.

Waite, L. J., and Bachrach, C. (Eds.). (1999). *The Ties That Bind: Perspectives on Marriage and Cohabitation.* New York: Aldine de Gruyter. Discusses marriage, unmarried couples, and domestic relations and the social changes that have occurred in these relationships.

Whyte, M. K. (1990). *Dating, Mating, and Marriage.* New York: Aldine de Gruyter. Provides a popular discussion.

Williams, M. (1990). *The Mexican-American Family: Tradition and Change.* Dix Hills, NY: General Hall. Provides a helpful discussion.

CHAPTER 10

LEARNING OBJECTIVES

After reading the chapter, you should be able to:

Discuss various criteria of a successful marriage, including durability, approximation of ideals, fulfillment of needs, and satisfaction.

Identify what makes some marriages happy and others miserable, according to John Gottman.

Identify and explain the 12 qualities of successful marriages that are described in the textbook: communication; admiration and respect; companionship; spirituality and values; commitment; affection; the ability to deal with crises and stress; responsibility; unselfishness; empathy and sensitivity; honesty, trust, and fidelity; and adaptability, flexibility, and tolerance.

Describe the seven types of marriages identified using the ENRICH assessment: devitalized, financially focused, conflicted, traditional, balanced, harmonious, and vitalized.

Qualities of a Successful Marriage

Learning Objectives

Criteria for Evaluating Marital Success
Durability
Approximation of Ideals
Fulfillment of Needs
Satisfaction

Happy Versus Unhappy Marriages
Family Issues: Patterns of Marital Relationships: What Type Fits You?

Twelve Characteristics of Successful Marriages
Communication
Admiration and Respect
Companionship

Spirituality and Values
Commitment
Affection
The Ability to Deal with Crises and Stress
Responsibility
Unselfishness
Empathy and Sensitivity
Honesty, Trust, and Fidelity
Perspective: Trust in Relationships
Adaptability, Flexibility, and Tolerance

Summary
Key Terms
Questions for Thought
Suggested Readings

This book is about relationships: marital relationships, family relationships, and intimate relationships between unmarried persons. We begin Part III on a positive note by discussing how we can get along with other people and live together in a harmonious, fulfilling way. Living together is an art, requiring important qualities of character, a high degree of motivation, and finely tuned personal and social skills.

The focus in this chapter is on the marital relationship. However, most of the principles discussed here can be applied to all intimate relationships and to interpersonal relationships in the larger family unit.

CRITERIA FOR EVALUATING MARITAL SUCCESS

Before we look at the various characteristics of a successful marriage, we need to consider what defines a successful marriage. Four different criteria of a successful marriage are discussed here—durability, approximation of ideals, fulfillment of needs, and satisfaction—but no one alone seems adequate. Instead of adopting a single criterion, we discuss 12 different characteristics of successful marriage in the next section.

Durability

What constitutes a successful marriage? One measure that has been used is durability. Many people would say that the marriage that lasts is more successful than the one that is broken (Heaton and Albrecht, 1991). In many cases, marital stability and marital quality do go together. However, some marriages last a lifetime and are filled with hatred, conflict, and frustration (Bohannan, 1984). Some spouses haven't spoken to each other, except through the children, for decades. For many of us, marital success involves criteria more important than the number of years a couple stays together, regardless of other aspects of the relationship.

Approximation of Ideals

Another way of evaluating marital success is the extent to which the marriage approximates a couple's ideals or fulfills their expectations. Both partners have their own concept of an ideal relationship. When asked, "What is your concept of a good marriage?" one student replied:

> A good marriage is one in which two people love one another, get along well together, in which they think alike on important issues, share common goals and interests, enjoy each other's company and have fun together, in which they are really good friends, are able to talk to one another to work out problems together.

Other students add to this fairly typical reply, describing a good marriage in these terms:

> One that allows you to be yourself and to be completely honest with one another

> Fifty-fifty, where partners share everything

> One that allows you freedom to do your own thing and to grow

> One where your partner is your best friend

Other students add different characteristics that are important to them. Marital success, in their view, is determined by the extent to which idealistic expectations are fulfilled.

One problem with this way of assessing the success of a marriage is that some people have very unrealistic expectations in the first place. The standards by which they judge their marriage are impossible to achieve. Expectations need to be realistic, not just romantic fantasy.

Fulfillment of Needs

Another criterion of marital success is whether the marriage makes a sufficient contribution to individual needs, including the following:

- **Psychological needs**—for love, affection, approval, and self-fulfillment
- **Social needs**—for friendship, companionship, and new experiences
- **Sexual needs**—for both physical and psychic sexual fulfillment
- **Material needs**—for "room and board" and physical maintenance and services

This view assumes that partners are aware of each other's needs and willing and at least partly able to fulfill them (Tiggle, Peters, Kelley, and Vincent,

The number of years a couple stays together is not the most important indicator of marital success. Qualities such as empathy, respect, companionship, and affection are but a few of the characteristics of a successful marriage.

1982). Note the emphasis here on partial fulfillment. Marriage can never meet every need. Some needs will always have to be met apart from the marriage itself. One's job, friendships, hobbies, and recreational pursuits all contribute to need fulfillment. However, a successful marriage makes an acceptable contribution; any marriage that doesn't has failed in the eyes of most couples.

Two cautions need to be added. First, it is helpful if need fulfillment is mutual (Fowler, 1982). In relationships in which one person does all the giving and the other all the receiving, the giver often becomes exhausted. Second, mutual need fulfillment is most possible if needs fall within the limits of realistic expectations. A highly dependent, possessive person, for example, may demand so much love and approval that no one could possibly fulfill those needs. In this case, the marriage might not succeed, not because of the unwillingness of the giving person to fulfill needs, but because of the unreasonable demands of the insatiable partner.

Satisfaction

Much of the research on marriage success measures marital satisfaction: the extent to which couples are content and fulfilled in their relationship. According to this view, marital success is defined as the extent to which both partners in the relationship are satisfied that it has fulfilled reasonable expectations

and mutual needs (Hunsley, Pinsent, Lefedvre, James-Tanner, and Vito, 1995). This definition recognizes that there are individual differences in expectations and need requirements, so that what satisfies one couple might not satisfy another. Marital satisfaction includes marital quality, marital adjustments, and marital happiness (Heyman, Sayers, and Bellack, 1994). Marital satisfaction is a comprehensive concept and is the one accepted here as the criterion for marital success. It is important that *both* partners be satisfied. Sometimes one partner is very content with a relationship while the other is ready to file for divorce.

Obviously, there are degrees of success. Few marriages live up to *all* expectations and fulfill *all* needs all the time. Furthermore, successful couples strive for improvement. Their marriages are in the process of becoming, and few ever feel they have completely arrived. However, if they are satisfied with the progress they have made, they judge their effort as successful. We will discuss growth and fulfillment further in Chapter 11.

HAPPY VERSUS UNHAPPY MARRIAGES

What makes some marriages happy and others miserable? John Gottman has been studying this question for decades and has found the pattern of

Agreement about what needs to be done in the household and by whom directly contributes to a successful marriage.

communication in couples to be very important in marital happiness. In happy couples, when one partner makes a positive statement, it is reciprocated in a positive manner; in unhappy couples, partners often have no immediate response to a positive statement. In happy couples, after one partner makes a negative statement, the other offers no immediate response; in unhappy couples, both partners continue to reciprocate negatively. This **negative affect reciprocity** is a consistent characteristic of distressed couples (Gottman, 1998).

Some messages can be interpreted either positively or negatively. For example, the statement "Stop interrupting me" may be an attempt to repair an interaction, but it may also be said with irritation. Gottman believes that in a happy marriage there is a greater probability that the listener will focus on the repair aspect of the message and respond by saying, "Sorry, what were you saying?" In an unhappy marriage, there is a greater probability that the listener will respond only to the irritation in the message and say something like, "I wouldn't have to interrupt if I could get a word in edgewise." In this case, the message does not repair any part of the communication pattern, and the negativity bounces back and forth (Gottman, 1998).

Gottman also sees differences in how spouses in happy and unhappy marriages view positive and negative actions of their partner. In a happy marriage, if one partner does something negative, the other partner tends to think that the negativity is fleeting and situational. For example, negative behavior may be attributed to a tough day at work or a bad mood, as opposed to a fixed characteristic of the individual. Thus, the negativity is viewed as temporary and the cause as situational. In an unhappy marriage, however, the same behavior is likely to be interpreted as a sign of inconsideration, selfishness, and indifference and as internal to the partner. The same pattern exists for positive behavior. Happy couples interpret positive behavior as internal to the partner, whereas unhappy couples are likely to interpret the same positive behavior as a fluke and to not believe that it will last (Gottman, 1998).

The "demand-withdraw" (or "pursuer-distancer") pattern is another characteristic of unhappy marriages. With this pattern, it is usually the woman who raises and pursues the issues and the man who attempts to avoid the discussion and tends to withdraw. Research suggests that in unhappy marriages with high negative affect men withdraw emotionally and women do not (Gottman and Levenson, 1988).

Furthermore, in two longitudinal studies, Gottman (1994) found that it was not anger that led to

Patterns of Marital Relationships: What Type Fits You?

The degree of marital satisfaction depends partially on the congruence between marital expectations and accomplishments. Yet expectations differ markedly among different couples. What one couple expects marriage to be is not necessarily what another expects it to be.

In one study, a reliable and clinically useful assessment tool, ENRICH, was used to assess marriages across multiple external and internal dimensions of the relationships of 8,385 couples (Lavee and Olson, 1993). Seven types of couples were identified: devitalized (40%), financially focused (11%), conflicted (14%), traditional (10%), balanced (8%), harmonious (8%), and vitalized (9%). Devitalized, financially focused, and conflicted couples are stuck in utilitarian marriages in which the partners stay together for convenience or because of their lack of a better alternative. The other types of couples can be termed intrinsic; that is, the partners stay together because of the relationship itself.

Devitalized couples are typified by pervasive unhappiness with all relationship issues. A couple may have had a meaningful marriage at one time, but the marriage has declined in satisfaction over the years. Although the partners may have children, community activities, and work that they enjoy and that keep them busy, the marriage relationship itself lacks excitement and interest.

Financially focused couples demonstrate overall dissatisfaction with the marriage, with adjustment in only one marital dimension: money management. The partners seem to devote themselves to their careers rather than to the relationship.

Conflicted couples have fallen into a pattern of nearly constant fighting and arguing. These couples seem to thrive on conflict. Nagging, attacking, bickering, and arguing have become a way of life, and yet these partners stay married for a lifetime. Either the pattern of conflict has become a habit, or they have adopted a pattern that they learned in their own families of origin.

Traditional couples seem to have characteristics of both intrinsic and utilitarian marriages. Internal relationship issues, such as communication, conflict resolution, and sexuality, are a source of distress, but religious life and interaction with the extended family provide personal resources. These partners are not as critical of each other's personality as are those in conflicted couples, and they show considerably less distress with the marriage than do other utilitarian married couples. Their marriage seems to be as stable as those of other intrinsic couples.

Balanced couples express satisfaction with both internal and external couple issues despite some specific areas of difficulty. Partners may have some disagreements in specific areas, but overall they experience a strong and positive relationship.

Harmonious couples are well adjusted in their intimate relationship but demonstrate less satisfaction with some external aspects (for example, financial) of marital life. As in balanced couples, the partners experience strong and positive relationships.

Vitalized couples are characterized by a high degree of satisfaction with all aspects of the marriage. The partners get along very well with each other, they resolve difficulties, and they are satisfied with their relationship. The key to the vitalized marriage relationship is that partners are intensely bound together psychologically in important life matters.

This typology of marital types enables us to recognize that not all marriages are alike. Marital problems can arise when the scripts of the two partners are mismatched—that is, when they have different expectations and their partner is not able to fulfill them. The first three types of marriage (devitalized, financially focused, and conflicted) have few areas of strength and are most distressed. The traditional couples have a base of strength to build on, but the partners lack communication and conflict resolution skills. The last three marital types (balanced, harmonious, and vitalized) rarely have serious problems unless some traumatic experience unexpectedly arises, such as an affair or a crisis with a child (Lavee and Olson, 1993).

unhappy marriages and reliably predicted divorce, but rather four processes that he called "the Four Horsemen of the Apocalypse": criticism, defensiveness, contempt, and "stonewalling" or listener withdrawal. Other researchers added "belligerence"—a behavior that is provocative and is designed to escalate the conflict ("What can you do if I do go out tonight? What are you gonna do about it? Just try to stop me")—as a likely predictor of divorce. These findings were replicated in a recent study which found that contempt, belligerence, and defensiveness are common negative behaviors during conflict (Gottman, Coan, Carrere, and Swanson, 1998).

Based on a national study of 21,501 married couples, family science researcher David Olson has found that happy and unhappy couples differ in five key areas: (1) how well partners communicate, (2) how flexible they are as a couple, (3) how emotionally close they are, (4) how compatible their personalities are, and (5) how they handle conflict. When given Olson's 165-question inventory, happy couples identified those five areas (communication, flexibility, emotional closeness, compatibility, and conflict resolution) as strengths; unhappy ones did not. For example, about 75% of happy couples agreed on the high quality of their communication, whereas only 11% of unhappy couples did. Similarly, 75% of happy couples agreed that they can change and adapt when necessary, whereas only 20% of unhappy couples believed this to be true. Olson believes that spouses must feel they can adapt to change and feel close and connected in order to have a happy marriage.

He also identified five other areas that affect a couple's happiness: (1) the sexual relationship, (2) the choice of leisure activities, (3) the influence of family and friends, (4) the ability to manage finances, and (5) agreement on spiritual beliefs. He advises that, in order to build strength as a couple, partners should pay the same sort of attention to the relationship that they did when they were dating and praise the other partner for the positive things, instead of focusing on what bothers them about the partner (Olson, 2000).

TWELVE CHARACTERISTICS OF SUCCESSFUL MARRIAGES

Numerous research studies have delineated the qualities of successful marriage. In their research, Spanier and Lewis (1980) listed 87 probable factors that are related to marital quality. Some of these are background factors, some outline qualities of the relationship, and others emphasize personality characteristics. Some couples would emphasize particular criteria more than others. Additional factors may exist that research has not yet delineated.

Other chapters discuss family background factors that influence marital success, such as attitudes toward intimacy and sex, gender roles, values, patterns of communication, age, ethnicity, and length of acquaintance. Thus, we are concerned in this chapter with a mixture of personality charac-

teristics of the partners and characteristics of the relationship itself, which together constitute qualities important to marital success. Twelve of these important qualities are described in this chapter.

Table 10.1 compares the findings of four representative studies on the 12 characteristics of successful marriages. Study 1, by Bell, Daly, and Gonzalez (1987), described the strategies married couples use to maintain the quality of their bonds. Data were obtained from two groups. The first group (130 females and 32 males) consisted of 144 married people and 18 individuals cohabiting with their romantic partner. The second group comprised 109 married females (median age 33.9 years) in graduate courses at an eastern U.S. university. Ninety-five of these women were in their first marriage; 12 had been married once before; 2 were in their fourth marriage. Participants completed measures of marital quality and evaluated the frequency and importance of each strategy used.

Study 2, by Lauer and Lauer (1985), was a survey of 351 couples with enduring marriages. The study summarized the factors that kept the couples together. Three hundred of the couples said they were happily married; both partners in 19 couples said they were unhappily married but were staying together for a variety of reasons, such as "for the sake of the children." Among the remaining 32 couples, only one partner reported unhappiness in the marriage.

Study 3, by Curran (1983), reported on the responses of 500 professionals who work with families to questions designed to determine the qualities of "healthy" families.

Study 4, by Stinnett and DeFrain (1985), reported on a survey of 1,000 families across the United States in a Family Strength Research Project. Some South American families were also questioned.

Four characteristics of successful marriages were mentioned in all four studies: communication, admiration and respect, companionship, and spirituality. Three characteristics of successful marriages were delineated by three of the studies: commitment, affection, and ability to deal with stress and crises. Three characteristics of successful marriages were described in two of the studies: responsibility, unselfishness, and empathy and sensitivity. Two characteristics of successful marriages were each described in only one of the studies:

Table 10.1   Characteristics of Successful Marriages: Summary of Findings from Four Studies

Marital Quality	Study			
	1. Bell, Daly, and Gonzalez: Strategies Used by Couples	2. Lauer and Lauer: Factors That Keep Couples Together	3. Curran: Qualities of Healthy Families	4. Stinnett and DeFrain: Family Strengths
Commitment	—	Viewing marriage as long-term commitment; wanting marriage to succeed	Being committed to family	Being committed to family; investing time/energy in family
Honesty, trust, fidelity	Being honest, truthful, sincere	—	—	—
Responsibility	Being dependable	—	Sharing responsibilities	—
Adaptability, flexibility, tolerance	—	—	—	Being adaptable, flexible; believing people can change, adjust
Unselfishness	Assisting partner whenever possible; giving nice things to partner	—	Helping each other	—
Communication	Listening; self-disclosing; polite conversation	Confiding in spouse; calm discussions, stimulating exchange of ideas	Listening to, responding to, respecting others' feelings, thoughts; avoiding turn-offs and put-downs	Developing good communication technique; spending time talking, listening; having fair arguments
Empathy, sensitivity	Being warm, caring, sensitive	—	—	Having compassion for others
Admiration, respect	Building partner's self-esteem; supporting partner in endeavors	Liking spouse as a person; finding spouse interesting, taking pride in spouse's accomplishments	Respecting differences, privacy, property, institutions of society; admiring and supporting each other	Expressing appreciation for one another; making one another feel good
Affection	Showing physical and verbal affection	Agreeing on expression of affection, sex	—	Expressing mutual affection, caring
Companionship	Sharing enjoyable social activities, closeness	Being best friends; laughing together; sharing interests	Spending quality time together	Wanting to spend time together
Ability to deal with crises, stress	Being cheerful, optimistic	—	Expecting problems to be normal part of life; developing problem-solving skills	Being able to weather storms of life
Spirituality, values	Sharing spiritual activities, beliefs, values	Viewing marriage as sacred; agreeing on goals, values, philosophy of life	Having strong values manifested in religious behavior, sense of right and wrong	Having strong value system, high degree of religious orientation, involvement

Note: Adapted from "Affinity-Maintenance in Marriage and Its Relationship to Women's Marital Satisfaction" by R. A. Bell, J. A. Daly, and M. C. Gonzalez, 1987, *Journal of Marriage and the Family, 49*, pp. 445–454; "Marriages Made to Last" by J. Lauer and R. Lauer, 1985, *Psychology Today, 19*, pp. 22–26; *Traits of a Healthy Family* by D. Curran, 1983, New York: Ballantine; and *Secrets of Strong Families* by N. Stinnett and J. DeFrain, 1985, Boston: Little, Brown.

Can this couple talk about anything? Are the two able to share their feelings? Does either one hold back from the other? Answers to such questions about communication in a relationship can tell a lot about how long the relationship is likely to last.

honesty, trust, and fidelity, and adaptability and flexibility.

Communication

According to numerous studies, good communication is one of the most important requirements in a successful marriage (Curran, 1983; Robinson and Blanton, 1993). Couples who are able to communicate effectively report that they do the following:

We can talk about everything.

We are able to talk about our problems and to work them out.

We're able to share our feelings.

We each try to listen when the other is talking.

We don't believe in holding things in.

We talk about things and it clears the air. (Student comments to author)

Talking helps us to understand one another and keeps us close. (Honeycutt, 1986)

When marriages are troubled, it is often because of poor communication. Poor communication results in increasing anger, tension, and frustration at the difficulty in getting others to listen and to understand. One wife commented:

I try to talk to him, but he doesn't seem to care. Finally, I get so upset that I scream and holler at him and start to cry. He just walks away and says to me, "I'm not going to talk to you if you holler at me." There's no way to get through to him. (Author's counseling notes)

Effective communication involves the ability to exchange ideas, facts, feelings, attitudes, and beliefs so that a message from the sender is accurately heard and interpreted by the receiver, and vice versa. However, not all communication is helpful to relationships. Communication can be either productive or destructive to a relationship. Saying critical, hurtful things in a cold, unfeeling way may worsen a relationship. One member of a couple who openly shares negative feelings the other can't handle may increase tension and alienation. Thus, politeness, tact, and consideration are required if communication is to be productive. The issue of communication is so important that a part of Chapter 14 of this book is devoted to a detailed discussion of it.

Admiration and Respect

One of the most important human needs is for acceptance and appreciation. The most successful marriages are those in which these needs are partly fulfilled in the relationship (Cousins and Vincent,

1983). Two people who like each other, who admire and support each other in their respective endeavors, who are proud of each other's achievements, who openly express appreciation of each other, and who build each other's self-esteem are fulfilling their emotional needs and building a satisfying relationship (Bell, Daly, and Gonzalez, 1987; Lauer and Lauer, 1985). Respect in marriage encompasses respect for individual differences and respect for the other person as an important human being (Curran, 1983).

Partners who are able to meet these needs are usually emotionally secure people themselves. They don't have to criticize each other or put each other down to build themselves up. They like expressing appreciation and giving compliments. Their approval is not conditional, requiring the partner to do certain things before it is granted. Rather, their approval is what psychologists call **noncontingent reinforcement.** It is **unconditional positive regard.** They don't try to change their spouse but are able to accept him or her as he or she is. If they have any complaints, they voice them in private, not in front of other people. They are not threatened by a competent, high-achieving spouse and so avoid destructive competition. They like themselves and each other and express their approval in word and deed.

Companionship

One important reason for getting married is companionship. Successful married couples spend sufficient time together—and quality time. The partners enjoy each other's company, share common interests and activities, and have a lot of laughs together. They are interested in each other's hobbies and leisure time preferences. Furthermore, they try to be interesting companions to each other. They consider their spouse their best friend. (See Chapter 13 for more about companionship in marriage.)

It is unrealistic to expect partners to do everything together or to have all their interests in common. Most people want some separateness in their togetherness; they want to be able to do some things with their own friends. But it is helpful to have interests and friends in common. Problems arise when partners continue to enjoy most of their social life with friends they knew before marriage rather than spend time together. Some couples drift

Successful married couples share common interests and activities; they enjoy each other's company.

apart simply because the partners seldom see each other. Curran (1983) goes so far as to state, "Lack of time together may be the most pervasive enemy the healthy family has." Marital interaction and happiness seem to go together. An acceptable degree of interaction contributes to marital happiness, and marital happiness tends to increase the amount of interaction (Zuo, 1992).

People also differ on how close a companion they want their spouse to be. When one wants close companionship and the other doesn't, it can become a source of tension and conflict. Mace and Mace (1974) likened the marriage relationship to the dilemma of two porcupines settling down to sleep on a cold night. If the porcupines get too close, their quills prick each other. If they move too far apart, they can't benefit from each other's body heat. So the porcupines shift back and forth, first together and then apart, until they arrive at a position in which they can achieve the maximum amount of warmth with a minimum amount of hurt.

Spirituality and Values

Another factor that contributes to successful marriage is shared spirituality and values (Hatch, James, and Schumm, 1986). Successful couples share spiritual activities; the partners have a high degree of religious orientation and similar beliefs and values that are manifested in religious behavior. They have a strong value system and similar goals, and they share a philosophy of life. They try to live up to their own high ideals. They have a strong sense of right and wrong and a desire to help other people.

Filsinger and Wilson (1984) conducted a study of marital adjustment of 208 married couples selected from a cross section of both fundamental and liberal Protestant churches in a large southwestern metropolitan area. They found that religiosity (measured in terms of religious belief, ritual, experience, knowledge, and the social consequences of religion) was the most consistent and strongest predictor of marital adjustment. This finding is in agreement with other studies that show religiosity to be correlated with marital adjustment, with marital satisfaction (Bell, Daly, and Gonzalez, 1987), with marital success (Curran, 1983; Stinnett and DeFrain, 1985), and with marital stability (Glenn and Supancic, 1984; Lauer and Lauer, 1985).

Religious couples indicate that their religion contributes to their marriage in a number of ways. They derive social, emotional, and spiritual support from their faith. In some cases, church involvement provides friends and activities for the couples to share. Religious faith also encourages marital commitment through the value that is placed on the marital bond and through spiritual support in times of difficulties. Some people point to the increased intimacy that results in sharing such an intimate thing as one's religious faith. Many married couples turn to their faith for moral guidance in making decisions and dealing with conflict (Robinson and Blanton, 1993).

Commitment

Successful marriage requires a high degree of motivation: the desire to make the marriage work and a

Successful couples commonly share spiritual activities and similar beliefs. Studies find such shared values to be a consistent predictor of marital adjustment, regardless of how liberal or conservative the couple's beliefs are.

willingness to expend time and effort to make sure it does. Some couples encounter so many serious problems in their relationship that one wonders how the marriage will ever succeed. But, through extraordinary motivation and determination, they overcome their obstacles, solve their problems, and emerge with a satisfactory relationship. Other couples give up after very little effort; some of these people really didn't want to be married in the first place, so they never worked at the marriage (Nock, 1995a; Surra and Hughes, 1997).

Marital success is more attainable if the commitment is mutual. One person can't build a relationship or save a marriage, no matter how much he or she tries. In their research on 301 married persons, Sabatelli and Cecil-Pigo (1985) found that partners who were participating equally in the relationship and who experienced maximum interdependence were also the most committed. People aren't going to put forth their best effort if their partner is not equally involved.

One of the important questions is, To whom and to what is the commitment? The commitment is really threefold:

1. **The commitment is of the self, to the self.** This involves the desire to grow, to change, and to be a good marriage partner. Some people who come for marriage counseling want their partner to change, but they are unwilling to change themselves or to assume any personal responsibility for making things better. None of us can really change other people if they don't want to change, but we can change ourselves if we need to. It's not easy, but it can be done.

2. **The commitment is to each other.** When people say "I do" in a marriage ceremony, they make a personal promise or pledge to each other: to love, honor, cherish, and be faithful under all circumstances of life. Their commitment is a highly personal one (Quinn, 1982).

3. **The commitment is to the relationship, the marriage, and the family.** Mace and Mace (1980) define commitment as a willingness to support "ongoing growth in their relationship." When children are involved, the commitment goes beyond the couple relationship to include the whole family unit.

Stanley and Markman (1992) make a distinction between personal dedication and constraint commitment. Personal dedication refers to the desire of an individual to maintain or improve the quality of his or her relationship for the joint benefit of the couple. It is evidenced by a desire, not only to continue in the relationship, but also to improve it, to sacrifice for it, to invest in it, to link personal goals to it, and to benefit the partner as well as oneself.

In contrast, constraint commitment refers to forces that compel individuals to maintain relationships regardless of their personal dedication to them. Constraints may arise from either external or internal pressures, and they promote relationship stability by making termination of the relationship more costly economically, socially, personally, and psychologically.

But what happens if there is conflict between commitments? Is the commitment to the marriage and the family or to one's partner more important? Mae West famously described marriage as an institution but asked, "Who wants to live in an institution?" Indeed, who does, unless it serves the needs of those in it? Some people are able to work out troubled relationships because marriage is sacred to them and they want to preserve the family unit. In so doing, they may find individual and couple fulfillment. For other people, however, commitment to "save the marriage" may come at great cost to themselves and the children.

One of the most basic challenges is maintaining a sense of autonomy while also experiencing a sense of relatedness to one's partner (Rankin-Esquer, Burnett, Baucom, and Epstein, 1997). Partners in successful couples have mastered the art of losing themselves in their relationship without losing their sense of self. This requires a well-developed identity and high self-esteem. Figure 10.1 depicts three types of relationships. In A, two people maintain their individual identities but make little effort to achieve oneness as a married couple. In B, two people lose their separate identities, which become swallowed up in the relationship. In C, there is

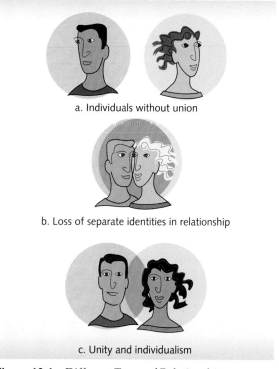

a. Individuals without union

b. Loss of separate identities in relationship

c. Unity and individualism

Figure 10.1   Different Types of Relationships.

sufficient commitment to form a union, but enough separateness for each to maintain a sense of self.

Commitment is also enhanced if it is made with an assumption of permanence, which is the ideal according to our religious and cultural values. One survey of more than 5,000 students in four universities revealed that 92% viewed marriage as a commitment for life (Martin and Martin, 1984). Certainly, partners are more highly motivated to work out marital problems if they expect their relationship to last forever.

Affection

One important expectation of most married partners is they will meet each other's need for love and affection. This need varies from couple to couple, depending on the way the partners are socialized. Some people have a higher need for emotional intimacy than others. But most expect their needs to be met in their marriage (Dandeneau and Johnson, 1994; Kenny and Acitelli, 1994).

Several related factors are important. Lauer and Lauer (1985) stress the importance of spouses' agreeing on how to show affection and how often. Some people want a lot of physical contact: hugging, kissing, cuddling, touching, caressing. Others are satisfied with an occasional kiss. Some people are very uninhibited in sexual expression and desire playful sex. Others are more restrained. There also may be differences in the desired frequency of intercourse. In successful marriages, couples are able to work out such differences.

In their research, Bell, Daly, and Gonzalez (1987) found that both physical and verbal affection were important to successful marriage. As one wife put it, "I know he loves me, but I want him to tell me." Words that express warmth, appreciation, endearment, and approval, that raise low spirits, and that boost damaged egos can be as essential as physical contact and sexual intimacy.

Interestingly, even though fulfillment of affectional and sexual needs is important to marital success, strong feelings of romantic love are not a requirement. Romantic love is one of the most important factors in emotional attraction and in motivating couples to want to be together. In successful marriages, love may continue to grow, but it changes over the years, with fewer components of romanticism and stronger bonds of attachment and affection. Emotional bonding and affective expression are important ingredients in successful marriages (Anderson, 1986; Carstensen, Gottman, and Levenson, 1995; Kinston, Loader, and Miller, 1987).

The Ability to Deal with Crises and Stress

All couples, both those who achieve marital success and those who do not, experience problems and stress in and outside their relationship. One of the factors that distinguishes the two groups is that spouses who have successful marriages are able to solve their problems and manage stress in a creative fashion. Stinnett and DeFrain (1985) found that successful couples are "able to weather the storms of life." These partners expect problems as a normal part of life and develop problem-solving skills so they can cope (Curran, 1983). They often interpret crises as an opportunity to move in a positive direction. They feel they have grown from struggling through and coping with the crisis. In one study of strong families, 77% felt that something positive had developed as a result of coping with a crisis (Stinnett, Knorr, DeFrain, and Rowe, 1981). One of the characteristics of strong families is that family members turn to one another for strength and assistance. This enhances family unity, cohesiveness, and commitment.

Successful couples also have a greater tolerance for frustration than do unsuccessful couples. In this sense, the partners are more emotionally mature and stable. They have learned healthy, constructive ways of dealing with anger, rather than taking it out on other family members (Hardy, Orzek, and Heistad, 1984).

Research evidence also suggests that the degree of depression is a strong predictor of marital quality. Depression both arises from and creates marital dissatisfaction. Persons who are unhappy in their marriage report relatively high levels of depression, and depressed persons and their spouses report stressful, unsatisfying marriages (McLeod and Eckberg, 1993).

Responsibility

Responsibility involves being accountable for one's own behavior within the context of the family. It also means assuming responsibility for family maintenance (Fincham and Bradbury, 1992). Successful marriage depends on the mutual assumption, sharing, and division of responsibility in the family. Typical complaints brought to marriage counselors include the following:

My partner is completely irresponsible.

My partner never does anything around the house. I do everything, inside and outside work both.

My partner is irresponsible in handling money.

My spouse doesn't like to work. He'd rather be out with friends partying and having a good time.

My spouse doesn't take enough responsibility for cleaning the house. She knows that if she doesn't do it, eventually I'll get it done.

My partner doesn't show any interest in taking care of the children. He feels that because he brings home a paycheck, that is the end of his responsibilities. He leaves everything else to me.

I have to make all the decisions and plans for our social life. I wish my spouse would assume some of this responsibility. (Author's counseling notes)

In marriages in which couples report a high degree of satisfaction, two conditions exist in relation to the division of responsibility. First, the partners feel there is a fairly equal division of labor. In situations in which one partner is working 100 hours a week and the other works little, the working spouse rightfully resents the uneven distribution of responsibility. Women in particular are dissatisfied when they perceive unfairness in the performance of household chores and in the spending of money (Blair, 1993). Consider this account:

Ed worked hard all his life building up a cleaning business. He was very successful and decided to retire at age 60. He spends his time playing golf at the country club and playing cards at the Elks club. Since the family needs the money and the business needs attention, his wife Edith spends her days managing the company. She resents deeply the fact that she is still working and her husband isn't. (Author's counseling notes)

Numerous studies reveal that an inequitable division of household and child-care responsibilities causes conflict in families. Despite changes in gender attitudes and the increased participation of women in the workforce, women still do the majority of the housework (Shelton, 1992). The research on household task performance provides little evidence of egalitarianism in marriage when it comes to housework, as employed women do nearly twice as much as men. This lack of equity is a major source of dissatisfaction for many women.

Second, in successful marriages, gender-role performance matches gender-role expectations. Many couples have set ideas about who should perform what tasks. Thus, if a man expects his spouse to perform traditional feminine roles in the family—caring for children, taking care of the home, attending to his needs—but she's more interested in pursuing her career, conflict develops. If the woman expects her spouse to be the primary breadwinner and an all-around handyman at home and he doesn't live up to her expectations, she may become very dissatisfied with the relationship.

Unselfishness

Ours is an age of individualism in which many try to find happiness through self-gratification and narcissistic **selfism.** Selfism in marriage lessens each partner's responsibility for the success of the relationship. Social exchange theory emphasizes that people seek relationships in which the cost-benefit ratio is satisfactory and fair. From this perspective, decreased investment on the part of one spouse decreases the likelihood that the other will receive the rewards deemed sufficient to continue the relationship. The result is marital instability, because associations are continued only if each partner feels he or she is receiving what is deserved and expected.

It is not surprising, therefore, that the most successful marriages are based on a spirit of mutual helpfulness, with each partner unselfishly attending to the needs of the other, as well as to his or her own (Bell, Daly, and Gonzalez, 1987). One woman explained:

My husband is the most generous, giving man I have ever known. He will give you the shirt off his back. Every day he does so many little things for me. When we go out, he always makes sure that I'm having a good time. He insists on bringing my coffee while I'm in bed in the morning. He helps me around the house all the time. He never seems to think about himself. He's too busy thinking about the rest of us. (Author's counseling notes)

It is not evident in the quotation, but the woman was just as giving and unselfish as her spouse. They had a wonderful marriage, primarily because the unselfishness was reciprocal. She had come in for counseling because she was concerned about a friend who was having marital problems.

Paradoxically, people who are self-centered and self-serving are less likely to feel as fulfilled or as happy as those who seek to meet the needs of others. Psychologist Bernard Rimland at the Institute for Child Behavior Research in San Diego asked 216 college students to write the names of up to 10 persons whom they knew best and after each name to write either *H* for happy or *N* for unhappy. Then they were asked to go down the list again and write either *S* for selfish or *U* for unselfish. Only 78 people whom the students rated as selfish were also rated happy, while 827 whom the students rated as happy were also rated unselfish. By definition, selfish people are devoted to bringing themselves happiness. Judged by others, however, they seem to succeed less often than do people who work at bringing happiness to others (Cox, 1982).

Empathy and Sensitivity

Empathy refers to the ability to identify with the feelings, thoughts, and attitudes of another person (Wampler and Powell, 1982). It is the vicarious sharing of the experiences of another person. Kagan and Schneider (1987) call this ability **affective sensitivity** and describe its development in five steps:

- **Phase 1: Perception.** Developing empathy begins with contact and interaction during which someone perceives the thoughts, feelings, memories, anticipations, and aspirations of another person and the emotional tones associated with them.
- **Phase 2: Experiencing.** The observer resonates to, or vicariously experiences, the emotions of the other.
- **Phase 3: Awareness.** Awareness is the process of acknowledging to oneself that one has perceived and resonated to the emotions of another individual.
- **Phase 4: Labeling.** Awareness is acknowledged verbally; the observer speaks of having sensitivity to what another person has communicated.

- **Phase 5: Stating.** Empathy requires a person to communicate verbally or by some other means that he or she has perceived another person's message. Communication may be nonverbal, such as touching. The purpose of this final phase is to let the other person know that one understands.

According to the research, empathy is an important ingredient in a successful marriage (Bell, Daly, and Gonzalez, 1987). An empathetic person is someone who listens, understands, and cares (Sprecher, Metts, Burleson, Hapfield, and Thompson, 1995).

Honesty, Trust, and Fidelity

According to the research of Bell, Daly, and Gonzalez (1987), the old-fashioned virtues of honesty, trust, and fidelity are important ingredients in contemporary successful marriages. Sincerity, truthfulness, faithfulness, and trust are the cement that bind people together. Partners know they can accept each other's word, believe in each other, and depend on each other to keep promises and to be faithful to commitments that are made. One young woman comments:

> I never have to worry about my husband. When he tells me something I know it's true. He's a very sincere, up-front person. I know just where I stand with him all the time. He always keeps his word. If he promises the kids something, he never disappoints them. He travels a lot, but I trust him completely. I know he's faithful to me. He isn't the kind of man to sneak around. If two people can't believe in one another, or depend on one another, they don't have much of a relationship in my opinion. (Student comments to author)

When two people first start going out together, one of the things each seeks to discover is whether the other is honest and sincere about the relationship. In marriage itself, once one spouse begins to doubt the honesty, sincerity, and faithfulness of the other, he or she will feel increasingly insecure and vulnerable. In fact, the future of the relationship may be threatened. Once trust is broken, developing it again involves a willingness to forgive. When one partner does something that hurts the other but is truly sorry for what has happened, the relationship can be rebuilt only if

Several research studies have focused on the meaning and importance of trust in relationships (Larzelere and Huston, 1980; Rotter, 1980).

The Meaning of Trust

Trust is the degree of confidence people feel when they think about their relationship. Trust means that they feel a person is predictably dependable, that they can count on that individual in times of need. Trust is generalized expectancy that the promise, the word, or the written or verbal statement of another person can be relied upon.

Characteristics of Trusters

People who trust others are more dependable themselves and more likely to be trustworthy. Conversely, those who score low on trust are less trustworthy and actually more likely to lie and cheat themselves. People who feel other people cannot be trusted also feel they themselves can lie and cheat because others are doing it; they see it as a necessary defensive reaction. Furthermore, if they are dishonest themselves, they project their faults onto others.

High trusters are more likable than others and are rated as happier, more ethical, more attractive to the opposite sex, and more desirable as a close friend. Psychologists rate them as better adjusted than low trusters. High trusters tend to base their code of ethics on conventional morality.

High trusters are not more gullible or less intelligent than low trusters. When they have evidence that others are deceiving them, they are not more trusting than are low trusters (Rotter, 1980).

Broken Trust

Once trust has been violated, it becomes difficult to reestablish. Even if a partner promises to change and begins to work at rebuilding the trust, doubt remains because to be fooled again would hurt too much. Any error becomes evidence that the new effort is merely a sham and that nothing has changed. This cycle of doubt and distrust can be changed, but considerable motivation and care are required if a once-solid relationship is to be rebuilt.

---

the person who has been hurt is willing to forgive the other (Hargrave and Sells, 1997).

Adaptability, Flexibility, and Tolerance

Spouses whose marriages are successful are usually adaptable and flexible (Wilcoxon, 1985). They recognize that people differ in their attitudes, values, habits, thought processes, and ways of doing things. They recognize that their own preferences are not necessarily the only viable ones, so they accept individual and group differences. They don't insist that everyone they live with be a carbon copy of themselves.

They recognize as well that life is not static, that situations and circumstances change as we go through various stages of the life cycle. They are able to accept change as the norm and are willing to adjust to varying circumstances (deTurck and Miller, 1986). They also are willing to grow with the relationship as time passes (Anderson, 1986).

Adaptability and flexibility require a high degree of emotional maturity. People have to be secure enough to let go of old thoughts and habits that are no longer functional or appropriate. But to let go requires some confidence that the new will

work as well as the old. Flexible people are not threatened by change. In fact, they welcome new challenges because they offer a chance to grow and develop. Marcus (1983) wrote:

> One person's capacity to adapt to another requires a degree of security. . . . Instead of feeling threatened by flexibility, they . . . feel proud of their capacity to be flexible. Because marriage requires a series of adaptations, it is of itself a stimulus toward achieving mature adult status. (p. 120)

The most difficult people to deal with are perfectionists, who have only one rigid standard by which they judge everyone and everything. Perfectionists have no tolerance for imperfection. They have impossibly high standards for themselves and others and are completely inflexible in the way they think. Since they believe that they are always right and others wrong, they insist that any changes in a relationship have to be made by someone else. As one man said, "When my wife and I discuss anything, I'm right ninety-nine percent of the time, and she's wrong" (author's counseling notes). Certainly, it's very difficult to work out problems with a person who is so arrogant and rigid in his thinking. (Barrow and Moore, 1983).

229

Because perfectionists fear appearing foolish and inadequate and are afraid that their thoughts and feelings will not be acceptable to others, they inhibit self-disclosure and are unable to communicate effectively. This further deprives them of the warmth and unconditional acceptance they crave but cannot earn through accomplishment. Marital closeness becomes difficult, because they never let other people really get to know them (Burns, 1980).

SUMMARY

1. A successful marriage has been defined as one that is durable, approximates ideals, fulfills mutual needs, and is satisfying.

2. Marital success reflects the extent to which both partners in a relationship are satisfied that it has fulfilled reasonable expectations and mutual needs.

3. In happy marriages, after one partner makes a negative statement, the other partner is likely not to respond immediately, whereas in unhappy marriages, both partners continue to reciprocate negatively.

4. In happy marriages, if one partner does something negative, the other partner tends to think that the negativity is fleeting and situational. In unhappy marriages, however, the same behavior is likely to be interpreted in terms of overall inconsideration, selfishness, and indifference.

5. The "demand-withdraw" pattern is characteristic of unhappy marriages. In this pattern, it is usually the woman who raises and pursues the issues and the man who attempts to avoid the discussion and to withdraw.

6. The presence of criticism, defensiveness, contempt, and stonewalling on the part of one or both partners is characteristic of unhappy marriages.

7. Seven types of marital patterns have been identified: devitalized, financially focused, conflicted, traditional, balanced, harmonious, and vitalized. This typology enables us to recognize that not all marriages are alike.

8. Twelve characteristics of successful marriage are communication; admiration and respect; companionship; spirituality and common values; commitment; affection; the ability to deal with crises and stress; responsibility; unselfishness; empathy and sensitivity; honesty, trust, and fidelity; and adaptability, flexibility, and tolerance.

KEY TERMS

negative affect reciprocity

devitalized couples

financially focused couples

conflicted couples

traditional couples

balanced couples

harmonious couples

vitalized couples

noncontingent reinforcement

unconditional positive regard

selfism

affective sensitivity

QUESTIONS FOR THOUGHT

1. How would you describe a successful marriage, and how does this description differ from, or how is it similar to, the definitions discussed in the textbook?

2. For single students brought up in two-parent families: Did your parents have a successful marriage according to your views? Why or why not?

3. For single students brought up in a one-parent family: Select a married couple that you know well. Is this a successful marriage according to your views? Why or why not?

4. For married students: Do you have a successful marriage according to your views? Why or why not?

5. Select the four most important qualities for a successful marriage according to your views, discuss them, and tell why you feel they are so important.

SUGGESTED READINGS

Burr, W. R., Klein, S. R., and Associates. (1995). *Reexamining Family Stress: New Theory and Research.* Thousand Oaks, CA: Sage. Discusses family stress responses as determined by the level of stress.

Cutrona, C. E. (1996). *Social Support in Couples: Marriage as a Resource in Times of Stress.* Thousand Oaks, CA: Sage. Surveys theoretical issues confronting researchers in studying social support in the context of marital relationships.

Golden, L. B. (2000). *Case Studies in Marriage and Family Therapy.* Upper Saddle River, NJ: Merrill. Utilizes actual cases to discuss therapy practices for couples and families.

Gottman, J. (1994). *Why Marriages Succeed or Fail.* New York: Simon & Schuster. Argues that marital stability and satisfaction result from teachable conflict management skills.

Gottman, J. (1999). *The 7 Principles for Making Marriage Work.* London: Weidenfeld & Nicolson. Provides a research-based guide to revitalizing and strengthening marriages.

Gray, J. (1999). *Mars and Venus: 365 Ways to Keep Passion Alive.* London: Vermilion. Gives practical advice for maintaining an exciting and intimate relationship.

Gray, J. (2000). *Mars and Venus in Touch.* New York: HarperCollins. Explores how communication between men and women can increase passion and intimacy in a relationship.

Hughes, M. (1991). *Marriage Counseling: An Essential Guide.* New York: Continuum. Although intended for professional therapists, is equally suitable for lay readers interested in understanding and dealing with marital concerns.

Mackey, R. A., and O'Brien, B. A. (1995). *Lasting Marriages: Men and Women Growing Together.* Westport, CT: Praeger. Explores why some marriages last while others fail.

McKenry, P. C., and Price, S. J. (Eds.). (1994). *Families and Change: Coping with Stressful Events.* Thousand Oaks, CA: Sage. Focuses on family stress theory.

Scarf, M. (1987). *Intimate Partners: Patterns in Love and Marriage.* New York: Random House. Examines the variety of relational patterns.

CHAPTER 11

LEARNING OBJECTIVES

After reading the chapter, you should be able to:

Understand the basic stages of the family life cycle in an intact marriage and in a family in which there is divorce and remarriage.

Describe the various trends in marital satisfaction, from the honeymoon stage to late adulthood.

Summarize the major marital adjustment tasks and problems early in marriage.

Describe how gay and lesbian families are different from and similar to other types of families.

Describe the adjustments to parenthood.

Discuss the major adjustments during middle adulthood, including the postparental years.

Summarize the major adjustments during late adulthood, including divorce.

Discuss problems of family relationships for the elderly and the widowed, including alternatives for caring for the elderly.

Marital Relationships over the Family Life Cycle

Learning Objectives

Marriage and Personal Happiness

The Family Life Cycle

Data on Family Life Cycles

Changes in Marital Satisfaction

The Curvilinear Pattern

Gay and Lesbian Families

Adjustments Early in Marriage

Marital Adjustment Tasks

Problems During Three Early Stages

Adjustments to Parenthood

Parenthood as Stress

Parenthood and Psychological Well-Being

Adjustments During Middle Adulthood

Marital Adjustments

The Postparental Years

Adjustments During Late Adulthood

Developmental Tasks

Perspective: Postretirement Employment

Marital Satisfaction

Divorce

Parent–Adult Child Relationships

Widowhood

Family Issues: Who Cares for the Elderly?

Summary

Key Terms

Questions for Thought

Suggested Readings

Marriage relationships are never static but rather are constantly changing, developing, and growing. Sometimes relationships are frustrating, unsatisfying, and troublesome; other times they are fulfilling and vital.

The adjustments that people face early in marriage are unique because the relationship is so new. The adjustments during parenthood and middle age relate to the aging process and to children growing older and leaving home. Late adulthood requires establishment of new roles in the family as a couple, as older parents of adult children, and as grandparents. The elderly have to make peace with their past and be able to accept their life as they have lived it.

Most people face the prospect of separation from their spouse for some part of their lives. A small percentage of older people get divorced at this stage of life (which will be discussed in Chapter 20); more live out their lives as widows or widowers. Being alone requires special adjustments that couples do not face.

The extent to which the elderly are able to overcome their problems and make the adjustments that life requires will determine their levels of well-being and life satisfaction during this stage of life. Each phase of life has its own joys and its own problems. Knowing what some of these are

helps everyone pass through each stage more successfully.

MARRIAGE AND PERSONAL HAPPINESS

The positive link between satisfaction with marriage and family life and psychological well-being is well established (Mills, Grasmick, Morgan, and Wenk, 1992). Few married people would disagree with the idea that the quality of their marriage has a strong effect on their happiness and satisfaction with life (Zollar and Williams, 1987). An unhappy marriage can have a negative effect on life satisfaction and subjective well-being (Haring-Hidore, Stock, Okun, and Witler, 1985). People who are having severe marital problems may not be able to eat properly or to sleep; and so they can become quite debilitated.

Marital relationships are seldom static. Partners may report a period of harmony during which everything seems fine, only to have "all hell break loose" to the point at which the couple is talking about divorce. The more unstable the couple, the more variable the relationship. Most couples have some ups and downs in their relationship. What is important, however, is the general quality of the

The quality of marriage has a strong effect on personal happiness and life satisfaction. Since the marital relationship is seldom static, most couples will experience periods of both instability and harmony.

relationship over time and the extent to which partners report satisfaction with it.

THE FAMILY LIFE CYCLE

One of the most helpful ways of examining marital relationships over time is in terms of various phases of the family life cycle. The **family life cycle** divides the family experience into phases, or stages, over the life span and seeks to describe changes in family structure and function during each stage. The cycle can also be used to show the challenges, tasks, and problems that people face during each stage, as well as the satisfactions derived.

Data on Family Life Cycles

Figure 11.1 shows the traditional family life cycle of spouses in an intact marriage. The ages of the spouses are median ages for the U.S. population. Thus, the man is married at 26, the woman at 24. They wait 2 years before having the first of two children. The man is 50 and the woman 48 when the youngest child is 20 and leaves home. The empty-nest years until retirement are from age 50 to 65 for the man and age 48 to 65 for the woman. The man dies at age 74 while the woman lives to age 79, spending her last years as a widow (U.S. Bureau of the Census, 1999a).

The family life cycle is different for divorced couples. Figure 11.2 shows separate cycles of spouses who marry, have two children, and divorce; each remarries a spouse with two children. The children reside with their mother after the divorce. Note that the median age of first marriage for couples who divorce is 1 year younger than for couples who never divorce. The man is 32 and the woman 30 when they divorce. Their children are 3 and 5 years old. The father remarries 4 years later, at age 36, to a woman who is 33, with two children 6 and 8 years old who reside with her and her new spouse. The father is 50 when his youngest stepchild is 20 and moves out of the house. He and his spouse have 15 empty-nest years until he retires at age 65 and an additional 8 years together before he dies at age 74.

The woman is 30 when she divorces. Her two children are ages 3 and 5. She remarries 3 years later, when her children are 6 and 8. She is 47 years old when her youngest child is 20 and moves out of the house. She spends 18 empty-nest years with her spouse until she retires at age 65 and has 9 more years with him until he dies at age 74. She spends the last 8 years of her life, from age 71 to 79, as a widow (U.S. Bureau of the Census, 1999a).

Of course, the family life cycle is different for everyone, and these graphs do not represent the life cycle of all types of families. However, they do give

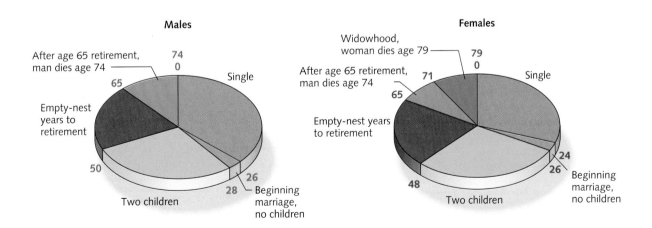

Numbers around circumferences are ages in years.

Figure 11.1   Family Life Cycle—Intact Marriage (*Note:* Data from *Statistical Abstract of the United States, 1999* by U.S. Bureau of the Census, 1999, Washington, DC: U.S. Government Printing Office.)

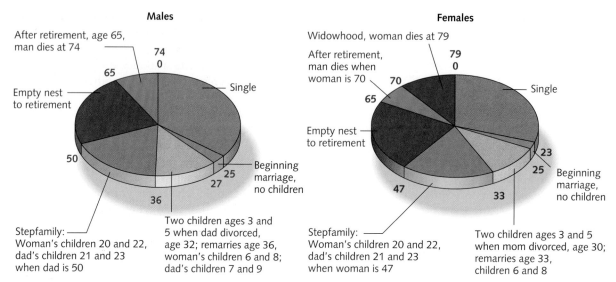

Figure 11.2   Family Life Cycle—Marriage, Divorce, Remarriage; Children Reside with Wife (*Note:* Data from *Statistical Abstract of the United States, 1999* by U.S. Bureau of the Census, 1999, Washington, DC: U.S. Government Printing Office.)

us a sense of what happens to the majority of people in the United States. Exceptions to the two basic life cycles include those who remarry more than once, those who have much larger families, gay and lesbian families, and single-parent families. Twenty-seven percent of White families, 36% of Hispanic families, and 62% of African American families are one-parent families (U.S. Bureau of the Census, 1999a). In general, African Americans are less likely to marry than Whites, and those who marry do so at an older age than Whites. Greater percentages of African Americans than Whites get divorced. Divorce takes place after about the same length of marriage as for Whites, but Blacks typically wait longer to remarry, so Black stepparents begin the postparental stage at a later age than White stepparents. On average, African Americans live 7 years less than Whites: men to age 66 and women to age 74 (U.S. Bureau of the Census, 1999a).

Changes in Marital Satisfaction

How does marital satisfaction change over various phases of the family life cycle? The answer depends on the particular family. Family patterns differ. The most helpful model of what happens over long-term marriage has been outlined by Weishaus and

Field (1988), who describe six different types of long-term marriage:

1. **Stable/positive.** These partners have stable but not static marriages, maintaining moderately high to high satisfaction and generally positive affection and interaction throughout the years.

2. **Stable/neutral.** These partners never experience emotional closeness but marry for other reasons. They are generally comfortable with each other and are without excessive conflict.

3. **Stable/negative.** These partners experience primarily negative emotions throughout marriage, manifested as hostility or indifference. Lack of any positive feeling is apparent. There is little joy, only the feeling that duty has been performed.

4. **Curvilinear.** For these partners, satisfaction is high early in marriage, drops during the middle years, and rises again after the children have left home.

5. **Continuous decline.** These partners experience gradual and more or less continuous eroding of marital satisfaction.

6. **Continuous increase.** These partners derive increasing satisfaction as the years pass.

The Curvilinear Pattern

The most common pattern of change in marital satisfaction is curvilinear: high satisfaction at the time of marriage, lower during the child-rearing years, and higher again after the youngest child has passed beyond the teens (Anderson, Russell, and Schumm, 1983). Marital happiness has been found to decrease as the newness of the relationship wears off (Johnson, Amoloza, and Booth, 1992). Some studies show the decline in satisfaction lasting only until all the children have started school (Belsky and Rovine, 1990). However, these studies are based on cross-sectional or retrospective data. Other longitudinal studies show no ∪-curved change in marital satisfaction over the life course. They do show some deterioration in the woman's reported marital satisfaction during the 31st to 45th years of marriage (Vaillant and Vaillant, 1993).

The common assumption that spouses, particularly women, are affected negatively by the children's leaving home cannot be substantiated by research. In fact, data from six U.S. national surveys indicate that women whose children have left home are happier, enjoy life more, and have greater marital satisfaction than do women whose children are still at home (Glenn and McLanahan, 1982).

The most plausible explanation for why marital satisfaction is at an ebb when the children are of school age seems to be that the demands placed upon the couple during these years are at their greatest. The couple is under increased financial pressure because of the needs of a growing family. Usually, job responsibilities outside the home are at a maximum. The children make increasing demands as they get older, and community responsibilities also increase during the middle years of marriage. Specifically, the intensity and number of social roles gradually increase until the middle years. As a result, the partners experience greater role strain because they cannot perform all these roles as well as they and others might expect. This role discrepancy results in less satisfaction with the marital relationship. After the children are grown, however, role expectations and strain decrease, with a concomitant increase in marital satisfaction (Olson et al., 1983).

The increased satisfaction continues for a while, but as the problems of growing older increase, marital satisfaction begins to decline again. In spite of

Some couples breathe a sigh of relief when the last child leaves home, and many couples report a noticeable increase in marital satisfaction.

the decrease in marital satisfaction, however, divorce rates are not higher late in marriage. The lower divorce rate for older marriages occurs because couples have more barriers and fewer alternatives from which to choose.

Gay and Lesbian Families

Most of the research and discussion of gay and lesbian families have focused on how they differ from other, "more traditional" family forms. However, they share many similarities with other family types and in most respects are like all other families. As Laird (1993) observed:

> They must negotiate their relationships with the larger community and their families of origin, forging social networks and establishing boundaries

between themselves and the outside world, as well as negotiating relationships and roles, developing problem-solving strategies, mediating conflicts, and marking boundaries inside the family. They must decide who will do what, when, where, and how in order to meet the particular needs of the family as a whole and of individual family members, whose interests at times may conflict or compete. Like all families, they face possibilities for conflict over divisions of labor, the use of money, space, and time, their sexual and intimate relationships, issues of closeness and distance, dominance and subordination, child-rearing ideologies, and so on. (p. 308)

However, Laird went on to point out that gay and lesbian families differ from others in at least two important ways. First, most families are headed by same-sex couples, although some are headed by single gay or lesbian parents and others by multiple parenting figures. Second, these families are often stigmatized as inappropriate family forms, which presents them with unique challenges. For example, although gay and lesbian single parents face the same issues of finances, time constraints, and dating as most heterosexual single parents, the prospect of forming new long-term relationships and families is complicated by society's judgment of gay and lesbian families. Two-parent gay and lesbian families with children from previous marriages often share similar situations and deal with similar important issues as stepfamilies. However, there have been child custody cases in which custody or visitation rights were not granted to a parent on the sole basis of his or her sexual orientation. This kind of discrimination can have a powerful influence on the decision-making process of gay and lesbian individuals and families. Imagine the stress of living with the fear of losing your children due to your sexual orientation or of having your children ridiculed because of your family form. Unfortunately, that is a reality for many gay and lesbian parents and often causes them to be more private and secretive than they would like to be.

Some researchers believe that gay and lesbian families go through different life stages than other families because of their sexual orientation and the discrimination they face. For example, the "coming out" process is a unique experience to gays and lesbians. Minton and McDonald (1983/1984) suggested that this is a developmental process that

often covers the life span and eventually leads to personal acceptance and management of a positive gay self-image. In fact, the whole identity of being "gay" appears to represent a relatively new and unique cultural category in history (Herdt, 1992), particularly gay and lesbian families. While there are many socially prescribed roles for males/fathers and females/mothers in families, same-sex couples lack clear traditions or guidelines for role and task decision making. This has its benefits in that it allows for tremendous role flexibility for members of gay and lesbian families. However, it also introduces more uncertainty and complexity into role negotiation, and it can be frustrating to continually challenge prevailing notions of family structure and function.

Traditionally, gay and lesbian families were not child-centered if one or both partners had not been previously married. This is changing somewhat with what has been labeled the "lesbian baby boom," as more lesbians are opting to have children through known or unknown donor insemination. In some cases, both women in the relationship are choosing to bear children. For gay couples, adoption is still difficult as some states have enacted prohibitive agency policies to discourage gays and lesbians from adopting children. Florida remains the only state that bans same-sex couples from adopting, after New Hampshire repealed a similar law in 1999. However, research consistently has shown that gay and lesbian families are just as successful at carrying out normal family roles and tasks and raising healthy children as other types of families (see Patterson, 1992, for a review of this literature).

As in all family types, there is tremendous diversity within gay and lesbian families in terms of family patterns, forms, and membership. No two families are ever alike, however similar they may seem superficially. Much of the literature to date on gay and lesbian families has chosen to stress the differences between them and heterosexual families and has emphasized each's commonalities as a group rather then their diversity (Laird, 1993). Certainly, gay and lesbian families have special strengths, raising families so well despite oppression and discrimination. As Laird (1993) stated, this suggests that we need to know more about their secrets to success and their ways of overcoming the lack of socially sanctioned rituals such as marriage, as well as the lack of other social and legal sanctions such as spousal rights and benefits. Boxer and Cohler (1989) observed that, in order to understand the life course of gays and lesbians, it is crucial to understand how gay and lesbian families remain strong and resilient in the face of so much discrimination.

ADJUSTMENTS EARLY IN MARRIAGE

All partners discover that the marriage cannot live up to all of their expectations. As a result, they go through a series of adjustments in which they try to modify their behavior and relationship to achieve the greatest degree of satisfaction with a minimum degree of frustration.

Marital adjustment may be defined as the process of modifying, adapting, and altering individual and couple patterns of behavior and interaction to achieve maximum satisfaction in the relationship. According to this definition, adjustment is not an end in and of itself, but a means to an end: satisfaction in and with the marriage. It is quite possible for spouses to "adjust" to each other but still be quite unhappy and dissatisfied with the relationship. For example, people who like sex may come to accept the fact that their mate seldom wants to go to bed with them. They learn to adjust to this situation, but this does not mean that they really like it or are satisfied with this accommodation. Or people may learn to "adjust" to a mate's bad temper and try to overlook it, but this does not mean they approve. They have learned how to avoid overt conflict, but this adjustment gives them very little real comfort or joy. The goal of adjustment is to achieve the greatest degree of marital satisfaction and success.

Sometimes a particular adjustment may not be the best that one would like, but it may be said to be successful to the extent that it provides the highest satisfaction possible under the circumstances. Obviously, adjustment is not static, not a step taken just once. It is a dynamic, ongoing process that takes place throughout a couple's married life.

Marital Adjustment Tasks

All couples discover that they have to make adjustments in order to live together harmoniously. The areas of adjustment might be called **marital adjustment tasks;** 12 categories are shown in Table 11.1. The extent to which couples need to make adjustments after marriage will depend partially on the extent to which some of these tasks are confronted during courtship.

All couples who enter into a serious relationship are faced with most of the adjustments listed in Table 11.1. Some couples make many of them before marriage and so have fairly smooth sailing afterward. Other couples make few adjustments ahead of time and so are faced with nearly all of these marital adjustment tasks after marriage. These tasks can be overwhelming if encountered all at once. This situation often leads to a period of disillusionment and disenchantment in couples who have not realized what marriage involves.

Problems During Three Early Stages

One longitudinal study investigated the problems of 131 couples during three stages of the early years of their relationship (Storaasli and Markman, 1990): (1) before marriage, (2) during the first year of marriage, and (3) after the birth of their first child. Table 11.2 shows the results.

Note that money was the number one problem at all three stages of the relationship. Jealousy was a big problem before marriage but declined thereafter. Relatives were a problem before marriage and again after the first child was born. Communication and sex became greater problems after marriage and after the first child was born. Relationships with friends, religion, and alcohol and drugs were more of a problem before marriage. Problems having to do with recreation declined in importance after marriage and then rose after the first child was born.

ADJUSTMENTS TO PARENTHOOD

"First pregnancy," says a respected psychiatrist, "is a nine-month crisis. Thank God it takes nine months, because a child's coming requires enormous changes in a couple's ways of adjusting to each other" (Maynard, 1974, p. 139). Getting used to living with another adult in a committed

Table 11.1   Marital Adjustment Tasks

Emotional fulfillment and support	**Social life, friends, recreation**
Learning to give and receive affection and love	Learning to visit, entertain as a couple
Developing sensitivity, empathy, closeness	Deciding on type, frequency of social activities as individuals and as a couple
Giving emotional support, building morale, fulfilling ego needs	Selecting, relating to friends
Sexual adjustment	**Family, relatives** (Fischer, Sollie, Sorell, and Green, 1989)
Learning to satisfy, fulfill each other sexually	Establishing relationships with parents, in-laws, relatives
Working out mode, manner, timing of sexual expression	Learning how to deal with families
Finding, using acceptable means of birth control	
	Communication
Personal habits	Learning to disclose and communicate ideas, worries, concerns, needs
Adjusting to each other's personal habits, speech, cleanliness, grooming, manners, eating, sleeping, promptness (Larson, Crane, and Smith, 1991)	Learning to listen to each other and to talk to each other in constructive ways
Reconciling differences in smoking, drinking, drug habits	
Eliminating or modifying personal habits that annoy each other	**Power, decision making**
Adjusting to differences in body rhythms, schedules	Achieving desired balance of status, power
Learning to share space, time, belongings, work	Learning to make, execute decisions
	Learning cooperation, accommodation, compromise
Gender roles	
Establishing spousal roles in and outside the home	**Conflict, problem solving**
Working out gender roles in relation to income production, housekeeping, household maintenance, homemaking, child care	Learning to identify conflict causes, circumstances
	Learning to cope with conflict constructively
Agreeing on division of labor	Learning to solve problems
	Learning where, when, how to obtain help if needed
Material concerns, finances (Rice, 1986)	
Finding, selecting a residence: geographic area, neighborhood, type of housing	**Morals, values, ideology**
Equipping, maintaining a household	Understanding, adjusting to individual morals, values, ethics, beliefs, philosophies, life goals
Earning adequate income, managing money	Establishing mutual values, goals, philosophies
	Accepting each other's religious beliefs, practices
Work, employment, achievement	Making decisions in relation to religious affiliation, participation
Finding, selecting, maintaining employment	
Adjusting to type, place, hours, conditions of employment	
Working out schedules when one or both are working	
Arranging for child care when one or both are working	

relationship is challenging, but adding a third member to the family, an infant who is totally dependent, is a stressful transition in the family life cycle—and one of the most rewarding (Hackel and Ruble, 1992).

Parenthood as Stress

In recent years, there has been a tendency to refer to the addition of a first child less as a crisis and more as a period of stress and transition. The more

Table 11.2 Relationship Problems During Three Early Stages

Mean Problem Intensity*

Before Marriage		First Year of Marriage		After Birth of First Child	
Money	48.6	Money	42.3	Money	39.0
Jealousy	25.0	Communication	21.2	Sex	33.5
Relatives	22.7	Sex	19.8	Communication	32.4
Friends	18.5	Relatives	19.7	Relatives	23.9
Communication	17.8	Friends	16.7	Recreation	13.7
Sex	14.2	Children	15.3	Children	12.8
Religion	13.8	Jealousy	13.2	Friends	12.5
Recreation	12.8	Recreation	11.3	Jealousy	9.1
Children	11.8	Alcohol/drugs	8.8	Religion	7.6
Alcohol/drugs	11.8	Religion	6.4	Alcohol/drugs	6.5

*0 indicates no problem; 100 indicates a severe problem.

Note: Data from "Relationship Problems in the Early Stages of Marriage" by R. D. Storaasli and H. J. Markman, 1990, *Journal of Family Psychology,* 4, pp. 80–98.

stressful a couple's marriage before parenthood, the more likely it is that they will have difficulty in adjusting to the first child. Changes in marital quality and marital conflicts were explored in a longitudinal study of White and African American couples who made the transition to parenthood within the first 2 years of marriage. All the couples, regardless of ethnic group, reported lower marital happiness and more frequent conflicts after the transition than before (Crohan, 1996).

Sometimes stress arises if the pregnancy was not planned (Snowden, Schott, Awalt, and Gillis-Knox, 1988). Part of the stress comes from the fact that most couples are inadequately prepared for parenthood. As one mother stated, "We knew where babies came from, but we didn't know what they were like." Many new parents have no experience in caring for infants. Couples who prepare for parenthood by attending classes, reading books, and so forth find greater satisfaction in being a parent than do those who do not prepare. In addition, the level of stress during the transition to parenthood is reduced for couples who are socialized for their roles as parents by attending parenting classes (Gage and Christensen, 1991).

Part of the stress arises because of the abrupt transition to parenthood. Stress will vary from child to child depending on each child's temperament and how easy each child is to care for. Some children never give any trouble. Others, such as hyper-active or sickly children, require an abnormal amount of care.

Stress is greater if parents are young and immature. Over half a million teenagers become parents each year. Eighty-six percent of teenage fathers have female partners ages 15–19. Thirteen percent of all babies born have at least one teenage parent; 4% have parents who are both under 20. A majority of these parents have not even finished high school. It is highly unlikely that significant numbers of these teenagers are ready for parenthood (Landry and Forrest, 1995).

The economic status of the family has been found to be a factor in parents' level of distress. It affects both spouses' parenting-related stress, as well as their psychological well-being. Parents who are struggling to make ends meet feel higher levels of stress in raising their children than do parents with greater economic resources (Lavee, Sharlin, and Katz, 1996).

The transition to parenthood ushers in many life changes and adjustments, as well as new patterns, responsibilities, and routines. Much research has focused on the transition to parenthood and on what concurrent variables in a parent's life are associated with competent parenting. Many variables, including social support from family and spouse, are associated with the degree of warmth and sensitivity a parent exhibits toward the infant. Social support is associated with the adaptation to parenthood and

The birth of a first child is a period of transition and stress, but successful adjustments are measures of parenting readiness.

with positive parent-infant interactions. For example, women who receive support during pregnancy experience more positive mental and physical health outcomes during labor, delivery, and the postpartum period than do women who do not receive support (Goldstein, Diener, and Mangelsdorf, 1996).

Parenthood and Psychological Well-being

The research shows that children may have a positive effect on marital adjustment and the well-being of parents (Umberson, 1987), or a negative impact (Ross and Huber, 1985), or a minimal impact (McLanahan and Adams, 1987; Menaghan, 1989; Umberson and Gove, 1989). Wallace and Gotlib (1990) found that marital satisfaction for couples increased from the middle of pregnancy to 1 month postpartum but decreased rapidly over the next 5 months. (Assessment was not made after 6 months.) In other words, after the initial excitement of having a baby wore off, marital satisfaction declined. Other research has found that the transition to parenthood is not an inescapable detriment to marital quality, but it does require a realignment of men's and women's marital roles. Any mismatch between marital role expectations and enactment following parenthood may cause conflict and erode feelings of love between spouses (Crnic and Booth, 1991; MacDermid, Huston, and McHale, 1990).

In terms of psychological well-being, much depends on the individual parent's situation (McLanahan and Adams, 1987; Menaghan, 1989; Umberson and Gove, 1989). Being a single parent, for example, may be more emotionally taxing than being one of two parents taking care of a child (Garfinkel and McLanahan, 1986; Hughes, 1989). Other research has shown that women experience greater parental strain than men because of their greater responsibilities (Scott and Alwin, 1989; Wethington and Kessler, 1989). Also, the greater the number of children, the greater the strain on the parents while the children are young (Goldsteen and Ross, 1989).

ADJUSTMENTS DURING MIDDLE ADULTHOOD

The most noticeable changes of middle adulthood are physical ones. These changes are gradual, but increasing wrinkles, graying hair, and balding heads remind us of the aging process. Muscle tone declines, weight increases, and strength and endurance ebb. "Body monitoring" increases as individuals concern themselves with the dimensions of their middle-aged bodies. Physical exercise becomes more necessary to keep in shape and to offset the decrease in the body's metabolism, which results in the tendency to put on weight (Poehlman, Melby, and Badylak, 1991).

Health concerns become increasingly related to life satisfaction (Willits and Crider, 1988). Perhaps for the first time, adults are confronted with their own mortality (Kercher, Kosloski, and Normoyle, 1988). Previously, they have counted the years past, but now they begin to count the years ahead. The midlife transformation is precipitated by the awareness that one's years are numbered. Paradoxically, people are entering the prime of life and the period of greatest life fulfillment. In any case, the physical reminders of aging pale when compared to the dramatic confrontation with one's own mortality, as parents and even peers begin to die.

This personalization of mortality leads to an awareness that time is finite, that life is a race against time; there is a sense of urgency to accomplish all that one wants to achieve. Oles (1999) created a model of midlife transition in men and suggested that during midlife a man begins to examine his unrealized goals and strivings and begins to wonder about the meaning of his life. There are both similarities and differences between men in midlife crises and people with depression (Oles, 1999). Both groups have a similar depressed mode, but people with depression have a decrease in productivity and activity, whereas middle-aged men show an increase, possibly caused by a new sense of urgency. Thus, many middle-aged men, and women, intensify efforts to live life while they can, before it is too late.

This crucial shift of time orientation in the life cycle may lead to introspection, self-analysis, and self-appraisal. Middle-aged people engage in an existential questioning of self, values, and life itself. They ask, Who am I? What have I done with my life? Where is my life going? What is the purpose of life? What am I here for? Is there anything else for me? These identity issues are an important source of marital dissatisfaction during the middle years (Steinberg and Silverberg, 1987).

This assessment of self extends to an examination of responsibilities, career, and marriage. As one middle-aged individual put it, "I'm tired of doing what is expected, what I'm supposed to do. I'd like to find out what I want to do, and start thinking of me for a change" (author's counseling notes). Financial responsibilities tend to be heavy in middle age. Some men at midlife become obsessed with financial security for themselves and their family in retirement. Family income becomes an important

contributor to feelings of mastery and power over one's life.

Many middle-aged people are under considerable stress. This is the time of heaviest responsibilities at work and in the community. The main stresses for men are related to work and finances (Levinson, 1978), and job burnout may occur during this time (Arthur, 1990). Middle-aged women typically feel stress over the lack of companionship with their spouses, their own work, and the possibility of their young adult children making poor personal and professional choices. As far as work is concerned, however, employment of middle-aged women is also a buffer against other stresses in their lives.

Thus, midlife is a time when personal, practical, and existential issues are all in focus. It can become a time for reexamination, a time to chart new courses in life.

Marital Adjustments

As we have discussed, marital satisfaction tends to be at its lowest ebb when the children are of school age or in their teenage years. On average, the woman is 41 and the man 43 when the youngest child is 13 (see Figure 11.1). If the partners have been busy working and raising children and being active in community affairs, they may have drifted apart, spending less time communicating, playing, and simply being together. It is easy for spouses to get so absorbed with other activities that the marriage suffers from lack of attention. Parents who stay together until their children are grown now feel freer to dissolve their relationship—and some do.

For others, however, middle age can become a time for revitalizing a tired marriage, for rethinking the relationship, and for deciding that they want to share many things in life together. It has been suggested that there are three cycles in most marriages—falling in love, falling out of love, and falling back in love—and that the last cycle is both the most difficult and the most rewarding. If spouses can learn to communicate and express tender feelings, especially feelings of love and affection that they have neglected, they can develop greater intimacy than they have experienced in a long time. This improved communication can also uncover and resolve troublesome issues and lead to improved companionship and togetherness.

Middle-aged people differ greatly in their ability to make necessary changes during this period of life. Researchers talk about **ego resiliency** (ER), or the generalized capacity for flexible and resourceful adaptation to stressors. It is an important personality resource that enables individuals to competently and adaptively negotiate their life under changing conditions such as those of the midlife transition. Adults entering midlife with high levels of ER are likely to view midlife as an opportunity for change and growth, whereas individuals with lower levels of ER are likely to experience it as a time of stagnation or decline (Klohnen, Vandewater, and Young, 1996).

Some middle-aged people are called upon to assume another role—that of caregiver to an impaired parent or parent-in-law (Dwyer and Coward, 1991; Seccombe and Ishii-Kuntz, 1991). Over 40% of people in their late fifties have at least one parent still alive (Seccombe and Ishii-Kuntz, 1991). Although the elderly today are less likely to live with their children than they were 40 years ago, grown children, especially daughters or daughters-in-law, still bear primary responsibility for aged parents (Dwyer and Coward, 1991). Thus, many women are called upon to assist or supervise elderly relatives in shopping, preparing meals, and so on. The majority of these women assuming the caregiving role also work and face their own family responsibilities. The role strain is often considerable, as women juggle the demands of the competing roles of worker, wife, homemaker, mother, grandmother, and caregiving daughter or daughter-in-law.

One research study stressed both the rewards and the stresses of assuming this caregiver role (Stephens, Franks, and Townsend, 1994). Rewards included knowing that the care recipient was well cared for. The caregiver usually received a great deal of satisfaction from assuming this role if the care recipient showed affection or appreciation, if the relationship became closer and the care recipient's health improved, if he or she was cooperative and not demanding, and if his or her good side came through despite illness.

But caregiving also created a number of stresses, especially if the care recipient was critical or complained, was unresponsive or uncooperative, was agitated, was in declining health, asked repetitive questions, or was forgetful. All of these conditions were sources of stress. If caregivers did not receive help from family or friends or if considerable extra expenses were involved in the caregiving, these factors became additional sources of stress.

Because they are caught between caregiving responsibilities for their children and for their elderly parents, middle-aged adults are sometimes called the **sandwich generation.** One study investigated whether multigenerational caregiving roles adversely affected middle-aged caregivers' marital quality, psychological well-being, financial resources, satisfaction with leisure time pursuits, and perceived fairness of the household division of labor (Loomis and Booth, 1995). Drawing on a national sample of married persons, the researchers found, perhaps surprisingly, that the change in family responsibilities had little or no effect on caregivers' well-being. The researchers concluded that there is probably a selection effect whereby those most able to take on the responsibilities of caregiving do so. Those who have strong marriages tend to assume multigenerational caregiving responsibilities and are probably generous caregivers in their own marriage. Also, individuals who take on additional care responsibilities may be more proficient at balancing time allocations for family, work, and personal needs. People who take on such responsibilities place a high value on caring for others. Meeting the additional obligations may be a source of fulfillment that offsets any negative effects on well-being imposed on the caregiver.

The researchers explained that they do not wish to imply that caring for an elderly parent, particularly one who is disabled or in very poor health, does not sometimes adversely affect family caregivers. In general, however, the effects of assuming significant obligations to parents appear to be minimal. They conclude that assuming multigenerational responsibilities does not develop into an especially difficult situation for most middle-aged adults (Loomis and Booth, 1995).

The Postparental Years

The term **postparental years** usually refers to the period between the last child's leaving home and the parents' retirement. Some writers prefer the term the *empty-nest years,* because once children are born, one is always a parent (Raup and Myers, 1989). As shown in Figure 11.1, if the woman gets married at the median age of 24 and has two chil-

When the last child leaves home, the postparental years begin. Although most couples report a noticeable increase in marital satisfaction, today's empty nest doesn't always stay empty. What effect might a returning child have on marital satisfaction?

dren, she will be 48 when the last child leaves home. The man who marries at age 26 and has two children will be 50 when the last child leaves.

Many parents find it especially upsetting when the last child leaves home (Lewis, Volk, and Duncan, 1989). However, there is considerable evidence that adults in the postparental period are happier than are those earlier or later in life (Lee, 1988b). The period has been described as "a time of freedom."

One postscript needs to be added: Unmarried children continue living with their parents for a longer period of time than they used to. This is due partly to the delay of marriage (Goldscheider and Goldscheider, 1989). Moreover, once the children leave, the empty nest may not stay that way; that is, grown children may return to the nest. High divorce rates and financial need have resulted in increasing numbers of adult children returning home to live with their parents. Today's generation of young adults has been referred to as the "boomerang kids" since they may leave home and return several times (Mitchell and Gee, 1996).

This has important ramifications for parents, their adult children, and the grandchildren. Most parents do not welcome the return of their children and view their stay as a short-term arrangement (Clemens and Axelson, 1985). The sources of potential conflict include everyday maintenance of self and clothing, the upkeep of house and yard, the use of the family car, and the life-style of the child, in-

cluding sexual expression, drinking, drugs, and friends. Furthermore, although most grandparents love their grandchildren, they find it difficult to assume the role of frequent babysitter while the parent goes out to work or play. Sometimes the adult child reverts to the role of dependent child, and the parents return to superordinate roles of earlier times. Increasing evidence points to a lessening of life satisfaction for all parties involved (Clemens and Axelson, 1985).

ADJUSTMENTS DURING LATE ADULTHOOD

Late adulthood brings a number of major life changes. These changes affect not only the aging individual but also his or her spouse and other family members. Because late adulthood can extend over a 30-year period and dramatic physiological, psychological, and sociological changes can take place during these years, late adulthood is often divided into three stages. People ages 65–74 are sometimes referred to as the young-old, those 75–84 are the middle-old, and those 85 and over are the oldest-old. The developmental tasks these three groups face may be quite different. For example, people age 85 and over are more likely than people under 85 to be in poor health; to need assistance in dressing, bathing, eating, and other activities of

Older people dread physical problems that impair mobility and independence. One of the developmental tasks of late adulthood is to stay physically healthy.

Developmental Tasks

The major **developmental tasks,** or adjustments, facing elderly people can be grouped into nine categories: (1) staying physically healthy and adjusting to limitations, (2) maintaining adequate income and means of support, (3) adjusting to revised work roles, (4) establishing acceptable housing and living conditions, (5) maintaining identity and social status, (6) finding companionship and friendship, (7) learning to use leisure time pleasurably, (8) establishing new roles in the family, and (9) achieving integrity through acceptance of one's life. We'll discuss each of these tasks briefly before turning to a more detailed discussion of the marriage and family relationships of the elderly.

Staying Physically Healthy and Adjusting to Limitations The task of staying physically healthy becomes more difficult as people age. It requires good health habits and the practice of preventive medicine. Getting enough exercise and proper nutrition is especially important for maintaining health in old age. Older people dread physical problems that impair their mobility, their senses, and their ability to care for themselves (Quinn, 1983). As a consequence, maintaining good health is one of the most important predictors of life satisfaction in the elderly (Baur and Okun, 1983; Heidrich and Ryff, 1993).

Maintaining Adequate Income and Means of Support Many adults face the problem of having inadequate income in their old age. Socioeconomic resources vary tremendously among the elderly, with age itself being an important correlate of resource level. In 1997, 10.5% of people 65 and over lived below the poverty level. The older the people were, the greater the percentage who lived in poverty. There is also a difference in economic resources according to gender. Seven percent of males but 15% of females 65 and over live below the poverty level (U.S. Bureau of the Census, 1999c). There are also differences according to ethnicity. Among African Americans, 26% of those 65 and over live below the poverty level, as opposed to only 9% of older White people.

One study revealed that elderly people who felt they were better off financially than their relatives

daily living; and to need home health care (Seccombe and Ishii-Kuntz, 1991).

Late adulthood involves some major transitions: from marriage to widowhood, from living with a family member to living alone, and from physical independence to physical dependence. The transitions in marital status and household structure are likely to occur around the mid-seventies, usually some years before the onset of any disabilities. The timing of these transitions is significant for long-term survivors. By the time they reach the age when their family would be an important source of assistance, they are unlikely to have a surviving spouse, and a large proportion live alone. As many as one-third of the very old have no live-in family members who can respond to their needs (Johnson and Troll, 1996).

reported higher life satisfaction than did those who were not as well off (Usui, Keil, and Durig, 1985). Those with financial problems experience diminished feelings of control over their lives. Financial strain and diminished feelings of control are related to increased stress (Krause and Baker, 1992). Most older adults want financial independence, but this requires careful long-term planning (Strate and Dubnoff, 1986).

Adjusting to Revised Work Roles   Retirement at age 65 is no longer compulsory, but many workers must retire at 70. Forced retirement has been ranked among the top 10 crises in terms of the amount of stress it causes the individual (Sarason, 1981). People who elect retirement, plan for it, and look forward to it feel they have directed their own lives and are not being pushed or manipulated (Kilty and Behling, 1985, 1986). This is not the case for the many people who must delay retirement because they do not have the means to finance it (Richardson and Kilty, 1992), nor for those who are forced to retire before they intended because of health limitations (Henretta, Chan, and O'Rand, 1992). Those most satisfied with retirement are those who have been preparing for it for a number of years. This is an important point, since the quality of the retirement experience influences marital satisfaction after retirement (Higginbottom, Barling, and Kelloway, 1993). Chronological age, health, and self-perception of the ability to adjust to retirement are all important influences on planned retirement age (Taylor and Shore, 1995).

One study listed four primary reasons for retirement: (1) job stress, (2) pressure from employer, (3) desire to pursue one's own interests, and (4) circumstances, such as age or health. Those who retired to escape job stress found relatively greater rewards from the reduced stress in retirement. Those who were pressured by their employer to retire were more likely to report a difficult transition, less satisfaction with retirement, fewer sources of enjoyment in retirement, and poor function in physical, social, and leisure activities than were people who retired voluntarily. Voluntary retirees who retired to pursue their own interests reported an easier transition to retirement and higher satisfaction with, more sources of enjoyment in, and positive adjustment to retirement. The reaction to retirement

of those who retired because of circumstances, for example, age or health, depended on whether they really wanted to retire (Floyd et al., 1992). Certainly, retirement should be retirement to, not from, something. Retirees who are most satisfied seem to be those most involved in meaningful activity following retirement.

Employment serves as an important power resource for many spouses. Retirement, therefore, can undermine a spouse's status in the marriage and alter both spouses' relative power in the relationship. The effect of retirement is partly dependent on the employment status of the other spouse, as well as on both spouses' gender-role attitudes. The man's loss of a provider role undermines his status in the marriage and makes him more dependent on the marriage itself. The woman's employment status, by contrast, seems to have little impact on dependence perception. For example, women whose spouse has retired see themselves as relatively less dependent on the marriage regardless of whether they themselves are employed or retired (Szinovacz and Harpster, 1993).

Using longitudinal data from a national sample of married couples, one study (Myers and Booth, 1996) explored a wide range of contextual factors that influenced the effect of retirement on marital quality. Characteristics of the man's job, the division of labor within the marriage, social support, health, and marital quality are preretirement factors that affect the influence of retirement on marital quality. Leaving a high-stress job improves marital quality, whereas gender-role reversals, declines in health, and reduced social support associated with the retirement adversely affect marital quality. Furthermore, the effects of retirement vary according to the number of changes that accompany retirement.

Other findings of the study suggest that the division of labor within and outside the household is one of the most troubling areas. Given that a substantial number of women are in the labor force and are younger than their spouses, it follows that men increasingly find themselves retiring before their mate does. Men's persistent resistance to performing housework, coupled with feeling threatened by their spouse's occupational success, suggests that couples in which men retire first will have poorer quality marriages (Myers and Booth, 1996).

Establishing Acceptable Housing and Conditions   For some older people, being able to keep their own home is of great importance. It allows them independence and usually more satisfactory relationships with their children. However, they may experience difficulty in home maintenance. Income has a marked effect on the quality and quantity of home upkeep (Reschobsky and Newman, 1991).

Statistics from 1998 reveal that almost 82% of households maintained by people age 65 and older were owned by them. In the remaining households, the elderly were renting. Of course, many older people (about 1 out of 10 men and 1 out of 5 women 65 and older) are not heads of households, since they live with their children. Forty-two percent of people age 75 and older live with their spouse (U.S. Bureau of the Census, 1999a).

Maintaining Identity and Social Status   The aged have high status and prestige in many societies because they possess the greatest knowledge of skills, traditions, and ceremonies considered essential for group survival. For example, the elderly have had high status in agricultural societies because they controlled the property, had the greatest knowledge of farming skills, were able to perform useful tasks, and were the leaders of the extended family. But as our society became more industrialized and modern, the elderly lost their economic advantages and their leadership roles both in industry and in the extended family. Consequently, they lost their status and prestige (Ishii-Kuntz and Lee, 1987).

Part of the loss of status comes when people retire, as many people find status through their occupation (Hurst and Guldin, 1981). When they leave that role, they have the feeling that they have lost their main identity. For example, a former mechanic is no longer a mechanic—occupationally, he or she is nothing. Those who are able to develop a meaningful identity through avocations, social life, marriage, children, or other activities adjust more easily.

Finding Companionship and Friendship   Loneliness is one of the most frequent complaints of older people, especially of the formerly married (Essex and Nam, 1987). Their challenge is to find meaningful relationships with others (Hatch and Bulcroft, 1992). Developing and maintaining friendships

with peers seems to be more important to the emotional well-being of the elderly than does interaction with kin. The elderly who are able to find dating partners can likely satisfy their need for companionship and emotional fulfillment (Adams, 1985). One 73-year-old woman stated:

> It was a lot harder when my boyfriend, Ted, died than when my husband of forty years passed away. I needed Ted in a way I never needed my husband. Ted and I spent so much time together; he was all I had. And at my age I know it will be hard to find someone else. . . . I would like to date someone like Ted again . . . but, well, let's face it; how many men want a seventy-three-year-old woman? (Bulcroft and O'Connor, 1986, p. 401)

Learning to Use Leisure Time Pleasurably   Late adulthood offers most people an opportunity to

Late adulthood offers an opportunity to pursue leisure activities. Enjoying pleasurable activities is key to life satisfaction for older people.

Data from the Retirement History Study (RHS) of the Social Security administration provide insight into the employment behaviors of individuals after retirement (Myers, 1991). Some 8,131 men were followed over a 10-year period. The study examined the alternative employment choices of older workers who had decided to leave full-time employment in their career job. Four career job exits were found: (1) part-time employment in their career job, (2) part-time employment in a new job, (3) full-time employment in a new job, and (4) full-time retirement. The majority of workers (74% of this sample) made the traditional retirement decision of complete withdrawal from the labor force. The remainder (26.2% of this sample) worked at some time after leaving full-time employment. The most likely change in employment was to a new full-time job (11%). The second most likely was to work part-time at a new job (10%). The least common was to work part-time on the career job (5%).

Economic variables affected the different decisions. Higher market wages were found to increase the probability of full-time employment, while personal wealth was found to reduce the probability of full-time employment. Employer pension benefits were found to reduce the probability of any type of future employment, while Social Security benefits led to an increase in the probability of part-time work. Thus, the response of those who left their career jobs differed with age, wealth, eligibility to receive employer pension and Social Security benefits, and changes in Social Security benefits. In addition, the training and job opportunities available were important determinants of the postcareer labor force behavior (Myers, 1991).

---

enjoy themselves. As work roles decline, more leisure time is available for preferred pursuits. Life satisfaction in late adulthood is very much dependent on social activity. People need worthwhile, pleasurable activities to help them feel good about themselves and about life in general.

Establishing New Roles in the Family   Several events bring about the adjustment of family roles: children marrying and moving away, grandparenthood, retirement, the death of a spouse, or dependence on one's children. All of these circumstances require major adjustments and a realignment of family roles and responsibilities (Brubaker, 1990). Family relationships during late adulthood will be discussed in more detail later in this chapter.

There is some reversal of gender roles in relation to authority in the family as people get older. The man who retires loses some status and authority in family governance, and the woman often assumes a more dominant role as an authority figure (Liang, 1982). This is especially true in relation to planning activities for herself and her mate and to assuming a nurturing role that has not been possible since the children left home.

Achieving Integrity Through Acceptance of One's Life   Erikson (1959) stated that the development of ego integrity is the chief psychosocial task of the final stage of life. This includes reviewing one's life, being able to accept the facts of one's life without regret, and being able to face death without great fear. It entails appreciating one's own individuality, accomplishments, and satisfactions, as well as accepting the hardships, failures, and disappointments one has experienced. Ultimately, it means contentment with one's life as it is and has been (Reker, Peacock, and Wong, 1987).

Marital Satisfaction

As the health and longevity of the elderly increase, an increasing proportion of adults over age 65 are still married and living with their spouse (Giordano, 1988). In 1998, 79% of men ages 65–74 and 69% of men 75 and older were married. Figures for women of comparable ages were 55% and 29.5%, respectively. Obviously, there are far greater numbers of widowed women than men. Table 11.3 shows the figures (U.S. Bureau of the Census, 1999a).

For many older adults, marriage continues to be a major source of life satisfaction. Marital happiness and satisfaction usually increase during a second honeymoon stage after the children leave home and after retirement. The spouses usually have more leisure time to spend with each other and with adult children and grandchildren, and they depend more on each other for companionship. As one wife remarked, "I feel closer to Bill than I have for years. We had forgotten what it meant to have real companionship" (author's counseling notes). Marital satisfaction tends to be high among those whose spouse is also the most important confidant (Lee, 1988a).

249

Table 11.3 Marital Status of Older Americans, by Age and Gender, in Percentages, 1998						
	Male			Female		
Marital Status	**55–64**	**65–74**	**75+**	**55–64**	**65–74**	**75+**
Never-married	5.4	4.1	3.4	4.6	4.3	5.1
Married	80.2	79.2	69.2	67.8	54.8	29.5
Widowed	2.6	8.8	23.7	13.2	31.9	60.4
Divorced	11.9	7.8	3.7	14.4	8.9	5.0

Note: From *Statistical Abstract of the United States, 1999* (p. 55) by U.S. Bureau of the Census, 1999, Washington, DC: U.S. Government Printing Office.

Sometimes during the last stages of old age, marital satisfaction again declines (Gilford, 1984). Some women complain that their spouses are always underfoot and expect to be waited on. Keating and Cole (1980) report that women are busier than ever completing and reorganizing household tasks, so they have little time to respond to their spouse's needs as well. Much of a retired man's time at home is spent in his own pursuits and not necessarily on additional household tasks. So although the retired couple is together more, retirement does not ensure that the woman will have much additional leisure time.

At some point, declining physical health and financial resources usually begin to take their toll. Spouses often find it harder to cope with their life situation as they grow older. Declining status and involuntary disengagement from society result in increasing discontent. Spouses may have fewer physical, social, and emotional resources with which to reward each other in mutual marital exchange, and marital satisfaction declines. Figure 11.3 shows the trend.

Divorce

Divorce at any time of life is a distressing experience. If it comes during late adulthood, it is even more difficult. Chiriboga (1982) found that the proportion of divorced adults who are unhappy increases steadily with age. In comparison to those who are middle-aged at the time of divorce, adults who are over 60 are lower in morale and overall happiness. They exhibit more symptoms of psychological disturbance and report they are troubled by the separation.

The effects of later-life parental divorce on the relations between parents and young adult children were explored in a sample of 3,281 young adults who had grown up in intact families. Family dissolution that occurred after children were grown had sizable effects on parent–adult child relations. Later-life parental divorce lowered the relationship

Most older people have strong ties to their children and grandchildren. Becoming a grandparent brings about a welcome new status.

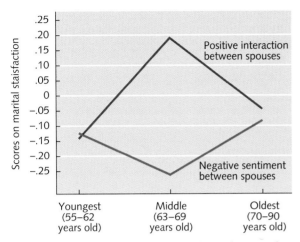

Figure 11.3   Mean Levels of Marital Satisfaction of Older Couples, by Age Group (*Note:* From "Contrasts in Marital Satisfaction Throughout Old Age: An Exchange Theory Analysis" by R. Gilford, 1984, *Journal of Gerontology, 39,* p. 331.)

quality and level of contact between adult children and parents, especially between fathers and children. The effects of later-life marital dissolution on the exchange of health-related support and financial assistance differed by sex of the child and parent. Divorce disrupted parent-son support exchange more than parent-daughter (Aquilino, 1994).

Parent–Adult Child Relationships

The image of parents growing older without contact with their adult children does not coincide with the facts. A national survey by Shanas (1980) revealed that half of the aged people with children had seen one of them on the day of the interview or the day before. If the time period covered the previous week, the proportion of elderly parents in contact with children increased to three-fourths (Kovar, 1986). Thus, most older people are *not* isolated from their children (Dorfman and Mertens, 1990).

Aldous (1987) examined the relationships between 124 older couples and their adult children. The couples were in their early and mid-sixties; some were retired, and some were not. On average, the couples had been married 30 years or more. About a third of the fathers had professional, technical, or managerial careers. The parents had an average of 3.6 children, most of whom had left home and lived, on average, 487 miles away. The parents'

relationships with their children exhibited certain common characteristics.

First, contacts were frequent. Parents and children kept in touch with one another by letter or telephone more than weekly in the previous year. They visited in one another's homes more than once a month and celebrated holidays together at least once every 2 months.

Second, they helped one another. Because parents had greater resources than children, parents had made loans, given gifts, or paid bills for each child about once every 2 months. They also provided child care, house care, shopping, transportation, and help in times of illness. Parents were most in touch with adult children who were most in need. For example, the never-married and divorced were of special concern to parents. Divorced daughters with children most often received household help and child care from parents.

Third, the children reciprocated as they were able. They provided gifts and financial aid of $50 or less in value about four times a year. They were most able to provide help requiring physical energy, giving assistance with house and yard work six times a year.

Fourth, both mothers and fathers reported some disagreement with their adult children over the rearing of grandchildren, treatment of siblings, treatment of themselves, and frequency of get-togethers. Generally, however, both parents and adult children were very satisfied with their relationship.

Other studies have reported the following important factors in parent–adult child relationships:

- Frequency of contact is not the key factor in satisfactory relationships.

- Emotional support is important and can be more significant than whether adult children provide financial support (Houser and Berkman, 1984).

- The morale of the elderly is higher if they feel they can reciprocate some of the help their children or friends give them (Roberto and Scott, 1986; Stoller, 1985).

- Although moderate amounts of intergenerational support are beneficial to older adults, excessive support received from adult children actually may do harm by eroding feelings of competence and imposing excessive demands on the older person. In the beginning, support from children is much appreciated by older parents, but as time passes, greater support begins to depress them and make them feel bad about their situation (Silverstein, Chen, and Heller, 1996).

- Providing extensive care for severely functionally impaired parents causes extreme stress and hardship for the caregivers. Community personal care services, day care, home nursing, and homemakers' services are needed. Nevertheless, the most important resource an elderly person can have is responsible and caring children (Matthews and Rosner, 1988; Walker, Shin, and Bird, 1990).

WIDOWHOOD

The death of a spouse is one of life's most traumatic events at any age. Loss of a loving partner is a painful and stressful human experience. A deeply felt loss is intrinsically linked to the disruption of personal identity. The survivor often confronts emotional, economic, and physical problems precipitated by a spouse's death.

Couples who married and had children in the 1980s and whose marriages are not broken by divorce or separation can expect to live together for 45 years. From birth, the female's life expectancy is 79 and the male's is 74, but the man is 2 years older than the woman when they marry, so she can expect to be a widow for 7 years (U.S. Bureau of the Census, 1999a). The greater longevity of women means that the number of widows exceeds that of widowers at all age levels. Table 11.4 shows the ratios at different ages (U.S. Bureau of the Census, 1999a). Partly as a result of these ratios, the remarriage rate for widows is lower than for widowers. The older a person is when a mate dies, the lower the chances of remarriage.

Older people, especially widows, have a consistently high degree of contact with other family members, including married children. Usually, the elderly woman is closer to her children, especially daughters, than is the elderly man. However, the woman is more likely to depend on them for material aid. The more dependent elderly people become and the more helping roles are reversed, the

Table 11.4 Ratio of Widows to Widowers at Different Ages, 1998

Age	Ratio of Widows to Widowers
45–54	4.6 to 1
55–64	5.5 to 1
65–74	4.5 to 1
75 and older	4.0 to 1

Note: Adapted from *Statistical Abstract of the United States, 1999* by U.S. Bureau of the Census, 1999, Washington, DC: U.S. Government Printing Office.

lower their morale. All research findings stress the importance of peer support in helping widows and widowers adjust. Morale is positively associated with involvement with friends.

In addition to the psychological stress of spousal loss and the need to reconstruct a new sense of self, widows have to solve some practical, everyday problems of living (DeGarmo and Kipson, 1996). The most frequently cited problem is loneliness. Some widows idealize their spouse, making it even harder to get over their loss. Widows miss their husbands as companions and partners in activities. This problem is accentuated if the woman has a low income and cannot afford many social activities outside the home. Widows report that social participation is a problem because so many activities are couple-oriented (Keith, 1986). Sexual frustration is also common among the widowed. The problem of loneliness is accentuated because large numbers of widows live alone. The problem is minimized if the widow has peers, friends, and confidants who are available as social companions (Balkwell, 1985). Friends are more important than spouses or children in minimizing the experience of loneliness for unmarried older adults (Hall-Eston and Mullins, 1999). Those who are married but have neither children nor friends experience greater loneliness than their unmarried or widowed counterparts who do have children or friends.

A second problem cited by widows is home maintenance and car repair. Younger widows also cite decision making, child rearing, and financial management. Widows in the oldest group mention problems such as ignorance of basic finances, lack of transportation, and fear of crime. The only

Who Cares for the Elderly?

As longevity increases, the number of elderly people increases, and the question of who takes care of the physically limited elderly becomes more important. The majority of elderly care for themselves and for one another. Only 8% of people ages 65–74 need the help of another person in at least one activity of daily living, but 22% of the middle-old cohort (ages 75–84) and 54% of the oldest-old (85 and older) need assistance. The need for highly personalized care, such as assistance with bathing or using the toilet, increases threefold between the middle-old cohort and the oldest-old group, which is also the group most likely to need long-term care. When a spouse is not available, a child, especially a daughter or daughter-in-law, is usually the major source of support for an impaired elderly person (Johnson and Troll, 1992).

When elderly people become incapable of caring for themselves, alternative living and care arrangements may be necessary. Most elderly prefer to remain in their own homes for as long as possible because they value their independence and their privacy. Most also prefer not to live with their children, but to live close enough that visiting is easy. These preferences should be taken into consideration before the decision is made to move an elderly person into a relative's home or a nursing home.

In many cases, with a variety of kinds of support, the elderly person can function where he or she is. Living quarters may be made safer; for example, extra lighting may be provided on stairways, and handrails installed in the bathroom. Arrangements can be made for assistance with strenuous activities, such as housecleaning and laundry, and for transportation to stores, church, and bank. "Meals on wheels" programs deliver hot meals to the homebound elderly, visiting nurse programs tend to their physical needs, home health aides and volunteer companions make home visits, and volunteer networks keep the elderly in touch by telephone. Home care offers a great many medical and psychological benefits. Individuals are more comfortable in their own home than in a hospital environment; they eat better, feel better, and sleep better. They take more responsibility for their own care at home and are less prone to become dependent on others. Certainly, it is wise to first try to find solutions for small problems before uprooting an elderly person to a relative's or a nursing home.

Although some elderly individuals are so incapacitated that they require care in a special residential facility, others are there only because they have no other help or nowhere else to go. Many elderly people are admitted to institutions far before they really need to be. In 1997, there were over 1.5 million people in nursing homes in the United States, or 4% of all people 65 years of age and older (Kramarow, Lentzner, Rooks, Weeks, and Saydah, 1999).

Nursing homes vary considerably in quality and in goals. Some are no more than excessively costly warehouses for the elderly and dying, where residents are looked after by poorly trained and sometimes uncaring staff members in inadequate, unclean, and unsafe facilities. In 1990, more than one-third of the nation's nursing homes failed to meet federal standards for clean food, and nearly a quarter did not administer drugs properly. About 67% of homes in the United States are privately owned and operated for profit, so the administrators may try to keep costs as low as possible, sometimes by skimping on necessary care (Gabrel and Jones, 2000).

Many nursing homes are attractive and do a fine job. The physical plant is pleasant and clean, and it has adequate safety measures: ramps for wheelchairs, a sprinkler system in case of fire, nonskid floor coverings, bathrooms modified for safety, and grab bars in appropriate locations. The staff consists of well-trained professionals: physicians, registered nurses who are on call at all times, certified physical therapists, and dietitians. Most of the residents are out of bed, dressed, and well groomed, and they participate in a variety of recreational activities. They have privacy for phone calls, visits, and dressing, and they are allowed to decorate their rooms with personal belongings. In short, in the best nursing homes, residents are treated with warmth and dignity. Unfortunately, these homes are tremendously costly and may not be covered by Medicare/Medicaid or private insurance.

Certainly, there are no easy answers for the care of the physically limited aged. Family members need to think carefully and explore a variety of options—and, above all, consult the elderly person about his or her preferences (Timko and Moos, 1991).

Loneliness is the most frequently cited problem of widowhood and is most extreme for widows whose social activities were highly couple-oriented.

advantage of widowhood, mentioned by younger women, is increased independence.

Financial problems plague both widows and widowers. In every age category, however, widows have a lower income than widowers. Recent research suggests that most widows ride an "economic roller coaster," moving in and out of poverty for many years following the death of their spouse (Zick and Smith, 1991b). The most impoverished females are widows older than 65, even though they may be receiving Social Security or pensions of some sort (Warlick, 1985). Minorities in rural areas or inner cities are the poorest. If they are to have the basic necessities of life, a variety of social supports are needed. Changes in financial status and an increase in physical disabilities pressure older persons to relocate, which compounds the problems of adjustment to widowhood (Bradsher, Longino, Jackson, and Zimmerman, 1992).

Widows indicate that one of their major adjustments is related to role changes. Widowhood, at any age, changes the basic self-identity of a woman.

This is especially true of the traditionally oriented woman whose role of wife has been central to her life. Such women have to reorient their thinking to find other identities. Specific role changes depend on what roles were emphasized before widowhood.

Whether the adjustments for widowers are easier or more difficult than for widows is a matter of dispute. Because some widowers have not been as close to their families as have their spouses, they have fewer contacts with them and receive less social support from them following the death of their spouse. Men with dependent children may have difficulty caring for them. Widowers without parental responsibilities, however, have a greater degree of freedom than do widows without dependent children. The major adjustment is to the loss of their spouse's companionship and love (Clark, Siviski, and Weiner, 1986). Loneliness is the major problem for widowers; accepting the loss of their spouse and going places and doing things alone are of secondary importance (Clark, Siviski, and Weiner, 1986).

SUMMARY

1. The quality of marriage has an important effect on happiness and satisfaction with life, but marriage relationships are seldom static. Their quality varies over time.

2. The family life cycle divides the family experience into phases, or stages, each with its own challenges, tasks, and problems.

3. Weishaus and Field describe six different models of long-term marriage: stable/positive, stable/neutral, stable/negative, curvilinear, continuous decline, and continuous increase. The most common pattern of marital satisfaction is curvilinear: high at the time of marriage, lowest during the child-rearing years, and higher again after the youngest child is beyond the teen years.

4. Research consistently shows that gay and lesbian families are just as successful at carrying out family roles and tasks and raising healthy children as other types of families.

5. Marital adjustments may be defined as the process of modifying, adapting, and altering individual and couple patterns of behavior and interaction to achieve maximum satisfaction in the relationship. The goal of adjustment is to achieve the greatest possible degree of marital satisfaction and success.

6. Marital adjustment tasks early in marriage may be grouped in a number of different categories: emotional fulfillment and support; sexual adjustment; personal habits; gender roles; material concerns; work, employment, and achievement; social life, friends, and recreation; family and relatives; communication; power and decision making; conflict and problem solving; and morals, values, and ideology.

7. Beginning marriage may lead to a period of disillusionment if the spouses do not realize ahead of time what marriage involves.

8. One longitudinal study of marriage satisfaction during three early stages of marriage found that money was the biggest problem. Problems relating to jealousy, friends, religion, and alcohol and drug abuse declined in importance, while problems relating to communication and sex increased in importance. Relatives were a greater problem for couples before marriage and after the birth of the first child.

9. The transition to parenthood may have a positive, negative, or minimal effect on marital satisfaction. For many, it is a time of stress and requires considerable adjustment.

10. Midlife issues include adjusting to physical changes and to the increasing awareness of one's mortality. This leads to a shift in time orientation; to introspection, self-analysis, and self-appraisal; and to basic questions about the purpose of and goals in life.

11. The assessment of self extends to an examination of the responsibilities of one's career and marriage. Midlife can become a time for reexamination, for charting new courses in life.

12. Middle age can also be a time for revitalizing a tired marriage, for rethinking the relationship, and for deciding what things in life partners want to share.

13. Some middle-aged couples must care for aging parents.

14. The postparental years are usually happier for couples, who now have a greater chance to do what they want without the responsibility of children.

15. Sometimes the empty nest doesn't stay that way. Children move back home for various reasons, resulting in potential conflict.

16. The task of staying physically healthy becomes more difficult as people age. It requires good health habits and the practice of preventive medicine.

17. Many adults face the problem of having inadequate income in their old age. Most people face a significant drop in income when they retire.

18. Forced retirement creates stress. People ought to be able to decide for themselves when they should retire. Partial retirement with part-time employment is a happy solution for some people. Certainly, retirement need not be a time of idleness and uselessness. People are happier if they retire to, not from, something; they need worthwhile things to do after retirement.

19. Having acceptable housing and living conditions is a problem for many elderly. Many want their own residence, which allows them independence.

20. Maintaining identity and social status after retirement becomes a problem when their identity and status were rooted in the work people performed. The elderly need to find identity through avocations, social events, marriage, their children, or other activities.

21. Finding companionship and friendship is one important key to life satisfaction in late adulthood.

22. Learning to enjoy leisure time contributes to well-being in late adulthood.

23. Roles in the family change as people get older, but new ones need to be established in relation to grown children and grandchildren.

24. The achievement of ego integrity through a life review and acceptance of one's life as it has been is the chief psychosocial task of the last stage of life.

25. Marital happiness and satisfaction usually increase after the children leave home and immediately after retirement and then decrease again as age takes its toll.

26. Divorce is more stressful in late adulthood than it is earlier in life.

27. The image of parents growing older out of contact with their adult children does not coincide with the facts. Contacts are frequent. Emotional support is more important than financial help, and morale is higher if the elderly can reciprocate. Considerable stress is created if adult children have to provide extensive care for severely functionally impaired parents.

28. The death of a spouse is one of life's most traumatic events. Because of the greater longevity of women, and because men are, on average, 2 years older than women when they marry, the average married woman can expect to live the last 7 years of her life as a widow.

29. Widows face a number of problems, including loneliness, home maintenance and car repair, finances, and role changes in the family.

30. Widowers are usually not as close to their families as widows are and so have less social support.

31. As longevity increases and more people are living longer, the question arises, Who is going to care for them as they get older? The majority of them care for themselves or for one another. The elderly value their independence, and a great majority prefer not to live with their children. Socioeconomic resources influence greatly the amount and kind of care that is given the elderly. When a spouse is not available, a child (especially a daughter or daughter-in-law) is usually the major source of support for the impaired.

32. When elderly people become incapable of caring for themselves, alternative living arrangements must be made. The older person's own home can be adapted to his or her special needs, and community support services of various kinds can be used. If it is necessary for the elderly person to be put in a nursing home, the home ought to be chosen with great care because nursing homes differ so drastically in quality. Family members need to consult the elderly themselves and to explore a variety of options before committing themselves to any particular type of care.

KEY TERMS

family life cycle

marital adjustment

marital adjustment tasks

ego resiliency

sandwich generation

postparental years

developmental tasks

QUESTIONS FOR THOUGHT

1. During which stage of the family life cycle is marital satisfaction usually highest? During which stage is it usually lowest? Explain.

2. From your point of view, which marital adjustments will be most difficult early in marriage? Why?

3. How do the adjustments during middle adulthood compare to those in late adulthood?

4. How do marriage and family relationships change as people become older?

5. What differences can having a baby make in the lives of a couple?

SUGGESTED READINGS

Bengtson, D. L. (Ed.). (1996). *Adulthood and Aging: Research on Continuity and Discontinuity.* New York: Springer. Explores the theme of continuity or discontinuity as individuals negotiate the changes over their life course.

Bowen, G. L. (1991). *Navigating the Marital Journey.* New York: Praeger. Discusses making marriage consistent with the goals and ideals of marriage.

Carter, E. A., and McGoldrick, M. (Eds.). (1999). *The Expanded Family Life Cycle: Individual, Family, and Social Perspectives.* Boston: Allyn & Bacon. Focuses on diversity and families whose life cycles vary from the traditional.

Clarke, A. M. (2000). *Early Experience and the Life Path.* London: Jessica Kingsley. Addresses the "nature-nurture" debate and the concept of shaping and reshaping development of children who have experienced adversity.

Cowan, C. P., and Cowan, P. A. (1992). *When Partners Become Parents: The Big Life Change for Couples.* New York: Basic Books. Examines the transition to parenthood.

Ekerdt, D. J., and Vinick, B. A. (Eds.). (1992). *Families and Retirement.* Newbury Park, CA: Sage. Focuses on the effect of retirement on whole families.

Marshak, L. E. (1999). *Disability and the Family Life Cycle.* New York: Basic Books. Discusses the life span of families with a disabled family member, with each chapter focusing on a different stage.

McCubbin, H. I. (Ed.) (1998). *Stress, Coping, and Health in Families: Sense of Coherence and Resiliency.* Thousand Oaks, CA: Sage. Explores how the sense of coherence affects families at risk, immunology, and aging.

Rubenson, E. F. (2000). *When Aging Parents Can't Live Alone: A Practical Family Guide.* Los Angeles: Lowell House. Provides a guide for families faced with caring for aging parents.

Sussman, M. B., Steinmetz, S. K., and Peterson, G. W. (Eds.). (1999). *Handbook of Marriage and the Family.* New York: Plenum Press. Addresses such topics as family diversity, theory and methods of the family, changing family patterns, and the family and other institutions.

LEARNING OBJECTIVES

After reading the chapter, you should be able to:

Understand the criteria by which men judge whether they have successfully fulfilled their role as provider for the family, the conflicts that many men experience in fulfilling both work and family roles, and the effects on family members of the father's participation in child care.

Understand basic facts about the employment and careers of married women: their search for life satisfaction, their family members' ethics and value systems, the role conflict and strain they experience, and the marital adjustments they face.

Describe basic facts about dual-career families as compared to dual-earner families: the types of women and men who are in such families; the benefits they realize; issues of potential

conflict, including moving, traveling for their job, child care, household responsibilities and scheduling, and identity and competitiveness; and the quality of marriage.

Understand basic facts about money and the family: the financial needs of families, the relationship between money and marital satisfaction, and money management as a source of harmony or discord.

Describe effects of poverty on family life.

Explain the concept of the feminization of poverty.

Describe how the welfare program has changed and discuss the advantages and disadvantages of these changes.

Work, Family Roles, and Material Resources

Learning Objectives

Work and the Family

The Provider Role

 Family Issues: Who Supports the Family?

Work, Stress, and the Family

 Perspective: Navy Officer Wives

The Parents' Child-Care Role

Employed Women and the Family

Ethics and Value Systems

Role Conflict and Strain

 Perspective: Graduate Student Management of Family and Academic Roles

Marital Adjustment

Dual-Career Families

Benefits of a Dual-Career Marriage

Issues for Dual-Career Couples

 Perspective: First-Time Mothers' Styles of Integrating Parenting and Employment

The Quality of Dual-Career Marriages

Material Resources

Financial Needs

The Gender Wage Gap

 Perspective: X Marks the Spot: Generation X College Students Speak Out on Goals for the Future

Money and Marital Satisfaction

Poverty and Family Life

The Poverty Line

The Effects of Poverty

The Feminization of Poverty

The Effects of Poverty on Children

The Widening Gap Between the Rich and the Poor

 Family Issues: Welfare and the Family

Summary

Key Terms

Questions for Thought

Suggested Readings

I n the majority of today's families, both spouses are employed outside the home. Employment has a profound effect on family life, as well as on personal satisfaction. In turn, family life can influence the work environment.

In this chapter, we explore the relationship between work and family living to show how each influences the other. We are particularly concerned with the effects of employment on family life, when parents are taking on multiple roles: spouse, parent, employee. What are the effects on life satisfaction and marital adjustments, and what roles might spouses play to increase personal well-being and that of their family?

We are also concerned here with dual-career families—both the benefits realized and the adjustments required. What are some of the advantages of a dual-career family, and what are the major problems that dual-career couples face? And what effects do dual-career marriages have on the spousal relationship and on the family?

Finally, we are concerned with material resources and the family: the relationship between money and marital satisfaction, the financial needs of families, the effects of poverty on family life, and some principles of money management.

WORK AND THE FAMILY

Traditionally, men have had the responsibility for supporting their family, and women have had the responsibility for nurturing the family. Thus, many men, especially those who hold traditional gender values, define success in terms of their work, and that is where they invest most of their time and energy, sometimes to the detriment of their family.

The Provider Role

While there have been many gender-role changes over the years, most men still consider one of their primary roles to be a provider for their family. The male who successfully fulfills that role is more likely to be happy with himself and to feel adequate as a husband and father than is the male who feels he is not a good provider. Draughn (1984) found that men judge their own job competence and satisfaction according to four criteria:

The "good provider" role can be rewarding, but it can be stressful if it takes time away from the marital relationship.

1. **Personal achievement:** the extent to which they feel important, capable, and adequately rewarded; have received pay raises; have promotion opportunities and a sense of achievement; and find their job interesting

2. **Income achievement:** the extent to which they feel their level of income is satisfactory, compares favorably with others', reflects their personal worth, includes cost-of-living raises, and enables them to save money

3. **Task and work environment:** the extent to which they are challenged, but not burdened, by job difficulty and job pressure; and the extent to which they are satisfied by the physical surroundings and facilities in which they work, the other people on the job, and the amount of time the work requires

4. **Perception of spouse and friends:** the extent to which their spouse makes a favorable assessment of their success, salary, and workplace; the extent to which their friends assess their accomplishments favorably; and the impact of home problems on the job and of job problems on the marriage

Feelings of inadequacy in fulfillment of the provider role are likely to be disastrous for both the man and his family (Draughn, 1984). It is difficult for a man to feel good about himself or his role performance if he wants to but can't supply the bare necessities of life. If family housing is a dilapidated apartment, if the children have to go to school in shabby clothes, if the family can't afford a depend-

The proportion of families in which men are the sole bread-winner is declining. In 1960, 42% of all families were supported solely by a male householder. By 1997, this proportion had declined to 15% (U.S. Bureau of the Census, 1999a, Table 755). Married men's labor force participation has declined, so the number of families not supported solely by men has increased. The decline in the family breadwinner role is greatest among men who are older, have less education, or are minorities. In addition, as more young men have become unable to earn enough to support a family above the poverty level, more women and other family members have joined the work force. The number of single-parent, female-headed families has increased as well.

Several factors have contributed to the decline in labor force participation among older men. First, changes in the U.S. economy, which have affected industrial workers especially, have increased the chance that older workers will be laid off. Displaced older workers are less likely than younger workers to move on to new employment opportunities or to retrain for new jobs. Second, disability insurance has been used by an increasing percentage of men since the mid-1960s. Third, more older men today than in the past are eligible for Social Security or other retirement income when they are not in the labor force. Not only have Social Security benefits increased, but they have been supplemented by private pension plans. As the level of support provided by retirement benefits has risen, retirement has become an increasingly attractive alternative to labor force participation for older workers.

There has also been a decrease in labor force participation of younger men. Since 1960, the labor market demand for better educated workers has led to a decline in the labor force participation of younger men with low education. There are several reasons men with less education have lower labor force participation rates than other men. First, they have greater difficulty gaining employment through-

out their life, which increases the likelihood of their dropping out of the labor force. Second, they generally have poorer health and are likely to have jobs that are physically demanding; thus, they are more likely to stop working sooner. Third, they have less career commitment because their work is likely to be less interesting, less pleasant, and less financially rewarding. Labor market demands for better educated workers have also contributed to a decline in the labor force participation of younger men by encouraging them to postpone marriage and go to school longer. Young, single men are only half as likely as married men to be in the labor force, presumably because single men are much more likely than married men to receive financial support from their parents. Thus, the entry of young men into the labor force has been delayed even as educational demands have postponed marriage.

Changes in men's income have also contributed to the decline in families supported solely by male householders. A decreasing number of men in the primary family-building ages of 20 to 34 earn enough to support a family of four above the poverty level. The decreased ability to support families is associated with the decrease in the marriage rate of young men, a rise in the proportion of young mothers who do not marry, and a decline in marital fertility.

Finally, men's declining earning power may have contributed indirectly to the rise in the number of families with no male present by increasing the likelihood of divorce or separation. Married women are less economically dependent on their husbands today than in the past. Women's increased earnings and the availability of government aid have created a greater degree of financial independence, which may contribute to their ability to end unsatisfactory marriages. Increasing divorce rates, coupled with the legal tradition of awarding postdivorce custody of minor children to the mother, have contributed to the rise in the proportion of families with no male present (Wilkie, 1991).

able car or birthday presents, men may feel they have failed in the principal area in which others expect them to be competent: that of provider. Women have not been socialized to this great an extent to provide financially for the family.

In their study of the relationship between marital adjustment and work identity of blue-collar men, Gaesser and Whitbourne (1985) found that satisfaction with extrinsic work factors (wages, security, work setting and hours, and company policies) is the most important consideration

related to marital adjustment. Workers who are satisfied with their job have more energy to devote to the marital relationship.

Work, Stress, and the Family

Job stress affects the parents' marriage and relationship with their children (Kinnunen, Gerris, and Vermulst, 1996). Jobs that are particularly stressful for the family include those that are so difficult that one is under constant strain at work and hard to live

Navy life is a prototypical example of an upper-middle-class career that requires the wife's total involvement. The Navy depends on the services of the Navy wife as an adjunct to her officer husband and as a supporter of his career ambitions. She is required to perform a double-duty role when the demands of her husband's career prevent him from sharing home duties. She is expected to maintain the status of her husband's rank, to perform publicly and formally at military functions, and to be his intellectual partner. Indeed, the military expends many resources to define and sustain the division of labor that maximizes the efficiency of support of the career officer, because the military relies on families to allow the officer to perform the duties of his role. Navy families must endure frequent moves, long separations, irregular and long work hours, and hazardous duty assignments. Navy wives say that the Navy "owns" their husbands and that somehow their families must go along with that arrangement. "Going along" implies that wives accept the heavy demands of the Navy on both the husbands and themselves.

The Navy secures the wife's involvement by making the Navy an all-encompassing community in which her family can reside in Navy housing, shop, receive legal advice and medical care, and engage in leisure time activities. Even friendships are largely determined by the Navy. The husband's duty station provides wives with a ready-made circle of friends with whom they are encouraged to interact. Wives telephone one another with messages relating to the welfare of the ship, ship parties, and functions at the Officers' Club. They frequently get together informally and depend on one another to help out, especially when their husbands' ships are at sea.

Entertaining ranks high on the list of Navy activities, the burden of which falls on the wives, particularly those whose husbands are high ranking, such as admirals' wives, captains' wives, and commanders' wives, who frequently host several parties per year. The military, in fact, depends on such parties and other functions as a means of disseminating information about the command and to promote social cohesion (Mederer and Weinstein, 1992).

with at home. Stressful jobs also include those that require periods of separation and that are so time-consuming that one can't spend any quality time with family.

When people experience stress on the job, their partner is also likely to experience psychological distress (Rook, Dooley, and Catalano, 1991). In fact, the partner may experience as much distress over the other person's job as if it were her or his own job. Interestingly, women in untroubled marriages feel the greatest concern and suffer more from their spouse's job misfortune than do women in troubled marriages or in marriages in which the spouses are not so close. Men with high dual commitments to job and family and who perceive their spouse as very supportive of their work and parenting activities report less role strain than men with a less supportive spouse (O'Neil and Greenberger, 1994).

The person who is a workaholic and who devotes 80 hours a week to a job has no time or energy left for family. The partners seldom go out together or spend time alone; they seldom communicate; they seldom make love. The workaholic hardly knows the children since he or she is rarely home during their waking hours. The more ambitious the person is and the harder he or she works, the less

likely he or she is to take the time to develop close family relationships.

In some cases, the compulsion to work so hard and long comes from within the person. True workaholics are compelled to succeed, often for personal ego fulfillment, to bolster their self-image as they try to become a "somebody." They are perfectionists who demand complete mastery and control over a situation. They become absorbed with details and are unable to delegate responsibility. When they fail to reach unrealizable goals, they suffer anxiety, guilt, anger, and depression, which they attempt to overcome by further attempts at control. They may become irritable and abusive toward their spouse, children, and fellow employees. Leisure time is a burden, an empty period during which nothing is accomplished. Workaholics show signs of anxiety and depression if they are deprived of something to do for even a few hours. This work addiction may contribute to high blood pressure or heart disease.

Certainly, there are ways of finding fulfillment in life other than through work. Meaningful family relationships can meet real needs, too. People need to sort out their priorities and ask themselves if their job is worth sacrificing their family for. Marriages and family relationships, like anything else worthwhile, require time and attention to maintain. In other cases, the pressure to work long hours comes from the employer, who displays a callous disregard for employees' mental health and personal life. These people have to satisfy their boss or lose their job.

One barrier to family closeness is a job schedule that makes it difficult for family members to be together. Some jobs require rotating shifts (White and Keith, 1990). If the spouses work on different shifts, they rarely have any time to be together. Working the same shift can be important in maintaining a relationship. One study found that divorce is common among couples in which one spouse works nights (Presser, 2000). Fathers who work nights are six times more likely to divorce than are fathers who work days, and mothers who work nights triple their odds of divorce. Other jobs, such as that of a police officer, are very stressful in and of themselves and require a lot of work on weekends and holidays. Some work, such as the armed services and merchant marine, requires long periods of separation. Conflict between family and job demands becomes a source of individual and family stress.

The Parents' Child-Care Role

The decisions that parents make about work and family, especially about how they care for their children, help shape their children's intellectual development, social behavior, and personalities. In everything they do, from the jobs they choose to the way they allocate household chores, parents provide powerful models of male and female behavior for their children. Parents, inadvertently or intentionally, prepare their children for similar future roles in the workplace and the family.

Today, unlike a decade or so ago, most fathers are expected to share in the responsibilities of child care, especially in dual-earner families. As of 1993, 13% of fathers were the primary caregiver during their spouse's working hours (Casper, 1997). Of these men, the fathers of preschoolers were more likely to be the main care provider, due to the younger age of the children and the necessity of adequate care. As the children grew older, the role of fathers as caregivers shrank.

Mothers benefit from fathers' participation in raising children. Fathers who assume responsibility for child care ease the burden of employed mothers and reduce the maternal stress associated with work overload, anxiety, and a shortage of time for rest and leisure. Fathers who are actively involved in caring for their children enjoy the positive effects of multiple roles, which include enhanced marital relations and closer father-child bonds. Men—like women—who combine different life roles such as parent, worker, and spouse may be better off emotionally than men with fewer life roles.

Parents' work schedules have significant repercussions for how they coordinate and organize family life. Data from the National Childcare Survey 1990 indicate that fathers are more likely to care for their children when they work different hours than their spouse does (Hofferth, Brayfield, Deich, and Holcomb, 1991). Fathers are more likely to be the primary caregiver for a preschool-age child if they work a night shift; they are more likely to be the primary caregiver for a school-age child if they work a day shift.

Certain employment schedules make family life especially difficult. Mothers and fathers with unconventional work schedules are hard-pressed to keep their family life in sync with "normal" society. For example, parents who work evenings, late afternoons, or weekends may routinely miss their children's extracurricular activities. It is nearly impossible to find child-care centers or other formal arrangements that are available at night or on weekends. Thus, parents who are employed at odd hours have fewer choices in caring for their children.

How women and men allocate their time across multiple roles affects how they combine and juggle the competing responsibilities of employment, parenthood, and marriage. Conflicting work schedules may contribute to marital stress and role conflict. For example, men may spend more time with their children at the expense of time with their spouse (Brayfield, 1995).

Most dual-earner couples admit that they have to budget their time very carefully. If the individual has considerable flexibility in controlling his or her work schedule, it is easier to mesh job and home responsibilities. For self-employed individuals, scheduling may be considerably easier. Some businesses have **flextime** that allows workers to choose the 8 hours during the day when they will work (Meer, 1985a).

Many spouses also try to arrange their schedules so that one or the other is available to care for

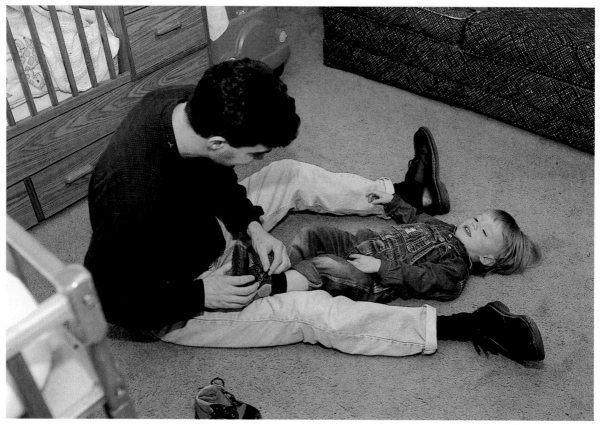

Increasing numbers of fathers participate in child care as part of their family responsibilities. A father's involvement in child rearing benefits his children's academic achievement, social competence, and self-esteem.

children and so that they can spend time together as a couple. Some couples work different shifts so that one partner or the other is always available to care for children (Presser, 1988). Most couples admit that they have to give up a number of activities just to have time for necessary things. Dual-earner couples usually do not entertain as often as some others do. Nor is there as much time for involvement in community activities or for such pastimes as gardening or reading.

One recent study found that many middle-class dual-earner couples are coping with the dual demands of work and family by "scaling back" (Becker, 1999). That is, the partners place limits on the number of hours they work, reduce expectations for career advancement, decide to have a one-job/one-career marriage, or trade family and job responsibilities over the life course, although women do the most scaling back. The results of this study suggest that if both spouses are employed they must make compromises with regard to time and effort in order to achieve success at home.

EMPLOYED WOMEN AND THE FAMILY

The number and percentage of women in the labor force are increasing (see Chapter 1; Menaghan and Parcel, 1990). In 1998, 62% of all married women over age 16, 76% of women with the youngest child ages 6–13, and 64% of married women with the youngest child under age 6 were in the labor force (U.S. Bureau of the Census, 1999a). In the same year, 62% of married women with babies 1 year old or younger were also in the labor force. In fact, the greatest increase in the number of working mothers over the past decade has been in the group with infants under 12 months of age (Volling and Belsky, 1993). The effect on children will be discussed in detail in Chapter 17.

Women report that their experience of mothering is altered significantly when they work outside the home, and they often must address new variations of problems concerning time pressures and conflicting role demands. Mothers who are employed not only have less time to spend with their children but also spend fewer hours on household chores such as meal preparation and cleaning. For example, in 1965, the average woman spent 27 hours a week on cooking and cleaning; in 1995, she spent only 15½ hours a week (Robinson, Godbey, and Jacobson, 1999). All women experienced this decrease, whether they were employed or unemployed, single or married, or young or old. Although modern conveniences have reduced the time needed for housework, much of the decrease is attributed to the fact that working women simply have less time available to maintain the household.

Like women who remain at home, however, employed mothers perform most of the household chores and care activities. Women employed full-time may reduce the amount of time they spend on household tasks, but not the range of their responsibilities. This led some researchers to refer to employed mothers as "supermoms"—mothers who remain heavily involved with family responsibilities while also meeting the demands of paid employment (DeMeis and Perkins, 1996).

But what about the impact of paid employment on women's lives? Are employed wives more fulfilled, more satisfied with life, and just plain happier than housewives? Work has been described as an alienating force in the lives of men, but it is somehow transformed into a liberating force in the lives of women. This position assumes that any sort of paid employment is preferable to full-time home-making. The research on life satisfaction of mothers who work outside the home versus those who do not shows slightly greater satisfaction among those working outside the home, but the results depend on a number of variables (Benin and Nienstedt, 1985; Freudiger, 1983; Tiedje et al., 1990).

Ethics and Value Systems

Part of the effect of the women's employment on the marriage depends on the ethics and value systems of the couple. Many couples find themselves torn between two ethics: the ethic of equity, defined as a relatively fair division of household labor, and the ethic of care, defined as the desire to be attentive and responsive to the needs of individual family members. Many women's satisfaction with the division of labor appears contingent on the time spent and the number of tasks performed by them and by their spouse. Women often complain about imbalances in the division of household labor and feel that the divisions are unfair. Many women put the ethic of care—being sensitive to the needs of various family members—first. This ethic is demonstrated through preparing meals, shopping for food, cleaning house, washing clothes, and caring for children. Employed women with this ethic routinely perform a proportionately greater share of daily household tasks than do their partners (Stohs, 1994).

Role Conflict and Strain

One important consideration in the life satisfaction of working mothers is whether they have been able to integrate their work life with their home life. A number of factors influence the role strain of working women. Basically, there are three major sources of strain: (1) individual (those that originate within the individual), (2) family-related (those that come from the family), and (3) work-related (those that originate from the work situation; Kelly and Voydanoff, 1985). The combination of family structure and responsibilities, work time, and job demands is related to the degree of role strain (Voydanoff, 1988).

One individual source of role strain is the woman's own conflict over the fact that she is working (Greenberger and O'Neil, 1990). If she prefers being at home but has to work for various reasons, her ambiguous feelings become a source of internal conflict and tension. Conversely, women who have nontraditional gender-role attitudes but who fill a traditional homemaker role evaluate their situation more negatively than do other women (McHale and Crouter, 1992). One mother remarked, "I hate working. I'd rather be home, but George and I can't make it financially unless I do, so I have no choice" (author's counseling notes).

A family-related source of strain for working mothers is the presence of young children in the family (Eggebeen, 1988). The more young children

Many graduate students are married, and some are also parents. Thus, they are confronted with the responsibilities of their family role in addition to their academic role. Often, they also work at least part-time. Interrole conflict exists when expectations in one of these roles are incompatible with the expectations of the other (Dyk, 1987).

Greenhaus and Beutell (1985) have identified two major forms of interrole conflict: time-based and strain-based. **Time-based conflicts** arise when time pressures from one role make it physically impossible to meet expectations arising from another. Time-based conflicts may arise from any one or more of the following sources: workaholism, children, spousal absence, job and academic demands, and traditional gender-role expectations. **Strain-based conflicts** arise when strain in the student role affects participation in the family role, or vice versa. There is a negative emotional spillover from work to nonwork. Stressful events in school such as the pressure of assignments, exams, or term papers affect family life; child-care responsibilities at home or marital conflict may affect schoolwork.

Beutell and Greenhaus (1980) have identified two coping strategies: structural role redefinition and personal role redefinition. **Structural role redefinition** involves attempts to lessen the conflict by mutual agreement on a new set of expectations. Thus, the graduate student spouse and parent might give up part of a role—such as reducing the course load, limiting volunteer efforts with organizations outside the home, sharing study with other students, coordinating child care with other parents who take turns, hiring assistance for domestic chores or for baby-sitting, or enlisting the help of other family members. The goal is to reduce the load the student carries personally.

Personal role redefinition involves reducing the standards of role performance. It may be done in at least three ways: prioritization, compartmentalization, and reduction of standards. Individuals first set priorities for school, work, and family and perform only those tasks with the highest priority. Identifying short-range and long-range priorities helps uncover those things that must be done now, versus those things that may be done later. Compartmentalization involves not attending to one role while performing another. Thus, a student blocks out family demands while focusing on studies but puts the books aside while spending time with the family. Reduction of standards at school means deciding to do what one can to be well prepared and leaving the rest. At home, it may mean lowering one's standards of household cleanliness.

in the family, the more stress is introduced. Some women feel guilty about leaving their children, especially when the children are small. However, mothers feel less stress if they are satisfied with the quality of substitute child care. The maternal leave law, which allows pregnant women to take a leave of absence from work to have their baby, is a help for some in eliminating the conflict between having to work and wanting to stay home and care for a newborn (Trzcinski and Finn-Stevenson, 1991). The level of the mother's stress also depends partially on the willingness of the father to become involved during infancy in caring for his child (Nugent, 1991; Volling and Belsky, 1991).

Another source of conflict is the strain of having to fulfill too many roles at once (Voydanoff and Donnelly, 1989b). Most working mothers recognize that they do not have as much time for child care, housework, and leisure time activities as they would if they were not working (Firestone and Shelton, 1988). If a mother works full-time, is raising one or more children, and tries to be a good spouse, she has taken on the responsibility of at least two and a half full-time jobs. If her job is demanding and her spouse is not very sympathetic and helpful at home, or if he, along with the children, demands a lot from her, she is under constant pressure to give and give. If she feels she can't fulfill her own or her family's expectations, she may become upset or depressed (Keith and Schafer, 1985).

The job itself may also be a source of stress and strain. One study found that changes in job-role quality were significantly associated with psychological distress (Barnett, Marshall, and Singer, 1992). Difficult job demands and assignments, inconvenient schedules, long hours, and pressures to produce all create strain (Wethington and Kessler, 1989). If a boss or coworkers are hard to get along with or if the job requires unreasonable hours and has a lot of responsibilities, the woman is exhausted by the time she gets home. The last thing she needs is to have to spend the rest of her waking hours trying to satisfy the demands of spouse and children.

Although balancing commitments to children, partner, and career can often be demanding and difficult, many working mothers would not choose anything less.

This is why assistance from a partner, older children, or hired help is so important. One woman remarked, "I'd love to be able to come home from work and have someone have *my* supper on the table for *me*" (author's counseling notes).

For many women, however, working outside the home enhances their lives, especially if they love their job and have a spouse and children who help or are able to hire some assistance. Some women are more relaxed at work than at home and may even go to work to get away from their families. One mother remarked, "I can't wait to get out of the house in the morning. Work is the only place I have any peace and quiet. I'd go absolutely crazy if I had to stay home all day. My children could drive me crazy" (author's counseling notes). One study of middle-aged and older Black women revealed that employment contributed significantly to their well-being (Coleman, Antonucci, Adelmann, and Crohan, 1987). Many women return to work after their children have left home, and they find their employment fulfilling (Moen, 1991).

There are all kinds of people and all kinds of needs. Some women are far better wives and mothers because they go to work. They're more patient, more giving, and more attentive during the time they are home than they would be if their only full-time job was that of wife, homemaker, and mother (Menaghan and Parcel, 1991).

Marital Adjustment

Social science has devoted considerable effort to comparing employed and nonemployed women to determine effects on spousal relationships. Some investigators report a positive relationship between women's employment and marital adjustment. For example, one study found that increases in women's income do not significantly affect marital discord, but, interestingly, marital discord increases women's income by increasing the likelihood that they will enter the workforce (Rogers, 1999). The additional income a woman brings in seems to have a stabilizing effect on the marriage (Greenstein, 1990) and to reduce the strain of one person having to provide all the financial resources.

However, the effect of women's employment on marital quality depends partially on the number of children in the household. One study found that, as the number of children in the household increases, so do their demands, and full-time employment of the mother thus is associated with less marital happiness and more marital conflict. This finding is consistent with previous research reporting that work-family role strain was heightened for employed mothers and that marital interaction and quality were compromised when dual-earner families had children (Rogers, 1996).

In mother-stepfather families, the relationship between maternal employment and marital quality is more complicated. When the family is small, the mother's full-time employment is associated with less marital happiness and more marital conflict. This suggests that combining the demands of full-time employment and family has negative effects on the marital relationship that outweigh the potential benefits. When family size increases, however, the mother's full-time employment is associated with greater marital happiness and less marital conflict. The mother's contributions to the family income are likely to ease economic strain and increase marital quality.

A comprehensive review of findings from 27 studies summarized 2,018 comparisons between spouses of employed and nonemployed women and 2,584 comparisons between employed and nonemployed women to determine the degrees of marital adjustment (Smith, 1985). Marital adjustment was divided into five categories: physical, companionship, communication, tensions and regrets, and a global (overall) measure. Most of the comparisons showed no difference in adjustment between male groups and female groups. The very few differences tended to favor the nonemployed groups. However, when the results were controlled according to women's educational level, family income, and social class, the presence and age of children in various stages of the life cycle, and their spouse's education, the basic finding of little difference between employed and nonemployed groups remained. What this means is that the women's employment status alone appears to have little or no effect on marital adjustment (Spitze, 1988). This does not mean there aren't problems in dual-earner families. Certainly, there may be. For example, a stressful job seems to be correlated with higher levels of stress and lower levels of marital adjustment (Sears and Galambos, 1992). But it does mean that whether the woman works is not *the* key to marital adjustment. Other factors are more significant. For example, one study found that a couple's belief in their ability to resolve disagreements, not the woman's work status, is the best predictor of marital adjustment (Meeks, Arnkoff, Glass, and Notarius, 1986). Another study found that an equitable relationship—that is, one in which there is a fair balance of rewards and constraints for both spouses—is the key factor in marital adjustment (Rachlin, 1987). Thus, both single-earner and dual-career couples may have either poor or good marriages.

Gender-role attitudes and role expectations may be much more important in determining the quality of a marriage than is the woman's employment status. The man's attitudes are more important to the experience of marital quality for both spouses than are the attitudes of the woman. His role expectations, gender-role identity, and support are important, as are his spouse's perceptions of his expectations and support. The marital quality experienced by both spouses is also strongly affected by the ability to give and receive support. Men with sensitive personalities produce a higher quality of marriage for their spouse. Women also experience higher marital quality the more egalitarian they believe their spouse's expectations to be (Vannoy and Philliber, 1992).

In analyzing marital power according to gender, Tichenor (1999) concluded that the dynamics of power within a marriage may not necessarily be tied to earnings. Even when the woman earns more than her spouse, he still usually holds more power in the relationship, and her actions often serve to reinforce the pattern of male dominance in the relationship. This finding suggests that marital power is tied more to gender than to status or income.

DUAL-CAREER FAMILIES

There are two basic types of two-income families: dual-career and dual-earner. The **dual-earner family** is one in which both spouses are involved in the paid labor force (Rachlin, 1987). Ordinarily, merely having a job does not involve as extensive a commitment, as much continuity of employment, or as much responsibility as the pursuit of a career.

The **dual-career family**, also called a dual-professional family (Hiller and Dyehouse, 1987), is a specific subtype of the broader category of dual-earner families (Rachlin, 1987). The dual-career family has two career-committed individuals, both of whom are trying to fulfill professional and family roles. But the pursuit of a career requires a high degree of commitment and continuous development. Individuals pursue careers by undergoing extensive education and preparation and then moving upward from one job level to another. A career ordinarily requires full-time employment, especially if one is working for someone else. The greater the responsibility and the higher the position achieved, the greater the commitment required of the individual—leaving less time to devote to mate and child. The dual-career marriage is actually a minority pattern and, from a strictly managerial standpoint, is difficult to achieve. It is difficult to balance husband-wife and father-mother role relationships and responsibilities, to find adequate child care help in a society that expects parents to assume the major burden, and to maintain the expected spousal intimacy and companionship so that the marriage itself remains a viable relationship. Nevertheless, many couples succeed in pursuing careers and in being good mates and parents. Other couples try to succeed at all three roles and fail.

One solution being considered by increasing numbers of career couples is to remain childless (Cooney and Uhlenberg, 1989). This decision actually makes a dual-career marriage easier (Reading and Amatea, 1986).

Benefits of a Dual-Career Marriage

There are some real satisfactions and benefits in a dual-career marriage. The financial rewards in a dual-career marriage are considerable, especially if both spouses are earning salaries as professional people (Hanson and Ooms, 1991). The standard of living is relatively high, with the couple able to afford costly leisure activities and go on expensive vacations. In addition, the extra career-related expenses for clothes, transportation, domestic help, and child care make it necessary for the couple to have a relatively high income. This high income contributes to marital quality.

One frequently mentioned reason any highly qualified woman wants a career in addition to a family is the need for creativity, self-expression, achievement, and recognition. A woman who is trained for a profession wants the satisfaction of using that training. Many such women are dissatisfied with confining their energies to their spouse and children, with simply being "John's wife" or "Kala's mother," and they find a large part of their identity in their career life. There are also indirect benefits to the spouse and the family. A woman with a rewarding, satisfying career will be a happier mate and mother.

The most successful dual-career marriages are those in which the spouses treat each other as equal

If both members of a couple are career-committed individuals, they will face special challenges in trying to balance professional and family roles.

partners. As a result, they share not only in earning the income but also in caring for children and in performing household tasks. Women are far less satisfied and under more strain in marriages in which the responsibility for homemaking tasks rests primarily on their shoulders.

Issues for Dual-Career Couples

Role Strain The strains of a dual-career marriage are considerable (Galambos and Silbereisen, 1989). One source of strain is overwork. The demands of the marriage, children, career, and home are great and often leave couples tense and exhausted. Factors related to role strain include flexibility of work schedule, the age of the youngest child, and the number of children. Flexibility of work schedule is significantly correlated with role strain, especially for men. The number of hours worked has no significant relationship to stress, provided there is a high level of marital equality for both men and women. In such marriages, the partners do favors for each other, listen and offer advice, and alter habits and ways of doing things to please each other. Both men and women report that the number of children is the most critical factor in stress levels. Both men and women with larger families report higher levels of distress (Guelzow, Bird, and Koball, 1991).

When spouses each have a career in addition to home responsibilities, they often need to work out difficult compromises. If one spouse is offered a promotion that means moving to another town, what will be the effect on the other spouse's career? The pressure to move frequently while one's career is becoming established can present difficulty for the two-career family (Kilpatrick, 1982).

Some couples commute long distances if their home and their career base are in different locations. They may work all week in separate places and get together on weekends. A study of commuting and noncommuting dual-career couples showed that commuters are more satisfied with their work life and with the time they have for themselves but are more dissatisfied with their family life, their partner relationships, and life as a whole (Bunker, Zubek, Vanderslice, and Rice, 1992). They do not report more stress than do single-residence, dual-career couples. In short, the commuting life-style has both rewards and costs, and in some ways the single-residence, dual-career life-style might be the more stressful and dissatisfying one.

Travel   The issue of travel arises in dual-career marriages because professionals often attend out-of-town meetings or conferences or consult with others in different locales. Professionals are frequently expected to go on business trips, usually from 2 to 10 days. Some have to travel monthly or more often; a few have to make extended trips abroad. Generally, men travel even more than women; some may be away for long periods of time each year.

How does each feel about the other traveling far from home on business trips? What child-care arrangements work out best? What is the minimum

For the dual-earner family, finding quality child care can be a big problem. Ensuring the availability of quality day care for children is becoming recognized as a national concern.

level of housekeeping that both partners can live with? How can they best budget their time? Will the spouses be competing for success? These are some important issues.

Child Care   The difficulties involved in combining a career with parenthood become apparent after the first child is born. In the nuclear family, the spouses and children live in their own household separate from their relatives, so there is no other family member available to care for the children while the parents are working. This fact, added to job pressures and work loads, encourages the couple to make alternative arrangements for child care (Peterson and Gerson, 1992).

Parents can send their child to a day-care center if one is available, but care is generally provided only during the day. The child must still be taken to

First-Time Mothers' Styles of Integrating Parenting and Employment

First-time mothers can be grouped into four categories according to their feelings about combining motherhood, employment, and child care for their infant: enamored, managers, distressed, and disengaged (Shuster, 1993). Table 12.1 lists the characteristics of the mothers in the four categories.

Enamored mothers interact most sensitively with their infant and see themselves as their infant's primary caregiver, strongly believing that no one can care for their baby as well as they can. They do not view the child-care provider as a replacement for themselves and are comfortable discussing their ambivalent feelings about combining parenting with employment and using a caregiver for their child.

Mothers in the second group, the managers, seem to focus their attention on successfully organizing their multiple roles. They see their infant's child-care provider as an equal member in a mutual caregiving team and are comfortable sharing their parenting role with the provider. A majority of these mothers want to work.

Distressed mothers seem to be struggling in their efforts to combine parenting and employment. They describe their belief in the exclusivity of their mothering role. They also express fear of being replaced by the care provider, with whom they anticipate feeling competitive, and they worry that their babies will become more attached to the caregiver than to themselves. The majority of these mothers would rather be at home with their infant than working. Some seem to compensate for their own anxieties about being separated from their infant by expressing distress that their child-care provider is "spoiling" their baby with too much holding and playing. In discussing their infant's care arrangements, they focus on their own frustrated desires, which are compounded by their feelings of competition with their child-care provider. "I wish I could be home" is the favorite comment.

Mothers in the fourth group, the disengaged, seem disconnected from their infant. Describing their pregnancy, they express feelings of insecurity: "I was shocked . . . the whole time I was in disbelief," and "I was worried that I wouldn't be a terrific mother as I thought I would be." These women's primary feelings about mothering include anger, distress, depression, and desire to escape the limitations placed on their abilities to meet their own needs. A disengaged mother remarked, "I don't like babies . . . babies are pretty ugly." These mothers seem to avoid taking the role of their baby's primary provider and instead assign this role to their child-care provider or other available adults. These women also report a much higher percentage of unplanned pregnancies and score much lower on the measurement of the quality of interactions with their infant (Shuster, 1993).

the center and brought back home each day, an arrangement that further complicates the lives of two busy career people, especially if they have to drive miles each way. What happens when one parent is out of town? Usually, one or the other parent is available, but providing transportation is only part of the problem. The parent who is home must still get the child ready for day care and care for him or her after the center has closed. What if a child is sick or the parent has an important evening meeting?

One crucial consideration, of course, is the kind of care provided to the child when parents are at work. The quality and consistency of the care provided are paramount. In one study, 93 adolescents who grew up in dual-career families were asked to rate their families on various components of family strength (appreciation, concern, respect, support, esteem, commitment, positive communication, and conflict management). Sixty-eight percent said they were satisfied or very satisfied with their families on these components of family strength, and 83% were satisfied or very satisfied with having grown up in a dual-career family (Knaub, 1986). Apparently, their parents didn't do such a bad job in combining careers with child rearing.

Household Responsibilities To help ease the strain of overwork, most dual-career couples try to hire some sort of domestic help on a regular basis (Oropesa, 1993). Couples report considerable difficulty in getting competent help, however. Some become so discouraged with the hired help that they decide to split the work between themselves. Most try to purchase various labor-saving devices such as dishwashers, food processors, and bread machines to cut down on the time required. Some use other means for increasing the efficiency of housework and for streamlining tasks. For example, they buy more prepared foods and clothing that doesn't need ironing. Others report that they have lowered their standards of housekeeping and cleanliness. Some, however, are disturbed by their own untidiness. Some couples assign definite chores to the children. One study found that adolescent daughters

Table 12.1   A Typology of Employed, First-Time Mothers

Type	Maternal Belief System	Expectations for Nonparental Caregiver	Quality of Mother-Infant Interactions
Enamored	Incontrovertible supremacy of mother as primary caregiver	Caregiver as supplemental to mother; meeting infant's needs	Sensitive, contingent caregiving
Managers	Mother as organizer	Caregiver as equal partner; meeting family's organizational/scheduling needs	Acceptable, responsive caregiving
Distressed	Exclusivity of the primary caregiver, not necessarily mother	Caregiver as competitor who spoils infant; preference to be at home with baby	Acceptable, responsive caregiving coupled with distancing, avoidance, inappropriate independence expectations
Disengaged	Anger, rejection of motherhood	Caregiver as primary provider replacing mother	Disconnection from parenting role; insensitive, noncontingent caregiving

Note: From "Employed First-Time Mothers: A Typology of Maternal Responses to Integrating Parenting and Employment" by C. Shuster, 1993, *Family Relations, 42,* pp. 13–20.

in such families were assigned more chores than adolescent sons. In practice, dual-career families were more sexist than traditional families in this regard (Benin and Edwards, 1990).

The Quality of Dual-Career Marriages

Like any marriage, dual-career marriages can be of high or low quality, depending on many factors. Thomas, Albrecht, and White (1984) divided marital quality into two major components: (1) satisfaction with life-style and (2) rewards from spousal interaction. Satisfaction with life-style included four requirements for marital quality: (1) socioeconomic adequacy, (2) satisfaction with the woman working, (3) optimal household composition (older children in the family rather than younger), and (4) community embeddedness (maintaining an adequate and desired level of satisfying social life).

Rewards from spousal interaction included five requirements for marital quality: (1) positive regard from one's spouse, (2) emotional gratification (expression of affection, sexual satisfaction, encouragement of personal growth from the spouse, and congruence between ideal and actual spouse), (3) effective communication, (4) role fit (absence of role conflict and presence of role complementarity and role sharing), and (5) an acceptable amount of interaction (sharing activities and companionship).

The researchers emphasized that marital quality for dual-career couples depends on the extent to which the spouses find that these requirements are met in their life-style and their relationship.

One study of Black dual-career couples revealed that marital happiness contributes significantly to overall happiness and psychological well-being (Thomas, 1990). Another study also found that both spouses' perceptions of marital quality are affected primarily by marital characteristics rather than by employment characteristics. Overall, work-related factors seem to have only a slight effect on marital quality as perceived by either spouse (Blair, 1993).

MATERIAL RESOURCES

While some women are employed for personal fulfillment and satisfaction (Cotton, Antill, and Cunningham, 1989), in most cases, financial necessity and the desire to improve the family's standard of living remain the most important motives for working (Eggebeen and Hawkins, 1990).

Financial Needs

The financial needs of today's families are great. Figure 12.1 shows the percentage of families at different income levels; the figures represent gross

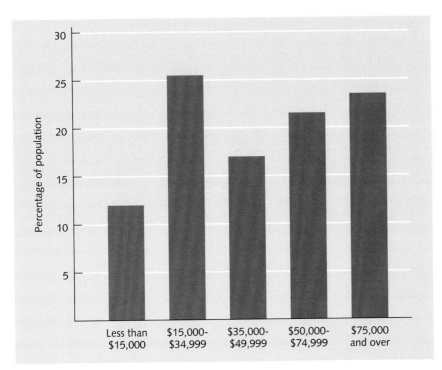

Figure 12.1   Gross Income Distribution of Families in the United States, 1997 (*Source:* From *Statistical Abstract of the United States, 1999* [p. 478] by U.S. Bureau of the Census, 1999, Washington, DC: U.S. Government Printing Office.)

income (before deductions). The median family income level was $44,568 in 1997, meaning that 50% of all families were above and 50% were below that figure (U.S. Bureau of the Census, 1999c).

In spite of the rise in family income over the years, however, real income, or purchasing power, has remained fairly constant (Aldous, Ganey, Trees, and Marsh, 1991). Because of inflation, the cost of living has increased as much as wages have increased during the past 15 years, so families are no better off now than they were 15 years ago (U.S. Bureau of the Census, 1999c).

Various estimates have been given of how much it costs to bear and rear a child to maturity. In 1999, the cost of raising a child to age 18 in a middle-class family was about $160,140, according to the U.S. Department of Agriculture's annual report, *Expenditures on Children by Families* (see Figure 12.2; Lino, 2000). This figure was up 13 percent from 1960, after adjusting for inflation. In 1999, a family with two children could expect to spend over $320,000 to rear them to age 18. If college costs are added, the total will be over $380,000 if both children go to a state university for 4 years and over $465,000 if both children go to more expensive private colleges. The College Board estimated in 1999 that average annual tuition and fees were $3,274 for a 4-year

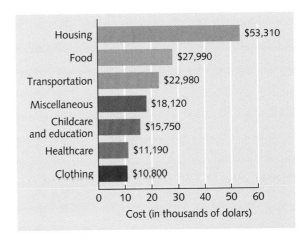

Figure 12.2   The Average Costs of Raising a Child to Age 18, 1999 (*Source:* From *Expenditures on Children by Families, 1999* [Miscellaneous Publication No. 1528-1999] by Mark Lino, 2000, Washington, DC: U.S. Department of Agriculture, Center for Nutrition Policy and Promotion.)

public college and $12,894 for a 4-year private college. Room and board accounted for another $4,474 for a public institution and $5,224 for a private one. For many parents, child support continues after college; 47 percent of parents in their fifties support children over the age of 21 (Lino, 1999).

Housing still ranks as the biggest expense for families, accounting for about one-third of expenses, just as it did 40 years ago. In some cities, families earning as much as $70,000 a year can't afford decent housing without spending more than half their income (Stegman, Quercia, and McCarthy, 2000). For example, in Boston in 1998, almost 31,000 families could afford to buy a $100,000–$125,000 home, but only 1,255 homes in that price range were available. Nationally, in 1997, 3 million moderate-income families had critical housing needs, which was 17% more than in 1995. Of these 3 million families, 76% spent more than half their income on housing, and the rest lived in substandard housing (Stegman, Quercia, and McCarthy, 2000).

The Gender Wage Gap

Although President Kennedy signed the Equal Pay Act in 1963, outlawing wage discrimination based on gender, women in the United States still only earn 73–75¢, on average, for every dollar a man earns (U.S. Bureau of the Census, 1999c). Title VII of the Civil Rights Act of 1964 was an even broader attempt to correct the inequity. However, women still consistently earn lower wages than men, many times even when doing the same work. A 1998 analysis of census data found that, even during women's and men's peak earning years (ages 45–54), women earned 68% of what men earned. So why is it that the phenomenon continues?

Some would suggest that the wage gap is partly a result of differences in education. But the data show that when education levels are taken into account there is still an inequity in salaries (see Figure 12.3; U.S. Bureau of the Census, 1999c). In 1998, on average, women with professional degrees earned $35,193 less than men with professional degrees, female college graduates earned $14,574 less than male college graduates, and Black college-educated women earned $3,777 less than White males with only a high school diploma (National Committee on Pay Equity, 1998).

Work experience is also cited as a determining factor in the gender wage gap, but again the argument is weakened by specific examples in which equal qualifications do not mean equal pay. Surveys conducted by the National Committee on Pay Equity (n.d.) show that in the field of public relations women with less than 5 years of experience make

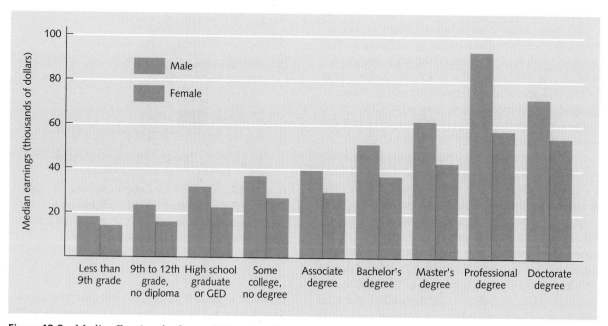

Figure 12.3   Median Earnings by Sex and Educational Attainment, Full-Time, Year-Round Workers, Age 25 and Older, 1998 (*Note:* From Current Population Survey, March 1999, by U.S. Bureau of the Census, 1999, Washington, DC: U.S. Government Printing Office.)

X Marks the Spot: Generation X College Students Speak Out on Goals for the Future

Four hundred and sixty-two college students from four schools were asked to think ahead 10 years and rate the importance of success in various life domains and indicate any obstacles to achieving them (Eskilson, 1997). Here are some key findings:

- Women students attached greater importance than men to attaining family goals.

- Men and women students did not differ in the importance they attached to economic success.

- Women of all races and minority students of both sexes named discrimination as a future obstacle.

- Students of color rated economic success as more important than did White students.

- Students whose parents were less well educated expressed concern that difficulties with "connections," money, and the right education might hinder their future success.

- Most students believed that they would achieve their life goals.

No relationship was found between college academic performance and the importance attached to future material success. This suggests that students' hopes for the future may not be rooted in present accomplishments.

$29,726 a year, while men with the same amount of experience make $48,162. And when the experience level increases to 15–20 years, women average $49,270 and men average $69,120. A similar example can be found in the field of purchasing: Professional purchasers with 3 or fewer years of experience make $35,900 if they are women and $47,700 if they are men.

Evidently, other factors are at least partly responsible for the continued gender wage gap. Three reasons can be attributed to women themselves: (1) They choose to work in lower-paying industries, (2) they don't work as many hours per week as men, and (3) they don't "fight" for their own pay. Whole sections of the economy are traditionally women's jobs and have always been paid less—for example, nursing, secretarial work, and teaching. A study released by the National Bureau of Economic Research showed that a "sizable fraction" of the gender pay gap is caused by women's concentration in lower-paying industries and in lower-paying jobs within higher-paying industries (Krotz, 1999). Because women typically take on more family responsibilities than men, such as picking the children up from school or day care, they tend to put in less overtime and are less willing to travel on business. Some argue that men advance more quickly in companies because of their willingness to work longer hours, particularly if they have a spouse who assumes responsibility for child care. It is also well known among corporate headhunters that women aren't always prepared for compensation negotiations and, more often than not, take the offer on the table. That is, they often sell themselves short—and companies know it.

Various equal-pay measures have been debated in Congress, including the Fair Pay Act, which prohibits wage discrimination on the basis of race, national origin, and sex, and the Paycheck Fairness Act, which goes one step farther and forbids employers to penalize workers who share salary information. Several companies have paid settlements in recent years after government audits or their own investigations revealed violations of the Equal Pay Act. Texaco agreed to pay $3.1 million to 186 female employees found to be systematically underpaid. Trigon Blue Cross Blue Shield paid $264,901 in back pay to 34 female managers, and US Airways agreed to pay $390,000 in back pay and salary adjustments to 30 female managers (National Committee on Pay Equity, n.d.). Experts, including economists, academics, and Labor Department officials, have varying opinions on how soon the wage gap will close—with answers varying from 1 year to never. Pay consultant James Brennan has tracked women's compensation for three decades and has calculated that, based on current and past rate extrapolations, the wage gap will close in 2050 (Krotz, 1999).

Money and Marital Satisfaction

Family income has a close relationship to marital satisfaction (Schaninger and Buss, 1986). Financial complaints are consistently cited as a major problem by couples seeking divorce. However, marital satisfaction is not always greatest when income is

Although a high income makes it easier for a family to weather life's crises, satisfaction with family life also depends on whether people feel that the family's income is adequate.

highest. For most couples, marital satisfaction is dependent on partners' feelings that income is adequate (Berry and Williams, 1987). A study of the marital quality of Black couples expands on this observation: Subjective indices such as perceived economic adequacy are more closely related to all aspects of marital quality than are objective measures such as income, education, or occupation (Clark-Nicolas and Gray-Little, 1991). That is, if spouses are not earning as much as they feel they need, and if they feel their earnings aren't adequate, their marital satisfaction is lessened because of financial pressures and tensions over money.

Income is important for both marital and individual satisfaction. High incomes within marriage can increase security and provide the necessary means for healthy life-styles. Income affects mortality through its effects on the physical, social, and psychological environment. High incomes improve people's housing, health behavior, and access to quality health care (Rogers, 1996).

Harmony or Discord   Even more than the level of income, the management of money is a major source of harmony or discord in the marital relationship. Couples who can agree on handling finances report more satisfactory marriages than do couples who have conflict over money (Berry and Williams, 1987). When conflict occurs, it arises because of immature attitudes or unrealistic expectations toward earning, saving, or spending money. Money is also sometimes used as a tool for personal attacks. The emotional use of money to control or punish a spouse or to compensate for inadequacies, guilt, or an inability to give love also causes difficulty. Money can be a valuable resource for the marital system, but it can also be a source of irritation.

Reasons People Go into Debt   No matter how much money they make, some people are always in debt. They estimate that if they had a little more each month they would be able to balance their budget, but when that "little more" is obtained, they still can't make do. They never seem able to meet all their obligations. The more their income increases, the greater indebtedness they incur.

The families that are most in debt are not the poor but those in middle-income brackets. The poor less frequently have mortgages, charge accounts, or large installment debts, although they might if they were able to establish credit. Level of income is not the reason couples do or do not go into debt. The reasons relate more to the life-style of the partners and their ability to manage their money wisely.

Couples go into debt for various reasons. For example, many people go into debt because of excessive and unwise use of credit. Credit can be help-

Spouses who have been able to agree about earning, saving, and spending patterns have overcome one of the biggest obstacles to a harmonious, happy marriage.

ful: Few couples can afford to pay cash for a home, automobile, or other large purchases. But habitual and unthinking use of credit often leads to excessive indebtedness.

Many people go into debt because of crisis spending. Unexpected events can throw the family budget off completely and force people to go into debt to meet the emergency. Unemployment is the most common crisis; illness is another one. Some couples, such as farm couples, have variable incomes; they never know from one year to the next what their earnings will be, so it is very hard to plan ahead.

Many people go into debt because they buy things carelessly or impulsively. As a possible consequence, they pay more than is necessary, get merchandise of inferior quality that doesn't last as long as it should, or purchase things they don't really need. Some people buy things without stopping to think whether they can afford them. One woman reported:

> My husband loves to go to auctions. Whenever he reads about someone selling the contents of their home in an auction, he always shows up. He loves the crowds and the excitement, but he gets carried away. Once he brought home a cement mermaid. I don't know what he expected to do with it since we don't have a fish pond or swimming pool. But he likes it.

It's still down in the family room where he put it. (Author's counseling notes)

Some people are compulsive buyers. Their buying habits may be an expression of their emotional insecurity; they can't say no to a salesperson for fear of hurting that person's feelings or are afraid that person won't like them. Or they buy to try to gain status and recognition. Another woman reported:

> My husband Frank is a compulsive collector. He spends a fortune on his coin collection, will travel hundreds of miles to see a rare coin, and will always end up outbidding everyone else to buy it. He shows his collection to everyone who comes into the house and derives great satisfaction from owning a coin that other collectors have never seen. (Author's counseling notes)

Money Management There is no right or wrong money management system. The best system is what works for the individual couple. Who actually manages the money is not as important as the skill with which it is done and the extent of the responsibility and agreement of both spouses in relation to its use. The person who has the most interest and skill in money management might be the one to exercise the most control, as long as the other person is in agreement. Marital adjustment is smoother when couples adopt a "we" attitude in relation to making financial decisions.

POVERTY AND FAMILY LIFE

Obviously, millions of people will never reach median income levels. In 1998, 12.7% of families were below the poverty level, which was $16,660 for a non-farm family of four (U.S. Bureau of the Census, 1999c). For these families, daily life is a struggle merely to pay rent and to buy groceries, a pair of shoes, a winter coat, or a TV set.

The Poverty Line

The poverty line was originally intended to establish the household income that a family required to afford basic necessities. The first threshold was tied to the spending of the average American family in 1955, starting with the proportion of the budget spent on food. In 1955, that proportion was about one-third. The formulation of the poverty line was based on the smallest amount of money necessary to provide adequate nutrition for one family member, multiplied by three, since food was considered to be one-third of a family's expenses. In 1964, the poverty line was adjusted due to a rise in food costs, and it has been adjusted for inflation every year since.

Critics of the current poverty line argue that the costs of many necessities have outpaced inflation and that many of the common expenses families incur today were not part of family life in 1955. Although food prices have risen since 1955 at practically the same rate as inflation, food today accounts for barely one-sixth of the average family budget, rather than the third on which the original poverty line was based. Schwarz (1998) offered the following outline of annual expenses for a family of four, providing for no more than the barest necessities:

Food	$4,576
Two-bedroom apartment (government-approved, low-cost) including minimum utilities and phone	$6,144
10-year-old car (operating, insuring, maintaining)	$3,700
Clothing	$250/family member
Medical, pharmaceutical, dental	$2,000
Personal/household (ranging from toothpaste to repairs)	$3,900
Taxes (federal, state, Social Security)	$3,270
Total	$24,590

Note that this budget does not include child care, emergency funds, or savings and that the food budget is only $88 per week, which comes to $1.05 per person per meal. Then compare the total to the 1998 poverty threshold for a family of four: $16,660. Today the poverty line doesn't measure the poor, but rather the very poor (Schwarz, 1998).

Not only has the poverty line become distorted, but the minimum wage that many people living below the poverty line rely on has also lost its value. The minimum wage in 1950 paid about 110% of the amount required for a family of four with two full-time workers and two children to survive (Schwarz, 1998). This used to be enough to raise a family into the middle class, but by the 1970s, the minimum wage for two full-time workers had fallen to 90% of necessary income, and it now stands at 70%. Today, the poorest families are likely to be the largest ones, ones headed by women alone, or ones in which the father has little education.

The Effects of Poverty

The effects of poverty on the family include (1) increased tension and unhappiness in the marital relationship, (2) high rates of children born to single mothers, (3) desertion, separation, and divorce, and (4) children brought up without a stable father figure in the home (Booth and Edwards, 1985). Low income results in cultural and social deprivation, with accompanying lower aspirations and educational levels (Rank, 1987). Limited resources also leave few opportunities for contacts with the outside world, resulting in isolation. Increased problems and the lack of resources result in much higher rates of mental and physical illness. Limited alternatives and feelings of helplessness and powerlessness leave little hope for the future or few prospects for getting ahead. And the poor are at the mercy of life's unpredictable happenings: sickness, injury, job loss, legal problems, and school difficulties (Spencer, Dobbs, and Swanson, 1988). These situations may arise because of factors over which those affected have no control: problems in the economy, the changing nature of jobs, political trends and government policies, business practices, and racism and sexism in society (Chilman, 1991). Family members living in poverty strive for security because they never feel certain about their lives (Rank, 1987). Coping is especially difficult for parents with very low income, who have to care for themselves and their children. Many are never able to free themselves from their situation. The task is made even more difficult when they are forced to raise their children in crime-ridden, dangerous neighborhoods (Bowen and Chapman, 1996).

Many families of low socioeconomic status (SES) live in America's inner cities. Since the 1970s, people with low incomes in search of jobs and affordable housing have become increasingly likely to live in metropolitan areas and in neighborhoods with a high concentration of low-income people (Klebanov, Brooks-Gunn, and Duncan, 1994). Neighborhood poverty is associated with a poorer home environment. Other poor families live in rural areas or are migrant workers, moving from place to place in search of seasonal employment (Morrison and Lichter, 1988).

A growing number of poor families are homeless, living on the streets or staying temporarily in homeless shelters (Axelson and Dail, 1988; Bode, 1987). According to the Urban Institute, 1 of every 100 Americans used a homeless service (such as an emergency shelter or soup kitchen) during 1996 (Burt et al., 1999). And the number of homeless nearly doubled over 10 years, from 1.4–1.8 million in 1987 to 2.3–3.5 million in 1996. Nearly 25% of homeless people who receive services are children, up from about 15% in 1987. Over the course of a given year, at least 38% of the entire homeless population are children. Researchers at the Urban Institute believe rising housing costs are the main reason for the increase in homelessness.

The Feminization of Poverty

The population living in poverty in the United States increasingly is becoming one of women, irrespective of ethnicity or age. This process is known as the **feminization of poverty.** Women have higher poverty rates than men for two main reasons: (1) Women's economic resources do not approach parity with those of men, and (2) women are more likely than men to be single custodial parents dur-

ing their working lives and to be unmarried and living alone in their later years. For these reasons, poverty is more likely to be a chronic problem among female-householder families (Starrels, Bould, and Nicholas, 1994). Figure 12.4 compares the income levels of households headed by women with those of households headed by married couples.

Many female-headed households are forced into poverty when the father defaults on child support payments. The failure of absent fathers to support their children economically has long-term consequences because mothers have fewer material resources to invest in their children (Paasch and Teachman, 1991). Large numbers of these mothers work, leaving their children under the care of relatives, friends, or whomever they can afford. Lack of adequate and affordable child care is one of the major reasons more mothers do not work outside the home (Joesch, 1991).

Opportunities for economic advancement are limited for people living in poverty. For single mothers, poverty reduces their chances of completing school, decreases their opportunities for marriage, and increases the likelihood that they will need public assistance to feed and house their family (Orthner and Neenan, 1996). Single mothers with little education are often under severe economic pressure and are prone to experience negative life events (poor schooling for children, more stress, illness, and crime victimization) and low social support, which, in turn, are associated with psychological distress and ineffectual parenting practices (Simons, Beaman, Conger, and Chao, 1993b). Their sons in particular are at greater risk for antisocial behavior problems (Bank, Forgatch, Patterson, and Fetrow, 1993). In addition, low-income single mothers of young children are exposed to especially high levels of daily stress and, not surprisingly, are prone to depression and feelings of hopelessness (Olson and Banyard, 1993).

The Effects of Poverty on Children

Millions of American children are being raised in poverty, and the number is growing. For children, poverty is associated with poor school performance, higher school dropout rates, more teen pregnancies, and a greater likelihood of remaining in poverty when they are adults. Emancipation from family comes early and is often psychologically premature.

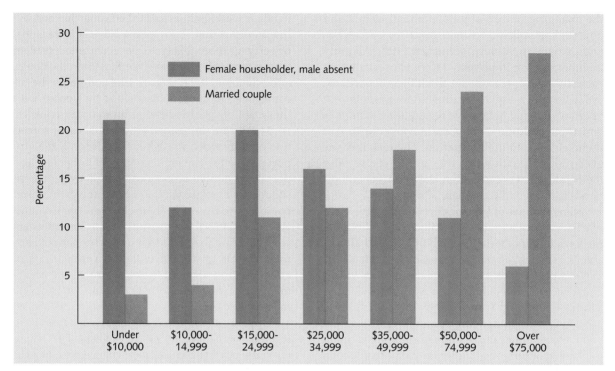

Figure 12.4   Income Distribution of Selected Household Types, 1997 (*Note:* From *Statistical Abstract of the United States, 1999* [Table No. 744] by U.S. Bureau of the Census, 1999, Washington, DC: U.S. Government Printing Office.)

These youths frequently are not ready to take their place in the adult world, and many turn to peers to replace family ties.

Dropout rates from school are high among low-SES youths (Rice, 1993). Although parents usually want their children to have more education than they did, there is often pressure on adolescents to get a job to help support the family; this pressure may contribute to adolescents dropping out of school after they reach the legal age to do so. Furthermore, many low-SES youths feel the prejudices of middle-class society and so experience isolation from mainstream school activities. If they are doing poorly academically, they often can't wait to quit school entirely. Of course, doing so perpetuates the cycle of poverty and cultural deprivation.

Low-SES families tend to be larger than average, and sometimes little attention is paid to the older children because the younger ones require immediate care. Guidance and discipline take the form of orders, absolutes, and physical punishment. Child-rearing patterns tend to emphasize obedience, respect for parents, conformity to exter-nally imposed standards, and avoidance of trouble rather than personal growth and the development of creativity, curiosity, independence, and self-direction. Some families exercise greater control over daughters than sons, so the daughters may use early marriage to escape from home (Abell, Clawson, Washington, Bost, and Vaughn, 1996).

Fathers of low-SES families are often less emotionally and behaviorally involved with their adolescent children than are fathers who are better off financially. However, a father's involvement, when it exists, can enhance youths' achievements and emotional well-being; and reduce delinquency (Harris and Marmer, 1996).

Research generally supports the concept that parental reasoning complexity is an important predictor of parents' behavior in interactions with their children. Reasoning complexity and behavior are significantly related to educational level and occupation, with more complex reasoning corresponding to higher educational levels. More complex reasoning also is related to an authoritative style of child rearing, to the use of indirect positive controls,

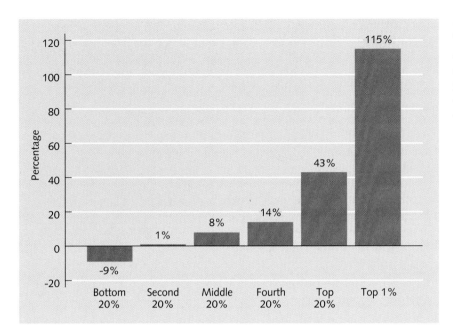

Figure 12.5 Change in After-Tax Family Income, 1977–1999 (*Note:* From *The Widening Income Gulf* by Center on Budget and Policy Priorities, September 4, 1999, Washington, DC: Congressional Budget Office.)

and to parental warmth, acceptance, and support. Less complex reasoning is typically expressed through authoritarian patterns and restrictiveness. Thus, how parents interpret the parent-child relationship and resolve the tasks of parenting depends to a large degree on the complexity of their reasoning (Dekovic and Gerris, 1992).

The Widening Gap Between the Rich and the Poor

The late 1990s were characterized by economic growth, a booming stock market, and the lowest unemployment rate in decades. Median earnings rose 5% in 1999, translating into an average weekly wage of $549 (U.S. Bureau of Labor Statistics, 2000). But a closer look reveals a problem that clouds this image—income inequality. On average, women earned $473 a week in 1999, while men earned $618. Salaries increased 10–20% in the information technology sector but only 4–5% in traditional industries. Numerous reports, cited by the Economic Policy Institute, concluded that the gap between the rich and the poor was greater than ever at the end of the century.

Research by the Congressional Budget Office supports this conclusion; the top 20% of households showed a 43% increase in after-tax income between 1977 and 1999, while the middle 20% had only an 8% increase, and the bottom 20% had a 9% drop (see Figure 12.5). In fact, income disparity has widened to the degree that in 1999 the richest 1% of the population were projected to receive as much after-tax income as the bottom 38%. In other words, the earnings of the 2.7 million richest Americans would equal those of the poorest 100 million combined.

There were other indicators of the increasing disparity during the 1980s and 1990s. For instance, in 1989, there were 66 billionaires and 31.5 million people living below the poverty line; by 1999, there were 268 billionaires and 34.5 million people living below the poverty line. The disparity can also be seen when comparing the pay of CEOs to that of workers. This pay gap quintupled from the early 1990s to the end of the decade—making it 10 times wider than it had been in the early 1980s. In 1998, CEOs made 419 times as much as workers (Collins, Hartman, and Sklar, 1999). Table 12.2 lists representative salaries for a cross-section of occupations.

This growing disparity in income is relevant for several reasons and affects society as a whole. According to a recent survey by the Fannie Mae Foundation, urban historians, planners, and architects identified the income gap as the single most important factor influencing the shape of American

When people hear the word *welfare,* they show different reactions. People who are on welfare or who have been on it find it demeaning (Jarrett, 1996), but they admit that they are very glad to get it because the financial assistance is much needed. When people who have never been on welfare hear the word, they often assume recipients are lazy and do not want to work or look for a job since they're able to live off the state and the federal government.

The important question we will consider here is how the present welfare system affects the family. In 1996, the welfare system in the United States changed dramatically with the passage of the Personal Responsibility and Work Opportunity Reconciliation Act. The bipartisan welfare reform plan requires work in exchange for time-limited assistance. The new Temporary Assistance to Needy Families (TANF) program replaced the Aid to Families with Dependent Children (AFDC) and Job Opportunities and Basic Skills Training (JOBS) programs.

TANF brought an end to entitlement to federal assistance, allowing states, territories, and tribes to operate their own assistance programs. The federal government provides block grants to cover the costs of benefits, administrative expenses, and services, but the states determine eligibility and benefit levels. States, territories, and tribes are given enormous flexibility, provided that the programs they design accomplish the purposes of TANF, which are (1) to provide assistance to needy families so that children may be cared for in their own homes, (2) to reduce dependency by promoting job preparation, work, and marriage, (3) to prevent out-of-wedlock pregnancies, and (4) to encourage the formation and maintenance of two-parent families. Basic stipulations of TANF include the following: (1) Recipients must work after 2 years on assistance; (2) recipients who are not working must participate in community service 2 months after they start receiving benefits; (3) recipients must participate in unsubsidized or subsidized employment, on-the-job training, community service, or vocational training, or they must provide child care for individuals participating in community service; and (4) families who have received assistance for 5 cumulative years are ineligible for cash aid.

All states offer basic health services to certain very poor people: individuals who are pregnant, aged, disabled, or blind and families with dependent children. One of these programs is Medicaid. Medicaid eligibility is automatic for almost all cash welfare recipients in the United States. Many people who are eligible go on welfare simply because they need some kind of medical insurance and services and can-

not afford private health insurance. Some states extend Medicaid to certain other persons who qualify, such as people with medical expenses that when subtracted from their income reach a "medically needy" level. Within federal guidelines, each state determines its own Medicaid eligibility criteria and the health services to be provided under Medicaid. The cost of providing Medicaid services is jointly shared by the federal government and the states.

The federal Supplemental Security Income (SSI) program administered by the Social Security Administration provides benefits to the aged, the blind, and the disabled. The SSI program provides a minimum income for these persons and establishes uniform national basic eligibility requirements and payment standards. Most states supplement the basic SSI payments.

In 1997, 13.3% of all people in the United States were below the poverty line, and 7% of the population was receiving some form of assistance (U.S. Bureau of the Census, 1999c). Data reported by the U.S. Department of Health and Human Services in January 1999 showed a 43% drop in the number of families receiving assistance, with 5.4 million fewer recipients in June 1999 than in August 1996 (see Figure 12.6). The percentage of decline ranged from 82% in Wisconsin to 12% in Rhode Island.

But some researchers and welfare reform critics point to failings in the system and distortion in these statistics. Mary Jo Bane, former secretary for Children and Families in the Department of Health and Human Services, resigned from her position when President Clinton signed the welfare bill because of her concerns for the well-being of needy children. Her concerns mainly stemmed from Title IV of the act, which barred most legal immigrants from most federal benefit programs, and from Title VIII, which provided across-the-board cuts in food stamp benefits. Bane (1997) reported:

> *Analyses produced by the Department of Health and Human Services and by the Urban Institute before the bill was enacted predicted that upward of a million children would be pushed into poverty as a result of the bill, and that some eight million families with children would lose income. The poverty effects result mostly from the cuts in food stamps, supplemental security income, and immigrant benefits, since many families potentially affected by the cuts have incomes right on the edge of poverty.*

The Children's Defense Fund released findings from its analysis of government data in 1999 that showed an in-

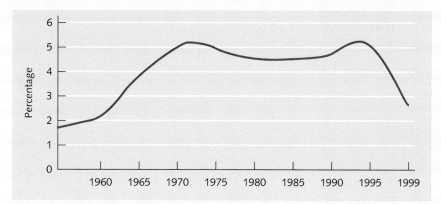

Figure 12.6 Percentage of U.S. Population on Welfare, 1960–1999 (*Note:* From U.S. Welfare Caseloads Information, by U.S. Department of Health and Human Services, the Administration for Children and Families, 1999; retrieved February 1, 2000, from the World Wide Web: http://www.acf. dhhs.gov/news/stats/6090_ch2. htm)

crease of almost half a million children living in extreme poverty just 1 year after enactment of the welfare reform act (Sherman, 1999). The report defined "extreme poverty" as households in which income was below half of the poverty line. Among single-mother families, the group hardest hit by welfare reform, the number of children living in extreme poverty jumped 26% between 1996 and 1997.

Sheldon Danziger, professor of social work and public policy at the University of Michigan, addressed the issue of whether the caseload is a false indicator of the act's success during a 1999 congressional briefing, "Is Welfare Reform Working? The Impact of Economic Growth and Policy Changes" (Consortium of Social Science Associations, 1999). Danziger argued that more attention should be fo-

cused on how recipients are faring and less on the declining number of cases. One example he cited is the number of cases in West Virginia that have been eliminated because SSI benefits have made them ineligible for TANF, not because the recipients have found employment. Danziger noted that research has shown that even during good economic times approximately one-third of those no longer receiving welfare are not working and that many who go off welfare do not earn more than they did while receiving aid, thus dooming a large group of children to live in poverty. For the current welfare system to protect children in poverty, more research is needed to determine the true reasons for current caseload decline.

The population in poverty in the United States is becoming increasingly composed of women. Food stamps enable many women and children to buy groceries that they would otherwise not be able to afford.

Table 12.2 What People Earn	
Job	**Salary**
CEO, Major technical company	$90,000,000
University president	325,000
Vice president, Internet company	125,000
Architect	90,000
Trucker	65,000
Psychologist	60,000
Information technology specialist	55,000
Restaurant manager	45,000
Massage therapist	40,000
Children's book author/lecturer	40,000
Owner, home day care	37,000
Director, nonprofit agency	35,000
Web site designer	34,000
High school teacher	33,000
Radio show host	30,000
Personal fitness trainer	28,000
Accountant	26,000
Bartender	16,000
Private, U.S. Army	13,404

Note: From "What people earn," February 27, 2000, *Parade.*

metropolitan areas over the next 50 years. Disparity in income is related to the achievement gap between White and minority students, with a greater percentage of minority students living in poverty than their White counterparts. Our democratic institutions are also influenced by the income gap, with 80% of all political contributions coming from less than 1% of the population.

Many experts believe that the gap will continue to widen, with the rich getting richer and the poor getting poorer. It is a challenging situation to address, and there is much disagreement as to how to remedy the problem. One approach, suggested by the organization United for a Fair Economy (UFE), is an "asset-building agenda," which recommends actions that could help close the gap. Examples include tax-exempt savings programs, expanded earned-income credits, a higher minimum wage, increased access to homeownership, and a higher capital gains tax. Others believe that changes in the welfare program will help families out of poverty and that the prosperity of the rich has a positive effect on other aspects of the economy that directly benefit poor and working-class families. They believe that a higher minimum wage and increased capital gains taxes would only hurt the economy and ultimately take its toll on poor and working-class families. However, regardless of political ideology, no one disagrees that living in poverty is detrimental to the health and well-being of families, particularly children.

SUMMARY

1. In our society, the key male role traditionally is the provider role. Feelings of inadequacy as a provider can be problematic for some men.

2. Job stressors negatively affect the emotional health of families.

3. Some types of work are particularly stressful for the family, including work that is difficult, work that requires periods of separation from the family, and work that is too demanding of a person's time.

4. The workaholic's compulsion to work comes from within. Workaholics have a strong need to succeed for ego fulfillment. They are perfectionists who drive themselves to try to find importance in and control over their life.

5. Sometimes the demand to work long hours comes from an employer who has a callous disregard for the employee's mental health and personal life. One of the barriers to family closeness is a job schedule that makes it difficult for family members to be together.

6. Parents provide models of male and female behavior for their children. More fathers are helping with child care, which helps in forming closer father-child bonds, eases the mother's burden, and strengthens the spousal relationship. In many cases, work hours and schedules affect child-care roles. Dual-earner couples have to schedule their time carefully.

7. The number and percentage of married women in the labor force are increasing. The

research on life satisfaction of employed mothers versus that of those who do not work outside the home shows slightly greater satisfaction among those who are employed.

8. Many couples are caught in a quandary between the ethic of equity, defined as a fair division of labor, and the ethic of care, in which couples try to be sensitive to the needs of family members.

9. One of the most important determinants of the life satisfaction of working mothers is whether they are able to integrate their work life with their home life. Working outside the home enhances the lives of many women. The maternal role has the most potential for conflicts with employment outside the home.

10. There are a number of major sources of role strain on working mothers: individual sources, family-related sources, and work-related sources. One individual source is the woman's own conflict over working. Family-related sources include the presence of young children in the family and the strain of having to fulfill too many roles at once. The job itself may also be a source of stress and strain.

11. Some research shows that as the number of children in the family increases, full-time employment of the woman lowers marital happiness and increases marital conflict. Other research has found that gender-role attitudes and expectations may be more important for the quality of a marriage than the woman's employment status.

12. Married graduate students experience two major forms of interrole conflict: time-based and strain-based. The two most effective ways of coping with these conflicts are structural role redefinition and personal role redefinition.

13. Participation in the labor force is decreasing among men and increasing among women, with greater numbers of women supporting the family.

14. A specific subtype of the dual-earner family is the dual-career, or dual-professional, family, in which both spouses' jobs usually require a high degree of commitment and continuous development.

15. The benefits of a dual-career marriage include financial rewards; an outlet for creativity, self-expression, achievement, and recognition; and shared child-care and household tasks.

16. Problems that may arise in dual-career marriages include experiencing pressures to give all for one's career and to put it ahead of family; having to move frequently; making the decision of whose career takes precedence; having to find jobs for both spouses; traveling frequently; finding adequate substitute child care; and assigning household responsibilities.

17. There are four categories of responses of first-time mothers to combining parenting and employment: enamored, managers, distressed, and disengaged.

18. Like any marriage, dual-career marriages can be of high or low quality, depending on many factors. Marital quality arises from two major components: satisfaction with life-style and rewards from spousal interaction.

19. Financial necessity and the desire to improve the family's living standard are the most important motives for married women with children to work.

20. The financial needs of today's families are considerable. In spite of rising income, however, real income remains about constant because of inflation.

21. Women earn 73–75¢ for every dollar that men earn. This gender wage gap cannot be accounted for by differences in education or job qualifications.

22. Family income has a close relationship to marital satisfaction, but satisfaction depends most on the feeling that income is adequate, not on having a high income.

23. Money management is also a source of harmony or discord in the family. The best money management system is what works for the individual couple.

24. People go into debt because of credit spending, crisis spending, careless or impulsive spending, and compulsive spending.

25. About 12.7% of families in the United States have incomes below the poverty level. The effects of poverty on families include high

rates of children born to single mothers; desertion, separation, and divorce; tensions and unhappiness in the marital relationship; and higher rates of stress and physical illness.

26. Women have higher poverty rates than men, irrespective of ethnicity and age. The reasons for this feminization of poverty are women's fewer economic resources and the greater likelihood that they will be single custodial parents and that they will live alone in old age.

27. The number of American children in poverty has been growing. Effects of poverty include poor grades, high dropout rates, and greater likelihoods of teenage pregnancy and of remaining in poverty throughout adulthood.

KEY TERMS

flextime

time-based conflicts

strain-based conflicts

structural role redefinition

personal role redefinition

dual-earner family

dual-career family

feminization of poverty

QUESTIONS FOR THOUGHT

1. For men: Would you want your spouse to work outside the home? Explain. For women: Would you like your spouse to stay home raising the children? Explain.

2. For women: Do you intend to work outside the home after you have children? Why or why not?

3. What problems do dual-career couples face to which you can relate?

4. If you were in a dual-career marriage and your spouse was offered a job at twice the salary in another part of the country, what would you do?

5. What are some strategies for having a happy marriage, two children, and a full-time career? Explain.

6. How important are material resources for a happy marriage? Explain.

SUGGESTED READINGS

Bassin, D., Honey, M., and Kaplan, M. M. (Eds.). (1994). *Representations of Motherhood.* New Haven, CT: Yale University Press. Offers provocative reinterpretations of motherhood.

Eckenrode, J., and Gore, S. (Eds.). (1990). *Stress Between Work and Family.* New York: Plenum. Presents a series of articles on types of stressors across work, family, and social roles.

Galinsky, E. (1999). *Ask the Children: What America's Children Really Think About Working Parents.* New York: Morrow. Gives a detailed report based on interviews with children about how parents address the responsibilities of work and home.

Gill, G. K. (1998). *The Third Job: Employed Couples' Management of Household Work Contradictions.* Aldershot, England; Brookfield, VT: Ashgate. Discusses housework in a dual-career family, considering both external (such as lack of affordable child care) and internal (such as tension over division of chores) factors.

Hays, S. (1996). *The Cultural Contradictions of Motherhood.* New Haven, CT: Yale University Press. Contrasts motherhood and work.

Hochschild, A., with Anne Machung. (1989). *The Second Shift: Working Parents and the Revolution at Home.* New York: Viking Press. Examines two-job marriages, family care, and household tasks.

Hoffman, L. W. (1999). *Mothers at Work: Effects on Children's Well-being.* Cambridge: Cambridge University Press. Examines the effects of the mother's employment on family life and the well-being of the children, based on a study of 369 families with third- or fourth-graders in a midwestern city.

Hoffnung, M. (1992). *What's a Mother to Do? Conversations on Work and Family.* Pasadena, CA: Trilogy Books. Explores women's experiences in negotiating the conflicting expectations of paid work and motherhood.

Keller, K. (1994). *Mothers and Work in Popular American Magazines.* Westport, CT: Greenwood Press. Discusses how women's magazines act as moral guides for readers.

Lewis, S., Izraeli, D. N., and Hootsmans, H. (Eds.). (1992). *Dual-Earner Families: International Perspectives.* London: Sage. Presents thirteen articles on the state of dual-earner families in several nations.

Mackey, W. P. (1996). *The American Father: Biocultural and Developmental Aspects.* New York: Plenum. Takes a cross-cultural approach.

Neal, M. B., Chapman, N. J., Ingersoll-Dayton, B., and Emlen, A. C. (1993). *Balancing Work and Caregiving for Children, Adults, and Elders.* Newbury Park, CA: Sage. Examines working family members who occupy multiple caregiving roles.

Parcel, T. L., and Menaghan, E. D. (1994). *Parents' Jobs and Children's Lives.* New York: Aldine de Gruyter. Discusses how mothers' and fathers' employment experiences affect children's cognitive and social development.

Rubin, L. B. (1992). *Worlds of Pain: Life in the Working-Class Family.* New York: Basic Books. Gives insight into family life and gender roles.

Rubin, L. B. (1994). *Families on the Fault Line: America's Working Class Speaks About the Family, the Economy, Race, and Ethnicity.* New York: HarperCollins. Reprints interviews with 162 working-class and lower-middle-class families in various studies across the United States.

CHAPTER 13

LEARNING OBJECTIVES

After reading the chapter, you should be able to:

Understand the importance of companionship in marriage and identify the styles of companionship that characterize relationships and individual differences in the need for closeness.

Understand the meaning of loneliness, the reasons people feel lonely, and the types of people who are most likely to be lonely.

Identify patterns of interaction in the family.

Discuss companionship in leisure time activities as it relates to the need for recreation, types of sports and leisure activities, vacations, television, and computers.

Discuss basic considerations in relation to friendships outside the family, including personality characteristics and social life, gender differences, and same-sex and opposite-sex friendships.

Companionship in and outside the Family

Learning Objectives

Companionship and the Family

Companionship as a Motive for Marriage

Styles of Companionship

Togetherness Versus Separateness

Loneliness

Family Issues: No Time for Love

Family Interaction

Companionship in Leisure Time Activities

Sports and Other Recreational Activities

Vacations

Television

Computers

Beyond the Family

Friendships

Gender Differences

Same-Sex and Opposite-Sex Friendships

Summary

Key Terms

Questions For Thought

Suggested Readings

In an impersonal world, the family becomes an even more important source of companionship and love. It is here that family members seek fulfillment of their basic human needs for affection and belongingness.

In this chapter, we are concerned with family interaction and togetherness versus separateness. We are concerned also with companionship in leisure time activities, the need for recreation, the types of activities people enjoy, and the effects of personality differences on social life as related to marital satisfaction. Family vacations, television viewing habits, and computer use are discussed as they affect family relationships. Finally, we look beyond the family to friendships and examine some basic male-female differences in relationships with friends and some of the benefits and pitfalls of same-sex and opposite-sex friendships.

COMPANIONSHIP AND THE FAMILY

We all need companionship—the company of someone to love, to talk to, and to share life experiences with, both positive and negative. Most of life's happiest experiences are more enjoyable when we are in the company of someone else. Most of life's saddest moments are less difficult if we have a companion to help ease the burden.

Companionship as a Motive for Marriage

If we were to ask partners why they want to get married, most would say "for love and companionship."

Research indicates that partners who share interests, who do things together, and who share some of the same friends and social groups derive more satisfaction from their relationship than do partners who are not mutually involved. However, it's not just the amount of time spouses spend together that is a key criterion of marital satisfaction, but the quality of the relationship they enjoy when they are together. Marital satisfaction increases when communication is high during shared leisure time (Holman and Jacquart, 1988).

Styles of Companionship

Researchers have identified three different styles of companionship that characterize relationships: joint, parallel, and segregated.

What is the greatest advantage of being married? Some studies show that both married and single people answer that sharing and companionship are important motives for marriage.

Joint companionship is characterized primarily by jointly shared interests and activities (Rogler and Procidano, 1986). The emphasis is on interaction during leisure pursuits, and there is close emotional involvement as well. One man described his situation: "It just so happens that my wife is also my best friend. We do everything together and have most things in common. I can't understand people who get married and then go their separate ways" (author's counseling notes).

Parallel companionship is characterized by different activities in the company of each other. These partners want to be together, but they each want to do their own thing. Watching TV, reading, doing individual household projects, and pursuing hobbies are all examples of activities of parallel companionship. There may be some conversation, visiting, or playing with the children, but most of the couple's attention is focused on individual pursuits. While it is nice to have company, if there is little meaningful conversation or real involvement, there will be little emotional closeness.

Segregated companionship is characterized by activities performed primarily outside the dyadic relationship. Each spouse spends time with his or her own circle of friends or kin, excluding the other from activities. One woman observed:

> When my husband bought a boat, I thought it would be something we could do together. He takes his friends sailing, but he doesn't want me along. He really doesn't want to be with me. One reason may be because I don't drink and his friends do. He knows I disapprove of their behavior. (Author's counseling notes)

In such relationships, home may be little more than a meeting place where spouses pass each other on their way to other activities.

There are advantages and disadvantages to each of these companionship styles, depending on what couples expect. Those who want joint companionship but are segregated may become disenchanted. As one woman put it, "If I wanted to be alone all the time, I would never have gotten married" (author's counseling notes).

Togetherness Versus Separateness

As discussed in Chapter 5, people differ in their need for closeness. Partners who want close companionship will be miserable if separated. In fact, some spouses give up promotions or change jobs so they won't have to be separated so much.

Generally, people who have utilitarian marriages and who stay together for convenience, for the sake of the children, or for financial or social reasons rather than for companionship don't mind enforced separation. In fact, some spouses *want* to spend a lot of time away from each other. But partners who really enjoy each other's company, who have a fulfilling sex life, and who seek a vital, close relationship enjoy the time they have together.

There is a difference between closeness and possessiveness, however. Some people want to possess their spouse so much that they cannot tolerate any gaps in their togetherness.

Loneliness

Loneliness is not simply being alone. It's being alone when we'd rather be with someone; or it's the feeling we have when we are with someone and do not feel close to him or her or when we would rather be with someone else. Loneliness is the distressing feeling we have when there is a discrepancy between the kind of social relations we want and the kind of social relations we have. It involves dissatisfaction with our present social relations (Brehm, 1985). Loneliness can be due to either social isolation or emotional isolation. Social isolation is situational (being geographically separated), whereas emotional isolation is relational (feeling estranged from a person who is physically nearby).

In their survey, Rubenstein and Shaver (1982) found five major reasons people gave for feeling lonely:

1. **Lack of attachment**—having no spouse, having no sexual partner, breaking up with spouse or lover
2. **Alienation**—feeling different, being misunderstood, not being needed, having no close friends
3. **Aloneness**—coming home to an empty house
4. **Forced isolation**—being housebound, being hospitalized, having no transportation
5. **Dislocation**—being far from home, starting in a new job or school, moving too often, traveling too often

Although people say they choose to marry for companionship, marriage counselors hear couples complaining over and over, "We never spend any time together," or "We don't talk to each other," or "We don't have any interests in common," or "We've drifted apart." These comments come from couples who in the beginning of their marriages said the primary reason for getting married was "companionship and love."

Obviously, something has gone wrong. Usually, one of several things has happened:

- One or both spouses spend most of their time on the job, with little left over for the family. It's easy under these circumstances to drift apart.

- One or both spouses have separate friends and spend most of their leisure time with their own friends rather than with joint friends as a couple.

- One or both spouses have individual hobbies and leisure time activities that they pursue separately rather than together. If these activities take up most of the leisure time, the couple are separated during leisure hours. One man described his situation: "My wife is a marathon runner. She works out several hours a day and works full-time in addition. It doesn't leave us any time together as a couple" (author's counseling notes).

- The spouses spend most of their free time attending movies, concerts, or athletic events, and they spend little time alone together just talking. They are in each other's company, but they are not finding real intimacy based on emotional closeness.

- One or both spouses spend their free time with the children rather than devoting some of it to being together as a couple. One man complained, "Since the baby was born, my wife's whole life has been wrapped up in Sarah. My wife has no time for me" (author's counseling notes).

- One or both spouses don't enjoy being together. They are embarrassed by what the other person does when they do go out, and often argue when in each other's company. One man explained, "When we go to another couple's house, my wife totally monopolizes the conversation. She interrupts. She turns the conversation around to talk about something she's interested in. It's very embarrassing" (author's counseling notes).

In each of these situations, the couple doesn't spend enough quality time together. When the partners are together, their activities are not conducive to companionship, which doesn't help to strengthen their relationship. Although people in intimate relationships need time for themselves, they also need to set time aside for the "we" in the relationship. Planning ahead and scheduling this time in advance, as one often does with other priorities, can help ensure that companionship needs in a marriage will be met. For example, some couples hire a baby-sitter at regular intervals in order to go out on a "date." These dates can even be set up several months in advance to make sure that both partners' schedules are clear, as opposed to being together as a couple only in whatever time is left at the end of the day.

Loneliness may be due not only to social or emotional isolation but also to personality attributes, to the kind of people we are. For example, lonely people may have low self-esteem and feel unworthy and unlovable; as a result, others have difficulty accepting them because they cannot accept themselves. Lonely people may be passive and shy and seldom take the initiative in social situations. Or they engage in relatively little self-disclosure that would allow others to get to know them (Solano, Batten, and Parish, 1982).

A consistent finding in research has been that for adults the absence of a mate or prospective mate is associated with loneliness. However, loneliness occurs within marriage as well. Tornstam (1992) found that 40% of married people reported being lonely "often" or "sometimes," 16% said they felt lonely even when they were with others, and 7% said they were lonely all the time. In the same study, however, very few people reported having no friends at all. A typical pattern is that spouses of lonely women tend to be less self-disclosing, whereas spouses of lonely men tend to feel less liking for and less intimacy with their mate (Sadava and Matejcic, 1987). There appear to be gender differences in loneliness among marrieds. When people are asked about loneliness, women are more likely to indicate feeling lonely than are men, particularly married women ages 20–49 (Tornstam, 1992). Women may simply be more willing to admit to feelings of loneliness, or they may have higher expectations for companionship within marriage that are not being met.

Loneliness is the distressing feeling of being alone when we do not want to be alone. Why are some people lonely? What can they do?

Family Interaction

Most married people need privacy and time to pursue their own interests as individuals. They also need time together as a married couple. And they need time to be with their children as a whole family. It's not easy to keep things in balance. When the children are young, it's easy to become absorbed in taking care of them and neglect the marital relationship. Marriage relationships have to be nurtured to stay alive.

One study of family interaction in 126 families with one, two, or three children ages 6–11 found that there was four times as much interaction between parents and children as there was between spouses (see Figure 13.1; Davey and Paolucci, 1980).

What type of activities did family members participate in? Sixty-two percent of interaction involved socializing. The next most frequent activity was eating (15% of the total interaction). Ten percent of all family interaction involved household work: meal preparation and cleanup, house and yard care, ironing and laundry, and marketing. Most of the remainder of the time was spent caring for family members.

According to one study on parent-adolescent relationships, there is a 21% decrease in the amount of time children spend with their families over their

adolescent years. On average, 5th-graders spent 35% of their waking hours with their families, while 12th-graders spent only 14% (Larson, Richards, Moneta, Holmbeck, and Duckett, 1996). This research indicates that intrafamily relations become less positive and less affectionate during this stage and do not improve until the end of adolescence. Other adolescent trends, such as the desire to be alone during early adolescence and to be outside of the home during later adolescence, do not appear to be the result of a change in family dynamics.

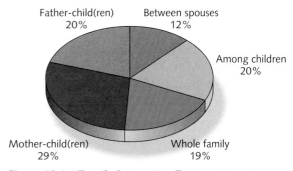

Figure 13.1 Family Interaction Patterns (*Note:* Data from "Family Interaction: A Study of Shared Time and Activities" by A. J. Davey and B. Paolucci, 1980, *Family Relations, 29,* pp. 43–49.)

It is not so important what type of recreation people prefer, as long as it affords a break from work-related activity, a change from one's usual routine, and a chance to do something enjoyable.

Instead, they seem to be a consequence of factors outside of the family, such as the desire to spend more time with friends and on after-school activities (Larson et al., 1996). Although the amount of family time decreased between the 5th and 12th grades, just as much time was spent in conversations with family members, indicating the attempt to actively maintain family relationships. In some cases, 5th-graders and 12th-graders actually spent the same amount of one-on-one time in conversation with their parents. Thus, while adolescence often marks a period of decreased family togetherness and more negativity toward the family, it also involves more one-on-one interaction, which eventually leads to positive family relationships (Larson et al., 1996).

COMPANIONSHIP IN LEISURE TIME ACTIVITIES

Recreation is a necessary part of a balanced life. Its purpose is to re-create, to refresh body and spirit, to soothe jangled nerves and relieve tension, to provide relaxation and pleasure away from the cares of the world. It really is not so important what type of recreation people prefer, as long as it affords a break from work-related activity, a change from one's usual routine, and a chance to do something different that one enjoys.

Sports and Other Recreational Activities

A national sample revealed the percentage of people 7 years of age or older who participated in different sporting activities. Walking (32%), swimming (25%), bicycling (19%), exercise (20%), and camping (19%) were the top five activities. Figure 13.2 shows the results of the survey (U.S. Bureau of the Census, 1999a).

In addition to sports, other leisure activities—such as gardening, hobbies, handicrafts, reading, and shopping—can be shared by the whole family or can be done alone. Their effect on family dynamics can be either harmful or helpful. The father who spends all his free time playing golf or watching sports on television in order to avoid interacting with his family is putting leisure time activities in the way of family relationships. But the parents who are always in the cheering section at their child's soccer match or Little League game or reading Harry Potter books aloud with their child are building family solidarity and giving their child important emotional support.

Vacations

Vacations enable family members to relax and enjoy one another's company and a variety of activities. Vacations enable people to get away from

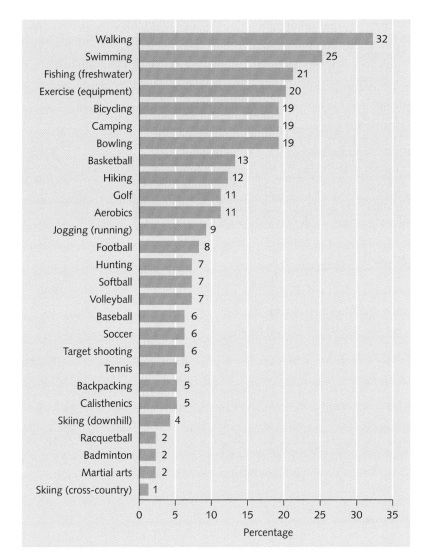

Figure 13.2 Participation in Selected Sports by People Age 7 or Older, 1999 (*Note:* Data from *Statistical Abstract of the United States, 1999* by U.S. Bureau of the Census, 1999, Washington, DC: U.S. Government Printing Office.)

the pressures of their everyday lives and to have fun doing some of the things they don't usually have time for. Most vacationers return home refreshed and rejuvenated and ready to assume responsibilities once more.

Vacations can be a great help in building companionship if family members get along when they are together and if they enjoy similar types of experiences. However, marriage counselors often hear from couples who have just come back from a miserable vacation. What was designed for fun and relaxation turned out to be a source of conflict and upset.

One of the problems with vacations is that family members aren't used to being together 24 hours a day. When they're home and working or in school, they don't see one another much and may get along

reasonably well. But when family members are forced to be together continuously, unresolved issues may come up that they have previously avoided. If they aren't used to communicating or solving problems, tensions may worsen and tempers flare.

Television

One of the most common family pastimes is watching television. The communications industry reports that the typical American home has the TV set turned on for 1,561 hours per year, or 30 hours per week (U.S. Bureau of the Census, 1999a). In some families, the set is turned on the first thing in the morning and is not turned off until late at night. This does not mean family members are always

The average American family watches 30 hours of TV a week. Effects of TV viewing include a decrease in communication and interaction among family members.

watching it; sometimes it's there for background noise. However, a 1999 Nielsen survey indicated that the average American child ages 2–5 views television almost 14 hours per week ("Average Television Viewing Time," 1999).

The effects on the family are of some concern. One negative effect of watching TV is that it decreases communication and interaction among family members (Christopher, Fabes, and Wilson, 1989). The more TV family members watch, the less they talk. Fathers especially seem to become absorbed in TV viewing, and the quality of their interaction with their children and spouse may suffer (Hopkins and Mullis, 1985).

Watching television is a passive activity. Absorption in the "boob tube" may result in a decrease in family communication, a decrease in frequency of sexual relations, less time devoted to activities and work around the house, and less physical activity and social interaction among children. In one experiment, families who voluntarily gave up TV viewing reported that their children played and read more, siblings fought less, family activities became more common, and mealtimes lasted longer (Chira, 1984). Other effects of TV viewing on children are discussed in Chapter 7. Research has shown that the way children watch TV is related to the age of their parents (Weissman, 1999). Baby boomers feel more guilt about plunking their children down in front of the TV, whereas Gen Xers have a more accepting attitude about their children

watching TV. As a result, children watch more television in households with Gen X parents than in those with baby boom parents. In one study, Gen X households were almost twice as likely over a 6-month period to have tuned into the Cartoon Network than were baby boom households, and they were 54% more likely to have watched Nickelodeon. David Morrison, director of TwentySomething, a Gen X research firm, believes that baby boomers seem less willing or able to acknowledge that when it comes to children there's such a thing as good TV and bad TV, whereas Gen Xers believe that TV can be both entertaining and educational (Weissman, 1999). Through proper mediation and guidance, parents can minimize some of the harmful effects of television and still make it readily available as a positive source of learning (Abelman and Pettey, 1989).

Computers

Of all the technological advances in recent years, none has had as profound an effect as the computer. Since the introduction of the first personal computer in 1980, computer use has skyrocketed. In a recent year, 30.3% of the U.S. population were using home computers, including 8.5% of children under age 5 and 5.9% of adults 70 and older (U.S. Bureau of the Census, 1999a). Considered a luxury item just a few years ago, the home computer is becoming almost a necessity.

One of the most important reasons for using the computer has been the introduction of the Internet. The Internet is open 24 hours a day, 365 days a year. It is a way to meet people, share ideas and experiences, and search for a friend. In 1999, 42% of adults had access to the Internet either at home or at work (U.S. Bureau of the Census, 1999a). Once online, users can e-mail friends and relatives, play games, visit chat rooms, or browse through hundreds of articles and magazines. The splendor of *National Geographic,* for example, can come to life on the screen, complete with not only still photographs but also sound and video clips. Users who log on to the Internet can browse their way through art and science museums or bookstores and music catalogs.

On the downside, however, many children and adolescents spend hours every day online, playing games and browsing the Internet. In fact, many parents complain that their children are spending even more time online than they used to watching television. When computer use becomes excessive, children miss out on person-to-person contact with others, including their own family. Instead, these computer users form their own communities, inhabiting electronic villages. Thus, some primary face-to-face relationships have been superseded by computer relationships (Pipher, 1996).

Another interesting result of the computer revolution is that a technology gap between some parents and their children has developed as a result of parents' slower assimilation of computer knowledge. Many parents don't understand computers and are even afraid of them. In contrast, their children may use computers on a daily basis.

BEYOND THE FAMILY

The quality and type of social life people participate in depends partially on their personalities and individual preferences. Some people are gregarious and outgoing, make friends easily, like to be with others, and feel comfortable in a variety of social situations. Other people are shy and withdrawn and avoid many kinds of social involvement.

Filsinger and Lamke (1983) found that interpersonal competence in general social relationships is a predictor of interpersonal competence on marriage. This means that those who score low on social anxiety tests score high on marital adjustment

measures. Filsinger and Wilson (1983) found that both individual social anxiety and couple social anxiety were related to marital adjustment; the higher the social anxiety, the lower the adjustment to marriage. Apparently, the characteristics that enable people to feel comfortable in social situations also help people get along in marriage.

Friendships

No family is a self-contained social unit that can exist apart from other people. No matter how well developed the companionship within the family, family members need friends. Children need friends their own age; couples need friends to talk to and to do things with. Life is more interesting and fun when it involves compatible friends. Friends also call on one another for both instrumental and emotional support (Roberto and Scott, 1986). One study of the chief sources of life satisfaction revealed that friends ranked third in importance, after spouse and parents (Argyle and Furnham, 1983). Studies of dimensions of psychological health have revealed that achieving mutual friendship is one of the most important components of mental health.

Making friends is not always easy, especially if the couple move to a city where neither spouse knows anyone. Industrialization and urbanization have resulted in an anonymous environment such that people can live alongside one another for months without ever really getting acquainted (Allan, 1985). Some people are not likely to take the social risks necessary to form more friendships even when they would like to (Duck, 1991).

The challenge is to overcome the anonymity of city life by developing friendship networks—if not with one's neighbors, then with people whom one meets through work, through other people, through one's children, through social organizations, or through activities. One study of 92 graduate students who moved either to New York City or to upstate rural areas revealed that 2 months after their arrival students who had moved to small towns had, on average, twice as many friends as those who had moved to New York City. Seven months later, however, the numbers were about the same. The newcomers in both environments got together with most of their friends at least once a week (Horn, 1981). In the beginning, the urban students reported higher levels of fear, distrust, and uncertainty in meeting strangers. As they became acquainted, however, the city people were more likely to invite friends home. One city student explained, "You need close relationships because of the cold nature of the city" (Horn, 1981, p. 100).

In a study of social networks of both Black and White rural families, the Black mothers reported significantly fewer support networks than White mothers (Gaudin and Davis, 1985). In comparison to the Black mothers, the White mothers reported over twice as many neighbors they could call on. The primary social network of the Black mothers consisted of their relatives. In general, the Black families had more relatives living close by.

Field (1999) studied older adults to try to understand how friendships change in old age. Participants were interviewed twice, once as young-old adults ages 60–74 and again when they were at least 75. The study found that acquaintances and casual friends became less and less important in old age but that close friends and relatives remained very important. Casual friends were no longer as useful, and so contact with them decreased. However, there were gender differences in older-generational friendships. Women were more involved in friendships than were men, while men had less desire to make new friends and had less intimate contact with friends. These gender differences were less pronounced at the young-old stage and more pronounced at the older stage (Field, 1999).

Gender Differences

There is a difference between friendships based primarily on emotional sharing and those based on engaging in common activities. Though all close friendships have both elements, female friendships are characterized more by emotional sharing and male friendships more by engaging in common activities. The following examples illustrate the differences:

> Sally and Susan were good friends. They would tell one another all about their boyfriends, how they felt about them and details of their relationships. Whenever they had problems, they called one another to discuss the situation. They asked one another's advice and gave consolation and moral support.

> Chuck and Hank were good friends. They played racquetball together, worked on their old cars in one another's garages, attended movies, went to bars together, and always called one another to plan something to do or when they needed a ride. (Student comments)

In these examples, the women shared feelings and intimacies; the men shared interests and activities. Men seldom talk about personal, intimate things with their friends. Wright (1982) observed that females have "face-to-face" friendships, while male friendships are "side-by-side." When men do talk about intimate things, it is usually with women, since men feel less anxiety and less competition with women than with other males. Many men still have the notion that revealing emotions is unmanly. Women are more at ease than men with emotional intimacy in friendships.

Friendships tend to change when people go from being single to being part of a couple. Although newlyweds often claim that nothing has changed with regard to their friendships since their marriage, researchers have noted considerable changes. For example, Hause (1995) found that, on average, contacts with friends decreased by about 50% after marriage. Males, especially, tended to lose their single friends as the new couple turned more and more to mutual friends, who tended to be couples as well.

Same-Sex and Opposite-Sex Friendships

One study revealed that for married people same-sex friendships are more satisfactory than opposite-sex friendships. For women, same-sex friends may be able to share more interests, to do things together, and to give emotional support. However, another study revealed that men generally express more satisfaction with their opposite-sex friendships, whereas women are likely to be equally satisfied with their same-sex and opposite-sex friendships (Elkins and Peterson, 1993).

One spouse may become jealous of the other's opposite-sex friends. Certainly, most spouses will not tolerate opposite-sex friendships that include sexual intimacy. Suspicion of extramarital emotional or physical involvement is one of the most frequent problems presented to marriage coun-

Same-sex friends typically share interests, do things together, and give emotional support to each other. Why are the same behaviors sometimes problematic in friendships between people of the opposite sex?

selors. The spouse may insist that the other person is "just a friend." In some cases, this is true; but other times, the spouse is lying, and there has been an involvement that goes beyond friendship. Spouses can usually tell when there is romantic interest that goes beyond friendship. One woman remarked:

> My husband has a good friend, Pauline, whom he met at work. He says they are just friends, but he really sparkles when he talks about her. I've seen the way they look at one another when they are together. I don't think he's slept with her, but he certainly is attracted to her. He has lunch with her several times a week, by themselves, and I'm getting very upset by it. (Author's counseling notes)

In this case, the man had slept with Pauline, and the wife had cause for concern.

In other situations, an opposite-sex relationship is platonic or strictly a business relationship and certainly is no threat to the marriage; but the other spouse is almost pathologically jealous and accuses his or her mate of affairs with every acquaintance of the other sex. Such jealousy is very destructive and usually arises from deep-seated insecurities and anxieties that require therapeutic intervention. One man said, "My wife accuses me of being attracted to every woman I see. If I even talk to a woman, whether at work or in the neighborhood, she gets very angry and upset and accuses me unjustly" (author's counseling notes).

Fifty percent of the people in the world are of the other sex, and some of them will be friends—at work, in the neighborhood, and in community organizations. People can do several things to prevent opposite-sex relationships from causing difficulty in their marriage:

1. Keep business relationships on a professional basis.
2. Make a point of introducing friends to your partner.
3. Let your partner know of occasions when you have seen or met with the other person, whether at a business lunch or on a social occasion.
4. Never try to hide anything from your partner, and don't have anything to hide.
5. Avoid one-on-one dates for social purposes.
6. Prefer groups of mixed company rather than dyadic encounters.
7. Recognize that many affairs develop without people intending things to happen, simply because people place themselves in compromising situations.
8. Make certain that other people whom you meet know your monogamous attitude.

9. As a couple, develop your social life with other couples whom you both enjoy.

10. If you're having marital difficulties, get help from a professional. Many extramarital affairs develop because of a series of unresolved problems in the marriage, making the partners vulnerable to outside encounters and relationships.

Since successful marriage involves sexual exclusiveness and commitment to one person only, these steps may prove useful. To ignore them and allow friendships to go beyond the just-friends stage is to court problems.

SUMMARY

1. The primary motive for marriage in our culture is love and companionship. Partners who share interests, do things together, and share some of the same friends and social groups derive more satisfaction from their relationship than do partners who are not mutually involved.

2. Three different styles of companionship characterize relationships: joint companionship, parallel companionship, and segregated companionship. There are advantages and disadvantages to each of these companionship styles.

3. People differ in their need for closeness, which is not the same as possessiveness.

4. Sometimes companionship doesn't develop in a marriage. There are various reasons: One or both spouses spend most of their time on the job, spend most of their leisure time with separate friends, pursue individual hobbies or leisure time activities, spend most of their free time out of the house attending paid amusements, spend their free time with their children rather than with each other, vegetate in front of the TV, or simply don't enjoy being together.

5. Loneliness is not simply being alone; it is the distressing feeling that there is a discrepancy between the kind of social relations we want and those we have. Loneliness can be due to either social isolation or emotional isolation. Social isolation is situational; emotional isolation is relational.

6. There are five major reasons for being lonely: lack of attachment, alienation, being alone, forced isolation, and dislocation. Loneliness may also result from negative personality attributes.

7. Married people need to maintain some privacy and to do things on their own. They also need time together as a couple and to be with their children.

8. Recreation is a necessary part of a balanced life. It is important to achieve a healthy balance between physical and nonphysical activities.

9. According to a national survey, the five most popular sporting activities are walking, swimming, bicycling, exercising, and camping.

10. Vacations can help build companionship if family members get along when they're together and if they can enjoy similar types of experiences. However, some family members fight because they aren't used to being together so much, and unresolved problems flare up while they are on vacation.

11. One of the most common family pastimes is watching television. There are some negative effects of excessive TV watching, the most important being less communication and interaction among family members.

12. Computers have had a profound effect on our lives. Through the Internet, the whole world is now at our fingertips. But excessive use of computers may interfere with social relationships with friends and family. Because many parents do not understand computers, a technology gap is developing between children and parents.

13. Having friends is one of the chief sources of life satisfaction and is important to psychological and social well-being. Making friends is not easy, especially if couples move to a city where they do not know anyone. The challenge is to overcome the anonymity of city life by developing friendship networks.

14. There are some differences between the friendships men develop and those women develop. Female friendships are characterized by emotional sharing, and male friendships by shared interests and activities.

15. There is the possibility of spousal jealousy over opposite-sex friendships. Certainly, most spouses will not tolerate extramarital sexual intimacy.

KEY TERMS

joint companionship   parallel companionship   segregated companionship

QUESTIONS FOR THOUGHT

1. According to research, companionship is one of the most important motives for marriage, but there are individual differences in the type of companionship and the degree of closeness desired. How important is companionship in marriage to you? What type of companionship do you want, and for what occasions? What degree of closeness do you desire, and how should it be expressed?

2. What sort of leisure time and recreational activities would you like to share with a mate? Would you marry someone whose leisure time preferences were different from yours? Explain. If you discovered after marriage that your leisure time preferences were different, what would you do?

3. How would you feel about your spouse having opposite-sex friends after you were married? Would you encourage him or her to see that person without you along? Explain your views and the reasons for them.

4. If your spouse objected to your wanting to spend a lot of time with your single friends whom you had known for years, what would you do? What would you do if you and your spouse could not agree on your choices of couples for friends?

SUGGESTED READINGS

Blieszner, R., and Adams, R. G. (1992). *Adult Friendship.* Newbury Park, CA: Sage. Examines close friendships over the life cycle.

Bryant, J. (Ed.). (1990). *Television and the American Family.* Hillsdale, NJ: Lawrence Erlbaum. Discusses the use of television, the portrayal of families on TV, the effects of TV on families, ways to mediate these effects, and some public policy issues.

Nardi, P. M. (1999). *Gay Men's Friendships: Invisible Communities.* Chicago: University of Chicago Press. Discusses gay political organizations and the bonds between gay men.

Oliker, S. J. (1989). *Best Friends and Marriage: Exchange Among Women.* Berkeley: University of California Press. Presents interviews with women on close friendships.

Price, J. (1999). *Navigating Differences: Friendships Between Gay and Straight Men.* New York: Haworth. Explores how different sexual orientations impact the way men maintain friendships, cope with sexual struggles, and open communication channels.

Rawlins, W. K. (1992). *Friendship Matters: Communications, Dialectics, and the Life Course.* New York: Aldine de Gruyter. Focuses on theory and research on personal relationships.

LEARNING OBJECTIVES

After reading the chapter, you should be able to:

Define power and family power.

Outline the different units of family power.

Explain why people want power as it pertains to self-actualization, social expectations, family-of-origin influences, and psychological needs.

Describe the sources of power in families.

Describe the four types of marital power patterns: egalitarian, male-dominant, female-dominant, and anarchic.

Describe power tactics—that is, the ways power is applied.

Discuss the consequences of power struggles for individuals and for marital satisfaction, and explain why equity is needed.

Define communication, both verbal and non-verbal, and tell why it is important in marriage.

Identify the major barriers to communication: physical and environmental, situational, cultural, gender-based, and psychological.

Describe the requirements for improving communication skills: motivation, concern, self-disclosure, clarity, feedback and reciprocity, and arguing constructively.

Power, Decision Making, and Communication

Learning Objectives

The Meaning of Power

Why People Want Power
Self-Actualization
Social Expectations
Family-of-Origin Influences
Psychological Need

Sources of Power
Cultural Norms
Gender Norms
Economic Resources
Education and Knowledge
Personality Differences
Communication Ability
Emotional Factors
Physical Stature and Strength
Life Circumstances
Children

Marital Power Patterns

Power Processes
Power Tactics That Help
Power Tactics That Can Help or Harm
Power Tactics That Harm

Consequences of Power Struggles
Perspective: Power Neutralization Strategies

Communication
Family Issues: Women's Empowerment
Verbal and Nonverbal Communication
Barriers to Communication

Improving Communication Skills
Motivation and Concern
Self-Disclosure
Perspective: I-Statements in Family Communication
Clarity
Feedback and Reciprocity
Arguing Constructively

Summary
Key Terms
Questions for Thought
Suggested Readings

The marital ideology among educated, middle-class people in the United States emphasizes an egalitarian exercise of family power. That is, partners are equal and should share everything 50–50. But exactly what does this mean in relation to making decisions, influencing each other, and governing the family? In fact, this ideology isn't often worked out in practice. Some people want more power and control than others. Even when partners are equals, they usually don't share all decisions and control.

We are concerned here with patterns of power and with what gives some people power over others. We are concerned as well with the applications of power, the processes of power, and the ways power is applied in intimate relationships. And we are concerned with the outcomes of power: the effects of various power patterns on individuals and on marital satisfaction.

One of the most important requirements for a satisfying relationship is the ability to communicate. We aren't born with this ability; rather communication is a fine art that must be learned. Thus, in this chapter, we are also concerned with improving communication skills.

THE MEANING OF POWER

In perhaps the most popular conceptualization among social scientists, **power** in intimate relationships is defined as the ability to influence one's partner to get what one wants (Beckman, Harvey, Satre, and Walker, 1999). Power may be exercised in social groups and organizations and in all kinds of interpersonal relationships. We are concerned here only with family power. The power exerted by various family members is partly derived from social power—that which society exerts or delegates. Power within the family can be marital power, parental power, offspring power, sibling power, or kinship power. There can also be combinations of power units, such as father-son, mother-daughter, or mother-son (Feldman, Wentzel, and Gehring, 1989). We are especially interested in marital power—the power relationship in the marital dyad—and to a lesser extent in power exercised by children over parents.

WHY PEOPLE WANT POWER

Some people always seem to need to be in control, whereas others always seem to avoid taking charge. What causes these differences in people's desire for power?

Self-Actualization

Most people want to feel that they have some control over their own life, that they have the power to change, influence, or direct what happens to them personally. People who are unwilling or unable to use power condemn themselves to a life of frustration. They never get to do what they really want to do, to realize their own desires, or to carry out their own plans. Indeed, hundreds of seminars and classes are conducted yearly to teach people how to become more assertive or empowered.

The person who asserts him- or herself eventually will lock horns with someone else who has other ideas, and a power struggle may ensue to see whose wishes are carried out. Even people who are not ordinarily combative find that they sometimes have to exert power over other people to be able to fulfill themselves. Without some personal power, it's difficult to survive as an independent individual. Even toddlers need to learn how to say no and how to influence parents if they are to grow up to be autonomous adults.

Social Expectations

Often people exert power because that is what they feel they are supposed to do, and they want to avoid criticism for not fulfilling expectations. Each society has its own institutionalized norms that prescribe spouses domains of authority. This kind of power is referred to as **legitimate power,** or power bestowed by society on men and women as their right according to social prescription. What society prescribes may not always be fair, but it still may exert considerable influence on the behavior of individuals.

Family-of-Origin Influences

Patterns of power can often be traced to experiences in one's family of origin. Children tend to model their behavior after their parents'. For example, a son growing up under the influence of a dominant father may adopt the same pattern of behavior and have difficulty establishing a more democratic relationship with his spouse. Galvin and Brommel (1986) quoted one man:

> My German father and my Irish mother both exercised power over us in different ways. My father used to beat us whenever we got out of line, and that power move was very obvious. On the other hand, my mother never touched us, but she probably exercised greater power through her use of silence. Whenever we did something she did not approve of, she just stopped talking to us—it was as if we did not exist. Most of the time the silent treatment lasted for a few hours, but sometimes it would last for a few days. My brother used to say it was so quiet that "you could hear a mouse pee on a cotton ball." I hated the silence worse than the beatings. (p. 135)

The family of origin serves as the first power base from which the child learns to function. Methods used there are often repeated in the child's adult life. Certain types of power applications, such as physical violence and abuse, may be passed from generation to generation. Even techniques of control, such as silence, are learned behavior.

Psychological Need

Sometimes the need for power and the way it is expressed go far beyond ordinary limits. People who have deep-seated feelings of insecurity and inferiority may try to hide them or to compensate for them by becoming autocratic and dictatorial. They can't let their partner win an argument or get her or his way, for fear of feeling weak and ineffective. Their facade of power depends upon not letting any cracks develop in their armor.

Three theoretical frameworks are often used to explain the need for power: attachment theory, social control theory, and feminist theory (Ehrensaft, Langhinrichsen-Rohling, Heyman, O'Leary, and Lawrence, 1999). According to attachment theory, aggression against an attachment figure, at any age, is a control strategy for regaining either emotional or physical closeness to a person when the bond with that person is perceived to be endangered. Individuals who are insecurely attached to their primary attachment figure are more likely to perceive subjective threats to the bond with that person than

are individuals who are securely attached (Bowlby, 1977; Hazan and Shaver, 1987). This could explain why some partners are intensely jealous of their partner's interactions with others and try to limit and control those interactions.

According to social control theory, using power (or violence) as a response to an upsetting behavior by others serves three functions: (1) a means to manage conflict in a relationship, (2) an expression of grievances, and (3) a form of social control. Consistent with this theory, most marital assaults occur in the context of a disagreement (O'Leary et al., 1989). Social control theory can help explain why male batterers sometimes suggest that their partner deserved to be beaten for perceived offenses such as attempts at autonomy, failure to perform household chores, or disrespectful behavior (Ehrensaft et al., 1999).

According to feminist theory, the patriarchal hierarchy in families allows the use of male-female violence as a way of maintaining male power within the marriage. Consistent with this theory, rates of spouse abuse are lower in societies in which women have economic power within the marriage than in those in which women have little or no economic power (Levinson, 1988). Family violence is also lower in families in which men expect to share power with their spouse (O'Kelly and Carney, 1986).

SOURCES OF POWER

Various efforts have been made to sort out the origins of power (Sexton and Perlman, 1989). What gives husbands and wives power in the marital relationship? Various sources have been identified, including cultural norms, gender norms, economic resources, education and knowledge, personality differences, communication ability, emotional factors, physical stature and strength, and life circumstances. We will examine each of these bases of power as they relate to marriage partners. We will also briefly look at ways children may exercise power over their parents.

Cultural Norms

The power structure of families varies among different social classes and ethnic groups. Most studies indicate that men in lower socioeconomic status families try to be more dominant and authoritarian than do their middle-class counterparts. They are often concerned about their masculine image and so demand deference as men and rely on tradition to support their patriarchal authority. They often use physical force and coercion in maintaining control. In actual practice, however, although higher status men espouse an egalitarian philosophy, they also control more resources, have greater prestige, and are voluntarily given more deference and control than are lower status men. Thus, they tend to exercise more power than the men in blue-collar families.

Traditionally, the African American family has been considered matriarchal, with women dominant. But recent research tends to contradict this view. African American marriages tend to be more egalitarian than White marriages, with middle-class Black families more egalitarian than middle-class White families. However, African American marriages cannot be stereotyped any more than White marriages can. African American couples show variations in power structure within each socioeconomic level, just as White couples do.

Puerto Rican and Mexican American families have traditionally been considered patriarchal. The Mexican American male was expected to prove his "machismo" (manhood) by being dominant over his spouse and children (see Chapter 3). Mexican American families do emphasize male dominance, but the most prevalent pattern is one in which the partners share in decision making as equals. Thus, the concept of Mexican American patriarchy lacks validity.

An intensive study of decision making in Puerto Rican families in the New York City area also contradicted the male-dominant image of Latino families (Cooney, Rogler, Hurrell, and Ortiz, 1982). A substantial majority of spouses shared decisions regarding their place of residence, insurance, vacation plans, and home improvements. Roughly one-third also shared decisions regarding the man's job or the woman's employment.

Gender Norms

Power relationships are also influenced by stereotyped gender norms (Enns, 1988). Gender-role socialization that emphasizes women's passivity, submissiveness, and dependence reinforces patriarchal power structures and reduces women's authority.

Traditional gender norms often specified a rigid division of responsibility. The man made financial decisions, while the woman cared for the children; the man did heavy outdoor chores, while the woman did maintenance inside the house. As more egalitarian gender norms develop and as interest spheres and power domains overlap, more family issues become subject to negotiation and compromise.

Smith and Beaujot (1999) examined three groups of men (traditional, intermediate, and liberal) and asked them open-ended questions about the woman's place in the family and whether women prefer to stay at home or be in the workforce. The traditional respondents unanimously thought that women prefer to stay at home cooking, cleaning, and caring for the children and that men should be in the workforce and should discipline the children. All of the traditional men believed that, if a sacrifice was needed in the family, the woman's career should go first because it was secondary to her job as wife and mother. The intermediate group was split on the issue of whether women prefer to stay at home or that go to work. This group still held many of the beliefs of the traditional group, including the idea that women are more nurturing and should therefore be more responsible for the children and that men should be more responsible for the finances. Most of the liberal respondents believed that women were split between the idea of staying at home and that of working outside the home. These men believed that household work, marital power, and important decisions should be shared.

In general, in male-dominated societies, more men than women possess power in the form of resources, social status, respect, positive self-regard, and physical authority (Pratto, 1996). Researchers have found females to be less likely to have access to valued resources across the life span. Girls are even less likely than boys to gain access to scarce resources in a play situation in the absence of adults (Powlishta and Maccoby, 1990). This gender gap is carried over to the intimate relationships between men and women (Galliher, Rostosky, Welsh, and Kawaguchi, 1999).

Economic Resources

According to resource theory, those who control valued resources needed by other family members hold power over them (deTurck and Miller, 1986).

Money and property are two valued economic resources. Some men who are the primary breadwinner feel have a right to dictate family decisions. One man remarked, "It's my money, I earned it; therefore, I have the right to spend it as I please" (author's counseling notes).

Women who have no source of income of their own may not have equal power in their marriage if it is not relegated by their spouse and if they don't demand it (Klagsbrun, 1985). When the woman is gainfully employed, she usually gains more power in decision making in the family.

Tichenor (1999) examined the power differences between traditional families, in which the man made more money than the woman, and status-reversal families, in which the woman earned significantly more than the man. Status-reversal women did receive more help around the house, yet they still were responsible for a larger part of domestic labor than the men in traditional families. In fact, no man in either group who was employed full-time did over half of the domestic labor. One sentiment common to most of the status-reversal women was that they were not doing enough. Although these women earned the bulk of the money—and sometimes all of the money—they constantly felt that they were not helping out enough around the home. Many of these women spoke with awe of the great job that their partner was doing in raising the children and getting work done around the house. In contrast, none of the men in traditional families spoke this way about their spouse. These findings suggest that power in families has more to do with gender than money. The status-reversal women often tried to downplay the amount of money they earned and emphasized that all money was shared. None of these women claimed that because they made more money they deserved more power, as is often the case in traditional families.

Education and Knowledge

In a society in which education is valued, a person who has superior education has an important source of power. This type of power is referred to as **expert power,** whereby a person is acknowledged as generally superior in intelligence. The influence of education on power depends partly on the cultural context and partly on the relative difference between the man and the woman.

The greater the woman's education and earnings, the more likely she is to share decision-making power with her partner.

Knowledge is also a source of power. One man commented, "My wife decorates the house. She knows much more about these things than I do" (author's counseling notes). This type of power is referred to as **informational power** because it involves superior knowledge of a specific area.

According to the **theory of primary interest and presumed competence,** the person who is most interested in and involved with a particular choice and who is most qualified to make a specific decision will be more likely to do so. Often, these two aspects, interest and competence, go together. For example, if the woman will be using the kitchen utensils more than her partner, is more interested in which ones to buy, and has had more experience in the use of different utensils, presumably she will be the one who will exert the most influence on buying utensils. If the man does most of the barbecuing, presumably he will take more interest in and exert more influence on choosing what barbecue equipment to buy.

Personality Differences

Personality characteristics also influence power. A considerable age difference between spouses affects power, with the older spouse exerting power over the younger one. Regardless of age, some people seem to be more domineering and forceful than others, exerting considerable influence on all with whom they come in contact.

The degree of power depends partly on how motivated people are to gain strength and control. Some people strive for power to overcome inner feelings of weakness and insecurity. The converse also occurs: Those with the greatest relational power also report higher levels of self-esteem (de-Turck and Miller, 1986). The two seem to go together. Then, too, charming people with a great deal of charisma may be natural leaders whom others follow readily.

Communication Ability

Some people are better talkers than others. They have superior verbal skills and are able to explain their ideas clearly and to convince others through the power of their words. Males seem to take more active control over conversation than do females. Some men, however, are relatively nonverbal, sometimes because they have been brought up in a home in which problems were never discussed. Some people do all the talking and complain that their partner doesn't talk to them.

Emotional Factors

Partners have an important source of psychological power: the ability to bestow or withhold affection. Some spouses use sex as a weapon, withholding it if their partner does not do what they want. For example, one woman would delay going to bed until her partner had fallen asleep in order to send the message that she was not interested in sexual intimacy with him until he became less distant with her.

Of course, love or sex must be valued before it can become a power source. When love dies, so does its power. According to social exchange theory, those with the greatest love and emotional need have the least power. Because they are so dependent, they have the most to lose if the relationship ends. They are so afraid of losing love that they often do everything possible to please their partner (Warner, Lee, and Lee, 1986).

Physical Stature and Strength

Coercive power is based on the belief that one spouse can punish the other for noncompliance. One type of coercion is the threat of physical punishment. One woman commented:

> My husband is a big man, and very strong. When he gets mad I never know what he's going to do. I'm afraid he'll hurt me. He once threw me down the front steps, just because I didn't have his lunch ready. (Author's counseling notes)

This woman realized what her spouse could do to her if he decided to strike her. The physical beating of a partner is used by some men as a means of punishment or control. On rare occasions, women use physical violence against their mate as a means of getting their own way.

Life Circumstances

The more limited their alternatives, the less power people have in relationships. If a man feels that his partner can't leave because she has no one to turn to, no place to go, and no money to support herself, he has more power in the relationship than he would otherwise. The stage in the family life cycle is an important consideration. Women who have the most dependent children or who are the most dependent economically and socially have less power over their situation than do women who are not yet parents or whose children are grown.

Circumstances may change power balances, or a crisis may result in a realignment of power in a relationship. Physical incapacitation or illness of one spouse may force an otherwise submissive partner to take a more dominant role. Egalitarian couples, because they are more fluid and flexible, are able to shift and exchange roles in order to meet the demands of a stressful situation.

Children

Children themselves have sources of power. That is, children exert considerable influence over their parents and other family members. Even the cry of a baby has considerable influence. An older child

Coercive power is based on the belief that one spouse can punish the other for noncompliance.
An economically dependent spouse is more likely to stay in a severely abusive situation.

can render parents powerless if he or she can get them to disagree. For this reason, therapist Jay Haley (1982) emphasized the need for parents to discuss issues with each other and to present a united front to avoid confusion.

MARITAL POWER PATTERNS

Marital power patterns can be divided into four types: egalitarian, male-dominant, female-dominant, and anarchic. In an egalitarian power pattern, power is distributed equally between the partners. In a male-dominant pattern, the man has more power than the woman; in a female-dominant pattern, the pattern is reversed. In an anarchic power pattern, both partners have power and seek to exercise it in a random manner, disregarding all rules in governing the total family. Male-dominant couples are congruent with a traditional norm, while egalitarian couples are congruent with a more modern norm of balanced power between the spouses.

Most research on family power focuses on the distribution of power between spouses and examines the association between power distribution and marital adjustment. Studies of the relationship between power and marriage satisfaction have consistently shown two results: (1) Shared power (an egalitarian power pattern) is associated with the highest level of reported marital satisfaction, and (2) female-dominant couples are, on the whole, less satisfied than egalitarian or male-dominant couples. Egalitarian couples have a higher level of agreement on the desired distribution of power than couples with hierarchical relationships. Violence occurs least often in marriages in which power is shared.

High rates of dissatisfaction have been found in female-dominant relationships. Most spouses in such relationships view dominance by the woman as undesirable. Some argue the level of satisfaction in such marriages is low because the man cannot adequately exercise power, leaving the woman to assume more authority than desired by either spouse and causing dissatisfaction in both. The woman in a female-dominant marriage may be especially demanding because of a wish to force her spouse to take on a leadership role. When she confronts his unwillingness and resistance, she may use more control tactics than both a couple in which partners share power and a dominant man with role expectations and tradition on his side. The high-power woman may more frequently resort to demanding, negative communication, which may lead to marital dissatisfaction. Interestingly, therapy appears to be more successful for female-dominated couples than for couples with other power patterns (Gray-Little, Baucom, and Hamby, 1996).

An association between negative behaviors—such as complaints, hostile comments, and whining—and low marital satisfaction is one of the best established findings in the literature on marital interaction. There is also a greater incidence of minor violence in both male- and female-dominant marriages than in egalitarian ones. And unhappy partners are more likely to disagree with each other about who has responsibility for what decisions.

Any kind of functional authority pattern may be better than none. Couples with little agreement will have different points of view, resulting in interactions that are anarchic. Anarchic couples exhibit more negative behavior than either male- or female-dominant couples. The lack of decision-making structure is detrimental to marital functioning. Partners who share power can reach mutually acceptable decisions based on compromise. When an anarchic couple is faced with a decision, however, there is neither an expressed norm nor an implicit understanding of who will exercise control. Each spouse contests the other's authority. As a result, the anarchic couple is caught up in a struggle in which each partner tries to control the other while resisting the other's influence.

Spouses who are able to negotiate compromises or who are willing to make accommodations to their partner's position seem to have higher levels of marital adjustment than spouses who are habitually confrontational (Gray-Little, Baucom, and Hamby, 1996).

POWER PROCESSES

We have discussed power bases, that is, the sources of power and power patterns. **Power processes** are the ways power is applied. A distinction needs to be made between orchestration power and implementation power. **Orchestration power** is the power to make the important decisions that determine family life-styles and the major characteristics and features of the family. **Implementation power** sets these decisions in motion. For example, one spouse may decide how much money can be spent on a new appliance, but the other spouse is the one who actually makes the purchase. Conflicts arise when the implementing spouse tries to modify the guidelines and boundaries established by the orchestrating spouse.

Power Tactics That Help

Power tactics are the means that people use to get others to do what they want them to do. Some tactics help build better relationships.

Discussing, Explaining, Asking, or Telling   Discussing, explaining, asking, and telling are positive methods of power implementation. Partners who can explain things in a rational, intelligent way, or who ask questions directly and clearly, are using a gentle, or "soft," form of power that is effective. It also builds positive feelings of satisfaction in the relationship (Kipnis, 1984).

Bargaining and Negotiating   Bargaining is the process by which two parties decide what each will give and receive in arriving at a decision. The process involves quid pro quo, which means "something for something." The purpose of bargaining is to reach an agreement or compromise solution to a problem. Bargaining is a process of position modification and convergence.

Power Tactics That Can Help or Harm

Some power tactics are helpful under some circumstances but harmful in others.

Persuading   Persuasion is stronger than discussion. Its purpose is to try to convince the other person to believe or do something that he or she is reluctant to. Sometimes, the person is genuinely convinced and accepts willingly; at other times, the person acquiesces, but against his or her inclinations. Consider this example:

> Bill wanted to go to Hawaii on his vacation. Sally was reluctant because she did not want to go so far away. Bill got all the brochures and for months talked to his

wife about how wonderful it would be to go to Hawaii. He finally convinced her that Hawaii was *the* place to go. Sally went to Hawaii, but resented Bill for not considering her feelings. (Author's counseling notes)

Being Nice   Being exceptionally attentive and considerate when one wants something may put people in a good mood and make them feel so grateful that they can't refuse a request. Some spouses are better at "buttering up" their partner than others. Sincere flattery and consideration are appreciated. But false efforts to win favors are deceitful and create distrust.

Power Tactics That Harm

When power tactics are used to maintain or increase the imbalance of power in a relationship, they are destructive.

Acting Helpless or Dependent   Some people try to exert control by acting helpless or dependent. If they present themselves as powerless or unable to do something, they may evoke the sympathy of the other person, who is glad to show off his or her expertise. Some spouses play the weak, helpless role to evade responsibility, as this example shows:

> Don hates yard work, house repairs, painting, and every kind of physical chore in and outside the house. Several times, his wife asked him to do something. He was all thumbs, completely inept, and did such a terrible job that his wife took over and did it herself. Don explained, "If she knows I'll do a terrible job, she doesn't ask me." (Author's counseling notes)

But this role has its downside. For instance, some women have no respect for a man who is not capable in many areas, especially in doing traditional men's chores.

Some men are flattered by "coming to the rescue" of dependent females. For this reason, some women have been brought up to pretend to be helpless. Other women find such tactics demeaning to themselves and to all women.

Overprotecting   The overprotective man or woman does not allow his or her spouse to mature or become independent, thus rendering the spouse powerless. An example is the woman who plays mother hen to her spouse, treating him like a helpless child so she can "rule the roost."

Deceiving, Lying, or Outwitting   Some people seek to control others by deceiving them, lying to them, or outwitting them. They make promises they don't intend to keep in exchange for concessions. They pretend to be what they are not. They become habitual liars to try to avoid responsibilities. For example, "Harry told Sylvia that he didn't want to discontinue their affair and that he would divorce his wife and marry her. Five years have passed, and he has never filed divorce papers" (author's counseling notes).

Criticizing   One of the most personally destructive ways of gaining power is the constant use of criticism to undermine and demean the other person. Some spouses wait until other family members or company are present and then point out the wrongdoings and failures of their spouse. It's difficult for the criticized spouse to defend him- or herself without creating an embarrassing scene. One woman complained, "According to my husband, I never do anything right. It doesn't matter how hard I try, or what I do, he finds fault. He's beaten me down so I don't have any self-respect or self-confidence at all anymore" (author's counseling notes). Comparing one person with another—with a friend or a sibling, for example—is another way of making someone feel inept and inadequate.

Scapegoating   Scapegoating is a way of blaming someone else for every bad thing that happens. The goal is to make the other person feel responsible and guilty so that the controller doesn't have to accept the blame. For example, "Mary is married to an insensitive, cruel husband. When she decides to leave, he blames her for separating him from his infant daughter. He insists it's all her fault that she is leaving" (author's counseling notes).

Gaslighting   The term **gaslighting** comes from the movie *Gaslight,* in which the husband attempts to drive his wife insane by turning down the gaslights and then telling her she's imagining things when she says they are growing dimmer. In gaslighting, one partner denies the truth of what the other is saying, sarcastically criticizes the other for his or her feelings or opinions, or turns things around to make the other partner feel guilty for having any doubts. Consider this example:

A husband is having an affair that the wife suspects. He stays away all night Friday and has become very indifferent toward his wife. When she questions him, he accuses her of imagining things and claims that the only thing wrong with their marriage is that she doesn't trust him. He tells his wife that she is too jealous, too suspicious, and tries to possess him and run his life, and that if she gives him more freedom maybe things would work out. He insists she's imagining things and that the affair is all in her mind. (Author's counseling notes)

Punishing Some spouses use a variety of punishments to influence the behavior of the other. For example, using the silent treatment can be very punishing. Some couples live in silence for days as tension continues. Silence, however, prevents reconciliation and perpetuates misunderstandings (Galvin and Brommel, 1986).

Blackmailing Threatening blackmail is a coercive tactic that creates fear and anger, as this example suggests:

Bill's parents hated alcoholic beverages and told him and their other children that if they ever drank they would disown them. Bill wanted to divorce his wife Shirley, but she threatened to tell his parents about his drinking if he ever left her. (Author's counseling notes)

Expressing Anger Emotionally unstable people may become violent, throw temper tantrums, punch out walls, break furniture, or use other power tactics to try to get their own way. For example, 'When Dick found out that his wife wanted to divorce him, he started throwing furniture around the house. "If you leave me, there won't be anything left of this house. You'll get nothing," he threatened' (author's counseling notes).

Acting Cruel or Abusive The most extreme form of control is cruel and abusive treatment. The man who beats up his spouse terrorizes her so that he can maintain control over her. It takes a strong woman to separate herself from such treatment, especially if her partner tries to make her believe that it is all her fault and that she deserves it. Sometimes it is the woman who is cruel and abusive to her spouse.

CONSEQUENCES OF POWER STRUGGLES

One of the most important considerations in evaluating patterns of power in the family is the effect that different patterns have on individuals and their relationships. Some people strive to gain control, but at what cost? If they gain the upper hand at the cost of alienating their partner, provoking anger and hostility, or destroying their relationship, what's the point? Some spouses are so intent on winning the battle that they lose the marriage.

Generally, extreme imbalances of power between two people tend to have a negative effect. Lack of power is associated with psychological distress for both men and women. At the other extreme, high levels of power can also be destructive, because power can corrupt. This means that power produces strong psychological changes in power holders, and they start to exploit those they control. They can become self-centered and selfish, as well as unfeeling and abusive. The person dominated becomes an "it" to use rather than a person to cherish.

One of the consequences of power imbalances in relationships is that the person who feels coerced or manipulated and who often gives in becomes frustrated and resentful. A person may accept coercion for a while, but as frustrations and hostility increase, the relationship worsens. Couples who habitually deal with decisions on a win-or-lose basis often discover that a "victory" in a marital conflict is illusory. The victory turns into a loss for both partners when feelings of anger and hurt develop between them.

Marital satisfaction is maximized when couples achieve a balance of power that is acceptable to both partners. This balance varies with different couples (Henggeler, Edwards, Hanson, and Okwumabua, 1988; Whisman and Jacobson, 1990). Although dominance by one partner works for some couples, an extreme imbalance of power usually causes dissatisfaction.

Social science research emphasizes that equitable relations tend to be more stable and satisfying. In a study of Puerto Rican families, marital satisfaction of the women was closely associated with egalitarian gender roles (Rogler and Procidano, 1989a). Women who feel they have power to control the outcome of marital conflicts are more satis-

Power Neutralization Strategies

People can use various strategies to neutralize the power of another person. Many of these strategies, however, achieve only temporary solutions.

1. **Refuse to do it.** Listen; don't argue or disagree, but don't take any action.

2. **Change the subject, refuse to listen, or show no interest.** One woman complained that every time she'd bring up her partner's drinking he'd start to do something else or walk away. Of course, couples never really solve anything using these tactics.

3. **Become emotionally detached from the situation.** If a spouse threatens to leave, the other spouse's attitude will be, "Go ahead, there's the door." The threat is neutralized, but the problem remains.

4. **Obtain the needed services elsewhere.** For example, if a partner refuses to paint the kitchen, hire someone else to do it.

5. **Resign oneself to do without or find a substitute.** If an insensitive partner threatens to withdraw love and affection, the other partner can neutralize his action by saying, "I really don't need your affection. I get all I need from the children." This really doesn't solve the problem except to prevent the partner from using withdrawal of love and affection as a weapon.

6. **Change the balance of power through self-improvement.** One man treated his spouse badly when she was obese and dependent and as long as he felt she was powerless in the relationship. She went on a diet and lost 55 pounds, returned to school, earned her degree, and got a job earning more money than he did. Now, he's very nice to her because he's afraid she's going to leave him.

7. **Beat the other person at his or her own game.** This means responding with coercive tactics or withholding a reward until the other complies. Sometimes this tactic works. It may be the only way of preventing the other person from bullying. At other times, this kind of power struggle will create a standoff, with neither partner willing to give in. Two stubborn people playing this game can wreck a relationship.

fied with their marriages than are women who have little control. If women blame their spouse for the conflict and have little control over the situation, they find their marriage very unsatisfying. Exchange theorists suggest that satisfaction in marriage hinges on the perception of fairness or equity in exchanges, rather than on the existence of a particular power structure.

COMMUNICATION

Sharing control is an important element in marital satisfaction (Honeycutt, 1986). Satisfaction also depends on the extent and nature of the communication between the partners (Allen and Thompson, 1984). Many authorities contend that good communication is the key to intimacy and to family interaction and is the lifeblood of the marital relationship (Stephen, 1985). One couple wrote:

> There is no area of our married life that isn't affected by communication: our bed, our job, our children, our social life, our leisure time, our relationship with relatives and friends. All could become potential areas of discontent and friction when there isn't good communication between us. (Herrigan and Herrigan, 1973, p. 149)

Communication between human beings may be defined as a message one person sends and another receives. It involves both content and process (Boland and Follingstad, 1987). Content is what is communicated; process is the means by which feelings, attitudes, facts, beliefs, and ideas are transmitted between people. Communication is not limited to words but also occurs through listening, silence, glances, facial expressions, gestures, touch, body stance, and all other nonlanguage symbols and cues used to give and transmit meaning. In short, it may include all the messages sent and received and all the means by which people exchange feelings and meanings as they try to understand and influence one another.

One study examined 30 nondistressed couples and 30 distressed couples with respect to differences in communication skills and marital satisfaction. They found that distressed and nondistressed couples had the same communication skills level; however, the partners in the distressed couples used their skills with more negative intentions and

The traditional concept of power is described as a struggle of individuals or groups for control over another person or group. Any increase in power for one of the parties leads to a decrease in power for the other. This usually results in inequality, and in dominance and submission, with the stronger prevailing over the weaker. One of the solutions suggested here is to strive for equity—equality and fairness—so that both parties are satisfied with the result.

Another solution, according to feminist theorists, is to strive for personal power—empowerment—to improve one's capacities and develop one's own abilities (Lips, 1991). This kind of power does not require the submission of others or the domination of them. For this reason, it is beneficial both to the self and to others. Feeling powerful in this sense implies the freedom and ability to direct one's energies outward in creative effort rather than being forced to express it in the struggle to dominate.

To be able to do this, women need to be freed from the burden of inferiority, to recognize that the feminine qualities of sensitivity and understanding—which cause women to be labeled as the weaker sex—are strengths that enable them to relate to others and to solve important problems in relationships and society. Being concerned and sensitive resolves far more personal issues than does acquiring enough power to coerce others in order to get one's own way.

---

ill will. In other words, it is not always a lack of communication skills that makes a marriage go awry. Rather, it can be the intentions of a partner that cause a marriage to be distressed (Burleson and Denton, 1997).

Verbal and Nonverbal Communication

Nonverbal communication comes in many forms. **Body language** involves physical reactions such as posture, facial expression, still or tense muscles, blushing, movement, panting, tears, sweating, shivering or quivering, an increased pulse rate, and a thumping heart. The message "I love you" may be communicated by facial expression (pleasant), touch (gentle and caring), eyes (attentive), speed of speech (slow), tone of voice (soft), and gesture (outstretched arms). The manner of dressing and the use of cosmetics are also forms of communication.

Both verbal and nonverbal communication are strongly associated with good marital adjustment. However, nonverbal communication, the language of signs and signals, is more subject to misinterpretation. One study found that when men were able to read their spouse's nonverbal cues, the women were more satisfied with their marriage than when the men were not able to interpret them (Gottman and Porterfield, 1981).

Direct actions are another form of communication; that's why florists remind us, "Say it with flowers." Some nonverbal communication is symbolic communication. A surprise gift can send a message of care and love.

One of the most important uses of words is what has been called the "stroking function." This refers to words that soothe; that give recognition, acceptance, and reassurance; and that fulfill emotional needs. Words can heal hurt egos and satisfy deep longings. What man is immune to the words "I think you're a handsome, wonderful guy"? Words are also used to solve problems, to convey information, or to reveal emotions. One of the most important functions of words is to provide companionship; as the poet John Milton wrote, "In God's intention, a meet and happy conversation is the chiefest and the noblest end of marriage."

Sometimes the verbal and nonverbal messages are contradictory. A woman may say to her partner, "I'm listening, I'm listening," but she's sitting in front of the television set and paying close attention to it. Or a man may tell his partner "I love you" over and over, but she wonders if he means it because he seldom makes love to her, never wants to spend time with her, and refuses to do little things to help her. Inconsistent words and actions, often referred to as **double-bind communication,** cause stress between partners to increase as anxiety grows (Roy and Sawyers, 1986).

Barriers to Communication

Barriers to communication may be grouped under four categories: physical and environmental, situational, psychological, and gender.

Physical and Environmental Barriers   There is a close relationship between physical proximity and

314

Good communication is the key to intimacy and family interaction and is the lifeblood of the marital relationship.

social interaction. In general, closer physical distances are associated with more intimate relationships. This means that factors such as the size and arrangement of living spaces and the location of furniture in those spaces influence interaction. The closer people sit around a table, the more likely they are to be friendly, talkative, and intimate. Whether couples sleep together in the same bed or in separate bedrooms influences the extent of their interaction.

Physical confinement is associated with accelerated self-disclosure, particularly in intimate areas of exchange. This means the closer couples are physically, the greater the possibility that intimacy will develop. Of course, there is also the possibility that conflict and tension will arise.

Situational Barriers   Situations can also enhance communication or make it more difficult. If employment separates couples frequently or for long periods of time, the tendency is for communication to break down, with a resultant loss of intimacy. When couples live together with others, lack of privacy becomes a major factor in making intimate communication more difficult. The situational context changes during different periods of marriage and affects communication. For example, men may make great efforts to give emotional support to

their spouse during pregnancy; following childbirth, however, they may feel that their spouse does not require the same special support. The closeness reported during pregnancy then declines, resulting in the increased dissatisfaction that some women feel after childbirth.

Psychological Barriers   The most important barriers to communication are psychological: fear of rejection, ridicule, failure, or alienation and lack of trust between two people. Partners will not share experiences that are unrewarding, threatening, or painful if they are not sure of an empathetic reply.

Gender Barriers   Some barriers to communication are a result of socialized masculine-feminine differences. Gender differences in communication and power can be seen across the life span. In general, research on peer interactions in childhood has shown that girls and boys have different behaviors related to exerting power. For example, boys tend to use more aggressive conversational tactics, such as initiation and attention-getting devices, which are associated with higher status in our society; girls tend to use more subtle strategies, such as reinforcing what was already said (Berghout-Austin, Salehi, and Leffler, 1987). The same pattern can be seen in classroom settings, with boys using more direct attempts to influence their interaction partners and being more successful than girls in getting their way (Serbin, Sprafkin, Elman, and Doyle, 1982). By adolescence, girls in mixed-sex pairs are more likely to relinquish decision-making control to their male partner in problem-solving tasks (Lind and Connole, 1985). Not surprisingly, similar patterns persist in adult intimate relationships.

Deborah Tannen (1982, 1994) has written many books on conversation styles and their relationship to gender. According to Tannen, men and women grow up in two different sex-separated cultures and learn different styles of interacting, which they practice and which are reinforced. Specifically, men inhabit a hierarchical social order in which conversation serves as a negotiating device that they use to maintain their independence and avoid failure. Women, in contrast, communicate for the central purpose of building connections with others and providing mutual support.

Although there may be hierarchies in women's communities, Tannen observed, their collectives are designed to sustain intimacy and to ward off social isolation. Thus, men and women have different perceptions of and assumptions about communication and use distinctively different ways to communicate. Men tend to perceive social relations in a hierarchical fashion, employing conversational styles that are competitive and fact-oriented. Women perceive social relations as egalitarian and often use conversation as a means of sharing feelings and promote intimacy. Women, for example, are inclined to express their preferences in the form of questions ("Would you like to go see a movie?"), whereas men tend to express their feelings in the form of definitive statements ("Let's go see a movie").

Tannen also identified gender differences related to the meaning given to verbal behavior. For example, when one woman offers to help another, she is likely to perceive the offer as a gesture of friendship and support. In contrast, when men offer help to one another, the one being offered help is more likely to perceive it as an act of condescension or a message that he is incompetent and thus needs help. Tannen did not draw conclusions about the origins of these gender distinctions. She suggested environmental origins but did not argue for them in any detail, noting only that differences in conversational styles can be seen in very young children (Franzwa and Lockhart, 1998).

IMPROVING COMMUNICATION SKILLS

Skill in communication has four requirements: (1) a positive feeling between partners who value and care for each other and are motivated to want to develop sympathetic understanding, (2) a willingness to disclose one's own attitudes, feelings, and ideas, (3) an ability to reveal attitudes, feelings, and ideas clearly and accurately, and (4) a reciprocal relationship in which disclosure and feedback originate with both partners, who listen carefully and attentively to each other. Successful communicators also know how to argue constructively.

Motivation and Concern

Communication is most possible when partners really show they care about each other and when they are motivated to try to understand each other. It is not just the communication itself that is important but also the spirit behind the message and the partners' feelings for each other. The tone of voice used and the words selected are important as well. Most researchers also talk about the importance of empathy—experiencing the feelings, thoughts, and attitudes of another person. Some people are sensitive to the feelings and wishes of others and try to understand them and act accordingly (Floyd, 1988). Partners who frequently make positive statements about each other have much higher marital satisfaction than do those who are very negative or disparaging in what they say. In addition, supportive communication stimulates reciprocal supportiveness, increasing the degree of marital integration.

Self-Disclosure

Communication depends partly on people's willingness to disclose their real feelings, ideas, and attitudes. People cannot really get to know others unless they are willing to talk about themselves. Some people can be classified as high revealers, and others as low revealers. High revealers are more prone to disclose intimate facets of their personalities and to do so earlier in their relationships than are low revealers. They are also able to more accurately assess the intimate attitudes and values of their friends than are low revealers. In general, dyads in which both persons are high revealers are more

I-statements are declarative sentences that describe a feeling, thought, or experience in a first-person singular manner (Burr, 1990). Some examples are "I'm very pleased at what has happened"; "I'm angry when . . ."; and "I feel like making love." I-statements can be used to describe ideas, beliefs, attitudes, hopes, feelings, reactions, and so forth. They communicate the feelings or concerns of the person making the statement.

There are a number of advantages to using I-statements:

- They are not threatening and so are less apt to provoke resistance and rebellion.

- They show that the individual assumes responsibility for his or her behavior.

- They promote intimacy, honesty, and openness in relationships.

- They are specific rather than general and focus on problems rather than personalities.

- Appreciative I-messages can express positive feelings.

- Preventive I-messages are designed to inform others ahead of time about things that are needed or desired.

In contrast to I-statements, you-statements focus a thought, problem, feeling, or experience on someone else. Examples are "You make me mad" and "You're being unreasonable." You-statements place the blame on others and usually create defensiveness and resistance. You-statements tend to exacerbate a situation rather than move a family toward a solution.

---

compatible than are pairs of low revealers or pairs that differ in the level of disclosure.

However, it's not just the amount of disclosure that is important, but also what is said, when, and how (Schumm, Barnes, Bollman, Jurich, and Bugaighis, 1986). People who are feeling hostile may be wise not to talk until they can discuss the situation more rationally. Satisfied partners infrequently discuss negative feelings pertaining to their mate. Feelings about their partner are usually positive and pleasant.

Clarity

Partners differ in their ability to convey messages clearly and accurately. Some people have few verbal skills and so make greater use of nonverbal techniques. You can learn to say what you mean and to accurately interpret what others say by doing the following:

1. Avoid "double-level" messages in which words say one thing and actions and innuendos another.

2. Speak clearly and to the point, and say what you really mean; avoid vagueness, ambiguity, and indirect approaches.

3. Avoid both exaggeration and understatement.

4. Avoid flippant, kidding remarks that mask your true feelings and opinions. How many times have you heard, "I didn't really mean that. I was only joking. Don't take everything so literally"?

5. Ask the other person to repeat what was said if there is any doubt about it or if it may have been misinterpreted.

6. Talk about important things when there is a minimum of distraction and when you both can focus your attention completely on what is being said.

Feedback and Reciprocity

Feedback involves responding to what the other person has said, as well as disclosing one's own feelings and ideas. This type of marital interaction has been correlated with marital satisfaction. In technical terms, feedback means receiving the output of a computer and feeding it additional information to correct its errors (Sollie and Scott, 1983). In human communication, feedback means paraphrasing the other person's statement to make sure it is understood, asking clarifying questions, and then giving one's own input or response. Accurate feedback also requires open listening and hearing, and giving one's undivided attention to what is said.

Arguing Constructively

Many couples repeatedly argue about the same issues without ever resolving them. At the heart of these quarrels may be issues of closeness and control (Christensen and Jacobson, 2000). For many people, these issues define the relationship, affirm their self-image, and determine in large part their satisfaction with the relationship. When issues of control and closeness arise, partners tend to overreact, and quarrels erupt.

Christensen and Jacobson (2000) endorsed something called "acceptance therapy" for couples in conflict. According to their research, a partner is not likely to change, and some conflicts simply can't be resolved. Thus, people need to learn to accept a partner, give up trying to change him or her, and instead work on changing themselves. Gottman (2000) reported that many quarrels in relationships are the same fight over and over again and that in these situations partners would do better to stop trying to "solve" that problem and come to accept both it and each other. Such problems may have their roots in childhood and different family backgrounds. These differences may never be resolved, and even if they are, the behavior is often not easy to change. For example, a couple may argue over and over again about closeness and intimacy issues. The man may have been raised in an unemotional household, while the woman was raised in one that was boisterous and filled with laughter. The difference creates conflict in their relationship. The two partners may both move to the middle, but it is unlikely that one can shift entirely to the other's point of view. Acceptance of a partner's different traits does not mean giving in due to fear or intimidation, but rather being strongly committed to a more fulfilling and satisfying relationship.

Christensen and Jacobson (2000) suggested several guidelines for arguing constructively:

1. Develop a "third side" of the argument that incorporates both your own and your partner's view; this can help the two of you see the problem more objectively.

2. See the problem as a difficulty the two of you have, rather than as something your partner does to you.

3. Demonstrate that you have heard your partner by summarizing what he or she has to say; ask your partner to do the same.

4. While arguing, do something positive for your partner with no strings attached.

5. Focus on one problem at a time, not a parade of them.

6. Focus on the painful reactions each of you experiences rather than on your partner's negative actions.

7. Recognize that your partner's hurtful actions may be a defense mechanism to mask pain.

8. Don't insist that yours is the only way.

9. Remember that the only person you can change is yourself.

10. Try less of "the same" in the argument and more of something different to help reduce the level of conflict.

11. Rather than arguing the same way every time, do something different, such as sending an e-mail, making a cassette tape, or writing a letter, which can help prevent you from getting caught up in the argument, escalating it, or raising your voice.

SUMMARY

1. Power has been defined as the ability of an individual within a social relationship to carry out his or her will, even in the face of resistance by others.

2. People desire power for a variety of reasons: because they want to have control over their life, because society expects them to have it, because they are following the pattern modeled by their parents, or because of a psychological need to compensate for feelings of inferiority and insecurity. Three theoretical frameworks explain the need for power: attachment theory, social control theory, and feminist theory.

3. Power is based on cultural norms, gender norms, economic resources, education and knowledge, personality differences, communication ability, emotional factors, physical stature and strength, and circumstances. Children as well as adults have sources of power.

4. Marital power patterns can be divided into four types: egalitarian, male-dominant, female-dominant, and anarchic. Egalitarian power patterns have been associated with the greatest degree of marital satisfaction, anarchic with the least. Female-dominant power patterns are also associated with marital dissatisfaction.

5. Power processes are the ways power is applied. Orchestration power is the power to make the important decisions that determine family life-styles and the major characteristics and features of the family. Implementation power sets these decisions in motion.

6. People use various means to get what they want. Some of these tactics help build better relationships; others do not.

7. Helpful power tactics include discussing, explaining, asking, telling, and bargaining and negotiating.

8. Power tactics that can help or harm include persuading and being nice.

9. Power tactics that harm include being helpless and dependent as a means of control; overprotecting to keep people from gaining power; deceiving, lying, and outwitting; criticizing to keep a person subjugated; scapegoating; gaslighting (destroying a person's validity and integrity); punishing; blackmailing; and controlling through anger, temper, cruelty, or abuse.

10. There are various means for neutralizing power: refusing to cooperate, not listening, becoming emotionally detached, obtaining services elsewhere, resigning oneself to do without or finding a substitute, changing the balance of power through self-improvement, and beating the other person at his or her own game. The problem with some of these methods is that they don't completely solve the problem, or they lead to a power struggle that results in a standoff, with neither party willing to give in. Two stubborn people playing this game can wreck a relationship.

11. One important consideration is what effect power relationships have on individuals and on marital satisfaction. Generally, extreme imbalances of power between two people tend to have a negative effect. Lack of power is associated with psychological distress for both men and women. At the other extreme, high

levels of power can be destructive, resulting in negative psychological changes in the power holder and in harm to the power subject.

12. Marital satisfaction is maximized when partners achieve a balance of power that is acceptable to them. This balance may vary with different couples. What is important is that spouses feel that the power relationships they have achieved are fair and equitable according to their expectations.

13. One way for women to gain equity in a relationship is through empowerment: improving their capacities and abilities and recognizing that the feminine traits of sensitivity and caring are sources of strength rather than of weakness.

14. Good communication is the key to intimacy, family interaction, and marital satisfaction.

15. Communication may be defined as a message one person sends and another receives. It is accomplished through both verbal and nonverbal means. It is one of the most important requirements for marital satisfaction, but it can be helpful or harmful depending on how it is conducted.

16. Barriers to communication can be grouped into four categories: physical and environmental, situational, gender, and psychological.

17. According to Deborah Tannen, men and women grow up in two different sex-separated cultures, in which they learn different styles of interacting, which are then practiced and reinforced. Men inhabit a hierarchical social order in which conversation serves as a negotiating device for preserving independence and avoiding failure. Women, in contrast, communicate for the central purpose of building connections and promoting mutual support.

18. The four requirements of good communication are motivation and concern, willingness to disclose oneself, the ability to transmit messages clearly, and the use of feedback to clarify what is being transmitted.

KEY TERMS

power	coercive power	gaslighting
legitimate power	power processes	communication
expert power	orchestration power	body language
informational power	implementation power	double-bind communication
theory of primary interest and presumed competence	bargaining	feedback
	scapegoating	

QUESTIONS FOR THOUGHT

1. How do you exercise power in your family of origin? How much power do you hold in comparison to other family members?

2. If you are married, what are the major sources of power you have in relation to your spouse? What are your spouse's sources of power in relation to you?

3. If you are single and going with someone, what are the major sources of power you have in relation to your partner? What are your partner's sources of power in relation to you?

4. What do you view as the most constructive way to exercise power in a family? Discuss.

5. How do you think a couple can best achieve a balance of power?

6. What are some reasons you've observed for people's inability to communicate with others?

7. How would you classify yourself in terms of your degree of self-disclosure in intimate relationships with the following people: your best friend, your mother, your father, and your spouse or a close friend or partner?

SUGGESTED READINGS

Bradbury, T. N. (Ed.). (1998). *The Developmental Course of Marital Dysfunction.* Cambridge: Cambridge University Press. Presents recent research by leading scholars on how marriages develop, deteriorate, and change.

Cummings, E. M., and Davies, P. (1994). *Children and Marital Conflict: The Impact of Family Disputes and Resolution.* New York: Guilford Press. Gives information about the impact of marital conflict on children.

Cupach, W. R., and Spitzberg, D. A. (Eds.). (1994). *The Dark Side of Interpersonal Communication.* Hillsdale, NJ: Lawrence Erlbaum. Explores undeveloped areas of research in interpersonal relationships.

Derlega, V. J., Metts, S., Petronio, S., and Margulis, S. T. (1993). *Self-Disclosure.* Newbury Park, CA: Sage. Examines self-disclosure in close relationships.

Duck, S. (1994). *Meaningful Relationships: Talking Sense and Relating.* Thousand Oaks, CA: Sage. Discusses how talk is the primary vehicle through which individuals establish, maintain, and even withdraw from personal relationships.

Elgin, S. H. (1997). *How to Disagree Without Being Disagreeable.* New York: Wiley. Focuses on improving communication.

Kalbfleisch, P. J., and Cody, M. J. (Eds.). (1995). *Gender, Power, and Communication in Human Relationships.* Hillsdale, NJ: Lawrence Erlbaum. Deals with the interrelations of gender and power in social interaction.

Lingren, H. G. (1999). *Fighting Fair in Marriage.* Lincoln: Institute of Agriculture and Natural Resources, University of Nebraska–Lincoln. Gives strategies for recognizing and resolving marital conflicts through negotiation and exploration of alternatives.

McKie, L., Bowlby, S. R., and Gregory, S. (Eds.). (1999). *Gender, Power, and the Household.* New York: St. Martin's Press. Discusses gender roles and power issues in the household.

Olson, D. H. (2000). *Empowering Couples: Building on Your Strengths.* Minneapolis: Life Innovations. Presents guidelines for building practical relationship skills by helping couples identify their strengths.

Socha, T. J., and Diggs, R. C. (Eds.). (1999). *Communication, Race, and Family: Exploring Communication in Black, White, and Biracial Families.* Mahwah, NJ: Lawrence Erlbaum. Explores how family communication influences perceptions of race and how improving family communication can improve society.

Tannen, D. (1991). *You Just Don't Understand: Women and Men in Conversation.* New York: Morrow. Examines the different communication styles of men and women.

Tannen, D. (1994). *Talking Nine to Five: Women and Men in the Workplace: Language, Sex, and Power.* New York: Morrow. Explores how gender differences in communication affect who gets heard, how someone gets credit, and what gets done at work.

Tannen, D. (1995). *Gender and Discourse.* New York: Oxford University Press. Explains theories of miscommunication between men and women.

Tannen, D. (1999). *The Argument Culture: Stopping America's War of Words.* New York: Ballantine Books. Discusses the ways in which young boys and girls express disagreement or aggression and provides constructive ways for dealing with conflict.

Wright, H. N. (2000). *Communication: Key to Your Marriage.* Ventura, CA: Regal Books. Gives guidelines to help spouses understand each other at new and deeper levels.

LEARNING OBJECTIVES

After reading the chapter, you should be able to:

Outline the reasons for family planning.

Discuss basic facts about oral contraceptives: how they prevent conception; types and administration; effectiveness, advantages, and health benefits; risks; and side effects.

Discuss basic facts about other forms of hormonal contraceptives, such as progestin implants and injections and RU-486 (Mifepristone).

Understand basic facts about the use of vaginal spermicides as contraceptives.

Describe the use of IUDs and other mechanical devices or barrier methods: condoms, female condoms, diaphragms, and cervical caps.

Describe the processes of male and female sterilization: vasectomy and tubal ligation.

Discuss methods of birth control without the use of devices, including fertility awareness methods, coitus interruptus, and noncoital stimulation.

Summarize the considerations in choosing which method to use.

Discuss the legal, physical and medical, moral, social and realistic, and psychological and personal considerations in relation to abortion.

Summarize the basic facts about infertility: causes, infertility and subjective well-being, treatments, and alternative means of conception.

Discuss basic issues in relation to adoption.

Discuss the basic issues and trends in relation to childlessness, smaller families, and delayed parenthood.

Summarize the reasons for having children.

Summarize the reasons for choosing a child-free marriage.

Identify the effects of children on parents' happiness.

Discuss the process of deciding whether to have children.

Family Planning and Parenthood

Learning Objectives

The Importance of Family Planning

Hormonal Control
Oral Contraceptives
 Perspective: Why Some People Don't Use
Contraceptives
Other Forms of Hormonal Contraceptives
 Family Issues: RU-486 (Mifeprex): The Abortion Pill

Vaginal Spermicides

Intrauterine Devices

Barrier Methods
Condoms
 Perspective: Condom Availability in U.S. Schools
Diaphragms
Cervical Caps
 Perspective: Mistakes People Make with
Contraceptives

Sterilization
Vasectomy
Tubal Ligation

Birth Control Without Devices
Fertility Awareness Methods
Coitus Interruptus
Noncoital Stimulation

Choosing a Method of Contraception

Abortion
Legal Considerations
Physical and Medical Considerations
Moral Considerations
Social Considerations
Psychological and Personal Considerations
 Perspective: Facts About Abortion

Infertility
Causes of Infertility
Infertility and Subjective Well-Being
Treatment of Infertility
Alternative Means of Conception
The Adoption Option

To Parent or Not to Parent
Delayed Parenthood
Reasons for Having Children
Choosing a Child-Free Marriage
Effects of Children on Parents' Happiness
The Decision to Have or Not to Have Children

Summary
Key Terms
Questions for Thought
Suggested Readings

We are fortunate to live at a time when efficient and safe methods of contraception are available. Without birth control, couples would have to resign themselves to having one child after another or to avoiding sexual relations after they'd had the number of children they desired. A walk through an old cemetery reveals the difference that family planning has made. Dozens of tombstones contain the names of women who died at young ages from the burden of bearing one child after another. Beside them are the names of many of their children who also did not get a chance at life because of ill health.

Contraception has improved the lives of millions of people. Most important, it helps them to plan the number of children they want and to have them at the time that is best for all concerned. An additional option for couples is to have no children.

To acquaint couples with the options available, this chapter includes an overview of contraceptive methods and their use and discusses special treatments available to couples who have problems with fertility. The chapter also examines abortion and the decision of whether to parent. But first, we explore the importance of family planning.

THE IMPORTANCE OF FAMILY PLANNING

In 1994, 49% of all pregnancies were unintended. Forty-eight percent of women ages 15–44 had had at least one unplanned pregnancy sometime in their lives, 28% had had one or more unplanned births, 30% had had one or more abortions, and 11% had had both (Henshaw, 1998). In other words, almost half of American women experience an unintended pregnancy at least once in their life, and almost half of all pregnancies are unplanned. Low-income and minority women have greater difficulty than other women in avoiding unplanned pregnancy. For women with a family income of less than 150% of the poverty line (in 1999, $16,895 for a family of four), 74% of pregnancies are unplanned, compared to 52% of those among women with higher income (Forrest and Frost, 1996).

There are several compelling reasons for **family planning.** The most urgent one is to protect the health of the mother and the children. Births to mothers who are too young or too old or births that

are close together pose increased health risks for both mothers and children (Wineberg and McCarthy, 1989). For example, infants conceived within a few months of the preceding birth have a higher-than-average risk of low birth weight, preterm birth, and neonatal death. Family planning experts suggest that birth intervals should be at least 2 years (Miller, 1991).

Timing is important, since when childbirth occurs is a major determinant of its effect on the family. The timing of fatherhood in men's lives affects the way they fill the role of father (Cooney, Pedersen, Indelicato, and Palkovitz, 1993). Older fathers are more likely to be positively involved in their children's upbringing. By delaying parenthood, men evidently are able to invest themselves more readily in the role and to feel good about their involvement. Also, delaying parenthood promotes marital satisfaction for men and women.

Family planning is necessary for the good of the marriage and the family. The negative psychological impact on the mother and father is lessened considerably if parenthood is chosen and welcomed. Having children imposes strains on the marriage; having children early in a relationship adds additional stress. Unfortunately, the younger the partners, the more likely the woman is already pregnant; and brides who are pregnant have the poorest prognosis for marital success. Because both premarital pregnancy and early postmarital pregnancy are associated with a higher-than-average divorce rate, many of these children grow up in a single-parent household. Furthermore, women whose pregnancy is unwanted or mistimed are four times as likely as women with an intentional pregnancy to be physically assaulted by their partner (Gazmararian et al., 1995). In addition, unwanted children are more likely to be neglected and abused (Zuravin, 1988).

In the United States in 1995, an estimated 1.65 million pregnancies among females ages 15–19 were avoided through the use of contraceptives. Teenage contraceptive use prevents pregnancies that could have significant societal costs, making their use a critical public health strategy (Kahn, Brindis, and Glei, 1999).

Not only do young couples begin having children at an early age, but they have more children. The more they have, the greater the strain on them and on their marriage (Abbott and Brody, 1985). Also, the more children in a family, the less higher education they are likely to receive (Witwer, 1989). Children,

Training programs and community support have helped many teenagers adjust to their roles as new parents.

especially girls, born as a result of unwanted pregnancy experience some negative effects on their social development and psychological health (Remez, 1995). Family planning is necessary to give children the best possible start in life (Heuvel, 1988).

As noted in Chapter 12, it costs about $160,140 to raise a child to age 18, and college will cost an additional $60,000–$145,000. It doesn't take much imagination to realize that having a large number of children places a great strain on the family budget.

In recent years, much emphasis has been placed on the humanitarian and ecological importance of family planning. At the present rate of population growth, the world will have 7.5 billion people by the year 2020. The world now has over 6 billion people. Can it support almost 2 billion more in 2 decades? More than half the world's people live in poverty, and cities like Calcutta, Delhi, Mexico City, and São Paulo have become urban nightmares. Family planning thus has become one of the most important humanitarian issues facing humankind.

HORMONAL CONTROL

The invention of birth control pills, or oral contraceptives, in the 1960s was a major advancement in contraceptive technology. The pill was more effective than any previous method in preventing pregnancy, and it was a no-mess, no-fuss alternative to condoms and diaphragms. Other forms of hormonal

birth control have now been developed and tested, and some are becoming available to the public.

Oral Contraceptives

Oral contraceptives contain two synthetically produced female sex hormones that are chemically similar to ones the woman already produces in her body to regulate ovulation and the menstrual cycle. These natural hormones are estrogen and progesterone (progestin is the artificially produced equivalent). By manipulating the amount of these two hormones in the woman's bloodstream, these pills prevent conception in three ways:

1. Ovulation is prevented in about 90% of the menstrual cycles.

2. The cervical mucus remains thick and sticky throughout the month, blocking the entrance to the uterus and making penetration by the sperm difficult.

3. The endometrium, the inner lining of the uterus, is altered so that successful implantation and nourishment of a fertilized ovum are difficult (Guttmacher, 1983).

Types of Oral Contraceptives   There are several types of pills. **Combination pills** contain estrogen and progestin. Because the pill is a prescription drug, it should never be taken without a prior physical examination and a doctor's prescription and guidance. A woman takes the pill for 21 days and

Why Some People Don't Use Contraceptives

DAVID A. GRIMES *(1984) has identified some of the reasons people fail to use contraceptives:*

- **Lack of knowledge.** These people do not know what contraceptives are available, how efficient they are, and when and how to use them.

- **Lack of preparedness.** Some people think they are immoral if they plan to have intercourse and prepare for it.

- **Denial.** These people believe that "it won't happen to me."

- **Lack of personal responsibility.** These people are unwilling to take responsibility because of immaturity or the desire to put the responsibility on the partner.

- **Intentional risk taking.** Some people play the game of "coital chicken" in pursuit of a not-so-cheap thrill.

- **Guilt or hostility.** These people have a subconscious desire for pregnancy as a punishment of self or partner.

- **Shame and embarrassment.** These people fear that family members or others will find out.

- **Gamesmanship.** Some people attempt to control a sexual relationship.

- **Problem with sexual identity.** Here, fertility is equated with sexuality, and vice versa.

- **Nihilism.** These people are fatalistic about their plight in life and socioeconomic status, feel hopeless and helpless, and have a poor self-concept (Winter, 1988).

- **Fear of side effects, health consequences, and loss of control of sexual drive.**

- **Lack of understanding.** Some people don't recognize the need to take prompt action when there has been a contraceptive omission or failure.

- **Lack of access to contraceptive services** (Radecki and Bernstein, 1990).

- **Unstable relationships.** People in less stable relationships are less likely to use effective contraceptives than are those in longer-term relationships (Harvey and Scrimshaw, 1988).

- **Not enough money to obtain contraceptives.**

then stops doing so for 7 days. Some brands have a different color pill, a **placebo** (sometimes containing iron), which the woman takes for 7 days before recommencing the 21-day regimen.

If a woman forgets to take a single pill, she should make it up by taking it as soon as she remembers. If she misses two pills, she should either take both at once or take one additional pill each of the next two days, depending on the type of pill. (The manufacturer's insert in each package contains directions.) If she misses more than two pills, it is generally recommended that a backup method be used for a month or so, until the hormone-regulated menstrual cycle is reestablished (Williams-Deane and Potter, 1992).

Another form of pill, called the **minipill** because it contains only progestin, is also available. This pill is taken daily with no break. The minipill does not prevent either ovulation or menstruation, but it greatly reduces the likelihood of impregnation by maintaining a mucous barrier in the cervix, altering the sperm cells within the tubes, or interfering with the passage of the egg down the tube. Although minipills have fewer side effects, they have a slightly higher failure rate than the combination pills. They are prescribed infrequently at the present time.

Some kinds of oral contraceptives are prescribed as **emergency contraceptives** to prevent pregnancy following unprotected sexual intercourse. A woman may require emergency contraception because the contraceptive method she was using failed (for example, a condom broke or a diaphragm slipped), she neglected to use a contraceptive method, or she was sexually assaulted.

Emergency contraception is used extensively in some countries. In the United States, however, emergency contraception is prescribed primarily for rape victims treated in emergency rooms, college health centers, or family planning clinics (Grossman and Grossman, 1994). Emergency contraception may be the best kept contraceptive secret in America. Students remark on how seldom emergency contraception is discussed and call for routine education about the method. Low utilization of emergency contraception is partly attributable to health care providers' lack of knowledge about the method. In a survey of 167 physicians with expertise in adolescent health, 84% said they prescribed contraceptives to adolescents, but only 80% of these prescribed emergency contraception, generally a few times a year at most (Gold, Schein, and Coupey, 1997). One survey of 235 women who had received emergency contraceptives found that 91% were satisfied with the treatment. More than two-thirds of the women were using contraceptives before receiving emergency treatment, with 45% reporting problems with the condom and 23% reporting having unplanned sex. Twenty-nine percent of the sample believed that emergency contraceptives should be made available over the counter. As this study suggests, emergency contraceptives are positive options for women, but they should not be a substitute for regular contraceptive use (Harvey, Beckman, Sherman, and Petitti, 1999).

The most common method, the Yuzpe method, involves taking four combined estrogen/progestin pills: two tablets within 72 hours of unprotected coitus (preferably as soon as possible) and two more 12 hours later. Use of these emergency contraceptive pills (ECPs) reduces the expected number of pregnancies by more than 75%. However, repeated use of ECPs is not recommended because ECPs are not 100% effective and repeated use may pose health risks and cause unpleasant side effects. Another postcoital therapy less frequently used is insertion of a copper-releasing IUD (Hatcher et al., 1998).

Advantages of Oral Contraceptives   The combination birth control pill is one of the most effective contraceptives. Since some users are careless, however, the estimated typical user's failure rate is 3.8% (Kost, Forrest, and Harlap, 1991). The failure rate is the percentage of users (ages 15–44) who get pregnant during the first year of use. The pill is convenient and easy to use; all that is required is remembering to take a pill every day.

The birth control pill is a reversible contraceptive; that is, after the woman stops taking it, her fertility returns. However, some women who stop taking the pill because they want to become pregnant take slightly longer to conceive than do those who haven't been on the pill (Turner, 1990). A minority of women who have been on the pill become more fertile after ceasing to take it, usually because of more regular menstruation and ovulation.

There are also some noncontraceptive health benefits associated with oral contraceptives. Too often these beneficial effects have been ignored, especially by the media, which seem to emphasize the negative. The pill's positive effects on the following health problems are well documented:

- **Benign breast disease.** Oral contraceptives reduce benign breast disease. The longer the pill is used, the lower the incidence of the disease.
- **Cysts of the ovary.** The combination pills suppress ovarian activity and reduce ovarian cysts.
- **Iron-deficiency anemia.** Oral contraceptive users suffer approximately 45% less iron-deficiency anemia than do nonusers.
- **Pelvic inflammatory disease (PID).** Pill users have only half the risk of developing pelvic inflammatory disease. When the pill is used for 1 year or longer, the rate is 70% (Witwer, 1990c).
- **Ectopic pregnancy.** Current users of oral contraceptives have nearly complete protection against this condition.

The pill also seems to offer protection against rheumatoid arthritis, endometriosis, and osteoporosis (Hatcher et al., 1998). Although the evidence is not yet conclusive, pill users appear to be only half as likely to develop these conditions. Women who have used oral contraceptives appear to be about half as likely to develop ovarian and endometrial cancer as are women who have never used the pill (Kost, Forrest, and Harlap, 1991). The protective effects of the pill against two of the most common cancers in American women appear to be long-lasting (Coker, Harlap, and Fortney, 1993).

Disadvantages of Oral Contraceptives   Birth control pills do not protect against STDs, including AIDS, although they do lower the risk of pelvic inflammatory diseases (Hatcher et al., 1998). Regular use of condoms is recommended for women taking oral contraceptives unless they are in a monogamous relationship with an uninfected partner. One of the most serious concerns associated with the birth control pill is that it may cause blood clots (thrombosis). There is a slight increase in risk with age (Klitsch, 1996). Pill users who are younger than 50, do not smoke, and have no history of hypertension have a very low risk of blood clots, which cause strokes (Hatcher et al., 1998). For women who smoke heavily (more than 25 cigarettes per day), the risk of death from thromboembolism is nine times greater than for nonsmokers. If women who use the pill did not smoke, most of the deaths could be averted (Kost, Forrest, and Harlap, 1991).

Another drawback of the combination pill is the possible increased risk of breast cancer. However, the current consensus is that the risk is small and that the tumors spread less aggressively than they would in women who were not on the pill (Hatcher et al., 1998). In fact, the increased risk may be due not to the pill but to the greater likelihood that women taking the pill will have their tumor diagnosed. However, women who have a family history of breast cancer may wish to discuss alternative contraceptives with their doctor. All women, whether they use oral contraceptives or not, are urged to get annual breast examinations (Coker, Harlap, and Fortney, 1993) and to perform self-exams monthly.

There may be an increase in the risk of cervical cancer among pill users, especially among long-term users who started having sex early and have had multiple sex partners (Donovan and Klitsch, 1995; Hatcher et al., 1998). It is difficult to sort out variables. Those women who have been sexually active the longest and have sex the most frequently and with the most partners have increased risk. But it has also been shown that pill users have intercourse more frequently than those who don't use the pill, so which is the cause of cervical cancer—the pill or the sexual activity? This is why it is necessary for researchers to consider the sexual histories of the women in their research population (Lincoln, 1984). Doctors still recommend that women receive annual examinations, including Pap smears, to help detect cervical cancer.

The effect of taking the pill on sexual drive and frequency of intercourse is variable. There seems to be some evidence that for some women the pill alters vaginal secretions and decreases levels of free testosterone, which may decrease sexual drive (Hatcher et al., 1998). However, women who feel more comfortable and secure in their sexual relationships are more likely to make the commitment to an ongoing sexual relationship that is implied by oral contraceptive use (Bancroft, Sherwin, Alexander, Davidson, and Walker, 1991).

Other side effects of the pill, depending on the particular combination of ingredients, can include nausea, weight gain, swollen breasts, headaches, and nervousness. Many of the unpleasant side effects disappear after a woman's metabolism adjusts to the pill or after her doctor alters brands or dosage.

Other Forms of Hormonal Contraceptives

In recent years, scientists have been working to improve hormonal contraception. Since the main reason for the pill's failure as a contraceptive is failure to take it every day, one of the main focuses of this research has been on methods of safely delivering the hormones in longer-lasting doses. One promising method is the **progestin implant,** which is inserted under the skin of the upper arm (Weisman, Plichta, Tirado, and Dana, 1993). Flexible, non-biodegradable tubes filled with hormones and placed under the skin release regular doses of synthetic progestin (Tanfer, 1994). Progestin implants come in various forms. Norplant, which was approved by the FDA in December 1990, provides sustained release of progestin directly into the bloodstream for 5 years (Darney, 1990). It is free of estrogen, and because it is administered subcutaneously rather than orally, it avoids possible liver damage and side effects such as nausea (Potts, 1988). It is a highly convenient method; once it is inserted, the user does not have to remember to do anything else, as she does if she is on the pill (Frank, Poindexter, Johnson, and Bateman, 1992).

The failure rate of implants is less than 0.1% for women in general. Adolescent mothers who choose hormonal contraceptive implants such as Norplant as their contraceptive method are less likely to have a subsequent pregnancy than are their counterparts who use oral contraceptives (Hollander, 1995b).

Implants' apparent disadvantages include the fact that, like the pill, they provide no protection against sexually transmitted diseases. Insertion and removal must be done by a doctor in a minor surgical procedure; removal can be difficult if the implants were placed too far beneath the skin. Some users experience inflammation or infection of the insertion site and thus need to have the implants removed (Remez, 1996). Side effects can include an irregular menstrual pattern, breast tenderness, and depression.

Progestin injections have also been developed (Westfall, Main, and Barnard, 1996). Depo-Provera is the one most commonly used in the United States. One injection lasts 3 months, although in some cases ovulation may not start again for 9 or 10 months after the last shot. The probability of pregnancy among typical users is extremely low—only 0.3%. Side effects, including menstrual irregularity,

After first being approved for use by the French in 1988, the drug formerly known as RU-486 was recently approved for use in the United States by the Food and Drug Administration. Mifepristone, marketed as Mifeprex, is a drug used for the termination of early pregnancy, defined as 49 days or less from the beginning of the last menstrual period. It has not been approved for use as a "morning-after pill" or as a means to end pregnancy after 49 days (or 7 weeks after the start of the last period).

Mifeprex works by blocking production of the hormone progesterone, which is necessary to maintain a pregnancy. The FDA-approved regimen requires three visits to a doctor's office; they can begin as soon as the woman becomes pregnant. During the first visit, she takes three tablets of Mifeprex. Two days later, she visits the doctor to take two pills of a prostaglandin called misoprostol, which help the uterus expel the embryo. A third visit to the doctor's office or clinic is required 12 days later to confirm that the pregnancy has been terminated (U.S. Department of Health and Human Services, 2000).

Nearly all women using Mifeprex experience at least one of its side effects, which include bleeding, cramps, and nausea. Bleeding and spotting usually occur for 9 to 16 days, and about 1 in 100 women experiences bleeding heavy enough to require a surgical procedure to stop it (U.S. Department of Health and Human Services, 2000).

Mifeprex can be distributed only through qualified doctors and will not be available through pharmacies (Center for Drug Evaluation and Research, 2000). To be qualified, doctors must be able to accurately determine the duration of a pregnancy, detect whether it is an ectopic (tubal) pregnancy, and verify that they will be able to provide surgical intervention in case of an incomplete abortion or severe bleeding.

More than 620,000 European woman have used mifepristone since its approval in France. It has also been approved in the United Kingdom and Sweden (U.S. Department of Health and Human Services, 2000).

are similar to those of Norplant; weight gain seems to be somewhat greater than with Norplant. Disadvantages include lack of protection against sexually transmitted diseases, significant drops in high-density lipoprotein (HDL) cholesterol levels, and decreases in bone density for long-term users, especially if they smoke. Although there was once a concern that Depo-Provera might increase the risk of breast and other cancers, a number of international studies have found the risk to be minimal or nonexistent (Hatcher et al., 1998).

In a recent study of 965 university students on their knowledge of Norplant and Depo-Provera, researchers found that most knew little about the implants and injections. Higher levels of knowledge coincided with the greater likelihood of future use of both methods of contraceptives. Overall, the study revealed a need to educate the public on the benefits of these contraceptive devices, which are largely underutilized (Sawyer and Pinciaro, 1998).

VAGINAL SPERMICIDES

Spermicides, or chemicals that kill sperm, come in the form of contraceptive foam, suppository, cream, jelly, and, most recently, film. They work in two ways: (1) by blocking the entrance to the uterus and (2) by immobilizing the sperm. To be most effective, they must be inserted in the very back of the vagina, over the cervix (as illustrated in Figure 15.1), not more than 5–15 minutes before ejaculation. Spermicides lose their effectiveness within about an hour, so they must be reapplied each time intercourse is repeated.

The effectiveness of spermicides varies greatly; it has been estimated that the average failure rate is 26% for typical use and 6% for correct use at every act of intercourse over the course of a year (Hatcher et al., 1998). Foam can be used alone because it spreads more evenly and blocks the cervix more adequately than other spermicides. Creams and jellies are usually used in conjunction with a diaphragm, cervical cap, or condom.

Vaginal contraceptive film (VCF) is a newer product; once the transparent 2-inch square is inserted, it dissolves into a gel over the cervix. It is less messy than foams and jellies, which usually create some vaginal discharge, and it seems less irritating for those people who have an allergic reaction to other forms of spermicides.

In addition to being available without a prescription, a benefit of spermicides, especially those with nonoxynol-9, is that they provide moderate

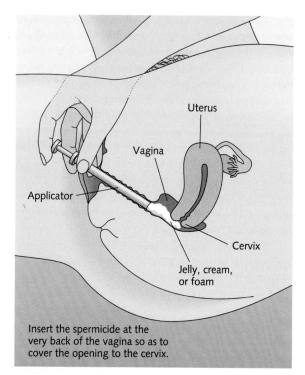

Insert the spermicide at the very back of the vagina so as to cover the opening to the cervix.

Figure 15.1   Insertion of Spermicidal Preparation with a Plastic Applicator

protection against some bacterial STDs. However, they do not protect against HIV and, because they can irritate vaginal tissues, may even increase the risk (Hatcher et al., 1998). Both men and women may experience burning or other adverse reactions to the chemicals, including urinary tract infections in some women, especially if the spermicide is used with a diaphragm. Allergic responses can sometimes be alleviated by switching to another type or brand of spermicide.

INTRAUTERINE DEVICES

The **IUD,** or intrauterine device, is made of plastic and sometimes metal; it is placed in the uterus to prevent pregnancy. IUDs alter the chemical environment in the uterus and inhibit fertilization; they also interfere with the implantation of fertilized eggs.

The IUD must be inserted by a physician. He or she loads the IUD in an inserter that resembles a plastic straw and threads it through the cervical canal and into the uterine cavity. The IUD is "unwound" into a straight line while in the inserter but resumes its former shape when released in the uterus. A thin plastic thread extends from the lower end of the IUD through the cervical canal and into the upper vagina. The physician trims the thread to about 1 or 1.5 inches long. Periodically, the woman checks the length of the thread to make sure that the IUD is still in place.

IUDs were quite popular in the United States in the late 1960s and early 1970s. In the mid-1970s, however, information began to appear about a high incidence of pelvic infections and infertility and even some deaths among users of a type of IUD called the Dalkon Shield. A number of lawsuits were filed against the manufacturer, and the Dalkon Shield was withdrawn from the market. Other types of IUDs, such as the Lippes Loop, the Copper 7, and the Copper T, had much better safety records, but because of the widespread publicity about the Dalkon Shield, as well as occasional medical problems with other IUDs, women became increasingly apprehensive. IUD manufacturers were concerned about expensive lawsuits and insurance costs and withdrew all but one type, the hormone-releasing Progestasert, from the market (Forrest, 1986). In 1989, another IUD, the Copper-T 380A, or ParaGard, was approved for use. It has more copper than the earlier Copper 7 or Copper T, which increases its effectiveness (Klitsch, 1988b). A copper-containing IUD is also sometimes used as a form of emergency contraception by women who have had unprotected sexual intercourse (Grossman and Grossman, 1994).

IUDs are more reliable than the pill; they have a failure rate of 2.5% for women who can retain them (Kost, Forrest, and Harlap, 1991; Reinisch and Beasley, 1990). Once an IUD is inserted, it requires no attention except periodic checking of the string to make sure it has not been expelled. The hormone-releasing Progestasert has to be replaced every year; the Copper-T 380A can remain in the uterus for 10 years (Hatcher et al., 1999).

The spontaneous expulsion rate is about 7% for women who have never been pregnant and about 3% for women who have had children (Reinisch and Beasley, 1990). Other potential disadvantages of IUDs include a heavier menstrual flow, stronger cramps, and a slightly increased risk of pelvic inflammatory disease (PID). In addition, IUDs do

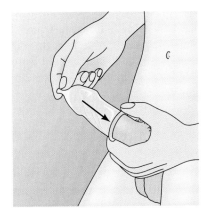

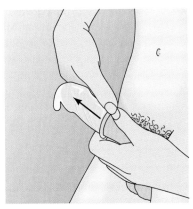

1. When penis is hard, place rolled-up condom at head of penis and squeeze air from tip of condom. This leaves room for semen.

2. Still holding tip, unroll condom all the way down to hair at base of penis. Gently smooth out air bubbles, the main reason why condoms break.

3. To prevent leakage after ejaculation, hold condom rim while carefully withdrawing from partner. Then roll condom off penis, away from partner, being careful not to spill semen.

Figure 15.2   Correct Way to Use a Condom

not protect against STDs. The risk of serious PID might be lowered by careful selection of users, meticulousness in insertion of the device, and close monitoring for early signs of infection (Petitti, 1992). If an IUD is in place when a pregnancy is diagnosed, there is a significant chance of spontaneous abortion.

BARRIER METHODS

Some of the earliest forms of contraception were barrier methods designed to prevent the meeting of sperm and ovum. The condom was in use as early as the sixteenth century in Italy, primarily to provide protection against syphilis. Reusable diaphragms and cervical caps were in use in Europe in the 1800s (Hatcher et al., 1998).

Although condoms used with vaginal spermicides are more effective than other barrier methods in preventing pregnancy, all barrier methods are less effective than hormonal methods or IUDs. However, they have few adverse side effects, and they offer some protection against STDs, especially when used with vaginal spermicides. When used correctly, latex condoms can provide protection against HIV (Hatcher et al., 1998). Barrier methods may increase the risk of urinary tract infections in women (Althaus, 1997; Hollander, 1996a).

Condoms

The **condom** is usually made of thin, strong latex rubber or, less frequently, of polyurethane or natural membranes. It is placed over the end of the erect penis and then unrolled to enclose the penile shaft (see Figure 15.2). Condoms come in different styles and colors. Some have a teat on the end to receive the ejaculate. If the condom doesn't have this feature, it can be unrolled on the penis so as to leave a half-inch space at the end to receive the semen. One style has an adhesive to seal the top of the condom to the penis, thus preventing leakage of semen. Other models come packaged singly in fluid, which provides lubrication and allows the penis to be inserted into the vagina easily. If a condom is not lubricated, a contraceptive jelly or cream may be used to aid penetration and to prevent the condom from tearing on insertion. Vaseline, baby oil, and other petroleum- or oil-based products should never be used, because they cause the condom to deteriorate.

The failure rate of condoms used alone as a contraceptive has been calculated at about 14% (Hatcher et al., 1999). When failure occurs, it is due to one or more of several reasons: (1) The condom has a hole in it, (2) it ruptures, or (3) it slips off. The most common reason for failure of condoms is slipping off the shaft of the penis during either intercourse or withdrawal, allowing the semen to leak out (Althaus, 1992). Slippage is more likely when

School condom availability programs have been promoted as a way to increase condom use among students. A survey of key individuals involved in school condom programs across the United States found that, as of January 1995, at least 431 public schools in 50 U.S. school districts made condoms available to students. In about half of the schools in the survey, students obtained more than one condom per student per year, on average. In 14% of the schools, students obtained more than six condoms per student per year. In smaller schools and in alternative schools, condoms were made available in baskets. Schools with health clinics dispensed more condoms per student per year than did other schools, presumably because health clinics made sexually active students more aware of the need to use condoms (Kirby and Brown, 1996).

additional lubrication is used (Trussell, Warner, and Hatcher, 1992). To prevent leakage or the condom's slipping off, users should hold on to the top of the condom when the penis is withdrawn. Educational programs would help ensure that more people know how to use a condom correctly (Cohen, Dent, and MacKinnon, 1991).

If a condom and a spermicidal foam, jelly, or cream are used together, the failure rate among typical users is about 2.5%. This level of efficacy compares favorably with the failure rate among typical users of oral contraceptives (Kestelman and Trussell, 1991).

Since the onset of the AIDS epidemic, the use of condoms has increased significantly, especially among young men (Sonenstein, Pleck, and Ku, 1989). Condoms are sometimes used in addition to other methods of birth control to prevent the spread of AIDS (Santelli, Davis, Celentano, Crump, and Burwell, 1995). Usage rates are still much too low, however. Recent findings show that women adopting long-term hormonal contraceptive methods decrease their use of condoms and increase their risk of contracting HIV/AIDS and other STDs (Cushman et al., 1998). A national AIDS behavioral survey in 1991 indicated that only 17% of men with multiple sex partners and 13% with high-risk sexual partners use condoms all the time (Turner, 1993). In another study of patients at an STD clinic in Baltimore, men who had had more than four partners in the previous year were less likely to use condoms than those who had had fewer partners, and women age 20 or older were less likely to use condoms than were women younger than 20. Only 17% of the men and 15% of the women had used condoms during their last sexual intercourse (Edwards, 1992a). A study of 210 undergraduate men and women on the association between dating relationships and condom use found that the length of the relationship was the only factor that independently predicted condom use. More serious and committed relationships and higher levels of love were associated with less condom use and a higher risk of contracting STDs (Civic, 1999).

Condoms have been widely promoted as the best method, except abstinence, of preventing the spread of STDs. The type and quality of the condom used are important. For example, lambskin condoms, often preferred for their sensitivity, allow the leakage of AIDS, herpes, and hepatitis B viruses through the membrane itself. Syphilis and gonorrhea bacteria are too large to pass through. A latex condom does not allow leakage of small viral organisms unless the condom is torn or improperly used. According to findings from a New Zealand study involving family planning clinic clients, condoms break, slip, or leak during active intercourse 11% of the time. All told, 40% of the clients reported at least one instance of a condom break, slip, or leak. These problems were more common among couples who were young or relatively inexperienced in using condoms. Oral and anal sex were 4.2 times more likely than vaginal intercourse to result in a condom break and 2.6 times more likely to result in a slip. Vigorous sex was perceived by respondents to have been the cause of some condom breaks. Vaginal dryness was mentioned as a cause of breakage in some cases, and tearing by fingernails was the cause in other instances. Leaving the condom on too long was the most frequently mentioned explanation for a condom slip. A condom was more likely to break or slip if the respondent reported that it was either too small or too large (Donovan, 1994). Dr. Gerald Bernstein, who worked on a government-funded condom evaluation, said, "Using condoms is not what people are talking about

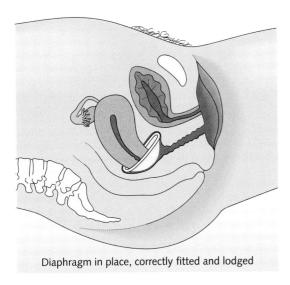

Diaphragm in place, correctly fitted and lodged

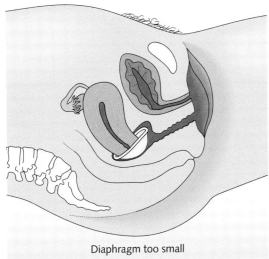

Diaphragm too small

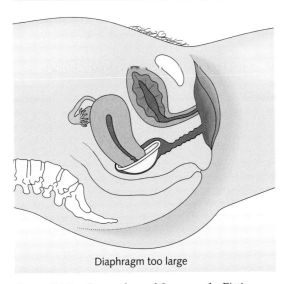

Diaphragm too large

Figure 15.3 Correctly and Incorrectly Fitting Diaphragms

when they say 'safe sex.' It may be safer sex, but I think it's a misnomer to say condoms are 'safe' sex" (Parachini, 1987).

A female condom is somewhat like a polyurethane plastic bag with a flexible ring at the closed end and another at the open end. The upper ring helps with insertion and keeps the upper end of the condom in place over the cervix; the lower ring keeps the condom from being pushed inside the vagina and also covers part of the vulva, thus protecting a larger genital area from STDs than does the male condom. A female condom (marketed under the brand name Reality) was approved by the FDA in 1993 to reduce the risk of unwanted pregnancy and the transmission of STDs, including HIV. Effectiveness rates for the female condom range from 79% to 95%. Worldwide acceptability data indicate that women are often eager to try a device that is under their control. The vast majority of studies report that partners have acquiesced to its use and sometimes have preferred the device to a male condom (Gollub, Stein, and El-Sadr, 1995).

Diaphragms

The **diaphragm** is a thick, rubber latex, dome-shaped cap stretched over a collapsible metal ring, designed to cover the cervical opening. It comes in a variety of sizes and must be fitted to each woman by a physician. A snug fit is especially important, since the diaphragm's effectiveness as a contraceptive depends on its forming an impenetrable shield over the entrance to the uterus (see Figure 15.3). If the fit is not right, the sperm can get around the edges of the diaphragm and enter the cervix. For this reason, the largest diaphragm a woman can wear comfortably is advised, since sexual excitement causes the back portion of the vagina to enlarge (Masters and Johnson, 1966). After childbirth, a woman always requires a larger diaphragm. Also, a size change may be in order whenever a woman gains or loses 15 pounds.

To add to its effectiveness as a contraceptive, a spoonful of spermicidal cream or jelly is smeared in the cup fitting against the cervix and about the rim to create a protective seal. For additional protection, foam may be inserted into the vagina after the diaphragm is in place and before each act of intercourse (Tyrer, 1984). When fitted and placed

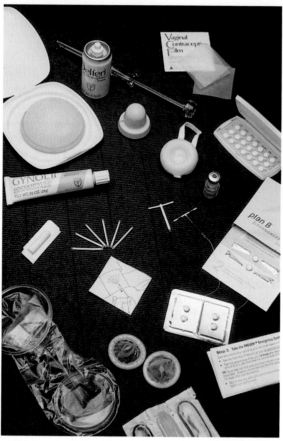

The variety of contraceptives from which to choose is considerable. How does one make the best choice? What are the risks of pregnancy and the health risks associated with each type of contraception?

correctly, and when used in conjunction with a spermicide, the failure rate is 6% (Hatcher et al., 1999). Overall, however, the actual failure rate for typical users is 20% (due primarily to incorrect placement or dislodgement during intercourse). The diaphragm should not be removed until at least 6 hours after intercourse.

Cervical Caps

After nearly a decade-long delay, the FDA finally approved use of the **cervical cap** in 1988 (Klitsch, 1988a). The cervical cap is a small, rubber, thimble-shaped barrier that fits tightly across the cervix and prevents sperm from entering the uterus. Like the diaphragm, it is used with a spermicide and inserted shortly before intercourse. It is approximately

as effective as the diaphragm for women who have not had children, with a 9% failure rate for correct use and a 20% failure rate for typical use. For women who have had children, the failure rate is higher: 26% for correct use and 40% for typical use (Hatcher et al., 1999). Because initial use may cause changes in cervical cells, wearers should get a Pap smear after the first 3 months. The cap is recommended only for women with a normal Pap smear.

STERILIZATION

In 1995, an estimated 15 million women ages 15–44 in the United States had chosen **sterilization** as their means of birth control. This was 1.4 times the number that had chosen the pill (U.S. Bureau of the Census, 1999a). More women have been sterilized than men, although the acceptance of vasectomy is increasing.

Vasectomy

Male sterilization, or **vasectomy,** has become increasingly popular as a means of birth control. It is a simple operation, requiring only 15–30 minutes in a doctor's office, is relatively inexpensive, and is effective in 90% of cases (Hatcher et al., 1999). It involves either cutting and tying or cauterizing the vas deferens and is performed under local anesthetic (Althaus, 1995).

When failure occurs, it is due to (1) a spontaneous rejoining of the two severed ends of the vas deferens (the duct that carries sperm from the testicle to the penis), (2) a failure on the part of the doctor to tie an accessory vas (some men have three or four), or (3) intercourse without using other contraceptives while there are still residual sperm in the tubes. As a means of fertility control, vasectomy is usually effective, is less costly and less complicated than tubal ligation (female sterilization), and has fewer long-term health risks. Yet U.S. men are less likely than women to seek sterilization (Forste, Tanfer, and Tedrow, 1995).

There are a number of misconceptions regarding vasectomies. A vasectomy does not involve **castration,** which is the removal of the testicles. With a vasectomy, the man continues to ejaculate semen, but it contains no sperm. His physical ability to

Mistakes People Make with Contraceptives

The following are some of the common errors in using various contraceptives.

The Pill

- Forgetting to take the pill for one or more days
- Taking the pill only at the time of intercourse
- Running out of pills and being unable to fill prescription
- Taking the wrong pills on particular days
- Discontinuing taking the pills because of side effects, such as spotting

IUD

- Failing to detect expulsion
- Confusing the pain from PID with pain caused by the IUD
- Failing to notify a physician if pregnancy occurs so that the IUD can be removed

Condoms

- Using deteriorated condoms
- Failing to put them on soon enough
- Failing to withdraw soon enough after ejaculation, so the penis becomes flaccid and the condom slips off
- Reusing a soiled condom
- Using petroleum jelly, which breaks down rubber, as a lubricant

Diaphragm

- Having an improper fit
- Inserting the diaphragm improperly
- Removing the diaphragm too soon after coitus, or if additional spermicidal jelly is desired, removing the diaphragm to put more in
- Using the wrong kind of jelly (petroleum jelly or other nonspermicidal jelly)

Spermicides

- Applying or inserting it improperly
- Confusing feminine hygiene suppositories and spermicidal suppositories
- Not waiting long enough for the suppository to melt

---

have sexual relations is in no way affected; he still has erections, orgasms, and ejaculation as usual. In addition, his voice, body hair, musculature, beard growth, and so on remain unchanged. And he still produces male hormones that are released by the testicles into the bloodstream. Research indicates no adverse health consequences of vasectomy. It appears unlikely to raise men's chances of developing either prostate or testicular cancer (Hatcher et al., 1999).

Vasectomy should be considered permanent, since the chances of rejoining the vas through surgery (vasovasostomy) are uncertain. The effectiveness of microsurgery to reverse the vasectomy depends on the type of vasectomy and the skill of the surgeon, but it can result in pregnancy rates of at least 50% and in the return of sperm to the ejaculate of 90% of the men (Hatcher et al., 1999). Some men who decide to have a vasectomy have some of their sperm frozen in a sperm bank. An overwhelming majority of males who have had vasectomies report they are glad they did and would recommend it to their friends.

Tubal Ligation

Tubal ligation is female sterilization by severing or closing the fallopian tubes, or both, so that mature egg cells and sperm cannot pass through the tube. Since the ovaries and the secretion of female hormones are in no way disturbed, there is no change in the woman's physique, menstrual cycle, sexual interest, or sexual capacity. In most cases, her interest in sex and her sexual responsiveness improve because the fear of unwanted pregnancy has been removed. Women who have undergone tubal ligation also have a reduced risk of contracting ovarian cancer (Edwards, 1994; Rind, 1992c).

Depending on the method of ligation and the surgeon's skill, tubal ligation is reversible in 60–80% of cases, but reversal is not easily accomplished since it requires a second major operation (Hatcher et al., 1999). Most women who request reversal were sterilized young and subsequently divorced and remarried ("Requests," 1984).

The most widely used method of tubal ligation is **laparoscopy**. With this method, the physician introduces a tubular instrument through the abdominal wall, usually through the navel, and closes the fallopian tubes with tubal rings or a spring-locked clip, or through electrocautery.

Existing literature indicates that approximately 0.8–3.7% of women will get pregnant during the first year after the operation, depending on the method of ligation (Hatcher et al., 1999). When pregnancy occurs, it is due to one of three reasons: (1) The woman had an undetected pregnancy at the time of the operation, (2) the surgery was performed improperly, or (3) the tubes reopen as a result of the body's healing process. Younger women have higher failure rates (Hatcher et al., 1999).

Women in the United States who are sterilized at age 30 or younger and those who obtain the procedure postpartum are twice as likely as others to regret the decision over the next 14 years. While this represents a significant portion of those sterilized, the majority are happy with the outcome and have few regrets about their decision (Hillis, 1999).

BIRTH CONTROL WITHOUT DEVICES

Some people, for religious or philosophical reasons, do not want to use artificial means of birth control. The advantages of "natural" methods are that they are free and do not require a trip to the drugstore or the doctor's office. However, they are much less reliable than any other method of birth control, and they provide no protection against STDs.

Fertility Awareness Methods

The **rhythm method,** or calendar method, of birth control relies on timing coitus so that it occurs only during the so-called safe period of the month—that period when the woman is most likely to be infertile. Although authorities differ in their time estimates, we can say with reasonable certainty that the ovum can be fertilized up until 48 hours after it is released and that the sperm can fertilize an ovum up until 48 hours after being ejaculated. However, to be safe, we should add an extra 24 hours to these figures. The average woman ovulates 14 days before her next menstrual period, with a common range of 12–16 days. A few women ovulate regularly outside of this common range; other women

ovulate outside of this range occasionally. Some have very irregular ovulation. For these reasons, for some women, it is difficult to detect a completely "safe period" of the month when pregnancy can't occur. The failure rate during any 1 year is estimated at around 26% (Jones and Forrest, 1992).

A woman can use a variety of physical signs (such as consistency of cervical mucus or body temperature) and the calendar (after recording six menstrual cycles) to determine when she ovulates. Careful attention to one's individual cycle, by whatever means, can only minimize the possibility of pregnancy. Figure 15.4 illustrates the schedules of fertile and infertile periods of women on regular 26- and 31-day cycles and the schedule of a woman whose cycle varies from 26 to 31 days. Since the woman whose schedule is irregular never knows exactly when ovulation occurs nor when her next period will be, she is safer to abstain for 15 days instead of the usual 10. A woman whose cycle is irregular from 24 to 33 days can never find any "safe" period except during menstruation. Of course, these are only statistical calculations. As has been mentioned, one can't really be sure of any infertile period during any cycle. As can be seen in Figure 15.4, possible times for intercourse are severely limited, especially on the irregular cycle.

There are, however, two principal methods by which couples can improve upon the rhythm method. One is the basal body temperature method. This method relies on the fact that body temperature rises a fraction of a degree at the time of ovulation and remains higher for the rest of the cycle. The woman records her temperature daily, looking for the rise. However, such a temperature rise can occur 72 hours prior to ovulation and up to 72 hours afterward. This method is not specific in pinpointing ovulation, but it indicates that ovulation is in process and that, by the third sustained day of the rise, it is in fact complete.

The cervical mucus ovulation detection method relies on cervical mucus as the predictor of ovulation. Sometime before the middle of the menstrual cycle, cervical mucus becomes detectable at the vulva when follicular estrogen rises. At this point, the mucus is sticky and gummy and appears yellow or white. With progressive ripening of the follicle, the mucus becomes increasingly slippery, clear, and stringy, like raw egg white. The vagina becomes increasingly lubricated. The last day of

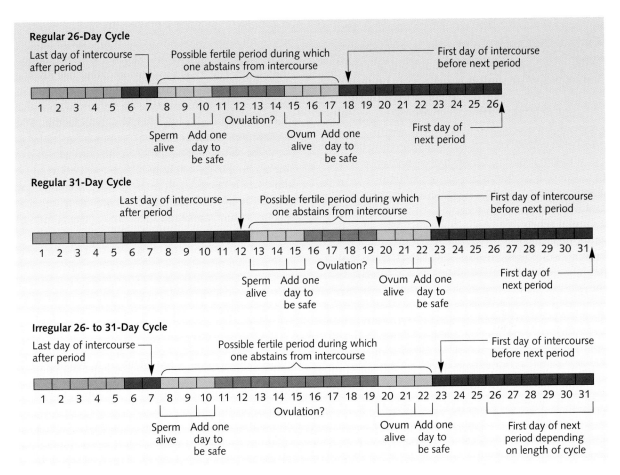

Figure 15.4   Fertile and Infertile Periods During a 26-Day, 31-Day, and Irregular (26- to 31-Day) Cycle

lubrication is called the "peak" and is followed no more than 24 hours later by ovulation. Abstinence is required from the first day of mucus discharge until the fourth day after the peak (Klaus, 1984). There are also a number of ovulation predictor kits on the market that attempt to pinpoint the time of ovulation. The possibility of intercourse and the risk of pregnancy during forbidden times is so great that the method cannot be considered ideal for most couples who want reliable contraception (Trussell and Grummer-Strawn, 1990).

These fertility awareness methods are not very reliable as contraceptive techniques, but they can be helpful in conceiving. Physicians often advise couples who are having difficulty conceiving to use a combination of the basal body temperature method and the cervical mucus method. By having

intercourse daily when the woman is most likely to be ovulating, a couple can greatly enhance the likelihood of conception. The probability of conception is highest on the day of ovulation and drops sharply immediately thereafter. Because it is difficult to determine exactly when ovulation takes place, the possibility of conception is increased when intercourse occurs daily during the most probable times (Hollander, 1996d).

Some people think that sperm can be flushed from the vagina by **douching** with water or some other liquid. However, douching is not effective as a means of contraception, because (1) sperm move very quickly and have probably already entered the cervix by the time the woman begins douching and (2) the jet of water may propel sperm still in the vagina up into the cervix.

Coitus Interruptus

Coitus interruptus refers to the practice of withdrawing the penis from the vagina before ejaculation occurs. Although this method is better than nothing, its success depends on a high degree of self-control on the part of the man. When sexually aroused, the normal man reaches a point beyond which ejaculatory control is impossible. If he doesn't withdraw in time, he will ejaculate whether he wants to or not. Also, before orgasm, the male discharges a small amount of lubrication fluid that has been secreted by the Cowper's glands, although he is not aware of when this preejaculate is discharged. Because this fluid often contains sperm cells that have been residing in the urethra, the sperm may be deposited before the man withdraws. Even though the sperm count is low and fertilization is less likely than with actual orgasm, it can occur. Depending on the care and timing of the man, withdrawal has a failure rate ranging from 4% to 19% (Hatcher et al., 1999). The greatest disadvantage to coitus interruptus is its interference with the sexual satisfaction and pleasure of both the man and the woman.

Noncoital Stimulation

Couples can use techniques of stimulation to orgasm other than intercourse. Mutual masturbation has been used for years as a substitute for intercourse. If the man gets semen on his fingers and introduces sperm into the vaginal canal, however, conception can occur. Interfemoral stimulation is a method whereby the man places his penis between the woman's closed thighs and rubs back and forth along the length of the clitoris. Climax may be reached in this way, but if the male ejaculates near the vaginal opening, there is a possibility the sperm may find their way inside. Oral-genital stimulation is sometimes used, not only as a method of precoital love play but also as a technique of arousal to orgasm.

CHOOSING A METHOD OF CONTRACEPTION

The ideal contraceptive would be (1) 100% effective, (2) inexpensive, (3) convenient to use, without interfering with lovemaking, and (4) without any risk or adverse side effects. Currently, no one method meets all these criteria. Even with contraceptive use, about 1 in 10 women experience an accidental pregnancy. Inconsistent and incorrect use are the main reasons for this high level (Tew and Kirchgaessner, 1999). In deciding on a method, couples might consult their physician, weigh all factors, and make an informed decision.

What contraceptive methods are currently in use among women in the United States? In 1995, the National Center for Health Statistics (NCHS) collected nationally representative data on contraceptive practices among women ages 15–44. The results of the survey are shown in Table 15.1. Sterilization was the most popular contraceptive method among married women and their husbands. The pill was the second most popular method, and the condom was third (U.S. Bureau of the Census, 1999a).

Contraceptive status and method of choice of never-married and previously married women differed sharply from those of married women. Sexually active, never-married women were less likely than married women to practice contraception and were more likely to choose the pill when they did. Previously married women were also less likely than married women to practice contraception but, when using a method, were more likely than either married or never-married women to use an IUD.

ABORTION

If contraceptives are not used or a given method fails, then a woman or a couple is faced with an unplanned pregnancy. One of the alternatives is **abortion.** Abortion raises some difficult questions to which there are no simple answers. Abortion issues may be divided into five categories, which are discussed in the following sections: (1) legal, (2) physical and medical, (3) moral, (4) social and realistic, and (5) psychological and personal.

Legal Considerations

Abortion law is rather complex in the United States. On January 22, 1973, the U.S. Supreme Court ruled that a state could not inhibit or restrict a woman's right to obtain an abortion during the first trimester of pregnancy (the first 12 weeks) and that the decision to have an abortion was the woman's own in

Table 15.1 Number and Percentage Distribution of Women Ages 15–44 Practicing Contraception, by Current Method, According to Marital Status, 1995

Method	Number (in Thousands) and Percentage			
	Total	Never Married	Currently Married	Formerly Married
	60,201	22,679	29,673	7,849
Sterilization (male and female)	24.8	4.8	37.0	36.7
Total sterile	29.7	6.9	43.2	45.1
Pill	17.3	20.4	15.6	14.6
IUD	0.5	0.3	0.7	0.4
Diaphragm	1.2	0.5	1.8	0.9
Condom	13.1	13.9	13.3	10.1
Rhythm/periodic abstinence	1.5	0.6	2.3	0.7
Other methods*	3.9	4.6	3.3	3.9
Seeking pregnancy	4.0	1.5	6.4	2.1
Nonsurgically sterile	1.7	1.1	2.0	2.2
Nonusers				
Never had intercourse	10.9	28.9		
No intercourse in past month	6.2	11.5	0.5	12.7
Had intercourse in past month	5.2	6.4	4.2	5.7
Pregnant, postpartum	4.6	3.1	6.4	1.9
Withdrawal	2.0	1.5	2.3	1.8

Note: Data from *Statistical Abstract of the United States, 1999* (p. 84) by U.S. Bureau of the Census, 1999, Washington, DC: U.S. Government Printing Office.
*Includes implants, injectables, morning after pill, suppository, and less frequently used methods.

consultation with her doctor (*Doe v. Bolton*, 1973; *Roe v. Wade*, 1973; Sarvis and Rodman, 1974). The major ground for the Court's decision was the woman's right to privacy.

The Court further declared that during the second trimester of pregnancy (weeks 13–26)—when abortion is more dangerous—"a state may regulate the abortion procedure to the extent that the regulation relates to the preservation and protection of maternal health" (*Roe v. Wade*, 1973). Reasonable regulation might include outlining the qualifications or licensure of the person who performs abortions or the licensing of the facility where the abortion is performed. The Court went on to say that the state's interest in protecting the life of the fetus arises only after viability (after 24–28 weeks, when the fetus is potentially capable of living outside the mother's womb). However, the state "may go so far as to proscribe [forbid] abortion during that period except when it is necessary to preserve the life or health of the mother" (Reed, 1975, p. 205). The reasons the Court rejected the state's interest in protecting human life from the moment of conception were (1) that the "unborn have never been recognized in the law as persons in the whole sense" and (2) that the rights extended to the unborn, in law, are contingent upon live birth, so (3) a state's interest in protecting fetal life cannot override the woman's right to privacy (Sarvis and Rodman, 1974).

In 1997, Congress passed the Hyde Amendment, sharply restricting the use of federal Medicaid funding to pay for abortions for low-income women. This ban on federal funding of abortions has been renewed every year since. The Supreme Court has also ruled that a state may require an unmarried minor who seeks an abortion to notify or obtain the consent of her parents; if she does not wish to do so, she must be able to obtain permission from a judge ("The Supreme Court," 1990). The judge's authorization is based on a determination either that the minor is mature enough to make her own decision or that it is in the minor's best interest to have the abortion without informing her parents (Rodman, 1991).

This decision, which took effect in 1982 and was upheld in 1990, has had wide-ranging implications. Ideally, all unmarried minors should get parental advice about their pregnancy. But it is precisely because of the lack of good family relationships that minors refuse to talk to their parents. Agencies in three states report that 20–55% of their minor patients are going to court rather than confiding in their parents ("The Supreme Court," 1990). In Minnesota, which requires minors to notify both parents or to get permission of a judge to have an abortion, 43% of minors used the court bypass rather than tell their parents (Blum, Resnick, and Stark, 1990). This puts these minors through an emotionally difficult and sometimes traumatic experience.

Based on a nationally representative sample of more than 1,500 unmarried minors who had gotten an abortion, the most common reasons given for not telling their parents were wanting to preserve their relationship with their parents and wanting to protect the parents from stress and conflict. Of those who did not tell their parents, 30% had experienced violence in their family, feared that violence would occur, or were afraid of being forced to leave home (Henshaw and Kost, 1992). Another study, this one of Black urban teenagers, revealed that most adolescents voluntarily told one or both of their parents, usually their mother, when they became pregnant, and most involved their mother in their decisions. Even when a young woman did not confide in either parent, she generally sought support from a specific person, usually an adult who had served as a parent surrogate. If the respondent did not turn to her mother, it was often because they did not live together (Zabin, Hirsch, Emerson, and Raymond, 1992). Even if an adolescent did not confide in an important adult in her life as soon as she suspected she was pregnant, she was likely to do so at some time between the pregnancy test and her final decision.

In 1989, the U.S. Supreme Court agreed to hear a case brought to it by the state of Missouri (*Webster v. Reproductive Health Services,* 1989). The Court was asked to rule on four sections of a 1986 act passed by the Missouri legislature:

1. A preamble stating that "the life of each human begins at conception" and that state laws be interpreted to provide unborn children "with all the rights, privileges, and immunities available to other persons, citizens, and residents of this state," subject to the Constitution and the Court's precedents

2. A prohibition on the use of public facilities or employees to perform abortions

3. A prohibition on public funding of abortion counseling

4. A requirement that physicians conduct viability tests prior to performing abortions

In a 5–4 decision, the Court upheld the constitutionality of sections 2 and 4 of the Missouri act and returned to the states the right to place restrictions on abortion. The Court refused to acknowledge the constitutionality of the preamble and contended that it represented only a value judgment of the state of Missouri that did not restrict abortions in any way.

According to the Supreme Court, Missouri and other states may pass laws ensuring that public hospitals or other taxpayer-supported facilities not be "used for the purpose of performing or assisting an abortion not necessary to save the life of the mother." In addition, states may make it "unlawful for any public employee within the scope of his employment to perform or assist an abortion, not necessary to save the life of the mother." This latter ruling is not intended to direct the conduct of any physician or health care provider, private or public, but "is directed solely at those persons responsible for expending public funds" (*Webster v. Reproductive Health Services,* 1989). The Court did not declare illegal, as such, the performance of abortions in privately supported facilities by physicians who are paid privately. However, critics do point out that the decision severely restricts the availability of abortions to the poor.

One of the most controversial parts of the *Webster* decision is the rejection of the trimester provisions of *Roe v. Wade* (1973) and the acceptance of medical tests for viability as one possible substitute. According to the Court, a state may make it mandatory for medical tests to be performed on any fetus thought to be at least 20 weeks old to determine its viability before an abortion can be performed. The Court reaffirmed the provision in *Roe v. Wade* that states may pass laws regulating or proscribing abortion after viability "except where it is necessary . . . for the preservation of the life or health of the mother."

This decision has been criticized because, according to some, determination of viability is expensive, can be unreliable and inaccurate, and may pose significant health risks for both the pregnant woman and the fetus. Various tests can be done to find gestational age, fetal weight, and lung maturity. However, at 20 weeks of age, no fetus is viable or can be made viable. Tests of lung maturity cannot provide the necessary information until a fetus is 28–30 weeks old in gestational age; tests before this age are imprecise ("The Court Edges Away," 1989). Furthermore, the standard measure used by physicians to calculate the length of pregnancies is based on the woman's report of the onset of her last menstrual period. But using the first day of the last menstrual period as the beginning marker for terminated pregnancies is misleading because the calculations then include the 2 weeks that precede fertilization. Hence, the length of pregnancy is estimated by physicians as always 2 weeks more than the actual developmental age of the fetus (Santee and Henshaw, 1992).

In defending its position, the majority of the Court said, "We are satisfied that the requirement of these tests permissibly furthers the State's interest in protecting potential human life" (*Webster v. Reproductive Health Services*, 1989). Opponents argue that regardless of the tests' outcome the decision eliminates the woman's right to choose whether she will have an abortion.

Both right-to-choose and right-to-life advocates predicted that the Court's decision would lead to a 50-state battle to determine whether additional restrictions will be enacted. Faye Wattleton, then president of the Planned Parenthood Federation of America, commented, "Now a woman's access to abortion will become hostage to geography as states enact a patchwork of laws and regulations aimed at blocking abortions" (Dionne, 1989, p. 1). Archbishop John May, president of the National Conference of Catholic Bishops, observed, "The biggest winners today are the tiniest people of all— children within the womb" (Dionne, 1989, p. 1).

A recent case heard by the U.S. Supreme Court was *Planned Parenthood of Southeastern Pennsylvania v. Casey* (1992). The Court reaffirmed the essential holding in *Roe v. Wade* that prior to fetal viability a woman has a constitutional right to obtain an abortion. After viability, a state may prohibit an abortion, but only if it provides exceptions when the woman's life or health is at risk. At the same time, however, the Court discarded *Roe*'s trimester framework, which severely restricted a state's power to regulate abortion in the early stages of pregnancy, stating that the trimester framework "undervalues" the state's interest in potential life, which exists throughout pregnancy. The Court held that the state may regulate abortion throughout pregnancy as long as it does not impose an "undue burden" on a woman's right to terminate her pregnancy. The Court defined "undue burden" as a regulation that "has the purpose or effect of placing a substantial obstacle in the path of a woman seeking an abortion of a nonviable fetus."

Applying the undue burden standard, the Court upheld several provisions of the Pennsylvania abortion law, including a 24-hour waiting period that follows completion of specific informed-consent requirements and reporting and record-keeping rules—provisions that were virtually identical to conditions the Court had declared unconstitutional just a few years earlier. The Court upheld the law's parental consent provision but struck down, as an undue burden, the requirement that a married woman notify her spouse of her intent to have an abortion ("Court Reaffirms *Roe* but Upholds Restrictions," 1992). The U.S. Supreme Court has already agreed to hear other cases, so the stage has been set for further battles.

The most recent controversy in abortion law has been over partial-birth abortions. Partial-birth abortions often get confused with late-term abortions, but the two are not necessarily the same. "Late-term" refers only to the time the abortion takes place, after week 26 and in the third trimester of pregnancy; "partial-birth" refers to the method used in aborting the fetus. Partial-birth abortions are performed in the second and third trimesters of pregnancy, through a procedure known as intact dilation and extraction, which involves inducing a breech delivery with a forceps (Abortion Law Homepage, 2000). Laws to ban the partial-birth abortion procedure have been passed in at least 30 states. Supporters of the bans have argued that this procedure is not so much abortion as infanticide, which is illegal. If the partial-birth delivery used in the procedure is indeed a "birth," then a person exists and has constitutional rights. Opponents of the law reject this idea and focus on the fact that other abortion procedures traditionally upheld by the Court can involve the delivery or partial delivery of a live but nonviable fetus that dies as a result of the procedure. They argue that these laws only serve to restrict a woman's right to an abortion (Sykes, 2000).

In sum, according to current Supreme Court rulings, states can regulate abortion in five ways: (1) ban elective abortions after the fetus is viable, (2) require parental consent or notice or a judge's bypass before a minor can obtain an abortion, (3) require informed consent or counseling before an abortion, (4) require certain kinds of record keeping for each state, and (5) require waiting periods, usually 24–48 hours, before an abortion.

Physical and Medical Considerations

Certainly, from every viewpoint, if a pregnancy is to be terminated, it should be terminated as soon after conception as possible. This is of special necessity from a biological and medical point of view. Many physicians and hospitals refuse to perform abortions on women who are more than 12 weeks pregnant. Many physicians and other adults who approve of abortion in the first trimester of pregnancy find so-called partial-birth abortions, performed later in pregnancy, unacceptable (Winikoff, 1995).

What are the possible aftereffects of abortion on the mother's health and future childbearing? Overall, induced abortion is safer for women than childbirth itself ("Researchers Confirm," 1982). In general, abortion doesn't impair the ability of women to become pregnant again ("Abortion Doesn't Impair," 1985).

Moral Considerations

Much of the controversy about abortion has centered on moral issues. For many individuals and religious denominations, abortion is wrong because it represents the murder of a human being. According to this point of view, the soul enters the body at the moment of conception, so the new life is immediately a human. The Christian Church in the centuries after Christ forbade abortion under all conditions from the beginning of pregnancy.

Opponents of this view argue that to say that a group of human cells, however highly differentiated at the early stages of growth, is a person is to stretch the point. These cells have neither consciousness nor any distinctly human characteristics and traits. Advocates of this view point to the teachings of the thirteenth-century theologian and philosopher Thomas Aquinas, who said that there was neither life nor ensoulment until the fetus moved, so abortion was not sinful in the first 16 weeks of pregnancy. Three centuries later, the Church fixed ensoulment at 40 days after conception, following Aristotle's teaching. Abortion during the first 40 days of pregnancy was not considered sinful until the First Vatican Council in 1869, when it was once more ruled that life begins at the time of conception and that abortion at any time is a grave sin. This view was reaffirmed by the Second Vatican Council and made official Catholic doctrine by Pope Paul

VI in 1965. In recent times, Protestant thought has become more liberal, permitting abortion under certain circumstances.

Members of the right-to-life movement and others emphasize the right to life of the fetus and say that no individual or state should deprive the fetus of its constitutional and moral right to live. Legally, of course, the Supreme Court has never established the fact that the fetus is a person, enjoying full protection under the Constitution and the Bill of Rights. Right-to-choose proponents emphasize that the moral and legal rights of other parties must also be considered, not just those of the fetus. What about the rights of the mother, the father, and other family members (Finlay, 1981)? Should these lives be sacrificed for the sake of the fetus?

The Supreme Court ruling establishes the legal principle that the mother's rights take precedence, at least before viability. Obviously, the moral dilemmas raised by the abortion issue are not easy to solve (Allgeier, Allgeier, and Rywick, 1981; Silber, 1980).

Social Considerations

Those advocating the right to choose emphasize the fact that strict laws against abortion, such as those that permit abortion only when the mother's physical life is threatened, have never worked. A current example can be found in Ireland, where abortion law is very restrictive. The law forbids information about access to abortion and permits abortion only when a woman's life is threatened (directly or indirectly) by a pregnancy. Nonetheless, thousands of Irish women travel to England, where abortion law is less restrictive, for abortions each year (Francome, 1992).

If a woman is determined not to have her baby, she may attempt, however foolishly (and sometimes futilely), to abort her own fetus. Or she may go to an unqualified person and get an illegal abortion that may threaten her life. Various estimates place the number of illegal abortions before 1967 at around 1 million per year, or about 20% of total pregnancies. Maternal death rates from illegal abortions in New York City were about 19 times higher than those from legal abortions. Legalized abortion, therefore, saves lives by reducing the number of illegal attempts (Guttmacher, 1983).

In reply to these social considerations, right-to-life groups emphasize their fears that without any

The Supreme Court has repeatedly been asked to consider when life begins. Who has the right to decide when and if a pregnancy can be terminated? The dilemmas raised by the abortion issue are not easily solved by anyone.

restriction, except the individual woman and her conscience, an "abortion mentality" develops so that abortions become too commonplace. The majority of abortions today are not for medical reasons, but for personal, social, and economic reasons (Belsky, 1992). The highest abortion rate occurs among White women aged 18 19, followed by White women aged 20–24 (Henshaw, 1992). Women who live with a partner outside of marriage or who have no religious identification are 3½ to 4 times as likely as women in the general population to have an abortion (Henshaw and Kost, 1996).

Most thoughtful advocates of abortion agree that it should be only a backup measure, not the primary method of birth control. They urge fuller use of contraceptives among all sexually active people.

Psychological and Personal Considerations

Right-to-life proponents have often pointed to the negative psychological effects on the woman who has had an abortion. But the incidence of psychological aftereffects is a major subject of dispute. Both sides cite facts to support their views. Those advocating the right to choose point to the fact that many women are far more depressed before the abortion is performed than they are afterward. One study found that depression and anxiety decreased after abortion (Rind, 1991). When abortions were illegal, much of the anxiety was over the illegality of the act, so these feelings have been eliminated. Other studies have shown that an abortion does not appear to have an adverse effect on women's self-esteem or psychological well-being (Klitsch, 1992a).

In contrast, right-to-life proponents point to the fact that some women do suffer psychological scars in the aftermath of an abortion. For this reason, abortion counseling, which assists the woman in working through her feelings ahead of time (and afterward if needed), is important. For some, abortion provides great relief with little if any disturbance; for others, the experience is upsetting. The key factor seems to be whether the woman wants

Facts About Abortion

Incidence of Abortion

- Forty-nine percent of pregnancies among American women are unintended; one-half of these are terminated by abortion.

- In 1996, 1.37 million abortions took place, down from an estimated 1.61 million in 1990. From 1973 through 1996, more than 34 million legal abortions occurred.

- Each year, 2 out of every 100 women ages 15–44 have an abortion; 47% of them have had at least one previous abortion, and 55% have had a previous birth.

- An estimated 43% of women will have at least one abortion by the time they are 45 years old.

- Each year, an estimated 50 million abortions occur worldwide. Of these, 20 million procedures are obtained illegally.

Who Has Abortions

- Fifty-two percent of U.S. women obtaining abortions are younger than 25. Women ages 20–24 obtain 32% of all abortions, and teenagers obtain 20%.

- While White women obtain 60% of all abortions, their abortion rate is well below that of minority women. Black women are more than three times as likely as White women to have an abortion, and Hispanic women are roughly two times as likely.

- Catholic women are 29% more likely than Protestants to have an abortion but are about as likely as all women nationally to do so.

- Two-thirds of all abortions are among never-married women.

- On average, women give at least three reasons for choosing abortion. Three-fourths say that having a baby would interfere with work, school, or other responsibilities; about two-thirds say they cannot afford a child; and one-half say they do not want to be a single parent or are having problems with their spouse or partner.

- About 14,000 women have abortions each year following rape or incest.

Contraceptive Use

- Fifty-eight percent of women having abortions in 1995 had used a contraceptive method during the month they became pregnant.

- Eleven percent of women having abortions have never used a method of birth control; nonuse is greatest among those who are young, unmarried, poor, Black, Hispanic, or poorly educated.

- Nine in 10 women at risk for unintended pregnancy are using a contraceptive method.

- Forty-nine percent of the 6.3 million pregnancies that occur each year are unplanned; 53% of these occur among the 7% of women at risk for unintended pregnancy who do not practice contraception.

Providers and Services

- Ninety-three percent of U.S. abortions are performed in clinics or doctors' offices.

- The number of abortion providers declined by 14% between 1992 and 1996 (from 2,380 to 2,042). Eighty-six percent of all U.S. counties lacked an abortion provider in 1996. These counties were home to 32% of all 15–44-year-old women.

- Forty-three percent of all abortion facilities provide services only through the 12th week of pregnancy.

- Forty-two percent of nonhospital facilities provided abortions to women less than 6 weeks pregnant in 1996, a 27% increase since 1992, when only one-third (33%) provided such early abortions.

- In 1997, the cost of a nonhospital abortion with local anesthesia at 10 weeks of gestation ranged from $150 to $1,535, and the average amount paid was $316.

- In nonhospital facilities offering both surgical and medical abortion in 1997, the cost of medical abortion ranged from $100 to $1,250, and the average was $401; the average cost of a surgical abortion was $355.

- About 4,200 medical abortions were performed in 1996 and 4,300 in the first half of 1997; these procedures involved the use of mifepristone and methotrexate (in clinical trials or off-label use).

- Twelve percent of all nonhospital abortion providers offered their patients medical abortion in 1997 (163 providers).

- Forty-three percent of nonhospital facilities indicated in 1997 that they would probably provide medical abortions within the next year if the Federal Drug Administration approved mifepristone; 29% said they would do so even in mifepristone were not approved, by using methotrexate.

- Nine in 10 managed-care plans routinely cover abortion or provide limited coverage.

Safety of Abortion

- The risk of abortion complications is minimal; less than 1% of all abortion patients experience a major complication, such as serious pelvic infection or a hemorrhage requiring a blood transfusion or unintended major surgery.

- The risk of death associated with abortion increases with the length of pregnancy, from 1 death for every 530,000 abortions at 8 or fewer weeks to 1 per 17,000 at 16–20 weeks and 1 per 6,000 at 21 or more weeks.

- The risk of death associated with childbirth is about 10 times as high as that associated with abortion.

- Almost half of the women having abortions beyond 15 weeks of gestation say they were delayed because of problems in affording, finding, or getting to abortion services.

- Teens are more likely than older women to delay having an abortion until after 16 weeks of pregnancy, when medical risks associated with abortion increase significantly.

Law and Policy

- In the 1973 *Roe v. Wade* decision, the Supreme Court ruled that women, in consultation with their physician, have a constitutionally protected right to have an abortion in the early stages of pregnancy—that is, before viability—free from government interference.

- In 1992, the Court upheld the right to abortion in *Planned Parenthood v. Casey*. However, the ruling significantly weakened the legal protections previously afforded women and physicians by giving states the right to enact restrictions that do not create an "undue burden" for women seeking abortion.

- The most common restrictions in effect are parental involvement requirements, mandatory counseling and waiting periods, and limitations on public funding.

- Thirty-one states currently enforce parental consent or notification laws for minors seeking an abortion: AL, AR, DE, GA, IA, ID, IN, KS, KY, LA, MA, MD, MI, MN, MO, MS, NC, ND, NE, OH, PA, RI, SC, SD, TN, TX, UT, VA, WI, WV, and WY. The Supreme Court ruled that minors must have the alternative of seeking a court order authorizing the procedure.

- Forty-five percent of minors who have abortions tell their parents, and 61% undergo the procedure with at least one parent's knowledge. The great majority of parents support their daughter's decision.

Public Funding

- The U.S. Congress has barred the use of federal Medicaid funds to pay for abortions, except when the woman's life would be endangered by a full-term pregnancy or in cases of rape or incest.

- About 14% of all abortions in the United States are paid for with public funds, virtually all of which are state funds. Sixteen states (CA, CT, HI, ID, IL, MA, MD, MN, MT, NJ, NM, NY, OR, VT, WA, and WV) pay for abortions for some poor women.

- Without publicly funded family planning services, an estimated 1.3 million additional unplanned pregnancies would occur annually; about 632,300 would end in abortion—at least a 40% increase in the incidence.

Note: From "Induced Abortion" by Alan Guttmacher Institute, February 2000, *Facts in Brief* [Fact sheet]. Retrieved from the World Wide Web: http://www.agi-usa.org/pubs/fb_induced_abortion.html.

an abortion or is reluctant to obtain one. Being refused an abortion and forced to bear an unwanted child can lead to psychological problems such as depression. But the woman who has health problems and has to have an abortion, or who is persuaded to have an abortion against her better judgment, is also likely to have negative psychological reactions. If the decision is the woman's, adverse psychological reactions are minimized.

INFERTILITY

In 1995, an estimated 15% of women ages 15–44 sought services for infertility (U.S. Bureau of the Census, 1999a). With help, about half of infertile couples are able to conceive (Collins, Wrixon, Janes, and Wilson, 1983).

Causes of Infertility

About 40% of infertility is a result of the male having problems. For a male to impregnate a woman, he must (1) be able to maintain an erection long enough to ejaculate sperm within the vagina, (2) have an unobstructed pathway through the vas deferens and the urethra, allowing the sperm and semen to pass through, (3) secrete semen in adequate amounts and with the right chemical composition to keep sperm alive and healthy and to transport it to the ovum, and (4) produce healthy sperm in sufficient numbers. Male infertility is caused by a number of psychological as well as physiological factors. The most common factor is impaired sperm production due to environmental toxins, heat, undescended testes, abnormal veins in the scrotum (varicocele), testicular atrophy, drugs (alcohol abuse, chronic marijuana use, and others), prolonged fever, and endocrine disorders affecting the production of sex hormones. Sometimes antibodies in the male or female are detrimental to sperm, or there is an obstruction in the seminal tract preventing the sperm from passing through. Defective delivery of sperm into the vagina may be due to functional or organic impotence or to premature ejaculation before penetration, or it may result from surgery to the bladder or prostate.

About 40% of infertility cases involve the woman. There are a number of causes of infertility in women (Ansbacher and Adler, 1988; Malinak and Wheeler, 1985), including the following:

(1) disorders of the reproductive organs, ovaries, fallopian tubes, uterus, cervix, (2) vaginitis, (3) sexually transmitted diseases, (4) endocrine disorders of the pituitary, thyroid, ovaries, and adrenals, (5) systemic diseases such as diabetes mellitus, (6) genetic disorders, and (7) immunologic causes such as formation of antibodies detrimental to sperm. Women who smoke cigarettes also may have difficulty becoming pregnant when they wish to; the amount that they smoke appears to be related to the waiting time until conception. Research indicates that the median waiting time to achieve conception is approximately 1 month longer for women who smoke more than 10 cigarettes a day than for women who do not smoke (Hollander, 1996b). Age is also important to fertility: Fertility decreases gradually after age 35 and ceases at menopause.

About 20% of infertility is caused by factors that involve both partners. Negative factors include too frequent or infrequent intercourse, the use of petroleum jelly or another lubricant that damages the sperm, intercourse only during infertile periods of the month, and advanced age or poor health.

Infertility and Subjective Well-Being

Infertility causes stress and negatively affects women's and men's subjective well-being. The greater the stress, the lower the partners' self-esteem and internal control and the greater their interpersonal conflict (Abbey, Andrews, and Halman, 1994). They may feel they have failed, they may blame each other for their infertility, and they may experience considerable anxiety when they are striving to conceive. In addition, visits to the doctor can interfere with their ability to fulfill their job responsibilities. Uncertainty about future parenting makes it difficult for people to initiate endeavors such as a new job or additional schooling. The cost of fertility treatment can create a financial burden as well. Relationships with friends and family frequently are strained, either because the partners keep their situation a secret or because others' reactions to their problem are not helpful. Thus, infertility affects a variety of different aspects of men's and women's well-being, and this is reflected in its strong negative relationship to life quality (Andrews and Halman, 1992).

One study found that the great stress associated with infertility undermines the marital adjustment of both spouses. A man is better able to adjust to an involuntarily childless marriage if his partner is employed or has high earnings. A woman's marital adjustment diminishes with the length of marriage and the course of treatment for infertility. The stress women experience as a result of infertility influences the perception of their marriage and may undermine their ability to get the support they need in adjusting to nonparenthood (Ulbrich, Coyle, and Llabre, 1990).

In another study, significant increases in stress and decreases in marital functioning were experienced by subjects as the treatment progressed. Furthermore, greater levels of marital stress were observed in couples who did not conceive. Nonpregnant women experienced a substantially higher level of stress and lower levels of sexual satisfaction than women who became pregnant. In general, the women experienced greater stress than the men as treatment progressed (Benazon, Wright, and Sabourin, 1992). Another study found that infertility treatments significantly affected both marital and sexual satisfaction after treatment was terminated, as well as during the treatment itself (Pepe and Byrne, 1991).

Treatment of Infertility

Partners older than 35 should see a doctor after 6 months of unsuccessful attempts to conceive. Younger couples can wait as long as a year. Older couples need help sooner because of physical and psychological factors that work against conception the longer treatment is postponed. Also, some methods are not available to couples after they reach a certain age.

Treatment for infertility will depend on the cause. Surgical and hormonal treatments are most common. The partners will also probably be instructed in fertility awareness methods (described earlier in the chapter) so that they can have intercourse when there is the greatest likelihood that the woman is ovulating. If these treatment methods are not successful, the couple may want to consider alternative means of conception that have become available through recent breakthroughs in medical technology.

Alternative Means of Conception

Artificial insemination is the injection of sperm into the woman's vagina or uterus for the purpose of inducing pregnancy (Cushner, 1986). **Homolo-**gous insemination, or **AIH** (artificial insemination–husband), is artificial insemination using the man's sperm. His sperm is collected, frozen, and stored until a sufficient quantity is available; then it is thawed and injected. AIH is usually chosen to try to resolve problems with the man's sperm (such as a low sperm count), but the rate of conception is only about 5%. **Heterologous insemination,** or **AID** (artificial insemination–donor), is more effective (Tagatz, Bigson, Schiller, and Nagel, 1980).

In vitro fertilization (**IVF**) involves removing an egg cell from a woman, fertilizing it with sperm in the laboratory, growing it for 3 or 4 days, and then implanting one or more of the subsequent blastocysts (preembryos) in the uterine wall. Up to four blastocysts may be returned to the womb, since using multiple blastocysts increases the chance of pregnancy. With in vitro fertilization, there is about a 25% pregnancy rate. IVF offers the reward of a biological child, but it entails extremely high financial, emotional, and physical costs (L. S. Williams, 1992). The procedure is used when the fallopian tubes are blocked, so that the sperm can't reach the ovum. The procedure is opposed by those who feel it is immoral in that it tampers with nature.

Cryopreservation, or the freezing of blastocysts, is fast becoming commonplace as a way of augmenting in vitro fertilization. Cryopreservation makes it possible to store the extra blastocysts (preembryos)for later use in the event that earlier attempts at implantation are unsuccessful. Cryopreservation further allows for the possibility of blastocyst adoption. It is estimated that frozen blastocysts may be kept potentially viable for 600 years and perhaps even 10,000 years (Edwards, 1991).

Embryo transplant, in comparison to IVF, is relatively simple, less invasive, and more successful, because the embryo is over 14 days developed. This method has the added advantage of being nonsurgical; the transfer from donor to recipient is accomplished by a specially designed catheter. The use of the procedure need not be confined to infertile women. It can allow fertile women who are concerned about adverse genetic transmissions to bear a child (Edwards, 1991).

In a **gamete intrafallopian transfer** (**GIFT**), the egg and sperm are inserted directly into the fallopian tube, where normal conception takes place. "GIFT is what nature really does, with a little help from us," says Dr. Ricardo Asch, professor of gynecology and obstetrics at the University of California

These babies are living examples of the success of in vitro fertilization. One hundred sixty-eight babies and their parents attended this party to celebrate the 10th anniversary of in vitro fertilization worldwide.

at Irvine (Ubell, 1990). The success rate is 40%—double that of in vitro fertilization.

In an **ovum transfer,** a volunteer female donor is artificially inseminated with sperm from the infertile woman's partner. The **zygote** is removed after 5 days and transplanted to the mother-to-be, who carries the child during pregnancy (Dunn, Ryan, and O'Brien, 1988).

A **surrogate mother** agrees to be inseminated with the semen of the father-to-be, to carry the fetus to term, and to give the child to the couple along with all rights. There are many unresolved legal questions relating to the rights of the child and to the legitimacy of surrogate agreements. Sometimes the surrogate mother changes her mind and decides not to give up the child. Surrogate mothers give

three reasons for serving in this capacity: (1) compassion and a desire to help a childless couple, (2) enjoyment of pregnancy, and (3) money. In one study, half of surrogate mothers were married and already had children of their own (Sobel, 1981).

The Adoption Option

Strictly speaking, adoption is not a cure for infertility, since over half of all women who have adopted have also given birth to a child. Furthermore, it is more likely that adoption follows giving birth than the other way around (Bachrach, London, and Maza, 1991).

The number of adoptions per year in the United States increased steadily over the decades and reached a peak of 175,000 in 1970. The number has been declining steadily since then; in 1992, it was about 100,000 (U.S. Bureau of the Census, 1992). There are fewer infants available for adoption today because of more effective contraceptives, more unmarried mothers keeping their babies (Donnelly and Voydanoff, 1991), and legalized abortion. About half of those who petition for adoption are related to the child they wish to adopt. Among women who have ever married, adoption is more common among Whites than among Blacks or Hispanics, among those with at least a high school education, and among those in higher income brackets. In 1991, about 8% of adoptions were of orphans from foreign countries, with Romanian children constituting over one-fourth the number and smaller numbers coming from Korea, Colombia, India, the Philippines, Peru, and other countries (U.S. Bureau of the Census, 1992). Orphans from Russia were first brought to the United States for adoption in 1992 (personal conversation with a client). Interracial adoptions of minority children in the United States have declined because of the influence of minority group advocates and social workers who are concerned about identity problems in the children.

Among petitioners not related to the child, about 40% of placements are through public agencies, 30% are through private agencies, and another 30% are through independent sources (U.S. Bureau of the Census, 1992). In recent years, there has been a dramatic increase in the percentage of adoptions arranged privately (Daly and Sobol, 1994). Because there are long waiting periods to adopt a child through established agencies, some adoptive parents turn to independent sources: the mother herself or an agent (usually a lawyer) specializing in open adoption. In **open adoption,** the birth mother is permitted to meet and play an active role in selecting the adoptive parents. She may continue to have contact with her child and the adoptive parents after her child has been placed, depending on the agreement. Open adoption is usually expensive, involving lawyer fees and birth expenses. Six states forbid private adoptions, but other states, such as California and Texas, support them. Many authorities claim that open adoption eases the pain for the birth mother and is in the best interests of the child (Kallen, Griffore, Popovich, and Powell, 1990). Other specialists claim the opposite, saying that it

is not in the child's best interests to tell him or her of the adoption unless asked, much less let the child know who the birth mother and biological father are. Some states have laws allowing adoptees to get copies of their original birth certificates.

Family practitioners in North America once believed that successful adoption outcomes required complete severance of adopted children's biological ties. Original birth records were sealed, and adoptees received little background biological information. Although many people now challenge this view, thousands of adoptees have been raised under this secrecy rule. Recently, increasing numbers of adoptees have searched for and contacted their birth mother. These reunions have created an unforeseen social event called the adoption reunion, which can pose several problems. Birth mothers may not have told others that they had had the child. They may marry, have another child, and pretend their second child is their first. Keeping the secret can create anxiety in birth mothers over the years; then the existence of a child they gave up for adoption is revealed. Mothers and children can't help but wonder whether they will be accepted by the other person. Some birth mothers and some adopted children are glad that they have had the reunion; others are not satisfied with the contact outcome (March, 1997).

Until the 1970s, adoption in the United States was shrouded by secrecy and stigma. Members of the adoption triad (adoptive parents, birth parents, and adopted child) were protected from one another in the belief that all benefited from confidentiality. Birth mothers allowed their parental rights to be terminated, transferring those rights to adoption agencies, which then placed the children with adoptive parents. Adoptive parents and birth parents never met, and adopted children usually were not given the opportunity to meet their birth parents. This secrecy was the result of the stigma that the culture had placed upon adoption: Birth parents had children out of wedlock, and so adopted children were "illegitimate." In recent decades, there have been noticeable changes in the confidentiality rules once commonplace in agency-facilitated adoptions. Adoption practices now lie on a continuum of openness that allows for different levels of communication between adoptive parents and birth parents. In confidential adoptions, there is no communication between the adoptive family and the birth parents. In fully disclosed, or open, adoptions, the adoptive family and the birth parents maintain direct, ongoing communication. In mediated adoptions, communication between the adoptive family and the birth parents is relayed through a third party without the exchange of identifying information.

Many adoptive families move along the continuum throughout their life cycle, making significant changes in levels of openness. For example, adoptions that begin as confidential may evolve into relationships involving direct correspondence and full disclosure. Conversely, some adoptions move in the opposite direction, decreasing in openness over time. Changes in adoption openness are potentially stressful to the family system; they are often a response to one or more members' dissatisfaction with the current level of openness. For example, a child can become unhappy with the lack of information regarding his or her background. Lack of basic genealogical or background information interferes with the process of developing a coherent identity and sense of self. Adoptive parents, too, can be dissatisfied with their ability to provide the child with a birth history and related information. Consequently, changes in adoption openness are often made in response to a problem or an issue the family needs to address.

The very act of increasing adoption openness can be stressful. When a family moves toward more openness, it must extend its boundaries to include someone often perceived as threatening. The media sometimes portray birth parents as attempting to reclaim adopted children if given the opportunity. And adopted children may be portrayed as being very upset if their birth parents do not measure up to their idealized image. Once an adoption reunion takes place, the birth parents and the adopted child must arrive at some arrangement whereby they maintain contact in a manner satisfactory to all concerned. Continuing to negotiate boundaries that maintain a level of comfort for all members of the triad requires significant skill. Experience has shown that relationships work best when they evolve over time, with any changes in openness being mutually determined by all parties involved (Mendenhall, Grotevant, and McRoy, 1996).

An important consideration is how the adoptive parents feel about having adopted children and how the adoptees themselves turn out. As in other families, the family environment is a crucial factor in adoptees' adjustment (Stein and Hoopes, 1986). Although school and behavior problems are more prevalent in adopted children during the elementary years, most adopted children do not show any such problems, especially by adolescence (Brodzinsky, Schechter, Braff, and Singer, 1984). In a study of adoptive parents and their adolescents, parents acknowledged disadvantages of adoption yet reported that their lives and those of their children were no different from those of biological families (Kaye and Warren, 1988). The adolescents themselves acknowledged disadvantages of adoption even less than their parents. Some adoptees become aware of negative reactions to them because others characterize their parents as different from the norm. Secrecy about biological kinship ties prevents adoptees from being able to respond to others' questions about their parents. After a reunion with birth parents, adoptees generally have a higher perception of self and feel more socially acceptable (March, 1995).

TO PARENT OR NOT TO PARENT

Couples today can decide when to have children, how many children to have, and even whether to have children. These choices have become possible because adequate means of contraception are available to prevent unwanted pregnancies and because sociocultural norms relating to parenting are undergoing profound changes (Neal, Groat, and Wicks, 1989).

In a 1995 population survey, an examination of lifetime birth expectations of all married women ages 18–34 revealed that the number of births to date was 1.1 per woman and that 48% did not expect any future births (U.S. Bureau of the Census, 1996/1997). Among those surveyed, 9.3% expected to have no children at all. Having children is still favored over not having children, although the number of children desired is declining.

Delayed Parenthood

In recent decades, the timing of the birth of the first child has been delayed. In 1998, the median age for women at first birth was 24.3, compared to 22.0 in

In a recent survey, the larger proportion of women who had their first baby after age 30 were highly educated, professional women in dual-career marriages.

1972. Birthrates for women in their thirties increased 2% in 1998 to 87.4 per 1,000, up 67% since its low in 1975. The number of births to women ages 35–39 reached a record high in 1998 of 424,890. In 1998, the proportion of all first births to women 30 and older was 23% compared to just 5% in 1975 (Ventura, Martin, Curtin, Mathews, and Park, 2000). This delay in parenthood may be attributed to delayed marriage, financial considerations, increased pressure for women to get more education and get started in a career, and desire for personal development. However, according to one study, there were no differences in marital adjustment or self-esteem between delayed childbearers and those having children at younger ages (Roosa, 1988).

The long-term effect of delaying first birth is decreasing fertility, because women who delay childbearing end up having fewer children. The effect on families is probably positive. Partners have more time to adjust to marriage before becoming parents. They are usually more emotionally mature, stable, and responsible. Late childbearers are more settled in jobs and careers and more likely to have greater insight, own their own homes, and have more savings. They are usually better able to handle the competing demands of work and parenthood. Thus, a new stage appears to be developing: a transition stage between marriage and parenthood during which partners are free to pursue personal development, to build a stable marriage, and to be-

come financially secure before taking on the responsibility of children.

The trend toward delayed parenthood may or may not be accompanied by increased health risks. Assuming adequate health care during pregnancy, childbirth, and the postpartum period, infants born to women ages 30–39 appear to be just as healthy at birth as those born to younger women (Witwer, 1990a). However, there does seem to be greater risk of spontaneous abortions, chromosomal abnormalities, and multiple gestations among women over 30 than among those younger. If the mother is 40 or older, the infant is at higher risk for low birth weight and infant death during the first year than if the mother is younger ("Children of Older Women," 1988).

Reasons for Having Children

The arguments couples give for having children are very personal ones (Neal, Groat, and Wicks, 1989):

> My life would not be complete without having children. Children help you feel fulfilled. I never felt like an important person until I became a parent.

> I've always wanted a family of my own. When you have children, it gives you someone to do things with, to provide companionship, fun, and love.

> I think I'd be very lonesome if I and my spouse were all alone. Life could get pretty boring.

I don't think you really become a mature adult until you have children. I know I never really grew up until after the kids were born. You learn responsibility and to think of someone beside yourself. It helps us to be better people.

Unless you have children, people think there's something wrong with you. I think it's only natural to feel you want to be a parent and that you can be a good one too.

I've always wanted someone to love and who loves me.

I think children help to bring you together and to have something in common. It gives you something to work for.

Children are a part of you. When you're gone, they're still here, an extension of you, carrying on your life and family.

I think one of the reasons for marriage is to have children. It's part of finding spiritual fulfillment. (Author's counseling and teaching notes)

Couples who desire children recognize that there are disadvantages, but for them the advantages far outweigh the negative factors (Goldsteen and Ross, 1989). They'd rather have children than extra money to spend or extra time for leisure, travel, or new interests and hobbies. They put having children before being able to come and go as they wish, having an orderly household, working full-time, or being alone with their spouse.

In addition to personal reasons for having children, childless couples experience social pressures to become parents. One source of pressure is the negative attitude some people have toward those who are childless (Callan, 1985). Women report that they are stigmatized to some extent because they do not have children. Other people try to make them feel that they are abnormal, selfish, immoral, irresponsible, immature, unhappy, unfulfilled, or nonfeminine. Women also report that family members and friends generally accept their childlessness for the first 12 months. Then, after the first year, the pressure to have a baby grows, reaching a peak during the third or fourth year. After the fifth year, the pressure diminishes; family and friends give up trying to persuade them.

Choosing a Child-Free Marriage

While the vast majority of couples want to have children, voluntary childlessness is increasing.

About 9% of women ages 15–44 expect to have no children, and about 6.6% of all women remain voluntarily childless (National Center for Health Statistics, 1995). One survey revealed that women who had a post–high school education were far less likely to have children than were those who had less education. Ethnicity was not a significant determinant of childlessness, but childhood residence was. Rural women were less likely to remain childless than were those who grew up in nonrural areas (U.S. Bureau of the Census, 1987). Other research revealed little difference in happiness in the family of origin between those who wanted to remain childless and those who did not. However, the childless were less traditional and less sexist in their views of women (Feldman, 1981).

Surveys among youths have yielded similar results: Women who wanted to remain childless had higher social mobility goals, were less likely to want to be "housewives only," and were more likely to prefer an urban residence and to expect to marry at later ages than women who wanted children (Kenkel, 1985). Interestingly, another survey among Black and White adolescents revealed that both Black and White males placed more value on having children than did their female counterparts (Thompson, 1980).

Couples who are voluntarily childless have some convincing arguments against having children. One study of 600 couples in the early years of marriage listed the following disadvantages of children (Neal et al., 1989): Child care takes too much time; children cause too much worry and tension; they have a negative effect on one's health and stamina; they cause too much disorder in the household; they cost too much; they require a drastic change in life-style; they make it difficult for a woman to work outside the home; and having children contributes to the population problem.

Let's look at some of the arguments against having children. Problems of overpopulation do continue to increase (Donaldson and Keely, 1988). They will not, however, if couples reproduce only themselves, that is, if they have only two children.

Some childless couples frankly admit that they worry about how their children will turn out and they don't want to take the gamble.

Another of the principal arguments against having children is the restriction on freedom that rearing children entails. Having children means readjusting one's life-style to take into account their

For many people, one reason for having children is to perpetuate the family. From their older relatives, the children learn family history, values, and traditions to pass on to future generations.

needs and activities. A mother from Ann Arbor, Michigan, commented, "Suddenly I had to devote myself to the child totally. I was under the illusion that the baby was going to fit into my life, and I found that I had to switch my life and my schedule to fit him" (author's counseling notes). It's a simple fact that no children means no childwork and less housework. No children means more freedom for the partners to do what they please.

There is no question that the woman who is seeking self-fulfillment through a career of her own finds it much easier when she doesn't have children (Faux, 1984). As a result, women brought up to find personal fulfillment primarily through career pursuits may not feel dissatisfied or threatened if they do not also have children (Reading and Amatea, 1986). It depends on what women are socialized to do and become.

For many couples, the decision not to have children right away gradually evolves into a decision not to have children at all. In her study of 52 voluntarily childless couples, Veevers (1974a, 1974b) found that only one-third of the couples had agreed *before* marriage not to have children. For the other two-thirds, remaining childless came not as an agreement ahead of time but as a series of postponements that took place in four stages.

In the first stage, couples postponed having children for a definite period because they were working, graduating from school, traveling, buying a house, saving a nest egg, or adjusting to marriage.

During the second stage, the couple remained committed to parenthood but postponed the event indefinitely, perhaps because they "couldn't afford it now" or needed "to feel more ready." In the third stage, there was open acknowledgment that they might remain permanently childless, since they had already experienced many of the social, personal, and economic advantages of remaining childless. In the fourth stage, the couple had made a definite decision not to have children. For some, this involved a change in attitude or a recognition that an implicit decision had already been made and that it now ought to be acknowledged openly.

Effects of Children on Parents' Happiness

One of the motherhood and marital myths is that married women with children are happier than women in childless couples. Children can have either a positive or a negative effect on individual psychological well-being depending on the situation (Goldsteen and Ross, 1989; Menaghan, 1989). One study found that childless women were generally as happy and well adjusted as mothers (Callan, 1987). Another study found that the voluntarily child-free couples displayed higher levels of cohesion and marital satisfaction than did couples who were parents. They also perceived themselves to be negatively stereotyped by relatives and friends (Somers, 1993).

It is helpful if prospective mates choose each other partially on the basis of their desire to have children or not.

The effect on marriage of having children is variable. As discussed in Chapter 11, marital satisfaction is at its lowest ebb during the child-rearing years (Schumm and Bugaighis, 1986). Couples who expect that the presence of children will solve their marital problems are in for a rude awakening. Having children usually aggravates marital tensions.

Judging from the thousands of cases of child abuse in the United States each year, large numbers of people should not become parents. Many people have neither the interest nor the aptitude to be parents; the resultant performance of the parental role is at best marginally competent and at worst blatantly irresponsible.

One of the arguments people offer for having children is that they don't want to be alone in their old age. There is some evidence that widows who are childless report a lower sense of well-being than those who are not (Beckman and Houser, 1982). However, friendship with people of the same age is far more important to the happiness of older adults. The decision to have children should not be based on the assumption that parenthood will lead to psychological rewards in old age.

The Decision to Have or Not to Have Children

The decision to have children is an important one. It is helpful if prospective mates can choose each other partially on the basis of whether they want children (Callan, 1983; Oakley, 1985). Couples who are trying to decide whether they want children can find various types of help (Skovholt and Thoen, 1987). Couples who search for information and thoroughly discuss alternatives before making parenthood decisions are more likely to make decisions they can live with afterward than are those couples who never really consider the alternatives.

SUMMARY

1. Planned parenthood means having children by choice and not by chance; it means having the number wanted when they are wanted. Family planning is necessary to protect the health of the mother and children, to reduce the negative psychological impact and stress of parenthood, to maintain the well-being of the marriage and the family and its quality of life, and to avoid contributing to global overpopulation.

2. Oral contraceptives are effective, convenient, and easy to use. They are of several types: combination pills containing estrogen and progestin, the minipill (progestin only), and the emergency contraceptive pill (hormonal pills taken in large doses postcoitally). RU-486, the "abortion pill," is a new option.

3. Combination pills have a number of positive health effects: They reduce the risk of benign breast disease, ovarian cysts, iron-deficiency anemia, PID, ectopic pregnancy, rheumatoid arthritis, and endometrial and ovarian cancer. Overall, if women are under 50, don't smoke, and are in good health, they can use oral contraceptives with only a very small risk.

4. Users of combination pills worry about thromboembolism (a small risk, especially for smokers), cancer (a small risk of breast cancer and cervical cancer), fertility (little effect), and various other potential side effects.

5. Other hormonal contraceptives include progestin implants and progestin injections.

6. Contraceptive foam, suppositories, creams, jellies, and film are vaginal spermicides that are used to prevent conception by blocking the entrance to the uterus and by immobilizing and killing the sperm.

7. Mechanical contraceptive devices include the IUD, condom, diaphragm, and cervical cap.

8. About 25 million sterilizations (more female than male) had been performed in the United States as of 1995. Male sterilization, or vasectomy, is easier to perform, is cheaper, and is highly effective, with no adverse health consequences. Tubal ligation for women is now most often done by laparoscopy.

9. Methods of birth control without devices include various fertility awareness techniques, which rely on limiting intercourse to the so-called safe period of the month, when the woman can't get pregnant (there is really no completely safe period); coitus interruptus (withdrawal); and various means of noncoital stimulation. Douching has no value as a contraceptive technique.

10. Sterilization is the most popular contraceptive method among married women, with the pill second and the condom third.

11. The pros and cons of abortion include legal, physical and medical, moral, social, and psychological and personal considerations. The abortion controversy and dilemma have no easy answers.

12. About 15% of women have sought medical help to conceive. About half of them conceive with help.

13. Infertility may be the result of problems of the man, the woman, or the couple.

14. Treatment for infertility will depend on the causes. Surgical and hormonal treatments are most common. The couple may also be instructed in fertility awareness methods to enhance the possibility of conception.

15. Alternative means of conception include artificial insemination (either AIH or AID), in vitro fertilization (IVF), embryo transplant, gamete intrafallopian transfer (GIFT), ovum transfer, and surrogate mothers.

16. Couples who are not able to have children of their own may want to consider adoption. Placements may be made through public agencies, private agencies, or independent sources.

17. In open adoption, the birth mother is permitted to meet and play an active role in selecting the new parents and to have a role in her child's life after placement.

18. At one time, adoption was shrouded in secrecy and stigma: The adoptive parents and adopted child were prevented from knowing the birth history of the child. Adoption practices now lie on a continuum of openness, allowing for different levels of communication between adoptive parents, birth parents, and child. Adoption reunions are not without risk, since either the birth and adoptive parents or the child may be hurt.

19. The crucial factor in how adopted children turn out is the family environment in which they are brought up.

20. Couples today can decide when to have children, how many children to have, and even whether to have children.

21. The number of children desired by U.S. families is declining, with most couples wanting no more than two.

22. More women are delaying parenthood so that they can complete their education, get established in their jobs, have more time to adjust to marriage, and have greater opportunity for personal freedom before having their first baby.

23. The arguments for having children are very personal ones: to make life complete, to have a family of one's own, to avoid boredom, to feel like a mature adult, to meet society's expectations, to have someone to love and to be loved by, to have something to share with one's spouse, or to find spiritual fulfillment. Moreover, society, friends, and parents still put a great deal of pressure on couples to have children.

24. Women who want to remain childless are more likely to be well educated, urban, less traditional in their gender roles, upwardly mobile, and professional; they are also more likely to marry at a later age than women who want children.

25. There are a number of arguments against having children, such as world overpopulation and restrictions on personal freedom. Without children, there is less work at home, more opportunity for self-fulfillment, less strain on the marriage, less worry and tension, less expense, and fewer obstacles to the pursuit of a career.

26. Having children is not a guarantee of personal or marital happiness, especially for those who lack the interest or aptitude for parenthood.

27. The decision to have children is one that couples should thoughtfully consider.

KEY TERMS

family planning

oral contraceptives

combination pills

placebo

minipill

emergency contraceptives

progestin implant

progestin injection

spermicides

IUD

condom

diaphragm

cervical cap

sterilization

vasectomy

castration

tubal ligation

laparoscopy

rhythm method

douching

coitus interruptus

abortion

artificial insemination

homologous insemination (AIH)

heterologous insemination (AID)

in vitro fertilization (IVF)

embryo transplant

gamete intrafallopian transfer (GIFT)

ovum transfer

zygote

surrogate mother

open adoption

QUESTIONS FOR THOUGHT

1. Do you believe in family planning? Why or why not?

2. What are the pros and cons of using the usual birth control pill containing a combination of estrogen and progestin?

3. Would you want to use a spermicide as a contraceptive? Which ones would you use or not use? Why?

4. Assume you are an unmarried person; which of the following types of contraception would you use: condom, diaphragm, or oral contraception? Explain the reasons for your preference.

5. Assume you are married and have all the children you want; would you consider sterilization for yourself (vasectomy if you are a man, tubal ligation if you are a woman)? Explain the reasons for your decision.

6. For you, what is the basic issue, if any, in judging the morality of abortion? Explain.

SUGGESTED READINGS

Butler, J. D., and Walbert, D. F. (Eds.). (1992). *Abortion, Medicine and the Law* (4th ed.). New York: Facts on File. Reprints 30 articles on legal, medical, and ethical aspects of abortion.

Critchlow, D. T. (1999). *Intended Consequences: Birth Control, Abortion, and the Federal Government in Modern America.* New York: Oxford University Press. Takes a comprehensive look at the debate over birth control and abortion in America, both before and after the pill and *Roe v. Wade.*

Foge, L. (1999). *The Third Choice: A Woman's Guide to Placing a Child for Adoption.* Berkeley, CA: Creative Arts Book. Provides a guide for birth mothers considering adoption and discusses pregnancy, birth, relinquishment, and grief and recovery.

Groze, P. (1996). *Successful Adoptive Families: A Longitudinal Study of Special Needs Adoptions.* Westport, CT: Praeger. Examines how special needs' adoptions are characterized by the existence of some unique qualities about either the adoptive child or the circumstances surrounding the adoption.

Hatcher, R. A., et al. (1994). *Contraceptive Technology* (16th rev. ed.). New York: Irvington. Represents the bible of contraception.

Lasker, J. N., and Borg, S. (1994). *In Search of Parenthood: Coping with Infertility and High-Tech Conceptions* (Rev. ed.). Philadelphia: Temple University Press. Examines infertility and gives an introduction to some of the new reproductive options available to infertile couples.

Lunneborg, P. (1992). *Abortion: A Positive Decision.* New York: Bergin & Garvey. Offers a right-to-choice view.

McFarlane, D. R. (2000). *The Politics of Fertility Control: Family Planning and Abortion Policies in the American States.* New York: Chatham House. Discusses the political controversy surrounding fertility control and the reasons the debate is so important.

Ragone, H. (1994). *Surrogate Motherhood: Conception in the Heart.* Boulder, CO: Westview Press. Gives in-depth interviews with program directors, surrogate mothers, and commissioning couples.

Siegel, J. E., and McCormick, M. C. (2000). *Prenatal Care: Effectiveness and Implementation.* Cambridge: Cambridge University Press. Evaluates the effectiveness of prenatal care interventions and discusses the issue from a broader perspective of public and long-term health issues.

Winstein, M. (1999). *Your Fertility Signals: Using Them to Achieve or Avoid Pregnancy Naturally.* St. Louis: Smooth Stone Press. Explains ovulation and the natural methods of temperature and other signals to reduce or eliminate the need for contraceptives.

CHAPTER 16

After reading the chapter, you should be able to:

Describe the signs and symptoms of pregnancy, discuss the use of pregnancy tests, and calculate the birth date.

Discuss the emotional reactions to prospective parenthood and pregnancy and the developmental tasks of pregnancy.

Understand basic facts about prenatal medical and health care, some of the minor side effects and major complications of pregnancy, and the issues of sexual relations and mental health during pregnancy.

Identify the stages of prenatal development and ways to avoid birth defects.

Discuss prepared childbirth and the Lamaze method of natural childbirth.

Understand basic information about labor, options for delivery, induced or accelerated labor, the use of anesthesia, and cesarean sections.

Discuss the following topics in relation to postpartum care, decisions, and adjustments: care of the newborn, bonding, rooming in, breast- versus bottle-feeding, postpartum adjustments, and returning to work.

Pregnancy and Childbirth

Learning Objectives

Pregnancy

Signs and Symptoms of Pregnancy

Tests for Pregnancy

Calculating the Birth Date

Emotional Reactions to Pregnancy

Prenatal Care

The Importance of Prenatal Care

Minor Side Effects of Pregnancy

Major Complications of Pregnancy

Sexual Relations During Pregnancy

Perspective: Developmental Tasks of Pregnancy

Mental Health

Perspective: Avoiding Birth Defects

Prenatal Development

The Germinal Period

The Embryonic Period

The Fetal Period

Prepared Childbirth

The Lamaze Method

Labor and Delivery

The Duration of Labor

Stages of Labor

The Use of Anesthesia

Perspective: Options for Delivery

Induced, or Accelerated, Labor

Cesarean Section

The Postpartum Period

Care of the Newborn

Parent-Infant Contact and Bonding

Rooming In

Breast- Versus Bottle-Feeding

Family Issues: Preterm and Small-for-Gestational-Age Babies

Postpartum Adjustments

Returning to Work

Sexual Relations After Childbirth

Summary

Key Terms

Questions for Thought

Suggested Readings

Most couples want to have children sometime in their lives. But expectant parents are faced with a number of important questions: How does a couple know if the woman is pregnant? How can the birth date be calculated? What are some typical reactions to parenthood and pregnancy, and what major adjustments do men and women face? What do they need to know to protect the health of the baby? What are the possible complications of pregnancy? How can couples prepare themselves for the experience of childbirth? What happens during labor and childbirth itself? What about the use of anesthesia? What about natural childbirth methods? What about induced, or accelerated, labor? Or delivery by cesarean section? What do couples need to know before and after the baby is born? These are some of the important questions discussed in this chapter.

PREGNANCY

Most women suspect they are pregnant before medical tests confirm the fact. They can feel subtle changes in their body, and they begin to think about the changes in their life that a baby will bring. And they wonder how their partner will react to the news.

Signs and Symptoms of Pregnancy

One of the first questions the prospective mother asks is, "How do I know for certain that I'm pregnant?" The signs and symptoms of pregnancy can be divided into three categories. **Presumptive signs** indicate a possibility of pregnancy. They are the first signs that are noticed by the woman, but they are subjective and may be caused by conditions other than pregnancy, so she may only assume pregnancy from them. The presumptive signs are (1) cessation of menstruation, (2) morning sickness (nausea and possibly vomiting at any time of day), (3) an increase in the size, tenderness, and fullness of the breasts, along with a darkening of the areolas (the ring around the nipple), (4) frequent urination, (5) quickening, or the feeling of fetal movement by the mother, and (6) overpowering sleepiness.

Probable signs of pregnancy are more objective than are presumptive signs, since they must be interpreted by the physician. Some of them occur later in pregnancy than the presumptive signs, but they still are not absolute proof. The probable signs include (1) a positive pregnancy test, (2) darkening of vaginal tissues and of cervical mucous membranes (the so-called Chadwick's sign), (3) softening of cervical tissue (the Hegar's sign), (4) enlargement of the abdomen and uterus, (5) mapping of the fetal outline manually, (6) intermittent contractions of the uterus, and (7) an increase in the basal body temperature (from 98.8° F to 99.9° F for more than 16 days).

Positive signs of pregnancy are indisputable, since no other condition except pregnancy causes them. There are six of them. The examiner can (1) feel the fetus move, (2) hear the fetal heartbeat, (3) get an electrical tracing of the fetal heart, (4) detect a doubling of HCG levels, (5) map the fetal outline by means of special ultrasonic equipment, and (6) detect the fetal skeleton by X ray. When any of these signs are discovered, the mother and her physician *know* she is pregnant. Because of the dangers of radiation to the developing fetus, doctors use X rays only in rare circumstances.

Tests for Pregnancy

The sooner the woman knows she is pregnant, the earlier she can begin prenatal care. Since most women don't want to wait several months to determine if they are pregnant, pregnancy tests are administered. The two basic categories of tests are biologic and immunologic. There are numerous types of tests in each category, but all are based on detecting the presence of **HCG (human chorionic gonadotropin)**, which is secreted by the placenta. In the older biologic tests, a woman's urine was administered to test animals such as mice, frogs, toads, or rabbits. If HCG was present in the urine, it caused ovulation in female animals. Pregnancy was detected by killing the animal and examining the ovaries. The disadvantages were that pregnancy could not be detected until 4–6 weeks after the last menstrual period and that many animals were killed.

The immunologic tests are easier to perform and yield results more quickly. They involve adding the woman's urine to anti-HCG chemicals to see the reaction. The immunologic tests are easier to administer than the biologic tests, but they are not 100% accurate, especially in the first few weeks

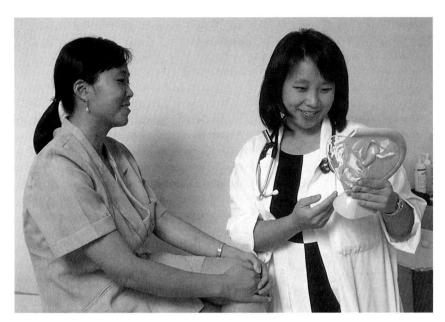

How does a woman know when she might be pregnant? What signs may tell her that she is? Signs of pregnancy can be detected, interpreted, and confirmed by a physician.

of pregnancy. They can give either false positive or false negative readings. Furthermore, these tests will not detect ectopic pregnancies. A woman with a negative test who does not menstruate within another week should repeat the test.

Home pregnancy tests sold under various brand names are immunologic tests designed to measure the presence of HCG. These tests are convenient and relatively inexpensive. Manufacturers claim 99% accuracy when the tests are performed correctly.

Calculating the Birth Date

The duration of the pregnancy is ordinarily estimated at 280 days, or 40 weeks, from the beginning of the last period. Of course, these are average figures. One study showed that 46% of women had their babies either the week before or the week after the calculated date, and 74% within a 2-week period before or after the date. Occasionally, pregnancy is prolonged more than 2 weeks beyond the calculated date; usually, an error in calculation is involved. At the most, 4% of pregnancies actually last 2 weeks or more beyond the average time (Guttmacher, 1983).

The expected date of birth may be calculated using **Naegele's formula** as follows: subtract 3 months from the first day of the last menstrual

Home pregnancy tests are convenient and relatively inexpensive. Most home pregnancy test kits advise women to see their physician after they have examined the results of the test.

period and then add 7 days. Thus, if the date of the first day of the last period was November 16, subtracting 3 months gives the date August 16, and adding 7 days gives the birth date as August 23. This is really a shortcut for counting 280 days from any fixed date. In other words, a woman ordinarily delivers her baby 9 months and 7 days after the first day of her last menstrual period (Guttmacher, 1983).

Emotional Reactions to Pregnancy

Becoming a parent can be one of the most exciting and meaningful experiences in life (Cowan and Cowan, 1995). How men or women react to prospective parenthood depends on a number of factors. A very important one is whether the pregnancy is planned (Snowden, Schott, Awalt, and Gillis-Knox, 1988). Do the partners want a child at this time? Do they feel ready to accept the responsibilities? Are the mother and father of appropriate ages?

Another important factor is the status of the couple's relationship. Do they have a harmonious relationship? (The more stressful the relationship, the more difficulty the couple will have adjusting to parenthood.) Are they married? If not, how do they feel about raising a child out of wedlock? Does the woman want to be a single or unmarried parent? Does the woman want to bear his child? Does the man want her to bear his child? Will they assist each other in the rearing of the child? Will he accept responsibilities as a father? Will she as a mother? How will the child affect their relationship? Unpartnered women have been found to experience greater psychological risk and more complications during their pregnancies because of inadequate social support (Liese, Snowden, and Ford, 1989).

May (1982) studied 100 expectant fathers and their partners to determine what factors were important to a subjective sense of readiness for pregnancy and fatherhood. She found four factors that were most important to these men:

1. Whether they had intended to be a father at some time in their lives
2. Stability in the couple's relationship
3. Relative financial security
4. A sense of closure to the childless period of their lives; in other words, they had to feel they had achieved most of the goals they wanted to accomplish before fatherhood

The timing of the pregnancy was extremely important to the men in this study, just as it is important to women.

Pregnancy affects the man and the woman differently. The woman has to carry the child for 9 months, accompanied by varying degrees of physical discomfort or difficulties and sometimes by anxiety about impending childbirth. Many women want to be mothers but hate the period of pregnancy. One woman commented, "I don't like being pregnant. I feel like a big toad. I'm a dancer, used to being slim, and can't believe what I look like from the side. I avoid mirrors" (Boston Women's Health Book Collective, 1998, p. 440). Other women are extremely happy during pregnancy. As one woman noted, "I was excited and delighted. I really got into eating well, caring for myself, getting enough sleep. I liked walking through the streets and having people notice my pregnancy" (Boston Women's Health Book Collective, 1998, p. 440).

Part of the woman's reaction to her pregnancy depends on the reaction of her partner to her and her changing figure. One study emphasized that a woman accepts her pregnancy when it brings her closer to her partner but rejects pregnancy when she feels it serves to distance her from her partner. The woman's reaction to pregnancy is also strongly related to the financial and emotional support and help she receives from her partner.

PRENATAL CARE

The Importance of Prenatal Care

Ordinarily, the fetus is well protected in its uterine environment, but the expectant mother needs to put herself under the care of a physician as soon as she suspects she is pregnant (Fingerhut, Makuc, and Kleinman, 1987). Prenatal care is essential to maintain the health of the expectant mother ("Larger Share," 1987). Time is of the essence, because the first 3 months of fetal development are crucial to the health of the child. Furthermore, inadequate prenatal nutrition increases the likelihood of low birth weight and infant death (Jamieson and Buescher, 1992). Babies of poor women seem to be at special risk for low birth weight (Turner, 1992b). Young maternal age is also a very high risk factor for poor pregnancy out-

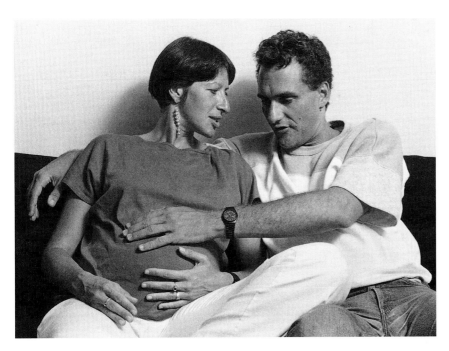

The woman's reaction to pregnancy is strongly related to the emotional support and help she receives from her partner.

come. In both cases, part of the reason is inadequate prenatal care (Brown, 1989).

Data in the 1988 National Survey of Family Growth (NSFG) were obtained from 8,450 women ages 15–44 (of whom 63% were White, 33% Black, and 4% members of other groups). The interviews covered the women's fertility history and intentions, contraceptive use, and prenatal care, as well as socioeconomic and demographic characteristics. Ninety-eight percent of the respondents obtained prenatal care, but only 65% initiated care within the first trimester. In 1997, 82.5% of mothers began prenatal care in the first trimester, while 3.9% of mothers did not begin prenatal care until the third trimester or had no care at all (U.S. Bureau of the Census, 1999a). Most of the women who get little or no prenatal care lack health insurance coverage (Klitsch, 1990b). Young women are significantly less likely than older women to receive early prenatal care. Teenagers are more likely to delay care until at least the fifth month or to receive no care at all. Additionally, women who intended to become pregnant are more likely to seek early care than are women whose pregnancies were unwanted (Hollander, 1995c). Women who do not want anyone to know about the pregnancy have significantly higher odds of receiving inadequate prenatal care (Cook, Selig, Wedge, and Gohn-Baube, 1999).

Data from other studies indicate the importance of family structure and its effect on prenatal care. Hispanic married women living with the father of the expected child are substantially more likely to receive adequate prenatal care than are women of other groups. Hispanic women living alone or with their mother are significantly more likely to receive inadequate prenatal care (Albrecht, Miller, and Clarke, 1994).

Initial visits to the doctor include a complete physical examination. It is helpful if the prospective father goes along, because he needs to be involved. The physician will take a complete medical history, perform various tests, and make recommendations regarding nutrition, health care during pregnancy, sexual relations, potential minor complications, and danger signs to watch for in avoiding major complications. Many expectant mothers are concerned about too much weight gain, but too little weight gain can be just as harmful, resulting in underweight infants and premature birth (Witwer, 1990b). Low birth weight seems to run in families. That is, infants whose mothers were below normal weight at birth or infants who have a low-birth-weight sibling are more likely to have low birth weight themselves (Mahler, 1996b).

Because the baby receives his or her nutrients and oxygen from the mother's bloodstream via the placenta and umbilical cord, everything the mother consumes affects the fetus. If the mother's diet is nutritionally inadequate, the baby will not receive vital nutrients, and the mother's health will also suffer. Rest and moderate exercise are also important to the well-being of both the pregnant woman and the fetus. Pregnant women need more sleep and rest because the energy demands on their body are so great. Moderate exercise won't harm the fetus because it is cushioned by the amniotic fluid, and toned-up muscles will aid delivery and help the woman regain her nonpregnant shape afterward.

Minor Side Effects of Pregnancy

No pregnancy is without some discomfort. Expectant mothers may experience one or several of the following discomforts to varying degrees and at various times during pregnancy: nausea (morning sickness), heartburn, flatulence, hemorrhoids, constipation, shortness of breath, backache, leg cramps, uterine contractions, insomnia, minor vaginal discharge, and varicose veins. Because of the physical and hormonal changes in their body, expectant mothers also often experience lethargy and mood swings.

Major Complications of Pregnancy

Major complications arise only infrequently, but when they do they present a more serious threat to the health and life of the baby than do the minor discomforts already mentioned. For example, pernicious vomiting is prolonged and persistent vomiting. One patient in several hundred suffers from this condition to such an extent that hospitalization is required.

Toxemia is characterized by waterlogging of connective tissue (edema), as indicated by swollen limbs and face or rapid weight gain, protein in the urine, headache, and blurring of vision. The placenta may not grow properly and may not be able to provide adequate oxygen and nourishment to the baby. Treatment for mothers experiencing toxemia includes rest and possibly medication to reduce high blood pressure. Toxemia is more common in first pregnancies and is linked to a family history of the condition. If toxemia goes unchecked,

it can lead to convulsions (eclampsia), which can be very dangerous for both mother and child (Pasquariello, 1999).

Spontaneous abortion, or miscarriage, may be indicated by vaginal bleeding. Spontaneous abortion is fairly common, occurring in one out of every five or six pregnancies, often before the 12th week of pregnancy. Early miscarriage can be nature's way of screening out future problems, indicating an irregularity in development (Boston Women's Health Book Collective, 1998). About 85% of all first-trimester miscarriages are due to genetic abnormalities of the fetus. The primary causes of second-trimester miscarriages are maternal factors, including structural problems of the uterus, acute infections, cervical abnormalities, hormonal imbalances, environmental toxins, and undue stress (Boston Women's Health Book Collective, 1998). Almost all women who have had a miscarriage will be able to go on to have successful pregnancies, and 70% of women who have had two miscarriages will be able to carry subsequent pregnancies to term.

Abruptio placentae, the premature separation of the placenta from the uterine wall, happens in about 1 out of every 200 pregnancies, usually in the third trimester. In **placenta previa,** the placenta is growing partly over or all the way over the opening to the cervix (Remez, 1992a). Painless bleeding occurs from week 28 because the placenta is partially or completely blocking the baby's exit by covering the cervix. In cases of heavy bleeding, a premature delivery by cesarean section may be required. If the placenta is still covering the cervix after the 38th week, a cesarean section is needed, but sometimes vaginal birth is possible if the placenta only extends close to the cervix (Pasquariello, 1999). Women who smoke during the first two trimesters of pregnancy are almost three times as likely as women who do not to have their pregnancy complicated by placenta previa (Rind, 1992a).

Ectopic pregnancy occurs when the fertilized ovum attaches itself and grows somewhere other than the uterus. It may be a **tubal pregnancy,** with the ovum attached to the wall of the fallopian tube and growing there rather than within the uterus. Or the pregnancy may be situated in the ovary, abdomen, or cervix. Figure 16.1 shows possible im-

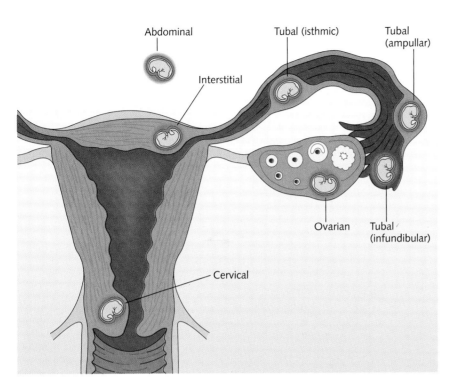

Figure 16.1 Possible Implantation Sites for Ectopic Pregnancy

plantation sites; all such pregnancies have to be terminated by an operation. Data indicate that the number of such pregnancies has been climbing steadily. This may be due to a number of factors: the postponement of childbearing, during which time the fallopian tubes age; previous abortion; pelvic inflammatory disease (PID); sexually transmitted diseases; frequent douching with commercial preparations; or previous surgery. Any condition that affects the fallopian tubes and impedes transport of the fertilized ovum will contribute to an ectopic pregnancy ("Increasing Rates," 1984, p. 14). In spite of the increase in such pregnancies, the mortality rates have fallen, indicating that women are getting prompter and better treatment ("Annual Ectopic Totals," 1983).

Rh incompatibility is determined during an initial prenatal exam. The Rh factor is a protein found in the blood. Because some of a baby's red blood cells cross the placenta and enter the mother's bloodstream during pregnancy and delivery, an Rh-negative mother will develop antibodies to the blood cells of an Rh-positive baby. If she has another Rh-positive baby, the antibodies in her blood

will pass through the placenta and destroy the baby's red blood cells, possibly causing jaundice, anemia, mental retardation, and even death. Fortunately, a serum called anti-Rh gamma globulin was developed in the 1960s. When administered to an Rh-negative mother within a few hours of giving birth to an Rh-positive baby, it prevents the development of antibodies. Or it may be given at about week 28 of the pregnancy; the antibodies are gradually destroyed (Berkow, 1987). If tests of the amniotic fluid (amniocentesis) reveal that the fetus may already be affected, intrauterine blood transfusions may be given into the fetal abdominal cavity.

Sexual Relations During Pregnancy

Pregnancy is a major life transition and generally results in a change in sexual activity. Most researchers studying sexuality during pregnancy have reported a decrease in sexual desire and frequency of sexual intercourse from the first to the third trimester, with a sharp decline in the frequency of coitus from the second to the third trimester (Hyde, DeLamater, and Plant, 1996). However, a classic

According to Valentine (1982), every pregnancy requires prospective parents to perform a significant amount of psychological work to prepare themselves physically and emotionally for the arrival of their new child. She described developmental tasks that must be mastered before postpartum adjustment and parental roles are accomplished.

Valentine outlined four developmental tasks confronted by the expectant woman and four others confronted by the expectant father. The pregnant woman's tasks are these:

- **Development of an emotional attachment to the fetus.** The facilitation of this process affects later maternal feelings toward the new infant.

- **Differentiation of self from the fetus.** This enhances her commitment to her child as an individual.

- **Acceptance and resolution of the relationship with her own mother.** If the woman's relationship with her mother is problematic, her relationship with her child may be affected adversely.

- **Resolution of dependency issues.** These are centered on the relationship with her mother and her partner. At some point, she needs a shift in dependency from

those of primarily daughter/wife to the attainment of role as mother.

The developmental tasks of the expectant father are these:

- **Acceptance of the pregnancy and attachment to the fetus.** This is necessary in finding a satisfactory role as father before parenting responsibilities begin.

- **Evaluation of practical issues.** These include financial responsibilities and living arrangements. This is necessary in the development of a sense of being a good provider for one's family.

- **Resolution of dependency issues.** Some men have a heightened sense of dependency during pregnancy and develop greater anxiety about rejection or being unimportant because they receive less of the woman's attention or because sexual relations lessen.

- **Acceptance and resolution of the relationship with his own father.** A father's feelings toward his own father condition his own ability to express loving and tender feelings toward his own child.

---

study by Masters and Johnson (1966) found a marked increase in sexual interest in the second trimester, followed by a decline in the third trimester. These findings were substantiated by a longitudinal study of couples expecting their first child. The women reported a decrease in sexual desire, frequency, and satisfaction throughout pregnancy, but most commonly in the third trimester. Among the men, this decrease was common only during the third trimester (Bogren, 1991).

Many reasons have been given for this decline in sexual interest during pregnancy, including chronic exhaustion, the feeling of being less sexually attractive, physical discomfort associated with intercourse, concern for the pregnancy, and fear of causing harm to the fetus by intercourse or orgasm (Bogren, 1991). However, most doctors believe that sexual intercourse causes no harm to the fetus, although many recommend curtailing sexual intercourse in the last 4 weeks of pregnancy. There are several conditions that may make intercourse late in pregnancy unsafe, including a previous miscarriage, some dilation of the cervix, vaginal or uterine bleeding, rupture of the bag of water, and premature labor.

Mental Health

Most expectant mothers experience some stress during pregnancy. A moderate amount of stress has no harmful effect on the fetus, but prolonged nervous and emotional disturbance of the mother is associated with low birth weight, infant hyperactivity, feeding problems, irritability, and digestive disturbances (Istvan, 1986). Women who experience stressful events during pregnancy appear to be at increased risk for premature delivery (Mahler, 1996c). Rini, Dunkel-Schetter, Wadhwa, and Sandman (1999) studied prenatal psychosocial predictors of infant birth weight and length. They found that women with more resources had higher-birth-weight babies, whereas those reporting more stress had shorter gestations. Factors such as being married, having higher income and education, and giving birth for the first time were associated with lower stress. Emotional disturbance may also have negative effects on the mother herself. Women who suffer from pernicious vomiting during pregnancy have been found to be under considerable emotional stress, usually be-

Birth defects result from three factors: (1) heredity, (2) prenatal environment, and (3) birth injuries.

Only 20% of birth defects are inherited. If there are any birth defects in your family and you wonder if a defect may be passed along to an offspring, get genetic counseling. Various tests, such as amniocentesis and chorionic villi sampling, can be performed to check for genetic abnormalities.

You can also control the prenatal environment in which the fetus is developing. Take the following proactive steps:

1. Avoid taking drugs of any kind without medical approval. This includes commonly abused drugs such as alcohol (National Institute on Alcohol Abuse and Alcoholism, 1986), nicotine (Nieburg, Marks, McLaren, and Remington, 1985), narcotics, cocaine, sedatives, analgesics, and marijuana (Fried, Watkinson, and Willan, 1984; Klitsch, 1992b). Even aspirin or mild tranquilizers may be harmful. Smoking cigarettes increases the risk of spontaneous abortion, low birth weight, and premature birth; drinking alcoholic beverages increases the risk of spontaneous abortion, congenital musculoskeletal defects, and mental retardation, depending on the amount drunk. Even drinking coffee slightly increases the risk of spontaneous abortion, premature birth, and possibly congenital defects (Edwards, 1992d).

2. Avoid industrial chemicals, heavy metals, and environmental pollutants, such as dioxin, PCB, and lead.

3. Avoid radiation from any source.

4. Avoid exposure to maternal diseases such as rubella, toxoplasmosis (found in fecal matter of cats and other animals), and sexually transmitted diseases. Other diseases, such as poliomyelitis, diabetes, tuberculosis, and thyroid disease, have also been implicated in problems of fetal development.

5. Follow scrupulously your physician's recommendations regarding diet, exercise, health habits, and care.

6. Get the best medical care possible. Some birth injuries can be avoided by proper care during delivery.

cause of conflict between wanting and not wanting the unborn child.

There is a close relationship between severe emotional trauma and spontaneous abortion (Berkow, 1987). Women who are prone to bearing premature infants may show similar emotional distress. Emotional disturbance has also been shown to be related to difficult and prolonged labor and to physical complications of pregnancy such as toxemia.

Pregnancy is not always the euphoric, blissful experience that romantic literature describes. It can be a happy, healthful time, but it can also be a period of stress and anxiety, especially for the immature and unprepared. That is why preparation for childbirth and for parenthood is so important.

PRENATAL DEVELOPMENT

Prenatal development takes place during three periods:

1. **The germinal period**—from conception to implantation (attachment to the uterine wall), about 14 days

2. **The embryonic period**—from 2 weeks to 8 weeks after conception

3. **The fetal period**—from 8 weeks through the remainder of the pregnancy

The mother's experience of the pregnancy changes from period to period as the baby grows inside her. All of the major body structures are formed during the first two periods, the time when the baby is most vulnerable to harmful drugs, environmental pollutants, and radiation (see Figure 16.2). By the end of the fourth or fifth month, the mother can usually feel fetal movement. The last several months of pregnancy are most uncomfortable for the mother because the growing fetus crowds her internal organs and strains the muscles of her back.

The Germinal Period

The fertilized ovum, called a zygote, is propelled down the fallopian tubes by hairlike cilia. About 30 hours after fertilization, the process of cell division begins. One cell divides into two, two into four, and so on. Every time the cells divide, they become smaller, allowing the total mass, called the blastula, to pass through the fallopian tubes.

Three to 4 days after fertilization, the newly formed blastocyst begins to attach itself to the inner lining of the uterus in a process called implantation.

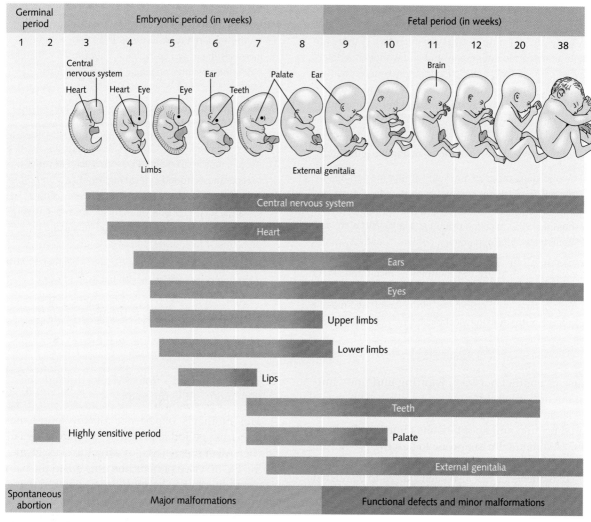

Figure 16.2 Sensitive Periods of Development (*Note:* From *Human Development: A Life-Span Approach* by F. P. Rice, 1992, New York: Macmillan.)

Implantation is complete about 10 days after the blastula enters the uterus.

The Embryonic Period

The embryonic period begins at the end of the second week, with the embryo developing around the layer of cells across the center of the blastocyst. At 18 days, the embryo is about one-sixteenth of an inch long. During its early weeks, the human embryo resembles those of other vertebrate animals, as Figure 16.3 illustrates. The embryo has a tail and traces of gills, both of which soon disappear. The

head develops before the rest of the body. Eyes, nose, and ears are not yet visible at 1 month, but a backbone and vertebral canal have formed. Small buds that will develop into legs and arms appear. The heart forms and starts beating, and other body systems begin to take shape.

Hormonal changes in the mother's body begin as soon as the egg is fertilized and may be accompanied by sleepiness, fatigue, and emotional upset. Hormonal changes also cause nausea, or morning sickness, in about two-thirds of pregnant women. Morning sickness usually disappears by the 12th week.

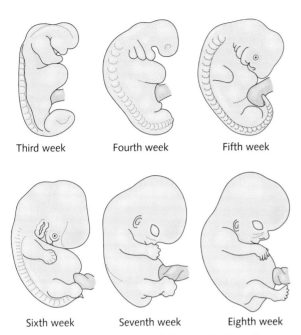

Third week   Fourth week   Fifth week

Sixth week   Seventh week   Eighth week

Figure 16.3   Development of Human Embryo from the Third Week to Eighth Week After Conception
(*Note:* From *Human Development: A Life-Span Approach* by F. P. Rice, 1992, New York: Macmillan.)

The Fetal Period

By the end of the embryonic period (2 months), the fetus has developed the first bone structure and distinct limbs and digits that take on human form. Major blood vessels form, and internal organs continue to develop. By the end of the first trimester (one-third the length of pregnancy), the fetus is about 3 inches long; most major organs are present, the head and face are well formed, and a heartbeat can be detected with a stethoscope. Fetal movement can usually be detected by the fourth or fifth month. At the end of the fifth month, the fetus weighs about 1 pound and is about 12 inches long. It sleeps and wakes, sucks, and moves its position. Eyes, eyelids, and eyelashes form at the end of the sixth month. The eyes are light-sensitive, and the fetus can hear uterine sounds.

During the third trimester, the head and body of the fetus become more proportionate. Fat layers form under the skin. By the end of the eighth month, the fetus weighs about 5 pounds and is about 18 inches long. The nails have grown to the ends of the fingers and toes by the end of the ninth

month. The skin becomes smoother and is covered with a protective waxy substance called vernix caseosa. The baby is ready for delivery.

PREPARED CHILDBIRTH

The term **prepared childbirth,** as used here, means physical, social, intellectual, and emotional preparation for the birth of a baby. Physical preparation involves the mother's taking care of her body to provide the optimal physical environment for the growing fetus and physically conditioning her body so that she is prepared for labor and childbirth. Prepared childbirth also involves social preparation of the home, partner, and other children so that the proper relationships exist within the family in which the child will be growing up. Prepared childbirth involves intellectual preparation: obtaining full knowledge and understanding of what the process of birth entails and what to expect before, during, and after delivery, including adequate instruction in infant and child care. Finally, prepared childbirth involves psychological and emotional conditioning to keep fear, anxiety, and tension to a minimum and to make the process as pleasant and pain-free as possible.

Prepared childbirth does not exclude drugs and medication during labor and delivery, if the mother desires to use them. In other words, the focus is not just on unmedicated childbirth (often referred to as natural childbirth, when in fact all childbirth is natural), but on whether the woman, her partner, and her family are really prepared for the experience of becoming parents.

The Lamaze Method

One of the most popular childbirth training methods is the **Lamaze method,** which originated in Russia and was introduced to the Western world in 1951 by Fernand Lamaze (1970), a French obstetrician (Samuels and Samuels, 1996). The important elements of the Lamaze method include the following:

- Learning about birth, including the importance of relaxing uninvolved muscles.

- Exercising to get in good physical condition.

- Learning controlled breathing and ways to relax the muscles and release muscular tension. These

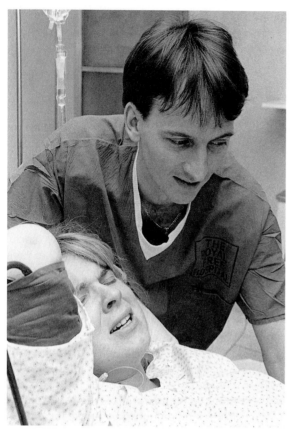

Expectant fathers are encouraged to attend birth preparation classes and to act as coaches during labor and delivery. Fathers who are present at delivery tend to show more interest in their infants and to talk to them than do fathers who are not present.

techniques are useful in pain prevention, which can minimize the need for pain-relieving drugs.

■ Offering emotional support to the woman during labor and delivery, primarily by teaching the man how to coach her during the process. The importance of the partners' relationship and communication are emphasized. In this method as well as other prepared childbirth methods, the attendance of the father or another support person in childbirth education classes and during labor and delivery is essential. Research has shown that the presence of a supportive companion or labor coach during labor lessens women's need for obstetric intervention (Turner, 1991).

An important feature of the Lamaze method is that the mother is taught that she can be in control during the experience of childbirth (Felton and Segelman, 1978).

LABOR AND DELIVERY

Real **labor** is rhythmic contractions that recur at fixed intervals, usually about 15–20 minutes apart at first and decreasing to 3- to 4-minute intervals when labor is well under way. In addition, the total length of each muscular contraction increases from less than half a minute to more than a minute. One sign that labor is about to begin or has already begun is the discharge of the blood-tinted mucus plug that has sealed the neck of the uterus. The plug is dislodged from the cervix and passes out of the vagina as a pinkish discharge known as **show.** Its appearance may anticipate the onset of labor by a day or more, or it may indicate that dilation has already begun (Berkow, 1987).

Sometimes the first indication of the impending labor is the rupture of the **bag of water (amniotic sac),** followed by a gush or leakage of watery fluid from the vagina. In one-eighth of all pregnancies, especially first pregnancies, the membrane ruptures *before* labor begins. When this happens, labor usually will commence in 6–24 hours if the woman is within a few days of term; 80% go into labor within 48 hours. If she is not near term, labor may not commence for 30–40 days or longer. This delay is actually necessary, because the longer the fetus has to develop completely, the greater the chance of the baby being born healthy. When the membrane ruptures more than 24 hours prior to labor, there is an increase in the risk of infection. It is important at this stage to guard against infection by not taking baths, refraining from sexual intercourse, and remaining well rested and hydrated. Practitioners or physicians may also advise monitoring body temperature while waiting for labor to begin to make sure there is no infection (Boston Women's Health Book Collective, 1998). About half the time, however, the bag of water doesn't rupture until the last hours of labor.

The Duration of Labor

Bean (1974) reported a study of 10,000 women who delivered at a Baltimore hospital. The study showed the total length of labor of each woman, from the

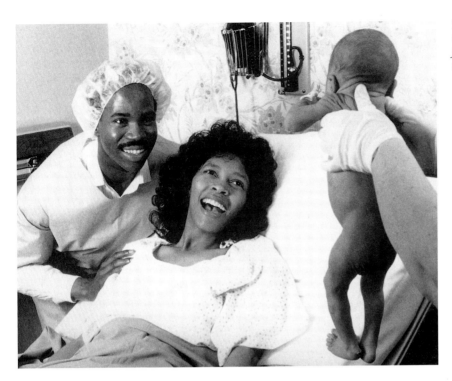

The second stage of labor ends with the birth of the baby. Within the next few minutes, the baby's physical condition will be carefully evaluated.

onset of the first contraction until the expulsion of the afterbirth. The median number of hours of labor for primiparous women (first labor) was 10.6; for multiparous women (all labor subsequent to the first), it was 6.2. One woman in 100 may anticipate that her first child will be born following less than 3 hours of labor, while 1 woman in 9 requires more than 24 hours.

The physician will give instructions as to when he or she wants to be notified. Most want to be called as soon as rhythmic contractions are established. The physician will also determine when the mother should go to the hospital or birthing center.

Stages of Labor

The actual process of labor can be divided into three phases. The first stage is the dilation stage, during which the force of the uterine muscles pushing on the baby gradually opens the mouth of the cervix, which increases from less than four-fifths of an inch in diameter to 4 inches. This phase takes longer than any other. There is nothing the mother can do to help except relax as completely as possible to allow the involuntary muscles to do their work.

The second stage begins upon completion of dilation and ends with the birth of the baby. It involves the passage of the baby through the birth canal. During the phase when hard contractions begin, the mother alternately pushes and relaxes to help force the baby through the birth canal. After the baby is delivered and tended to, the obstetrician again turns his or her attention to the mother for the third stage of labor.

The third stage involves the passage of the placenta, or afterbirth. The mother may be kept in the delivery room for an hour or so after delivery while her condition is checked. When her condition is considered normal, she is usually placed in a recovery room for a while before being returned to her own room.

The Use of Anesthesia

Anesthesia used to alleviate pain in childbirth can be divided into two categories: general anesthesia and local or regional anesthesia. General anesthesia affects the whole body by acting on the central nervous system. It can slow or stop labor and lower maternal blood pressure. It crosses the placental barrier and affects the fetus as well

In the early 1900s, about 95% of babies were born at home. Birthing was a family event. By the 1950s, that ratio had been reversed, with 95% of babies being born in hospitals. The switch was at the urging of physicians, who prefer delivery in the sterile, well-equipped, more convenient hospital setting. In the 1970s, the "medicalization" of childbirth began to be criticized. Some expectant parents and some medical practitioners objected to the rigidity, impersonality, and expense of hospital delivery practices. They felt that family members should have the choice of being present during delivery and that women should have more control over the childbirth process. These dissatisfactions led to the development of new options for delivery. In some states, nurse-midwives, rather than physicians, provide prenatal care and often assist in or perform routine deliveries. Some hospitals now provide alternatives to sterile and impersonal delivery rooms.

Birthing rooms are lounge-type, informal, cheerful rooms within the hospital itself. Medical equipment is available but unobtrusive. Both labor and delivery take place in the birthing room, attended by the father and medical personnel. The mother is encouraged to keep her baby with her after delivery to encourage bonding. Unfortunately, the advantages of birthing rooms cannot fully counterbalance the trend toward ever briefer hospital stays.

Birthing centers offer an alternative to the traditional hospital setting. They are separated from but near a hospital, offering a homelike environment with the medical backup of the hospital. They provide complete prenatal and delivery services and emphasize childbirth as a family-centered event, giving both parents maximum involvement (Eakins, 1986). The parents learn about infant care while still in the center.

Some couples opt for home birth. Supervised by a physician or nurse-midwife, home births are less expensive than hospital deliveries. At home, a woman can labor and give birth in a comfortable environment, surrounded by loved ones. Statistics show that home birth is as safe as hospital birth for low-risk women with adequate prenatal care and a qualified attendant. Typically, the midwife interviews the pregnant woman to determine if a high-risk situation exists (diabetes, blood disorders, **breech birth, transverse birth,** multiple births). If they do determine that a high-risk situation exists or may develop, the midwife and family decide whether home birth is a viable option. Occasionally, there will be complications during home delivery. A midwife is trained to recognize the early stages of complications and to take the appropriate action. Transport to the hospital during the course of the birthing process may be necessary for the health of either the baby or the mother. Some midwives require the mothers to preregister at a nearby hospital in case any complications arise.

Each type of delivery has advantages and disadvantages, which the couple must weigh carefully. The overriding consideration, however, must be the health and well-being of mother and baby.

as the mother, decreasing the responses of the newborn infant. Local or regional anesthesia blocks pain in specific areas and has minimal effect on the fetus.

Induced, or Accelerated, Labor

There are various reasons physicians sometimes induce labor with drugs: Rh blood problems, diabetes, toxemia, an overdue baby, ruptured membranes, and labor that stops too soon. Physicians also want to ensure that trained personnel will be available, especially in remote areas. In 1978, the FDA recommended against elective induction (that which is solely for the woman's or physician's convenience). Risks of induced labor include internal hemorrhaging, uterine rupture, hypertension, oxygen deprivation to the fetus, premature birth, and excessive labor pain (Berkow, 1987).

Cesarean Section

Medical complications may require a **cesarean section,** which is direct removal of the fetus by incision of the abdomen and uterine wall. Some medical indications of the need for a cesarean include a small pelvic opening, difficult labor, breech or other malpresentation, placenta previa, heart disease, diabetes, or a sexually transmitted disease in the mother. Although cesareans are major surgery, the risk of maternal death is less than 2%. It is regarded as one of the safest of all abdominal surgeries. However, the cesarean section rate quadrupled between 1970 and the 1980s, to a rate that some authorities felt was too high because not all the cesareans performed were justified or necessary ("C-section Rates," 1989; Ryan, 1988). Today, the cesarean section is the most common operation performed in the United States. In

1968, there were an average of 5% of cesarean sections; that figure rose to 25% in 1987 and dropped to 22% in 1999 (National Center for Health Statistics, 2000b). There used to be an attitude of "once a cesarean, always a cesarean." Current understanding is that at least three-quarters of women who have had a previous cesarean section may be able to have a subsequent vaginal delivery (Remez, 1994). Another reason is the introduction of programs to augment and induce labor (Hollander, 1996e).

THE POSTPARTUM PERIOD

Just as prospective parents have a number of decisions to make about the delivery of the baby, so new parents have a number of decisions to make about the period right after the birth. Different physicians and hospitals have different policies about the amount of contact between the parents and the newborn, about how long the hospital stay should be, and about when and whether to start breast-feeding. Because caring for a newborn can be exhausting and challenging for new parents, planning ahead for the postpartum period can make the transition easier for both the parents and the infant.

Care of the Newborn

As soon as the baby emerges, the most important task is to get him or her breathing, if he or she does not do so on his or her own. The physician or midwife swabs or suctions the nose and mouth with a rubber bulb to remove any mucus. The **umbilical cord** is clamped in two places—about 3 inches from the baby's abdomen—and cut between the clamps. There are no nerve endings in the cord, so neither the infant nor the mother feels the procedure. Drops of an antibiotic or silver nitrate are put in the infant's eyes to prevent bacterial infection, since the infant could be blinded by gonorrhea bacteria if the mother is infected. An exemption may sometimes be obtained if the physician is certain there is no gonorrhea.

One minute after delivery and again at 5 minutes, the baby is evaluated by a widely used system developed by pediatrician Virginia Apgar and called the **Apgar score.** The test assigns values for various signs and permits a tentative, rapid diagnosis of the baby's physical condition. The five signs of the baby's condition at birth that are measured are heart rate, respiratory effort, muscle tone, reflex response (response to breath test and to skin stimulation of the feet), and color. Each sign is given a score of 0, 1, or 2 (Greenberg, Bruess, and Sands, 1986). Thus, the maximum score on the scale is 10, which is rare. A score of 0 may indicate neonatal death. A score of 1–3 indicates that the infant is very weak; 4–6, moderately weak; and 7–10, in good condition.

Parent-Infant Contact and Bonding

There is some evidence that parent-infant contact during the early hours and days of life is important for bonding (Klaus and Kennel, 1982). Studies at Case Western Reserve University in Cleveland confirmed the traditional belief that the emotional bonds between mother and infant are strengthened by intimate contact during the first hours of life. This is referred to as **bonding.**

Rooming In

To avoid separating newborns from their parents, most hospitals are equipped with **rooming-in** facilities, where the baby is cared for most of the time by the mother in her own room or in a room the mother shares with several others. One advantage to rooming in is that the new father and siblings can share in the baby's care, so that child care is family-centered from the beginning. Another advantage is that new mothers can learn much about infant care while still in the hospital, thus reducing the anxiety and even panic that may occur if they are given the total responsibility all at once upon their return home. Most mothers return home on the second day after birth.

Breast- Versus Bottle-Feeding

One of the questions every mother faces is whether to breast-feed her baby. If the decision to breast-feed is made during pregnancy, the mother can massage her nipples and toughen them for the experience. One consideration is how the mother feels about nursing. Both bottle- and breast-fed babies do well emotionally, depending on the parents' relationship

Preterm and Small-for-Gestational-Age Babies

A preterm baby is one that is less than 37 weeks of gestational age. While a small-for-gestational-age baby may be preterm, mature, or postterm, the infant's birth weight is in the bottom 10th percentile for gestational age (Singer, Davillier, Bruening, Hawkins, and Yamashita, 1996).

Remarkable advances have been made in caring for preterm and small-for-gestational-age infants (Hollander, 1995b). Highly specialized incubators called neonatal-intensive-care units (NICUs) have been developed to take over for various functions of organ systems of the body that are not sufficiently mature to sustain life on their own. The NICU monitors respiration, heartbeat, brain waves, and other vital signs and provides medicines, oxygen, and food. The infant lies on a vibrating water bed in an incubator that carefully controls humidity and temperature.

Researchers have found that even when confined to incubators these tiny infants need normal skin contact, singing, talking, cuddling, handling, and rocking from caregivers and parents. Such contacts facilitate development. The survival rate for premature and small-for-gestational-age infants closely correlates with their birth weight. In the best equipped and best staffed hospitals, 80–85% of infants weighing 2.2–3.2 pounds survive. Remarkably, a number of those weighing 0.5–1.6 pounds survive and are not impaired. Care for the smallest infants has advanced so rapidly that many of those who used to die or be seriously handicapped now develop to be normal babies (Rice, 1995).

School-age children who were born weighing 5½ pounds or less are at greater risk for a number of physical problems, including asthma, cerebral palsy, and learning disabilities, than are children born at normal birth weight. The lower a child's birth weight, the more likely he or she is to have physical problems, including asthma, seizures, epilepsy, hydrocephalus, cerebral palsy, mental retardation, blindness or difficulty seeing, deafness or difficulty hearing, learning disabilities, hyperactivity, emotional problems or mental illness, meningitis, encephalitis, lead poisoning, heart problems, and anemia. Low-birth-weight children are also at significant risk for behavioral problems, compared with children of normal birth weight (Turner, 1992a).

with their child. Each child needs physical contact and warmth, the sound of a pleasant voice, and the sight of a happy face. A warm, accepting mother who is bottle-feeding her baby helps her infant feel secure and loved. The important thing is the total parent-child relationship, not just the method of feeding.

Whatever type of milk is given has to be of sufficient quantity and has to agree with the baby. Most doctors would agree that there is usually nothing nutritionally better for the baby than mother's milk, provided the supply is adequate (Eiger and Olds, 1987). Babies less frequently develop allergies to the mother's milk and have a lower incidence of intestinal infections and a lower incidence of crib death (Palti, Mansbach, Pridan, Adler, and Palti, 1984). Mother's milk also contains antibodies that protect the baby against infectious diseases. Sometimes, however, the mother's supply is not adequate, or her nipples become so cracked and sore that nursing becomes too painful. Because of the effort involved, nursing mothers may become excessively fatigued by 3 months postpartum. Such problems can usually be overcome. One way is to supplement the breast with a bottle (Spock and Rothenberg, 1985). Most nutritionists feel that babies are ready for supplementary solid foods at 6 months of age, and earlier in many cases. It is important also that the nursing mother watch her diet carefully, since the baby receives necessary nutrients from her. Furthermore, drugs taken by her may be passed along to the baby in her milk. AIDS may also be transmitted (Rogers, 1985).

Beyond the benefits to the baby, women who breast-feed reduce their risk of breast cancer. Results of a Mexican case-control study suggested that the longer the woman breast-feeds, the lower her risk may be (Hollander, 1996c).

Some women find breast-feeding to be a challenge, and they become very upset if they can't manage it; others really want to breast-feed. Many mothers do not breast-feed their babies because they have full-time employment outside the home. Women who are employed part-time are more likely to breast-feed and to breast-feed longer than are women employed full-time, suggesting that conflicts between breast-feeding and working at a job vary according to the intensity of the employment (Lindberg, 1996).

Each mother should follow her best instincts and do what she really wants to do and what seems best for the baby. If needed, mothers can receive support

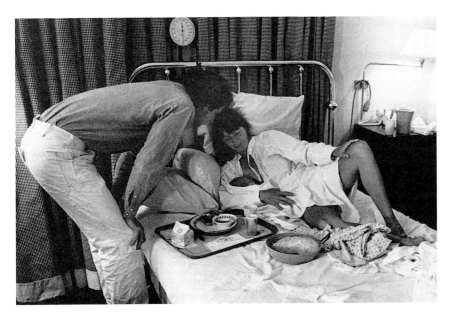

One advantage of rooming-in arrangements is the new father's opportunity to share in the baby's care from the very beginning.

and advice from the La Leche League, which has chapters all over the world and which gives advice and help to breast-feeding mothers. Overall, after two decades of decline, there has been a definite increase in the percentage of mothers who are breast-feeding their babies, especially among middle- and upper-class mothers (Eiger and Olds, 1987).

Postpartum Adjustments

The period following childbirth is one of conflicting feelings. The long period of pregnancy is over, which is a source of feelings of relief. If the baby is wanted and healthy, considerable happiness and elation are felt. Within several days after delivery, however, the woman may experience various degrees of "baby blues," or postpartum depression, characterized by feelings of sadness and by tears, depression, insomnia, irritability, and fatigue (Hopkins, Marcues, and Campbell, 1984).

These feelings have numerous causes (Pfost, Stevens, and Matejcak, 1990). Biological factors, including genetics, variation in hormone levels, diminished thyroid activity, and sleep deprivation, may play a role (Albright, 1993). The mother may have been under emotional strain while she anxiously awaited her baby. Once the tension is over, a letdown occurs, resulting in feelings of exhaustion and depression. Childbirth itself may impose considerable physical strain on her body, which requires

a period of rest and recovery. Following childbirth, there is a rapid decline in levels of estrogen and progesterone in the bloodstream, which may have a negative effect on her. Research has found that the best predictor of postpartum depression is the level of depression during pregnancy. For example, chronic stressors such as frequent conflict with support network members, maternal health problems, and lack of social support have been linked to postpartum depression (Seguin, Potvin, St-Denis, and Loiselle, 1999). Apparently, some postpartum depression is a current manifestation of previously existing depression (Albright, 1993).

After the birth, the mother feels the strain of wanting to do everything right in caring for the baby. One young mother remarked, "I never imagined that one small baby would require so much extra work. I'm exhausted" (author's counseling notes). If the mother does not have much help from her partner, or if the partner continues to make personal demands upon her, she may become exhausted from a lack of sleep, from the physical and emotional strain of caring for the baby, from the work around the house, and from caring for other children, in addition to attending to her partner's needs. Clearly, she needs help and understanding and a great deal of social support. Conscientious partners who do everything they can to assist are also affected by a lack of sleep, interference with regular work, and the strains imposed on them.

The experience of rearing a child can be more negative than, more positive than, or similar to what was expected prior to the child's birth. Perhaps the most important opportunity for divergence between expectations about and experiences with child rearing occurs after the birth of the first child. This discrepancy between expectations and experiences may affect the ease of new parents' adjustment to parenthood. One study of a sample of 473 married, middle-class, White women pregnant with their first child indicated that the women expected things to be better at 1 year postbirth than they actually were. The discrepancy significantly affected the ease of their adjustment to motherhood. Adjustment was more difficult when parenting expectations exceeded experiences in the mother's relationship with her spouse, her sense of physical well-being, her sense of maternal competence, and her maternal satisfaction. In addition, high expectations regarding child-care assistance from spouse and support from extended family were associated with more difficult periods of adjustment (Kalmuss, Davidson, and Cushman, 1992).

Returning to Work

Among the considerations following childbirth are whether the mother or father will return to work and, if so, the timing of that return. One study found that close to 20% of women interrupted their paid work for 1 month or less after giving birth, 53% had begun to work by the 6th month, and 61% had returned to work by the beginning of the 12th month. Financial considerations seemed to play an important role in the timing of the women's return to employment after childbirth. In particular, women from families that owned a home and therefore had to make mortgage payments and those with higher tax rates, as well as women who worked during pregnancy, returned to work sooner. Higher family income from sources other than the woman's earnings had the opposite effect: The women were more likely to stay home longer. Access to quality nonparental child care was also an important consideration. The decision to return to work requires adequate provision for care of the child while the parent is absent (Joesch, 1994).

The Family and Medical Leave Act of 1993 enables parents to take time off from work without pay and without losing their job. Parents can take up to 12 weeks of unpaid family leave providing they do not work in a company with fewer than 50 employees. They are entitled to return to work without penalty. The act lengthens the break from employment to some degree, since health benefits are covered by the employer during the leave. More important, the law guarantees the same or a comparable position upon return from leave, reducing the cost associated with finding a new job and thus lowering the cost of staying at home (Monroe, Garand, and Teeters, 1995).

Sexual Relations After Childbirth

What about sexual interest and activity after childbirth? There is less consistency in the research findings on the time when most people resume sexual activity following childbirth (Reamy and White, 1987). In one study, Kenney (1973) found that at 4 weeks postpartum 75% of women had returned their sexual activity to prepregnancy levels. Grudzinskas and Atkinson (1984) interviewed 328 women at 5–7 weeks after childbirth and found that only 50% had resumed intercourse. Masters and Johnson (1966) reported that all 101 women they studied had resumed sexual intercourse 6–8 weeks after childbirth. Hyde et al. (1996) studied 570 women and 550 of their partners and found that on average couples resumed sexual intercourse approximately 7 weeks postpartum. Interestingly, breast-feeding women reported significantly less sexual activity and less sexual satisfaction after childbirth than women who were not breast-feeding—a finding that has been reported by other researchers as well. There are three possible explanations for this. First, breast-feeding causes significant biological changes in the body. Estrogen production is suppressed, which decreases vaginal lubrication, making intercourse uncomfortable. And high levels of prolactin, coupled with decreased levels of testosterone, may contribute to reduced sexual desire. Second, breast-feeding mothers may have their needs for intimate touching met by breast-feeding and thus show less interest in sexual expression with their partner. Third, breast-feeding mothers may be fatigued from the drain on their bodies and the responsibility of feeding. Of course, it may be a combination of all three of these factors (Hyde et al., 1996).

SUMMARY

1. The signs and symptoms of pregnancy can be divided into three categories: presumptive signs, probable signs, and positive signs. Suspicions of pregnancy can also be confirmed by a pregnancy test, the most common of which are immunologic tests.

2. The birth date can be calculated by using Naegele's formula, a short way of counting 280 days from the beginning of the last menstrual period.

3. How men and women react to prospective parenthood and pregnancy depends on a large number of factors, including their desire and readiness to be parents and the status of their relationship. The timing of the pregnancy is extremely important. Some women hate being pregnant; others are extremely happy during pregnancy. Part of the woman's reaction to pregnancy depends on the reaction of her mate to her and her changing figure. The developmental tasks of pregnancy for a couple consist of developing an emotional attachment to the fetus; solving practical issues, such as financial and living arrangements; resolving dependency issues in relation to each other; and resolving the relationships with their parents. In addition, the woman needs to learn to differentiate herself from her fetus.

4. Couples are wise to get good prenatal care as soon in the pregnancy as possible. Women may experience minor discomforts early in pregnancy. Major complications such as pernicious vomiting, toxemia, threatened spontaneous abortion, placenta previa, ectopic pregnancy, Rh incompatibility, and certain illnesses require expert medical help. Sexual relations usually continue during pregnancy up until the later part of the third trimester. The mental health of the mother is also important during pregnancy since her emotional state affects the pregnancy, the childbirth experience, and the emotions of the child.

5. Prenatal development takes place during three periods: the germinal period, the embryonic period, and the fetal period.

6. Birth defects result from three factors: heredity, the prenatal environment, and birth injuries. Couples can do much to prevent birth defects.

7. Couples can prepare themselves for childbirth; physical, social, intellectual, and emotional preparation for the baby is necessary. Preparations may include learning about birth, exercising to get in good physical condition, learning relaxation techniques and proper breathing, and preparing the man to give emotional support and help to the woman during labor and delivery. The most popular prepared childbirth method is the Lamaze method.

8. Couples may want to consider all factors before deciding where to give birth, whether in a hospital, at home, or at a birthing center.

9. Labor may be divided into three stages: dilation, childbirth, and passage of the afterbirth. Anesthesia may be general, which affects the mother's whole body and that of the baby, or local or regional, which blocks pain locally or regionally and doesn't have as much negative effect on the fetus. Induced, or accelerated, labor and cesarean sections are warranted only if sufficient medical reasons are present.

10. Remarkable advances have been made in saving the lives of preterm or small-for-gestational-age babies.

11. Bonding between parent and child is more likely if parents maintain intimate contact with their infant from the time of birth. Rooming in allows the mother and the father to have this contact and to take care of the baby themselves.

12. Either breast- or bottle-feeding, properly done, may meet both the physical and the emotional needs of the baby. However, breast-feeding offers several medical benefits to both the child and the mother.

13. Postpartum blues are common.

14. Adjustments to parenthood depend partly on the degree to which actual experiences coincide with expectations.

15. Among the considerations following childbirth are whether the parent will return to work and, if so, the timing of the return.

KEY TERMS

presumptive signs

probable signs

positive signs

HCG (human chorionic
   gonadotropin)

Naegele's formula

toxemia

abruptio placentae

placenta previa

ectopic pregnancy

tubal pregnancy

Rh incompatibility

prepared childbirth

Lamaze method

labor

show

bag of water (amniotic sac)

cesarean section

umbilical cord

Apgar score

breech birth

transverse birth

bonding

rooming in

QUESTIONS FOR THOUGHT

1. How can a woman determine if she is pregnant?

2. What are some major and minor side effects of pregnancy?

3. What are the usual effects on sexual relations of being pregnant?

4. If you were having a baby, or your partner were having a baby, would you consider the Lamaze method of childbirth? Why or why not?

5. What are your views on bottle-feeding versus breast-feeding? Explain the reasons for your views.

6. If you were having a baby, or your partner were having a baby, would you consider a home birth? Why or why not?

SUGGESTED READINGS

Armstrong, P., and Feldman, S. (1990). *A Wise Birth.* New York: Morrow. Discusses the effects of medical technology and technological thinking on modern childbirth.

Boston Women's Health Book Collective. (1998). *The New Our Bodies, Ourselves.* New York: Touchstone/Simon & Schuster. Represents an updated edition of a classic.

Card, J. J. (Ed.). (1993). *Handbook of Adolescent Sexuality and Pregnancy: Research and Evaluation Instruments.* Newbury Park, CA: Sage. Gives an overview of adolescent pregnancy and pregnancy prevention.

Eisenberg, A., Hathaway, S., and Merkoff, H. E. (1991). *What to Expect While You're Expecting* (Rev. ed.). New York: Workman. Is a readable encyclopedia for expectant and new parents.

Freedman, L. H. (1999). *Birth as a Healing Experience: The Emotional Journey of Pregnancy Through Postpartum.* Binghamton, NY: Harrington Park Press. Examines the emotional and spiritual aspects of pregnancy and the postpartum period and discusses consequences of cesarean sections and other medical interventions.

Lanham, C. (1999). *Pregnancy After a Loss: A Guide to Pregnancy After a Miscarriage, Stillbirth or Infant Death.* Berkeley, CA: Berkeley Publishing Group. Provides guidance for devastated couples dealing with a subsequent pregnancy.

Nilsson, L. L. (1990). *A Child Is Born.* New York: Delacorte/Seymour Lawrence. Serves as a helpful book for adults and children alike, with beautiful photographs.

Otte, T. (2000). *The Illustrated Guide to Pregnancy and Birth.* Los Angeles: Lowell House. Represents a standard parents' guide to pregnancy, birth, and newborn care.

Spencer, P. (1999). *Parenting Guide to Pregnancy and Childbirth.* New York: Ballantine Books. Answers the typical questions of parents-to-be.

Stoppard, M. (1999). *The New Parent.* North York, Ontario: Elan. Serves as a practical guide to being a first-time parent and addresses the needs of working and stay-at-home parents, single parents, and adoptive or stepparents.

Parent-Child Relationships

Learning Objectives

Philosophies of Child Rearing
Parental Differences
Parent-Child Differences
Cultural Differences
Life Circumstances
Differences in Children

Parental Roles
Meeting Children's Needs
■ **Perspective:** Constructive Versus
Destructive Parenting
Sharing Responsibilities

Fostering Cognitive and Intellectual Growth
Parental Contributions
■ **Perspective:** Children's Home Environments
Language Development and Cultivation
Education Defining and Modeling

Meeting Emotional Needs
Emotional Attachments
Effects of Separation and Rejection
Child Care

Autonomy

Socialization and Discipline
Meaning and Goals of Discipline
Principles of Discipline
Corporal Punishment

One-Parent Families
Unmarried Teenage Mothers
Family Structure and Children's Adjustments
Special Issues in the Female-Headed Family
■ **Perspective:** Children's Contributions
to Household Work
Special Issues in the Male-Headed Family
Family Work

Summary
Key Terms
Questions for Thought
Suggested Readings

Being parents has many rewards and pleasures. For some people, living childless—even with a loving mate—is unthinkable. They want children as a creative expression of themselves: to love and to be loved by them. They find their own lives enriched by having children.

But parenting is not an easy task. New parents soon learn that taking care of an infant involves long hours of physical labor and many sleepless nights. One mother commented, "No one told me a baby wakes up four or five times a night." Parents soon learn that their life as a couple isn't the same. They don't have the same freedom of movement and the opportunities to do what they want to do. Parenting is an ongoing 24-hour-a-day job 7 days a week for years and, once begun, is irrevocable. You can't give the baby back. A baby changes things. In fact, the baby changes everything, so parents should give considerable thought to the responsibilities involved. If they devote themselves to learning how to be the best possible parents, they and their children are better able to enjoy the experience (Vukelich and Kliman, 1985).

PHILOSOPHIES OF CHILD REARING

Most parents have idealized notions of the best way to raise children, but the reality may not coincide with the ideal (Dressel and Clark, 1990). Child-rearing philosophies—like fashions—seem to go in cycles. Yesterday's parents, feeling their own parents were too strict, turned to self-demand schedules, child-centered homes, progressive education, and more indulgent concepts of child rearing (Alwin, 1990). Now some parents are worried that today's children are too spoiled and are reacting to what they feel has been overpermissiveness. Child-rearing philosophies change from one generation to the next and parents often have to sort out conflicting advice (Dail and Way, 1985). What is important is the quality of the parent-child relationship and the overall climate of the family setting, not the particular philosophy of child rearing that the parents follow.

Parental Differences

Parents often differ in their basic philosophies of child rearing, a situation that can create marital conflict and confusion for the child. Each parent may feel that the way he or she was reared is the "right way" and that other methods will not be as effective. Mothers and fathers convey their parenting beliefs to their children by means of their parenting practices. When these children are grown, their parenting behavior may be patterned after their own parents' practices (Simons, Beaman, Conger, and Chao, 1992). Or parents may repudiate the methods by which they were reared and resolve to do differently with their own children (Reis, Barbara-Stein, and Bennett, 1986). Differences between fathers and mothers are common (Coleman, Ganong, Clark, and Madsen, 1989). Fathers tend to emphasize intellectual development more and social development less than mothers do. Both mothers and fathers emphasize intellectual development more for boys than for girls. Moreover, fathers tend to be less sensitive than mothers to their infant's communications and respond slowly or nonappropriately to their infant's signals (McGovern, 1990). Some research suggests that fathers in our culture tend to be stricter disciplinarians, while mothers tend to be more nurturing (Starrels, 1994). The point is that parents differ in their parenting philosophies and capabilities. Some parents know a lot about child development; others know little (Glascoe and MacLean, 1990).

Parent-Child Differences

Several studies have shown that children and parents have overlapping but different perceptions of their relationship and of each other's behavior; that is, children's reports of their parents' behavior may not agree with how the parents perceive themselves. From a developmental point of view, parent-child agreement can be seen as one of the characteristics of effective parenting. People's thoughts and actions often are based on their definition of a situation. Children are influenced by their perceptions of parental attitudes and behaviors rather than by actual parental attitudes. When perceptions are not in agreement, misunderstandings and disagreements result. One of the challenges of child rearing is to communicate so that children and parents can better understand each other and can come to some sort of mutual agreement on child-rearing practices (Tein, Roosa, and Michaels, 1994).

In 1971, Bengtson and Kuypers hypothesized that differences in perceptions of closeness between generations reflect the developmental perspectives of parents and adult children. They argued that parents, heavily invested in their children, emphasize continuity between generations. The young adult children, striving for independence, emphasize the differences, reflecting their needs for autonomy and individuation. This phenomenon is referred to as developmental stake. More recently, Giarrusso, Stallings, and Bengtson (1995) proposed a revision of developmental stake theory, suggesting that the term **intergenerational stake** better represents family perceptions of closeness. In their reconceptualization, the emphasis shifts from a focus on individual development to life course concerns that characterize each generation. Moreover, this reconceptualization extends the focus on young adults and middle-aged parents to include middle-aged adults and their aging parents. Intergenerational stake, or the divergence in perceptions of closeness between generations, appears to be greatest among young adults and then later in the life course.

Cultural Differences

Cultural differences also play an important role in philosophies of child rearing. One study examined the beliefs about child rearing, intelligence, and education among parents from different ethnic backgrounds. Immigrant parents from Cambodia, Mexico, the Philippines, and Vietnam and U.S.-born Anglo-American and Mexican American parents responded to questions about what is most important for first- and second-graders to learn in school and what characterizes an intelligent child. Immigrant parents rated conformity to external standards as more important than development of autonomous behavior. In contrast, U.S.-born parents favored autonomy over conformity. Parents from all groups except Anglo-Americans indicated that noncognitive characteristics, such as motivation, social skills, and practical school skills, were as important as or more important than cognitive characteristics, such as problem-solving skills, verbal ability, and creative ability. Thus, parents from different cultural backgrounds have different ideas about what it means to be intelligent, what kind of skills children need in order to do well in school, and what practices will promote their children's development (Okagaki and Sternberg, 1993).

Using data from the National Survey of Families and Households, a study of cultural variations in parenting among White, African American, Hispanic, and Asian American mothers and fathers, researchers assessed parents in terms of parenting attitudes, behaviors, and involvement. However, even taking differences in socioeconomic status into consideration, the researchers found more similarities than differences between and among the four parenting groups. Among the various cultural groups, White parents placed less general emphasis on the children's exercising self-control and succeeding in school than did African American, Hispanic, and Asian American parents (Julian, McKenry, and McKelbey, 1994).

Life Circumstances

Not only is family background important in the way parents relate to their children, but life circumstances also affect parent-child relationships (Pittman, Wright, and Lloyd, 1989). The level of marital satisfaction has a significant effect upon parenting practices (Simons, Whitbeck, Conger, and Melby, 1990), as does the level of parental mental health and self-esteem. Parents who experience a great deal of stress in their lives, such as economic stress, often have more difficulty being patient and relaxed with their children. One study found that African American and Hispanic mothers who were on welfare were less emotionally and verbally responsive to their children, spanked them more, and were generally more likely to impose restrictions and punishment than were those not on welfare (Philliber and Graham, 1981). However, welfare was not the cause, per se; rather, it was the overall frustration of their lives that affected the quality of parenting. These parenting behaviors are found more frequently among parents with less education and lower maternal age. Other studies have shown that more mothers than fathers feel the stress of parenting, primarily because of the heavier burden and greater responsibilities placed upon them (Dodson, 1998; Scott and Alwin, 1989). The total circumstances of parents' lives influence the quality of parenting. The quality of family relationships in the parents' families of origin also has both direct and indirect influences on their psychological and physical health. These, in turn, influence the parents' relationships with their own children (Harvey, Curry, and Bray, 1991).

Another life circumstance affecting parenting is maternal age at first birth. The older a mother is when she has her first child, the more likely she is to give praise and physical affection to her child. The younger a mother at first birth, the more likely she is to criticize her child and use physical punishment (Conger, McCarty, Yang, Lahey, and Burgess, 1984). When pregnancy occurs in the early teen years, it may have long-term negative consequences for the young mother's social, psychological, and material well-being and for her child. Teenage fathers often are not involved in the care of their children, particularly when they are not married to the mother. Common obstacles to teenage father involvement is a strained relationship with the child's mother (Allen and Doherty, 1996) and a disinterest in child rearing (Rhein et al., 1997). Teen fatherhood is related to a variety of risk factors, such as low educational performance, risky sexual behavior, and drug use (Thornberry, Smith, and Howard, 1997). Because of immaturity and life circumstances, many teenage parents have a great deal of difficulty meeting their children's total needs.

Differences in Children

Biological influences play a much larger role in child-rearing practices than is sometimes admitted. For example, there are biological bases for intelligence and personality (Miller, 1993). For this reason, no one method of child rearing can be considered "best" for all children. Children are individuals; what works for one may not work for another. Some children want close attachments with parents, for example, while others do not (Rosen and Rothbaum, 1993). Some children are more difficult to raise than others (Simons et al., 1990). Children who are temperamentally easy to raise have a positive effect on healthy family functioning (Stoneman, Brody, and Burke, 1989).

PARENTAL ROLES

Although all children are different, they all go through the same developmental stages and have the same basic growth needs. No matter what child-rearing strategy the parents follow, they must meet these needs.

Meeting Children's Needs

The parental role sounds simple: to meet the needs of children so that they can grow (Amato and Ochiltree, 1986). Within all children are the seeds of growth, that is, a natural inclination to develop to maturity. Parents don't have to teach children to grow physically, for example. The tendency to grow is so strong that only by extreme physical deprivation can parents prevent physical development, and even then some development takes place. The parental task is to discover the physical needs of the child and to fulfill those needs.

Similarly, the parental task is to fulfill emotional needs so that children become emotionally secure and stable people. If children's needs for love, affection, security, understanding, and approval are met, they are more likely to develop positive feelings. But if their emotional needs are unmet, children may become fearful, hostile, insecure, anxious, and rejecting.

The quality of children's attachment to their parents has been studied extensively. For example, children's early positive attachments show themselves later in more frequent, sociable, and positive interactions with parents and peers. Conversely, children with insecure attachments are more likely to cling to their parents, interact negatively with them and with their peers, and show signs of anxiety around their parents. Children form secure attachments to their parents through positive, reciprocal interactions over time. When attachments with parents are severed by separation, children feel threatened, which can be detrimental to their self-esteem and interpersonal relations (Bullock, 1993).

Children also have social needs. They are naturally gregarious, and they want to be with others, generally like other people, and ordinarily try to please them and be accepted by them. But these natural tendencies are unsophisticated. Children want to make friends but don't know how to relate; they want others to like them but don't know how to please. Their need, therefore, is for socialization—to build on their normal desire to belong and to relate by learning group mores, customs, manners, and habits so that they can fit into the group. The parental task is to provide their children with the necessary opportunities for socialization so that they can become a part of society. Further-

The parental role sounds so simple—to meet the needs of children so they can grow. In what ways does a child need to grow? What must parents do to satisfy all of the child's needs?

more, certain parental practices, such as a high degree of parental affection and authoritative child rearing, may stimulate a child's positive orientation toward others and influence the child's acceptance by a peer group. In other words, parental reactions to their child's need for help are related to their child's prosocial behavior and social confidence (Dekovic and Janssens, 1992).

The capacity for intellectual growth is also inborn. Children are born naturally curious: They want to learn about everything, and they desire a variety of new experiences by which this learning can take place. The parental role is to encourage cognitive growth and to fulfill these intellectual needs by providing sensory stimulation and a variety of learning experiences. Parents facilitate intellectual growth by providing opportunities for observation, reading, conversation, and contact with others and with the natural world. When a child's environment is stimulating, curiosity is encouraged, and his or her cognitive development will proceed very rapidly. But if a child's surroundings are sterile, unchanging, and uninteresting, or if his or her human contacts and experiences are limited, growth will stop or slow down because of intellectual deprivation.

According to a study of the children of White, Black, and Hispanic adolescent mothers, the early home environment and the mother's level of education seem to be the most important influences on cognitive attainment among their children (Edwards, 1992b). Parental encouragement in response to children's grades and support for children's autonomy also help children to be intrinsically motivated and to perform better in school (Ginsburg and Bronstein, 1993).

Children have the capacity to grow morally as well as intellectually. They are born trusting and become mistrusting only when they learn that they cannot depend on people around them. They are born with a capacity to develop a conscience and to distinguish different moral values. But their ability is only a potential one; it has to be developed through educated reasoning, imitation of the example of others, and simple trial and error. The parental role here is to fulfill their children's moral needs for trust and for values to live by.

Sometimes, of course, children's needs aren't met because parents either can't or won't fulfill them. The children do not receive proper food and rest; they are not loved or socialized; and they are deprived intellectually and spiritually. When this happens, growth stops or slows down, and the children become physically, emotionally, socially, intellectually, or morally limited. Growth takes place when needs are fulfilled; development is delayed because of deprivation.

Any type of parenting can be constructive if it has a positive effect on children's development. Constructive parenting is characterized by warmth, inductive reasoning (which gives children choices of alternatives), clear communication, and developmentally appropriate expectations (Wenk, Hardesty, Morgan, and Blaire, 1994). It tends to promote cognitive functioning, social skills, moral development, and psychological adjustment (Reed and Dubow, 1997).

Destructive parenting lacks warmth, good communication, and supervision; it includes hostility, coercion, abuse, and neglect of the child. Positive rewards, such as affection and companionship, so important for the development of appropriate behavior, tend to be inconsistent, inadequate, or absent. Destructive parenting is associated with negative developmental outcomes, such as delinquency, psychopathology, academic failure, and substance abuse (Simons et al., 1990).

Sharing Responsibilities

In many societies, the man's primary family role is that of economic provider. Traditionally, women assume responsibility for the day-to-day care and supervision of children and are more likely to provide children with emotional and physical comfort. Yet children benefit if both parents share in meeting their needs (Atkinson, 1987). The needs of dependent children are not easily met by the mother or father alone, especially if there is more than one child. Having only one parent to fulfill the role of both parents is exhausting and potentially overwhelming.

Every parent brings strengths and weaknesses to the role. Like most mothers, the best fathers are almost indispensable (Hanson and Bozett, 1987). One mother related:

> I do an awful lot for the children, but there are some things that John can do better. He can put the baby to bed, rock her, and get her to sleep a lot more calmly and easily than I can. I'm too impatient. He teaches our oldest son how to fish, roller skate, and play baseball. I never could do those things. And John is very affectionate. He hugs and kisses Maurine and holds her. I do too, but not like John. She is in seventh heaven when she is in his arms. You don't have to tell me that my children need their father. I know they do. (Author's counseling notes)

Closeness to their fathers adds to children's happiness and life satisfaction and minimizes psychological stress. Closeness to stepfathers also contributes to children's well-being. Overall, these findings indicate that fathers are important figures in the lives of children and young adults (Amato, 1994b). Moreover, the fathers also benefit from caring for their children, and paternal involvement also increases marital satisfaction (Ishii-Kuntz, 1994; Kalmijn, 1999).

Despite these benefits, fathers with preschool children participate, on average, in only 26% of child-care activities (Ishii-Kuntz, 1994). Other studies indicate that in two-parent families in which the mother is not employed fathers spend about 20–25% as much time as the mothers do in child-care activities. In two-parent families with employed mothers, the level of paternal engagement is substantially higher. But this does not necessarily mean that fathers are doing more; it may mean that mothers are doing less. Fathers are proportionally more involved when mothers are employed, but their level of involvement in absolute terms may not differ significantly. Other studies have found that fathers spend much more time on child care when there are younger children in the family and that they are more involved with their sons than with their daughters, particularly when the children are of school age (Ishii-Kuntz, 1994).

Although middle-class fathers take a more active role than lower-class fathers, the major responsibilities for child care still fall most heavily on the mother. However, many fathers wish to increase the time they spend with their children, but numerous cultural, occupational, family, and personal barriers may stand in their way. For example, some fathers are too consumed with achieving economic success to pay much attention to their children (LaRossa and Reitzes, 1993). At least when residing in the home, fathers are more involved in the rearing of their children than were fathers a generation or two ago. The gap between men's and women's participation in child rearing appears to be shrinking. As a result, today's fathers report feeling closer to their children than their own fathers were to them. Social attitudes toward fathering have also shifted. Perhaps more than ever before, fathers are acknowledged as important to the intellectual and emotional well-being of their offspring. Not surprisingly, research supports the notion that fathers can enhance their children's social, emotional, and cognitive development (Woodworth, Belsky, and Crnic, 1996).

There is increasing recognition that fathers can and should participate in child rearing and that if they do not their children miss much, and they themselves miss out on a chance for self-actualization (Barnett and Baruch, 1987). One observation of child care in public places, such as parks, revealed that 43% of the children had men as the primary caregiver (Amato, 1989). Some of the men may have been noncustodial fathers, but all were taking children on excursions and participating in their children's growth and development. Concurrently, demographers are noting that a small but growing number of fathers are limiting their work hours to spend more time with their children. Others are leaving the workforce entirely and becoming stay-at-home fathers so that their children receive consistent in-home care and so that they can enjoy and participate in their children's growth and development.

In sum, there have been increases over time in the average degree of paternal involvement with children. However, mothers continue to spend more time with their children than do fathers and to take responsibility for most of their day-to-day care, regardless of their employment status. Many working women, therefore, are engaged in a second shift of taking care of their family after returning from a day of paid work (Ishii-Kuntz, 1994). At the same time, the father's involvement is increasingly recognized as a benefit to the child and the father and to marital harmony.

Parents' employment and responsibilities outside the home sometimes result in their children's becoming **latchkey children:** unsupervised youngsters who care for themselves before or after school, on weekends, and during holidays while the parents work. It is estimated that 5 million children in the United States ages 5–13 are home regularly without direct adult supervision while the parents work (Tirozzi, 1998). They commonly carry keys to let themselves in their homes—hence the term *latchkey children.* Some parents cite benefits of self-care: independence, self-reliance, less stereotyped gender-role views of mothers, peer interaction, greater participation in household duties, and greater ability to care for self. Other parents believe that such claims reflect attempts to ease parents' guilty feelings.

Numerous studies emphasize the negative aspects of self-care. Children frequently mention that they experienced fear and apprehension at being left alone (Council for Children, 1984). Overall, the environmental context is the single most important factor in how well latchkey children adjust to self-care. Whether the children are in a relatively safe, crime-free setting or in an environment in which the potential for crime is higher makes a difference in fear levels (Robinson, Rowland, and Coleman, 1986).

Contrary to popular opinion, most latchkey children are not the children of low-income single parents who cannot afford stable child-care arrangements (Cain and Hofferth, 1989). Most are older, White, middle-class children who live in suburban or rural areas. More than 28 million school-age children have both parents or their only parent in the workforce (Chaddock, 1999), and these parents are usually still at work when the school day ends. Because of this, most Americans (93%) want school-based after-school programs in their community. In response to parents' demands, Congress in 1997 set aside $1 million to fund pilot after-school programs. The subsequent demand was so great that Congress increased the sum to $40 million in 1998 and to $200 million in 1999 (Chaddock, 1999).

FOSTERING COGNITIVE AND INTELLECTUAL GROWTH

The word **cognition** (derived from the Latin *cognoscere,* "to know") refers to the process of becoming acquainted with the world and objects in it, including ourselves. We do this by taking in information through the senses of vision, touch, taste, hearing, and smell; processing this information; and acting on it. This process goes on constantly, so an infant is developing cognitively all the time.

Parental Contributions

Parents can assist their children's cognitive development in several ways. One way is by providing secure human relationships from which exploration

The family environment, especially the prevailing attitudes or emotional tone of parent-child interactions, has long been recognized as an important factor in child development. Home environment is related to a variety of developmental variables, including independence, self-esteem, moral development, anxiety, conduct problems, and school adaptation and achievement.

One study examined the home environments employed mothers provided for their young children and investigated the impact of current employment experiences, current family conditions, and maternal and child-caring characteristics on children's home environments. The findings suggest that maternal characteristics—age, education, ethnicity, self-esteem, and locus of control—are the most critical predictors of the home environments the mothers created. Age and educational resources are very important. Within the relatively narrow age range of the mothers studied (21–28), older mothers and better educated mothers drew on more developed cognitive and problem-solving skills to create stronger home environments. Mothers who worked in occupations with more complex work activities created home environments that were more cognitively enriching and more affectively and physically appropriate than those created by mothers who worked in occupations with less complex activities. Home environments, in turn, had a major impact on the children's verbal facility.

Individual resources were as important as current conditions in shaping family environments. Mothers who perceived that they controlled their own lives more consciously created positive home environments than mothers who felt they had less control. Similarly, mothers with stronger self-esteem attempted to impart feelings of competence and self-worth to their children, in part, by providing a positive home environment (Menaghan and Parcel, 1991).

can take place. Cognitive development proceeds faster when the child feels emotionally secure.

In addition to providing a secure base, parents can enhance cognitive development by offering a stimulating and intellectually rich environment (Parks and Smeriglio, 1986). This means talking and singing to babies; playing music; offering objects that vary in shape, texture, size, and color; propping babies up so that they can see more; taking them places so as to expose them to a variety of sights, sounds, and people; and offering playthings to look at, hold, squeeze, suck, bite, taste, smell, hear, and examine. It means offering toddlers playthings they can climb onto, crawl under, push, pull, drag, ride, swing, jump on, float, and splash.

Children who are environmentally deprived do much more poorly on IQ tests because of cognitive delays. With this in mind, the Head Start program was created. Head Start is a federally funded program offering early education, health care and social services, and nutrition to children from low-income families. The goal of the Head Start program is to compensate for this cultural deprivation by offering an environment rich in sensorimotor experiences. Head Start does help, and there has been some effort to extend it to younger children. Specifically, intervention by age 18 months is recommended for infants who are markedly environmentally deprived.

Language Development and Cultivation

In the beginning, human babies produce vowel-like sounds that are expressions of emotional distress or comfort. Between 9 and 12 months, babies show that they understand words and respond and adjust to them. For example, a baby may open his or her mouth in response to the word "cracker" or accept a glass of water in response to the word "drink." The median age for uttering the first word is 11 months. By 12 months, the average vocabulary is two words. Between 12 and 18 months, babies begin to combine words. The earliest sentences are usually two words: a noun and a verb, such as "Daddy gone."

Language development has a definite connection to environment and human relationships. Parents who read stories to their children and talk to them enable them to produce significantly more sounds and thus to learn to talk earlier than do other infants. Both the amount and the warmth of the vocalization of parents with their infants are related to their children's vocalization. Furthermore, communication skills that parents teach their children have a definite effect on the children's peer acceptance. In other words, there is a positive relationship between children's popularity in their peer group and their communication skills (Burleson, Della, and Applegate, 1992).

Education Defining and Modeling

As children get older, parents serve as models and definers of their children's educational aspirations and attainment (Cohen, 1987). Parents transmit their educational values to their children. Parents who are well educated serve as examples of what they hope their children will achieve. Those who take an interest in their children's schooling are teaching them that education is important and that they are expected to do well. In his study of parents as educational models and definers, Cohen (1987) found that mothers and fathers were about equal in their modeling influence, although whichever parent had more education tended to have more influence. Because of their higher levels of education, white-collar parents were usually more effective educational models than were blue-collar parents.

MEETING EMOTIONAL NEEDS

The basic emotional needs of children are for security, trust, love, and affection, as well as self-esteem. The psychoanalyst Erik Erikson (1959) concluded that developing trust is the basic **psychosocial task** during the first year of life. If infants are well-handled, nurtured, and loved, they develop trust and security and a basic optimism. Badly handled, they become insecure and mistrustful. Overall, infant affect (positive emotion) is positively correlated with the quality of the home environment in which they are brought up (Luster, Boger, and Hannan, 1993).

During the first year of life, parents can best meet these emotional needs by fostering their children's feelings of dependency, helping them feel totally secure. This is accomplished in several ways. The home environment is important. If it is fairly relaxed and free of tension and anxiety, if it is a pleasant, happy place, children develop a feeling of well-being merely by living there. The emotional tone that parents convey is also important. Warm, loving, pleasant parents who are themselves calm and relaxed convey these feelings to their children. Being able to depend on parents for need fulfillment, whether it be for food when hungry or for comfort when upset, also develops infants' sense of security and trust. Physical contact and closeness are also important. Infants feel secure when held

Children's performance at school is enhanced if their parents often read to them and provide other early literary experiences.

close to their parent's warm body, when they can feel their hand on their parent's face, or when they feel the comfort of loving arms. Infants also need several hours of sucking daily apart from their nutritional activities. Above all, children need to feel they are wanted and accepted, that their parents truly like and approve of them. These feelings, when transmitted to them, build their own sense of self-esteem. Several studies have found that children who are exposed to high levels of negative parental emotions are less well accepted by their peers, while high levels of positive parental emotions are associated with greater peer acceptance (Boyun and Parke, 1995).

Parental support in the form of praise and affection is extremely important in developing self-esteem (Felson and Zielinski, 1989). As children enter adolescence, parental criticism, shaming, and belittling are

If the home environment is relaxed and free of tension and anxiety and if the home is a pleasant, happy place, children develop a feeling of well-being.

associated with low self-esteem and high levels of depression, substance abuse, and various forms of emotional disturbance (Robertson and Simons, 1989).

Emotional Attachments

Research has shown that children begin to make emotional attachments very early in their development. Even though many babies are able to distinguish their mother from other people by 1 month of age, they begin to develop emotional attachments to people in general before they become attached to one person. Half of the specific attachments, including attachments to mother, occur between 25 and 32 weeks. Securely attached infants have been found to have mothers who respond quickly to their indications of need.

Attachment is measured by the intensity of the child's distress when the object of attachment, usually the mother, leaves him or her alone or with a stranger. Securely attached children are less upset by the mother's disappearance and more easily soothed. The child whose attachment is less secure will be more upset by the mother's departure and, if soothed, will be more likely to become upset and possibly angry when the mother returns. Soothing takes longer, and the child, wary that the mother may leave again, may need visual or physical contact to remain calm.

Initial research on attachment focused on infants and very young children. Now researchers are investigating the effects of attachment at later ages and in different situations. For example, attachment has been related to coping styles. This research indicated that the experience of early rejection may heighten a child's sensitivity to rejection and increase his or her likelihood of experiencing difficulties with and rejecting playmates (Downey, Lebolt, and Rincon, 1998). In addition, Shapiro and Levendosky (1999) found that the psychological distress of childhood sexual abuse is mediated by secure attachment. Furthermore, studies of family relationships across several generations have documented connections between the quality of attachment relationships in childhood and later intimate adult relationships (Cohn, Silver, Cowan, Cowan, and Pearson, 1992) and in late-life parent-child relations (Ceglian and Gardner, 1999).

Effects of Separation and Rejection

The research findings regarding attachment mean that, if a parent has to absent her- or himself from a child in the early months of the infant's life, the child will be less upset if there is a competent substitute, especially one to whom the infant has also formed an attachment. Distress can be avoided by leaving children only with sitters to whom they have become attached.

Whether a child is upset at a parent's departure depends partially on the parent's level of anxiety. If a mother has to go to work, for example, and is quite anxious about leaving her infant, the infant is likely to sense her anxiety and be more upset. Mothers who are less anxious on departure, who enjoy their work, and who are more autonomous and less anxious on reunion with their infants find that their infants accept the situation more readily. When a mother's experiences of a role—whether as employed mother or homemaker—are negative, there are detrimental effects on herself and on her children. If she experiences personal strain in her daily life, this personal strain is bound to affect her parenting behavior, which, in turn, affects her child's behavior (MacEwen and Barling, 1991).

Child Care

The use of friends, relatives, and neighbors as caregivers has declined as working parents increasingly use organized group care in the form of child-care centers and family day-care homes (Camasso and Roche, 1991). However, as Figure 17.1 shows, Hispanics still use more family care than organized group care (U.S. Bureau of the Census, 1999a).

Some authorities and parents feel that group care is more appropriate after ages $2\frac{1}{2}$–3, when the child appreciates contact with peers. If day care at younger ages is necessary, however, it is less upsetting if the child is cared for at the center by the same adult each day (Wille, 1992).

For children under age $2\frac{1}{2}$, a change in caregivers can be detrimental to the teacher-child relationship. After that age, relationship quality with caregivers tends to be stable regardless of whether the person changes. Thus, it is especially important for young children to have the same caregiver every day (Howes and Hamilton, 1992b).

The quality of the day care is also important. The relationship between child-care quality and children's social and cognitive development has been well established. Children who experience high-quality child care score higher on a variety of child development measures than children who experience low-quality child care. Child-care facilities that meet Federal Interagency Day Care Requirements (FIDCR) have low pupil-to-caregiver

ratios and small group sizes. Children in facilities rated as good or very good in caregiving are more likely to be securely attached to caregivers. And securely attached children are more likely to be confident with peers. Children in facilities rated high in activities are more likely to orient to both adults and peers (Howes, Phillips, and Whitebook, 1992). Moreover, the relationship with the caregiver, as well as with the parents, is a powerful predictor of children's later social development (Howes and Hamilton, 1992a).

Margolian (1991) did a study of factors related to abuse and neglect by nonparental children's caregivers. The strongest correlates of neglect were the child's age, the caregiver's age, and the child-care setting. Babies under the age of 1 year were three times more likely to be neglected; adolescent caregivers were twice as likely to be neglectful; male caregivers were more abusive and neglectful than female caregivers; and home-based care was the setting with the greatest risk.

Several factors influence the type of child care parents choose. One is cost and the ability to pay. Child care at home is certainly less expensive than in a day-care center. Parents with more than one child are more likely to choose home care than care in a day-care center. The availability of other adults in the household influences a parent's choice of child care, because these other adults can provide a convenient, relatively inexpensive source of care. Older siblings may provide inexpensive, convenient care for a preschool child, especially if only brief and occasional care is needed. The quality of child care available and the parents' goals are important influences on the choice of care. Parents who value developmental characteristics more often choose a day-care center over family day care or home care. Parents who value their child's knowing the caregiver more often choose family day care than a day-care center. Parents to whom hours, location, and cost of care are important are more likely than others to choose home care. Highly educated parents' choice of day-care centers depends on the importance they place on care that stimulates child development. Day-care centers with developmentally appropriate programs and trained staff promote child development, at least for preschoolers 3 years old and older (Johansen, Leibowitz, and Waite, 1996).

A study of families in the Detroit area investigated the determinants of type of child care used

Figure 17.1   Type of Child-Care Arrangements for Children Under Age 6, by Ethnicity, 1995 (*Note:* Adapted from *Statistical Abstract of the United States, 1999* [Table 639] by U.S. Bureau of the Census, 1999, Washington, DC: U.S. Government Printing Office.)

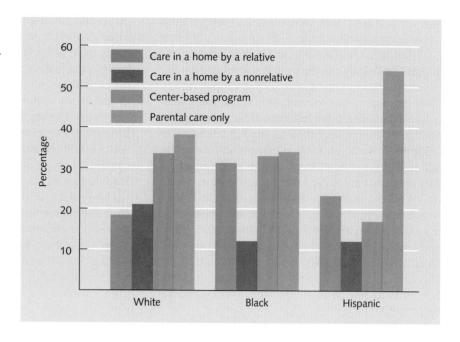

by mothers of preschool-age children. For employed mothers, four factors influenced whether they used professional child care: (1) the child's age, (2) the availability of relatives, (3) income, and (4) child-care preferences. Among non–African Americans, level of education was also a factor in choosing nonrelative care. Professional child care becomes more common the older the child, the fewer the relatives available locally, the higher the family income, the higher the mother's educational level, and the weaker her preference for exclusive parental care of children. The child-care choices of employed mothers are influenced by their preferences, not just by economic factors. For nonemployed mothers, only two factors were significantly related to the use of nonmaternal child care: (1) the child's age and (2) family income. The great majority of nonemployed users of child care choose formal group care such as nursery schools or preschools (Kuhlthau and Mason, 1996).

Autonomy

Children start developing their emotional need for autonomy at about 18 months, and that need is foremost for the next 2 years. **Autonomy** is the need to assert independence and self-will (Erikson, 1959). "No, I don't want to" becomes a familiar sound during this period.

If children are to function as individuals, they must learn to do things for themselves: to walk, to pick up and manipulate objects, to feed themselves, to hang on to things to prevent themselves from falling. As soon as children can move around, they will push adults away. This is the child's way of trying to become independent. "Me do" is the key phrase during this period.

Since toddlers are not as capable as they would like to be, frustration and anger are frequent, and temper outbursts increase. Anger outbursts peak during the second year and decline thereafter. Physical factors can influence anger responses—for example, hunger before mealtime and illness, even slight colds or constipation.

The parent's role is to encourage independence in things such as eating, playing with toys, and walking and to guide through substitution, distraction, and tactful control, trying to avoid direct confrontation as much as possible.

SOCIALIZATION AND DISCIPLINE

Socialization is the process by which people are taught the ways of society or social groups so that they can function appropriately. One dictionary defines *socialize* as "to make fit for life in companionship with others." Children are taught social roles and norms through contact with already-socialized individuals, initially the family.

Social roles are culturally defined positions such as mother, father, grandparent, supervisor, or student. Expectations for particular roles may vary cross-culturally and change over time. **Social norms** are expectations for behavior as one performs his or her role. Norms vary by age, gender, and social class, and they differ within societies and change over time. For example, in the United States during the 1950s, norms informed the mother that she must see that the children were clean, appropriately dressed, and on time for school. She was expected to see that the house was tidy and that meals were served at reasonable times. However, today, the woman may be expected to share equally in the financial support of the family and to be a partner in the management of the home. Later in life, when the children are gone and her partner has retired, she may elect to continue employment outside the home while the man assumes the household responsibilities.

Among the many tasks that parents undertake, the socialization of young children is one of the most important. Through the socialization process, attitudes and behaviors necessary for effective functioning in society are transmitted. If parents are absent from the home a great deal, other adults may exert more socializing influence on small children than do the parents. As the children grow older and maintain contacts with their peers, the peer group may begin to exert more influence in developing values. Bronfenbrenner (1975) suggested that in many urban and suburban homes, where the parents of school-age children are not often home and the children themselves are with their peers most of the time, peers have the greatest influence on values. Ordinarily, it is adults who are able to teach values such as cooperation, unselfishness, consideration for others, and responsibility. Peer values for boys often emphasize aggressive, antisocial behavior. In an interview, Bronfenbrenner commented,

> If parents begin to drop out as parents even before the child enters school, you begin to get children who become behavior problems because they haven't been "socialized." . . . They haven't learned responsibility, consideration for others. You learn that from adults. There's no way that you can learn it from kids of your own age. (1975, p. 49)

Bronfenbrenner was pointing to an important trend—the trend in which fewer parents spend the necessary time with their children to make their influence felt. When this happens, other people or groups become more important influences.

Meaning and Goals of Discipline

The word **discipline** comes from the same root as the word *disciple,* which means "a learner." Discipline, therefore, is a process of learning, of education, a means by which socialization takes place. The purpose of discipline is to instruct in proper conduct or action rather than to punish. The ultimate goal of discipline is to sensitize the conscience of children so that they develop the self-control that will enable them to live in accordance with the rules, regulations, and standards established by the group.

Toddlers' growing capacity to explore their environment opens up new dangers to themselves and to their parents' prized possessions. As a consequence, the proportion of parent-child interactions that focus on prohibition increases from about 10 months of age to 2 years of age, when children begin to be aware of the connection between actions and consequences (Larzelere, Amberson, and Martin, 1992).

In the beginning, control over the child is established by external authority, by setting standards and rules of behavior (Gralinski and Kopp, 1993). But children gradually are encouraged to adopt these principles for themselves, not because they have to but because they want to. When this happens, these internalized truths become their own standard of conduct.

At very young ages, discipline may be accomplished through wise management: providing interesting toys and activities; equipping sections of the residence, such as a play room or play yard; and child-proofing the house by placing dangerous objects out of reach. Young children may be disciplined through distraction and offering substitute activities. Sometimes the wisest discipline is through environmental manipulation: removing the child from the situation or the situation from the child. Parents can discuss issues with older children and arrive at joint decisions, whereas instruction to preschoolers necessarily involves more imperatives. Even then, explanations and reasons can be helpful, depending upon the child's level of understanding. A combination of reasoning and mild punishment is recommended (Larzelere and Meranda, 1994).

Principles of Discipline

If discipline is to accomplish the goal of development of inner controls, a number of principles need to be followed. These may be summarized as follows:

- **Children respond more readily to parents within the context of a loving, trusting relationship of mutual esteem.** Children who receive nurturance and emotional support from parents show lower levels of aggression than do those who do not receive this support (Zelkowitz, 1987). The most effective discipline favors an ideology that balances control with warmth, and judicious demands with responsiveness (Baumrind, 1996).

- **Discipline is more effective when it is consistent rather than erratic and when behavioral expectations are clearly specified** (Coombs and Landsverk, 1988). Both overly harsh discipline and inconsistent discipline have been linked to a wide range of negative outcomes including poor peer relationships, a high incidence of rebellious behavior, poor performance in school, and delinquency (Fisher and Fagot, 1993).

- **Learning is enhanced if responses involve rewards and punishments.** That is, reinforcement is both positive and negative.

- **Discipline is more effective when it is applied as soon after the offense as possible.**

- **Severe punishment, especially if it is cruel and abusive, is counterproductive.** It merely serves to stimulate resentment, rejection, and similar harsh, cruel behavior on the part of children (Rohner, Kean, and Cournoyer, 1991; Simons, Beaman, Conger, and Chao, 1993a; Weiss, Dodge, Bates, and Pettit, 1992).

- **Discipline becomes less effective if it is too strict or too often applied.** A parent who continually criticizes a child no matter what the child does is teaching the child that it is impossible to please the parent.

- **Discipline must be developmentally appropriate, depending on the child's age and level**

Discipline is most effective in the context of a loving, trusting relationship. Time-outs and discussions about appropriate behavior are constructive discipline methods to use with young children.

of understanding. All children want and need external controls in the beginning, since they are not yet mature enough to exert control over their own behavior. Appropriate methods of discipline will vary according to the child's age and level of understanding. However, extremes of either permissiveness or authoritarianism are counterproductive.

- **The internalization of appropriate social and moral norms is the result of successful socialization.** It is a major means by which social order and control are maintained in a society, because it involves the individual's voluntary compliance. Effective socialization motivates the child to behave in accordance with society's values and norms by making these values an important part of the child's self-concept (Abell and Gecas, 1997).

- **Methods of discipline to be avoided are those that threaten the child's security or development of self-esteem.** Some examples are threatening to give children away if they aren't good or to call a policeman to put them in jail. Similarly, threatening to withdraw love if children aren't good is a harmful means of disciplining, but it is one that middle-class parents often employ in subtle ways to control their children's behavior. It may work to temporarily control behavior, but it is devastating to the child's sense of security if regularly employed.

- **In general, authoritative methods of discipline, those that give children choices, are more effective than more authoritarian methods.** Mothers and fathers who use authoritative methods of discipline stimulate prosocial behavior on the part of their children (Hart, De-Wolf, Wozniak, and Burts, 1992).

Corporal Punishment

Corporal punishment—the use of physical force with the intention of causing pain but not injury for the purpose of correction or control—is legal in every state. Over 90% of parents use corporal punishment on toddlers (Giles-Sims, Straus, and Sugarman, 1995). Moreover, parents who use corporal punishment tend to do so frequently. In fact, 7½% of the mothers of children ages 3–5 interviewed for the National Longitudinal Study of Youth hit their child during the interview. Just over half of parents continue corporal punishment into their children's adolescence; in one study, parents had hit their teenagers an average of eight times during the previous 12 months (Straus and Donnelly, 1993). A majority of Americans seem to feel that a good, hard spanking is sometimes necessary.

More attention needs to be paid to the possible harmful effects of corporal punishment. Corporal punishment of children is associated with aggression toward other children and a less well developed conscience. A number of studies have also found a link between corporal punishment and physical abuse by parents. Most cases of physical abuse occur at the end of a continuum that begins with verbal threats, escalates to corporal punishment, and gets out of hand (Davis, 1996). Thus, corporal punishment increases the risk of physical abuse (Straus and Yodanis, 1996). Social learning theories suggest that children learn to use and value violence by observing and modeling the behavior of their parents, especially when the violence is in the form of corporal punishment of children. Since corporal punishment is a socially approved behavior, parents' use of corporal punishment to correct and teach contains hidden messages. Two of the hidden lessons are (1) that violence can and should be used to secure positive ends and (2) that the moral rightness of violence is permissible when other things don't work. Corporal punishment teaches children that, when someone misbehaves and won't listen to reason, it is appropriate to use violence. Lessons learned in childhood may persist in adulthood and affect marital relations. It is almost inevitable that, sooner or later, the spouse will "misbehave" and "not listen to reason" as the partner sees it. Partners who as adolescents were hit for misbehavior are more likely as adults to hit a spouse who goes against their wishes (Straus and Yodanis, 1996).

ONE-PARENT FAMILIES

So far, the discussion in this chapter has implied that there are two people at home who are able and willing to meet children's needs. In many families this is not the case. In 1998, 4% of children were living with neither parent, and 28% of all children were living at home with only one parent, at least temporarily. Of this total number, 84% were maintained by mothers; only 16% were maintained by fathers. The number of one-parent families continues to grow (U.S. Bureau of the Census, 1999a), and high divorce rates mean that one-parent families will increase even more in the years ahead. The one-parent family represents a major segment of the population, and disproportionately so for African Americans and the poor. Sixty-four percent of all Black children under age 18 are currently living with only one parent or neither parent as compared with 26% of White children under 18 (U.S. Bureau of the Census, 1999).

Single parents have special needs, especially for support and education that will help them succeed as parents and heads of households. Research has indicated that single-parent families, like other types of families, may be healthy or unhealthy, depending on the total situation.

Unmarried Teenage Mothers

Over 96% of unmarried teenage mothers decide to keep their babies (Hanson, 1992; Namerow, Kalmuss, and Cushman, 1993). Some let their parents or relatives adopt their babies, but the remainder want to raise the children themselves, assisted by whatever family or community members are available. White teenage mothers tend to receive financial support from their families, whereas African American teenage mothers tend to receive social support from their families.

Adolescent mothers tend to perceive their babies as "more difficult" than do either older mothers or the babies' grandmothers. Such maternal perceptions may put the children at risk for subsequent behavioral problems. Teenage parents also tend to be less able to socialize and educate their children (Tiesel and Olson, 1992).

Many people view unmarried motherhood of teenage girls as a disadvantage (Christman, 1990; Ohannesian and Crockett, 1993). According to a longitudinal survey, early childbearing limits the educational attainment of young women. Women who have a child before age 20 have on average almost 3 years less schooling than women who do not have children until later (Klepinger, Lundberg, and Plotnick, 1995). Giving birth as a teenager reduces the likelihood of high school completion by 50% (Ahn, 1994).

According to national surveys, one-quarter of teenage mothers have a second child within 24 months of their first child. The likelihood of a closely spaced second birth is greatest among women who first gave birth before age 17 (Kalmuss and Namerow, 1994). One program sought to delay repeat pregnancy among a sample of 3,400 first-time teenage mothers who were on welfare. Half the young mothers were selected for a special program of enhanced services, including family planning information and counseling. Although the majority of the young mothers were using contraception, half had become pregnant again within 2 years of the birth of their first child. An analysis of the effects of providing enhanced services showed that these programs did little or nothing to delay subsequent pregnancies (Maynard and Rangaragan, 1994). This finding is consistent with others which show that encouraging sexually active adolescents to begin or to continue using contraception is a major challenge for health and social service providers (Brindis, Starbuck-Morales, Wolfe, and McCarter, 1994).

Unmarried teenage mothers are a diverse population. Once they have had their first child, their entire life script is not necessarily written. Some are able to gain valuable work experience; others are not. Some are able to finish their education or postpone additional childbearing. Some get married; others remain single. These factors have a significant influence on teenage mothers' ability to become self-sufficient. Analysis shows that a woman's behavior after an early pregnancy is quite important. Although giving birth as a teenager can be a handicap, these young mothers have many options for reducing the negative consequences. Gaining work experience is an important way for a woman to increase her ability to be self-sufficient later. However, for a single mother, this requires adequate child care and other supports. Pursuing education and delaying additional childbearing also can improve a young woman's chances to be self-sufficient in the future (Sandfort and Hill, 1996).

Family Structure and Children's Adjustments

Overall, the quality of parenting and family relationships strongly affects children's social, psychological, and academic adjustments in both traditional and nontraditional families. However, some research suggests that children from families with two biological parents are more likely to be well adjusted than are children from other family configurations (Gringlas and Weinraub, 1995). It is important to remember that situational factors in many nontraditional family types, such as single-parent, have a strong effect on child outcomes. Situational factors identified in single-parent families (family dissolution, reduced family supports, increased stress, lower incomes, disruptive parenting) are similar to those found in families following a divorce or the death of a spouse. These stressful life events and their influence on maternal psychological well-being affect the single-parent child in ways that they may not affect children from two-parent families. The combination of single-parent family status and frequent stressful events appears to have especially strong negative effects on child behavior.

For example, in comparison to children in families with two biological parents, single-parent chil-

Noncustodial parents need to be concerned about spending enough time with their children.

dren in divorced families score higher on measures of problem behavior and lower on measures of social competence, academic achievement, and self-concept. Children in mother-only households show more adolescent deviance, higher susceptibility to peer pressure, and increased substance abuse. Single parents are more likely to have reduced finances and excessive levels of stress. Their parenting tends to be less effective; specifically, they are likely to be less affectionate and less consistent in discipline and to have poorer control of their children (Gringlas and Weinraub, 1995). However, children in single-parent families are rated no differently than children in two-parent families when maternal stress level does not differ (Gringlas and Weinraub, 1995).

It must be emphasized that, because children, parents, and circumstances all differ, the effects of the one-parent family structure on children are not always the same. A study of a random sample of Baltimore schoolchildren during their first 2 years of school found no effect of parental configuration on marks or test score gains in reading and math, with one exception: African American children in single-mother families in which other adults were present got higher marks in reading at the beginning of the first grade than did their counterparts in mother-only or mother-father families. Children whose families had more economic resources and whose parents had higher expectations for their school performance consistently outperformed other children in reading and math (Entwisle and Alexander, 1996).

Special Issues in the Female-Headed Family

One of the most important problems of the female-headed family is limited income (Pett and Vaughn-Cole, 1986; Richards and Schmiege, 1993). The median income of families headed by a woman, whether never-married or divorced, is 45% of the income of married-couple families. As a consequence, 35% of persons in these families live below the poverty line (U.S. Bureau of the Census, 1999a) Economic hardship seems to have a more negative influence on children than a single-parent family structure (Demo, 1992). Although disruptions in family structure (through parental separation, divorce, remarriage, or cohabitation) are associated with more problematic parenting and poorer outcomes for children, socioeconomic factors do appear to have a stronger impact on the quality of parenting in single-mother households than either family disruption or the absence of a partner (Bronstein, Klauson, Stoll, and Abrams, 1993).

Single mothers also struggle with inadequate child care. Care in another person's home and care in the child's own home are the most common types of care provided for children under age 5.

After the first year or so following separation, problems of communicating, showing affection, and spending time together tend to diminish for the custodial parent and the children.

Twenty-three percent of children under age 5 are cared for in day care, group-care centers, nursery schools, kindergartens, and grade schools combined. Nine percent of children are cared for by women at work. A few children are left alone to care for themselves.

The mother who is rearing children alone may have difficulty performing all family functions well (Burden, 1986; Goldberg, Greenberger, Hamill, and O'Neil, 1992). Role strain is very common among these mothers (Campbell and Moen, 1992). There may be little time or energy left to perform household tasks, which means either the house is not as well kept, there is little time available for food preparation, or the physical and emotional care of the children is neglected (Quinn and Allen, 1989). Part-time work is a common strategy used by mothers of preschool children in order to manage both financial and child-care responsibilities (Folk and Beller, 1993).

Some solitary parents seek social outlets outside the home through a variety of groups. Parents Without Partners was organized not only to help parents with problems with their children but also to meet the social and emotional needs of adults who are alone. Single parents also establish a variety of social networks and receive social support from their family of origin, friends, and extended family networks (Gladow and Ray, 1986). These networks are important to their psychological well-being.

Nevertheless, a father-present home is not necessarily always better for the children than a father-absent home. Some fathers, though home, spend little time caring for their children or relating to them (Levant, Slattery, and Loiselle, 1987). In such families, father absence would not have as much effect as in homes in which the father spends more time with his children. Some fathers as well as mothers are also inappropriate models.

The effect of paternal absence on the mother is crucial in determining the influence on the children. Many father-absence studies have failed to take into account the mother's changed position following a divorce, a separation, or the death of her spouse. If the mother is quite upset, if her income is severely limited, if her authority and status in the eyes of the children are significantly reduced, if she must be away from home frequently because she has to work, or if she has inadequate care for her children when she is gone, the children are going to be affected—not because of their father's absence, as such, but because of the subsequent effect on their mother and their relationship with her. However, the presence of surrogate father figures exerts a modifying influence on both boys and girls.

For both boys and girls, the economic contribution of the nonresident father is fundamental to their well-being, and its lack may underlie some of

Children's Contributions to Household Work

Most parents feel that appropriate expectations and responsibilities for tasks promote their children's growth and development. Consistent with this view, younger children are given less complicated tasks, such as picking up their toys or putting their clothes away; older children are asked to mow the lawn, perform light housekeeping, or prepare meals.

More middle-income and working-class parents depend on their children to help perform routine household tasks and care for younger siblings. Research indicates that when middle-income and working-class mothers work full-time both parents contribute less to household tasks; children in these families shoulder more of the responsibility (Antill, Goodnow, Russell, and Cotton, 1996). By assuming these responsibilities, children make meaningful contributions to the family economy (Morrow, 1996).

Several studies indicate that girls outperform boys in routine tasks (Antill et al., 1996; Gill, 1998). This is especially the case with gender-specific tasks; that is, girls do more "women's work" than boys do "men's work." Moreover, the assignment of tasks is influenced by the parent's level of education and beliefs about gender roles. Those with less education and more traditional ideas about gender roles direct their children to more gender-specific tasks. A parent's influence appears to be greater with same-sex children (Blair, 1992).

---

the differences in educational and occupational attainment mentioned earlier (Nock and Kingston, 1988). Father absence is not the opposite of father presence; most fathers, although absent from the child's home, are not absent from the child's life. What happens during the visit is of greater importance than the frequency of contact, and authoritative parenting is very important. Nonresident fathers may indulge and entertain their children, but this may be at the child's expense. Fathers, both resident and nonresident, who are responsive and encouraging and who are involved in everyday problem solving promote well-being and competence in their children, whether they are boys or girls (Amato and Gilbreth, 1999). Overall, the implications of father absence must be viewed in relation to the child's age, the recency and duration of the absence, and the quality of the home environment before and after the father's departure.

Special Issues in the Male-Headed Family

The proportion of children living in father-only households has quadrupled in the past 30 years. The fathers in father-only households are increasingly likely to be younger than 30 and never-married and to have low income. Solo fathers usually do not suffer poverty to the same extent as do solo mothers. However, financial pressure is still one of the most common complaints. Most single fathers have a larger income than do single mothers but still not as large an income as that of married men (U.S. Bureau of the Census, 1999a).

Like single mothers, most single fathers are concerned about not spending enough time with their children (Risman, 1986). If the children are of preschool age, fathers are faced with the same dilemma as solo mothers who must work—that of finding adequate child-care services. Even if the man can afford household help and child care, he experiences a profound change in his daily maintenance and care and that of the children. Single fathers undergo considerable intrapersonal stress as they take on the responsibility of raising their children alone. Marital separation often gives rise to feelings of anger, loss, loneliness, failure, and lack of self-esteem and self-confidence. Single fathers are under additional intrapersonal pressure to prove their competency as parents. Part of their stress arises because they are often forced to change their circle of friends and to rebuild their social life (Greif, 1988).

Overall, however, the evidence suggests that many are satisfied with their new life-styles. They tend to be stable, rather traditional, and established men with a strong motivation to be with their children. Most feel comfortable and competent as single parents (Risman, 1986).

Family Work

Much has been written about one-parent families, but there has been little written about how to handle household work. Single parenting may be more difficult for those who are unaccustomed to the full burden of family labor. Do single fathers assume all responsibility for their children? Do single fathers perform the same household tasks as single mothers? Women in single-parent households spend more time with children and in performing traditionally female household tasks than do men in single-parent households. Family work in one-parent households, like family work in two-parent households, is gendered. Mothers in two-parent families make vastly greater contributions to child care than do their spouses. Regardless of family structure, however, fathers do more family work when mothers are not around. The less available mothers are, the more fathers do. Thus, at least with respect to household work, families with single-parent mothers or fathers are very similar to two-parent families (Hall, Walker, and Acock, 1995).

SUMMARY

1. Child-rearing philosophies change from one generation to the next, so parents need to sort out conflicting advice. Men and women often differ on basic philosophies of child rearing.

2. Parents and children often disagree in their perceptions of each other's behavior.

3. Cultural differences play an important role in parents' priorities.

4. Life circumstances affect parent-child relationships, particularly the amount of stress people experience. Maternal age at first birth affects the degree of supportive maternal behavior.

5. Children are different, so no one method of discipline can be considered best for all children.

6. The parental role is to meet the physical, emotional, social, intellectual, and moral needs of children. Growth takes place when needs are fulfilled; development is hindered by deprivation.

7. Constructive parenting is characterized by warmth, clear communication, and inductive reasoning; destructive parenting is characterized by lack of communication, hostility, neglect, and abuse.

8. The home environment has important effects on children.

9. Children benefit if both parents share in meeting their needs.

10. Both parents are important in the lives of children. While many fathers are involved in child care, they are not as involved as mothers.

11. The term *latchkey children* refers to unsupervised children who care for themselves while parents work. Self-care has both positive and negative effects.

12. Cognition means knowing and understanding. Parents can assist in cognitive development by providing secure human relationships from which exploration can take place and by offering a stimulating and intellectually rich environment. Environmental deprivation retards cognitive development. Language development is enhanced by talking and reading to children. Parents also serve as models and definers of children's educational aspirations and attainment.

13. The infant's emotional needs include trust, love, affection, security, and self-esteem. Children's self-esteem develops in relation to the home environment, the emotional tone between parents and child, and the willingness of parents to fulfill emotional needs, to offer physical contact and closeness, and to help children feel wanted and accepted.

14. Infants begin developing emotional attachments to people in general before developing specific attachments to caregivers. Infants are upset by separation from or rejection by primary caregivers unless they are attached to the substitute caregiver.

15. Some authorities feel that group care for children is more appropriate after ages 2½–3.

16. The type of child care parents choose is related to cost, availability of other adults, parental goals, quality of caregiving, and the range of child-care alternatives available.

17. Autonomy is a fundamental emotional need for children. Striving for autonomy begins at 18 months and continues for the next 2 years.

18. Socialization is the process by which people are taught the ways of a given society or social group; it conveys the norms, roles, and values

necessary for living within the society. Parents enhance children's socialization by maintaining close, affectionate relationships with them and by providing appropriate role models.

19. The purpose of discipline is to teach. It is a means by which socialization takes place. The goal is to sensitize their consciences so that children internalize truths and standards.

20. Twenty-eight percent of all families with children living at home are maintained by one parent. This figure continues to rise. Eighty-four percent of single-parent homes are maintained by mothers and 16% by fathers. Larger percentages of Black children than White children are growing up in one-parent families.

21. Unmarried teenage motherhood heightens the risk that young women will be caught in a cycle of failure to finish school, repeat pregnancies, inability to establish a stable family life, and dependence on others for support. Those who are able to further their education, gain work experience, and postpone subsequent pregnancies create brighter futures, both for themselves and for their children.

22. The quality of parenting is strongly associated with children's total adjustments. The effects of one-parent families on children differ; these effects are largely related to socioeconomic differences.

23. Special problems of single mothers are limited income, inadequate child care, role strain, difficulty in communicating with and controlling children, and lack of time to spend with children.

24. Parents Without Partners and other social networks and social supports can be important sources of help for single parents.

25. Father-present homes are not always better than father-absent homes. Some fathers, though at home, spend little time with their children or are inappropriate role models for children. The effect of paternal absence on the mother is crucial in determining the influence on the children. The more negatively the mother is affected, the more negative the effect on the children.

26. Single fathers, like single mothers, face a number of problems: financial pressure, housework, not enough time with the children because of work responsibilities, finding adequate child-care services, and intrapersonal stress and pressure arising from marital failure and separation, from proving competency as a parent, and from having to change their circle of friends and rebuild their social life.

KEY TERMS

intergenerational stake

latchkey children

cognition

psychosocial task

attachment

autonomy

socialization

social roles

social norms

discipline

corporal punishment

QUESTIONS FOR THOUGHT

1. What are the basic emotional needs of children? Do these match with what you remember as your needs as a child?

2. What are the needs of children for socialization and discipline? Do you believe in spanking children? Why or why not?

3. What are some strategies for single parents, both mothers and fathers, to manage their many responsibilities?

4. What are some things parents can do to promote their children's emotional and intellectual development?

SUGGESTED READINGS

Adler, L. L., and Denmark, F. L. (Eds.). (1994). *Violence and the Prevention of Violence.* Westport, CT: Praeger. Provides individual readings on different aspects of social and family violence.

Angel, R. J., and Angel, J. L. (1994). *Painful Inheritance: Health and the New Generations of Fatherless Families.* Madison: University of Wisconsin Press. Represents an encyclopedic review of the literature on the health consequences for children of living in families without a biological father.

Bigelow, B. J., Tesson, G., and Lewko, J. H. (1996). *Learning the Rules: The Anatomy of Children's Relationships.* New York: Guilford Press. Examines what relationships mean to children and how children manage them.

Blankenhorn, Z. (1995). *Fatherless: Confronting Our Most Urgent Social Problem.* New York: Basic Books. Argues that father absence causes all major social problems and that only one type of fatherhood can serve children.

Burns, A., and Scott, C. (1994). *Mother-Headed Families and Why They Have Increased.* Hillsdale, NJ: Lawrence Erlbaum. Describes and explains the prevalence of mother-headed families in world perspective.

Cicirelli, B. G. (1995). *Sibling Relationships Across the Life Span.* New York: Plenum. Discusses the influence of lifelong sibling relationships and gives up-to-date reviews of research literature.

Daly, K. (1996). *Families and Time.* Thousand Oaks, CA: Sage. Explores the family's use of time.

Dodson, L. (1999). *Don't Call Us Out of Name: The Untold Lives of Women and Girls in Poor America.* Boston: Beacon Press. Gives poor women's stories of work, family, and poverty and their demeaning experiences with the social service system.

Dongen, M., van Frinking, G., and Jacobs, M. (Eds.). (1995). *Changing Fatherhood: An Interdisciplinary Perspective.* Amsterdam: Thesis. Examines fatherhood from many perspectives.

Dunn, J. (1993). *Young Children's Close Relationships: Beyond Attachment.* Newbury Park, CA: Sage. Discusses children's relationships with parents, siblings, and friends.

Harkness, S., and Super, C. M. (Eds.). (1996). *Parents' Cultural Belief Systems: Their Origins, Expressions, and Consequences.* New York: Guilford Press. Focuses on the beliefs parents have about children.

Luster, T., and Okagaki, L. (Eds.). (1993). *Parenting: An Ecological Perspective.* Hillsdale, NJ: Lawrence Erlbaum. Explores social networks and their influence upon families.

Murray, S. A. (1994). *Beating the Devil Out of Them: Corporal Punishment in American Families.* New York: Lexington Books. Summarizes 30-plus years of research on the occurrence and effects of violence inflicted on children.

Phoenix, A., Woollett, A., and Lloyd, E. (Eds.). (1991). *Motherhood: Meanings, Practices, and Ideologies.* London: Sage. Offers essays on motherhood.

Rivdens, J. (1994). *Mothers and Their Children: A Feminist Sociology of Child Rearing.* London: Sage. Argues for the need to reexamine caregiving principles.

Rossi, A., and Rossi, P. (1990). *Of Human Bonding: Parent-Child Relations Across the Life Course.* New York: Aldine de Gruyter. Examines how relations between children and parents vary across the life course.

Sigel, I. E., McGillicudy, D. E., Lisi, A. V., and Goodnow, J. J. (Eds.). (1992). *Parental Belief Systems: The Psychological Consequences for Children* (2nd ed.). Hillsdale, NJ: Lawrence Erlbaum. Discusses parental cognition.

Wood, B., and Beck, R. J. (1994). *Home Rules.* Baltimore: Johns Hopkins University Press. Focuses on parental expectations for children.

Wrigley, J. (1995). *Other People's Children: An Intimate Account of the Dilemmas Facing Middle-Class Parents and the Women They Hire to Raise Their Children.* New York: Basic Books. Discusses in-home caregivers and parents' relationships with them.

Yablonsky, L. (1990). *Fathers and Sons: The Most Challenging of All Family Relationships.* New York: Gardner Press. Reports the results of surveys and interviews with fathers and sons.

Zucchino, D. (1997). *The Myth of the Welfare Queen.* New York: Touchstone Books. Portrays a year in the lives of two women as they navigate the patchwork of federal and state programs to support their families.

LEARNING OBJECTIVES

After reading the chapter, you should be able to:

Understand that family-of-origin experiences while growing up continue to exert an influence after marriage.

Discuss the causes of and alternatives to parental disapproval of mate choice.

Identify some of the effects of positive and negative identification with parents and the way these affect a person in adulthood.

Understand the realities of care provided by families to their elderly family members.

Discuss important considerations relating to intergenerational bonds—in particular, mother–grown daughter relationships and father-son support networks.

Discuss important issues in relation to conflicts between parents and adult children.

Summarize some of the basic information about relationships with in-laws, including the relationship of in-law adjustment to marital happiness and the causes of and alternatives to in-law conflict.

Identify considerations in living with extended families during middle age.

Discuss relationships with grandparents: how grandparents are different today than in former generations, what grandparents can do for grandchildren, how adolescents and young adults relate with grandparents, what grandchildren can do for grandparents, and how grandparents parent their grandchildren.

Parents and Extended Family Relationships

Learning Ojectives

Parent–Adult Child Relationships

When Parents Disapprove of Choice of Partner

Children's Identification with Parents

Interdependence Between Generations

Mother-Daughter Relationships

Father-Son Support Networks

Conflict Between Parents and Adult Children

Parent–Adult Child Relationships
and Psychological Functioning

In-Laws

Successful In-Law Relationships

The Roots of Conflict

Family Issues: Adult Child Contact with Elderly
Black Parents

Living with Parents or In-Laws

Effects of Coresidence

Sources of Stress

Extended Families During Middle Age

Sharing Residence with the Elderly

Grandparents

What Grandparents Can Do for Grandchildren

Family Issues: Grandparents Who Parent
Their Grandchildren

Adolescents, Young Adults, and Grandparents

What Grandchildren Can Do for Grandparents

Summary

Key Terms

Questions for Thought

Suggested Readings

The couple relationship in marriage does not exist in isolation. Not only do the spouses continue to maintain relationships with their own parents, but each has also acquired a whole new set of in-laws. How the spouses relate to their own parents and to their parents-in-law has important influences on their marriage and their children.

In this chapter, we are concerned with these extended family relationships and their effect on the couple. We are also concerned with some special situations: problems created by parental disapproval of choice of partner, positive and negative parental identification, interdependence between generations, mother-daughter and father-son support networks, and conflict between parents and adult children.

Special attention is given to in-law and grandparent relationships. What kinds of in-laws and grandparents do people like? What are important roots of conflict? What are some special considerations when couples live with in-laws or grandparents? What are some positive aspects of such relationships? What can grandparents do for children, and what can children do for grandparents? In answering all these questions, this chapter emphasizes working out harmonious relationships among generations.

PARENT–ADULT CHILD RELATIONSHIPS

The relationship a child experienced with his or her parents while growing up continues to exert a profound influence on that person as an adult. If the relationship with the parents has been satisfying, pleasant emotional reactions and memories are carried into adulthood. However, disruptive relationships involving frustration, deprivation, fear, or hurt produce unpleasant emotional experiences and memories that reemerge from time to time, producing varying amounts of stress. In some cases, time moderates the distress; in others, parent-child misunderstandings emerge and influence the family relationships across the life span.

When Parents Disapprove of Choice of Partner

Parent–young adult child relationships become particularly important in the mate selection process.

Parental influence may begin when the adolescent first starts dating (Johnson and Milardo, 1984). The parents are appropriately interested in their child's choice of friends and dating partners. The key to maintaining a harmonious relationship and to continuing dialogue with their adolescent lies in how they express that concern. If the parents object to the choice, the couple are sometimes pushed into each other's arms for comfort and solace. This "Romeo and Juliet" effect may result in a hasty, poor partner choice that would not have been made if the relationship had been allowed to evolve or dissolve naturally.

Parental objections are usually based on one or more of the following reasons:

- **The parents don't like the person their son or daughter has chosen:** "He's rude." "She's crude." "He's impolite." "She has a bad reputation." "He's not a very nice person." "She's too domineering." These objections are based on dislike of the other person's personality.

- **The parents feel the other person has a problem:** "He drinks too much." "She's too emotional." "He can't hold a steady job." "She can't get along with anybody."

- **The other person is different from the parent's family:** "Her family are rather common people." "He's not educated." "She's not of our faith." "Why couldn't he have picked some nice Italian (or Irish, Jewish, African American, or Latino) girl?"

- **There is a significant age difference:** "She's too young." "He's too old for him."

- **The person has been married once or more before:** "This is his third time around." "She has three children by a previous marriage. Why does he want to get stuck with her?"

- **They're in too much of a hurry:** "They've only known each other for three months." "They don't even know each other." "We don't even know him (her)."

Some families would object no matter whom their son or daughter selected. Such families may be possessive of their offspring and unwilling to let them leave home or grow up. Or they want to keep their children home to help the family. An only daughter who was still at home was expected to care for her widowed mother. She explained:

The relationship a child experiences with his or her parents while growing up continues to exert a profound influence on that person as an adult.

I had to take my mother into consideration. No, I couldn't do anything. She had to be my prime concern. . . . So there was just no question about it. . . . It was my responsibility because my older brother was married, and my other brother was in school, so I was elected. (Allen and Pickett, 1987, p. 522)

Parental disapproval may be expressed in a number of ways. Parents who object before marriage may not be able to back off after the wedding, so they continue to object and criticize, exerting an adverse influence. Parents may come between the partners by taking sides in disputes. For the children's part, choosing a spouse in opposition to parental acceptance may be indicative of problems in the parent–young adult relationship, which may find disruptive expression in the marriage. Furthermore, the selection of a partner to whom parents object is often motivated by a desire to rebel against

parental values, a motivation that impairs judgment in choosing a partner.

Of course, young adults can try to get their parents to like their partner. If objections are based on lack of knowledge, given time and opportunity to get acquainted, some parents end up approving. But parents are not always wrong. If there are serious differences, this may be a warning signal to go slowly, to take more time and not rush into marriage. Premarital counseling may also help the couple clarify issues.

The time to resolve problems is before marriage, if possible, or else troublesome issues will carry over into the marriage. One woman explained,

When my husband was courting me, I tried in every way to get his parents to like me, but they would never accept me. They seemed to resent everything I did. I knew I was going to have in-law problems after marriage, and we certainly did. (Author's counseling notes)

Children's Identification with Parents

As we have seen, in healthy families, children form close emotional attachments to parents. In the process, gender-role socialization takes place. That is, girls learn what it is like to be a spouse and mother, and boys learn what it is like to be a spouse and father. Each child also forms expectations of what traits and behaviors to expect from the opposite sex based on the role models they have observed. This identification, particularly with parents, influences marital expectations and behavior. However, identification may be positive or negative.

Positive identification is the attachment of the child to images of desired loving behavior. In this situation, the young adult child seeks to duplicate family-of-origin relationships in his or her own marriage. Such situations become troublesome when the spouse is not like the beloved parent—for example, when the woman cannot be like her mate's mother or the man like his mate's father. As one man said, "I'm not like your father, so don't expect me to be." The man who expects his partner to play the same role in their marriage that his mother did in hers is suggesting, "I can only love you if you're like my mother." People may develop unrealistic expectations from the example set by their own parents.

Negative identification results in an effort to avoid being like the parent. In situations of negative identification, differences rather than similarities underlie mate selection and facilitate marital harmony. For example, a man reared by a demanding mother might always be wary lest a female dominate him. A woman may avoid men who drink because, as a child, she was frightened when her father came home drunk. She may find her partner's restraint particularly appealing. In marriage, two personalities interact. How they deal with the mate's conscious and unconscious needs will partly determine the success of the marriage.

Interdependence Between Generations

For many years, the myth grew that elderly people were alienated from their families, especially from their adult children, that families did not care for their elderly relatives, and that children had abandoned their elderly parents to institutions for care. Families as primary social units were believed to be

dying out, or at least were seen as irresponsible toward elderly members. The myth was substantiated by the decrease in family size and the geographical mobility of families (understood as widening the generation gap), the development of an advanced society that supported nonworking members, and the proliferation of nursing homes and hospitals to care for chronically ill and frail elderly persons.

We now know that the myth is indeed just that. While independence and autonomy remain a cultural ideal, families are typified by interdependence. Interdependence refers to cooperation between persons and groups; one benefits from the contributions of others even as they contribute to one's own well-being. Families tend to maintain varying degrees of interdependence throughout the life course. The flow of resources typically is from the older generations to the younger ones even when elderly members are receiving some form of assistance. Families were and still are a major source of help to the elderly. Families often go to great lengths to care for their elderly members and do not lightly enter into decisions to institutionalize them. They also maintain strong bonds with older members and visit the older relatives who are institutionalized and mentally or physically impaired. Nevertheless, the myth constituted a serious indictment of families. Only after several decades of research on the part of gerontologists was this myth laid to rest (High, 1991).

Research has shown that some late-life events are associated with increased intergenerational involvement. Using data from the National Survey of Families and Households, Roan and Raley (1996) examined the effects of mothers' widowhood on intergenerational relations. Their longitudinal analysis revealed that coresidence was not common but that adult children were more likely to coreside with their mothers if their mothers were widowed. Moreover, the mothers' widowhood increased intergenerational contact because parents and adult children shared their grief and offered mutual support. Although Blacks were less likely to provide financial assistance to kin, they had a higher likelihood than Whites of coresiding with or frequently contacting kin (Roan and Raley, 1996).

Despite social changes such as geographic mobility, divorce, and women's participation in the labor force, adult children, especially daughters, remain the most reliable source of instrumental social support for their parents. There are two major reasons for support: (1) the ties of affection and (2) the sense of responsibility. Strong affectional ties are powerful motivating factors in providing support. Daughters are more likely to be directly motivated to act by feelings of emotional intimacy. Sons are more inclined to help parents out of a sense of obligation regardless of the quality of their relationship.

Economic factors, such as anticipation of an inheritance, are also strong motivating factors. While affection appears to motivate daughters to increase the amount of support provided to mothers, anticipation of a potential inheritance, for both daughters and sons, plays a role with respect to support of fathers. Indeed, inheritance is a more powerful predictor of support for fathers than is affection. These patterns reflect traditional gender-based motivations: sentiment-induced support of mothers and financial incentive–induced support of fathers (Silverstein, Parrott, and Bengtson, 1995).

Dependence between generations is not limited to what the middle-aged generation does for the older generation, however. It includes the contributions that the older generations make to younger family members as well. These contributions are sizable and take the form of shared meals, loans for household appliances and furnishings, transfers of deeds and titles, and bargain-rate sales of homes, businesses, and vehicles. Some grandparents cosign loans for their children and grandchildren or save money for the grandchildren's tuition. Others provide child care or other services that allow the parents to work or do other things. Gifts are also common. Overall, more resources flow down the generations than flow up.

The social support patterns between middle-aged parents and their adult children differ according to marital status. Parents in first marriages are more likely overall than parents in other marital situations to report giving support. Middle-income widows are also inclined to help their children financially through gifts, loans, and asset transfers (Eggebeen, 1992). Giving social support to children, whether reciprocated or not, is associated with better psychological well-being than is only receiving social support from children. Parents benefit psychologically by being able to give support as well as receive it (Marks, 1995).

Mother-Daughter Relationships

Parental and filial sentiment and responsibility persist into adulthood, with the mother-daughter relationship the most enduring and active of intergenerational bonds. Typically, married daughters see their mothers more often than sons do (Guinzburg, 1983), and maternal grandparents see their grandchildren more than paternal grandparents do. L. R. Fischer (1983) found that the mother-daughter bond becomes even closer after the daughter has a baby. Living nearby is associated with less conflict between daughters and mothers, but more conflict with mothers-in-law. Daughters are much more likely to ask their mothers than their mothers-in-law for child-rearing advice. Daughters with children, compared with those without children, are more likely to have more contact with their mothers—more telephone contact with mothers both near and far and more visits with near mothers (L. R. Fischer, 1983).

Daughters invest time and money in their aging mothers, giving significant aid both to dependent mothers and to mothers who are self-sufficient. The aid is generally tailored to the elderly mothers' needs (Guberman, Maheu, and Maille, 1992; Walker and Pratt, 1991). Moreover, daughters are more likely than sons to adjust their visiting or helping behavior in accordance with the contributions of their siblings (Spitze and Logan, 1991).

When there is strain in the mother-daughter relationship, it is usually because of the mother's criticism of the daughter: her weight, temper, or past and present behavior. Mothers also sometimes criticize their daughter for home management issues, such as the way the daughter keeps house or cooks. Mothers also like to give their daughters advice on child rearing—what to feed a child or how to toilet train a child. Sometimes the mother's criticism focuses on the daughter's partner. However, in L. R. Fischer's (1983) study, 42% of daughters reported no sources of irritation or annoyance with their mothers. Generally, mothers and daughters report strong, positive feelings in their relationship, although these feelings are stronger for mothers than for daughters. Most mothers praise daughters while discussing their faults or choose not to discuss their faults at all (Fingerman, 1996).

An investigation of the sources of tension between aging mothers and adult daughters revealed some interesting findings (Fingerman, 1996). One source of tension in the mother-daughter relationship is conflicting ideas of inclusion and exclusion. Most mothers and daughters consider the other person important in their life, yet mothers seem to feel emotionally closer to their daughters than daughters feel to their mothers. Mothers are more likely to name their daughter as their preferred confidante or the person with whom they most enjoy spending time. Differences in sources of tension may stem from these differences in emotional investment. If daughters find their mother intrusive, their complaints may be related to their mother's investment in the relationship. Daughters feel intruded upon, whereas mothers feel excluded.

Another major source of conflict is concern about mothers' well-being. Tension may arise from discrepancies in perceptions of the mothers' needs. Daughters are often concerned about their elderly mothers' self-care—for example, the mother's exerting herself unnecessarily or her refusal to get a flu shot. Daughters are solicitous about their mothers' physical well-being regardless of the mothers' actual health status.

Similarity in education and values between mothers and daughters enhances communication, intimacy, and understanding (Welsh and Stewart, 1995). Not surprisingly, well-educated mothers are more likely to react favorably to their married daughters' return to school than are less educated mothers, and well-educated mothers are consistently more likely to be used as confidantes (Suitor, 1987). Less educated mothers are more likely to express disapproval of their daughters' pursuit of an education. One daughter whose mother had only an elementary education reported:

> She doesn't care for [my going to school]. She feels I should be home where I belong. . . . I wouldn't have any trouble if I was home here all of the time. (Wouldn't have any trouble with what sorts of things?) Marriage, kids, any problems. She attributes anything that goes wrong [to my being away from home]. . . . I'm married, so my husband should feed me and clothe me and I should sit home and have dinner ready on the table. (Suitor, 1987, p. 439)

Other factors affect mother-daughter attachments. One of these is the aid pattern between the two generations. Thompson and Walker (1984) identified four basic patterns of aid exchange between mothers and daughters:

1. **Mother-dependent:** The flow of assistance is greater from daughter to mother than from mother to daughter.

2. **High-reciprocity:** Mother and daughter exchange high levels of aid.

3. **Low-reciprocity:** Mother and daughter exchange low levels of aid.

4. **Daughter-dependent:** The flow of assistance is greater from mother to daughter than from daughter to mother.

Research suggests that aid patterns may be developmental, changing as the mother and daughter age and change. Researchers studied two sets of mother-daughter relationships: (1) young adult women (students) and their middle-aged mothers, and (2) these same middle-aged women and their mothers. They found that the typical aid patterns from parent to child continue until the elderly parent is unable to contribute. Among younger pairs, the daughter-dependent pattern is the model, but it is the least typical pattern among older pairs. As mothers get older, they come to depend more and more on their daughters for assistance, which sometimes causes role strain for the daughters, particularly if they work full-time in addition to taking care of their own households and families (Scharlach, 1987). Another study investigated the emotional strain associated with caregiving as experienced by both Black and White daughters. Because extended Black families typically help in the caregiving for elderly relatives, Black daughters reported less role strain overall, but the caregiver's personal and social life is a predictor of stress in both groups (Mui, 1992).

The aid patterns also are significantly related to the degrees of mother-daughter attachment. In general, among young pairs, those most materially dependent (usually the younger daughters) report lower levels of attachment. In other words, middle-aged mothers usually provide more aid and report more positive evaluations of attachment than their daughters, who may be rebelling against parental authority. Among older pairs, high reciprocity of aid is most conducive to attachment for both mothers and daughters, and high material interdependence is associated with high emotional interdependence. However, among all groups, the need to maintain independence continues throughout life. The ability to give aid remains more important to attachment than receiving aid (Thompson and Walker, 1984). In the most satisfying arrangement, the mother-daughter relationship is mutual and interdependent (Boyd, 1989). Even the aid patterns in intergenerational caregiving between mothers and daughters may be perceived as reciprocal. Mothers report that they are not uncomfortable with their dependence on their daughters because of their earlier contribution to their children. Daughters, too, note the importance of their mothers in their lives, especially in providing emotional support. In turn, the daughters are willing to provide assistance to their mothers (Walker, Pratt, Martell, and Martin, 1991).

Father-Son Support Networks

In comparison to mother-daughter relationships, father-son association is less frequent, and adult sons seem to play a relatively minor role in the support network of older fathers (Kivett, 1988). The extent of support by adult sons depends partly on proximity—how near they live to their fathers and how obligated they feel. Most contacts are prescribed by birthdays, family reunions, and other family ceremonies, as well as by emergencies. In a study of rural older fathers and their adult sons, at least one son lived within 60 minutes of his father (Kivett, 1988). Sons who were closest were most able to provide emergency assistance. Other adult sons in this study made contact through telephone calls. In general, however, direct help was infrequent and of the essential type, such as transportation and health care. This was due partly to the fact that fathers were in moderately good health, had adequate income, and were married, receiving support and help from their spouses. The primary need for support from adult children was emotional, not physical or financial (Myers, 1988). When older parents become more feeble, they are less able to care for themselves, so the need for all types of aid and support increases.

Conflict Between Parents and Adult Children

Conflict can arise when the adult children do not follow socially approved behavior that the parents have taught. Even after the children are grown and have left their parents' home, the elderly parents still expect their offspring to live according to the way the parents want them to live. Fisher, Reid, and Melendez (1989) asked 55 elderly adults to describe situations that provoked anger between them and their adult children, who were now living separately. Figure 18.1 shows the major sources of conflict. Parents were most angry at their adult children for failure to live up to role expectations: failure to act like a good spouse or parent or a successful professional. The second greatest source of parental dismay was failure of adult children to conform to social rules as taught by parents: meeting family obligations within the adult child's own family, such as helping the spouse with chores; coming home to the family instead of socializing with colleagues after work; keeping appointments; and following rules of behavior, such as those relating to drinking, drug taking, or reckless driving. Over 20% of adult parents also were upset over failure to reach consensus on values and opinions. Some elderly parents expressed disappointment as well over the extent of their contact with adult children, affectional support, and helping behavior.

Adult children were most angry at the lack of consensus with parents and at the lack of help their parents gave them; they were unhappy to a lesser extent with differences in role expectations and were disappointed by failure to provide empathy, fairness, respect, love, or trust or by infrequent contact. It is apparent that these elderly parents and their adult children still had certain expectations of each other (Fisher, Reid, and Melendez, 1989).

Parent–Adult Child Relationships and Psychological Functioning

Adult children's lives can affect their parents' well-being. No matter how old their children are, parents continue to worry about them. When the children have marital problems, financial difficulties, health problems, vocational difficulties, or other problems, their parents are bound to be affected. For example, the marital conflict of adult children is related to higher levels of anger, sadness, and pessimism in mothers (Hall and Cummings, 1997).

Parents remain heavily invested in their children's lives throughout the life course. All parents hope that their children will grow up and establish themselves as successful, functioning adults. If the children do not do so, parents become concerned

Figure 18.1 Distribution of Conflict Issues Between Parents and Adult Children (*Note:* From "Conflict in Families and Friendships of Later Life" by C. B. Fisher, J. D. Reid, and M. Melendez, 1989, *Family Relations, 38,* p. 85.)

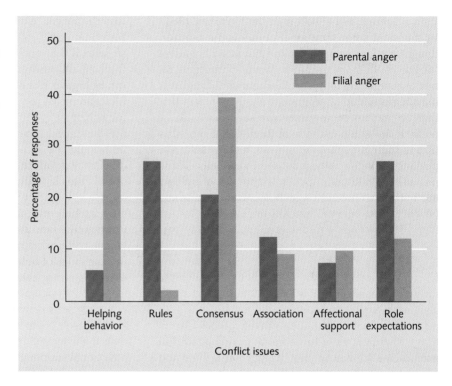

and upset. Children who have not successfully negotiated leaving their parents' home and who have not become independent serve as a reminder that parents have not achieved their task of socialization. Generally, parents whose adult children have mental, physical, or stress-related problems experience greater depression than parents of children who do not have these problems (Pillemer and Suitor, 1991).

The relationships between adult children and their parents have psychological consequences for the younger generation, too. Sons whose relationships with their parents are positive have lower levels of psychological distress than do sons whose relationships are negative. It is important to note that positive relationships with mothers and with fathers are significant predictors of adult sons' psychological distress. The more positive the relationships with their mothers or fathers, the lower the level of distress (Barnett, Marshall, and Pleck, 1992).

Similarly for daughters, having a positive relationship with a parent is associated with a high sense of well-being and low levels of distress. Distress is often conditioned by family-role patterns. For example, having a poor relationship with one's mother is associated with psychological distress,

particularly among daughters who are single or childless (Barnett, Kibria, Baruch, and Pleck, 1991). Thus, the quality of the relationships between adult children and their parents is associated with the psychological functioning of both generations (Umberson, 1992).

IN-LAWS

In-law disagreements are more common in the early years of marriage. Some young couples are able to work out their relationships with in-laws, including the spouse's parents, siblings, and other relatives, so that good accommodations are reached. Others settle into a permanent state of friction with their in-laws. This friction may not break up the marriage, but it can cause unhappiness (L. R. Fischer, 1983).

Successful In-Law Relationships

One of the most comprehensive studies on in-laws was reported in the book *In-laws: Pro and Con* by Duvall (1954). Her study is an old one, but it is still a rich source of relevant information. Her findings form the basis for the discussion that follows.

About one-fourth of all couples have a fine relationship with each partner's family. How important are in-laws to marital success?

About one-fourth of all couples in Duvall's study had a very fine relationship with their in-laws. Couples give the following reasons for liking their in-laws:

- "They are the kind of people we admire: sincere, interesting, young in spirit, good-natured, pleasant and fun, generous, tolerant, and understanding."

- "They do many things to help us" (Goetting, 1990). "They take care of the baby." "They help us when we're sick or when my husband is away." "They give us so many things, like furniture, clothes, and money."

- "They are more like parents to me than my own parents." Orphans and people who are estranged from their own parents may be especially close to their in-laws.

- "They are the parents of my spouse, who is a fine person."

- "We're in-laws ourselves so we can appreciate what it means." Such couples objected to stereotyped prejudices against in-laws, which they felt were unfair.

The Roots of Conflict

There are many reasons for in-law conflicts. Sometimes the problem is with the parents-in-law. More frequently, it is with the partners themselves, who in most cases are more critical of their in-laws than the in-laws are of them.

Immaturity of the married couple may contribute to conflict with in-laws. In fact, there is a negative correlation between age at marriage and in-law adjustment. Those who marry young take longer to achieve accommodations with in-laws and have more frequent disagreements than do those who marry later.

It is not surprising that young couples are more vulnerable to in-law problems than older couples. Young partners still rebelling against their parents may transfer a part of this rebellion against authority to their in-laws. A lack of confidence and experience invites more parental interference or help. Young parents may not be able to carry the full financial responsibility for their family, and the responsibility shifts back to parents.

It takes time for young partners to shift their primary loyalties from parents to each other. If the marriage is to succeed, however, their first loyalty must be to each other. Young partners also need time to get used to the different behavioral patterns and habits of other family members. In sum, good relationships with parents-in-law require maturity, time, and patience.

Some parents create problems because they resent the mate their son or daughter married. Some parents find it hard to accept a son- or daughter-in-law who comes from a different national, religious, economic, or social background. Others resent any-

Adult Child Contact with Elderly Black Parents

Feelings of affection and frequency of contact are reciprocally linked; that is, the more parents and children see each other, the greater affection they will have for each other, and vice versa (Lawton, Silverstein, and Bengtson, 1994). Older African Americans are highly involved in a network of family support. They are often considered the backbone of the Black family system. Older women, in particular, fill familial support roles and have a very important role in intergenerational assistance. Elderly Black parents are also more likely than elderly parents of other groups to live in extended families.

However, the literature on the Black elderly has largely ignored issues of gender. The mother-daughter bond is said to be particularly salient among Blacks, as it is among Whites; a few studlies have reported on the influence of gender on the interaction between parents and children.

A study of 575 Black respondents examined gender differences and levels of contact with children among Black middle-aged and elderly persons. Men, especially those who lived alone, experienced substantially fewer visits and phone calls per year than did women. This means there was a subgroup of Black men who were not currently married, who lived alone, who were less involved with their children, and whose needs for both contact and assistance were unmet (Spitze and Miner, 1992).

A later study based on the National Survey of Black Families examined gender differences in relation to intergenerational patterns of support. Four hundred and eighty-seven young adult fathers and mothers cited grandmothers as the person to whom they turn for parenting support. Mothers are more likely to seek both help with child care and advice, whereas fathers are more likely to seek assistance with child care only. As has been found in other studies of grandparenthood, residential proximity is fundamental to contact between generations (Hunter, 1997).

one a son or daughter married because the mate "is not the right one" or "is not good enough." In these cases, the intolerance of the parents is the primary problem.

Parents may have difficulty adjusting to the "loss" of their child and create problems by being overprotective and meddling. Sometimes the dependent child encourages this overprotection and continues to look to parents rather than to the mate for guidance. In such cases, the mate rightly feels left out and finds it unbearable to have to play "second fiddle" to the in-laws.

LIVING WITH PARENTS OR IN-LAWS

Coresidence by parents and adult children is not uncommon. Research has indicated that it typically reflects the housing needs of adult children, rather than the caregiving needs of parents, and that coresidence does not generally have negative effects on parent–adult child relationships (Ward and Spitze, 1992). When adult children live with their parents, it's usually because of the adult children's needs and circumstances (Ward, Logan, and Spitze, 1992). Most young couples do not want to live with either partner's parents after marriage, but the younger they are when they get married, the greater the likelihood that they will do so for a while, since they cannot afford living quarters of their own. This "doubling" sometimes adds to the stress of family relationships (Kleban, Brody, Schoonover, and Hoffman, 1989).

Effects of Coresidence

Coresident young adults give, receive, and perceive more support from their parents than nonresident adult children but report significantly less affectionate relationships with their parents. The effects of coresidence are more positive when the children are older, employed, or in school (White and Rogers, 1997).

According to the National Survey of Families and Households, parental satisfaction with the presence of adult children (ages 19–34) in the home was highly related to parent–adult child conflict and to the level of positive social interaction between parent and child. The negative consequences of dependency are also influenced by the children's marital and parental status. Parents whose adult children move back home after marital breakups report more negative effects of coresidence than do parents of never-married children. Also, supporting adult children who are unemployed and who are continually financially dependent becomes more burdensome as the share of adult children's basic needs paid for by parents increases. Supporting grandchildren as well as adult children exerts additional negative influence on parental experiences (Aquilino, 1991). However, many parents are highly satisfied with the coresident living arrangement and describe mostly positive relationships with their adult children.

Sources of Stress

The type of living arrangement affects the amount of stress. If doubling up takes place under one roof but in two separate apartments or living quarters, the situation is not any more stressful than if the two families lived next door to each other. But when families live in the same house or apartment and share living space, the likelihood of conflict is greater. Some families even end up sharing the same sleeping quarters. If at all possible, it is helpful if each couple has at least one room they can call their own and to which they can retreat, when necessary, for privacy.

When it is not possible to be completely separate, conflict is less likely if families develop a clear understanding of financial and household obligations ahead of time. Who is to pay for what, and how much? What household and yard work are family members expected to do? The division of household labor and responsibilities is a particularly challenging area for coresiding families. In the National Survey of Families and Households, adult children reported doing substantial amounts of weekly housework; parents reported doing lower amounts. Adult children did more housework in one-parent households than in two-parent households and did increasing amounts with age. Daughters spent somewhat more time on household work than did sons. Also, when a parent was in poor health, the adult children did more housework. Some adult children might have been doing extra housework that they themselves generated, so they were probably not relieving their parents of any substantial amount of housework in exchange for living in the house (Spitze and Ward, 1995).

Another potentially stressful situation is created when parents and adult children share responsibilities for a family business. A study of two-generation farm families revealed differences in family satisfaction between the older generation and their married sons and daughters-in-law (Weigel and Weigel, 1990). The older generation held most of the power over decision making and money. Very often, the younger generation supplied labor but had very little control, as well as consistently lower income. The older generation wanted more family togetherness, while the younger generation wanted more independence, freedom, and equality. The overlapping of work and family roles creates a special dilemma for family members who not only live together or close by but also work together.

Extended Families During Middle Age

Living in an extended household sometime during middle age is not a rare phenomenon in the United States. About one-third of White women and two-thirds of Black women will live with their parents at some time as they pass through middle age (Beck and Beck, 1989). Usually, the arrangement is temporary, but middle-aged people may be called upon to help an aging parent or one or more adult children through a crisis or period of need. These middle-aged individuals have been termed the "sandwich generation" because they simultaneously help their parents and their children.

Sharing Residence with the Elderly

When elderly parents and adult children live together, it is usually the parent who shares a residence with the adult child rather than the other way around (Aquilino, 1990; Suitor and Pillemer, 1987). There has been an increase in the number and percentage of people who accept the idea of an elderly person sharing a home with an adult child (Okraku, 1987). In general, the younger the age group, the more approval of multigenerational coresidence. Evidently, younger adults have become more sensitized to the plight of elderly people and see shared residence as a viable option for assisting elderly parents and especially for keeping them out of institutions (Poulshock and Deimling, 1984). However, the young adults are addressing a situation that is more likely to involve their parents and grandparents; it is less likely to directly affect them, and they may not yet foresee a time when

Many elderly people will give up their independence and share a residence with an adult child. One advantage, confirmed by research, is the unique emotional attachments between grandparents and grandchildren.

their own parents might need their help. Their acceptance of the idea of sharing resources with older generations may reflect their own economic situation, and they welcome the benefits of pooled resources and assistance in domestic and child-rearing tasks (Okraku, 1987).

Older people may give up their independence and share residence with an adult child only when forced to do so by circumstances, such as divorce or widowhood (Cooney, 1989). Autonomy and the freedom to make their own decisions are also important to older people (Pratt, Jones, Shin, and Walker, 1989). Perhaps surprisingly, parents report low levels of conflict with their coresident adult children (Suitor and Pillemer, 1988). Even though there has been some softening in attitudes, in actuality fewer generations double up today than did

so several generations ago. Today, only 7% of males and 17% of females 65 years of age and over live with other relatives (including children; Federal Interagency Forum, 2000).

GRANDPARENTS

Recent demographic trends have contributed to a rise in the number of grandparents and to fewer grandchildren per grandparent. For most, grandparenthood begins in middle age and spans several decades, lasting well into the grandchild's adulthood. More people living longer means that adults today can expect to share their role as grandparent with other grandparents and that some can expect to be great-grandparents (Szinovacz, 1998).

In recent years, we have seen a dramatic increase in the number of grandparents serving as primary caregivers to their grandchildren and great-grandchildren. Approximately 4 million U.S. children currently live with their grandparents or other relatives, up from just over 2 million in 1980. In approximately a third of these homes, neither parent is present, suggesting that the grandparent may well be serving as the sole or primary caregiver (Minkler, Roe, and Price, 1992; U.S. Bureau of the Census, 1999a).

Today's grandparents are usually much different from the stereotypic image. For example, the modern grandmother is far less likely to be wrapped in her shawl, rocking idly before the fireplace. She is more apt to be youthful, vigorous, alert, and energetic, with plenty of ideas and enthusiasm. She's also likely to be employed. In a recent national study, one-third of grandmothers who were babysitting were also job holders themselves (Aldous, 1995).

Today's grandparents are different from previous cohorts in a number of ways. Increasingly, each generation of grandmothers and grandfathers will span a greater range of ages because of teen births and delayed parenthood (Szinovacz, 1998). Improved nutrition and medical care have made it possible for people to stay healthier longer. The life expectancy of today's woman in the United States is 79; of today's man it is 74.

Modern grandparents have a chance to be younger in mind and spirit. Many middle-income grandparents can, if they so choose, keep up in appearance, taste, vitality, and knowledge with their children and children-in-law. They can continue to think creatively and to take refresher courses in their fields of knowledge. Modern mass media and increasing opportunities for adult education in the community help middle-aged and older citizens keep up with modern trends and ideas. Moreover, grandparents are motivated by their grandchildren to send e-mail, view films, visit Web sites, and read books, keeping them current with new ideas and technology. Many grandparents also learn a great deal by traveling.

Finally, modern grandparents are different from the grandparents who preceded them because they are more likely to have intergenerational lineages. Today, grandparents may have living parents and even grandparents. When the age at first birth is during early adolescence for a number of generations in a row, intergenerational lineages are more likely. Although not numerous, grandmothers can be in their late twenties and have living mothers and grandmothers (Burton, 1995; Stack, 1974). Conversely, when young adults delay the age of first birth, the time between generations increases, and intergenerational lineages are less likely (Szinovacz, 1998).

What Grandparents Can Do for Grandchildren

During the past decade, there has been an increasing recognition of the importance of grandparents (Whitveck, Hoyt, and Huck, 1993). In fact, social scientists have referred to grandparents as central to family dynamics and as a valuable family resource (Ingersoll-Dayton and Neal, 1991). The emotional attachments between grandparents and grandchildren have been described as unique because the relationship is exempt from the psychoemotional intensity and responsibility that exist in the parent-child relationship (Barranti, 1985). However, the relationship between grandchildren and grandparents is mediated by the parents. Usually, the connections with the maternal grandparents are stronger than those with the paternal grandparents. However, if the parents align more closely with the paternal grandparents, the grandchildren are likely to do so as well (Chan and Elder, 2000). The relationship between grandparents and grandchildren also is influenced by changes in family life, such as a move or a divorce. Following a parental divorce

or separation, contact between grandchildren and maternal grandparents often increases or at least is maintained, while contact with paternal grandparents often declines (King and Elder, 1995).

Grandparents can do a number of things for children (Denham and Smith, 1989). For example, they can help children feel secure and loved (Kivett, 1993). Children can never have too much of the right kind of love—love that helps them grow and develop and that eliminates anxiety, tension, and emotional pain. Love that adds security and trust, that accepts and understands, is always needed. The role of modern grandparents is associated less with authority and power and more with warmth and affection (Wilcoxon, 1987). Many grandparents continue to play an important role in the lives of grandchildren even after the parents have divorced (Gladstone, 1988; Johnson and Barer, 1987).

Grandparents can play a crucial role during family transitions, such as divorce. They are a source of family continuity and stability. Because of their function in maintaining the family system, grandparents may be seen as "family watchdogs." Although they usually play a relatively passive role in the family, during crisis grandparents often become actively involved in the family. A large percentage of divorced adult children, for example, are dependent on their parents for help. Contact between grandchildren and grandmothers usually increases after the separation or divorce of an adult child. In addition, grandmothers report that they provide more support (baby-sitting, teaching family history and tradition, giving advice) after the separation or divorce (Ingersoll-Dayton and Neal, 1991; Purnell and Bagby, 1993). They play an even more important role in families in which there are unwed teenage mothers. One study found that babies were more secure when their grandmothers took over responsibility for their care and gave directions to the teenage mother (Oyserman, Radin, and Benn, 1993).

Grandparents can help children learn to know, trust, and understand other people. Children can learn that their grandmother's arms can be just as comforting as their mother's. They can discover that their grandfather's house is a safe and happy home away from home. They learn how to be flexible and to adjust to the ways their grandmother thinks, feels, and behaves, which are different from the ways their mother does.

Grandparents can be important in the lives of adolescents and young adults. Research shows that grand-parents share family history and help the young understand their parents.

Grandparents help children to bridge the gap between the past and the present, to give children a sense of history. Most children enjoy hearing grandparents talk about what life was like when they were growing up. By sharing their rich heritage with children, grandparents give them a deeper, broader foundation upon which to base their own lives and to build new knowledge (Martin, Hagestad, and Diedrich, 1988). This knowledge about their cultural and family heritage helps adolescents' identity development.

Grandparents can provide children with experiences and supervision that their parents do not have time or money to provide. In this sense, the grandparent acts as a surrogate parent (Presser, 1989). This is especially important given the increase in one-parent families and the increase in time spent at work.

Grandparents can give children a sense of values and a philosophy of life that is the result of years of living. Valuable life experiences and lessons need to be shared; in this regard, grandparents play the traditional role of valued elder.

Grandparents may play the role of arbitrator between their adult children and grandchildren. Grandparents may be the negotiators between the young and the middle-aged regarding behaviors and values. They may serve as interpreters in help-

Grandparents Who Parent Their Grandchildren

The media refer to some grandparents as the "silent saviors," "the second line of defense," and "the safety net." These terms are used to describe grandparents who thought their child-rearing days were over and who now find themselves raising their children's children. In interviews with 114 grandparents who provided daily care to their grandchildren, researchers identified three categories of caregiving: (1) custodial grandparents, whose grandchildren live with them and with whom they have a legal relationship; (2) grandparents whose grandchildren live with them but with whom there is no legal relationship; and (3) grandparents whose grandchildren do not live with them but for whom they provide day care.

As a group, the grandparents who provided care to grandchildren were solvers of what seemed to be insoluble problems. Custodial grandparents attempted to provide a stable environment for their grandchildren, sometimes when their own children were drug- and alcohol-addicted. Grandparents, especially day-care grandparents, attempted to provide their grandchildren with a stable day-care environment when parents worked and day-care costs were prohibitive. Grandparents evidenced strength in the face of adversity and coped with their situations, apparently because they felt they must.

As was discussed in Chapter 1, grandchildren altered their caregivers' lives, both positively and negatively, especially when they lived with their caregivers. Caregivers responsible for a child's daily personal and legal (decision-making) care felt profoundly the effect of providing such care. Granted the legal right to the grandchild by the court, custodial grandparents assumed the responsibility for both the daily care of the grandchild and decision making for the child's upbringing. In essence, they assumed the functions typically linked to parenthood. Although rearing grandchil-

dren sometimes seemed burdensome, almost two-thirds of the custodial grandparents reported having more of a purpose for living because of providing care to their grandchild; the grandchild kept them active and "in shape."

The living-with grandparents assumed some, if not all, of the daily physical care for the grandchild, but they did not have legal custody. There were at least two categories of living-with grandparents: those who had the grandchild's parents living with them and those who did not. These grandparents never knew when the grandchild's parents would take the grandchild back, and they had no way of protecting the child from an unsuitable or even dangerous parent.

A three-generational household raised other issues. Grandparents reported feeling that they "walked a thin line" in trying to provide a stable environment for their grandchildren without overstepping parental boundaries. The parent retained decision-making responsibilities but often left the grandparent with the physical care of the grandchild. Such a relationship gave the grandparent great responsibility without any authority. These grandparents also reported a strain between their beliefs about what grandparenting would be like and how it actually was.

Day-care grandparents assumed responsibility for the regular care of their grandchildren and assumed no legal responsibility. Although these grandparents arranged their schedules around their grandchild's day, they were least affected by their caregiving role because the children went home at the end of the day. Some day-care grandparents were thrilled to be taking care of their grandchildren; others resented the assumption that they wished to spend their days in this way. Of the three categories, however, these grandparents tended to function more according to our societal definition of grandparents than of parents (Jendrek, 1993).

ing each generation understand the other's perspective, and they may provide a refuge for both adult children and grandchildren (Ingersoll-Dayton and Neal, 1991).

Finally, grandparents can give children a wholesome attitude toward old age. In Western culture especially, in which youthfulness is almost worshipped, children need to know and learn to respect their elders. Older people who have lived rich, fruitful, meaningful lives are a good example for children. They are role models for the future role of grandparent, for aging, and for family relationships.

Adolescents, Young Adults, and Grandparents

Grandparents can be important in the lives of adolescents and young adults (Kennedy, 1990). They can tell adolescents and young adults about the family history and help them understand their parents. Grandparents also function as confidants and provide outlets when parent-teen relations become tense. By observing grandparents and talking with them, adolescents are better able to understand the behavior and attitudes of their parents.

Research on the relationship between college-age men and women and their grandparents revealed that, when there is high contact between generations, the maternal grandmother–granddaughter bond is the strongest (Uhlenberg and Hammill, 1998). In addition, maternal grandmothers describe a closer relationship with grandchildren than do grandfathers. Grandfathers often have a narrower view of what they have to offer children than do grandmothers and perceive granddaughters as not needing or wanting their advice. However, paternal grandfathers and grandsons have a more intense bond than do maternal grandfathers and grandsons (Kivett, 1985).

What Grandchildren Can Do for Grandparents

The grandparent-grandchild relationship is not a one-way street, with benefits flowing only from grandparent to grandchild (Ashton, 1996). Grandchildren can enhance the lives of their grandparents in several ways (Baranowski, 1983). First, grandchildren are a source of biologic continuity and living evidence that the family will endure. All individuals wish a part of themselves to survive after death, and grandchildren are in a perfect position to play this part. In a sense, grandchildren allow a grandparent to glimpse his or her own immortality. Second, grandparents' self-concept is enhanced by playing the role of mentor, historian, and resource person. Third, the lives of some older people are enhanced by the presence of grandchildren. Grandchildren can help keep grandparents up-to-date by introducing them to the new ideas, customs, and traditions of the younger generation. Finally, grandchildren who have grown past early childhood can provide a variety of types of assistance to help grandparents maintain an independent life-style. Adolescents can help their grandparents with lawn care, household chores, and other tasks related to maintaining a home. Such help plays a crucial role in enabling older adults to stay in their homes as long as possible.

SUMMARY

1. The relationship a child experiences with his or her parents while growing up continues to exert a profound influence on that person as an adult. Both satisfying and disruptive memories and emotions may be carried into marriage.

2. Parent-child relationships become particularly important in the mate selection process. Parents may try to influence choice of mate. Parental objections to a choice of mate may drive the couple into each other's arms. Rebellion against parents also impairs judgment in choosing a mate.

3. People can do several things when parents disapprove of mate choice. They can try to get their parents to like their mate and can give their parents time and opportunity to get acquainted. They can discuss the situation with their parents, and they can get premarital counseling. And if the problems are left unresolved, they can carry over into the marriage.

4. In healthy families, children identify with the roles of their parents and learn what mother, father, and spouse are like from their parents. Identification may be positive or negative.

5. Children who form overly dependent, neurotic attachments to their parent of the opposite sex weaken the primary marriage relationship through conflicting loyalties and by the interference of parents.

6. In spite of myths to the contrary, families are a major source of help to the elderly.

7. The mother-daughter relationship is the most enduring and active of intergenerational bonds. When there is a strain in the mother-daughter relationship, it is usually because of the mother's criticism of the daughter as a person, her home management, the way she raises her children, or her spouse.

8. Conflicting ideas of inclusion and exclusion are a source of tension in mother-daughter relationships. Daughters may feel mothers are intrusive; mothers may feel excluded. Another source of tension is anxiety over the mother's well-being.

9. Similarity in educational attainment and values between mothers and daughters enhances communication, intimacy, and understanding.

10. Aid patterns are significantly related to the degree of mother-daughter attachment, with those giving the most aid reporting the closest attachment. Four basic patterns have been identified: mother-dependent, high-reciprocity, low-reciprocity, and daughter-dependent.

11. Parents benefit psychologically by both giving support and receiving it.

12. Adult sons play a relatively minor role in the support network of their fathers, but the amount of help and support depends on proximity and the health of the older parent. The primary need for support from adult children is emotional, not physical or financial.

13. Conflicts between older parents and adult children most often arise over helping behavior, rules, consensus, association, affectional support, and role expectations.

14. Conflicted relationships between adult children and parents can be a source of stress for all the generations, including children.

15. About one-fourth of all couples have a fine relationship with in-laws and like them for a variety of reasons. In-law disagreements are most common in the early years of marriage.

16. The roots of in-law conflict may include the following: partners' negative conditioning to expect trouble, their immaturity, the parents' resentment of the mate selected, and emotionally insecure parents who can't let their child go and who are overprotective and meddling.

17. Most young couples do not want to live with their parents after marriage, and parents don't want to live with them. When doubling up is necessary, harmony is more likely when each couple has their own space and when obligations and responsibilities have been discussed ahead of time.

18. There has been an increase in the number and percentage of young people who accept the idea of sharing a home with an elderly relative, but older people give up their independence and share residence with an adult child only when forced to by circumstances. In actuality, fewer generations double up today than previously.

19. Living in an extended family sometime during middle age is not a rare experience in the United States. Middle-aged individuals and couples may be called upon to help members of both older and younger generations in need of a home.

20. When elderly parents and adult children live together, it is usually the parent who shares a residence with the adult child.

21. Demographic trends have resulted in more living grandparents and fewer grandchildren per grandparent.

22. Today's grandparents are healthier and live longer than their predecessors and are often open to continued growth, experiences, and development well into late life.

23. Many couples appreciate grandparents for all they do for them and their children.

24. Grandparents can help children feel secure and loved; play a crucial role during family transitions such as divorce; help children learn to know, trust, and understand other people; give children a sense of history; provide children with supervision and experiences that parents do not have the time or money to do; give children a sense of values and a philosophy of life based on their years of living; play the role of arbitrator between adult children and grandchildren; and give children a wholesome attitude toward old age.

25. Grandparents can also be important in the lives of adolescents and young adults. The maternal grandmother–granddaughter bond is the strongest of the grandparent-grandchild bonds, but paternal grandfathers and grandsons have a more intense bond than do maternal grandfathers and grandsons. Parents heavily influence the grandparent-grandchild relationship.

26. Grandchildren can also do many things for grandparents: provide a source of biologic continuity and a sense that the family will endure, enhance grandparents' self-concept, help grandparents overcome social isolation, and provide physical assistance.

27. Grandparents provide care to grandchildren as custodial grandparents, grandparents who have no legal status but who have grandchildren living with them, and day-care grandparents.

KEY TERMS

positive identification   negative identification

QUESTIONS FOR THOUGHT

1. What are some important family-of-origin experiences you have had, and how have they influenced you or how may they influence you after marriage?

2. To what extent and in what ways have your parents influenced your mate selection (either present or future)? What characteristics would your parents like to see in your "ideal" mate? How does your parents' "ideal" view compare with your own view?

3. After marriage, what are some of the approaches you would use to build a healthy relationship with your in-laws?

4. Would you want to live with your in-laws after marriage, or would you want them to live with you? Explain your reasons and feelings.

5. What have been the major characteristics of your relationships with your grandparents?

SUGGESTED READINGS

Bassoff, E. (1988). *Mothers and Daughters: Living and Letting Go.* New York: Plume/Penguin. Gives guidelines for promoting growth and development for women and their daughters as the daughters enter adulthood.

Bengtson, V. L., Schaie, W. K., and Burton, L. M. (Eds.). (1995). *Adult Intergenerational Relations: Effects of Societal Change.* New York: Springer. Presents and discusses research on intergenerational solidarity in late life.

Conrad, R. K. (1993). *What Should We Do About Mom? A New Look at Growing Old.* Bradenton, FL: Human Services Institute. Examines the challenge to families when older members grow old and need specialized care.

Cotterill, P. (1994). *Friendly Relations? Mothers and Their Daughters-in-Law.* London: Taylor & Francis. Presents interviews with 35 women that reveal the relationships between mothers and their daughters-in-law.

Kahana, E., Biegel, B. E., and Wyale, M. L. (Eds.). (1994). *Family Caregiving Across the Life Span.* Thousand Oaks, CA: Sage. Discusses a broad spectrum of chronic illnesses that necessitate family caregiving throughout the life span and the responses to these challenges by both caregiving families and caregiving systems.

Knipsheer, C. P. M., Gierbeld, J. J. deJohn, VanTilburg, T. G., and Dykstra, P. A. (Eds.). (1995). *Living Arrangements and Social Networks of Older Adults.* Amsterdam: B.U. University Press. Explores Dutch family structures and functions in later life.

Logan, J. R., and Spitze, G. D. (1996). *Family Ties: Enduring Relations Between Parents and Grown Children.* Philadelphia: Temple University Press. Focuses on relationships between parents and their grown children.

Pfeifer, S. P., and Sussman, M. B. (Eds.). (1991). *Families: Intergenerational and Generational Connections.* New York: Haworth Press. Presents essays on parent-child relations, caregiving to dependent relatives, grandparenthood, and other generational and intergenerational topics.

Piper, M. (1999). *Another Country: Navigating the Emotional Terrain of Our Elders.* New York: Riverhead Books. Explores issues in aging and parent–adult child relations.

CHAPTER 19

LEARNING OBJECTIVES

After reading the chapter, you should be able to:

Understand that conflict is inevitable in family relationships.

Identify the sources of conflict in the family: personal, physical, interpersonal, and situational or environmental.

Discuss the effects of conflict on children.

Discuss methods of dealing with conflict.

Describe the meaning of family crises and the definable stages of coping with one.

Understand the reasons for infidelity and the crisis it creates.

Discuss the crisis of economic distress, the effects on individuals and family relationships, and means of coping with it.

Describe the crisis of violence and abuse in the family; the factors related to violence; the facts about spouse abuse and child abuse, including sexual abuse; and the treatment for spouse and child abuse.

Discuss death as a family crisis, the varying circumstances of death, and people's reaction to them.

Describe the stages of grief and people's reactions during each stage.

Conflict, Family Crises, and Crisis Management

Learning Objectives

Conflict and Children
The Family Environment
Interparent Conflict
Older Children and Adolescents

Sources of Conflict
Personal Sources
Physical Sources
Interpersonal Sources
Situational or Environmental Sources

Methods of Dealing with Conflict
Avoidance
Ventilation and Catharsis
Constructive Conflicts
Destructive Conflicts
Perspective: Spouses' Rules for Marital Conflict
Means of Ending Conflict

Family Crises
Stage 1: Onset
Stage 2: Disorganization
Stage 3: Reorganization

The Crisis of Infidelity
Reasons for Infidelity
Affairs as Crises for Married People
Perspective: Investing in Your Relationship

Family Issues: Extramarital Affairs

The Crisis of Economic Distress
Types of Economic Distress
Effects on Individuals and on Family Relationships
Coping with Economic Distress

The Crisis of Violence and Abuse
A Cycle of Violence
Factors Related to Violence
Spouse Abuse
Perspective: Men Who Abuse
Child Abuse
Treatment for Spouse and Child Abuse
Sexual Abuse of Children
Family Issues: Sexual Abuse and the Criminal Justice System

The Crisis of Death and Grief
Uncertain Death
Certain Death
Premature Death
Unexpected Death
Calamitous Death
Grief

Summary
Key Terms
Questions for Thought
Suggested Readings

A certain amount of conflict and discord is a normal part of every relationship. Two people will never agree on everything. Tensions build up and misunderstandings occur in the process of living. The numerous decisions that couples must make and the disappointments, frustrations, and adjustments they must face will result, at some time, in a hurt look, an angry word, or a more overt quarrel. Some couples have more conflict than others, and some are able to deal with it more constructively than others, but the potential for conflict is present in every human relationship. In fact, those partners who are the closest to each other and have the greatest potential for satisfaction in their relationship also have the greatest potential for conflict.

How conflict is managed, rather than how much conflict there is, distinguishes satisfied from dissatisfied couples (Jones and Gallois, 1989). Although some conflict may be inevitable, that does not mean it is always desirable or helpful. Conflict can destroy love and even an otherwise good marriage. But it can also relieve tensions, clear the air, and bring two people closer together than ever before. It depends on the total circumstances, the focus of the conflict, the way it is handled, and the ultimate outcome.

In this chapter, we look closely at conflict—its causes, its functions in marriage, some ways couples deal with it, and its effects on children. After looking at conflict, we discuss typical patterns of family adjustment to crises and describe the processes of adjustment. In addition, we discuss four major crises that families may face: infidelity, economic distress, violence and abuse, and death.

CONFLICT AND CHILDREN

When children are involved, conflict necessitates additional considerations. How are children affected by conflict? Are older children and adolescents affected to the same extent as younger children? Should parents quarrel in front of the children? Is it best to try to hide marital problems from them? These are all questions of great significance for families' and children's well-being.

The Family Environment

As we discussed in Chapter 3, when the family environment is characterized by positive affect—love, warmth, faith, trust, consideration, and empathy—

children thrive. Such an environment helps them to feel good about themselves and to know that they are loved and wanted. Conversely, researchers have found that child-rearing environments in which interpersonal relations are characterized by anger and conflict placed children at risk for the development of behavioral and emotional problems (Jaycox and Repetti, 1993).

A general family atmosphere of anger and discord has a greater impact on children than marital discord. Some parents who have discordant marriages may maintain the image of a harmonious relationship and keep their disputes hidden from their children. However, children are very observant, and it is impossible for them to escape a general climate of anger and conflict in the home. The effects of conflict on children are less if they can withdraw when their parents are fighting, even if they cannot withdraw completely from a negative home environment.

Interparent Conflict

Exposure to interparent conflict is a source of stress for children and is predictive of problems in child adjustment (Kerig, 1996). The more disruptive of family functioning parental conflicts are, the more likely they are to be perceived by children as stressful and to reduce children's reliance on the family as a safe emotional environment in which their needs can be met. Consistent with this, empirical evidence has confirmed that children who perceive their parents' fights as frequent and intense also have a higher incidence of maladjustment and behavior problems.

Quarrels between parents that are directly related to their children, such as disagreements about child-rearing practices, have a more negative impact on parenting and child development than quarrels that are not related to the children. Children begin to see themselves as a source of conflict and to blame themselves for their parents' difficulties. As a result, they are more disturbed than if the conflict does not involve them. Furthermore, parents who quarrel with each other may take out their anger on their children. Sometimes older children are drawn into the argument and try to take sides or to keep their parents from fighting. Failure to achieve peace is disturbing to them, and, here again, children blame themselves for not being able to do anything about their family's difficulties.

Some conflict and discord may be a normal part of every relationship. Research suggests that couples who are closer and have the greatest potential for satisfaction in their relationship also have the greatest potential for conflict.

Moreover, the effects of family conflict are heightened by direct exposure to conflict and aggression. Ninety two-parent families with a child 9–13 years of age participated in a study which showed that repeated conflict in the family sensitized children to interparent aggression, with the result that subsequent conflict affected them more than if it had not been experienced so frequently before. Consistent with a sensitization hypothesis, interparent physical aggression during the previous year was related to child withdrawal and anxiety (Gordis, Margolin, and John, 1997). Children who are exposed to interparent aggression tend to have a higher incidence of emotional and behavioral problems (Rogers and Holmbeck, 1997).

Marital conflicts that include physical aggression seem to be especially distressing to children and to have a lasting effect on how they react to subsequent interadult conflicts. Tensions between spouses may become intertwined with tensions among other family members, especially the children. Dysfunctional families are characterized by the spread of tensions from one subsystem to another, particularly from the parents to the children (Margolin, Christensen, and John, 1996).

Older Children and Adolescents

Frequent or intense conflict between parents is often associated with a wide range of indicators of adolescent maladjustment, including negative acting-out behavior, emotional upset, and poor academic performance (Buehler, Krishnakumar, Anthony, Tittsworth, and Stone, 1994). An analysis of the effects of marital and parent-child conflict on older children and on grandmothers indicated that older children reported relatively intense, defensive, and emotional reactions (anger, fear) to the conflict. Grandmothers reported feeling sad because of the conflict, but they did not feel a sense of threat as did the older children (Hall and Cummings, 1997). One investigation showed that tense family conflict may increase adolescent suicidal ideation. That is, adolescents may be more likely to think about suicide when they experience tension in the family (Shagle and Barber, 1993).

SOURCES OF CONFLICT

Conflict may have its origin in (1) personal sources, (2) physical sources, (3) interpersonal sources, or (4) situational or environmental sources (Rice, 1983).

Personal Sources

Personal sources of conflict are those that originate within the individual when inner drives, instincts, and values pull against each other. The conflict is not with one's partner but with oneself, and tensions arise from the internal battle. As a result of these inner tensions, the individual has disagreements or gets into quarrels in situations that heighten that tension. Consider this case:

> Mr. M. was brought up by parents who rejected him and made him feel unwanted and unloved as a child. As a result, he became the kind of man who was afraid to show love for his wife or to let her get close to him. He needed her and wanted her attention and companionship; but whenever she tried to develop a close, loving, intimate relationship, he became anxious and fearful and would end up rejecting her or pushing her away. She was very hurt and became frustrated and angry, which, in turn, made him mad. They always ended up in a fight when they started getting close to each other. (Author's counseling notes)

In this example, the man had deep-seated fears of being too distant, but also anxiety about being too close (Israelstam, 1989).

Irrational fears and anxieties and neurotic needs can be the basic sources of spousal friction. For example, a spouse who has a deep-seated fear of losing his or her partner becomes extremely jealous, even for only superficial contacts. Emotional illness is another source of friction and arguments. For example, when a spouse is depressed, the couple may experience disruptive and hostile behavior when the partners interact with each other (Schmaling, Whisman, Fruzzetti, and Truax, 1991). Premarital depression is also associated with subsequent deterioration of marital relationships (Beach and O'Leary, 1993). Even emotionally healthy men and women have mood swings that influence their behavior.

The basic cause of personal conflicts lies deep within the psyche of the individuals involved. Usually, the anxieties have their origins in childhood experiences and early family relationships. For this reason, troubles that arise in marriage because of these previous experiences are difficult to deal with. Permanent solutions can be found when the internal tensions within the individual are relieved.

Physical Sources

Physical sources of conflict are inner tensions having a physical origin. Physical fatigue is one such source. Fatigue causes irritability, emotional upset, impatience, distorted reasoning, and a low toler-

ance for frustration. It causes people to say and do things that they wouldn't say or do ordinarily. Hunger, overwork, and a low level of blood sugar are also potential sources of tension. A painful headache may be just as much a source of conflict as a serious disagreement.

Interpersonal Sources

Interpersonal sources of conflict are those that occur in relationships between people. All couples have marital problems, but unhappily married people are more likely to complain of neglect and lack of love, affection, sexual satisfaction, understanding, appreciation, and companionship than are the happily married. Furthermore, their self-image suffers; their mate may magnify their faults, belittle their efforts, and make false accusations. They feel worthless, and the complaints become the focus of the conflict that ensues. Lack of communication, inability to resolve differences, and withdrawal from each other also perpetuate the difficulties (Dhir and Markman, 1984).

The intimate interaction patterns and relationships between partners far outweigh other major sources of conflict. Couples begin to feel hurt, resentful, and frustrated when the partners are not meeting each other's sociopsychological needs. Relationships with kin, the community, or others outside the family do not affect the partners as much as their relationship with each other does. They expect that their sociopsychological needs for understanding, communication, love, affection, and companionship will be met. If they are not, the couple may become dissatisfied and discontented.

It is difficult to sort out the cause and effect of conflict because of the interrelationship of multiple problems. Marriage counselors know that the problems couples complain about in the beginning of counseling may be only symptoms of the focal point of conflict. The real causes of difficulties often run much deeper. For example, a spouse's lack of sexual interest may be correlated with quarreling, lack of communication, dislike of the partner, mental health problems, infidelity, or general alienation. Sometimes, the couple may not realize the basic reasons for the difficulties. These causes often are found in the psyche of one of the individuals or in the pattern of the couple's interpersonal relationship.

Situational or environmental sources of conflict include things such as living conditions, societal pressures on family members, cultural strains among minority group families, such as discrimination and assimilation (Vega, Kolody, and Valle, 1988), and unexpected events that disturb family functioning. A study in Sweden showed that disharmonious mother-child and father-child relations increased as the children grew older, with the disharmony peaking in late childhood (Stattin and Klackenberg, 1992).

Sometimes a marital relationship remains in a state of relative equilibrium until some traumatic event occurs to disrupt the relationship. Sometimes a long-standing marriage suddenly becomes conflictual. For example, one man could not work through his feelings of isolation and deprivation following the death of his father, so he felt he had been an undutiful son and withdrew from his spouse and family while he struggled with his guilt and neediness. In this instance, a specific event triggered the conflict, although the seeds of tension were already present in the relationship. Unexpected events such as unemployment, change of jobs, disaster, illness, pregnancy, death, or a forced separation or move may be enough to trigger a crisis. Couples who are emotionally insecure or unstable usually have far more difficulty coping than do other couples. Couples characterized by high levels of tension have even more conflict when their time together increases because of vacations, retirement, illness, or reduced hours of employment.

METHODS OF DEALING WITH CONFLICT

It is not the existence of conflict per se that is problematic for the family, but the methods of managing and resolving the conflict. The methods discussed in this section include avoidance, ventilation and catharsis, and constructive and destructive arguments. As we discussed in Chapter 14, some couples have a lot of conflict but keep it under control and resolve their tensions and problems. Other couples are unable to minimize tension or solve anything, so small problems grow into big ones.

Stressful living conditions or unexpected events that disturb family functioning affect every member of the family, not just the adults. The more children in a family, the more strain, stress, and conflict are naturally introduced.

Avoidance

Some couples try to deal with conflict through **avoidance.** That is, they try to prevent conflict by avoiding the people, situations, and issues that stimulate it. The following comments illustrate avoidance techniques: "My husband really growls when he gets up in the morning, so it's better if we don't say anything," and "My wife is very sensitive about her kinky hair, so I never say anything" (author's counseling notes). In each case, the couple is trying to avoid conflict.

In some instances, however, couples try to avoid discussing controversial issues even though they are important in the marriage. In these cases, keeping quiet might be counterproductive. By so doing, the couple avoids conflict but also fails to resolve the problem (Bowman, 1990). Partners who never address important issues in their efforts to avoid controversy gradually withdraw from each other. Gradual disengagement and alienation occur when partners stop communicating with and caring about each other. As a result, there is increased loneliness, less reciprocity in attempting to settle issues, a loss of intimacy, and a decline in other forms of interaction, such as sexual intercourse.

One of the most common complaints of women is that their spouse won't talk to them about problems. These men seek to prevent conflict by avoiding issues. As a result, the women become even more frustrated and either exert pressure in efforts to confront their spouse with the problem or withdraw more and more. The problems are not solved.

Sometimes, however, temporarily avoiding conflict is the wisest choice. Positive solutions can be found only after intense negative feelings have subsided and people can think straight. Thus, upset individuals might want to engage in physical activity, go to a movie, visit a neighbor, or discuss things with a counselor before confronting the problem.

Ventilation and Catharsis

The opposite of avoiding conflict is ventilating it. **Ventilation** means expressing negative emotions and feelings. This concept has been used in psychotherapy for years. It involves encouraging people who are upset to talk out or to act out their feelings to get them in the open; only then can the individuals scrutinize their feelings, understand them, and channel them in less destructive directions. This therapeutic approach, which emphasizes the importance of "letting it out," is based on the idea of **catharsis,** or draining off negative emotions and feelings so that they can be replaced by more positive ones. This assumes that people have a tendency toward aggression that cannot be bottled up. If they attempt to repress this tendency, it will only result in a more destructive expression at some later time. Therefore, it is better to let out the aggression through a series of minor confrontations than to let negative feelings accumulate until they become a potential relationship bomb.

This approach to dealing with conflict can be helpful psychotherapy for people with feelings of hostility and emotional problems. But venting one's hostilities on the psychiatrist's couch, in the coun-

seling center, or in other psychotherapeutic environments, and in the presence of a trained therapist, is far different from doing the same in one's own home, where the hostilities are directed toward one's spouse or children. In therapy, the hostilities toward family members are given verbal expression or, in the case of children, physical expression in the presence of the therapist, but not actually in the physical presence of the person. Telling a therapist "I hate my spouse" is far different from actually telling the person "I hate you." In the first instance, the hostilities may have been drained off harmlessly, so that when the individual gets back home he or she feels less hateful; but in the second instance, even though the individual feels better, the spouse feels worse and will usually retaliate in some fashion. This may result in an increase of hostile feelings between the two people.

Almost no research supports the idea of catharsis in the family and some shows the reverse; that is, opportunities to observe or to give vent to anger, hostility, and violence tend to produce greater subsequent levels of aggression and violence (Tavris, 1982). The reason is that the family is an intimate, closely confined group, with members intensely involved with one another. If excessive hostility is directed at other family members, they feel angry, hurt, or misunderstood. If this reactive emotion is not dealt with, additional disagreements arise and tension mounts, sometimes to intolerable levels. Furthermore, family members can't get away from the source of friction without splitting up the family, even if only temporarily. Of course, tolerance for verbal aggression ranges widely. What one person finds to be excessive aggression may be completely acceptable behavior to another. Of critical importance here is the fact that when verbal aggression becomes excessive it can lead to physical aggression (Phelps, Meara, Davis, and Patton, 1991).

In a revealing piece of research, Straus (1974) found a strong, positive association between the level of verbal and physical aggression between spouses. He discovered that as the level of verbal aggression increases the level of physical aggression accelerates even more rapidly. Figure 19.1 shows the relationship. The study found no evidence of any beneficial effects of "letting it out," releasing inhibitions, or expressing one's anger toward one's mate. On the contrary, the results suggested that "gut-level communication," rather

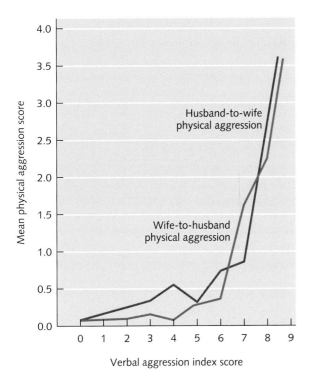

Figure 19.1 Relationship Between Verbal and Physical Aggression (*Note:* From "Leveling, Civility, and Violence in the Family" by M. A. Straus, 1974, *Journal of Marriage and the Family, 36,* p. 17. Copyright 1974 by the National Council on Family Relations. Reprinted by permission.)

than helping avert physical aggression, is associated with physical violence (Straus, 1974). Furthermore, the more often aggression is expressed, the more often it is likely to occur in the future. The partners are learning to assume aggressive roles.

One study of over 5,000 couples found that men and women engaged in about equal amounts of verbal aggression toward their partners. This aggression tended to decrease with age and with increasing numbers of children in the family and to increase with alcohol abuse and the use of other drugs. Socioeconomic status and race were not found to be related to verbal aggression (Straus and Sweet, 1992).

What about more intellectual, rational approaches to problem solving? Straus's evidence suggests that families that take the calm, rational, intellectual, emotion-suppressing approach have much lower levels of physical violence. This is even more true for working-class families than for middle-class families. Intellectual approaches that observe "civility" and "etiquette" in interpersonal relationships are more helpful in the long run in promoting marital harmony and stability and in resolving conflicts (Martin, Schumm, Bugaighis, Jurich, and Bollman, 1987).

Constructive Conflicts

A distinction must be made between conflicts that are constructive and those that are destructive. **Constructive arguments** are those that attack the problems, stick to the issues, and lead to a more complete understanding and to consensus, compromise, or other acceptable solutions to the problem. They minimize negative emotions, foster respect and confidence, and bring a couple closer together. They take place in a nonhostile, trusting atmosphere in which honest disagreements may be discussed and understood and in which the argument progresses according to fair rules. They involve a low level of negative verbal responses.

Destructive Conflicts

Destructive arguments are those that attack the other person rather than the problem. They seek to shame, belittle, or punish the other person through name calling or by attacking sensitive issues in a spirit of ill will, hatred, revenge, or contempt (Halford, Hahlweg, and Dunne, 1990). They frequently rely on criticism and negative personal comments in attempts to influence the other person. Destructive arguments are characterized by a lack of genuine communication and by suspicion, and they often rely on interpersonal strategies that involve threat or coercion. The argument brings up many side issues, and it seeks to relieve the attacker's own tensions at the expense of the other person. Destructive arguments elevate tension levels; increase resentment and hostility toward the other person; undermine confidence, trust, friendship, and affectionate feelings; result in loss of companionship; and engender greater alienation.

One of the characteristics of destructive arguments is the way they get off the track and raise irrelevant issues. The following example is a recapitulation of a family fight on a Sunday morning following a Saturday night dance:

In two studies, married people were asked to generate important rules of communication in marital conflicts (Jones and Gallois, 1989). The rules outlined were divided into five categories. Only some of the rules are included in the lists that follow.

Consideration

- Avoid belittling, humiliating, or using character-degrading words about the other person.
- Regard the other person's issue as important.
- Acknowledge and try to understand the other person's point of view.
- Speak to the other person as an adult.
- Avoid using sarcasm or mimicking the other person.
- Try to understand the other person's faults and avoid criticism and judgment.
- Be kind to the other person.
- Avoid making the other person feel guilty.
- Listen carefully and attentively to the other person.
- Avoid talking too much or dominating the conversation.
- Avoid interrupting.

Self-Expression

- Keep to the point and don't get involved in other issues.
- Get to the point quickly.
- Be honest and say what is on your mind.
- Be specific; don't generalize.
- Clarify the problem.

- Express your feelings about the topic.
- Explain reasons for your point of view.
- Avoid exaggeration.

Conflict Resolution

- Explore alternatives.
- Make joint decisions.
- Be prepared to compromise.
- Be able to say you're sorry.
- Resolve the problem so that both people are happy with the outcome.

Rationality

- Try not to get angry.
- Avoid raising your voice.
- Avoid aggressive language or losing your temper.
- Try to keep calm and not get upset.

Positivity

- Try to relieve the tension in arguments through jokes and laughter.
- Use receptive body language.
- Look at each other.
- Be supportive and give the other person praise where due.

Note: Adapted from "Spouses' Impressions of Rules for Communication in Public and Private Marital Conflicts" by E. Jones and C. Gallois, 1989, *Journal of Marriage and the Family, 51,* pp. 957–967.

Beth (sarcastically): You were quite a ladies' man at the party last night.

Jason (casually): What do you mean?

Beth (raising her voice): Get off it. You know damned good and well what I mean. You danced with Joan half the night. I thought you'd squeeze her so hard you'd smash her boobs.

Jason (cuttingly): Well, at least she's got some to squeeze; that's more than some people I know.

Beth (starting to yell): Look who's talking, lover boy. You couldn't even make it last night, could you? What's the matter, losing your zip?

Jason (angrily): Not really; you're getting so goddamn fat, you're disgusting to look at. Why in

the hell don't you go see your doctor and lose some weight?

Beth (very sarcastically): Speaking of doctors, your mother says it's time for your annual checkup. Can't you even go to your doctor without mama reminding you? When are you going to grow up and do something yourself for a change? I never heard of a grown man who calls his mama every day the way you do.

Jason (stomping out of the room): You s.o.b.; every time we get into a discussion, why do you have to bring in my mother? I'm going to play golf.

Beth (yelling after him): Maybe you can score at the country club. You sure can't in bed.

Certainly, this quarrel did not solve any problems. Beth was jealous and hurt by Jason's dancing with Joan, but he did nothing to relieve her anxiety or hurt. Instead, he attacked her ego by trying to belittle her. She struck back, using destructive approaches, bringing up completely different problems. Such a quarrel only increased their misunderstanding, tension, hostility, and alienation.

Marital satisfaction has been shown to be positively related to the frequency with which each spouse uses constructive strategies to resolve conflict and negatively related to the frequency with which each spouse uses destructive strategies to resolve conflict (Kurdek, 1995).

Means of Ending Conflict

A study of 52 families revealed the outcome of conflict among family members on 64 different occasions around the family dinner table. The study asked who started and stopped the conflict and what the outcome was (Vuchinich, 1987). Conflicts were initiated almost equally by mothers, fathers, sons, and daughters. Conflict was stopped most often by the mother and least often by the father. Daughters stopped conflict more often than sons.

Although the women may have been functioning as peacemakers, conflicts were not often resolved. Sixty-one percent of the conflicts ended in a standoff, with family members dropping the conflict without any resolution. In 21% of the conflicts, the conflict ended with one person's agreeing or going along with another (submission). In 14% of the conflicts, participants each gave a little ground and accepted a compromise. In 4% of the conflicts, one party withdrew by refusing to talk or by leaving the room. About a third of the conflicts were "nipped in the bud" before they started, either by accepting corrections or by ignoring challenges.

FAMILY CRISES

A **crisis** may be defined as a drastic change in the course of events; it is a turning point that affects the trend of future events. It is a time of instability, necessitating decisions and adjustments. Sometimes the crisis develops because of events outside the family: a hurricane, earthquake, flood, war, eco-

nomic depression, or plant closure. At other times a crisis occurs within the family system: divorce, alcoholism, the loss of a family member, or conflict that erupts in violence (Weigel, Weigel, and Blundall, 1987). Internal crises tend to demoralize a family, increasing resentment, alienation, and conflict. Sometimes a crisis develops out of a series of smaller external and internal events that build up to the point at which family members can't cope. Broderick (1984) explained:

> Even small events, not enough by themselves to cause any real stress, can take a toll when they come one after another. First an unplanned pregnancy, then a move, then a financial problem that results in having to borrow several thousand dollars, then the big row with the new neighbors over keeping the dog tied up, and finally little Jimmy breaking his arm in a bicycle accident, all in three months, finally becomes too much. (p. 310)

Broderick calls this situation **crisis overload.**

During a family crisis, families go through three stages before reaching a new level of organization (Boss, 1987; Lavee, McCubbin, and Patterson, 1985; Walker, 1985). This may be higher or lower than the level before the crisis.

Stage 1: Onset

The first stage is the onset of the crisis and the increasing realization that a crisis has occurred (see Figure 19.2). An initial reaction may include disbelief. Family members may define a situation differently; what is a major crisis to one person may not be to another. One spouse, for example, may be on the verge of asking for a divorce; the other may refuse to accept the fact that there is a problem, believing that the spouse is "making too big a deal out of it." The first step, therefore, is to define the problem and gradually accept that a crisis exists—for example, gradually recognizing and accepting a child's disability. The impact of the crisis will depend on the nature of the precipitating event and the interpretation and cognitive perception of it, the degree of hardship and stress the crisis produces, and the resources available to handle the problem.

Stage 2: Disorganization

The second stage is a period of disorganization. Shock and disbelief may make it impossible to

Figure 19.2 Family Adjustment to a Crisis

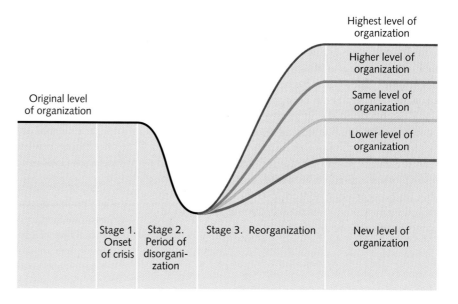

function or to think clearly in the beginning (see Figure 19.2). "I don't know what I'm going to do" is a common reaction. The period of disorganization may last for only a few hours, or it may stretch into days or weeks. During this period, the family's normal functioning is disrupted. Tempers are short, loyalties are strained, tension fills the air, friction increases, and family morale declines. Child and spouse abuse is more likely to develop during the time of maximum disorganization than at any other time.

When Mount Saint Helens erupted on May 18, 1980, thousands of people felt the stress. Associated Press reports from Washington after the eruption indicated that locally criminal assaults rose 25%, suicide threats and attempts doubled, and the number of cases of battered women increased 45% (Blumenthal, 1980). The situation was particularly stressful because of the violence of the explosion (500 times the force of the atom bomb dropped on Hiroshima) and the uncertainty of subsequent explosions. People did not know what would happen next or how long the catastrophe would last. The effects of stress were delayed, however. The greatest increase in spouse abuse cases did not occur until about 30 days after the major eruption.

Other studies have shown that the use of alcohol and other drugs sharply increases during times of stress and may lead to a deeper level of disorganization or serve to handicap the individual's and family's capacity to bounce back from the crisis (Anisman and Merali, 1999; Miller, Turner, and Kimball, 1981).

Stage 3: Reorganization

The third stage is one of gradual reorganization during which family members try to take remedial action (see Figure 19.2). If the crisis is a financial one, family members may borrow money, sell the family car, or cash in some savings. Other family members may get temporary employment to help out, or a former wage earner may start drawing unemployment. If the financial crisis persists, the stock of resources begins to run out. The family has to think about taking out a second mortgage, selling the house, or moving to another neighborhood.

Once the family "hits bottom," things begin to improve. The unemployed wage earner gets a new job, and bills are gradually paid off; the family begins to recoup its emotional and physical resources. Eventually, after a period that may range from days to months, the family is reorganized at a new level. Sometimes the new level is not as satisfactory as the old; at other times the level of organization is superior to the old. For example, in the case of a financial crisis, family money management improves or total income is higher, or both. At any rate, the level is high enough and stable enough to mark the end of the period of crisis.

Families who experience crises, such as the loss of their home due to a natural disaster, will pass through the predictable stages of disbelief, disorganization, and reorganization before they begin rebuilding their lives.

Crisis theory, such as that just described, is helpful as a model for understanding what happens when families have various kinds of crises. While this theory can be applied to a wide variety of crises, we have selected four types for detailed discussion here: (1) infidelity, (2) economic distress, (3) violence and abuse, and (4) death and grief.

THE CRISIS OF INFIDELITY

The majority of Americans still enter marriage expecting and committed to sexual fidelity. Americans place a high value on sexual exclusiveness as important to a healthy marriage. The National Health and Social Life Survey found that 80% of married women and 65–85% of married men of every age reported that they had no partners other than their spouse while married (Michael et al., 1994). Ninety percent of married adults had had only one sex partner in the previous 12 months. These figures reflect the fact that a large majority of married Americans are faithful; here we will discuss those who are not.

Reasons for Infidelity

Why do adults become involved in extramarital affairs even though they say they don't believe in them? There are a variety of reasons.

Emotional Need For some people, extramarital affairs represent an effort to fulfill emotional needs. Affairs are an expression of personality problems. A woman may unconsciously seek an older father figure (who is already married) to comfort her and love her and to replace the father whom she lost in childhood or who rejected her as a child. A man may want an older woman who will mother him because he never felt loved and cared for by his mother while he was growing up.

Extramarital affairs can be an important validation of attractiveness and self-esteem. Affairs may result from fear about one's self-worth or sexual attractiveness. The affairs become an attempt to feel better about oneself. Elbaum (1981) observed:

> The need for validation that is absent in marriage is a common cause of extramarital coitus. In fact, some affairs are not sexual in nature but revolve around a man or woman seeking affection and comfort from a significant other. (p. 491)

Infidelity may be a symptom of emotional difficulties in the individual and an attempt to resolve these difficulties.

Unresolved Marital Problems Infidelity can also be a symptom of unresolved problems in the marriage itself. These problems build up year after year and are not successfully addressed. An affair encourages a spouse to divert energy away from the marital relationship (Pittman, 1993).

Unresolved issues, such as the lack of communication, the efforts of one person to dominate the other, the failure to show affection, and the lack of social life and companionship, build up over the years. People repress their feelings because they don't like to be upset and frustrated all the time. Eventually, they shut off their positive feelings of warmth and affection as well. The marital partners may be at a stalemate, able neither to revive the marriage nor to end it. However, they are still vulnerable and will respond to those people who fulfill the needs not being met in their primary relationship. In these situations, a spouse may cultivate a marital arrangement—that is, participate in an affair that meets some immediate needs without disrupting the marriage further (Pittman, 1993).

If hostility builds up between marital partners, an extramarital affair becomes a way of balancing the animosity felt toward a spouse or a way of getting even for the hurts suffered in the marriage. Most people are not interested in extramarital relationships when everything is going smoothly in their marriage. For this reason, an affair can be a symptom of problems rather than the problem itself, even though it sometimes stabilizes but usually compounds the difficulties.

Ambivalence About Marriage   Single people who are ambivalent about getting married may seek sexual partners who are already married because they feel "safer" knowing they won't have to make a permanent commitment. They escape the responsibilities of being a spouse but gain the benefits of having a lover.

Pleasure and Excitement   Some people have affairs simply because they want the excitement of sexual variety. Other people enjoy the sense of competition with a married spouse, and the married person's unavailability only serves to increase the challenge. They like the excitement of illicit sex. There is risk, of course. One is the possibility that they might become emotionally involved whether they intended to or not. To other people, a one-night stand provides excitement and freedom from the responsibilities of an emotional commitment.

The risks here include the possibility of AIDS or another sexually transmitted disease and the negative effects on the marriage because marital vows have been violated.

A new relationship may seem more exciting than an old one, primarily because it is different and new. But once the initial flush of intense emotions declines, the lovers may feel empty unless something deeper has developed in the meantime.

Permissive Values   Some individuals don't really see anything wrong with extramarital sex—as long as their spouses don't find out or "it doesn't hurt anyone." Some people have numerous partners before marriage and continue to do so afterward because permissiveness is a part of their value system. One married man became involved with another woman with whom he continued to have sex. He couldn't understand why his spouse was so upset when she found out. As far as he was concerned, he ought to have been allowed to have both a spouse and a mistress.

Ulterior Motives   Having a lover who is also a supervisor or mentor sometimes offers other advantages. One management trainee explained, "I know he gave me special help and attention he wouldn't have otherwise. That's why I've been able to move up so fast" (Richardson, 1986, p. 26). Having an affair with a married person who is in a position of authority is one way an individual may advance a career, but it may also jeopardize his or her job. Of course, some people may not think of these things and may simply want to be allied to someone who is wealthier and more powerful. Some married men opt for affairs with single, younger women. The men get an ego boost and they enjoy sexual activity without the responsibilities of marriage.

Affairs as Crises for Married People

Extramarital affairs have varying effects on married people and their marriages. Both men and women have affairs, and some marriages are never the same afterward. A sense of betrayal and the ensuing distrust are common. One woman remarked, "I don't know if I can ever trust him again. Every time he's out of town I wonder what he is doing and who he's with" (author's counseling notes). An-

The following guidelines are helpful in building a healthy marital partnership (Stayton, 1983; Voth, Perry, McCranie, and Rogers, 1982):

1. Keep the lines of communication open. Share feelings, disappointments, and unmet expectations, as well as positive emotions. Major problems arise usually as the result of a series of small, unresolved issues that build up over time. Solve small problems as they arise by learning to discuss them rationally, calmly, and sympathetically.

2. Find out what the needs of your partner are, take them seriously, and strive to meet them.

3. Learn to be loving and affectionate, frequently expressing warmth and physical affection. Hugging, cuddling, kissing, and caressing are as important to emotional fulfillment as is sexual intercourse.

4. Get therapy to help you work through any unresolved personality faults and problems.

5. Strive for variety and imagination in your lovemaking. If your sexual relationship has become too routine,

spruce it up, perhaps by changing the time, place, manner, and mode of sexual expression.

6. Resolve to make your sexual relationship a mutually satisfying experience by being concerned about each other's preferences and desires and by giving as well as receiving pleasure.

7. Commit yourself to your relationship and your partner, and live by that commitment.

8. Show respect and appreciation for and approval and acceptance of your spouse.

9. Avoid situations that are conducive to extramarital involvements. Keep your business associations on a professional basis. Avoid one-to-one meetings for social purposes. Avoid compromising situations. Recognize that people sometimes say and do things when they have been drinking alcohol or taking other drugs that they wouldn't ordinarily say and do.

10. When you find yourself physically attracted to a person not your spouse, tell your mate and discuss the situation. Be honest, and don't try to hide anything.

---

other woman commented, "All I can think of is that he was doing this with that other woman. I can't give myself to him" (author's counseling notes). In such cases, extramarital affairs may be a major factor in precipitating divorce.

Sometimes, however, the crisis of an affair stimulates the couple to finally accept the fact that their marriage is in deep trouble and that they need help. One woman explained:

I've been trying to tell my husband for years that I was unhappy in our marriage, but he didn't listen. Now, I've met someone else, and for the first time my husband is listening and is willing to go to a marriage counselor. (Author's counseling notes)

In this case, the affair had a positive value.

Some marriages are not affected very much by an affair. One of the spouses is having an affair, but the other doesn't care. These are often marriages in which the emotional bonds between the spouses are already broken, so the extramarital relationship is simply evidence of the fractured marriage. These people have either lost or never had a meaningful relationship with each other. In still other

marriages, the spouses may agree that one or both of them has the freedom to have affairs. And in some situations, one spouse discovers that the other has been unfaithful but chooses not to confront the situation because they have children and do not want to divorce or separate for their sake.

Affairs that are most threatening to the marriage are ongoing ones that include emotional involvement, as well as sexual relations. Women are much more likely than men to be emotionally invested in the relationship (Penn, Henandez, and Bermudez, 1997). People who believe that they have fallen deeply in love don't want to give up the affair; the affair seems so meaningful and exciting. One person involved in an affair remarked, "I haven't felt like this for years. I can't give up something that makes me feel alive again" (author's counseling notes). Of course, what people don't realize in the beginning is that the intense emotional excitement will pass. If the relationship is to endure, the couple need to have many other things going on in the relationship.

From many points of view, extramarital relationships become a crisis in the marriage that requires considerable effort to resolve.

The research on extramarital affairs has been scarce, but those studies that have appeared reveal some interesting things. Three types of extramarital affairs have been identified in the literature: (1) sexual but not emotional, (2) sexual and emotional, and (3) emotional but not sexual. More women than men were found to have had emotional affairs, and twice as many men as women were found to have had sexual affairs. Most extramarital sex does not involve love and appears to be sporadic, with sexual intercourse usually occurring not more than five times a year. Extramarital involvement that is either only sexual or only emotional appears to detract significantly from the marriage. However, affairs that are both sexual and emotional are the most damaging, and most first-time divorces are at least partly the result of an affair (Penn, Hernandez, and Bermudez, 1997; Pittman, 1993).

Most studies focus on marital quality as the primary factor behind extramarital sexual involvement, and very little attention has been paid to the role that individual attitudes and characteristics play. Thompson (1984) examined both individual characteristics and marital quality as correlates of extramarital sexual involvement. He determined that individual characteristics (alienation, the need for intimacy, emotional independence, and egalitarian gender roles) were stronger correlates of extramarital sex than quality of the marriage.

One study investigated factors that influenced a woman's decision to end an extramarital sexual relationship. Sex attitudes were related to a woman's decision to end the relationship. As predicted, the more positive her attitudes toward sex, the longer she remained in an extramarital affair. If a woman continued an affair, the power of her emotions appeared to override her attitudes toward sex in determining if and when to end the relationship. Also, the longer a woman continued an extramarital relationship, the more difficult the shared experiences and emotional investment seemed to make it for her to end the affair. Finally, the extent of love for the affair partner and the length of time they had known each other prior to sexual intercourse influenced the affair's duration (Hurlbert, 1992).

THE CRISIS OF ECONOMIC DISTRESS

Many families have to face the crisis of economic distress due to employment instability or uncertainty; underemployment; declining income due to demotion, cutbacks, or retirement; or the inability to earn an adequate income because of lack of education and skills, disability, or health problems (Chilman, 1991). Economic distress has profound effects on individual and family functioning. In this section, we will examine some of these effects.

Types of Economic Distress

The effects of an economic crisis depend on the type of crisis and its duration. For example, a permanent closure of one's office or plant is more stressful than a temporary cut in hours.

Employment Instability   Even during prosperous times, the unemployment rate in the United States hovers at around 5% of the labor force. During periods of recession, the percentage increases considerably. As of 1998, the overall unemployment rate was 4.5%. The rates are always highest among minority groups and among both males and females under 20 years of age (U.S. Bureau of the Census, 1999a). During recessions, unemployment rates are usually higher in the construction and agricultural industries. People with the least education and seniority have the highest rates of attrition (U.S. Bureau of the Census, 1999a).

The effect of unemployment on individuals and families depends partly on how long it lasts, whether it involves permanent job displacement or a temporary layoff, whether other comparable or replacement jobs are readily available, and whether there is more than one wage earner in the family. Young couples and single mothers with a number of children, especially young children, are most affected by unemployment. Many have minimal skills and resources, so they have to turn to others for help.

Employment Uncertainty   Some families feel the stress of employment uncertainty for long periods of time (Wilson, Larson, and Stone, 1993). For example, when a corporation like General Motors announces that it is closing an assembly plant, families may wait for months to learn whether the plant to be closed is in Michigan or Texas. Individuals and families wait while the armed services decide which base to close. Workers in a particular plant are told to expect layoffs but don't know which workers will be let go. Those already unemployed endure the uncertainty of not knowing where and when they will find another job (Voydanoff, 1990).

Underemployment   Underemployment is also a source of economic distress. It may involve working at a job below one's skills and training or working fewer hours or at lower pay than one would like. During the recessions of the early 1980s and early 1990s, many white-collar workers—even those at middle-management levels—and highly skilled blue-collar workers were laid off and forced to accept whatever type of employment they could find.

Declining Income   Another source of economic distress is a decline in personal or family income due to a demotion, cut in hours and pay, declining sales or profits (Johnson and Booth, 1990), forced retirement (Hanks, 1990), or divorce or widowhood (Choi, 1992). Adverse economic changes require families to adjust to a lower income by changing their life-style, reducing their consumption, or increasing their income by changing jobs or by having another family member go to work (Elder, Conger, Foster, and Ardelt, 1992). Typically, the custodial parent and children experience a decline in income following divorce, whereas the noncustodial parent enjoys an increase. Noncustodial parents do not share a fair proportion of their earnings with their former spouse to help support the children (Weitzman, 1985), and women whose marriages fail face increasing odds of becoming poor (Arendell, 1987; Morgan, 1989). Farm families typically have varied and uncertain incomes from year to year and in poor crop years are faced with a substantial financial crisis of undetermined duration (Meyer and Lobao, 1997).

Effects on Individuals and on Family Relationships

Economic distress has a significant effect on the individuals and families involved. Unemployment and employment uncertainty are associated with depression, anxiety, psychophysiological distress, and mental hospital admissions (Dooley, Catalano, and Rook, 1988; Ensminger and Celentano, 1988). The level of economic status affects mortality; the advent of poverty, for example, increases the haz-

ard of dying for both men and women (Zick and Smith, 1991a). Men's unemployment is associated with increased psychological distress for their spouses (Liem and Liem, 1988). In fact, women show more anxiety and depression when their spouse is unemployed than when they are unemployed themselves (Voydanoff and Donnelly, 1989a). Some studies show that unemployment lowers self-esteem, which, in turn, is related to a lower level of self-mastery and to an increase in depression (Perrucci, Perrucci, Targ, and Targ, 1988; Shamir, 1986).

The effect of economic distress on families is extensive and wide ranging. For one thing, families need a minimum level of income and employment stability to function. Without it, many find themselves subject to separation and divorce (Liem and Liem, 1988). In a study of farm families, Johnson and Booth (1990) found that economic hardships were strongly related to thoughts about divorce. One study of White, middle-class couples found that those who were under economic pressure had lower marital quality because of an increase in hostility and a decrease in warmth among family members (Lorenz, Conger, Simon, Whitbeck, and Elder, 1991). Other studies have shown that income loss and economic strain are negatively associated with marital quality and family satisfaction due to financial conflicts, the man's psychological instability, marital tensions and hostility, and lack of warmth and support (Conger et al., 1990). Mounting economic pressure makes men more irritable and short-tempered, increasing their hostility in the marital relationship and causing them to behave more punitively in their parent role (Elder, Conger, Foster, and Ardelt, 1992; McLoyd, 1989). These patterns are repeated in farm families. Those with employed wives had higher debt loads than did those with nonemployed wives; the women also worked longer hours in all production (including paid work, farm production, and household production) and were less satisfied with their marital relationships. Not surprisingly, the men had lower levels of life satisfaction (Godwin, Draughn, Little, and Marlowe, 1991).

A study of 429 inner-city families traced the effects of economic pressure on the emotional status and parenting behavior of African American and Anglo-American parents. Family hardship and strong economic pressure diminished the sense of parental competency among both Blacks and Whites. Parents became depressed and demoralized under economic pressure and lost confidence in their parenting ability. Black parents suffered more emotional distress than did White parents. One possible explanation is that the African American families had fewer economic resources to begin with, so any economic distress directly diminished their confidence in their ability to effectively meet their children's needs (Elder, Eccles, Ardelt, and Lord, 1995).

Problems within marriage can also spill over to work, resulting in loss of income. One study found that marital distress is associated with work loss—particularly among men in their first 10 years of marriage. Based on the average earnings of participants, work loss associated with marital problems translated into a loss of approximately $6.8 billion per year. Preventing marital problems may thus result in important psychological and economic benefits for society (Forthofer, Markman, Cox, Stanley, and Kessler, 1996).

Coping with Economic Distress

Individuals and families use various strategies in coping with economic distress. Avoidance coping involves keeping one's feelings to oneself, refusing to believe the economic crisis is real, and eating, drinking, and smoking to relieve tensions. Avoiding the problem may allow more positive interaction with one's spouse and fewer arguments about finances and partially lessen the impact of financial distress (Wilhelm and Ridley, 1988); however, it doesn't solve the problem. Instead of ignoring or avoiding the problem, families are better served in the long run by developing skills in conflict management and problem solving. A more positive approach is to cut back on expenditures wherever possible and postpone major expenditures, such as buying a new car or starting orthodontic treatment (Elder et al., 1992). Selling property or possessions is sometimes necessary. Some families rent rooms, take in boarders, or supply child care for others. Many families have to borrow from savings or life insurance policies. Finding part-time or temporary employment may be possible. Teenagers or other family members may have to go to work. Other families start small businesses at home. Skills such as sewing or carpentry

can be tapped to earn additional income. Generally, married men spend significantly less time unemployed than do single men, probably because of the realization that they need income to help support their families (Teachman, Call, and Carver, 1994).

Before their resources are exhausted, families may turn to relatives, friends, coworkers, neighbors, self-help groups, human service professionals, or helping agencies. Informal support, especially from family members, is used more often than support from professionals and agencies (Buss and Redburn, 1983). A study of African American families revealed that both family and nonkin were important sources of emergency assistance (Taylor, Chatters, and Mays, 1988). Major types of support may include money, goods, services, emotional support, baby-sitting, transportation, job-hunting aid, and advice and feedback. There are also many types of social and government programs designed to help people who are in financial distress. However, many families find these sources of help frustrating and humiliating to access and use, so they avoid them as much as possible (Dodson, 1998).

Instead, family members frequently seek the social support of relatives and friends as they try to cope with economic distress. External support can reduce the stress of individuals, but it may also generate costs for the persons involved. These contrasting effects may be operating in families with unstably employed men whose spouses seek emotional support outside the immediate family. In theory, for example, the woman's support from external sources reduces her stress, but it can also affirm the man's sense of failure as a breadwinner and evoke more negativity on his part in family relationships. In families headed by a man with an unstable work history, the woman's support from relatives and friends is positively associated with the man's negativity toward his spouse (Robertson, Elder, Skinner, and Conger, 1991).

THE CRISIS OF VIOLENCE AND ABUSE

Family violence generally refers to any rough or extended use of physical force or aggression or of verbal abuse by one family member toward an-

Violence may or may not result in physical injury of another person. Family violence refers to any rough or extended use of physical force or aggression or of verbal abuse by one family member toward another.

other. Violence may or may not result in the physical injury of another person. Thus, a man who throws and breaks dishes, destroys furniture, or punches out walls when he is angry may not injure his spouse or children, but he is certainly being violent. Family violence is not easily defined, however, because there are disagreements over what use of force, if any, is appropriate, and because there is often a discrepancy between spouses' perceptions of family violence.

Attitudes toward violence have a significant effect on whether people act violently toward a spouse or children. In our society, men are more often socialized to accept violence. Early in their lives, boys are encouraged to behave belligerently and aggressively and to use physical force (Scher and Stevens, 1987). The legitimation of violence increases the probability that violence will occur in relationships (K. R. Williams, 1992).

In Sweden, a parent can be imprisoned for a month for striking a child; in contrast, many Americans believe that spanking children is normal and necessary, and even good. In fact, as we saw in Chapter 17, a high percentage of families use corporal punishment to discipline their children. But many spankings verge on beatings.

Some men and women believe that it is acceptable for a man to hit his spouse under some circumstances. Most woman beaters deny they have "beaten" anyone; "I just pushed her around a little bit, but I didn't really hurt her" is a common assertion. Yet many of these women are badly injured. Even civil authorities hesitate to interfere in family quarrels, because of the different beliefs about legitimate force and illegitimate violence in the family. As violence continues, however, public tolerance seems to be declining, and people are demanding preventative and remedial action (Gross and Robinson, 1987).

Some writers argue that there are two distinct forms of couple violence taking place within families. Data gathered from women's shelters suggest that some families suffer from occasional outbursts of violence from either spouse (common couple violence), while other families are terrorized by systematic male violence (patriarchal terrorism; Johnson, 1995). It must not be assumed that common couple violence is unimportant. Suggesting that only severe, repeated violence "counts" seems to come disturbingly close to normalizing minor violence. There is evidence that minor violence is associated with depression and poor family functioning. It is also associated with a greater risk of severe future assaults (Hamby, Poindexter, and Gray-Little, 1996).

Spouse abuse and *child abuse* are more limited and specific terms than *family violence*; they usually refer to acts of violence that have a high probability of injuring the victim. An operational definition of **child abuse,** however, may include not only physical assault that results in injury but also malnourishment, abandonment, neglect (defined as the failure to provide adequate physical and emotional care), emotional abuse, and sexual abuse (Finkelhor and Araji, 1986; Hodson and Skeen, 1987). Sexual abuse by a relative is incest (Nelson, 1986). **Spouse abuse** may include not only battering but sexual abuse and marital rape as well. Violence often starts during courtship and continues after marriage (Bernard, Bernard, and Bernard, 1985; Flynn, 1987; Makepeace, 1986, 1987; Roscoe and Benaske, 1985). Studies of both victims and perpetrators of courtship violence reveal a higher likelihood of violence among minority groups and among people without strong religious beliefs or affiliations or infrequent church attendance, people with very low or very high income, people who experience social stress or isolation, people from disrupted homes, people who have had emotionally distant and harsh parenting, people who start dating early, and people who have problems with school, employment, or substance abuse (Makepeace, 1987).

A Cycle of Violence

Studies of family violence show that individuals who had violent, abusive childhoods are more likely to become child and spouse abusers than are individuals who experienced little or no violence in their childhood years (O'Leary and Curley, 1986). Also, teenagers who are exposed to violence are more likely to use violence against their parents (Peek, Fischer, and Kidwell, 1985). Violence begets violence, which means it may be learned from generation to generation (Giles-Sims, 1985). For example, a man who becomes involved in dating violence is likely to have been severely abused by his father (Alexander, Moore, and Alexander, 1991).

Both men and women are more likely to accept violence against women if they observed their father hitting their mother. Data from a nationally representative sample of 2,143 adults showed that the modeling of marital aggression did not appear to be sex-specific. That is, observing one's father hitting one's mother increased the likelihood that sons would be victims as well as perpetrators and that daughters would be perpetrators as well as victims of severe marital aggression (Kalmuss, 1984). Some batterers have experienced abuse not only from parents but from siblings as well. The greater the frequency of violence, the greater the chance that the victims will grow up to be violent parents or partners.

Factors Related to Violence

Family violence is a multifaceted phenomenon that can best be understood from a multidisciplinary perspective. Indeed, no single theory or discipline has been adequate in explaining it (McKenry, Julian, and Gavazzi, 1995).

Family violence may be related to stress of one kind or another. When stressors are uncontrollable, unpredictable, or chronic the likelihood of substance abuse increases (Anisman and Merali, 1999). Although alcohol and drug use may initially be used to decrease the anxiety of stressful life events, substance use itself can become a stressful event and violence may follow.

Unplanned pregnancies and premarital pregnancies can also cause emotional stress and place a strain on the limited financial resources of both the mother and the father. Women report being the victims of beatings before and after the birth of their child. Attacks during pregnancy are especially brutal, with women being kicked or punched in the stomach.

Financial problems, unemployment, or job dissatisfaction that men perceive as evidence of incompetency in fulfilling their role as provider are linked to child abuse and woman beating. Social isolation also raises the risk that severe violence will be directed at children or spouses (Coley and Beckett, 1988). Families who lack close personal friendships and who are poorly integrated into the community lack support networks during times of stress. They also are less influenced by the social expectations of friends and family. Certainly, an abusive man will discourage his spouse from becoming friendly with neighbors out of embarrassment or fear of discovery, and this isolation increases her vulnerability and compounds her problem.

Despite violent family histories, men who develop strong attachments to and perceive threats of negative sanction from significant others (partners, friends, relatives) are less likely to be violent with their female partner. The last thing abusers want is for other people to know about their abuse (Lackey and Williams, 1995). This indicates that abusive behavior can be modified or changed.

Domestic violence is found among families of all socioeconomic and ethnic groups (Hampton, Gelles, and Harrop, 1989). Physical abuse between spouses occurs in middle- and upper-class marriages, but it seems more frequent among lower-class families (Lockhart, 1987). This may be due partly to the underreporting of violence among middle- and upper-class families. Furthermore, lower-class women are more dependent economically on their spouses and so feel locked into an abusive relationship. Middle- and upper-class families have many more resources to mediate stress, such as greater financial resources, better access to contraception and abortion and to medical and psychological personnel, and more opportunities to utilize baby-sitters, nursery schools, and camps to provide relief from family responsibilities.

Spousal incompatibility with respect to status contributes to marital dissatisfaction and to violence. Couples in which the woman's educational attainments are low relative to the man's experience a high incidence of spousal violence. Similarly, couples in which the woman is more successful than the man also experience marital dissatisfaction and a high incidence of spousal violence. Either extreme creates tensions.

A lot of family violence is related to alcohol and drug abuse. Some people are not abusive until they are under the influence. The question arises, Do they lose control because of the alcohol or drugs, or do they drink or take drugs to give them an excuse for their abusive behavior? Either one or both may be true.

Family violence is more likely in divorced and remarried households than in first-time marriages (Kalmuss and Seltzer, 1989). Divorced and remarried households are more likely to contain individuals socialized in violent families. The cumulative stress of experiencing multiple family transitions heightens the risk of family conflict (Kalmuss and Seltzer, 1989). However, even though conflict and

violence are more likely, they are not inevitable (Heyman, O'Leary, and Jouriles, 1995).

Spouse Abuse

Spouse abusers may seem to be ordinary citizens in other aspects of their lives, but a positive social facade frequently conceals disturbing personality characteristics. Spouse abusers have been described as having Jekyll-and-Hyde personalities. They typically have poor self-images, which they express by being violent (Goldstein and Rosenbaum, 1985). Excessive jealousy and alcohol or drug abuse are also common among abusers. Because they are insecure individuals who do not feel good about themselves, abusers typically seek a partner who is passive and compliant, whom they can bully, and whom they can blame for all of their own problems. Their abused partner becomes their scapegoat, because the abusers cannot accept responsibility for their own actions.

Controlled studies indicate that men who physically abuse their spouses are characterized by generalized aggressive tendencies, impulsive and defiant personality styles, an external locus of control, type A behavior, rigid authoritarian attitudes, a traditional role identity, and low self-esteem and self-concepts. They perceive their spouse as less physically attractive than do men in distressed but nonabusive marriages. Abusers report lower levels of marital satisfaction and significant problems in communication. Anger, verbal attacks, and withdrawal appear to dominate the problem-solving interactions in abusive marriages. Abusive relationships have also been found to be associated with sexual dysfunction. Abusive men evidence significantly lower relationship closeness and less sexual assertiveness and sexual satisfaction in their marriages than do nonabusive men. They demonstrate more negative attitudes toward sex and greater sexual preoccupation (Hurlbert and Apt, 1991). In addition, they have very negative attitudes toward women and lower levels of rational thinking (Eisikovits, Edleson, Guttmann, and Sela-Amit, 1991).

A contemporary study of American couples conservatively documented that one in every eight men had committed a violent act against his spouse during the preceding year. A comprehensive review of recent studies revealed the reported

Figure 19.3   Control Chart. This chart uses the wheel as a symbol of the relationship of physical abuse to other forms of abuse. Each spoke represents a tactic used to control or gain power, which is the hub of the wheel. The rim that surrounds and supports the spokes is physical abuse. It holds the system together and gives it strength. (*Note:* From Domestic Abuse Intervention Project [206 West Fourth Street, Duluth, MN 55806], [n.d.]. Used by permission.)

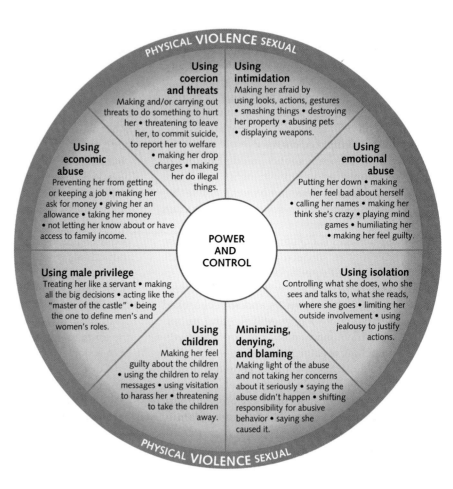

rate of woman abuse in the United States to be between 11% and 22% (Hoffman, Demo, and Edwards, 1994).

Abusers are not only males. A number of studies indicate that women, particularly those who are younger, inflict more verbal and physical aggression than men (Morse, 1995; O'Leary et al., 1989; Stets, 1990; Swinford, DeMaris, Cernkovich, and Giordano, 2000). However, these studies highlight the importance of distinguishing between the frequency of aggressive acts and the severity. The greater strength and average size of men enable them to do more injury. Women are likely to use violence against men in self-defense, causing physical harm or injury in retaliation against their spouse. A woman who kills her spouse is often reacting to his abuse (Goetting, 1987). Women use violence predominantly in self-defense, whereas males use violence predominantly to intimidate their partner (Flynn, 1990).

Figure 19.3 shows the primary tactics and behaviors male abusers manifest to get and maintain control in relationships. Battering is an intentional act used to gain power and control over another person. Physical abuse is only one part of a whole system of abusive behavior that an abuser uses against his partner. Violence includes not only the acts of physical aggression but also patterns of oppression occurring over time, including events leading up to and following the use of force itself. The most widely held theory of the pattern or cycle of violence outlines at least three phases—the tension-building phase, the acute battering phase, and the loving contrition phase—that ensnare women in a web of punishment and deceit (Wolf-Smith and LaRossa, 1992).

In trying to understand abuse, people often wonder, What about the women who are abused? What are they like, and why do they allow themselves to be mistreated? These questions denigrate

Men who abuse their partners tend to share both characteristics and tactics.

Characteristics of Abusive Men

- High rates of violence in childhood, both as victim and perpetrator
- A resort to violent means more readily than by nonabusive men
- Jealousy
- Marital maladjustment
- A tolerant attitude toward spousal abuse
- Impulsive behavior
- Anger that is greater in duration, intensity, and frequency than that in nonabusive men
- Abandonment anxiety
- Sleep disturbance
- Depression

Tactics of Abusive Men

- Social isolation
- Verbal abuse
- Emotional abuse
- Economic dependence
- Intermittent undermining
- Manipulation
- Intense anger and demandingness

Abusive behavior increases in severity in relation to the characteristics just listed. The tactics are usually employed intermittently. This keeps the victims on guard, wary of when the next round of abuse will occur and never knowing how severe the next attack will be. However, abused individuals have seen and experienced enough to be afraid. In fact, the fear can become so intense that it is almost disabling (Dutton and Haring, 1999; Hanson, Cadsky, Harris, and Lalonde, 1997).

the victim and assume that she (or he) is lacking in some way. Women from any background can find themselves in abusive relationships. The onset of abuse is insidious and intermittent, leaving the woman with mixed messages and an unclear picture of her situation. Some abused women have experienced childhood abuse, which has been shown to elevate the probability that they will become the victims of domestic assault. Women subjected to abusive parenting tend to develop hostile, rebellious orientations and are likely to affiliate with and marry men with similar characteristics who engage in a variety of deviant behaviors, including violence toward their spouse (Simons, Johnson, Beaman, and Conger, 1993). Yet whether or not the woman comes from an abusive family history, she becomes confused about herself and her partner. Sometimes her partner is nice to her and says he loves her and needs her; at other times he is abusive. He tries to make her feel that the reason he becomes violent and abusive is that she has done something wrong. She comes to feel that he's abusing her to try to make her a better person. She comes to accept the blame for what happens and to feel that it is her fault (Andrews and Brewin, 1990). She does not want to be hurt (she's not a masochist), so she searches for the right way to behave so her partner

will be consistently loving. She feels that he's good and she's bad. She doesn't confront him or question his behavior. Her security depends on his approval, so she acts compliant and renounces her own wishes. She gives up her freedom if he demands that she quit her job or give up her activities, interests, and friends. Every part of her life is affected by his control. Her self-confidence and self-esteem continue to diminish because he makes her feel that she is a bad person and everything is her fault. She doesn't leave him because she hopes things will change, she feels that if she just tries harder everything will be all right, she's afraid she'll lose his love, and she's fearful of what he might do to her (DeMaris and Swinford, 1996; Forward, 1986). Women who remain in abusive relationships report that there is little or no change in the frequency or severity of abuse or the amount of love and affection expressed, and they often report that their relationship is not as bad as it could be (Herbert, Silver, and Ellard, 1991).

Child Abuse

Early studies attempted to show that abusive parents suffered from mental or emotional illness, that the reason people abused their spouse or children was that they suffered from psychoses, neuroses, or

stop using words that hurt.

Start using words that help.
Words can hit a child as hard as a fist. And leave scars that last a lifetime. Even when you're upset...stop! Think about what you're saying. For helpful information, write: National Committee for Prevention of Child Abuse, Box 2866E, Chicago, IL 60690.

Whether verbal or physical, child abuse is usually due to the parents' inability to cope with the frustrations of their lives and to their lack of knowledge about children and parenting. For their own sake and for the sake of their children, abusive parents need to be encouraged to seek out the many kinds of help available to them.

psychopathic problems of one kind or another. More recent research has shown that child abusers are not necessarily emotionally ill. However, they usually exhibit more psychological problems than other parents do. Abusive behavior can be triggered by the child's irritating behavior, which the parents neither expect nor understand. They often have negative concepts of self, which they project onto the child. When parents feel negative about themselves, the abuse is magnified. Once begun, abuse continues because of the parents' continuing lack of knowledge about children and parenting and their growing contempt for themselves. Abusive parents see themselves as unworthy people and so allow the abuse to continue as a method of validating their unworthiness.

Abuse of children may also be a spillover from stress and conflict in the parents' lives. Financial difficulties or a lack of parenting skills result in a high level of stress, with the child becoming the target of parental frustration. Repeated incidences of abuse result in reduced feelings of personal control, with outcomes no longer contingent upon one's own efforts (Kugler and Hanson, 1988). Very young, single, poor parents are particularly prone to child abuse, since their immaturity and inexperience and inability to cope create feelings of helplessness and anger that they are not able to control (Young and Gately, 1988).

Parent-child interaction is reciprocal; one affects the other. Children with certain characteristics have a greater potential for being recipients of parental abuse than do others. Those who are hardest to take care of and who provoke the greatest stress in the parents are most likely to be abused. The same is true for those who are perceived to be "different," such as premature babies and those of low birth weight, who are more likely to be restless and fretful and who require intensive care, and children who have physical handicaps or are mentally retarded or whose development is delayed. Parents with more children than their resources can adequately support are more likely to abuse them (Zuravin, 1991). If there is a lack of emotional-attachment behavior between parents and child, the child is more likely to be abused. Some evidence suggests that children who live with one or more nonbiological parents are at greater risk for violence and abuse than are children who are cared for by biological parents (Gelles and Harrop, 1991). In families characterized by extreme battering, substantial variability exists in the level of aggression directed toward children. Some children in such families are not physically victimized by the parents at all; others are beaten frequently and severely. In families characterized by extreme battering, boys are more often victims of aggression than are girls (Jouriles and Norwood, 1995).

Child abuse takes two main forms: attack and neglect (Gelles and Conte, 1990). The effects caused by parents who physically attack and hurt their children may be devastating both emotionally and physically. The battered child may suffer fractures, lacerations, burns, hemorrhages, and bruises to the brain or internal organs.

The negative effects of child abuse are compounded because abuse has a detrimental effect on children's emotional and social relationships. Because abused children are likely to exhibit a higher level of negative behavior and to be behaviorally disturbed, less socially competent (Trickett, 1993), more aggressive, and less cooperative, they are likely to be less well liked by their peers (Haskett and Kistner, 1991; Salzinger, Feldman, and Hammer, 1993). Teachers may view them as disturbed. Abused children have more discipline referrals and suspensions and often perform poorly academically (Eckenrode, Laird, and Doris, 1993). Adults who were abused as children may show increased use of alcohol and drugs and higher incidence of HIV infection than adults who were not abused. Apparently, they engage in self-destructive behavior that reflects very low self-esteem (Allers and Benjack, 1991). Other research indicates that not only is the child who is abused affected, but his or her siblings are affected as well (Jean-Gilles and Crittenden, 1990). Moreover, abused children who have adjustment problems in adolescence are more likely to perpetuate violence in their adult intimate relationships (Swinford et al., 2000). The potential for emotional rehabilitation of abused children depends on the damage done. There are cases of battered children blossoming into happy people after being adopted by loving parents. However, if the abuse was sexual, residual trauma may continue to plague even older adults and disrupt their ability to function (Allers, Benjack, and Allers, 1992).

Treatment for Spouse and Child Abuse

Three major treatment approaches are used to help abusive families. The psychiatric approach uses individual, family, and group therapy (Willbach, 1989). Those who have been abused may exhibit psychological symptoms such as **posttraumatic stress disorder** (PTSD) and high levels of depression, avoidance, and anxiety, as well as showing borderline psychotic and passive-aggressive behavior patterns. Many of the aftereffects of trauma hamper an individual's ability to function in relationships. Common problems include an inability to trust, difficulty in sharing emotions, sexual dysfunction, poor parenting skills, a hot-tempered personality, and an aversion to members of the opposite sex (Busby, Steggell, Glenn, and Adamson, 1993).

The sociological approach to treatment for abuse emphasizes family planning programs, family life

education, and support services such as day-care centers, nursery schools, and homemaker services.

The social situation approach focuses on modifying distressing social situations and changing interaction patterns among family members.

Crisis shelters (Berk, Newton, and Berk, 1986), transition houses, "hot-line" services, police intervention teams, the legal system, trained social service workers, family therapy services and teams (Gelles and Maynard, 1987), and many other organizations are involved in dealing with abuse. Considerable progress has been made in treating both the abused and the abusive, and every effort ought to be made to get professional help for these people.

Authorities, such as medical personnel, and the general public are being encouraged to report cases of child or spouse abuse so that intervention can begin as soon as possible. The natural inclination of people not to interfere allows much abuse to go unreported and untreated. However, in recent years, the media have focused increasing attention on spouse and child abuse. Estimates of the incidence of childhood sexual abuse range from 15% to 22% for female children and from 3% to 8% for male children (Haverkamp and Daniluk, 1993). Each year there are approximately 500,000 reported cases of children in the United States who have been sexually abused (Luster and Small, 1997).

Sexual Abuse of Children

Symptoms of Child Sexual Abuse It is important that adults recognize symptoms of child sexual abuse (Banyard and Williams, 1996). Child sexual abuse may be a causative factor in many severe disorders, including dissociative, anxiety, eating, and affective disorders, and sexual and substance abuse problems. It may also be a contributing factor in many other conditions, such as paranoid, obsessive-compulsive, and passive-aggressive disorders. Many studies have found sexual abuse victims to have high levels of anxiety and depression, suicidal tendencies, and difficulty with intimate relationships. Mood disturbances (depression, guilt, and low self-esteem) are frequent. Depression is the most common symptom, and victims tend to be more self-destructive and suicidal than are nonabused depressed individuals. They can suffer from anxiety attacks and phobias and experience sleep and appetite disturbances. They may suffer from all kinds of somatic disorders, especially gastrointestinal problems. They may have significantly more medical complaints than nonabused persons, especially of chronic pelvic pain, headaches, backaches, skin disorders, and genitourinary problems (Ratican, 1992).

Pedophilia   One type of child sexual abuse is called **pedophilia.** The *Diagnostic and Statistical Manual of Mental Disorders* of the American Psychiatric Association (1994) defines pedophilia as "recurrent, intense sexually arousing fantasies, sexual urges, or behaviors involving sexual activity with a prepubescent child or children (generally age 13 or younger)" and lasting over a period of at least 6 months. All pedophiles are child sexual abusers, but not every person who is involved in the sexual abuse of children is a pedophile. The true pedophile can be sexually aroused only by sexual activity with children, whereas other adults who sexually abuse children may not find the activity a primary source of sexual arousal and may have other motivations.

One of the myths concerning child sexual abuse is that child molesters are usually unknown to their victims. In fact, the opposite is true. In 80–90% of the cases, the offender is someone in the child's immediate family whom the child loves and trusts (England and Thompson, 1988). Because of its prevalence and importance, the discussion of sexual abuse of children here will be limited to a discussion of incest.

Incest: Definition and Offenders   Incest is sexual activity between people who are closely related. The relationships that are forbidden by law vary from state to state. Most social scientists consider all forms of sexual contact, sexual exploitation, and sexual overtures initiated by any adult who is blood-related or surrogate family to the child as incest. In other words, the abuse is considered incestuous if the adult shares a primary relationship with the child, whether they are related or not.

In the United States, incest occurs in one in six families; about 100,000 new cases are reported each year. Perpetrators are members of the victims' nuclear and extended families (Gilgun, 1995). The most prevalent form of incest is between siblings, not parent-child, grandparent-grandchild, or stepparent-stepchild as is often supposed.

Brother-Sister Incest   Some brother-sister sexual activity involves sexual play while both are young. In other cases, an older sibling is involved with a young child in sexually exploitative behavior. In a study of 796 college students who had experienced sibling incest, one-fourth said that the sexual contacts were exploitative (Finkelhor, 1980). Occasionally, "blackmail" is involved: The older sibling threatens to tell the parents something the younger sibling has done unless he or she allows sexual contact.

Reactions to brother-sister sexual contact are varied. With increased sibling age differential, the chances of exploitative relationships increase. Occasional experiences are less significant than a series of incidents over years. When an older sibling blackmails, bribes, or forces a younger one to comply, the victim's reactions are quite negative. When it involves mutual consent of siblings of similar age, the participants may realize that parents would disapprove and so feel guilty, but few long-term effects result.

Father-Daughter Incest   Much of the research has focused on father-daughter relationships. Such incest usually takes place in unhappy and disorganized family contexts. The father is often a shy, insecure man who is socially incompetent and has a poor employment record. He may be rigid, moralistic, authoritative, and conservative in sexual matters. He usually holds very traditional family values and expects children to be subservient to adults, and females to be subservient to males (Alexander and Lupfer, 1987). If his spouse works to help support the family, she may be away from home for the day, leaving him alone with the children. In most cases, the spouses' sexual relationship is unsatisfactory, so the man turns to his daughter for affection and sex, often initiating the relationship when the daughter begins to mature. In these cases, the sexual abuse of his daughter is not basically a sexual problem, but rather represents the sexual expression of nonsexual problems, such as depression, low self-esteem, and feelings of inadequacy (Gelles and Conte, 1990).

The incestuous contact is usually premeditated and initiated by the father and passively tolerated by the daughter. The father begins by cuddling, hugging, and kissing his daughter, which both may enjoy. The contact expands to include touching

Sexual Abuse
and the Criminal Justice System

In recent years, there has been a sharp increase in the number of reported cases of child sexual abuse and in the number of child sexual abuse cases adjudicated through the criminal justice system. At the same time, there has been renewed speculation about the impact that the criminal justice system itself might have on the trauma experienced by the child victims. Concerned parties have recommended changes in the approach of the criminal justice system and in the policies of the investigatory agencies in order to reduce the traumatic nature of the process and still guarantee the legal rights of the accused.

Prosecuting cases of child sexual abuse that depend on the testimony of the children abused is difficult for four main reasons. First, the evidence in the case often is dependent on the degree to which the child's testimony is believable. Although false reports, particularly from very young children, are rare, adults are often skeptical when children report having been molested.

Second, many people believe that sexual abuse is caused by mental disorders and should be dealt with within the mental health system rather than the criminal justice system. The criminal justice system is seen as being too punitive, providing little in the way of therapeutic intervention to change the offending behavior.

Third, many people fear that the child will be traumatized by the process, that prosecution will only further victimize the child. This is especially true when the perpetrator of the abuse is a family member or trusted friend. Criminal prosecution may result in the withdrawal of economic and emotional support for the victim or the rest of the victim's family.

Finally, many prosecutors are reluctant to undertake a case that rests primarily on the child's testimony without corroborating physical evidence. In some cases, U.S. criminal courts may allow hearsay testimony to be presented. In one Supreme Court decision, White v. Illinois (1992), the Court did not require a 4-year-old child to testify and allowed the testimony of her investigating officer, her mother, her baby-sitter, an emergency room nurse, and a doctor. The Court held that this information was admissible under state law. In another recent U.S. Supreme Court case, Idaho v. Wright (cited in Myers, 1990), the pediatrician's testimony about what a 2½-year-old child had disclosed was allowed.

The Supreme Court has also addressed issues relating to reducing the trauma that children experience when they testify. In *Maryland v. Craig* (1990), it held that the child witness could testify by means of one-way video because the witness, if forced to testify in court, would suffer serious emotional distress that would prevent her from reasonably communicating. Although this ruling is sometimes challenged on Sixth Amendment grounds, many states have laws that allow for child testimony in sexual abuse cases by closed-circuit television, videotape, pretrial testimony, or some combination of these methods (Martin, 1992).

(such as feeling the daughter's buttocks or breasts), playful wrestling, prolonged kissing, or genital caressing. It usually takes place without any force being used and may develop into full intercourse. Occasionally, a father may abuse his daughter if he gets angry or drunk or wants to punish her or "teach her what she ought to know."

The relationship may continue over many years, until the daughter is old enough to understand, resist, or leave home. She may tell her mother, another family member, or a friend, but she rarely goes to the police. The relationship is often broken off if she gets a boyfriend.

If the mother knows but chooses not to do anything, the relationship is even more damaging. The mother may even encourage the relationship because it relieves her of having to fulfill her partner's emotional and sexual needs. Long-term effects on the victim can be severe. The girl may carry a burden of guilt, shame, bitterness, anger, and low self-esteem for years. She may be at greater risk for divorce or low marital satisfaction than women who have not been sexually abused (Gelster and Feinauer, 1988).

Another of the serious aspects of parent-child incest was revealed in a study of incestuous fathers and stepfathers who were in treatment: 49% of them also abused children outside of the family, and 18% of them were raping adult women at the same time they were abusing their own children (Abel, Becker, Cunningham-Rathner, Mittlemen, and Rouleau, 1988).

Stepfather-Stepdaughter Incest More stepfathers have incestuous relationships with their stepdaughters than do biological fathers with their daughters. It has been estimated that a stepfather is five times more likely than a biological father to approach a child sexually. The higher percentage is probably due to a lower incest taboo and to a more distant relationship between stepfathers and stepdaughters than between biologically related fathers and daughters (Giles-Sims and Finkelhor, 1984).

The effects on stepdaughters may be both short- and long-term. Possible short-term effects are primarily emotional, as the girl may feel fearful, angry, humiliated, confused, trapped, or used. The stepfather may try to prevent her from dating boys and may become violent if she attempts to halt the incestuous relationship (Vander Mey and Neff, 1982). As with other incestuous relationships, possible long-term effects may include antisocial and acting-out behavior, such as drug abuse, delinquency, and prostitution. The girl may become depressed or suicidal or may have difficulty functioning sexually or maternally.

Intervention   Intervention is difficult in cases of incest, partly because authorities are seldom made aware of the problem. A relationship may go on for years, often until the young woman becomes pregnant. Most states require professionals who may come in contact with it to report cases of suspected sexual abuse. Treatment of sexual abusers is difficult at best, and the professionals who treat them need specialized training (Priest and Smith, 1992).

THE CRISIS OF DEATH AND GRIEF

Another type of family crisis is death. Death, especially of a spouse, child, or other close relative, is among life's most stressful events. It creates considerable physical, mental, and emotional stress and tension, which may take a long time to subside.

There are various circumstances of death. They include (1) uncertain death, (2) certain death, at either a known or an unknown time, and (3) untimely death, which may include premature death, unexpected death, and calamitous death (Pattison, 1977). We will discuss each of these circumstances and their effects on the family.

Uncertain Death

Everyone will die, but the exact time is uncertain for most people. Studies of groups of adults reveal variations in attitudes toward death among different age groups. Middle-aged respondents, ages 45–54, express the greatest fear of death; the elderly, ages 65–74, express the least. Middle-aged adults are more frightened of death because they are becoming aware of the finitude of their lives. Older adults are much less likely to fear death, and many are ready for it when it comes. In surveys among institutionalized and noninstitutionalized persons ages 61–97, 51% said they were absolutely unafraid of death, and 40% were indifferent to it. Only 1% said they had a strong fear of death. The one fear expressed was that death would be painful (Myska and Pasewark, 1978).

The circumstance of uncertain death can be very stressful, however, if people have been badly injured and are in critical condition, or if they have had radical surgery with the result uncertain. During such times, the patient and family members must live through a continuing period of acute crisis. Indeed, the most difficult part about such uncertainty is the waiting: dreading a setback, hoping for improvement, waiting anxiously for other family members to arrive. The patient needs to avoid panic, to relax, and to let healing take place. The spouse and family need relief from the continued anxiety and worry; they need sleep and reassurance that their loved one will be all right.

The question of whether the patient will live or die is resolved eventually. In the meantime, however, there may be long-term uncertainties, such as in cases of cancer that may or may not have been arrested. Ambiguity may remain for years; and long years of waiting can be difficult. However, some people learn not to worry about what might happen and to be as happy and optimistic as possible.

Certain Death

Certain death requires a different adjustment. The approximate time of death may be known or unknown or may only be surmised. Such might be the case in a deadly disease, such as cancer of the pancreas. Whether the approximate time of death is known or not, the adjustments to terminal illness are difficult.

Elisabeth Kübler-Ross (1969, 1974), a psychiatrist at the University of Chicago, spent consider-

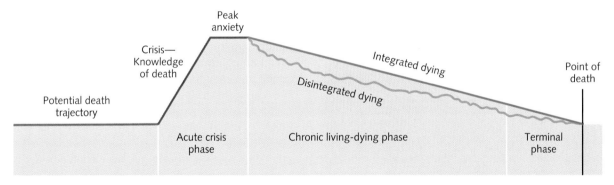

Figure 19.4   The Living-Dying Trajectory (*Note:* Adapted from "The Experience of Dying" by E. M. Pattison, 1977, in *The Experience of Dying* [pp. 43–60] ed. by E. M. Pattison, Englewood Cliffs, NJ: Prentice-Hall. Used by permission of the publisher.)

able time talking with 200 dying patients to try to understand and describe their reactions to terminal illness. She found considerable resistance among medical personnel to the idea of talking with patients about dying, but she also found that the patients were relieved to share their concerns.

Kübler-Ross identified five stages of dying, which do not necessarily occur in a regular sequence. In fact, she said, "Most of my patients have exhibited two or three stages simultaneously and these do not always occur in the same order" (Kübler-Ross, 1974). The five stages are denial, anger, bargaining, depression, and acceptance.

In the denial stage, the patient says, "No, not me. It can't be true." Some accuse their doctor of incompetence, and some think a mistake was made in the lab or in diagnosis. Others seek out other physicians, faith healers, or miracle cures. Some simply deny the reality of impending death and proceed as if nothing were wrong. Only a few people maintain denial to the very end; most accept reality gradually.

As they acknowledge reality, their next reaction is one of anger. The person demands, "Why me? It's not fair it should be happening to me." People in this stage become very hostile, resentful, and irritable, often quarreling with doctors, nurses, and loved ones.

As terminally ill people begin to realize that death may be coming, they try bargaining to win a reprieve. The person propositions God, the medical staff, and family, sometimes just to live a while longer to attend a wedding or complete a task. The person says to God, "If you'll give me six more months, I'll leave most of my money to the church."

If the person lives beyond the bargained-for period, however, the agreement is usually broken.

Once people lose hope that life is possible and accept death as inevitable, depression may set in. Depression may be caused by regret at leaving behind everything and everybody that one loves. It may be caused by guilt over one's life. It may result from shame over bodily disfigurement or an inability to die with dignity. Some people need to express their sorrow in order to overcome it. Others need cheering up and support to improve their morale and to regain their self-esteem.

The final stage of the dying process is acceptance. The person has worked through denial, anger, depression, and fear of death; he or she is now exhausted and weak. This is the time for friends or family members to sit quietly holding the person's hands, to show that death is not such a frightening experience (Rice, 1986).

Pattison (1977) presented the dying process in a somewhat different way. He suggested that all of us project a **trajectory of life;** we anticipate a certain life span within which we arrange our activities and our lives. And then we are abruptly confronted with a crisis—the crisis of knowledge of death (see Figure 19.4). Our potential trajectory is suddenly changed. We will die in days, weeks, months, or several years. Our life has been foreshortened, so our activities must be rearranged. We cannot plan for the potential; we must deal with the actual. The period between the "crisis and knowledge of death" and the "point of death" is the **living-dying interval.** This interval is divided into three phases: (1) the acute crisis phase, (2) the chronic

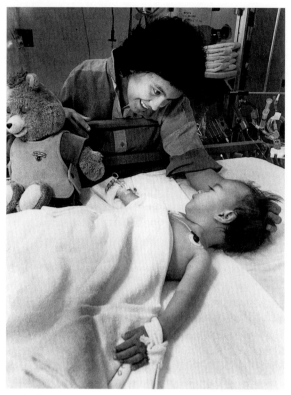

Medical crises can severely test a family's ability to adjust. When a child's life is threatened or lost, initial reactions can be disbelief or refusal to accept the situation; these reactions may be followed by a stage of disorganization lasting for days or weeks.

living-dying phase, and (3) the terminal phase. Family members can help the person respond to the acute crisis so that it does not result in a chaotic disintegration of the person's life during the chronic living-dying phase.

Premature Death

The psychological reactions to death are more extreme when death occurs in childhood or at a comparatively young age. People have trouble accepting a child's death and understanding it. It seems so unfair, because the child has not had a chance at life. It is difficult to reconcile what *is* with what *might have been* (Goodman, Rubinstein, Alexander, and Luborsky, 1991).

Sudden infant death syndrome (SIDS), or **crib death**, is one such unexpected death that shocks and disorganizes the family system. Family members experience intense grief that causes physical upset and emotional pain. Parents may experience despondency, concentration difficulties, time confusion, loss of appetite, and insomnia. They may dread being alone and fear the responsibilities of caring for other children. They may feel helpless or angry, and they often blame themselves.

Most families survive the loss of a child, although a small percentage of spouses divorce as a result. Some family members come to believe that a great deal of good can emerge from such a tragedy. Many of these same people also believe that life will never be the same. Life, for many, takes on a deeper meaning. Life is beautiful, many bereaved family members conclude, and life is fragile. We inherit the earth for a few precious moments, and then we are gone (DeFrain, 1991).

The helping relationships of married couples following miscarriage and infant death are varied. Couples reactions range from a well-synchronized sharing at one extreme to profoundly separated grieving and virtually no mutual support at the other. Most couples, however, provide at least some support to each other. When the woman needs more emotional support than the man can provide, she may be able to obtain support from people outside the marriage. Fathers are less likely than mothers to seek or to find emotional support outside the marriage, and they vary considerably in their desire for outside emotional support.

Emotional support is the most important kind of support spouses provide for each other. This includes talking, listening, holding hands, hugging, crying, and making eye contact that lets each person know that the other understands. In addition, men provide instrumental support for their partner, doing household chores that usually are the woman's responsibility. When she resumes these activities, both spouses are likely to interpret her doing so as supportive of the man. In the stressfulness of infant loss, women may experience their spouse's lack of verbal expressiveness as poor support, but men may simply feel too grief-stricken to speak. Most low-expressive men, however, stated the opinion that they should be strong for their spouse (Smart, 1992).

Unexpected Death

Unexpected death is the sudden death of a healthy person. The emotional impact upon survivors is gauged by how vital, alive, and distinctive the person was at the time of death. The more vital and alive the person, the harder it is to imagine him or her dead. When a young adult dies, relatives react with frustration, disappointment, and anger. Career, marriage, children, and home were yet to come. The unexpected death of a middle-aged individual can also be tragic, but for different reasons. This person has assumed responsibilities for a family, job, and home, as well as in the community. Financial obligations are at a peak. There is extensive involvement with spouse, children, relatives, business associates, and friends. Death leaves the survivors with continuing obligations and no one to assume the responsibilities. Coping with dying involves coping with the obligations.

Calamitous Death

Calamitous death is not only unpredictable but can also be violent, destructive, demeaning, and even degrading. It includes accidents, involuntary manslaughter, homicide, and suicide.

Accidents Accidents are the leading cause of death in the United States among people under age 40, including children (U.S. Bureau of the Census, 1999a). Most accidents have identifiable causes and are preventable, so family members are left with the knowledge that the accidental death need not have happened. The revelation of death comes as a shock, causing an extended period of disorganization before relatives can manage living their lives without their loved one.

Involuntary Manslaughter **Involuntary manslaughter** is the unintentional killing of another human being, most often while driving a car and less often in situations such as hunting accidents. Consider this real-life example:

> Mrs. A. was driving her car at night while very drunk. She swerved over the yellow center line into an oncoming car, killing the woman driver. She was convicted of involuntary manslaughter and sentenced to 2 years in prison. During this period of time, her husband came for counseling as preparation for the time when his wife would be released from prison. After her discharge from prison, the couple both came for therapy to try to put their lives back together. (Author's counseling notes)

In this case, several other factors were significant. In the beginning, the man gave his spouse no moral support. During the 6 months' trial, the couple never talked about what had happened, because he didn't want to. He slept on the couch; she described her pain as terrible. She wanted to reach out to her spouse, but he was not there when she needed him. When she said she wanted a divorce, he finally broke down and cried and said he didn't want one. After her imprisonment, he got therapy.

The man was very lonesome during the period of separation and used periodic therapy as a means of support. He mentioned in one session that he had been brought up by an abusive alcoholic father, so he had a number of factors in his background that he dealt with in therapy during the time of separation from his spouse. He also admitted that there were many unaddressed issues in their marriage, and he was anxious to do something about them. He was able to gain a lot of insight into their problems as a couple.

Some of the more important marital problems included a lack of communication, different goals in life, a lack of companionship (the man was a TV addict), and differences in sexual appetite. The woman wanted more love and affection in their relationship. But the major problem in the marriage was her chronic alcoholism. She entered a treatment and education program for her alcoholism while in prison, and she was able to recover.

Following her release from prison, the woman was ecstatic for about 2 weeks. But then she suffered a posttraumatic stress disorder: She cried daily, languished in bed, and couldn't force herself to go to work. The simplest tasks—like going grocery shopping—overwhelmed her. Through therapy, she was able to relive some of her past experiences and overcome them. Jail had been a nightmare for her, and it had taken her 6 months to accept the fact that she was doing time.

Three months after the woman's discharge from prison, the spouses' communication had improved. The man had become more loving and attentive. The woman was off antidepressants and had entered an educational program for certified nurses' aides. The lives of the two people were slowly coming together.

This case history illustrates the process of disorganization and reorganization that often takes

The emotional impact of an unexpected death, such as that of a young mother, is gauged by how alive and distinctive the person was at the time of death. Responsibilities often shift suddenly and heavily onto surviving family members.

place after a severe crisis, one that is devastating to the whole family. Incidentally, Mr. and Mrs. A. now have a child and are doing well in their marriage.

Suicide   Suicide is one of the most devastating of family crises because it leaves family members feeling so remorseful, guilty, confused, and hurt. Survivors inevitably ask, "Why did he or she do it?" "Why didn't I sense that something was wrong?" and "Why didn't I do something to prevent it?" Survivors who are left with dependent children, large financial responsibilities, and other obligations are also justifiably resentful, demanding, "How could he do such a thing?" and exclaiming, "I hate him for doing this and leaving me all the responsibility of caring for the children."

If family members blame themselves for letting suicide happen, for not preventing it from happening, or for causing it to happen, it may take considerable therapy for them to get over the self-recrimination. Compared with that of family members of someone who has died a natural death, the process of bereavement is more difficult for family members of someone who has committed suicide (Farberow, Gallagher-Thompson, Gilewski, and Thompson, 1992). Group therapy can be very helpful in moving the family members through the grieving process (Freeman, 1991).

Grief

No matter how long the death of a loved one has been anticipated, it still comes as a shock. In fact, people who have watched loved ones suffer through chronic illness before dying are sometimes affected as much as or more than those whose loved ones died after a short illness.

Hiltz (1998) described three stages of grief. The first is a short period of shock during which the surviving family members are stunned and immobilized with grief and disbelief. The second is a period of intense suffering during which individuals experience intense physical and emotional symptoms. Physical reactions may include disturbed sleep, stomach upset and loss of appetite, weight loss, loss of energy and muscular strength, and shortness of breath or tightness in the chest (Rosenbloom and Whittington, 1993). Emotional reactions may include anger, guilt, depression, anxiety, and preoccupation with thoughts of the deceased. During this stage of intense grief, people need to talk with friends or family about their loss. But since grief and death are uncomfortable subjects, this opportunity is often denied, and recovery from the loss is more difficult and prolonged. Finally, in the third stage, there is a gradual reawakening of interest in life.

One common reaction to bereavement is to purify the memory of the deceased by mentally downplaying that person's negative characteristics. The bereaved tend to remember the good things about the deceased and to forget negative traits or events. If this idealization continues, it can prevent the formation of new intimate friendships. Extended bereavement can result in a sentimentalized, nostalgic, and morose style of life.

Men and women may respond differently to bereavement. Men find it more difficult to express grief, but they can accept the reality of death more quickly. Women are better able to continue working during bereavement than are men. After the death of a spouse, men are more apt to describe their loss as the loss of part of themselves; women may frame their loss in terms of being deserted, abandoned, and left to fend for themselves.

The negative impact of bereavement and the loss of a loved one cannot be overstated. Damage to the self accompanies widowhood, for example, if the spouse was important in the life of the partner. The degree and duration of this damage depend on the intensity of the involvement with the departed and the availability of significant others. Daughters who were caregivers to their elderly mothers compared their bereavement feelings at 2 months and 6 months following the mother's death. During this period, the daughters reported decreases in feelings of emotional shock, anger, and helplessness. But bereavement feelings are often complex and sometimes contradictory. For example, daughters reported feeling relatively high levels of psychological strength in coping with their mother's death while simultaneously reporting feelings of shock, anger, and guilt.

Clearly, the loss of a parent, particularly a mother for whom the daughter had been caring, involves significant distress (Pratt, Walker, and Wood, 1992). The death of a family member often affects the health and well-being of other family members. It also affects the structure and dynamics of the family, including the relationships between survivors, possibly leading to increased closeness or to strain in these relationships.

One of the most common deaths faced by adults is the death of a parent. Demographers report that the death of a father is most likely to occur when adult children are ages 35–54 and that the death of a mother is most likely to occur when they are ages 45–64. The death of a parent is a common life transition for adults and may be a significant predictor of change in marital quality. It may affect adult children's marital relationships, which, in turn, affect individuals' well-being. The death of a parent may place a great deal of strain on many marital relationships. The decline in marital quality may occur because the partner fails to provide emotional support, cannot comprehend the significance and meaning of the loss, or is disappointed by the bereaved individual's slow recovery. Some partners feel imposed upon by the continuing stress and depression of the bereaved person. Compared with nonbereaved individuals, people who have recently experienced the death of a mother express a greater decline in social support from their partner and an increase in their partner's negative behavior. Those who have recently experienced the death of a father express a greater increase in relationship strain and frequency of conflict and a greater decline in relationship harmony.

The period following a parent's death may be a time when individuals are in particular need of support from their partner. Their partner's failure to provide support or any strains that are initiated by their partner may lead to a decline in marital quality for recently bereaved individuals (Umberson, 1995).

SUMMARY

1. Conflict is part of every relationship. It arises from various sources: personal, physical, interpersonal, and situational or environmental.

2. Conflict and a negative family environment may have a negative effect on children and place them at increased risk for behavioral and emotional problems.

3. Frequent and hostile conflict in the family is associated with emotional upset and negative acting-out behavior on the part of adolescents.

4. Avoidance is a method of dealing with conflict. The opposite of avoidance is ventilation and catharsis: letting out all feelings in an unrestrained manner. Rational, tactful, thoughtful, and considerate approaches to solving conflict work better.

5. Conflict is constructive if it sticks to issues, generates solutions, and builds better feelings between people. Conflict is destructive if it attacks the ego rather than the problem or if the discussion gets off track, increases tension and alienation, and leaves the initial issue unresolved or unaddressed.

6. A crisis may be defined as a drastic change in the course of events; it is a turning point during which the trend of future events is affected.

7. Researchers identify three stages in family adjustment to crises: (1) the onset of the crisis, (2) a period of disorganization, and (3) reorganization. After reorganization, the new level of family organization may be lower, at the same level, or higher than it was before the crisis.

8. Infidelity is a crisis in many marriages because Americans enter marriage expecting and committed to sexual fidelity. People get involved in extramarital affairs for a variety of reasons.

9. Spouses enrich their marriages by communicating honestly and openly, by committing to each other, and by assuming the perspective of the other.

10. Extramarital affairs have varying effects on married people: Some marriages are never the same afterward; some are ended by divorce; some spouses are stimulated to solve the problems of their own marriage; and some

marriages in which the emotional bonds are already broken are not affected very much by the affair.

11. In some situations, a partner discovers that the other is unfaithful and chooses not to confront the other regarding the infidelity. The affairs that are most threatening to marriage are ongoing affairs that include emotional involvement as well as sexual relations.

12. Many families have to face the crisis of economic distress due to employment instability or uncertainty, underemployment, or declining income.

13. Economic distress is associated with both physiological distress and psychological distress, and it has far-reaching effects on families. It increases the possibility of divorce because of lower levels of consensus, poorer communication, disharmony, and stress in the relations between spouses and between parents and children.

14. Individuals and families use various methods for coping with economic distress: avoiding the issue, cutting back on expenditures, selling property, renting rooms, supplying child care, borrowing money, finding part-time or temporary employment, starting home businesses, or turning to various social supports.

15. Family violence is any rough and extended use of physical force or aggression or of verbal abuse by one family member toward another.

16. Couple violence can take the form of common couple violence or patriarchal terrorism. Common couple violence may escalate into severe violence.

17. Child abuse may include not only physical assault but also neglect, emotional abuse, and sexual abuse.

18. Individuals who experienced violent, abusive childhoods are more likely to grow up and become child and spouse abusers than are those who experienced little or no violence in their childhood years. Family violence is related to stress of various kinds.

19. Abusers are likely to have a poor self-image, rank higher in general aggression, be jealous, abuse alcohol and drugs, and be insecure individuals who need a scapegoat for their problems.

20. Although both women and men use verbal and physical aggression against their spouse, men are more likely to inflict injury because of their size and strength.

21. Abused women accept the blame for the abuse because their partner tries to make them believe it is their fault.

22. Child abusers exhibit more psychological problems than nonabusers, have a negative self-concept, lack knowledge of parenting, overreact to stress in their life, and—because of immaturity and inexperience—are unable to cope.

23. Children who are born prematurely or are fretful, handicapped, or otherwise very difficult to care for are more likely to be abused. The effects can be devastating.

24. There are three major treatment approaches to help child-abusing families: the psychiatric, sociological, and social situation approaches.

25. Pedophilia is a form of child sexual abuse. The great majority of those who sexually abuse children are people in the child's immediate family whom the child loves and trusts.

26. Incest is sexual activity between people who are closely related or are surrogate family members. The most prevalent incestuous relationships are between siblings. Brother-sister incestuous relationships are most damaging if they involve an older sibling exploiting a younger one. Father-daughter incestuous relationships usually take place in unhappy and disorganized family situations in which a maladjusted father turns to his daughter for affection and sex and as a sexual expression of nonsexual problems such as depression, low self-esteem, and feelings of inadequacy. Stepfather-stepdaughter incestuous relationships are five times more frequent than those between biological fathers and daughters. Mother-son incest does not occur frequently and is usually limited to stimulation of a son while young.

27. Intervention in incestuous relationships is difficult because authorities are rarely made aware of the problem. Professionals are required to report suspected incidences. Sexual abuse cases of children are hard to prosecute, especially if they require testimony by the child.

28. The death of a family member is among life's most stressful events. There are various circumstances of death: uncertain death, certain death (at either a known or an unknown time), and untimely death, which includes premature death, unexpected death, and calamitous death. Middle-aged people are more fearful of death than the elderly.

29. In instances of certain death, the time may be known or unknown. Kübler-Ross identified five stages of adjustment in certain death: denial, anger, bargaining, depression, and acceptance.

30. Pattison presented the dying process as part of our trajectory of life, divided into three phases: the knowledge of death and the acute crisis that follows, the chronic living-dying phase, and the terminal phase.

31. The psychological reactions of family members are more extreme when a death occurs in childhood or at a comparatively young age.

32. Unexpected death refers to the sudden death of a healthy person. It requires a wide variety of adjustments in the family of the deceased.

33. Calamitous death is unpredictable and often violent, destructive, demeaning, and even degrading. It includes accidents, involuntary manslaughter, homicide, and suicide. Suicide is one of the most upsetting of family crises because it leaves family members feeling remorseful, guilty, confused, and hurt.

34. The three stages of grief include a first period of shock, a second stage of intense suffering, and finally a gradual reawakening of interest in life.

KEY TERMS

personal sources of conflict

physical sources of conflict

interpersonal sources of conflict

situational or environmental
  sources of conflict

avoidance

ventilation

catharsis

constructive arguments

destructive arguments

crisis

crisis overload

family violence

child abuse

spouse abuse

posttraumatic stress disorder

pedophilia

incest

trajectory of life

living-dying interval

sudden infant death syndrome
  (crib death)

involuntary manslaughter

QUESTIONS FOR THOUGHT

1. What were the major sources of conflict in your family of origin? What were the effects on you? On other family members?

2. If family members could take to help the grief-stricken person overcome grief?you are married, what are the major sources of conflict in your relationship with your spouse? What can be done to minimize this conflict?

3. If you are single but committed to someone, what are the major sources of conflict in your relationship? What can be done to minimize this conflict?

4. Suppose you were married and found out that your spouse was having an affair. What effect would it have on you and your marriage? What would you do, and why?

5. As a parent or potential parent, what are some of the precautions you could take to protect your child from sexual abuse?

6. Knowing what you do about the stages of grief and people's reactions during different stages, what would be some positive steps that the grief-stricken person could take to overcome grief? What would be some positive steps that other

SUGGESTED READINGS

Buchanan, C. M., Maccoby, E. E., and Dornbusch, S. M. (1996). *Adolescents After Divorce*. Cambridge, MA: Harvard University Press. Uses the commentary of adolescents themselves to describe the situations that foster and impede adolescent adjustment to their parents' divorce.

Canary, D. J., Cupach, W. R., and Messman, S. J. (1995). *Relationship Conflict*. Thousand Oaks, CA: Sage. Provides an overview of contemporary research on conflict in interpersonal relationships.

Candib, L. M. (1995). *Medicine and the Family: A Feminist's Perspective*. New York: Basic Books. Addresses problems of physicians related to their interaction with families.

Cardarelli, A. P. (Ed.). (1997). *Violence Between Intimate Partners: Patterns, Causes, and Effects*. Boston: Allyn & Bacon. Proposes a model for understanding power and violence in an array of intimate relationships.

Cook, P. W. (1997). *Abused Men: The Hidden Side of Domestic Violence*. Westport, CT: Praeger. Presents data and qualitative evidence to argue that the abuse of men, although significant, is ignored.

Dutton, R. G. (1998). *The Abusive Personality*. New York: Guilford Press. Builds on leading models of abuse to describe the structure of the abusive personality.

Gelles, R. (1996). *The Book of David: How Preserving Families Can Cost Children's Lives*. New York: Basic Books. Focuses on one boy, David, who is exposed to family violence and on how social institutions protect children who have been exposed to violence in their home.

Gelles, R. J., and Loseke, D. R. (1993). *Current Controversies on Family Violence*. Newbury Park, CA: Sage. Offers twenty-three chapters written by respected experts in family violence research.

Goldman, L. (1994). *Life and Loss*. Bristol, PA: Accelerated Development. Helps parents and teachers assist children in dealing with their feelings of loss.

Hamptom, R. L. (Ed.). (1991). *Black Family Violence: Current Research and Theory*. Lexington, MA: Lexington Books. Represents a compilation of research findings.

Kirkwood, C. (1993). *Leaving Abusive Partners*. Newbury Park, CA: Sage. Gives voice to 30 formerly abused women.

Knudsen, D., and Miller, J. L. (Eds.). (1991). *Abused and Battered: Social and Legal Responses to Family Violence*. New York: Aldine de Gruyter. Examines a variety of forms of family violence.

Lyons, R. F., Sullivan, M. J., and Ritvo, P. D., with James Coyne. (1995). *Relationships in Chronic Illness and Disability*. Thousand Oaks, CA: Sage. Focuses on family relationships.

Stacey, W. A., Hazelwood, L. R., and Shute, A. (1994). *The Violent Couple*. Westport, CT: Praeger. Examines the dynamics of domestic violence and the mutuality of violence in marriage.

Worden, J. W. (1996). *Children and Grief: When a Parent Dies*. New York: Guilford Press. Summarizes the findings from the Harvard Bereavement Study.

Wyly, M. B. (1997). *Infant Assessment. Developmental Psychology Series*. Boulder, CO: Westview Press. Represents a basic guide.

CHAPTER 20

LEARNING OBJECTIVES

After reading the chapter, you should be able to:

Summarize social and demographic factors that increase individual probability of divorce.

Summarize the causes of divorce as identified by divorced men and women.

Describe the process of disaffection.

Describe the important factors to consider in making a decision about whether to get divorced.

Discuss marriage counseling, marriage enrichment, and structured separation as alternatives to divorce.

Discuss ways to get divorced—no-fault divorce and mediation—in terms of property and finances, child support, legal fees, and children.

Understand the major adjustments that adults make after divorce.

Discuss the following in relation to children and divorce: child custody, child support, visitation rights, and the reactions of children.

The Troubled Family and Divorce

Learning Objectives

Probability of Divorce: Social and Demographic Factors

Marital Age

Religion and Socioeconomic Status

Geographic Area

Parental Divorce

The Presence of Children

Causes of Marital Breakup

Spouses' Perceptions

The Marital Disaffection Process

The Divorce Decision

Alternatives to Divorce

Marriage Counseling

Marriage Enrichment

Separation

Family Issues: Why Marriage Counseling Sometimes Does Not Succeed

No-Fault Divorce and Mediation

Perspective: Marital Separation Contract

Adult Adjustments After Divorce

Emotional Trauma

Societal Attitudes Toward Divorce

Loneliness and Social Readjustment

Adjustments to Custody Arrangements

Finances

Realignment of Responsibilities and Work Roles

Contacts with the Ex-Spouse

Kinship Interaction

Children and Divorce

Child Custody

Child Support

Visitation Rights

Reactions of Children

Summary

Key Terms

Questions for Thought

Suggested Terms

The United States has one of the highest divorce rates of any country in the world. The divorce rate surged during the 1960s and 1970s as the baby boomers came of age. Rates of divorce declined slightly during the 1980s and were stable but high through the 1990s (Goldstein, 1999). Divorce trends suggest that about half the couples who married between 1981 and 1990 will stay married (Edmondson, 1997). The increasing numbers of divorced people have resulted in numerous books on the subject—books that discuss everything from do-it-yourself divorce to divorce as a creative experience. With the books has come increasing interest in examining divorce laws, which in their old forms created much suffering for millions of couples and their children. Most state legislatures have now changed their laws and encourage reconciliation counseling, divorce mediation, and no-fault divorce.

All of the statistics, laws, court cases, and individual efforts involve human beings: parents and children who are trying to make the best of difficult situations, each in his or her own way. We need, therefore, to take a careful look at the facts and causes of divorce, at our divorce laws, and at children's reaction to divorce and its effects on them. We also need a more sympathetic understanding of what couples go through and how they struggle to adjust following a divorce.

Divorce is a stressful and troubling experience for everyone involved.

PROBABILITY OF DIVORCE: SOCIAL AND DEMOGRAPHIC FACTORS

In looking at divorce rates, let us examine first those social and demographic factors that increase or decrease the probability of divorce. Divorce rates vary from group to group and relate to factors such as age at marriage, religion, occupation, income, education, ethnicity, geographic area, and parental divorce (Glick, 1990; Lester, 1999). These factors will not pinpoint which individuals are going to get divorced, but they do indicate statistical probabilities for different groups. Let's look at some of the more important social and demographic correlates of divorce and separation in the United States.

Marital Age

Age at first marriage is one of the most important predictors of marital success (Trent and South,

1989). People who marry quite young are more likely to divorce than are those who wait until they are older (Booth and Edwards, 1985). In fact, Martin and Bumpass (1989) concluded that age at marriage is the strongest predictor of divorce in the first 5 years of marriage and that the negative effects of youthful marriage last far into marriage. Figure 20.1 shows the relationship between age at first marriage and the percentage of White men and women who have ever been divorced or legally separated, according to combined data from seven U.S. national surveys conducted from 1973 to 1980 (Glenn and Supancic, 1984). As the figure shows, the percentage of those divorced or legally separated who were 15–17 years of age or younger at the time of first marriage was about three times the percentage of those divorced or legally separated who were 24–26 years of age at the time of first marriage. Except for ages 27–29, the percentage of males who divorced was higher than the percentage of females (Glenn and Supancic, 1984). However, the age at first marriage has been increasing since the mid-

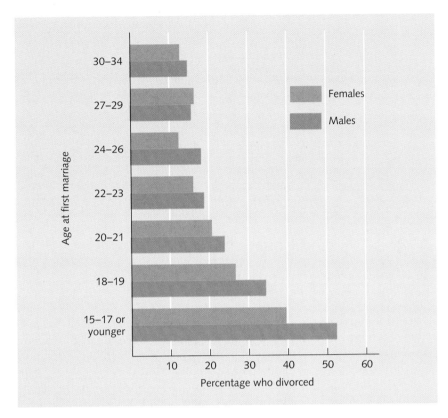

Figure 20.1 Percentage of Ever-Married White People Who Have Ever Been Divorced or Legally Separated, by Age at First Marriage and Gender (*Note:* Adapted from "The Social and Demographic Correlates of Divorce and Separation in the United States: An Update and Reconsideration" by N. D. Glenn and M. Supancic, 1984, *Journal of Marriage and the Family, 46,* pp. 563–575. Copyright © 1984 by the National Council on Family Relations. Reprinted by permission.)

1950s. This relative delay in marrying is a result of people staying in school longer, women entering the workforce in greater numbers, and rates of cohabitation increasing dramatically.

Religion and Socioeconomic Status

Frequency of attendance at religious services is correlated strongly and negatively with divorce or separation. That is, those who attend church regularly are less likely to divorce or separate. Religious teachings can be powerful factors in motivating couples to try to make their marriage succeed. The 1987–1988 National Survey of Families and Households indicated that one-third of women attempting reconciliation were still married more than 1 year after reconciliation began. Religion was most strongly correlated with the success of their reconciliation. Those who had strong religious beliefs were more likely to reconcile when difficulties arose (Wineberg, 1994).

Socioeconomic status includes education, income, and occupation. Figure 20.2 shows the relationships between education level and divorce rate.

Earlier studies had shown that rates of divorce or separation were higher at lower socioeconomic levels (South and Spitze, 1986). Newer studies, however, find a relationship between education, gender, and divorce indicating that women with higher levels of education are more likely to divorce than are women with less education (Glick, 1994). These newer studies are based in a period of increased education and employment opportunities for women. Overall, socioeconomic variables do not correlate with the possibility of divorce as much as do age at first marriage and frequency of attendance at religious services (Glenn and Supancic, 1984).

Geographic Area

Divorce rates vary across different regions of the country. In general, rates by states increase from east to west and from north to south (Glenn and Shelton, 1985). Divorce rates are highest in the West and next highest in the South. Figure 20.3 shows the differences. Divorce rates also tend to be higher in large cities and lower in small cities or rural areas, even when adjusted for other variables

Figure 20.2   Percentage of Ever-Married White People Who Have Ever Been Divorced or Legally Separated, by Gender and Years of School Completed (*Note:* Adapted from "The Social and Demographic Correlates of Divorce and Separation in the United States: An Update and Reconsideration" by N. D. Glenn and M. Supancic, 1984, *Journal of Marriage and the Family, 46,* pp. 563–575. Copyright © 1984 by the National Council on Family Relations. Reprinted by permission.)

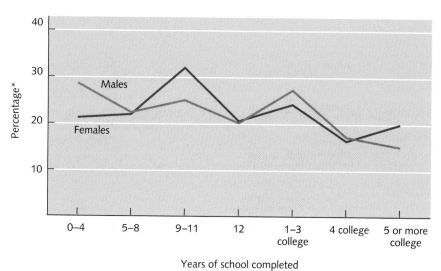

such as ethnic, religious, and socioeconomic differences. This is explained partly by the higher levels of residential mobility among people in large cities and urban areas than among people in small cities and rural areas. Rapid economic growth, demographic changes (birth rates, death rates, proportion of elderly), and employment rates are all correlated with divorce rates (Lester, 1997, 1999). Overall, geographic movement places demands on the family that challenge both directly and indirectly the viability of the family system (Lester, 1999).

Parental Divorce

It is commonly believed that people whose parents are divorced are more susceptible to divorce themselves. A longitudinal study of the intergenerational transmission of divorce found that prior to 1975 people from divorced families were 2.5 times more likely to divorce than were those from intact families; by 1995, however, the likelihood of divorce for the children of divorced parents had fallen to less than 50% (Wolfinger, 1999), with divorce more likely for girls than for boys from divorced families (Amato, 1996). Much of this difference is attributable to the tendency of girls from divorced families to marry younger and to have less education (Feng, Giarrusso, Bengston, and Frye, 1999).

If both spouses experienced parental divorce, their risk of divorce is increased. The risk of divorce is particularly high if parental divorce occurred when the spouses were 12 years of age or younger. Spouses whose parents divorced are more likely to have problems with anger, jealousy, hurt feelings, communication, infidelity, and so on. As children, they may have been exposed to poor models of behavior and may not have learned the skills and attitudes that facilitate successful functioning within their married role. Therefore, they may be more likely to become divorced themselves (Amato, 1996).

The Presence of Children

The risk of marital dissolution is highest among childless couples, probably because they are not constrained to stay together by the presence of children (Heaton, 1990). There are differences in the risk of marital dissolution depending on the ages and number of children. The likelihood of marital dissolution decreases as the number of children rises to a maximum of four. Once couples have five or more children, the likelihood of marital dissolution increases. The rates of divorce are relatively low when the youngest child is under age 3 but rise sharply when that child reaches the mid-teens and decline substantially after he or she reaches age 17. Thus, children's stabilizing effect on marriage is strongest when they are very young or when they have reached adulthood. One of the most interesting findings is that parents of sons are less likely to

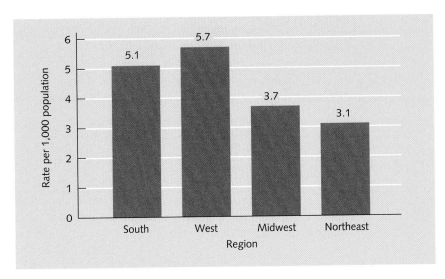

Figure 20.3   Divorce and Annulment Rates by Regions, 1994 (*Note:* Data from *Statistical Abstract of the United States, 1996/1997* [p. 107] by U.S. Bureau of the Census, 1996/1997, Washington, DC: U.S. Government Printing Office.)

divorce than are parents without sons (Morgan, Lye, and Condran, 1988). This is attributed to the father's greater involvement with sons than with daughters (Seccombe and Lee, 1987). Other research has found that, if the family includes at least one son, fathers spend increased time with their children. If there is more paternal involvement in family life, through either the father's investing more time with the children or doing household chores, the woman has a greater perception of fairness in the relationship and is more satisfied with the marriage (Kalmij, 1999; Katzev, Warner, and Acock, 1994).

CAUSES OF MARITAL BREAKUP

Social and demographic factors indicate the probability of divorce, but they don't reveal the actual causes of marital breakup. Causes may be determined by studying people who are divorcing in order to find out their perceptions of the reasons their marriages have failed.

Spouses' Perceptions

The results of three different studies on the reasons people give for divorcing have been summarized in Tables 20.1 and 20.2. Table 20.1 summarizes the women's perception of the causes of divorce, and Table 20.2 summarizes the men's perception of the

causes. Only the top 20 causes are listed. Since the study populations were different and the instruments varied in design, there are some differences as well as some similarities in results from the three studies. A composite picture has been obtained by averaging the percentage of respondents from each study who mentioned each cause. The results show remarkable consistency in the perceptions of spouses.

Based on the research on divorce and marital satisfaction, there appear to be two critical times in a marriage when divorce is most likely: (1) the first 7 years of marriage, during which half of all the divorces occur, and (2) at midlife, when people often have young teenage children. The latter period has been described by some researchers as possibly the lowest point in marital satisfaction during the life course (see, for example, Adelman, Chadwick, and Baerger, 1996; Orbuch, House, Mero, and Webster, 1996). Gottman and Levenson (2000) studied the predictors of divorce in these two critical periods of a marriage. They found that different sets of variables predicted early divorce and later divorce. Negative affect during conflict (for example, criticism, contempt, defensiveness) predicted early divorcing, but it did not predict later divorcing. By contrast, the lack of positive affect in discussing the events of the day (for example, being excited or showing interest in what a spouse had to say) predicted later divorcing, but it did not predict early divorcing. Thus, it could be the case that marriages characterized by criticism,

Table 20.1 Women's Perceptions of Causes of Marital Breakup

Rank	Cause	Average	Percentage Mentioning Problem		
			Cleek, Pearson Study	Kitson, Sussman Study	Burns Study
1	Basic unhappiness	59.9	59.9	—	—
2	Emotional abuse	55.5	55.5	—	—
3	Communication problems	47.3	69.7	32.0	40.0
4	Incompatibility, different backgrounds	36.7	56.4	17.0	—
5	Sexual problems	36.0	32.0	—	40.0
6	No sense of family, husband's lack of time at home	30.5	—	15.0	46.0
7	Man's alcohol abuse	29.0	30.0	21.0	36.0
8	Financial, employment problems	28.0	32.9	15.0	36.0
9	Man's infidelity	27.7	25.2	21.0	37.0
10	Woman's lack of interest	26.0	—	—	26.0
11	Untrustworthiness, immaturity	21.0	—	21.0	—
12	Man out with "the guys"	20.0	—	20.0	—
13	Changes in interests, values	19.0	—	19.0	—
14	Disagreements over children	14.0	8.9	—	19.0
15	Gender-role conflict; women's liberation movement	13.5	3.0	24.0	—
16	Inadequate housing	13.0	—	—	13.0
17	In-laws, relatives	12.9	10.7	7.0	21.0
18	Man's lack of interest	12.0	—	—	12.0
18	Emotional, personal problems; instability	12.0	—	12.0	—
18	Stubbornness	12.0	—	12.0	—
18	Not enough social life	12.0	—	12.0	—
18	Too young at time of marriage	12.0	—	12.0	—
18	Arguments, lack of agreement	12.0	—	12.0	—
19	Physical, psychological abuse; cruelty	11.9	21.7	10.0	4.0
20	Woman's infidelity	8.0	3.9	—	12.0

Note: Data from "Perceived Causes of Divorce: An Analysis of Interrelationships" by M. G. Cleek and T. A. Pearson, 1985, *Journal of Marriage and the Family, 47,* pp. 179–183; "Marital Complaints, Demographic Characteristics, Symptoms of Mental Distress in Divorce" by G. C. Kitson and M. B. Sussman, 1982, *Journal of Marriage and the Family, 44,* pp. 87–101; and "Perceived Causes of Marriage Breakdown and the Conditions of Life" by A. Burns, 1984, *Journal of Marriage and the Family, 46,* pp. 551–562.

contempt, and intense fighting dissolve sooner than do those without positive affect. In marriages without positive affect, people may stay together but become emotionally detached and postpone divorce until their loneliness becomes unbearable and they no longer feel the need to remain married for the sake of the children (Gottman and Levenson, 2000).

Showing positive affect may be one of the most important aspects of a successful marriage. Gigy and Kelly (1992) found that the most common reasons for divorcing, cited by nearly 80% of all men and women in their study, were a gradual growing apart, a loss of a sense of closeness, and a lack of feelings of being loved and appreciated. Severe and intense fighting was cited by only 40% of the couples. Dolan and Hoff-

Table 20.2 Men's Perceptions of Causes of Marital Breakup

		Percentage Mentioning Problem			
Rank	Cause	Average	Cleek, Pearson Study	Kitson, Sussman Study	Burns Study
1	Basic unhappiness	46.9	46.9	—	—
2	Sexual problems	43.1	30.2	—	56.0
3	Communication	42.1	59.3	26.0	41.0
4	Incompatibility, different backgrounds	31.4	44.7	18.0	—
5	Woman's lack of interest	25.0	—	—	25.0
6	Emotional abuse	24.7	24.7	—	—
7	Woman's infidelity	22.8	10.5	—	35.0
8	No sense of family, husband's lack of time at home	20.5	—	13.0	28.0
9	Physical abuse, cruelty	20.3	3.6	—	37.0
10	Financial problems	20.2	28.7	8.0	24.0
11	In-laws, relatives	18.2	11.6	14.0	29.0
12	Not sure what happened	18.0	—	18.0	—
13	Gender-role conflict	17.8	14.5	21.0	—
14	Changes in interests, values	17.0	—	17.0	—
15	Man's lack of interest	15.0	—	—	15.0
16	Man's alcohol abuse	13.2	9.4	—	17.0
16	Differences over children	13.2	4.4	—	22.0
17	Too young at time of marriage	13.0	—	13.0	—
17	Overcommitment to work	13.0	—	13.0	—
17	Woman's ill health	13.0	—	—	13.0
17	Not enough social life	13.0	—	13.0	13.0
18	Man's infidelity	11.6	6.2	—	17.0
19	Jealousy	11.0	—	11.0	—
20	Untrustworthiness, immaturity	10.0	—	10.0	—

Note: Data from "Perceived Causes of Divorce: An Analysis of Interrelationships" by M. G. Cleek and T. A. Pearson, 1985, *Journal of Marriage and the Family, 47,* pp. 179–183; "Marital Complaints, Demographic Characteristics, Symptoms of Mental Distress in Divorce" by G. C. Kitson and M. B. Sussman, 1982, *Journal of Marriage and the Family, 44,* pp. 87–101; and "Perceived Causes of Marriage Breakdown and the Conditions of Life" by A. Burns, 1984, *Journal of Marriage and the Family, 46,* pp. 551–562.

man (1998) found that, regardless of women's socioeconomic status, lack of emotional support and incompatibility were the most frequently cited determinants of divorce. Gottman and Levenson (2000) suggest, "Perhaps changing the affective nature of the way couples discuss such mundane topics as the events of their day, in which they either make an emotional connection upon reunion or fail to do so, could affect the way they resolve conflict, and possibly the future course of the marriage" (p. 743).

The Marital Disaffection Process

The loss of intimacy and love is a major component of marital dissolution (Kersten, 1990). Kingsbury and Minda (1988) identified marital disaffection as an indicator of whether couples plan to continue or terminate their relationship. Marital disaffection involves the gradual loss of emotional attachment, a decline in caring, emotional estrangement, and an increasing sense of apathy and indifference. Positive feelings are replaced over time by neutral or even negative feelings. However, it is important to emphasize that mutual disaffection is the result of other problems in the relationship, rather than the initial cause. Spouses report they want a divorce because they don't love each other, but falling out of love is usually a consequence of years of unresolved tensions in the relationship.

One of the most revealing descriptions of the development of marital disaffection is given by Kersten (1990), who divides the process into three phases: (1) a beginning phase, (2) a middle phase, and (3) an end phase. The beginning phase is characterized by increased disappointment, disillusionment, and feelings of hurt and anger. One partner's (or both partners') thoughts begin to center on the other partner's negative traits because that partner's behavior is not what was expected. The partners are still optimistic about the future of their marriage and attempt to solve the problems by asserting their feelings or by attempting to please their spouse.

During the middle phase, anger and hurt increase in frequency and intensity. Spouses expect their partner to behave in certain negative ways, and apathy increases. Some partners begin to weigh whether to stay in or leave the marriage as they sort out factors relating to the children, finances, or religion. Attempts to please the partner decrease, but problem-solving attempts (such as entering a drug treatment program) increase.

During the end phase, anger again is the most frequent feeling. Feelings of trust decline, and apathy and a sense of helplessness increase. The following is a typical expression of apathy: "I've just put up with the same behavior so long now—I just want out because I don't see him ever changing. . . . It's too late to rekindle the feelings. . . . I don't want to try" (Kersten, 1990, p. 261). The most frequent thoughts during this stage concern wanting to end the marriage and determining exactly how it can be dissolved. However, there may still be some ambivalence. Before this stage, counseling is infrequently pursued, but now many couples seek marital therapy in a last attempt to save the marriage or to get assistance in leaving it.

Basic to the dissolution of the relationship is the perception that the costs of staying together outweigh the rewards. Partners focus on the negative traits of their spouse, so it is very difficult to change their feelings. To do so requires the partner to make drastic changes. Sometimes changes are made and feelings do become positive again, but it takes a lot of hard work. If the marriage is dissolved, the disaffected spouse continues to focus on the negative traits of the ex-spouse, convincing him- or herself that dissolution was justified (Kersten, 1990).

THE DIVORCE DECISION

The decision to divorce is a difficult one for most people. Few couples are able to make such a decision easily and quickly; rather, they usually agonize for months or years before finally deciding. Even then, the partners may change their mind a number of times, repeatedly separating and then moving back together. Many couples file a petition for divorce, only to withdraw it. Others even go to court and then change their mind at the last minute.

From a counselor's point of view, it's hard to predict who will or will not get divorced. Some couples have relatively minor problems but give up easily. Other couples seem to be likely candidates for divorce but through intense effort and motivation overcome all obstacles and end up with a good marriage. The outcome depends partially on the motivation and commitment of the partners.

There are, of course, some couples who never divorce, but not necessarily because the two people love each other or are compatible. Consider this case:

> Mr. and Mrs. P. have been married 43 years. He's 79 and she's 76. They absolutely hate each other. They say and do horrible things to each other. They constantly criticize each other and are in chronic conflict. They have no companionship, never share any social activities together. He's gay, has male lovers on the side, and never has intercourse with her. He's intellectual, verbal, and artistic. She's none of these things. He's a dreamer, she's practical. The only reason they give for living together is to have two social security checks instead of one. (Author's counseling notes)

According to exchange theory, reconciliation is more likely when the costs of divorce are high, the barriers to getting out of the marriage are great, and the alternatives are few. Levinger (1979) proposed a three-factor theory of marital cohesion, identifying three basic considerations in deciding whether to remain married:

1. **Satisfaction with or attractions of the marriage.** These are the forces that strengthen the marriage bond. They may include sexual fulfillment, emotional bonding, care, concern, and need (even neurotic need) for each other. Attractions may also include socioeconomic rewards: a better income, an improved standard of living, superior social status, a nice house, more economic security, or the need for the physical services that a spouse can provide.

2. **Barriers to getting out of the marriage.** These are the forces that prevent marriage breakdown. In one study, three perceived barriers were cited most often by participants as being very important: (1) the possibility of children suffering (50.1%), (2) the threat of losing a child (46%), and (3) religious beliefs (41.4%). About 33% of married individuals felt that their dependence on their spouse was very important in keeping their marriage intact, while 31% cited their spouse's dependence on them as very important. While married couples perceived financial security to be important, it was not important enough to keep them from divorcing (Knoester and Booth, 2000). When the perceived barriers were analyzed as to how well they actually deter divorce, only two decreased the odds of divorce: (1) the importance of religious beliefs and (2) dependence on one's spouse. When responses were separated by gender, it became evident that women rank perceived dependence on their spouse and religious beliefs as more essential barriers to divorce and that men rank more highly the threat of losing a child and the influence of family and friends. Responses to other barriers did not differ significantly between women and men. Neither of the perceived barriers that involve children were found to be deterrents to divorce. Overall, although many people perceive certain barriers to divorce and value them as important, these barriers apparently do not keep couples together (Knoester and Booth, 2000).

3. **The attractiveness of alternatives to the marriage.** These include an evaluation of personal assets: sexual attractiveness, appearance, age, and other factors that influence the possibilities

of remarrying, if desired. Individuals with high socioeconomic status marry spouses of the same status. Attractive men and men with high socioeconomic status marry women who are the most attractive. People with high self-esteem and a sense of personal competence are more likely to feel that they can get along on their own (Dreman, Orr, and Aldor, 1989). Spouses with good education, high income, and intelligence realize that even if they are cut off from their spouse's earning power they still are capable of living the good life.

A powerful motivating force in divorce is the desire to leave one's spouse to marry another person. A person who is involved in an ongoing emotional and sexual relationship outside of marriage may not be as hesitant about getting a divorce as a person who has no one else on the side. While an extramarital affair is often a result of an unhappy marriage, it also may be the added incentive to terminate the marriage.

A fourth factor affects the decision to stay married or get divorced. This factor was not discussed by Levinger, but it is an important one: the intensity of the emotional pain generated by an unhappy marriage. Some people don't really believe in divorce, but they can't tolerate the unhappiness of the marriage any longer. One man explained:

> I've remained in the marriage for twenty-eight years because I didn't believe in divorce and because I didn't want to desert my children. But I can't take it any longer. My wife hates me and takes every occasion to let me know she does. She tells me she hopes I'll die so she can collect my life insurance. There is no love, companionship, or anything positive left in our relationship. (Author's counseling notes)

A woman commented:

> You can't imagine what it was like being married to my alcoholic husband. He was completely irresponsible. I did literally everything around the house, yard, and in raising our five children. Yet, he wouldn't admit that he had an alcohol problem. (Author's counseling notes)

In these situations, there was no question in the minds of the individuals that divorce was the only acceptable course.

ALTERNATIVES TO DIVORCE

When spouses are dissatisfied with their marriage, they might consider marriage counseling, marriage enrichment programs, and separation.

Marriage Counseling

Some couples need to consider that there may be alternatives to divorce. One important alternative is marriage counseling. Couples cannot be expected to live together unhappily, but breaking up the marriage may not always be the best or only option. Divorce often substitutes one set of problems for another. Another option is to see if, with professional help, the unhappy marriage can become a satisfying one. Couples are often skeptical about the outcome of counseling—especially if they have never been to a counselor before or if they have had unhappy experiences with therapists. Not all therapists are equally competent. One summary of the efficacy of marital and family therapy found that therapy involved beneficial outcomes in about two-thirds of the cases, that there is a greater chance of a positive outcome when spouses are treated together rather than individually, and that positive results typically occur in treatments of short duration—from 1 to 20 sessions (Piercy and Sprenkle, 1990). Analysis of the effects of marital and family therapy indicated very definitely that it works (Shadish, Ragsdale, Glaser, and Montgomery, 1995). Other research has indicated that marital therapy is effective, at least in the short term, in reducing marital conflicts. In addition, research has shown marital therapy to be effective over the long term in promoting marital stability, reducing marital conflicts, and preventing divorce (Bray and Jouriles, 1995; Pinsof and Wynne, 1995).

Some states *require* **conciliation counseling** before a divorce may be granted. Even when it is required rather than chosen, counseling may help. One study in Iowa compared 12 couples who were ordered by the court to get counseling with 12 couples who had done so voluntarily (Sampel and Seymour, 1980). Five (42%) of the 12 couples in court-ordered conciliation counseling decided against marital dissolution and agreed to work on their marriages. This compared to 9 (75%) of the 12 couples in the voluntary counseling group who decided against marital dissolution. It appears that conciliation counseling did have some of the effect intended by the Iowa legislature when it added this component to its divorce laws. Similarly, other research on conciliation counseling has shown that it increases the percentage of marital reconciliations (Sprenkle and Storm, 1983). The most important thing is for partners to give their marriage their best shot.

From a clinical point of view, the earlier couples in a troubled marriage seek counseling, the more likely it will succeed. As discussed, many couples never seek therapy until the relationship has deteriorated to the point at which it's very difficult to straighten things out. Actually, couples need help the most during the first year of marriage. Mace (1982) suggested that professional practitioners schedule monthly sessions with newlyweds (either as couples or as groups of couples) during the first year of marriage.

Marriage Enrichment

Marriage enrichment programs combine education with group discussion to assist couples in improving marital communication, relationships, and problem solving. Programs are conducted in groups shortly before or after the wedding or any number of years after it. The central purpose of such programs is preventative: to address issues before they become unmanageable conflicts (Guerney and Maxson, 1990; Mace, 1987).

One such program, the Prevention and Relationship Enhancement Program (PREP), was designed to teach partners skills and ground rules for handling conflict and promoting intimacy. It is crucial that couples learn constructive ways to handle differences and negative affects, such as anger and frustration. PREP is educational; it is not presented as therapy or counseling. Leaders outline the course themes in brief lectures. PREP couples practice key techniques in sessions with trained consultants and in homework. Specific readings are also assigned (Stanley, Markman, St. Peters, and Leber, 1995).

Separation

A trial separation is another alternative before divorce. Couples ask, "Do you think if we separated for a while it would help us to decide what we

Some states require conciliation counseling before a divorce may be granted. Can voluntary counseling be more effective?

should do?" Separation can be an effective treatment method in some instances, especially if the separation is carefully structured and if marital therapy continues during the separation. Separation is not to be taken lightly. It is a time of emotional upheaval and extreme stress—for spouses and for children—and it has both potential benefits and risks.

Structured separation may be defined as a time-limited approach in which the couple terminates cohabitation, commits to regularly scheduled therapy with a therapist, and agrees to regular interpersonal contact, with a moratorium on a final decision to either reunite or divorce. The objective of the separation is change; it is designed to interrupt old interactional patterns through the creation of an environment conducive to change. It is characterized by ambivalent feelings between the spouses and toward the marriage. The anticipated result is that spouses will move either closer together or farther apart (Morgan, 1989).

A number of different situations may support the decision to consider structured marital separation as a treatment method (Granvold and Tarrant, 1983):

■ **Extreme conflict.** The frequency, intensity, and duration of conflict is so overwhelming that the couple cannot tolerate it. Physical or emotional abuse and verbal aggressiveness may be so

debilitating that no positive change can take place in the relationship.

■ **Absence of spousal reinforcement.** There is little or no reward, pleasure, or satisfaction from the marital relationship, and separation may help raise the level of mutual positive exchange.

■ **Feeling constricted or smothered.** One or both partners need more personal and emotional space, relief from spousal control and jealousy, and an opportunity for personal growth and individual freedom while they restructure their relationship.

■ **A situational or midlife transition.** Situational transitions may include loss of a loved one, a job change, a move to a new community, or children leaving home. A midlife transition is characterized by evaluation of one's achievements relative to one's goals. It may result in increased satisfaction with the status quo, recalibration of one's current direction, or the identification of entirely new goals. In extreme cases, it can include disillusionment, depression, a sense of stagnation, self-doubt, directionlessness, and emotional upheaval. For these individuals, respite from the marital relationship may allow them to deal with the crisis before they are confronted with an intense effort to change the marriage.

Why Marriage Counseling Sometimes Does Not Succeed

Marriage counseling may fail to preserve the marriage for any combination of the following reasons (author's counseling notes):

- **One of the spouses doesn't want the counseling to succeed.** They may have become so tired of the marriage that they absolutely don't want it to continue. They may not believe that counseling will succeed, so they do everything possible to sabotage it. They may have somebody else that they want to marry, so they want to break up this marriage.

- **Counseling helps, but not by preserving the marriage.** Sometimes the counseling helps to dissolve the relationship. As the couple learns more effective communication skills, it may become clear that divorce is the better alternative.

- **The couple lack commitment to the counseling process.** They don't really try. There is no motivation. Without spouses' strong willingness to try to do their very best, counseling cannot succeed.

- **Each spouse blames the other and refuses to take personal responsibility.** Each spouse believes that the entire problem lies with the other person. Or they refuse to admit there is a problem. If they are not both willing to take responsibility for part of the problem, and for making the solution, the counseling will not succeed.

- **One of the spouses is rigid and inflexible.** Sometimes counseling can go on for years, but if one of the spouses is not willing to make the changes necessary for the relationship to work, then it won't work.

- **The spouses are incompatible.** They may be perfectly decent people, but they have different philosophies, values, habits, and ways of doing things. It's not that they don't want to live together, but they find that they simply cannot.

- **One of the spouses is too immature.** A spouse may be so insecure, unstable, irresponsible, or angry or hostile that he or she causes a great disruption in the relationship and destroys anything valuable in it. Personality problems prevent the person from working out relationship problems.

- **One of the spouses is mentally ill.** The person who is depressed, paranoid, or manic is not capable of living together in a positive way with another person. Unless the mental illness can be treated, the marriage will not succeed.

- **The couple don't come to counseling long enough to achieve success.** They may expect instant results and quit coming before the counseling can be of permanent help.

- **The spouses possess poor communication skills.** One person won't talk; the other monopolizes the conversation; they get in highly destructive arguments; they won't stick to the subject; or they are not able to discuss issues in a positive way, so they never resolve any problems.

- **The spouses' pasts constantly intrude on the present.** Dysfunctional family backgrounds are carried over into the present relationship. Without resolving issues in their respective parent-child relationships, they will be unable to work out their present relationship.

- **Spouses listen to wrong advice from family or friends.** Instead of making their own decisions, they try to follow what other people tell them to do. Many times, the advice is exactly the wrong way for them to work out the relationship.

- **The couple selected the wrong counselor.** Each counselor has particular skills, qualifications, education, and specialties. The couple needs to select the person with the appropriate education, background, and interests to deal with their particular problems.

The counselor's task is to motivate and assist the couple in overcoming these impediments to success. To do this, the counselor must motivate the couple's commitment to the counseling process. Counseling can encourage a commitment, motivate the couple to take personal responsibility, encourage change, and improve communication. In some instances, it may not be possible to help, but only by giving counseling a chance can its potential benefits be discovered.

■ **Indecision regarding divorce.** If couples can't decide, a structured marital separation may effect a break in the decision-making dilemma.

Some couples want a separation in order to pursue other sexual relationships. One man explained, "I have to be free to find out if my love for Sarah [the other woman] is genuine and will last." In this situation, his spouse was understandably upset: "You want to see if it's going to work out, then if it doesn't, you're coming home to me. I'm not going to be anybody's second choice" (author's counseling notes).

Few spouses will agree to a separation to free the other to pursue extramarital affairs. If the couple is really serious about straightening out the marriage, it is most helpful to first give up the affair and work on the marriage. If the spouse pursues the affair, there usually isn't any marriage left to come back to.

NO-FAULT DIVORCE AND MEDIATION

A divorce is a legal method of ending a marriage. Legally, following the divorce, (1) the parties can marry someone else, (2) their property is divided, as are their debts, and (3) if children are involved, their care and custody are decided. In some circumstances, spousal support on a permanent or rehabilitative basis is awarded. These issues can be very difficult to negotiate even if both parties want the divorce.

Traditionally, divorce was granted only if one party could be found guilty of some type of marital misconduct, such as adultery or physical abuse. The party accused of being guilty was punished by getting a smaller share of the couple's property or being denied custody of their children while the other spouse was rewarded for being faithful to the vows of marriage. In 1970, California passed the first **no-fault divorce** legislation, and currently all 50 states have a no-fault divorce law.

The essence of no-fault divorce laws is that they do not attribute fault and thus do not require one of the spouses to be considered "innocent" and the other "guilty." No-fault divorce laws recognize the breakdown of the marriage and the inability of the spouses to function as a married

couple. The possibility for vengeance is removed when no-fault divorce is the only alternative offered. The law removes all fault (the question of who is to blame) and reduces the grounds to irreconcilable differences or an irremediable breakdown of the marriage. Consent of both spouses is not required; rather, one spouse can decide unilaterally to divorce. No-fault divorce laws are gender-neutral in that both spouses are responsible for spousal and child support and both spouses are eligible for child custody. Financial rewards in terms of spousal support, child support, and property distribution are linked not to issues of fault or blame, but rather to the spouses' current financial needs and resources. Probably the most important feature of no-fault divorce laws is that they improve the sociopsychological and communication climate of divorce by abolishing the concept of fault and by tempering the adversarial process surrounding divorce proceedings.

There are those who feel that this approach makes divorce too easy. Divorce may be extremely easy to get if it is not contested, requiring only a superficial hearing in court. But it is the process of trying to work out the settlement that is often challenging. Couples may still fight bitterly, and the adversarial nature of divorce is hardly eliminated.

It is debatable whether no-fault divorce has led to an increase in divorce rates. Some researchers believe it has, particularly among couples of median family income (Nakonezny, Shull, and Rodgers, 1995). Others believe that no-fault divorce was a response to the already-occurring loosening of divorce restrictions and has not caused a significant increase in the divorce rate (Glenn, 1999). Almost everyone who wanted to divorce and who was willing to pay the costs was probably able to divorce even before the implementation of no-fault provisions (Glenn, 1999). But the removal of high attorney fees from the adversarial process of divorce may have made divorce more financially attainable for many unhappy couples and eliminated a great deal of human suffering (Nakonezny, Shull, and Rodgers, 1995).

One of the most helpful solutions to property, spousal support, custody, child support, and other issues is to employ a mediator to help resolve differences (Emery, 1995; Teachman and Polonko, 1990b). Both private mediators and public or court-appointed mediators provide services throughout

I, (Tom/Jan) Smith, agree to a marital separation from my spouse for six weeks during which time I will not make any final decisions to either divorce or remain married. I agree to the following stipulations:

Therapy—I will attend weekly conjoint marital therapy sessions for the duration of this contract. I will initiate individual therapy as I prefer and in consideration of Dr. _____ 's recommendations.

Contact with spouse—I will spend time with my partner on two occasions per week. I will have telephone contact with my spouse only to arrange our "dates" and in the case of an emergency. I will make no effort to see my spouse more frequently than the designated rate.

Sexual contact with my spouse—I understand that my partner and I may continue having sexual contact with one another and that either of us has the right to initiate sexual activity.

Dating—I understand that neither of us is eligible to date others.

Sexual contact with others—I understand that neither of us is eligible to have sexual relations with others during the contracted separation period.

Privacy—I will make no effort to oversee the activities of my spouse, drop in, or telephone except as specified above.

Contact with children (Tom)—I agree to spend individual time with my children at least weekly. I will arrange to take my children overnight unless travel for my job prevents me from doing so.

Financial support—It is agreed that Tom will pay the house and car payments and $350.00 monthly to cover utilities, child-related expenses, etc.

Homework—I will make every effort to carry out the homework assignments to which I have agreed during therapy sessions. I understand that my marital relationship is to have priority during this separation period. I will use only positive methods to encourage my spouse to participate in doing homework.

Renegotiation—I will participate in renegotiating the separation contract at the end of this contract period should my spouse and I, in collaboration with our therapist, prefer to sustain the separation period. Furthermore, should either my partner or I wish to alter any part of this contract at any time, it is to be discussed and renegotiated during a therapy session with Dr. _____ .

Signed _____

Date _____

Note: Adapted from "Structured Separation for Marital Treatment and Decision-Making" by D. K. Granvold, 1983, *Journal of Marital and Family Therapy, 9,* pp. 403–412. Copyright © 1983 American Association for Marriage and Family Therapy. Reprinted by permission.

Note: The therapist is not responsible for the specific terms identified in this contract but has served as a mediator/counselor in developing the contract.

---

the United States. One advantage of using mediators is that they can objectively represent the interests of both parents and of the children. Their role is fourfold:

1. To gain a commitment to mediation and establish ground rules for the discussion.

2. To define the issues and elicit facts and all pertinent information, including the needs, desires, and feelings of the partners.

3. To process the issues by employing solutions and maintaining positive momentum, managing emotions, encouraging empathy, and narrowing differences.

4. To help the couple reach a settlement and ensure its implementation. The decisions that are made can be drawn up by a lawyer in the form of a legal agreement, signed by all parties, and presented to the court as the basis for settlement (Vanderkooi and Pearson, 1983).

Mediators of property and money settlements can ask for complete financial disclosure, get a property appraisal if needed, and even hire an accountant if many assets are involved. Settlements that are agreed on do not become binding until approved by the court. One advantage of a mediated settlement is that the partners are more likely to comply with decisions that are made jointly than with financial judgments that are ordered by the court against the will of the couple. Disputes regarding child custody and visitation rights and responsibilities ideally are settled on the basis of the best interests of the children. Research has shown that people who use divorce

mediation have better relationships with their ex-spouses, are generally more satisfied with the outcomes of divorce, have less need for relitigation, and feel more satisfied with the process and the results (Marlow and Sauber, 1990). They also report better relationships with their children (Beck and Blank, 1997).

The process of no-fault divorce requires less extensive litigation (many couples file without benefit of attorneys), reduces legal expenses, and makes a "friendly" divorce easier than under the old adversary system. It has partially removed from the legal process the punitive element of moral condemnation that pervaded divorce for centuries.

Some other changes bring up further questions. One of the changes has been an increase in the percentage of men who have filed the petition once they no longer had to make public accusations against their spouse. At the same time, with the threat of reprisals removed, spousal support has been awarded less frequently, for shorter periods of time, and for smaller amounts. In addition, household property and furniture are less likely to be awarded exclusively to the woman, and attorney's fees are more likely to be paid by both spouses. Fewer women are awarded full custody, and joint custody arrangements have increased. The effect on child support payments to the custodial parent has been variable. Overall, the loss of bargaining power by the woman has resulted in a less favorable finan-cial settlement to many women, particularly older homemakers. Those who do not have substantial earning power of their own are affected greatly, with many having to reduce their standard of living significantly because of inadequate support from their ex-spouse. So, although no-fault divorce has many advantages, it has also created some inequities and contributed to economic hardship for many custodial parents and their children.

ADULT ADJUSTMENTS AFTER DIVORCE

The problems of adjustment after divorce may be grouped into a number of categories: (1) getting over the emotional trauma of divorce, (2) dealing with the attitudes of society, (3) loneliness and the problem of social readjustment, (4) adjustments of the noncustodial spouse, (5) finances, (6) realignment of responsibilities and work roles, (7) contacts with the ex-spouse, and (8) kinship interaction.

Emotional Trauma

Under the best circumstances, divorce is an emotionally disturbing experience. Under the worst conditions, it may result in a high degree of shock and disorientation. Divorce is often an emotional crisis triggered by a sudden loss. The process of divorce may involve emotional turmoil before and during the divorce, the shock and crisis of separation, mourning as the relationship is laid to rest, and disruption as one attempts to regain balance and reorganize. A drawn-out and bitter legal battle tends to heighten the emotional trauma of divorce. In these cases, the actual divorce decree comes as a welcome relief from a long period of pain.

The trauma is greater when one spouse wants the divorce and the other doesn't, when the idea comes unexpectedly, when one spouse continues to be emotionally attached to the other after the divorce, or when friends and family disapprove.

For most couples, the decision to divorce is viewed as an "end of the rope" decision that is reached, on average, over a period of about 2 years. One spouse usually wants a divorce more than the other, and spouses who want the marriage to end are likely to view divorce differently than those who would like the marriage to continue (Emery, 1994). Wang and Amato (2000) found that spouses who wanted and initiated the divorce exhibited less attachment to their ex-spouse and better overall divorce adjustment. Thus, the partner who leaves experiences less postdivorce distress than the partner who is left (Emery, 1994).

Most studies reveal that during the pre- and postseparation periods both men and women report a decline in psychological adjustment (Doherty, Su, and Needle, 1989; Gove and Shin, 1989). The early postseparation period is the hardest time for some, as they struggle to come to grips with the loss of their spouse and with the personal cost that loss entails. The time of greatest trauma for others is at the time of final separation. After that comes a long period of realization that the relationship is over emotionally as well as legally. An examination of the relationship between divorce and psychological stress in adult women showed that stress and depression increased significantly soon after the divorce and then diminished over the next 3 years, although not to the same levels reported by married women (Lorenz et al., 1997). The fact that physical health is poorer, alcohol consumption is higher, (Mastekaasa, 1994), and the suicide rate is much greater for divorced men and women than for married people indicates that getting divorced can be traumatic (Stack, 1990).

Societal Attitudes Toward Divorce

Part of the trauma of divorce stems from the attitudes of society toward divorce and divorced persons. In the eyes of some, divorce reflects moral failure or personal inadequacy. It takes a lot of courage to let it be known publicly that one has failed. "Friends," one woman remarked bitterly, "they drop you like a hot potato." However, negative attitudes are lessening as divorce becomes more common. One reason is that people today who recall their parents' marriage as being unhappy or who experienced parental divorce have more accepting attitudes toward the possibility of their own and other people's divorce (Amato and Booth, 1991).

In general, people who hold negative attitudes toward divorce are likely to view their own divorce as a moral failure. People who hold positive, accepting attitudes toward divorce when they are married report less attachment to the ex-spouse following divorce and better postdivorce adjustment than do people who hold negative, rejecting attitudes (Wang and Amato, 2000).

Loneliness and Social Readjustment

Even if two married people did not get along, at least they knew that someone else was in the house. After divorce, they begin to realize what it is like to live alone. This adjustment is especially hard on those without children or those whose children are living with the other spouse. Holidays can be particularly difficult.

Numerous authorities suggest that the friendship and companionship of other people are among the most essential ingredients for a successful readjustment after divorce, so getting involved with others is important. Finding new relationships that are positive and supportive helps undo the psychological injury caused by the divorce. Several studies have shown that social network size is a significant predictor of postdivorce adjustment: the more friends one has, the better one adjusts (Coysh, Johnston, Tschann, Wallerstein, and Kline, 1989; DeGarmo and Forgatch, 1999).

The strongest predictor of divorce adjustment seems to be involvement in an intimate relationship. People with a new dating (or cohabiting) partner report better overall adjustment, less attachment to their ex-spouse, and a more positive outlook on life (Wang and Amato, 2000). Remarriage also leads to better overall adjustment and a more positive appraisal of life (Marks and Lambert, 1998; Wang and Amato, 2000). Remarriage is likely to help people adjust not only by providing a confidant and a regular sexual partner but also by increasing economic security (Shaprio, 1996).

There seems to be some difference in the social readjustment of divorced people according to their age at the time of divorce, with older individuals having a more difficult time adjusting than do younger individuals (Wang and Amato, 2000). Older women in particular have a hard time readjusting. Fewer women than men over age 40 at the time of divorce remarry. Many women have inadequate income to support themselves and their children. Many people are moderately or severely lonely and depressed shortly after a divorce. Among people who do not remarry, loneliness represents one of the grave consequences of divorce (Fischman, 1986).

Adjustments to Custody Arrangements

Adjustments to custody arrangements vary. Caring parents miss their children and often seek every opportunity to be with them. They often suffer from anxiety and guilt that they can't be with their children more and do more for them. Other parents virtually abandon their children, never seeing, calling, or writing them or remembering holidays and birthdays. A third category of parents would like to see their children more often but are prevented from doing so by geographical distance or other circumstances. Overall, research shows that divorce reduces the closeness between noncustodial parents and their children and that there are fewer contacts between older divorced parents and their adult offspring later in life (Cooney and Uhlenberg, 1990).

King and Heard (1999) studied family interactions following divorce, based on 1,565 responses from divorced mothers to the National Survey of Families and Households. They considered father visitation, mother satisfaction with the visitation, and the parental conflict that surrounds the visitation. Overall, they found that mothers prefer involved fathers even if some conflict occurs as a result. Only a small number of mothers were content to have the fathers relatively absent from involvement with them and the children. Interestingly, this study did not find an association between father involvement and child well-being, nor was conflict a predictor of child outcomes. Instead, mother satisfaction appeared to play an influential role in child outcomes: Child well-being suffered when mothers were dissatisfied, whatever the arrangements.

Shapiro and Lambert (1999) examined the National Survey of Families and Households to identify the effects of divorce on the quality of the father-child relationship over time. Father well-being was also observed. They found that divorced fathers with custody perceive poorer relationship quality with their children than do continuously married fathers. Fathers with joint physical custody (coresident) continue daily involvement with their children but usually have to fight to get it. They feel more in control, and the role of father is likely to be highly salient to them. Nonresident fathers perceive the poorest relationships, have the least contact with their children, and probably feel a loss of control. However, both coresident and nonresident fathers experience higher levels of depression and unhappiness than continuously married fathers (Shapiro and Lambert, 1999).

Finances

In spite of some advances, women still earn less income than males, given the same occupation, education, experience, and hours. Furthermore, the mother still ends up with primary custody of the children in 85% of cases. Some mothers receive only a little or irregular support from their ex-spouse. Although most divorced mothers work, their incomes are lower, and mothers with custody of their children often experience serious economic hardship (Shapiro, 1996). In a study of divorcees, 71% said that financial difficulties were their major problem (Amato and Partridge, 1987). Even if the marriage is disrupted after the children have left home, the economic position and life-style of women are seriously eroded (Morgan, 1989).

It is estimated that divorced women with custody of the children experience a 71% decline in family income in the year immediately following the divorce (Glick, 1990). According to a 1996 Census Bureau survey, 61% of divorced mothers and 40% of custodial fathers who were awarded child support received full or partial payment. In 1996, mothers who received their full child support payments had incomes 25% lower than those of fathers who received their full payment. Twenty-three percent of mothers received no payment even though they were supposed to (U.S. Bureau of the Census, 1996/1997). As a result, the typical divorced father had more money to support himself than his ex-spouse had to support both herself and the children.

Many divorced female retirees also find themselves struggling financially. According to government data, 22% of divorced female retirees live in poverty compared to 18% of widows. This situation will probably become more serious because the number of retirement-age women will increase by 84% in the next 20 years to 9.6 million (U.S. Bureau of the Census, 1999a). Part of this problem stems from divorce settlements that do not take into account retirement and pension benefits for women. Also, many women negotiate to keep the house and primary custody of the children in the divorce settlement, but the house becomes too costly to maintain on their own income and thus becomes a financial drain, preventing them from saving for retirement. Many women do not get a share of their ex-spouse's pension benefits or retirement plans, and women who have stayed at home to raise a family typically have no pension plan of their own. Imagine a scenario in which a couple decides that the woman will stay home to raise the children while the man will work outside the home. After 20 years of this arrangement, they decide to divorce. She is forced to go to work outside of the home at age 45, while he maintains his job status and has a 20-year jump on his retirement savings. Given their uneven work history and lower salaries than men, older women are particularly vulnerable to poverty in later life.

Realignment of Responsibilities and Work Roles

The divorced parent with custody of the children is faced with the prospect of an overload of work. Now one parent must perform all the family functions that were formerly shared by two people. She or he also has to readjust the parenthood role to include taking over functions formerly fulfilled by the noncustodial parent. As a consequence, less time is devoted to the children, they listen less, and there are more problems controlling and guiding them. So, whether male or female, the solo parent has to fulfill all family functions and may have little relief from that responsibility.

Contacts with the Ex-Spouse

Understandably, many partners are so angry at their spouse when they divorce that they carry these feelings through the divorce process and sometimes for many years after. This anger needs to be dealt with both for the partner's sake and for the children's, so that they are not exposed to it unendingly and are not drawn into the fight between their parents (Isaacs and Leon, 1988a).

The more upsetting the divorce has been and the more vindictive the spouse, the less the other person wants to have any postdivorce contact. This is particularly true in cases of remarriage. Most second wives or husbands object to contacts with former spouses, because this usually leads to resentment and conflicts, especially if a bitter ex-spouse tries to cause trouble for the new couple.

When contacts are maintained, it is usually in relation to the children or support money or both (Bloom and Kindle, 1985). When the children have problems, both parents need to be involved and to correspond or talk to each other about the problems. In this case, an amicable relationship helps them work things out and makes things easier on the children (Tschann, Johnston, and Wallerstein, 1989). Sometimes, however, couples have to turn to the courts to settle disputes after the divorce.

Most postdivorce disputes are related to visitation rights and child support. Some communities have "Father's Day" in court, when fathers are taken to task for not making support payments on time. Other disputes may occur if a former spouse seeks to reduce spousal support payments or to increase them.

Some spouses have difficulty breaking emotional attachments following divorce. This increases the subjective stress experienced (Berman, 1988). The greater the attachment, the more difficulty spouses have in adjusting to divorce.

In contrast to these situations, some couples remain friends. One woman commented:

> My former husband and I get along better now than when we were married. He came over for dinner the other night; I cooked, and we had a pleasant evening. It's strange, but when we were married, we fought all the time. Now we are really good friends. (Author's counseling notes)

Kinship Interaction

Both divorced men and women rely on kin in times of divorce, especially for practical support but also for social-emotional support to relieve psychological distress. Most parents are active in easing the strains in the lives of their divorcing adult children and their grandchildren (Johnson, 1988). Men are more likely to rely on kin in the early stages of divorce, and women over longer periods of time (Gerstel, 1988).

Divorce is a multigenerational process that affects parents and other kin, as well as the divorcing couple and their children (Ferreiro, Warren, and Konanc, 1986). Positive support from parents can have an important effect on the divorcing person's adjustment. Helpful behavior includes the following:

- **Emotional support.** This involves listening, showing empathy, and affirming love and affection.
- **Child care.** This might mean occasional baby-sitting or taking the grandchildren for weekends.
- **Good, rational advice.** Examples include being able to talk over decisions with parents.
- **Respect for autonomy and regression.** Divorcing people have contrasting needs. Some want autonomy in decision making; others want to regress to dependency for a while (Lesser and Comet, 1987).

The effects of divorce differ between adult sons and daughters. In general, divorced daughters with child custody have more contact with parents and receive more help from parents than do married daughters. Sons, by contrast, have more contact with parents and receive more baby-sitting help when they are married than they do in other situations (Spitze, Logan, Deane, and Zerger, 1994).

Overall, continued contact with former in-laws after divorce is not frequent. Women are more likely than men to maintain ties with ex-kin. Most of the positive relationships with ex-kin involve grandchildren, with custodial parents maintaining more contact than noncustodial parents. Relationships with ex-kin that are not sustained tend to end abruptly after separation, with little chance of subsequent resumption (Ambert, 1988a).

CHILDREN AND DIVORCE

There has been growing concern over the number of children exposed to parental divorce. Several studies indicate that children from divorced families are referred to mental health facilities at least as frequently as and sometimes more often than their counterparts from intact families. Furthermore, custodial parents are virtually unanimous in reporting that their children evidence emotional and behavioral difficulties both at school and at home following divorce. There is a need to discuss the whole subject of children and divorce in more detail (Lee, Picard, and Blain, 1994).

Child Custody

The term **custody** refers to both legal custody (who holds decision-making rights) and physical custody (where the children will live). In **sole legal custody,** the noncustodial parent forfeits the right to make decisions about the children's health, education, or religious training; in effect, the custodial parent is given control over child rearing. In **joint legal custody,** custody is shared between the two parents, with parental rights and obligations left as they were during the marriage. There are advantages and disadvantages to both arrangements.

Traditionally, sole custody of the children has been granted to the mother unless it can be established that she is unfit. In some cases, the mother may not be competent or may have a poor relationship with her children (Lowery, 1985). In 1997, 85% of the 13.7 million custodial parents were women (U.S. Bureau of the Census, 1999a). However, 2.1 million men were custodial parents. More and more, therefore, the overriding consideration is what the court considers the best interests of the children.

In cases of custody dispute, a mediator may be employed or a child development expert appointed to investigate the family situation and to recommend custody arrangements to the court. The wishes of older children are usually taken into consideration in deciding with whom they will reside.

In some cases, joint custody is awarded, with both parents responsible. The children typically reside with one parent and visit the other often. In joint custody, children have access to both parents, and both are responsible for the welfare of the children. Important decisions are made jointly. Joint custody fathers are more likely to be actively involved in parenting than are noncustodial fathers (Bowman and Ahrons, 1985). Joint custody also takes the pressure off one parent to assume total responsibility. Some research indicates that joint custody increases parental self-esteem, lessens depression, diminishes anxiety, and ameliorates parents' feelings of disruption (Coysh et al., 1989).

Joint custody arrangements require maturity and forbearance on the part of both parents; otherwise, numerous squabbles create continual tension (Lowery and Settle, 1985). Bringing together two people who want to be apart and who don't get along can perpetuate all the squabbles of the unhappy marriage. Some parents also experience great stress when they interact with social institutions, family, and friends. For example, the desire of both parents to receive school announcements, report cards, or results of doctor's examinations commonly meets with resistance. Friends and family members may view a friendly relationship as deviant and pressure the ex-spouses not to have anything to do with each other. There is general agreement, however, that joint custody, if desired and amicably managed by both parents, is a good solution to a difficult problem.

Child Support

Providing for continued support of children is one of the obligations of parenthood. Under law, this is an obligation of both the mother and the father, whether the parents are married or not. Since 85% of custodial parents are women, child support awards are the most common mechanism by which noncustodial fathers are required to transfer economic resources to their children. These transfers are often very critical to the well-being of the children.

As the number of single-parent families has risen, so has the importance of collecting child support as a public policy issue. According to 1998 U.S. Census Bureau data, 28% of all children under age 18 resided in single-parent homes, and over 30% of single-parent families (compared to 16% of all families) lived below the poverty line. The poverty rate for custodial mothers (33%) was more than twice as high as that for custodial fathers (14%). Approximately 58% of the 13.7 million custodial parents had child support awards (61% of custodial moth-

ers and 40% of custodial fathers). Often custodial parents are not awarded child support payments because the other parent is judged unable to pay. Seventy percent of the mothers and 57% of the fathers with awards received at least a portion of the money (Scoon-Rogers, 1999). It is estimated that only a quarter of custodial parents receive the full amount awarded (Lin, 2000).

There are essentially three systems for determining the amount of child-support awards: (1) specifying a straight percentage of the noncustodial parent's income based on the number of dependent children; (2) calculating support according to the combined income of both parents, with each paying the percentage that is their share of the combined income; and (3) taking both parents' incomes into consideration but allowing for exemptions such as taxes, work-related expenses, or new dependents of a noncustodial parent. Investigators have concluded that many noncustodial parents can afford to pay substantially more child support than is awarded under any of these three systems (Klitsch, 1989).

In an attempt to establish fairer standards for child support obligations, federal lawmakers passed legislation requiring that each state establish standards for determining child support, and judges who deviate from this standard must provide grounds, in writing, for doing so. This legislation gave the courts less discretion than they previously had held, but it has still resulted in widely varying standards from state to state (Klawitter, 1994). Coleman, Ganong, Killian, and McDaniel (1999), in studying child support obligations, found little agreement about how much money parents should pay for child support, with a large discrepancy between what states recommended and what parents thought was fair. Many parents felt that there should be a reduction in the father's obligation if the mother remarried but not if only the father remarried. Thus, a reduction of financial support appears to relate mostly to the mother's perceived increased income, and not to additional financial responsibilities assumed by the father (Coleman et al., 1999).

The legal system has three approaches to promote compliance with support orders. The deterrence-based approach uses legal punishment to ensure payment of support. It can be either specific, which involves punishing an individual who is delinquent in payment in order to prevent future delinquency, or general, which involves punishing offenders in order to discourage others from becoming delinquent (Sorensen and Halpern, 1999). These punishments include interception of tax refunds, liens on property, and jail time. There is some statistical evidence that the deterrence-based approach does increase child support payments (Sorensen and Halpern, 1999).

Another approach is based on compliance. Rather than relying on punishment after the fact, this approach intervenes before the law is broken (Reiss, 1984). The compliance approach uses random checking, or checking of potential offenders, resulting in funds being withheld from earnings before a child support payment is missed. This approach has also been shown to have a positive effect on payments (Sorensen and Halpern, 1999).

Finally, the consensus-based approach relies not on fear of punishment or on payment regulation, but on societal acceptance and concurring norms. There are two strategies for establishing the proper norm: (1) enforcing the law consistently until behavior changes and (2) using the media to convince the public that the norm has merit. Establishing standards for determining child support and encouraging judges to use consistent criteria when awarding child support are two examples of the consensus-based approach.

Studies have shown that compliance with support orders is positively affected by both income withholding and the father's perception of fairness. They have also revealed that, once a parent feels that the order is fair, withholding no longer has an impact on compliance, and that withholding does not reduce compliance among those who perceive the order to be fair. These results suggest that policymakers should focus on improving perceptions of fairness while continuing to promote income withholding in efforts to improve compliance (Lin, 2000).

Making regular child support payments is very important to children's welfare. It lets the children know that they are cared for by both parents. It better enables the children to have the necessities of life, to live in better neighborhoods and housing, and to have adequate food, clothing, and education. It prevents the children from being penalized because of the actions of parents. They need to be loved and nurtured by both parents, regardless of their parents' marital status.

Visitation Rights

Ordinarily, visitation rights are granted to the noncustodial parent. These rights may be unlimited—allowing visitation at any time—or they may be restrictive—limiting visitation only to specific times. In 1999, about 10.6 million (77%) of the 13.7 million parents who were not living with their children (noncustodial parents) had joint custody and/or visitation rights for contact with their children (U.S. Bureau of the Census, 1999a). A vindictive spouse can make life miserable by managing to be away with the children when it's time for the other parent to visit, by poisoning the children's minds against the other parent, by refusing to allow the children to phone or write, or by using visitation rights as a club to wield over the other parent's head.

According to the provisions of the Uniform Marriage and Divorce Act of 1979,

> (A) A parent not granted custody of the child is entitled to reasonable visitation rights unless the court finds, after a hearing, that visitation would endanger the child's physical health or significantly impair his [or her] emotional development.
>
> (B) The court may modify an order granting or denying visitation rights whenever modification would serve the best interests of the child; but the court shall not restrict a parent's visitation rights unless it finds that the visitation would endanger a child's physical health or significantly impair his [or her] emotional development. (Cited in Franklin and Hibbs, 1980, p. 289)

Although increased visitation is believed to reflect a good noncustodial parent-child relationship, this association is mediated by the postdivorce parental relationship.

Reactions of Children

Using national longitudinal data to examine parent-child relationships before and after parental divorce, researchers found that parents report escalating problems in their relationships with their children as early as 8–12 years prior to divorce. The low quality of the parents' marriage largely accounted for this association. Low quality in the parents' marriage when children were 10 years old on average was a predictor of low parental affection for the children when they were

18 years old. Divorce further eroded affection between fathers and children, indicating that the quality of the parents' marriage had both direct and indirect long-term consequences for parent-child affection.

Why should low marital quality translate into problematic parent-child relations? Marital discord may preoccupy and distract parents, leaving them emotionally unavailable and unable to deal with their children's needs. It also may cause parents to be irritable and hot-tempered in dealing with their children. At the same time, marital discord may increase children's behavior problems, making them more difficult to manage. The result could be a situation in which parent-child relationships spiral downward (Amato and Booth, 1996).

The conflict and difficulties that lead to divorce are set in motion well before the family separates. The roughly 2 years that follow disruption have been described as a "crisis period" characterized by dramatic changes in children's day-to-day lives. Consequently, any effects of divorce on children may reflect not only the stress of the breakup and its aftermath but also dysfunctional family processes, marital conflict, or problems children have prior to the breakup (Booth, 1999; Morrison and Cherlin, 1995).

A growing number of clinicians emphasize that children perceive divorce as a major negative event that stimulates painful emotions, confusion, and uncertainty. Some clinicians feel that the majority of children regain psychological equilibrium within a year or so and resume a normal curve of growth and development (Hetherington and Stanley-Hagen, 1999). Two studies show no significant association between adult self-esteem and the experience of parental divorce as a child. However, both studies show a lowered sense of power in later life, primarily because of lower educational attainment (Amato, 1988; Glenn and Kramer, 1985).

Other researchers feel that, for a substantial portion of children, the upheaval in their lives will interfere with normal social-emotional growth. This view is substantiated by Judith Wallerstein in a 25-year study of 60 divorced families, involving 130 children, living in Marin County, California (Wallerstein and Lewis, 1998). Wallerstein found that 10 years after divorce, half the women and one-third of the men were still so angry at their former spouse that this anger colored their relationship with their children. The children in her study had memories of abandon-

ment, terror, and loneliness. They felt that they had been denied the basic security with which to grow and that they had "lost" their childhood by feeling compelled to assume responsibility for their parents' well-being. And the effects of divorce did not disappear over time, but instead appeared to be cumulative. High levels of alcohol abuse, promiscuity, and delinquency showed up 10–15 years after the parents' divorce. Half the children entered adulthood as underachieving, self-deprecating young men and women. Financial support for college was often missing, as few fathers offered consistent financial support throughout childhood and toward higher education. Overall, Wallerstein concluded from decades of research that divorce causes serious harm to children who experience it (Wallerstein and Lewis, 1998).

Wallerstein's sample came from an affluent area during years of rapid social change in the United States. There was no control group with which to compare findings. No study was done of how tension prior to divorce affected children. So whether these findings can be applied to other children from divorced families is not certain.

The effects of divorce on children depend on many variables: whether divorce improves or reduces the quality of parenting, whether divorce improves or worsens the emotional atmosphere of the home, whether the divorce is amicable or bitter, what the effect of divorce is on the parents, and what custody and living arrangements are worked out.

In the time immediately surrounding the divorce, children may go through a period of mourning and grief, and the mood or feeling may be one of sadness and dejection. One 7-year-old described divorce as "when people go away" (Rice, 1979). Other common reactions are a heightened sense of insecurity. Children feel that "if you really loved me, you wouldn't go away and leave me." Some become very afraid that their custodial parent will also leave, and the child may become very possessive of that parent. One mother remarked, "Since the divorce, Tommy has been very upset when I go to work or when he goes to school. I think he's afraid that he'll come home and not find me there" (Rice, 1979, p. 304).

Another common reaction of children is to blame themselves. If the children are a major source of conflict for the couple, the children may feel they are responsible. Some children think that the departing parent is abandoning them because they haven't been "good boys or girls." Yet another com-

mon reaction is for children to try to bring their parents together. They wish that everyone could live together and be happy. The longing for a reunited family may go on for a long time, until children fully understand the realities of the situation and the reason for the separation.

After children get over the initial upset of divorce, one common reaction is anger and resentment, especially against the parent they blame for the divorce. Sometimes this is directed against the father—especially if they feel he has deserted the family. When the father comes to visit, he may be surprised to find that his children remain cold and aloof. They have been hurt, so they have erected defenses, shut off their emotions, and tried to remain unfeeling (Rice, 1979).

The resentment or hostility may also be directed at the mother, especially if the children blame her for the divorce. One 5-year-old blamed her mother for her father's absence: "I hate you, because you sent my daddy away." (Actually, the mother hadn't wanted the divorce.) An older girl, age 12, asked her mother, "Why did you leave my father all alone?" It was obvious that the girl did not understand the reason for the divorce (Rice, 1979, p. 305).

Children have other adjustments to make. They need to adjust to the absence of one parent, often one on whom they depended deeply for affection and for help. One teenage girl remarked, "The hardest thing for me was to get used to living without my father. I never really realized how much I needed him until he left" (author's counseling notes).

Older children may also be required to assume more responsibility for family functioning: cooking, housekeeping, even earning money to support the family. This is usually a maturing experience for them, but it's also a difficult adjustment. Some children, used to having everything, have a difficult time realizing that money is short and that they can't buy the clothes and other things they used to.

Research consistently finds that children whose parents are separated or divorced are more likely to have behavioral problems. However, children in intact families with high levels of parental conflict also have high levels of problem behaviors. Thus, while divorce is clearly disruptive to children, living with two quarreling parents appears to be equally problematic. Increasingly, researchers conclude that parental conflict poses a greater threat to children's well-being than does family structure per se (Buehler et al., 1998; Wandewater and Lansford, 1998).

Of course, special adjustments are necessary for children of divorced parents. For example, when the parent caring for the children begins to date again and to become emotionally involved with another person, the children must share their parent with another adult. If the parent remarries, as the majority do, the children are confronted with readjustment to a stepparent and perhaps stepsiblings.

SUMMARY

1. A number of factors affect the probability of divorce: age at first marriage, early child-bearing, frequency of attendance at religious services, socioeconomic status, ethnic background, geographic area, parental divorce, and the number of children in the family.

2. Studies of the perceptions of men and women of the causes of marital breakup revealed the following: According to the women, the 10 most important were basic unhappiness, emotional abuse, communication problems, incompatibility and different backgrounds, sexual problems, the man's lack of sense of family and lack of time at home, his alcohol abuse, financial or employment problems, the man's infidelity, and the woman's lack of interest in the marriage. The men listed 9 of the 10 causes that the women had listed (although not in the same order), with the exception being their alcohol abuse.

3. Disaffection, or the loss of intimacy and love, is a major component of marital dissolution. It develops in three phases, during which feelings of anger, disappointment, apathy, and hopelessness grow until the costs of staying together are perceived as outweighing the rewards. Finally, one spouse, who now focuses only on the negative traits of the partner, wants to end the relationship.

4. The decision to divorce is a difficult one. There are four basic considerations in deciding whether to remain married: satisfaction with or attractions of the marriage, barriers to getting out of the marriage, the attractiveness of alternatives to the marriage, and the intensity of the emotional pain generated by the unhappy marriage.

5. There are three major alternatives to divorce: marriage counseling, marriage enrichment programs, and structured separation, during which couples try to resolve their problems.

6. Five types of situations may support a couple's decision to consider structured marital separation: extreme conflict, absence of spousal reinforcement, feelings of being constricted or smothered, a situational or midlife transition, and indecision regarding divorce.

7. In no-fault divorce, the spouses petition for divorce on the basis of irremediable breakdown of the marriage or irreconcilable differences.

8. Sometimes spouses fight over property and finances, spousal support, child support, and child custody, using the children as pawns to win concessions. Such actions are particularly upsetting to the children.

9. One of the most helpful solutions to property, custody, child support, and other issues is to employ a mediator to help resolve differences.

10. Many of the effects of no-fault divorce have been helpful: less extensive and less expensive litigation, the greater possibility of friendly divorce, and partial elimination of the punitive element of moral condemnation that pervaded divorce for centuries.

11. Some effects of no-fault divorce are not always helpful. More men are filing, because the threat of recrimination has been removed. While this may be of some advantage to them, their spouses have been placed at a disadvantage in trying to attain fair financial and property settlements. Overall, men may be better off financially after the divorce; many women and their children are forced to live in poverty.

12. The major adjustment problems of adults after divorce involve emotional trauma, the negative attitudes of society, loneliness and social readjustment, adjustments of the noncustodial spouse, finances, realignment of responsibilities and work roles, contacts with the ex-spouse, and kinship interaction.

13. The mother's satisfaction with the father's involvement following divorce is an important predictor of children's well-being.

14. Custodial fathers report better relationship quality with their children than do noncustodial fathers. However, continuously married fathers report the highest level of relationship quality with their children.

15. The term *custody* refers to both legal and physical custody. In the past, the mother traditionally got sole custody of the children. Today, the courts strive to consider the best interests of the children.

16. In joint legal custody, the responsibility for parenting is given to both parents. They both have parental rights and responsibilities for child rearing, as they did during the marriage. Joint custody requires the active cooperation and responsibility of both parents, as well as the ability to get along with each other.

17. Providing for continued support of the children is the responsibility of both the mother and the father even if they are not married. But only 58% of custodial parents get child support awards, and only 70% of mothers and 57% of fathers actually receive even a portion of the award. There are different systems for calculating the amount of child support payments. Laws have been enacted to force delinquent fathers to pay. Making regular child support payments is important to children's welfare.

18. Ordinarily, the parent not given custody has visitation rights. While frequent visitation is associated with good noncustodial parent-child relationships and benefits the child, the association is mediated by the quality of the postdivorce parental relationship.

19. Many parents have problems in their marriage that begin years before a divorce. This marital discord affects children negatively because parents are unable to meet their children's needs.

20. Children perceive divorce as a major negative event that stimulates painful emotions, confusion, and uncertainty. The effects of divorce on children depend on many variables.

21. Wallerstein found long-term negative effects of divorce on children that continued to show up in adulthood.

KEY TERMS

conciliation counseling

structured separation

no-fault divorce

custody

sole legal custody

joint legal custody

QUESTIONS FOR THOUGHT

1. Assume that you are married. What problems in marriage would you consider most damaging to your marital relationship? Explain the reasons for your selection.

2. Do you believe in divorce? Why or why not? Are there any circumstances under which you definitely would or would not get a divorce?

3. What factors would you want to consider in deciding whether to get a divorce?

4. In your opinion, why does marriage counseling at times *not* succeed? Contrast your views with what is presented in the Family Issues box "Why Marriage Counseling Sometimes Does Not Succeed."

SUGGESTED READINGS

Arendell, T. (1995). *Fathers and Divorce.* Thousand Oaks, CA: Sage. Presents in-depth interviews with a volunteer sample of 75 divorced fathers on their personal experiences.

Cohen, A. (1999). *Happily Ever After: Can You Be Friends After Lovers?* Carlsbad, NM: Hay House. Examines the pathways for maintaining friendship when the sexual interest is lost.

Cummings, E. M., and Davies, P. (1994). *Children and Marital Conflict. The Impact of Family Disputes and Resolutions.* New York: Guilford Press. Compiles research on the impact of interparental conflict on child developmental outcomes.

Everett, S. D., and Everett, P. A. (1994). *Healthy Divorce.* San Francisco: Jossey-Bass. Takes a constructive approach to divorce.

Greif, G. L., and Hegar, R. L. (1994). *When Parents Kidnap: Families Behind the Headlines.* New York: Prepress. Focuses on child custody and abduction.

Guttman, J. (1993). *Divorce: Theory and Research.* Hillsdale, NJ: Lawrence Erlbaum. Gives a comprehensive view of divorce.

Kayser, K. (1993). *When Love Dies: The Process of Marital Disaffection.* New York: Guilford Press. Asks, How do we fall out of love, and what can we do about it?

Kingma, D. R. (2000). *Coming Apart: Why Relationships End and How to Live Through the Ending of Yours.* Berkeley, CA: Conari Press. Examines marital breakup and the healing process.

Kurtz, D. (1995). *For Richer, for Poorer, Mothers Confront Divorce.* New York: Routledge. Analyzes divorce in the United States and presents a troubling picture of the situation of divorced women and their children.

Larson, D., Swyers, J., and Larson, S. (1995). *The Costs and Consequences of Divorce: Assessing the Clinical, Economic, and Public Health Impact of Marital Disruption in the United States.* Rockville, MD: National Institute for Health Care Research. Represents a relatively nontechnical presentation of the consequences of divorce.

McGraw, P. C. (2000). *Relationship Rescue: A Seven-Step Strategy for Reconnecting with Your Partner.* New York: G. K. Hall. Gives self-help tips for mending relationships.

Prager, K. J. (1995). *The Psychology of Intimacy.* New York: Guilford Press. Provides a conceptualization of intimacy that organizes and stimulates theory and research and represents what we know or do not know about intimacy.

Quick, B. (2000). *Still Friends: Living Happily Ever After . . . Even If Your Marriage Falls Apart.* Berkeley, CA: Wildcat Canyon Press. Promotes civility and balance after a divorce.

Stevenson, M. R., and Black, K. M. (1995). *How Divorce Affects Offspring: A Research Approach.* Madison, WI: Brown & Benchmark. Examines child outcomes.

Vaughan, D. (1990). *Uncoupling: Turning Points in Intimate Relationships.* New York: Vintage Books. Depicts patterns of turning points in intimate relationships.

Coming Together: Remarriage and Stepparenting

Learning Objectives

Remarriage

Divorce and Success in Remarriage

Courtship and Mate Selection in Remarriage

Perspective: Successful Remarriages

Carrying Expectations from One Marriage to Another

Finances

Relationships with the Ex-Spouse

Stepfamilies

Family Issues: Stepfamily Turning Points

Stepparent-Stepchild Relationships

Child Well-Being in Stepfamilies

Facilitating Bonds Between Stepparents and Stepchildren

Cohabiting with a New Partner

Coparents and Parenting Coalitions

Family Issues: Ten Major Issues for Families of Remarriage

Stepsibling Relationships

Summary

Key Terms

Questions for Thought

Suggested Readings

According to the cultural ideal, marriage lasts until "death do us part." Historically, this marital commitment was largely borne out, and most marriages ended with the death of a spouse, often when young children were still present (Glick, 1976). As life expectancy has increased and as cultural norms for divorce and remarriage have changed, more marriages are ended by divorce than by death. Whether the marriage ends by divorce or death, remarriage and the formation of stepfamilies have become quite common (Coontz, 2000).

Today, 46% of all marriages are remarriages, and the largest proportion of the remarried population is divorced people who have married other divorced people (U.S. Bureau of the Census, 1998, Table 157). In fact, approximately two-thirds of people who divorce each year remarry eventually. Furthermore, remarriage occurs fairly quickly. The median interval between divorce and remarriage is 3 years for women and 4½ years for men (U.S. Bureau of the Census, 1996/1997). Rates vary by ethnic background. Blacks remarry more slowly than Whites, and Hispanics are less likely to remarry at all than are Blacks or Whites. For example, 44% of White women remarry within 3 years of a divorce, compared to 20% of Black women and 23% of Latino women (U.S. Bureau of the Census, 1998, Table 161).

The average duration of a remarriage that ends in divorce is 7.4 years for men and 7.1 years for women (National Center for Health Statistics, 1995). On average, men are approximately 42 years old and women 39 years old when their second marriage ends in divorce. If it is a third or later marriage ending in divorce, men are about 46, and women 42 (National Center for Health Statistics, 1995). Research has also revealed that couples with remarried women are almost twice as likely to divorce as those with remarried men, in part because of the 50% higher rate of divorce in marriages in which children are present (Tzeng and Mare, 1995).

Vital questions are: To what extent are remarriages successful? How might couples increase the chances of success? What special challenges do remarrieds face? Also, how do primary families differ from stepfamilies? How are stepmother and stepfather roles defined? What challenges do stepparents face? What are the reactions and adjustments of different stepchildren? What do we need to know about stepsibling relationships? What is it like growing up in a stepfamily?

REMARRIAGE

Remarried families (sometimes called binuclear families) may be grouped into categories according to family configuration. Couples with one remarried spouse include families with (1) no children, (2) children-in-common only, (3) her children (stepfather families), (4) his children (stepmother families), (5) children-in-common plus her children (natural parent plus stepfather), (6) children-in-common plus his children (natural parent plus stepmother), and (7) children of both spouses (two stepparents—either the man or the woman had a child out of wedlock). Couples with two remarried spouses include families with (1) no children, (2) children-in-common only, (3) her children (stepfather families), (4) his children (stepmother families), (5) children-in-common plus her children (natural parent plus stepfather), (6) children-in-common plus his children (natural parent plus stepmother), (7) children of both spouses (two stepparents), (8) children-in-common plus their children (natural parents plus two stepparents), (9) custodial children of the mother plus relationships with the father's children on a noncustodial basis, and (10) custodial children of the father plus relationships with the mother's children on a noncustodial basis.

Family relationships can become quite complicated in remarriages when one or both spouses bring children from a previous marriage, especially since half of all women who remarry will bear a child with their new spouse (Wineberg, 1990). Children may have natural parents plus stepparents, both natural siblings and stepsiblings, both natural grandparents and stepgrandparents, and natural aunts and uncles plus step-aunts and step-uncles, not to mention cousins and other relatives. Adult spouses relate to each other, to their own natural parents and grandparents, to their new parents-in-law and grandparents-in-law, and to their new brothers- and sisters-in-law. They may also continue to relate to their former parents- and grandparents-in-law, to their former brothers- and sisters-in-law, and to other family members. It is no wonder that family integration is sometimes challenging.

Divorce and Success in Remarriage

The majority of survey studies have revealed that the probability of divorce is slightly greater in remar-

Family relationships can become quite complicated in remarriages when one or both spouses bring children from a previous marriage and the remarried couple then have children of their own.

riages than in first marriages (Booth and Edwards, 1992). This means that half the children whose parents divorce and remarry will experience a second parental divorce (Coleman and Ganong, 1990).

From one point of view, remarriage should be more successful than first marriage. Remarrieds are older, more mature and experienced, and often highly motivated to make their marriage work. One study showed that, relative to other couples, spouses in remarried and stepfather families reported higher relationship quality and stronger motivations to be in the relationship (Kurdek, 1989a). According to self-reports of remarried couples, differences in marital satisfaction or quality of the marital relationship are rarely found, and when they are, they tend to be small in magnitude (Ganong and Coleman, 1994). Overall, research has shown that remarriage are just as happy as first marriage, with little difference in partners' well-being (Demo and Acock, 1996b; Ihinger-Tallman and Pasley, 1997). While spouses in long-established stepfamilies

view their marital relationship as just as happy as their first marriage, they also view their second marriage as more egalitarian in terms of housework and child care (Hetherington, 1999a), more open and pragmatic, and less romantic, and they are more willing to confront conflict (Hetherington et al., 1992). Although the risk of divorce is higher for remarried couples, many eventually establish strong, positive marital relationships and an adaptive, well-functioning parenting environment (Hetherington and Stanley-Hagan, 1999).

For some couples, remarriage introduces challenges that were not present in their first marriage. The biggest challenge can be children. Remarried couples with children from prior marriages are more likely to divorce than are remarried couples without stepchildren (Tzeng and Mare, 1995). Since mothers still most often get custody, their children are likely living with her and her new spouse, who becomes a stepfather. A divorced parent and the children may be a "closed system" of social interaction, which is difficult for a new stepparent to enter. In general, men more often feel excluded in the face of mate-child relationships than do women (Hobart, 1987). The man's children are usually living with his ex-spouse, creating family ties with her household, and the potential for conflict and resentment. The woman's ex-spouse as non-custodial father usually sees his children, so he has contact with both his ex-spouse and her new partner, also allowing the possibility of conflict and problems. Being a stepparent is a far more difficult task than being a biological parent, because children often have difficulty accepting a substitute parental figure. The spouse of a noncustodial parent must try to develop a friendly relationship with stepchildren from visits. All of the adults are co-parenting, with three or four parent figures as opposed to two. The children are continually reacting to and dealing with growing up in two households, with three or four adult figures, and with two or more models of relationship patterns with the opposite sex. Both adults and children must contend with the attitudes and influences of other family members. Thus, blending families can be complicated and challenging.

Stepsibling relationships can also pose challenges. Sometimes there is competition between the new spouse's and the partner's children. They each may become jealous of the time and attention their own parent gives to the stepchildren. However, researchers have found that most adolescents view their custodial parent's remarriage as positive (Anderson, Greene, Hetherington, and Clingempeel, 1999). The most frequent word that adolescents used to describe their reactions to remarriage was *happy*, followed by *satisfied* and *pleased*. Mothers also rated the reaction of their adolescents to their remarriage as positive. One reason given by adolescents who viewed their custodial parents' remarriages as positive was that their family had fewer money problems (Anderson et al., 1999).

Courtship and Mate Selection in Remarriage

There are a number of ways that courtship and mate selection in remarriage are different from those in first marriage. For one thing, the two people typically are older. The median age at remarriage is 37.8 for men and 34.2 for women (U.S. Bureau of the Census, 1998, Table 159). Overall, people who remarry are likely to be more emotionally mature and more experienced than when they married the first time around. For another thing, the majority have children. The median ages of two children at the time of remarriage are 6 and 8 years. This means that a custodial parent may evaluate a potential mate in terms of his or her potential as a stepparent (Church, 1999).

Sometimes ex-spouses and families become involved in the courtship of the couple. In some situations, the ex-spouse may try to break up the relationship, turn the children against the new partner, exert a negative influence on family members so that they won't accept the newcomer, and create jealousy and tension between the new partners. If family members liked the first spouse and sympathize with him or her, they may have a difficult time accepting the newcomer (Kurdek, 1989b). Potential mates of formerly married people are often introduced to other family members only after there is some assurance of commitment by the couple. The announcement of the new involvement may come as a surprise, with family members not having enough time or exposure to get used to the new relationship. New partners enter a family system that has an established history, and there are no guidelines for how they should fit in. Consequently, there may be several false starts in attempting to build relationships with the family, the children, and possibly the ex-spouse.

There are differences in the length of courtship among remarrieds. Generally, the length of the courtship before the second marriage is similar to that before the first marriage. That is, people with very brief courtships the first time around have very brief courtships before remarrying. However, age is an important variable. Males over 30 experience second courtships about half as long as those of younger males. At all ages, women with lower income and education marry sooner than women with higher income and education, whereas men with higher income and education marry sooner than those with lower income and education (Glick, 1990). The median number of years between divorce and remarriage is about 3 years for women and 4½ years for men, although this varies by age, race/ethnicity, the presence and number

How are happily remarried couples able to succeed? Many factors enter in, of course, but couples who succeed seem to have five factors in common.

The first factor is that the partners have given themselves time to get to know each other well. Like any marriage, remarriages are more complete if each member of the couple really knows the other well beforehand.

Second, happily married couples resist the many pressures to remarry before they are ready. These pressures stem from society itself and from friends and relatives who can't tolerate others being unmarried for very long and who fix them up with dates. And then there are the pressures of loneliness and the need for love and companionship.

Remarriage is also sometimes used as a reparative measure—to try to make it up to the children for the hurts and anguish caused by the death of the other parent or by divorce. Such motivations may backfire; instead of helping the children, a troubled marriage or a difficult stepparent relationship may actually make the situation worse.

Not all reasons for remarriage are desirable. Some divorced people remarry on the rebound as a way of hurting their former spouse by showing that they are still desirable. Remarriage can also become a reenactment of an earlier, neurotic relationship that, although unhealthy, nevertheless supplied certain needs. The partners must sort out what

they most seek in their relationship and be certain that they are not pressured into marriage for the wrong reasons or before they are ready.

Third, partners are able to discuss every aspect of their relationship before marriage. If they haven't done so before, then they do so afterward.

Fourth, partners have learned from past mistakes. Before remarriage, they need to ask themselves: Do I understand what went wrong the first time? What were the underlying causes of my marital problems? Have I gained insight into the shortcomings, and am I able to overcome them?

Finally, partners put their marriage first. These couples have learned that the basis for sound parent-child relationships is a sound marriage. The partners' primary loyalty is to each other, and secondarily to their children.

There will be numerous forces inside and outside their homes that will be trying to pull couples apart. Unless their bond is secure, the marriage can be broken. Immature children and stepchildren may try to weaken their bond, as may ex-spouses. Even other family members who resent the divorce or the remarriage may try to sow seeds of distrust or suspicion between the partners.

The happier the remarriage, the more secure and loving will be the environment in which children are reared (Ganong and Coleman, 1984; Rice, 1978).

---

of children, and income (Lampard and Peggs, 1999; Wineberg, 1999). During the period of emotional turmoil before and after a divorce, people are very vulnerable to the attention of others who are nice to them. Sexual intimacy usually commences early in a relationship, which tends to intensify the emotional involvement and the feeling of being in love. However, parents may hesitate to cohabit or to begin a partnered relationship if they feel it will negatively affect their children (Lampard and Peggs, 1999).

There may also be subtle psychological influences at work in the mate selection process. Some people want to marry a person who they believe resembles a spouse to whom they were married before. When people are divorced by a spouse against their will and remain emotionally attached to that spouse, or when a former spouse has died, they may seek another mate who reminds them of their former one. Of course, no two people are alike, so trouble arises in the remarriage when one or both

spouses discover that their new mate is *not* like their former spouse or when they try to pressure their new mate to be like the former one.

Even if people don't like some characteristics of a former spouse, they may seek out a new mate with similar traits, because the reasons they were initially attracted to that type of person still exist. Consider this example:

> Joe was brought up by a very domineering mother whom he rebelled against. His first wife, Joan, reminded him of his mother. He and his wife fought frequently; the conflict became so upsetting that Joe divorced her. He vowed never to have anything to do with that kind of woman again. But a year later, he was remarried to the same kind of woman all over again. Even though he rebelled against that kind of woman, it was the only type of relationship he knew. It brought him a sense of security. It was the one norm that he patterned his subsequent relationships after. (Author's counseling notes)

Many different motivations may be involved when there are large age discrepancies between mates, and many of these marriages are quite successful. In fact, overall, there are no significant differences in marital quality among couples from various age groups.

Carrying Expectations from One Marriage to Another

Remarried couples face many of the same expectations as first-married couples. But in addition to these expectations, remarried couples usually have other expectations unique to their status as people who have been married more than once. One expectation is that being married to the second spouse is going to be similar in some ways to being married to the first one. However, these expectations may be not only unrealistic but also unfair to the second spouse. One result is that spouses replicate the mistakes of their first marriage in remarriage, because they expect that the situation will be the same (Kalmuss and Seltzer, 1986).

One potential problem is rooted in pain experienced in the previous marriage. People who were married before remember all too well the problem behaviors of their former spouse, such as alcohol abuse, extramarital affairs, belittling comments, violent outbursts, rancorous arguments, irresponsibility, selfishness, and a lack of love and affection. As a result, these people enter a second marriage with a real fear that the problems and hurts they experienced before will happen again. This fear may make them oversensitive to anything their new partner does or says that reminds them of the difficulties they had before. One man explained his feelings:

> My first wife hated sex and rejected me most of the time over the many years of our marriage. As a result, I'm very sensitive to anything that my second wife does which seems to be rejection. If she's tired or sick and doesn't feel like intercourse, I'm hurt by her lack of desire, even though she really doesn't mean to reject me. Actually, she's very affectionate, and loves to make love. I even had trouble accepting that. I couldn't believe that she really liked it. Gradually, though, I accepted the fact that she really wanted me, so that now I'm not upset by those rare occasions when she is not willing. (Author's counseling notes)

Sensitivity to many forms of behavior develops. One woman became very sensitive to criticism because her first spouse had frequently berated her, especially in relation to her role as a mother. She became upset whenever her second spouse made suggestions for changing some of her methods of handling the children. The last thing she wanted was similar treatment from this man. Many other examples could be given. In each case, the reaction of the remarried person is quite understandable, but it can create problems if it is so extreme that it interferes with the new spousal relationship.

Another problem in remarriage involves confusion over role expectations. This confusion arises because of the difficulty in sorting out what one's second spouse expects from what one's first mate required. Both men and women in remarriages tend to base some of their expectations of spousal roles on the role performance of former spouses, even if the first marriage was quite unhappy. This is unfair to the current spouse, who may not be at all like the former mate. The key is to relate to one's spouse as a unique individual, not as a person whom one expects to be like someone else.

Problems may also arise when people want their new partner to play a role completely different from that played by the former spouse. This happens when a person has developed an intense dislike of things a former spouse did and, consequently, expects the second spouse to behave in a completely different manner. This can lead to some interesting behavior. Here is one such example:

Ann was first married to a husband who expected her to wait on him hand and foot. To keep the peace, she did so for 25 years, even though she became more and more resentful of having to do so. Finally she could stand it no longer and got a divorce. She vowed that she never wanted anything to do with that type of man again.

Hank was first married to a wife who never assumed any responsibility for the house, the children, or for earning income. He did virtually everything for the whole family, because he couldn't stand a dirty house, unkempt children, and living in poverty. After 25 years he grew to resent it and divorced his wife. He vowed he would never marry that type of woman again.

Ann and Hank met and fell in love. Ann was very impressed that Hank was the kind of man who had always done everything at home. At last, she would be married to the kind of husband she had always wanted. Hank was delighted when he found out that Ann had waited on her husband for all those years. At last, he would have a wife who would do things for him for a change.

But in the beginning, both Ann and Hank were very much disappointed. Hank became resentful because Ann asked him to do the same things he had resented doing for his first wife. Ann was disillusioned because she found out that Hank expected her to serve him just as she had done for her first husband. It took some time before they each understood the feelings and needs of the other and before they learned to compromise in meeting those needs. (Author's counseling notes)

It can be quite unfair to expect one's spouse to fulfill needs that were not met in a previous marriage, but one naturally might want important needs met that were not fulfilled before. The key is *mutual* fulfillment, not a situation in which one person does all the giving and the other does all the receiving.

Finances

Financial problems can be particularly bothersome for remarried couples (Mason, Skolnick, and Sugarman, 1998). A divorced father who remarries usually has to pay child support. If he is also helping to support his new wife's children, there is a double financial burden, particularly if her ex-spouse does not keep up with child support payments. However, for a female-headed single-parent family, remarriage is one of the fastest routes out of economic hardship (Zill, Morrison, and Coiro, 1993).

Fishman (1983) described the two basic economic patterns that stepfamilies adopt: (1) "Common-pot" families pool all their resources for household expenses, whereas (2) "two-pot" families safeguard individual resources for personal use or for their biological children. Fishman found that a common-pot system unifies the stepfamily, while the two-pot economy encourages biological loyalties and personal autonomy. The common-pot approach is illustrated in Figure 21.1. In the fictional Becker-Robinson stepfamily, Mike and Fran live together with his two children and her three children. Fran works full-time, and Mike owns a shoe store. They bought a house in both their names. All earnings are pooled together in a joint account. Fran receives sporadic child support from her ex-spouse, which she puts in the common pot. Resources of time, services, goods, and cash are distributed according to individual family members' needs, not biological relationship. This is not always simple to do. Sacrifices are necessary, and tensions arise. For example, Fran's daughter Ann is going to college, and her expenses come from the common pot. This means that the money is not available for other things (Fishman, 1983).

In the two-pot approach, each marital partner contributes a specific amount to the ongoing maintenance of the household, but children are supported by their biological parents. This approach is illustrated in Figure 21.2. In the fictional Marshall-Linton stepfamily, Harry and Sheila live together with Sheila's three children. She receives $200 a week in child support. Harry's older daughter, Greta, is away at college; his younger daughter, Ginny, lives with her mother and new stepfather. Ginny visits regularly; Greta's visits are sporadic. Harry gives Sheila $50 per week for his share of food and small expenses. The house is in Harry's

Figure 21.1   The Common-Pot Approach (*Note:* From "The Economic Behavior of Stepfamilies" by B. Fishman, 1983, *Family Relations, 32*, pp. 359–366. Copyright © 1983 by the National Council on Family Relations. Reprinted by permission.)

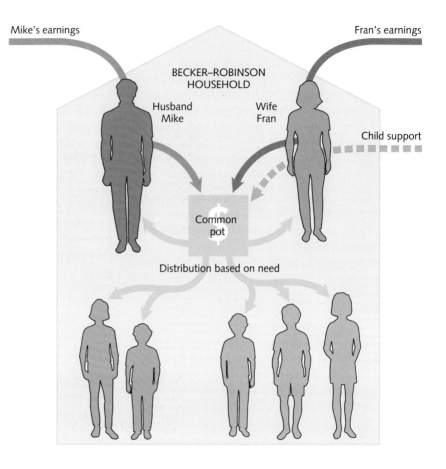

name, and he pays the fixed expenses—mortgage, gas, and electric. He also sends his ex-spouse a monthly stipend for Ginny's support and pays for Greta's college expenses. Sheila adds the $200 a week she gets for child support to the $50 Harry gives her and deposits the money in her personal account. Out of this, she runs the house and pays for clothes and incidentals for her children and herself. Harry and Sheila have no joint checking or savings account. Obviously, in this two-pot system, the financial arrangement indicates a tenuous bond in the marriage. Harry's ex-spouse was a "spendaholic" who was always buying and who left him and sued for alimony and divorce. He is fearful to trust another woman again. Sheila tries to be a good spouse. She is a homebody who does not spend much on herself, but Harry still criticizes her when she does spend. The bond between them is weak.

These examples illustrate that a financial commitment to a new spouse comes slowly; and still more slowly, if at all, comes financial commitment to stepchildren. The challenge for each stepfamily is to build the interpersonal bonds, sense of group commitment, and economic system that meet both family and individual needs and that reflect family members' commitment to one another (Fishman, 1983).

Relationships with the Ex-Spouse

In reality, divorced people seldom have affectionate feelings toward the former spouse but rather usually have a long list of complaints. However, individuals who divorce typically have to develop a new relationship with the ex-spouse when children are involved. This new relationship can be a difficult one, particularly in the early stages of divorce as ex-spouses deal with feelings of ambivalence, anger, attachment, and remorse, as well as sometimes fighting viciously and even reconciling passionately (Masheter, 1997).

Even when ex-spouses seem to hate each other, they probably have developed an emotional attachment that does not end when the marriage ends. In the first stages of separation, signs of continued at-

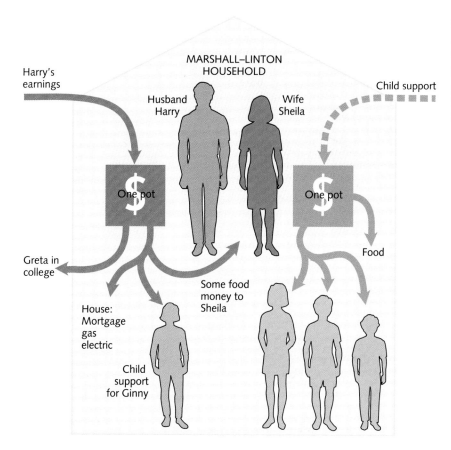

Figure 21.2 The Two-Pot Approach (*Note:* From "The Economic Behavior of Stepfamilies" by B. Fishman, 1983, *Family Relations, 32,* pp. 359–366. Copyright © 1983 by the National Council on Family Relations. Reprinted by permission.)

tachment between ex-spouses, such as continually calling the other person or needing to know his or her whereabouts, are not uncommon. Four actions characteristic of continued attachment are (1) spending a lot of time thinking about the former relationship, (2) wondering what the ex-partner is doing, (3) doubting that the divorce really happened, and (4) feeling that one will never recover from the marital breakup (Kitson, 1982). Preoccupation with the ex-spouse is usually characteristic of a problematic relationship with the individual (Masheter, 1997), which often includes hostility, particularly among depressed women (Thabes, 1997). Partners often blame each other for their hurt feelings and feel justified in their aggression and hostility. In a longitudinal study, Ambert (1988b) concluded that postdivorce harmony is rare, although after 6 years most divorced people—especially nonparents—have rather indifferent feelings toward their ex-spouse. Particularly after remarriage, interaction between the ex-spouses tends to decrease (Christensen and Rettig, 1995).

Buunk and Mutsaers (1999) examined how the nature of one's relationship with a former spouse is related to satisfaction in remarriage by focusing on three aspects of the relationship with the ex-spouse: attachment, hostility, and friendship. After 6 years of remarriage, on average, there was little continued attachment to or friendship with the ex-spouse, although there were still feelings of hostility, particularly when children were involved. In general, positive feelings toward the ex-spouse were quite rare. The relationship with the ex-spouse was more positive among the more highly educated and among those who did not have children from the former marriage. Continued attachment to the ex-spouse was especially problematic in relation to current marital satisfaction. Men who still felt attached to a former spouse reported that their current spouse had problems with the relationship with the ex-spouse. The more attached men still felt to the former spouse, the less happy the second marriage. In addition, the more their current spouse reported feelings of continued attachment to a

A recent study examined what members of stepfamilies perceived to be turning points in their family development. The researchers focused on the first 4 years of stepfamily living and defined a turning point as a positive or negative event that altered family relationships in a significant way (Baxter, Braithwaite, and Nicholson, 1999).

The study identified five turning points that members perceived as altering their sense of feeling like a family: (1) changes in household/family composition, (2) conflict or disagreement, (3) holidays or special celebrations, (4) quality time, and (5) family crises. Household composition is an important turning point because the structure of a blended family is often inconsistent and unstable, with children's visitation and change of residence posing a continual challenge (Kelley, 1992; Whisett and Land, 1992). For about two-thirds of the reported household composition turning points, respondents noted a positive effect on their feeling of a sense of family, suggesting that the majority of respondents were adaptable to their frequently changing circumstances. In contrast, the conflict-related turning points were overwhelmingly perceived as negative events, involving stepparent-stepchild and spousal relationships (Baxter et al., 1999). Holidays and special events were perceived as positive turning points by most respondents, although about one-third reported them as negative experiences. While family celebrations offer opportunities for emotional bonding among family members (Visher and Visher, 1990), some family members reported stress associated with conflicting obligations to various constituencies, and others noted feelings of loss associated with memories of past celebrations. Quality-time events were universally perceived as positive turning points. Activities such as watching a football game or going shopping together promoted a sense of family. Stepfamilies in this study also often perceived family crises as having a positive effect on family identity. These turning points represented times of need when the family came together and in some instances represented the first time a family member, especially a stepchild, recognized that other members of the new family cared about them personally.

Identifying these turning points helps to reveal the moments and experiences that are significant to stepfamilies in forming an identity and may help family members and others involved to gain insight into the complex and sometimes confusing process of becoming a new family (Baxter et al., 1999).

former spouse, the less happy these women were. One possible reason for this gender difference is that women are more sensitive about their spouse's feelings of continued attachment than are men. Among women, hostility toward and/or friendship with a former spouse was dependent on their current spouse's attitude toward this type of relationship. These findings may reflect a higher interpersonal sensitivity of women to the attitudes of their spouse, but they may also indicate that women express their hostility toward their former spouse more so than do men, which may make their current spouse develop a negative attitude toward the friendship with that former spouse (Buunk and Mutsaers, 1999).

In general, relationships between ex-spouses seem to reach a low level of intensity after a number of years, with most remarried individuals not feeling a need to maintain a close relationship with the former spouse. This suggests that most individuals eventually get over the severe hostility characteristic of many relationships between ex-spouses during the initial stages of separation (Buunk and Mutsaers, 1999).

STEPFAMILIES

Many couples expect stepfamily relationships to be similar to those of primary families, and they may be disappointed, surprised, and bewildered if they find differences (Bray and Berger, 1993). Research suggests that expecting or forcing a stepfamily to be like a traditional biological family can lead to new problems or exacerbate existing ones (Bray and Berger, 1993). Stepfamilies need to recognize that building a sense of family takes time, that family boundaries must be flexible to accommodate existing ties to noncustodial parents and extended family, and that stepparents cannot replace biological parents and may need to develop a separate, nontraditional parenting role (Hetherington and Stanley-Hagan, 1999).

Disappointment may occur if stepparents have unrealistically high expectations of themselves and their new family. Having been married before and been parents before, they expect that they will be able to step right into the stepparent role. They may be shocked to discover that their stepchildren don't take to them the way they do to their biological parents. This may cause feelings of anxiety, anger, guilt, and low self-esteem. They may feel that there is something wrong with them, or they may blame the children. They need to realize that it may take several years to develop satisfactory relationships.

There is usually an initial period of disequilibrium associated with divorce and remarriage, followed by the eventual restabilization of the new family system, which typically takes 2–3 years (Hetherington, 1989). However, some researchers have estimated that restabilization in stepfamilies may take as long as 5–7 years (Cherlin and Furstenberg, 1994). After stepfamilies have been together for 5 or more years, restabilization seems to have taken place, and it is then that we see more similarities than differences in the ways in which families function. Thus, in long-term stable stepfamilies, relationship patterns become more like those in nondivorced families (Bray and Kelly, 1998). This transition or restabilization is somewhat dependent on family history. Children whose parents had a highly conflictual marital relationship show a decrease in behavioral problems following divorce, whereas those from families with little conflict experience an increase in problems following divorce (Amato, Loomis, and Booth, 1995).

Parents and stepparents sometimes enter into their new family with a great deal of guilt and regret over their failed marriage. They feel sorry for their children, whom they have put through an upsetting experience. This has several effects. Usually, parents and stepparents tend to be overindulgent, are not as strict as they might otherwise be, and have more trouble guiding and controlling the children's behavior (Amato, 1987). Often, they try to buy the children's affection and cooperation. One stepfather reported:

> I would get angry at something my stepdaughter did and feel guilty afterward, so I'd take her to the store and buy her a present. One day after a similar episode, she asked, "What are you going to buy me today?" I realized she had caught on very quickly and had learned how to use my guilt to her own advantage. (Author's counseling notes)

Stepparents' roles are ill-defined (Church, 1999; Mason et al., 1998). Stepparents are neither parents nor friends. Efforts to try to be parents may be rejected by older children. Stepparents can't be mere friends; as responsible adults, they need to make a contribution to the lives of stepchildren. They are required to assume many of the responsibilities of parents, such as providing financial support and physical care, offering recreational opportunities and companionship, and going to school meetings, athletic events, and so on. Yet, in the beginning especially, they may have few of the privileges and satisfactions of parenthood. Clinicians advise stepparents to focus initially on nurturing stepchildren and developing feelings of affection before attempting to discipline. Too often, stepparents do not spend enough time building trust and friendships before they start disciplining, which typically leads to resistance and negative reactions from stepchildren (Visher and Visher, 1996).

Stepparents must attempt to deal with children who have already been socialized by another set of parents. Stepparents may not agree with the way their stepchildren were brought up, but their suddenly stepping in and trying to change things is deeply resented. Stepparents may have to gradually introduce changes. Or they may need to accept the differences in the way that children are brought up and recognize that their way is not the only "right" way (Visher and Visher, 1989).

Stepparents expect gratitude for what they do, but they may get rejection and criticism instead. They take for granted the responsibility to support and care for their own biological children but feel they are being very generous and helpful by offering the same support to stepchildren. Indeed, the move from a single-parent family to a stepfamily may result in improved financial resources, and another adult can provide emotional support for the biological parent (Zill, 1994). However, a new stepparent may be viewed by a stepchild as an intruder in and a threat to an existing close relationship with the biological parent (Hetherington and Jodl, 1994), regardless of emotional or financial support. Stepchildren may take the emotional and financial support for granted and ask for more, offering little appreciation for what is done for them. One stepfather complained, "I don't expect the world, but it would help to have a little thanks once in a while." Actually, however, both biological children and stepchildren tend to take help for granted. Stepchildren are really not that different from biological children.

Stepparents must deal with a network of complex kinship relationships: with their own biological family members, with their stepchildren, with their ex-spouse's family members, and with their new spouse's family members. Instead of two major family groups, they have four family groups to contend with.

Stepparents must cope with stepsibling feelings and relationships. Stepchildren may not be helpful to one another in coping with the strains of the divorce period. Instead, there may be stepsibling rivalry and competition for the attention of parents (Amato, 1987).

Finally, family cohesion tends to be lower in stepfamilies than in intact families (Pill, 1990). Life in stepfamilies may be chaotic and stressful during the years following remarriage. Even if life in stepfamilies settles down over time, it still remains less cohesive than in intact families as far as children are concerned (Thomson, McLanahan, and Curtin, 1992). Research has shown that stepfamilies, in comparison to first-marriage families, are less cohesive, have less clear role expectations, and are more flexible in response to change (Bray and Berger, 1993). This may be an adaptive approach that allows for more open family boundaries. Less closeness among family members and decreased bonding may promote adaptation to the unique challenges confronted by stepfamilies (Bray and Hetherington, 1993; Ganong and Coleman, 1994), such as living with different sets of parents and siblings at different times of the year.

Some of the differences in closeness between stepfamilies and first-marriage families have to do with biological relatedness. Both mothers and fathers have been found to be warmer with, more supportive of, and more involved with their biological children than with their stepchildren. Even when stepparents have a long period of time in which to become attached to their stepchildren, they remain more distant, are less warm and involved, and have less rapport with their stepchildren than parents do with their biological children in either first-marriage families or stepfamilies. In addition, children have more distant, less affectionate relationships with stepparents than with biological parents, even in long-established stepfamilies. This suggests that, although many stepparents and stepchildren have the opportunity to establish close relationships, bonding is more difficult between nonrelated parents and children (Hetherington, 1999a).

It must be emphasized, however, that although it may take time to solve problems, stepfamily relationships can become a real source of joy and satisfaction for many couples. Skills training programs for parents and stepfamilies and remarriage education programs can help people who are remarrying prepare for all the new experiences they are about to encounter (Kaplan and Hennon, 1992; Nelson and Levant, 1991).

STEPPARENT–STEPCHILD RELATIONSHIPS

Generally, biological parents see themselves as having higher quality relationships with their children than stepparents report having with their stepchildren (Fine, Voydanoff, and Donnelly, 1993). Part of the problem of living in stepfamilies is that the positive roles of stepparents are not clearly defined (Church, 1999). Instead, negative stereotypes of stepparents increase the difficulty of functioning in a positive manner (Coleman and Ganong, 1994). Fairy tales and folklore have developed the stereotype of the cruel stepmother, a myth that is hard to overcome. The stepmother role may be more difficult than that of stepfather because the mother has more responsibilities for direct care of the children (Hetherington and Stanley-Hagan, 1999; Sauer and Fine, 1988). Stepfathers appear to have more of an option to remain disengaged and participate less in child care than do biological fathers and stepmothers, as most divorced custodial fathers expect the new stepmother to participate actively in housework and in child care (Hetherington and Henderson, 1997). In general, mothers in all families assume more responsibility for household tasks and child care than fathers do, but fathers participate more actively in the care of their own children than in the care of their stepchildren (Hetherington, 1999b). Stepmothers, more often than stepfathers, experience greater difficulty in rearing their stepchildren than in rearing their biological children, regardless of whether their biological children are from a previous marriage or from the current one (MacDonald and DeMaris, 1996).

Generally, the stepparent-stepchild relationship is one of the most stressful and problematic relationships in stepfamilies (Ganong and Coleman, 1994). Because of the potential for conflict, the development of positive stepparent-stepchild relationships is one of the major tasks of remarried family life (Visher and Visher, 1996). Along with the challenges and conflicts, the relationships also introduce positive life changes, new resources, and opportunities for new fulfilling family relations that contribute to the well-being of parents and children (Hetherington and Stanley-Hagan, 1999).

Child Well-Being in Stepfamilies

In general, according to research that has compared the adjustment of children in stepfamilies to that of children in first-marriage families, children in stepfamilies tend to be less well adjusted, to exhibit more behavioral or emotional problems, to have poorer academic achievement, and to have lower social competence and social responsibility (Amato, 1994a; Anderson et al., 1999; Hetherington and Jodl, 1994; Hetherington et al., 1992; Zill, 1994). Girls from stepfamilies are at a higher risk for teenage childbearing, dropping out of school (McLanahan and Sandefur, 1994), and leaving home at an earlier age (Cherlin and Furstenberg, 1994; Hetherington, 1998), which is usually attributed to family conflict. There is a higher incidence of sexual abuse of girls in stepfamilies and a higher incidence of running away or dropping out of school for boys in stepfamilies (Bray and Kelly, 1998). Stepchildren also have more problems in relationships with their parents and siblings and with their own spouses when they are adults (Hetherington, 1997). They tend to be less satisfied with their lives; to have more adjustment problems, greater marital instability, and lower socioeconomic attainment; and to be more likely to be on welfare (Amato and Keith, 1991; Hetherington, 1998; McLanahan and Sandefur, 1994). However, it is important to understand that child adjustment and well-being in stepfamilies is related to a variety of factors (Hetherington and Stanley-Hagan, 1999).

Research has shown that, the younger the child at the time of remarriage, the more easily the child establishes an attachment to a new stepparent (Hetherington, 1993; Perry, 1995), which helps in terms of adjustment and well-being. The remarriage transition appears to be more difficult for early adolescents than for younger children, especially those who have not experienced multiple family transitions before (Perry, 1995). Relationship problems between a biological custodial parent and

Part of the problem of living in stepfamilies is that positive step-parenting roles are not clearly defined.

a child are more common when the remarriage occurs when the child is an adolescent, even in parent-child relationships that previously had been relatively close and constructive (Hetherington and Jodl, 1994). Thus, we see that adolescents are more likely to exhibit behavioral problems and deficits in social responsibility and academic competence (Hetherington et al., 1992).

Gender differences in terms of adjustment are minimal, but they do occur in children's relationships with parents and stepparents. Boys, especially preadolescent boys, are more likely to accept and to adapt more quickly to a stepparent (Brand, Clingempeel, and Bowen-Woodward, 1988), whereas adolescent girls experience greater conflict and negativity with their stepparents (Hetherington and Jodl, 1994). A close relationship with a supportive stepfather is more likely to facilitate the well-being and achievement of stepsons than that of stepdaughters (Hetherington, 1993; Zill, Morrison, and Coiro, 1993), and boys are more likely than girls to

Psychologically, if a biological parent is alive and showing interest in a child, the child will not want a new parent and will often resent any attempts to replace the biological parent.

change custody from biological mothers to fathers during adolescence (Bray and Kelly, 1998). Girls in stepfamilies exhibit more defiant, aggressive, and disruptive behavior toward both biological mothers and stepfathers, and withdrawn, avoidant, noncommunicative behavior is more common between adolescent stepdaughters and stepfathers (Hetherington, 1993). One study found that adolescent stepdaughters spoke to their stepfathers 30% less than did daughters to their biological nondivorced fathers (Vuchinich, Hetherington, Vuchinich, and Clingempeel, 1991).

The number of transitions children experience also seems to affect adjustment. Typically, children entering stepfamilies have experienced many family transitions: conflict in the previous marriage, parental separation and divorce, possible cohabitation of the custodial biological parent and future stepparent or other partners before remarriage, and

then the transition into a stepfamily. Some children also experience the remarriage of their noncustodial parent. Adolescents experiencing their custodial parent's remarriage usually encounter a number of concurrent life transitions, such as moving to a new home, starting a new school, or adjusting to a new sibling. While most adolescents do not perceive these events as negative (Anderson et al., 1999), they are often difficult adjustments. In a longitudinal study of adolescents from divorced families, the cumulative impact of multiple transitions was evident: The lowest levels of adolescent social competence were observed in children who experienced the most family transitions. Thus, the number of family transitions clearly matters for adolescent social competence (Anderson et al., 1999).

Also, research points to a positive relationship between perceived marital quality and the perceived quality of the stepparent-stepchild relationship (Fine and Kurdek, 1995), which affects overall stepchild well-being. Most studies have found that a harmonious, satisfying marital relationship is associated with competent parenting and more positive relations between children and parents (Bray, 1999; Hetherington and Jodl, 1994). However, exceptions to this pattern have been found in stepfamilies with preadolescent girls. Resistance and negativity toward stepfathers are often exhibited by preadolescent girls, particularly early in the remarriage if the parents are happy together (Hetherington, 1993). This difference could be related to the onset of puberty and sexual concerns in early adolescence, and resistance toward stepfathers and a happy marriage may be perceived by both the adolescent and parents as a protective buffer against inappropriate intimacy between stepfathers and stepdaughters (Hetherington and Jodl, 1994). Biologically related fathers and daughters also have difficulty dealing with affection, especially physical affection, as the daughter becomes sexually mature. But these tensions and concerns about appropriate expression may be even more intense with nonbiologically related stepdaughters and stepfathers (Hetherington and Stanley-Hagan, 1999).

Another common explanation for why children in stepfamilies show more behavioral problems is related to a change in parenting styles. Research on parenting often shows the benefits to children's well-being of an authoritative parenting style (high levels of warmth and responsiveness, effective monitoring and control of children's behavior, enforcement of rules, low levels of manipulation and conflict). In stepfamilies, such parenting-related processes often become disrupted, particularly during the period of adjustment to a remarriage. Many studies, in fact, find temporary increases in conflicts and overall negativity between children and parents during the first year of adjustment to remarriage (Anderson et al., 1999).

While children in stepfamilies experience higher rates of negative outcomes than children in biological families (Crosbie-Burnett and Giles-Sims, 1994), many children get along very well with their stepparents. Communication with stepparents is the key and is an important predictor of well-being in children in stepfamilies (Collins, Newman, and McKenry, 1995). In fact, most stepchildren view their stepparents positively, although usually not as positively as children view their biological parents (Hetherington and Jodl, 1994).

It is important to remember that, while stepchildren may show more behavioral problems, they are not suffering from a mental or behavioral disorder (Bray, 1999). Studies have found that 70–80% of children in stepfamilies function in the nonclinical range (not suffering from mental or behavioral disorders) and only 20–30% in the clinical range (suffering from such disorders) (Bray, 1999). In contrast, 85–90% of children in nondivorced families function in the nonclinical range. Although statistically the risk is double, most children in stepfamilies seem to function normally (Bray, 1999). And while problems may reemerge or develop in late adolescence and adulthood, the percentage of children who experience severe, lasting problems is relatively small (Hetherington and Stanley-Hagan, 1999). Thus, most children in divorced families and stepfamilies do not develop behavioral problems, are quite resilient through all the transitions, and become competent and well-adjusted individuals (Emery and Forehand, 1996). Also, many studies do not consider length of time in a family when comparing children of first-married families and stepfamilies. Studies often compare long-established nondivorced families to stepfamilies in early stages of family formation, with negative conclusions drawn about stepfamilies (Hetherington and Clingempeel, 1992).

Most family scholars who study divorce and remarriage today conclude that what happens inside a family is more important than family type or structure in influencing children's adjustment (Amato, 1994a; Avenevoli, Sessa, and Steinberg, 1999; Demo and Acock, 1996a; Zill, 1994). Children appear to be at greater risk for behavioral problems when they grow up in highly conflictual first marriages, more so than in well-functioning, supportive single-parent or remarried families (Amato, 1993). Children, regardless of the family structure (nondivorced nuclear families, single-parent families, stepfamilies), exhibit greater well-being, achievement, socially responsible behavior, and social competence and fewer behavior problems when they are raised in a loving, harmonious, supportive family environment (Anderson et al., 1999; Hetherington, 1999b; Hetherington and Stanley-Hagan, 1999).

Facilitating Bonds Between Stepparents and Stepchildren

Most stepparents want to get along with their stepchildren, but, as stated previously, this relationship can be difficult and problematic. Recent research has examined the challenges faced by stepparents in developing bonds with stepchildren, and some common styles and strategies have emerged.

One study revealed three common patterns of behavior among stepparents in forming a relationship with their stepchild: (1) nonseekers of affinity with children, (2) early affinity seekers, and (3) continuous affinity seekers (Ganong, Coleman, Fine, and Martin, 1999). Affinity-seeking strategies are intentional actions by people who are trying to get other people to like them or feel positive toward them (Ganong et al., 1999). Nonseekers were not mean or neglectful, but they mainly interacted with the children in order to become closer to the parent, not to win the children's affection. They did very little or nothing intentionally to get their stepchildren to like them and usually did not think a lot about this. Early seekers pursued a relationship with the children prior to living with them. Although they sought to bond with the children, they had other motivations, such as getting the children to respond to their discipline as they filled a new role of replacement parent. These stepparents stopped seeking affinity soon after they began living with the stepchildren. Continuous affinity seekers actively pursued the children's affection early in the relationship and continued to do so after the remarriage. They deliberately tried to get their stepchildren to like them and purposefully engaged in activities that stepchildren liked to do. Stepparents who were affinity seekers also described themselves as liking children in general. None of the nonseekers described themselves in this way. Stepparents who were continuous affinity seekers had the strongest bonds with their stepchildren because it was important to them to continue working on the relationship after becoming a stepfamily (Ganong et al., 1999).

Certain characteristics of both stepparents and stepchildren have been found to contribute to the development of a close relationship. Personality appears to be an important characteristic of successful stepparents. Stepparents who are successful at establishing a close relationship with their stepchildren tend to be more "laid back" and less eager to establish control or fill a role as a disciplinarian. Although they make attempts to become friends with their stepchildren, they have less need to be in control of the relationship and do not need to have a friendship develop immediately (Ganong et al., 1999). Overall, the friendship style of stepparenting seems to be the most successful in facilitating bonding with stepchildren (Erera-Weatherley, 1996). As for stepchildren, those who have something in common with their stepparent and those who want the stepparent to function as a parent experience a stronger bond with the stepparent. Stepchildren who think the stepparent had something to do with their parents' separating and remaining separated typically reject the stepparent's attempts at bonding (Ganong et al., 1999).

Common activities stepparents use to get their stepchildren to like them include doing fun things as a family, going on family outings, playing games, nonverbally expressing feelings, spending money on things the stepchildren want, and spending time talking together. Although stepchildren may have fun doing things as a family, group activities do not necessarily offer many opportunities for stepparents and stepchildren to interact directly with each other. One-on-one activities, such as playing board games, going fishing, and having conversations between just the stepparent and stepchild, appear to be the most effective means for bonding (Ganong et al., 1999).

Cohabiting with a New Partner

One of the issues that many divorced people face is whether to live together with a new partner before remarriage. If either partner has children, the effects on them need to be considered. Isaacs and Leon (1988b) studied the adjustment of children of divorced mothers under four different circumstances: (1) The mother remarried, (2) she lived with a partner but was not remarried, (3) she was seriously involved but not living with a partner, and (4) she was not seriously involved. The children whose mothers were not remarried but were living with their new partner had substantially more behavioral problems than did any of the other groups. The most well-adjusted group was children whose mothers were not involved, followed by those whose mothers had remarried. This suggests that divorced parents should take children into consideration when deciding the degree of commitment and the living arrangement.

Coparents and Parenting Coalitions

An ideal for cooperative postdivorce parenting is coparenting by divorced parents and a parenting coalition when there are more than two parenting adults after remarriage (Visher and Visher, 1989). In **coparenting,** the two divorced parents cooperate rather than compete in the task of raising their children. In a **parenting coalition,** the biological parents (now divorced and remarried) plus the stepparents cooperate in rearing their own children and any stepchildren. The children have contact with both of their parents and with their stepparents.

There are a number of advantages to these kinds of cooperative parenting. The children's needs, as well as the needs of adults, can be met more adequately than if there is continued antagonism between adults. The children are not caught in a web of hostility, and their chances of becoming messengers between two households are greatly reduced, as is their fear of losing a parent. The power struggles between households are lessened as well. The children's self-esteem is enhanced, so they are easier to be with. Not only that, but the parents' responsibilities are lessened since the task of rearing the children is shared.

Frequently, adults are not aware of the pain they are causing their children by their hostile behavior.

For many decades, the primary model for "normal" family life was the nuclear family: two "natural" parents and their children. This model is no longer the normative structure in our society. Remarried families are quickly becoming the dominant family structure, raising many new questions for today's families. Following are 10 major issues described by Walsh (1992):

1. **Labels for the new parent.** The problem of what to call "the woman who is married to daddy" or "my partner's children" remains unresolved.

2. **Affection for the new parent and the absent parent.** Expressing love for the new stepparent seems to be intimately involved with feelings of loyalty or allegiance. It is not uncommon for children to believe that to love anyone else as one's mother or father means being disloyal to one's natural parent. Children in reconstituted families believe, and often rightfully so, that their noncustodial biological parent will be angry or hurt if they express affection for the stepparent. This divided loyalty is frequently a source of stress.

3. **Loss of a natural parent.** The loss of a parent usually triggers a grief reaction, whether the loss is due to death, desertion, or divorce. Stepfamily members may mourn the loss of their primary family, and working through their grief is a prelude to creating a successful reconstituted family.

4. **Instant love of new family members.** Because two adults love each other and choose to marry is no guarantee that they will love each other's children or that the children will love them. Yet this expectation is the source of considerable stress in reconstituted families.

5. **Fantasy about re-creating the primary family.** Children of divorced parents are disappointed when the fantasy of parental reconciliation is not realized. These fantasies are common and may be present even when the divorce occurred years before.

6. **Discipline by the stepparent.** Conflicts over discipline and child rearing rank first on the list of problems in remarriage. However, discipline works only when the person receiving it cares about the reactions of and the relationship with the person who disciplines. Establishing a good relationship with the stepchildren is a prerequisite to being able to positively influence their behavior.

7. **Confusion over family roles.** Confusion over role assignment in reconstituted families is common. Socialized to be in charge, men may find themselves in the awkward position of enforcing discipline when they have no apparent authority. Socialized to fulfill the needs of others, women often try to take on the burdens of the entire family. Feeling that they have little voice in decision making while being forced to discipline, stepmothers have expressed frustration with their ambivalent roles.

8. **Sibling conflict.** Sibling rivalries are typical in any family. In stepfamilies, rivalries may be a major source of dispute, especially if they remain unresolved.

9. **Competition for time and attention.** Increased competition for the attention of the custodial parent by all of the children can lead to disciplinary problems. The children may be jealous of the stepparent when they see him or her as a rival for the attention of their natural parent. The greater the amount of contact between the nonresidential parent and the child, the less disruption in their relationship, which decreases stress in the remarriage family.

10. **Sexual conflicts.** One of the most difficult issues for reconstituted family members is sexuality. Sexual boundaries in remarriage families are less clear-cut than in biological families.

If they decide to control the anger, the children benefit from the new atmosphere of cooperation (Visher and Visher, 1989). However, despite evidence that a positive relationship is beneficial for children's adjustment and well-being, most ex-spouses do not get along well, which results in many nonresidential fathers eventually withdrawing and having limited or no contact with their children (Hetherington and Jodl, 1994). In contrast to fathers, nonresidential mothers are almost twice as likely to remain in contact with their children following divorce, and stepmothers and biological mothers are more likely to get into competitive relationships that lead to loyalty conflicts in children (Hetherington and Jodl, 1994). It is important to remember that mothers have been referred to as the gatekeepers to relationships of other people with their children. This is especially noticeable in children's relations with both noncustodial fathers and stepfathers (Hetherington and Stanley-Hagan, 1999).

In a stepfamily, instead of obtaining one new brother or sister at a time, a child may get several at once. The child may also be confronted with the parent's having to share attention with stepsiblings.

STEPSIBLING RELATIONSHIPS

Sibling relationships in stepfamilies that are warm and supportive are associated with greater social competence and responsibility in children, whereas sibling rivalry and aggression are associated with antisocial behavior (Hetherington and Jodl, 1994). The term **sibling rivalry** refers to the competition of brothers and sisters for the attention, approval, and affection of parents. The problem arises because of envy and fear that one brother or sister is receiving more physical or emotional care and benefits from parents.

Sibling rivalry is often exaggerated in the stepfamily. Instead of obtaining one new brother or sister, a child may get several all at once. And the stepsiblings may not be helpless infants, but children of similar or older ages who can be very demanding of the child's own parent. From the children's point of view, a tendency to be jealous is quite understandable. The children may have become used to living with one parent and to seeking out that parent for help, comfort, and advice. Then they are confronted with their parent's turning his or her attention to a new spouse and stepchildren. Stepsiblings may also be forced to share living quarters, and even their own bedroom, as well as all other spaces such as bathrooms and playrooms. They may find their toys broken, their things messed up, their clothes borrowed, and so on. However, on average, relationships among stepsiblings are less contentious than among biologically related siblings, particularly in adolescence. This may be due to ambiguity in the stepsibling role and to the lack of connection and involvement among many stepsiblings. It is also possible that children can more easily understand that a different relationship exists with their siblings based on biological relatedness of parent and child (Hetherington and Stanley-Hagan, 1999).

About half of all women who remarry give birth in their second marriage (Wineberg, 1990). Sibling rivalry in the blended family becomes more complex than in the biological family. Biological parents may have a tendency to show preferential treatment, either favoring their own offspring or overcompensating for the absence of biological ties and favoring their stepchildren (Hobart, 1987).

The initial reactions of stepsiblings or future stepsiblings to one another are not always indicative of the degree of problems in the future. Children who seem suspicious and distant from one another at first can grow into loyal and trusting friends. Stepsiblings have been known to become very proud of one another. Younger children often idolize older stepsiblings, who may become very protective of younger stepsiblings. Learning to share with one another and to live with others who have not been part of one's immediate family is a broadening, enriching experience and helps children, who otherwise tend to be egocentric and selfish, to share and to be tolerant of others. It is easier to build positive relationships when the children are young. Generally, younger children are more trusting and accepting than older children and more flexible in making adjustments. Also, families with harmonious relationships between the spouses show less sibling rivalry than do families in which the marriage is troubled, indicating the effect of the total marriage on the children in the family.

Some couples who have children of their own report that having a baby improves stepsibling relationships. One study reported that the birth of a new sibling in stepfamilies was universally positive, with none of the children in the sample rating it as negative (Anderson et al., 1999). The new baby can serve as a bond between the two groups of children. It gives them something in common and something to care for besides themselves and can unite them around a mutual interest.

SUMMARY

1. Marrying more than once has become quite common. The majority of divorced people also have children; when they remarry, new stepfamilies are created.

2. Remarried families may have one or two remarried spouses, each with or without children. Family relationships and integration become quite complicated and difficult in reconstituted families.

3. The probability of divorce is slightly greater in remarriages than in first marriages, but successful remarrieds state that their new marriage is better than their first marriage. Overall, research indicates few differences in marital satisfaction between first marriages and remarriages.

4. Remarriage introduces some complexity not present in first marriage. The biggest challenge is children. Relationships with ex-spouses and stepsiblings can also pose problems.

5. Courtship and mate selection in remarriage are different from those in first marriage. The couple is older. The majority of remarrieds have children. Ex-spouses and family members may become involved in the courtship of the couple. Some people want to marry someone like their ex-spouse, or they try to pressure their new mate to be like the former one.

6. Couples carry expectations from one marriage to another. One expectation is that being married to a second spouse is going to be similar in some ways to marriage to the first spouse. One result is that spouses replicate the mistakes of their first marriage in remarriage or have real apprehension that the problems and hurts that they experienced before will happen again. This fear makes them oversensitive and reminds them of the difficulties they had before.

7. Another challenge may arise because of confusion over role expectations and enactment. A person may desire a spouse to play a role similar to or completely different from the one played by a former spouse.

8. Financial problems may emerge in remarriage because of the necessity of supporting both the new family and the children from the previous family.

9. Some remarrieds pool all of their resources in a "common pot," distributing them according to each individual family member's needs. Other remarrieds use a "two-pot" system in which each partner contributes a specific amount to the ongoing maintenance of the household, with the children supported by their biological parents.

10. Individuals who divorce typically have to develop a new relationship with the former

spouse when children are involved. This new relationship is often a difficult one, particularly in the early stages of divorce, as ex-spouses deal with feelings of ambivalence, anger, attachment, and remorse, as well as sometimes viciously fighting and passionately reconciling. In general, relationships between ex-spouses seem to reach a low level of intensity after a number of years, with most remarried individuals not feeling a need to maintain a close relationship with the former spouse.

11. In the short term, there is less conflict in remarriages than in first marriages, but conflict increases as new problems arise.

12. In successful remarriages, spouses give themselves time to know each other well, resist the many pressures to remarry before they are ready, discuss every aspect of their relationship before marriage, have learned from past mistakes, and put their marriage first.

13. Many couples expect stepfamily relationships to be like those of primary families. Many are disappointed, because stepfamily and primary family relationships are not the same.

14. Part of the problem of living in a stepfamily is that positive roles of stepparents are not clearly defined.

15. Most family scholars who study divorce and remarriage today conclude that what happens inside a family is more important than family type or structure in influencing children's adjustment. Children, regardless of the family structure, exhibit greater well-being, higher achievement, more socially responsible behavior and social competence, and fewer behavioral problems when they are raised in a loving, harmonious, supportive family environment.

16. Overall, the friendship style of stepparenting seems to be the most successful in facilitating bonding with stepchildren.

17. Children whose mothers cohabit with their new partner before marriage have more behavior problems than those whose mothers are not living with a boyfriend, whose mothers are remarried, or whose mothers are not involved in a relationship.

18. Stepchildren are all individuals. They can't all be treated alike any more than can all biological children or stepparents be treated alike.

19. Coparenting by divorced parents involves cooperating in the task of raising the children. A parenting coalition involves the biological parents and the stepparents in raising their own children and any stepchildren. Coparenting and parenting coalitions after divorce are advantageous to children and parents alike.

20. Sibling rivalry refers to the competition of siblings for the attention, approval, and affection of parents. The situation is often aggravated in the stepfamily.

21. Couples can be encouraged by the fact that the initial reactions of stepsiblings or future stepsiblings to one another are not always indicative of the degree of problems in the future. Many become very close and loyal friends. Couples report that having a baby of their own improves stepsibling relationships, although it can also lead to sibling rivalry.

KEY TERMS

coparenting   parenting coalitions   sibling rivalry

QUESTIONS FOR THOUGHT

1. If you were divorced at age 30 with two school-age children in your custody, would you want to remarry? Why or why not? If you did remarry, what are some of the problems you would be most likely to encounter? If you did not remarry, what are some of the problems you would be most likely to encounter?

2. What do you believe would be the differences between being a parent and being a step-parent as far as relationships with children are concerned?

3. If you divorced, what sorts of things would you try to do that would be in the best interests of your children?

4. If you divorced and wanted to remarry, what would you do to ensure that your remarriage was successful?

SUGGESTED READINGS

Booth, A., and Dunn, J. (Eds.). (1994). *Stepfamilies: Who Benefits? Who Does Not?* Hillsdale, NJ: Lawrence Erlbaum Associates. Compiles papers presented at the National Symposium on Stepfamilies in 1993 at Pennsylvania State University.

Bray, J. H., and Kelly, J. (1999). *Stepfamilies: Love, Marriage, and Parenting in the First Decade.* New York: Broadway Books. Gives guidelines for problem solving in stepfamilies.

Depner, C. E., and Bray, J. H. (Eds.). (1993). *Nonresidential Parenting: New Vistas in Family Living.* Newbury Park, CA: Sage. Gives an overview of noncustodial parenting.

Ganong, L. H., and Coleman, M. (1994). *Remarried Family Relationships.* Thousand Oaks, CA: Sage. Focuses on couple and parent-child relationships.

Kelley, P. (1995). *Developing Healthy Stepfamilies: Twenty Families Tell Their Story.* New York: Hayworth. Examines health and strength in stepfamilies.

Kirkness Norwood, P., and Wingender, T. (1999). *The Enlightened Stepmother: Revolutionizing the Role.* New York: Morrow/Avon. Helps individuals prepare for the role for which most women are overwhelmingly unprepared.

Pasley, K., and Ihinger-Tallman, M. (Eds.). (1994). *Stepparenting: Issues and Theories, Research, and Practice.* Westport, CT: Greenwood Press. Covers a broad range of topics.

Shomberg, E. F. (1999). *Blending Families: A Guide for Parents, Step-Families, Step-Grandparents and Everyone Building a Successful New Family.* New York: Berkely Publishing Group. Focuses on the complexity of intergenerational stepfamilies.

Thoele, S. P. (1999). *Courage to Be a Stepmom: Finding Your Place Without Losing Yourself.* Berkeley, CA: Wildcat Canyon Press. Addresses the emotions felt by stepmothers and offers suggestions for meeting individuals' needs while building relationships with stepchildren.

Glossary

abortion The expulsion of the fetus. Can be either spontaneous or induced.

abruptio placentae The premature separation of the placenta from the uterine wall.

affective sensitivity Empathy, or the ability to identify with the feelings, thoughts, and attitudes of another person.

affinity A relationship formed by marriage without ties of blood.

altruistic love Unselfish concern for the welfare of another.

androgyny A blending of male and female characteristics and roles; especially, a lack of gender-typing with respect to roles.

Apgar score A widely used system to evaluate the physical condition of the newborn, named after the originator, Virginia Apgar.

artificial insemination Injection of sperm cells into the woman's vagina or uterus for the purpose of inducing pregnancy.

attachment theory Theory suggesting that early interactions with parents lead to the formation of attachments that reflect children's perceptions of their own self-worth and their expectations about intimate relationships.

autonomy The need of people to assert their independence and self-will.

avoidance Method of dealing with conflict by avoiding the people, situations, and issues that stimulate it.

bag of water (amniotic sac) Sac containing the fluid in which the fetus is suspended.

balanced couples Couples in which partners have some disagreements but are generally satisfied with both internal and external couple issues.

bargaining The process by which two parties decide what each shall give and receive in arriving at a decision.

barrios Residential ghettos in urban areas in which some Hispanics live.

bilateral descent Inheritance is passed through both the male and the female line.

binuclear family A new family formed by the marriage of two persons, at least one of whom has been married before.

blastocyst The mass of cells 3–4 days after fertilization takes place that grows into an embryo.

blended, or reconstituted, family A family formed when a widowed or divorced person, with or without children, marries another person who may or may not have been married before and who may or may not have children.

B-love Term used by Maslow for being-love, which is love for the very being and uniqueness of another person.

body language Posture, facial expression, still or tense muscles, blushing, panting, tears, sweating, shivering, increased pulse rate, thumping heart, and other bodily reactions that convey feelings and reactions.

bonding Development of emotional attachment between the mother and newborn immediately after birth.

breech birth When the buttocks or feet are the first part of the baby to pass through the vagina.

bundling A courting practice in colonial America that allowed a couple to share a bed without undressing.

castration Removal of the testicles.

catharsis Venting negative emotions to rid oneself of them so that they can be replaced by more positive ones.

cervical cap A small, rubber, thimble-shaped barrier that fits over the cervix and prevents the sperm from entering the uterus.

cesarean section Removal of the fetus by incising the abdominal and uterine wall.

child abuse May include not only physical assaults on a child but also malnourishment, abandonment, neglect, emotional abuse, and sexual abuse.

chlamydia A family of infections caused by a bacterium leading to nongonococcal urethritis and epididymitis in men, and cervical infections and pelvic inflammatory disease (PID) in women.

coercive power The threat of physical force or other types of punishment to force compliance.

cognition Literally, the act of knowing; the act of becoming acquainted with the world and the objects, people, and conditions in it.

cognitive developmental theory A theory suggesting that gender roles and identities cannot be learned until children reach a certain stage of intellectual development.

cohabiting family Two people of the opposite sex living together and having sex, who are committed to their relationship without formal legal marriage.

cohort A group of people born during the same period of time.

coitus interruptus Withdrawal of the penis from the vagina prior to ejaculation; used as an attempt at birth control.

combination pills Oral contraceptives containing estrogen and progestin.

common-law marriage A marriage by mutual consent, without a license, recognized as legal under certain conditions by some states.

communication A message one person sends and another receives.

compadres/comadres Mexican American godparents.

companionate love A low-key emotion with feelings of affection and deep attachment.

compatibility The capability of living together in harmony.

conciliation counseling Marriage counseling ordered by the court in which spouses try to decide whether they want to dissolve their marriage or agree to try to solve their problems.

condom A rubber sheath worn over the penis to prevent sperm from being ejaculated into the vagina; also prevents venereal disease.

conflicted couples Couples in which the partners are constantly fighting.

conflict theory A theory that family conflict is normal and that the task is not to eliminate conflict but to learn to control it so that it becomes constructive.

conjoint therapy Therapy with both partners present.

consanguinity The state of being related by blood; having descent from a common ancestor.

conscious love Rational, reasoning love.

constructive arguments Arguments that stick with the issues, that attack the problem and not the other person, that employ rational methods, and that result in greater understanding, consensus, compromise, and closeness between two people.

consummate love A term used by Sternberg to describe love as a combination of intimacy, passion, and commitment.

corporal punishment Physical or bodily punishment with the intention of inflicting pain.

crisis A drastic change in the course of events; a turning point that affects future events.

crisis overload A series of crises occurring one after another until they become more than a person can handle.

culture The sum total of ways of living, including the values, beliefs, aesthetic standards, linguistic expressions, patterns of thinking, behavioral norms, and styles of communication a group of people has developed to ensure its survival in a particular physical and human environment.

cunnilingus Stimulation of the female genitals with the mouth.

custody A term that refers to both legal custody (the parent's right to make decisions regarding the welfare of the child) and physical custody (the parent's right to have the child living with him or her).

date rape Forcing involuntary sexual compliance on a person while on a date.

dating A courting practice in which two people meet in order to get to know each other better and participate in activities together.

dependent love Love that develops for someone who fulfills one's needs.

desire stage The first stage of the human sexual response cycle according to Kaplan.

destructive arguments Arguments that attack the other person rather than the problem; that increase resentment and hostility and undermine trust, friendship, and affectionate feelings; that result in greater alienation; and that do not solve the problem.

developmental tasks Growth responsibilities that arise at various stages of life.

devitalized couples Couples in which the partners once had a satisfying relationship but who have since become unhappy with all aspects of the marriage.

diaphragm A thick, dome-shaped latex cap that is stretched over a collapsible metal ring, designed to cover the cervical opening to prevent sperm from entering the uterus.

digital foreplay Stimulation of the sexual organs with the fingers.

discipline A means by which socialization takes place; the process of instruction in proper conduct or action.

D-love Term used by Maslow for deficiency-love, which develops when another person meets one's needs.

dopamine A neurotransmitter that functions in the parts of the brain that control emotions and bodily movement.

double-bind communication Conflicting messages sent when verbal messages and body language don't agree.

douching Squirting liquid containing vinegar or another substance into the vagina; sometimes used to try to wash out sperm after intercourse.

dual-career family Also called dual-professional family; a subtype of the dual-earner family in which there are two career-committed partners, both of whom are trying to fulfill professional roles that require continuous development.

dual-earner family A family in which both partners are in the paid labor force.

dyspareunia Painful intercourse.

ectopic pregnancy Attachment of the blastocyst and growth of the embryo in any location other than inside the uterus.

ego resiliency The generalized capacity for flexible and resourceful adaptation to stressors.

ejaculatory inhibition Inability of the male to reach a climax.

embryo transplant The process of removing an embryo from the uterus of a donor and implanting it into the uterus of another woman.

emergency contraceptives Oral contraceptives taken after intercourse to prevent unwanted pregnancy.

endorphins Chemical neurotransmitters that have a sedative effect on the body.

equity theory A subcategory of exchange theory holding that people seek a fair and balanced exchange in which the partners can mutually give and take what is needed.

erectile dysfunction Inability of the male to maintain an erection so that coitus can take place.

erection Swelling and firming of the sexual organs when they are stimulated.

erogenous zones Sexually sensitive regions of the body.

erotic love Sexual, sensuous love.

ethnicity The way people define themselves as part of a group through similarities in ancestry and cultural heritage.

evolutionary theories of gender Theories suggesting that genetic heritage is more important than social learning in the development of gender roles.

exchange theory The theory that people choose relationships in which they can maximize their benefits and minimize their costs.

excitement phase The initial phase in the human sexual response cycle according to Masters and Johnson, and the second phase according to Kaplan.

expert power Power that is given because a person is considered superior in knowledge of a particular subject.

expressive role The role of the family in meeting the emotional and social needs of family members.

extended family An individual, possibly a mate, any children, and other relatives who live in the household.

extradyadic sexual activity Sexual activity outside the dyadic, or couple, relationship.

familism Emphasis on the needs of the family above those of the individual.

family Any group of people united by ties of marriage, blood, or adoption, or any sexually expressive relationship, in which (1) the people are committed to one another in an intimate, interpersonal relationship, (2) the members see their individual identities as importantly attached to the group, and (3) the group has an identity of its own.

family developmental theory A theory that divides the family life cycle into phases, or stages, over the life span and emphasizes the developmental tasks that need to be accomplished by family members at each stage.

family life cycle The phases, or stages, of the family life span, each of which is characterized by changes in family structure, composition, and functions.

family of origin The family into which you are born and in which you are raised.

family of procreation The family you establish when you have children of your own.

family planning Having children by choice and not by chance; having the number of children wanted at the time planned.

family violence Any illegitimate use of physical force or aggression or verbal abuse by one family member toward another.

feedback Response to the message another has sent and disclosure of one's own feelings and ideas.

fellatio Stimulation of the male genitals with the mouth.

femininity Personality and behavioral characteristics of a female according to culturally defined standards of femaleness.

feminist theory Theory or perspective that focuses on male dominance in families and society and examines how gender differences are related to power differentials between men and women.

feminization of poverty The trend toward increasing proportions of women, regardless of ethnicity or age, living in poverty.

filtering process A process by which mates are sorted by filtering out ineligibles according to various standards.

financially focused couples Couples in which the partners are involved in only one aspect of the marriage: money management.

flextime A company policy that allows employees to choose the most convenient hours for them to work during the day, selected from hours designated by the employer.

friendship love A love based on common concerns and interests, companionship, and respect for the partner's personality and character.

gamete intrafallopian transfer (GIFT) The process of inserting sperm cells and an egg cell directly into the fallopian tube, where fertilization is expected to occur.

gaslighting The process by which one person destroys the self-confidence, perception, and sense of reality of another person.

gay or lesbian family Two people of the same sex living together, having sex, and being mutually committed.

gender The psychosocial components that characterize one as masculine or feminine.

gender identity A person's personal, internal sense of maleness or femaleness, which is expressed in personality and behavior.

gender role The outward manifestation and expression of maleness or femaleness in a social setting.

gender-role congruence Agreement between partners' gender-role expectations and their performance.

gender schema theory A theory suggesting that people have very definite ideas about how males and females should look and behave, based on the framework of logic and ideas used to organize information and make sense of it.

gender stereotypes Assumed differences, norms, attitudes, and expectations about men and women.

generational transmission The process by which one generation passes knowledge, values, attitudes, roles, and habits on to the next generation.

gonorrhea A sexually transmitted disease caused by the gonococcus bacterium.

harmonious couples Couples in which the partners have an intimate relationship and get along well together.

HCG (human chorionic gonadotropin) A hormone produced by the placenta that, if present in the mother's urine, is an indication of pregnancy.

hepatitis B An infectious disease of the liver.

herpes simplex A sexually transmitted disease caused by a virus.

heterogamy The selection of a partner who is different from oneself.

heterologous insemination (AID) Artificial insemination by using the sperm of a donor.

HIV/AIDS Acquired immune deficiency syndrome; a sexually transmitted disease caused by the human immunodeficiency virus and characterized by irreversible damage to the body's immune system and, eventually, death.

homogamy The selection of a partner similar to oneself.

homologous insemination (AIH) Artificial insemination by using the sperm of the man.

human papillomavirus (HPV) (genital warts) A sexually transmitted disease that causes genital warts to appear.

hypergamous union Marriage in which the woman marries upward on the social ladder.

hypoactive sexual desire disorder Sexual arousal and self-initiated sexual activity less frequent than once every 2 weeks, or the absence or marked decrease in frequency of sexual fantasy.

hypogamous union Marriage in which the woman marries beneath herself on the social ladder.

ideal mate theory A theory that people tend to marry someone who fulfills their fantasy of what an ideal mate should be like, based partly on early childhood experiences.

imaging The process of playacting to present oneself in the best possible manner.

implementation power Power that sets decisions in motion.

incest Sexual activity between two people who are closely related.

informational power Power acquired because of extensive knowledge of a specific area.

instrumental role The role of the family in meeting the needs of society or the physical needs of family members.

intergenerational stake Refers to family members' perceptions of closeness, especially as they relate to life course concerns that characterize each generation.

interpersonal sources of conflict Those tensions that occur in the relationships between people.

in vitro fertilization (IVF) Removing the egg cell from the mother, fertilizing it with the partner's sperm in the laboratory, and then implanting the fertilized egg in the uterine wall.

involuntary manslaughter The unintentional killing of another human being, such as while driving an automobile.

involuntary stable (permanent) singles Never-marrieds and previously marrieds who wanted to marry, who have not found a mate, and who have more or less accepted being single.

involuntary temporary singles Never-marrieds and previously marrieds who have actively been seeking a mate but have not found one.

IUD Intrauterine device; a device that is inserted into the uterus and worn there as a means of preventing pregnancy.

joint companionship Relationship in which a couple shares interests and activities.

joint legal custody Custody shared by both parents, both of whom are responsible for child rearing and for making decisions regarding the child.

labor Rhythmic muscular contractions of the uterus that expel the baby.

Lamaze method A popular childbirth training and delivery method in which the woman comes to be in control of the childbirth experience by getting in good physical shape, learning controlled breathing and muscle relaxation techniques, and receiving emotional support from her partner.

laparoscopy Procedure whereby a tubular instrument is passed through the abdominal wall and the fallopian tubes are severed and/or closed as a sterilization technique.

latchkey children Unsupervised children who care for themselves before or after school, on weekends, or during holidays while their parents work. They commonly carry keys to let themselves in the house or apartment.

legitimate power Power that is bestowed by society on men and women as their right according to social prescription.

limerence A term used by Tennov to describe the intense, wildly emotional highs and lows of being in love.

living-dying interval The period of time between the knowledge of the imminence of death and death itself.

lubrication Inner secretions from the vaginal walls in the female or from the Cowper's glands in the male.

machismo Spanish for "manhood"; masculinity.

marital adjustment The process of modifying, adapting, and altering individual and couple patterns of behavior and interaction to achieve maximum satisfaction in the relationship.

marital adjustment tasks Areas of concern in marriage in which adjustments need to be made.

marriage gradient Differences in age, social status, class, education, and financial assets between the spouses.

masculinity Personality and behavioral characteristics of a male according to culturally defined standards of maleness.

matriarchal family A family in which the mother is head of the household with authority over other family members.

matrilineal descent Inheritance that is traced through the female line.

matrilocal residence A residential pattern in which newlyweds reside with or near the woman's family.

minipill An oral contraceptive containing progestin only.

myotonia Involuntary contractions of muscles.

Naegele's formula A method of calculating the expected date of birth by subtracting 3 months from the first day of the last period and adding 7 days.

narcissistic love Love of self; selfish, self-centered love.

needs theories Theories of mate selection proposing that we select partners who will fulfill our own needs—both complementary and instrumental.

negative affect reciprocity A pattern of communication in unhappy couples whereby partners respond negatively to each other's statements.

negative identification The effort on the part of the child not to be like the parent.

neolocal residence A residential pattern in which newlyweds leave their parents' home and reside in a new location of their choice rather than with either family.

nocturnal emissions Male ejaculation during sleep.

no-fault divorce A legal approach that eliminates fault as a precondition for access to courts and recognizes the right of individuals to petition for divorce on the grounds of irretrievable breakdown of the marriage or irreconcilable differences.

noncontingent reinforcement Unconditional approval of another person.

norepinephrine A hormone secreted by the adrenal glands that has a stimulating effect on blood pressure.

norms Expectations for behavior as one performs social roles.

nuclear family A father, a mother, and their children.

observational modeling The process by which children observe, imitate, and model the behavior of others around them.

open adoption A system of adoption in which the birth mother is permitted to meet and play an active role in selecting the adoptive parents and to maintain some form of contact with her child depending on the agreement reached.

oral contraceptives Contraceptive pills taken orally.

orchestration power The power to make the important decisions that determine family life-style.

orgasm The sudden discharge of neuromuscular tension at the peak of sexual arousal.

orgasm dysfunction The inability of the woman to reach a sexual climax.

orgasm phase According to Masters and Johnson, the third phase in the human sexual response cycle, in which there is a sudden discharge of neuromuscular tension.

ovum transfer The process of artificially inseminating a volunteer female with sperm from an infertile woman's partner and removing the zygote after 5 days and transplanting it to the mother-to-be, who carries the child during pregnancy.

parallel companionship When people do things in each other's company and engage in parallel activities.

parental identification and modeling The process by which the child adopts and internalizes parental values.

parent image theory A theory of mate selection that a person is likely to marry someone resembling his or her parent of the opposite sex.

patriarchal family A family in which the father is head of the household with authority over other family members.

patrilineal descent Inheritance that is traced through the male line.

patrilocal residence A residential pattern in which a newlywed couple resides with or near the man's family.

pedophilia A sexual perversion in which a person's primary or exclusive method of achieving sexual arousal is by fantasizing about or engaging in sexual activity with prepubertal children.

personal role redefinition Reduction of the standards of role performance as a means of reducing conflict.

personal sources of conflict Those that originate within the individual when inner drives, instincts, and values pull against one another.

pheromones Hormonal secretions of the body with an odor that is supposed to be sexually arousing.

physical sources of conflict Inner tensions having a physical origin, such as fatigue, hunger, or a headache.

placebo A pill having no pharmacological effect.

placenta previa The placenta growing partly or all the way over the opening to the cervix, usually causing abruptio placentae.

plateau phase According to Masters and Johnson, the second phase in the human sexual response cycle, characterized by a high degree of sexual excitement and by a leveling off of sexual tension.

polyandrous family A woman married to more than one husband.

polygamous family A single family unit based on the marriage of one person to two or more mates.

polygynous family A man married to more than one woman.

positive identification The attachment of a child to positive images of desired loving behavior.

positive signs Signs of pregnancy detected by the physician that indicate positively that the woman is pregnant.

postparental years The period between the last child leaving home and the spouses' retirement; also called the empty-nest years.

posttraumatic stress disorder Severe stress reactions that occur after a person has suffered a trauma.

power The ability of an individual within a social relationship to carry out his or her will, even in the face of resistance by others.

power processes The ways in which power is applied.

premature ejaculation A man's inability to delay ejaculation long enough for intercourse to take place, or for his partner to have an orgasm 50% of the time.

prepared childbirth Physical, social, intellectual, and emotional preparation for the birth of a baby.

presumptive signs Signs by which the mother presumes she is pregnant.

primary erectile dysfunction The inability to have an erection, where the condition has always existed.

probable signs Signs detected by the examining physician that indicate pregnancy is probable.

progestin implant A capsule containing progestin that is implanted under the skin and can remain in place for several years to prevent pregnancy.

progestin injection An injection of progestin to prevent pregnancy.

propinquity In mate selection, the tendency to choose someone who is geographically near.

psychosocial task The skills, knowledge, functions, and attitudes individuals need to acquire at different periods in their lives.

pubic lice Parasitic insects occupying hairy regions of the body that suck blood from their human hosts, causing itching.

rape Legally, sexual intercourse, with actual penetration of a woman's vagina by the man's penis, without consent and accomplished through force, threat of violence, or intimidation.

reciprocal parent-child interaction The influence of the parent on the child and the child on the parent so that each modifies the behavior of the other.

resolution phase According to Masters and Johnson, the final phase in the human sexual response cycle, characterized by a gradual return of the body to its unaroused state.

Rh incompatibility A condition in which the mother has Rh negative blood and the fetus has Rh positive blood or vice versa.

rhythm method A method of birth control whereby the couple have intercourse only during those times of the menstrual cycle when the woman is least likely to get pregnant.

rites of passage Ceremonies by which people pass from one social status to another.

roles Culturally defined social positions such as mother, grandparent, supervisor, or student.

romantic love A profoundly tender or passionate affection for another person, characterized by intense feelings and emotion.

rooming in Method of postpartum care in which the mother and father care for their newborn themselves in an area of the hospital assigned to them.

sandwich generation Middle-aged adults caught between caregiving for their children and for their elderly parents.

scabies A parasitic infection of mites that burrow into the skin, lay eggs, and cause itching.

scapegoating Blaming someone else for every bad thing that happens.

secondary erectile dysfunction The inability to have an erection under certain circumstances or situations that have not always existed.

segregated companionship When people participate primarily in activities outside the dyadic relationship.

selfism A personal value system that emphasizes that the way to find happiness is through self-gratification and narcissism.

serotonin A chemical neurotransmitter that has a stimulating effect on the body.

sex flush The appearance of reddish, spotty, rashlike color on the skin during sexual arousal.

sexual dysfunction A malfunction of the human sexual response system.

sexually transmitted disease (STD) Disease transmitted through sexual contact.

show Blood-tinged mucus that is passed when the mucus plug is expelled; an early sign of labor.

sibling rivalry The competition of brothers and sisters for the attention, approval, and affection of parents.

single-parent family A parent, who may or may not have been married, and one or more children.

situational or environmental sources of conflict These include living conditions, societal pressures, cultural strains, and unexpected events.

socialization The process by which people learn the ways of a given society or social group so that they can function within it.

social learning theory A theory emphasizing that boys develop "maleness" and girls develop "femaleness" through exposure to scores of influence—including parents, peers, television, and schools—that teach them what it means to be a man or a woman in their culture.

social structure/cultural theories of gender Theories suggesting that most of the differences between male and female gender roles are established because of the status, powler, and division of labor in a given society.

sole legal custody Situation in which the noncustodial parent forfeits the right to make decisions about the children's health, education, or religious training.

spermicides Chemicals that are toxic to sperm and used as a contraceptive in the form of foam, suppository, cream, jelly, or film.

spouse abuse Physical or emotional mistreatment of one's spouse.

steady dating Dating one person exclusively.

stepfamily A remarried man and/or woman plus children from a former marriage.

sterilization The process of rendering a person infertile, by performing either a vasectomy in the male or tubal ligation in the female.

strain-based conflicts Conflicts that arise when strain in the role outside the home affects participation in the family role, or vice versa.

structural-functional theory A theory that emphasizes the function of the family as a social institution in meeting the needs of society.

structural role redefinition Attempts to lessen conflict by mutual agreement on a new set of role expectations.

structured separation A time-limited approach in which partners terminate cohabitation, commit themselves to regularly scheduled therapy with a therapist, and agree to regular interpersonal contact—with a moratorium on a final decision either to reunite or to divorce.

sudden infant death syndrome, crib death The sudden, unexpected death of an infant, the exact cause of which is uncertain but is thought to be due to respiratory malfunction.

surrogate mother A woman who agrees to be artificially inseminated with the semen of a father-to-be, to carry the fetus to term, and then to give the child to the couple along with all parental rights.

symbolic interaction theory A theory that describes the family as a unit of interacting personalities communicating through symbols.

syphilis A sexually transmitted disease caused by a bacterium called a spirochete.

systems theory A theory that emphasizes the interdependence of family members and how they affect one another.

theory A tentative explanation of facts and data that have been observed.

theory of primary interest and presumed competence The theory that the person who is most interested in, most involved with, and best qualified to make a particular choice will be more likely to do so.

time-based conflicts Conflicts that arise when time pressures from one role make it physically impossible to meet expectations arising from another.

toxemia A serious disease of pregnancy.

traditional couples Couples in which the partners have problems with internal issues but draw satisfaction from external sources and maintain a stable marriage.

trajectory of life Projection of a certain life span and the activities individuals are going to experience during it.

transgendered Refers to people who have difficulty establishing their gender identity.

transsexual A person who has the genitals of one sex but the gender identity of the other.

transverse birth When the shoulder and arm of the baby are the first parts seen at the opening of the vagina.

tubal ligation Female sterilization by severing and/or closing the fallopian tubes so that the ovum cannot pass down the tube.

tubal pregnancy Attachment of the blastocyst and growth of the embryo in the fallopian tube.

umbilical cord The hollow cord connecting the circulation system of the fetus to the placenta.

unconditional positive regard Acceptance of another person as he or she is.

vaginismus Involuntary contraction and spasming of the muscles of the vagina.

vasectomy Male sterilization whereby the vas deferens are cut and tied to prevent the sperm from being ejaculated out of the penis.

vasocongestion Engorgement of the sexual body parts with blood, causing erection.

ventilation The process of airing, or expressing, negative emotions and feelings.

vitalized couples Couples with a high degree of satisfaction with all aspects of marriage.

voidable marriage A marriage that can be set aside by annulment under certain prescribed legal circumstances.

void marriage A marriage considered invalid in the first place because it was illegal.

voluntarily childless family A couple in which the partners decide not to have children.

voluntary stable (permanent) singles Never-marrieds and previously marrieds who choose to be single.

voluntary temporary singles Never-marrieds and previously marrieds who are not opposed to the idea of marriage but are not currently seeking mates.

wet dreams Erotic dreams while the man sleeps, leading to ejaculation.

zygote A fertilized egg cell.

Bibliography

Abbey, A., Andrews, F. M., and Halman, L. J. (1994). Psychosocial predictors of life quality. *Journal of Family Issues, 15,* 253–271.

Abbott, D. A., and Brody, G. H. (1985). The relation of child age, gender, and number of children to the marital adjustment of wives. *Journal of Marriage and the Family, 47,* 77–84.

Abel, G. G., Becker, J., Cunningham-Rathner, J., Mittlemen, M., and Rouleau, J. L. (1988). Multiple paraphiliac diagnosis among sex offenders. *Bulletin of the American Academy of Psychiatry and Law, 16,* 153–168.

Abell, E., Clawson, M., Washington, W. N., Bost, K. K., and Vaughn, B. E. (1996). Parenting values, attitudes, behaviors, and goals of African American mothers from a low-income population in relation to social and societal context. *Journal of Family Issues, 17,* 593–613.

Abell, E., and Gecas, B. (1997). Guilt, shame, and family socialization. *Journal of Family Issues, 18,* 99–123.

Abelman, R., and Pettey, G. R. (1989). Child attributes as determinants of parental television-viewing mediation. *Journal of Family Issues, 10,* 251–266.

Abortion doesn't impair the ability of women to become pregnant. (1985). *Family Planning Perspectives, 17,* 39, 40.

Abortion Law Homepage. (2000, April 10). *Partial-Birth Abortion Laws.* Retrieved from the World Wide Web: http://members.aol.com/abtrbng/pbal.htm

Abramson, P. R. (1983). Woman attracted to man she couldn't be happy with. *Medical Aspects of Human Sexuality, 17,* 141.

Adams, R. G. (1985). People would talk: Normative barriers to cross-sex friendships for elderly women. *The Gerontologist, 25,* 605–611.

Adelman, P. K., Chadwick, K., and Baerger, D. R. (1996). Marital quality of Black and White adults over the life course. *Journal of Social and Personal Relationships, 13,* 361–384.

Agocha, V., and Cooper, M. (1999). Risk perceptions and safer-sex intentions: Does a partner's physical attractiveness undermine the use of risk-relevant information? *Personality and Social Psychology Bulletin, 25*(6), 746–759.

Ahmeduzzaman, M., and Roopnarine, J. L. (1992). Sociodemographic factors, functioning style, social support, and fathers' involvement with preschoolers in African-American families. *Journal of Marriage and the Family, 54,* 699–707.

Ahn, N. (1994). Teenage childbearing and high school completion: Accounting for individual heterogeneity. *Family Planning Perspectives, 26,* 17–21.

Ahrons, C. R., and Rodgers, R. (1987). *Divorced Families: A Multidisciplinary View.* New York: Norton.

Ahuvia, A. C., and Adelman, M. B. (1992). Formal intermediaries in the marriage market: A typology and review. *Journal of Marriage and the Family, 54,* 452–463.

Albrecht, S. L., Miller, N. K., and Clarke, L. L. (1994). Assessing the importance of family structure in understanding birth outcomes. *Journal of Marriage and the Family, 56,* 987–1003.

Albright, A. (1993). Postpartum depression: An overview. *Journal of Counseling and Development, 7,* 316–320.

Aldous, J. (1977). Family interaction patterns. *Annual Review of Sociology* (pp. 105–135). Palo Alto, CA: Annual Review.

Aldous, J. (1987). New views on the family life of the elderly and near-elderly. *Journal of Marriage and the Family, 49,* 227–234.

Aldous, J. (1995). New views of grandparents in intergenerational context. *Journal of Family Issues, 16,* 104–122.

Aldous, J., Ganey, R., Trees, S., and Marsh, L. C. (1991). Families and inflation: Who was hurt in the last high-inflation period? *Journal of Marriage and the Family, 53,* 123–134.

Alexander, M. C., Moore, S., and Alexander, E. R., III. (1991). What is transmitted in the intergenerational transmission of violence? *Journal of Marriage and the Family, 53,* 657–668.

Alexander, P. C., and Lupfer, S. L. (1987). Family characteristics and long-term consequences associated with sexual abuse. *Archives of Sexual Behavior, 16,* 235–245.

Allan, G. (1985). *Family Life.* Oxford: Basil Blackwell.

Allen, A., and Thompson, T. (1984). Agreement, understanding, realization, and feeling understood as predictors of communicative satisfaction in marital dyads. *Journal of Marriage and the Family, 46,* 915–921.

Allen, K. R., and Pickett, R. S. (1987). Forgotten streams in the family life course: Utilization of qualitative retrospective interviews in the analysis of lifelong single women's family careers. *Journal of Marriage and the Family, 49,* 517–526.

Allen, S., and Hawkins, A. (1999). Maternal gatekeeping: Mothers' beliefs and behaviors that inhibit greater father involvement in family work. *Journal of Marriage and the Family, 61*(1), 199–212.

Allen, W., and Doherty, W. (1996). The responsibilities of fatherhood as perceived by African American teenage fathers. *Families in Society, 77*(3), 142–155.

Allers, C. T., and Benjack, K. J. (1991). Connections between childhood abuse and HIV infection. *Journal of Counseling and Development, 70,* 309–313.

Allers, C. T., Benjack, K. J., and Allers, N. T. (1992). Unresolved childhood sexual abuse: Are older adults affected? *Journal of Counseling and Development, 71,* 14–17.

Allgeier, A. R., Allgeier, E. R., and Rywick, T. (1981). Orientations toward abortion: Guilt or knowledge? *Adolescence, 16,* 273–280.

Althaus, F. (1991). Young adults choose alternatives to marriage, remain single longer. *Family Planning Perspectives, 23,* 45–46.

Althaus, F. (1992). Study finds low condom breakage rate, ties most slippage to improper use. *Family Planning Perspectives, 24,* 191–192.

Althaus, F. (1993). A postcoital contraceptive, Mifepristone has few side effects and high efficacy. *Family Planning Perspectives, 25,* 48–49.

Althaus, F. (1995). Most vasectomies are performed in urology practices by physicians using ligation and local anesthesia. *Family Planning Perspectives, 27,* 220–221.

Althaus, F. (1997). Women who use barrier methods with spermicide may have higher risks of urinary tract infections. *Family Planning Perspectives, 29,* 48–49.

Alwin, D. F. (1990). Cohort replacement and changes in parental socialization values. *Journal of Marriage and the Family, 52,* 347–360.

Amato, P. R. (1987). Family process in one-parent, stepparent, and intact families: The child's point of view. *Journal of Marriage and the Family, 49,* 327–337.

Amato, P. R. (1988). Long-term implications of parental divorce for adult self-concept. *Journal of Family Issues, 9,* 201–213.

Amato, P. R. (1989). Who cares for children in public places? Naturalistic observation of male and female caregivers. *Journal of Marriage and the Family, 51,* 981–990.

Amato, P. R. (1993). Children's adjustment to divorce: Theories, hypothesis, and empirical support. *Journal of Marriage and the Family, 55,* 23–38.

Amato, P. R. (1994a). The implications of research findings on children in stepfamilies. In A. Booth and J. Dunn (Eds.), *Stepfamilies: Who Benefits? Who Does Not?* (pp. 81–87). Hillsdale, NJ: Erlbaum.

Amato, P. R. (1994b). Father-child relations, mother-child relations, and offspring's psychological well-being in early adulthood. *Journal of Marriage and the Family, 56,* 1031–1042.

Amato, P. R. (1996). Explaining the intergenerational transmission of divorce. *Journal of Marriage and the Family, 58,* 628–640.

Amato, P. R., and Booth, A. (1991). The consequences of divorce for attitudes toward divorce and gender roles. *Journal of Family Issues, 12,* 306–322.

Amato, P. R., and Booth, A. (1996). A perspective study of divorce in parent-child relationships. *Journal of Marriage and the Family, 58,* 356–365.

Amato, P. R., and Gilbreth, J. G. (1999). Nonresident father and children's well-being: A meta-analysis. *Journal of Marriage and Family, 61,* 557–573.

Amato, P. R., and Keith, N. (1991). Parental divorce and the well-being of children: A meta-analysis. *Psychology Bulletin, 110,* 26–46.

Amato, P. R., Loomis, L. S., and Booth, A. (1995). Parental divorce, marital conflict, and offspring well-being during early adulthood. *Social Forces, 73*(3), 895–915.

Amato, P. R., and Ochiltree, G. (1986). Family resources and the development of child competence. *Journal of Marriage and the Family, 48,* 47–56.

Amato, P. R., and Partridge, S. (1987). Women and divorce with dependent children: Material, personal, family, and social well-being. *Family Relations, 36,* 316–320.

Ambert, A. (1988a). Relationships with former in-laws after divorce: A research note. *Journal of Marriage and the Family, 50,* 679–686.

Ambert, A. (1988b). Relationship between ex-spouses: Individual and dyadic perspectives. *Journal of Social and Personal Relationships, 5,* 327–346.

American Psychiatric Association. (1994). *Diagnostic and Statistical Manual of Mental Disorders* (4th ed.). Washington, DC: American Psychiatric Association.

American Social Health Association. (2000, April). Untreated chlamydia can lead to infertility; routine testing is critical, especially for young women. Retrieved from the World Wide Web: http://www.ashastd.org/press/040100.html

Anderson, E., Greene, S., Hetherington, E., and Clingempeel, W. (1999). The dynamics of parental remarriage. In E. M. Hetherington (Ed.), *Coping with divorce, single parenting, and remarriage: A risk and resiliency perspective* (pp. 295–319). Mahwah, NJ: Erlbaum.

Anderson, S. A. (1986). Cohesion, adaptability, and communication: A test of an Olson circumplex model hypothesis. *Family Relations, 35,* 289–293.

Anderson, S. A., Russell, C. S., and Schumm, W. R. (1983). Perceived marital quality and family-life cycle categories: A further analysis. *Journal of Marriage and the Family, 45,* 127–139.

Andersson, L., and Stevens, N. (1993). Associations between early experiences with parents and well-being in old age. *Journal of Gerontology, 48,* P109–P116.

Andre, T., Whigham, M., Hendrickson, A., and Chambers, S. (1999). Competency beliefs, positive affect, and gender stereotypes of elementary students and their parents about science versus other school subjects. *Journal of Research in Science Teaching, 36*(6), 719–747.

Andrews, B., and Brewin, C. R. (1990). Attributions of blame for marital violence: A study of antecedents and consequences. *Journal of Marriage and the Family, 52,* 757–776.

Andrews, F. M., and Halman, L. J. (1992). Infertility and subjective well-being: The mediating roles of self-esteem, internal control, and interpersonal conflict. *Journal of Marriage and the Family, 54,* 408–417.

Anisman, H., and Merali, Z. (1999). Understanding stress: Characteristics and caveats. *Alcohol Research and Health, 23,* 241–249.

Annual ectopic totals rose steadily in 1970s but mortality rates fell. (1983). *Family Planning Perspectives, 15,* 85, 86.

Ansbacher, R., and Adler, J. P. (1988). Infertility workshop and sexual stress. *Medical Aspects of Human Sexuality, 22,* 55–63.

Anson, O. (1989). Marital status and women's health revisited: The importance of a proximate adult. *Journal of Marriage and the Family, 51,* 185–194.

Antill, J. K., Goodnow, J. J., Russell, G., and Cotton, S. (1996). The influence of parents and family context on children's involvement in household tasks. *Sex Roles, 34,* 215–236.

Aquilino, W. S. (1990). The likelihood of parent, adult-child coresidence: Effects of family structure and parental characteristics. *Journal of Marriage and the Family, 52,* 405–419.

Aquilino, W. S. (1991). Predicting parents' experiences with coresident adult children. *Journal of Family Issues, 12,* 323–342.

Aquilino, W. S. (1994). Later life parental divorce and widowhood: Impact on young adults' assessment of parent-child relations. *Journal of Marriage and the Family, 56,* 908–922.

Arendell, T. J. (1987). Women and the economics of divorce in the contemporary United States. *Signs, 13,* 121–135.

Argyle, M., and Furnham, A. (1983). Sources of satisfaction and conflict in long-term relationships. *Journal of Marriage and the Family, 45,* 481–493.

Arthur, N. M. (1990). The assessment of burnout: A review of three inventories useful for research and counseling. *Journal of Counseling and Development, 69,* 186–189.

Ashton, V. (1996). A study of mutual support between Black and White grandmothers and their adult grandchildren. *Journal of Gerontological Social Work, 26,* 87–100.

Atkinson, A. M. (1987). Fathers' participation and evaluation of family day care. *Family Relations, 38,* 146–151.

Atkinson, M. P., and Glass, B. L. (1985). Marital age heterogamy and homogamy, 1900 to 1980. *Journal of Marriage and the Family, 47,* 685–691.

Avenevoli, S., Sessa, F. M., and Steinberg, L. (1999). Family structure, parenting practices, and adolescent adjustment: An ecological examination. In E. M. Hetherington (Ed.), *Coping with Divorce, Single Parenting, and Remarriage: A Risk and Resiliency Perspective* (pp. 65–90). Mahwah, NJ: Erlbaum.

Average television viewing time. (1999). *The World Almanac and Book of Fact, 2000* (p. 189). Mahwah, NJ: World Almanac Books.

Axelson, L. J., and Dail, P. W. (1988). The changing character of homelessness in the United States. *Family Relations, 37,* 463–469.

Baber, K. M., and Allen, K. R. (1992). *Women and Families: Feminist Reconstructions.* New York: Guilford Press.

Bachrach, C. A., London, R. A., and Maza, P. L. (1991). On the path to adoption: Adoption seeking in the United States, 1988. *Journal of Marriage and the Family, 53,* 705–718.

Backover, A. (1991). Native Americans: Alcoholism, FAS puts a race at risk. *Guidepost, 37,* 1–9.

Bahr, S. J. Chappell, C. B., and Leigh, G. K. (1983). Age at marriage, role enactment, role consensus, and marital satisfaction. *Journal of Marriage and the Family, 45,* 795–803.

Baize, H., and Schroeder, J. (1995). Personality and mate selection in personal ads: Evolutionary preferences in a public mate selection process. *Journal of Social Behavior and Personality, 10,* 517–536.

Baley, R. K. (1995). Black-White differences in kin contact and exchange among never married adults. *Journal of Family Issues, 16,* 77–103.

Balkwell, C. (1985). An additudinal correlate of the timing of a major life event: The case of morale in widowhood. *Family Relations, 34,* 577–581.

Ball, R. E., and Robbins, L. (1986a). Black husbands' satisfaction with their family life. *Journal of Marriage and the Family, 48,* 849–855.

Ball, R. E., and Robbins, L. (1986b). Marital status and life satisfaction among Black Americans. *Journal of Marriage and the Family, 48,* 389–394.

Bancroft, J., Sherwin, B. B., Alexander, G. M., Davidson, D. W., and Walker, A. (1991). Oral contraceptives, androgens, and the sexuality of young women: II. The role of androgens. *Archives of Sexual Behavior, 20,* 121–135.

Bandura, A. (1976). *Social Learning Theory.* Englewood Cliffs, NJ: Prentice-Hall.

Bane, M. J. (1997, January/February). Welfare as we might know it. *American Prospect, 30.* Retrieved June 30, 2000, from the World Wide Web: http://www.prospect.org/archives/30/fs30bane.html

Bank, L., Forgatch, M. S., Patterson, G. R., and Fetrow, R. A. (1993). Parenting practices of single mothers: Mediators of negative contextual factors. *Journal of Marriage and the Family, 55,* 371–384.

Banyard, L., and Williams, L. N. (1996). Characteristics of child sexual abuse as correlates of women's adjustment: A prospective study. *Journal of Marriage and the Family, 58,* 853–865.

Baranowski, M. D. (1983). Strengthening the grandparent-grandchild relationship. *Medical Aspects of Human Sexuality, 17,* 106–126.

Barber, B. K., and Thomas, D. L. (1986). Dimensions of fathers' and mothers' supportive behavior: The case for physical affection. *Journal of Marriage and the Family, 48,* 783–794.

Barich, R. R., and Bielby, D. D. (1996). Rethinking marriage. *Journal of Family Issues, 17,* 139–169.

Barnes, G. E., Greenwood, L., and Sommer, R. (1991). Courtship violence in a Canadian sample of male college students. *Family Relations, 40,* 37–44.

Barnett, R. C., and Baruch, G. K. (1987). Determinants of fathers' participation in family work. *Journal of Marriage and the Family, 49,* 29–40.

Barnett, R. C., Kibria, N., Baruch, G. K., and Pleck, J. H. (1991). Adult daughter–parent relationships and their associations with daughters' subjective well-being and psychological distress. *Journal of Marriage and the Family, 53,* 29–42.

Barnett, R. C., Marshall, N. L., and Pleck, J. H. (1992). Adult son–parent relationships and their associations with sons' psychological distress. *Journal of Family Issues, 13,* 505–525.

Barnett, R. C., Marshall, N. L., and Singer, J. D. (1992). Job experiences over time, multiple roles, and women's mental health: A longitudinal study. *Journal of Personality and Social Psychology, 62,* 634–644.

Barranti, C. C. R. (1985). The grandparent-grandchild relationship: Family resource in an era of voluntary bonds. *Family Relations, 34,* 343–352.

Barrett, A. (1999). Social support and life satisfaction among the never married. *Research on Aging, 21*(1), 46–72.

Barrow, J. C., and Moore, C. A. (1983). Group interventions with perfectionistic thinking. *The Personnel and Guidance Journal, 61,* 612–615.

Bassoff, E. S. (1984). Relationships of sex-role characteristics and psychological adjustment in new mothers. *Journal of Marriage and the Family, 46,* 449–454.

Battaglia, D. M., Datteri, D., and Lord, C. (1998). Breaking up is (relatively) easy to do: A script for the dissolution of close relationships. *Journal of Social and Personal Relationships, 15*(6), 829–845.

Baumeister, R., and Bratslavsky, E. (1999). Passion, intimacy, and time: Passionate love as a function of change in intimacy. *Personality and Social Psychology Review, 3*(1), 49–67.

Baumeister, R., Wotman, S., and Stillwell, A. (1993). Unrequited love: On heartbreak, anger, guilt, scriptlessness, and humiliation. *Journal of Personality and Social Psychology, 64,* 377–394.

Baumrind, D. (1996). Parenting: Discipline controversy revisited. *Family Relations, 45,* 405–414.

Baur, P. A., and Okun, M. A. (1983). Stability of life satisfaction in late life. *The Gerontologist, 23,* 261–265.

Baxter, L. A. (1984). Trajectories of relationship disengagement. *Journal of Social and Personal Relationships, 1,* 29–48.

Baxter, L. A. (1990). Dialectical contradictions in relationship development. *Journal of Social and Personal Relationships, 7,* 69–88.

Baxter, L. A., Braithwaite, D. O., and Nicholson, J. H. (1999). Turning points in the development of blended families. *Journal of Social and Personal Relationships, 16*(3), 291–313.

Baxter, L. A., and Montgomery, B. M. (1997). Rethinking communication in personal relationships from a dialectical perspective. In S. Duck (Ed.), *Handbook of Personal Relationships* (pp. 325–349). New York: Wiley.

Baxter, L. A., and Simon, E. P. (1993). Relationship maintenance strategies and dialectical contradictions in personal relationships. *Journal of Social and Personal Relationships, 10,* 225–242.

Beach, S. R. H., and O'Leary, K. B. (1993). Dysphoria and marital discord: Are dysphoric individuals at risk for marital maladjustment? *Journal of Marital and Family Therapy, 19,* 355–368.

Bean, C. (1974). *Methods of Childbirth.* New York: Dolphin.

Beck, J. G., Bozman, A. W., and Qualtrough, T. (1991). The experience of sexual desire: Psychological correlates in a college sampling. *The Journal of Sex Research, 28,* 443–456.

Beck, R., and Blank, N. (1997). Broadening the scope of divorce mediation to meet the needs of children. *Mediation Quarterly: Journal of the Academy of Family Mediators, 14*(3), 179–185.

Beck, R. W., and Beck, S. H. (1989). The incidence of extended households among middle-age Black and White women: Estimates from a 15-year panel study. *Journal of Family Issues, 10,* 147–168.

Becker, P. (1999, November). Scaling back: Dual-earner couples' work-family strategies. *Journal of Marriage and the Family, 61,* 995–1007.

Beckman, L., Harvey, S., Satre, S., and Walker, M. (1999). Cultural beliefs about social influence strategies of Mexican immigrant women and their heterosexual partners. *Sex Roles, 40*(11/12), 871–892.

Beckman, L. J., and Houser, B. B. (1982). The consequences of childlessness on the social-psychological well-being of older women. *Journal of Gerontology, 37,* 243–250.

Bell, R. A., Daly, J. A., and Gonzalez, M. C. (1987). Affinity-maintenance in marriage and its relationship to women's marital satisfaction. *Journal of Marriage and the Family, 49,* 445–454.

Bell, W., and Garner, J. (1996). Kincare. *Journal of Gerontological Social Work, 25,* 11–20.

Belsky, J. (1992). Medically indigent women seeking abortion prior to legalization: New York City, 1969–1970. *Family Planning Perspectives, 24,* 129–134.

Belsky, J., and Rovine, M. (1990). Patterns of marital change across the transition to parenthood: Preparing to three years postpartum. *Journal of Marriage and the Family, 52,* 5–19.

Belsky, J., Youngblade, L., Rovine, M., and Volling, B. (1991). Patterns of marital change and parent-child interaction. *Journal of Marriage and the Family, 53,* 487–498.

Bem, S. L. (1985). Androgyny and gender schema theory: A conceptual and empirical integration. In T. B. Sondereg-ger (Ed.), *Nebraska Symposium on Motivation: Psychology of Gender* (pp. 179–226). Lincoln: University of Nebraska Press.

Benazon, N., Wright, J., and Sabourin, S. (1992). Stress, sexual satisfaction, and marital adjustment in infertile couples. *Journal of Sex and Marital Therapy, 18,* 273–284.

Benedikt, M. (1999). *Values.* Austin: University of Texas Press.

Bengtson, V. L., Cutler, N. E., Mangen, D. J., and Marshall, V. W. (1985). Generations, cohorts and relations between age groups. In R. H. Binstock and E. Shanas (Eds.), *Handbook of Aging and Social Sciences* (pp. 304–338). New York: Van Nostrand Reinhold.

Bengtson, V. L., and Kuypers, J. A. (1971). Generational differences and the developmental stake. *Aging and Human Development, 2,* 249–260.

Benin, M., and Keith, D. M. (1995). The social support of employed African-American and Anglo mothers. *Journal of Family Issues, 15,* 275–297.

Benin, M. H., and Edwards, D. A. (1990). Adolescents' chores: The difference between dual- and single-earner families. *Journal of Marriage and the Family, 52,* 361–373.

Benin, M. H., and Nienstedt, B. C. (1985). Happiness in single- and dual-earner families: The effect of marital happiness, job satisfaction, and life cycle. *Journal of Marriage and the Family, 47,* 975–984.

Bennett, N. T., Blanc, A. K., and Bloom, D. E. (1988). Commitment and the modern union: Assessing the link between premarital cohabitation and subsequent marital stability. *American Sociological Review, 53,* 127–138.

Benson, M. J., Arditti, J., Reguero DeAtiles, J. T., and Smith, S. (1992). Intergenerational transmission: Attributions in relationships with parents and intimate others. *Journal of Family Issues, 13,* 450–464.

Benson, M. J., Larson, J., Wilson, S. M., and Demo, D. H. (1993). Family of origin influences on late adolescent romantic relationships. *Journal of Marriage and the Family, 55,* 663–672.

Berardo, D. H., Shehan, C. L., and Leslie, G. R. (1987). A residue of tradition: Jobs, careers, and spouses' time in housework. *Journal of Marriage and the Family, 49,* 381–390.

Berghout-Austin, A. M., Salehi, M., and Leffler, A. (1987). Gender and developmental differences in children's conversations. *Sex Roles, 16*(9/10), 497–510.

Bergstrom-Walan, M., and Nielsen, H. H. (1990). Sexual expression among 60- to 80-year-old men and women: A sample from Stockholm, Sweden. *The Journal of Sex Research, 27,* 289–295.

Berk, R. A., Newton, P. J., and Berk, S. F. (1986). What a difference a day makes: An empirical study of the impact of shelters for battered women. *Journal of Marriage and the Family, 48,* 481–490.

Berkow, R. (Ed.). (1987). *The Merck Manual* (15th ed.). Rahway, NJ: Merck, Sharp and Dohme Research Laboratories.

Bernard, J. L., Bernard, S. L., and Bernard, M. L. (1985). Courtship violence and sex-typing. *Family Relations, 24,* 573–576.

Berry, R. E., and Williams, F. L. (1987). Assessing the relationships between quality of life and marital income satisfaction: A path analytic approach. *Journal of Marriage and the Family, 49,* 107–116.

Berscheid, E., and Walster, E. (1974). Physical attractiveness. *Experimental Social Psychology, 7,* 157–215.

Beutell, N. J., and Greenhaus, J. H. (1980). Some sources and consequences of interrole conflict among married women. *Proceedings of the Annual Meeting of the Eastern Academy of Management, 17,* 2–6.

Billingham, R. E. (1987). Courtship violence: The patterns of conflict resolution across seven levels of emotional commitment. *Family Relations, 36,* 283–294.

Bird, G. W., Stith, S. M., and Schladale, J. (1991). Psychological resources, coping strategies, and negotiation styles as discriminators of violence in dating relationships. *Family Relations, 40,* 45–50.

Blackwell, D. L., and Lichter, D. T. (2000). Mate selection among married and cohabiting couples. *Journal of Family Issues, 21*(3), 275–302.

Blair, S. L. (1992). The sex-typing of children's household labor: Parental influence on daughters and sons. *Youth and Society, 24,* 178–203.

Blair, S. L. (1993). Employment, family, and perceptions of marital quality among husbands and wives. *Journal of Family Issues, 14,* 189–212.

Blaisure, K. R., and Allen, K. R. (1995). Feminists and the ideology and practice of marital equality. *Journal of Marriage and the Family, 57,* 5–19.

Blee, K. M., and Tickamyer, A. R. (1995). Racial differences in men's attitudes about women's gender roles. *Journal of Marriage and the Family, 57,* 21–30.

Bloom, B. L., and Kindle, K. R. (1985). Demographic factors in the continuing relationships between former spouses. *Family Relations, 34,* 375–381.

Blum, R. W., Resnick, N. C., and Stark, T. (1990). Factors associated with the use of court bypass by minors to obtain abortions. *Family Planning Perspectives, 22,* 158–160.

Blumstein, P., and Schwartz, P. (1983). *American Couples: Money, Work, Sex.* New York: Morrow.

Bode, J. (1987). Testimony before the U.S. House of Representatives select committee on Children, Youth, and Families. In *The Crisis of Homelessness: Effects on Children and Families.* G. Miller (Chair). Washington, DC: U.S. Government Printing Office.

Bogren, L. Y. (1991). Changes in sexuality in women and men during pregnancy. *Archives of Sexual Behavior, 20,* 35–45.

Bohannan, P. (1984). *All the Happy Families.* New York: McGraw-Hill.

Bohannon, J., and White, P. (1999). Gender role attitudes of American mothers and daughters over time. *Journal of Social Psychology, 139*(2), 173–179.

Boland, J. P., and Follingstad, D. R. (1987). The relationship between communication and marital satisfaction: A review. *Journal of Sex and Marital Therapy, 13,* 286–313.

Bolig, R., Stein, P. J., and McKenry, P. C. (1984). The self-advertisement approach to dating: Male-female differences. *Family Relations, 33,* 587–592.

Booth, A. (1999). Causes and consequences of divorce: Reflections on recent research. In R. Thompson and P. Amato (Eds.), *The postdivorce family: Children, parenting, and society* (pp. 29–48). Thousand Oaks, CA: Sage.

Booth, A., and Amato, C. R. (1994). Parental gender role nontraditionalism and offspring outcomes. *Journal of Marriage and the Family, 56,* 865–877.

Booth, A., and Edwards, J. N. (1985). Age at marriage and marital instability. *Journal of Marriage and the Family, 47,* 67–75.

Booth, A., and Edwards, J. N. (1992). Starting over. Why remarriages are more unstable. *Journal of Family Issues, 13,* 174–179.

Booth, A., and Johnson, D. (1988). Premarital cohabitation and marital success. *Journal of Family Issues, 9,* 255–272.

Boss, P. G. (1987). Family stress. In M. B. Sussman and S. K. Steinmetz (Eds.), *Handbook of Marriage and the Family* (pp. 695–723). New York: Plenum.

Boston Women's Health Book Collective. (1998). *Our Bodies, Ourselves for the New Century: A Book by and for Women.* New York: Touchstone Books.

Botwin, M. D., Buss, D. M., and Shackelford, T. K. (1997). Personality and mate preference: Five factors in mate selection and marital satisfaction. *Journal of Personality, 65,* 108–136.

Bowen, G. L. (1989). Marital sex-role incongruence and marital adjustments. *Journal of Family Issues, 10,* 409–415.

Bowen, G. L., and Chapman, M. B. (1996). Poverty, neighborhood danger, social support, and the individual adaptation among at-risk youth in urban areas. *Journal of Family Issues, 17*, 641–666.

Bowen, G. L., and Orthner, D. K. (1983). Sex-role congruency and marital quality. *Journal of Marriage and the Family, 45*, 223–230.

Bowlby, J. (1977). The making and breaking of affectional bonds. *British Journal of Psychiatry, 130*, 201–210.

Bowman, M. E., and Ahrons, C. R. (1985). Impact of legal custody status on fathers' parenting postdivorce. *Journal of Marriage and the Family, 47*, 481–488.

Bowman, M. L. (1990). Coping efforts and marital satisfaction: Measuring marital coping and its correlates. *Journal of Marriage and the Family, 52*, 463–474.

Boxer, A. M., and Cohler, B. J. (1989). The life course of gay and lesbian youth: An immodest proposal for the study of lives. *Journal of Homosexuality, 17*(3/4), 315–355.

Boyd, C. J. (1989). Mothers and daughters: A discussion of theory and research. *Journal of Marriage and the Family, 51*, 291–301.

Boykin, A. W., and Toms, R. D. (1985). Black child socialization: A conceptual framework. In H. P. McAdoo and J. L. McAdoo (Eds.), *Black Children: Social, Educational, and Parental Environments* (pp. 35–51). Newbury Park, CA: Sage.

Boyum, L. A., and Parke, R. D. (1995). The role of emotional expressiveness in the development of children's social competence. *Journal of Marriage and the Family, 57*, 593–608.

Bozman, A. W., and Beck, K. G. (1991). Covariation of sexual desire and sexual arousal: The effects of anger and anxiety. *Archives of Sexual Behavior, 20*, 47–60.

Brackbill, R. M., Sternberg, M. R., and Fishbein, M. (1999, January/February). Where do people go for treatment of sexually transmitted diseases? *Family Planning Perspective, 31*(1), 10–15.

Bradsher, J. E., Longino, C. F., Jr., Jackson, D. J., and Zimmerman, R. S. (1992). Health and geographic mobility among the recently widowed. *Journal of Gerontology, 47*, S261–S268.

Brand, E., Clingempeel, W. G., and Bowen-Woodward, K. (1988). Family relationships and children's adjustment in stepmother and stepfather families. In E. M. Hetherington and J. D. Arasteh (Eds.), *Impact of Divorce, Single-Parenting, and Stepparenting on Children* (pp. 299–324). Hillsdale, NJ: Erlbaum.

Bray, J. (1999). Step families: The intersection of culture, context, and biology. *Monographs of the Society for Research in Child Development, 64*(4), 210–218.

Bray, J. H., and Berger, S. H. (1993). Developmental issues in stepfamilies. Research project: Family relationships and parent-child interactions. *Journal of Family Psychology, 7*, 76–90.

Bray, J. H., and Hetherington, E. M. (1993). Families in transition: Introduction and overview. *Journal of Family Psychology, 7*, 3–8.

Bray, J. H., and Jouriles, E. N. (1995). Treatment of marital conflict and prevention of divorce. *Journal of Marital and Family Therapy, 21*, 461–473.

Bray, J. H., and Kelly, J. (1998). *Stepfamilies: Love, Marriage, and Parenting in the First Decade.* New York: Broadway Books.

Brayfield, A. (1995). Juggling jobs and kids: The impact of employment schedules on fathers' caring for children. *Journal of Marriage and the Family, 57*, 321–332.

Brecher, E. M. (1984). *Love, Sex, and Aging.* Boston: Little, Brown.

Brehm, S. S. (1985). *Intimate Relationships.* New York: Random House.

Bretschneider, J. G., and McCoy, N. L. (1988). Sexual interest and behavior in healthy 80- to 102-year-olds. *Archives of Sexual Behavior, 17*, 109–129.

Brindis, C., Starbuck-Morales, S., Wolfe, A. L., and McCarter, B. (1994). Characteristics associated with contraceptive use among adolescent females in school-based family planning programs. *Family Planning Perspectives, 26*, 160–164.

Broderick, C. B. (1984). *Marriage and the Family* (2nd ed.). Englewood Cliffs, NJ: Prentice-Hall.

Broderick, C. B., and Smith, J. (1979). The general systems approach to the family. In W. R. Burr, R. Hill, F. I. Nye, and I. L. Reiss (Eds.), *Contemporary Theories About the Family* (Vol. 2, pp. 112–129). New York: Free Press.

Brody, C. J., and Steelman, L. C. (1985). Sibling structure and parental sex-typing of children's household tasks. *Journal of Marriage and the Family, 47*, 265–273.

Brody, G. H., Stoneman, D., Flor, D., and McCrary, C. (1994). Religion's role in organizing family relationships: Family process in rural, two-parent African-American families. *Journal of Marriage and the Family, 56*, 878–888.

Brody, L., Copeland, A., Sutton, L., Richardson, D., and Guyer, M. (1998). Mommy and daddy like you best: Perceived family favoritism in relation to affect, adjustment and family process. *Journal of Family Therapy, 20*(3), 269–291.

Brodzinsky, D., Schechter, D., Braff, A., and Singer, L. (1984). Psychological and academic adjustment in adopted children. *Journal of Consulting and Clinical Psychology, 52*, 582–590.

Broman, C. L. (1988). Satisfaction among Blacks: The significance of marriage and parenthood. *Journal of Marriage and the Family, 50,* 45–51.

Broman, C. L. (1991). Gender, work-family roles, and psychological well-being of Blacks. *Journal of Marriage and the Family, 53,* 509–520.

Broman, C. L. (1993). Race differences in marital well-being. *Journal of Marriage and the Family, 55,* 724–732.

Bronfenbrenner, U. (1975). Liberated women: How they're changing American life. Interview conducted for *U.S. News & World Report,* p. 49.

Bronstein, P., Klauson, J., Stoll, M. F., and Abrams, C. L. (1993). Parenting behavior and children's social, psychological, and academic adjustment in diverse family structures. *Family Relations, 42,* 268–276.

Brown, L. M., and Gilligan, C. (1992). *Meeting at the Crossroads: Women's Psychology and Girls' Development.* New York: Random House.

Brown, S. L., and Booth, A. (1996). Cohabitation versus marriage: A comparison of relationship qualities. *Journal of Marriage and the Family, 58,* 668–678.

Brown, S. S. (1989). Drawing women into prenatal care. *Family Planning Perspectives, 21,* 73–80.

Brubaker, T. H. (1990). Families in later life: A burgeoning research area. *Journal of Marriage and the Family, 52,* 959–981.

Brumberg, J. J. (1997). *The Body Project: An Intimate History of American Girls.* New York: Vintage Books.

Bryant, Z. L., and Coleman, M. (1988). The Black family as portrayed in introductory marriage and family textbooks. *Family Relations, 37,* 255–259.

Bryson, K. R., and Casper, L. M. (1999, May). *Coresident Grandparents and Grandchildren.* (*Current Population Reports,* Series P23-198). Washington, DC: U.S. Bureau of the Census.

Buckner, L. P., and Salts, C. J. (1985). A premarital assessment program. *Family Relations, 34,* 513–520.

Buehler, C., Krishnakumar, A., Anthony, C., Tittsworth, S., and Stone, G. (1994). Hostile interparental conflict in youth maladjustment. *Family Relations, 43,* 409–416.

Buehler, C., Krishnakumar, A., Stone, G., Anthony, C., Pemberton, S., Gerard, J., and Barber, B. K. (1998). Interparental conflict styles and youth problem behaviors: A two-sample replication study. *Journal of Marriage and the Family, 60,* 119–132.

Buehler, R., Griffin, D. W., and Ross, M. (1995). It's about time: Optimistic predictions in work and love. In W. Stroebe and M. Hewstone (Eds.), *European Social Review of Psychology, Vol. 6* (pp. 1–32). Chichester, UK: Wiley.

Bulcroft, K., and O'Connor, M. (1986). The importance of dating relationship on quality of life for older persons. *Family Relations, 35,* 397–401.

Bullock, J. R. (1993). Children's loneliness and their relationships with family and peers. *Family Relations, 42,* 46–49.

Bumpass, L. L., Martin, T. C., and Sweet, J. A. (1991). The impact of family background and early marital factors on marital disruption. *Journal of Family Issues, 12,* 22–42.

Bumpass, L. L., and Sweet, J. A. (1989). National estimates of cohabitation. *Demography, 26,* 615–625.

Bumpass, L. L., Sweet, J. A., and Cherlin, A. (1991). The role of cohabitation in declining rates of marriage. *Journal of Marriage and the Family, 53,* 913–927.

Bunker, B. B., Zubek, J. M., Vanderslice, V. J., and Rice, R. W. (1992). Quality of life in dual-career families: Commuting versus single-residence couples. *Journal of Marriage and the Family, 54,* 399–407.

Burden, D. S. (1986). Single parents and the work setting: The impact of multiple job and homelife responsibilities. *Family Relations, 35,* 37–43.

Burgess, E. W., and Locke, H. J. (1953). *The Family: From Institution to Companionship.* New York: American Book.

Buriel, R. (1993). Child-rearing orientations in Mexican-American families: The influence of generation and sociocultural factors. *Journal of Marriage and the Family, 55,* 987–1000.

Burleson, B., and Denton, W. (1997). The relationship between communication skill and marital satisfaction: Some moderating effects. *Journal of Marriage and the Family, 59,* 884–902.

Burleson, B. R., Della, J. G., and Applegate, J. L. (1992). Effects of maternal communication in children's social-cognitive and communication skills on children's acceptance by the peer group. *Family Relations, 41,* 264–272.

Burns, D. D. (1980). The perfectionist's script for self-defeat. *Psychology Today, 14,* 34–52.

Burns, D. D. (1983). The spouse who is a perfectionist. *Medical Aspects of Human Sexuality, 17,* 219–230.

Burr, J., and Mutchler, J. (1999). Race and ethnic variation in norms of filial responsibility among older persons. *Journal of Marriage and the Family, 61*(3), 674–687.

Burr, W. R. (1990). Beyond I-statements in family communication. *Family Relations, 39,* 266–273.

Burt, M., Aron, L. Y., Douglas, T., Valente, J., Lee, E., and Iwen, B. (1999, December 7). *Homelessness: Programs and the People They Serve: Findings from the National Survey of Homeless Assistance Providers and Clients.* Washington, DC: Urban Institute. Retrieved June 30, 2000, from the World Wide Web: http://www.urban.org/housing/homeless/homeless.html

Burton, L. M. (1995). Intergenerational patterns of providing care in African-American families with teenage childbearers: Emergent patterns in an ethnographic study. In V. L. Bengtson, K. W. Schaie, and L. M. Burton (Eds.), *Adult Intergenerational Relations: Effects of Societal Change* (pp. 79–98). New York: Springer.

Busby, T. M., Steggell, G. L., Glenn, E., and Adamson, D. W. (1993). Treatment issues for survivors of physical and sexual abuse. *Journal of Marital and Family Therapy, 19,* 377–392.

Buscaglia, L. (1982). *Living, Loving, and Learning.* New York: Fawcett Columbine.

Buss, D. M., and Schmitt, D. P. (1993). Sexual strategies theory: An evolutionary perspective on human mating. *Psychological Bulletin, 2,* 204–232.

Buss, T. F., and Redburn, F. S. (1983). *Shutdown at Youngstown.* Albany: State University of New York Press.

Buunk, B. P., and Mutsaers, W. (1999). The nature of the relationship between remarried individuals and former spouses and its impact on marital satisfaction. *Journal of Family Psychology, 13*(2), 165–174.

Byers, E. S. (1988). Effects of sexual arousal on men's and women's behavior in sexual disagreement situations. *The Journal of Sex Research, 25,* 235–254.

Byers, E. S., and Demmons, S. (1999). Sexual satisfaction and sexual self-disclosure within dating relationships. *Journal of Sex Research, 36*(2), 180–189.

Byers, E. S., and Lewis, K. (1988). Dating couples' disagreements over the desired level of sexual intimacy. *The Journal of Sex Research, 24,* 15–29.

Cain, V. S., and Hofferth, S. L. (1989). Parental choice of self-care for school-age children. *Journal of Marriage and the Family, 51,* 65–77.

Call, B., Strecher, S., and Schwartz, P. (1995). The incidence and frequency of marital sex in a national sample. *Journal of Marriage and the Family, 57,* 639–652.

Callan, V. J. (1983). Childlessness and partner selection. *Journal of Marriage and the Family, 45,* 181–186.

Callan, V. J. (1985). Perceptions of parents, the voluntary and involuntary childless: A multidimensional scaling analysis. *Journal of Marriage and the Family, 47,* 1045–1050.

Callan, V. J. (1987). The personal and marital adjustment of mothers and of voluntarily and involuntarily childless wives. *Journal of Marriage and the Family, 49,* 847–856.

Camasso, M. J., and Roche, S. E. (1991). The willingness to change to formalized child care arrangements: Parental considerations, cost and quality. *Journal of Marriage and the Family, 53,* 1071–1082.

Cameron, S., and Collins, A. (1998). Sex differences in stipulated preferences in personal advertisement. *Psychological Reports, 82,* 119–123.

Campbell, A. (1981). *The Sense of Well-Being in America.* New York: McGraw-Hill.

Campbell, N. L., and Moen, P. (1992). Job-family role strain among employed single mothers of preschoolers. *Family Relations, 41,* 205–211.

Caplan, P. J. (1986, October). Take the blame off mother. *Psychology Today, 20,* 70–71.

Cargan, L., and Melko, M. (1982). *Singles: Myths and Realities.* Beverly Hills, CA: Sage.

Carroll, J. L., and Bagley, D. H. (1990). Evaluation of sexual satisfaction in partners of men experiencing erectile failure. *Journal of Sex and Marital Therapy, 16,* 70–78.

Carstensen, L. L., Gottman, J. M., and Levenson, R. W. (1995). Emotional behavior in long-term marriage. *Psychology and Aging, 10,* 140–149.

Carter, S., and Sokol, J. (1987). *Men Who Can't Love.* New York: M. Evans.

Casas, J. M., and Ponterotto, J. G. (1984). Profiling an invisible minority in higher education: The Chicana. *Personnel and Guidance Journal, 62,* 349–353.

Casper, L. M. (1997, September). My daddy takes care of me! Fathers as care providers. (*Current Population Reports: Household Economic Studies,* Series P70-59). Washington, DC: U.S. Bureau of the Census.

Casper, L. M., and Bryson, K. R. (1998). *Co-Resident Grandparents and Their Grandchildren: Grandparent Maintained Families.* (Population Division Working Paper No. 26). Washington, DC: U.S. Bureau of the Census.

Cate, R. M., Henton, J. M., Koval, J., Christopher, P. S., and Lloyd, S. (1982). Premarital abuse: A social psychological perspective. *Journal of Family Issues, 3,* 79–90.

Cate, R. M., and Koval, J. E. (1983). Heterosexual relationship development: Is it really a sequential process? *Adolescence, 18,* 507–514.

Cate, R. M., Long, E., Angera, J. J., and Draper, K. K. (1993). Sexual intercourse and relationship development. *Family Relations, 42,* 158–164.

Ceglian, C. P., and Gardner, S. (1999). Attachment style: A risk for multiple marriages? *Journal of Divorce and Remarriage, 31,* 125–139.

Center for Drug Evaluation and Research. (2000, September 30). Mifepristone questions and answers. Retrieved from the World Wide Web: http://www.fda.gov/cder/drug/infopage/mifepristone/mifepristone-qa.htm

Chaddock, G. (1999). Learning: K-12: Say goodbye to "latch-key" kids. *Christian Science Monitor, 91*(245), 14.

Chan, C. G., and Elder, G. H. (2000). Matrilineal advantage in grandchild–grandparent relations. *The Gerontologist, 40,* 179–190.

Chatters, L. M., Taylor, R. J., and Neighbors, H. W. (1989). Size of informal helper network mobilized during a serious personal problem among Black Americans. *Journal of Marriage and the Family, 51,* 667–676.

Cheal, D. (1993). Unity and difference in postmodern families. *Journal of Family Issues, 14,* 5–19.

Cheng, C. (1999). Gender-role differences in susceptibility to the influence of support availability on depression. *Journal of Personality, 67*(3), 439–467.

Cherlin, A., and Furstenberg, F. F. (1994). Stepfamilies in the United States: A reconsideration. In J. Blake and J. Hagen (Eds.), *Annual Review of Sociology* (pp. 359–381). Palo Alto, CA: Annual Reviews.

Children of older women at highest risk of low birth weight, infant death. (1988). *Family Planning Perspectives, 20,* 242–243.

Chilman, C. (1991). Working poor families: Trends, causes, effects, and suggested policies. *Family Relations, 40,* 191–198.

Chira, S. (1984, February 11). Town experiment cuts TV. *New York Times.*

Chiriboga, D. A. (1982). Adaptation to marital separation in later and earlier life. *Journal of Gerontology, 37,* 109–114.

Choi, N. G. (1992). Correlates of the economic status of widowed and divorced elderly women. *Journal of Family Issues, 13,* 38–54.

Christensen, A., and Heavey, C. L. (1990). Gender, power, and marital conflict. *Journal of Personality and Social Psychology, 59,* 73–85.

Christensen, A., and Jacobson, N. (2000). *Reconcilable Differences.* New York: Guilford Press.

Christensen, D. H., and Rettig, K. D. (1995). The relationship of remarriage to post-divorce coparenting. *Journal of Divorce and Remarriage, 24,* 73–88.

Christmon, K. (1990). Parental responsibility of African-American unwed adolescent fathers. *Adolescence, 25,* 645–654.

Christopher, F., Madura, M., and Weaver, L. (1998). Premarital sexual aggressors: A multivariate analysis of social, relational, and individual variables. *Journal of Marriage and the Family, 60,* 56–69.

Christopher, F. S. (1988). An initial investigation into a continuum of premarital sexual pressure. *The Journal of Sex Research, 25,* 255–266.

Christopher, F. S., Fabes, R. A., and Wilson, P. M. (1989). Family television viewing: Implications for family life education. *Family Relations, 38,* 210–214.

Christopher, R., Owens, L., and Strecker, H. (1993). Exploring the dark side of courtship: A test of a model of male premarital sexual aggression. *Journal of Marriage and the Family, 55,* 469–479.

Church, E. (1999). Who are the people in your family? Stepmothers' diverse notions of kinship. *Journal of Marriage and Divorce, 31,* 83–105.

Civic, D. (1999). The association between characteristics of dating relationships and condom use among heterosexual young adults. *AIDS Education and Prevention, 11*(4), 343–352.

Clark, C., Shaver, P., and Abrahams, M. (1999). Strategic behaviors in romantic relationship initiation. *Personality and Social Psychology Bulletin, 25*(6), 707–720.

Clarke, S. C. (1995, July 14). Advanced report of final marriage statistics, 1989 and 1990. *Monthly Vital Statistics Report, 43*(12).

Clark-Nicolas, P., and Gray-Little, B. (1991). Effect of economic resources on marital quality in Black married couples. *Journal of Marriage and the Family, 53,* 645–655.

Clemens, A. W., and Axelson, L. J. (1985). The not-so-empty nest: The return of the fledgling adult. *Family Relations, 34,* 259–264.

Cohen, D., Dent, C., and MacKinnon, D. (1991). Condom skills education and sexually transmitted disease reinfection. *The Journal of Sex Research, 28,* 139–144.

Cohen, J. (1987). Parents as educational models and definers. *Journal of Marriage and the Family, 49,* 339–351.

Cohn, D. A., Silver, D. H., Cowan, C. P., Cowan, P. A., and Pearson, J. (1992). Working models of childhood attachment and couple relationships. *Journal of Family Issues, 13,* 432–449.

Coke, M. M. (1992). Correlates of life satisfaction among elderly African-Americans. *Journal of Gerontology, 49,* P316–P320.

Coker, A. L., Harlap, S., and Fortney, J. A. (1993). Oral contraceptives and reproductive cancers: Weighing the risks and benefits. *Family Planning Perspectives, 25,* 17–21.

Coleman, L. M., Antonucci, T. C., Adelmann, P. K., and Crohan, S. E. (1987). Social roles in the lives of middle-aged and older Black women. *Journal of Marriage and the Family, 49,* 761–771.

Coleman, M., and Ganong, L. H. (1990). Remarriage and stepfamily research in the 1980s: Increased interest in an old family form. *Journal of Marriage and the Family, 52,* 925–940.

Coleman, M., and Ganong, L. H. (1991). Remarriage and stepfamily research in the 1980s. In A. Booth (Ed.), *Contemporary Families: Looking Forward, Looking Back* (pp. 192–207). Minneapolis: National Council on Family Relations.

Coleman, M., Ganong, L. H., Clark, J. M., and Madsen, R. (1989). Parenting perceptions in rural and urban families: Is there a difference? *Journal of Marriage and the Family, 51,* 329–335.

Coleman, M., Ganong, L. H., Killian, T., and McDaniel, A. K. (1999). Child support obligations: Attitudes and rationale. *Journal of Family Issues, 20*(1), 46–68.

Coley, S. M., and Beckett, J. O. (1988). Black battered women: A review of empirical literature. *Journal of Counseling and Development, 66,* 266–270.

Collins, C., Hartman, C., and Sklar, H. (1999). *Divided Decade: Economic Disparity at the Century's Turn.* Boston: United for a Fair Economy.

Collins, J. A., Wrixon, W., Janes, L. B., and Wilson, E. H. (1983). Treatment-independent pregnancy among infertile couples. *New England Journal of Medicine, 309,* 1201–1209.

Collins, N. L., and Read, S. J. (1994). Cognitive representations of attachment: The structure and function of working models. In K. Bartholomew and D. Perlman (Eds.), *Advances in Personal Relationships, Vol. 5: Attachment Processes in Adulthood* (pp. 53–90). London: Jessica Kingsley.

Collins, P. H. (1987). The meaning of motherhood in Black cultural and Black mother/daughter relationships. *Sage: A Scholarly Journal on Black Women, 4,* 3–10.

Collins, W. E., Newman, B. M., and McKenry, P. C. (1995). Intrapsychic and interpersonal factors related to adolescent psychological well-being in stepmother and stepfather families. *Journal of Family Psychology, 9,* 433–445.

Coltrane, S. S., and Ishii-Kuntz, M. (1992). Men's housework: A life course perspective. *Journal of Marriage and the Family, 54,* 43–57.

Conant, M., Spicer, C., and Smith, C. (1986). Herpes simplex virus transmission: Condom studies. *Sexually Transmitted Diseases, 11,* 94–95.

Conger, R. D., Conger, K. J., Elder, G. H., Lorenz, R. O., Simons, R. L., and Whitbeck, L. B. (1992). A family process model of economic hardship and adjustment of early adolescent boys. *Child Development, 63,* 526–541.

Conger, R. D., Elder, G. H., Jr., Lorenz, F. O., Conger, K., Simons, R. L., Whitbeck, L. B., Huck, S., and Melby, J. N. (1990). Linking economic hardship to marital quality and instability. *Journal of Marriage and the Family, 52,* 643–656.

Conger, R. D., McCarty, J. A., Yang, R. K., Lahey, B. B., and Burgess, R. L. (1984). Mother's age as a predictor of observed maternal behavior in three independent samples of families. *Journal of Marriage and the Family, 46,* 411–424.

Consortium of Social Science Associations. (1999, March 12). *Is Welfare Reform Working? The Impact of Economic Growth and Policy Changes: Executive Summary, COSSA Congressional Seminar.* Washington, DC: COSSA. Retrieved June 30, 2000, from the World Wide Web: http://members.aol.com/socscience/welfareseminar.htm

Cook, C., Selig, K., Wedge, B., and Gohn-Baube, E. (1999). Access barriers and the use of prenatal care by low-income, inner-city women. *Social Work, 44*(2), 129–139.

Cook, E. P. (1985). Androgyny: A goal for counseling. *Journal of Counseling and Development, 63,* 567–571.

Cook, E. P. (1990). Gender and psychological distress. *Journal of Counseling and Development, 68,* 371–375.

Coombs, R. H., and Landsverk, J. (1988). Parenting styles and substance use during childhood and adolescence. *Journal of Marriage and the Family, 50,* 473–482.

Cooney, R. S., Rogler, L. H., Hurrell, R. M., and Ortiz, V. (1982). Decision making in intergenerational Puerto Rican families. *Journal of Marriage and the Family, 44,* 621–632.

Cooney, T. M. (1989). Co-residence with adult children: A comparison of divorced and widowed women. *The Gerontologist, 29,* 779–784.

Cooney, T. M., and Hogan, D. P. (1991). Marriage in an institutionalized life course: First marriage among American men in the 20th century. *Journal of Marriage and the Family, 53,* 178–190.

Cooney, T. M., Pedersen, F. A., Indelicato, S., and Palkovitz, R. (1993). Timing of fatherhood: Is "on-time" optimal? *Journal of Marriage and the Family, 55,* 205–215.

Cooney, T. M., and Uhlenberg, P. (1990). The role of divorce in men's relations with their adult children after mid-life. *Journal of Marriage and the Family, 52,* 677–688.

Cooney, T. M., and Uhlenberg, P. (1991). Changes in work-family connections among highly educated men and women, 1970 to 1980. *Journal of Family Issues, 12,* 69–90.

Coontz, S. (2000). Historical perspectives on family studies. *Journal of Marriage and the Family, 2,* 283–297.

Cotton, S., Antill, J. K., and Cunningham, J. D. (1989). The work motivations of mothers with preschool children. *Journal of Family Issues, 10,* 189–210.

Council for Children. (1984). *Taking Action for Latchkey Children.* Charlotte, NC: Council for Children.

The court edges away from Roe v. Wade. (1989). *Family Planning Perspectives, 21,* 184–187.

Court reaffirms Roe but upholds restrictions. (1992). *Family Planning Perspectives, 24,* 174–185.

Cousins, P. C., and Vincent, J. P. (1983). Supportive and adversive behavior following spousal complaints. *Journal of Marriage and the Family, 45,* 679–682.

Cowan, C. C., and Cowan, P. A. (1995). Intervention leads to transition to parenthood. *Family Relations, 44,* 412–423.

Cox, C. (1982). A golden rule test. *Psychology Today, 16,* 78.

Coysh, W. S., Johnston, J. R., Tschann, J. M., Wallerstein, J. S., and Kline, M. (1989). Parental postdivorce adjustment in joint and sole physical custody families. *Journal of Family Issues, 10,* 52–71.

Craig, M. E., Kalichman, S. C., and Follingstad, D. R. (1989). Verbal coercive sexual behavior among college students. *Archives of Sexual Behavior, 18,* 421–434.

Crispell, D. (1996, July). Empty nests are getting fuller. *The Numbers News.* Retrieved July 17, 2000, from the World Wide Web: http://www.demographics.com/publications/fc/96_nn/9607_nn/9607NN11.htm

Crnic, K. A., and Booth, C. L. (1991). Mothers' and fathers' perceptions of daily hassles of parenting across early childhood. *Journal of Marriage and the Family, 53,* 1042–1050.

Crohan, S. E. (1996). Marital quality and conflict that crossed the transition to parenthood in African-American and White couples. *Journal of Marriage and the Family, 58,* 933–944.

Crohan, S. E., and Veroff, J. (1989). Dimensions of marital well-being among White and Black newlyweds. *Journal of Marriage and the Family, 51,* 373–383.

Crosbie-Burnett, M., and Giles-Sims, J. (1994). Adolescent adjustment of stepparenting styles. *Family Relations, 43,* 394–399.

Crystal, S., and Beck, P. (1992). A room of one's own: SRO and the single elderly. *The Gerontologist, 32,* 684–692.

C-section rates remain high, but postcesarean vaginal births are rising. (1989). *Family Planning Perspectives, 21,* 36–37.

Csikszentmihalyi, M. (1999, October). If we are so rich, why aren't we happy? *American Psychologist,* 821–827.

Csikszentmihalyi, M., and Schneider, B. (2000). *Becoming Adult: How Teenagers Prepare for Work.* New York: Basic Books.

Curran, D. (1983). *Traits of a Healthy Family.* New York: Ballantine Books.

Curtin, S. C., and Martin, J. A. (2000, August 8). Births: Preliminary data for 1999. *National Vital Statistics Report, 48*(14).

Cushman, L. F., Romero, D., Kalmuss, D., Davidsong, A. R., Heartwell, S., and Rubin, M. (1998). Condom use among women choosing long-term hormonal contraception. *Family Planning Perspectives, 30*(5), 240, 243.

Cushner, I. M. (1986). Reproductive technologies: New choices, new hopes, new dilemmas. *Family Planning Perspectives, 18,* 129–132.

Dail, P. W., and Way, W. L. (1985). What do parents observe about parenting upon prime time television? *Family Relations, 34,* 491–499.

Dalla, R. L., and Gamble, W. C. (1997). Exploring factors relating to parenting competence among Navaho teenage mothers: Dual techniques of inquiry. *Family Relations, 46,* 113–121.

Daly, K. J., and Sobol, M. P. (1994). Public and private adoption. *Family Relations, 43,* 86–93.

Dandeneau, N. L., and Johnson, F. N. (1994). Facilitating intimacy: Interventions and effects. *Journal of Marital and Family Therapy, 20,* 17–33.

Darling, C. A., Davidson, J. K., Sr., and Cox, R. P. (1991). Female sexual response and the timing of partner orgasm. *Journal of Sex and Marital Therapy, 17,* 3–21.

Darling, C. A., Davidson, J. K., Sr., and Jennings, D. A. (1991). The female sexual response revisited: Understanding the multiorgasmic experience in women. *Archives of Sexual Behavior, 20,* 527–540.

Darney, P. D. (1990). Acceptance and perceptions of NOR-PLANT among users in San Francisco, U.S.A. *Studies in Family Planning, 21,* 152.

Davey, A. J., and Paolucci, B. (1980). Family interaction: A study of shared time and activities. *Family Relations, 29,* 43–49.

Davidson, J. (1989). Longevity blooms with younger grooms. *Psychology Today, 21,* 72.

Davies, L. (1995). A closer look at gender and distress among the never married. *Women and Health, 23,* 13–30.

Davis, K. E. (1985). Near and dear: Friendship and love compared. *Psychology Today, 19,* 22–30.

Davis, P. W. (1996). Threats of corporal punishment as verbal aggression: A naturalistic study. *Child Abuse and Neglect, 20*(4), 289–304.

Davis-Brown, K., Salamon, S., and Surra, C. A. (1987). Economic and social factors in mate selection: An ethnographic analysis of an agriculture community. *Journal of Marriage and the Family, 49,* 41–55.

Deacon, S. (1999). Explore your family: An experiential family-of-origin workshop. *Family Therapy, 26*(2), 87–102.

Deater-Deckard, K., and Scarr, S. (1996). Parenting stress among dual-earner mothers and fathers: Are there gender differences? *Journal of Family Psychology, 10*(1), 45–59.

Deaux, K., and Major, B. (1987). Putting gender into context: An interactive model of gender-related behavior. *Psychological Review, 94,* 369–389.

DeFrain, J. (1991). Learning about grief from normal families: SIDS, stillbirth, and miscarriage. *Journal of Marriage and Family Therapy, 17,* 215–232.

DeGarmo, D. S., and Forgatch, M. S. (1999). Contexts as predictors of changing maternal parenting practices in diverse family structures. In E. M. Hetherington (Ed.), *Coping with Divorce, Single Parenting, and Remarriage: A Risk and Resiliency Perspective* (pp. 227–252). Mahwah, NJ: Erlbaum.

DeGarmo, D. S., and Kipson, G. C. (1996). Identity relevance and disruption as predictors of psychological stress for widowed and divorced women. *Journal of Marriage and the Family, 58,* 983–997.

DeGenova, M. K. (1997). *Families in Cultural Context.* Mountain View, CA: Mayfield.

Dekovic, M., and Gerris, J. R. M. (1992). Parental reasoning complexity, social class, and child-rearing behaviors. *Journal of Marriage and the Family, 54,* 675–685.

Dekovic, M., and Janssens, J. M. A. M. (1992). Parents' child-rearing style and child's sociometric status. *Developmental Psychology, 28,* 925–932.

DeMaris, A. (1987). The efficacy of a spouse-abuse model in accounting for courtship violence. *Journal of Family Issues, 8,* 291–305.

DeMaris, A. (1990). The dynamics of generational transfer in courtship violence: A biracial exploration. *Journal of Marriage and the Family, 52,* 219–231.

DeMaris, A., and MacDonald, W. (1993). Premarital cohabitation and marital instability: A test of the unconventionality hypothesis. *Journal of Marriage and the Family, 55,* 399–407.

DeMaris, A., and Rao, K. B. (1992). Premarital cohabitation and subsequent marital stability in the United States: A reassessment. *Journal of Marriage and the Family, 54,* 178–190.

DeMaris, A., and Swinford, S. (1996). Female victims of spousal violence. *Family Relations, 45,* 98–106.

DeMeis, D. K., and Perkins, H. W. (1996). "Super moms" of the nineties. *Journal of Family Issues, 17,* 777–792.

Demo, D. H. (1992). Parent-child relations: Recent changes. *Journal of Marriage and the Family, 54,* 104–117.

Demo, D. H., and Acock, A. C. (1996a). Family structure, family process, and adolescent well-being. *Journal of Research on Adolescence, 6*(4), 457–488.

Demo, D. H., and Acock, A. C. (1996b). Singlehood, marriage, and remarriage. *Journal of Family Issues, 17,* 388–407.

Demo, D. H., and Acock, A. C. (1997). Family diversity and the division of domestic labor: How much have things really changed? *Family Relations, 42,* 323–331.

Denham, T. E., and Smith, C. W. (1989). The influence of grandparents and grandchildren: A review of the literature and resources. *Family Relations, 38,* 345–350.

The denial of Indian civil and religious rights. (1975). *Indian Historian, 8,* 43–46.

Denny, N., Field, J., and Quadagno, D. (1984). Sex differences in sexual needs and desires. *Archives of Sexual Behavior, 13,* 233–245.

Desmarais, S., and Curtis, J. (1999). Gender differences in employment and income experiences among young people. In J. Barling and E. Kelloway (Eds.), *Young Workers' Varieties of Experiences* (pp. 59–88). Washington, DC: American Psychological Association.

deTurck, M. A., and Miller, G. R. (1986). The effect of husbands and wives social cognition on their marital adjustment, conjugal power and self-esteem. *Journal of Marriage and the Family, 48,* 715–724.

Dhir, K. S., and Markman, H. J. (1984). Application of social judgment theory to understanding and treating marital conflict. *Journal of Marriage and the Family, 46,* 597–610.

Diener, E., Horwitz, J., and Emmons, R. A. (1985). Happiness of the very wealthy. *Social Indicators, 16,* 263–274.

Dietz, C. L. (1995). Patterns of intergenerational assistance within the Mexican-American families. *Journal of Family Issues, 16,* 344–356.

Dionne, E. J., Jr. (1989, August 3). Poll finds ambivalence on abortion persists in U.S. *New York Times,* p. 1.

Dodson, L. (1998). *Don't Call Us Out of Name: The Untold Lives of Women and Girls in Poor America.* Boston: Beacon Press.

Doe v. Bolton, 410 U.S. 179 (1973).

Doherty, W. J., Su, S., and Needle, R. (1989). Marital disruption and psychological well-being. *Journal of Family Issues, 10,* 72–85.

Dolan, M. A., and Hoffman, C. D. (1998). Determinants of divorce among young women: A reexamination of critical influences. *Journal of Divorce and Remarriage, 28*(3/4), 97–106.

Dolcini, M. M., Catania, J. A., Coates, T. J., Stall, R., Hudes, E. S., Gagnon, J. H., and Pollack, L. M. (1993). Demographic characteristics of heterosexuals with multiple partners: The national AIDS behavioral surveys. *Family Planning Perspectives, 25,* 208–214.

Donaldson, P. J., and Keely, C. B. (1988). Population and family planning: An international perspective. *Family Planning Perspectives, 20,* 307–311.

Donnelly, B. W., and Voydanoff, P. (1991). Factors associated with releasing for adoption among adolescent mothers. *Family Relations, 39,* 311–316.

Donovan, C. (1997). Confronting the hidden epidemic: The Institute of Medicine's report on sexually transmitted diseases. *Family Planning Perspectives, 29,* 87–89.

Donovan, C., and Klitsch, N. (1995). Oral contraceptive users may be at some increased risk of cervical carcinoma. *Family Planning Perspectives, 27,* 134–136.

Donovan, P. (1994). Condom breaks and slips occur more often among less experienced users. *Family Planning Perspectives, 26,* 283–284.

Donovan, P. (1995). Midwestern teenagers who have many partners are more likely than others to drink often and have low grades. *Family Planning Perspectives, 27,* 40–41.

Dooley, D., Catalano, R., and Rook, K. S. (1988). Personal and aggregate unemployment and psychological symptoms. *Journal of Social Issues, 47,* 107–123.

Dorfman, L. T., and Heckert, D. A. (1988). Egalitarianism in retired rural couples: Household tasks, decision making, and leisure activities. *Family Relations, 37,* 73–78.

Dorfman, L. T., and Mertens, C. E. (1990). Kinship relations in retired rural men and women. *Family Relations, 39,* 166–173.

Doten, D. (1938). *The Art of Bundling.* New York: Farrar.

Dowling, C. (1983). The relative explosion. *Psychology Today, 17,* 54–59.

Downey, G., Lebolt, A., and Rincon, C. (1998). Rejection sensitivity and children's interpersonal difficulties. *Child Development, 69,* 1074–1091.

Downie, J., and Coates, R. (1999). The impact of gender on parent-child sexuality communication: Has anything changed? *Sexual and Marital Therapy, 14*(2), 109–121.

Doyle, J. A. (1985). *Sex and Gender.* Dubuque, IA: Brown.

Draughn, P. S. (1984). Perceptions of competence in work and marriage of middle-age men. *Journal of Marriage and the Family, 46,* 403–409.

Dreman, S., Orr, E., and Aldor, R. (1989). Competence or dissonance? Divorcing mothers' perceptions of sense of competence and time perspective. *Journal of Marriage and the Family, 51,* 405–415.

Dressel, P. L. (1980). Assortive mating in later life. *Journal of Family Issues, 1,* 379–396.

Dressel, P. L., and Clark, A. (1990). A critical look at family care. *Journal of Marriage and the Family, 52,* 769–782.

Dubroff, L. M., and Papalian, M. M. (1982, June). Syphilis and gonorrhea in pregnant patients. *Medical Aspects of Human Sexuality, 16,* 85–90.

Duck, S. W. (1982). A topography of relationship disengagement and dissolution. In S. W. Duck (Ed.), *Personal Relationships. 4: Dissolving Personal Relationships* (pp. 1–29). London: Academic Press.

Duck, S. W. (1991). *Understanding Relationships.* New York: Guilford Press.

Duff, C. (1994, September 12). Cool pad, fab food, one catch: Mom lives there, too. *Wall Street Journal.*

Duncan, S., Box, T., and Silliman, B. (1996). Racial and gender effects on perceptions of marriage preparation programs among college-educated young adults. *Family Relations, 45,* 80–90.

Dunn, P. C., Ryan, I. J., and O'Brien, K. (1988). College students' acceptance of adoption and five alternatives fertilization techniques. *Journal of Sex Research, 24,* 282–287.

Dupre, A. R., Hampton, H. L., Morrison, H., and Meeks, G. R. (1993). Sexual assault. *Obstetrical and Gynecological Survey, 48,* 640–648.

Dutton, D., and Aron, A. P. (1974). Some evidence of heightened sexual attraction under conditions of high anxiety. *Journal of Personal and Social Psychology, 30,* 510–517.

Dutton, R. K., and Haring, M. (1999). Perpetrator personality effects on post-separation victim reactions in abusive relationships. *Journal of Family Psychology, 14,* 193–204.

Duvall, E. M. (1954). *In-Laws: Pro and Con.* New York: Association Press.

Duvall, E. M. (1977). *Marriage and Family Development* (5th ed.). Philadelphia: Lippincott.

Dwyer, J. W., and Coward, R. T. (1991). A multivariate comparison of the involvement of the adult sons versus daughters in care of impaired parents. *Journal of Gerontology, 46,* S259–S269.

Dyk, P. A. H. (1987). Graduate student management of family and academic roles. *Family Relations, 36,* 329–332.

Dyk, P. A. H. (1990). Healthy family sexuality: Challenge and assessment. *Family Relations, 39,* 216–220.

Eakins, P. S. (Ed.). (1986). *The American Way of Birth.* Philadelphia: Temple University Press.

Easley, N. J., and Epstein, N. (1991). Coping with stress in a family with an alcoholic parent. *Family Relations, 40,* 218–224.

East, P. L., Felice, M. E., and Morgan, M. C. (1993). Sisters' and girlfriends' sexual and childbearing behavior: Effects on early adolescent girls' sexual outcome. *Journal of Marriage and the Family, 55,* 953–963.

Eckenrode, J., Laird, N., and Doris, J. (1993). School performance and disciplinary problems among abused and neglected children. *Developmental Psychology, 29,* 53–62.

Edmondson, B. (1997, November/December). Golden opportunities. *Marketing Tools.* Retrieved from the World Wide Web: http://www.demographics.com/publications

Edwards, J. N. (1987). Changing family structure and youthful well-being. *Journal of Family Issues, 8,* 355–372.

Edwards, J. N. (1991). New conceptions: Biosocial innovations and the family. *Journal of Marriage and the Family, 53,* 349–360.

Edwards, J. N., and Kluck, P. (1980). Patriarchy: The last universe. *Journal of Family Issues, 1,* 317–337.

Edwards, S. (1992a). Among high-risk adults, men with more than four partners, women older than 19 used condoms less. *Family Planning Perspectives, 24,* 283–284.

Edwards, S. (1992b). Early environment and mothers' intellectual ability affect cognitive attainment of adolescents' children. *Family Planning Perspectives, 24,* 89–90.

Edwards, S. (1992c). Heterosexual transmission of HIV facilitated by anal sex and sex during menses. *Family Planning Perspectives, 24,* 237–238.

Edwards, S. (1992d). Use of coffee, alcohol, cigarettes raises risk of poor birth outcomes. *Family Planning Perspectives, 24,* 188–189.

Edwards, S. (1994). Women who have undergone a tubal sterilization have a reduced risk of contracting ovarian cancer. *Family Planning Perspectives, 26,* 90–91.

Eggebeen, D. J. (1988). Determinants of maternal employment for White preschool children: 1960–1980. *Journal of Marriage and the Family, 50,* 149–159.

Eggebeen, D. J. (1992). Family structure and intergenerational exchanges. *Research on Aging, 14,* 427–447.

Eggebeen, D. J., and Hawkins, A. J. (1990). Economic need and wives' employment. *Journal of Family Issues, 11,* 48–66.

Ehrensaft, M., Langhinrichsen-Rohling, J., Heyman, R., O'Leary, K., and Lawrence, E. (1999). Feeling controlled in marriage: A phenomenon specific to physically aggressive couples. *Journal of Family Psychology, 13*(1), 20–32.

Eigen, L., and Rowden, D. A. (1995). A methodology and current estimate of the number of children of alcoholics in the United States. In *Children of Alcoholics: Selected Readings.* Rockville, MD: National Association for Children of Alcoholics.

Eiger, M. S., and Olds, S. W. (1987). *The Complete Book of Breastfeeding.* New York: Workman.

Eisikovits, Z. C., Edleson, J. L., Guttmann, E., and Sela-Amit, M. (1991). Cognitive styles and socialized attitudes of men who batter: Where should we intervene? *Family Relations, 40,* 72–77.

Ekman, P., Levenson, R. W., and Friesen, W. V. (1983). Autonomic nervous system activity distinguishes among emotions. *Science, 221,* 1208–1210.

Elbaum, P. L. (1981). The dynamics, implications and treatment of extramarital sexual relationships for the family therapist. *Journal of Marital and Family Therapy, 7,* 489–495.

Elder, G. H., Conger, R. D., Foster, E. M., and Ardelt, M. (1992). Families under economic pressure. *Journal of Family Issues, 13,* 5–37.

Elder, G. H., Jr., Eccles, J. S., Ardelt, M., and Lord, S. (1995). Inner-city parents under economic pressure: Perspectives on strategies of parenting. *Journal of Marriage and the Family, 57,* 771–784.

Eliminating Syphilis from the United States. (n.d.). Washington, DC: U.S. Department of Health and Human Services. Retrieved from the World Wide Web: http://www.cdc.gov/stopsyphilis/FactPDF/USfact.pdf

Elkins, L. E., and Peterson, C. (1993). Gender differences in best friendships. *Sex Roles, 29,* 497–508.

Elliot, F. R. (1986). *The Family: Change or Continuity?* Atlantic Highlands, NJ: Humanities Press International.

Ellis, B. J., and Symons, D. (1990). Sex differences in sexual fantasy: An evolutionary psychological approach. *The Journal of Sex Research, 27,* 527–555.

Ellison, C. G. (1990). Family ties, friendships, and subjective well-being among Black Americans. *Journal of Marriage and the Family, 52,* 298–310.

Elman, M. R., and Gilbert, L. A. (1984). Coping strategies for role conflict in married professional women with children. *Family Relations, 33,* 317–327.

Emery, R. E. (1994). *Renegotiating Family Relationships: Divorce, Child Custody, and Mediation.* New York: Guilford Press.

Emery, R. E. (1995). Divorce mediation: Negotiating agreements and renegotiating relationships. *Family Relations, 44,* 377–383.

Emery, R. E., and Forehand, R. (1996). Parental divorce and children's well-being: A focus on resilience. In R. J. Haggerty, L. R. Sherrod, N. Garmezy, and M. J. Rutter (Eds.), *Stress, Risk, and Resilience in Children and Adolescents: Processes, Mechanisms, and Interventions* (pp. 64–99). New York: Cambridge University Press.

England, L. W., and Thompson, C. L. (1988). Counseling child sexual abuse victims: Myths and realities. *Journal of Counseling and Development, 66,* 370–373.

Enns, C. Z. (1988). Dilemmas of power and equality in marital and family counseling: Proposal for a feminist perspective. *Journal of Counseling and Development, 67,* 242–248.

Ensminger, M. E., and Celentano, D. D. (1988). Unemployment and psychiatric distress. *Social Science Medicine, 27,* 239–247.

Entwisle, D. R., and Alexander, K. L. (1996). Family type and children's growth in reading and math over the primary grades. *Journal of Marriage and the Family, 58,* 341–355.

Erera-Weatherley, P. I. (1996). On becoming a stepparent: Factors associated with the adoption of alternative stepparenting styles. *Journal of Divorce and Remarriage, 25*(3/4), 155–174.

Erikson, E. H. (1959). *Identity and the Life Cycle.* New York: International Universities Press.

Erikson, J. (1991, November 19). La Frontera, its Indian AIDS grant. *Arizona Daily Star.*

Erkut, S., Fields, J., Sing, R., and Marx, F. (1996). Diversity in girls' experiences: Feeling good about who you are. In B. Leadbeater and N. Way (Eds.), *Urban Girls.* New York: New York University Press.

Eskilson, A. (1997). Solving for the X. *Journal of Youth and Adolescence, 28*(1), 51–70.

Essex, M. J., and Nam, S. (1987). Marital status and loneliness among older women: The differential importance of close family and friends. *Journal of Marriage and the Family, 49,* 93–106.

The Expanded Guide to the AIDS Antibody Test. (1991). (Available from San Francisco AIDS Foundation, P.O. Box 6182, San Francisco, CA 94101-6182).

Fagan, J., and Browne, A. (1994). Violence between spouses and intimates. In A. Reiss and J. Roth (Eds.), *Understanding and Preventing Violence, Vol. 3: Social Influences* (pp. 115–292). Washington, DC: National Academy Press.

Farberow, N. L., Gallagher-Thompson, D., Gilewski, M., and Thompson, L. (1992). Changes in grief and mental health of bereaved spouses of older suicides. *Journal of Gerontology, 47,* P357–P366.

Fass, P. S. (1977). *The Damned and the Beautiful.* New York: Oxford University Press.

Faux, M. (1984). *Childless by Choice.* Garden City, NY: Doubleday.

Federal Interagency Forum on Aging-Related Statistics. (2000). Older Americans 2000: Key indicators of well-being. Retrieved from the World Wide Web: http://www.agingstats.gov/chartbook2000/population.html#indicator5

Feeney, J. A. (1999a). Issues of closeness and distance in dating relationships: Effects of sex and attachment style. *Journal of Social and Personal Relationships, 16*(5), 571–590.

Feeney, J. A. (1999b). Romantic bonds in young adulthood: Links with family experiences. *Journal of Family Studies, 5*(1), 25–46.

Feeney, J. A., and Noller, P. (1991). Attachment style and verbal descriptions of romantic partners. *Journal of Social and Personal Relationships, 8,* 187–215.

Feeney, J. A., and Noller, P. (1996). *Adult Attachment.* Thousand Oaks, CA: Sage.

Feingold, A., and Mazzella, R. (1998). Gender differences in body image are increasing. *Psychological Science, 9*(3), 190–195.

Feldman, C. M. (1997). Childhood precursors of adult interpartner violence. *Clinical Psychology: Science and Practice, 4,* 307–334.

Feldman, H. (1981). A comparison of intentional parents and intentionally childless couples. *Journal of Marriage and the Family, 43,* 593–600.

Feldman, S. S., Mont-Reynaud, R., and Rosenthal, D. A. (1992). When East moves West: Acculturation of values of Chinese adolescents in the United States and Australia. *Journal of Research on Adolescence, 2,* 147–173.

Feldman, S. S., Wentzel, K. R., and Gehring, T. M. (1989). A comparison of the views of mothers, fathers, and preadolescents about family cohesion and power. *Journal of Family Psychology, 3,* 39–60.

Felson, R. B., and Zielinski, M. A. (1989). Children's self-esteem and parental support. *Journal of Marriage and the Family, 51,* 727–735.

Felton, G., and Segelman, F. (1978). Lamaze childbirth training and changes in belief about personal control. *Birth and Family Journal, 5,* 141–150.

Feng, D., Giarrusso, R., Bengtson, V. L., and Frye, N. (1999). Intergenerational transmission of marital quality and marital instability. *Journal of Marriage and the Family, 61,* 451–463.

Ferguson, S. J. (1995). Marriage timing of Chinese-American and Japanese-American women. *Journal of Family Issues, 16,* 214–243.

Ferree, M. M. (1990). Beyond separate spheres: Feminism and family research. *Journal of Marriage and the Family, 52,* 866–884.

Ferree, M. M. (1991). The gender division of labor in two-earner marriages. *Journal of Family Issues, 12,* 158–180.

Ferreiro, B. W., Warren, N. J., and Konanc, J. T. (1986). ADAP: A divorce assessment proposal. *Family Relations, 35,* 439–449.

Field, D. (1999). Continuity and change in friendships in advanced old age: Findings from the Berkeley Older Generational Study. *International Journal of Aging and Human Development, 48,* 325–346.

Filsinger, E. E., and Lamke, L. K. (1983). The lineage transmission of interpersonal competence. *Journal of Marriage and the Family, 45,* 75–80.

Filsinger, E. E., and Thoma, S. J. (1988). Behavioral antecedents of relationship stability and adjustment: A five-year longitudinal study. *Journal of Marriage and the Family, 50,* 785–795.

Filsinger, E. E., and Wilson, M. R. (1983). Social anxiety and marital adjustment. *Family Relations, 32,* 513–519.

Fincham, F. D., and Bradbury, T. N. (1992). Assessing attributions in marriage: The relationship attribution measure. *Journal of Personality and Social Psychology, 62,* 457–468.

Finding Answers and Support for Herpes. (1999). Research Triangle Park, NC: American Social Health Association. Retrieved from the World Wide Web: http://www.ashastd.org/herpes/hrc/educate.html

Fine, M., and Hovestadt, A. J. (1984). Perceptions of marriage and rationality by levels of perceived health in the family of origin. *Journal of Marriage and Family Therapy, 10,* 193–195.

Fine, M. A., and Kurdek, L. A. (1995). Relation between marital quality and (step)parent-child relationship quality for parents and stepparents in stepfamilies. *Journal of Family Psychology, 9*(2), 216–223.

Fine, M. A., McKenry, P. C., Donnelly, B. W., and Voydanoff, P. (1992). Perceived adjustment of parents and children: Variations by family structure, race, and gender. *Journal of Marriage and the Family, 54,* 118–127.

Fine, M. A., Voydanoff, P., and Donnelly, B. W. (1993). Relations between parental control and warmth and child well-being in stepfamilies. *Journal of Family Psychology, 7,* 222–232.

Fingerhut, L. A., Makuc, D., and Kleinman, J. C. (1987). Delayed prenatal care and place of first visit: Differences by health insurance and education. *Family Planning Perspectives, 19,* 212–214.

Fingerman, K. L. (1996). Sources of tension in the aging mother and adult daughter relationship. *Psychology and Aging, 11,* 591–606.

Finkelhor, D. (1980). Sex among siblings: A survey on prevalence, variety, and effects. *Archives of Sexual Behavior, 9,* 171–194.

Finkelhor, D., and Araji, S. (1986). Explanations of pedophilia: A four factor model. *The Journal of Sex Research, 22,* 145–161.

Finkelhor, D., Mitchell, K., and Wolak, J. (2000). *Online Victimization: A Report on the Nation's Youth.* Washington, DC: National Center for Missing and Exploited Children.

Finlay, B. A. (1981). Sex differences in correlates of abortion: Attitudes among college students. *Journal of Marriage and the Family, 43,* 571–581.

Firestone, J., Harris, R., and Lambert, L. (1999). Gender role ideology and the gender based differences in earnings. *Journal of Family and Economic Issues, 20*(2), 191–215.

Firestone, J., and Shelton, B. A. (1988). An estimation of the effect of women's work on available leisure time. *Journal of Family Issues, 9,* 478–495.

Fischer, J. L., Sollie, D. L., Sorell, G. T., and Green, S. K. (1989). Marital status and career stage influence on social networks of young adults. *Journal of Marriage and the Family, 51,* 521–534.

Fischer, L. R. (1983). Mothers and mothers-in-law. *Journal of Marriage and the Family, 45,* 187–192.

Fisher, C. B., Reid, J. D., and Melendez, M. (1989). Conflict in families and friendships of later life. *Family Relations, 38,* 83–89.

Fisher, P. A., and Fagot, B. I. (1993). Negative discipline in families. A multidimensional risk model. *Journal of Family Psychology, 7,* 250–254.

Fishman, B. (1983). The economic behavior of stepfamilies. *Family Relations, 32,* 359–366.

Fitzgerald, B. (1999). Children of lesbian and gay parents: A review of the literature. *Marriage and Family Review, 29*(1), 57–75.

Fitzgerald, H. E., Sullivan, L. A., Ham, H. P., Zucker, R. A., Bruckel, S., and Schneider, A. M. (1993). Predictors of behavior problems in three-year-old sons of alcoholics: Early evidence for the onset of risk. *Child Development, 64,* 110–123.

Fletcher, G., Simpson, J., Thomas, G., and Giles, L. (1999). Ideals in intimate relationships. *Journal of Personality and Social Psychology, 76*(1), 72–89.

Floge, L. (1989). Changing attitudes toward family issues in the United States. *Journal of Marriage and the Family, 51,* 873–893.

Floyd, F. J. (1988). Couples' cognitive/affective reactions to communication behaviors. *Journal of Marriage and the Family, 50,* 523–532.

Floyd, F. J., Hanes, S. N., Doll, E. R., Winemiller, D., Lemsky, C., Burgy, T. M., Werle, M., and Heilman, N. (1992). Assessing retirement satisfaction and perceptions of retirement experiences. *Psychology and Aging, 7,* 609–621.

Flynn, C. P. (1987). Relationship violence: A model for family professionals. *Family Relations, 36,* 295–299.

Flynn, C. P. (1990). Relationship violence by women: Issues and implications. *Family Relations, 39,* 194–198.

Folk, K. F., and Beller, A. H. (1993). Part-time work, child-care choices for mothers of preschool children. *Journal of Marriage and the Family, 55,* 146–157.

Follingstad, D. R., Wright, S., Lloyd, S., and Sebastian, J. A. (1991). Sex differences in motivations and effects in dating violence. *Family Relations, 40,* 51–57.

Forrest, J. D. (1986). The end of IUD marketing in the United States: What does it mean for American women? *Family Planning Perspectives, 18,* 52–57.

Forrest, J. D., and Frost, J. J. (1996). The family planning attitudes and experiences of low-income women. *Family Planning Perspectives, 28,* 246–277.

Forste, R., Tanfer, K., and Tedrow, L. (1995). Sterilization among currently married men in the United States, 1991. *Family Planning Perspectives, 27,* 100–122.

Forthofer, M. S., Markman, H. J., Cox, M., Stanley, S., and Kessler, R. C. (1996). Associations between marital distress and work loss in a national sample. *Journal of Marriage and the Family, 58,* 597–605.

Forward, S. (1986). *Men Who Hate Women: The Women Who Love Them.* New York: Bantam Books.

Fossett, M. A., and Kiecolt, K. J. (1993). Mate availability and family structure among African-Americans in U.S. metropolitan areas. *Journal of Marriage and the Family, 55,* 288–302.

Foster, D., Klinger-Vartabedian, L., and Wispe, L. (1984). Male longevity and age differences between spouses. *Journal of Gerontology, 39,* 117–120.

Fowers, B. J., Montel, K. H., and Olson, D. H. (1996). Predicting marital success for premarital couple types based on PREPARE. *Journal of Marital and Family Therapy, 22,* 103–119.

Fowers, B. J., and Olson, D. H. (1986). Predicting marital success with PREPARE: A predictive validity study. *Journal of Marital and Family Therapy, 12,* 403–413.

Fowers, B. J., and Olson, D. H. (1989). ENRICH Marital Inventory: A discriminant Validity and Cross-Validation Assessment. *Journal of Marital and Family Therapy, 15,* 65–79.

Fowler, C. R. (1982). How to destroy marriage. *Medical Aspects of Human Sexuality, 16,* 16–31A.

Francome, C. (1992). Irish women who seek abortions in England. *Family Planning Perspectives, 24,* 265–268.

Frank, N. L., Poindexter, A. N., Johnson, N. L., and Bateman, L. (1992). Characteristics and attitudes of early contraceptive implant acceptors in Texas. *Family Planning Perspectives, 24,* 209–213.

Franklin, D. L. (1988). The impact of early childbearing on developmental outcomes: The case of Black adolescent parenting. *Family Relations, 37,* 268–274.

Franklin, D. L., Smith, S. E., and McMiller, W. E. C. (1995). Correlates of marital status among African-American mothers in Chicago neighborhoods of concentrated poverty. *Journal of Marriage and the Family, 57,* 141–152.

Franklin, R. L., and Hibbs, "B." (1980). Child custody in transition. *Journal of Marital and Family Therapy, 6,* 285–291.

Franzwa, G., and Lockhart, C. (1998). The social origins and maintenance of gender: Communication styles, personality types and grid-group theory. *Sociological Perspectives, 41*(1), 185–208.

Fredericks, C. (1999). HIV testers and non-testers at a university student health center: A study of college student sexual risk-taking. (Doctoral dissertation, University of Southern California, 1999). *Dissertation Abstracts International, 60,* 2-A.0346.

Freeman, S. J. (1991). Group facilitation of the grieving process with those bereaved by suicide. *Journal of Counseling and Development, 69,* 328–331.

Freud, S. (1953). *Three Essays on the Theory of Sexuality* (Standard ed.). Vol. 7. London: Hogarth, 1953.

Freudenberger, H. J. (1987). Today's troubled men. *Psychology Today, 21,* 46–47.

Freudiger, P. (1983). Life satisfaction among three categories of married women. *Journal of Marriage and the Family, 45,* 213–219.

Fried, P. A., Watkinson, B., and Willan, A. (1984). Marijuana use during pregnancy and decreased length of gestation. *American Journal of Obstetrics and Gynecology, 150,* 23–27.

Friedman, R., Hurt, S., Arnoff, M., and Clarkin, J. (1980). Behavior and the menstrual cycle. *Signs, 5,* 719–738.

Fromm, E. (1956). *The Art of Loving.* New York: Harper & Row.

Fu, H., Darroch, J. E., Haas, T., and Ranjit, N. (1999). Contraceptive failure rates: New estimates from the 1995 National Survey of Family Growth. *Family Planning Perspectives, 31*(2), 56–63.

Fu, H., and Goldman, N. (1996). Incorporating health in the models of marriage choice: Demographic and sociologic perspectives. *Journal of Marriage and the Family, 58,* 740–758.

Fuligni, A., Burton, L., Marshall, S., Perez-Febles, A., Yarrington, J., Kirsh, L., and Merriwether-DeVries, C. (1999). Attitudes toward family obligations among American adolescents with Asian, Latin American, and European backgrounds. *Child Development, 70*(4), 1030–1044.

Gabrel, C., and Jones, A. (2000). The National Nursing Home Survey: 1997 summary. *Vital Health and Statistics, 13*(147).

Gaesser, D. L., and Whitbourne, S. K. (1985). Work identity and marital adjustment in blue-collar men. *Journal of Marriage and the Family, 47,* 747–751.

Gage, M. G., and Christensen, D. H. (1991). Parental roles, socialization and transition to parenthood. *Family Relations, 40,* 332–337.

Galambos, N. L., and Garbarino, J. (1983). Identifying the missing links in the study of latchkey children. *Children Today, 12,* 2–4, 40.

Galambos, N. L., and Silbereisen, R. K. (1989). Role strain in West German dual-earner households. *Journal of Marriage and the Family, 51,* 385–389.

Galliher, R. V., Rostosky, S. S., Welsh, D. P., and Kawaguchi, M. C. (1999). Power and psychological well-being in late adolescent romantic relationships. *Sex Roles, 40,* 689–710.

Galvin, K. M., and Brommel, B. J. (1986). *Family Communication: Cohesion and Change* (2nd ed.). Glenview, IL: Scott, Foresman.

Ganong, L., and Coleman, M. (1984). The effects of remarriage on children: A review of the empirical literature. *Family Relations, 33,* 389–406.

Ganong, L. H., and Coleman, M. (1992). Gender differences and expectations of self and future partners. *Journal of Family Issues, 13,* 1, 55–64.

Ganong, L. H., and Coleman, M. (1994). *Remarried Family Relationships.* Thousand Oaks, CA: Sage.

Ganong, L. H., Coleman, M., Fine, M., and Martin, P. (1999). Stepparents' affinity-seeking and affinity-maintaining strategies with stepchildren. *Journal of Family Issues, 20*(3), 299–327.

Garcia, S., and Khersonsky, D. (1997). They are a lovely couple: Further examination of perceptions of couple attractiveness. *Journal of Social Behavior and Personality, 12*(2), 367–380.

Garfinkel, I., and McLanahan, S. S. (1986). *Single Mothers and Their Children.* Washington, DC: Urban Institute.

Garner, D. M. (1997, January/February). Body image. *Psychology Today,* 32–84.

Gary, L., Beatty, L. A., and Berry, G. L. (1986). Strong Black families: Models of program development for Black families. In S. Van Zandt et al. (Eds.), *Family Strengths 7: Vital Connections* (pp. 453–468). Lincoln, NE: Center for Family Strengths.

Gaudin, J. M., and Davis, K. B. (1985). Social networks of Black and White rural families: A research report. *Journal of Marriage and the Family, 47,* 1015–1021.

Gayles, G. (1984). The truths of our mother's lives: Mother-daughter relationships in Black women's fiction. *Sage: A Scholarly Journal on Black Women, 1,* 8–12.

Gazmararian, J. A., et al. (1995). The relationship between pregnancy intendedness and physical violence in mothers of newborns. *Obstetrics and Gynecology, 85,* 1031–1038.

Gelles, R. J., and Conte, J. R. (1990). Domestic violence and sexual abuse of children: A review of research in the eighties. *Journal of Marriage and the Family, 52,* 1045–1058.

Gelles, R. J., and Harrop, J. W. (1991). The risk of abusive violence among children with nongenetic caregivers. *Family Relations, 40,* 78–83.

Gelles, R. J., and Maynard, P. E. (1987). A structural family systems approach to intervention in cases of family violence. *Family Relations, 36,* 270–275.

Gelster, K. L. P., and Feinauer, L. L. (1988). Divorce potential and marital stability of adult women sexually abused as children compared to adult women not sexually abused as children. *Journal of Marital and Family Therapy, 14,* 269–277.

Gerstel, N. (1988). Divorce and kin ties: The importance of gender. *Journal of Marriage and the Family, 50,* 209–219.

Giarrusso, R., Stallings, M., and Bengtson. V. L. (1995). *The "Intergenerational Hypothesis" Revisited: Parent-Child Differences in Perceptions of Relationships 20 Years Later.* New York: Springer.

Gibbs, J. (1996). Health compromising behaviors in urban early adolescent females: Ethnic and socioeconomic variations. In B. Leadbeater and N. Way (Eds.), *Urban Girls.* New York: New York University Press.

Gigy, L., and Kelly, J. B. (1992). Reasons for divorce: Perspectives of divorcing men and women. *Journal of Divorce and Remarriage, 18,* 169–187.

Gil, V. E. (1990). Sexual fantasy experiences and guilt among conservative Christians: An exploratory study. *The Journal of Sex Research, 27,* 629–638.

Giles, D. (1994). Summer resorts: Black resort towns are enjoying a renaissance thanks to buppies and their families. *Black Enterprise, 25,* 90–91.

Giles-Sims, J. (1985). A longitudinal study of battered children of battered women. *Family Relations, 34,* 205–210.

Giles-Sims, J., and Finkelhor, D. (1984). Child abuse in stepfamilies. *Family Relations, 33,* 407–413.

Giles-Sims, J., Straus, M. A., and Sugarman, D. B. (1995). Child, maternal, and family characteristics associated with corporal punishment. *Family Relations, 44,* 170–176.

Gilford, R. (1984). Contrasts in marital satisfaction throughout old age: An exchange theory analysis. *Journal of Gerontology, 39,* 325–333.

Gilgun, J. F. (1995). We shared something special: The moral discourse of incest perpetrators. *Journal of Marriage and the Family, 57,* 265–281.

Gill, G. K. (1998). The strategic involvement of children in housework: An Australian case of two-income families. *International Journal of Comparative Sociology, 39,* 301–314.

Ginsburg, G. S., and Bronstein, P. (1993). Family factors related to children's intrinsic/extrinsic motivational orientation and academic performance. *Child Development, 64,* 1461–1474.

Giordano, J. A. (1988). Parents of the baby boomers: A new generation of young-old. *Family Relations, 37,* 411–414.

Gladow, N. W., and Ray, M. P. (1986). The impact of informal support systems on the well-being of low income single parents. *Family Relations, 35,* 123–125.

Gladstone, J. W. (1988). Perceived changes in grandmother-grandchild relations following a child's separation or divorce. *The Gerontologist, 28,* 66–72.

Glascoe, F. P., and MacLean, W. E. (1990). How parents appraise their child's development. *Family Relations, 39,* 280–283.

Glass, J. (1992). Housewives and employed wives: Demographic and attitudinal change, 1972–1986. *Journal of Marriage and the Family, 54,* 559–569.

Glenn, N. D. (1982). Interreligious marriage in the United States: Patterns and recent trends. *Journal of Marriage and the Family, 44,* 555–566.

Glenn, N. D. (1984). A note on estimating the strength of influences for religious endogamy. *Journal of Marriage and the Family, 46,* 725–727.

Glenn, N. D. (1991). The recent trend in marital success in the United States. *Journal of Marriage and the Family, 53,* 261–270.

Glenn, N. D. (1999). Further discussion of the effects of no-fault divorce on divorce rates. *Journal of Marriage and the Family, 61,* 800–802.

Glenn, N. D., and Kramer, K. B. (1985). The psychological well-being of adult children of divorce. *Journal of Marriage and the Family, 47,* 905–912.

Glenn, N. D., and McLanahan, S. (1982). Children and marital happiness: A further specification of the relationship. *Journal of Marriage and the Family, 44,* 63–72.

Glenn, N. D., and Shelton, B. A. (1985). Regional differences in divorce in the United States. *Journal of Marriage and the Family, 47,* 741–752.

Glenn, N. D., and Supancic, M. (1984). The social and demographic correlates of divorce and separation in the United States: An update and reconsideration. *Journal of Marriage and the Family, 46,* 563–575.

Glenn, N. D., and Weaver, C. N. (1988). The changing relationships of marital status to reported happiness. *Journal of Marriage and the Family, 50,* 317–324.

Glick, P. C. (1976). Updating the life cycle of the family. *Journal of Marriage and the Family, 39,* 5–13.

Glick, P. C. (1984). Marriage, divorce, and living arrangements: Prospective changes. *Journal of Family Issues, 5,* 7–26.

Glick, P. C. (1989). Remarried families, stepfamilies, and stepchildren: A brief demographic analysis. *Family Relations, 38,* 24–27.

Glick, P. C. (1990). American families: As they are and were. *Sociology and Social Research, 74,* 139–145.

Glick, P. C. (1994). Living alone during middle adulthood. *Sociological Perspectives, 37,* 445–457.

Godwin, D. D., Draughn, P. S., Little, L. F., and Marlowe, J. (1991). Wives' off-farm employment, farm family economic status, and family relationships. *Journal of Marriage and the Family, 53,* 389–402.

Goetting, A. (1987). Homicidal wives. *Journal of Family Issues, 8,* 332–341.

Goetting, A. (1990). Patterns of support among in-laws in the United States. *Journal of Family Issues, 11,* 67–90.

Gold, M. A., Schein, A., and Coupey, S. M. (1997). Emergency contraception: A national survey of adolescent health activity. *Family Planning Perspectives, 29,* 15–19.

Goldberg, W. A., Greenberger, E., Hamill, S., and O'Neil, R. (1992). Role demands in the lives of employed single mothers with preschoolers. *Journal of Family Issues, 13,* 312–333.

Goldman, A., and Carroll, J. L. (1990). Educational intervention as an adjunct to treatment of erectile dysfunction in older couples. *Journal of Sex and Marital Therapy, 16,* 127–141.

Goldscheider, F. K., and Goldscheider, C. (1989). Family structure and conflict: Nest-leaving expectations of young adults and their parents. *Journal of Marriage and the Family, 51,* 87–97.

Goldsteen, K., and Ross, C. E. (1989). The perceived burden of children. *Journal of Family Issues, 10,* 504–526.

Goldstein, J. R. (1999). The leveling of divorce in the United States. *Demography, 36,* 409–414.

Goldstein, L. H., Diener, N. L., and Mangelsdorf, S. C. (1996). Maternal characteristics and social support across the transition to motherhood: Associates with maternal behavior. *Journal of Family Psychology, 10,* 60–71.

Gollub, E. L., Stein, D., and El-Sadr, W. (1995). Short-term acceptability of the female condom among staff and patients at New York City Hospital. *Family Planning Perspectives, 27,* 155–158.

Gonorrhea/Neisseria. (2000, February 10). Atlanta: Centers for Disease Control. Retrieved from the World Wide Web: http://www.cdc.gov/ncidod/dastlr/gcdir/gono.html

Good, G. E., and Mintz, L. B. (1990). Gender role conflict and depression in college men: Evidence for compounded risk. *Journal of Counseling and Development, 69,* 17–21.

Goodman, M., Rubinstein, R. L., Alexander, B. B., and Luborsky, M. (1991). Cultural differences among elderly women in coping with the death of an adult child. *Journal of Gerontology, 46,* S321–S329.

Gordis, E. B., Margolin, G., and John, R. S. (1997). Marital aggression, observed parental hostility, and child behavior during triadic family interaction. *Journal of Family Psychology, 11,* 76–89.

Gordon, M. (1981). Was Waller ever right? The rating and dating complex reconsidered. *Journal of Marriage and the Family, 43,* 67–76.

Gottfried, A. E., Gottfried, A. W., Killian, C., and Bathurst, K. (1999). Maternal and dual-earner employment. In M. Lamb (Ed.), *Parenting and Child Development in "Nontraditional" Families* (pp. 15–37). Mahwah, NJ: Erlbaum.

Gottman, J. M. (1994). *What Predicts Divorce? The Relationship Between Marital Process and Marital Outcomes.* Hillsdale, NJ: Erlbaum.

Gottman, J. M. (1998). Psychology and the study of marital processes. *Annual Review of Psychology, 49,* 169–197.

Gottman, J. M. (2000). *Seven Principles of Marriage.* New York: Crown.

Gottman, J. M., Coan, J., Carrere, S., and Swanson, C. (1998). Predicting marital happiness and stability from newlywed interaction. *Journal of Marriage and the Family, 60*(1), 5–22.

Gottman, J. M., and Levenson, R. W. (1988). The social psychophysiology of marriage. In P. Noller and M. A. Fitzpatrick (Eds.), *Perspective on Marital Interaction* (pp. 182–200). Philadelphia: Multilingual Matters.

Gottman, J. M., and Levenson, R. W. (1992). Marital processes predictive of later dissolution: Behavior, physiology, and health. *Journal of Personality and Social Psychology, 63,* 221–233.

Gottman, J. M., and Levenson, R. W. (2000). The timing of divorce: Predicting when a couple will divorce over a 14-year period. *Journal of Marriage and the Family, 62,* 737–745.

Gottman, J. M., and Porterfield, A. (1981). Communicative competence in the nonverbal behavior of married couples. *Journal of Marriage and the Family, 43,* 817–824.

Gove, W. R., and Shin, H. (1989). The psychological well-being of divorced and widowed men and women. *Journal of Family Issues, 10,* 122–144.

Gralinski, J. H., and Kopp, C. B. (1993). Everyday rules for behavior: Mothers' requests to young children. *Developmental Psychology, 29,* 573–584.

Granvold, D. K., and Tarrant, R. (1983). Structured marital separation as a marital treatment method. *Journal of Marital and Family Therapy, 2,* 189–198.

Graves, K. L., and Leigh, B. C. (1995). The relationship of substance use with sexual activity among young adults in the United States. *Family Planning Perspectives, 27,* 18–22.

Gray-Little, B., Baucom, D., and Hamby, S. (1996). Marital power, marital adjustment, and therapy outcome. *Journal of Family Psychology, 10*(3), 292–303.

Green, G. (1964). *Sex and the College Girl.* New York: Dial.

Green, K. L., Cameron, R., Polivy, J., Cooper, K., Liu, L., Leiter, L., and Heatherton, T. (1997). Weight dissatisfaction and weight loss attempts among Canadian adults. *Canadian Medical Association Journal, 157,* S17–S25.

Greenberg, J. S., Bruess, C. E., and Sands, D. W. (1986). *Sexuality: Insights and Issues.* Dubuque, IA: Brown.

Greenberger, E., and O'Neil, R. (1990). Parents' concerns about their child's development: Implications for fathers' and mothers' well-being and attitudes toward work. *Journal of Marriage and the Family, 52,* 621–635.

Greenblat, C. (1983). The salience of sexuality in the early years of marriage. *Journal of Marriage and the Family, 45*(2), 289–299.

Greenhaus, J. H., and Beutell, N. J. (1985). Sources of conflict between work and family roles. *Academy of Management Review, 10,* 76–88.

Greenstein, T. N. (1990). Marital disruption and the employment of married women. *Journal of Marriage and the Family, 52,* 657–676.

Greenstein, T. N. (1996). Husbands' participation in domestic labor: Interactive effects of wives' and husbands' gender ideology. *Journal of Marriage and the Family, 68,* 585–595.

Greif, G. L. (1986). Mothers without custody and child support. *Family Relations, 35,* 87–93.

Grimes, D. A. (1984). Conception after tubal sterilization. *Medical Aspects of Human Sexuality, 18,* 95.

Gringlas, M., and Weinraub, M. (1995). The more things change . . . Single parenting revisited. *Journal of Family Issues, 16,* 29–52.

Gross, D. R., and Robinson, S. E. (1987). Ethics, violence, and counseling: Hear no evil, see no evil, speak no evil? *Journal of Counseling and Development, 65,* 340–344.

Grossman, R. A., and Grossman, B. D. (1994). How frequently is emergency contraception prescribed? *Family Planning Perspectives, 26,* 270–271.

Grudzinskas, J. G., and Atkinson, L. (1984). Sexual function during the puerperium. *Archives of Sexual Behavior, 13,* 85–91.

Guberman, N., Maheu, P., and Maille, C. (1992). Women as family caregivers: Why do they care? *The Gerontologist, 32,* 607–617.

Gubrium, J. F., and Holstein, J. A. (1993). Family discourse, organizational embeddedness, and local enactment. *Journal of Family Issues, 14,* 66–81.

Guelzow, M. G., Bird, G. W., and Koball, E. H. (1991). An exploratory path analysis of the stress process for dual-career men and women. *Journal of Marriage and the Family, 53,* 151–164.

Guerney, B., and Maxson, P. (1990). Marital and family enrichment research: A decade review and look ahead. *Journal of Marriage and the Family, 52,* 1127–1135.

Guinzburg, S. (1983). Mothers and married sons. *Psychology Today, 17,* 14.

Gurak, D. T., Falcon, L., Sandefur, G. D., and Torrecilha, R. (1989, March). *A Comparative Examination of the Link Between Premarital Cohabitation and Subsequent Marital Stability.* Paper presented at the meeting of the Population Association of America, Baltimore.

Gutman, H. G. (1976). *The Black Family in Slavery and Freedom, 1750–1925.* New York: Pantheon Books.

Gutmann, M. C. (1996). *The Meanings of Macho: Being a Man in Mexico City.* Berkeley: University of California Press.

Guttmacher, A. F. (1983). *Pregnancy, Birth, and Family Planning* (Revised and updated by I. H. Kaiser). New York: New American Library.

Gwartney-Gibbs, P. A., Stockard, J., and Bohmer, S. (1987). Learning courtship aggression: The influence of parents, peers, and personal experiences. *Family Relations, 36,* 276–282.

Hackel, L. S., and Ruble, D. N. (1992). Changes in the marital relationship after the first baby is born: Predicting the impact of expectancy disconfirmation. *Journal of Personality and Social Psychology, 62,* 944–957.

Haggstrom, G. W., Kanouse, D. E., and Morrison, P. A. (1986). Accounting for the educational shortfalls of mothers. *Journal of Marriage and the Family, 48,* 175–186.

Hahn, B. A. (1993). Marital status in women's health: The effect of economic marital acquisitions. *Journal of Marriage and the Family, 55,* 495–504.

Hahn, J., and Blass, T. (1997). Dating partner preferences: A function of similarity of love styles. *Journal of Social Behavior and Personality, 12*(3), 595–610.

Haley, J. (1982). Restoring law and order in the family. *Psychology Today, 16,* 61–69.

Halford, W. K., Hahlweg, K., and Dunne, M. (1990). The cross-cultural consistency of marital communication associated with marital distress. *Journal of Marriage and the Family, 52,* 487–500.

Halgin, R. P., and Leahy, P. M. (1989). Understanding and treating perfectionistic college students. *Journal of Counseling and Development, 68,* 222–225.

Hall, D. R., and Zhao, J. D. (1995). Cohabitation and divorce in Canada: Testing the selectivity hypothesis. *Journal of Marriage and the Family, 57,* 421–427.

Hall, E. J., and Cummings, E. F. (1997). The effects of marital and parent-child conflicts on other family members: Grandmothers and grown children. *Family Relations, 46,* 135–143.

Hall, E. J., and Cummings, M. (1997). The effects of marital and parent-child conflicts on other family members: Grandmothers and grown children. *Family Relations, 46,* 135–143.

Hall, L. D., Walker, A. K., and Acock, A. T. (1995). Gender and family work in one-parent households. *Journal of Marriage and the Family, 57,* 685–692.

Hall-Eston, C., and Mullins, L. (1999). Social relationship, emotional closeness, and loneliness among older meal program participants. *Social Behavior and Personality, 27*(5), 503–517.

Hamby, S. L., Poindexter, D. C., and Gray-Little, V. (1996). Four measures of partner violence: Construct similarity and classification differences. *Journal of Marriage and the Family, 58,* 127–139.

Hamilton, K., and Waller, G. (1993). Media influences on body size estimation in anorexia and bulimia. *British Journal of Psychiatry, 162,* 837–840.

Hampson, R. B., Beavers, W. R., and Hulgus, Y. (1990). Cross-ethnic family differences: Interactional assessment of White, Black, and Mexican-American families. *Journal of Marital and Family Therapy, 16,* 307–319.

Hampton, R. L., Gelles, R. J., and Harrop, J. W. (1989). Is violence in Black families increasing? A comparison of national survey rates. *Journal of Marriage and the Family, 51,* 969–980.

Hanks, R. S. (1990). The impact of early retirement incentives. *Journal of Family Issues, 11,* 424–437.

Hansen, G. L. (1987). Extradyadic relations during courtship. *The Journal of Sex Research, 23,* 382–390.

Hanson, R. K., Cadsky, O., Harris, A., and Lalonde, C. (1997). Correlates of battering among 997 men: Family history, adjustment, and attitudinal differences. *Violence and Victims, 12,* 191–208.

Hanson, S. L. (1992). Involving families and programs for pregnant teens: Consequences for teens and their families. *Family Relations, 41,* 303–311.

Hanson, S. L., and Ooms, T. (1991). The economic costs and rewards of two-earner, two-parent families. *Journal of Marriage and the Family, 53,* 622–634.

Hanson, S. M. H., and Bozett, F. W. (1987). Fatherhood: A review and resources. *Family Relations, 36,* 333–340.

Hardesty, C., and Bokemeier, J. (1989). Finding time and making do: Distribution of household labor in non-metropolitan marriage. *Journal of Marriage and the Family, 51,* 253–267.

Hardy, G., Orzek, A., and Heistad, S. (1984). Learning to live with others: A program to prevent problems in living situations. *Journal of Counseling and Development, 63,* 110–112.

Hare, J., and Richards, L. (1993). Children raised by lesbian couples: Does context of birth affect father and partner involvement? *Family Relations, 42,* 249–255.

Hare-Mustin, R. T. (1988). Family change and gender differences: Implications for theory and practice. *Family Relations, 37,* 36–41.

Hargrave, T. D., and Sells, J. N. (1997). The development of a forgiveness scale. *Journal of Marital and Family Therapy, 23,* 21–62.

Haring-Hidore, M., Stock, W. A., Okun, M. A., and Witler, R. A. (1985). Marital status and subjective well-being: A research synthesis. *Journal of Marriage and the Family, 47,* 947–953.

Harlow, H. F. (1958). The nature of love. *The American Psychologist, 13,* 673–685.

Harris, K. F., and Marmer, J. K. (1996). Poverty, paternal involvement, and adolescent well-being. *Journal of Family Issues, 5,* 614–640.

Harris, K. M., and Morgan, S. P. (1991). Fathers, sons, and daughters: Differential paternal involvement in parenting. *Journal of Marriage and the Family, 53,* 531–544.

Hart, C. H., DeWolf, D. M., Wozniak, P., and Burts, D. C. (1992). Maternal and paternal disciplinary styles: Relations with preschoolers' playground behavioral orientations and peer status. *Child Development, 63,* 879–892.

Hartman, W., and Fithian, M. (1984). *Any Man Can: Multiple Orgasmic Response in Males.* Paper presented at the Regional Conference of the American Association of Sex Education, Counselors, and Therapists, Las Vegas.

Harvey, D. M., Curry, C. J., and Bray, J. H. (1991). Individuation and intimacy in intergenerational relationships and health: Patterns across two generations. *Journal of Family Psychology, 5,* 204–236.

Harvey, S. M., Beckman, L. J., Sherman, C., and Petitti, D. (1999). Women's experience and satisfaction with emergency contraception. *Family Planning Perspectives, 31*(5), 237–240, 260.

Harvey, S. M., and Scrimshaw, S. C. M. (1988). Coitus-dependent contraceptives: Factors associated with effective use. *The Journal of Sex Research, 25,* 364–378.

Haskett, M. E., and Kistner, J. A. (1991). Social interactions and peer perceptions of young physically abused children. *Child Development, 62,* 979–990.

Hatch, L. R., and Bulcroft, K. (1992). Contact with friends in later life: Disentangling the effects of gender and marital status. *Journal of Marriage and the Family, 54,* 222–232.

Hatch, R. C., James, D. E., and Schumm, W. R. (1986). Spiritual intimacy and marital satisfaction. *Family Relations, 35,* 539–545.

Hatcher, R. A., Trussell, J., Stewart, F., Cates, W., Stewart, G. K., Guest, F., and Kowal, D. (1998). *Contraceptive Technology* (17th ed.). New York: Ardent Media.

Hatcher, R. A., Zieman, M., Watt, A. P., Nelson, A., Darney, P. A., and Pluhar, E. (1999). *A Pocket Guide to Managing Contraception.* Tiger, GA: Bridging the Gap Foundation.

Hause, K. S. (1995). *Friendship After Marriage: Can It Ever Be the Same?* Paper presented at the conference of the International Network on Personal Relationships, College of William and Mary, Williamsburg, VA.

Haverkamp, B., and Daniluk, J. C. (1993). Child sexual abuse. Ethical issues for the family therapist. *Family Relations, 42,* 134–139.

Hayes, B. C., and Pittelkow, Y. (1993). Religious belief, transmission, and the family: An Australian study. *Journal of Marriage and the Family, 55,* 755–766.

Hazan, C., and Shaver, P. (1987). Romantic love conceptualized as an attachment process. *Journal of Personality and Social Psychology, 52,* 511–524.

Hearst, N., and Hulley, S. B. (1988). Preventing the heterosexual spread of AIDS: Are we giving our patients the best advice? *Journal of the American Medical Association, 259,* 2428.

Heaton, T. B. (1990). Marital stability throughout the child-rearing years. *Demography, 27,* 55.

Heaton, T. B., and Albrecht, S. L. (1991). Stable unhappy marriages. *Journal of Marriage and the Family, 53,* 747–758.

Heaton, T. B., and Jacobson, C. K. (1994). Race differences in changing family demographics in the 1980s. *Journal of Family Issues, 15,* 290–308.

Heaton, T. B., and Pratt, E. L. (1990). The effects of religious homogamy on marital satisfaction and stability. *Journal of Family Issues, 11,* 191–207.

Heidrich, S. N., and Ryff, C. D. (1993). Physical and mental health in later life: The self-system as mediator. *Psychology and Aging, 8,* 327–338.

Heilbrun, A. B., and Loftus, M. P. (1986). The role of sadism and peer pressure in the sexual aggression of male college students. *The Journal of Sex Research, 22,* 320–332.

Heiman, J. (1980). Female sexual response patterns. *Archives of General Psychiatry, 37,* 1311–1316.

Heiman, J. R., Rowland, D. L., Hatch, J. P., and Gladue, B. A. (1991). Psychophysiological and endocrine responses to sexual arousal in women. *Archives on Sexual Behavior, 20,* 171–186.

Henggeler, S. W., Edwards, J. J., Hanson, C. L., and Okwumabua, T. H. (1988). The psychological functioning of wife-dominant families. *Journal of Family Psychology, 2,* 188–211.

Henker, F. O. (1984). Sudden disappearance of libido. *Medical Aspects of Human Sexuality, 18,* 167–172.

Henley, N., and Freeman, J. (1995). The sexual politics of interpersonal behavior. In J. Freeman (Ed.), *Women: A Feminist Perspective* (5th ed., pp. 79–91). Mountain View, CA: Mayfield.

Henninger, D., and Esposito, N. (1971). Indian schools. In D. Gottlieb and A. L. Heinsohn (Eds.), *America's Other Youth: Growing Up Poor.* Englewood Cliffs, NJ: Prentice-Hall.

Henretta, J. C., Chan, C. G., and O'Rand, A. M. (1992). Retirement reason versus retirement process: Examining the reasons for retirement typology. *Journal of Gerontology, 47,* S1–S7.

Henshaw, K. (1998). Unintended pregnancy in the United States. *Family Planning Perspectives, 30*(1), 24–29, 46.

Henshaw, S. K. (1992). Abortion trends in 1987 and 1988: Age and race. *Family Planning Perspectives, 24,* 85–86.

Henshaw, S. K., and Kost, K. (1992). Parental involvement in minors' abortion decisions. *Family Planning Perspectives, 24,* 196–207.

Henshaw, S. K., and Kost, K. (1996). Abortion patients in 1994–1995: Characteristics in contraceptive use. *Family Planning Perspectives, 28,* 140–158.

Henton, J., Cate, R., Koval, J., Lloyd, S., and Christopher, S. (1983). Romance and violence in dating relationships. *Journal of Family Issues, 4,* 467–482.

Hepatitis B. (1998). Research Triangle Park, NC: American Social Health Association. Retrieved from the World Wide Web: http://www.ashastd.org/std/hepb.html

Herbert, T. B., Silver, R. C., and Ellard, J. H. (1991). Coping with an abusive relationship: I. How and why do women stay? *Journal of Marriage and the Family, 53,* 311–325.

Herdt, G. (1992). *Gay Culture in America: Essays from the Field.* Boston: Beacon Press.

Herold, E., and Milhausen, R. (1999). Dating preferences of university women: An analysis of the nice guy stereotype. *Journal of Sex and Marital Therapy, 25,* 333–343.

Herold, E. S., and Way, L. (1988). Sexual self-disclosure among university women. *The Journal of Sex Research, 24,* 1–14.

Herrigan, J., and Herrigan, J. (1973). *Loving Free.* New York: Grosset & Dunlap.

Hetherington, E. M. (1989). Coping with family transitions: Winners, losers and survivors. *Child Development, 60,* 1–14.

Hetherington, E. M. (1993). An overview of the Virginia longitudinal study of divorce and remarriage with a focus on early adolescence. *Journal of Family Psychology, 7,* 1–18.

Hetherington, E. M. (1997). Teenaged childrearing and divorce. In S. Luthar, J. A. Burack, D. Cicchetti, and J. Weisz (Eds.), *Developmental Psychopathology: Perspective on Risk and Disorders* (pp. 350–373). New York: Cambridge University Press.

Hetherington, E. M. (1998). Social capital and the development of youth from nondivorced, divorced, and remarried families. In A. Collins (Ed.), *Relationships as Developmental Contexts: The 29th Minnesota Symposium on Child Psychology.* Mahwah, NJ: Erlbaum.

Hetherington, E. M. (1999a). Family functioning in nonstepfamilies and different kinds of stepfamilies: An integration. *Monographs of the Society for Research in Child Development, 64*(4), 184–191.

Hetherington, E. M. (1999b). Family functioning and the adjustment of adolescent siblings in diverse types of families. *Monographs of the Society for Research in Child Development, 64*(4), 1–25.

Hetherington, E. M., and Clingempeel, W. G. (1992). Coping with marital transitions. *Monographs of the Society for Research in Child Development, 57*(2/3), Chicago: University of Chicago Press.

Hetherington, E. M., Clingempeel, W. G., Anderson, E. R., Deal, J., Stanley-Hagan, M., Hollier, E. A., and Lindner, M. (1992). Coping with marital transitions: A family systems perspective. *Monographs of the Society for Research in Child Development, 57*(2/3).

Hetherington, E. M., and Henderson, S. H. (1997). Fathers in stepfamilies. In M. E. Lamb (Ed.), *The Role of the Father in Child Development* (3rd ed., pp. 212–226). New York: Wiley.

Hetherington, E. M., and Jodl, K. M. (1994). Stepfamilies as settings for child development. In A. Booth and J. Dunn (Eds.), *Stepfamilies: Who Benefits? Who Does Not?* (pp. 55–79). Hillsdale, NJ: Erlbaum.

Hetherington, E. M., and Stanley-Hagan, M. M. (1999). Stepfamilies. In M. Lamb (Ed.), *Parenting and Child Development in "Nontraditional" Families* (pp. 137–159). Mahwah, NJ: Erlbaum.

Heuvel, A. V. (1988). The timing of parenthood and intergenerational relations. *Journal of Marriage and the Family, 50,* 483–491.

Heyman, R. E., O'Leary, K. D., and Jouriles, E. M. (1995). Alcohol and aggressive personality styles: Potentiators of serious physical aggression against wives? *Journal of Family Psychology, 9,* 44–57.

Heyman, R. E., Sayers, S. L., and Bellack, A. S. (1994). Global marital satisfaction versus marital adjustment: An empirical comparison of three measures. *Journal of Family Psychology, 8,* 432–446.

Higginbottom, S. F., Barling, J., and Kelloway, E. K. (1993). Linking retirement experience and marital satisfaction: A mediational model. *Psychology and Aging, 8,* 508–516.

High, D. M. (1991). A new myth about families of older people? *The Gerontologist, 31,* 611–618.

Hill, G., and Hill, K. (1997). *The Real Life Dictionary of the Law.* Santa Monica, CA: General Publishing Group.

Hill, M. (1988). Class, kinship density, and conjugal role segregation. *Journal of Marriage and the Family, 50,* 731–741.

Hiller, D. V., and Dyehouse, J. (1987). A case for banishing dual-career marriages from research literature. *Journal of Marriage and the Family, 49,* 787–795.

Hillis, S. D. (1999). Women who are sterilized at age 30 or younger have increased odds of regret. *Family Planning Perspectives, 93*(6), 889–895.

Hiltz, S. R. (1978). Widowhood: A roleless role. *Marriage and Family Review, 1,* 1–10.

Hite, S. (1981). *The Hite Report: A Nationwide Study of Female Sexuality.* New York: Dell.

HIV and Its Transmission. (1999, July). Atlanta: Centers for Disease Control and Prevention. Retrieved from the World Wide Web: http://www.cdc.gov/hiv/pubs/fact/transmission.htm

Ho, D. Y. F. (1989). Continuity of variation in Chinese patterns of socialization. *Journal of Marriage and the Family, 51,* 149–163.

Hobart, C. (1987). Parent-child relations and remarried families. *Journal of Family Issues, 8,* 259–278.

Hodson, D., and Skeen, P. (1987). Child sexual abuse: A review of research and theory with implications for family life educators. *Family Relations, 36,* 215–221.

Hofferth, S., Brayfield, A., Deich, S., and Holcomb, P. (1991). *The National Childcare Survey, 1990.* Washington, DC: Irving Institute Press.

Hofferth, S. L. (1985). Updating children's life course. *Journal of Marriage and the Family, 47,* 93–115.

Hoffman, K. L., Demo, D. H., and Edwards, J. N. (1994). Physical wife abuse in a non-Western society: An integrated theoretical approach. *Journal of Marriage and the Family, 56,* 131–146.

Hoge, D. R., Petrillo, G. H., and Smith, E. I. (1982). Transmission of religious and social values from parents to teenage children. *Journal of Marriage and the Family, 44,* 569–580.

Hollander, D. (1995a). Births while cohabiting most common for Blacks and disadvantaged Whites. *Family Planning Perspectives, 27,* 180–181.

Hollander, D. (1995b). Improvements in neonatal care have increased survival rates for very low birth weight infants. *Family Planning Perspectives, 27,* 182–183.

Hollander, D. (1995c). Young, minority, and disadvantaged women exhibit least favorable pregnancy-related health behavior. *Family Planning Perspectives, 27,* 259–260.

Hollander, D. (1996a). Barrier methods may protect some women against cervical chlamydia, but pill use does not affect risk. *Family Planning Perspectives, 28,* 37–38.

Hollander, D. (1996b). Conception may take a long time among women who smoke. *Family Planning Perspectives, 28,* 181–182.

Hollander, D. (1996c). Long-term breast feeding, especially a first child, lowers breast cancer risks. *Family Planning Perspectives, 25,* 239.

Hollander, D. (1996d). Monthly probability of conception is highest during the six days ending on the day of ovulation. *Family Planning Perspectives, 28,* 127–128.

Hollander, D. (1996e). Programs to bring down cesarean rates proved to be successful. *Family Planning Perspectives, 28,* 182–184.

Hollander, D. (1997a). 1995 U.S. fertility rates were lower than any since the mid 1980s. *Family Planning Perspectives, 29,* 47–48.

Hollander, D. (1997b). Pill-related stroke risk is low, especially if users lack other risk factors. *Family Planning Perspectives, 29,* 95–96.

Holman, T. B., and Burr, W. R. (1980). Beyond the beyond: The growth of family theories in the 1970s. *Journal of Marriage and the Family, 42,* 729–741.

Holman, T. B., and Jacquart, M. (1988). Leisure-activity patterns and marital satisfaction: A further test. *Journal of Marriage and the Family, 50,* 69–77.

Holman, T. D., and Dao Li, B. (1997). Premarital factors influencing perceived readiness for marriage. *Journal of Family Issues, 18,* 124–144.

Holman, T. D., Larson, J. H., and Harmer, S. L. (1994). Premarital couples: The development and predictive validity of a new premarital assessment instrument: The Preparation for Marriage Questionnaire. *Family Relations, 43,* 46–52.

Holmes, E. R., and Holmes, L. D. (1995). *Other Cultures, Elder Years.* Thousand Oaks, CA: Sage.

Honeycutt, J. M. (1986). A model of marital functioning based on an attraction paradigm and social-penetration dimension. *Journal of Marriage and the Family, 48,* 651–667.

Hoopes, D. S. (1979). Intercultural communication concepts and the psychology of intercultural experiences. In M. Pusch (Ed.), *Multicultural Education: A Cross-Cultural Training Approach* (pp. 3–33). La Grange Park, IL: Intercultural Press.

Hopkins, J., Marcues, M., and Campbell, S. B. (1984). Postpartum depression: A critical review. *Psychological Bulletin, 95,* 498–515.

Hopkins, N. M., and Mullis, A. K. (1985). Family perceptions of television viewing habits. *Family Relations, 34,* 177–181.

Horn, J. C. (1981). In cities, fast friends come slowly. *Psychology Today, 15, 32,* 100.

Horowitz, R. (1983). *Honor and the American Dream.* New Brunswick, NJ: Rutgers University Press.

Horwitz, A. D., White, H. R., and Howell-White, S. (1996). Becoming married and mental health: A longitudinal study of cohorts of young adults. *Journal of Marriage and the Family, 58,* 895–907.

Houser, B. B., and Berkman, S. L. (1984). Aging parent/mature child relationships. *Journal of Marriage and the Family, 46,* 245–299.

Houts, R. M., Robins, E., and Huston, T. L. (1996). Compatibility and the development of premarital relationships. *Journal of Marriage and the Family, 58,* 7–20.

Hovell, M., Sipan, T., Blumberg, E., Atkins, C., Hofstetter, C. R., and Kreigner, S. (1994). Family influences on Latino and Anglo adolescents' sexual behavior. *Journal of Marriage and the Family, 56,* 972–986.

Howes, C., and Hamilton, C. E. (1992a). Children's relationships with caregivers: Mothers and child-care teachers. *Child Development, 63,* 859–866.

Howes, C., and Hamilton, C. E. (1992b). Children's relationships with child-care teachers: Stability in concordance with parental attachment. *Child Development, 63,* 867–878.

Howes, C., Phillips, D. A., and Whitebook, M. (1992). Thresholds of quality: Implications for the social development of children in center-based child care. *Child Development, 63,* 449–460.

Hoyt, M. F. (1986). Neuroticism and mate selection. *Medical Aspects of Human Sexuality, 20,* 11.

Hughes, M. (1989). Parenthood and psychological well-being among the formerly married. *Journal of Family Issues, 10,* 463–481.

Hunsley, J., Pinsent, C., Lefedvre, M., James-Tanner, S., and Vito, D. (1995). Assessment of couples, marriages, and families: Construct of validity of the short forms of the Dyadic Adjustment Scale. *Family Relations, 44,* 231–237.

Hunter, A. (1997). Counting on grandmothers: Black mothers' and fathers' reliance on grandmothers for parenting support. *Journal of Family Issues, 18,* 251–269.

Hunter, A. G., and Ensminger, M. E. (1992). Diversity and fluidity in children's living arrangements: Family transitions in an urban Afro-American community. *Journal of Marriage and the Family, 54,* 418–426.

Hurlbert, D. F. (1992). Factors influencing a woman's decision to end an extramarital sexual relationship. *Journal of Sex and Marital Therapy, 18,* 104–113.

Hurlbert, D. F., and Apt, C. (1991). Sexual narcissism and the abusive male. *Journal of Sex and Marital Therapy, 17,* 279–292.

Hurlbert, D. M. (1991). The role of assertiveness in female sexuality: A comparative study between sexually assertive and sexually nonassertive women. *Journal of Sex and Marital Therapy, 17,* 183–190.

Hurst, C. E., and Guldin, D. A. (1981). The effects of intra-individuals and inter-spouse status inconsistency on life satisfaction among older persons. *Journal of Gerontology, 36,* 112–121.

Hwang, S., and Saenz, R. (1997). Fertility of Chinese immigrants in the United States: Testing a fertility emancipation hypothesis. *Journal of Marriage and the Family, 59,* 50–61.

Hyde, J., DeLamater, J., and Plant, E. (1996). Sexuality during pregnancy and the year postpartum. *Journal of Sex Research, 32*(2), 143–151.

Ihinger-Tallman, M., and Pasley, K. (1997). Stepfamilies in 1984 and today: A scholarly perspective. *Marriage and Family Review, 26*(1/2), 19–40.

Increasing rates of ectopic pregnancies. (1984). *Medical Aspects of Human Sexuality, 18,* 14.

Ingersoll-Dayton, B., and Neal, M. B. (1991). Grandparents in family therapy: The clinical research study. *Family Relations, 40,* 264–271.

Isaacs, M. B., and Leon, G. (1988a). Divorce, disputation, and discussion: Communication styles among reunited separated spouses. *Journal of Family Psychology, 1,* 298–311.

Isaacs, M. B., and Leon, G. (1988b). Remarriage and its alternatives following divorce: Mother and child adjustment. *Journal of Marriage and Family Therapy, 14,* 163–173.

Ishii-Kuntz, M. (1994). Paternal involvement and perceptions toward fathers' roles: A comparison between Japan and the United States. *Journal of Family Issues, 15,* 30–48.

Ishii-Kuntz, M., and Lee, G. R. (1987). Status of the elderly: An extension of the theory. *Journal of Marriage and the Family, 49,* 413–420.

Israelstam, K. V. (1989). Interacting individual belief systems in marital relationships. *Journal of Marriage and Family Therapy, 15,* 53–63.

Istvan, J. (1986). Stress, anxiety, and birth outcomes: A critical review of the evidence. *Psychological Bulletin, 100,* 331–348.

Jaccard, J., Dittus, P. J., and Gordon, B. B. (1996). Maternal correlates of adolescent sexual and contraceptive behavior. *Family Planning Perspectives, 28,* 159–165.

Jackson, J., and Berg-Cross, L. (1988). Extending the extended family: The mother-in-law and daughter-in-law relationship of Black women. *Family Relations, 37,* 293–297.

James, B. E. (1983). When wives take sexual initiative. *Medical Aspects of Human Sexuality, 17,* 250.

Jamieson, D. J., and Buescher, P. A. (1992). The effect of family planning participation on prenatal care use and low birth rate. *Family Planning Perspectives, 24,* 214–218.

Jarrett, R. L. (1996). Welfare stigma among low-income, African-American single mothers. *Family Relations, 25,* 368–374.

Jayakody, R., Chatters, L. M., and Taylor, R. J. (1993). Family support to single and married African-American mothers: The provision of financial, emotional, and childcare assistance. *Journal of Marriage and the Family, 55,* 261–276.

Jaycox, L. H., and Repetti, R. L. (1993). Conflict in families and the psychological adjustment of preadolescent children. *Journal of Family Psychology, 7,* 344–355.

Jean-Gilles, M., and Crittenden, P. M. (1990). Maltreating families: A look at siblings. *Family Relations, 39,* 323–329.

Jedlicka, D. (1984). Indirect parental influences on mate choice: A test of the psychoanalytic theory. *Journal of Marriage and the Family, 46,* 65–70.

Jendrek, M. P. (1993). Grandparents who parent their grandchildren: Effects on lifestyle. *Journal of Marriage and the Family, 55,* 609–621.

Jocob, T. (1992). Family studies of alcoholism. *Journal of Psychology, 5,* 319–338.

Joe, T., and Yu, P. (1984). *The "Flip-Side" of Black Families Headed by Women: The Economic Status of Black Men.* Washington, DC: Center for the Study of Social Policy.

Joesch, J. M. (1991). The effect of price of child care on AFDC mothers' paid work behavior. *Family Relations, 40,* 161–166.

Joesch, J. M. (1994). Children and the timing of women's paid work after child birth: A further specification of the relationship. *Journal of Marriage and the Family, 56,* 429–440.

Johansen, A. S., Leibowitz, A., and Waite, L. J. (1996). The importance of childcare characteristics—the choice of care. *Journal of Marriage and the Family, 58,* 759–772.

John, D., Shelton, D. A., and Luschen, K. (1995). Race, ethnicity, gender, and perceptions of fairness. *Journal of Family Issues, 16,* 357–379.

Johnson, C. L. (1988). Postdivorce reorganization of relationships between divorcing children and their parents. *Journal of Marriage and the Family, 50,* 221–231.

Johnson, C. L., and Barer, B. M. (1987). Marital instability and changing kinship networks of grandparents. *The Gerontologist, 27,* 330–335.

Johnson, C. L., and Troll, L. (1992). Family functioning in late, late life. *Journal of Gerontology, 47,* S66–S72.

Johnson, C. L., and Troll, L. (1996). Family structure and the timing of transitions from 70 to 103 years of age. *Journal of Marriage and the Family, 58,* 178–187.

Johnson, D. R., Amoloza, T. O., and Booth, A. (1992). Debility and developmental change in marital quality: A three-wave panel analysis. *Journal of Marriage and the Family, 54,* 582–594.

Johnson, D. R., and Booth, A. (1990). Rural economic decline and marital quality: A panel study of farm marriages. *Family Relations, 39,* 159–165.

Johnson, M. P. (1995). Patriarchal terrorism in common couple violence: Two forms of violence against women. *Journal of Marriage and the Family, 57,* 283–294.

Johnson, M. P., and Milardo, R. M. (1984). Network interference in pair relationships: A social psychological recasting of Slater's theory of social regression. *Journal of Marriage and the Family, 46,* 893–899.

Jones, E., and Gallois, C. (1989). Spouses' impressions of rules for communication in public and private marital conflicts. *Journal of Marriage and the Family, 51*, 957–967.

Jones, E. F., and Forrest, J. D. (1992). Contraceptive failure rates based on the 1988 NSFG. *Family Planning Perspectives, 24*, 12–19.

Jorgensen, S. R. (1986). *Marriage and the Family: Development and Change.* New York: Macmillan.

Jouriles, E. N., and Norwood, W. B. (1995). Physical aggression toward boys and girls in families characterized by the battering of women. *Journal of Family Psychology, 9*, 69–78.

Julian, P. W., McKenry, P. C., and McKelbey, M. W. (1994). Cultural variations in parenting. *Family Relations, 43,* 30–37.

Julian, T., McKenry, R., Gavazzi, S., and Law, J. (1999). Test of family of origin structural models of male verbal and physical aggression. *Journal of Family Issues, 20*(3), 397–423.

Julien, E., and Over, R. (1988). Male sexual arousal across five modes of erotic stimulation. *Archives of Sexual Behavior, 17,* 132–143.

Kagan, N., and Schneider, J. (1987). Toward the measurement of affective sensitivity. *Journal of Counseling and Development, 65*, 459–464.

Kahn, J. G., Brindis, C. D., and Glei, D. A. (1999). Pregnancies averted among U.S. teenagers by the use of contraceptives. *Family Planning Perspectives, 31*(1), 29–34.

Kahn, S. S. (1983). *The Kahn Report on Sexual Preferences: What the Opposite Sex Likes and Dislikes—and Why.* New York: St. Martin's Press.

Kaiser Family Foundation/Glamour Survey of Men and Women on Sexually Transmitted Diseases. (1998). Menlo Park, CA: Kaiser Family Foundation.

Kallen, D. J., Griffore, R. J., Popovich, S., and Powell, V. (1990). Adolescent mothers and their mothers view adoption. *Family Relations, 39,* 311–316.

Kalmijn, M. (1999). Father involvement in childrearing and the perceived stability of marriage. *Journal of Marriage and the Family, 61*, 409–421.

Kalmuss, D. (1984). The intergenerational transmission of marital aggression. *Journal of Marriage and the Family, 46*, 11–19.

Kalmuss, D., Davidson, A., and Cushman, L. (1992). Parenting expectations, experiences, and adjustment to parenthood: A test of the violated expectations framework. *Journal of Marriage and the Family, 54*, 516–526.

Kalmuss, D., and Seltzer, J. A. (1986). Continuity of marital behavior in remarriage: The case of spouse abuse. *Journal of Marriage and the Family, 48*, 113–120.

Kalmuss, D., and Seltzer, J. A. (1989). A framework for studying family socialization over the life cycle. *Journal of Family Issues, 10*, 339–358.

Kalmuss, D. S., and Namerow, P. P. (1994). Subsequent child-bearing among teenage mothers: The determinants of a closely spaced second birth. *Family Planning Perspectives, 26*, 149–153.

Kane, S. (1990). AIDS, addiction, and condom use: Sources of sexual risk for heterosexual women. *The Journal of Sex Research, 27*, 427–444.

Kaplan, E. A. (1990). Sex, work, and motherhood: The impossible triangle. *The Journal of Sex Research, 27,* 409–425.

Kaplan, H. S. (1974). *The New Sex Therapy.* New York: Brunner/Mazel.

Kaplan, H. S. (1979). *Disorders of Sexual Desire.* New York: Simon & Schuster.

Kaplan, H. S. (1990). The combined use of sex therapy in intrapenile injections in the treatment of impotence. *Journal of Sex and Marital Therapy, 16*, 195–207.

Kaplan, L., and Hennon, C. B. (1992). Remarriage education: A personal reflections program. *Family Relations, 41*, 127–134.

Katz, M. H., and Piotrkowski, C. S. (1983). Correlates of family role strain among employed Black women. *Family Relations, 32*, 331–339.

Katzev, A. R., Warner, R. L., and Acock, A. C. (1994). Girls or boys? Relationship of child gender to marital instability. *Journal of Marriage and the Family, 56*, 89–100.

Kaye, K., and Warren, S. (1988). Discourse about adoption in adoptive families. *Journal of Family Psychology, 1*, 406–433.

Keating, N. C., and Cole, P. (1980). What do I do with him 24 hours a day? Change in the housewife role after retirement. *The Gerontologist, 20*, 84–89.

Keenan, J., Gallup, G., Goulet, N., and Kulkarni, M. (1997). Attributions of deception in human mating strategies. *Journal of Social Behavior and Personality 12*(1), 45–52.

Keihani, K. (1999). Pornography and female sexual socialization. (Doctoral dissertation, Pacific Graduate School of Psychology, 1999). *Dissertation Abstracts International, 59*, 7-B.3735.

Keith, P. M. (1986). Isolation of the unmarried in later life. *Family Relations, 35*, 389–395.

Keith, P. M., and Nauta, A. (1988). Old and single in the city and the country: Activities of the unmarried. *Family Relations, 37*, 79–83.

Keith, P. M., and Schafer, R. B. (1985). Role behavior, relative deprivation, and depression among women in one- and two-job families. *Family Relations, 34*, 227–233.

Kelley, D. (1985). Sex, guilt, and authoritarianism: Differences in responses to explicit heterosexual and masturbatory slides. *Journal of Sex Research, 21,* 68–85.

Kelley H. H., and Thibaut, J. W. (1978). *Interpersonal Relations: A Theory of Interdependence.* New York: Wiley-Interscience.

Kelley, P. (1992). Healthy stepfamily functioning. *Families in Society, 73,* 579–587.

Kelly, R. F., and Voydanoff, P. (1985). Work/family role strain among employed parents. *Family Relations, 34,* 367–374.

Kenkel, W. F. (1985). The desire for voluntary childlessness among low-income youth. *Journal of Marriage and the Family, 47,* 509–512.

Kennedy, G. E. (1990). College students' expectations of grandparent and grandchild role behaviors. *The Gerontologist, 30,* 43–48.

Kennedy, J. (1999). Romantic attachment style and ego identity, attributional style, and family of origin in first-year college students. *College Student Journal, 33*(2), 171–180.

Kenney, J. A. (1973). Sexuality of pregnant and breastfeeding women. *Archives of Sexual Behavior, 2,* 215–229.

Kenny, D. A., and Acitelli, L. K. (1994). Measuring similarity in couples. *Journal of Family Psychology, 8,* 417–431.

Kercher, K., Kosloski, K. D., and Normoyle, J. B. (1988). Reconsideration of fear of personal aging and subjective well-being in later life. *Journal of Gerontology, 43,* P170–P172.

Kerig, P. K. (1996). Assessing the links between interparental conflict and child adjustment: The conflict and problem-solving scales. *Journal of Family Psychology, 10,* 454–473.

Kersten, K. K. (1990). The process of marital disaffection: Intervention at various stages. *Family Relations, 39,* 257–265.

Kestelman, P., and Trussell, J. (1991). Efficacy of the simultaneous use of condoms and spermicides. *Family Planning Perspectives, 23,* 226–227.

Kilpatrick, A. C. (1982). Job change in dual-career families: Danger or opportunity. *Family Relations, 31,* 363–368.

Kilty, K. M., and Behling, J. H. (1985). Predicting the retirement intentions and attitudes of professional workers. *Journal of Gerontology, 40,* 219–227.

Kilty, K. M., and Behling, J. H. (1986). Retirement financial planning among professional workers. *The Gerontologist, 26,* 525–530.

King, P. (1989). Living together: Bad for kids. *Psychology Today, 21,* 77.

King, V., and Elder, G. H. (1995). American children view their grandparents: Linked lives across three rural generations. *Journal of Marriage and the Family, 57,* 165–178.

King, V., and Heard, H. E. (1999). Nonresident father visitation, parental conflict, and mother's satisfaction: What's best for child well-being? *Journal of Marriage and the Family, 61,* 385–396.

Kingsbury, N. M., and Minda, R. B. (1988). An analysis of three expected intimate relationship states: Commitment, maintenance, and termination. *Journal of Social and Personal Relationships, 5,* 405–422.

Kinnunen, U., Gerris, J., and Vermulst, A. (1996). Work experiences and family functioning among employed fathers of children of school age. *Family Relations, 45,* 449–455.

Kinsey, A. C., Pomeroy, W., and Martin, C. (1948). *Sexual Behavior in the Human Male.* Philadelphia: Saunders.

Kinsey, A. C., Pomeroy, W., Martin, C., and Gebhard, P. (1953). *Sexual Behavior in the Human Female.* Philadelphia: Saunders.

Kinston, W., Loader, P., and Miller, L. (1987). Quantifying the clinical assessment of family health. *Journal of Marriage and Family Therapy, 13,* 49–67.

Kipnis, D. (1984). The view from the top. *Psychology Today, 18,* 30–36.

Kirby, B. B., and Brown, N. L. (1996). Condom availability programs in U.S. schools. *Family Planning Perspectives, 28,* 196–202.

Kitano, H. H., Yeung, W., Chai, L., and Hatanaka, H. (1984). Asian-American interracial marriage. *Journal of Marriage and the Family, 46,* 179–190.

Kitson, G. C. (1982). Attachment to the spouse in divorce: A scale and its applications. *Journal of Marriage and the Family, 44,* 379–393.

Kivett, V. R. (1988). Older rural fathers and sons: Patterns of association and helping. *Family Relations, 37,* 62–67.

Kivett, V. R. (1993). Racial comparisons in the grandmother role. *Family Relations, 42,* 165–172.

Klagsbrun, F. (1985). *Married People Staying Together in the Age of Divorce.* New York: Bantam Books.

Klaus, H. (1984). Natural family planning. *Medical Aspects of Human Sexuality, 18,* 59–70.

Klaus, M., and Kennel, J. (1982). *Parent-Infant Bonding* (2nd ed.). St. Louis: Mosby.

Klawitter, M. (1994). Child support awards and the earnings of divorced non-custodial fathers. *Social Service Review, 68,* 351–368.

Kleban, M. H., Brody, E. M., Schoonover, C. B., and Hoffman, C. (1989). Family help to the elderly: Perceptions of sons-in-law regarding parent care. *Journal of Marriage and the Family, 51,* 303–312.

Klebanov, P. K., Brooks-Gunn, J., and Duncan, G. J. (1994). Does neighborhood and family poverty affect mothers' parenting, mental health, and social support? *Journal of Marriage and the Family, 56,* 441–455.

Kleiner, H. S., Hertzog, J., and Targ, D. B. (1998). *Grandparents Acting as Parents.* Paper presented at the national satellite video conference Grandparents Raising Grandchildren: Implications for Professionals and Agencies, Purdue University Cooperative Extension Service.

Klepinger, D. A., Lundberg, S., and Plotnick, R. T. (1995). Adolescent fertility and the educational attainment of young women. *Family Planning Perspectives, 27,* 23–28.

Klitsch, M. (1988a). FDA approval ends cervical cap's marathon. *Family Planning Perspectives, 20,* 137–138.

Klitsch, M. (1988b). The return of the IUD. *Family Planning Perspectives, 20,* 19–40.

Klitsch, M. (1989). Noncustodial fathers can probably afford to pay far more child support than they now provide. *Family Planning Perspectives, 21,* 278–279.

Klitsch, M. (1990a). Hispanic fertility rate 40 percent higher than rate of non-Hispanics. *Family Planning Perspectives, 22,* 136–137.

Klitsch, M. (1990b). Women who lack health insurance coverage are more likely to bear seriously ill newborns. *Family Planning Perspectives, 22,* 415.

Klitsch, M. (1992a). Abortion experience does not appear to reduce women's self-esteem or psychological well-being. *Family Planning Perspectives, 24,* 282–283.

Klitsch, M. (1992b). Maternal cocaine use raises delivery costs, need for neonatal care. *Family Planning Perspectives, 24,* 93–95.

Klitsch, M. (1996). New generation of progestins may raise oral contraceptive users' risk of blood clots. *Family Planning Perspectives, 28,* 33–34.

Klohnen, E. C., Vandewater, E. A., and Young, A. (1996). Negotiating the middle years: Ego-resiliency and successful midlife adjustment in women. *Psychology and Aging, 11,* 431–442.

Kluwer, E. S., Heesink, J. E. M., and Van DeBliert, E. (1996). Marital conflict about the division of household labor and paid work. *Journal of Marriage and the Family, 58,* 958–969.

Knaub, P. K. (1986). Growing up in a dual-career family: The children's perception. *Family Relations, 35,* 431–437.

Kniveton, B., and Day, J. (1999). An examination of the relationship between a mother's attitude toward the sex education of her children and her perception of her own parent's view. *Emotional and Behavioral Difficulties, 4*(2), 32–37.

Knoester, C., and Booth, A. (2000). Barriers to divorce. *Journal of Family Issues, 21,* 78–99.

Knox, D. (1985). *Choices in Relationships: An Introduction to Marriage and the Family.* New York: West.

Knox, D., and Wilson, K. (1983). Dating problems of university students. *College Student Journal, 17,* 225–228.

Korman, S. K. (1983). Nontraditional dating behavior: Date-initiation and date expense-sharing among feminists and nonfeminists. *Family Relations, 32,* 575–581.

Korman, S. K., and Leslie, G. (1982). The relationship between feminist ideology and date expense-sharing to perceptions of sexual aggression in dating. *The Journal of Sex Research, 18,* 114–129.

Koss, M. P., Dinero, T. E., and Seibel, C. A. (1988). Stranger and acquaintance rape: Are there differences in the victim's experience? *Psychology of Women Quarterly, 12,* 1–24.

Kost, K., Forrest, D., and Harlap, S. (1991). Comparing health risks and benefits of contraceptive choices. *Family Planning Perspectives, 23,* 54–61.

Kost, K., and Forrest, J. D. (1992). American women's sexual behavior and exposure to risk of sexually transmitted diseases. *Family Planning Perspectives, 24,* 244–254.

Kovar, M. G. (1986). Aging in the eighties: Age 65 years and over and living alone, contacts with family, friends, and neighbors. *Advance Data from Vital and Health Statistics,* no. 116 (DHHS Publication No. [PHS] 86-1250). Washington, DC: National Center for Health Statistics.

Kramarow, E., Lentzner, H., Rooks, R., Weeks, J., and Saydah, S. (1999). *Health, United States, 1999: Health and Aging Chartbook.* Hyattsville, MD: National Center for Health Statistics.

Krause, N., and Baker, E. (1992). Financial strain, economic values, and somatic symptoms in later life. *Psychology and Aging, 7,* 4–14.

Krissman, K. (1990). Social support and gender role attitude among teenage mothers. *Adolescence, 49,* 709–716.

Krotz, J. L. (1999, July/August). Getting even. *Working Woman, 24*(7), 42–46.

Kübler-Ross, E. (1969). *On Death and Dying.* New York: Macmillan.

Kübler-Ross, E. (1974). *Questions and Answers on Death and Dying.* New York: Macmillan.

Kugler, K. E., and Hanson, R. O. (1988). Relational competence and social support among parents at risk of child abuse. *Family Relations, 37,* 238–332.

Kuhlthau, K., and Mason, K. O. (1996). Market child-care versus care by relatives. *Journal of Family Issues, 17,* 561–578.

Kurdek, L. A. (1989a). Relationship quality for newly married husbands and wives: Marital history, stepchildren, and individual-preference predictors. *Journal of Marriage and the Family, 51,* 1053–1064.

Kurdek, L. A. (1989b). Social support and psychological distress in first-married and remarried newlywed husbands and wives. *Journal of Marriage and the Family, 51,* 1047–1052.

Kurdek, L. A. (1995). Predicting change in marital satisfaction from husbands' and wives' conflict resolution styles. *Journal of Marriage and the Family, 56,* 153–164.

Labov, T., and Jacobs, J. A. (1986). Intermarriage in Hawaii, 1950–1983. *Journal of Marriage and the Family, 48,* 79–88.

Lackey, C., and Williams, K. R. (1995). Social bonding and a succession of partner violence across generations. *Journal of Marriage and the Family, 57,* 295–305.

LaFramboise, T. D., and Bigfoot, D. S. (1988). Cultural and cognitive considerations of prevention of American Indian adolescent suicide. *Journal of Adolescence, 11,* 139–153.

Laird, J. (1993). Lesbian and gay families. In R. Walsh and L. D. Wynne (Eds.), *Normal Family Processes* (pp. 282–328). New York: Guilford Press.

Lally, C. F., and Maddock, K. W. (1994). Sexual meaning systems of engaged couples. *Family Relations, 43,* 43–60.

Lamaze, F. (1970). *Painless Childbirth.* Chicago: Regnery.

Lamb, M. (1998). Cybersex: Research notes on the characteristics of the visitors to online chat rooms. *Deviant Behavior: An Interdisciplinary Journal, 19,* 121–135.

Lampard, R., and Peggs, K. (1999). Repartnering: The relevance of parenthood and gender to cohabitation and remarriage among the formerly married. *British Journal of Sociology, 50,* 443–465.

Landers, A. (1985, June 11). Is affection more important than sex? *Family Circle.*

Landry, D. J., and Forrest, J. E. (1995). How old are U.S. fathers? *Family Planning Perspectives, 27,* 159–161.

Laner, M. R., and Thompson, J. (1982). Abuse and aggression in courting couples. *Deviant Behavior, 3,* 229–244.

Larger share of maternal deaths for Massachusetts women with poor prenatal care. (1987). *Family Planning Perspectives, 19,* 217.

LaRossa, R., and Reitzes, D. C. (1993). Continuity and change in middle-class fatherhood, 1925–1939: The culture-conduct connection. *Journal of Marriage and the Family, 55,* 455–468.

Larsen, A. S., and Olson, D. A. (1989). Predicting marital satisfaction using PREPARE: A replicator's study. *Journal of Marital and Family Therapy, 15,* 311–322.

Larson, J. H., Crane, D. R., and Smith, C. W. (1991). Morning and night couples: The effect of wake and sleep patterns on marital adjustment. *Journal of Marital and Family Therapy, 17,* 53–65.

Larson, J. H., and Holman, P. D. (1994). Premarital predictors of marital quality and stability. *Family Relations, 43,* 228–237.

Larson, R. W., Richards, M. H., Moneta, G., Holmbeck, G., and Duckett, E. (1996). Changes in adolescents' daily interactions with their families from ages 10 to 18: Disengagement and transformation. *Developmental Psychology, 32,* 744–754.

Larzelere, R. E., Amberson, T. G., and Martin, J. A. (1992). Age differences in perceived discipline problems from 9 to 48 months. *Family Relations, 41,* 192–199.

Larzelere, R. E., and Huston, T. L. (1980). The dyadic trust scale: Toward understanding interpersonal trust in close relationships. *Journal of Marriage and the Family, 42,* 595–603.

Larzelere, R. E., and Meranda, J. A. (1994). The effectiveness of parental discipline with toddler misbehavior: The different levels of child distress. *Family Relations, 43,* 480–488.

Lau, S., and Pun, K. (1999). Parental evaluations and their agreement: Relationship with children's self-concepts. *Social Behavior and Personality, 27*(6), 639–650.

Lauer, J., and Lauer, R. (1985). Marriages made to last. *Psychology Today, 19,* 22–26.

Lauer, R. H., and Lauer, J. C. (1991). The long-term relational consequences of problematic family backgrounds. *Family Relations, 40,* 286–290.

Lavee, Y., McCubbin, H. I., and Patterson, J. M. (1985). The double ABCX model of family stress and adaptation: An empirical test by analysis of structural equations with latent variables. *Journal of Marriage and the Family, 47,* 811–825.

Lavee, Y., and Olson, D. H. (1993). Seven types of marriage: Empirical typology based on ENRICH. *Journal of Marital and Family Therapy, 19,* 325–340.

Lavee, Y., Sharlin, S., and Katz, R. (1996). The effect of parenting stress of marital quality. *Journal of Family Issues, 17,* 114–135.

Lavine, H., Sweeney, D., and Wagner, S. (1999). Depicting women as sex objects in television advertising: Effects on body dissatisfaction. *Personality and Social Psychology Bulletin, 25*(8), 1049–1058.

Lawton, L., Silverstein, M., and Bengtson, B. (1994). Affection, social contact, and geographic distance between adult children and their parents. *Journal of Marriage and the Family, 56,* 57–68.

Lee, G. R. (1988a). Marital intimacy among older persons. *Journal of Family Issues, 9,* 273–284.

Lee, G. R. (1988b). Marital satisfaction in later life: The effects of nonmarital roles. *Journal of Marriage and the Family, 50,* 775–783.

Lee, G. R., Seccombe, K., and Shehan, C. L. (1991). Marital status and personal happiness: An analysis of trends and data. *Journal of Marriage and the Family, 53,* 839–844.

Lee, J. (1973). *The Colors of Love: An Exploration of the Ways of Loving.* Don Mills, Ontario: New Press.

Lee, J. (1977). A typology of styles of loving. *Personality and Social Psychology Bulletin, 3,* 173–182.

Lee, J. (1988). Love-styles. In R. J. Sternberg and M. L. Barnes (Eds.), *The Psychology of Love* (pp. 38–67). New Haven, CT: Yale University Press.

Lee, P. M., Picard, F., and Blain, M. D. (1994). A methodological and substantive review of intervention outcome studies for families undergoing divorce. *Journal of Family Psychology, 8,* 3–15.

Leigh, G. K., Holman, T. B., and Burr, W. R. (1984). An empirical test of sequence in Murstein's SVR theory of mate selection. *Family Relations, 33,* 225–231.

LeMasters, E. E. (1957). *Modern Courtship and Marriage.* New York: Macmillan.

Lentz, S., and Zeiss, A. (1984). Fantasy and sexual arousal in college women: An empirical investigation. *Imagination, Cognition, and Personality, 3,* 185–202.

Leong, F. T. L. (1991). Career development attributes and occupational values of Asian-American and White-American college students. *The Career Development Quarterly, 29,* 221–230.

Leslie, L. A., Anderson, E. A., and Branson, M. P. (1991). Responsibility for children. The role of gender and employment. *Journal of Family Issues, 12,* 197–210.

Leslie, L. A., Huston, T. L., and Johnson, M. P. (1986). Parental reactions to dating relationships: Do they make a difference? *Journal of Marriage and the Family, 48,* 57–66.

Lesser, E. K., and Comet, J. J. (1987). Help and hindrance: Parents of divorcing children. *Journal of Marital and Family Therapy, 13,* 197–202.

Lester, D. (1997). Correlates of worldwide divorce rates. *Journal of Divorce and Remarriage, 26,* 215–219.

Lester, D. (1999). Regional differences in divorce rates: A preliminary study. *Journal of Divorce and Remarriage, 30,* 121–124.

Levant, R. F., Slattery, S. C., and Loiselle, J. E. (1987). Fathers' involvement in housework and child care with school-age daughters. *Family Relations, 36,* 152–157.

Levin, I. (1993). Family as mapped realities. *Journal of Family Issues, 14,* 82–91.

Levin, I., and Trost, J. (1992). Understanding the concept of family. *Family Relations, 41,* 348–351.

Levine, J. A., and Pittinsky, T. L. (1997). *Working Fathers: New Strategies for Balancing Work and Family.* Reading, MA: Addison-Wesley.

Levine, S. B. (1991). Psychological intimacy. *Journal of Sex and Marital Therapy, 17,* 259–267.

Levinger, G. (1979). A social exchange view on the dissolution of pair relationships. In R. L. Burgess and T. L. Huston (Eds.), *Social Exchange in Developing Relationships* (pp. 169–193). New York: Academic Press.

Levinger, G. (1979). A social psychological perspective on marital dissolution. In G. Levinger and O. C. Moles (Eds.), *Divorce and Separation* (pp. 37–60). New York: Basic Books.

Levinson, D. (1988). Family violence in cross-cultural perspective. In V. B. Van Hasselt, R. L. Morrison, A. S. Bellack, and M. Hersen (Eds.), *Handbook of Family Violence* (pp. 435–455). New York: Plenum.

Levinson, D. J. (1978). *The Seasons of a Man's Life.* New York: Ballantine Books.

Lewis, K. G., and Moon, S. (1997). Always single and single again women: A qualitative study. *Journal of Marital and Family Therapy, 23,* 115–134.

Lewis, R. A., Volk, R. J., and Duncan, S. F. (1989). Stresses on fathers and family relationships relative to rural youth leaving and returning home. *Family Relations, 38,* 174–181.

Li, Q. (1999). Teachers' beliefs and gender differences in mathematics: A review. *Educational Research, 451*(1), 63–76.

Liang, J. (1982). Sex differences in life satisfaction among the elderly. *Journal of Gerontology, 37,* 100–108.

Lichter, D. T., Anderson, R. M., and Hayward, M. D. (1995). Marriage markets and marital choice. *Journal of Family Issues, 16,* 412–431.

Liebowitz, M. R. (1983). *The Chemistry of Love.* Boston: Little, Brown.

Liem, R., and Liem, J. H. (1988). Psychological effects of unemployment on workers and their families. *Journal of Social Issues, 44,* 87–105.

Liese, L. H., Snowden, L. R., and Ford, L. K. (1989). Partner status, social support, and psychological adjustments during pregnancy. *Family Relations, 38,* 311–316.

Lin, I. (2000). Perceived fairness and compliance with child support obligations. *Journal of Marriage and the Family, 62,* 388–398.

Lin, M. (2000, March). *Expenditures on Children by Families, 1999 Annual Report.* (Miscellaneous Publication No. 1528-1999). Washington, DC: U.S. Department of Agriculture, Center for Nutrition Policy and Promotion.

Lincoln, R. (1984). The pill, breast, and cervical cancer, and the role of progestogens in arterial disease. *Family Planning Perspectives, 16,* 55–63.

Lind, P., and Connole, H. (1985). Sex differences in behavioral and cognitive aspects of decision control. *Sex Roles, 12(7/8),* 813–823.

Lindberg, L. D. (1996). Women's decisions about breast feeding and maternal employment. *Journal of Marriage and the Family, 58,* 239–251.

Linz, D. (1989). Exposure to sexually explicit materials and attitudes toward rape: A comparison of study results. *The Journal of Sex Research, 26,* 50–84.

Lipkin, M. J., and Lamb, G. S. (1982). The couvade syndrome: An epidemiologic study. *Annals of Internal Medicine, 96,* 509–511.

Lips, H. M. (1991). *Women, Men, and Power.* Mountain View, CA: Mayfield.

Lips, H. M. (1997). *Sex and Gender: An Introduction* (3rd ed.). Mountain View, CA: Mayfield.

Littenburg, B., and Ransohoff, D. (1984). Hepatitis B vaccination. *American Journal of Medicine, 77,* 1023–1026.

Littlejohn, S. (1983). *Theories of Human Communication.* Columbus, OH: Merrill.

Lloyd, S. A. (1991). The dark side of courtship: Violence in sexual exploitation. *Family Relations, 40,* 14–20.

Lloyd, S. A., and Cate, R. M. (1984). Predicting premarital relationship stability: A methodological refinement. *Journal of Marriage and the Family, 46,* 71–76.

Lockhart, L. L. (1987). A reexamination of the effects of race and social class on the incidence of marital violence: A search for reliable differences. *Journal of Marriage and the Family, 49,* 603–610.

Long, E. C., Cate, R. N., Fehsenfeld, D. A., and Williams, K. M. (1996). A longitudinal assessment of a measure of premarital sexual conflicts. *Family Relations, 45,* 302–308.

Loomis, L. S., and Booth, A. (1995). Multigenerational caregiving and well-being: The myth of the beleaguered sandwich generation. *Journal of Family Issues, 16,* 131–148.

Loomis, L. S., and Landale, M. S. (1994). Nonmarital cohabitation and childbearing among Black and White American women. *Journal of Marriage and the Family, 56,* 949–962.

Lopata, H. Z. (1993). The interweave of public and private: Women's challenge to American society. *Journal of Marriage and the Family, 55,* 176–190.

Lopez, F. G., and Thurman, C. W. (1993). High-trait and low-trait angry college students: A comparison of family environments. *Journal of Counseling and Development, 71,* 524–527.

LoPiccolo, J. (1985, September 22). *Advances in Diagnosis and Treatment of Sexual Dysfunction.* Paper presented at the 28th annual meeting of the Society for the Scientific Study of Sex, San Diego.

Lorenz, F. O., Conger, R. D., Simon, R. L., Whitbeck, L. B., and Elder, G. H., Jr. (1991). Economic pressure and marital quality: An illustration of the method variance problem and the causal modeling of family processes. *Journal of Marriage and the Family, 53,* 375–388.

Lorenz, F. O., Simons, R. L., Conger, R. D., Elder, G. H., Jr., Johnson, C., and Chao, W. (1997). Married and recently divorced mothers' stressful events and distress: Tracing change across time. *Journal of Marriage and the Family, 59,* 219–232.

Lowe, G. D., and Witt, D. D. (1984). Early marriage as a career contingency: The prediction of educational attainment. *Journal of Marriage and the Family, 46,* 689–698.

Lowery, C. R. (1985). Child custody in divorce: Parents' decisions and perceptions. *Family Relations, 34,* 241–249.

Lowery, C. R., and Settle, S. A. (1985). Effects of divorce on children: Differential impact on custody and visitation patterns. *Family Relations, 34,* 455–463.

Lowry, R., et al. (1994). Substance use and HIV-related sexual behaviors among U.S. high school students: Are they related? *American Journal of Public Health, 84,* 1116–1120.

Lueptow, L. B., Guss, M. B., and Hyden, C. (1989). Sex role ideology, marital status, and happiness. *Journal of Family Issues, 10,* 383–400.

Luster, T., Boger, R., and Hannan, K. (1993). Infant affect and home environment. *Journal of Marriage and the Family, 55,* 651–661.

Luster, T., and Small, S. A. (1994). Factors associated with sexual risk-taking behaviors among adolescents. *Journal of Marriage and the Family, 56,* 622–632.

Luster, T., and Small, S. A. (1997). Sexual abuse history and problems in adolescence: Exploring the effects of moderating variables. *Journal of Marriage and the Family, 59,* 131–142.

Lutwak, N. (1985). Fear of intimacy among college women. *Adolescence, 77,* 15–20.

MacDermid, S., Huston, R. L., and McHale, S. M. (1990). Changes in marriage associated with transition to parenthood: Individual differences as a function of sex-role attitudes and changes in the division of household labor. *Journal of Marriage and the Family, 52,* 475–486.

MacDermid, S., Jurich, J., Myers-Walls, J., and Pelo, A. (1992). Feminist teaching: Effective education. *Family Relations, 41(1),* 31–38.

MacDonald, T., and Ross, M. (1999). Assessing the accuracy of predictions about dating relationships: How and why do lovers' predictions differ from those made by observers. *Personality and Social Psychology Bulletin, 25*(1), 1417–1419.

MacDonald, W. L., and DeMaris, A. (1996). Parenting stepchildren and biological children. *Journal of Family Issues, 17,* 5–25.

Mace, D. (1982). *Close Companions: The Marriage Enrichment Handbook.* New York: Continuum.

Mace, D. (1987). Three ways of helping married couples. *Journal of Marriage and Family Therapy, 13,* 179–185.

Mace, D., and Mace, V. (1974). *We Can Have Better Marriages If We Really Want Them.* Nashville: Abingdon.

Mace, D., and Mace, V. (1980). Enriching marriages: The foundation stone of family strength. In N. Stinnett et al. (Eds.), *Family Strengths: Positive Models for Family Life.* Lincoln: University of Nebraska Press.

MacEwen, K. E., and Barling, J. (1991). Effects of maternal employment experiences on children's behavior via mood, cognitive difficulties, and parenting behavior. *Journal of Marriage and the Family, 53,* 635–644.

Maddock, J. W. (1989). Healthy family sexuality: Positive principles for educators and clinicians. *Family Relations, 38,* 130–136.

Magana, J. R., and Carrier, J. M. (1991). Mexican and Mexican-American male sexual behavior and the spread of AIDS in California. *The Journal of Sex Research, 28,* 425–441.

Magdol, L., Moffit, T., Caspi, A., and Silva, P. (1998). Hitting without a license: Testing explanations for differences in partner abuse between young adult daters and cohabitors. *Journal of Marriage and the Family, 60,* 41–45.

Mahler, K. (1996a). Completed, premarital pregnancies more likely among cohabiting women than among singles. *Family Planning Perspectives, 28,* 179–180.

Mahler, K. (1996b). Risk of low birth weight rises among infants with mother and siblings with low birth weight. *Family Planning Perspectives, 28,* 129–130.

Mahler, K. (1996c). Stress during pregnancy may lead to premature delivery, but birth weight appears unaffected. *Family Planning Perspectives, 28,* 292–297.

Mahler, K. (1996d). Women with a history of forced sex initiate voluntary sex earlier. *Family Planning Perspectives, 28,* 130–131.

Makepeace, J. (1981). Courtship violence among college students. *Family Relations, 30,* 97–102.

Makepeace, J. M. (1986). Gender differences in courtship violence victimization. *Family Relations, 35,* 383–388.

Makepeace, J. M. (1987). Social factor and victim-offender differences in courtship violence. *Family Relations, 36,* 87–91.

Make the cover a sales tool. (1998, March 1). *Folio: The Magazine for Magazine Management.* Retrieved from the World Wide Web: http://www.foliomag.com/content/plus/1998/19980301.htm#3

Malamuth, N. M. (1989a). The attraction to sexual aggression scale: Part one. *The Journal of Sex Research, 26,* 26–49.

Malamuth, N. M. (1989b). The attraction to sexual aggression scale: Part two. *The Journal of Sex Research, 26,* 324–354.

Malinak, R., and Wheeler, J. (1985). Endometriosis. *Female Patient, 6,* 35–36.

Malkin, A. R., Wornian, K., and Chrisler, J. C. (1999). Woman and weight: Gendered messages on magazine covers. *Sex Roles, 40*(7/8), 647–655.

Mancini, J. A., and Orthner, D. K. (1988). The context and consequences of family change. *Family Relations, 37,* 363–366.

Maneker, J. S., and Ranking, R. P. (1985). Education, age at marriage, and marital duration: Is there a relationship? *Journal of Marriage and the Family, 47,* 675–683.

Mann, J. (1994). *The Difference: Growing up Female in America.* New York: Warner Books.

Manning, W. D. (1995). Cohabitation, marriage, and entry into motherhood. *Journal of Marriage and the Family, 67,* 191–200.

Manning, W. D., and Lichter, B. C. (1996). Parental cohabitation and children's economic well-being. *Journal of Marriage and the Family, 58,* 998–1010.

March, K. (1995). Perception of adoption as social stigma: motivation, search and reunion. *Journal of Marriage and the Family, 57,* 653–660.

March, K. (1997). The dilemma of adoption reunion: Establishing open communication between adoptees and their birth mothers. *Family Relations, 26,* 99–105.

Marcus, I. M. (1983). The need for flexibility in marriage. *Medical Aspects of Human Sexuality, 17,* 120–131.

Margolian, L. (1991). Abuse and neglect in nonparental child care: A risk assessment. *Journal of Marriage and the Family, 53,* 694–704.

Margolin, G., Christensen, A., and John, R. S. (1996). The continuance and spillover of everyday tensions in distressed and nondistressed families. *Journal of Family Psychology, 10,* 304–321.

Margolin, G., Talovic, S., Fernandez, V., and Onorato, R. (1983). Sex role considerations and behavior marital therapy: Equal does not mean identical. *Journal of Marital and Family Therapy, 9,* 131–145.

Margolis, M. (1984). *Mothers and Such: Views of American Women and Why They Changed.* Berkeley: University of California Press.

Markides, K. S., and Vernon, S. W. (1984). Aging: Sex-role orientation, and adjustment: A three-generation study of Mexican Americans. *Journal of Gerontology, 39,* 586–591.

Marks, N. F., and Lambert, J. D. (1998). Marital status continuity and change among young and midlife adults. *Journal of Family Issues, 19,* 652–686.

Markstrom-Adams, C. (1990). Coming-of-age among contemporary American Indians as portrayed in adolescent fiction. *Adolescence, 25,* 225–237.

Marlow, L., and Sauber, S. R. (1990). *The Handbook of Divorce Mediation.* New York: Plenum.

Marshall, L. L., and Rose, P. (1988). Family of origin violence and courtship abuse. *Journal of Counseling and Development, 66,* 414–418.

Marshall, S. K., and Markstrom-Adams, C. (1995). Attitudes on interfaith dating among Jewish adolescents. *Journal of Family Issues, 16,* 787–811.

Marsiglio, W. (1991). Paternal engagement activities with minor children. *Journal of Marriage and the Family, 53,* 973–986.

Martin, B. (1990). The transmission of relationship difficulties from one generation to the next. *Journal of Youth and Adolescence, 19,* 181–199.

Martin, D., and Martin, M. (1984). Selected attitudes toward marriage and family life among college students. *Family Relations, 33,* 293–300.

Martin, M. J. (1992). Child sexual abuse: Preventing continued victimization by the criminal justice system and associated agencies. *Family Relations, 41,* 330–333.

Martin, M. J., Schumm, W. R., Bugaighis, M. A., Jurich, A. P., and Bollman, S. R. (1987). Family violence and adolescents' perceptions of outcomes of family conflict. *Journal of Marriage and the Family, 49,* 165–171.

Martin, P., Hagestad, G. O., and Diedrich, P. (1988). Family stories: Events (temporarily) remembered. *Journal of Marriage and the Family, 40,* 533–541.

Martin, T. C., and Bumpass, L. L. (1989). Recent trends in marital disruption. *Demography, 26,* 37–51.

Maryland v. Craig, 110 S. Ct. 3157 (1990).

Masheter, C. (1997). Healthy and unhealthy friendship and hostility between ex-spouses. *Journal of Marriage and the Family, 59,* 463–475.

Maslow, A. H. (1962). *Toward a Psychology of Being.* Princeton, NJ: Van Nostrand.

Maslow, A. H. (1970). *Motivation and Personality* (2nd ed.). New York: Harper & Row.

Mason, M., Skolnick, A., and Sugarman, S. D. (Eds.). (1998). *All Our Families: New Policies for a New Century.* New York: Oxford University Press.

Mastekaasa, A. (1992). Marriage and psychological well-being: Some evidence on selection into marriage. *Journal of Marriage and the Family, 54,* 901–911.

Mastekaasa, A. (1994). Psychological well-being and marital disillusion: Selection effects. *Journal of Family Issues, 15,* 208–228.

Masters, W. H., and Johnson, V. E. (1966). *Human Sexual Response.* Boston: Little, Brown.

Masters, W. H., and Johnson, V. E. (1970). *Human Sexual Inadequacy.* Boston: Little, Brown.

Masters, W. H., and Johnson, V. E. (1979). *Homosexuality in Perspective.* Boston: Little, Brown.

Maticka-Tyndale, E. (1991). Sexual scripts and AIDS prevention: Variations in adherence to safer-sex guidelines by heterosexual adolescents. *The Journal of Sex Research, 28,* 45–66.

Matteo, S., and Rissman, E. (1984). Increased sexual activity during the midcycle portion of the human menstrual cycle. *Hormones and Behavior, 18,* 249–255.

Mattessich, P., and Hill, R. (1987). Life cycle and family development. In M. B. Sussman and S. K. Steinmetz (Eds.), *Handbook of Marriage and the Family* (pp. 437–469). New York: Plenum.

Matthews, S. H., and Rosner, T. T. (1988). Shared filial responsibility: The family as the primary caregiver. *Journal of Marriage and the Family, 50,* 185–195.

May, K. A. (1982). Factors contributing to first-time father's readiness for fatherhood: An exploratory study. *Family Relations, 31,* 353–361.

Maynard, F. (1974). Understanding the crises in men's lives. In C. E. Williams and J. F. Crosby (Eds.), *Choice and Challenge* (pp. 135–144). Dubuque, IA: Brown.

Maynard, R., and Rangaragan, A. (1994). Contraceptive use and repeat pregnancies among welfare-dependent teenage mothers. *Family Planning Perspectives, 26,* 198–205.

Mayseless, O. (1991). Adult attachment patterns in courtship violence. *Family Relations, 40,* 21–28.

Mazur, A. (1986). U.S. trends in feminine beauty and overadaptation. *The Journal of Sex Research, 22,* 281–303.

McCabe, M. (1999). The interrelationship between intimacy, relationship functioning, and sexuality among men and women in committed relationships. *Canadian Journal of Human Sexuality, 8*(1), 31–38.

McCabe, M. P. (1987). Desired and experienced levels of premarital affection and sexual intercourse during dating. *The Journal of Sex Research, 23,* 23–33.

McCandless, N. J., Lueptow, L. B., and McClendon, M. (1989). Family economic status and adolescent sex-typing. *Journal of Marriage and the Family, 51,* 627–635.

McCann, J. T., and Biaggio, M. K. (1989). Sexual satisfaction in marriage as a function of life meaning. *Archives of Sexual Behavior, 18,* 59–72.

McCarthy, B. W. (1990). Treating sexual dysfunction associated with prior sexual trauma. *Journal of Sex and Marital Therapy, 16,* 142–146.

McGovern, M. A. (1990). Sensitivity and reciprocity in the play of adolescent mothers and young fathers with their infants. *Family Relations, 339,* 427–431.

McHale, S. M., and Crouter, A. C. (1992). You can't always get what you want: Incongruence between sex-role attitudes and family work roles and its implications for marriage. *Journal of Marriage and the Family, 54,* 537–547.

McKenry, P. C., Julian, T. W., and Gavazzi, S. M. (1995). Toward a biopsychosocial model of domestic violence. *Journal of Marriage and the Family, 57,* 307–320.

McLanahan, S., and Adams, J. (1987). Parenthood and psychological well-being. *Annual Review of Sociology, 13,* 237–257.

McLanahan, S., and Sandefur, G. (1994). *Growing Up with a Single Parent: What Hurts, What Helps.* Cambridge, MA: Harvard University Press.

McLaughlin, D. K., Lichter, D. P., and Johnston, G. M. (1993). Some women marry young: Transitions to first marriage in metropolitan and nonmetropolitan areas. *Journal of Marriage and the Family, 65,* 827–838.

McLeod, B. (1986). The oriental express. *Psychology Today, 20,* 48–52.

McLeod, J. D., and Eckberg, D. A. (1993). Concordance for depressive disorders and marital quality. *Journal of Marriage and the Family, 55,* 733–746.

McLoyd, V. C. (1989). Socialization and development in a changing economy: The effects of paternal job and income loss on children. *American Psychologist, 44,* 293–302.

McLoyd, V. C., and Wilson, L. (1992). Telling them like it is: The role of economic and environmental factors in single mothers' discussion with their children. *American Journal of Community Psychology, 20,* 419–444.

McShane, D. (1988). An analysis of mental health research with American-Indian youth. *Journal of Adolescence, 11,* 87–116.

Mead, M. (1950). *Sex and Temperament in Three Primitive Societies.* New York: Merton Books.

Mederer, H. J., and Weinstein, L. (1992). Choice and constraints in a two-person career. *Journal of Family Issues, 13,* 334–350.

Meehan, P. J., Saltzman, L. E., and Sattin, R. W. (1991). Suicides among older United States residents: Epidemiologic characteristics and trends. *American Journal of Public Health, 81,* 1198–1200.

Meeks, S., Arnkoff, D. B., Glass, C. R., and Notarius, C. I. (1986). Wives' employment status, hassles, communication and relational efficacy: Intra- versus extra-relationship factors and marital adjustment. *Family Relations, 34,* 249–255.

Meer, J. (1985a). Flex-time and sharing. *Psychology Today, 19,* 74.

Meer, J. (1985b). Loneliness. *Psychology Today, 19,* 28–33.

Meisler, A. W., and Carey, M. P. (1991). Depressed affect and male sexual arousal. *Archives of Sexual Behavior, 20,* 541–554.

Menaghan, E. G. (1989). Psychological well-being among parents and nonparents. *Journal of Family Issues, 10,* 547–565.

Menaghan, E. G., and Parcel, T. L. (1990). Parental employment and family life: Research in the 1980s. *Journal of Marriage and the Family, 52,* 1079–1098.

Menaghan, E. G., and Parcel, T. L. (1991). Determining children's home environments: The impact of maternal characteristics in current occupational and family conditions. *Journal of Marriage and the Family, 53,* 417–431.

Mendelberg, H. E. (1984). Split and continuity in language use of Mexican-American adolescents of migrant origin. *Adolescence, 19,* 171–182.

Mendenhall, P. J., Grotevant, H. D., and McRoy, R. G. (1996). Adoptive couples: Communication and changes made in openness levels. *Family Relations, 45,* 223–229.

Messer, A. A. (1983). Continuation in adult life of parent-child relationships: Effect on marriage. *Medical Aspects of Human Sexuality, 17,* 28–43.

Meyer, K., and Lobao, L. (1997). Farm couples in crisis politics: The importance of household, spouse, and gender in responding to economic decline. *Journal of Marriage and the Family, 59,* 204–218.

Michael, R. T., Gagnon, J. H., Laumann, E. O., and Kolata, G. (1994). *Sex in America.* Boston: Little, Brown.

Miller, B. C. (1993). Families, science, and values: Alternative views of parenting effects in adolescent pregnancy. *Journal of Marriage and the Family, 55,* 7–21.

Miller, B. C., and Heaton, T. B. (1991). Age at first sexual intercourse and the timing of marriage and childbirth. *Journal of Marriage and the Family, 53,* 719–732.

Miller, J., Turner, J. G., and Kimball, E. (1981). Big Thompson flood victims: One year later. *Family Relations, 30,* 111–116.

Miller, J. E. (1991). Birth intervals and perinatal health: An investigation of three hypotheses. *Family Planning Perspectives, 23,* 62–70.

Miller, K. J., Gleaves, D. H., Hirsch, T. G., Green, B. A., Snow, A. C., and Corbett, C. C. (2000). Comparisons of body image dimensions by race/ethnicity and gender in a university population. *International Journal of Eating Disorders, 27*(3), 310–316.

Miller, N. E. (1944). Experimental studies of conflict. In J. M. Hunt (Ed.), *Personality and the Behavior Disorders: A Handbook Based on Experimental and Clinical Research* (pp. 431–465). New York: Ronald Press.

Mills, R. J., Grasmick, H. G., Morgan, C. T., and Wenk, D. (1992). The effects of gender, family satisfaction, and economic strain on psychological well-being. *Family Relations, 41,* 440–445.

Minkler, M. (1998). Intergenerational households headed by grandparents: Demographic and sociological contexts. In *Grandparents and Other Relatives Raising Children: Background Papers for Generations United's Expert Symposium* (pp. 3–18). Washington, DC: Generations United.

Minkler, M., Roe, K. M., and Price, M. (1992). The physical and emotional health of grandmothers raising grandchildren in the crack-cocaine epidemic. *The Gerontologist, 32,* 752–761.

Minton, H. L., and McDonald, G. J. (1983/1984). Homosexual identity formation as a developmental process. *Journal of Homosexuality, 9*(2/3), 65–77.

Mirowsky, J., and Ross, C. E. (1987). Belief in innate sex roles: Sex stratification versus interpersonal inference in marriage. *Journal of Marriage and the Family, 49,* 527–540.

Mitchell, B. A., and Gee, E. M. (1996). "Boomerang kids" and mid-life parental marital satisfaction. *Family Relations, 45,* 442–448.

Moen, P. (1991). Transitions in mid-life: Women's work and family roles in the 1970s. *Journal of Marriage and the Family, 53,* 135–150.

Molder, C., and Tolman, R. (1998). Gender and contextual factors in adolescent dating relationships. *Violence Against Women, 4,* 180–194.

Moltz, D. (1992). Abuse and violence: The dark side of the family: An introduction. *Journal of Marital and Family Therapy, 18,* 223–232.

Monroe, C. A., Garand, J. C., and Teeters, H. (1995). Family leave legislation in the U.S. House. *Family Relations, 44,* 46–55.

Montgomery, M. J., and Sorell, G. T. (1997). Differences in love attitudes across family life stages. *Family Relations, 46,* 55–61.

Mookherjee, H. N. (1997). A comparative assessment of life satisfaction in the United States: 1978–1988. *Journal of Social Psychology, 132,* 407–409.

Moore, K. A., Peterson, J. L., and Furstenberg, F. F. (1986). Parental attitudes and the occurrence of early sexual activity. *Journal of Marriage and the Family, 48,* 777–782.

Morgan, L. A. (1989). Economic well-being following marital termination. *Journal of Family Issues, 10,* 86–101.

Morgan, S. P., Lye, D., and Condran, G. (1988). Sons, daughters, and the risk of marital disruption. *American Journal of Sociology, 90,* 1053–1077.

Morrell, M., Dixen, J., Carter, C., and Davidson, J. (1984). The influence of age and cycling status on sexual arousability in women. *American Journal of Obstetrics and Gynecology, 148,* 66–71.

Morrison, B. R., and Cherlin, A. J. (1995). The divorce process and young children's well-being: A prospective analysis. *Journal of Marriage and the Family, 57,* 800–812.

Morrison, D. R., and Lichter, D. T. (1988). Family migration and female employment: The problem of underemployment among migrant married women. *Journal of Marriage and the Family, 50,* 161–172.

Morrow, V. (1996). Rethinking childhood dependency: Children's contributions to the domestic economy. *The Sociological Review, 44,* 58–77.

Morse, B. J. (1995). Beyond the Conflict Tactics Scale: Assessing gender differences in partner violence. *Violence and Victims, 10,* 251–272.

Mosher, D. L., and Tomkins, S. S. (1988). Scripting the macho man: Hypermasculine socialization and enculturation. *The Journal of Sex Research, 25,* 60–84.

Moss, B. F., and Schwebel, A. I. (1993). Marriage and romantic relationships. Defining intimacy in romantic relationships. *Family Relations, 42,* 31–37.

Moss, N. E., and Abramowitz, S. I. (1982). Beyond deficit-filling and developmental stakes: Cross-disciplinary perspectives on parental heritage. *Journal of Marriage and the Family, 44,* 357–366.

Moynihan, D. P. (1965). *The Negro Family: The Case for National Action.* Washington, DC: U.S. Government Printing Office.

Muehlenhard, C. L., and Cook, S. W. (1988). Men's self-reports of unwanted sexual activity. *The Journal of Sex Research, 24,* 58–72.

Mui, A. C. (1992). Caregivers' strain among Black and White caregivers: A role theory perspective. *The Gerontologist, 32,* 203–212.

Mullis, R. L., and McKinley, K. (1989). Gender-role orientation of adolescent females: Effects on self-esteem and locus of control. *Journal of Adolescent Research, 4,* 506–516.

Murdock, G. P. (1949). *Social Structure.* New York: Macmillan.

Murstein, B. I. (1980). Mate selection in the 1970s. *Journal of Marriage and the Family, 42,* 777–792.

Myers, D. A. (1991). Work after cessation of career job. *Journal of Gerontology, 46,* S93–S102.

Myers, D. G. (1993). *The Pursuit of Happiness.* New York: Avon.

Myers, J. E. (1988). The mid/late life generation gap: Adult children with aging parents. *Journal of Counseling and Development, 66,* 331–335.

Myers, J. E. B. (1990). Legal update: 1990—a bellwether year for the abused child in the U.S. Supreme Court. *Violence Update, 1,* 349.

Myers, S. M., and Booth, A. (1996). Men's retirement and marital quality. *Journal of Family Issues, 17,* 336–357.

Myska, M. J., and Pasewark, R. A. (1978). Death attitudes of residential and non-residential rural aged persons. Part II. *Psychological Reports, 43,* 1235–1238.

Nahmias, S. (1989). A model of HIV diffusion from a single source. *The Journal of Sex Research, 26,* 15–25.

Nakonezny, P. A., Shull, R. D., and Rodgers, J. L. (1995). The effect of no-fault divorce law on the divorce rate across the 50 states and its relation to income, education, and religiosity. *Journal of Marriage and the Family, 57,* 477–488.

Namerow, P. B., Kalmuss, D. S., and Cushman, L. F. (1993). The determinants of young women's pregnancy-resolution choices. *Journal of Research on Adolescence, 3,* 193–215.

National Center for Health Statistics. (1995). Advance report of final divorce statistics, 1989 and 1990. *Monthly Vital Statistics Report, 43*(9), Supplement. Retrieved from the World Wide Web: http://www.cdc.gov/nchs/releases/95facts/95sheets/fs_439s.htm

National Center for Health Statistics. (1995). Fertility, family planning, and women's health. National Survey of Family Growth. Retrieved from the World Wide Web: http://www.cdc.gov/nchs/nsfg.htm

National Center for Health Statistics. (2000a). *National Vital Statistics Reports, 48,* 12.

National Center for Health Statistics. (2000b). *National Vital Statistics Reports, 48,* 14.

National Center for Policy Analysis. (1998, October 7). *Social Policy: Intermarriage Blurs Racial Lines.* Retrieved August 2, 2000, from the World Wide Web: http://www.ncpa.org/pd/social/spaug98h.html

National Committee on Pay Equity. (1998). *The Wage Gap by Education.* (Fact sheet). Retrieved August 21, 2000, from the World Wide Web: http://feminist.com/fairpay/f_education.htm

National Committee on Pay Equity. (n.d.). *What the Opposition Says.* (Fact sheet). Retrieved August 21, 2000, from the World Wide Web: http://feminist.com/fairpay/f_talkingpoints.htm

National Institute on Alcohol Abuse and Alcoholism. (1986). *Media Alert: FAS Awareness Campaign: My Baby . . . Strong and Healthy.* Rockville, MD: National Clearinghouse for Alcohol Information.

National Women's Health Resource Center. (1998). *Women and Sexually Transmitted Diseases (STDs).* Retrieved February 14, 1998, from the World Wide Web: http://www.healthywomen.org/qa/std.html#1

Neal, A. G., Groat, H. T., and Wicks, J. W. (1989). Attitudes about having children: A study of 600 couples in the early years of marriage. *Journal of Marriage and the Family, 51,* 313–328.

Nelson, C., and Keith, J. (1990). Comparisons of female and male early adolescent sex role attitude and behavior development. *Adolescence, 25,* 183–204.

Nelson, J. A. (1986). Incest: Self-report findings from a nonclinical sample. *The Journal of Sex Research, 22,* 463–477.

Nelson, W. P., and Lavant, R. F. (1991). An evaluation of a skills' training program for parents and stepfamilies. *Family Relations, 40,* 291–296.

New Survey Reveals Americans Underestimate Their Risk for Contracting Genital Herpes. (2000). Research Triangle Park, NC: American Social Health Association. Retrieved from the World Wide Web: http://www.ashastd.org/press/042600.html

Nieburg, P., Marks, J. S., McLaren, N. M., and Remington, P. L. (1985). The fetal tobacco syndrome. *Journal of the American Medical Association, 253,* 2998–2999.

Nock, S. L. (1995a). Commitment and dependency in marriage. *Journal of Marriage and the Family, 57,* 503–514.

Nock, S. L. (1995b). A comparison of marriages and cohabiting relationships. *Journal of Family Issues, 16,* 53–76.

Nock, S. L., and Kingston, P. W. (1988). Time with children: The impact of couple's work-time commitments. *Social Forces, 67,* 59–85.

Noll, R. B., Zucker, R. A., Fitzgerald, H. E., and Curtis, W. J. (1992). Cognitive and motor functioning of sons of alcoholic fathers and controls: The early childhood years. *Developmental Psychology, 28,* 665–675.

Nordenberg, T. (1999, July/August). Chlamydia's quick cure. *FDA Consumer Magazine.* Retrieved July 25, 2000, from the World Wide Web: http://www.fda.gov/fdac/features/1999/499_std.html

Norton, A. J., and Glick, P. G. (1986). One-parent families: A social and economic profile: *Family Relations, 35,* 9–13.

Norton, A. J., and Moorman, J. E. (1987). Current trends in marriage and divorce among American women. *Journal of Marriage and the Family, 49,* 3–14.

Notarius, C. I., and Johnson, J. S. (1982). Emotional expression in husbands and wives. *Journal of Marriage and the Family, 44,* 483–489.

Nugent, J. K. (1991). Cultural and psychological influences on the father's role in infant development. *Journal of Marriage and the Family, 53,* 475–485.

Nye, F. I. (1978). Is choice and exchange theory the key? *Journal of Marriage and the Family, 40,* 219–233.

Oakley, D. (1985). Premarital childbearing decision making. *Family Relations, 34,* 561–563.

O'Brien, S. (1989). *American Indian Tribal Governments.* Norman: University of Oklahoma Press.

O'Carroll, R. (1991). Sexual desire disorders: A review of controlled treatment studies. *The Journal of Sex Research, 28,* 607–624.

Ohannesian, C. M., and Crockett, L. J. (1993). A longitudinal investigation of the relationship between educational investment and adolescent sexual activity. *Journal of Adolescent Research, 8,* 167–182.

Okagaki, L., and Sternberg, R. J. (1993). Parental beliefs in children's school performance. *Child Development, 64,* 36–56.

O'Kelly, C. G., and Carney, L. S. (1986). *Women and Men in Society: Cross-Cultural Perspectives on Gender Stratification.* Belmont, CA: Wadsworth.

Okraku, I. O. (1987). Age and attitudes toward multigenerational residence, 1973 to 1983. *Journal of Gerontology, 42,* 280–287.

O'Leary, K. D., Barling, J., Arias, I., Rosenbaum, A., Malone, J., and Tyree, A. (1989). Prevalence and stability of physical aggression between spouses: A longitudinal analysis. *Journal of Consulting and Clinical Psychology, 57,* 263–268.

O'Leary, K. D., and Curley, A. D. (1986). Assertion and family violence: Correlates of spousal abuse. *Journal of Marital and Family Therapy, 12,* 281–289.

Oles, P. K. (1999). Toward a psychological model of midlife crisis. *Psychological Reports, 84,* 1059–1069.

Olson, D. (2000). *Empowering Couples: Building on Your Strengths.* Minneapolis: Life Innovations.

Olson, D. H., Fournier, D. G., and Druckman, J. M. (1982). *PREPARE-ENRICH Counselors Manual* (Rev. ed.). Available from PREPARE-ENRICH, P.O. Box 1363, Stillwater, OK 74076.

Olson, D. H., McCubbin, H. I., Barnes, H., Larsen, A., Muyen, M., and Wilson, M. (1983). *Families: What Makes Them Work.* Beverly Hills, CA: Sage.

Olson, S. L., and Banyard, B. (1993). "Stop the world so I can get off for a while": Sources of daily stress in the lives of low-income single mothers of young children. *Family Relations, 42,* 50–56.

O'Neil, R., and Greenberger, E. (1994). Patterns of commitment to work and parenting: Implications for role strain. *Journal of Marriage and the Family, 56,* 101–118.

Orbuch, T. L., House, J. S., Mero, R. P., and Webster, P. S. (1996). Marital quality over the life course. *Social Psychology Quarterly, 59,* 162–171.

Oropesa, R. S. (1993). Using the service economy to relieve the double burden. *Journal of Family Issues, 14,* 438–473.

Ortega, S. T., Whitt, H. P., and William, J. A. (1988). Religious homogamy and marital happiness. *Journal of Family Issues, 9,* 224–239.

Orthner, D. K., and Neenan, P. A. (1996). Children's impact on stress and employability of mothers in poverty. *Journal of Family Issues, 17,* 667–687.

Osmond, M. W., and Thorne, B. (1993). Feminist theories: The social construction of gender in families and society. In P. G. Boss, W. J. Doherty, R. LaRossa, W. R. Schumm, and S. K. Steinmetz (Eds.), *Source of Family Theories and Methods* (pp. 591–622). New York: Plenum.

Oyserman, D., Radin, N., and Benn, R. (1993). Dynamics in a three-generational family: Teens, grandparents, and babies. *Developmental Psychology, 29,* 564–572.

Palti, H., Mansbach, I., Pridan, H., Adler, B., and Palti, Z. (1984). Episodes of illness in breast-fed and bottle-fed infants in Jerusalem. *Journal of Medical Sciences, 20,* 395–399.

Papp, P. (1983). *The Process of Change.* New York: Guilford Press.

Parachini, A. (1987, August 19). Condoms fail government tests. *Portland Press Herald.*

Parks, P. L., and Smeriglio, V. L. (1986). Relationships among parenting knowledge, quality of stimulation in the home, and infant development. *Family Relations, 35,* 411–416.

Pasquariello, P. (1999). *Book of Pregnancy and Child Care.* New York: Wiley.

Patterson, C. J. (1992). Children of lesbian and gay parents. *Child Development, 63,* 1025–1043.

Patterson, C. J., and Redding, R. (1996). Lesbian and gay families with children: Implications of social science research for policy. *Journal of Social Issues, 52*(3), 29–50.

Pattison, E. M. (1977). The experience of dying. In E. M. Pattison (Ed.), *The Experience of Dying* (pp. 43–60). Englewood Cliffs, NJ: Prentice-Hall.

Pawlowski, B., and Dunbar, R. (1999). Withholding age as putative deception in mate search tactics. *Evolution and Human Behavior, 20*(1), 53–69.

Peek, C. W., Fischer, J. L., and Kidwell, J. S. (1985). Teenage violence toward parents: A neglected dimension of family violence. *Journal of Marriage and the Family, 47,* 1051–1058.

Pelvic Inflammatory Disease (PID). (1996). Research Triangle Park, NC: American Social Health Association. Retrieved from the World Wide Web: http://www.ashastd.org/std/pidref.html

Penn, C. D., Hernandez, S. L., and Bermudez, J. M. (1997). Using a cross-cultural perspective to understand infidelity in couples therapy. *The American Journal of Family Therapy, 25,* 169–185.

Pepe, M. B., and Byrne, T. J. (1991). Women's perceptions of immediate and long-term effects of failed infertility treatment on marital and sexual satisfaction. *Family Relations, 40,* 303–309.

Perelman, M. A. (1998). Commentary: Pharmacological agents for erectile dysfunction and the human sexual response cycle. *Journal of Sex and Marital Therapy, 24*(4), 309–312.

Perrucci, C. C., Perrucci, R., Targ, D. B., and Targ, H. R. (1988). *Plant Closings.* New York: Aldine de Gruyter.

Perry, B. (1995). Step-parenting: How vulnerable are stepchildren? *Educational and Child Psychology, 12*(2), 58–70.

Petersen, J. R., Kretchner, A., Nellis, B., Lever, J., and Hertz, R. (1983, February and March). The Playboy readers' survey, Parts I and II. *Playboy.*

Petersen, L. R. (1986). Interfaith marriage and religious commitment among Catholics. *Journal of Marriage and the Family, 48,* 725–735.

Peterson, G. W., and Rollins, B. C. (1987). Parent-child socialization. In M. B. Sussman and S. K. Steinmetz (Eds.), *Handbook of Marriage and the Family* (pp. 471–507). New York: Plenum.

Peterson, R. R., and Gerson, K. (1992). The determinants of responsibility for childcare arrangements among dual-earner couples. *Journal of Marriage and the Family, 54,* 527–536.

Petitti, D. B. (1992). Reconsidering the IUD. *Family Planning Perspectives, 24,* 33–35.

Pett, M. A., and Vaughan-Cole, B. (1986). The impact of income issues and social status in post-divorce adjustment of custodial parents. *Family Relations, 35,* 103–111.

Pfost, K. S., Stevens, M. J., and Matejcak, A. J., Jr. (1990). A counselor's primer on postpartum depression. *Journal of Counseling and Development, 69,* 148–151.

Phelps, R. E., Meara, N. M., Davis, K. L., and Patton, M. J. (1991). Blacks' and Whites' perceptions of verbal aggression. *Journal of Counseling and Development, 69,* 345–350.

Philliber, S. G., and Graham, E. H. (1981). The impact of age of mother on mother-child interaction patterns. *Journal of Marriage and the Family, 43,* 109–115.

Pictman, J. S., and Blanchard, D. (1996). The effects of work history and timing of marriage on the division of household labor: A life-force perspective. *Journal of Marriage and the Family, 58,* 78–90.

Piercy, F. P., and Sprenkle, D. H. (1990). Marriage and family therapy: A decade review. *Journal of Marriage and the Family, 52,* 1116–1126.

Pill, C. J. (1990). Stepfamilies: Refining the family. *Family Relations, 39,* 186–193.

Pillemer, K., and Suitor, J. J. (1991). "Will I ever escape my children's problems?" Effects of adult children's problems on elderly parents. *Journal of Marriage and the Family, 53,* 585–594.

Pina, D. L., and Bengston, D. L. (1993). The division of household labor and wives' happiness: Ideology, employment and perceptions of support. *Journal of Marriage and the Family, 55,* 901–912.

Pinhas, L., Toner, B. B., Ali, A., Garfinkel, P. E., and Stuckless, N. (1999). The effects of the ideal of female beauty on mood and body satisfaction. *International Journal of Eating Disorders, 25*(2), 223–226.

Pinsof, W. M., and Wynne, L. C. (1995). The efficacy of marital and family therapy: An empirical overview, conclusion, and recommendation. *Journal of Marital and Family Therapy, 21,* 585–613.

Pipher, M. (1994). *Reviving Ophelia: Saving the Selves of Adolescent Girls.* New York: Ballantine Books.

Pipher, M. (1996). *The Shelter of Each Other. Rebuilding Our Families.* New York: Grosset/Putnam Books.

Pittman, F. (1993). Beyond betrayal: Life after infidelity. *Psychology Today, 26,* 32–38+.

Pittman, J. F., Wright, C. A., and Lloyd, S. A. (1989). Predicting parenting difficulties. *Journal of Family Issues, 10,* 267–286.

Planned Parenthood of Southeastern Pennsylvania v. Casey, 60 U.S. L. W. 4795 (1992).

Pleck, J. (1997). Paternal involvement: Levels, sources, and consequences. In M. E. Lamb (Ed.), *The Role of the Father in Child Development* (3rd ed., pp. 66–103). New York: Wiley.

Poehlman, E. T., Melby, T. L., and Badylak, S. F. (1991). Relation of age and physical exercise status on metabolic rate in younger and older healthy men. *Journal of Gerontology, 46,* B54–B58.

Pogash, C. (1992, April 14). Science vs. religion. *San Francisco Examiner Image,* pp. 6–15.

Ponzetti, J. L. (1990). Loneliness among college students. *Family Relations, 39,* 336–340.

Pope, G., Olivardia, R., Gruber, A., and Borowiecki, J. (1999). Evolving ideals of male body image as seen through action toys. *International Journal of Eating Disorders, 26*(1), 65–72.

Potts, M. (1988). Birth control methods in the United States. *Family Planning Perspectives, 20,* 288–297.

Poulshock, S. W., and Deimling, G. T. (1984). Families caring for elders in residence: Issues in the measurement of burden. *Journal of Gerontology, 39,* 230–239.

Powlishta, K. K., and Maccoby, E. E. (1990). Resource utilization in mixed-sex dyads: The influence of adult presence and task typ. *Sex Roles, 23*(5/6), 223–240.

Pratt, C. C., Jones, L. L., Shin, H., and Walker, A. J. (1989). Autonomy and decision-making between single older women and their caregiving daughters. *The Gerontologist, 29,* 793–797.

Pratt, C. C., Walker, A. A., and Wood, D. L. (1992). Bereavement among former caregivers to elderly mothers. *Family Relations, 41,* 278–283.

Pratto, F. (1996). Sexual politics: The gender gap in the bedroom, the cupboard, and the cabinet. In D. M. Buss and N. M. Malamuth (Eds.), *Sex, Power, Conflict: Evolutionary and Feminist Perspectives.* New York: Oxford University Press.

Presser, H. (2000, February). Nonstandard work schedules and marital instability. *Journal of Marriage and the Family, 62,* 93–110.

Presser, H. B. (1988). Shift work and child care among young dual-earner American parents. *Journal of Marriage and the Family, 50,* 133–148.

Presser, H. B. (1989). Some economic complexities of child care provided by grandmothers. *Journal of Marriage and the Family, 51,* 581–591.

Priest, R., and Smith, A. (1992). Counseling adult sex offenders: Unique challenges and treatment paradigms. *Journal of Counseling and Development, 71,* 27–32.

Przbyla, D., and Byrne, D. (1984). The mediating role of cognitive processes in self-regulated sexual arousal. *Journal of Research in Personality, 18,* 54–63.

Purnell, M., and Bagby, B. H. (1993). Grandparents' rights. Implications for family specialists. *Family Relations, 42,* 173–178.

Pyke, K., and Coltrane, F. (1996). Entitlement, obligation, and gratitude in family work. *Journal of Family Issues, 17,* 60–82.

Quinn, N. (1982). "Commitment" in American marriage: Cultural analysis. *American Ethnologist, 9,* 775–798.

Quinn, P., and Allen, K. R. (1989). Facing challenges and making compromises: How single mothers endure. *Family Relations, 38,* 390–395.

Quinn, W. H. (1983). Personal and family adjustment in later life. *Journal of Marriage and the Family, 45,* 57–73.

Raboch, J., and Raboch, J. (1992). Infrequent orgasms in women. *Journal of Sex and Marital Therapy, 18,* 114–120.

Rachlin, V. C. (1987). Fair vs. equal role relations in dual-career and dual-earner families: Implications for family interventions. *Family Relations, 36,* 187–192.

Radecki, S. E., and Bernstein, G. S. (1990). An assessment of contraceptive need in the inner city. *Family Planning Perspectives, 22,* 12–127.

Raley, E. K. (1995). Black-White differences in kin contact and exchange among never married adults. *Journal of Family Issues, 16,* 77–103.

Rank, M. R. (1987). The formation and dissolution of marriages in the welfare population. *Journal of Marriage and the Family, 49,* 15–20.

Rankin-Esquer, L. A., Burnett, C. K., Baucom, D. H., and Epstein, M. (1997). Autonomy and relatedness in marital functioning. *Journal of Marital and Family Therapy, 23,* 175–190.

Rapaport, K. R., and Posey, C. D. (1991). Sexually coercive college males. In A. Parrot (Ed.), *Acquaintance Rape: The Hidden Crime.* New York: Wiley.

Ratican, K. L. (1992). Sexual abuse survivors: Identifying symptoms and special treatment considerations. *Journal of Counseling and Development, 71,* 33–40.

Raup, J. L., and Myers, J. E. (1989). The empty nest syndrome: Myth or reality. *Journal of Counseling and Development, 68,* 180–183.

Reading, J., and Amatea, E. S. (1986). Role deviance or role diversification: Reassessing the psychosocial factors affecting the parenthood choice of career-oriented women. *Journal of Marriage and the Family, 48,* 255–260.

Reamy, K. J., and White, S. E. (1987). Sexuality in the puerperium: A review. *Archives of Sexual Behavior, 16,* 165–186.

Redfield, R., Markham, P., Salahuddin, S., Wright, D., Sarngadharan, M., and Gallo, R. (1985). Heterosexually acquired HTLV-III/LAV disease, AIDS-related complex and AIDS: +Epidemiologic evidence for female-to-male transmission. *The Journal of the American Medical Association, 254,* 2094–2096.

Reed, J. P. (1975). The current legal status of abortion. In J. G. Well (Ed.), *Current Issues in Marriage and the Family* (pp. 200–208). New York: Macmillan.

Reed, J. S., and Dubow, E. F. (1997). Cognitive and behavioral predictors in communication in clinic-referred and non-clinical mother-adolescent diads. *Journal of Marriage and the Family, 59,* 91–102.

Regan, P. C. (1998). Minimum mate selection standards as a function of perceived mate value, relationship context, and gender. *Journal of Psychology and Human Sexuality, 10,* 53–73.

Regan, P. C., and Berscheid, E. (1997). Gender differences in characteristics desired in a potential sexual and marriage partner. *Journal of Psychology and Human Sexuality, 9,* 25–37.

Regan, P. C., and Dreyer, C. (1999). Lust? Love? Status? Young adults' motives for engaging in casual sex. *Journal of Psychology and Human Sexuality, 11*(1), 1–24.

Reik, T. A. (1957). *Of Love and Lust.* New York: Straus & Cudahy.

Reinisch, J. M., and Beasley, R. (1990). *The Kinsey New Report on Sex.* New York: St. Martin's Press.

Reinisch, J. M., Hill, C. A., Sanders, S. A., and Ziemba-Davis, M. (1995). High-risk sexual behavior at a Midwestern university: A confirmatory survey. *Family Planning Perspectives, 27,* 79–82.

Reis, J., Barbara-Stein, L., and Bennett, S. (1986). Ecological determinants of parenting. *Family Relations, 35,* 547–554.

Reise, S. P., and Wright, T. M. (1996). Personality traits, cluster B personality disorders, and sociosexuality. *Journal of Research in Personality, 30,* 128–136.

Reiss, A. J., Jr. (1984). Selecting strategies of social control over organizational life. In K. Hawkins and J. M. Thomas (Eds.), *Enforcing Regulation.* Boston: Kluwer-Nijhoff.

Reiss, I. L. (1980). *Family Systems in America* (3rd ed.). New York: Holt, Rinehart & Winston.

Reiss, I. L., and Leik, R. K. (1989). Evaluating strategies to avoid AIDS: Number of partners vs. use of condoms. *The Journal of Sex Research, 26,* 411–433.

Reker, G. T., Peacock, E. J., and Wong, P. T. P. (1987). Meaning and purpose in life and well-being: A life-span perspective. *Journal of Gerontology, 42,* 44–49.

Remez, L. (1992a). Abruptio placentae rates increase significantly in U.S. from 1979 to 1987. *Family Planning Perspectives, 24,* 143–144.

Remez, L. (1992b). Infant mortality on an Oregon Indian reservation is almost three times higher than the overall U.S. rate. *Family Planning Perspectives, 24,* 138–139.

Remez, L. (1995). Unwantedness at birth may induce psychological, social problems for adults. *Family Planning Perspectives, 27,* 260–261.

Remez, L. (1996). Early implant removals most often requested because of side effects. *Family Planning Perspectives, 28,* 35–37.

Renshaw, D. C. (1984). Touch hunger—a common marital problem. *Medical Aspects of Human Sexuality, 18,* 63–70.

Requests for reversal of tubal sterilization linked with young age at surgery and marital disruption. (1984). *Family Planning Perspectives, 16,* 139–140.

Reschobsky, J. D., and Newman, S. J. (1991). Home upkeep and housing quality of older home owners. *Journal of Gerontology, 46,* S288–S297.

Researchers confirm induced abortion to be safer for women than childbirth; refute claims of critics (1982). *Family Planning Perspectives, 14,* 271–272.

Rexroat, C., and Shehan, C. (1987). The family life cycle and spouses' time in housework. *Journal of Marriage and the Family, 49,* 737–750.

Rhein, L., Ginsburg, K., Schwartz, D., Pinto-Martin, J., Zhao, H., Morgan, A., and Slap, G. (1997). Teen father participation in child rearing: Family perspectives. *Journal of Adolescent Health, 21*(4), 244–252.

Rice, B. (1981). Can companies kill? *Psychology Today, 15,* 78–85.

Rice, F. P. (1978). *Stepparenting.* New York: Condor.

Rice, F. P. (1979). *Working Mother's Guide to Child Development.* Englewood Cliffs, NJ: Prentice-Hall.

Rice, F. P. (1986). *Adult Development and Aging.* Boston: Allyn & Bacon.

Rice, F. P. (1989). *Human Sexuality.* Dubuque, IA: Brown.

Rice, F. P. (1993). *The Adolescent: Development, Relationships, and Culture* (7th ed.). Boston: Allyn & Bacon.

Rice, F. P. (1995). *Human Development, a Life-Span Approach* (2nd ed.). Englewood Cliffs, NJ: Prentice-Hall.

Richards, L. N., and Schmiege, C. J. (1993). Problems and strengths of single-parent families. Implications for practice and policy. *Family Relations, 42,* 277–285.

Richardson, B., and Kilty, K. N. (1992). Retirement intentions among Black professionals: Implications for practice with older, Black adults. *The Gerontologist, 32,* 7–16.

Ridgeway, C., and Smith-Lovin, L. (1999). The gender system and interaction. *Annual Review of Sociology, 25,* 191–215.

Rind, P. (1991). Depression and anxiety decrease after abortion, regardless of method. *Family Planning Perspectives, 23,* 237–238.

Rind, P. (1992a). Smoking and pregnancy nearly triple women's risk of placenta previa. *Family Planning Perspectives, 24,* 47–48.

Rind, P. (1992b). "Teens and Toddlers" aims to reduce child abuse among adolescent parents. *Family Planning Perspectives, 24,* 37–40.

Rind, P. (1992c). Tubal sterilization may confer some protection against ovarian cancer. *Family Planning Perspectives, 24,* 44–45.

Rini, C., Dunkel-Schetter, C., Wadhwa, R., and Sandman, C. (1999). Psychological adaptation and birth outcomes: The role of personal resources, stress, and sociocultural context in pregnancy. *Health Psychology, 18*(4), 333–345.

Risman, B. J. (1986). Can men "mother"? Life as a single father. *Family Relations, 35,* 95–102.

Roan, C. L., and Raley, R. K. (1996). Intergenerational coresidence and contact: A longitudinal analysis of adult children's response to their mother's widowhood. *Journal of Marriage and the Family, 58,* 708–717.

Roberto, K. A., and Scott, J. P. (1986). Equity considerations in the friendships of older adults. *Journal of Gerontology, 41,* 241–247.

Roberts, T. W. (1992). Sexual attraction and romantic love: Forgotten variables in marital therapy. *Journal of Marital and Family Therapy, 18,* 357–364.

Robertson, E. B., Elder, G. H., Jr., Skinner, M. L., and Conger, R. D. (1991). The costs and benefits of social support in families. *Journal of Marriage and the Family, 53,* 403–416.

Robertson, J. F., and Simons, R. L. (1989). Family factors, self-esteem and adolescent depression. *Journal of Marriage and the Family, 51,* 125–138.

Robinson, B. E., Rowland, B. H., and Coleman, M. (1986). Taking action for latchkey children and their families. *Family Relations, 35,* 473–478.

Robinson, J. P., Godbey, G., and Jacobson, A. J. (1999). *Time for Life: The Surprising Ways Americans Use Their Time.* University Park: Pennsylvania State University Press.

Robinson, L. C., and Blanton, P. W. (1993). Marital strengths in enduring marriages. *Family Relations, 42,* 38–45.

Rodgers, B. (1996). Social and psychological wellbeing of children from divorced families: Australian research findings. *Australian Psychologist, 31,* 174–182.

Rodman, H. (1991). Should parental involvement be required for minors' abortions? *Family Relations, 40,* 155–160.

Rodriguez, H. (1998, May). *Cohabitation: A Snapshot.* Washington, DC: Center for Law and Social Policy. Retrieved July 25, 2000, from the World Wide Web: http://www.clasp.org/pubs/familyformation/cohab.html

Roe v. Wade, 410 U.S. 113 (1973).

Rogers, M. F. (1985). AIDS in children: A review of the clinical, epidemiological and public health aspects. *Pediatric Infectious Disease, 4,* 230–236.

Rogers, M. J., and Holmbeck, G. N. (1997). Effects of interparental aggression on children's adjustment: The moderating role of cognitive appraisal and coping. *Journal of Family Psychology, 11,* 125–130.

Rogers, S. (1999, February). Wife's income and marital quality: Are there reciprocal effects? *Journal of Marriage and the Family, 61,* 123–132.

Rogers, S. J. (1996). Mothers' work hours and marital quality: Variations by family structure and family size. *Journal of Marriage and the Family, 58,* 606–617.

Rogler, L. H., and Procidano, M. E. (1986). The effect of social networks on marital roles: A test of the Bott hypothesis in an intergenerational context. *Journal of Marriage and the Family, 48,* 693–701.

Rogler, L. H., and Procidano, M. E. (1989a). Egalitarian spouse relations and wives' marital satisfaction in intergenerationally linked Puerto Rican families. *Journal of Marriage and the Family, 51,* 37–39.

Rogler, L. H., and Procidano, M. E. (1989b). Marital heterogamy and marital quality in Puerto Rican families. *Journal of Marital and Family Therapy, 51,* 363–372.

Rohner, R. P., Kean, K. J., and Cournoyer, D. E. (1991). Effects of corporal punishment, perceived caregiver warmth, and cultural beliefs on the psychological adjustment of children in St. Kitts, West Indies. *Journal of Marriage and the Family, 53,* 681–693.

Ronfeldt, H., Kimerling, R., and Arias, I. (1998). Satisfaction with relationship power and the perpetration of dating violence. *Journal of Marriage and the Family, 60,* 70–78.

Rook, K., Dooley, D., and Catalano, R. (1991). Stress transmission: The effects of husbands' job stressors on the emotional health of their wives. *Journal of Marriage and the Family, 53,* 165–177.

Roosa, M. W. (1988). The effect of age in the transition to parenthood: Are delayed childbearers a unique group? *Family Relations, 37,* 322–327.

Roosa, M. W., Tein, J., Croppenbacher, N., Michaels, N., and Dumea, L. (1993). Mothers' parenting behavior and child mental health in families with a problem-drinking parent. *Journal of Marriage and the Family, 55,* 107–118.

Roscoe, B., and Benaske, N. (1985). Courtship violence experienced by abused wives: Similarities in pattern of abuse. *Family Relations, 34,* 419–424.

Rosen, K. H., and Stith, S. M. (1993). Intervention strategies for treating women in violent dating relationships. *Family Relations, 42,* 427–433.

Rosen, K. S., and Rothbaum, F. (1993). Quality of parental caregiving and security of attachment. *Developmental Psychology, 29,* 358–367.

Rosen, R. C., Taylor, J. S., Leiblum, S. R., and Bachmann, G. A. (1993). *Journal of Sex and Marital Therapy, 19,* 171–188.

Rosenbloom, C. A., and Whittington, F. J. (1993). The effects of bereavement on eating behaviors and nutrient intakes in elderly widowed persons. *Journal of Gerontology, 48,* S223–S229.

Ross, C. E. (1995). Reconceptualizing marital status as a continuum of social attachment. *Journal of Marriage and the Family, 57,* 129–140.

Ross, C. E., and Huber, J. (1985). Hardship and depression. *Journal of Health and Social Behavior, 26,* 312–327.

Ross, C. E., Mirowsky, J., and Goldstein, K. (1990). The impact of family on health: The decade in review. *Journal of Marriage and the Family, 52,* 1059–1078.

Ross, C. E., and Van Willigen, M. D. (1996). Gender, parenthood, and anger. *Journal of Marriage and the Family, 68,* 572–584.

Rotter, J. B. (1980). Trust and gullibility. *Psychology Today, 14,* 35–42.

Rowland, D. L., Haensel, S. M., Blom, J. H. M., and Slob, A. K. (1993). Penile sensitivity in men with premature ejaculation and erectile dysfunction. *Journal of Sex and Marital Therapy, 19,* 189–197.

Roy, L., and Sawyers, J. K. (1986). The double-bind: An empirical study of responses to inconsistent communications. *Journal of Marital and Family Therapy, 12,* 395–402.

Rubenstein, C. M., and Shaver, P. (1982). *In Search of Intimacy.* New York: Delacorte.

Rubin, Z., Hill, C. T., Peplau, L. A., and Dunkel-Schetter, C. (1980). Self-disclosure in dating couples: Sex roles and the ethic openness. *Journal of Marriage and the Family, 42,* 305–317.

Rubinstein, R. L., Alexander, B. B., Goodman, M., and Luborsky, M. (1991). Key relationships of never-married, childless older women: A cultural analysis. *Journal of Gerontology, 5,* S270–S277.

Ruble, D. N., and Brooks-Gunn, J. (1982). The experience of menarche. *Child Development, 53,* 1557–1566.

Ryan, K. J. (1988). Giving birth in America, 1988. *Family Planning Perspectives, 20,* 298–301.

Sabatelli, R. M., and Cecil-Pigo, E. F. (1985). Relational interdependence and commitment in marriage. *Journal of Marriage and the Family, 47,* 931–937.

Sack, K. (1998, November 24). Georgia's high court voids sodomy law. *New York Times,* p. A14.

Sadava, S. W., and Matejcic, C. (1987). Generalized and specific loneliness in early marriage. *Canadian Journal of Behavioural Science, 19,* 56–66.

Sadker, M., and Sadker, M. (1985). Sexism in the schoolroom of the 80s. *Psychology Today, 19,* 54–57.

Salzinger, S., Feldman, R. S., and Hammer, M. (1993). The effects of physical abuse on children's social relationships. *Child Development, 64,* 169–187.

Sampel, D. D., and Seymour, W. R. (1980). A comparative analysis of the effectiveness of conciliation counseling on certain personality variables. *Journal of Marital and Family Therapy, 6,* 269–275.

Samuels, M., and Samuels, N. (1996). *The New Well Pregnancy Book.* New York: Simon & Schuster.

Sanchez, L., and Kane, E. W. (1996). Women's and men's constructions of perceptions of household fairness. *Journal of Family Issues, 17,* 358–387.

Sander, W. (1993). Catholicism and intermarriage in the United States. *Journal of Marriage and the Family, 55,* 1037–1041.

Sandfort, J. R., and Hill, M. S. (1996). Assisting young, unmarried mothers who become self-sufficient: The effects of different types of early economic support. *Journal of Marriage and the Family, 58,* 311–326.

Santee, B., and Henshaw, S. K. (1992). The abortion debate: Measuring gestational age. *Family Planning Perspectives, 24,* 172–173.

Santelli, J. S., Davis, M., Celentano, B. D., Crump, D., and Burwell, L. T. (1995). Combined use of condoms with other contraceptive methods among inner-city Baltimore women. *Family Planning Perspectives, 27,* 74–78.

Sarason, I. G. (1981). *The Revised Life Experiences Survey.* Unpublished manuscript, University of Washington.

Sarvis, B., and Rodman, H. (1974). *The Abortion Controversy.* New York: Columbia University Press.

Sauer, L. E., and Fine, M. A. (1988). Parent-child relationships in stepparent families. *Journal of Family Psychology, 1,* 434–451.

Sawyer, R. G., and Pinciaro, P. J. (1998). College students' knowledge and attitudes about Norplant and Depo Provera. *American Journal of Health Behavior, 22(3),* 163–171.

Scanzoni, J. (1987). Families in the 1980s. *Journal of Family Issues, 8,* 394–421.

Schachter, S., and Singer, J. F. (1962). Cognitive, social, and physiological determinants of emotional state. *Psychological Review, 69,* 379–399.

Schaninger, C. M., and Buss, W. C. (1986). A longitudinal comparison of consumption and finance handling between happily married and divorced couples. *Journal of Marriage and the Family, 48,* 129–136.

Scharlach, A. E. (1987). Role strain in mother-daughter relationships in later life. *The Gerontologist, 27,* 627–631.

Scher, M., and Stevens, M. (1987). Men and violence. *Journal of Counseling and Development, 65,* 351–355.

Schiavi, R. C. (1990). Chronic alcoholism and male sexual dysfunction. *Journal of Sex and Marital Therapy, 16,* 23–33.

Schlenker, J. A., Caron, S. L., and Halteman, W. A. (1998). A feminist analysis of *Seventeen* magazine: Content analysis from 1945–1995. *Sex Roles, 38*(1/2), 135–149.

Schmaling, K. B., Whisman, M. A., Fruzzetti, A. E., and Truax, P. (1991). Identifying areas of marital conflict: Interactional behaviors associated with depression. *Journal of Family Psychology, 5,* 145–157.

Schoen, R., and Weinick, R. M. (1993). Partner choices in marriage and cohabitations. *Journal of Marriage and the Family, 55,* 408–414.

Schoen, R., and Woolridge, J. (1989). Marriage choices in No. Carolina and Virginia, 1969–71 and 1979–81. *Journal of Marriage and the Family, 51,* 465–481.

Schumm, W. R., Barnes, H. L., Bollman, S. R., Jurich, A. P., and Bugaighis, M. A. (1986). Self-disclosure and marital satisfaction revisited. *Family Relations, 34,* 241–247.

Schumm, W. R., and Bugaighis, M. A. (1986). Marital quality over the marital career: Alternative explanations. *Journal of Marriage and the Family, 48,* 165–168.

Schwartz, R., and Schwartz, L. J. (1980). *Becoming a Couple.* Englewood Cliffs, NJ: Prentice-Hall.

Schwarz, J. E. (1998). The hidden side of the the Clinton economy. *The Atlantic Monthly, 282*(4), pp. 18–21.

Schwertfeger, M. M. (1982). Interethnic marriage and divorce in Hawaii: A panel study of 1968 first marriages. *Marriage and Family Review, 5,* 49–60.

Scoon-Rogers, L. (1999, March). Child support for custodial mothers and fathers: 1995. (*Current Population Reports,* Series P60-196). Washington, DC: U.S. Bureau of the Census.

Scott, J., and Alwin, D. F. (1989). Gender differences in parental strain: Parental role or gender role? *Journal of Family Issues, 10,* 482–503.

Sears, H. A., and Galambos, N. L. (1992). Women's work conditions and marital adjustment in two-earner couples: A structural model. *Journal of Marriage and the Family, 54,* 789–797.

Seccombe, K., and Ishii-Kuntz, M. (1991). Perceptions of problems associated with aging: Comparisons among four older-age cohorts. *The Gerontologist, 31,* 527–533.

Seccombe, K., and Ishii-Kuntz, M. (1994). Gender and social relationships among the never-married. *Sex Roles, 30,* 585–603.

Seccombe, K., and Lee, G. (1987). Female status, wives' autonomy, and divorce. A cross-cultural study. *Family Perspectives, 20,* 241–249.

Segraves, K. B., and Segraves, R. T. (1991). Hypoactive sexual desire disorder: Prevalent in comorbidity in 906 subjects. *Journal of Sex and Marital Therapy, 17,* 55–58.

Segraves, R. T., Saran, A., Segraves, K., and Maguire, E. (1993). Clomipramine versus placebo in the treatment of premature ejaculation: A pilot study. *Journal of Sex and Marital Therapy, 19,* 198–200.

Seguin, L., Potvin, L., St-Denis, M., and Loiselle, J. (1999). Socio-environmental factors and postnatal depressive symptomatology: A longitudinal study. *Women and Health, 29*(1), 57–72.

Seidman, S. M., Mosher, W. D., and Aral, F. O. (1994). Predictors of high-risk behavior in unmarried American women: Adolescent environment as a risk factor. *Journal of Adolescent Health, 15,* 126–132.

Semmens, J. P., and Tsai, C. C. (1984). Some gynecological causes of sexual problems. *Medical Aspects of Human Sexuality, 18,* 174–181.

Serbin, L. A., Sprafkin, C., Elman, M., and Doyle, A. (1982). The early development of sex-differentiated patterns of social influence. *Canadian Journal of Behavioral Science, 14,* 350–363.

Sexton, C. S., and Perlman, D. S. (1989). Couples' orientation, gender role orientation, and perceived equity as determinants of married power. *Journal of Marriage and the Family, 51,* 933–941.

Sexually Transmitted Diseases in America: How Many Cases and at What Cost? (1998, December). Menlo Park, CA: Kaiser Family Foundation. Retrieved from the World Wide Web: http://www.kff.org/content/archive/1447/std_rep.pdf

Shadish, W. R., Ragsdale, K., Glaser, R. R., and Montgomery, L. M. (1995). The efficacy and effectiveness of marital and family therapy: A perspective from meta-analysis. *Journal of Marital and Family Therapy, 21,* 345–360.

Shagle, S. C., and Barber, B. K. (1993). Effects of family, marital, and parent-child conflict on adolescent self-derogation and suicidal ideation. *Journal of Marriage and the Family, 55,* 964–974.

Shamir, B. (1986). Self-esteem and the psychological impact of unemployment. *Social Psychology Quarterly, 49,* 61–72.

Shanas, E. (1979). The family as a social support system in old age. *The Gerontologist, 19,* 169–174.

Shanas, E. (1980). Older people and their families: The new pioneers. *Journal of Marriage and the Family, 42,* 9–15.

Shapiro, A., and Lambert, J. D. (1999). Longitudinal effects of divorce on the quality of father-child relationship and on father's psychological well-being. *Journal of Marriage and the Family, 61,* 397–408.

Shapiro, A. D. (1996). Explaining psychological distress in a sample of remarried and divorced persons. *Journal of Family Issues, 17,* 186–203.

Shapiro, D. L., and Levendosky, A. A. (1999). Adolescent survivors of childhood sexual abuse: The mediating role of attachment style and coping in psychological and interpersonal functioning. *Child Abuse and Neglect, 23,* 1175–1191.

Shehan, C. L., Berardo, F. M., Bera, H., and Carley, S. M. (1991). Women in age-discrepant marriages. *Journal of Family Issues, 12,* 291–305.

Sheinberg, M., and Penn, P. (1991). Gender dilemmas, gender questions, and the gender mantra. *Journal of Marriage and Family Therapy, 17,* 33–44.

Shelton, B. (1992). *Women, Men and Time.* New York: Greenwood Press.

Sherman, A. (1999, August 22). *Extreme Child Poverty Rises Sharply in 1997.* Washington, DC: Children's Defense Fund.

Sherwin, R., and Corbett, S. (1985). Campus sexual norms and dating relationships: A trial analysis. *The Journal of Sex Research, 21,* 258–274.

Shuster, C. (1993). Employed first-time mothers: A typology of maternal responses to integrating parenting and employment. *Family Relations, 42,* 13–20.

Siegel, J. M. (1995). Looking for Mr. Right? *Journal of Family Issues, 16,* 194–211.

Signorielli, N. (1998, February). Television and the perpetuation of gender-role stereotypes. *AAP News,* 7–10.

Signorielli, N., and Bacue, A. (1999). Recognition and respect: A content analysis of prime-time television characters across three decades. *Sex Roles, 40*(7/8), 527–544.

Sigusch, V., Schmidt, G., Reinfeld, A., and Wiedeman-Sutor, I. (1970). Psychosexual stimulation: Sex differences. *Journal of Sex Research, 6,* 10–24.

Silber, T. (1980). Abortion in adolescence: The ethical dimension. *Adolescence, 15,* 461–474.

Silberstein, L. R., Striegel-Moore, R. H., Timko, C., and Rodin, J. (1988). Behavioral and psychological implications of body dissatisfaction: Do men and women differ? *Sex Roles, 19,* 219–232.

Silliman, B., and Schumm, W. (1995). Client interests in premarital counseling: A further analysis. *Journal of Sex and Marital Therapy, 21*(1), 43–56.

Silliman, B., and Schumm, W. (1995). Client interests in premarital counseling: A further analysis. *Journal of Sex and Marital Therapy, 21,* 43–56.

Silverstein, M., and Chen, X. (1999). The impact of acculturation in Mexican American families on the quality of the adult grandchild–grandparent relationship. *Journal of Marriage and the Family, 61,* 188–198.

Silverstein, M., Chen, X., and Heller, K. (1996). Too much of a good thing? Intergenerational social support and the psychological well-being of older parents. *Journal of Marriage and the Family, 58,* 970–982.

Silverstein, M., Parrott, T. M., and Bengtson, V. L. (1995). Factors that predispose middle-aged sons and daughters to provide social support to older parents. *Journal of Marriage and the Family, 57,* 465–475.

Simenauer, J., and Carroll, D. (1982). *Singles: The New Americans.* New York: Simon & Schuster.

Simkins-Bullock, J., Wildman, B. G., Bullock, W. A., and Sugrue, D. P. (1992). Etiological attributions, responsibility attributions, and marital adjustment in erectile dysfunction patients. *Journal of Sex and Marital Therapy, 18,* 83–103.

Simons, R. L., Beaman, J., Conger, R. D., and Chao, W. (1992). Gender differences in the intergenerational transmission of parenting beliefs. *Journal of Marriage and the Family, 54,* 823–836.

Simons, R. L., Beaman, J., Conger, R. D., and Chao, W. (1993a). Childhood experience, conceptions of parenting, and attitudes of spouse as determinants of parental behavior. *Journal of Marriage and the Family, 55,* 91–106.

Simons, R. L., Beaman, J., Conger, R. D., and Chao, W. (1993b). Stress, support, and antisocial behavior trait as determinants of emotional well-being and parenting practices among single mothers. *Journal of Marriage and the Family, 55,* 385–398.

Simons, R. L., Johnson, C., Beaman, J., and Conger, R. D. (1993). Explaining women's double jeopardy: Factors that mediate the association between harsh treatment as a child and violence by a husband. *Journal of Marriage and the Family, 55,* 713–723.

Simons, R. L., Whitbeck, L. B., Conger, R. D., and Melby, J. N. (1990). Husband and wife determinants of parenting: A social learning and exchange model of parental behavior. *Journal of Marriage and the Family, 52,* 375–392.

Singer, L. T., Davillier, M., Bruening, P., Hawkins, S., and Yamashita, T. S. (1996). Social support, psychological distress, and parenting strains in mothers of very low birth weight infants. *Family Relations, 45,* 343–350.

Skovholt, T. M., and Thoen, G. A. (1987). Mental imagery and parenthood decision making. *Journal of Counseling and Development, 65,* 315, 316.

Small, A., Teagno, L., and Selz, K. (1980). The relationship of sex role to physical and psychological health. *Journal of Youth and Adolescence, 9,* 305–314.

Small, S. A., and Kerns, B. (1993). Unwanted sexual activity among peers during early and middle adolescence: Incidence and risk factors. *Journal of Marriage and the Family, 55*, 941–952.

Small, S. A., and Luster, T. (1994). Adolescent sexual activity: An ecological, risk-factor approach. *Journal of Marriage and the Family, 56*, 181–192.

Smart, L. S. (1992). The marital helping relationship following pregnancy loss and infant death. *Journal of Family Issues, 13*, 81–98.

Smith, C. J., Noll, J. A., and Bryant, J. B. (1999). The effect of social context on gender self-concept. *Sex Roles, 40*(5/6), 499–512.

Smith, D., and Over, R. (1990). Enhancement of fantasy-induced sexual arousal in men through training in sexual imaging. *Archives of Sexual Behavior, 19*, 477–489.

Smith, D. E. (1993). The standard North American family: SNAF as an ideological code. *Journal of Family Issues, 14*, 50–65.

Smith, D. S. (1985). Wife employment and marital adjustment: A cumulation of results. *Family Relations, 34*, 483–490.

Smith, K. R., and Zick, C. D. (1986). The incidence of poverty among the recently widowed: Mediating factors in the life course. *Journal of Marriage and the Family, 48*, 619–630.

Smith, P., and Beaujot, R. (1999). Men's orientation toward marriage and family roles. *Journal of Comparative Family Studies*, 471–487.

Smith, R. E., Pine, C. J., and Hawley, M. E. (1988). Social cognitions about adult male victims of female sexual assault. *The Journal of Sex Research, 24*, 101–112.

Smock, P. J., and Manning, W. D. (1997). Nonresident parent's characteristics and child support. *Journal of Marriage and the Family, 59*, 798–808.

Snow, J. T., and Harris, M. B. (1989). Disordered eating in Southwestern Pueblo Indians and Hispanics. *Journal of Adolescence, 12*, 329–336.

Snowden, L. R., Schott, T. L., Awalt, S. J., and Gillis-Knox, J. (1988). Marital satisfaction in pregnancy: Stability and change. *Journal of Marriage and the Family, 50*, 325–333.

Snyder, D. K., Velasquez, J. M., and Clark, B. L. (1997). Parental influence on gender and marital role attitudes: Implication for intervention. *Journal of Marital and Family Therapy, 23*, 191–201.

Sobel, D. (1981, June 29). Surrogate mothers: Why women volunteer. *New York Times*, p. B5.

Solano, C. H., Batten, P. G., and Parish, E. A. (1982). Loneliness and patterns of self-disclosure. *Journal of Personality and Social Psychology, 43*, 524–531.

Sollie, D. L., and Kaetz, J. F. (1992). Teaching university-level family studies courses: Techniques and outcomes. *Family Relations, 41*, 18–24.

Sollie, D. L., and Scott, J. P. (1983). Teaching communication skills: A comparison of videotape feedback methods. *Family Relations, 32*, 503–511.

Solomon, J. C., and Marx, J. (1995). To grandmother's house we go: Health and school adjustment of children raised solely by grandparents. *The Gerontologist, 35*, 386–394.

Somers, M. D. (1993). A comparison of voluntarily child-free adults and parents. *Journal of Marriage and the Family, 55*, 643–650.

Sonda, L. P., Mazo, R., and Chancellor, M. B. (1990). The role of yohimbine for the treatment of erectile impotence. *Journal of Sex and Marital Therapy, 16*, 15–21.

Sonenstein, F. L., Pleck, J. H., and Ku, L. C. (1989). Sexual activity, condom use and AIDS awareness among adolescent males. *Family Planning Perspectives, 21*, 152–158.

Sorensen, E., and Halpern, A. (1999). Single mothers and their child support receipt: How well is child support enforcement doing? Unpublished manuscript. Washington, DC: Urban Institute.

South, S., and Spitze, G. (1986). Determinants of divorce over the marital life course. *American Sociological Review, 51*, 583–590.

South, S. J. (1991). Sociodemographic differentials in mate selection preferences. *Journal of Marriage and the Family, 53*, 928–940.

South, S. J. (1993). Racial and ethnic differences in the desire to marry. *Journal of Marriage and the Family, 55*, 357–370.

South, S. J., and Lloyd, K. M. (1992). Marriage opportunities and family formation: Further implications of imbalanced sex ratios. *Journal of Marriage and the Family, 54*, 440–451.

Spanier, G. B., and Lewis, R. A. (1980). Marital quality: A review of the seventies. *Journal of Marriage and the Family, 42*, 825–839.

Spencer, M. B., Dobbs, B., and Swanson, D. P. (1988). African American adolescents: Adaptational processes and socioeconomic diversity in behavioral outcomes. *Journal of Adolescence, 11*, 117–137.

Spitze, G. (1988). Women's employment and family relations: A review. *Journal of Marriage and the Family, 50*, 595–618.

Spitze, G., and Logan, J. R. (1991). Sibling structure and intergenerational relations. *Journal of Marriage and the Family, 53*, 871–884.

Spitze, G., Logan, J. R., Deane, G., and Zerger, S. (1994). Adult children's divorce and intergenerational relationships. *Journal of Marriage and the Family, 56*, 279–293.

Spitze, G., and Miner, S. (1992). Gender differences in adult child contact among Black elderly parents. *The Gerontologist, 32,* 213–218.

Spitze, G., and Ward, R. (1995). Household labor in intergenerational households. *Journal of Marriage and the Family, 57,* 355–361.

Spitzer, B., Henderson, K., and Zivian, M. (1999). Gender differences in population versus media body sizes: A comparison over four decades. *Sex Roles, 40*(7/8), 545–565.

Spock, B., and Rothenberg, M. B. (1985). *Dr. Spock's Baby and Child Care.* New York: Pocket Books.

Sporakowski, M. J. (1988). A therapist's views on the consequences of change for the contemporary family. *Family Relations, 37,* 373–378.

Sprecher, S., Metts, A., Burleson, G., Hapfield, E., and Thompson, A. (1995). Domains of expressive interaction in intimate relationships: Associations with satisfaction and commitment. *Family Relations, 44,* 203–210.

Sprenkle, D. H., and Storm, C. L. (1983). Divorce therapy outcome research: A substantive and methodological review. *Journal of Marital and Family Therapy, 9,* 239–258.

Stack, C. (1974). *All Our Kin.* New York: Harper & Row.

Stack, F. (1994). The effect of geographic mobility on premarital sex. *Journal of Marriage and the Family, 56,* 204–208.

Stack, S. (1990). New micro-level data on the impact of divorce on suicide, 1959–1980: A test of two theories. *Journal of Marriage and the Family, 52,* 119–127.

Stack, S., and Wasserman, R. (1995). The effect of marriage, family, and religious ties on African-American suicide ideology. *Journal of Marriage and the Family, 57,* 215–222.

Stafford, L., and Canary, D. J. (1991). Maintenance strategies and romantic relationship type, gender and relational characteristics. *Journal of Social and Personal Relationships, 8,* 217–242.

Stafford, L., and Reske, J. R. (1990). Idealization and communication in long distance premarital relationships. *Family Relations, 39,* 274–289.

Stanley, S. M., and Markman, H. J. (1992). Possessing commitment in personal relationships. *Journal of Marriage and the Family, 54,* 595–608.

Stanley, S. M., Markman, H. J., St. Peters, M., and Leber, B. D. (1995). Strengthening marriages and preventing divorce. New directions in prevention research. *Family Relations, 44,* 392–401.

Staples, R. (1981). *The World of Black Singles: Changing Patterns of Male-Female Relationships.* Westport, CT: Greenwood Press.

Staples, R. (1985). Changes in Black family structure: The conflict between family ideology and structural conditions. *Journal of Marriage and the Family, 47,* 1005–1013.

Starrels, M. E. (1994). Gender differences in parent-child relations. *Journal of Family Issues, 15,* 148–165.

Starrels, M. E., Bould, S., and Nicholas, L. J. (1994). The feminization of poverty in the United States. *Journal of Family Issues, 15,* 590–607.

Stattin, H., and Klackenberg, G. (1992). Discordant family relations in intact families: Developmental tendencies over 18 years. *Journal of Marriage and the Family, 54,* 940–956.

Stayton, W. R. (1983). Preventing infidelity. *Medical Aspects of Human Sexuality, 17,* 36C–36D.

Stegman, M. A., Quercia, R. G., and McCarthy, G. (2000, June). Housing America's working families. *New Century Housing, 1*(1). Retrieved July 6, 2000, from the World Wide Web: http://www.nhc.org/affiliates/chprpt.pdf

Stein, L., and Hoopes, J. (1986). *Identity Formation in the Adopted Child.* New York: Child Welfare League of America.

Stein, P. (Ed.). (1981). *Single Life: Unmarried Adults in Social Context.* New York: St. Martin's Press.

Steinberg, L., and Silverberg, S. B. (1987). Influences on marital satisfaction during the middle stages of the family life cycle. *Journal of Marriage and the Family, 49,* 751–760.

Steinman, D. L., et al. (1981). A comparison of male and female patterns of sexual arousal. *Archives of Sexual Behavior, 10,* 529–548.

Stephan, C. W., and Stephan, W. G. (1989). After intermarriage: Ethnic identity and mixed-heritage Japanese-Americans and Hispanics. *Journal of Marriage and the Family, 51,* 507–519.

Stephen, T. D. (1985). Fixed-sequence and circular-causal models of relationship development: Divergent views on the role of communication in intimacy. *Journal of Marriage and the Family, 47,* 955–963.

Stephens, M. A. P., Franks, M. N., and Townsend, A. L. (1994). Stress and rewards in women's multiple roles: Case of women in the middle. *Psychology and Aging, 9,* 45–52.

Sternberg, R. (1986). A triangular theory of love. *Psychological Review 93,* 119–135.

Sternberg, R., and Barnes, M. (1985). Real and ideal others in romantic relationships: Is four a crowd? *Journal of Personality and Social Psychology, 49,* 1589–1596.

Sternberg, R., and Barnes, M. (Eds.). (1988). *The Psychology of Love.* New Haven, CT: Yale University Press.

Stets, J. E. (1990). Verbal and physical aggression in marriage. *Journal of Marriage and the Family, 52,* 501–514.

Stets, J. E. (1991). Cohabiting and marital aggression: The role of social isolation. *Journal of Marriage and the Family, 53,* 669–680.

Stets, J. E. (1993). Control in dating relationships. *Journal of Marriage and the Family, 55,* 573–685.

Stets, J. E., and Henderson, D. A. (1991). Contextual factors surrounding conflict resolution while dating: Results from a national study. *Family Relations, 40,* 29–36.

Stevens, G., and Schoen, R. (1988). Linguistic intermarriage in the United States. *Journal of Marriage and the Family, 50,* 267–279.

Stinnett, N., and DeFrain, J. (1985). *Secrets of Strong Families.* Boston: Little, Brown.

Stinnett, N., Knorr, B., DeFrain, J., and Rowe, G. (1981). How strong families cope with crises. *Family Perspective, 15,* 159–166.

Stohs, J. H. (1994). Alternative ethics in employed women's household labor. *Journal of Family Issues, 15,* 550–561.

Stoller, E. P. (1985). Exchange patterns in the informal support networks of the elderly: The impact of reciprocity on morale. *Journal of Marriage and the Family, 47,* 335–342.

Stoneman, Z., Brody, G. H., and Burke, M. (1989). Sibling temperaments and maternal and paternal perceptions of marital, family, and personal functioning. *Journal of Marriage and the Family, 51,* 99–113.

Storaasli, R. D., and Markman, H. J. (1990). Relationship problems in the early stages of marriage. *Journal of Family Psychology, 4,* 80–98.

Storey, W. (2000). Children in married and common law relationships: Legal differences. *Parents News Magazine.*

Strate, J. M., and Dubnoff, S. J. (1986). How much income is enough? Measuring the income adequacy of retired persons using a survey based approach. *Journal of Gerontology, 41,* 393–400.

Straus, M. (1974). Leveling, civility, and violence in the family. *Journal of Marriage and the Family, 36,* 13–29.

Straus, M. A., and Donnelly, D. (1993). Corporal punishment of teenage children in the United States. *Youth and Society, 24,* 419–442.

Straus, M. A., and Sweet, S. (1992). Verbal/symbolic aggression in couples: Incidence rates and relationships to personal characteristics. *Journal of Marriage and the Family, 54,* 346–357.

Straus, M. A., and Yodanis, C. L. (1996). Corporal punishment in adolescence and physical assaults on spouses in later life: What accounts for the link? *Journal of Marriage and the Family, 58,* 825–841.

Strong, B., Wilson, S., Robbins, M., and Johns, T. (1981). *Human Sexuality* (2nd ed.). Minneapolis: West.

Strouse, J. S. (1987). College bars as social settings for heterosexual contacts. *The Journal of Sex Research, 23,* 374–382.

Stryker, S. (1972). Symbolic interaction theory: A review and some suggestions for comparative family research. *Journal of Comparative Family Studies, 3,* 17–32.

Stull, D. E., and Scarisbrick-Hauser, A. (1989). Never-married elderly: A reassessment with implications for long-term care policy. *Research on Aging, 11,* 124–139.

Suitor, J. J. (1987). Mother-daughter relations when married daughters return to school: Effects of status similarity. *Journal of Marriage and the Family, 49,* 435–444.

Suitor, J. J. (1991). Marital quality and satisfaction with the division of household labor across the family life cycle. *Journal of Marriage and the Family, 53,* 221–230.

Suitor, J. J., and Pillemer, K. (1987). The presence of adult children: A source of stress for elderly couples' marriages? *Journal of Marriage and the Family, 49,* 717–725.

Suitor, J., and Pillemer, K. (1988). Explaining intergenerational conflict when adult children and elderly parents live together. *Journal of Marriage and the Family, 50,* 1037–1047.

Sullivan, A. (1995). *Virtually Normal: An Argument About Homosexuality.* New York: Knopf.

The Supreme Court upholds parental notice requirements. (1990). *Family Planning Perspectives, 22,* 177–181.

Surra, C. A. (1990). Research theory on mate selection and premarital relationships in the 1980s. *Journal of Marriage and the Family, 52,* 844–865.

Surra, C. A., and Hughes, D. K. (1997). Commitment processes and an account of the development of premarital relationships. *Journal of Marriage and the Family, 59,* 5–21.

Swinford, S. P., DeMaris, A., Cernkovich, S. A., and Giordano, P. C. (2000). Harsh physical discipline in childhood and violence in later romantic involvements: The mediating role of problem behaviors. *Journal of Marriage and the Family, 62,* 508–519.

Sykes, M. (2000). "Late-term" confusion, "partial-birth" lies. *Pro-Choice Views.* Retrieved from the World Wide Web: http://prochoice.about.com/newsissues/prochoice/library/bllatetermconfusion.htm

Szinovacz, M., and Harpster, P. (1993). Employment status, gender-role attitudes, and marital dependence in later life. *Journal of Marriage and the Family, 55,* 927–940.

Szinovacz, M. E. (1998). Grandparents today: A demographic profile. *The Gerontologist, 38,* 37–52.

Tagatz, G., Bigson, M., Schiller, P., and Nagel, T. (1980). Artificial insemination utilizing donor semen. *Minnesota Medicine, 63,* 539–541.

Tanfer, K. (1987). Patterns of premarital cohabitation among never-married women in the United States. *Journal of Marriage and the Family, 49,* 483–497.

Tanfer, K. (1994). Knowledge, attitudes, and intentions of American women regarding their hormonal implant. *Family Planning Perspectives, 26,* 60–65.

Tannen, D. (1982). *You Just Don't Understand: Women and Men in Conversation.* New York: Morrow.

Tannen, D. (1994). *Talking Nine to Five: How Women's and Men's Conversational Styles Affect Who Get Heard, Who Get Credit, and What Gets Done at Work.* New York: Morrow.

Tavris, C. (1982). Anger diffused. *Psychology Today, 16,* 25–29.

Taylor, M. A., and Shore, L. M. (1995). Predictors of planned retirement age: An adaptation of Beehr's model. *Psychology and Aging, 10,* 76–83.

Taylor, R. J. (1985). The extended family as a source of support to elderly Blacks. *The Gerontologist, 25,* 488–495.

Taylor, R. J. (1986). Receipt of support from family among Black Americans: Demographic and familial differences. *Journal of Marriage and the Family, 48,* 67–77.

Taylor, R. J., Chatters, L. M., and Jackson, J. S. (1993). A profile of familial relations among three-generation Black families. *Family Relations, 42,* 332–341.

Taylor, R. J., Chatters, L. M., and Mays, V. M. (1988). Parents, children, siblings, in-laws, and non-kin as sources of emergency assistance to Black Americans. *Family Relations, 37,* 298–304.

Taylor, R. J., Chatters, L. M., Tucker, M. B., and Lewis, E. (1990). Developments in research on Black families: A decade review. *Journal of Marriage and the Family, 52,* 993–1014.

Teachman, J. D., Call, B. R. A., and Carver, K. P. (1994). Marital status in the duration of joblessness among White men. *Journal of Marriage and the Family, 56,* 415–428.

Teachman, J. D., and Polonko, K. A. (1990a). Cohabitation and marital stability in the United States. *Social Forces, 69,* 207–220.

Teachman, J. D., and Polonko, K. (1990b). Negotiating divorce outcomes: Can we identify patterns in divorce settlements? *Journal of Marriage and the Family, 52,* 129–139.

Tein, J., Roosa, M. W., and Michaels, M. (1994). Agreement between parent and child reports on parental behaviors. *Journal of Marriage and the Family, 56,* 341–355.

Tennov, D. (1979). *Love and Limerence: The Experience of Being in Love.* New York: Stein & Day.

Teti, D. M., and Lamb, M. E. (1989). Socioeconomic and marital outcomes of adolescent marriage, adolescent childbirth, and their co-occurrence. *Journal of Marriage and the Family, 51,* 203–212.

Teti, D. M., Lamb, M. E., and Elster, A. B. (1987). Long-range socioeconomic and marital consequences of adolescent marriage in three cohorts of adult males. *Journal of Marriage and the Family, 49,* 499–506.

Tew, S., and Kirchgaessner, C. (1999). *About One in 10 Women Using Contraceptives Experience an Accidental Pregnancy.* (News release). New York: Alan Guttmacher Institute.

Thabes, V. (1997). Survey analysis of women's long-term, postdivorce adjustment. *Journal of Divorce and Remarriage, 27,* 163–175.

Thayer, S. (1988). Close encounters. *Psychology Today, 22,* 31–36.

Thomas, A., and Speight, S. (1999). Racial identity and racial socialization attitudes of African American parents. *Journal of Black Psychology, 25*(2), 152–170.

Thomas, D. L., and Cornwall, J. (1990). Religion and family in the 1980s: Discovery and development. *Journal of Marriage and the Family, 52,* 983–992.

Thomas, S., Albrecht, K., and White, P. (1984). Determinants of marital quality in dual-career couples. *Journal of Applied Family and Child Studies, 33*(4), 513–521.

Thomas, V. G. (1990). Determinants of global life happiness and marital happiness in dual-career Black couples. *Family Relations, 39,* 174–178.

Thomason, T. C. (1991). Counseling Native Americans: An introduction for non–Native American counselors. *Journal of Counseling and Development, 69,* 321–327.

Thompson, A. P. (1984). Emotional and sexual components of extramarital relations. *Journal of Marriage and the Family, 46,* 35–42.

Thompson, J. K., and Heinberg, L. J. (1999). The media's influence on body image disturbance and eating disorders: We've reviled them, now can we rehabilitate them? *Journal of Social Issues, 55*(2), 339–353.

Thompson, K. S. (1980). A comparison of Black and White adolescents' beliefs about having children. *Journal of Marriage and the Family, 42,* 133–139.

Thompson, L. (1991). Family work. Women's sense of fairness. *Journal of Family Issues, 12,* 181–196.

Thompson, L., and Walker, A. J. (1984). Mothers and daughters: Aid patterns and attachment. *Journal of Marriage and the Family, 46,* 313–322.

Thompson, L., and Walker, A. J. (1995). The place of feminism in family studies. *Journal of Marriage and the Family, 57*(4), 847–865.

Thompson, R., and Zuroff, D. (1999). Development of self-criticism in adolescent girls: Roles of maternal dissatisfaction, maternal coldness, and insecure attachment. *Journal of Youth and Adolescence, 28*(2), 197–210.

Thomson, E., and Colella, U. (1992). Cohabitation and marital stability: Quality or commitment? *Journal of Marriage and the Family, 54*, 259–267.

Thomson, E., McLanahan, S. S., and Curtin, R. D. (1992). Family structure, gender, and parental socialization. *Journal of Marriage and the Family, 54*, 368–378.

Thornberry, T., Smith, C., and Howard, G. (1997). Risk factors for teenage fatherhood. *Journal of Marriage and the Family, 59*(3), 505–522.

Thornton, A. (1989). Changing attitudes toward family issues in the United States. *Journal of Marriage and the Family, 51*, 873–893.

Tichenor, V. J. (1999). Status and income as gendered resources: The case of marital power. *Journal of Marriage and the Family, 61*, 638–650.

Tiedje, L. B., Wortman, C. B., Downey, G., Emmons, C., Biernat, M., and Lang, E. (1990). Women with multiple roles: Role compatibility perceptions, satisfaction, and mental health. *Journal of Marriage and the Family, 52*, 63–72.

Tiesel, J. W., and Olson, D. H. (1992). Preventing family problems: Troubling trends and promising opportunities. *Family Relations, 41*, 398–403.

Tiggle, R. B., Peters, M. D., Kelley, H. H., and Vincent, J. (1982). Correlational and discrepancy indices of understanding and their relation to marital satisfaction. *Journal of Marriage and the Family, 44*, 209–216.

Timko, C., and Moos, R. H. (1991). A typology of social climates in group residential facilities for older people. *Journal of Gerontology, 46*, S160–S169.

Timnick, L. (1982). How you can learn to be likable, confident, socially successful for only the cost of your present education. *Psychology Today, 16*, 42–49.

Tirozzi, G. (1998). *Non-School Hours: Mobilizing School and Community Resources.* Washington, DC: U.S. Government Printing Office.

Took, W., and Camire, L. (1991). Patterns of deception in intersexual and intrasexual mating strategies. *Ethnology and Sociobiology, 12*, 345–364.

Tornstam, L. (1992). Loneliness in marriage. *Journal of Social and Personal Relationships, 9*, 197–217.

Trends in the HIV and AIDS Epidemic. (1998, December). Atlanta: Centers for Disease Control and Prevention. Retrieved from the World Wide Web: http://www.cdc.gov/hiv/stats/trends98.pdf

Trent, K., and South, S. J. (1989). Structural determinants of the divorce rate: A cross-societal analysis. *Journal of Marriage and the Family, 51*, 391–404.

Trent, K., and South, S. J. (1992). Sociodemographic status, parental background, childhood family structure, and attitudes toward family formation. *Journal of Marriage and the Family, 54*, 427–439.

Trepanier-Street, M. L., Romatowski, J. A., and McNair, S. (1990). Development of story characters in gender-stereotypic and non-stereotypic occupational roles. *Journal of Early Adolescence, 10*, 496–510.

Trickett, P. K. (1993). Maladaptive development of school-aged, physically abused children: Relationships with child-rearing context. *Journal of Family Psychology, 7*, 134–147.

Trost, J. (1993). Family from a dyadic perspective. *Journal of Family Issues, 14*, 92–104.

Trotter, R. J. (1986). The three faces of love. *Psychology Today, 20*, 46–54.

Trovato, F., and Lauris, G. (1989). Marital status and mortality in Canada: 1951–1981. *Journal of Marriage and the Family, 51*, 907–922.

Trussell, J., and Grummer-Strawn, L. (1990). Contraceptive failure of the ovulation method of periodic abstinence. *Family Planning Perspectives, 22*, 65–75.

Trussell, J., Rodriquez, G., and Vaughan, B. (1988). *Union disillusion in Sweden.* Paper presented at the Seminar on Event History Analysis sponsored by the International Union for the Scientific Study of Population, Paris.

Trussell, J., Warner, D. L., and Hatcher, R. A. (1992). Condom slippage and breakage rates. *Family Planning Perspectives, 24*, 20–23.

Trzcinski, E., and Finn-Stevenson, M. (1991). In response to arguments against mandated parental leave: Findings from the Connecticut survey of parental leave policies. *Journal of Marriage and the Family, 53*, 445–460.

Tschann, J. M., Johnston, J. R., and Wallerstein, J. S. (1989). Resources, stressors, and attachment as predictors of adult adjustment after divorce: A longitudinal study. *Journal of Marriage and the Family, 51*, 1033–1046.

Tuan, M. (1999). Neither real Americans nor real Asians? Multigenerational Asian ethnics navigating the terrain of authenticity. *Qualitative Sociology, 22*(2), 105–125.

Tubman, J. G. (1993). Family risk factors, parental alcohol use, and problem behaviors among school-age children. *Family Relations, 42*, 81–86.

Tucker, M. B., and Taylor, R. J. (1989). Demographic correlates of relationship status among Black Americans. *Journal of Marriage and the Family, 51*, 655–665.

Turkel, A. R. (1998). All about Barbie: Distortions of a transitional object. *Journal of the American Academy of Psychoanalysis, 26*(1), 165–177.

Turner, B. F., and Adams, C. G. (1988). Reported change in preferred sexual activity over the adult years. *The Journal of Sex Research, 25*, 289–303.

Turner, R. (1990). Delays in conception found among women who had used the pill. *Family Planning Perspectives, 22*, 139–140.

Turner, R. (1991). Companion during labor lessens women's need for obstetric intervention. *Family Planning Perspectives, 23*, 238–239.

Turner, R. (1992a). Low birth weight linked to physical, behavioral problems at school age. *Family Planning Perspectives, 24*, 279–280.

Turner, R. (1992b). Underweight births are equally likely among poor Blacks and Whites. *Family Planning Perspectives, 24*, 95–96.

Turner, R. (1993). Condom use is low among U.S. heterosexuals at risk of HIV infection; 15% of population has at least one risk factor. *Family Planning Perspectives, 25*, 43–44.

Turner, R. (1994). AIDS threat leads some U.S. women to change their sexual behavior. *Family Planning Perspectives, 26*, 93–95.

Turner, R. H. (1970). *Family Interaction.* New York: Wiley.

Tyrer, L. B. (1984). Precautions in diaphragm use. *Medical Aspects of Human Sexuality, 18*, 243, 247.

Tzeng, J. M., and Mare, R. D. (1995). Labor market and socioeconomic effects on marital stability. *Social Science Research, 24*, 329–351.

Tzeng, M. (1992). The effects of social economic heterogamy and changes on marital disillusion for first marriages. *Journal of Marriage and the Family, 54*, 609–619.

Ubell, E. (1990, January 14). You don't have to be childless. *Parade Magazine*, pp. 14, 15.

Uhlenberg, P., and Hammill, B. G. (1998). Frequency of grandparent contact with grandchildren sets: Factors that make a difference. *The Gerontologist, 38*, 276–285.

Ulbrich, P. M., Coyle, A. T., and Llabre, M. M. (1990). Involuntary childlessness and marital adjustment: His and hers. *Journal of Sex and Marital Therapy, 16*, 147–158.

Umberson, D. (1987). Family status and health behaviors: Social control as a dimension of social integration. *Journal of Health and Social Behavior, 23*, 306–319.

Umberson, D. (1992). Relationships between adult children and their parents: Psychological consequences with both generations. *Journal of Marriage and the Family, 54*, 654–674.

Umberson, D. (1995). Marriage as support or strain? Marital quality following the death of a parent. *Journal of Marriage and the Family, 57*, 709–723.

Umberson, D., and Gove, W. R. (1989). Parenthood and psychological well-being. *Journal of Family Issues, 10*, 440–462.

U.S. Bureau of Labor Statistics. (2000, January). Employment and household data, annual averages, Table 37. Retrieved from the World Wide Web: ftp://ftp.bls.gov/pub/special.requests/if/aat37.txt

U.S. Bureau of the Census. (1987). Fertility of American women: June 1986. (*Current Population Reports*, Series P-28,-421). Washington, DC: U.S. Government Printing Office.

U.S. Bureau of the Census. (1992). *Statistical Abstract of the United States, 1992* (112th ed.). Washington, DC: U.S. Government Printing Office.

U.S. Bureau of the Census. (1996/1997). *Statistical Abstract of the United States, 1996/1997* (116th ed.). Washington, DC: U.S. Government Printing Office.

U.S. Bureau of the Census. (1998a, October 26). *Census Bureau Facts for Features: American Indian Heritage Month* (No. CB98-FF.13). Retrieved July 11, 2000, from the World Wide Web: http://www.census.gov/Press-Release/cb98ff13.html

U.S. Bureau of the Census (1998b). *Statistical Abstract of the United States, 1998.* Washington, DC: U.S. Government Printing Office.

U.S. Bureau of the Census. (1999a). *Statistical Abstract of the United States, 1999* (118th ed.). Washington, DC: U.S. Government Printing Office.

U.S. Bureau of the Census. (1999b). Interracial couples. *Current Population Reports, March 1998* (Report MS-3). Washington, DC: U.S. Government Printing Office.

U.S. Bureau of the Census. (1999c). Money income in the United States. (*Current Population Reports*, Series P60-206). Washington, DC: U.S. Government Printing Office.

U.S. Bureau of the Census, Ethnic and Hispanic Statistics Branch, Population Division. (2000b). Table 1.2: Population by Age, Hispanic Origin and Race, and Sex, March 1999. *Current Population Survey, March 1999.* Retrieved June 27, 2000, from the World Wide Web: http://www.census.gov/population/socdemo/hispanic/cps99/tab01-2.txt

U.S. Bureau of the Census, Population Estimates Program, Population Division. (2000a). *Resident Population Estimates of the United States by Sex, Race, and Hispanic Origin, April 1, 1990 to July 1, 1999, with Short-Term Projection to April 1, 2000.* Retrieved June 29, 2000, from the World Wide Web: http://www.census.gov/population/estimates/nation/intfile3-1.txt

U.S. Department of Health and Human Services. (2000, September 30). FDA approves Mifepristone for the termination of early pregnancy. Retrieved from the World Wide Web: http://www.fda.gov/bbs/topics/NEWS/NEW00737.html

Usui, W. M., Keil, T. J., and Durig, K. R. (1985). Socioeconomic comparisons and life satisfaction of elderly adults. *Journal of Gerontology, 40*, 110–114.

Utter, J. (1993). *American Indians: Answers to Today's Questions.* Lake Ann, MI: National Woodlands.

Vaillant, C. O., and Vaillant, G. E. (1993). Is the U-curve of marital satisfaction an illusion? A 40-year study of marriage. *Journal of Marriage and the Family, 55,* 230–239.

Valentine, D. P. (1982). The experience of pregnancy: A developmental process. *Family Relations, 31,* 243–248.

Vanderkooi, L., and Pearson, J. (1983). Mediating divorce disputes: Mediator behavior, styles, and roles. *Family Relations, 32,* 557–566.

Vannoy, D. (1991). Social differentiation, contemporary marriage, and human development. *Journal of Family Issues, 12,* 251–267.

Vander Mey, B. J., and Neff, R. L. (1982). Adult-child incest: A review of research and treatment. *Adolescence, 18,* 717–735.

Vannoy, D., and Philliber, W. W. (1992). Wife's employment and quality of marriage. *Journal of Marriage and the Family, 54,* 387–398.

Veevers, J. E. (1974a). The life style of voluntarily childless couples. In L. Larson (Ed.), *The Canadian Family in Comparative Perspective.* Toronto: Prentice-Hall.

Veevers, J. E. (1974b). Voluntary childlessness and social policy: An alternative view. *The Family, 23,* 397–406.

Vega, W. A., Kolody, B., and Valle, R. (1988). Marital strain, coping, and depression among Mexican-American women. *Journal of Marriage and the Family, 50,* 391–403.

Ventura, S. J., Martin, J. A., Curtin, S. C., Mathews, T. J., and Park, M. M. (2000). Births: Final data for 1998. *National Vital Statistics Reports, 48*(3). Hyattsville, MD: National Center for Health Statistics.

Vera, H., Berardo, D. H., and Berardo, F. M. (1985). Age heterogamy in marriage. *Journal of Marriage and the Family, 47,* 553–569.

Vigorito, A. J., and Curry, T. J. (1998). Marketing masculinity: Gender identity and popular magazines. *Sex Roles, 39*(1/2), 135–152.

Vinje, D. (1996). Native American economic development on selected reservations: A comparative analysis. *American Journal of Economics and Sociology, 55,* 427–442.

Visher, E. B., and Visher, J. S. (1989). Parenting coalition after remarriage: Dynamics and therapeutic guidelines. *Family Relations, 38,* 65–70.

Visher, E. B., and Visher, J. S. (1990). Dynamics of successful stepfamilies. *Journal of Divorce and Remarriage, 14,* 3–12.

Visher, E. B., and Visher, J. S. (1996). *Therapy with Stepfamilies.* New York: Brunner/Mazel.

Vitousek, B. M. (1979). Mixed marriages are a mixed bag. *Family Advocate, 1,* 16–19, 37–38.

Volling, B. L., and Belsky, J. (1991). Multiple determinants of father involvement during infancy in dual-earner and single-earner families. *Journal of Marriage and the Family, 53,* 461–474.

Volling, B. L., and Belsky, J. (1993). Maternal employment: Parent, infant, and contextual characteristics related to maternal employment decisions the first year of infancy. *Family Relations, 42,* 4–12.

Voth, H. M., Perry, J. A., McCranie, J. E., and Rogers, R. R. (1982). How can extramarital affairs be prevented? *Medical Aspects of Human Sexuality, 16,* 62–74.

Voydanoff, P. (1988). Work role characteristics, family structure demands, and work/family conflict. *Journal of Marriage and the Family, 50,* 749–761.

Voydanoff, P. (1990). Economic distress and family relations: A review of the eighties. *Journal of Marriage and the Family, 52,* 1099–1115.

Voydanoff, P., and Donnelly, B. W. (1989a). Economic distress and mental health. *Lifestyles, 10,* 139–162.

Voydanoff, P., and Donnelly, B. W. (1989b). Work and family roles and psychological stress. *Journal of Marriage and the Family, 51,* 923–932.

Vuchinich, S. (1987). Starting and stopping spontaneous family conflicts. *Journal of Marriage and the Family, 49,* 591–601.

Vuchinich, S., Hetherington, E. M., Vuchinich, R. A., and Clingempeel, W. G. (1991). Parent and child interaction and gender differences in early adolescents' adaptation to stepfamilies. *Developmental Psychology, 27,* 618–626.

Vukelich, C., and Kliman, D. S. (1985). Mature and teenage mothers' infant growth expectations and use of child development information sources. *Family Relations, 34,* 189–196.

Wagstaff, D. A., Kelly, J. A., Perry, M. K., Sikkema, K. J., Solomon, L. J., Heckman, T. G., and Anderson, E. S. (1995). Multiple partners, risky partners, and high HIV risk among low-income urban women. *Family Planning Perspectives, 27,* 241–245.

Waite, L. J. (1995). Does marriage matter? *Demography, 32,* 483–507.

Walker, A., and Thompson, L. (1984). Feminism and family studies. *Journal of Family Issues, 5*(4), 545–570.

Walker, A. J. (1985). Reconceptualizing family stress. *Journal of Marriage and the Family, 47,* 827–837.

Walker, A. J., and Pratt, C. C. (1991). Daughters' help to mothers: Intergenerational aid versus caregiving. *Journal of Marriage and the Family, 53,* 3–12.

Walker, A. J., Shin, H., and Bird, D. N. (1990). Perceptions of relationship change and caregiver satisfaction. *Family Relations, 39,* 147–152.

Wallace, P. M., and Gotlib, I. H. (1990). Marital adjustment during the transition to parenthood: Stability and predictors of change. *Journal of Marriage and the Family, 52,* 21–29.

Waller, W. (1937). The rating and dating complex. *American Sociological Review, 2,* 727–734.

Wallerstein, J., and Lewis, J. (1998). The long-term impact of divorce on children: A first report from a 25-year study. *Family and Conciliation Courts Review Special Issue: A Commemoration of the Second World Congress on Family Law and the Rights of Children and Youth, 36*(3), 368–383.

Walsh, W. M. (1992). Twenty major issues in remarriage families. *Journal of Counseling and Development, 70,* 709–715.

Walster, E., and Walster, G. W. (1978). *A New Look at Love.* Reading, MA: Addison-Wesley.

Wampler, K. S., and Powell, G. S. (1982). The Barrett-Lennard Relationship Inventory as a measure of marital satisfaction. *Family Relations, 35,* 539–545.

Wandewater, E. A., and Lansford, J. E. (1998). Influences of family structure and parental conflict on children's well-being. *Family Relations, 47,* 323–330.

Wang, H., and Amato, P. R. (2000). Predictors of divorce adjustment: Stressors, resources, and definitions. *Journal of Marriage and the Family, 62,* 655–668.

Ward, J. (1996). Raising resisters: The role of truth telling in the psychological development of African American girls. In B. Leadbeater and N. Way (Eds.), *Urban Girls.* New York: New York University Press.

Ward, R., Logan, J., and Spitze, G. (1992). The influence of parent and child needs on coresidents in middle and later life. *Journal of Marriage and the Family, 54,* 209–221.

Ward, R. A., and Spitze, G. (1992). Consequences of parent-adult coresidence. *Journal of Family Issues, 13,* 553–572.

Ward, S. K., Chapman, K., Cohn, E., White, S., and Williams, K. (1991). Acquaintance rape and the college social scene. *Family Relations, 40,* 65–71.

Warlick, J. L. (1985). Why is poverty after 65 a woman's problem? *Journal of Gerontology, 40,* 751–757.

Warner, R. L., Lee, G. R., and Lee, J. (1986). Social organization, spousal resources, and marital power: A cross-cultural study. *Journal of Marriage and the Family, 48,* 121–128.

Washburn, W. E. (Ed.). (1988). *Handbook of North American Indians: History of Indian-White Relations.* Washington, DC: Smithsonian Institution.

Watson, R. E. L. (1983). Premarital cohabitation vs. traditional courtship: Their effects on subsequent marital adjustment. *Family Relations, 32,* 139–147.

Way, N. (1995). "Can't you see the courage, the strength that I have?" Listening to urban adolescent girls speak about their relationships. *Psychology of Women Quarterly, 19*(1), 107–128.

Webster v. Reproductive Health Services, 109 S. Ct. 3040 (1989).

Weigel, R. R., and Weigel, D. J., and Blundall, J. (1987). Stress, coping, and satisfaction: Generational differences in farm families. *Family Relations, 36,* 45–48.

Weis, D. L., Slosnerick, M., Cate, R., and Sollie, D. L. (1986). A survey instrument for assessing the cognitive association of sex, love, and marriage. *The Journal of Sex Research, 22,* 206–220.

Weishaus, S., and Field, D. (1988). A half century of marriage: Continuity or change? *Journal of Marriage and the Family, 50,* 763–774.

Weisman, C. S., Plichta, S. B., Tirado, D. E., and Dana, K. S. (1993). Comparison of contraceptive implant adopters and pill users in a family planning clinic in Baltimore. *Family Planning Perspectives, 25,* 224–226.

Weiss, B., Dodge, K. A., Bates, J. E., and Pettit, G. S. (1992). Some consequences of early harsh discipline: Child aggression and a maladaptive social information processing style. *Child Development, 63,* 1321–1335.

Weissman, R. (1999, March). It's not the boob tube anymore. *American Demographics.* Retrieved August 20, 2000, from the World Wide Web: http://www.demographics.com/publications/ad/99_ad/9903_ad/ad990308c.htm

Weitzman, L. (1985). *The Divorce Revolution: The Unexpected Social and Economic Consequences for Women and Children in America.* New York: Free Press.

Weller, L., and Rofe, Y. (1988). Marital happiness among mixed and homogeneous marriages and Israel. *Journal of Marriage and the Family, 50,* 245–254.

Wells, B. (1983). Nocturnal orgasms: Females' perceptions of a "normal" sexual experience. *Journal of Sex Education and Therapy, 9,* 32–38.

Welsh, W. N., and Stewart, A. J. (1995). Relationships between women and their parents: Implications for midlife well-being. *Psychology and Aging, 10,* 181–190.

Wenk, D., Hardesty, P. L., Morgan, C. S., and Blaire, S. L. (1994). The influence of parental involvement in the well-being of sons and daughters. *Journal of Marriage and the Family, 56,* 229–234.

Westfall, J. M., Main, D. S., and Barnard, L. (1996). Continuation rates among injectable contraceptive users. *Family Planning Perspectives, 28,* 275–277.

Wethington, E., and Kessler, R. C. (1989). Employment, parental responsibility, and psychological distress. *Journal of Family Issues, 10,* 527–546.

Whisman, M. A., and Jacobson, N. S. (1990). Power, marital satisfaction, and response to marital therapy. *Journal of Family Psychology, 4*, 202–212.

White v. Illinois, 60 L. W. 4094 (1992).

White, J. W., and Humphrey, J. A. (1991). Young people's attitudes toward acquaintance rape. In A. Parrot (Ed.), *Acquaintance Rape: The Hidden Crime.* New York: Wiley.

White, L., and Keith, B. (1990). The effect of shift work on the quality and stability of marital relations. *Journal of Marriage and the Family, 52*, 453–462.

White, L. K. (1990). Determinants of divorce: A review of research in the eighties. *Journal of Marriage and the Family, 52*, 904–912.

White, L. K., and Rogers, S. J. (1997). Strong support but uneasy relationships: Coresidence in adult children relationships with parents. *Journal of Marriage and the Family, 59*, 62–76.

Whitveck, L. B., Hoyt, D. R., and Huck, S. M. (1993). Family relationship history, contemporary parent-grandparent relationship quality, and the grandparent-grandchild relationship. *Journal of Marriage and the Family, 55*, 1025–1035.

Wiederman, M., and Hurd, C. (1999). Extradyadic involvement during dating. *Journal of Social and Personal Relationships, 16*(2), 265–274.

Wilcoxon, S. A. (1985). Healthy family functioning: The other side of family pathology. *Journal of Counseling and Development, 63*, 495–499.

Wilcoxon, S. A. (1987). Grandparents and grandchildren. *Journal of Counseling and Development, 65*, 289–290.

Wilcoxon, S. A., and Hovestadt, A. J. (1983). Perceived health and similarity of family of origin experiences as predictors of dyadic adjustment for married couples. *Journal of Marital and Family Therapy, 9*, 431–434.

Wilfley, E. E., and Rodin, J. (1995). Cultural influences on eating disorders. In K. K. Brownell and C. G. Fairburn (Eds.), *Body Images: Development, Deviance, and Change.* New York: Guilford Press.

Wilhelm, M. S., and Ridley, C. A. (1988). Stress and unemployment in rural nonfarm couples: A study of hardships and coping resources. *Family Relations, 37*, 50–54.

Wilkie, J. R. (1991). The decline in men's labor force participation and income and the changing structure of family economic support. *Journal of Marriage and the Family, 53*, 111–122.

Wilkinson, D. (1997). American families of African descent. In M. K. DeGenova (Ed.), *Families in Cultural Context.* Mountain View, CA: Mayfield.

Willbach, D. (1989). Ethics and family therapy: The case management of family violence. *Journal of Marriage and Family Therapy, 15*, 43–52.

Wille, D. E. (1992). Maternal employment: Impact on maternal behavior. *Family Relations, 41*, 273–277.

Williams, K. R. (1992). Social sources of marital violence and deterrence: Testing an integrated theory of assaults between partners. *Journal of Marriage and the Family, 54*, 620–629.

Williams, L., and Jurich, J. (1995). Predicting marital success after five years: Assessing the predictive validity of FOCCUS. *Journal of Marital and Family Therapy, 21*, 141–153.

Williams, L. S. (1992). Adoption actions and attitudes of couples seeking invitro fertilization. *Journal of Family Issues, 13*, 99–113.

Williams-Deane, M., and Potter, L. S. (1992). Current oral contraceptive use instructions: An analysis of patient package inserts. *Family Planning Perspectives, 24*, 111–115.

Williamson, D. (1991). *The Intimacy Paradox: Personal Authority in the Family System.* New York: Guilford Press.

Willits, F. K., and Crider, D. M. (1988). Health rating and life satisfaction in the later middle years. *Journal of Gerontology, 43*, S172–S176.

Wilson, S. N., Larson, J. H., and Stone, K. L. (1993). Stress among job, insecure workers and their spouses. *Family Relations, 42*, 74–80.

Winch, R. F. (1958). *Mate Selection: A Study of Complementary Needs.* New York: Harper & Row.

Winch, R. F. (1967). Another look at the theory of complementary needs in mate selection. *Journal of Marriage and the Family, 29*, 756–762.

Winch, R. F. (1971). *The Modern Family.* New York: Holt.

Wineberg, H. (1990). Childbearing after remarriage. *Journal of Marriage and the Family, 52*, 31–38.

Wineberg, H. (1994). Marital reconciliation in the United States: Which couples are successful? *Journal of Marriage and the Family, 56*, 80–88.

Wineberg, H. (1999). The timing of remarriage among women who have a failed marital reconciliation in the first marriage. *Journal of Divorce and Remarriage, 30*, 57–69.

Wineberg, H., and McCarthy, J. (1989). Child spacing in the United States: Recent trends and differentials. *Journal of Marriage and the Family, 51*, 213–228.

Winikoff, B. (1995). Acceptability of medical abortion in early pregnancy. *Family Planning Perspectives, 27*, 142–148.

Winter, L. (1988). The role of sexual self-concept in the use of contraceptives. *Family Planning Perspectives, 20*, 123–127.

Witwer, M. (1989). High school graduation is more likely for those from small families. *Family Planning Perspectives, 21*, 285–286.

Witwer, M. (1990a). Advanced maternal age poses no major health risk for first-born infants. *Family Planning Perspectives, 22,* 235–236.

Witwer, M. (1990b). Low rate of weight gain late in pregnancy may signal premature birth. *Family Planning Perspectives, 22,* 92–93.

Witwer, M. (1990c). Oral contraceptive use may protect against PID caused by Chlamydia. *Family Planning Perspectives, 22,* 239–240.

Wolfinger, N. H. (1999). Trends in the intergenerational transmission of divorce. *Demography, 36,* 415–420.

Woll, S. B., and Cozby, C. P. (1988). Videodating and other alternatives to traditional methods of relationship initiation. In W. H. Jones and D. Perlman (Eds.), *Advances in Personal Relationships* (Vol. 1, pp. 69–108). Greenwich, CT: JAI.

Wolf-Smith, J. H., and LaRossa, R. (1992). After he hits her. *Family Relations, 41,* 324–329.

Woll, S. B., and Young, P. (1989). Looking for Mr. or Ms. Right: Self-presentation in videodating. *Journal of Marriage and the Family, 51,* 483–488.

Woodworth, S., Belsky, J., and Crnic, K. (1996). The determinants of fathering during the child's second and third years of life: A developmental analysis. *Journal of Marriage and the Family, 58,* 679–692.

Wright, P. H. (1982). Men's friendships, women's friendships, and the alleged inferiority of the latter. *Sex Roles, 8,* 1–20.

Wyatt, G. E., and Dunn, K. M. (1991). Examining predictors of sex guilt in multiethnic samples of women. *Archives of Sexual Behavior, 20,* 471–485.

Xiaohe, X., and Whyte, M. K. (1990). Love matches and arranged marriages: A Chinese replication. *Journal of Marriage and the Family, 52,* 709–722.

Yau, J., and Smetna, J. G. (1993). Chinese-American adolescents' reasoning about cultural conflicts. *Journal of Adolescent Research, 8,* 419–438.

Yescavage, K. (1999). Teaching women a lesson. *Violence Against Women 5*(7), 796–812.

Young, G., and Gately, T. (1988). Neighborhood impoverishment and child maltreatment. *Journal of Family Issues, 9,* 240–254.

Young U.S. adults marry considerably later, live with parents longer than counterparts in the 1960s. (1988). *Psychology Today, 20,* 144–145.

Zabin, L. S., Hirsch, M. B., Emerson, M. R., and Raymond, E. (1992). With whom do inner-city minors talk about their pregnancies? Adolescents' communication with parents and parent surrogates. *Family Planning Perspectives, 24,* 148–154.

Zelkowitz, P. (1987). Social support and aggressive behavior in young children. *Family Relations, 36,* 129–134.

Zick, C. D., and Smith, K. R. (1991a). Marital transitions, poverty, and gender differences in mortality. *Journal of Marriage and the Family, 53,* 327–336.

Zick, C. D., and Smith, K. R. (1991b). Pattern of economic change surrounding the death of a spouse. *Journal of Gerontology, 46,* S310–S320.

Zill, N. (1994). Understanding why children in stepfamilies have more learning and behavior problems than children in nuclear families. In A. Booth and J. Dunn (Eds.), *Stepfamilies: Who Benefits? Who Does Not?* (pp. 97–106). Hillsdale, NJ: Erlbaum.

Zill, N., Morrison, D. R., and Coiro, M. J. (1993). Long-term effects of parental divorce and parent-child relationships, adjustment, and achievement in young adulthood. *Journal of Family Psychology, 7*(1), 91–103.

Zimmerman, K., and Cochran, L. (1993). Alignment of family and work roles. *Career Development Quarterly, 41*(4), 344–349.

Zollar, A. C., and Williams, J. S. (1987). The contribution of marriage to the life satisfaction of Black adults. *Journal of Marriage and the Family, 49,* 87–92.

Zuo, J. (1992). The reciprocal relationship between marital interaction and marital happiness: A three-way study. *Journal of Marriage and the Family, 54,* 870–878.

Zuravin, S. J. (1988). Fertility patterns: Their relationship to child physical abuse and child neglect. *Journal of Marriage and the Family, 50,* 983–993.

Zuravin, S. J. (1991). Unplanned childbearing and family size: Their relationship to child neglect and abuse. *Family Planning Perspectives, 23,* 155–161.

Zvonkovic, A. M., Greaves, K. M., Schmiege, C. J., and Hall, L. D. (1996). The marital construction of genders through work and family decisions: A qualitative analysis. *Journal of Marriage and the Family, 58,* 91–100.

Zwerling, P. (1989). A gay wedding. In B. Strong and C. DeVault, *The Marriage and Family Experience* (4th ed.). St. Paul, MN: West.

CREDITS

Text

Chapter 1 Figure 1.9 and 1.10 From *Sex in America: A Definitive Survey* by Robert T. Michael, et al. Copyright © 1994 by CSG Enterprises, Inc., Edward O. Laumann, Robert T. Michael, and Gina Kolata. Reprinted by permission of Little, Brown and Company (Inc.). **Chapter 5** Table 5.1 Reprinted with the permission of Scribner, a Division of Simon and Schuster from *Modern Courtship and Marriage* by E. E. Masters. Copyright © 1957 by Macmillan Publishing Company. Table 5.2 From *Marriage and the Family* by S. R. Jorgensen, 1986, New York: Macmillan, p. 260. Copyright © 1986 by Stephen R. Jorgensen. Reprinted by permission. Table 5.4 From "Gender Differences in Courtship Violence Victimization" by J. M. Makepeace. Copyright © 1986 by the National Council on Family Relations, 3989 Central Ave., NE, Suite 550, Minneapolis, MN 55421. Reprinted by permission. **Chapter 6** Figure 6.3 From *Motivation and Personality* by Maslow. Copyright © 1971 by Maslow. Reprinted by permission of Prentice-Hall, Inc., Upper Saddle River, NJ. Figure 6.4 From Marriage and Parenthood by F. Philip Rice. Copyright © 1979 by Allyn & Bacon. Reprinted by permission of the publisher. Figure 6.5 From "A Triangular Theory of Love" by R. Sternberg, *Psychological Review,* 1986, 93, pp. 119–135. Reprinted by permission of the author. **Chapter 8** Figure 8.1 From *Human Sexual Response* by W. H. Masters and V. E. Johnson. Reprinted by permission. Figure 8.2 and 8.4 From *Human Sexuality* by W. H. Masters and V. E. Johnson. Reprinted by permission. **Chapter 11** Figure 11.3 From R. Gilford, *Journal of Gerontology*, 1984, 39, p. 331. Reprinted by permission of the Gerontological Society of America. **Chapter 12** Table 12.1 From "Employed First-Time Mothers: A Typology of Maternal Responses to Integrating Parenting and Employment" by C. Schuster, *Family Relations*, 1993, 42, pp. 13–20. Copyright © 1993 by the National Council on Family Relations, 3989 Central Ave., NE, Suite 550, Minneapolis, MN 55421. Reprinted by permission of the publisher. **Chapter 16** Figure 16.2 From *Human Development: A Life-Span Approach*, Second Edition. Copyright © by Pearson Education. Reprinted by permission of Prentice-Hall, Inc., Upper Saddle River, NJ. **Chapter 18** Figure 18.1 From "Conflict in Families and Friendships of Later Life" By C. B. Fisher, J. D. Reid, and M. Melendez, *Family Relations*, 1989, 38, p. 85. Copyright © 1989 by the National Council on Family Relations, 3989 Central Ave., NE, Suite 550, Minneapolis, MN 55421. Reprinted by permission of the publisher. **Chapter 19** P. 432 From "Spouses' Impressions of Rules for Communication in Public and Private Marital Conflicts" by E. Jones and C. Gallois, *Journal of Marriage and the Family*, 1989, 51, pp. 957–967. Copyright © 1989 by the National Council on Family Relations, 3989 Central Ave., NE, Suite 550, Minneapolis, MN 55421. Reprinted by permission of the publisher. Figure 19.1 From "Leveling, Civility, and Violence in the Family" by M. A. Straus, Journal of Marriage and the Family, 1974, 36, p. 17. Copyright © 1974 by the National Council on Family Relations, 3989 Central Ave., NE, Suite 550, Minneapolis, MN 55421. Reprinted by permission of the publisher. Figure 19.3 From Domestic Abuse Intervention Project, 202 East Superior Street, Duluth, MN 55802. Reprinted by permission. Figure 19.4 Reprinted by permission of Simon & Schuster from *The Experience of Dying* by E. Mansell Pattison. Copyright © 1977 by Prentice-Hall, Inc. **Chapter 21** P. 505 From *Journal of Counseling and Development*, 1992, 70, pp. 709–715. Copyright © 1992 by ACA. Reprinted by permission. No further reproduction authorized without written permission of the American Counseling Association. Figure 21.1 From "The Economic Behavior of Stepfamilies" by B. Fishman, Family Relations, 1983, 32, pp. 359–366. Copyright © 1983 by the National Council on Family Relations, 3989 Central Ave., NE, Suite 550, Minneapolis, MN 55421. Reprinted by permission of the publisher.

Index

abortion, 338–346
  laws regarding, 338–342
  spontaneous, 331, 364, 366–367
  unmarried women and, 51
abuse, physical
  corporal punishment and, 395
  effects on children, 394
  family background and, 305
  in intimate relationships, 201
  of unwanted children, 324
abuse, sexual
  attachment and, 390
  of children
    effects of, 447
    incest, 442, 448–450
    incidence of, 447
    intervention, 450
    pedophilia, 448
    symptoms of, 447
  criminal justice system and, 448
  in marriage, 442
  victims of
    number of, 104
    singlehood among, 75
    vulnerability of, 105
abuse, spousal
  communication and, 443
  definition, 442
  incidence of, 443–444
  marital satisfaction and, 443
  perpetrators, 444–445
  power and, 305
  rates of, 305
  scapegoating and, 443
  self-esteem and, 443
  sexual dysfunction and, 443
  substance abuse and, 443
  treatment for, 447
  victims, 444–445
  by women, 444
acceptance therapy, 318
acculturation
  Chinese Americans and, 61
  Native Americans and, 58, 60
ACOA. See adult children of alcoholics
adjustment, marital
  communication and, 314
  definition, 239
  developmental tasks and, 239
  equity and, 268
  number of children and, 267
  predictors of, 268

satisfaction and, 239
social anxiety and, 297
women's employment and, 267–268
work identity and, 261.
          See also marriage, adjustments in
adoption, 83
  as alternative to childbearing, 348–350
  as family task, 21
  by gays/lesbians, 20
adult children of alcoholics, 32
adulthood, late, 245–252
adulthood, middle, 242–243
adults, single
  involuntary, 72
  never-married, 61, 70–72, 74
  voluntary, 71–72
adults, widowed
  by ethnicity, 70
advertisements, personal, 96–98
affection
  expression of, 37
  and marital success, 226
affinity, 206
African Americans
  childbirth among, 8, 51, 55
  children, 51–52
  definition, 48
  economic issues, 10, 48, 50–51, 54
  education, 48, 50–54
  elderly, 52
  expectations of, 50
  families, 48–54, 61, 236, 395
  gender and, 51–54
  household labor and, 52–53
  life expectancy of, 236
  marital status, 14, 51, 55, 70, 202
  marriage, 51–54, 193, 196, 236
  mate selection, 192–193
  networks among, 51–52, 298
  parenting and, 50, 52, 241
  problems of, 52–53
  religion and, 50, 52
  satisfaction of, 51–54, 149
  sexual behavior of, 16, 51
  slavery and, 48–50
  socialization of, 53, 149
  teens, 51, 53
  values of, 53
after-school programs, 387
agape, 131
age
  cohabitation and, 202

divorce and, 197, 462–463
income and, 246
living arrangements and, 81, 414
marriage and. See marriage, age and
mate selection and, 190, 196–197
oppression based on, 23
poverty and, 246
readiness for marriage and, 204–205
remarriage and, 252
retirement and, 247
sexual intercourse and, 80, 172
aggression
  communication and, 43
  corporal punishment and, 395
  in dating, 104–110
  interparental, 427
  substance abuse and, 431
  ventilation/catharsis and, 430–431
Aid to Families with Dependent
    Children (AFDC), 58
AIDS, 13, 208, 210
  incidence of, 81–82
  among Native Americans, 57
  premarital test for, 207
  protection against, 18
  spread of, 17
alcohol, use of
  casual sex and, 124
  courtship violence and, 109
  as relationship problem, 239
  sexual assault and, 107
alcoholism
  effects on family, 22, 32
  in Hispanic families, 32
  among Native Americans, 59, 60
  risk factors for, 32
  and sexual dysfunction, 176
amniotic sac, 370
androgyny, 152–154
anger
  communication and, 222
  gender and, 151
  media and, 147
  parenthood and, 151
  sexual dysfunction and, 176
annulment, 207
anorexia nervosa, 119
anxiety
  angry communication and, 43
  dating and, 101, 104
  emotional distance and, 126
  family background and, 34

575

anxiety, *(continued)*
  family dysfunction and, 126
  intimate relationships and, 201
  marital adjustment and, 297
  never-married adults and, 71
  romantic love and, 122, 123
  sexual abuse and, 447
  unattached people and, 34
Apgar score, 372
Asian/Pacific Islanders
  cultural identity of, 63
  definition, 48
  interracial marriage among, 193
assault, marital, 305
assault, sexual, 107, 326
assessment, premarital, 208–209
attachment, emotional
  father-fetus, 366
  infants and, 390
  mother-fetus, 366
attachment, social, 202
attachment, style of
  dating and, 104
  depression and, 35
  theories of, 123
attachment theory, 35–36, 123, 305
attitudes
  about careers, 40
  about childbearing, 40
  about divorce, 39, 476
  about elderly, 52, 54, 59
  about employment, 10
  family background and, 30, 34,
    37–39, 191
  about gender, 138
  about intimacy, 36–37
  about intimate partners, 34–36
  about marital roles, 10
  about marriage, 39, 40
  about media, 296
  media effect on, 138
  of parents about children, 32–34
  about sexuality, 10, 37–39, 205
  about STDs, 147, 149–150
  about unmarried motherhood, 39
attraction, 118–121
  mate selection and, 189–190
  romantic love and, 226
attractiveness
  personality-based, 120–121
  physical, 118–120
authenticity dilemma, 63
authority, family
  African Americans and, 50
  Chinese Americans and, 61
  elderly and, 249
  parents and, 12
autonomy, 392

B-love, 125–126

baby boom, 7, 8
baby boomers, 296
background, family
  anxiety and, 34
  attitudes and, 30, 34, 37–39, 191
  child rearing and, 191
  communication and, 36
  conflicted couples and, 219
  courtship violence and, 109
  effect on marriage, 30
  gender roles and, 39, 191
  intimate relationships and, 31, 34, 201,
    304–305
  marital satisfaction and, 191
  mate selection and, 188, 190–195
  power and, 304–305
  values and, 191
barrios, 54, 56
benefits, fringe
  bereavement leave, 11
  for gay/lesbian partners, 239
  health insurance, 12, 13
  maternal leave, 226
  sick leave, 11
BIA. *See* Bureau of Indian Affairs
bias, gender-based, 138–139
bigamy, 207
"biological clock," 199
birth control. *See* contraceptives
birth date, calculation of, 361
birth defects, avoidance of, 367
birth weight, low, 362, 363
  abuse of infants with, 446
  care of infants with, 374
  maternal stress and, 366
  problems associated with, 374
  smoking and, 367
birthrates
  among African Americans, 8, 55
  among Chinese Americans, 55
  and employment of women, 9
  among Hispanics, 8
  among Mexican Americans, 55
  among Native Americans, 55, 57, 59
  among teenagers, 18, 59, 83
  among unmarried women, 83
  among Whites, 8, 59
body dissatisfaction
  among girls, 119
  media and, 147
  among women, 120, 146, 147
body image
  distorted, 119
  by ethnic group, 149
  media and, 138, 145
  pornography and, 167
body monitoring, 242
body satisfaction
  among African Americans, 149
  among Hispanics, 149

bonding, parent-infant, 373
"boomerang kids," 245
Boy Scouts, 20
breast cancer, 328
breast-feeding, 373–375, 376
Brownies, 20
bundling, 92
Bureau of Indian Affairs, 56–59

care, long-term, 254
care, prenatal, 362–364, 373
career
  choice of, 196
  marriage and, 73
Cartoon Network, 296
cervical cap, 334
chastity, vows of, 73
child abuse, 13, 20
  definition, 442
  effects of, 446–447
  as family crisis, 434
  by nonparental caregivers, 391
  reasons for, 445–446
  treatment for, 447
child care
  African Americans and, 52
  day care, 391–392
  in dual-career families, 263–264
  in dual-earner families, 150, 151
  by extended family, 391
  family conflict and, 227
  fathers' participation in, 151–152,
    262–263, 386–387
  in female-headed families, 279
  gender roles and, 150–152, 153
  by grandparents, 251
  job schedule and, 263
  marital satisfaction and, 151
  maternal gatekeeping and, 151–152
  maternal stress level and, 266
  nonparental, 10, 391
  poverty and, 279
  responsibility for, 6, 10, 386
  role strain and, 150
  in single-earner families, 151
  in single-parent families, 397–399
  subsidized, 14
  wage gap and, 275
  women's employment and, 150, 376
child launching, 21
child neglect, 13, 20
child rearing
  African Americans and, 51, 52
  Chinese Americans and, 61–62
  cost of, 237, 325
  cultural differences in, 383
  egalitarianism and, 40
  family background and, 191
  family life cycle and, 20
  feminist theory of, 23

among gays/lesbians, 12
marital conflict regarding, 382
marital satisfaction and, 237
Mexican Americans and, 56
parent-child communication in, 382
philosophies of, 382–384
socioeconomic status and, 280
child support, 15, 204, 273, 279, 480–481
childbearing, 6
    attitudes about, 40
    cohabitation and, 202
    in family life cycle, 20
    as family task, 21
    among lesbians, 18, 20
    reasons for, 351–352
    among single women, 10, 18
childbirth
    delivery options, 373
    physical stress of, 375
    return to work after, 376
    sex after, 376
    support after, 375–376
childbirth, prepared, 369–370
childlessness, 2, 352–353
    divorce and, 464–465
    in dual-career families, 269
    single women and, 75
children
    abuse of. See child abuse
    attitudes about, 32–34
    care of. See child care
    in cohabiting households, 203–204
    cost of raising, 273, 325
    custody of, 12, 238, 477, 479–480
    depression among, 389–390, 477
    development of
        cognitive, 387–389
        day care quality and, 391
        home environment and, 388, 389
        language, 388
        psychological, 12
        self-esteem, 389–390
        social, 12
    family conflict and, 426–427
    needs of, 6, 20
        emotional, 384, 389–392
        intellectual, 385
        moral, 385
        physical, 384
        in single-parent families, 395–400
        social, 384–385
    neglect of. See child neglect
    number per family, 7
    nurture of, 20
    parents' happiness and, 353–354
    poverty and, 204
    power held by, 308–309
    rearing of. See child rearing
    socialization of, 20
        African Americans and, 53

by families, 20, 30
by community organizations, 20, 30
gender schema theory of, 141
by mass media, 30
Mexican Americans and, 56
by parents, 384–385
religious, 195
supervision of, 17
support of. See child support
television viewing and, 296
children of alcoholics (COA), 32
Children's Defense Fund, 282–283
Chinese Americans, 61–64
    birthrate among, 55
    interracial marriage among, 193
chlamydia, 181–182
Chocolate Singles, 98
Civil Rights Act of 1964, 274
civil rights movement, 5
closeness, emotional
    companionship style and, 291
    in dating, 103–104
    in family relationships, 126–127
    marital happiness and, 220
    need for, 291
clothing, gender-specific, 141
COA. See children of alcoholics
codependency, 75
coercion, sexual, 105–106
cognitive development theory, 140–141
cohabitation, nonmarital, 2, 200–204
    acceptance of, 7, 39, 72
    age and, 202
    children and, 202, 203–204
    domestic violence and, 201
    economic issues and, 200, 202
    educational level and, 202
    egalitarianism and, 202
    emotional support and, 202
    ethnicity and, 202
    household labor and, 200
    marriage and, 7, 201, 202–203
    mate selection and, 190, 199, 200
    monogamy and, 201
    patterns of, 200–201
    reactions to, 201–202
    reasons for, 201
    relationship quality and, 201, 202
cohesion, family, 37, 263
college attendance
    African Americans and, 50
    Chinese Americans and, 61
    Native Americans and, 59
"coming out," 238
commitment
    constraint, 225
    and marital success, 224–226
communication
    androgyny and, 153
    anger and, 222

anxiety and, 314
barriers to, 314–316
companionship and, 314
in dating, 36, 101, 104, 106, 199
definition, 313
within families, 41–43, 432
family background and, 36
feedback in, 317
gender and, 101, 141
improving, 316–318
intimacy and, 243
marital adjustment and, 313, 314
marital success and, 218–220, 222
nonverbal, 314
parent-child, 382
patterns of, 41–43
power and, 308
as relationship problem, 239, 243
in relationships, 304, 313–316
self-disclosure and, 230
sex and, 170
traditional couples and, 219
verbal, 314
companionship, 4
    communication and, 314
    dating and, 94
    elderly and, 248
    family and, 290–294
    friendship and, 297–298, 298–300
    gender differences and, 298
    importance of, 80
    in leisure activities, 292, 294–297
    and marital success, 223–224
    marriage and, 72, 269, 290, 292
    outside family, 297–300
    styles of, 290–291
compatibility
    and cohabitation, 201
    and mate selection, 190, 195–198
complementary needs, theory of, 188
Comstock Law, 8
conception
    alternate means of, 347–348
    increasing likelihood of, 337
condoms
    alcohol and use of, 82
    availability of, 332
    failure of, 331–332, 333
    nonuse of, 17
    prevention of STDs and, 180
    protection against AIDS, 332
    use of, 331–333
conflict, family, 22
    about child care, 227
    communication and, 432
    effects on children, 426–427
    interparent, 35, 426–427
    management of, 305, 429–433
    marital satisfaction and, 433
    marriage gradient and, 196

conflict, family, *(continued)*
  parent-child, 35, 411, 412
  as predictor of divorce, 219
  sources of, 427–429
  substance abuse and, 32
  systems theory of, 22
conflict, marital
  about child rearing, 382
  happiness and, 220
  parenthood and, 241, 242
  religion and, 224
  traditional couples and, 219
conflict, nonmarital, 173
conflict, theory of, 23
conflict, types of, 266, 431–432
consanguinity, 206
Constitution, United States
  Nineteenth Amendment to, 5
contact comfort, 36–37
continuous decline marital pattern, 236
continuous increase marital pattern, 236
contraceptives
  availability of, 8–9
  choosing, 338, 339
  failure of, 335
  laws regarding, 8–9
  natural birth control, 336–338
  nonuse of, 326
  parent-child discussion of, 17, 38
  teens and, 324
  types of
    barrier, 331–334
    cervical cap, 334
    condoms, 331–333
    diaphragm, 333–334
    IUDs, 330–331
    oral, 325–328
    progestin, 328–329
    spermicides, 329–330, 331–332
    tubal ligation, 335–336
    vasectomy, 334–335
  use of, 6, 18, 396
  See also condoms; contraceptives,
    oral
contraceptives, oral
  advantages of, 327
  disadvantages of, 327–328
  failure of, 326, 327
  sex drive and, 328
  STDs and, 332
  types of, 325–328
control factors, social
  as family task, 21
  teen sex and, 17
coparenting, 504–505
cost of living. *See* living, cost of
counseling
  marriage, 31, 470, 473
  premarital, 34, 191, 208–209, 407
  relationship, 111, 112

couples, types of, 219
courtship, 90, 239
crib death. *See* Sudden Infant Death
    Syndrome
crime, involvement in, 53
crisis, family, 433–434
Cub Scouts, 20
culture
  definition, 48
  Native American, 57, 58, 60
cunnilingus, 166
curvilinear marital pattern, 236–237
cybersex, 170

D-love, 125–126
Dalkon shield, 330
dating
  anxiety about, 101, 104
  attachment style and, 104
  choosing partners, 96–100, 120
  closeness/distance in, 103–104
  communication in, 36, 101, 104, 106,
    199
  companionship and, 94
  egalitarianism in, 94, 100, 101–102
  among elderly, 248, 249
  emergence of, 91–93
  gender roles in, 91, 94, 95, 100–102,
    104, 143
  gender-role compatibility and, 198
  imaging and, 101
  mate selection and, 90, 95–96
  patriarchy in, 102
  patterns of, 93, 94
  problems in, 101–104
  rape in, 104–105, 106–107
  reasons for, 94–96, 106
  self-disclosure in, 101–102, 106
  sex and, 93, 95, 100–101
  social status and, 91–92, 96
  socialization and, 94, 96, 102, 106
  socioeconomic status and, 93
  stages of, 93
  steady, 92–93
  systems of, 90
  violence in, 104–110
dating services, 98–100
death
  as family crisis, 450–456
  rates of, 57
death of spouse, 20
  family role adjustments, 249
  and happiness, 76
  and health, 76, 77
  psychological stress of, 252
debt, 276–277
dependency
  exaggerated, 34
  power and, 311
Depo-Provera, 328–329

depression
  in alcoholic families, 32
  androgyny and, 153
  attachment style and, 35
  among children, 389–390, 447
  media images and, 147
  among men, 32, 110
  mid-life crisis and, 243
  among never-married people, 71
  postpartum, 375
  poverty and, 279
  among unattached people, 34
  among White girls, 149
deprivation, emotional, 34
descent, line of
  bilateral, 6
  matrilineal, 5
  patrilineal, 4–5, 59
development, prenatal
  embryonic period, 368–369
  fetal period, 369
  germinal period, 367–386
developmental process theory, 189–190
diaphragm, 333–334
discipline
  definition, 393
  principles of, 394–395
  socialization and, 393
discrimination
  against African Americans, 52
  against gays/lesbians, 11, 12
diseases, sexually transmitted
  attitudes about, 147, 149–150
  birth defects and, 367
  incidence of, 81, 177
  premarital tests for, 207
  protection against, 18, 327–333
  risk factors for, 178, 179
  spread of, 17
  treatment of, 178
  types of, 178
dislocation, 291
disruption, marital
  age heterogamy and, 196–197
  educational heterogamy and, 193
  religion and, 195
dissatisfaction, marital
  marriage gradient and, 196
  sources of, 204
distress
  economic, 438–440
  marital, 219
  psychological, 32, 202
divorce
  adjustment after, 475
  age and, 195, 197, 462–463
  age at marriage and, 199, 204–205
  alternatives to, 470–472
  attitudes about, 39, 476
  Catholic Church and, 195

causes of, 465–468
child custody and, 477
childlessness and, 464–465
children's reaction to, 481–483
among elderly, 237, 250–251
in family life cycle, 235–236, 243
happiness and, 76
health and, 76, 77
income and, 439
job schedule and, 262
kin networks and, 479
living arrangements and, 79, 81, 245
marital happiness and, 234
no-fault, 472–475
parent-child relations and, 250–251
predictors of, 7–8, 208–209, 218–219,
    462–465
premarital pregnancy and, 324
previous cohabitation and, 202–203
rates of, 2, 4, 10, 12, 13, 14
    by ethnicity, 51, 55, 61, 70
    in hypergamous unions, 193
    in hypogamous unions, 193
    interfaith marriages and, 194
    interracial marriages and, 194
reasons for, 468–469
religion and, 463
socioeconomic status and, 463
work schedule and, 262
Divorce Act, 204
dopamine, 123
dreams, sexual, 169
drugs, illicit
    casual sex and, 124
    date rape and, 107
    as relationship problem, 239
    types of, 17
    use of, 13, 81
dying, stages of, 451
dysfunction, family
    patterns of, 34
    risks to children, 32
    treatment of, 22
dysfunction, sexual
    alcoholism and, 176
    causes of, 176
    in homosexuals, 174
    prevalence of, 175
    sexual trauma and, 176
    treatment of, 177
    types of, 174–176
dyspareunia, 175

eating disorders
    African Americans and, 53
    girls and, 145, 149
    sexual abuse and, 447
economics, family
    Native Americans and, 57–58
    never-married adults and, 74

education
    African Americans and, 50, 52
    Chinese Americans and, 61, 62
    costs associated with, 273
    Mexican Americans, 56
    Native Americans, 57, 58–59
    power and, 307
    premarital, 208
    of women, 6, 7
education, level of
    of African American women, 51, 54
    career and, 268
    in grandparent-headed house-
        holds, 13
    income and, 274
    mate selection and, 190, 192–193,
        196
    among nonmarital cohabitors, 202
    number of children and, 324
    parenthood and, 241
    poverty and, 279
    readiness for marriage and, 204
egalitarianism, 6
    African Americans and, 51, 52
    cohabitation and, 202
    in dating, 94, 100, 101–102
    gender-role expectations and, 40
    household labor and, 40, 151,
        227, 306
    marital satisfaction and, 309
    in marriage, 306
    Mexican Americans and, 56
    power and, 306
    in relationships, 304
    violence and, 309, 310
ego integrity, 249
ego resiliency, 244
ejaculation, premature, 174
eldercare, 408–409
    economic issues and, 244
    effects on caregivers, 244
    household labor and, 244
    leisure activities and, 244
    longevity and, 254
    marital quality and, 244
    Mexican Americans and, 54
    psychological well-being and, 244
    sources of, 254
    stress and, 252
elderly
    care of. *See* eldercare
    cultural attitudes about, 52, 54, 59
    dating among, 248, 249
    divorce among, 237, 250–251
    health of, 249, 250
    kin networks and, 298
    living arrangements of, 244
    loneliness and, 248
    personal identity of, 248
Electra complex, 188

eligibles, field of, 189
embryo, development of, 368, 369
embryo transplant, 347
emissions, nocturnal, 38, 169
empathy
    in communication, 316
    definition, 316
    and marital success, 228
employment
    attitudes about, 10
    gender-role stereotypes in, 144
    living arrangements and, 81,
        414–415
    opportunities for women and
        minorities, 8, 10, 60, 62
    postretirement, 249
    power and, 247
    pregnancy and, 204
    reasons for, 10
empty nest, 20, 235, 244–245
endogamy, 190
endorphins, 124
ENRICH, 219
Equal Opportunity Act of 1972, 139
Equal Pay Act, 274, 275
equality, marital, 149
equity theory, 23, 189
erection, 161–162
erogenous zones, 166
eros, 131
estrogen, 325
ethnicity, family, 48
evolutionary theory, 142
exchange theory, 22, 189, 313
exclusion acts, 61
exogamy, 190
expectations
    of community, 21
    of family, 266
    of kin network, 21
    about parenthood, 376
    of perfectionist parents, 33
expectations, gender-role
    egalitarianism and, 40
    marriage and, 197–198, 227
expectations, marital, 2, 4, 239
    for companionship, 292
    effects on marriage, 216, 219
    need fulfillment and, 217–218
expectations, parental, 41
    for adult children, 411
    African Americans and, 50
    Chinese Americans and, 62
expectations, societal, 21, 136–137, 146,
    260–261, 304, 393
Expenditures on Children by
    Families, 273
expression, sexual, 6, 20
    marital success and, 226
    parent-child discussions of, 38

families
    African American. *See* African Ameri-
        cans, families
    authority within, 3, 4, 5, 6
    characteristics of, 2
    communication in, 41–43
    definitions of, 2–3, 23
    dysfunctional, 127
    functions of, 4, 18–20, 235–239
    gay/lesbian, 238
    identity, 3
    maintenance of, 21
    Mexican American. *See* Mexican
        Americans
    Native American. *See* Native
        Americans
    needs of, 272–274
    number of, in U.S., 2
    philosophy of, 4–6
    power in, 22–23, 32, 55–56, 304–313
    relationships within, 16
    roles within, 5
    size of, 8–9, 280
    structures and forms of, 235–239
        binuclear, 3
        blended, 2, 3, 15–16
        childless, 3
        cohabiting, 4
        dual-career, 6
        dual-earner, 50, 150–151, 262–268
        extended, 2, 3, 20
        female-headed, 279
        matriarchal, 4
        multigenerational, 2
        nuclear, 3, 4, 18–20, 50, 55
        of origin, 3, 41
        patriarchal, 3
        polyandrous, 3
        polygamous, 3
        polygynous, 3
        of procreation, 3
        reconstituted, 2, 3
        single-earner, 151
        single-parent, 3, 10, 13, 236, 396–399
        step-, 3, 14
    theories of, 18–23
familism, 54–55
family, extended
    African American, 52
    elderly and, 248
    Mexican American, 54, 55
    Native American, 59
    traditional couples and, 219
family developmental theory, 20–21
family life cycle. *See* life cycle, family
Family and Medical Leave Act, 376
family planning, 324–325
Family Relations Act, 204
Family Strengths Research Project, 220
fatherhood

    readiness for, 362
    timing of, 324
fathers, participation of in child care,
        151–152, 386–387
feedback, 317
fellatio, 167
femininity
    concepts of, 40, 136
    nonconformity to standards, 146
    and powerlessness, 141
    stereotypes of, 143–145, 149
feminism
    in United States, 5
    views of marriage and, 72
feminist theory, 23–24, 305
fertility, rate of, 61
fertilization, in vitro, 347
fetal alcohol syndrome, 32, 57
fetus, development of, 369
filtering
    marriage gradient and, 196
    mate selection and, 190–191, 196
    nonmarital cohabitation and, 190
finances, family
    childrearing and, 237
    living arrangements and, 245
    marital happiness and, 220
    parenthood and, 241
    as relationship problem, 239
flexibility, marriage and, 219–220,
        229–230
flextime, 263
FOCCUS, 208–209
foreplay, digital, 166
foster care, 13, 59
"Four Horsemen of the Apocalypse," 219
Freud, Sigmund, 124, 188
friendship, 4
    companionship and, 297–300
    elderly and, 248, 298
    gender and, 298
    health and, 297
    intimacy in, 298
    marriage and, 223, 298
    sexual intercourse and, 298
Fromm, Erich, 127–128
frustration, sexual, 75

GHB (date rape drug), 107
G-spot, 167
gambling
    Chinese Americans and, 61
    Native Americans and, 58
gangs, involvement in, 53
gaslighting, 311
gays/lesbians
    adoption by, 20, 238
    child custody and, 238
    discrimination against, 11, 12, 238–239
    families, 237–239

    fringe benefits and, 239
    oppression of, 23
    parenting by, 12
    sexual activity of, 173–174
    See also lesbians, childbearing and
gender
    and anger, 151
    attitudes about, 138, 149–150
    communication and, 101, 141
    definition, 23, 136
    dysphoria, 136
    environmental influences, 136–140
    income and, 144, 146
    poverty and, 246, 279, 397
    power and, 141–142
    social construction of, 164
    stereotypes of, 136–137
    toys and, 136, 139, 143, 145, 147
gender bias. *See* bias, gender–based
gender differences
    in communication, 315–316
    companionship and, 298
    loneliness and, 292
    power disparities and, 23, 315
gender gap, 306
gender-role attitudes
    age and, 249
    household labor and, 227
    retirement and, 247
gender roles
    African Americans and, 51, 53–54
    Chinese Americans, 61
    cultural expectations and, 39, 40
    family background and, 39
    marriage and, 143, 198
    mate selection and, 197–198
    Mexican Americans and, 56
    patriarchy and, 306
    transmission of, 39–40
gender schema theory, 141
Generation X, 296
GIFT (gamete intrafallopian transfer),
        347–348
Girl Scouts, 20
goals, of college students, 276
gonorrhea, 182, 207, 208, 210, 372
grandparents
    child care by, 416, 417
    family role adjustment by, 249
    grandchildren and, 417–420
    parenting of grandchildren by, 419
    as role models, 418
grief, 455–456

happiness
    income and, 77
    marital status and, 76
    socioeconomic status and, 77
happiness, marital, 218–220, 223,
        234–235

Head Start, 388
health, mental
 androgyny and, 153
 friendship and, 297
health, physical
 contraceptive use and, 327
 as developmental task, 246
 divorce and, 76, 77
 elderly and, 249, 250
 marital quality and, 247
 of married people, 75–78
 of Native Americans, 57
 poverty and, 279
 pregnancy and, 362, 366–367
 retirement and, 247
 of single people, 75–78
 widowhood and, 76, 77
hepatitis B, 181
herpes simplex, 179–180, 207, 208, 210
heterogamy
 age, 196–197
 educational, 193
 mate selection and, 190
 marital stability and, 190
 and stress, 191–192
Hispanic Americans
 alcoholism among, 32
 birthrate among, 8
 body satisfaction among, 149
 divorce among, 70
 family structure, 10, 236
 interracial marriages among, 193
 prenatal care among, 363
 widowhood among, 70
HIV/AIDS, 178–180, 331
homelessness, 279
homemaking. See labor, household
homogamy
 educational, 192–193
 marital stability and, 190
 in mate selection, 190
homosexuality, incidence of, 13
 See also gays/lesbians; lesbians, childbearing and
householders, 82–83
households
 African American, 52, 54
 female-headed, 54, 55, 279
 grandparent-maintained, 13–14
 heads of, 4
 Mexican American, 55
 Native American, 58
 single-parent, 2
housework. See labor, household
housing, cost of, 274, 278
HPV/Genital warts, 181
human chorionic gonadotropin, 360
hunger, 57
hypoactive sex desire disorder,
  174–175

I-statements, 317
ideal mate, theory of, 188
Idealistic Distortion Scale, 208
ideals, approximation of, 216
identity, cultural
 African American, 53
 Asian American, 63
 Mexican American, 54
 Native American, 59
identity, gender
 definition, 136
 development of, 149
 parent-child relationship and, 138
 parental modeling and, 137–138
 societal expectations and, 136–137
 theories of, 140–142
identity, individual, 4, 248
illness, mental
 Chinese Americans and, 61
 intimate relationships and, 201
 Native Americans and, 57
 parents and, 32
 risk factors for, 32
images, media
 of African Americans, 53
 depression and, 147
 of marriage, 199
 of men, 147
 of physical attractiveness, 119
 of women, 146, 147
imaging, 101
immigration, 61
Immigration Act of 1882, 61
in-laws, relationships with, 412–414
in vitro fertilization, 19
incest, 442, 448–450
income
 African Americans and, 50–51
 age and, 246
 Chinese Americans and, 61
 debt and, 276
 developmental task, 246–247
 distribution of, 273
 divorce and, 439
 earned by wives, 6, 19
 educational level and, 274
 economic cooperation and, 19
 egalitarianism and, 40
 in female-headed families, 279, 281,
  397
 gender and, 146, 274
 gender-role stereotypes and, 144
 happiness and, 77
 household labor and, 248
 job satisfaction and, 260
 life satisfaction and, 52, 76
 in male-headed families, 399
 marital satisfaction and, 267–268, 275
 in married households, 82, 279, 281
 median, 273

Native Americans, 57
 power and, 307
 pregnancy and, 204
 race and, 274
 Whites, 51, 54
 of widows, 253
income gap, 284
Indian Education Act of 1972, 58–59
Indian Gaming Regulatory Act, 58
Industrial Revolution, 19, 91
inequality, gender-based, 146, 151
infertility, 330, 346–347
infidelity. See relationships, extramarital
inflation, 10
influence, parental, 30
influence, social, 30
inhibition, ejaculatory, 174
insemination, artificial, 12, 238, 347
instability, marital
 age at marriage and, 199, 204
 educational heterogamy and, 193
 See also stability, marital
Institute for Child Behavior
  Research, 228
insurance, health, 19, 282, 363
insurance, life, 19
interactions, family
 child care and, 293
 household labor and, 293
 patterns of, 293
interactions, parent-child
 adolescent children and, 293
 adolescent sexual activity and, 17
 reciprocal, 30
 substance abuse and, 32
intercourse, sexual
 age and, 80, 172
 arousal and, 171
 dating and, 95
 frequency of, 80, 160, 169, 171–173,
  226, 328, 366
 gender roles and, 105, 170
 mate selection and, 199
 multiple orgasms and, 165
 nonconsensual, 105, 107
 number of partners, 80, 99
 sexual response and, 164
interdependence
 of family members, 22
 fear of, 73
 intergenerational, 408, 414
 marital success and, 224–225
Internet, use of, 297
intimacy
 attitudes about, 36–37
 communication and, 243
 fear of, 73
 friendship and, 298
 value consensus and, 197
intimacy, emotional, 226

intimacy, psychological, 130
intimacy, sexual, 93, 100–101, 205, 298
intrauterine device (IUD), 330–331
isolation
　emotional, 4, 74, 280, 291
　social, 13, 78, 280, 291, 316

Japanese Americans, 193
jealousy, 239
Jewish Dating Service, 98
job schedule
　in dual-career families, 269–270
　effects on family, 262–263
Johnson, Lyndon Baines, 48

Korean Americans, 193

La Leche League, the, 375
labor, childbearing
　accelerated, 372
　cesarean section, 372
　definition, 370
　duration of, 370–371
　stages of, 371
labor, household
　African Americans and, 52–53
　child care and, 150
　children and, 62, 399–400
　Chinese Americans and, 62
　dual-career families and, 271–272
　egalitarianism and, 40, 151, 227
　eldercare and, 244
　over family life cycle, 152
　feminist theory of, 23
　gender roles and, 40, 150–152, 227
　income and, 248
　living arrangements and, 415
　men and, 53, 152, 247–248, 307
　nonmarital cohabitation and, 200
　responsibility for, 6, 10
　women and, 150, 227, 250, 307
labor, household, division of, 306
　conflict over, 150
　marital quality and, 227, 247
　marital satisfaction and, 150–151, 227
　in military families, 263
　satisfaction with, 150, 265
　sexism in, 271–272
laparoscopy, 335–336
"latchkey children," 387
Latinos, 48
leave, maternal, 266
leisure activities
　companionship in, 292, 294–297
　computers and, 296–297
　elderly and, 244, 249
　family relationships and, 294
　happiness and, 220, 223
　marriage and, 220, 223, 292
　as relationship problem, 239

retirement and, 249, 250
　sports, 294, 295
　television and, 295–296
　vacations and, 294–295
lesbians, childbearing and, 18, 20, 238
lice, pubic, 183
life cycle, family, 20–21
　data on, 235–236
　divorce and, 235–236, 243
　of gay/lesbian families, 237–239
　household labor and, 152
　of intact families, 235
　marital satisfaction and, 236, 249–250
　phases of, 235
　single-parent, 236
　stages of, 20–21, 244–245
　traditional, 20–21
life expectancy, 8
　of African Americans, 236
　age of spouse and, 197
　of men, 236, 252, 416
　of Native Americans, 57
　of Whites, 236
　of women, 236, 252, 416
ligation, tubal, 335–336
limerence, 122
living arrangements
　alone, 79
　elderly and, 78, 248, 415–416
　of men, 79–80
　with parents, 79–86, 206, 245,
　　414–415
living, cost of, 10
loneliness
　dislocation and, 291
　among elderly, 248
　gender differences and, 292
　marriage and, 81, 292
　reasons for, 291
　self-esteem and, 292
　singlehood and, 74, 79–81, 292
　among widows, 252
　among widowers, 253
love
　attitudes about, 132
　components of, 128–131
　definition, 121
　expression of, 37
　sexual desire and, 124
　styles of, 131
love, dimensions of
　altruistic, 128
　dependent, 125–127
　erotic, 124–125
　friendship, 127
　romantic, 121–123
love, types of
　companionate, 124
　conscious, 122
　narcissistic, 122, 124

lovemaking, principles of, 169–174
lubrication, 163, 164, 171
ludus, 131

machismo, 55, 306
malnutrition, 57
mania, 131
marriage
　adjustments in, 239, 243–244, 249
　alternatives to, 201
　attitudes about, 39, 40
　career and, 73
　cohabitation prior to, 7, 201–203
　disruption of, 52
　expectations for, 239
　family background and, 30
　fear of, 73, 83
　gender roles and, 143, 198
　happiness and, 234–235
　and health, 75–76
　income and, 82
　laws regarding, 206–207
　leisure activities in, 220, 223, 292
　loneliness and, 80, 292
　media images of, 199
　patterns of, 219, 236–237
　preparation for, 207–209
　problems in, 239
　rates of, 2, 6–7, 83
　readiness for, 204–206
　reasons for, 22, 34
　as rite of passage, 144
　roles in, 242
　and romantic love, 122–133
　satisfaction with. See satisfaction,
　　marital
　sexual abuse in, 442
　success in, 216–218, 220–230
　　See also success, marital
　support and, 84
　transition to, 204–209
　well-being and, 75–76
marriage, age and, 2, 6–8, 17, 73, 93, 196,
　　206, 235
　among African Americans, 236
　in-law adjustment and, 413
　among Whites, 236
marriage, delay of, 39, 70, 72, 245
　living arrangements and, 79–80
　media and, 147
　reasons for, 72
　socioeconomic status and, 72
　young adults and, 206
marriage, likelihood of
　for African Americans, 54, 236
　age and, 70
　field of eligibles and, 189
　poverty and, 279
　for Whites, 54, 236
marriage, types of

arranged, 90–91, 98
common-law, 207
commuter, 18
dual-career, 153, 269–272
group, 2
interfaith, 194–195
interracial, 193–194
long-term, 236
same-sex, 11
teen, 204
void/voidable, 207
marriage gradient, 196
marriage mandate, 144
"marriage squeeze," 73
Married Women's Property Act, 5–6
masculinity
concepts of, 40, 136
stereotypes, 141–142, 144–145
Maslow, Abraham, 125–126
masturbation, 38, 164, 165, 172
Matchmaker Dating Service of Maine, 99
mate, selection of
age and, 190, 196–197
attraction and, 189–190, 196, 199
"biological clock" and, 199
cohabitation and, 190, 199, 200, 202
compatibility and, 190, 195–198
dating and, 90, 95–96
economic issues in, 189, 192
education level and, 190, 192–193, 196
ethnicity and, 190, 192–194, 196
expectations and, 196
family background and, 188,
190–195
field of eligibles and, 189
filtering and, 190–191, 196
gender roles and, 197–198
heterogamy and, 190
homogamy and, 190
image and, 200
neurosis and, 200
parental pressure and, 199
personal habits and, 198
pregnancy and, 190, 199
propinquity and, 189, 190
regrets about, 198–199
religion and, 190, 194–195, 196
romantic love and, 128
sex and, 199
socioeconomic status and, 190,
191–192, 196
standards for, 120–121
substance abuse and, 200
theories of, 188–190
values and, 190, 197
Mead, Margaret, 136
media
attitudes about, 296
body image and, 138, 145
effect on attitudes, 138

gender bias in, 138
rape and, 107
socialization of children by, 30
Medicaid, 282
men
age at first sexual intercourse, 16
attributes desired in mates, 190
depression among, 32, 110
expectations of mates, 196
gender attitudes of, 149–150
household labor and, 53, 152, 247–248
life expectancy of, 236, 252, 416
living arrangements of, 79, 81
media images of, 147
number of widowers among, 249
personal ads by, 97
menstruation, 38, 325–326
and calculation of birth date, 362
cessation at pregnancy, 360
and sexual desire, 170–171
Mexican Americans, 54–56
mobility, upward, 50
modeling, observational, 30–31
"Modern Courtship and Marriage," 93
money, management of, 219, 276–278
monogamy, 51, 201
Mormons, dating among, 194
mortality, infant, 57
mortality, rates of
in ectopic pregnancies, 365
among married adults, 75
among single adults, 75
motherhood
African Americans and, 52
effects of, 83–84
Mexican Americans and, 56
Native Americans and, 59
motherhood mandate, 143–144
motherhood, single. *See* motherhood,
unmarried
motherhood, unmarried
attitudes about, 39
effects of, 83–84
reasons for, 82–83
mothers
divorced, 84
engagement levels of, 271
single, 52, 77, 82–84
surrogate, 348
teenage, 396
Moynihan, Daniel Patrick, 48, 51
myotonia, 163, 164

Naegele's formula, 361–362
National Bureau of Economic
Research, 275
National Center for Health Statistics, 338
National Childcare Survey, 263
National Health and Social Life Survey,
16–17, 18, 81, 166, 435

National Indian Gaming
Commission, 58
National Opinion Resource Center
General Social Surveys, 144
National Survey of Black Families, 414
National Survey of Families and Households, 172, 202–203, 383, 408, 414,
415
National Survey of Family Growth, 180,
363
Native Americans, 48, 56–60
culture, 57
definition, 56
geographical distribution, 56
migration to urban areas, 57
relocation of, 56, 57
reservations, 56
Navajo, 56
Navy wives, 263
needs, fulfillment of, 216–218
needs theory of mate selection, 188
negative affect reciprocity, 218
Negro Family: The Case for National Action,
The, 48
networks, kin, 21
African American, 51–52, 298
after divorce, 479
elderly and, 298
Mexican American, 54–55
Native American, 59
networks, social
African Americans, 298
Whites, 298
never-married adults. *See* adults, single
newborns, 372–373
Nickelodeon, 296
noncontingent reinforcement, 223
norepinephrine, 123
norms, cultural, 305–306
norms, gender, 306
norms, social, 393
Norplant, 327–328

obesity, 118
Oedipus complex, 188
Office of Indian Education, 59
Olympics, 140
oppression, 23, 146
based on age, 23
baced on race, 23
based on social class, 23
of homosexuals, 23
of women, 23, 146
orgasm, 124, 163–164
multiple, 164–166
nonachievement of, 174
phase of sexual response, 161
orientation, sexual, 12
ovulation, 325, 336–337
ovum transfer, 348

parent image theory, 188
parenthood
    adjustment to, 239–242
    anger and, 151
    delay of, 324, 350–351
    economic issues and, 241
    educational level and, 241
    expectations about, 376
    marital conflict and, 241, 242
    marital quality and, 241, 242
    preparation for, 241
    responsibilities of, 241, 242
    satisfaction and, 241–242
    single women and, 2, 398
    social support and, 241–242
    stress and, 240–242
    among teenagers, 241, 384, 396
    transition to, 241
    unplanned pregnancy and, 241
    well-being and, 242
parenting
    baby boomers and, 296
    constructive, 386
    destructive, 386
    gender bias in, 139
    by grandparents, 13–14
    skills, development of, 21
    socialization of children and, 384–385
    styles of, 56
Parents without Partners, 398
partners
    intimate, 34–36
    marital, 120–121, 406–407
    sexual, 17
patriarchy
    dating and, 102
    within families, 4, 5
    family violence and, 305
    gender roles and, 306
    in Mexican American families, 55–56, 306
    in Puerto Rican families, 306
Paycheck Fairness Act, 275
pedophilia, 448
perfectionism, 33, 229–230
personality traits, by gender, 40
plateau phase of sexual response, 160–161, 162, 163
polygyny, 3
population, United States
    African Americans, 48
    Asian/Pacific Islanders, 48
    divorced adults, 70
    females, 73
    Latinos, 48
    males, 73
    marital status of, 70
    Native Americans, 48, 56
    number of families in, 2
    by race and Hispanic origin, 48

    widowed adults, 70
pornography, 167
Positive Couple Agreement, 208
postparental years, 244–245
posttraumatic stress disorder, 447
poverty
    age and, 246
    child care and, 279
    children and, 204
    definition, 278
    educational level, 279
    effects of, 278–280
    ethnicity and, 246
    in female-headed households, 279
    feminization of, 279, 397
    gender and, 246
    in grandparent-headed families, 13
    health, 279
    homelessness, 279
    incidence of, 325
    isolation, 279
    low birth weight and, 362
    marital status and, 204, 278
    racism and, 279
    rural, 279
    sexism and, 279
    urban, 279
    wealth gap, 280–284
poverty line, 278–282
power
    division of labor and, 141
    economic, 5–6
    employment and, 247
    expert, 307
    within families, 22, 23, 32, 55–56, 304–313
    gender and, 141–142
    informational, 307
    lack of, 312
    legitimate, 304
    and mortality, 439
    need for, 305
    neutralization of, 313
    personality and, 308
    single-parent families and, 395
    in society, 23
power, coercive, 308
power, marital
    adjustment and, 309
    gender and, 268
    implementation of, 310
    orchestration of, 310
    sources of, 268
    tactics of, 310–312
power, marital, patterns of
    anarchic, 309, 310
    egalitarian, 309
    female-dominant, 309–310
    male-dominant, 309
power, personal, 304

pragma, 131
Preferred Singles, 98
pregnancy
    cessation of education and, 204
    complications of
        abruptio placentae, 364
        ectopic pregnancy, 361, 364–365
        placenta previa, 364
        Rh incompatibility, 365
        toxemia, 364
        tubal pregnancy, 364–365
    developmental tasks of, 366
    early marriage and, 204
    employment and, 204
    health during, 362, 366–367
    income and, 204
    within marriage, 5
    mate selection and, 190, 199
    nonmarital, 55, 190, 199
    nutrition during, 364
    postpartum period, 372–376
    premarital, 324
    rates of, 2
    reactions to, 362
    risk factors during, 362–363
    sex during, 365
    side effects of, 364
    signs of, 360
    stress during, 366
    support during, 242, 362
    among teens, 13, 17, 38–39, 53
    tests for, 360
    timing of, 362
    unpartnered women and, 362
    unplanned, 44, 363
        incidence of, 324, 338
        income and, 324
prejudice
    against Chinese Americans, 62
    against interracial marriage, 193, 194
    against Mexican Americans, 56
    against women, 82
Premarital Sexual Confidence Scale, 173
PREPARE, 208–209
progesterone, 325
property, ownership of, 4
propinquity, 189, 190
psychodynamic theory, 188
puberty, 38, 60
punishment, corporal, 395

quality, marital
    of African Americans, 275
    age at marriage and, 199
    age differential and, 196–197
    communication and, 272
    companionship and, 272
    depression and, 196
    in dual-career families, 267
    educational level and, 199

egalitarianism and, 268
eldercare and, 244
ethnicity and, 199
extroversion and, 196
gender roles and, 198, 268
habits and, 198
health and, 247
household labor and, 247
income and, 199
lifestyle and, 272
mental illness and, 196
occupation and, 199
parenthood and, 241, 242
positive regard and, 272
previous cohabitation and, 202–203
role conflict and, 272
quality of parents' marriage and, 198
socioeconomic status and, 199, 272
women's employment and, 272

race
courtship violence and, 109
marriage outside, 54
oppression and, 23
racism, 53, 54, 279
rape, 104–107
"Rating and Dating Complex," 91–92
redivorce, rates of, 14–15
rejection, parental, 34
relationships
dissolution of, 110–111
perceptions of, 316
problems in, 239, 243
sexual power in, 100, 102
relationships, anarchic, 310
relationships, extradyadic, 102–103
relationships, extramarital
and divorce, 437
effects on marriages, 298–299, 436–437
marital quality and, 438
Mexican Americans, 55
reasons for, 435–436
types of, 438
relationships, family
emotional closeness in, 126–127
leisure activities and, 294
repetition of patterns, 39
relationships, female-dominated,
309–310
relationships, intergenerational, 54
relationships, intimate
African Americans, 51
anxiety in, 201
childhood attachment and, 390
communication in, 41
danger signals in, 201
ending of, 110–112
family background and, 31, 34, 201
gender roles and, 144
relationships, male-dominated, 310

relationships, marital
African Americans, 51
effects of alcoholism on, 32
patterns of, 219
quality of, 35
    See also quality, marital
relationships, parent-child
adult children, 406–412
conflict in, 35, 411, 412
divorce and, 250–251
elderly and, 251–252
father-son, 411
gender and, 137–138
life circumstances and, 383
mother-daughter, 409–411
and mothers' self-esteem, 84
parent well-being, 411
reasoning complexity and, 280
satisfaction with, 251
relationships, spousal. See relationships,
    marital
religion
courtship violence and, 109
divorce and, 463
marital disruption and, 195
mate selection and, 190, 194–195, 196
Native Americans and, 60
as relationship problem, 239
socialization of children and, 195
traditional couples and, 219
religiosity
African Americans, 52
among children, 195
marital strength and, 25
marital success and, 224
mate selection and, 194–195
remarriage
among African Americans, 14, 51, 236
challenges in, 491–492
economic issues, 495–496
expectations, 494–495
in family life cycle, 235–236
among Hispanics, 14
issues in, 505
mate selection, 492–493
rates of, 2, 14–15
success in, 490–491, 493
among Whites, 14, 51, 236
repression, sexual, 38, 39
reproduction, 4, 19, 38
residence
common, 18–19
matrilocal, 5
neolocal, 6
patrilocal, 5
resolution phase of sexual response,
    161, 166
resource theory, 306–307
resources, economic, 306–307
responsibilities

community-related, 237
household, 227
job-related, 237
marital, 40
parental, 50
personal, 31, 35, 226–227
retardation, mental, 57
retirement
adjustment to, 247
delay of, 247
in family life cycle, 20–21, 235
family role adjustments due to, 249
gender and, 247
leisure activities in, 249, 250
loss of status due to, 249
marital power and, 247
marital quality and, 247
men's household labor and, 152
reasons for, 247
Retirement History Study, 249
rites of passage
engagement, 209–210
for gays/lesbians, 238
marriage, 144
wedding, 210–211
Rohyponol, 107
role concepts, 190
role models
African Americans, 51
male, 12, 83
parents as, 35, 40–41, 262, 389
role strain
child care and, 150
children and, 265, 270
in dual-career families, 269–270
eldercare and, 244
employment and, 265–267, 270
in gay/lesbian families, 12
among graduate students, 266
marital satisfaction and, 237
in single-parent families, 398
sources of, 265
spousal support and, 262
roles, family
changes over life cycle, 20–21
expressive, 4
instrumental, 4
in society, 18
roles, gender, 6, 23, 31, 39–40
anger and, 151
attitudes about, 138–139, 147, 149–150
behavior and, 145
body image and, 145–146
changes in, 154
child care and, 150–152, 153
compatibility and, 197–198
congruence of, 152
dating and, 91, 94–95, 100–102, 104,
    143, 198
definition, 136

roles, gender, *(continued)*
   ethnic variations in, 149–150
   in families, 145, 147–152
   family background and, 191
   family life cycle and, 152
   health and, 145
   household labor and, 150–152
   intimate relationships and, 144
   media images and, 138–139, 140, 146
   parent-child relationships and, 138
   parental modeling and, 137–138, 140
   "provider," 260–261
   psychological well-being and, 150
   schools and, 139–140
   and self-esteem, 145
   in sex, 105, 170
   societal expectations and, 136–137
   stress and, 145
   substance abuse and, 145
   suicide and, 145
   theories of, 140–142
roles, marital, attitudes about, 10
roles, parental, 384–387
roles, social, 2
   definition, 393
   marital satisfaction and, 237
roles, work-related, 40, 247–248
RU–486, 329

salary, occupation and, 281, 284
"sandwich generation," 244, 415
satisfaction, life
   of African Americans, 51–54
   of boomerang kids, 245
   of children, 386
   developmental tasks and, 20
   economic resources and, 246–247
   employment and, 76
   friendship and, 297
   gender roles and, 53–54
   health and, 243, 246
   income and, 52, 76
   marital status and, 52, 76
   mental health and, 76
   parenthood and, 241
   physical health and, 76
   role fulfillment and, 260
   sex and, 160
   of single adults, 71, 77
   social activity and, 249
   socioeconomic status and, 76
satisfaction, marital, 10
   of African American women, 51
   in arranged marriages, 98
   balance of power and, 312
   child care and, 151
   child rearing and, 237
   communication and, 290, 316
   companionship and, 290, 292
   conflict and, 433

   depression and, 226
   devitalized couples and, 219
   elderly and, 249–250
   family background and, 191
   family life cycle and, 249–250
   financially focused couples and, 219
   happiness and, 218
   household labor and, 151, 227
   income and, 275
   life satisfaction and, 234
   marital adjustment and, 218, 239
   in midlife, 243
   money management and, 275–277
   need fulfillment and, 218
   parenting practices and, 383, 386
   parenthood and, 241–242
   pattern of marriage and, 236
   patterns of change in, 236–237, 243
   in postparental years, 244–245
   previous cohabitation and, 202–203
   psychological well-being and, 234
   retirement and, 247, 249
   self-esteem and, 196
   socioeconomic status and, 191–192
   value consensus and, 197
   vitalized couples and, 219
   White women, 51
   of women, 237, 269
   work-related stress and, 261–262
satisfaction, sexual
   breast-feeding and, 376
   conflict and, 173
   frequency of intercourse and, 171–172
   gender roles and, 170
   predictors of, 175–176
   women and, 165
scabies, 183
scapegoating, 311
school dropout, 53, 280
security, economic, 4, 51
self-actualization, 304
self-concept
   African American children, 53
   attachment style and, 35
   of children, 22, 31, 37
   family background and, 32–34, 35
   perfectionist parents and, 33
self-employment, 263
self-disclosure, 316–317
   communication and, 230
   dating and, 101–102, 106
   loneliness and, 292
self-esteem
   androgyny and, 153
   of children, 149, 389–390
   criticism and, 311
   loneliness and, 292
   marital success and, 225
   mate selection and, 199
selfism, 227

sensitivity, affective, 228
separation, marital
   age at marriage and, 199, 204
   alternative to divorce, 470–472
   and happiness, 76
   and health, 76, 77
   living with parents and, 77
serotonin, 124
sex
   age at first experience, 16, 17
   communication and, 170
   following childbirth, 376
   intimacy and, 172–173
   marital happiness and, 160
   mate selection and, 199
   oral, 166–167
   parent-child discussion of, 38
   physical setting for, 171
   during pregnancy, 365
   reasons for engaging in, 16–17
   as relationship problem, 239
   teens and, 38
   timing of, 170–171
sex, attitudes about, 37–39
   Chinese Americans, 61
   Mexican Americans, 55
sex, casual, 124
sex education, 39
sex flush, 163, 164
sex, nonmarital, 17, 161, 173
   attitudes about, 16, 51, 72
   extradyadic, 102–103, 122
   Mexican Americans, 55
   among singles, 81–82
   variety in, 74
sexism
   in media, 138
   poverty and, 279
sexual arousal
   homosexuals and, 174
   sources of, 166–169
sexual behavior, high-risk, 81–82
   academic performance and, 17
   adolescents and, 17, 38
   African American teens and, 51
   alcohol consumption and, 17
   physical abuse and, 17
   sexual abuse and, 17
   suicide and, 17
sexual behavior, nonmarital, 16–18
sexual experience, predictors of, 17
sexual intercourse. *See* sex
sexual pressure, unwanted, 105
sexual response
   age and, 172
   desire phase of, 166
   excitement phase of, 160–161, 163
   phases of, 160–166, 174
   physiology of, 161–164
sexual stimulation, 163, 167–169

sexuality
    attitudes about, 10, 37–39
    traditional couples and, 219
singlehood
    adjustment to, 84–85
    advantages of, 74
    careers and, 74
    codependency and, 75
    companionship and, 77, 79
    disadvantages of, 74–75
    economic hardship and, 75
    among elderly, 77
    employment and, 81–82
    friendships and, 79
    happiness and, 76
    income and, 77, 81–82
    life satisfaction and, 77
    living arrangement and, 77
    loneliness and, 74, 79, 80, 292
    mortality and, 75
    perceptions of, 75
    and physical health, 77
    reasons for, 72–74
    sexual abuse and, 75
    social support and, 77, 79, 84
    standard of living, 75, 85
    well-being and, 75–76
singles bars, 96
slavery, 48–50
smoking, health risks of, 327, 364, 367
social control theory, 305
social exchange theory, 227, 308
social learning theory, 34–35, 36
    of corporal punishment, 395
    of gender identity, 140
    gender schema theory and, 141
Social Security Administration, 19, 249
social structure/cultural theory,
        141–142
socialization
    of African American girls, 149
    anticipatory, 96
    body image and, 167
    of children, 20, 393
    in dating, 94, 96, 102, 106
    definition, 392–393
    as family task, 21
    gender-role, 306, 408
    need for affection and, 226
    by television, 138–139
    of women, 102, 104, 261
sodomy, 174
sperm donor, 12
spermicides, 329–330, 331–332
stability
    family, 51
    marital, 190, 196, 216
standard of living, 10, 41
    of Native Americans, 57
    of single adults, 75

status, marital
    of African Americans, 70
    happiness and, 76
    health and, 75–78
    of Hispanics, 70
    living arrangements and, 414
    nomarital cohabitation and, 200–201
    poverty and, 204, 278
    of U.S. population, 70
    of Whites, 70
status, social, 4
    developmental tasks and, 248
    dating and, 91–92, 96
    elderly and, 248
status, socioeconomic
    child rearing and, 280
    courtship violence and, 109
    dating and, 93
    family size and, 280
    happiness and, 77
    isolation and, 280
    marital age differential and, 196
    mate selection and, 190, 191–192, 196
    oppression and, 23
    school dropout and, 280
stepfamilies, 498–503
    expectations, 498–499
    roles, 499
    child rearing, 499
     kin networks, 499–500
    cohesion, 500
    turning points, 498
    family relationships, 500–507
    child well-being, 501–503
stepparenting, 12
stereotypes
    of African Americans, 53
    of Chinese Americans, 61, 62
    gender-based
        cognitive development theory of,
            140–141
        in employment, 144
        femininity, 143–145, 149
        masculinity, 141–145
        media and, 138–139
        problems with, 144–145
        in school books, 139
        social learning theory of, 140
        weakening of, 150
sterilization, 334–336
storge, 131
strain, economic
    anger and, 151
    women's employment and, 268
strain, marital
    ideal mate fantasies and, 188
    number of children and, 324
stress
    in children of alcoholic families, 32
    courtship violence and, 109

divorce and, 84
eldercare and, 252
economic resources and, 247
forced retirement and, 247
living arrangements and, 415
parenthood and, 240–242
poverty and, 279
pregnancy and, 366
single parenthood and, 240–242
teen parenthood and, 241
stress, job-related
    effects on family, 261–262
    parent-child relationship and,
        261–262
    partner's distress and, 262
    retirement and, 247
stress, maternal, 263
structure, family
    African American, 52
    changes over life cycle, 20–21
    Native American, 59
structural-functional theory, 18–20
substance abuse
    African Americans and, 53
    among children
        home environment and, 389–390
        sexual abuse and, 447
        single-parent families, 397
        White girls, 149
    as danger signal in relationship, 201
    as family crisis, 434
    family conflict and, 32
    mate selection and, 200
    Native Americans and, 57
    risk factors for, 32
    spontaneous abortion and, 367
    spread of STDs and, 17
success, marital, 7–8
    affection and, 226
    approximation of ideals and, 216
    commitment and, 224–226
    communication and, 222
    companionship and, 223–224
    empathy, 228
    expectations and, 216, 227
    family background and, 198
    frequency of intercourse and, 226
    gender roles and, 227
    interdependence, 224, 225
    preparation for marriage and, 207
Sudden Infant Death Syndrome,
        451–452
suffrage, women's, 5
suicide
    as family crisis, 455–456
    among Native Americans, 57
    among never-married adults, 71
    and relationship termination, 112
    sexual abuse and, 447
    among White girls, 149

support, emotional
  anxiety and, 84
  depression and, 84
  friendship and, 297
  nonmarital cohabitation and, 202
  in parent-child relationship, 251
support, intergenerational, 251–252
support, social
  marital quality and, 247
  never-married adults and, 70–71
symbolic interaction theory, 21
syphilis, 182–183, 207, 208, 210
systems theory, 22

tasks, developmental, 20–21, 246–249
tasks, family, 21
technology gap, 297
teens
  birthrate among, 18, 59, 82
  contraceptive use among, 396
  parenthood, 241, 384, 396
  pregnancy among, 13, 17, 38–39, 53
  sex and, 17
television
  attitudes about, 296
  body image and, 145, 147
  family communication and, 295–296
  gender roles and, 138–139
  homemaking and, 296
  sexual relations and, 296
tests, premarital, 207
theory, definition of, 18
Title VII, 274
Title IX, 139–140
Together, 98
toxoplasmosis, 367
toys, gender-specific, 136, 139, 143–147
transgendering, 136
transition, midlife, 243–244
transsexuals, 136
trust
  between parents and children, 33
  relationships and, 229

unconditional positive regard, 223
underemployment
  African Americans and, 10
  Chinese Americans and, 61
  delay in marriage due to, 7
  as marital crisis, 439
  Native Americans and, 57
unemployment
  Chinese Americans and, 61
  debt and, 277
  living with parents and, 79
  among minorities, 438
  age and, 438
  education level and, 438
  depression and, 439
  rates of, 280
  self-esteem and, 439

United States Bureau of the Census, 2
United States Department of
  Education, 59
unmarried women, births to
  African Americans, 51
  Chinese Americans, 61
urbanization, 297

vaginismus, 175
values
  dating and, 197
  family background and, 30, 41, 191
  marital compatibility and, 197
  mate selection and, 190, 197
  media effect on, 138
  transmission of, 30
values, parental
  adolescent sex and, 17
vasectomy, 334–335
vasocongestion, 161, 164, 166
Viagra, 177
violence, courtship
  alcohol and, 109
  attitudes about, 108
  commitment and, 110
  factors contributing to, 108, 402
  family background and, 109
  forms of, 108
  progression of, 108–109, 402
  among young adults, 108
violence, domestic
  attitudes about, 108
  effects on children, 32
  nonmarital cohabitation and, 201
  roots in dating, 107–108
violence, family
  definition, 22, 440
  depression and, 441
  attitudes about, 442
  family background and, 305, 442
  patriarchy and, 305
  power and, 308, 312
  substance abuse and, 442, 443
  social isolation and, 442
  unemployment and, 442
  underreporting of, 443
  education and, 443
  in divorced/remarried families, 443
violence, marital
  family background and, 32, 35
Virgin Mary, the, 55
visitation rights, 481

wage gap, 274–275, 281
welfare
  attitudes about, 282–283
  Chinese Americans and, 61
  family and, 282–283
  in female-headed households, 51
  nonmarital cohabitation and, 200
  poverty and, 279

Whites, non-Hispanic
  abortion among, 51
  age differential in marriage, 196
  age at first sexual intercourse, 16
  age at marriage, 236
  birthrate among, 8, 59
  definition, 48
  depression among, 149
  divorce and, 55, 70, 236
  eating disorders and, 149
  elderly, 54
  income of, 51, 54
  interracial marriage among, 193
  life expectancy of, 236
  mate selection among, 192–193
  poverty among, 50
  single-parent families, 10, 51, 236
  social networks of, 298
  transition to parenthood, 241
  widowhood among, 70
widowhood, 252–253
  age of spouse and, 197
  child rearing and, 252–253
  duration of, 252
  elderly and, 252–253
  in family life cycle, 20, 235
  income and, 252
  intergenerational contact and, 408
  loneliness and, 252, 253
  Mexican Americans and, 55
  personal identity and, 252
  poverty and, 253
  remarriage and, 252
  sexual frustration and, 252
  Social Security benefits during, 253
  social supports and, 253
women
  age at first marriage, 7
  age at first sexual intercourse, 16
  attributes desired in mates, 189–190
  barriers to opportunities for, 23
  body image of, 120, 146, 147
  career options for, 8
  education of, 6, 7, 51, 54
  eldercare by, 244
  expectations of mates, 196
  health of, 77–78
  household labor and, 150, 227, 250
  life expectancy of, 236, 252, 416
  living arrangements of, 81
  media images of, 146, 147
  number of widows, 249
  oppression of, 23, 146
  participation in athletics, 140
  participation in labor force, 82
  power and, 196
  prejudice against, 83
  subordination of, 23
  weight and, 119
women, employment of
  attitudes about, 56

birthrate and, 9
breast-feeding and, 374
child care and, 150, 376
effect on family, 264–265
gender norms and, 306
gender-role attitudes and, 265
household labor and, 150, 227,
    265, 307
incidence of, 264
life satisfaction and, 53, 265
marital adjustment and, 267–268
motherhood and, 210, 265
power and, 307
perception of dependence and, 247
reasons for, 272
role strain and, 265–267

standard of living and, 272
television and, 138
wage gap and, 274–275, 281
women, empowerment of, 314
women, marital satisfaction of
    after childbirth, 315
    egalitarian gender roles and, 312
    household labor and, 227
    nonverbal communication and, 314
    power and, 312–313
    pregnancy and, 315
    Puerto Ricans, 312
women, unmarried
    childbearing among, 10, 18, 83
    childlessness among, 75
    parenthood and, 2, 398

women's equality movement
    dating and, 91, 100
    gender roles and, 149
women's rights convention, 5
women's rights movment.
    See feminism
work
    family and, 260–264
    gender segregation in, 144
    patterns of, 40–41
workaholism, 40–41, 262

YMCA, 20